# How to Spell Like a Champ

by Barrie Trinkle, Carolyn Andrews,
and Paige Kimble

WORKMAN PUBLISHING, NEW YORK

Library of Congress Cataloging-in-Publication Data is available.

ISBN-13: 978-0-7611-4369-7
ISBN-10: 0-7611-4369-6

Design by Barbara Balch
Illustrations by Robert Zimmerman

Workman books are available at special discounts when purchased in bulk for premiums and sales promotions as well as for fund-raising or educational use. Special editions or book excerpts can also be created to specification. For details, contact the Special Sales Director at the address below.

Workman Publishing Company, Inc.
225 Varick Street
New York, NY 10014-4381
www.workman.com

Printed in the U.S.A.

First printing October 2006

10 9 8 7 6 5 4 3 2 1

For all the kids who want
to spell every word right,
but especially for F-i-o-n-a
—B.T.

# Contents

# Acknowledgments

Thank goodness spelling bees are popular now. They've always been fun for some of us, but I'm glad we no longer have to wear the special jackets with GEEK stenciled on the back; mine was getting ratty after three decades, not to mention tight.

Something about spelling bees makes people friendly. Many spellers of all ages were willing to answer my nosy questions about their study habits and their memories of competitions past. The good people at Merriam-Webster generously allowed the use of their excellent materials, particularly some of the games in Chapter 7. Cybelle Weeks of the Scripps National Spelling Bee responded quickly and patiently to many requests for information.

Paige Kimble and Carolyn Andrews, the Scripps National Spelling Bee's director and word list manager, respectively, not only assisted with the writing of this book, but have also given me, among other things, a valid reason to keep my nose in the dictionary for several months of every year—which, if I didn't get paid to do it, would be my weird secret vice.

My husband, Miles Lane, our daughter, Fiona, and other members of our extended family tolerated my odd schedule with grace and kindness, which made it possible for me to finish this book.

Like most spellers, my greatest debt is to the people who taught me by example to love words. Thanks, Mom and Dad.

—Barrie Trinkle

*(continued)*

The Scripps National Spelling Bee's Web site celebrated its tenth birthday in January 2006. One of the features of our site is Carolyn's Corner, a study resource that I author. Through it, I have had the honor of reaching out to spellers and their families for more than a decade and have received much inspiration in the process. I am grateful for the questions asked and the interest shown.

Many dedicated spellers and their parents have fueled my contributions to this book. Special thanks go to "Georgie"—a faithful follower who visited Carolyn's Corner within an hour of its going online—and to Kerry—our most recent champion and a teacher's dream.

I am particularly indebted to my son, Ned, who rekindled my interest in words with his insatiable appetite for reading and learning when he was very young. Because of Ned, I have the privilege of sharing with you how to spell like a champion.

—Carolyn Andrews
word list manager, Scripps National Spelling Bee
author, Carolyn's Corner at www.spellingbee.com

# Introduction

My first word was *mango.*

It was my first spelling bee, in my school gymnasium. I was nine.

I knew the word. I had studied the word. Besides, it is spelled phonetically. So, with ease, the letters quickly rolled off my tongue.

"M-a-g-n-o."

A bell rang. Huh? I was in shock. What happened? It was not until I made it off the stage that my teacher explained my error. I bravely fought back tears and skulked back to the floor of the gymnasium with my schoolmates to watch the rest of the bee. I knew every word offered in that bee, and it stung to know that all I had to show for it was last place.

As a child, I developed an ever-growing fondness for words— words with shapes, textures, and tastes that delighted my senses and fueled my imagination. I devoured these words in library books while my father scoured the daily newspaper in search of interesting ones for me to learn.

One evening my family and I had stumbled upon a broadcast of the National Spelling Bee. I was captivated by the glorious, sometimes obscure words being offered to the young people on that stage and thrilled that I could spell some of the easier ones. And so my dream of participating in spelling bees was born, and there was nothing I wanted more than to go to the National Spelling Bee.

It might have been easy for me to drop my National Spelling Bee dream after the *mango* fiasco, but I was on fire about words. Time passed and my performance in spelling bees improved. My vocabulary and understanding of language patterns expanded greatly. There were disappointments, though, and more than once my parents asked, "Do you really want to do this?"

My answer was this: Finally, three years and three months after "m-a-g-n-o," I stood on a stage in Washington, D.C., and with a quivering voice, equal parts joy and nerves, correctly spelled the final word of the 1981 National Spelling Bee—*sarcophagus.*

A lot has changed since 1981. But instead of withering into antiquity, thanks to spellcheck, spelling bees are more popular than ever, saluted in documentaries like *Spellbound,* novels and movies like *Bee Season,* and even a Broadway musical entitled *The 25th Annual Putnam County Spelling Bee.* The publication of this book closely follows the release of another movie about spelling, *Akeelah and the Bee,* and James Maguire's book about our obsession with spelling, *American Bee.* This year, a whopping 274 spellers from all fifty states, as well as Guam, Puerto Rico, American Samoa, the Bahamas, Jamaica, Canada, and New Zealand converged on Washington, D.C., for the 79th Annual Scripps National Spelling Bee. That's not bad for a program that began with only nine finalists in 1925.

So kudos to the teachers and parents who inspire children to get it right, whether it's a math problem or a challenging spelling word. And kudos to the kids who have the motivation to study words, the spunk to spell in front of a crowd, and the courage to acknowledge and learn from their successes and failures.

—Paige Kimble

# CHAPTER 1

# A Great American Tradition

Did you feel a little tingle the first time you got a perfect score on a spelling test? Let's **extrapolate** (*Webster's Third New International Dictionary of the English Language, Unabridged:* "predict by projecting past experience or known data") and imagine that that perfect score had earned you a big cash prize, a guest spot on a hot late-night talk show, and your picture in every major newspaper in the country. Now we're talking more than a tingle. Most spelling bee champions would call it a pretty big buzz!

## Spelling Bees in Pop Culture, Past and Present

**1878:** **Bret Harte writes "The Spelling Bee at Angels," a humorous poem about a Saturday night spelldown between crusty prospectors in a gold rush saloon.**

**1941:** **Laura Ingalls Wilder publishes the autobiographical *Little Town on the Prairie*, depicting life in De Smet, South Dakota, in the 1880s. In a community spelling match—an impromptu entertainment on a cold winter evening—Laura misses *xanthophyll,* meaning "a red-orange crystalline carotenoid alcohol occurring especially in plants, usually with carotenes and chlorophylls, but also in animal fat, egg yolk, and corpus luteum." Her father spells it correctly to win the match. Those nineteenth-century farmers were no slouches!**

*(continued on page 6)*

The National Spelling Bee is really just a more public, more difficult, but much cooler spelling test, where a huge audience applauds every time you get a word right. So if you've already taken part in a spelling bee and want to keep working your way up the ladder or you've wondered what it would be like to be the last one standing—or rather, spelling—out of ten million American students who participate in the Scripps National Spelling Bee at the local level, read on. As Anurag Kashyap, the 2005 national champion, says:

> "I loved the experience and adrenaline rush I got at the microphone. . . . It was just an amazing feeling when all of my efforts and studying paid off in one big, climactic ending!"

## What Is a Spelling Bee, Anyway?

Have you ever turned on the TV and seen the climax of the Scripps National Spelling Bee? Two kids, usually looking as though they wished they hadn't eaten breakfast, face a pronouncer, a row of judges, a **phalanx** (*Webster's Third:* "a massed arrangement of persons, animals, or things") of cameras, and an anticipatory audience. Both spellers have spelled down

## The first national champion was 11-year-old Frank Neuhauser of Louisville, Kentucky, who in 1925 correctly spelled *gladiolus* to beat out eight other contestants.

not only the other spellers at the nationals, but also a series of peers at the school, local, and regional levels, and sometimes more. And no one in the audience, not even the seemingly omniscient pronouncer, knows which speller will take home the **colossal** (*Webster's Third:* "of very great size") trophy at the edge of the stage. It's reality TV, word-geek style. How did *this* odd form of entertainment come about? And what's the deal with its name?

**1925** *These nine students participated in the first National Spelling Bee. Can you spell "unfashionable"? Winner Frank Neuhauser is on the lower right.*

**1986:** *The Wonderful World of Disney* **airs a popular made-for-television movie,** *The Girl Who Spelled Freedom,* **based on the true story of Linn Yann, a Cambodian refugee who became a 1985 National Spelling Bee finalist just four years after escaping the brutal Khmer Rouge regime with her family.**

**2000: Myla Goldberg's first novel,** *Bee Season,* **becomes a word-of-mouth bestseller. The main character, Eliza Naumann, discovers she has a mystical facility for spelling; that, coupled with her father's unorthodox teaching methods, takes her to the National Spelling Bee finals.**

Spelling contests, often called "spelling matches" or "spell-downs," were a form of community entertainment throughout the nineteenth century, reaching a peak of popularity in the 1870s. In fact, there was quite a spelling craze during that decade, not unlike that of today. Education was still at a premium, and people with a facility for language were much admired, rather like television stars and hip-hop musicians are today. In the cities, particularly in the eastern United States, spelling matches were very serious business, often requiring entry fees. It wasn't until about 1875 that the term *spelling bee* came into common usage.

The first known recorded usage of the word *bee,* meaning "a community activity," dates from 1769. It was usually used for manual activities such as spinning, quilting, barn raising, corn husking, and other necessary tasks of rural life that were often shared among neighbors for social, as well as practical, reasons in far-flung frontier communities. Many people assume the word originally referred to the insect—after all, the bee is among the most social and industrious of creatures—but in recent years, **etymologists** ("word historians") have suggested that it's from a completely different word, the Middle English *bene,* meaning "a prayer or a favor." (Another word with the same ancestor, still in use in modern English, is *boon,* meaning "a timely benefit or blessing.") In England, a dialectal form of this word, *been* or *bean,* referred to "voluntary help given by neighbors toward the accomplishment of a particular task" *(Webster's Third). Bee* may simply be a shortened form of *been,* but no one is entirely certain.

## What Makes a Spelling Bee?

Not all spelling bees are alike; the difficulty of the words, the size of the audience, the rules, and the prizes vary widely. But all spelling bees, even written spelling bees, have a few essential elements: contestants, a word list, and a pronouncer who gives the words aloud. Most spelling bees also have judges who oversee the bee to make sure it is fair to all spellers.

A school spelling bee might choose one or two students to represent each class, or it might be open to all comers. Most often,

*Noah Webster, the father of the American dictionary.*

*"Bene . . . boon . . . been . . . bean . . . bee!"*

**2003:** *Spellbound,* a quirky documentary about several participants in the 1999 National Spelling Bee finals, becomes an art-house hit and is nominated for an Academy Award.

**2005:** *The 25th Annual Putnam County Spelling Bee,* adapted from the off-Broadway play *C-R-E-P-U-S-C-U-L-E,* becomes the first Broadway musical about you-know-what.

**2005:** *Bee Season* hits the big screen, starring Richard Gere, Juliette Binoche, and Flora Cross.

**2006:** *Akeelah and the Bee,* written and directed by Doug Atchison and starring Laurence Fishburne, Angela Bassett, and Keke Palmer, opens just before the National Spelling Bee finals.

**2006:** *American Bee: The National Spelling Bee and the Culture of Word Nerds* by James Maguire is published.

a teacher or principal serves as the pronouncer. There could be a separate judge or judges, or it might be up to the pronouncer to make sure that all students are given a fair chance to spell correctly. Homeschooled students might compete individually in a school spelling bee near their home, or they might spell against other homeschoolers to produce one or more homeschooling champions for an area.

As a speller moves ahead, spelling competition gets more serious. A local spelling bee can be written, oral, or a combination of both. Many spellers prefer competing in written bees. Since they take less time, why aren't all spelling competitions written? Spelling bees are held only partly for their educational value. They are also community events, and let's face it: Watching a roomful of kids writing on pieces of paper can be a snooze. Local and regional

*Victory of a school spelling bee.*

## Reason #9 to Enter a Spelling Bee: Classrooms that have 100 percent participation get to have pizza parties.

spelling bees that feed into the National Spelling Bee are usually sponsored by newspapers, and an oral spelling bee is more exciting and makes better news. If a regional bee is very large, there may be a written round before the oral finals just to winnow the field of contestants down to a number that will fit onstage.

Local and regional bees are usually a lot bigger than a school bee, although they may sometimes be held in a school auditorium. They can be a blast to watch! There are always parents and teachers in the audience, and so there is usually some entertainment. Often, a master of ceremonies gives a funny or interesting presentation before the spelling starts. Sometimes there are free cookies. Soon, though, everyone turns to the matter at hand: determining a champion (or sometimes multiple champions) who will represent the area at a larger bee, perhaps at the National Spelling Bee.

### Top Ten Reasons to Enter a Spelling Bee

10. There's an off-chance they'll make a movie about me.

9. Classrooms that have 100 percent participation get to have pizza parties.

8. Want to impress a geeky heartthrob in chem class.

7. My class will get an extra field trip.

6. Want to humiliate a really annoying classmate.

5. Need the trophy to keep my unmatched socks in.

4. Need a new dictionary.

3. Could use the T-shirt.

2. Will do anything to get out of class for an hour.

1. Mom is making me do it.

# In 1925, the first national champion won $500 in $20 gold pieces.

## Bee There

Most local spelling bees are open to the public. If you want to attend one near your home, contact your area's sponsoring newspaper to find out when and where its local or regional competition takes place. Direct your inquiry to the "spelling bee coordinator."

The National Spelling Bee finals are not open to the public; there simply isn't a room in Washington, D.C., big enough to hold all who would like to attend it. Media representatives need space for their equipment and a clear view of the contestants, and the finalists' families and friends take up the rest of the available seats. But the National Spelling Bee is always televised, so it's available to an audience of millions and is often rebroadcast again and again.

Of course, one of the best ways to see a spelling bee is from the stage—as a participant.

These bees typically have a more experienced pronouncer than school bees do. They also have one or more judges who pay careful attention to each contestant's spelling, determining whether the word has been spelled correctly. The judges also handle formal protests about the fairness of a speller's elimination and may reinstate a speller if they decide that it is the right thing to do, according to the rules of their contest.

The path to the National Spelling Bee is not the same for everyone. Some sponsoring newspapers are small, with a subscriber base that covers only one county, so some spellers win a school bee, then a county spelling title, and go from there straight to the national finals in Washington, D.C. Others must win or be in the top group of finishers in a county bee and then win a regional bee that covers multiple counties or even an entire state. At the national finals, contestants who represent a large area often arrive very well prepared, having competed several times over a few months— but that doesn't guarantee them a spot at the top! A number of national champions have represented small geographical areas.

# History of the National Spelling Bee

T he National Spelling Bee began in 1925 with nine contestants. It was sponsored by the Louisville *Courier-Journal,* which had conducted a statewide match to find the best grade-school spellers in Kentucky, and then decided to extend a challenge to other newspapers to choose their own champions to take part in a spelling showdown in Washington, D.C., to determine a national champion. The *Detroit News,* the *Akron Beacon Journal,* the *South Bend News-Times,* and the *Hartford Times* were also among the sponsors that first year.

In 1941, Scripps Newspapers took over sponsorship of the National Spelling Bee. There was no Scripps National Spelling Bee during the war years of 1943–45.

The first national champion was eleven-year-old Frank Neuhauser of Louisville, Kentucky, who in 1925 correctly spelled *gladiolus* to beat out eight other contestants and win $500 in $20 gold pieces. As national champion, he shook hands with President Calvin Coolidge. He went

# A number of national champions have represented small geographical areas.

## P-H-O-O-E-Y!

Each of the words below was misspelled at the end of a National Spelling Bee, making the difference between first and second place.

apotropaic

cervicorn

chrysanthemum

cortile

crescive

dyscalculia

farrago

geophagy

glitch

morigeration

oligarchy

onomastics

opsimath

parvenuism

philippic

prairillon

ratatouille

resipiscence

Roscian

schwarmerei

senescing

seriatim

sesquipedalian

trouvaille

velleity

virescence

on to study electrical engineering, and later he became a patent attorney. Mr. Neuhauser, who turned 92 in 2006, says that since his triumph he has always grown gladiolus in his garden.

## Hey, Maybe I Could Win!

Whether you're talking about your school bee, a local bee, or the National Spelling Bee finals in Washington, D.C., one thing's for sure—the person who *will* win one day is thinking the same thing right now: "It could be me!" But becoming a spelling champion doesn't mean spending a couple of afternoons with a computer game. It's a major project.

Scratch any spelling bee contestant and you'll find a regular kid, a cool kid—one who loves basketball, plays the trumpet, likes Mexican food, has a Labrador puppy, or dresses as Voldemort or Buffy the Vampire Slayer for Halloween. What do spelling bee winners do that's different from most kids? They read for fun—a lot—and they care about getting words right. Are you up for that?

As you go through this book, you'll likely see many new words. If some of them seem difficult, you're in good company, so don't be intimidated. You can learn them just as you learned the multiplication tables: by memorizing them. But just as math facts are interrelated, so are words, and the more you know about how they're related, the better you'll remember how to spell them. We'll show you how to get more information about the words you study.

If you're ready to become a word whiz, let's get started! First, a few tips: In this book, we sometimes use the term **phoneme,** meaning "the smallest unit of speech that distinguishes one utterance from another," when we discuss the various spellings of a sound. For example, the phoneme /f/ is usually spelled *f* or *ph* at the beginning of a word; but it can sometimes be spelled *gh,* as in *laugh,* at the end of a word. To indicate the **spelling** of example words, we use italic letters: *cat.* To show a **pronunciation** using phonemes, we use forward slashes: /kat/. (The linguist's term for that slash, by the way, is *virgule*—a word whose Latin root means "small rod.") Occasionally, we use quotes to designate

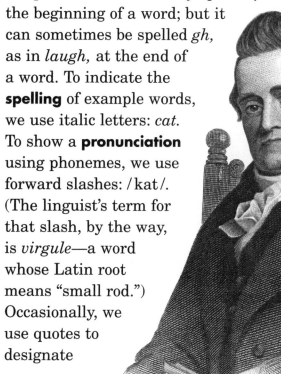

# So What's It Like to Be a Champion?

"**B**eing a spelling champion is a wonderful thing. It gives you two pillars of identity that will last you your whole life. First, you are a speller, a conscientious person who cares about the details, an authority that other people count on and turn to.

66*Fee fi phoneme. Words aren't always spelled like they seem.*99

Second, you are a champion, a hard worker, an ambitious performer who saw a thing through to the end and won the rewards, at whatever level."

—HENRY FELDMAN, *1960 National Spelling Bee champion (winning word: eudaemonic)*

# A Close Call

"I want to tell younger students that they should never give up. The spelling bee has a huge luck factor, and it's very likely that you'll be asked to spell words that you don't know. It's hard work to study for another year, but it's certainly worth it."

KERRY CLOSE,
*2006 National Spelling Bee champion*
(winning word: **Ursprache**)

some sounds, such as "uh" for the **schwa,** for which linguists would use a special symbol, or symbols, instead of English letters. If this sounds confusing now, it should all become clear somewhere around Chapter 3.

The CD that comes with this book takes you on a realistic journey from classroom bee to the National Spelling Bee. Along the way, the pronouncers will pronounce and give information about each word and then give you enough time to spell the word yourself. So when you've finished the book and are feeling good and ready, assemble your audience (dogs and hamsters just love this kind of thing), pop the CD into your player, and get ready to stand up and spell. Good luck!

# CHAPTER 2

# Becoming a Champion

*An investment in knowledge pays the best interest.*
—BENJAMIN FRANKLIN

"Okay, everybody, tomorrow is our classroom spelling bee and the winner will represent us in the school spelling bee next week."

The road that leads to the National Spelling Bee usually starts here, in a classroom bee. If you're reading this book, chances are you've already participated in one.

# Master Little Things, Get Bigger Things Right

"Spelling is terribly important. It is the essence of sincere attention to whatever you are doing. It gives you confidence and gratification to do a simple thing well and know that you got the right outcome. If you master the little things, then you may be able to get the bigger things right, and at the very least you will know that you got the details right repeatedly."

—HENRY FELDMAN,
*1960 National Spelling Bee champion*

*Henry, 1960.*

If you like to read and have already done well on spelling quizzes, you're an excellent candidate for spelling bee success. This chapter is all about increasing your chances of it!

There are two basic strategies for doing well in any spelling bee. First, **be prepared.** Find out exactly when and where your spelling bee will take place and put it on your calendar. Second, **set up your study area and get to work.** Even if your classroom bee is tomorrow, you can still put in some vocabulary study time and improve your chance of winning. Your teacher may decide to use spelling words you've had during the year, so look over your spelling tests and quizzes if you've saved them. Note the words you missed, and make sure you know them cold.

If you can, get a copy of the Scripps National Spelling Bee booklet *Spell It!* Your teacher or your school's spelling bee coordinator should be able to help you, or check the Scripps National Spelling Bee Web site, www.spellingbee.com. The words in this study booklet have been chosen specifically for the classroom and school level, so you will already know many of them. This makes it a great tool for practicing spelling aloud. See if you can get your parents, a sibling, or a friend to read the words for you to spell (bribe them, if you have to—chocolate works well). Maybe you and a friend or two can even set up and act out a mock spelling bee with real words, as you take turns being the pronouncer and making up sentences.

If you're preparing for a school spelling bee and you're already familiar with the words in *Spell It!,* keep studying! Start by carefully reading Chapter 5 in this book. When you look at the examples, try to think of some that aren't already represented. For instance, the rule may be, "Drop the final silent *e* of a word when adding a suffix that begins with a vowel, but keep the *e* if the suffix begins with a consonant." If the example given in the book is *advise / advising / advisement,* come up with a few others such as *leave / leaving / leaves* and *false / falsify / falsehood.*

❝*Keep the* e *when the suffix begins with a consonant!*❞

## The Four Types of Tricky Words

The words that most people misspell generally fall into four categories: exceptions to well-known spelling rules, like **seize;** words with double letters, like **accommodate;** words with silent letters, like **subpoena;** and words containing a schwa (the usually unstressed vowel sound "uh"), like **separate** ("SEP-uh-ruht"). Outside those main categories, a few words, like **fiery,** change the root spelling when a suffix is added; and some words, like **hypocrisy,** are just plain hard!

# You don't want to *memorize* the rules—you want them to become second nature so that you never have to think about them consciously.

**How the Octothorp Got Its "e"**

In 2002, *Webster's Third New International Dictionary* was updated. The only changes—the first since 1993—were in the addenda section, where most of the changes had to do with the addition of new words.

Octothorp, the name for the symbol that is commonly known as the pound sign (check out the bottom right button on your telephone), was updated with a variant spelling. In the 1993 version of the addenda section, the only listing was *octothorp.* Now two spellings are listed: *octothorp* and *octothorpe.*

Admittedly, this part may seem a little dull, but examples reinforce concepts. So come up with the snappiest, most memorable examples you can. If there are particular rules you have a hard time remembering how to apply, you can set yourself the task of writing a silly poem to illustrate a rule:

> The funniest boys have said,
> "Unless you've been dropped on your head,
> A single vowel *y*
> Means change it to *i*
> Before *-est, -ness, -hood, -ly,* or *-ed.*"

This particular ditty will never win any limerick prizes, but it contains the essential information: the rule

(when *y* is the lone vowel at the end of a word, it is changed to *i* before most suffixes); an example *(funny/funniest);* and an opposite example *(boy/boys,* where the *y* is not the only vowel at the end and so remains unchanged).

Of course, the work you do to come up with examples helps consolidate them in your mind. You don't want to *memorize* the rules—*way* too boring! You want them to become second nature so that you never have to think about them con-sciously. If you're already a good speller who has internalized many spelling rules, stretch yourself by finding exceptions to each rule. This is a good way to start studying some of the—drum roll, please—Weird Words in English,

starting of course with the word *weird,* which is an exception to the rule "*i* before *e,* except after *c* or when sounded like *a.*"

Next, read the front section of a city newspaper. Don't just skim it; pay close attention to the words used and to their spellings. Teachers like to keep education relevant to the larger world, so your school bee is very unlikely to be harder than the level of the average newspaper.

**1958** *Winner Jolitta Schlehuber of Topeka, Kansas, (winning word:* **syllepsis***) receives her check.*

## Weird Words

It gets a lot weirder than the rule-breaker word *weird*. What could be odder than a word that seemingly comes from nowhere? The words below have no known origin. Some of them are familiar and some are spelled the way they sound, but others leave you stranded without even a root word to hang on to.

**askarel**
**balderdash**
**bamboozle**
**bumicky**
**curmudgeon**
**flabbergast**
**gremlin**
**gyascutus**
**hobbledehoy**
**huckaback**
**humbug**
**jitney**
**kentledge**
**lobscouse**
**marrowsky**
**mumblebee**
**murre**
**quandary**
**scrivello**
**shenanigan**
**shrivel**
**tantivy**
**wingding**
**yegg**

Hand the newspaper to a friend or parent and ask this person to give you a short spelling quiz from it. Your questioner can select twenty or so words for you to spell aloud. If you haven't done this kind of spelling practice before, welcome to the world of *How to Spell Like a Champ.* Most spelling bee contestants spend part of their study time spelling aloud with another person giving them the words. It's one of the most effective ways to practice, because it gives you a feel for spelling aloud and doesn't allow you to fool yourself about knowing the words. If you can, do this for a few minutes each day before

*1992 Amanda Goad, 13, holds up her trophy after correctly spelling* **lyceum.**

# Try to have a strong mental picture of yourself correctly spelling each word aloud onstage.

the classroom bee. If words from the newspaper are easy for you, you're well on your way. If they're not, you just need to practice, practice, practice! Here's another thing you need to do: Practice!

You should also find a good list of commonly misspelled words (like the handy one in Chapter 5) and try to learn them all. *Doing this may be the smartest move of your entire spelling career.* Many a school spelling bee has hinged on an everyday word like *occurence, embarass,* or *athalete.* These words are in some ways harder to learn and remember than long, seemingly super-tough words—but they're used frequently, so get them right. (Hope you noticed that *occurrence, embarrass,* and *athlete* were misspelled. Just checking to see if you're paying attention!) Years from now, when you're in high school and are looking for jobs and applying to colleges, you'll be glad you studied commonly misspelled words, because misspelling a simple word can be very embarrassing. (People who use computers often spell-check their documents, but not that many spell-check their outgoing e-mail or thank-you notes to college admissions officers!) Ask your parents, teachers, and friends which words have been the hardest for them to learn to spell correctly, and learn those, too.

As you work through all of these steps, always keep a running list of the words you've

## All the News That's Fit to Spell

Here are nineteen school- or local-level spelling words, taken from the front page of *The New York Times* on an average day. Don't peek—just hand the book to someone who will read the words for you to spell. How did you do?

**adamantly**
**anonymity**
**catalytic**
**chaos**
**consolidate**
**cudgel**
**diaspora**
**dominance**
**evacuee**
**incumbent**
**memorandum**
**mosaic**
**ostensibly**
**polygraph**
**scenario**
**submission**
**subsidiary**
**tirade**
**transgressions**

## Bee Seasons

SCHOOL BEES:
**January–February**

LOCAL AND REGIONAL BEES:
**March**

THE SCRIPPS NATIONAL
SPELLING BEE: **late May or
early June**

had the most trouble learning. If you write them down and look at them often enough, you'll find they become the easiest words to remember.

Another strategy for doing well in spelling bees is to *chill.* Just relax. Follow a routine that makes you feel calm. Get a little exercise the day before the bee—play tennis or soccer, ride your bike, take a walk, whatever. Have a nice dinner, then do something fun. It's fine to have one last short study session before bed, but don't stay up late. As you study, try to have a strong mental picture of yourself correctly spelling each word aloud onstage in your school auditorium or wherever the spelling bee is being held. Then set the alarm to get you up with enough time to get ready for school without being rushed.

On the morning of the spelling bee, eat a good breakfast that includes some protein so that your blood sugar doesn't take a big dive after you get to school. If you want to look over your list of tricky words, spend just a little time with it before you leave home. You don't want to drag your list around with you and read it at the last minute before the bee starts; that will just make you feel desperate, not well prepared.

It's a good idea to go to the restroom well before the spelling bee begins so that you don't get rushed and distracted at the last minute. Look at yourself in the restroom mirror and see yourself as a champion! A positive attitude may not ensure spelling bee success, but it beats the effect that a pessimistic attitude can have.

If you've taken the above steps to study for your classroom or school bee, you can feel confident in your preparation. If you are nervous, stretch a little and take some deep breaths before spelling begins. Each time you sail through a word, try to enjoy the process as much as you can. The words may get harder as you go along, but competing will get easier.

## Moving Up the Ladder

If you win your school bee, you will be moving on to a city, county, or regional bee—perhaps all three. Usually, you will have at least a week, perhaps several, between your school bee and the next bee. Put all the details of the next bee—date, time, and place—on your calendar, and get your study tools in order. If you haven't started a spelling notebook yet, this is a good time to do it! See "Organizing a Spelling Notebook" in Chapter 3 for details on organizing and using it.

Decide now how much time you would like to spend preparing for your spelling bee participation.

## A Sort of Mental Scoreboard

"My main way of learning words was just to read as much as I could. I used to read a lot of books from English publishers, and I picked up some relatively obscure words from that. I used to read a lot of history books, too; still do, for that matter. One of the words I got in the national bee was **hussar,** which I had seen in one of the books I got from England. Another word I got in the contest was **chinook,** which I remembered from the salmon-egg bait we used to buy when we went trout fishing in Colorado. I had a mental trick that I used pretty effectively in the contest: Before I tried to spell a word I would visualize it appearing a letter at a time on a sort of mental scoreboard. That helped me avoid hasty mistakes."

—ROBIN KRAL,
*1972 National Spelling Bee champion*
(winning word: **macerate**)

# The Note Card Solution

"My mom prepared note cards for me to review whenever I had a spare moment. I also remember keeping note cards tucked in whatever books I was reading so that I could write down 'good words,' and I still do this!"

—PEG MCCARTHY,
*1978 National Spelling Bee champion*
(winning word:
**deification**)

*Peg, 1978.*

You're representing your school now, not just yourself, so if you don't try, you might disappoint others—especially your teachers, who are probably quite proud of you, as well as the student who would be representing your school if you hadn't participated in the first place. You don't want to have any regrets later about your performance, so determine how much time per day, or over the period of a week, is reasonable for you to dedicate to spelling. You can adjust this goal as your studying progresses. After a week or two, you will know whether you wish to increase or decrease your time. Try your best to stick to your goal until you decide that a different plan will suit you better.

It may seem as though you're giving up a lot for spelling, especially if you have to suspend other activities and turn down party invitations to study, but remember, it's only temporary (and some of those parties probably turned out  to be lame, anyway). School bees typically begin in January; local and regional bees must be completed by the beginning of April. In late May or early June a national champion is crowned.

# Can You Spell *arcuate fasciculus*?

Have you ever been called a "brain" by your friends? If you're a good speller, a better nickname might be "Broca" or "Wernicke." They're the two areas of the brain responsible for language functions, including spelling. Complex brain functions like spelling don't arise in a "center" or single area in the brain; rather, circuits connecting multiple areas of the brain are responsible for most complex behaviors.

When the pronouncer gives a word, the sound waves enter your ears and strike the tympanum (also known as the eardrum). This causes the three small bones of the inner ear to vibrate and pass the vibrations to the cochlea, where the vibrations are converted to bioelectric signals, or nerve impulses, inside the organ of Corti. The impulses travel through the eighth cranial nerve to the primary auditory cortex, then to Wernicke's area, where the word's phonemes and syllabic stresses are recognized. (Wernicke's area also processes written language—but in that case, the information comes from the optic nerve and the primary visual cortex.)

The information then travels along a pathway of nerve fibers, known as the arcuate fasciculus, to Broca's area, which interprets the information and formulates a response. Broca's area transmits a signal to the primary motor cortex, which controls the voluntary muscles, to produce speech (in an oral spelling bee) or writing (in a written bee).

To get the best performance out of your brain during a spelling bee, you need to start well ahead of time with a good diet and plenty of sleep and exercise. On competition day, eat a breakfast with complex carbohydrates (think fruit, oatmeal, or whole grain cereal), which have been shown to aid memory; and protein, which will help keep your blood sugar steady. Once the spelling bee is under way, drink water during the breaks, because your brain needs it to conduct electrical signals. If you get tired, stretch in your seat and take some deep breaths— oxygen is brain food.

# When Do I Eat and Sleep?

There's no question about it: The more study time you put in, the more you will learn, and the better you will do in spelling competition. However, there are definitely trade-offs! If you're studying hard, keeping a spelling notebook, and practicing spelling aloud, sometimes it may seem as though spelling has taken over your life. It's not easy to balance school, extracurricular activities, and practicing for any kind of big contest.

If you have athletics, music lessons, or other activities in addition to classes and homework, you may not have much time to sit down and study words for an uninterrupted period on a daily basis. If so, you'll need to find creative ways to fit numerous small bursts of spelling study into your schedule. Here are a few ideas:

- Have brief daily study sessions during the week, and a longer one (or two) on weekends.

- Keep a study list in your pocket or backpack that you can pull out and go over when you're waiting somewhere. Make sure you update this list frequently, so that you're not studying the same words over and over.

# Most spelling bee contestants spend part of their study time spelling aloud with another person giving them the words.

- Ask friends and neighbors to try a new word on you every time they see you and to keep track of the ones you miss so that they can ask you again. This is good practice for spelling words that come out of the blue!

- Ask teachers if you may study your word list quietly when you've finished your class work. They may be willing to let you, especially if you ask them to give you a list of good spelling words that pertain to their subject.

- Tape a short list of practice words to the bathroom mirror and go over it while you're brushing your teeth. Change this list every day. You might want to use this brief time to study a group of words that share a common root or affix or that have the same language of origin.

- If you have a computer, see if you can find a screensaver that will let you enter words that will scroll across your screen when your computer is idle. Enter a new set of "problem" words every couple of days. The more you see the correct spelling of these words, even when you aren't consciously thinking about them, the more they will become fixed in your memory.

# "This One Trivial Thing"

"My dad gave me some advice I will never forget. He first explained to me how proud he was of my achievements already. Then he said, 'You have to realize, Wendy, how much *chance* plays in the bee. You may know every other word in your round, but if you don't know the next one on the word list, you will be doomed. You are no less of a person, or a speller for that matter, for not knowing that one word. You have to think beyond this one trivial thing. What you have *learned* is most important. *That* is the ultimate measurement of whether you have truly won.'"

—Wendy Guey,
*1996 National
Spelling Bee champion*
(winning word:
**vivisepulture**)

Guess what? Your parents have been telling the truth all along. It turns out it really *is* important to eat well and get enough sleep. British studies have shown that teenagers who eat sugary foods in the morning perform like an average seventy-year-old on tests of memory and attention. Using the spelling bee as an excuse to grab dough-nuts instead of eating a real breakfast will backfire! And scientists at Harvard University and elsewhere have made a very interesting discovery: A good night's

sleep on the night after you've learned some-thing new will help you store that information in long-term memory; otherwise, the material may simply pass out of the brain. For your studying to pay off, you need to hit the hay on time every night. Making up for lost sleep on subsequent nights doesn't work, so don't try to pull all-nighters, even occasionally. Good habits are worth the time you put into them. It's hard enough winning spelling bees *without* having the brain of a seventy-year-old.

# CHAPTER 3

# Becoming More Serious

If you're just looking for tips on winning a school bee, and even thinking about the National Spelling Bee makes you nervous—skip this section! Do not under any circumstances read this! Are you reading this? No? Good. We wouldn't want to scare you off. But we have some great study tips for kids who are shooting for the stars.

Once upon a time, excellent spellers stood a reasonably good chance of making it to the national finals in their first year of competition. Well, that was then and this is now. Spelling itself may not have changed in the last few decades, but many other things have. Bigger prizes, more publicity, and a bit of Hollywood glamour have conspired to make spelling a very hot academic activity right now. There's tougher competition than ever before, so if you want to go to the National Spelling Bee, you need to start preparing as early as possible. It's increasingly common not only for national finalists to have competed in the national bee more than once (though a few newspaper sponsors have an eligibility rule limiting a speller to one trip to the nationals), but also for them to have competed at the local level for two years or more before they won a regional bee. You need to set goals that are both ambitious and realistic to keep progressing happily in your spelling career.

# Dictionaries

Let's get one thing straight: You're not getting to the finals without a dictionary. It's the one study tool you absolutely must

# Words in the addenda section of *Webster's Third* are frequently found on National Spelling Bee word lists. A word to the wise is sufficient.

have to advance beyond your school bee. You can find great study words in many places, but if you cannot look them up, you will learn nothing except how to spell them. The more you *know* about the words you study, the better you will remember them. If you don't have access to a dictionary at home, you may want to do your word study at the library.

If you are very serious about spelling bee competition, you may want to buy a new dictionary. In any case, you should know that the Scripps National Spelling Bee uses the most recent edition of *Webster's Third New International Dictionary of the English Language, Unabridged,* and its addenda section as the authority for the spelling of words. **Words not listed in this dictionary and its addenda will not appear on any word list used in Scripps National Spelling**

Words in the addenda section of *Webster's Third* are frequently found on National Spelling Bee word lists. A word to the wise is sufficient.

**❝*It's my* Third New International Dictionary, Unabridged, *or nothing.*❞**

## Waiting for Webster's Fourth

**W**ebster's Third New International Dictionary is a descriptive dictionary. Spellings listed in Webster's Third describe what is most often seen in print as a correct spelling. When the editors of Webster's Third updated the addenda section, they had seen enough examples of **octothorpe** in print to decide that the spelling of this word was just as acceptable as **octothorp.** Thus a variant spelling was added.

Bottom line: Be sure you're using the most recent version of Webster's Third New International Dictionary as you prepare.

Note of interest: The editors at Merriam-Webster are currently working on Webster's Fourth New International Dictionary. Changes will not be limited to the addenda section. When this dictionary becomes available (no date has been set), it will be the official dictionary of the Scripps National Spelling Bee.

**Bee competition.** You can certainly use another dictionary to study, because there is a great deal of overlap between dictionaries; but there will be some words in other dictionaries that are either not in Webster's Third or are listed with alternate spellings. Similarly, there are words in Webster's Third that do not appear in other dictionaries, particularly abridged dictionaries. Therefore, there will almost certainly be gaps in your preparation for advanced spelling bee competition if you do not have access to Webster's Third.

An excellent option for computer users is Webster's Third on CD-ROM. Using an electronic dictionary for your word study has some outstanding advantages. You can search the Webster's Third CD-ROM according to any of thirteen different criteria, either alone or in combination. For example, you can find words that entered English from Portuguese or narrow your search down to just adjectives that entered English from Portuguese. This will help you understand Portuguese spelling patterns. Another possibility is to find all words that contain a particular root or suffix. This flexibility has a huge impact on the way you study. When you find a word you don't know, it's easy to look up words that are related to it. When you see words presented in related groups, it's much easier to remember their meanings and spellings.

All national finalists receive a copy of *Webster's Third* before the finals in Washington, D.C., but if becoming a national finalist is your goal, start using this dictionary much earlier. By the time you become a national finalist and win a copy, the finals will be just around the corner. If you become the happy owner of a duplicate copy, you can always donate it to a friend, another speller, or your school library—or just keep an extra dictionary in the den or kitchen of your home. You never know where you'll be when the urge to look up a word strikes.

*Applauding the winners at a statewide Illinois "fingerspelling bee" for deaf students.*

# Read, read, read. Any magazine, book, or newspaper you pick up may contain your next spelling bee word.

Copies of *Webster's Third,* in hardcover and on CD-ROM, can usually be found at online bookstores or large chain bookstores for a discounted price. The Scripps National Spelling Bee will always take its words from the most recent edition, so check to be sure that the one you're getting is the "latest and greatest."

## Other Useful Tools

If you have a computer and use e-mail, get your parents' permission to sign up for a few free "word of the day" services. There are a number of good ones. You can subscribe to Merriam-Webster's Word of the Day at www.m-w.com. (In fact, you'll want to look this site over care-

**1926** *President Coolidge welcomes a group of school children who took part in the second National Spelling Bee. The winner was Pauline Bell of Louisville, Kentucky, who correctly spelled the word* **abrogate,** *winning two gold medals and $1,000.*

fully; it also has free crosswords and other vocabulary-building games. Merriam-Webster has a language arts site for students at www.wordcentral.com.) These services can be great vocabulary builders because they almost always offer some memorable pieces of information about the words.

Check with your school's spelling bee coordinator, who may have other materials that could help you, such as notes or word lists from previous local or regional bees. And remember: What goes around comes around. As you progress in spelling, it's a nice gesture to give a copy of any word lists you collect to the coordinator. The next student to represent your school in spelling bees will be very grateful.

Finally, the best thing you can do to hone your spelling is to read, read, read. Every magazine, book, or newspaper you pick up may contain your next spelling bee word.

## Organizing a Spelling Notebook

What kind of organizer are you? Do you enjoy putting together binders with colored divider tabs, colored paper, and colored labels down the spine? Or do you prefer creating and labeling nested folders on your computer and making a shortcut to them on

## Ibuprofen and Sousaphones

"Studying is important, but sometimes paying attention to the words in the world around you can help you just as much. For example, I knew how to spell **sousaphone** because I was in band and I knew about the instrument's connection to John Philip Sousa. I knew how to spell **ibuprofen** because I paid attention to commercials for cold medicine. I knew how to spell **kaolinic** because I had heard about how kaolin was used to make clay pipes when my parents took me on a trip to Busch Gardens and Colonial Williamsburg."

—JON PENNINGTON,
*1986 National Spelling Bee champion*
(winning word: **odontalgia**)

# Bee Lucky

"I'd advise kids who want to win to study all they can, to learn root words and word origins, and to practice guessing at words they don't know. I'd also advise them to be happy with however the results come out—there is an element of luck in winning spelling bees!"

—STEPHANIE PETIT,
*1987 National Spelling Bee champion*
(winning word:
**staphylococci**)

the computer desktop? Think hard about what comes naturally to you. If you're going to study seriously for a spelling bee, you may want to put together a spelling notebook—either a physical or a virtual one—and your system should reflect the way *you* learn best.

If you are a visual learner, you'll generally remember words you've seen once. (If you're very visual, you may have a photographic memory. You may even remember what page a word was on in a book you've read or where the word fell on the page!) In fact, you might find that all you need to study effectively is as many word lists as you can get and a partner to quiz you on them. Still, no one's perfect, and you'll want to keep track of any words you have trouble with so that you can review them a couple of times. The act of typing them into a file or writing them in a spiral-bound notebook once or a few times may be all you need to fix them in your memory.

Most people, however, don't have photographic memories, and a carefully planned notebook system can help them learn words much more efficiently than going over and over lists of words at random. Remember: The faster you

# Organization is a process, not a single act.

can learn words, the more words you can learn.

Don't worry if at first it seems like you're spending a lot of time organizing. As you study, the plan that suits you best will unfold. Organization is a process, not a single act. The advantage of setting up this kind of coordinated study is that having done it once for spelling, you'll know what works for you, and you'll be able to do it in the future for any other subject you decide you want to master.

There's an art to note-taking for your spelling notebook. When you take notes for school subjects, you probably start at the top of the page and keep taking notes until the class is over. The next time you take notes in that class, you probably just start where you left off and write some more. But you will learn more from your spelling note-taking if you designate areas in which to put different types of infor-mation, so that you can look them up easily later. If you like binders for organizing, use one that allows you to move pages and add paper. (You'll appreciate this flexibility if you decide halfway through your studying to change your organization scheme.) To start out, you might like to have one large binder and use dividers for each category of information. As your

**Letter Perfect**

D id you ever realize that the consonants of the alphabet have names that can be spelled?

**bee**
**cee**
**dee**
**ef**
**gee**
**aitch**
**jay**
**kay (also ka)**
**el**
**em**
**en**
**pee**
**cue**
**ar**
**ess (or es)**
**tee**
**vee**
**double-u (or double-you)**
**ex**
**wye (or wy)**
**zee**

spelling notebook grows, you might move it to several smaller binders, one for each category or group of categories.

If you have access to a computer at home and do most of your studying when a keyboard is within reach, you can take notes electronically. Assign a folder on the computer for each category or chapter of your notebook. When the occasion to take a note arises, you can click on the chapter to which you would like to add information. Or, if necessary, you can quickly create a new chapter for the note at hand. This electronic note-taking method saves space and might save time. It also allows for fast searching and instant alphabetization of words within a chapter.

*Mathew L. Roca, below right, lines up with 79 other New York City elementary school spelling bee contestants, in the final round of the 41st Annual* Daily News *New York Citywide Spelling Bee.*

The point is not necessarily to enter every word you study into the notebook. Rather, it's to record words that interest you, either because you find them difficult or because something about them strikes you as an interesting pattern. Initially, you will probably make lists of individual words that give you problems. As you begin to learn more about the composition of words, you may want to make lists of spelling rules and exceptions, root words and their derivatives, words that came to English from particular languages, and so forth. You can probably come up with more categories of your own. (Throw in some fun ones—"NBA Words," "Words from TV," "Palindromes," or words from your favorite series of books.) And you may want to add the same words to multiple categories—for example, *vinaigrette* might go into three categories: "French Words," "Food Words," and "Words Ending in *-et*/*-ette*."

When you are reading books, magazines, and newspapers for pleasure, you will frequently run across new words that fit into one of your categories or perhaps give you an idea for a new category for your notebook system. Carry a little notebook with you or keep some scratch

## Music
### LEVEL: Intermediate

adagio
allargando
allemande
animato
arabesque
Brahmsian
brillante
cadenza
clavier
coloratura
conjunto
doloroso
duple
flamenco
Handelian
libretto
ligature
mariachi
melomania
musicale
pastiche
polska
preludio
psalmist
reprise
schmaltz
sinistra
skirl
staccato
strophic
syncopate
tardo
tremolo
xylophone

# Finding Your Rhythm

"I tried a lot of different spelling speeds the first couple of years I competed—spelling slowly, spelling fast, spelling three letters at a time. I finally realized that when spelling aloud, I mentally 'see' the word on a blank page; it's as though I'm just reading off the letters. Once I knew that, I was able to settle into a natural rhythm when spelling. It's important to find your own rhythm and practice it consciously when you study, to help you retain the word. If you spell a word in competition with the same rhythm you use to successfully spell it in a practice session, it's hard to go wrong."

—BARRIE TRINKLE,
*1973 National Spelling Bee champion*
(winning word: **vouchsafe**)

paper handy [if you're not one of those kids who has a personal digital assistant (PDA) on hand at all times]; you can transfer the words to your notebook or computer later. You can use a cell phone or cell-phone camera to quickly store the spelling of an interesting word to add to your computer notebook later. You can also buy a miniature recorder just for this purpose at very low cost.

Here's a set of examples—one possible organization for your study notebook. Many of these grouping and category suggestions came from recent spelling bee contestants, but you'll certainly come up with more categories on your own, based on your personal interests and what kinds of words you find challenging.

Suffixes

words ending in *-ar/-er/-or*
words ending in *-ary/-ery/-ory*
words ending in *-ance/-ence* and *-ant/-ent*
words ending in *-yze/-ize/-ise*
words ending in *-gue/-g*
words ending in *-ean/-ian*
words ending in *-ese/-ise*
words ending in *-eous/-ious*
words ending in *-able/-ible*

## s Two

end avoiding
of memorizing
ts and asking
test you on the
e memorized.
y spelling bee
sk someone to
rds of *their*
ords that you
ven't studied. In
s you have to
of the officials'
ot your own, so
actice for that
on a regular
with the
l in time you
confidence.
ake you a better
those uncom-
ments in
n when you're
ell an unfamiliar

GE PIPKIN KIMBLE,
*National Spelling
Bee champion and
t Scripps National
elling Bee director*
(winning word:
**sarcophagus**)

words of unknown origin *(bamboozle,
bungee, quandary)*
words with an imitative origin *(froufrou,
hooroosh, kyoodle, whippoorwill)*

### Meaning

words from classical mythology and history
*(auroral, hector, iridescent, pegasus)*
words for different breeds of dogs
*(weimaraner, schnauzer, Chihuahua)*
words about games and sports *(badminton,
croquet, kibitzer, mancala, pinochle)*
food words [try organizing these under
various subcategories, such as vegetables
*(cassava, rutabaga, asparagus)*; cheeses
*(Gorgonzola, provolone, Wensleydale)*;
pasta shapes *(capellini, fusilli, tagliatelle)*;
beverages *(orangeade, mocha,
sarsaparilla)*; desserts *(ambrosia,
pandowdy, cannoli)*]

G-O-R-G-O-N

## Prefixes

words beginning with *dis-/dys-*
words beginning with *pari-/peri-*

## Languages

words from African languages *(tsetse, safari)*

words from French *(armoire, avalanche, bombardier)*

words with French suffixes *(-ure, -eur, -oir, -aise, -erie, -et/-ette)*

words from Japanese *(pachinko, tatami, sayonara)*

words from Portuguese *(sargasso, ipecac, mandarin)*

words from Spanish *(simpatico, hacienda, matador)*

**It Tak**

" I recomn
the rut
word li
someone to
words you'
Instead, pl:
every day..
give you w
choosing, '
possibly ha
spelling be
spell word:
choosing, i
why not pr
experience
basis? Stic
method an
will devel
That will i
thinker fo
fortable m
competiti
asked to s
word."

—P
198

curre
S

music words *(pizzicato, schottische, mariachi)*

words for flowers and plants *(geranium, epiphyte, bromeliad)*

words for dinosaurs *(ankylosaur, diplodocus, deinonychus)*

scientific words *(aerolithology, hydraulics, rhinolaryngology)*

words for occupations and careers *(magistrate, phlebotomist, amanuensis)*

geographical terms *(orography, guyot, estuary)*

names of diseases *(malaria, diphtheria, trichinosis)*

anatomy words *(viscera, pituitary, eustachian)*

*Bee nice.*

# Life Lessons

"In the months following my win, I learned many 'life skills': how to conduct myself in the public eye, how to interact with the media, and how to take compliment after compliment. But as much as I learned in those months, I learned even more from my two trips to the Comfort Room. Life is not holding the trophy aloft for a fleeting moment. Life is the Comfort Room and what surrounds it. You give it your best shot, you pause briefly to gather your strength, and you come back and try to do better than you did the time before. And no matter how well you do, there will always be someone better than you."

—NED ANDREWS,
*1994 National Spelling Bee champion*
(winning word:
**antediluvian**)

commonly confused homonyms *(stationary / stationery, complement / compliment)*

words with silent first letters *(ptarmigan, mnemonic, gnathic, knickerbocker)*

words that are often mispronounced *(mischievous, nuclear, pronunciation)*

capitalized words *(Armageddon, Britishism, Rubicon)*

interesting words from Shakespeare *(dastard, argosy, demesne)*

portmanteau words *(avionics, biodiversity, stagflation)*

eponyms *(begonia, nicotine, poinsettia)*

words that are illustrated in *Webster's Third*

words with double *i* *(foliiform, incurvariid, biischial)*

words with *oe* and *ae* combinations *(Croesus, chaeta)*

words with double *u* *(vacuum, continuum, duumvirate)*

exceptions to the "*i* before *e*" rule *(Anaheim, foreign, height, seismic, weird)*

verbs that end in *c* and add a *k* before *-ing* and *-ed* *(picnic, panic, bivouac)*

words with troublesome double letters *(aardvark, millennium)*

# Turn off the iPod and the phone, and disable Instant Messaging.

nouns that end in a vowel and *k (anorak, batik)* or a vowel and *c (ipecac, havoc)*

words whose root spelling changes when you add an affix *(pollen / pollinate)*

short but difficult words of three, four, and five letters *(aitch, mho, bloc)*

## The $64,000 Interrogatory

How long do serious spellers study every day? That's the $64,000 question. Well, it varies greatly. To study for a school bee, a speller might look over word lists for fifteen or twenty minutes per night for a week. Spellers who really want to win their local or regional bee often study at least an hour or two per day as their qualifying bees approach. Even more serious spellers who are heading for the National Spelling Bee may spend a month or more studying as much as four to six hours per day. Some feel they will learn the most if they

## Mail Order Words

If you know someone who is on mailing lists for catalogs, ask if you can have the catalogs after they've been read. Catalogs can be a gold mine of good spelling bee words.

Take **Limoges,** a 1998 National Spelling Bee word that appeared near the very end of the competition. Miniature hinged Limoges boxes made of porcelain, and relatively inexpensive takeoffs on the genuine, appear in many catalogs.

Item descriptions in catalogs can provide you many new words to study. Grab a stack of catalogs and start making a list of all the words you think would be good spelling bee words. Before you add them to your spelling notebook, though, look up each word in *Webster's Third*. Make sure that there is an entry for the word and that the word and its spelling meet the criteria listed in the National Spelling Bee rules.

# Portmanteau Math: Chuckle + Snort = Chortle

## Portmanteau Words

**P**ortmanteau is a fancy word for *suitcase*. It was originally French, and came from two words that meant "to carry" and "mantle" (a mantle is a large cloak)—much like *suitcase,* which is a case for a suit! The phrase *portmanteau word* means "a word composed of [1] parts of two words (as *chortle* from *chuckle* and *snort*), [2] all of one word and part of another (as *bookmobile* from *book* and *automobile*), or [3] two entire words, and characterized—invariably in the latter case and frequently in the two former cases—by single occurrence of one or more sounds or letters that appear in both the component words (as *motel* from *motor hotel,* *camporee* from *camp* and *jamboree, aniseed* from *anise seed*)." Have you noticed an interesting fact about *portmanteau*? It and its synonym *suitcase* are both portmanteau words!

spread their studying throughout the year; others like to start just before the school bee and work intensely for a few months.

However you decide to study spelling, you will learn better if you follow some common-sense study policies. First, do your formal studying in a quiet place where you won't be distracted. Turn off the iPod and the phone, and disable Instant Messaging (IM). Listening to music and trying to ignore IMs while you're concentrating on words is too much multitasking for your Broca's and Wernicke's areas.

You may want to break your studying into short sessions and do two of them per day. Or, if you have a number of brief times during the day when you look at a list of words—say at the breakfast table or on the bus—you may find it's enough to have just one formal sit-down study session per day. You should have at least one, though, so that you can take stock of what you've done and what you need to study next. It's hard to do that on the fly.

And don't forget to give yourself occasional rewards for a good study session. It'll keep you fresh and make you want to keep working. If it doesn't come naturally to you, you might even keep a list of fun things to do for ten minutes, such as a major IM session, returning a friend's phone call, playing with a pet, listening to a couple of favorite songs, or playing a game of solitaire—whatever floats your boat. Take a break to do one of these when you sense that you are getting tired. It will help you return energized to your studying for just a little longer.

# Getting Extra Help

If you have set your goals high, there may come a time when you feel you have done as much as you can on your own and would like access to an outside "word expert" to help you tackle learning a huge number of words in a logical way. There are several ways to go about this. First, though, talk to your parents and teachers and let them know how serious you are about spelling study and that you feel you need extra help to progress. Perhaps they can help you design a more ambitious and challenging study program and coach you themselves. If no one feels prepared to take on the role of spelling coach, someone may know another teacher, a local college professor, or a graduate student in English or linguistics who would be willing to coach you one or more times per week, either out of the goodness of his or her heart or at a price you and your family can afford.

**Food and Cooking**

**LEVEL: Intermediate**

adobo
antipasto
arugula
biscuit
brochette
calamari
carbonara
chimichanga
colcannon
collation
dashi
delicatessen
flummery
hibachi
hollandaise
kugel
mousse
napoleon
paprika
piccata
pistachio
porringer
preprandial
provender
samosa
seder
spaghetti
stroganoff
succotash
tahini
wasabi
zucchini

# When in Doubt, Envision It Out

"I did run into several words I had not studied or seen before the bees in which I participated. After many years of thinking about rules for spelling, I know a few, but at that time I used mostly intuition: I formed a mental picture of how I thought the word was spelled, a sort of theory or 'best guess,' and then spelled it. That's not blind luck, because I had pumped my brain full of words, and my brain unconsciously recognized patterns."

—JACQUES BAILLY,
*1980 National
Spelling Bee champion
(winning word:
elucubrate)*

If you feel you need a boost, but still want to work on your own, you may want to purchase spelling bee software or access to an interactive Web site. There is no need to spend a lot of money on spelling bee preparation unless you wish to do so—many people think you'll learn and retain more if you use your own practice methods, develop your own study lists, and spend your money on reference books you can use in school and at work for years to come— but there are some commercial spelling bee preparation products available, and one of them may be a very effective tool for you. Do an online search for "spelling bee software" and see what you find. Many of the spelling-tutor or "learn to spell" programs that you will see listed will be too elementary for your purposes, so be careful to check that what you are buying is for advanced spelling bee preparation.

Before you buy any program or Web site access, determine whether or not the software will run on your computer and that it is easy to  use. Search for user reviews of the software (not just on the company's Web site) to see how other spellers rate the product. To do your research thoroughly, go to the company's Web site and call the telephone number listed at the

"Contact Us" link. Ask the contact person at the company how long the software or Web site has been available and what evidence he or she can provide of customer success and satisfaction. Make sure you will get good value for the money you spend.

*V-I-S-U-A-L-I-Z-E.*

## Study Tools

### The Scripps National Spelling Bee Web site

If you have access to a computer, go to www.spellingbee.com, the official Web site of the National Spelling Bee, and start clicking. When you find out how great this site is for word study, you might even want to make it your home page. Carolyn's Corner includes tips

## Read. Rinse. Repeat.

Good readers make good spellers, and one of the hallmarks of good readers is that they would rather be reading than not. When they're in the shower and there's nothing else available, they'll read the shampoo bottle. So read the ingredients of everything, because it sometimes pays off! Here are a few words that have gone straight from product packaging to the finals of the Scripps National Spelling Bee:

| | | | |
|---|---|---|---|
| alkaline | emollient | lavender | quassia |
| antihistamine | enzyme | linseed | serum |
| arnica | eucalyptus | marjoram | silica |
| betony | exfoliative | marshmallow | surfactant |
| borage | glyceride | myrrh | verbena |
| chrysanthemum | henna | naphtha | wasabi |
| citronella | hibiscus | petroleum | whorlywort |
| desiccant | juniper | potassium | yarrow |
| echinacea | laurel | pyrethrum | yucca |

that are frequently updated from September to May. Some of the words discussed there are difficult, but the discussions are easy to understand. There are many advanced spelling tips for spellers who have won school and local bees and are moving on to regional and national finals.

The "Study Resources" link on the www.spellingbee.com home page leads to two of the best free tools at your disposal:

- **Merriam-Webster's *A Dictionary of Prefixes, Suffixes, and Combining Forms.*** This is a sixty-two-page PDF file that shows information for most of the prefixes, suffixes, and combining forms in the Scripps National Spelling Bee's official dictionary, *Webster's Third New*

*International Dictionary, Unabridged.*
If you watch the National Spelling Bee
on television, you can always tell which
spellers have used this—they're the
ones who ask ques-
tions like, "Does this
word contain the
Latin combining
form *pari-,* meaning
'equal'?" If you want
to be well prepared
for difficult words,
this is the way to go.

- **Consolidated Word List.**
  This is a compilation of more than one
  hundred Scripps National Spelling Bee
  word lists dating as far back as 1950.
  There are more than 20,000 words
  listed, with parts of speech, language
  origins, pronunciations, definitions,
  and sentences provided for more than
  half of them. Many of the words at
  local and regional spelling bees, as well
  as at the National Spelling Bee, appear
  on this list. It is shown as a series of
  PDF files.

If you're serious about progressing to the
National Spelling Bee finals in Washington,
D.C., you should study these two documents
thoroughly. It's handier to study them on the
computer than on a printout, because they are
automatically searchable. If you don't have a
computer to use at home, you can ask a teacher,

## Spell for Love

"I see that kids who have
done well in the past
relish the words they are
learning about. As athletes
are told to 'play for love of
the game,' I tell spellers to
'spell for the love of words.'
Find someone who will be
able to ask you lists of words
and work with this person
consistently. My mother was
my coach. A teacher or a
close friend helped as
well. Make sure you use
*Webster's Third.* Above all,
believe that you can win. I
was a supposed 'underdog,'
having ranked 81st in my
previous year of competition.
It's all about attitude!"

—Nupur Lala,
*1999 National Spelling
Bee champion*
(winning word: **logorrhea**)

## The Human Body

adductor
anthropometry
auricle
auriform
carcinoma
chromosomal
cilium
clavicle
cochlea
corpuscle
cutaneous
enteritis
febrile
fibrillation
ganglion
humerus
larynx
lumbago
lymph
palate
pancreatic
paralysis
patella
pericardial
peristalsis
physique
podology
pulmonary
tibia
trachea
tricuspid
venous
ventricle

principal, or librarian for extended study time on a school or library computer.

## Old Spelling Bee Lists and Study Booklets

Some of the best study tools are lists from earlier spelling bees and old National Spelling Bee study booklets. Over the years, the Scripps National Spelling Bee has produced several series of spelling study booklets. The first, *Words of the Champions,* was used until 1995. Words in *Words of the Champions* were grouped in three categories according to difficulty, and within each category, words were listed in alphabetical order. This booklet was replaced in 1995 by *Paideia,* in which words were categorized according to theme and grouped according to difficulty. If you have older siblings who studied for the spelling bee, you've probably seen a copy of *Paideia,* which contained about 4,000 words. It was discontinued in 2006; and the new study booklet, *Spell It!,* took its place.

The older study booklets are very useful, especially when you are competing at a high level. It is worth trying to borrow these from older students who may have used them in previous years. They may also be cataloged in your school library, so check with your librarian. Occasionally, they are even sold on eBay!

Some of the best advice always comes from someone who's been where you want to be. Scattered throughout this book are forty-five years worth of great spelling and life wisdom from some finalists and national champions.

CHAPTER 4

# Roots, Branches, Trees, and Forest

How many languages do you think are spoken in the world today—100, 500, 1,000? Try **6,912**—from Aari, a language of southern Ethiopia, to Zyphe, spoken in Myanmar. Two-thirds of them have no written representation and thus no spelling, but that hasn't stopped the English language from spending the last fifteen centuries borrowing words from around the world.

# Roots and Branches

If we imagine the world's languages as a great forest, one of the biggest trees in it would be the Indo-European family of languages, which includes English and most other modern European languages. The tree's trunk is a proto–Indo-European language spoken many thousands of years ago, around 5000 B.C.—long before recorded history. From that ancient tongue grew the Romance languages, such as French, Spanish, and Portuguese; the Germanic languages, including English; the Indo-Iranian languages, such as Sanskrit, Urdu, and Farsi; the Balto-Slavic languages, such as Russian, Polish, and Czech; the Celtic languages, such as Welsh, Breton, and Irish Gaelic; the Hellenic language, which became modern Greek; Albanian; Armenian; and a few other now extinct language groups, such as Anatolian, Thracian, and Illyrian. The Germanic, Romance, and Hellenic branches have contributed heavily to modern English.

The Germanic branch began as a common language about 3,000 years ago. After a thousand years, that language split into several subgroups: East Germanic, North Germanic, and West Germanic. No remnant of East Germanic remains today, but North Germanic is the ancestor of the

# What Are "Roots" and How Do You Study Them?

For our purposes, the word *root* has two meanings. It is the English base word from which we derive new words by adding prefixes, suffixes, or inflectional endings or substitutions—like the verb *tell,* which becomes *tells, telling,* and *told,* as well as *retell.* (Inflectional endings or substitutions are the letters you use to change the form of a part of speech, as when making a noun plural or conjugating a verb.)

More important to competitive spellers, the word *root* can also mean an element that is common to all the words of a group, such as *-gnostic* in *gnostic, agnostic,* and *diagnostic.* It may be all or most of what we call a "combining form," which is a word or part of a word borrowed from another language that helps us form new words in English. In the example above, *-gnostic* is a combining form that comes from Greek and means "knowing" or "characterized by knowledge." Few English words come from unique forms, unrelated to any other English word— most are derived from combining forms that are common to many words. That's why they're important to study.

Think of it this way: If spelling bees were adventure video games, combining forms would be the keys that would unlock the doors to the mystery words and get you closer to the trophy.

The National Spelling Bee worked with Merriam-Webster to create an excellent free resource, *A Dictionary of Prefixes, Suffixes, and Combining Forms.* It is posted as a PDF file on the National Spelling Bee Web site, www.spellingbee.com. The entries in this dictionary have been taken from *Webster's Third New International Dictionary* and put into a much easier form to help you study. It's probably the best freebie you'll run across in your quest for spelling excellence.

**A.D. 476 The Roman Empire falls; Jutes, Angles, and Saxons take over what is now Great Britain and bring their Germanic language along, crowding the Celtic languages into the corners of the British Isles.**

**596 St. Augustine brings Christianity to England and with it many words from Latin.**

**800–1000 Vikings whittle away Anglo-Saxon strongholds in Angleland (England) and eventually establish a kingdom and an influence on the language.**

*Viking ships brought a whole new set of words to the English language.*

modern Scandinavian languages of Danish, Norwegian, Swedish, and Icelandic. West Germanic eventually became modern German, Dutch, Flemish, Frisian (English's closest living relative), and English.

# The Queen's English (and How We Colonials "Improved" It)

The phrases "the Queen's English" and "the King's English" arose in the sixteenth century with the idea that the monarch's use of written and spoken English should be a model for the language of the commoners. With the birth of the printing press, literacy was on the rise; suddenly it was conceivable that a merchant—or even a servant—could read and speak English as well as the king.

Jolly good, but at the same time, adventuresome Europeans were beginning to show an interest in the New World. As the English populated the American colonies, they adopted many native American and New World Spanish words for things that had been unknown in Europe, such as *tobacco, potato, muskrat, toboggan,* and *hammock.* Even the vocabulary of the upper-class colonists—the ones who were able to speak as well as the king—was changing, becoming quite different from that used in the mother-land. It was becoming distinctly "American."

By 1783, American English had been thriving and changing for more than 150 years, a fact that did not escape Noah Webster, a Yale-educated schoolmaster from a middle-class family. Webster disliked the fact that the schoolbooks he used for teaching were published in England. He believed that American children should learn to read, write, and spell from American books—and not have to go around saying "Cheerio" all the time—so he decided to publish a new series of textbooks. In 1783, Webster's *A Grammatical Institute of the English Language,* more popularly known as the *Blue-Backed Speller,* was published. It was an immediate success and has never been out of print since! (Go ahead and look it up

**1066** The Norman Conquest of England makes Norman French popular among the English upper class.

**1337–1453** The Hundred Years' War between England and France precipitates the decline of French influence in England.

**1348–49** The Black Plague kills more than 30 percent of England's population; the surviving members of the working class are in such demand that, within a few years, their wages rise sharply, giving them greater power, and their language—English—even more influence.

**"***In my salad days, I added 1,700 words and phrases to the English language.***"**

**1362** First official recognition of English is enacted in Parliament.

**1474** William Caxton produces the first book printed in English, *The Recuyell of the Historyes of Troye.*

# Webster was a radical believer in simplified spelling: He argued for the omission of all silent letters.

**1564–1616** Shakespeare adds more than 1,700 popular words and phrases to the English language during his lifetime (like *bump, frugal, monumental, salad days,* and *too much of a good thing*) by reviving old words, making nouns from verbs, putting two words together to make a new word, and creating English words from Greek and Latin roots.

**1611** The King James Bible—the classic example of early modern English—is published.

**1755** Samuel Johnson (above) publishes his popular *Dictionary of the English Language* in London.

**1806** Noah Webster publishes the first American dictionary, followed in 1828 by an even bigger one.

online—it's available at many bookstores.) By the mid-1800s, it was selling a million copies per year and came in handy for those newfangled contests—called "spelling bees"—that more and more Americans seemed to enjoy.

But Noah Webster knew that American English lacked standard pronunciations and spellings, so he began to develop the first comprehensive American dictionary. Webster was a radical believer in simplified spelling: He argued for the omission of all silent letters. He didn't manage to popularize that idea, but he did establish what we now think of as American spelling—*color* instead of *colour, music* instead of *musick,* and so forth. He also brought the words that everyday Americans used for their tools, food, geography, and indigenous plants and animals firmly into the English language at last. Webster's magnum opus, *An American Dictionary of the English Language,* was published in 1828.

What would Noah Webster make of the language we speak and write today? Can you imagine what he would think of the following paragraph from a newspaper story?

Meanwhile, the space-junk problem is getting worse as the terrestrial world becomes more and more reliant on the sky: We increasingly depend on satellites for duties as diverse as cell-phone calls, TV broadcasting, military reconnaissance and guided hikes by global positioning systems. Satellites are used to track robotic minisubs in Antarctica and animals in the wild.

—Keay Davidson, "Space: The Final Junkyard," *San Francisco Chronicle*, March 12, 2006

Satellites, cell phones, broadcasting, robots, submarines, and global positioning systems were not only unknown in 1828, but didn't even exist until well into the twentieth century—and only a very small part of the Antarctic continent had been spotted in the 1820s. It's easy to see why the dictionary is updated from time to time.

Still, Webster understood that a living language is constantly changing to suit the needs of its speakers, so it's likely that he would be pleased to see how many new words

*(continued on page 62)*

## Oldfangled

Oddly enough, the word *newfangled* is a really old word in English. It comes from two Middle English words, *newe*, meaning "new," and *fangel*, which itself comes from an Old English word, *fangen*, meaning "taken."

"*I must be heard on the subject of silent letters!*"

# And Now a Word from Our Pronouncer...

*We asked Dr. Brian Sietsema, a pronunciation expert (who also happens to be the National Spelling Bee's associate pronouncer) to explain some of the basics of English pronunciation. This was his reply:*

Experts in human speech—linguists—use the term **phoneme** for the idea of a single sound in a given language. A phoneme can be spelled by one letter or a group of letters. Phonemes are often indicated in a special way, using slant marks and letters from different alphabets. For example, the phoneme /t/ expresses the idea of the "t" sound of English in the words _toot_, _stoop_, _later_, and _hit_ (even though there are slight differences in the way your mouth produces the /t/ among these words).

In purely physical terms, the sounds spelled with the underlined _t_ in each of those words are each a different sound, or **phone,** to use the precise linguistic label. The _t_ at the beginning of _toot_ is produced with a significant puff of air, unlike the _t_ of _stoop_. You can convince yourself of this difference by draping a tissue in front of your mouth as you pronounce the two words. The _t_ of _stoop_ is hardly distinguishable from

a _d;_ at normal rates of speaking, almost no one would notice if you were saying "sdoop" rather than _stoop._

The _t_ in _later_ is a kind of consonant that linguists call a "flap" or a "tap": It is formed by the tip of the tongue giving a swift tap on the roof of the mouth. This _t_ is the same as the sound of the _d_ in _ladder._

At normal rates of speaking in most dialects of English, the _t_ in _hit_ is completely different from the rest. Whereas the others are formed somewhere near the front of the mouth with the tip of the tongue involved, this _t,_ in a phrase like "hit my hand," is formed by a closure back in the throat, with no involvement of the tongue tip. Linguists call this kind of consonantal sound a "glottal stop."

Each of these phones is formed in different ways by the vocal organs in the mouth and throat, and they produce sound waves that are different from one another. While each of these sounds is spelled with the letter *t,* linguists would use a different character to indicate each phone: [tʰ] for *toot,* [t] for *stoop,* [ɾ] for *later,* and [ʔ] for hit. (Notice that phones are enclosed in square brackets, but phonemes in slashes.)

As speakers of English, we regard these different phones as being really just the expression of a single category of sound, the English phoneme /t/. In our language, therefore, [tʰ], [t], [ɾ], and [ʔ] are all allophones of the phoneme /t/. Speakers of other languages, however, may regard these phones as being distinct kinds of sound which are therefore to be spelled with different letters. Speakers of Hindi, for example, hear a clear distinction between [tʰ] and [t], and for them this difference makes for a difference in meaning. For them, these two phones belong to two different phonemes, /th/ and /t/. Speakers of Arabic, on the other hand, perceive the phones [p] and [b] as being essentially one and the same kind of sound, i.e., allophones of a single phoneme /p/; in English we regard [p] and [b] as expressions of two distinct phonemes /p/ and /b/ that consequently make for a difference in meaning, as in *pat* and *bat.*

A familiar example of how phones are perceived differently in different languages comes from comparing English and Spanish. In English, *den* and *then* begin with two different sounds, [d] and [ð], which are regarded as two distinct phonemes. In Spanish, however, these two sounds are both perceived as allophones of the Spanish phoneme /d/. These allophones occur in different phonetic contexts: [d] is found at the beginning of a word, but [ð] after a vowel, as in the phrase *de nada,* which to English speakers sounds like "day nah-thah."

*Samir Patel asks for languages of origin.*

## Transliteration, or How Do You Spell *sushi* in Japanese?

English words use the Roman or Latin alphabet, which is one of many alphabets. English has borrowed words from many languages, some of which use, or used, a different alphabet, but when we bring these words into English, we use our alphabet to represent them. The technical term for this process is *transliteration.* English words from Greek, Arabic, Japanese, Russian, Sanskrit, and many other languages have been transliterated.

and phrases American English has adopted since he published his dictionary—although it's hard to say if he'd be happy about *aerobicize, mall rat,* or the fact that *bad* can now mean "good."

**Hey, Get Your Hands off My Nouns!**

What do a ferret and the English language have in common? Both love to steal and stash whatever they can. The English language has a penchant for picking the pockets of other languages. Most of the words in the English language, in fact, belonged originally to other languages.

Languages often have signature spelling patterns for various sounds. You probably already know several of these patterns. The word *tortilla* looks and sounds Spanish, and the word *ballet* looks and sounds French. Knowing some spelling patterns associated with various languages has helped many spellers in competition. If a word is pronounced for you, and you are told the word's language of origin, your chances of ferreting out the correct spelling are much better.

So let's visit a few languages and take a look at some of the signature spellings of various sounds.

# Latin

Some sources indicate that almost 30 percent of the most commonly used English words have Latin in their history. Some students of Latin think of it as a difficult subject, but its spelling patterns are very consistent. As you learn to spell several words that have Latin as the language of origin, you gain a "feel" for how all words from Latin are spelled. Latin has few surprises.

Some notable sounds and spellings:

## LATIN

| SOUND<br>(what you hear) | SPELLING<br>(what you often see) | EXAMPLES |
|---|---|---|
| long *e* at end of plural noun | *ae* | algae, larvae, antennae (Note: Many of these words can also be pronounced with a long *i*.) |
| long *i* at end of plural noun | *i* | magi, fungi, cacti, alumni (Note: Some of these words can also be pronounced with a long *e*.) |
| "oo" as in *ooze* | *u* | recluse, revolution, nucleus, rumor, affluent, ruin |
| /y/ + "oo" as in *ooze* | *u* | commute, acute, municipal, nucleus, diffuse, tunic, deduce, cumulus |
| /y/ + schwa ("yuh") | *u* | deciduous, cellular, cumulus, argument, accurate |
| /gz/ | *x* | exist, exhume, auxiliary, exaggerate, exonerate, exhaust, examine |
| /k/ | c | candidate, execute, proclaim, constitution, college, locate, facsimile |

# The Letter of the Law

"I stuck with Latin throughout high school. In college, I majored in Latin and spent a semester in Rome. For a couple of years, I was a Teach for America fifth-grade teacher and a stickler for proper spelling; then I went to law school. There's no particular link in my mind between lawyering and spelling, but I did find studying for the bar strangely reminiscent of studying for the bee. I also think that surviving a spelling bee, or any other middle-school public performance, helps reduce kids' stage fright and public speaking anxiety when they go on to try other things."

—AMANDA GOAD,
*1992 National Spelling Bee champion*
(winning word: **lyceum**)

## Notes on Latin Spellings

Most of the time, /s/ is spelled *s* in words of Latin origin. Sometimes, however, /s/ is spelled *sc: muscle, rescind, descend, adolescent.*

The letter *z* is rare in words of Latin origin.

The letters *k* and *w* do not exist in English words of Latin origin unless the words have passed through another language before coming into English.

Because Latin words have no *rh*'s, *ph*'s, and *ch*'s—unless the Latin word got them from Greek—English words of Latin origin will not usually have *rh, ph,* or *ch* in their spellings.

Most of the time /m/ at the end of a word of Latin origin is spelled *m*. Sometimes, however, it is spelled *mb: aplomb, bomb, plumb.*

Sometimes /n/ at the end of a word of Latin origin is spelled *gn: design, benign, impugn, align, assign.*

The letter *i* is a vowel often used to connect two Latin word elements. If the connecting vowel sound is a schwa and you must guess at the spelling of this sound, the letter *i* might be a good guess: *florisugent, matrimonial, oviform, pediform, bacilliform, bilirubin, manicure, reniform.*

**Greek is frequently viewed as the language of science.**

# Greek

G reek is frequently viewed as the language of science. Because many good spelling bee words have definitions that relate to the various sciences, it is important for spellers to explore this language of origin and to learn its signature in words.

Some notable sounds and spellings are:

## GREEK

| SOUND<br>(what you hear) | SPELLING<br>(what you often see) | EXAMPLES |
| --- | --- | --- |
| /f/ | ph | alphabet, phase, philosophy, phonics, telegraph, diphtheria, phobia, amphibian, sphere |
| short i | y | abyss, dyslexia, synonym, sympathy, system, gymnasium, odyssey, Olympiad, onyx, syzygy |
| /k/ | c, k, or ch | carcinogen, cathode, democracy, kinetic, krypton, kaumographer, kaleidoscope, chrome, chloride, chaos, echo, chorus, technology, architect, character |
| /r/ | r/rh/rrh | parallel, periphery, theory, pyramid, thorax, rheostat, rhapsody, rhinoceros, rhythm, hemorrhage, cirrhosis |
| /z/ at beginning of word | x (from Greek letter xi) | xylophone, xanthic, xenial |
| /z/ at beginning of word | z (from Greek letter zeta) | zeal, zephyr, zetetic, zeugma |

# The Kiss of Success

"I recall telling ESPN that I knew all of my words when they asked me in front of the camera. It was because I felt I had known all of them instinctively, even though I hadn't previously encountered two of the words, **poimenics** and **bouchon**. What helped me arrive at the spelling of **bouchon** so quickly was that I had studied spelling patterns from Romance languages extensively. When Dr. Cameron gave me the proper French pronunciation, it clicked immediately and I had no trouble spelling the word. With **poimenics**, I used the 'Keep It Simple for Success' (KISS) rule. I just trusted my intuition on the word and didn't allow myself to stray from it. None of the clues given were helpful to me, but I just asked repeatedly for the pronunciation and tried to develop a feel for the word. It worked!"

—NUPUR LALA,
*1999 National
Spelling Bee champion*

## Notes on Greek Spellings

There are many ways to spell the same Greek sound in English. For example, /th/ can be spelled *th, phth,* and *chth* and /n/ can be spelled *n, gn, pn, mn,* and *cn.* Greek is full of surprises!

The long *u* can be spelled *u, eu,* and *ou.* If a word from Greek can be pronounced with an optional /y/ in front of a long *u* sound (as in *neurology*), or if the long *u* comes after /s/ (as in *pseudonym*), it is likely to be spelled *eu.* With Greek food words like *moussaka* and *souvlaki,* the long *u* is usually spelled *ou.*

While *y* is a telltale Greek spelling of a short *i,* the short *i* can also be spelled *i* in words of Greek origin: *hippopotamus, arithmetic, trichotillomania.* The letter *y* can also be used to spell a long *i: hygiene, cryogen, myelocyte.*

The letter *o* is the vowel most often used to connect two Greek word elements. If the connecting vowel sound is a schwa and you must guess at the spelling of this sound, the letter *o* is a very good guess: *xylophone, carcinogen, electrolyte, homonym, octopod, economist, atmosphere, geometric, gyroscope, hypnotist.*

Learning the meaning and spelling of Greek word elements takes the mystery out of many scientific words.

# Of the words most commonly used in English, as many have French in their histories as have Latin.

## English

Some sources indicate that around one fourth of the words in the English language were "born" as English words, but these represent a very large proportion of words we use in writing and speaking. Words whose origin is English are many of our basic, everyday words. Because of their familiarity, they are easy for us to spell—even if their spelling includes silent letters. Words such as *knowledge* and *writing* give us little trouble because we have seen and used them for almost as long as we can remember.

Generally speaking, though, words that have English as the language of origin do not contain tricky letter combinations. The safest approach to spelling a mystery word whose language of origin is English is to spell it exactly as it sounds, if no other clues are available.

## French

Of all the modern foreign languages that can be spotted in English words, French is *premier*. Of the words most commonly used in English, as many have French in their histories as have Latin. Do not, under any *circumstance,* be *insouciant* about the impact of French on spelling!

Some notable sounds and spellings are shown on the chart on the next pages:

## Advice en français

As you are *en route* to the top, it might be *une bonne idée* to try to develop a certain *sangfroid* toward the audience.

## FRENCH

| SOUND<br>(what you hear) | SPELLING<br>(what you often see) | EXAMPLES |
| --- | --- | --- |
| long *a* | *e* or *é* | carburetor, elite, regimc, dégringolade, decoupage, demarche, fete |
| long *a* | *ez* | suivez, rendezvous, oyez |
| long *a* at end of word | *et* | sachet, crochet, duvet, parquet, beignet, gourmet, chalet, ricochet, buffet, ballet, valet, piolet |
| long *a* at end of word | *e/ee* or *é/ée* | café, macrame, abbé, entrée, matinee, melee |
| /y/ + long *a* at end of word | *ier* | dossier, costumier, atelier, cahier, espalier, métier, pompier, tapissier, douanier |
| long *e* at end of word | *ee* | fricassee, marquee |
| long *e* at end of word | *ie* | papeterie, japonaiserie, bourgeoisie, menagerie, bijouterie, minauderie, jalousie, batterie, gaucherie, gaminerie, coterie, fourberie, sortie |
| long *i* | *aille* | rocaille, trouvaille, grisaille |
| long *o* | *aut* | auteur, soubresaut, hauteur, sauterne |
| long *o* | *eau* | eau, beau, trousseau, nouveau, chapeau, gateau, jambeau, plateau, heaume |
| long *o* | *eaux* (plural of words ending in -*eau*) | bordereaux, tableaux, Watteaux, morceaux |
| long *o* | *au* | mauve, taupe, paupiette, gaufrette, soubresaut |

| SOUND<br>*(what you hear)* | SPELLING<br>*(what you often see)* | EXAMPLES |
|---|---|---|
| /et/ | *ette* | banquette, estafette, layette, croquette, fanchonette, blanquette, lorgnette, noisette, marionette, pirouette |
| | | (Note: There are many words, such as *baronet, motet, annulet, coronet, flageolet, martinet,* and *bayonet,* that do not have the *-ette* spelling for /et/.) |
| "ahzh" at end of word | *age* | fuselage, garage, camouflage, sabotage, dressage, bavardage, espionage, persiflage, barrage, montage, maquillage, triage, vernissage |
| "odd" at end of word | *ade* | facade, croustade, ballade, chamade, persillade, glissade, roulade, levade |
| "air" at end of word | *aire* | doctrinaire, billionaire, legionnaire, solitaire, luminaire |
| "oo" as in *ooze* | *ou* | soufflé, boudoir, coup, bouquet, loupe, boutique, rouge, soubriquet, bouffant, bouillon, moulage, tourlourou, bijou, froufrou, rouleau |
| "oo" as in *ooze* | *u* | fondu, ecru, fichu, impromptu, menu, ormolu, parvenu, tutu |
| "oo" as in *ooze* | *ieu* | lieu, bondieuserie, purlieu, lieutenant, milieu |
| /sh/ at beginning of word | *ch* | chagrin, chablis, chevaline, chaise |
| /sh/ at beginning of word | *sh* | shallot, shalloon, shako, shagreen |

## FRENCH

| SOUND (what you hear) | SPELLING (what you often see) | EXAMPLES |
|---|---|---|
| /sh/ at end of word | *che* | gobemouche, brioche, cache, demarche, gauche, louche, panache, quiche, seiche, parfleche, potiche |
| /k/ at end of word | *que* | antique, grotesque, cinque, technique, mosque, arabesque, boutique, pique, claque, roque, clique |
| /g/ at end of word | *gue* | gigue, vogue, morgue, intrigue, fugue, fatigue, colleague, plague |
| "el" at end of word | *elle* | gazelle, mademoiselle, nacelle, belle, chandelle, jumelle (Note: A few words, like *noel* and *morel,* are spelled *el.*) |
| schwa + /l/ | *el* | bevel, estoppel, camel, cancel, caramel, enamel, gravel, kennel |
| /w/ + "oz" | *oise* | ardoise, dacquoise, bourgeoise, nicoise, reboise, genoise |
| /n/ + /y/ | *gn* | beignet, rognon, chignon, espagnole, vigneron, guignol, vignette, poignant, lorgnette, seigneur, champignon |
| /n/ + /w/ | *gnoi* | baignoire, peignoir |
| schwa + /r/ | *eur* | friseur, persifleur, jongleur, auteur, flaneur, fleuron, tiqueur (See note on *-er/-re* and *-or/-our* below.) |
| "il" at end of word | *ille* | coquille, escadrille, quadrille |

### Notes on French Spelling

French, true to its Latin heritage, tends to use *c* and avoid *k* for spelling the /k/ sound.

# One of Noah Webster's goals was to simplify the spelling of English words by making them more similar in appearance to the way that they sound.

Many words from French have silent consonants. Examples include *maillot, debut, picot, griot, ouvert* (silent *t*); *debris, Franglais, patois, coulis, apropos* (silent *s*); *champagne, bersagliere* (silent *g*); *roux, faux, bordereaux* (silent *x*); *coup* (silent *p*); *sangfroid* (silent *d*), and *email* (silent *l*—and it's French for "enamel").

A nasal vowel ("honk, honk") can be spelled many ways in English words of French origin. The nasal vowel results in various silent consonants:

- *-ent (denouement, battement)*
- *-ant (croissant, dansant)*
- *-on (frisson, garçon)*
- *-emps (contretemps)*
- *-in (boudin, baragouin)*
- *-en- (tendu, malentendu)*
- *-em- (croquembouche, embonpoint)*
- *-oint (embonpoint)*

One of Noah Webster's goals was to simplify the spelling of English words by making them more similar in appearance to the way that they sound. With words from French ending in

## Ooh la la!

Over the past several years, the French word *connoisseur* has been the most frequently used word on Scripps National Spelling Bee word lists.

schwa + /r/, such as *theatre* and *centre* and *colour* and *glamour,* he tried hard to change their spellings to *theater/center* and *color/glamor.* Many words were already firmly established in English, however, so what we have now are two acceptable spellings of each word. Some words such as *massacre* and *ogre* were so firmly established that they have only the traditional French spelling.

The *oi* letter combination is seen in many words of French origin and has many different sounds. Familiarize yourself with the sound and

**2005** *Scripps National Spelling Bee champion Anurag Kashyap, from San Diego, California, autographs another speller's hand.*

# Except for a few consonants, words from Spanish are often spelled just as you would think they should be.

spelling of words such as *foible, adroit, renvoi, moiré, chinoiserie, boudoir, coiffure, grimoire, avoirdupois, connoisseur, porpoise,* and *mademoiselle.*

## Spanish

English words from Spanish have very consistent spelling and the patterns are easy to memorize. Except for a few consonants (like *ll,* which sounds like /y/, and *j,* which sounds like /h/), words from Spanish are often spelled just as you would think they should be. If you are at the microphone and are asked to spell a mystery word of Spanish origin, it's best to spell it as it sounds. For example, if the final sound is a long *o,* spell it with an *o.* Don't pull out the French *-eau.* Don't try to put a fancy spin on the spelling of words from Spanish!

Some notable sounds and spellings are in the table on the next page.

### Notes on Spanish Spelling

The Spanish alphabet does not contain a *k.* The letter *k* is found in English words from Spanish only when Spanish has borrowed those words from some other language.

Don't use *ph* to spell the /f/ sound in English words from Spanish.

With the exception of *ll* and *rr,* double letters in words of Spanish origin are uncommon.

## Foreign Study Tips

Go to the library and find dictionaries or textbooks for other unusual foreign languages that use a Roman alphabet, such as Welsh, Gaelic, or Basque. Peruse them to see if any spelling patterns surface and check the pronunciations. This might give you a hint for spelling unusual words that have come from these languages to English.

If you have an electronic dictionary with a search feature, you can use it to search for all the words that have a particular language of origin. Look at each list of words from a given language and see if you can spot spelling patterns within this language.

## SPANISH

| SOUND<br>(what you hear) | SPELLING<br>(what you often see) | EXAMPLES |
| --- | --- | --- |
| long *a* | *e* | ceja, rejoneador, zarzuela, coleta, capeador, sevillana |
| /g/ + long *a* | *gue* | vargueno, malaguena |
| long *a* at end of word | *e* or *é* | suerte, padre, atole, baile, compadre, guanche, infante, jarabe, olé, jefe, molave, norte, pinche, sucre, tiple, hombre, amole, bisagre |
| long *e* at end of word | *i* | bonaci, Bribri, caji, guazuti, houvari, javali, mani, macabi, tecali, zemi, aguaji |
| long *e* at end of word | *e* | vigilante, amole, adobe, bisagre, casabe, cenote, jinete, chapote, chayote, mole, monte, pinole, rosinante, timbe, Apache, hombre |
| long *e* followed by "yuh"/"yoh" | *illa/illo* | banderilla, mantilla, tortilla, blanquillo, piloncillo, tomatillo |
| long *o* | *o* | desperado, pronto, rodeo, Latino, amigo, concho, diablo, gazpacho, tango, zocalo |
| /h/ | *j* | jicama, junta, aparejo, rejoneador, jacal |
| /k/ | *c* | cabana, cacao, cordovan, hurricane, cafeteria, cantina |
| /k/ | *qu* | ronquil, quiaquia, quinta, vaquero |
| "kay" | *que* | quesadilla, quebrada, quebracho |
| schwa at end of word | *a* | bonanza, bodega, hacienda, cabana, junta, plaza, fajita, chinchilla |

The letters *ch* and *ll* are considered single letters in Spanish. That's why these letter combinations pop up frequently in English words of Spanish origin.

Make lists of words that do not follow the "spell it like it sounds" guideline: for example, *tilde* (final schwa spelled with *e*).

A /th/ sound will be spelled with a *d* if it is surrounded by vowels. Examples: *rejoneador, toreador, cogida, capeador.*

# German

Historically, German has had an enormous influence on English, but words that have come from modern German can still look very unusual to us.

Some notable sounds and spellings are shown on the next page.

## Notes on German Spelling

German words love *k*'s, *ck*'s, and *ch*'s. They avoid *c*'s, except when the German word is borrowed from Greek or some other language that has an unusual preference for *c*'s. Remember: The letter *c* rarely appears alone in words of German origin; you'll almost always see it paired with *k* as in *glockenspiel,* or *h* as in *geistlich.*

## The Guttural /kh/

The German *ch* is often pronounced with a little gargle in the back of the throat. Try saying the word *book*. Now say it again—but this time, when you pronounce the *k*, allow your throat to stay slightly open and push a small amount of air through. This guttural sound is also present in other languages like Yiddish and Russian, though English often changes its pronunciation in adopted words to a safe, boring /k/.

## GERMAN

| SOUND (what you hear) | SPELLING (what you often see) | EXAMPLES |
| --- | --- | --- |
| long *e* | *ie* | vorspiel, glockenspiel, kunstlied, kriegspiel, blitzkrieg, volkslied, zwieback, wienerwurst, wiesenboden |
| long *i* | *ei* | abseil, Fahrenheit, gesundheit, gauleiter, leitmotiv, einkanter, gneiss, zeitgeist, Kneippism, schwarmerei, meister, ortstein, geige, poltergeist |
| /ch/ and /sh/ | *sch* | affenpinscher, gegenschein, schottische, kitsch, Nietzschean, schnitzel, putsch, austausch, bergschrund |
| "lick" (sort of!) | *lich* | geistlich, lieblich, schlich, frohlich (See sidebar on the guttural /kh/.) |
| /v/ | *w* | wenzel, edelweiss, wisent, weltpolitik, Weimaraner, wedel, leberwurst, wiesenboden |
| /k/ | *k* | einkorn, katzenjammer, einkanter, kohlrabi, lebkuchen, blitzkrieg, kipfel, randkluft, kuchen, nachtmusik, kitsch, steinkern, weltpolitik |
| /k/ | *ck* | pickelhaube, schnecke, zwieback, pumpernickel |
| /k/ | *ch* | echt |

# A Spelling Glitch

"At the 1980 national finals, when the competition was reduced to two spellers—Jacques Bailly and me—I was asked to spell **glitch**. *Glitch*, of course, means 'a mistake,' and it entered the English language with the space industry in the 1960s and became a commonly used word with the advent of personal computer usage in the 1980s. But in 1980 very few people had computers on their desks at work or in their homes, so *glitch* was not yet a common word. So, when I was asked to spell this simple-sounding word at the end of the Bee, I instantly thought that there must be a trick spelling. Then the pronouncer offered that its origin was German, and that bit of information confirmed my hunch that the spelling was g-l-i-t-s-c-h. I was wrong, of course, and the rest is history: Jacques Bailly corrected my misspelling of *glitch* and went on to spell **elucubrate** to win the Bee. In 1991, soon after being employed by Scripps to help run the National Spelling Bee, I had the privilege of examining the full word list for the 1980 bee. I was able to see that if I had spelled *glitch* correctly, my next word would have been **intonaco**, and I acknowledged that I probably would have misspelled that word, too. I never had any doubt that Jacques Bailly deserved the championship, but having the *intonaco* information helped me feel even better about the way things happened."

—Paige Pipkin Kimble,
*1981 National
Spelling Bee champion*

# Italian

Italian is a language that has given us many popular spelling bee words for beautiful music and yummy food. Some notable sounds and spellings:

## ITALIAN

| SOUND (what you hear) | SPELLING (what you often see) | EXAMPLES |
|---|---|---|
| long *a* at end of word | *e* | padre, volante, tagliatelle, pappardelle, ballabile, padrone, macrame, principe, scintillante |
| long *e* at end of word | *i* | spaghetti, salami, macaroni, perciatelli, ziti, Amati, brindisi, cannelloni, cannoli, calamari, literati, Carbonari, ravioli |
| long *e* at end of word | *e* | minestrone, torrone, fettuccelle, schiavone, brillante, campanile, canzone, pococurante, monte, lazzarone, pallone, panettone |
| long *e* + long *o* at end of word | *io* | impresario, atrio, punctilio, arpeggio, nuncio, oratorio, pistachio, studio, capriccio, intaglio |
| long *o* at end of word | *o* | alto, bravo, crescendo, bambino, fiasco, motto, maestro, libretto, largo, ghetto, graffito, inferno, incognito, palmetto, pesto, piano, piccolo, capriccioso, prosciutto, Reggio, soprano, tremolo, zero, amaretto |
| /y/ + long *o* at end of word | *io* | imbroglio, intaglio, bardiglio, latticinio, preludio, verdicchio |
| "eenie" at end of word | *ini* | rappini, spiedini, ditalini, spaghettini, zucchini, tortellini |

| SOUND<br>(what you hear) | SPELLING<br>(what you often see) | EXAMPLES |
|---|---|---|
| /ch/ | cc | breccia, carpaccio, capriccio, fettuccelle, mostaccioli, focaccia, fettuccine |
| /k/ before schwa or long *o* | cc | beccafico, spiccato, squacco, zocco, zoccolo, zacco, stucco, piccolo |
| /k/ before schwa, short *a,* or long *o* | c | cantata, pecorino, cambio, campanile, magnifico, giocoso, pococurante |
| /k/ before long *e,* short *e,* or long *a* | ch | chianti, chiaroscuro, marchesa |
| /ts/ | zz | pizza, intermezzo, mozzarella, palazzo, pizzicato |
| /ny/ | gn | agnolotti, signorina, Bolognese, malmignatte |
| /sk/ before long or short *e* | sch | maraschino, scherzo |
| schwa at end of word | a | regatta, bravura, buffa, camorra, durezza, fughetta, saltimbocca, sonatina, toccata, cantata, ocarina, piazza |

## Notes on Italian Spelling

Watch out for a silent *g* in a few words of Italian origin! Examples include *intaglio, gnocchi,* and *scagliola.*

Italian words seem to avoid using *k* to spell the /k/ sound. Note in the list above the three other ways to spell it!

## Japanese Doubles

Only seven words that have come to us directly from Japanese have double consonants:

**hokku**
**issei**
**momme**
**seppuku**
**shikken**
**tenno**
**teppanyaki**

## Japanese

Words from Japanese are relatively new in English, partly because Japan was closed to Western foreigners from the seventeenth through the nineteenth centuries. Now that Japanese culture has gone global, it's good to know some of these words—especially the food words! Some notable sounds and spellings can be found on the facing page.

## Turkish

It was **kismet** that Turkish and English would one day meet. Some notable sounds and spellings:

### TURKISH

| SOUND (what you hear) | SPELLING (what you often see) | EXAMPLES |
|---|---|---|
| long *e* at end of word | *i* | vali, Azeri, raki, effendi, kasseri |
| long *i* | *ai* | taiga, Bairam, serai |
| /k/ | *c* | canun, caza |
| /k/ | *k* | kilim, altilik, kismet, Mamluk, palanka, sanjak, moussaka, kasseri |
| /k/ | *kh* | khagan, khilafat, tarkhan |

## JAPANESE

| SOUND<br>*(what you hear)* | SPELLING<br>*(what you often see)* | EXAMPLES |
|---|---|---|
| long *a* | *ei* | reiki, geisha, issei, kibei, nisei, sensei |
| long *a* at end of word | *e* | yosenabe, urushiye |
| long *e* at end of word | *i* | Kabuki, odori, hibachi, origami, tsunami, wasabi, zori, Meiji, Romaji, dashi, kanji, awabi, odori, tatami, sashimi, chorogi, fuji, haori, koji, obi, randori, shikii, torii, shogi, sukiyaki, urushi, gi, surimi, sushi, tamari, teriyaki, umami, yakitori |
| long *e* at end of word | *e* | Kamikaze, momme, mume |
| long *i* | *ai* | bonsai, yamamai, mai, samurai, banzai, haikai, shintai, aikido, kaiseki |
| long *o* | *o* | mikado, pachinko, koto, miso, odori, genro, gyokuro, judo, kendo, mondo, sumo, tenno, dojo, zendo, gingko |
| "oo" as in *ooze* at the end of word | *u* | chanoyu, Bunraku, ayu, kudzu, haiku, hokku, shiatsu, zaibatsu, tofu, ansu, kwazoku, maru, Gagaku |
| /k/ | *k* | kakemono, bugaku, kana, kimono, haiku |
| schwa at end of word | *a* | ikebana, ama, katana, geisha, sayonara, kana, mana, ninja, soba |

# Portuguese

The Portuguese have always been sailors, and their language bears traces of their wide travels. Many English words from Portuguese have also passed through non-European languages, such as Sanskrit, Malay, Arabic, and various African tongues. It's important to remember the close relationship of Portuguese and Spanish, because there are many similarities in spelling, but words from Portuguese do have a few distinctive patterns.

## PORTUGUESE

| SOUND (what you hear) | SPELLING (what you often see) | EXAMPLES |
| --- | --- | --- |
| long *a* | *ei* | pareira, copoeira, barbeiro, feijoada, freijo, seringueiro |
| long *i* | *ai* | caixinha, coaita, pirai, saimiri, caique |
| long *u* | *u* | teju, munguba, murumuru, pirarucu |
| long *u* | *o* | choro, chocalho, fado |
| long *u* | *ou* | cachou, toucan, marabout, chibigouazou |
| /sh/ | *x* | maxixe, paxiuba, abacaxi, caixinha, guaxima, xarque |
| /sh/ at beginning of word | *ch* | chamade, chamiso, chocalho, chavante |
| /k/ | *c* | candiru, callimico, carambola |
| /k/ | *qu* | quica, jequitiba, macaque |
| /zh/ | *j* | feijoada, teju, acajou |

# Persian

Most words from Persian go through several languages before entering English, so you may notice some patterns shared by Hindi, Arabic, Turkish, and Sanskrit.

Some notable sounds and spellings are shown in the chart on the next page.

# Sanskrit and/or Hindi

Many of the words we immediately recognize as coming from the Indian subcontinent are Hindu religious terms such as *yoga, ashram,* and *karma.* However, Sanskrit and Hindi are both Indo-European languages and have donated many more common words to their distant cousin English—words like *pajama, bungalow, brother,* and *jungle.*

Some notable sounds and spellings are shown on the next page.

## Notes on Sanskrit/Hindi Spelling

English words from Sanskrit sometimes contain a silent *h:*

- /t/ can be spelled *th (kathakali)*
- /b/ can be spelled *bh (bhalu)*
- /d/ can be spelled *dh (dharma)*
- /k/ can be spelled *kh (gymkhana)*
- /p/ can be spelled *ph (phansigar)*

# Oh, the Horror!

"While I could make educated guesses based on roots for the vast majority of words I could not specifically remember, there remains one that truly confounded me. I remember that in one of the final rounds of the 2000 national finals I was asked to spell **emmetropia.** During the postmortem, I learned that I had been quizzed on it previously, but I had no recollection of it. I quickly closed my eyes and prayed that God would grant me the correct letters for this word. I could recall no rules for spelling it. All I knew was that the spelling *e-m-m-e-t-r-o-p-i-a* made sense, but I remember the horror I experienced as I reflected on the numerous other 'logically correct' spellings. But the chance had to be taken, and I had a sense of peace about the orthography I had chosen."

—GEORGE THAMPY,
*2000 National
Spelling Bee champion
(winning word:
demarche)*

## PERSIAN

| SOUND (what you hear) | SPELLING (what you often see) | EXAMPLES |
|---|---|---|
| long *e* at end of word | *i* | abbasi, Kabuli, kusti, tangi, Turki |
| /g/ | *g* | idgah |
| /g/ | *gh* | ispaghul, ghorkhar |
| /k/ | *c* | calean, carboy, caravan |
| /k/ | *k* | abkar, kamboh, kusti, Kabuli, karez, kran |
| /k/ | *kh* | Bakhtiari, dakhma, farsakh, ghorkhar, nakhoda |

## SANSKRIT AND/OR HINDI

| SOUND (what you hear) | SPELLING (what you often see) | EXAMPLES |
|---|---|---|
| long *e* at end of word | *i* | Hindi, amani, bibi, basmati, tandoori, begari, chakari, jungli, chhatri, dasturi, dhauri, granthi, kangri, koftgari, Pindari, lassi, poori, roti, pachisi, darzi, sabzi |
| schwa at end of word | *a* | mahatma, Buddha, karma, natya, chakra, pajama |
| schwa at end of word | *ah* | almirah, keddah, ayah, khankah, kajawah, numnah |
| "ana" as in British pronunciation of *banana* (sort of!) at end of word | *ana* | Nirvana, gymkhana, dhyana, jnana, rana, zenana |

# Miscellaneous Language Tidbits

These languages don't commonly lend words to English, and the words we do have from them tend to be somewhat unfamiliar. However—hint, hint—they're often good spelling bee words!

### In words of Afrikaans origin:

- Familiarize yourself with letter combinations in words such as *uintjie, Uitlander, uitspan, vaalhaai, volksraad, umfaan, aardvark, bobbejaan, geeldikkop, wildebeest, vetkousie.* Make a list of unusual spellings for various sounds.

### In words of Arabic origin:

- long *e* is sometimes spelled *ih: mihrab, ihram, faqih, tasbih, Lihyanic*
- many words are spelled more or less as they sound: *mancala, masjid, kemancha, albetad, azoth, bejel*
- there is sometimes a silent *h: madhab, dhimmi, dhikr, dukhn, fellagha*

### In words of Eskimo origin:

- /k/ is almost always spelled *k: Eskimo, komatik, manak, kooletah, muktuk, anorak, kamik, makluk, kashim*
- /k/ is sometimes spelled *q: qiviut*

### In words of Hawaiian origin:

- there are no silent letters such as the *e* in *hole*

## A Beastly Number of Malaysian Words

A number of unusual animal names *(teledu, cobego, cassowary, pangolin, siamang, bruang, gourami, kokam, linsang, lory, musang, simpai, tokay, tangilin)* come to us from the Malay language. Malay is spoken extensively not only in Malaysia, but also in parts of Thailand, Singapore, Brunei, the Philippines, and Borneo. The language is as rich and varied as the animal life in this part of the world—Malay has many dialects and, like English, has borrowed extensively from other languages such as Arabic and Sanskrit.

## Your Turn, Gospodin!

During the twentieth century, the Russian language gave English many new words. Some were used for political and social concepts pertaining to the now-defunct Soviet Union: *agitpunkt, agrogorod, apparatchik, cheka, commissar, glasnost, gulag, Kremlin, perestroika, refusenik, samizdat,* and *soviet*. Some were scientific and technical terms: *tokamak, sputnik, cosmonaut,* and even *reflexology*. But many English words from Russian have far older meanings: *steppe, nagaika, samovar, mammoth, kasha, balalaika, sobornost, feldsher, gospodin, troika, purga, babushka, chastushka, tundra*. Notice that there's still something identifiably "Russian" about these words. Look them up, and see if you can figure out some of the typical spelling patterns yourself!

- the only consonants used are *h, k, l, m, n, p,* and *w*
- consonants are never doubled
- the last letter is always a vowel

### In words of Hebrew origin:

- a final "ah" sound and a final schwa sound are often spelled *ah:* *bedikah, genizah, menorah, aliyah, takkanah, bamah, amidah, Asherah, neilah, taharah, parashah, gezerah, hashkabah, Jeremiah, kapparah, Jonah, kabbalah, mizpah, messiah*

- double consonants seem relatively common: *hosanna, kibbutz, shibboleth, Gehenna, akkum, kiddush, bikkurim, kapparah, kinnor, gabbai, koppa, messiah, hallel, Perizzite, rabbi, sabbath, shittah, takkanah, viddui*

### In words of Hungarian origin:

- /s/ can occasionally be spelled *s* or *tz* but is nearly always *sz: tzigane, Kuvasz, Lisztian, puszta, szaibelyite, veszelyite, szmikite, Szekler*

### In words of Polish origin:

- /v/ is usually spelled with a *w: kujawiak, krakowiak*

- /k/ is usually spelled with a *k: kielbasa, babka, oberek*

**In words of Russian origin:**

- /k/ is usually spelled with a *k: tokamak, apparatchik, zolotnik, bolshevik, chinovnik, gopak, gudok, kulak, obrok,*

## Test Your Expertise

**A**re you etymologically savvy now? Let's find out. Match each word in the left columns to one of the languages on the right. There are two words from Sanskrit, three from Greek, one from Persian, three from Japanese, four from French, three from German, five from Latin, four from Italian, and five from Spanish. Answers are on page 88.

| | | |
|---|---|---|
| **sensor** | **piatti** | Sanskrit _____ |
| **mythology** | **bushido** | Greek _____ |
| **penicillin** | **flotilla** | _____ |
| **ichthyoid** | **randori** | Persian _____ |
| **graffito** | **avalanche** | Japanese _____ |
| **simpatico** | **badinage** | French _____ |
| **enoki** | **duende** | _____ |
| **alameda** | **abduct** | German _____ |
| **phosphorus** | **Borsalino** | _____ |
| **meerschaum** | **karuna** | Latin _____ |
| **eigenvalue** | **antebellum** | _____ |
| **tantra** | **bonus** | _____ |
| **nouveau** | **avoirdupois** | Italian _____ |
| **quesadilla** | **spiel** | _____ |
| **toccata** | **percale** | Spanish _____ |
| | | _____ |

(For more games, see Chapter 7.)

**Answers to Quiz
from page 87**

duende
flotilla
quesadilla          avoirdupois
alameda             avalanche
simpático           badinage
SPANISH             nouveau
                    FRENCH
piatti
Borsalino           bushido
toccata             randori
graffito            enoki
ITALIAN             JAPANESE

bonus               percale
antebellum          PERSIAN
penicillin
sensor              phosphorus
abduct              ichthyoid
LATIN               mythology
                    GREEK
spiel
eigenvalue          karuna
meerschaum          tantra
GERMAN              SANSKRIT

*sputnik, kurgan.* Note: We have "*ck*'d"
some spellings such as *cossack.*

- /k/ + schwa is usually spelled *ka*:
  *babushka, burka, perestroika, balalaika,
  chastushka, nagaika, troika*

### In words of Scandinavian origin:

- Many borrowed Old Norse words contain
  the consonant group /sk/, which is still
  spelled *sk* as it was in Old Norse: *skid,
  skin, skip, skirl, skirt, skulk, skull, sky.*
  Other Old Norse words that had the consonant group /sk/ took a detour; when
  they landed in present day English, their
  /sk/ sounds were spelled *sc*: *scab, scale,
  score, scrape, scowl, scrimp.*

# Capitalized Words

The Scripps National
Spelling Bee began
using capitalized
words in 1997, which
increased the number of
good words they had to
draw from by several
thousand. The National
Spelling Bee rules state that the speller need
not specify that a letter is capitalized, so there's
no need to worry if you get one of these words—
as long as you've studied how to spell it! On
page 90 you will find just a few of the capitalized words that have appeared in recent
National Spelling Bees or on Scripps-published

# Neologisms often make excellent spelling bee words.

## Neologisms

Neologism is defined in *Webster's Third* as "a new word, usage, or expression." How new a word has to be in order to be considered a neologism is open to debate, but at some point in time, every word in the dictionary has been a neologism! Many neologisms start out as slang, but widespread and frequent use eventually gains them acceptance among linguistic traditionalists. *Note:* Several words below are not listed in *Webster's Third*.

| | | | |
|---|---|---|---|
| applet | extranet | jihadist | psychobabble |
| bioprospect | extremophile | kazillion | SARS |
| bioremediation | fashionista | latte | spam |
| biosolid | filovirus | mbaqanga | spinmeister |
| bioterror | Frankenfood | McJob | statin |
| blog | gangsta | megaplex | tatsoi |
| carjacking | gelcap | microarray | telomerase |
| chipotle | genomics | minitower | thirtysomething |
| cocooning | glasnost | multiculti | velociraptor |
| cohousing | greenwashing | nanomachine | wakeboard |
| cybercafe | Habanero | netiquette | webcast |
| cybernaut | heteroglossia | netizen | webmaster |
| cybrarian | hoodie | olestra | yoctosecond |
| defragmenter | hospitalist | perestroika | yottabyte |
| digerati | hyperlink | phytoplasma | zeptosecond |
| ecoterrorism | hyperther- | piehole | zettabyte |
| electronica | mophile | pikeminnow | zouk |
| emoticon | intranet | proteome | |

## The K's Have It

Look at the lists for each language and notice that there is something mentioned about the spelling of /k/ in almost every list. Correctly spelling the /k/ sound in English words is sometimes like flipping a coin. *If you must guess* how to spell the /k/ sound in a word that has a non–Western European language of origin, especially one that uses a non-Roman alphabet, *your safest guess is to spell it with a k.*

study lists. Look them up and note how many different language origins they represent:

| | | |
|---|---|---|
| **Abyssinian** | **Havarti** | **Tacitean** |
| **Afrikaans** | **Islamic** | **Tammanyism** |
| **Ananias** | **Jainism** | **Torquemada** |
| **Bauhaus** | **Krugerrand** | **Ulyssean** |
| **Berber** | **Latino** | **Unitarian** |
| **Boyg** | **Madagascar** | **Vatican** |
| **Camelot** | **Micawber** | **Vesuvian** |
| **Charleston** | **Nietzschean** | **Wednesday** |
| **Cimmerian** | **Nigerois** | **Wesak** |
| **December** | **Olympian** | **Yinglish** |
| **Doppler** | **Rankine** | **Zendo** |
| **Euterpean** | **Rastafarian** | **Zoroastrian** |
| **Geronimo** | **Sikkimese** | |
| **Hadean** | **Solomonic** | |

## Study Your Interests

What are your hobbies? Whether you like dogs, cats, or insects; collect coins, posters, or sneakers; enjoy music, sewing, or karate—you have a rich source of spelling bee words at your fingertips. People around the world enjoy many of the same activities, so the vocabulary that goes with your hobby may well be an international one. As you learn more about your hobby, make a note of good spelling words and look them up in the dictionary to find out more about where they came from. The very best hobby for a speller, though, may be learning foreign languages!

# CHAPTER 5

# A Few Good Rules and Many Annoying Exceptions

Spelling in English (and most other languages, for that matter) has two features that tend to drive many people crazy: rules and exceptions. (For our purposes, a rule is anything that constitutes a common English spelling pattern, and an exception is anything that doesn't seem to fit into a common English spelling pattern.)

# Keep in mind as you study this chapter that some of the "rules" you may already have learned are really more like guidelines with many exceptions.

## Don't Just Stand There— Ask!

I n the National Spelling Bee and in most other spelling bees, when you are given a word you are allowed to ask about its part of speech. This piece of information can be valuable because some suffixes and word parts sound alike but are spelled differently and belong to different parts of speech, like *-us* and *-ous*. It's always wiser to make absolutely sure of your information than to rush boldly into a spelling that may not be correct.

Since many spellers flounder on the rocks of similar-sounding affixes or are not sure when the affix affects the spelling of the root word, this chapter is devoted to presenting prefix and suffix spelling rules and exceptions as clearly as possible. After some general rules comes a short section on troublesome prefixes, which are actually few in number. The rest of the chapter focuses on the far greater number of rules and exceptions that apply to suffixes, which determine a word's part of speech, and we've sorted them that way.

Keep in mind as you study this chapter that some of the "rules" you may already have learned—like "*i* before *e* except after *c,* or when sounded like *a* as in *neighbor* and *weigh*" are really more like guidelines with many exceptions. Keep your mind, eyes, and ears open for examples that confirm patterns you know, as well as exceptions that you should write down.

## Some Very General Rules

L et's begin with the rules that apply across the board to words from every part of speech.

## Rule 1: Deleting the Silent *e*

Drop the final *e* before a suffix beginning with a vowel, unless all the following three criteria are met: (1) the word ends in *-ge* or *-ce*, (2) the suffix begins with *a* or *o*, and (3) the "soft" sound of *g* or *c* is to be retained. Examples: *alleging, intoning; advantageous, noticeable.*

## Rule 2: Doubling the Final Consonant

Double the final consonant before adding a suffix beginning with a vowel if the word has one syllable or an accent on the last syllable. If the accent shifts with the addition of the suffix, do not double the final consonant. Examples: *abetting, beginner, rappelled; conference, reference.*

1978 *A winner, a loser. Peg McCarthy of Topeka, Kansas, spells the word* **deification** *to win the 51st National Spelling Bee. Runner-up Lyn Sue Kahng from San Diego, California, hangs her head in defeat.*

## Future Fed Head Eliminated with "Edelweiss"

**B**en S. Bernanke, the chairman of the Federal Reserve Board and the nation's most visible economist, was once an eleven-year-old speller representing South Carolina at the National Spelling Bee. Unfortunately, Dr. Bernanke misspelled **edelweiss** and does not get to add the National Spelling Bee championship to his list of accomplishments.

## Rule 3: Changing *y* to *i*

Words that end in *y* usually change the *y* to *i* before a suffix, unless the *y* is the second of two vowels at the end of the word or the suffix begins with *i*. Examples: *happiness, silliest; grayness, boyish, flying.*

## Rule 4: Adding a Prefix

Whenever a prefix is added to a word, the spelling of the word itself remains the same. Examples: *mis- + shapen = misshapen; im- + mutable = immutable.* This is one of the simplest rules to follow because it has no exceptions!

## Rule 5: *i* before *e*

It may be what we call a "chestnut," but the *i*-before-*e* spelling rule really does work most of the time. In this two-vowel combination (linguists call it a *digraph* when the two letters make a single sound), put the *i* first unless the combination immediately follows a *c*, or has a long *a* sound. Examples: *believe; perceive, ceiling; vein, feint.* If the two vowels are pronounced separately, as in *science, concierge,* and *deity,* they should be spelled as pronounced rather than according to the rule. This rule also does not include nouns ending in *cy* that form a plural by changing *y* to *i* and adding *es*, like *vacancy/vacancies.*

Most of the remaining common exceptions are:

| | |
|---|---|
| **caffeine** | **plebeian** |
| **codeine** | **protein** |
| **counterfeit** | **reveille** |

| | |
|---|---|
| either | seismic |
| feisty | seize |
| foreign | sleight |
| forfeit | sovereign |
| heifer | stein |
| height | surfeit |
| heir | their |
| heist | veil |
| kaleidoscope | weir |
| leisure | weird |
| neither | |

Keep your eyes peeled for other exceptions as you study!

# A Few Pesky Prefixes

Most prefixes and combining forms have a distinct sound, but that won't help you if you just haven't studied *gnath-* and therefore don't know about the silent *g*. Merriam-Webster's *Dictionary of Prefixes, Suffixes, and Combining Forms,* available on the Scripps National Spelling Bee site (www.spellingbee.com), is your best bet for learning as many as you can. To give you a head start, we've pulled out a few common prefixes and combining forms that sound alike when placed at the front of a word,

## Creature Feature

Do you like weird monster movies—the ones with English dialogue dubbed in? Words for interesting creatures come from many different languages. Here are just a few—some familiar, others probably new to you.

Frankenstein
harpy
hircocervus
kraken
makara
marmennill
nix
onocentaur
orc
Sasquatch
snallygaster
sphinx
triton
whangdoodle

### anti- and ante-

*Ante-* is a Latin prefix meaning "before" or "prior." *Anti-* is also Latin but means "against."

| | |
|---|---|
| antebellum | anticyclone |
| antenatal | antifreeze |
| antescript | antigravity |

### cyno- and Sino-

*Cyno-* means "dog" and *Sino-* (which is usually capitalized, as in *Sinogram*) means "Chinese." The word *cynosure,* "a center of attention or interest," came from Latin and Greek roots that originally meant "a dog's tail."

### dis- and dys-

*Dys-* means "abnormal," "diseased," "difficult," "faulty," "impaired," "bad," or "unfavorable," and often comes at the beginning of scientific or medical terms. *Dis-* means "opposite of," "contrary of," "absence of," "not," or "completely." Confusingly, it can also sometimes mean "dys-," so it's worth looking up the words that start with *dys-* in the dictionary.

| | |
|---|---|
| dysentery | disadvantage |
| dyslexia | disagree |
| dyspeptic | disheveled |

### em-, en-, im-, and in-

These are not really homophones, but do sound somewhat alike. Be careful when spelling them aloud in competition. *Em-/en-* means "put into or on to," "cause to be," "provide with," or "thoroughly" (often in verbs whose meaning is not

very different without the prefix, as *tangle/entangle).* *Em-* is used before *b, m,* or *p* and *en-* is used in all other circumstances: *embrace, enable, enslave.* *Im-/in-* also follows that rule (and adds two more: *il-* is used before *l* and *ir-* is used before *r).* It means "not" *(immutable, imprudent)* or "in," "inward," "toward," "on" *(inculcate, impound).*

### fluor-/fluoro- and flori-

Any word having to do with flowers or blooming plants may contain the combining form *flori-,* as in *floriculture* and *florisugent. Fluor-/fluoro-* refers to the element fluorine—which is not a fragrant substance at all, but a poisonous gas at room temperature! *Fluorescent* light bulbs contain hydrogen fluoride, which gives them a cool glow. Something that is *florescent* is blooming or flourishing.

### par-/para- and peri-

*Peri-* means "surrounding," "around," or "near," and is often used in scientific words like *perihelion, periocular,* and *periodontal. Par-/para-* means "beside" (as in *paramedic,* who works in cooperation with a doctor), "beyond," "faulty or abnormal," and also has two scientific meanings ("derived from an original sediment," used in geological terms, and "isomeric or polymeric

## The Prepared Mind

" I n my opinion, it's impossible to be over-prepared. I remember a common saying from the national finals: 'I knew every word except the one I got!' But with respect to competition advice, chance favors the prepared mind. Greek and Latin roots are invaluable, but the prepared speller also knows the words that do not conform and knows when to break the rules. I made a compendium of words I hadn't heard of from several different library books, then con-firmed each one in *Webster's Third New International.* It was a very tedious process, but there's a lot of serendipity in the process."

—GEORGE THAMPY, *2000 National Spelling Bee champion* (winning word: **demarche**)

# I Could Spell That in My Sleep

"My mom and sister used to drill me for hours in the weeks before the state and national competition. My sister, Anne, and I rode a bus up to the ski slopes. She would drill me the whole way up and back. My mom would drill me all the way until bedtime. More than once, family members caught me spelling in my sleep."

—Katie Kerwin McCrimmon, *1979 National Spelling Bee champion (winning word: maculature)*

with," used in chemistry). Its meaning is a little hard to trace in the many words that contain it, like *paragon, parasite,* and *paraphrase,* so try to learn as many *peri-* and *para-* words as you can. If you do nothing else, at least learn the difference between *parameter* and *perimeter*—two words that are often confused.

### techno- and tekno-

Words with the combining form *techno-* are very common and have to do with the application of knowledge to practical matters. There are only two English words that use *tekno-,* which comes from the Greek *teknon,* meaning "child": *teknonymy* and *teknonymous,* both referring to the naming of children for their parents.

# Verbs

Standard verb endings are *-s, -es, -ing,* and *-ed.* For the most part, verb inflections (how you change the ending of the verb to match the subject and tense of the sentence) follow the general rules above. There are a few additional rules:

**Rule:** If the verb ends in *s, z, x, sh,* or *ch,* add *-es* to form the third person present: *caress/caresses, fizz/fizzes, coax/coaxes, crash/crashes, march/marches.*

**Rule:** If the verb ends in a single vowel *y*, change it to *i* before adding *-es* for third person present or *-ed* for past tense: *marry/marries/married, beautify/beautifies/beautified.* Do not change the *y* before the present participle ending *-ing: beautifying.* If the verb has a vowel before the *y*, treat it as you would a consonant ending: *annoy/annoys/annoyed, survey/surveys/surveyed.*

**Rule:** If the verb ends in *c*, add a *k* before *-ed* or *-ing* (*bivouac/bivouacked/bivouacking, panic/panicked/panicking, picnic/picnicked/picnicking, traffic/trafficked/trafficking*).

**Rule:** For one-syllable verbs ending in *ye* or *oe*, keep the final *e* before *-ing*, but drop it before *-ed*. Examples: *eye/eyeing/eyed, shoe/shoeing/shoed.*

**Rule:** If the verb ends in *ie* or *ee*, drop the final *e* before *-ed: belie/belied, free/freed.* If the verb ends in *ie*, change it to *y* before adding *-ing: tying, vying.*

## Last In, First Out

When you are given an unfamiliar word that originated in one language but went through another language or languages, use spelling guidelines from the most recent language—i.e., the one it went through just before coming into English.

*❝Be thankful that in English a noun's form stays the same no matter what its role in a sentence.❞*

**There are three words that end in *z* preceded by a vowel in which the *z* is doubled before adding -es: *quiz/quizzes*, *spaz/spazzes*, *whiz/whizzes*.**

## The Sad and Lonely Q

There are just a very few words in English that use Q without its friend U:

faqih
Inupiaq
nastaliq
Qatari
qintar
qiviut
qiyas
taqlid
zindiq

## -ise, -ize, or -yze?

Most verbs that end in the "eyes" sound have Latin roots and are spelled *-ize*. Those that are spelled *-ise* generally (though not always) come from Old French or Middle French. There aren't very many of them. If you don't see a few you expect (like *surprise*) on this list, it's because they can be spelled either *-ise* or *-ize*.

| | |
|---|---|
| abscise | improvise |
| advise | incise |
| chastise | previse |
| compromise | reprise |
| demise | revise |
| despise | rise |
| devise | surmise |
| disguise | televise |
| exercise | vise |
| franchise | wise |

The Latin noun combining form *-lysis* has led to the verb combining form *-lyze,* which means "to produce or undergo disintegration or dissolution" and is used in the following verbs (and similar verbs with prefixes, like *psychoanalyze* and *electrodialyze*):

| | |
|---|---|
| acetolyze | electrolyze |
| ammonolyze | hemolyze |
| analyze | hydrolyze |

| | |
|---|---|
| autolyze | paralyze |
| catalyze | pyrolyze |
| cytolyze | solvolyze |
| dialyze | |

So if you hear an *l* before the "eyes" sound, first check to see if it is a variant of one of these verbs; if it is not, go ahead and spell it *-lize*.

# Nouns

Nouns are the building blocks of a language, the first words most of us learn. Many nouns came directly into English from another language; others were made by modifying another noun *(neighborhood = neighbor + -hood)* or a verb *(aspirant = aspir(e) + -ant)*. Luckily for us, the form of a noun stays the same in English, no matter what function it plays in the sentence. Many folks in the world aren't so lucky.

## Plural Nouns

There are rules for forming plural nouns and many exceptions to the rules. Some of these arise when a word has hung on desperately to a historical plural that belongs to the language it came from or to an older form of English.

Regular English plurals are formed by adding *-s* to the singular: *lemur/lemurs.* If the singular noun ends in *s, x, z, ch,* or *sh,* the

**Food and Cooking**

LEVEL: Advanced

aioli
avgolemono
beignet
bouillon
cannoli
choucroute
chipolata
espagnole
focaccia
fricassee
jambalaya
kaiseki
lyonnaise
madrilene
mamaliga
milchig
mostaccioli
moussaka
paella
pansit
persillade
raclette
rotisserie
roux
sarsaparilla
schnecke
tagliarini
tandoori
tempeh
tiramisu
vichyssoise
vindaloo
yosenabe

# No Blurting!

"Words suddenly seem much harder and more confusing when you receive them onstage at a bee than at home from your mom! I would encourage spellers to try to stay completely focused on the pronouncer and the word and to block out all other distractions. Take your time with an unfamiliar word to explore all possible spellings and resist the temptation to blurt out your first instinct!"

—PEG MCCARTHY,
*1978 National Spelling
Bee champion*

ending *-es* is added to form the plural: *quartz/ quartzes.* This adds a syllable to the pronunciation and makes it actually possible to pronounce the plural! There are three words that end in *z* preceded by a vowel in which the *z* is doubled before adding *-es: quiz/quizzes, spaz/spazzes, whiz/whizzes.*

If the noun ends in a vowel or *l* plus *f*, we usually change the *f* to a *v* and add *-es: loaf/ loaves, thief/thieves, calf/calves, shelf/shelves.* There are some exceptions, including *aperitifs, beliefs, chefs, chiefs, clefs, massifs, motifs, proofs.* Both forms exist for some words: *hand-kerchieves/handkerchiefs, rooves/roofs, scarves/scarfs.* Note: This change is also made for a few nouns that have a silent *e* after the *f: knife/knives, life/lives, wife/wives.*

If the singular noun is a common noun (i.e., not a name) and ends in a single vowel *y*, the plural is formed by changing the *y* to *ie* and adding *-s: blueberry, blueberries.* If *y* is the second of two vowels, we keep it and add *-s: boys, monkeys.* If it is a name, we just add *-s* to form a plural: *Avery, Averys.* Note that this is properly used when speaking of more than one person in the same family: *The Averys have moved in next door.* (Never use an apostrophe to form

a plural noun! The right time to use an apostrophe is when forming a possessive or a contraction. The possessive form of *Avery* is *Avery's,* and the possessive form of the plural is *Averys': Lauren Avery's poodle will sit up and shake hands with red-haired girls. People say the Averys' broom closet is haunted.* Adding the apostrophe and *-s* effectively turns the noun into an adjective because it gives information about the noun that follows it. In a contraction, the apostrophe stands in for a missing letter: *Susan's* [Susan is] *going to Hawaii next week with her grandparents. They're* [They are] *planning to go surfing.*

Some nouns of Latin origin have kept the Latin form in the plural. Latin nouns that end in *a* typically add *-e* to form the plural:

| | |
|---|---|
| **alumna** | **alumnae** |
| **stria** | **striae** |
| **regina** | **reginae** |
| **petechia** | **petechiae** |
| **medusa** | **medusae** |
| **vertebra** | **vertebrae** |

Latin nouns that end in *us* usually form the plural by removing the *us* and adding *-i:*

| | |
|---|---|
| **alumnus** | **alumni** |
| **oculus** | **oculi** |
| **torus** | **tori** |
| **cubitus** | **cubiti** |
| **cumulus** | **cumuli** |
| **euripus** | **euripi** |
| **magus** | **magi** |
| **stimulus** | **stimuli** |

*Sammy Totino of Chesterland, Ohio, misspells the word* **ocarina** *during the 74th Annual National Spelling Bee.*

S ome words, called onomatopoeia, origi- nated as an imitation of natural sounds—in fact, some linguists have devel- oped a theory (sometimes known as the "bow-wow theory") that this is how all spoken language began. There are onomatopoeia in every language.

Latin nouns that end in *-um* or *-on* often replace that ending with *-a* to form the plural:

| | |
|---|---|
| **addendum** | **addenda** |
| **bacterium** | **bacteria** |
| **curriculum** | **curricula** |
| **datum** | **data** |
| **criterion** | **criteria** |
| **noumenon** | **noumena** |
| **phenomenon** | **phenomena** |

Latin- and Greek-based nouns that end in *-sis* usually form the plural just by changing the *i* to an *e:*

| | |
|---|---|
| **analysis** | **analyses** |
| **basis** | **bases** |
| **catharsis** | **catharses** |
| **crisis** | **crises** |
| **ellipsis** | **ellipses** |
| **emphasis** | **emphases** |
| **exegesis** | **exegeses** |
| **genesis** | **geneses** |
| **paralysis** | **paralyses** |
| **parenthesis** | **parentheses** |
| **synthesis** | **syntheses** |
| **synopsis** | **synopses** |

Other nouns of Latin origin have taken on the regular English plural forms *-s* and *-es* exclusively, like *dementia/dementias, echidna/ echidnas, trapezius/trapeziuses, tinnitus/tinni- tuses, exodus/exoduses.* Still others offer the choice of forming their plurals in either the Latin or English way, as shown in this table:

| SINGULAR | LATIN PLURAL | ENGLISH PLURAL |
| --- | --- | --- |
| alga | algae | algas |
| formula | formulae | formulas |
| nebula | nebulae | nebulas |
| nova | novae | novas |
| patina | patinae | patinas |
| persona | personae | personas |
| scapula | scapulae | scapulas |
| cactus | cacti | cactuses |
| fungus | fungi | funguses |
| nimbus | nimbi | nimbuses |
| nucleus | nuclei | nucleuses |
| octopus | octopi | octopuses |
| opus | opera | opuses |
| radius | radii | radiuses |
| thymus | thymi | thymuses |
| crisis | crises | crisises |
| eclipsis | eclipses | eclipsises |
| cerebellum | cerebella | cerebellums |
| plectrum | plectra | plectrums |
| podium | podia | podiums |

A small number of nouns from Latin end in *-ix* or *-ex,* and these sometimes form the plural by changing *x* to *-ces: genetrix/genetrices.* Others use the regular English formation and add *-es* to the word: *crucifix/crucifixes.* Most of the *-ix* nouns, however, offer a choice: *appendix/appendices/appendixes, matrix/matrices/matrixes.*

A few nouns from Latin maintain the same form of the word whether singular or plural: *series, species.* As with English nouns that form the plural this way (*moose, sheep, aircraft*), there are not very many.

There are a few nouns of French origin ending in *-eau* that can form the plural by adding *-x* (which can either be silent or pronounced /z/): *bandeau/bandeaux, bureau/bureaux, eau/eaux,* for example. Some of these also offer the English plural form *-s: chapeau/chapeaux/chapeaus,* and some have

**2004** *While National Spelling Bee champion David Scott Tidmarsh addressed his school, Edison Intermediate School in South Bend, Indiana, Edison students stood with cards spelling out his winning word,* **autochthonous.**

# A few nouns from Latin maintain the same form of the word whether singular or plural, like *series* and *species*.

only the *-s* form: *jetteau/jetteaus, rideau/rideaus*. Confusingly, the *-s* ending is also pronounced /z/, so proceed cautiously when spelling one of these plurals.

Some nouns ending in *o* add *s* for the plural ending (*albedos, logos, pianos, solos*), and some (*echoes, heroes, potatoes, tomatoes, torpedoes*) add *-es*. Many accept either spelling: *pinto/pintos/pintoes, stucco/stuccos/stuccoes, volcano/volcanos/volcanoes*. If there is another vowel before the *o*, the ending is usually *-s: cameos, studios, duos*. Otherwise, there doesn't appear to be a pattern to nouns ending in *o,* so it's best to memorize as many of these plurals as you can.

There are other nouns in English, mostly those with a Middle English/Old English heritage, that have irregular plurals, like *child/ children, goose/geese, man/men, mouse/mice, ox/oxen, tooth/teeth, woman/women*. Others are plurals that have no unique singular: *cattle, police*. Fortunately, most of these are very common and quite easy to spell.

## Noun Suffixes

Suffixes that are unstressed and contain a schwa are often confusing because they could be spelled multiple ways. We'll address these first.

**-er, -or, or -ar?** To make a "person or thing that performs an action" noun from a verb, we

## How the Birdies Sing

Some onomatopoeically-named birds talk about themselves all the time! Listen to the **bobwhite, cuckoo, curlew, dickcissel, kiwi, motmot, siskin, towhee, whippoor-will,** and **willet.**

# From Bee to Bar

usually add *-er* or *-or.* Unfortunately, there aren't any hard-and-fast rules that govern which one is used, but there are some general guidelines. The suffix *-er* is Middle English/Old English,  and *-or* is its Latin cousin. Often, if the verb that forms the noun comes from Middle English, we use *-er.* These are what we usually think of as our simple "doer" nouns: *farmer, greeter, hunter, invader, miner.* If the verb in question has a Latin root, we often add *-or* to form the noun: *director, incubator, moderator, perpetrator, sculptor, separator.* Note that in both cases, any silent *e* at the end of the verb is dropped, as it is before any suffix beginning with a vowel.

For nouns that are not formed from verbs, the "ur" ending is somewhat more likely to be spelled *-er* as in *barber, milliner,* and *monster.* It's worth memorizing some common exceptions like *doctor, gladiator, mentor,* and *sector.*

The suffix *-er* is also used in adjectives to show a comparative degree, as in *fleecier* and *brasher.* The adjectival ending *-ar,* which means "of or belonging to," "resembling," or "being" (as in *molecular, triangular,* and *vascular*), is also easy to confuse with *-er* and *-or.*

These are two of the reasons why it's impor-tant to know whether you're spelling an adjective

# For nouns made from Middle English/Old English verbs use -er; use -or for nouns formed from a Latin verb.

or a noun! Also, there are some nouns ending in *-ar* that are spelled the same way as the adjective that describes them, such as *tubercular*, which is both an adjective meaning "relating to or affected by tuberculosis" and a noun meaning "a person having tuberculosis."

There are a few other common nouns that end in *-ar*, and you should make a point of memorizing them. Some are compound words formed from the one-syllable nouns *bar, car, star,* and *war.* Others are:

| | |
|---|---|
| agar | circular |
| alegar | collar |
| altar | commissar |
| antimacassar | dollar |
| beggar | feldspar |
| burglar | liar |
| calendar | poplar |
| caterpillar | scholar |
| cedar | sugar |
| cheddar | tartar |
| cigar | vicar |
| cinnabar | vinegar |

**-ant or -ent, -ance or -ence?** The suffixes *-ant* and *-ent* can be used to create nouns and adjectives, and they sound alike when pronounced. The suffixes *-ance* and *-ence* can be used to create nouns. They, too, sound alike when pronounced.

**1997** *Rebecca Sealfon of Brooklyn, New York, wins the 70th Annual National Spelling Bee. Sealfon overcame a bad case of nerves and 244 other contestants to win the bee by correctly spelling the word* **euonym.**

## A Few Spicy Words

The terms for many popular Mexican foods, like **tamale** and **chipotle,** and even some foods that we don't necessarily think of as Mexican, like **avocado** and **chocolate,** come from Nahuatl, the language spoken by the Aztecs when the Spanish explorer Hernán Cortés arrived in 1519.

There is no rule that can help you with most of the words that have these endings. What can you say about the formation of *fragrant/fragrance* vs. *eminent/eminence,* for example? *Resistant/resistance* vs. *persistent/persistence*? Memorizing the spelling of words with these endings seems to be the best solution.

The following rules help out with a very small number of the words that have these endings. Try to remember these rules, and one of them just might be applicable when you must decide whether to use an *a* or an *e* to spell a word that calls for *-ant/-ance* or *-ent/-ence* as its final syllable.

**Rule:** After a soft *c* or a soft *g,* use *-ent/-ence.* After a hard *c* or a hard *g,* use *-ant/-ance.* (Note: Few words have a hard *c* or a hard *g* near the end.)

**Examples:**

*Words with soft* c *or* g *near the end:*

> **candescent/candescence**
> **convergent/convergence**
> **dehiscent/dehiscence**
> **diligent/diligence**
> **florescent/florescence**
> **fluorescent/fluorescence**
> **indulgent/indulgence**
> **innocent/innocence**
> **intelligent/intelligence**
> **magnificent/magnificence**
> **negligent/negligence**
> **quiescent/quiescence**

renascent/renascence

resurgent/resurgence

reticent/reticence

rubescent/rubescence

senescent/senescence

submergent/submergence

tumescent/tumescence

*Words with hard* c *or* g *near the end:*

elegant/elegance

extravagant/extravagance

mitigant/mitigance

significant/significance

**Rule:** If the verb form of the word ends in *-fer* and is accented on the final syllable, then the suffix will be *-ent* or *-ence.* With these words, if the suffix used is *-ent,* the addition of the suffix *-ial* is usually required to make the word complete.

**Examples:**

| *Verb form* | *+ ent* | *+ ence* |
|---|---|---|
| defer | deferential | deference |
| infer | inferential | inference |
| prefer | preferential | preference |
| refer | referential | reference |

## Any Alternate Pronunciations?

Asking for alternate pronunciations of nouns ending with the "us" sound can some-times be a huge help. If the ending of the noun is pronounced with only a regular schwa, the ending is often -*us*. Examples include **circus** and **hocus-pocus**. (Make a list of exceptions such as **fracas**.)

If the pronunciation of the ending of the noun is indicated with a dotted schwa, there will be at least two pronunciations: one with schwa and one with more of a short *i* sound. These words will often end in either -*ice* or -*ace*. Examples include **notice** and **populace**. (Make a list of exceptions such as **tennis**). But keep in mind that some words ending with a dotted schwa can have yet another pronunci-ation, one that can give away that pesky vowel indi-cated by the dotted schwa. For example, the endings of the following words can be

*(continued on next page)*

**Rule:** If the verb form of the word has an *a* in the final syllable, then the suffix will be -*ant* or -*ance*.

**Examples:**

| *Verb form* | + *ant* | + *ance* |
|---|---|---|
| **defoliate** | **defoliant** | |
| **delegate** | **delegant** | |
| **deviate** | **deviant** | **deviance** |
| **dominate** | **dominant** | **dominance** |
| **evacuate** | **evacuant** | |
| **hesitate** | **hesitant** | **hesitance** |
| **radiate** | **radiant** | **radiance** |
| **react** | **reactant** | **reactance** |
| **resonate** | **resonant** | **resonance** |
| **tolerate** | **tolerant** | **tolerance** |

Remember to add these and similar words to your lists or spelling notebook as you run across them in your studying. Word familiarity will likely be the biggest help to you when you have to decide whether to use -*ant*/-*ance* or -*ent*/-*ence*.

**-us, -ice, or -ace?** Nouns ending in the "us" sound are almost always spelled with the end-ing -*us*, like *abacus, cubitus, cumulus, hiatus, nexus, tetanus*. However, there are a number of nouns whose pronunciation ends in a sound very close to "us" that have the spelling -*ice* (like *accomplice, armistice, avarice, bodice, chalice, hospice, lattice, malefice, office, orifice, pumice*) or -*ace* (like *boniface, bullace, furnace, grimace, solace, surface, terrace*). The difference in the phoneme is that the schwa is dotted, giv-ing a vowel a sound a little closer to a short *i*.

# Word familiarity will be your best friend when you have to decide whether to use *-ant* or *-ent*.

Look up some of these words and practice this subtle difference in pronunciation. This has tripped up many spellers in spelling bees around the country, as well as at the national finals! And remember: When you hear the "us" sound at the end of a word, it is extremely important to determine whether you are being asked to spell a noun or an adjective.

*(continued from previous page)*

pronounced with either a schwa, a short *i* associated with the dotted schwa, or the gift of a long a: **grimace** and **boniface**. Bottom line: Ask for all of the pronunciations!

## Adjectives

Most adjective endings in English are fairly straightforward to spell and not easily confused, such as *-al, -ic, -ive,* and *-less.* A small number of them, however, cause a large number of misses in spelling bees. Here are a few tips to help you when the going gets rough:

**-ful** Even though *-ful* does mean "full of," it is always spelled with one *l* when you attach it to a word: *guileful, respectful.*

### -able or -ible?

• Say the word minus the suffix out loud. If an actual English word remains, the

## Remember that there are about five times as many words that end in *-able* as in *-ible*.

suffix is more likely to be spelled *-able: accept/acceptable, inhabit/inhabitable, respect/respectable, work/workable.* This is usually, but not always, true, so memorize some of the most common exceptions:

| | |
|---|---|
| **combustible** | **exhaustible** |
| **contemptible** | **flexible** |
| **convertible** | **forcible** |
| **corruptible** | **responsible** |
| **deductible** | **sensible** |
| **digestible** | **suggestible** |

- If the root is an English word ending in *e,* drop the *e* before adding *-able,* unless the consonant before the *e* is *g* or *c: perceive/perceivable, excite/excitable, embrace/embraceable, change/changeable.* If the ending is *-ible,* always drop the *e*

*The sound you don't want to hear.*

ending in the root: *forcible, responsible.*

- Words that are not formed directly from an unchanged English word are more likely to have the *-ible* ending: *divisible, fungible, irascible.*

- If the root ends in a long *i* sound, the suffix will be *-able: friable, viable.*

- There are a number of words that can be spelled with either ending, like *condensable/condensible, ignitable/ ignitible, possessable/possessible.* Be aware of these, but don't spend a lot of time worrying about them.

- Finally, if you really have no clue whether to use the *-able* or *-ible* ending, just remember that there are about five times as many words that end in *-able* as in *-ible.* In fact, it's a good idea to memorize at least the most common *-ible* words, because there aren't that many of them. Some good ones to know are:

| | |
|---|---|
| audible | intelligible |
| compatible | legible |
| credible | negligible |
| edible | permissible |
| eligible | plausible |
| fallible | possible |
| feasible | reprehensible |
| gullible | susceptible |
| horrible | terrible |
| incorrigible | transmissible |
| indelible | visible |

# Bar-Bee-Q

"**N**umber one: Work hard. Winning will not come without work and effort put into it. Number two: Have fun. I didn't participate in the spelling bee because I hated it. I loved the adrenaline rush I got at the microphone. I loved the National Spelling Bee because there were so many fun things I could do—the barbecue, tours, or just socializing with my friends. It was a wonderful experience— one to last a lifetime. So ENJOY IT!"

—Anurag Kashyap, *2005 National Spelling Bee champion* (winning word: *appoggiatura*)

# KISS

"At the bee, keep it simple for success! If you have to spell a word you don't remember seeing before, always remember that words are, by and large, spelled the way they sound. At home, remember that the most important thing you will win from studying for a spelling bee is knowledge, not prizes or fame."

—JACQUES BAILLY,
*1980 National Spelling Bee champion and current Scripps National Spelling Bee pronouncer*

**-eous or -ious?** Most of the words that end in *-eous* and *-ious* come from Latin, and the Latin roots tend to determine what the ending will be. Without going too far into Latin spelling rules, we can make some simple generalizations:

- Adjectives related to material composition or to sciences like biology, chemistry, and geology usually end in *-eous: cutaneous, herbaceous, osseous, vitreous.*

- Words related to taxonomic matters like phylum, class, order, family, genus, or species often have the ending *-aceous: liliaceous, pomaceous.*

- Adjectives related to human feelings, qualities, or actions usually end in *-ious: harmonious, laborious, malicious, suspicious.* There are some obvious exceptions, *courteous, erroneous, righteous,* and *spontaneous* are among them.

- If you can think of a related word ending in *-ion,* the correct ending is usually *-ious: ambition/ambitious, caution/cautious, infection/infectious, rebellion/rebellious, religion/religious.*

**-cious or -tious?** There are approximately equal numbers of words with these endings in *Webster's Third,* but when you remove the entries that are obsolete or have alternate spellings, *-cious* has the edge. If you know whether the noun that is the basis of the word ends in *-cion* or *-tion,* you're in business when it comes to forming the adjective. Here are some of the most common *-cious* and *-tious* adjectives:

# *-cious* vs. *-tious*

| | | | |
|---|---|---|---|
| audacious | judicious | salacious | fictitious |
| atrocious | loquacious | spacious | flirtatious |
| auspicious | lubricious | specious | fractious |
| autoecious | luscious | stenecious | infectious |
| avaricious | malicious | suspicious | licentious |
| bibacious | mendacious | tenacious | nutricious |
| bodacious | meretricious | velocious | obreptitious |
| capacious | minacious | veracious | oppositious |
| capricious | mordacious | vicious | ostentatious |
| conscious | nugacious | vivacious | pretentious |
| contumacious | officious | voracious | propitious |
| delicious | pernicious | ...................... | rambunctious |
| edacious | perspicacious | adventitious | repetitious |
| efficacious | pertinacious | ambitious | scrumptious |
| fallacious | pervicacious | bumptious | seditious |
| feracious | precious | captious | stillatitious |
| ferocious | precocious | cautious | superstitious |
| fugacious | prejudicious | circumlocutious | suppositious |
| gracious | procacious | conscientious | surreptitious |
| hellacious | pugnacious | contentious | tendentious |
| heteroecious | rapacious | expeditious | tralatitious |
| homoecious | sagacious | factitious | vexatious |

**-us or -ous?** The schwa-plus-*s,* or "us" sound, at the end of many adjectives is *almost* always spelled *-ous: membranous, scrupulous, vainglorious, vociferous.* Some exceptions to this rule are words such as *Columbus, Damascus, Mauritius*—adjectives that mean "of or from" a particular place, where the place name happens to end in *-us.* Others are Latin adjectives that have retained the Latin form *-us,* often because they are part of a scientific or academic vocabulary that has historically leaned heavily on

1977 *Rhonda Jones of Harmony, North Carolina, anxiously waits to be called for the 50th Annual National Spelling Bee.*

# Commonly Misspelled Words

L isted below are some of the most commonly misspelled non-homonymic English words. Getting them right in life—on school papers, college applications, and resumes—will mark you as detail oriented, literate, and smart. Make a list of them in your spelling notebook and add to it when you find other everyday misspellings. Look online for lists of other commonly misspelled words and ask your teachers what some of their favorites are.

| | | | |
|---|---|---|---|
| accidentally | disappear | lieutenant | recommend |
| accommodate | disappoint | marshmallow | refrigerator |
| accordion | dissipate | millennium | renown |
| accumulate | drunkenness | miniature | rhythm |
| acquaintance | dumbbell | miscellaneous | ridiculous |
| acquire | ecstasy | mischief | sacrilegious |
| acquit | embarrass | mischievous | sandal |
| amateur | exercise | misogyny | savvy |
| believe | exhilarate | missile | seize |
| breath | existence | misspell | sensible |
| breathe | Fahrenheit | necessary | separate |
| broccoli | fiery | occasion | sergeant |
| calendar | grammar | occurrence | sheriff |
| camouflage | guttural | odyssey | siege |
| Caribbean | handkerchief | parallel | similar |
| cartilage | harass | parliament | sorcerer |
| cemetery | height | pastime | subpoena |
| commemorate | hypocrisy | pharaoh | tariff |
| congratulations | immediately | playwright | threshold |
| consensus | inadvertent | poinsettia | tongue |
| Dalmatian | incidentally | prejudice | tragedy |
| defendant | incredible | presumptuous | tyranny |
| definite | independent | privilege | until |
| desiccate | infinite | pronunciation | vacuum |
| desperate | inoculate | pursue | vicious |
| deterrence | irresistible | raspberry | weird |
| dilemma | lavender | receipt | |
| diorama | liaison | receive | |

# Homonyms:
# Be Discreet, Not Discrete

Many homonyms (words that sound alike but have different meanings and often different spellings) and near homonyms (like *conscience*/*conscious*) seem to be misspelled more often than not! This is by no means a complete list of homonyms, but the ones shown here are some of the most common and therefore the most commonly misspelled. Some of them are not generally used in spelling bees because they are contractions and have an apostrophe, but they are included here because they are very important to know. As a good speller, you should make a special point of using common homonyms correctly.

| | | | | |
|---|---|---|---|---|
| accept | boarder | die | metal | pedal |
| except | border | dye | mettle | peddle |
| ad | brake | discreet | morning | principal |
| add | break | discrete | mourning | principle |
| affect | cellar | eminent | muscle | role |
| effect | seller | imminent | mussel | roll |
| allowed | cereal | immanent | naval | stationary |
| aloud | serial | forth | navel | stationery |
| altar | climb | fourth | overdo | than |
| alter | clime | hear | overdue | then |
| band | coarse | here | palate | their |
| banned | course | heroin | pallet | there |
| bare | complement | heroine | palette | they're |
| bear | compliment | it's | passed | threw |
| basis | conscience | its | past | through |
| bases | conscious | lightening | peace | who's |
| basses | currant | lightning | piece | whose |
| bridal | current | loose | peak | yore |
| bridle | desert | lose | peek | you're |
| | dessert | medal | pique | your |
| | | meddle | | |

# Just add *-ly* to the adjective to make the adverb.

Latin: *anticus, camus, castellatus, emeritus, intermedius, mammatus, maximus, minimus, omnibus, pararectus, redivivus, solus.* There are a very few other exceptions like *antivirus, bogus, Celsius,* and *interstimulus.*

See the discussion of *-ace, -ice,* and *-us* in the nouns sidebar on page 112 for further related information.

## Adverbs

Most adverbs end in *-ly*. A few that do not have retained an adverb ending from another language, like the following:

### Latin

*-im (literatim, passim, seriatim, verbatim)*
*-ad (aborad, anteriad, frontad, mediad, palmad)*

### Italian

(these are typically musical terms)
*-issimo (dolcissimo, fortissimo, pianissimo)*
*-mente (furiosamente, rapidamente, soave-mente)*

There are also several adverb endings that come from Middle English: *-ward/-wards, -ways,* and *-wise: southward, throneward, stern-ways, clockwise, lengthwise.* They are almost always applied to root words that also come from Middle English, and so the resulting words are usually very easy to spell.

## Adverbial Politics

Note that *politicly* and *politically* have different meanings! *Politicly* is formed from *politic,* and it means "craftily" or "shrewdly." *Politically,* which is formed from *political,* means "from a point of view related to politics."

## Duly Noted

In a handful of adverbs, a final letter is dropped before adding -*ly*. These are **duly, illy,** and **truly.**

**-ly or -ally?** The confusion around these two adverb endings is easily eliminated by using a very simple rule: Just add -*ly* to the adjective to make the adverb! If the related adjective ends in -*al,* the adverb form will end in -*ally: accidental/accidentally, musical/ musically, nominal/nominally, operational/ operationally, social/socially.* Where the root adjective ends in *c,* an optional -*al* adjective ending has historically been applied before adding -*ly: fantastic/fantastically, symbolic/ symbolically.* However, in all but a few of these words, the endings -*ally* and -*ly* are both permissible. The exceptions are *anticly, fantastically, politically, politicly,* and *romantically.*

# CHAPTER 6

# The Thrill of a Bee

All spelling bees are fun and exciting, but the buzz and excitement at a National Spelling Bee are unique. Everyone knows that the spellers onstage are the very best out of the ten million hopeful spellers who started out at the classroom level not very many months before. And in only two days, those onstage spellers will wrestle with six hundred or so mind-bendingly difficult words, and one champion will emerge.

The first thing people usually notice at the National Spelling Bee finals is how big the stage is. It has to be because there will be more than 135 spellers sitting on it at the beginning of Round Two! The second round, which is the first oral round, is completed in two parts for exactly that reason: There are always too many contestants to put them all onstage at once.

*"Are we ready at the records desk? Are the tapes rolling and recording? Are you ready, Dr. Bailly? Speller number one, Laura Ann Brown, representing the Birmingham Post-Herald of Birmingham, Alabama, you may approach the microphone."*

The spellers onstage are seated in numerical order. Each speller wears his or her number on a placard, which also shows the city and state of the sponsoring newspaper. Numbers are assigned alphabetically, according to the name of the state and city. Sometimes there are late entries, in which case the new contestants are usually added to the end of the numerical list.

# At the end of each round, staffers print out the round results and take them to the press desk for distribution to the public and to news media.

The microphone is center stage. The records desk is near the stage, in front of the audience. On it are several

computers where National Spelling Bee staff members record how the contestants spell their words. The large media screens at the front of the auditorium are controlled from the records desk. Usually, one screen shows a running list of the words as they are spelled, and the other shows a photograph and brief bio of the speller at the microphone. At the end of each round, staffers print out the round results and take them to the press desk for distribution to the public and the news media.

Also near the stage is a podium for the pronouncer and assistant pronouncer, allowing the speller at the microphone to see their faces clearly (and vice versa). The judges' desk is directly in front of the microphone, ensuring a clear view of the speller. Occasionally, other Scripps National Spelling Bee officials sit at this desk as well.

There are two platforms at the rear of the auditorium, one for television equipment and

## Curious Minds

Folks back home can also get a copy of the round results. All they need to do is log on to www.spellingbee.com during the competition and click on Round Results.

Results are posted in real time, so curious minds don't have to wait until the end of a round to find out how their favorite spellers are faring. If access to the television broadcast is not an option, following along on the Web is the next best thing to being there!

# The process of arriving at a finished word list begins nearly one year before.

Repetition is the Key. Repetition is the Key. Repetition . . .

"Heel, toe, heel, toe, slide, slide, slide, slide. . . ."

If you've ever done any line dancing, you're familiar with those words of the caller. If your memory is any good, it's not too long before you're saying the commands to yourself and no longer need the caller's prompt.

Some spellers learn new words in a similar way—repetition. They write a new word ten or so times, usually in a vertical line. This repetition seems to stamp the pattern of the word in the brain. Writing the word over and over sends a cadence to the brain that enables the speller to correctly spell the word.

the other for the National Spelling Bee's sound recording equipment. If there is an appeal of the judges' decision to eliminate a speller, it can be played directly into the judges' headphones or, in rare cases, into the room's sound system so that the entire audience can hear the replay.

## How the Words Are Chosen

A three-member word panel chooses words for the Scripps National Spelling Bee from the current *Webster's Third New International Dictionary*. A typical list contains approximately one thousand words divided into sections: separate sections for each of the first ten or so rounds, another section for higher rounds, and a final section for Championship Words. The first round is a written test consisting of twenty-five items of increasing difficulty. All spellers take the same test.

The process of arriving at a finished list begins nearly one year before the list is used in competition. The panelists begin with a tentative list of words, often chosen from their everyday reading, news stories, and subjects of personal interest; other words are chosen directly from *Webster's Third*. The proposed words are checked against *Webster's Third* to make sure they are compatible with the official bee rules. If a proposed word is not listed in *Webster's Third,* it is removed from consideration. Word panelists DO NOT consult the *Consolidated Word List*—a nearly comprehensive list of words used in the Scripps National Spelling Bee since 1950—in choosing words for the new list.

Next, word panelists use information provided in *Webster's Third* to compose concise dictionary entries for their words. Each entry includes the word, its pronunciation, the part of speech, a definition, and a sentence illustrating the use of the word. Another bee official provides the language of origin information for each word, drawing heavily from information provided in *Webster's Third*.

Once the dictionary entries

**"***If it's not in Webster's Third, it's not in the bee!***"**

## A Gift, Not a Guide

**R**emember: The word panelists DO NOT consult the *Consolidated Word List* when selecting words for word lists. Spellers who happen to receive a word that is on the *Consolidated Word List* do so purely by coincidence. It's a good guess that there has never been a round in national competition in which all the words in that round were on the *Consolidated Word List*. It's best to view the *Consolidated Word List* as a "study gift," *not* as a "study guide."

# Members of the word panel meet in the autumn to review the rough draft.

## For a Spelling Bee Word, No News Is Good News

A word's difficulty is often a sign of the times. If a word has recently been in the news quite a bit, the word's familiarity will cause it to receive a lower difficulty rating than it might otherwise receive, and will appear, if at all, earlier in the National Spelling Bee competition. For example, the word **cortege** experienced a big drop in difficulty in the year following Princess Diana's death because it had appeared in many news stories. In recent years, **cortege** has crept up in difficulty level because spellers have not had as many opportunities to encounter it.

are complete, the word list manager consolidates the information and produces a rough draft of the word list. Members of the word panel, along with some of the other bee officials, meet in the autumn to review the rough draft. This group revises many of the word entries and deletes some words from the list. During this meeting, each word is given a rating according to the panelists' and officials' best estimation of difficulty. When rating a word, consideration is given to the word's relative level of familiarity, the degree to which it can be spelled phonetically, and the degree to which the correct spelling may be deduced from knowledge of word roots and language patterns. A word's length in letters or number of syllables is sometimes a factor.

After the meeting, the word list manager edits the list again, reorders it according to the averaged ratings, and divides it into rounds. During another word panel meeting in the late winter before the national competition, the list is again discussed and some word placements are shifted if there is a consensus.

The final word list is sent to the pronouncer, who begins the process of researching each word's various pronunciations and compiling detailed notes on them. In May, the list is given to the judges for their review. Finally, one day before the competition begins, bee officials (pronouncers, judges, word panelists, word list manager, and the director) meet to review the word list, air any last-minute concerns, and make deletions, if needed.

After this lengthy process, which has incorporated many different meetings and levels of review, the list is deemed ready for use in competition.

# The Written Round

T he written, multiple-choice Round One has been a part of the national finals since 2002. It was adopted primarily because of the bee's time constraints, but most spellers like it because it gives them a chance to really show their stuff. Before 2002, spellers who were eliminated early in the bee had spelled only one or two words, but now every speller gets to make choices for the twenty-five items on the written test, plus spell at least one more word; even the spellers whose written test score will prevent passing the threshold of elimination spell one word—orally—in Round Two.

Each item on the written test counts for one point. The passing threshold is determined after

**Music**

LEVEL: Advanced

aubade
bariolage
cantabile
cantillate
celestina
decrescendo
diapason
divertissement
embouchure
euterpean
farandole
feroce
fortississimo
gamelan
glockenspiel
guaracha
lacrimando
larghetto
maestoso
misterioso
Orphean
ossia
pedaliter
piacevole
ridotto
risoluto
schottische
sfogato
solmizate
tacet
tarogato
tiralee
vide
vorspiel

## Special Circumstances

The Scripps National Spelling Bee accommodates spellers with physical challenges involving sight, hearing, speech, or movement. If you have any condition that might impede your performance in either the written or oral rounds, let your sponsoring newspaper know right away. It is very important that you do this if you know of any reason that would cause you to have difficulty in reading, writing, getting to the microphone, understanding the pronouncer, or making the judges understand you. Make sure your sponsor or official escort informs the National Spelling Bee headquarters as soon as possible, or by the deadline listed in the rules, at the latest. Don't be embarrassed about doing this; bee officials will be sensitive and discreet. They will inform you privately of any special procedures that they or you will need to follow, and it's likely that other spellers and audience members will remain completely unaware that any accommodation is being made for you.

the tests are graded (they are scored electronically) and is selected so as to allow ninety or more spellers to advance to Round Three of the finals.

Spellers should keep in mind that Round Two gives them a chance to overcome a less-than-stellar performance in Round

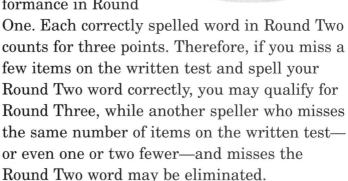

One. Each correctly spelled word in Round Two counts for three points. Therefore, if you miss a few items on the written test and spell your Round Two word correctly, you may qualify for Round Three, while another speller who misses the same number of items on the written test— or even one or two fewer—and misses the Round Two word may be eliminated.

Round One takes place in a very large room, usually the auditorium where the oral rounds of the bee are held. Spellers sit in assigned seats at long rows of tables. Each speller is given several No. 2 pencils, an eraser, a couple of blank sheets of paper, and a sealed envelope containing an official test form and an answer sheet with twenty-five multiple-choice items. The test form is preprinted with the speller's name and number. Spellers are allowed to bring extra No. 2 pencils and a sweater or jacket, but nothing else—no paper, purses, bags, or hats.

At the start of the round, the head judge instructs spellers to remove their test materials from the envelopes and check the identifying information. Then the pronouncer announces the start of a period of silence. This is the time to look over the items on the answer sheet and think about which words you know how to spell and which ones are a challenge.

For each word for which there are multiple spellings, the pronouncer will provide all the pronunciations listed in *Webster's Third*. He will also provide the part of speech, language of origin, definition, and a sentence. The pronouncer will pause for a few seconds, then repeat all of the information. No questions will be accepted from either the spellers or the audience. Spellers have five choices for each

*The Written Round.*

# A Real Nail-Biter

"The first year I participated in the national finals, I was eleven years old. I was a little nervous and fidgety and had a terrible nail-biting habit. Well, a wire service photographer took a series of pictures of me doing things like scratching my eyebrow, biting my thumbnail, staring at the ceiling, and running my hand through my hair. That little series of four pictures ran in newspapers all over the country! I looked like a little blonde chimp, and I think my mother was a bit embarrassed. It taught me that what happens near a camera can be seen anywhere by nightfall, and I was much more careful after that."

—BARRIE TRINKLE,
*1973 National
Spelling Bee champion*

item and are given a reasonable amount of time to darken the circle corresponding to the correct choice. Then the pronouncer moves to the next item on the list. At the end of the list, the pronouncer will repeat the twenty-five items one more time and announce the start of another period of silence, during which spellers can check and change any answers.

The following tips should help you do well in the written round:

- Follow all directions.

- Don't open your test envelope until instructed to do so.

- Check to make sure you have the right test sheet; if not, raise your hand to let a staff member know immediately.

- Fill in the circles neatly; don't make stray marks on the paper.

- For each item, quickly eliminate the choices you know to be wrong, and choose from the remaining possible answers.

- You are allowed to change your answers at any time during the test period. Be sure to erase prior answers *completely*.

- Be careful! During the period of silence at the end of the test, you should check

# Stay aware of your seatmates so you will know that you are sitting in the right place.

## Lucky Charms

Don't hesitate to bring your rabbit's foot along to the competition. In fact, many spellers carry something to reassure them that all will turn out well, often something they happened to be wearing the first time they won a bee, like special T-shirts, bracelets, earrings, or socks. One speller confessed that she always has a small piece of craft putty in her pocket, because she had one there when she won her first school bee! Others carry items that were given to them specifically for good luck like shamrocks, horseshoe key chains, wishbones, or coins. All of those are fine. Just keep it small—no MP3 player or your lucky pocket dictionary!

in two segments. In 2006, there were 140 and 134 spellers onstage for each of the two segments of Round Two, 97 for each of Round Three, and 86 for Round Four. It may take as long as two hours to finish each of the early rounds.

There are flat risers on the stage, so each row of chairs is slightly higher than the one in front of it. This gives your parents a good view of you and photographers a better chance to take pictures. (It also means that you're always visible to everyone, so you will want to be aware of what your onstage behavior looks like! You

*Theodore Yuan watches fellow competitors during Round Six of competition at the 2006 Scripps National Spelling Bee.*

the answer sheet with the choices *and* your test form with the filled-in circles side by side. The written round is scored by computer, so accidentally skipping a line will throw off all the answers after it and could turn a threshold-breaking answer sheet into one that will not qualify you for Round Three.

- Obviously, you should not leave your seat without permission or talk to anyone during the written test. Don't risk disqualification!

Spellers will be allowed to leave the testing room but will not be allowed to return to complete the test. You should leave only in the direst emergency because doing so means that only the part of the test you have completed will be scored and you will likely be eliminated from the bee. The entire test takes about 45 minutes to an hour, so plan on remaining in your seat for that period of time.

## What It's Like Onstage

Traditional oral spelling competition begins in Round Two. At some point on Wednesday of Bee Week, you will take your seat on the stage of the Scripps National Spelling Bee, take a deep breath, and wait for your Round Two word.

During most of your time onstage, you'll be sitting down. In the early rounds, there will be many spellers onstage. Round Two is completed

## Word of the Year

The American Dialect Society (ADS) was born in 1889, but has been voting on the "word of the year" only since 1990. However, ADS members Allan Metcalf and David Barnhart have researched the linguistic past and retroactively handed out "word of the year" awards to a new word every year since 1900, when the word of the year was "phony." Here's a sample:

1906: teddy bear
1928: athlete's foot
1938: teenager
1945: showbiz
1957: role model
1965: affirmative action
1976: couch potato
1989: virtual reality

never know when your picture is being taken.) As each contestant spells, the next one or two contestants line up well behind him or her on the risers, out of the way but ready to move forward at the appropriate time.

A bee staffer will explain your path to the microphone. During longer breaks, staffers sometimes remove the extra chairs onstage and rearrange the remaining ones, so your path may change. Stay aware of your seatmates so you will know that you are sitting in the right place. Also, make sure your placard with the number on it is facing outward. This will help the judges and other bee staff keep everyone in order.

The auditorium can be chilly, especially first thing in the morning or if you're feeling a little nervous. Bring a light sweater or jacket.

## Staying Sane

If you're feeling nervous on the morning of the competition, you should say so. Don't dwell on it, but let your family and friends know that you could use some encouragement. All the other spellers are feeling nervous too, even the "favorites." (In fact, they may feel more nervous, because they feel more pressure

## Get Mental

"It's obvious that you need to have knowledge of word roots and language patterns in order to figure out unfamiliar words. Less obvious is the fact that you need to have poise and a mental routine in order to *apply* that knowledge to figuring out unfamiliar words. The worst mental state you can be in prior to participating in a spelling bee is the 'I sure hope I get words I know' mindset. You're best off accepting that you *are* going to get a word or words that are unfamiliar. If you expect the unfamiliar, you'll be more likely to become the word sleuth you know you can be."

—Paige Pipkin Kimble, *1981 National Spelling Bee champion*

to do well.) Experience and skill are no protection against butterflies in the stomach. If you put it out there in the open when you talk to other spellers and share a joke about it, you'll feel calmer.

Here are a few quick tips for competition day:

- Your best hedge against the jitteriness that affects your performance is plenty of sleep the night before. A good night's sleep will recharge your batteries and help you concentrate on the words.

- Don't pass up breakfast! Your brain needs food. If you're feeling too nervous to eat much, at least take a breakfast or energy bar with you and nibble it before you go onstage.

- Plan for success. Assume that you'll stay in the contest and will therefore be onstage for several hours. You will get some breaks; always take the opportunity to go to the restroom and get a drink before you return to your seat. Talk to your parents or legal guardian before the bee and arrange for them to have quick snacks ready for you during the breaks in case you feel

# Don't try to absorb a big list of words at the last minute. The chance that you'll actually get one of those words is minuscule!

hungry. You won't be allowed to take food and drinks onstage.

- Don't try to absorb a big list of words at the last minute. The chance that you'll actually get one of those words is minuscule! Your time would be better spent meditating or talking to friends or enjoying some other pleasantly distracting activity that will help you relax and focus. (Some kids vouch that video games are great for this.)

## Getting Your Parents to Chill

You can't do much to control your parents' feelings, but the calmer you are, the calmer they'll probably be. You might try giving them a small gift as a little joke before the bee: a fidget stone, worry beads, or a crochet hook and a ball of yarn. If they are really nervous, they might be better off not watching you

## Spelling Trick

**"Stationary"** is being still while **"stationery"** is something you mail. Just remember that *stationary* has an a for *stay*, whereas *stationery* has an e for *envelope*.

# Tip on the Slip from a Champ

"I am about as nervous as anyone onstage. I get distracted by the weird lighting, unfamiliar people and furniture, faces in the audience, and a lot of feelings that have no words for them. These are prime conditions for a slip of the tongue. No matter how many times you *think* the correct spelling in your brain, when it comes to actually vocalizing, your mouth may have a mind of its own. So here is what I did to avoid tragedy: I would rehearse the spelling in a quiet whisper, out loud but under my breath, a good distance away from the microphone. Then I would step up to the mike and do it again, louder. An immediate repetition of almost the same action has a pretty good chance of success. There is no perfect defense against slipping up, but I can say that, in four years of this kind of tight-rope walking, I never suffered the catastrophe of saying *g* for *j*."

—HENRY FELDMAN,
*1960 National
Spelling Bee champion*

*Official Pronouncer Jacques Bailly, left, and Associate Pronouncer Dr. Brian Sietsema.*

spell—at least not all the time. Let them know that it's okay for them to leave the auditorium, even when it's your turn. When they return, you can give them a discreet thumbs-up to let them know you are hanging in there just fine.

Probably the best thing you can do for someone who is nervous is to let this person do something for you. So put Mom or Dad in charge of something you need. Ask nicely if one of them would be willing to call a few of your friends after each round, get you your favorite beverage and have it ready when the round is over, or plan a special family outing for when the bee is over.

If you're with both parents and they're both nervous, take each of them aside separately before the bee starts and ask one to keep the other a little distracted.

# A L T—ask, listen, think. Give yourself the best possible chance to spell the word correctly.

## Your Turn to Spell

Sooner or later, it will be your turn to spell. Be sure to follow the instructions you were given about the flow of traffic onstage. Move to the microphone quickly and calmly, and adjust it so that you can speak into it easily without stooping or standing on tiptoe. Then watch the pronouncer give you your word.

## Asking Questions

Asking good questions and listening carefully to the answers are two skills that a serious speller *must* develop. With so many competitors, the National Spelling Bee must place time constraints on them, so your time at the microphone is limited. Spend it wisely. Use the mnemonic **A L T—ask, listen, think.** Give yourself the best possible chance to spell the word correctly.

The official National Spelling Bee rules state the following:

In oral competition, the speller may ask the pronouncer to pronounce the word again, define it, use it in a sentence, or provide the language origin. In addition, if the speller wishes to ask if the dictionary lists a specific root word as the root of the word to be spelled, the speller must specify a pronunciation of the root (not a

## Don't Show Off!

Do ask genuine questions you might have about the word you have been asked to spell, but *don't* ask questions just to call attention to yourself. The audience will smell show-off behavior from a mile away—and find it annoying.

Moreover, in national competition, asking unnecessary questions or making observations to draw attention to yourself eats away at your valuable time limit at the microphone. Familiarize yourself with Rule 11 of the Contest Rules of the Scripps National Spelling Bee, which begins: "A speller is expected to spell familiar words without delay and to refrain from routines that employ unnecessary or repetitive questioning." This rule spells out the amount of time national finalists have at the microphone. Familiarity with the details of this rule is extremely important for national finalists. See the complete rule at www.spellingbee.com.

# Even though the rules don't require it—you should *always* pronounce the word you are given.

## More Words of the Year

The American Dialect Society has designated the following words as the "word of the year":

- 1903: highbrow
- 1920: normalcy
- 1921: media
- 1937: groovy
- 1949: cool
- 1967: ripoff
- 1977: loony tunes
- 1985: rocket scientist
- 1992: not!

spelling), its language, and its definition. . . . A speller is expected to spell familiar words without delay and to refrain from routines that employ unnecessary or repetitive questioning.

When they get a word they think they know, some spellers launch into the spelling immediately. This practice is very risky, because a speller who mistakes one easy word for another and spells the wrong word will hear the dreaded *ding!* of the judges' bell.

When you first receive your word, you should mentally center yourself. Take a deep breath if you need to. Then repeat the word clearly into the microphone, facing

the judges and using the exact pronunciation that was given. This helps them know that you have heard your word correctly. If *you* are not sure whether you've heard it correctly, ask the pronouncer to re-pronounce the word.

Probably no one in your life will listen to your every utterance as closely as the National Spelling Bee judges will. There's nothing that makes them feel worse than the plight of a speller who has inserted an extra syllable, misunderstood the sound /th/ as /f/, or simply spelled the wrong word, even though the responsibility of making sure of the pronunciation belongs to the speller. You must give the judges a reasonable chance to correct you, so—even though the rules don't require it—you should *always* pronounce the word you are given. If the judges think you have mispronounced the word, they will ask you to pronounce it again. If they still believe you are not saying the word correctly, they will ask the pronouncer to pronounce it again for you. If this happens, you should listen very carefully, then re-pronounce the word into the microphone, just as the pronouncer gave it to you. Once everyone is satisfied that you are saying the word correctly, you can get down to the business of figuring out the correct spelling.

*Stephanie Baer spells her first word in the 2003 National Spelling Bee.*

# Can You Spell "Life Lesson"?

"Looking back, as hard as it is to believe, I am glad I did not win—because I learned lessons I badly needed to learn through not obtaining my goal. You see, my mistake in 1996 was not that I didn't know how to spell the word **dispel**. It was that I thought I knew how to spell everything. . . . I now understand that humility is what makes an accomplishment worthwhile. If you don't expect to win, the surprise of doing so is all the more rewarding. And if you don't win but have a humble attitude from the start, disappointment is minimized and you can focus on others rather than on yourself. This lesson has made the rest of my life, up to this point, much happier than the hours following my elimination from the 1996 National Spelling Bee."

—CORRIE LOEFFLER, *National Spelling Bee finalist, 1994, 1995, and 1996; press desk, Scripps National Spelling Bee*

# When you first receive your word, you should mentally center yourself.

## Word Mystery: The Curious Case of the Missing C

Many words from Romance languages (French, Spanish, Italian, Portuguese, and Catalan) have Latin roots, but their spelling may have changed. For example, **brocade** comes from Spanish, Catalan, and Italian words, and further back from the Latin word *broccus*, meaning "projecting (like a tooth)." How it lost the extra *c* is a mystery to which the dictionary entry alone offers no solution.

Remember: *Ask, listen, think.* Sometimes spellers are a little shell-shocked when they receive a word they've never heard, so they'll go through the motions of asking questions—but the answers go in one ear and out the other. Again, mentally center yourself, and tell yourself that you *can* figure out this word.

Ask first for a definition and really listen to the answer. If the word is a homonym, the pronouncer should tell you that fact at the beginning. If you think it is a homonym and the pronouncer hasn't mentioned it, ask, "Is this word a homonym?" If it is, the definition will be the most useful piece of information you can get. If the word ends with a sound that could belong to several different endings, such as the sound "us," ask for the part of speech so that you know whether it might be an adjective ending in -*ous* or a noun ending in -*us*. Asking for a sentence lets you hear the word in context, which is just one more piece of insurance. If you feel sure of the word, you can now safely spell it.

However, if you're not entirely sure you know the word, you should next ask for the language of origin. This can help you figure out some letter combinations quickly. For example, knowing that *pharos* comes from Greek will help you spell the /f/ phoneme with a *ph*. (See Chapters 3 and 4 for more on language origins and spelling patterns.)

If you think the word may contain a particular root, you may ask, but you must know from what language it is and what it means. This question is most useful when you are trying to decide between two or more possible spellings, as when there is an unstressed syllable containing a schwa. Phrase your question something like this: "Does *nectariferous* contain the Greek combining form *-phor,* meaning "bearing"? The pronouncer will check the dictionary entry and

## Rich in Words

"Your mind is like your body: It needs to be exercised to keep in shape. Learning and memorizing words has helped to keep my mind fit. I've added many of those words I learned for the spelling bee to my vocabulary. I still use them, and they've made me a better journalist and a better writer. Learning a word makes it yours—exactly like putting money in your pocket— and it makes you rich in a way that money can't."

PATT MORRISON, *National Spelling Bee finalist, 1966;* Los Angeles Times *columnist, Emmy-winning television host, PBS and NPR commentator*

*The judges confer.*

give you an answer. Sometimes the answer will be "No" or "I don't see that listed here." Keep trying. "Does it contain the Latin combining form -*fer,* meaning 'bearing'?" Remember that a "no" answer does not *necessarily* mean that you are on the wrong track with the spelling. Sometimes the root you've asked about doesn't come from the language you indicated or doesn't mean what you think, and the pronouncer has no choice but to answer your question in the negative. Remember: Diligent root-word study often pays off big-time!

While you are entitled to ask questions, you should always remember that you are subject to a time limit that is strictly enforced. If you waste time in unnecessary pursuits—for example, trying to extract an unnatural pronunciation from the pronouncer in order to guess at the spelling of a schwa— you may exhaust your time limit and be forced to spell the word imme- diately. Once you have done this, you may be subject to a shorter time limit for subsequent rounds.

# Stuck in the Middle with *U*

The Scripps National Spelling Bee has a time-honored rule that many other spelling bees also follow: Even after hav- ing started to spell, a speller is allowed to stop

# Pretend that the rest of the audience is on Mars, and that you and the judges are sitting in your living room having a conversation.

and start over, retracing the spelling from the beginning, as long as there is *no change* to the letters that were already spelled or the order they were given in.

Have you ever gotten lost in the middle of spelling a word? It happens all the time. Many people get confused when they stop to think about the next letter or syllable, so if you hesitate on a spelling for more than a few seconds, it's a good idea to start over and spell the word all the way through. Do let the judges know

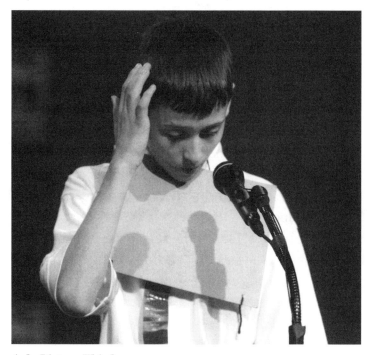

*Ask. Listen. Think.*

## Don't E-M-B-A-double R-A-double S Yourself

Have you ever heard anyone spell the word *Mississippi* "*M - i* - crooked letter - crooked letter - *i* - crooked letter - crooked letter - *i* - humpback - humpback - *i*"? Your grandparents probably know that jingle! Perhaps you have heard "*M - i* - double *s - i* - double *s - i* - double *p - i*."

P-l-e-a-s-e don't spell double letters this way in a spelling bee! The judges will expect you to spell each letter separately, and if you don't, you are likely to confuse yourself as well as them. Also, you'd be in deep trouble if you tried to spell a word like *vacuum* or *muumuu* by saying "double *u*"!

# A word beginning with the /k/ sound is statistically more likely to be spelled with the letter c than with the letter k.

## Sussing It Out

Sometimes you can figure out a word using word roots that you know, but there are times when the best you can do is guess at the spelling using whatever mental associations you have. Anurag Kashyap, 2005 National Spelling Bee champion, and a maestro of both techniques:

"At the nationals, I successfully spelled **priscilla, pompier,** and **ornithorhynchous** despite not studying the words. I correctly guessed **priscilla** by thinking of Priscilla Presley. **Pompier** means something to do with firefighters, so I thought of the fiery volcano at Pompeii, and remembered that the 'ee-yay' sound in French is *-ier.* I guessed **ornithorhynchous** using the Greek roots of *ornithos,* 'bird,' and *rhynchos,* 'beak.'

that you are starting the word over, and if you want to be especially cautious, wait for a nod from them. Waiting for the judges' acknowledgment of your plan is not necessary, but it is a safety measure. It makes crystal clear what letter sequence you want the judges to use when they evaluate your spelling.

## The Judges

The judges at the National Spelling Bee typically have many years of experience. Some of them have served as regional spelling bee judges for years before moving up to the national level, and others have served the National Spelling Bee in other capacities before becoming judges. They are very good at what they do, which is understanding spellers—even those with strong national or regional accents, quiet voices, or speech impediments. However, you should always keep in mind that the judges are the *most* important people in the room to communicate with. The easier you can make

their job, the less chance there is that you will have to endure an agonizing delay as they try to determine whether you gave the correct spelling.

Pretend that the rest of the audience is on Mars and that you and the judges are sitting in your living room having a conversation. Look straight at them when you spell, speak as clearly as you can, and don't hesitate to address them directly: "Judges, am I saying the word correctly?" or "I'm going to start my spelling over now, okay?" Doing this will not only get you the information you need, but will also help you feel in charge of your time at the microphone. And that can boost your confidence, which can get you through some majorly tough words.

## Using Your Instinct: KISS

Let's imagine for a moment that you are standing at the microphone on the National Spelling Bee stage and you have just been given a word that you have never heard before. You inquire about the word's meaning and its origin. You rule out all root words that seem like possibilities. Not a single

## Can Do

"I competed in the National Spelling Bee twice, and both times I thought it was the most unusual and interesting week of my life. I expected everyone to be just like me. Instead, I met more than a hundred kids who shared my love of words, but were different from me in so many ways that sometimes I forgot exactly why we had all come to Washington that week. Years later, I realized that the best lesson I got from being a contestant was that what you *can* do well is far more important than what you can't."

—VICTOR HASTINGS, *National Spelling Bee finalist, 1973 and 1974; attorney*

## Behind the Scenes

There are many people working at a National Spelling Bee, although spellers can see only a few of them from the stage. The press desk, the records desk, the sound recording table, the Comfort Room, and other positions are busy all the time during the spelling. These positions are often staffed by former spellers. So take comfort in knowing that there are many people present who know exactly how you're feeling onstage and are working to make your bee experience the best it can be.

answer to your questions gives you even a hint of a clue. In a nutshell, you know absolutely nothing about this word.

What should you do? Consider employing the KISS rule—<u>K</u>eep <u>I</u>t <u>S</u>imple (for) <u>S</u>uccess. Just spell the word the way it sounds as simply as you can—no fancy spins or silent letters thrown in.

You will have to use your own judgment about what KISS means to you. Some people might go ahead and spell the word completely phonetically, and they might be right. However, English has certain common spelling patterns that aren't phonetic. For example, a word beginning with the /k/ sound is statistically more likely to be spelled with the letter *c* than with the letter *k*. So you may want to work out a commonsense approach, using a combination of phonetics and well-known spelling patterns. For any given word, you might be wrong, but you could just as easily be right.

If you are leery about this, observe a spelling bee and test it out. You can visit another school's spelling bee, a regional spelling bee, a corporate spelling bee, or just watch a National Spelling Bee rerun on television. Spell silently along with the other spellers as they receive their words. Use the KISS rule when there is no information that can help you with the correct spelling of the word. Tally how many times your spelling is

# One of the best things you can do for yourself is to think about what it will be like when you miss a word.

right when you use the KISS rule and how many times your spelling is wrong when you use it. Then you can decide for yourself whether this approach will be effective for you.

In the end, all you really have to go on for a "mystery word" is your instinct. It's best to have tested your crunch-time instinct before you need it!

## What Happens If You Miss a Word?

We all know the first sign of having missed a word: *Ding!* If you happen to be the speller, first you'll hear the head judge ring a bell. Then the pronouncer will give the correct spelling. A National Spelling Bee staff member (often a former national finalist) will then greet you and walk offstage with you to the Comfort Room, a special lounge for spellers who have been eliminated. Your parents are allowed to meet you there, if you want them to. You can stay in the Comfort Room as long as you like—sitting in the comfy chairs, looking up your word in the dictionary, eating snacks,

DING

## Drunk on Words

Spelling bees are no longer just for kids. Bee fever has caught on in bars and clubs across the country. One Brooklyn, New York, bar even holds bimonthly bees, thanks to the successful combination of alcohol and orthography. Though the atmosphere lacks the formality and suspense of a National Spelling Bee, adult spellers still face fierce competition and—ahem—a **cornucopia** of challenging words. The grownups win free drinks, not college scholarships, which means the more **bibulous** participants may get a little sloppy as the evening wears on.

# The chance that the pronouncer has mispronounced a word in the National Spelling Bee finals is almost nil.

and chatting with staff members and other eliminated spellers. If you feel more than a little upset, the Comfort Room staff will make sure you have tissues, a shoulder to cry on, and privacy and quiet. You can leave the Comfort Room whenever you are ready. It's possible that a member of the news media will be outside in the hallway and will ask to talk to you about your bee participation. The bee encourages you to speak with this individual if you choose. This is your fifteen minutes of fame!

Some spellers who make it to the national finals have never missed a spelling word in

*W-H-E-E-L-B-A-R-R-O-W:*
*Finalists at play.*

competition. If you are such a speller, take a moment to imagine that bell ringing for you, because it most likely will. Every speller who makes it to the National Spelling Bee finals dreams of winning, but one of the best things you can do for yourself is to think about what it will be like when you miss a word. You will still be disappointed when it happens, but you'll be able to bounce back emotionally and enjoy the rest of the week with your new friends if you've prepared yourself to hear that *ding!*

## Appealing: When, Why, and How

An appeal of the judges' decision is the responsibility of your parent(s) or legal guardian. Appeals are usually made if the speller can show that there is an accepted alternate spelling or if the pronouncer gave the speller a homonym but did not clarify that it was a homonym. If you feel that you correctly spelled a version of the word that the pronouncer gave you—and the pronouncer did not give you a meaning of the word you were to spell—an appeal is in order. Ask an adult who has accompanied you to go to the judges before it would be your turn to spell again if you were

# The Fundamentals

"A newspaper reporter asked me how I felt. I said, 'T-I-R-E-D.' The National Spelling Bee has a physical endurance component in addition to the intellectual component. Generally, the simple rules apply. Get a good night's sleep. Eat a good breakfast and lunch. And whenever there's a bathroom break, take advantage of it, even if you don't think you need to."

—JON PENNINGTON,
*1986 National
Spelling Bee champion*

# Where are they now?

As you might expect, National Spelling Bee champions typically go on to succeed in other areas. Many have become doctors, attorneys, teachers, engineers, journalists, university professors, and business executives. The 1941 champion, Louis Edward Sissman (1928–1976), was a celebrated poet. His book *Hello, Darkness* won the National Book Critics Circle Award for poetry in 1978. Below are some of the professions practiced by champions of the last half century.

| | | |
|---|---|---|
| 1951 | Irving Belz | Psychiatrist, Conroe, Texas |
| 1954 | William Cashore | Professor of pediatrics, Brown University School of Medicine, Providence, Rhode Island |
| 1960 | Henry Feldman | Medical statistician, Boston, Massachusetts |
| 1961 | John Capehart | Thoracic surgeon, Dallas, Texas |
| 1971 | Jonathan Knisely | Physician and associate professor of radiology at Yale University School of Medicine, New Haven, Connecticut |
| 1972 | Robin Kral | Biotechnology executive, Dallas, Texas |
| 1973 | Barrie Trinkle | Editor and writer, Seattle, Washington |

still in the bee. Follow the bee's guidelines about filing appeals. This is applicable to any spelling bee. At the National Spelling Bee, your parent or legal guardian will need to fill out a paper form explaining the disagreement with the judges' decision.

Appeals have rarely resulted in the reinstatement of a speller, so don't waste time with a frivolous appeal. If you appeal your elimination, you will be reinstated *only* if the judges decide that you have correctly spelled an acceptable form of the word you were given. You will not be reinstated if you misunderstood the word

| 1974 | Julie Ann Junkin Bedsole | Third-grade teacher, Northport, Alabama |
| 1977 | John Paola | Veterinarian, Annapolis, Maryland |
| 1978 | Peg McCarthy | Psychologist, Topeka, Kansas |
| 1979 | Katie Kerwin McCrimmon | Reporter, *Rocky Mountain News,* Denver, Colorado |
| 1980 | Jacques Bailly | Associate professor of classics, University of Vermont; Scripps National Spelling Bee pronouncer |
| 1981 | Paige Pipkin Kimble | Director, Scripps National Spelling Bee, Cincinnati, Ohio |
| 1983 | Blake Giddens | Civil engineer, Alexandria, Virginia; Scripps National Spelling Bee judge |
| 1985 | Balu Natarajan | Sports medicine physician, Chicago, Illinois |
| 1986 | Jon Pennington | Editor, Arlington, Virginia |
| 1987 | Stephanie Petit | Attorney, San Francisco, California |
| 1988 | Rageshree Ramachandran | Physician and medical researcher, San Francisco, California |
| 1991 | Joanne Lagatta | Physician, Chicago, Illinois |
| 1992 | Amanda Goad | Attorney, New York, New York |
| 1996 | Wendy Guey | Investor relations associate, New York, New York |

and spelled a different word! It is *always* your—and only your—responsibility to make sure you have understood your word.

Occasionally, spellers appeal on the basis of the pronouncer's having "mispronounced" the word. This kind of appeal is also doomed to failure. The pronouncer can give only pronunciations listed in *Webster's Third New International Dictionary.* Sometimes spellers are accustomed to hearing a nonstandard pronunciation and are confused by the dictionary pronunciations, or their dictionaries may list pronunciations that *Webster's Third* doesn't have. That's too bad, but that argument won't get a speller back into the bee: What *Webster's Third* says goes. And by the time of the national finals, the pronouncer has pronounced every word on the list many times and at least twice in front of other officials and word panelists. The chance that the pronouncer has mispronounced a word in the National Spelling Bee finals is almost nil.

So now you may be wondering what constitutes an "accepted alternate spelling." The official rules of the National Spelling Bee state:

*Samir Sudhir Patel gets it right in Round Six of the 2006 National Spelling Bee.*

*Webster's Third New International Dictionary* and its addenda section . . . shall serve as the final authority for the spelling of words. If more than one spelling is listed for a word that the pronouncer has provided for the speller to spell, any of these spellings shall be accepted as correct if all of the following three criteria are met: ***(1) The pronunciations of the words are identical, (2) the definitions of the words are identical,*** and ***(3) the words are clearly identified as being standard variants of each other.*** Spellings at other locations having temporal labels (such as *archaic, obsolete*), stylistic labels (such as *substand, nonstand*), or regional labels (such as *North, Midland, Irish*) that differ from main entry spellings not having these status labels shall not be accepted as correct.

For example, both *broccoli* and *brocoli* would be acceptable spellings but *abbaye* (an archaic variant of *abbey*), *thoro* (a nonstandard spelling of *thorough*), and *cieling* (an obsolete variant of *ceiling*) would not.

Realistically, it's not likely that you'll see words like these in the National Spelling Bee— the word panel tends not to include words with alternate spellings on the list—but now you know what kinds of alternate spellings are defensible.

## Great Rewards

"Right after spelling the winning word, I was totally stunned and I felt as if I were the luckiest person on Earth. I remember thinking that I would be able to sit on a dais with all of the top spellers at the awards banquet, and that was such a big reward to me. Nothing else registered until later because I was so shocked at the time!"

—NUPUR LALA, *1999 National Spelling Bee champion*

# A Journalist Is Born

"At the press conference after I won, the reporters asked what I wanted to be when I grew up. I spontaneously answered that I wanted to be a journalist. I think I sensed the excitement of covering an event like the bee. I eventually became a reporter for my sponsoring newspaper, the *Rocky Mountain News*."

—KATIE KERWIN McCRIMMON, *1979 National Spelling Bee champion* (winning word: **maculature**)

# When It's Down to a Few, Then Two

Often, there is a short break when there are only a few spellers left, and parents of these spellers are invited to take a seat at the side of the stage. A speller who misses in these higher rounds will join his or her parents in these seats rather than leaving the stage. This way, it is easy for spellers to be reinstated into the bee if all of the spellers in a single round misspell their word, and it is also easier for the media to interview and take pictures of top finalists and their families at the end of the bee.

When there are two spellers remaining in the National Spelling Bee, the rules become slightly more complex. Prior to 1991, when one of the two remaining spellers misspelled a word, the other speller had to spell that word correctly plus one more to win the championship. This rule could be somewhat problematic because the second speller, having eliminated one spelling possibility, was often able to guess the spelling correctly even if he or she had never heard the word. Moreover, the speller with the lower placard number of the two remaining spellers had to correctly spell three more words than the second-place speller in order to win, while the speller with the higher placard number had to produce only two more correctly spelled words than the other speller.

Nowadays, the rule has been adjusted and simplified: When one of the two remaining spellers misses a word, the other speller is given the next word on the list rather than the misspelled word, and the winning speller must correctly spell two more words than the second-place speller, regardless of their relative positions onstage. So if speller number 21 spells correctly and speller number 137 misses a word in Round Nineteen, speller number 21 is given an entirely new word in Round Twenty and need spell only that word to win the bee.

*2005 National champion Anurag Kashyap spells it out.*

## Match These

English has borrowed onomatopoeic words from many languages. Can you match these words to their meaning and language of origin?

1. cachinnate (Latin)
2. flicflac (French)
3. clinquant (Middle French)
4. rataplan (French)
5. ululate (Latin)
6. reboant (Latin)

a. to laugh usually loudly or convulsively
b. glittering especially with gold decoration
c. to utter a loud mournful usually protracted and rhythmical sound
d. reverberating
e. a brushing movement of the foot used in ballet as a connecting step
f. the iterative sound of beating

KEY: 1a, 2e, 3b, 4f, 5c, 6d

Some local and regional bees still use the older rule, so it is good to understand it thoroughly.

Before 1991, if there were 150 spellers in the National Spelling Bee, the first speller to miss a word got 150th place, the second got 149th place, and so on. Now, in the interest of fairness, all spellers who are eliminated in the same round are considered to have tied for the same place and therefore receive the same prize. In 2005, Samir Patel and Aliya Deri tied for second place behind champion Anurag Kashyap—the first time two spellers have shared that spot.

## Head-to-Head Contests

In the first few decades of the National Spelling Bee, when the word lists were easier, it wasn't terribly uncommon for two spellers to battle for many rounds before one was declared champion. In fact, there were three years—1950, 1957, and 1962—in which the word list was exhausted and co-champions were declared.

Nowadays, long head-to-head contests are rare once the contestants have been whittled to two, but in 1997, Rebecca Sealfon of New York City and Prem Trivedi of Howell, New Jersey, spelled against each other for eight rounds for the National Spelling Bee title. Here are their round results:

**Round Fifteen:**
Prem Trivedi: usufructuary
Rebecca Sealfon: niello
**Round Sixteen:**
Prem: supererogatory
Rebecca: duenna
**Round Seventeen:**
Prem: analemma (misspelled as *annalemma*)
Rebecca: dulcinea (misspelled as *dulcenilla*)
**Round Eighteen:**
Prem: holophytic
Rebecca: sufflaminate
**Round Nineteen:**
Prem: foudroyant
Rebecca: deliquesce
**Round Twenty:**
Prem: philhellene
Rebecca: bourgade
**Round Twenty-One:**
Prem: griffonage
Rebecca: anglophilia
**Round Twenty-Two:**
Prem: cortile (misspelled as *cortille*)
Rebecca: coterie
**Round Twenty-Three:**
Rebecca: euonym

In 2006, Katharine "Kerry" Close of Spring Lake, New Jersey, and Finola Mei Hwa Hackett of Tofield, Alberta, Canada, also battled for eight rounds. Kerry won the championship with *Ursprache*.

# Chomping Champ

"I chewed gum to calm my nerves a bit during the contest, but didn't have a chance to spit it out or swallow it after I won. That led to several widely published, rather embarrassing pictures of me holding the trophy, mouth wide open as I prepared to take another furious chomp on my gum. Adrenaline got the best of me."

—ROBIN KRAL,
*1972 National Spelling Bee champion*
(winning word: **macerate**)

# Practice Makes Perfect

"I repeated the word **ante-diluvian** (after spelling it). Judge Mary Brooks said, 'That is correct.' Someone cheered; in hindsight, it was probably my mother. I felt as if an electric current was running through me, as if my body was an electromagnet being drawn downward toward the ground, and it required all my strength to simply keep standing up. Scripps' Bill Burleigh handed me the trophy, and I knew exactly what I was going to do with it: one hand on the base, one hand wrapped around the back of the cup, arms in the air. I admit it: At home in my bedroom, I had practiced imitating—and improving upon—the winners in photos from *Words of the Champions* and *Bee Week Guides* of bygone years. I never expected to be one of them."

—NED ANDREWS,
*1994 National Spelling Bee champion*

# Winning

If you're one of the last few spellers onstage, you'll be concentrating on the words so hard that you probably won't give any thought to what will happen at the end of the bee. So, just to prepare you for the distant but enticing possibility of winning, here's the basic rundown.

Once the last word has been spelled, there will be a lot of noise. The champion will be presented the trophy, and the winner's parents will likely present some hugs and kisses! A TV reporter will probably interview the winner for the TV cameras, and many, many pictures will be taken.

If you win, you should expect to be busy for a while. Everyone understands that you've been under a lot of pressure for the previous few hours, and that you may feel very emotional. Take a few moments to compose yourself and ask for a glass of water or some tissues if you need them.

It's exciting and sometimes a little scary to be interviewed by so many people. If you're that lucky speller, you may find that things will go more easily in your exhilarated state if you're ready for a few obvious questions you will certainly be asked—how you studied, whether you knew all the words you got, what you want to be when you grow up, and what you plan to do with the prize money.

The winner and his or her parents often spend much of the day (and night) that follow the bee in television studios or on the telephone, but somehow, in the midst of all that excitement, the winner also finds time to prepare a short speech for the awards banquet. If the National Spelling Bee finals are the climax of the week, the awards banquet is its denouement (a good word to add to your spelling bee notebook!). It's a memorable evening of fun, companionship, delicious food, and heartfelt thank-yous to the parents, coaches, and sponsors who made a first-place finish at the National Spelling Bee possible.

**2006** *2006 winner, Kerry Close, gets ready for her close-up. This was the first year the National Spelling Bee was broadcast on primetime televison.*

# Subtlety and Specificity

" The legacy has been an appreciation for subtlety and specificity, for taking care to use the right word the right way. Understanding how words are constructed, how they're related, how easily you can misunderstand them—all this I came to appreciate as I crammed for the contests. I'm no grammar snob, despite my career as a copy editor. But I appreciate simple, direct communication."

—DARIENNE HOSLEY STEWART, *National Spelling Bee finalist, 1985; copy editor*

# What's Next?

After Bee Week is over and you've gone home, you'll have some thinking to do. If this was your last year to compete, it's time to kick back, enjoy your summer, and start looking for a new challenge! Your hard work and your ability to stand up under pressure will have long-term benefits that you'll continue to reap even after you've put your spelling notebook on the shelf and turned to rock climbing, integral calculus, superhero training, or whatever your next bold undertaking is.

If (1) you didn't win the National Spelling Bee this year, (2) you won't turn sixteen or finish the eighth grade before next year's national finals, and (3) your local sponsor will allow you to compete again, ask yourself: Did I learn a lot? Was it fun? Do I want to come back and improve my ranking next year? If the answers are "Yes," give yourself a big pat on the back—then put your good buddy, the dictionary, where you can get to it easily.

After all, there are only about 362 days until the next National Spelling Bee. . . .

# Fun with Words

Y ou've probably already enjoyed multiplayer games like Scrabble, Boggle, or Balderdash, or solo word activities like crosswords, cryptograms, or anagrams. There's something particularly satisfying about learning a new word this way, which makes it more likely that you'll remember and use it. There's an excellent chance you'll remember the words you learn in the puzzles that follow, because although some are easy, you'll have to work pretty hard to solve others. You're definitely going to want a dictionary nearby.

Don't forget to add new words to your spelling notebook!

# Add Diction

The object here is to start with the letters at the top and add letters from the list at the bottom to complete five words. Each word builds on the letters of the word before it. The order of the existing letters will not change, but new letters can be inserted into the middle of the word or added to either end.

## Puzzle #1

**S I**

S I N — Religious offense

S I N G — Warble

_ _ _ _ _ Employing

_ _ _ _ _ _ One form of school transportation

_ _ _ _ _ _ _ Putting to an improper use

**U   A   N   B   G**

## Puzzle #2

**O N**

O N I Charged particle

L I O N Regal animal

_ _ _ _ _ _ Principal unit of the Roman army

_ _ _ _ _ _ _ _ Embassy

_ _ _ _ _ _ _ _ _ _ Assertion

**G   L   L   I   E   T   A   A**

# Puzzle #3

**I L**

\_ \_ \_ Feel sick
*I l l*

\_ \_ \_ \_ Hammer's target
*n a i l*

\_ \_ \_ \_ \_ Slow creature
*s n a i l*

\_ \_ \_ \_ \_ \_ \_ Like a serpent

\_ \_ \_ \_ \_ \_ \_ \_ With sarcasm

**Y  N  R  A  S  K**

# Puzzle #4

**H O**

\_ \_ \_ Monopolize

\_ \_ \_ \_ Kong

\_ \_ \_ \_ \_ \_ Wishing

\_ \_ \_ \_ \_ \_ \_ Jumping

\_ \_ \_ \_ \_ \_ \_ \_ Type of mall

**P  S  N  P  G  I**

# Puzzle #5

**D D**

\_ \_ \_ Took action

\_ \_ \_ \_ Expired

\_ \_ \_ \_ \_ Plunged headfirst

\_ \_ \_ \_ \_ \_ \_ Separated

\_ \_ \_ \_ \_ \_ \_ \_ Stockholder's reward

**I  V  I  E  D  N**

## Puzzle #6

**I E**

— — — Deceive

— — — — Food label fad word

— — — — — Metric measure

— — — — — — One who catalogues

— — — — — — — Get too much sun

**T L B R S**

## Puzzle #7

**O B**

— — — Hold up

— — — — Dressing gown

— — — — — Investigate

— — — — — — — Kind of court

— — — — — — — — Exploratory

**T E R V P A I**

## Puzzle #8

**N D**

— — — Moreover

— — — — Hourglass filler

— — — — — Reviewing platform

— — — — — — Unit of hair

— — — — — — — Beached

**E S A T D R**

## Puzzle #9

**R E**

— — — Regret

— — — — Bumpkin

— — — — — Muscovite money

— — — — — — Gang event

— — — — — — — Disintegrate

**M L C U B**

## Puzzle #10

**A E**

— — — Flying hero

— — — — "Chantilly _____"

— — — — — Cavalry weapon

— — — — — — — Decorative drape

— — — — — — — — — Landslide

**H A L V A C N**

**❝**Bumpkin *originally comes from a Dutch word for 'small cask,'* bommekijn.**❞**

# Dictionary Devil

T he Dictionary Devil has mixed up these words and their meanings. Even worse, he's taken some words from the definitions and jumbled them at the bottom of each puzzle. The Dictionary Devil thinks he's pretty clever. But he's not as clever as you. Match the words to the definitions and fill in the blanks from the words at the bottom of each puzzle.

## Puzzle #1

**angstrom** \_\_\_
(1) an unusually short _____

**baccarat** \_\_\_
(2) lamentation, _____

**pegasus** \_\_\_
(3) a unit of _____ equal to one ten-billionth of a _____

**homily** \_\_\_
(4) a _____ _____ horse

**quadruped** \_\_\_
(5) a _____ game played especially in _____ casinos

**picayune** \_\_\_
(6) a show of daring or _____

**plaint** \_\_\_
(7) an _____ having four feet

**bravura** \_\_\_
(8) something _____

**brilliance   European   sermon   meter
animal   trivial   fabulous   wail   length   winged   card**

# P u z z l e  #2

**crenation** ___
(1) a long _____ marked usually by many _____ of fortune

**funicular** ___
(2) any of a _____ of small swift slender dogs that are used for

_____

**loge** ___
(3) one of the rounded _____ on an edge (as of a coin)

**marquetry** ___
(4) a small _____

**macle** ___
(5) _____ work of wood, shell, or _____ (as on a table or cabinet)

**odyssey** ___
(6) a twinned _____

**quarto** ___
(7) a cable_____ ascending a _____

**whippet** ___
(8) the size of a piece of _____ cut four from a _____

**railway  inlaid  racing  mountain  changes  breed  compartment
ivory  crystal  wandering  paper  projections  sheet**

## Puzzle #3

**audit** ___
(1) a pointed witty _____

**vesicant** ___
(2) a _____ horse or _____

**zinger** ___
(3) an agent that causes _____

**acknowledgment** ___
(4) a _____ preparation used in styling _____

**depot** ___
(5) a _____ of anxiety, apprehension, or _____

**angst** ___
(6) _____

**mousse** ___
(7) a _____ examination and _____

**pinto** ___
(8) a thing done or _____ in recognition of something _____


**review  remark  pony  foamy  insecurity  spotted  methodical
feeling  given  hair  storehouse  received  blistering**

# Puzzle #4

**abjection** ___
(1) a _____ chain or _____ hanging between two points

**peer** ___
(2) separation or _____ into two parts or connected _____

**festoon** ___
(3) a fictitious _____

**pseudonym** ___
(4) any of the _____ of various carnivorous _____ (as a dog)

**remuda** ___
(5) one that is of _____ standing with _____

**seine** ___
(6) the herd of _____ from which those to be used for the day are chosen

**bifurcation** ___
(7) a low or downcast _____

**whelp** ___
(8) a large _____ _____ net

**another young weighted segments strip state mammals branching decorative equal name horses fishing**

# Puzzle #5

**firebrand** ___
(1) an interrogative _____ or clause

**tundra** ___
(2) a young _____

**visage** ___
(3) a _____ plain of arctic and subarctic _____

**question** ___
(4) a professional _____ of epic _____

**mithridate** ___
(5) _____

**butte** ___
(6) an _____ against _____

**cygnet** ___
(7) the _____ or countenance of a _____ or sometimes an animal

**rhapsodist** ___
(8) an isolated steep _____


**person   poems   hill   swan   poison   sentence   reciter   treeless
agitator   antidote   regions   face**

# Puzzle #6

**unabridged** ___
(1) of very high _____

**deprecatory** ___
(2) marked by _____ enthusiasm and often intense uncritical

_____

**superlative** ___
(3) _____

**edentulous** ___
(4) contemptuously _____ of _____ nature and motives

**eloquent** ___
(5) being the most _____ of its _____

**synthetic** ___
(6) _____ to avert _____

**cynical** ___
(7) _____ or movingly _____ or revealing

**fanatic** ___
(8) produced _____


**distrustful   devotion   class   toothless   quality   excessive   human
vividly   complete   approval   seeking   artificially   expressive**

## Puzzle #7

**pastiche** ___

(1) disagreeably _____ or _____

**debutante** ___

(2) a _____ made of _____ from different works

**plaiting** ___

(3) a small _____ sockeye salmon

**raucous** ___

(4) a very large swift-footed _____ _____ of Africa and Arabia

**ostrich** ___

(5) _____ _____ and enthusiasm

**vim** ___

(6) a man holding a rank of honor below a _____ but above a

_____

**kokanee** ___

(7) a young _____ making her _____ entrance into society

**baronet** ___

(8) the _____ of strands


**robust   bird   selections   energy   baron   formal   knight   harsh
flightless   interlacing   composition   landlocked   woman   strident**

# Puzzle #8

**trilby** __

(1) a _____ turn used for altering the direction of hill descent

**christie** __

(2) a green or _____ _____ that forms on copper, brass, or bronze

**populace** __

(3) pasta made in long _____ _____ smaller in diameter than spaghetti

**vermicelli** __

(4) a woman's _____ room, bedroom, or _____ sitting room

**proclivity** __

(5) an inclination or _____ toward _____

**boudoir** __

(6) the _____ of fat from the back of a hog cured by _____ and salting

**fatback** __

(7) the _____ people

**verdigris** __

(8) a soft _____ hat with indented crown


**deposit   common   felt   strings   solid   dressing   skiing   tendency
something   strip   private   drying   bluish**

## Puzzle #9

**kudu** ___
(1) a large or _____ _____

**tendency** ___
(2) a sauce made _____ of oil, vinegar, and _____

**gourmand** ___
(3) _____ repartee

**gaff** ___
(4) a _____ to a _____ kind of thought or action

**badinage** ___
(5) a _____ used to take fish or turtles

**apocalypse** ___
(6) one who is excessively _____ of eating and _____

**tome** ___
(7) a grayish brown African _____ with large spirally twisted horns

**vinaigrette** ___
(8) a writing prophesying a _____ in which _____ forces are destroyed

**fond  evil  typically  antelope  drinking  seasonings  particular
book  proneness  playful  cataclysm  spear  scholarly**

# Puzzle #10

**tirade** ___
(1) a _____ _____ with a curved blade and thick back

**biotite** ___
(2) a man practicing the _____ _____

**saber** ___
(3) a dark _____ containing _____, magnesium, potassium, and aluminum

**warlock** ___
(4) a _____ purplish-blue _____

**affenpinscher** ___
(5) ground _____

**carabid** ___
(6) a place, scene, or state of _____ and confusion

**sapphire** ___
(7) a _____ speech of _____ or condemnation

**bedlam** ___
(8) any of a breed of _____ dogs with a wiry black, red, tan, or gray coat

**mica   small   dark   prolonged   arts   cavalry   uproar   black   abuse
color   iron   beetle   sword**

# Synonym City

In Synonym City, words of a feather need to stick together. Can you sort the words with identical or similar meanings into groups? Try it without using the dictionary. Part of the first puzzle is done for you as an example. Note: There may be extra blank columns for some of these puzzles.

## Puzzle #1

|  | alibi | trace | dale | imprecation |
|---|---|---|---|---|
| **alibi** | _____ | _____ | _____ | _____ |
| **trace** | _____ | _____ | _____ | _____ |
| **dale** | _____ | _____ | _____ | _____ |
| **imprecation** | _____ | _____ | _____ | _____ |
| **track** | _____ | _____ | _____ | _____ |
| **profanity** | _____ | _____ | _____ | _____ |
| **excuse** | _____ | _____ | _____ | _____ |
| **valley** |  |  |  |  |
| **glen** |  |  |  |  |
| **vestige** |  |  |  |  |
| **blasphemy** |  |  |  |  |
| **curse** |  |  |  |  |

## P u z z l e   # 2

| | | | | |
|---|---|---|---|---|
| **reproduction** | reproduction | duplicate | copy | replica |
| **prowess** | | | | |
| **capitulation** | | | | |
| **facsimile** | | | | |
| **replica** | | | | |
| **gallantry** | | | | |
| **duplicate** | | | | |
| **valor** | | | | |
| **gradation** | | | | |
| **copy** | | | | |
| **surrender** | | | | |
| **nuance** | | | | |

## P u z z l e   # 3

| | | | | |
|---|---|---|---|---|
| **relinquish** | | | | |
| **stroll** | | | | |
| **surrender** | | | | |
| **abandon** | | | | |
| **saunter** | | | | |
| **resign** | | | | |
| **amble** | | | | |
| **mosey** | | | | |
| **scar** | | | | |
| **yield** | | | | |
| **cicatrize** | | | | |
| **waive** | | | | |

## Puzzle #4

altitudinous

warlike

lofty

vintage

traditional

adventitious

martial

elevated

supervenient

bellicose

extraneous

classic

## Puzzle #5

reprove

deposit

grieve

admonish

reproach

cache

bemoan

reprimand

lament

weep

bank

rebuke

## Puzzle #6

inciter _____ _____ _____

fate _____ _____ _____

aide-de-camp _____ _____ _____

fomenter _____ _____ _____

coadjutant _____ _____ _____

destiny _____ _____ _____

lot

instigator

doom

portion

assistant

lieutenant

## Puzzle #7

adventure _____ _____ _____

outline _____ _____ _____

morsel _____ _____ _____

contour _____ _____ _____

exploit _____ _____ _____

savory _____ _____ _____

feat

enterprise

silhouette

delicacy

tidbit

profile

# Puzzle #8

habitat      _____   _____   _____

crotchet      _____   _____   _____

caprice      _____   _____   _____

locality      _____   _____   _____

wharf      _____   _____   _____

home      _____   _____   _____

haunt

whim

dock

quay

vagary

pier

# Puzzle #9

slip      _____   _____   _____

lapse      _____   _____   _____

vituperation      _____   _____   _____

mistake      _____   _____   _____

triumph      _____   _____   _____

error      _____   _____   _____

billingsgate

blunder

obloquy

jubilance

exultation

invective

## Puzzle #10

divert      _____ _____ _____ _____

evoke      _____ _____ _____ _____

foreordain      _____ _____ _____ _____

amuse      _____ _____ _____ _____

educe      _____ _____ _____ _____

predestine      _____ _____ _____ _____

atonement

predetermine

extract

reparation

propitiation

elicit

# Classical Gas

L isted below are definitions or hints for twelve words that are built from the Greek combining forms and affixes listed at the end of this puzzle. Put together the word elements to create a word that fits the definition or hint. A few of the answers have neither a prefix nor a suffix, but are simply the combination of two combining forms. Use *Webster's Third* to confirm that you have created actual words.

1. Mr. Potato Head's numerous proboscides make it a cinch for you to perform this surgical procedure on him. Clueless? A special kind of "job" desired by Michael Jackson, among many others. ___rhinoplasy___

2. With this condition, a cat would have little chance getting away from a dog. _____

3. Because of this creature's "skin condition," it would be hard to hurt his feelings. ___dermapachy___

4. A condition in which there is wasting away because of lack of nourishment. ___trophophobe___

5. A condition in which there is no memory. ___amnemsia___

6. Without these "containers," we'd all be able to cry only crocodile tears.

   _____

7. "Madam, I'm Adam" is a well-known one of these. (It reads backward as well as forward.) _____

8. Another word for the act of drooling. ___Ptyalism___

9. A person with this condition could never be successful if he or she lived by the motto "No pain, no gain." _____

10. A state of lawlessness. ___anomoia___

11. One who maintains that he has no knowledge of a god or any ultimates. ___ancephalo___

12. Poor Marie Antoinette died in this state, her head in the basket.

_ancephaly_

| PREFIX | MEANING |
|---|---|
| **a-, an-** | not; without |

| GREEK COMBINING FORM | MEANING |
|---|---|
| **onych-, onycho-** | nail of the finger or toe; claw |
| **ptyal-, ptyalo-** | saliva |
| **troph-, tropho-** | nutrition |
| **drom-, dromo-** | course; running |
| **pachy-** | thick |
| **mnem-, mnemo-** | memory |
| **dacry-, dacryo-** | of a tear or tears; lacrimal |
| **-plasty** | plastic surgery |
| **alg-, algo-** | pain |
| **rhin-, rhino-** | nose |
| **-gnosis** | knowledge; cognition |
| **nomo-** | law |
| **derm-, derma-, dermo-** | skin |
| **pali-** (from Greek **palin**) | again; back |
| **phob-, phobo-** | fear; avoidance |
| **cephal-, cephalo-** (transliterated version of Greek **kephal-, kephalo-**) | head |
| **cyst-, cysti-, cysto-** (transliterated version of Greek **kyst-, kysto-**) | sac; pouch |

| SUFFIX | MEANING |
|---|---|
| **-ia** | quality, state, condition; pathological condition |
| **-y** | state, condition, quality |
| **-ism** | act, practice, process |
| **-ic** | one having the character or nature of |

# Magic Square

A magic square is a square of letters that reads the same across (along the rows) and down (along the columns). An example is:

| C | A | L | M |
|---|---|---|---|
| A | R | I | A |
| L | I | A | R |
| M | A | R | E |

In this puzzle, choose three of the combining forms shown below and use them to form a magic square.

| | | | | | |
|---|---|---|---|---|---|
| **axi-** | axis | **tri-** | three | **myc-** | fungus |
| **epi-** | upon | **nas-** | nose | **mal-** | bad |
| **xen-** | guest; foreigner | **gyr-** | circle | **ino-** | fiber |
| **pre-** | earlier than | **syn-** | together | **uni-** | one |

Was that too easy? Try it with a four-row square. You might think it would only be a little harder, but you may be surprised. Good luck!

**zygo-** yoke     **hyps-** height     **phos-** light
**sten-** close; narrow     **meli-** honey     **kino-** motion; action
**goni-** corner     **oste-** bone     **pter-** wing
**cyan-** dark blue     **tera-** trillion     **hist-** tissue

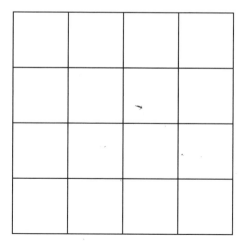

# Where in the World?

Think you know a lot about geography? These forty-five words—whose meanings, figuratively speaking, are all over the map—are all derived from place names. See if you can match the word to the place its name refers to (which is not necessarily related to its language of origin!).

**arcadia**       An inlet between Canada and the United States
                  _____

**assisi**        Mosul, Iraq _____

**attic**         A region in northern France _____

**axminster**     A mountain in China _____

**bayonet**       A village in the Netherlands _____

**blarney**       A city in the province of Toledo, Spain _____

**bougie**        A river in Scotland _____

**brummagem**     A region of ancient Greece _____

**calico**        A mine in South Africa _____

**castile**       A large city in the English Midlands _____

**chautauqua**    A region of central Spain _____

**cordovan**      A city on the Elbe River in Germany _____

**denim**         A district of ancient Palestine _____

**Edam**          A castle near Cork, Ireland _____

**glengarry**     A large city of northern Morocco _____

**guinea**        A city in southeastern France _____

**hantavirus**    A former province of Japan _____

**hardanger**     A pastoral area of ancient Greece _____

**huapango**      A state in central Mexico _____

**jeans**          A village in western France _____

**leghorn**        Genoa, Italy _____

**limerick**       A town in the Perugia province of Italy _____

**lisle**          China's largest city _____

**madrilene**      A river in Ontario, Canada _____

**magenta**        A seaport in southern Italy _____

**magnet**         A river in South Korea _____

**massasauga**     A leading resort on the French Riviera _____

**Meissen**        A fishing village in Yucatan, Mexico _____

**milliner**       A port city in the Tuscany region of Italy _____

**muslin**         A town near Veracruz, Mexico _____

**Nicoise**        A city in India _____

**Percheron**      An ancient city in Thessaly, Greece _____

**poblano**        A city in southwest Ireland _____

**quoddy**         A region in west Africa _____

**samaritan**      A town in Devon, England _____

**satsuma**        A district in Norway _____

**shanghai**       A lake in western New York state _____

**sisal**          A town in northern Italy _____

**soubise**        An Algerian seaport _____

**sunglo**         A valley in Inverness-shire, Scotland _____

**Talavera**       A French city near the Belgian border _____

**tangerine**      A city of the French Basque area _____

**tarantula**      The capital city of Spain _____

**tweed**          A city in the Andalusian region of Spain _____

**wesselton**      Milan, Italy _____

# Anagram Fest

An anagram is a word made by transposing the letters of another word, like **anemic** and **cinema**. Below are a number of definitions in pairs, with the number of letters given. Fill in the words and add the numbered letters to the appropriate blanks at the bottom of the puzzle. When all the letters are filled in, you'll see the name of a famous English wordsmith.

*Example:*

(6 letters)     perceive with the ear          L I S T E N
                making no utterance            S I L E N T

(8 letters)     occurring before birth         p r e _ _ _ _ _
                                                     2

                of or relating to a father     p _ _ _ _ _ _ _

(5 letters)     not tamed or domesticated : wild   f _ _ _ _
                                                    4

                flame up brightly              f _ _ _ _

(7 letters)     being in the state of matrimony    m a r r i g e

                one who esteems or regards
                highly                         a _ _ _ _ _ _

(6 letters)     more wicked                    e _ _ _ _ _

                address or assail with opprobrious
                language                       r _ _ _ _ _
                                               15

(5 letters)   the whole body of salt water that covers nearly three-fourths of the globe   o c e a n

a long narrow boat that is sharp at both ends and has curved sides   c a n o e

(6 letters)   characterized by warmth or heat of emotion   a _ _ _ _ _ / 11

declaimed in a bombastic fashion   r _ _ _ _ _

(6 letters)   having rhythmic fall   c _ _ _ _ _

pour (as wine) from the original bottle into another container   d _ _ _ _ _

(5 letters)   a person deprived of rights and privileges and often exploited   h _ _ _ _

inn   h o t e l / 10

(7 letters)   balcony : deck   t _ _ _ _ _ _

one who arranges food and service for a social affair   c a t e r e r

(9 letters)   one of three terms into which the academic year is divided   t _ _ _ _ _ _ _ _

persons who send a sum of money to another person   r _ _ _ _ _ _ _ _

(8 letters)    a writing (as a book or article) that treats a subject     t _ _ _ _ _ _ _

most wet or stained with tears     t _ _ _ _ _ _ _

(7 letters)    the fifteenth letter of the Greek alphabet     o _ _ _ _ _ _
<br>                                               3

like or having the capability of a feebleminded person     m _ _ _ _ _ _

(8 letters)    marked with stripes or lines (as on the skin)     s _ _ _ _ _ _ _

most delayed : latest     t _ _ _ _ _ _ _

(5 letters)    one that consumes food     e _ _ _ _
<br>                                               7

the sum of good qualities that make character     a _ _ _ _

(8 letters)    outward manner     d _ _ _ _ _ _ _

inflamed with love     e _ _ _ _ _ _ _

(8 letters)    of, relating to, or marked by reaction     r _ _ _ _ _ _ _
<br>                                               13

given to creation     c _ _ _ _ _ _ _

(7 letters)    varied     d _ _ _ _ _ _

amended : improved     r _ _ _ _ _ _

(7 letters)    of or relating to any area
conventionally designated as east    e _ _ _ _ _

closest    n _ _ _ _ _
      14

(8 letters)    treat with medicine    m _ _ _ _ _ _ _

destroy a considerable part of    d _ _ _ _ _ _ _

(9 letters)    inflammation of an artery    a _ _ _ _ _ _ _ _

incites impatience, anger,
or displeasure    i _ _ _ _ _ _ _ _

(7 letters)    forms or checks indicating a credit
against a future purchase    c _ _ _ _ _ _

a little bit    s _ _ _ _ _ _

(10 letters)    a substance that prevents the
growth or action of microorganisms    a _ _ _ _ _ _ _ _ _
      9

of or relating to parrots of the
family Psittacidae    p _ _ _ _ _ _ _ _

(8 letters)    of, relating to, or situated in Asia    o _ _ _ _ _ _

the act of telling or recounting    r _ _ _ _ _ _

(8 letters)    divided into chambers    c _ _ _ _ _ _ _

cause (solid matter) to become
soft by steeping in fluid    m _ _ _ _ _ _ _

(7 letters)    a protein or carbohydrate
               substance stimulating the
               production of an antibody          a _ _ _ _ _ _
                                                        1

               a fall-blooming North American
               plant having tubular blue flowers   g _ _ _ _ _ _

(9 letters)    having a high proportion of debt
               relative to equity                 l _ _ _ _ _ _ _ _

               a swampy grassland especially
               in southern Florida                e _ _ _ _ _ _ _ _

(7 letters)    of, relating to, or appropriate
               to slaves                          s _ _ _ _ _ _

               those who impose or collect by
               legal process or by authority      l _ _ _ _ _ _

(9 letters)    government in accordance
               with a system of law               n _ _ _ _ _ _ _ _
                                                                  8

               government by a single person      m _ _ _ _ _ _ _ _

(7 letters)    freed from guilt or blame          c _ _ _ _ _ _
                                                            6

               make known publicly, formally,
               or explicitly                      d _ _ _ _ _ _

(9 letters)    murder of a mother by her son
               or daughter                        m _ _ _ _ _ _ _ _

               completely opposed or opposite     d _ _ _ _ _ _ _ _

(7 letters)    executed in a drawn-out manner :
sustained      s __ __ __ __ __ __
                                                         12

             having little substance or strength    t __ __ __ __ __ __

(7 letters)    emotionally out of control : frenzied   f __ __ __ __ __ __
                                                                    5

             break : violate                    i __ __ __ __ __ __

$$\frac{\quad}{1}\ \frac{\quad}{2}\ \frac{\quad}{3}\ \frac{\quad}{4}\ \frac{\quad}{5}\ \frac{\quad}{6}\ \frac{\quad}{7}\ \frac{\quad}{8}\ \frac{\quad}{9}\ \frac{\quad}{10}\ \frac{\quad}{11}\ \frac{\quad}{12}\ \frac{\quad}{13}\ \frac{\quad}{14}\ \frac{\quad}{15}$$

# Word Search:

## *-able* Was I Ere I Saw *-ible*

There are twenty common words ending in *-able* and *-ible* buried in the word search puzzle below. See if you can find all of them.

| | | | |
|---|---|---|---|
| divisible | excusable | exhaustible | affable |
| invincible | fungible | adaptable | risible |
| transmissible | equitable | detestable | negotiable |
| indelible | deductible | locatable | educable |
| omissible | mandible | friable | irresistible |

| | | | | | | | | | | | |
|---|---|---|---|---|---|---|---|---|---|---|---|
| e | q | t | r | a | n | s | m | i | s | s | i | b | l | e |
| a | x | e | l | b | a | t | p | a | d | a | r | i | n | e |
| b | a | h | e | l | b | i | t | s | i | s | e | r | r | i |
| l | m | o | a | f | f | a | b | l | e | s | l | b | n | n |
| e | a | m | i | u | r | p | p | b | l | r | b | l | e | v |
| e | n | i | n | n | s | i | y | l | i | e | r | e | g | i |
| l | d | s | d | g | y | t | a | s | l | p | l | e | o | n |
| b | i | s | e | i | e | t | i | b | l | e | o | l | t | c |
| i | b | i | l | b | l | b | a | b | l | o | c | b | i | i |
| t | l | b | i | l | l | c | i | b | l | e | a | a | a | b |
| c | e | l | b | e | u | x | i | b | l | e | t | s | b | l |
| u | d | e | l | d | a | s | b | l | e | t | a | u | l | e |
| d | e | t | e | s | t | a | b | l | e | i | b | c | e | b |
| e | l | b | a | t | i | u | q | e | y | b | l | x | w | l |
| d | i | v | i | s | i | b | l | e | m | l | e | e | p | e |

# Wordmeister Challenge:
# A Very Verbose Verbigram

These thirty-seven words are themselves all about words and language. To help you out, some of the letters have already been filled in. There are a few tough words, so remember, the dictionary is your friend! When you've found them all, the letters in the boxes, written in order, will form a quotation by the most famous Roman of all time.

*Example:*

a long narrative poem recounting the deeds of a legendary or historical hero

e   p   [i]   c

versed in the use of language: ready with words   f   [ ]   _   e   _   t

a word or phrase that must be spoken by a person before he is allowed to pass a barrier or guard   p   a   s   s   w   [o]   r   d

to make briefer   a   _   b   _   _   [ ]   _   _   _   e

the vocabulary of a language, of an individual speaker, of a set of documents, of a body of speech, or of an occupational or other group

l   [ ]   x   _   _   n

a particular form of expression   l   _   c   _   [ ]   _   _   n

an untrue assertion especially when intentional

f   _   _   s   _   [ ]   _   _   d

a transposition of usually initial sounds of two or more words that generally creates a comic effect   s   p   _   _   _   [ ]   _   _   s   m

one that renders from one language or system to another

t    __   □   __   __   __   __   __   o   r   __

a tale traditional among a people and characteristically anonymous, timeless, and placeless   f   o   __   __   __   □   __   e

a polite, tactful, or less explicit term used to avoid the direct naming of an unpleasant, painful, or frightening reality   e   __   p   __   __   □   __   s   m

marked by the brief expression of a comprehensive matter

c   o   __   __   □   __   d   __   __   u   s

the use of a new word or expression or of an established word in a new or different sense   n   __   □   l   __   __   __   y

the characteristic language of official statements

o   f   □   __   __   __   __   __   s   e

give the meaning of (a work or passage) in other words

p   __   r   __   __   □   __   __   s   e

the science of sound

__   h   □   __   i   __   __

a formula of words chanted or recited in a magic ritual for their special virtues or particular effects   i   __   c   __   □   __   __   __   __   o   n

the mark (') used to indicate omission of one or more letters or figures

a   p   __   __   __   □   __   e

to tell or recite the happenings of (a story)   n   __   r   □   __   __   e

the characteristic system or the preferred system of inflections and syntax of a language  g __ __ □ __ __ r

the naming of a thing or action by a more or less exact reproduction of the sound associated with it  o __ n __ o __ __ __ □ __ __ __ __ a

the act or instance of stealing and passing off as one's own the ideas or words of another  p __ l __ __ __ __ __ □ __ s __ m

a local or regional variety of language distinguished by features of vocabulary, grammar, and pronunciation from other local or regional varieties  d __ __ __ □ c __ t

the art or practice of writing or speaking as a means of communication or persuasion often with special concern for literary effect
__ r __ h __ □ __ __ __ c __

to incite by argument or advice  e __ x __ □ __ __ t

any particular set of letters with which one or more languages are written
__ a __ __ p __ □ __ t __

the act or process or an instance of naming
n __ o __ □ __ __ __ t __ r __ e

to avoid committing oneself in what one says
__ e __ q __ □ __ __ __ t __ e

a term of address that conveys respect  h __ __ n __ __ __ □ __ c

an ungrammatical combination of words in a sentence
__ s __ o __ □ __ __ s __ m

an often prolonged parley usually between persons of different levels of
culture or sophistication  p  a  __  ☐  v  __  r

the use of an unnecessarily large number of words to express an idea
__  c  __  i  __  ☐  __  c  __  __  __  __  __  __  __  __  __  n  __

very long words (literally, words a foot and a half long)
__  s  __  e  __  q  __  __  __  __  __  ☐  __  __  __  a  __

in a manner capable of being understood or comprehended
__  i  __  t  ☐  __  __  __  __  __  b  __  y  __

a writing composed of words not having a certain letter
__  l  __  i  __  __  g  __  ☐  m  __

able to read and write  l  __  ☐  __  __  __  t  e

of or relating to correct spelling
__  o  __  r  __  ☐  __  g  __  __  __  __  c  __

**Quotation:** __  __  __  __  __  __  __  __  __  __  __  __  __

__  __  __  __  __  __  __  __  __  __  __  __  __  __  __  __

__  __  __

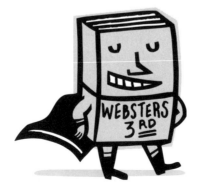

# Wordmeister Super Challenge: Greek Word Search

There are thirty English words that came from Greek hidden up, down, sideways, and diagonally in this puzzle. Check the definition to see if you can figure out the word, then find it in the grid. The word's length and first letter are given as an extra clue. Use your dictionary to help you! If you have access to the dictionary on CD-ROM, consider this a chance to practice using the search features.

| r | t | c | i | c | a | r | o | h | t | i | s | o | n | o | m | y | o | s | y |
|---|---|---|---|---|---|---|---|---|---|---|---|---|---|---|---|---|---|---|---|
| n | z | d | i | c | o | s | a | h | e | d | r | o | n | c | e | r | x | i | s |
| a | e | w | d | y | s | p | t | b | g | r | y | l | e | a | o | o | y | s | k |
| x | r | o | s | e | p | o | i | l | l | a | c | n | b | o | m | l | l | o | r |
| e | s | t | p | m | d | l | m | i | m | e | t | i | c | i | s | o | e | b | y |
| m | r | s | n | h | i | b | a | g | d | t | y | i | n | o | i | c | m | m | p |
| u | u | c | a | o | y | b | r | h | r | v | r | x | a | z | m | e | y | o | t |
| m | n | i | u | n | r | t | r | e | t | e | c | a | r | d | e | t | t | r | o |
| e | p | n | t | y | m | c | e | u | m | n | h | l | i | t | h | i | c | h | n |
| h | s | e | i | s | o | x | u | o | x | y | e | d | z | l | p | c | e | t | u |
| t | r | h | l | a | m | p | h | i | b | i | o | u | s | o | u | l | v | t | s |
| n | l | t | u | s | c | i | r | r | e | l | l | k | i | v | e | x | a | d | s |
| a | o | s | s | g | h | r | q | l | d | h | i | m | g | c | w | e | n | r | a |
| s | g | i | c | a | r | e | o | w | n | p | n | r | t | n | o | r | g | d | i |
| y | o | l | n | d | e | t | b | p | z | a | x | r | y | l | x | o | e | m | n |
| r | m | a | v | m | s | p | x | t | o | t | o | m | p | b | u | s | l | c | o |
| h | a | c | o | y | a | h | r | c | u | l | i | r | h | y | n | i | i | g | n |
| c | c | y | s | e | r | y | n | r | y | y | i | d | u | e | r | s | z | t | i |
| t | h | n | a | t | d | s | o | t | d | i | o | s | s | o | l | g | e | m | o |
| m | y | r | i | a | d | e | e | p | s | t | a | l | a | g | m | i | t | e | k |

1. the upper fortified part of an ancient Greek city (9)

   a _ _ _ _ _ _ _ _

2. able to live both on land and in water (10)

   a _ _ _ _ _ _ _ _ _

3. the habit of unconsciously gritting or grinding the teeth, especially in situations of stress or during sleep (7)  b _ _ _ _ _ _

4. systematic exercises performed usually in rhythm and often in a group without apparatus or with light hand apparatus to improve the strength, suppleness, balance, and health of the body (12)

   c _ _ _ _ _ _ _ _ _ _ _

5. a musical instrument consisting of a series of crude steam or air whistles used on riverboats and in circuses and carnivals (8)

   c _ _ _ _ _ _ _

6. the soil water available for plant growth (8)  c _ _ _ _ _ _ _

7. a large genus of perennial herbs that are widely distributed in the Old World and that include many plants derived chiefly from two species, which are probably Asiatic though known only in cultivation and are cultivated for their showy often double and brightly colored flower heads (13)  c _ _ _ _ _ _ _ _ _ _ _ _

8. a substance (as an acid, base, or salt) that when dissolved in a suitable solvent (as water) or when fused becomes an ionic conductor (11)

   e _ _ _ _ _ _ _ _ _ _

9. a thermodynamic quantity that is the sum of the internal energy of a body and the product of its volume multiplied by the pressure (8)

   e _ _ _ _ _ _ _

10. the substitution of an agreeable or inoffensive word or expression for one that is harsh, indelicate, or otherwise unpleasant or taboo (9)

    e _ _ _ _ _ _ _ _

11. to preach the gospel (10)  e _ _ _ _ _ _ _ _ _

12. resembling a tongue (8)  g _ _ _ _ _ _ _

13. of or relating to the Greek poet Homer, his age, or his writings (7)
    H _ _ _ _ _ _

14. a polyhedron having twenty faces (11)  i _ _ _ _ _ _ _ _ _ _

15. equality before the law (7)  i _ _ _ _ _ _

16. intimate spiritual communion and participative sharing in a common
    religious commitment and spiritual community (8)
    k _ _ _ _ _ _ _

17. a colorless inert gaseous element that occurs in air to the extent of
    about one part per million by volume and in gases from thermal springs
    and other natural gases, that is obtained by separating from liquid air,
    and that is used in electric lamps (7)  k _ _ _ _ _ _

18. of or relating to stone (6) l _ _ _ _ _

19. a dispute over or about words (9) l _ _ _ _ _ _ _ _

20. having an aptitude for or a tendency toward mimicry (7)
    m _ _ _ _ _ _

21. an immense number (6)  m _ _ _ _ _

22. any of several cephalopod mollusks of the southern Pacific and Indian
    oceans that constitute a genus and that are contained in the outermost
    chamber of a spiral chambered shell with an outer porcelaneous layer
    and an inner pearly layer (8)  n _ _ _ _ _ _ _

23. a young or inexperienced practitioner or student (8)
    n _ _ _ _ _ _ _

24. a deposit of crystalline calcium carbonate, more or less like an inverted
    stalactite, formed on the floor of a cave by the drip of water saturated

with calcium bicarbonate and often uniting with a stalactite in a complete column (10)  s _ _ _ _ _ _ _ _ _

25. the contraction of the heart by which the blood is forced onward and the circulation kept up (7)  s _ _ _ _ _ _

26. of, relating to, located within, or involving the thorax (8)
    t _ _ _ _ _ _ _

27. the formation or presence of a blood clot within a blood vessel (10)
    t _ _ _ _ _ _ _ _ _

28. a severe febrile disease characterized by high fever, stupor alternating with delirium, intense headache, and a dark red rash and caused by a rickettsia (*Rickettsia prowazekii*) that is transmitted especially by body lice (6)  t _ _ _ _ _

29. abnormal dryness of a body part or tissue (as the skin or conjunctiva) (7)  x _ _ _ _ _ _

30. a complex tissue in the vascular system of higher plants typically constituting the woody element (5)  x _ _ _ _

# Wordmeister Super Challenge:
# French Word Search

There are forty English words that came from French hidden up, down, sideways, and diagonally in this puzzle. Check the definition to see if you can figure out the word, then find it in the grid. The word's length and first letter are given as an extra clue. Use your dictionary to help you! If you have access to the dictionary on CD-ROM, consider this a chance to practice using the search features.

| | | | | | | | | | | | | | | | | | | | |
|---|---|---|---|---|---|---|---|---|---|---|---|---|---|---|---|---|---|---|---|
| e | t | o | c | s | i | n | q | u | e | s | p | l | a | n | a | d | e | i | r |
| l | u | p | o | p | i | e | w | n | p | a | e | n | o | t | o | l | e | p | s |
| v | t | p | e | g | a | l | e | s | u | f | n | i | l | e | n | y | u | j | h |
| a | p | o | r | l | r | t | t | a | j | l | t | c | i | f | j | g | l | a |   |
| u | m | u | n | t | i | j | t | r | t | h | a | a | a | h | u | f | i | o | u |
| d | o | s | r | r | p | u | e | o | v | e | i | r | n | h | e | b | a | r | t |
| e | r | e | d | n | e | l | u | p | y | v | g | a | m | e | l | a | n | g | e |
| v | p | a | j | u | k | i | q | p | z | s | e | f | t | n | u | i | r | n | u |
| i | m | v | t | a | f | e | o | a | o | z | o | u | a | v | e | r | r | e | r |
| l | i | a | e | q | u | n | c | r | o | u | p | i | e | r | e | u | k | t | f |
| l | o | l | i | z | a | n | g | a | y | n | r | e | u | e | u | q | l | t | c |
| e | r | u | k | l | m | e | a | m | u | e | i | v | o | q | e | u | e | e | l |
| a | m | m | n | c | l | r | i | u | v | n | o | i | j | e | t | a | f | h | y |
| v | o | i | o | n | t | o | i | r | b | i | v | l | e | p | t | t | v | c | e |
| r | l | n | h | i | h | e | t | i | b | a | e | n | r | a | e | o | i | i | u |
| i | u | a | c | l | l | n | v | a | f | r | d | a | v | t | s | r | e | u | a |
| l | m | i | o | e | a | o | u | o | r | e | n | e | u | o | i | z | r | q | e |
| t | i | r | b | v | u | m | o | d | i | s | t | e | e | i | o | a | e | t | d |
| e | l | e | a | a | r | e | c | n | a | i | c | u | o | s | n | i | s | s | i |
| r | i | s | c | j | t | o | l | c | l | i | m | o | u | s | i | n | e | v | r |

1. a song or poem greeting the dawn (6)  a _ _ _ _ _

2. an encampment under little or no shelter usually for a short time (7)
   b _ _ _ _ _ _

3. an uncut gem somewhat polished (8)  c _ _ _ _ _ _ _

4. a woman who endeavors without affection to attract men's amorous attention (8)  c _ _ _ _ _ _ _

5. a representative of a gambling house or casino who officiates at a gaming table (8)  c _ _ _ _ _ _ _

6. an act or conduct that may be required or expected of one (6)
   d _ _ _ _ _

7. a level open stretch of paved or grassy ground (9)
   e _ _ _ _ _ _ _ _

8. an aimless and usually self-centered and superficial person (7)
   f _ _ _ _ _ _

9. the central body portion of an airplane designed to accommodate the crew and the passengers or cargo (8)  f _ _ _ _ _ _ _

10. a marked, especially social or diplomatic, blunder or clumsy mistake (5)
    g _ _ _ _

11. a firm fabric in plain weave usually of silk or rayon and a heavy cotton filling that forms pronounced crosswise ribs (9)
    g _ _ _ _ _ _ _ _

12. arrogant or condescending manner (7)
    h _ _ _ _ _ _

13. made, done, or formed on or as if on the spur of the moment (9)
    i _ _ _ _ _ _ _ _

14. freedom from concern or care (11)  i _ _ _ _ _ _ _ _ _ _

15. a slender shaft of wood not less than 260 centimeters long, tipped with iron or steel, and intended to be thrown for distance as an athletic feat or exercise (7)  j _ _ _ _ _ _

16. cut in long thin strips—used especially of vegetables and fruit (8)
    j _ _ _ _ _ _ _

17. a military cap having a close-fitting band, a round flat top sloping toward the front, and a visor (4)  k _ _ _

18. a large luxurious sedan, especially one for hire and seating five persons behind the driver (9)  l _ _ _ _ _ _ _ _

19. a pair of eyeglasses or opera glasses with a handle (9)
    l _ _ _ _ _ _ _ _

20. a complete lighting unit including lamp, shade, reflector, fixture, and other accessories (9)  l _ _ _ _ _ _ _ _

21. a consommé flavored with tomato and served hot or cold (9)
    m _ _ _ _ _ _ _ _

22. a woman's one-piece, usually strapless, bathing suit (7)
    m _ _ _ _ _ _

23. a mixture of heterogeneous and often incongruous elements (7)
    m _ _ _ _ _ _

24. one who makes and sells fashionable dresses and hats for women (7)
    m _ _ _ _ _ _

25. a small piece of lean meat (as the eye of a chop or a small slice of tenderloin) (8)  n _ _ _ _ _ _ _

26. a substantial body of work constituting the lifework of a writer, an artist, or a composer (6)  o _ _ _ _ _

27. a brass made to imitate gold and used in mounts for furniture and for other decorative purposes (6)  o _ _ _ _ _

28. a dialect other than the standard or literary dialect (6)
    p _ _ _ _ _

29. the main body of riders in a bicycle race (7)  p _ _ _ _ _ _

30. a poem resembling a sonnet but lacking strict sonnet structure (10)
    q _ _ _ _ _ _ _ _

31. to line up or wait in a line especially of persons or vehicles (5)
    q _ _ _ _

32. a baked custard pie usually having an added savory ingredient (as chopped ham, seafood, or vegetables) (6)  q _ _ _ _ _

33. relation characterized by harmony, conformity, accord, or affinity (7)
    r _ _ _ _ _ _

34. a small ridge or mound of earth (6)  r _ _ _ _ _

35. a person with detailed knowledge in some specialized field (as of science or literature) (6)  s _ _ _ _ _

36. an oscillation of the surface of a lake or landlocked sea that varies in period from a few minutes to several hours (6)  s _ _ _ _ _

37. a brownish gray that is paler and slightly yellower than chocolate, duller and slightly redder than mouse gray, and duller and slightly redder than castor (5)  t _ _ _ _

38. an alarm bell or the ringing of a bell for the purpose of alarm (6)
    t _ _ _ _ _

39. a stage entertainment especially popular in theaters in the early decades of the twentieth century that consisted of various unrelated acts following one another in succession (10)  v _ _ _ _ _ _ _ _ _

40. one of a body of French infantry originally composed of Algerians that is characterized by a colorful uniform and by a very quick and spirited drill (6)  z _ _ _ _ _

# Chapter 7 Answer Key

## Add Diction

1. sin sing using busing abusing
2. ion lion legion legation allegation
3. ail nail snail snakily snarkily
4. hog Hong hoping hopping shopping
5. did died dived divided dividend
6. lie lite liter lister blister
7. rob robe probe probate probative
8. and sand stand strand stranded
9. rue rube ruble rumble crumble
10. ace lace lance valance avalanche

## Dictionary Devil

1. angstrom: a unit of length equal to one ten-billionth of a meter
   baccarat: a card game played especially in European casinos
   pegasus: a fabulous winged horse
   homily: an unusually short sermon
   quadruped: an animal having four feet
   picayune: something trivial
   plaint: lamentation, wail
   bravura: a show of daring or brilliance

2. crenation: one of the rounded projections on an edge (as of a coin)
   funicular: a cable railway ascending a mountain
   loge: a small compartment
   marquetry: inlaid work of wood, shell, or ivory (as on a table or cabinet)
   macle: a twinned crystal
   odyssey: a long wandering marked usually by many changes of fortune

quarto: the size of a piece of paper cut four from a sheet

whippet: any of a breed of small swift slender dogs that are used for racing

3. audit: a methodical examination and review

vesicant: an agent that causes blistering

zinger: a pointed witty remark

acknowledgment: a thing done or given in recognition of something received

depot: storehouse

angst: a feeling of anxiety, apprehension, or insecurity

mousse: a foamy preparation used in styling hair

pinto: a spotted horse or pony

4. abjection: a low or downcast state

peer: one that is of equal standing with another

festoon: a decorative chain or strip hanging between two points

pseudonym: a fictitious name

remuda: the herd of horses from which those to be used for the day are chosen

seine: a large weighted fishing net

bifurcation: separation or branching into two parts or connected segments

whelp: any of the young of various carnivorous mammals (as a dog)

5. firebrand: agitator

tundra: a treeless plain of arctic and subarctic regions

visage: the face or countenance of a person or sometimes an animal

question: an interrogative sentence or clause

mithridate: an antidote against poison

butte: an isolated steep hill

cygnet: a young swan

rhapsodist: a professional reciter of epic poems

6. unabridged: being the most complete of its class
   deprecatory: seeking to avert approval
   superlative: of very high quality
   edentulous: toothless
   eloquent: vividly or movingly expressive or revealing
   synthetic: produced artificially
   cynical: contemptuously distrustful of human nature and motives
   fanatic: marked by excessive enthusiasm and often intense
      uncritical devotion

7. pastiche: a composition made of selections from different works
   debutante: a young woman making her formal entrance into society
   plaiting: the interlacing of strands
   raucous: disagreeably harsh or strident
   ostrich: a very large swift-footed flightless bird of Africa and Arabia
   vim: robust energy and enthusiasm
   kokanee: a small landlocked sockeye salmon
   baronet: a man holding a rank of honor below a baron but above
      a knight

8. trilby: a soft felt hat with indented crown
   christie: a skiing turn used for altering the direction of hill descent
   populace: the common people
   vermicelli: pasta made in long solid strings smaller in diameter
      than spaghetti
   proclivity: an inclination or tendency toward something
   boudoir: a woman's dressing room, bedroom, or private sitting room
   fatback: the strip of fat from the back of a hog cured by drying and
      salting
   verdigris: a green or bluish deposit that forms on copper, brass,
      or bronze

9. kudu: a grayish brown African antelope with large spirally twisted horns

tendency: a proneness to a particular kind of thought or action

gourmand: one who is excessively fond of eating and drinking

gaff: a spear used to take fish or turtles

badinage: playful repartee

apocalypse: a writing prophesying a cataclysm in which evil forces are destroyed

tome: a large or scholarly book

vinaigrette: a sauce made typically of oil, vinegar, and seasonings

10. tirade: a prolonged speech of abuse or condemnation

biotite: a dark mica containing iron, magnesium, potassium, and aluminum

saber: a cavalry sword with a curved blade and thick back

warlock: a man practicing the black arts

affenpinscher: any of a breed of small dogs with a wiry black, red, tan, or gray coat

carabid: ground beetle

sapphire: a dark purplish-blue color

bedlam: a place, scene, or state of uproar and confusion

## Synonym City

| | | | |
|---|---|---|---|
| 1. alibi<br>excuse | trace<br>track<br>vestige | dale<br>valley<br>glen | imprecation<br>profanity<br>blasphemy<br>curse |
| 2. reproduction<br>facsimile<br>replica<br>copy<br>duplicate | prowess<br>gallantry<br>valor | capitulation<br>surrender | gradation<br>nuance |

3. relinquish    stroll     scar
   surrender    saunter   cicatrize
   abandon     amble
   resign       mosey
   waive
   yield

4. altitudinous   warlike    vintage     adventitious
   lofty        martial    traditional   supervenient
   elevated     bellicose   classic     extraneous

5. reprove    deposit    grieve
   admonish   cache     bemoan
   reproach    bank      lament
   reprimand          weep
   rebuke

6. inciter     fate       aide-de-camp
   fomenter   destiny    coadjutant
   instigator   lot        assistant
             doom     lieutenant
             portion

7. adventure   outline    morsel
   exploit     contour    savory
   feat       silhouette   delicacy
   enterprise   profile     tidbit

8. habitat    crotchet    wharf
   locality    caprice    dock
   home      whim      quay
   haunt     vagary     pier

9. slip     vituperation     triumph
    lapse     billingsgate     jubilance
    mistake     obloquy     exultation
    error     invective
    blunder

10. divert     evoke     foreordain     atonement
     amuse     educe     predestine     reparation
         extract     predetermine     propitiation
         elicit

## Classical Gas

1. rhinoplasty

2. anonychia

3. pachyderm

4. atrophy

5. amnesia

6. dacryocyst

7. palindrome

8. ptyalism

9. algophobia, analgesia

10. anomie, anomia, anomy

11. agnostic

12. acephalous

## Magic Square

| A | X | I |
|---|---|---|
| X | E | N |
| I | N | O |

| P | H | O | S |
|---|---|---|---|
| H | I | S | T |
| O | S | T | E |
| S | T | E | N |

## Where in the World?

| | |
|---|---|
| arcadia | A pastoral area of ancient Greece |
| assisi | A town in the Perugia province of Italy |
| attic | A region of ancient Greece |
| axminster | A town in Devon, England |
| bayonet | A city of the French Basque area |
| blarney | A castle near Cork, Ireland |
| bougie | An Algerian seaport |
| brummagem | A large city in the English Midlands |
| calico | A city in India |
| castile | A region of central Spain |
| chautauqua | A lake in western New York state |
| cordovan | A city in the Andalusian region of Spain |
| denim | A city in southeastern France |
| Edam | A village in the Netherlands |
| glengarry | A valley in Inverness-shire, Scotland |

| | |
|---|---|
| guinea | A region in west Africa |
| hantavirus | A river in South Korea |
| hardanger | A district in Norway |
| huapango | A town near Veracruz, Mexico |
| jeans | Genoa, Italy |
| leghorn | A port city in the Tuscany region of Italy |
| limerick | A city in southwest Ireland |
| lisle | A French city near the Belgian border |
| madrilene | The capital city of Spain |
| magenta | A town in northern Italy |
| magnet | An ancient city in Thessaly, Greece |
| massasauga | A river in Ontario, Canada |
| Meissen | A city on the Elbe River in Germany |
| milliner | Milan, Italy |
| muslin | Mosul, Iraq |
| Nicoise | A leading resort on the French Riviera |
| Percheron | A region in northern France |
| poblano | A state in central Mexico |
| quoddy | An inlet between Canada and the United States |
| samaritan | A district of ancient Palestine |
| satsuma | A former province of Japan |
| shanghai | China's largest city |
| sisal | A fishing village in Yucatan, Mexico |
| soubise | A village in western France |
| sunglo | A mountain in China |
| Talavera | A city in the province of Toledo, Spain |
| tangerine | A large city of northern Morocco |
| tarantula | A seaport in southern Italy |
| tweed | A river in Scotland |
| wesselton | A mine in South Africa |

# Anagram Fest

prenatal/paternal

feral/flare

married/admirer

eviler/revile

ocean/canoe

ardent/ranted

cadent/decant

helot/hotel

terrace/caterer

trimester/remitters

treatise/teariest

omicron/moronic

striated/tardiest

eater/arete

demeanor/enamored

reactive/creative

diverse/revised

eastern/nearest

medicate/decimate

arteritis/irritates

coupons/soupcon

antiseptic/psittacine

oriental/relation

camerate/macerate

antigen/gentian

leveraged/everglade

servile/leviers

nomocracy/monocracy

cleared/declare

matricide/diametric

soutenu/tenuous

frantic/infract

*Answer: Geoffrey Chaucer*

# Word Search: -*able* Was I Ere I Saw -*ible*

| e |   | t | r | a | n | s | m | i | s | s | i | b | l | e |
|---|---|---|---|---|---|---|---|---|---|---|---|---|---|---|
|   | x | e | l | b | a | t | p | a | d | a |   |   |   |   |
|   |   | h | e | l | b | i | t | s | i | s | e | r | r | i |
|   | m | o | a | f | f | a | b | l | e |   |   |   | n | n |
|   | a | m | i | u | r |   |   |   | r |   |   |   | e | v |
| e | n | i | n | n | s | i |   |   | i | e |   |   | g | i |
| l | d | s | d | g |   | t | a | s | l |   | l | e | o | n |
| b | i | s | e | i |   |   | i | b |   |   | o | l | t | c |
| i | b | i | l | b |   | b | a | b | l |   | c | b | i | i |
| t | l | b | i | l | l | c |   |   | l | e | a | a | b |
| c | e | l | b | e | u |   |   |   | e | t | s | b | l |
| u |   | e | l | d |   |   |   | a | u | l | e |
| d | e | t | e | s | t | a | b | l | e |   | b | c | e |
| e | l | b | a | t | i | u | q | e |   |   | l | x |
| d | i | v | i | s | i | b | l | e |   |   | e | e |

# Wordmeister Challenge: A Very Verbose Verbigram

epic

fluent

password

abbreviate

lexicon

locution

falsehood

spoonerism

translator

folktale

euphemism

compendious

neology

officialese

paraphrase

phonics

incantation

apostrophe

narrate

grammar

onomatopoeia

plagiarism

dialect

rhetoric

exhort

alphabet

nomenclature

equivocate

honorific

solecism

palaver

circumlocution

sesquipedalia

intelligibly

lipogram

literate

orthographic

"I love the name of honor more than I fear death." —Julius Caesar

# Wordmeister Super Challenge: Greek Word Search

acropolis
amphibious
bruxism
calisthenics
calliope
chresard
chrysanthemum
electrolyte

enthalpy
euphemism
evangelize
glossoid
Homeric
icosahedron
isonomy
koinonia

krypton
lithic
logomachy
mimetic
myriad
nautilus
neophyte
stalagmite

systole
thoracic
thrombosis
typhus
xerosis
xylem

| | | c | i | c | a | r | o | h | t | i | s | o | n | o | m | y | | s | |
| n | | | i | c | o | s | a | h | e | d | r | o | n | | | | x | i | |
| | e | | | y | | | | | | | | | | | y | s | k | | |
| | | o | | e | p | o | i | l | l | a | c | | | m | | l | o | r | |
| | | | p | | | l | m | i | m | e | t | i | c | | s | | e | b | y |
| m | | s | n | h | | | a | | | | i | | | i | | m | m | p | |
| u | | c | a | | y | b | | h | | | r | | | m | | | o | t | |
| m | | i | u | | | t | r | | t | e | | | | e | | | r | o | |
| e | | n | t | | | e | u | m | n | | l | i | t | h | i | c | h | n | |
| h | | e | i | | | | o | x | | e | | | p | | e | t | | | |
| t | | h | l | a | m | p | h | i | b | i | o | u | s | | u | l | v | | |
| n | l | t | u | | c | | | e | | s | | | | e | x | a | | | |
| a | o | s | s | | h | r | | l | | | m | | c | | e | n | | a | |
| s | g | i | | | r | | o | | | | | t | | | r | g | | i | |
| y | o | l | | | e | t | | p | | | r | y | | | o | e | | n | |
| r | m | a | | | s | | | | o | | o | | p | | s | l | | o | |
| h | a | c | | y | a | | | | l | | | h | | | i | i | | n | |
| c | c | | s | | r | | | y | | i | | u | | | s | z | | i | |
| | h | | | | d | | t | d | i | o | s | s | o | l | g | e | | o | |
| m | y | r | i | a | d | | e | | s | t | a | l | a | g | m | i | t | e | k |

# Wordmeister Super Challenge: French Word Search

| | | | | |
|---|---|---|---|---|
| aubade | fuselage | kepi | noisette | rapport |
| bivouac | gaffe | limousine | oeuvre | rideau |
| cabochon | grosgrain | lorgnette | ormolu | savant |
| coquette | hauteur | luminaire | patois | seiche |
| croupier | impromptu | madrilene | peloton | taupe |
| devoir | insouciance | maillot | quatorzain | tocsin |
| esplanade | javelin | mélange | queue | vaudeville |
| flaneur | julienne | modiste | quiche | zouave |

| | | | | | | | | | | | | | | | | | |
|---|---|---|---|---|---|---|---|---|---|---|---|---|---|---|---|---|---|
| | t | o | c | s | i | n | | | e | s | p | l | a | n | a | d | e | |
| | u | | | | | | n | p | | e | n | o | t | o | l | e | p | |
| v | t | | e | g | a | l | e | s | u | f | | i | | e | n | | | h |
| a | p | | | | l | t | t | a | | l | | c | i | f | | | l | a |
| u | m | | | i | j | t | r | t | | | a | a | h | | f | | o | u |
| d | o | | r | p | u | e | o | | | r | n | | e | | | a | r | t |
| e | r | | d | | e | l | u | p | | | g | | m | e | l | a | n | g | e |
| v | p | a | | k | i | q | p | | s | | | | | u | | | n | u |
| i | m | | | e | o | a | o | z | o | u | a | v | e | r | | e | r |
| l | i | a | | n | c | r | o | u | p | i | e | r | | | t | | |
| l | o | l | i | | n | g | | | r | e | u | e | u | q | | t | |
| e | r | u | | l | | e | a | | | i | | | e | u | | e | |
| | m | m | n | | l | | | u | | o | | | t | a | | h | |
| | o | i | o | n | | o | | b | | v | | e | p | t | t | | c |
| | l | n | h | i | | t | i | | a | e | | r | a | e | o | | i | u |
| | u | a | c | l | | n | v | | d | | v | t | s | r | | u | a |
| | | i | o | e | a | o | | | | e | u | o | i | z | | q | e |
| | | r | b | v | u | m | o | d | i | s | t | e | e | i | o | a | | d |
| | | e | a | a | | e | c | n | a | i | c | u | o | s | n | i | | i |
| | | s | c | j | | | l | i | m | o | u | s | i | n | e | | r |

# Notes

**Barrie Trinkle** has served on the Scripps National Spelling Bee's word panel since 1997. She was the 1973 National Spelling Bee Champion (her word was *vouchsafe*).

**Carolyn Andrews** is the word list manager for the Scripps National Spelling Bee. Her son, Ned, was the 1994 National Spelling Bee Champion (his word was *antediluvian*).

**Paige Kimble** is the director of the Scripps National Spelling Bee. She was the 1981 National Spelling Bee Champion (her word was *sarcophagus*).

# The Hornbook

Dr. Johnson described the hornbook as "the first book of children, covered with horn to keep it unsoiled." Pardon's New General English Dictionary (1758) defined it as "A leaf of written or printed paper pasted on a board, and covered with horn, for children to learn their letters by, and to prevent their being torn and daubed."

It was used throughout Europe and America between the late 1400s and the middle 1700s.

Shaped like an old-fashion-ed butter paddle, the first hornbooks were made of wood. The paper lesson the child was to learn was fastened to the wooden paddle and covered with a piece of horn. The transparent strip of horn was made by soaking a cow's horn in hot water and peeling it away at the thickness of a piece of celluloid. The horn was necessary to protect the lesson from the damp and perhaps grubby hands of the child. Hornbooks commonly contained the alphabet, the vowels, and the Lord's Prayer. Later hornbooks were made of vari-ous materials: brass, copper, silver, ivory, bronze, leather, and stone.

As the art of printing advanced, the hornbook was supplanted by the primer in the book form we know today. Subsequently West Publishing Company developed its "Hornbook Series", a series of scholarly and well-respected one volume treatises on particular areas of law. Today they are widely used by law students, lawyers and judges.

# FEDERAL INCOME TAXATION OF INDIVIDUALS

With Diagrams for Easy
Understanding of the
Leading Cases and Concepts

## Third Edition

By

### Daniel Q. Posin

*Professor of Law*
*Tulane University School of Law*

**HORNBOOK SERIES®**

**WEST PUBLISHING CO.**
ST. PAUL, MINN., 1997

COPYRIGHT © 1983, 1989, 1993 WEST PUBLISHING CO.

COPYRIGHT © 1997 By WEST GROUP
              610 Opperman Drive
              P.O. Box 64526
              St. Paul, MN 55164–0526
              1–800–328–9352

**Library of Congress Cataloging-in-Publication Data**

Posin, Daniel Q., 1941–
    Federal income taxation of individuals with diagrams for easy
  understanding of the leading cases and concepts  /  by Daniel Q.
  Posin. — 3rd ed.
      p.    cm. — (Hornbook series)
      Includes index.
      ISBN 0–314–06667–5  (softcover)
      1. Income tax—Law and legislation—United States.    I. Title.
  II. Series.
  KF6369.P67    1997
  343.7305'2—dc21
                                                      97–22405
                                                          CIP


**ISBN** 0–314–06667–5

TEXT IS PRINTED ON 10% POST
CONSUMER RECYCLED PAPER

*For my wife Kathe and
our children,
Kimberly, Rick & John*

\*

*"Where this is an income tax, the just man will pay more and the unjust less on the same amount of income."*
—Plato, The Republic, bk K, 343-D

*"Taxes are what we pay for civilized society."*
—Oliver Wendell Holmes, Jr., Compania de Tabacos v. Collector, 275 U.S. 87, 100 (1904)

\*

# Special Note and Acknowledgments

For gramatical convenience I have frequently referred to taxpayers in this book as "he." This obviously ignores the fact that many taxpayers are women. Moreover, it also ignores the fact that the overwhelming majority of tax returns filed are husband and wife joint returns. Rather than trying to cover all these possibilities by continually using the phrase "he, she, or they," throughout this book, I have stayed with the grammatically simpler "he." No offense is intended to the many women who take the course in federal income taxation and the many women who pay substantial amounts of federal income taxes.

I would like to thank Professor Michael Rose at the Ohio State University College of Law for his extremely helpful comments on this edition of the book. I would also like to thank two student research assistants, Dennis Grossman and Jay Chadda for their help.

\*

# Highlights

Analysis of the cases and concepts of the leading casebooks. Explanations often amplified with diagrams. Extensive treatment of time value of money issues throughout. In addition to comprehensive treatment of the standard course material, discussion of "real world" tax planning techniques, such as:

* Exotic Wall Street Techniques Employed by the Wealthy to Avoid Capital Gains: Of ESOP Sales, Upreits, Equity Swaps, Shorting Against the Box, Swap Funds, DECS and the like, explained in clear language.

* How the equity swap works: The Autotote deal.

* How the Estee Lauder insiders avoided $95 million in capital gains taxes when they sold their stock to the public.

* Exotic compensation techniques used by corporate executives.

* How John Welch, chief executive officer at General Electric deferred taxes on $1 million and increased his take by $263,000 within five years.

* Deferred compensation goes better with Coke: A case study of how Roberto C. Goizueta, the CEO of the Coca-Cola Company, amassed $1 billion of compensation between 1979 and 1996 and paid tax on it at a rate of 5%.

* How top executives of Morris Knudsen, Carter Hawley, and Woodward & Lothrop protected millions of dollars in supposedly risky pension rights in connection with their company's bankruptcy.

* How former Treasury Secretary William Simon and his partners made $700 million in profits on the sale of the Avis car rental agency less than two years after they bought it and paid no taxes.

* How real estate developers like Sam Zell combine tax-free swaps of property and an "umbrella partnership" to avoid millions of dollars in taxes: the upreit technique.

* A Bird's Eye View of sophisticated estate planning for upper income taxpayers.

* The 1996 tax return of Bill and Hillary Clinton.

\*

# WESTLAW® Overview

Federal Taxation offers a detailed and comprehensive treatment of legal principles and issues relating to federal taxation. To supplement the information contained in this book, you can access WESTLAW, a computer-assisted legal research service of West Publishing. WESTLAW contains a broad library of legal research resources, including case law, statutes, expert commentary, current developments and various other types of information.

Learning how to use these materials effectively will enhance your legal research. To help you coordinate your book and WESTLAW research, this volume contains an appendix listing WESTLAW databases, search techniques and sample problems.

THE PUBLISHER

\*

# Summary of Contents

\*

# Table of Contents

# Table of Illustrations

*

# FEDERAL INCOME TAXATION OF INDIVIDUALS

## With Diagrams for Easy Understanding of the Leading Cases and Concepts

### Third Edition

\*

# I. PROLOGUE: THE MIRACULOUS EFFECTS OF THE TIME VALUE OF MONEY

*Table of Sections*

-------

## 1.1  Cornering the Virginia Lottery

In February of 1992, a syndicate based in Australia attempted to corner the Virginia lottery. The lottery payoff had reached $27 million over the course of several weeks because there were no winners. The Virginia lottery requires the player to correctly pick 6 numbers from 1 to 44. The number of possible combinations is seven million. The syndicate's idea was to buy seven million $1 tickets and select all possible combinations. Thus it would have a sure thing: a net profit of $20 million

This attempt caused a sensation, gaining international press coverage. Many Virginia residents complained that these massive block purchases were unfair to the small player. The Virginia Lottery Board considered proposals to Governor L. Douglas Wilder to limit block purchases of lottery tickets.

What does all this have to do with federal income taxation?

A great deal, as we will see.

I put you this question. Was this scheme by the Australian syndicate a good idea? Let us think about this problem in a hard-nosed way.

Consider the numbers on such a scheme: At first blush, it looks like a lead-pipe cinch. You pay $7 million, you get $27 million.[1] But, as in the

-------

1. Because of logistical difficulties, the Australian syndicate actually only managed to purchase 5 million of the 7 million tickets needed to win. To keep the discussion clear as a matter of principle the text discusses the case where 7 million tickets are purchased.

Apparently one reason the syndicate selected the Virginia lottery was the relatively small number of tickets that needed to be purchased. Because of the peculiarities of the laws of probability, Virginia's 7 million possibilities on a 44 number game are half that of Florida's 14 million possibilities on a 49 number game. California has 51 numbers and New York has 54.

1

case of most lotteries, it turns out you do not really get your winnings up front. The Virginia lottery pays its winnings out at a rate of $1.35 million a year for 20 years. Is that still a good deal? Once again at first blush it still looks good. $1.35 million for 20 years equals $27 million.

But it turns out there are some complications. There's a tax bite. Assume the maximum rate of 33% federal tax plus 7% state tax gives us a total tax hit of 40%.[2] To what will this 40% bite be applied? It appears at first that it would be applied to the $1.35 million per year. But the $7 million payment for tickets is deductible since gambling losses are deductible against gambling winnings.[3] The $7 million is certainly a legitimate expense of this venture. Let us assume this $7 million deduction is also spread out over the 20 year period in which the income will be paid. This is almost certainly what the IRS would require.[4] Seven million dollars spread out over 20 years is $350,000 per year. Therefore, instead of $1.35 million per year the *taxable* amount of the payment is $1 million. Note that in order to ascertain a sensible amount on which to impose the tax we need to allow deduction of the reasonable expenses of buying the tickets.[5]

With that said we can see that the tax per year will be 40% of $1 million per year or $400,000. Thus the after tax amount of **cash** coming in each year is $1,350,000 minus $400,000 or $950,000.

We are now in a position to make a cash flow analysis (as they say in business school). As a matter of cash going out and coming in here is what has happened: In the first year $7 million went out and $950,000 came back in. In the next 19 years $950,000 comes back in. Another way of saying it is that the syndicate pays $7 million out up front and gets $950,000 per year for 20 years.

Is that a good deal? Another way to phrase it is to say what is $950,000 per year for 20 year worth? At first blush it appears to be worth simply $950,000 × 20 or a cool $19 million.

---

The discussion in the text assumes that the lottery winnings are subject to tax either in the U.S. or in Australia. In fact in a subsequent lawsuit the Australian syndicate hit the jackpot again, successfully arguing that the United States and the state of Virginia cannot withhold taxes on the $27 million lottery jackpot, because of the provisions of the U.S.-Australian income tax treaty. Article 7(1) of the treaty provides that the business profits of an enterprise of one contracting state are taxable in that state only if the enterprise carries on business in the other contracting state through a permanent establishment. Thus federal and state withholding on the lottery winnings was permanently enjoined. The state of Virginia decided not to appeal. The winnings were still subject to Australian tax, however. See International Lotto Fund v. Virginia State Lottery Department, et al., 800 F.Supp. 337 (E.D.Va.1992).

For pedagogical purposes the text assumes the syndicate was a U.S.-based syndicate of law students, therefore subject to U.S. federal and state tax.

**2.** The Virginia lottery does withhold federal and state taxes from the annual payouts.

**3.** § 165(d).

**4.** The taxpayer might wish to argue that the losses should be deducted sooner, but the IRS could be expected to maintain that the deduction should be spread out over the period of the winnings. See the treatment of annuities and installment sales later in the book.

**5.** The other expenses of hiring people to run around buying the tickets and keeping track of them would also be deductible in this venture, but we will ignore such expenses for purposes of the discussion.

But is $950,000 per year really worth $19 million right now? If the syndicate had $19 million right now, it would certainly grow to be worth a lot more than that over the years in that it would earn interest.

A simple yet profound insight is that an amount to be received in the future is not worth as much as that amount in the present. Because the amount received in the present can be invested to earn interest. The amount to be received in the future cannot be (since we don't have our hands on it yet).

The process of determining the value of a stream of payments to be paid in the future is called "present value analysis." In order to perform present value analysis (explained in detail below) on the $950,000 per year we need to have a realistic interest rate to use in our calculations.

Since the annual payment is backed by the state of Virginia, it may be regarded as almost as good as Treasury Bills issued by the federal government. (States, however, have been known to threaten to default on their obligations, and at this writing Virginia is in some financial difficulty). A reasonable interest rate taking into account the high degree of security of this payment is 9%. Since we are dealing with after-tax results, we will want to take the after-tax interest rate based on that 9%. We have agreed that the combined federal and state rate is 40%. Thus the after-tax interest rate based on 9% is 5.4% (i.e. 60% of 9%). Employing an after-tax interest rate of 5.4%, the present value of $950,000 per year for 20 years can be calculated (using a computer).

That present value is about $12 million. From a cash flow perspective the syndicate puts out $7 million and winds up with a deal worth $12 million, after all taxes are taken care of. Thus we seem to have a profit of $5 million. This is a lot less than the profit of $20 million that this venture appeared to offer at first blush. Applying tax and time value of money principles to this venture showed it to be worth substantially less than it appeared to be, albeit it still was profitable. A "sure thing" worth a $5 million profit on a $7 million investment is a lot different from a "sure thing" worth $20 million profit on a $7 million investment.

There are various practical risks to this venture that do not appear in the probability numbers. These risks loom a lot higher if the profit is only $5 million instead of $20 million. For example, there is the sheer logistical problem of buying seven million $1 lottery tickets. The syndicate may not be able to acquire that many. The syndicate might not know that it failed to get them until it had already spent 4 or 5 million dollars.

Indeed, that is exactly what happened to the syndicate. They actually only managed to acquire 5 million tickets in the Virginia lottery. Thus they were in for $5 million and still had 2 million possibilities not covered. In fact they did win.[6] They were lucky. So instead of a sure

**6.** The winning numbers were 8, 11, 13, 15, 19 and 20.

thing win of $20 million they were lucky to win $7 million[7]—and lucky not to lose $5 million.

Moreover, there is a further problem. That is, there may be more than one winner. Let us say there is another winner besides the syndicate. Not someone who also bought $7 million of tickets but someone who just got lucky buying one ticket. That is how one normally wins lotteries after all, getting lucky. If there were one other winner, then that winner and the syndicate split the jackpot. In that event the syndicate's payoff (before tax) is $675,000 per year for 20 years. Subtracting the $350,000 annualized expenses of the $7 million ticket purchase produces a taxable amount of $325,000. Paying a tax of 40% on that produces a tax on each payment of $130,000. Thus the after-tax cash payment is $675,000 − $130,000 = $545,000.

We therefore come to the nub question of what is the value of $545,000 per year for 20 years, with an after-tax interest rate of 5.4%. The computer cranks out the answer of $6.9 million. Now we are losing about $100,000. If there were two other winners, so that the syndicate gets one-third of the $27 million jackpot a similar set of calculations cranks out a present value of $5.2 million. Thus $1.8 million is lost on the venture because of multiple winners. Where does the $1.8 million go (not an inconsiderable sum)? Part of it fattens up the pot for the other multiple winners, who let us say bought just one or a few tickets. The rest of the $1.8 million goes to Virginia.

What are the chances of multiple winners? The larger the jackpot, the more tickets will be bought. The more tickets will be bought, the greater the likelihood there will be multiple winners. Of the 16 jackpots in the Virginia lottery worth over $10 million between 1990 and February 1992, 3 were shared. As our calculations above indicate, if it were shared by several people there would be a several million dollar loss to the syndicate.

Thus the arrangement, which appeared at first blush to be a sure thing, was highly risky.

We can learn several things that will be useful to us in this course from this frolic. I suggest the following list, in no particular order; you may think of some others:

Tax Lessons From This Story:

    1) Gambling winnings are taxable

    2) Gambling losses are deductible to the extent of gambling winnings

    3) Expenses paid up front to produce income over a period of years usually have to be deducted over that period of years instead of immediately. This is to match deductions with income.

---

**7.** The $7 million is roughly the $12 million present value less the $5 million spent on tickets. This calculation ignores the syndicate's other administrative expenses and the amounts of lesser prizes that might be won.

4) Time value of money analysis drastically affects the present value of payments of income over time.

We also learned some things about this attempt to corner the Virginia lottery.

Lessons about the attempt to corner the Virginia Lottery:

1) The syndicate's strategy was poor. Instead of an apparent sure win of $20 million, they wound up with at best a chance to win $7 million and, as it played out, a substantial chance of suffering a multi-million dollar loss. The approach the syndicate took was seriously in error, particularly when it is considered that they were playing with other people's money.

2) The resentment of other players to the syndicate's attempt to corner the lottery was utterly misplaced. The syndicate was in effect pumping heavy bucks into the pot. There was a significant chance of multiple winners. Anyone who was a multiple winner with the syndicate would have eaten the syndicate's lunch. Obviously it is a long shot for anyone to be a multiple winner with the syndicate. But since the odds are already 7 million to 1 against winning the pot at all, what is the problem?

3) The state of Virginia's hysterical reaction to this attempt was also misplaced. The syndicate is pumping money into the lottery, a substantial portion of which is raked off by the state. These speculators in lottery pots should be welcomed by the state with open arms. That's why they're running a lottery, isn't it?

There is a larger lesson here. Note the critical importance of understanding the time value of money. It was time value of money analysis that enabled us to see that the syndicate's strategy was misguided. In sophisticated financial transactions, one wants to be able to make this same sort of analysis for clients. And time value of money analysis has come, in recent years, to be of major importance in the field of federal income taxation. In the sections that follow we learn how to do it. And we see some more examples of its miraculous effects.

## 1.2 Background on Time Value of Money

There's some stuff in this prologue you're just not going to believe. You may think tax is dull, conjuring up visions of people in green eye-shades hunched over forms. Well, I do admit that I look pretty good in a green eye-shade, but I also want to tell you there are some spectacular moves available in this field: Moves harnessing some tremendously powerful forces, leading to some unbelievable results. These are things that just don't happen in other fields of law, because other fields of law are just not tapped into these very powerful forces. It all has to do with timing. In other fields of law, except for statute of limitations purposes, it does not really matter too much when a particular tort, contract, or crime occurs. But in tax, *when* something happens is of signal importance. And these effects are not just of academic interest. There are results in this chapter that can make you and your clients some very big money. Let's start out by looking at some of the basic ideas. Once we get through them, you're going to see some stuff you're just not going to believe.

### 1.3  Basic Concepts: Growth of Capital

One of the most fundamental concepts in the field of federal income taxation is the time value of money. The question in the field is not only how much is income or how much is deductible, the question is also when is the item income or deductible. To the student first approaching the field, it would not seem to matter especially much in what year something is income or deductible. But, as the discussion below will show, the timing of an item of income or deduction can have an astonishing impact.

As a way of approaching this subject consider that it is a fundamental economic fact of life that capital grows. Consider in particular—an example economists frequently use—a grove of trees that will produce lumber. If you buy the grove for $100,000 and the trees grow annually at 7%, the grove will have a value of $107,000 at the end of one year. Since you can always have this deal, why invest in something that does not grow?

We can expand this idea to include all of agriculture. Since agricultural crops and farm animals grow, why invest in something that does not grow, since the agricultural option is always available? Thus the value of an investment in an industrial activity must grow over time or it will not receive attention from investors. Of course, there are short-term fluctuations in the values of investments and some companies go broke, but over the longer term overall investments in industrial productions produce positive returns.

This return on investment can be in the form of interest, dividends, or increase in the value of the investment. The example of the trees growing by 7% is an example of increase in the value of the investment. If the 7% of the trees were cut and sold at the end of the year, with the proceeds used to pay stockholders in the company owning the trees, then the growth would be represented by dividends. If the proceeds of the cut trees were used to pay interest to those who had lent money to the tree-growing business, then the growth would take the form of interest.

It is this inevitable growth of capital over time that is fundamental to our study of time value of money in taxation.

While, as discussed above, capital growth can take the form of dividends, interest, or capital appreciation, in the tax field we focus primarily on interest. This is because the nature of the obligation to pay taxes to the government is one of debt. When the payment of debt is deferred—as it often is in the tax field—we become concerned about the concept of interest. Also, interest is the most convenient way to focus on the impact of time on capital growth. We can speak of a risk-free rate of return (generally the interest rate on short-term government bonds). When we speak of dividends or capital appreciation, there will inevitably be some risk involved. When risk is involved people need a higher rate of return to make up for the risk. So the risk factor complicates the analysis. Also the variable returns on riskier investments make our calculations cumbersome.

Thus when we speak of the time value of money, we will usually be talking about relatively secure short-term interest.

## 1.4  Interest

### 1.4.1  Present Value Analysis

If you were offered $100 today or $100 one year from today, which would you take? Think about this one for a while. Don't just plunge ahead reading in a hurry before you go to class. Which would you take? The answer is in the next paragraph.

Clearly the $100 today is more valuable, because it can be put in a savings account at, say, 6% interest and grow to $106. So if you take the $100 today, you will have $106 one year from now instead of $100 a year from now.[8] So, $100 today is worth $106 a year from now, whereas $100 a year from now is, of course, worth $100 a year from now.

Having said that, we can now push things just a little further. We're going to take one more step. We're going to get somewhere now. If you take this next step, you've got the rest of this course made in the shade. I guarantee you at least a B:

We have already figured out what $100 today is worth one year from now—namely $106. Let us instead figure out just what $100 one year from now is worth today. Get me? What would you pay today for the right to get $100 a year from now. Suppose (with an interest rate of 6%) somebody offered you the right to receive $100 a year from now. Suppose he said you could have that right for 37 cents? Would you take the deal? You'd jump at it right? You don't need a Ph.D. in mathematics to figure out that that's a heck of a deal. Suppose he offered it to you for $90? That's less clear, but just eyeballing it, it looks like a good deal. Suppose he offered it to you for $103? Would you take that? You know that's wrong. $103 this year will grow to be worth over $109, as our analysis above has already indicated.

What is the right price for the right to get $100 one year from now (with a prevailing 6% interest rate)? That right has got to be worth less than $100. Let us formulate the question. What is the question to be asked here? Try it? If you get the question right, I guarantee you at least a B+ in the course. The appropriate question is in the next paragraph.

8. Note that we are not considering that that $6 profit could be subject to tax, which would reduce it. We're just talking about basic time value of money concepts right now. We're not talking about taxes at this point. (Who wants to talk about taxes anyway!)

The appropriate question is what amount of money today would grow, at 6% interest, to $100 one year from today. That is the question. It may be a little tricky to make the computation, but the principle is clear. It looks like something like $94 or $95. We are not going to ask you to make a lot of computations, just understand the ideas involved. Wouldn't we be able to set up the equation like this, if X is the amount we're looking for:

$$X \times 1.06 = \$100$$
$$X = \$100/1.06$$
$$X = \$94.34$$

There, that didn't hurt too much now did it. We have just done something that people go to business school for two years to try to learn to do (and many never do get it). We have "discounted a future payment to its present value." This jargon is just another way of saying that we have asked ourselves what is the amount now that would grow to $100 in one year at 6% interest?

If you will read the preceding two paragraphs over forty times I guarantee you at least an A— in the course.

This is a surprisingly powerful computation. We have valued the present value of a payment of money at some time in the future. We have figured out that $100 a year from now, with a 6% interest rate, is worth $94.34 now.

Thus, in the preceding section, when you were offered $100 today or $100 a year from today, what you were really offered (given 6% interest) was $100 today or something worth $94.34 today. The choice was clear.

### 1.4.2  Simple and Compound Interest

Suppose you leave the $100 we were talking about in the preceding section in the bank for two years instead of one. Suppose further that you leave the interest of $6 in the account as well. The bank will then compute the 6% interest they will pay in the second year based on the $106 rather than $100. Why will they include the extra 6% in their computation? They have to or lose your business, that's why.

If they do not do it, you will take the $6 out and put it in another bank in a savings account. That $6 may be interest as far as the first bank is concerned, but it is principal as far as the second bank is concerned. The second bank will then give you 6% interest on your $6. The first bank knows you will do this. So rather than lose your business they will calculate the second year's 6% interest on the full $106 (no use everybody running around redepositing their interest payments as principal in other banks). Six percent interest on $106 cranks out to be $112.36.

What is the most powerful part of that number—the $112 or the 36 cents? Think that one over. This is another big-time concept in this field. The answer is once again in the next paragraph.

The $112 is certainly a lot more money than the 36 cents. But it's the 36 cents that is the power. With that 36 cents you have a tiger by the tail. The reason that the second year's computation gave us $6.36 instead of just $6 was that we were getting interest on the previous year's interest as well as interest on our original principal. The extra 36 cents may not seem like much, but try leaving that $100 in place compounding at 6% for 40 years and see what happens.

As a matter of fact, let's see what happens if you do just that. What happens is that that $100 grows to a cool $1,028.57, more than a ten-fold increase. This is demonstrated in the accompanying figure:

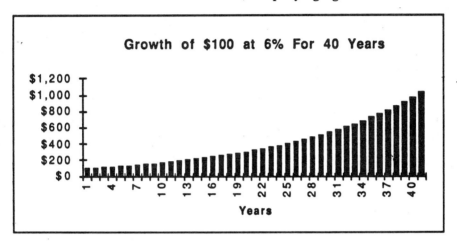

Notice the particularly powerful effects of compounding in the later years. Indeed, the interest on the accumulated amount for the 41st year is $61.71, more than 60% of the original principal. You are now getting more than 60% interest on your original principal. Forty years is a long time, of course, but on the other hand you have not had to do anything with it. You could have been drunk the whole time (although I don't recommend it). You've just let this money sit.

To juice it up a little bit, let us take a look at the investment if it pays 18% interest rather than 6%. How much larger will the $100 be when compounded at 18% rather than 6%? Take a guess. The 18% is, after all, triple the 6%. So would we be talking about the principal growing to around $3,000, about triple the principal grew to at 6%? Maybe a little more? Well, it turns out that $100 compounded annually at 18% for forty years blossoms to a nifty $75,037.83.

Although the interest rate was only triple, the amount the principal grew to was 75 times as much as it grew to when compounded at 6%. It grew to be over 750 times larger than the original principal. This is demonstrated in the next figure, where we compare the 6% interest compounded and the 18% interest compounded.

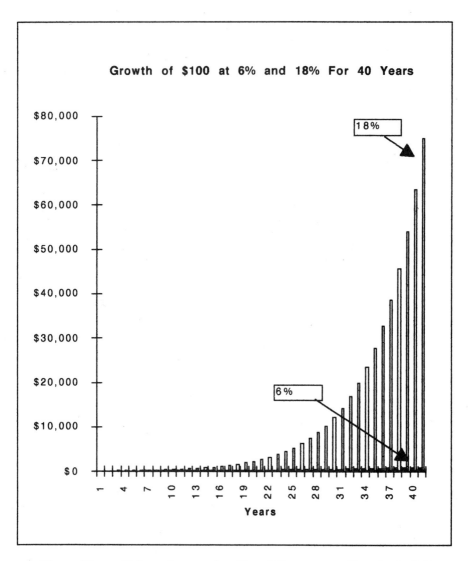

Growth of $100 at 6% and 18% For 40 Years

You will recall how impressive that 6% compounding looked from Figure 2.1 (and indeed it was impressive). Nevertheless, when compared to the 18% compounding in Figure 2.2, you can hardly see the 6% compounding.

As another example of what's happened, note that for the 41st year, the 18% interest on the $75,037.83 would amount to $13,506.81. This interest payment is 135 times larger than the original principal. This gives us a feel for the raw power of compound interest. We do have a tiger by the tail. I don't mean to knock other courses, but you don't come across something like this in torts, contracts, or procedure.

Compare this compound interest to simple interest. Suppose we had collected simple interest—that is just interest on the principal—for 40 years at 18%. That would amount to 18% of $100 for forty years or an unimpressive $720. That $720 is not even as much as you get with compound interest at 6%. And it is a lot less than the over $74,000 in interest we collected when interest was compounding. Thus, a little piece of financial advice: if anybody offers you simple interest, laugh in his or her face.

Having learned our basic lessons about time value of money, it is now time to have some fun with it.

### 1.5 A Few Stunts

#### 1.5.1 General Implications

It will surprise you how often time value of money comes up in taxation. When it comes up, the foregoing analysis always tells you what is going on. For example, taking a deduction is better sooner than later. This is because it saves you taxes sooner rather than later, and you therefore get your hands on the tax money saved sooner rather than later. You can then earn (compound) interest on your money sooner rather than later and it will grow to more. Paying tax on an income item is better later rather than sooner, because you have to part with your money later rather than sooner. Keeping the money allows you to earn (compound of course) interest on the money and it will grow to more. Another way of looking at it is to say that you need to set aside less than the full amount of the tax due and the amount set aside will grow in time to the amount actually due.

But enough of this pedantic stuff, let's have some fun:

#### 1.5.2 Stunt No 1: How to Eliminate Tax

This is a truly astonishing result. What we are going to show here is that the simple ability to change the timing of paying tax on an investment has two amazing effects: 1) the tax on the income from the investment is eliminated; and 2) the *pre-tax* rate of return on the investment is actually increased. Talk about pulling a rabbit out of the hat! I think you should buy me a drink for this one. (Why this preoccupation with alcohol, you ask. I don't recommend it). Consider the following example:

**Example 2.1:** T, in the 50 percent bracket,[9] invests $100 in a drill bit. A special provision in the Internal Revenue Code allows an immediate deduction of the full $100, saving T $50 in taxes.[10] T

**9.** The 50% percent figure is used for mathematical convenience. If the rate is lower than that, the effects described in the text will not be quite so powerful. If the rate is higher than that, the effects described in the text will be even more powerful. Historically, the maximum marginal rate on individuals has ranged up as high as 90%. See Chapter 1. Under current law, the maximum rate is in the 39% area. Combined with the income tax imposed by many states, the maximum rate on individuals frequently reaches 50%.

**10.** Such a deduction is available for investment in the costs of drilling an oil well (so-called "intangible drilling costs,"). See § 263(c); Treas. Reg. § 1.612–4(a) (1965). The ability to take this deduction immediately is very favorable to the oil drilling industry. Ordinarily the expenses of creating a major income producing asset

reinvests that $50 in the same kind of asset. Deducting immediately that $50 saves T $25 (assuming T's income is so high that he remains in the 50 percent bracket despite these deductions) which he can then reinvest in an identical asset. T continues to deduct immediately and reinvest until a full $100 is invested. At that point T will own *and have fully paid for* assets worth $200. Where did the extra money come from? The tax savings from the deduction in effect gave T an interest-free loan from the government of $100. Let us assume these assets appreciate 10 percent a year (compounded annually). Since the asset is going up in value but not paying any interest or dividends, the annual increase is not taxed until the end of the 10 years when the asset is finally sold.[11] Thus this investment benefits in a second way from deferral of tax. Not only is the initial investment immediately deducted but the increase in value is not taxed until the asset is finally sold. With a 10% rate of return compounded, at the end of ten years T will be able to sell out for about $519. His tax cost would have been $0 because he deducted the amounts he invested (see Chapter 6 on depreciation). Thus his tax gain would be $519. The $519 would be taxed at the 50% rate, yielding a tax of $259.50. Thus he would be left with net proceeds of $259.50. Thus under these conditions when the dust clears, T's $100 grew to $259.50. That's an after tax gain of $159.50 ($259.50 minus the original $100).

Here's the corker, kids. That gain of $159.50 is what T would get with an annual rate of return of 10% with no tax. *T, by being able to deduct his investment and resulting tax savings in full, was able to in effect eliminate the tax.* This was true even though he made up for taking the deduction at the beginning of the investment by being taxed on the full amount of the sales proceeds at the end. As they say in figure skating, timing is everything.

Taking the polar opposite example, suppose T had invested his original $100 in a U.S. government bond that paid 10% interest. Holding that bond gives T no depreciation deduction at all.[12] In addition T is taxed at a 50% rate on the 10% interest each year when he receives it. He then reinvests the after-tax proceeds. At the end of 10 years with this bond investment (certainly an investment most people would consider to be perfectly reasonable), T would have the princely sum, principal and interest, of $163. This is a total after tax gain of $63.

Note that the tax rules under which T operated were the same in both cases except for timing. With the first asset, T did take a deduction

such as an apartment building or a factory are only deductible over the life of the asset as depreciation, see Chapter 6. Thus the ability to deduct immediately the expenses of digging an oil well, which is an asset that produces income over a long period of time, is highly attractive to the oil industry. Just how attractive is illustrated in the text.

**11.** This is because under basic tax rules there has not been a realizing event. See Chapter 4.

**12.** Holding a bond in the financial market does not generally give rise to a deduction in the nature of depreciation or amortization, see Chapter 6.

for the amount of his investment at the beginning, but he took that amount back into income at the end. So as a net matter there was no deduction for the investment. Also T did not pay tax every year on the appreciation in his investment but rather only paid tax on his gains from the investment at the end.

With the second asset T did not take a deduction for his investment at the beginning and therefore of course did not take the amount of his investment back into income at the end. So as a net matter there was no deduction for the investment. T also paid tax on his income from the investment but did so every year rather than at the end. These apparently innocuous timing differences led to the amazing differences in results.

In both cases T did nothing more or less than pay tax at the same rate on the income from his investment. Nevertheless the gain on the first asset was $159.50 and the gain on the second was $63.

Thus, "mere" deferral has increased T's after-tax gain by 253 percent in the first asset over the second asset.

What is happening here? How is this possible? See if you can answer this question yourself. If you cannot answer, the answer is given in the footnote at the end of this paragraph. But do not look too fast. You've got time; you won't be late to class. Try to answer it first—the answer has been alluded to in the preceding discussion.[13]

By contrast the *after tax* return on the U.S. government bond (where there were no up-front deductions and interest was taxed annually) was a measly 5%.

But, you scoff, this is nice work if you can get it, but unless you're an oil-driller (see note above) you cannot get it. Answer: wrong. This leads us smoothly into our next stunt.

### 1.5.3 Stunt No. 2: How You Can (and Probably Will) Become a Multimillionaire

All you need to do to get this is get a job which has a type of pension called a defined contribution plan. This type of plan is pretty widespread.

---

**13.** I take it you are just looking here to confirm your analysis. You are right. In the first investment, T was able to delay paying tax by both taking an early deduction and deferring tax on gains from the investment. This delay or temporary tax savings put extra funds in T's hands which T was able to also invest in the same tax advantaged fashion. In effect, T was able to enjoy an interest-free loan from the government. Naturally if you have an interest-free loan and are able to invest it for a profitable return, you are going to make money.

If T had been required to pay interest on his temporary tax savings he enjoyed in the first investment, his return on the first investment would have been the same as his return on the second. This is easily demonstrated. The extra $100 of temporary tax savings earned 10% per year. But if the government were charging T 10% interest, T would just have principal left after each year. T would not get compound interest. Indeed, T would not even be able to keep any interest at all. T would just be holding principal and then giving it back to the government, with no gain (or loss either) from holding it for 10 years. Thus he now has no advantage over the bond.

A similar analysis can be made with regard to the 10% per year appreciation in the value of the first investment. If T had to pay tax on the 10% per year at a 50% rate, T's after tax return would be 5% compounded for 10 years. That is exactly what T was getting on the bond.

Alternatively, you can use voluntary plans yourself to achieve the same result.[14] To see how this gravy-train works, we need to have a quick run-through of how pension plans work (no problem).

Dry Explanation: Pension Plans

In general, employers may establish qualified pension, profit-sharing, or stock bonus plans, which are tax favored in a number of ways.

There are two kinds of plans: defined benefit and defined contribution. Defined benefit plans require amounts to be put in that will be sufficient to produce a specified annual retirement amount after the expected number of years. Defined contribution plans just provide that the employer puts in a particular fixed amount every year and whatever it grows to is what the employee gets. Frequently the employee can decide what kind of investments to make with the defined contribution plan. Amounts paid into either type of plan are not taxed to the employees even if the employee rights are "vested." Vested means the benefits are payable even if the employee quits or is fired before retirement. Employees are taxed only when they actually receive payments on retirement.

Employers deduct amounts paid into the plan immediately, even though the employee is not taxed until retirement. That being true, the employer should be equally happy to pay salary to an employee directly or to put it into a plan. The employer will put it into a plan, because the employee prefers to get the benefit. Giving the employee the extra benefit may mean that the employer can then actually bargain to pay lower salary. After all, many employers say, you get this salary and look at all your benefits.

Earnings on funds paid into the plan are not taxed and they compound tax free. This leads to the kind of stunning results we have been talking about.[15]

The benefit from these pension plans sounds OK, but at first blush you would think it is nothing spectacular. But you're past the first blush, now. You've lost your innocence. You know this could be big time. Let's take a look at some numbers.

Suppose that your employer pays into a qualified defined-contribution plan, on your behalf, $12,000 per year for 40 years. Let's say these funds earn an annual return of 10 percent.[16] This will be tax free compounding. At the end of 40 years, the total of the contributions and

**14.** § 401(k) for business employees and § 403(b) for employees of educational institutions. Also IRA's.

**15.** See also the discussion in Chapter 8.

**16.** Note that the 10% figure for annual appreciation that I use for investments over long periods of time is well justified. Over the period 1960–1990, the S & P Stock market index appreciated 10.2% per year, see Slater, Long–Haul Investing: Riding out the Risk in Stocks, The Wall Street Journal, December 16, 1991 p. C1.

the earnings will be $5,311,111. They call that being a multimillionaire. But let's go further.

Let us say that at this point you retire and begin to receive payments. Assume your life expectancy at retirement is 20 years; assume also the amounts to be paid to you still earn 10 percent per year. The annual payment to you will be $623,841, all of which is taxable. All is taxable because none of it was taxable initially when it went into the plan. If you are taxed at a rate of 30 percent on the entire amount, the amount left after tax will be $436,689 annually.

Suppose that we now take away all the tax benefits. The employer pays an extra $12,000 each year directly to you. You are taxed on it at a 30% rate. That is a tax of $3,600. Thus you have left after tax $8,400. Let's assume (just for the sake of the argument) that you don't blow this money but invest it at a pre-tax rate of return of 10%. The rate of return after-tax rate will be 7 percent. This gives you, therefore, an investment of $8,400 per year which has a rate of return of 7 percent per year. That gives you a total accumulation at the end of 40 years of $1,676,935. Let us say this amount is used to buy an annuity. The payout is calculated assuming a rate of return of 10 percent. Again, let us say a life expectancy at retirement is 20 years. The payment each year will be $196,972. Of this annuity payment, $113,125 will be taxed, the rest being a return of what you invested. How is this calculated? By spreading the investment in the contract of $1,676,935 out over 20 years, under the annuity rules (see Chapter 3). That means a basis of $83,847 per year.[17] Taking the $83,847 from the $196,972 per year received gives you $113,125. $113,125 is taxed. If we assume a tax rate of 30 percent, you have a tax of 30% of $113,125 or $33,937. Thus your after tax amount is $196,972 less the tax of $33,937, leaving an after tax amount of $163,035 each year. This is 37 percent of the $436,689 after tax that you received when you had a qualified plan with the same numbers.

Note that all of this is due to deferral and compounding over long periods of time.

So get yourself a qualified plan and you will become a pension multimillionaire. There are plenty of people out there who are. Recall this was done on our numbers. Only a measly $12 thousand a year compounded over forty years leaves you with over $5 million. You get after tax pension annual payments for the rest of your life of over $436,000.

You are putting in $12 thousand a year and coming out after tax with $436 thousand for the rest of your life. I'll tell you the truth: I have hopes on this deal myself. If it works out, I'll drop you a line from Tahiti.

### 1.5.4   Stunt No. 3: Running Over Pedestrians for Fun and Profit

We now discuss a most extraordinarily useful stunt. Understanding this stunt takes you a step toward major insight into the mysteries of

---

17.  What we mean to say is $1,676,935 divided by 20 = $83,847.

time value of money. It is illuminating not only in itself but also because of the light it sheds on the field in general.

Consider Baxter Trucking Corporation, an accrual method taxpayer. Being on the accrual method means that items of income and deduction are given effect in the year when the right to them becomes fixed, even though cash has not changed hands.[18] An inevitable part of Baxter's business is that it runs over and injures pedestrians from time to time. It insures itself with respect to these accidents. In 1978 Baxter runs over a teen-ager Eileen Trabert severely injuring her. In settlement of the ensuing lawsuit Baxter agrees to pay Eileen $10 million. However, under the terms of the settlement agreement, Baxter will pay the money out as $250,000 cash per year for the next 40 years.[19]

Let us assume a combined federal and state flat tax rate of 45%, which applies both to Baxter and Eileen, and a prevailing interest rate of 12%, which is available both to Baxter and Eileen.

As discussed in Chapter 3, the amount of any damages received by virtue of personal injuries or sickness is excluded from the income of the victim.[20] Since Baxter is on the accrual method, its obligation to make the payment is now fixed. It therefore takes a $10 million deduction (even though it pays no cash out at that time). Under the law at that time the position was probably sustainable under accrual method accounting.[21] This $10 million deduction to a corporation in the 45% bracket saves it $4.5 million. Baxter takes this $4.5 million and invests it in intermediate U.S. bonds that pay interest of 12% per year. After the 45% tax bite Baxter's annual return will be 6.6% compounded.[22]

Now to understand Baxter's situation completely, we have to consider how Baxter is going to fund the obligation to pay Eileen $250,000 per year for the next 40 years. An illuminating way to look at that is to say that Baxter sets aside a fund which is large enough so that when it grows at the after-tax rate of 6.6%[23] compounded for 40 years it will be just large enough to pay $250,000 per year over 40 years. At the end of 40 years the fund should be exhausted. How much does Baxter need now

**18.** See discussion below.

**19.** $250,000 × 40 = $10 million. I promise to do all the math.

**20.** See § 104(a)(2) and Regs. § 1.104–1(c). The policy behind this is apparently some idea of sympathy for the victim, or else that on balance the victim is not really "enriched" by the entire experience.

**21.** See Ohio River Collieries Co. v. Commissioner, 77 T.C. 1369 (1981) (the full amount of surface mining reclamation costs that could be estimated with reasonable accuracy was properly accrued when the surface soil was removed); Treas. Reg. § 1.461–1(a)(2) (as amended in 1967). Crescent Wharf & Warehouse Co. v. Commissioner, 518 F.2d 772 (9th Cir.1975) (the full amount of the liability for uncontested workers' compensation claims could be de-

ducted in the year in which the injury occurs notwithstanding that medical services might be rendered and disability might occur in the future); New York City Bar Ass'n, Transactions Involving Deferred Payment of Accrued Liabilities, 20 TAX NOTES 699 (1983); McGown, Structured Settlements: Deduct Now and Pay Later, 60 TAXES 251 (1982).

**22.** This is, of course, 55% of the 12% return; we are subtracting the 45% tax bite. Baxter reinvests the interest at the continuing after-tax 6.6% rate.

**23.** Baxter of course is taxed on the funds that it has under its control, regardless of the fact that it may have earmarked the funds to finance a future liability.

to set aside to accomplish this goal under these conditions? The answer is $3,724,648.[24] Another way of interpreting this number is to say that $3,724,648 is the present value of a stream of payments of $250,000 per year for 40 years with a 6.6% interest rate.

Now let's look at Baxter's complete situation using a cash flow analysis over time: In the first year, the year of the settlement, Baxter is out of pocket up front $3,724,648 in the sense that it has to set that money aside, can't use it, and can't use the interest from it (otherwise it will fail to have the money for Eileen and get sued again).[25] However, Baxter takes a deduction of $10,000,000. This saves Baxter $4,500,000 in taxes. Thus, Baxter is ahead on this deal in the first year in the precise amount of $4,500,000 − $3,724,648 = $775,352. Once out in front, Baxter stays there. Baxter invests this $775,352 for the after-tax return of 6.6% compounded for 40 years. This winds up to be a cool $9,995,099. In short Baxter, as a result of incurring a liability for running over Eileen, is ahead $9,995,099.[26]

What could Baxter have done to come out even better than this already sensational result? You doubtless will recognize from the foregoing that Baxter made a serious error in its negotiation with Eileen's lawyer. It should have held out to pay $500,000 annually over 50 years instead of $250,000 over 40 years. In that event it could take a deduction for $500,000 times 50 or $25,000,000. Deducting this amount immediately would have saved it $11,250,000 in taxes. Since it has to set aside a fund to finance payments of $500,000 per year over 50 years instead of $250,000 over 40 years, it will have to set aside a larger fund. The present value of payments of $500,000 per year over 50 years with a 6.6% interest rate (i.e. the amount Baxter has to set aside) is $7,745,142. Once again setting aside this fund to take care of Eileen, it has left over the following: $11,250,000 (tax savings of 45%) − $7,745,142 (Eileen fund) = $4,501,386. Investing this amount at the after-tax compounded return of 6.6% for 50 years leads Baxter to wind up with a stupendous $85,611,215. To make the 40 year and 50 year cases comparable, we need to take Baxter's 40 year amount in the previous hypo and let it accumulate at 6.6% for another 10 years, so that we've got 50 years in both deals. Doing that to Baxter's 40 year accumulation of $9,995,099 brings it out to $18,939,092. It's not bad. But it is still a staggering

24. The calculations in this example assume that payments and tax savings occur at the beginning of the year for which they are due. If they were made at the end, the numbers would be slightly different but the principles under discussion would, of course, remain the same. This is a complex financial calculation which requires a computer or high-powered calculator. You would not be expected to make this calculation just sitting in the student lounge drinking coffee.

25. Whether Baxter actually sets aside the money in a separate account or not, the economic effect on Baxter of having to pay this sum is as described in the text.

26. See also Mooney Aircraft v. United States, 420 F.2d 400 (5th Cir.1969) (On selling each aircraft that the company manufactured it issued a $1,000 bearer bond to be paid when the aircraft was retired from service; the company took a deduction for the full $1,000 up front even though the aircraft would last 15 to 30 years; held: no deduction allowed because the "all events" test for accrual method accounting was not satisfied, see Chapter 8).

$66,672,123 less than Baxter winds up with when it has to pay Eileen $500,000 for 50 years instead of $250,000 for 40 years. Such are the perils of being a defendant in a major tort claim.

How can such mind-bending results occur? The problem, as you probably have ascertained, is that Baxter is getting much too large a deduction for this structured settlement. When you get a deduction that is larger than justified and take that deduction against other high income and the situation prevails over long periods of time, you are going to make out like gangbusters.

Our analysis has precisely calculated the excessive amount of Baxter's deduction. Let us concentrate on the 40–year deal (we can rest assured the 50–year deal will be even more egregious). We ascertained that the present value of $250,000 per year for 40 years was $3,724,648. An accurate accrual method of accounting would have limited the deduction to that amount, rather than allowing $10,000,000 to be deducted. Had only that $3,724,648 amount been allowed as a deduction, the tax savings would have been $1,676,092. Notice, very interestingly, that Baxter is now in a negative position in the first year. It needs to set aside $3,724,648 to fund Eileen's payments. Its tax savings are $1,676,-092. So it is negative in the year of the settlement in the amount of $2,048,556. That is, of course, the normal situation. Any time you have a deductible expense, the deduction, under normal circumstances, cannot save you more in taxes than the expense itself but will save you less. Thus a deductible expense of $100 at a tax rate of 45% saves you $45. The other $55 is still out of your pocket. It is only taxpayers like Baxter in the original hypothetical, playing this lunatic game of taking deductions far in excess of what is justified, that turn a deductible expense into fabulous profits.

Looking at the situation where we have limited Baxter's deduction to the present value of the stream of payments, we see that Baxter appropriately has a loss: *Baxter gets nothing out of this situation now or 40 years from now!* You cannot invest a loss. The structured settlement, together with the proper limited deduction, has put Baxter out of pocket up front. Therefore it has nothing to invest as a result of the transaction.[27] By getting the right amount of deduction for Baxter, we have picked its pocket of its entire $9,995,099. It's actually much worse than that. Baxter is actually out of pocket. As well it should be. Maybe that will encourage its drivers to be more careful from now on.

It turns out to be highly useful to carry the analysis to the bitter end. We calculate how much this out-of-pocket amount in the first year is going to cost Baxter in terms of foregone interest income over 40 years. Our inquiry here then would be what would the $2,048,556 that Baxter is out of pocket have earned over 40 years had Baxter not gotten

---

**27.** Some readers (not you of course) might argue that Baxter could still invest the $1,676,,092. And so it could. The trouble is that is has had to set aside $3,724,648 plus accumulated interest on this amount in order to be able to make this investment. A couple of more deals like this and Baxter will be broke.

into this mess and had to pay off. $2,048,556 over 40 years at 6.6% interest is $26,408,031.[28] **This is as it should be. Baxter was a bad little corporation in running over Eileen and it should be made to suffer.**

What did Congress do to prevent these fabulous profits from redounding to tort-feasors? Congress's cure for this problem was interesting. Under the law as it was amended in 1984, the dazzling results we saw above are no longer possible. In effect Baxter is put on the cash method, allowed only to deduct its payments as they are made.[29] What does this mean for Baxter? Is this the right answer?

Our present-value analysis will tell us. Under Congress's rule Baxter is on the cash method and can only deduct payments as they are actually made. That is, Baxter is not allowed to deduct the full amount up front and is also not allowed to deduct the discounted present value up front.

So, what happens to Baxter under Congress's rule? Baxter still has to set aside the $3,724,648 in the first year. Baxter still has to figure out a way to make the payments. However, Baxter cannot deduct that amount. Instead Baxter can only deduct the $250,000 out of that $3,724,648 it actually pays to Eileen in the first year. That $250,000 payment saves Baxter 45% of it in taxes or $112,500.[30] Thus Baxter's cash flow position in the first year is as follows: − $3,724,648 + $112,500 = − $3,612,148. In the remaining 39 years, Baxter's cash flow position is + $112,500: the amount deducting the $250,000 saves it in taxes. Note that from a cash flow standpoint, we do not go negative the $250,000 payment each year. We have already set aside the $3,724,648 to cover the $250,000 and thus need set aside no more cash. Baxter does enjoy the cash benefit of the deduction on our tax return when it sends her the check for $250,000, however.[31] Where does this experience leave Baxter at the end of 40 years? Baxter winds up with a loss of $23,282,-713. That is exactly the amount that Baxter was behind using our approach of deducting the full $3,724,648 present value of the arrangement up front, as the discussion accompanying note 27 above indicated.

So, Congress got it exactly right here as to Baxter. Limiting Baxter to the cash method on its deductions did not overtax or undertax Baxter. It gave Baxter the same result as allowing Baxter to deduct in the first

---

**28.** This is not lunch money. Thus, to beat the thing to death, we can say that limiting the deduction to the right amount cost Baxter over the course of 40 years the positive $9,995,099 plus put it in the hole $26,408,031. Getting the deduction right, instead of wrong then, gives Baxter a total negative swing of $36,403,136.

**29.** § 461(h)(2)(C). For a general discussion of tax accounting, see Chapter 9.

**30.** The $250,000, of course comes out of the $3,724,648, so we do not give Baxter an additional negative cash flow hit of $250,000.

**31.** An alternative way to analyze this problem, which gives the same answer, would be to say that Baxter does not set aside the $3,724,648, but rather just pays the $250,000 per year out of operating funds. Thus Baxter would be taking a cash flow hit of $250,000 per year for 40 years instead of $3,724,648 in the first year. Both have the same impact on Baxter's ultimate results since, as we have demonstrated in the text several times, $3,724,648 is equivalent to $250,000 per year for 40 years given a 6.6% interest rate.

year the discounted present value of its payments. And the result from deducting the present value in the first year is economically accurate.[32]

And what of Eileen?

To understand Eileen's situation, we take as a given that for policy reasons Eileen is allowed to exclude a payment for a personal injury in a tort suit. But what was the real amount of that payment to Eileen? To ask that question is to ask what is the present value of $250,000 per year for 40 years with the after-tax rate of 6.6%. That happens to be (as we have said a nauseating number of times) $3,724,648.

That amount is the amount of the payment to Eileen that should be excluded because, as a policy matter, we exclude payments on account of personal injuries. That is the present value of her deal. We can understand that. If she had in fact negotiated to have her payment up front (for whatever reasons she may have preferred it), Baxter would have been willing to pay her $3,724,648. That is the amount, as we have demonstrated, that Baxter would have had to set aside to earn enough at the after tax rate of return of 6.6% to be able to make the $250,000 annual payments to Eileen and come out even after 40 years.

Now, what is Eileen's actual picture with the structured settlement? She receives $250,000 per year for 40 years. She can exclude the full amount of each of these payments by virtue of § 104(a)(2) as amplified by Rev. Rul. 79–220.[33] Eileen reinvests the $250,000 payments at the same pre-tax rate of 12% as Baxter. Her after tax rate is the same 6.6%. After 40 years of this deal Eileen winds up with $48,014,605. Is this the "right" result for Eileen?

We can see by referring once again to economic truth. That is, let us see what happens if the parties had negotiated to make the payment up front. Suppose Eileen had indeed received her $3,724,648 up front and excluded it. Let us say she then invested this amount in a government bond with a pre-tax interest rate of 12% and yielding her 6.6% after tax.

---

**32.** Structured settlements are usually put together using three companies to get a tax free rate of return on the money set aside to pay the claim. Thus less money need be set aside. The technique involves three companies: the casualty insurance company makes a deductible lump sum payment to a structured settlement company, which assumes the liability to make the payments. The structured settlement company purchases an annuity (an agreement to make payments over time, see Chapter 3) from an annuity company that specializes in annuities for damage awards. The structured settlement company takes a deduction for that purchase which offsets the income from the original insurance company. The annuity company takes a reserve (or deduction) on its books equal to the amounts received. When the annuity company makes the payments, the structured settlement company deducts them. By shuffling things back and forth this way, the three companies produce among themselves the effect of a deduction for the money being set aside originally plus a deduction when each payment is made, when only one or the other of those deductions is justified. This in effect causes the earnings on the money set aside to fund the payment to be earning income at the pre-tax rate. Incidentally, some years ago my father was the recipient of a tort award and the companies involved were very anxious to set it up as a structured settlement of this kind.

**33.** 1979–2 C.B. 74, which holds that the full amount of payments received under a structured settlement are excluded under § 104(a)(2), not just the discounted present value of them.

Note that she is taxed on her investment earnings after she gets her tax free payment. She is not getting any further special breaks. At the end of 40 years Eileen's amount would then have grown to $48,014,605. This is the same result Eileen gets if she receives the payments stretched out over 40 years.[34]

What this shows is that the treatment of Eileen is absolutely accurate. Once you have decided to exclude the damage payments for personal injuries to Eileen, it is correct to exclude the full amount of payments made pursuant to a structured settlement.[35] The numbers above demonstrate this. This is what present value analysis really means. If the present value is the same thing (not identical of course but the same thing the way $100 worth of apples is the same thing as $100 worth of oranges) as the larger future value, then if you do not tax one, you should not tax the other.[36]

### 1.5.5 Stunt No. 4: Original Issue Discount—The Big One

This is the biggest stunt of all. It is of major importance in the field of federal income tax. This stunt has got it all. It deals with the subject of "original issue discount" (whatever that is, don't worry, we'll talk), which is the leading subject in the time value of money area. And the time value of money is the most important topic in the field of federal income tax. So you see the importance there. Original issue discount also is a marvelous illustration of time value of money and deferral principles, what deferral really means and why it is so important. Original issue discount also is a topic of importance in advanced corporate financial transactions.[37] This stunt requires a little work, but you will be amply rewarded for it. I have another little reward for you, too. I feel strongly you should work your way through this stunt. If you do, I have some lagniappe (as they say in my part of the country) for you. A little morsel, a little reward: That is given in Stunt No. 5, below. Remember,

**34.** You may wonder why Eileen gains more ($66,241,946) than Baxter loses ($36,-433,067). This is a result of the fact that by virtue of this arrangement, the parties have eliminated the tax on the stream of income used to make the payments to Eileen. Baxter deducted the amounts and Eileen did not enter them into income. This is true regardless of how the parties structure the timing of the transaction.

**35.** Thus Rev. Rul. 79-220, 1979-2 C.B. 74, supra note 33, is correct.

**36.** The reason the Treasury prefers the deferred deduction approach (i.e., deduct as the payments are made) of the 1984 legislation is that it does not require advance knowledge of the payment date, the payment amount, or the discount. See Hearings on S. 237 and S. 1006 Before the Subcomm. on Energy and Agricultural Tax-ation of the Senate Comm. on Finance, 98th Cong., 1st Sess. (statement of William S. McKee, Acting Deputy Assistant Treasury Secretary for Tax Policy), reprinted in DAI-LY TAX REP. (BNA) No. 100, at J-5 (May 23, 1983).

I would therefore, with all due respect, disagree with several leading commentators. These commentators argue that the present rules involve undertaxing Eileen and overtaxing Baxter to make up for it, or surrogate taxation. See, e.g. Halperin, Interest in Disguise: Taxing the "Time Value of Money," 95 Yale L.J. 506, at 526 (1986); Ginsburg, Teaching Tax Law After Tax Reform, 65 Wash. L. Rev. 595, at 616 (1990).

**37.** See, e.g. D. Posin, *Corporate Tax Planning: Takeovers, Leveraged Buyouts and Restructurings* (1990) and suppl. at 343-385.

you're not allowed to do Stunt No. 5 until you have done No.4. But No. 4 will be immensely rewarding in itself.

Here's stunt No. 4. Let us go back to the mid–1970's, an era of high interest rates. Birdsill Corporation, a major manufacturer of outdoor birdfeeding devices and traded on the New York Stock Exchange, wishes to raise some money in the financial markets in order to make an acquisition. It wishes to acquire Beeport Corporation, a maker of bee-keeping equipment and protective devices. The companies expect to get "synergies" from this transaction by putting together the birds and the bees.[38]

To get some up-front cash for this transaction Birdsill does something rather curious. It proposes to issue some long-term debt in the market place with a face amount of $100 million, payable in forty years. Birdsill, being a major corporation traded on the New York Stock Exchange, should have no trouble marketing this debt. There's just one weird thing about this debt. It does not provide for the payment of any interest. No interest at all. Shocking.

Suppose your best client Irving called you and asked whether he should take a slice of this action: Pay $10 million for the privilege of getting $10 million back in forty years. Irving asks you what you think of this investment. Seems reasonable to him. Put in $10 million, get $10 million back. At least you're not losing anything, he says. Having read the earlier part of this chapter, you are in a strong position to advise your client on this matter. You could tell him that it is one of the three or four dumbest ideas you have ever heard.

However, you as an advisor might be able to do better than that. After all, we don't want to inform our most well-heeled client that he is dumb as a post for even broaching the subject. That's not what we call the intelligent practice of law. So, like any savvy practitioner, you say, "Let's talk about it." You might not want to pay, you inform Irving, a full $10 million for $10 million face of debt that pays back principal in forty years with no interest. But maybe paying less than $10 million might work for the right to get $10 million in forty years. How much would we pay is, of course, a matter that would take some calculation. We can see just eyeballing it that we know we'd pay more than 65 cents for it.

But what is the right number? I don't expect you, sitting in the student lounge with some cold coffee, to come up with this major calculation. But formulate the question. What is the question? Think about it. The answer is in the next paragraph.

As you ascertained, the relevant question is: What is $10 million forty years from now worth now? The 1970's had some very high interest rates. Birdsill, with its business being highly subject to the weather, is a risky company. Let us say, therefore, in this environment of high interest rates and a risky company, that the rate of interest that

<hr>

**38.** Okay, this is not Letterman. Just keep reading, please.

Irving needs in order to make his investment in Birdsill worthwhile, compared to other investments with similar risk, is 9%.

That is, of course, the after-tax interest rate, which is the rate that is relevant to Irving. If we assume a combined state and federal tax rate of 40%, then this 9% after tax rate implies a pre-tax rate of interest of 15%. What we are saying here is that 40% of the interest Irving gets is taxed to him leaving him with 60% left. Sixty percent of 15% is 9%. It is the pre-tax interest rate that must be used to figure out how much Irving would be willing to spend to get the right to receive $10 million forty years from now. The tax consequences of receiving the $10 million 40 years from now will be taken care of when the amount is received, as we have formulated the problem.

Thus our question now is: what amount invested now would grow at a 15% rate compounded annually to equal $10 million? That can be computed using the approach demonstrated above. The answer is $37,- 332. This is a surprisingly small number. But forty years is a very long time. This demonstrates once again the power of compound interest over long periods of time. What we are saying, then, is that $37,332 at 15% compounded annually grows to $10 million after forty years.[39] Thus after discussion with Irving concerning relevant interest rates to use and so forth, you come to the conclusion that, yeah, buying $10 million face amount of this non-interest bearing paper is a good idea after all. Just pay $37,332 for it. You're a pretty sharp guy, Irving. Let's do lunch.

But wait! Will Birdsill sell $10 million of forty year debt for that price?

Yes, it will. Because everyone else is making the same calculation that you and Irving made.[40] So everything is jake now. Irving's got his Birdsill bonds; Birdsill's got its up front money;[41] and (last but far from least) you've got your substantial fee for explaining all this to Irving.

Now, how does this deal play out over the course of the next forty years? Let's say, to keep the calculations simple, that Irving bought the bonds on January 1 of 1976. What happens as far as Irving's taxes are concerned in 1976? He actually gets no interest during the course of the year. All that's actually going to happen, under the terms of the bond trust indenture, is that he will get $10 million on December 31, 2015.

**39.** You can verify this one for yourself, if you like. Take a simple calculator. Enter $37,332. Then multiply that by 1.15. Multiply the resulting number by 1.15 (you are compounding). Do that forty times and see if you don't hit in the area of $10 million. You won't hit $10 million right on the nose because of rounding but you'll be within a thousand or so of it.

**40.** Of course, some people may not regard Birdsill short-term paper as quite so risky a proposition as you and Irving do. Then they would use a lower interest rate and then they would bid more for Birdsill paper and perhaps then buy it all up. Then Irving wouldn't buy Birdsill and would have to look around for another investment. But since I don't want to construct, and you don't want to read, another hypothetical, let's stick with Birdsill.

**41.** Birdsill's total up front money would, of course, no longer be $40 million. Rather, its up front money would be 4 × $37,332 or $149,328. Once again the power of the time value of money is demonstrated.

Does Irving therefore pay no taxes until 2015? No. Congress, while not as sharp as you and Irving, has been at this problem a lot longer and by 1969 had come to similar conclusions. These bonds are said to have "original issue discount." This is because the bonds were originally issued at a discount from their face amount of $10 million (see this field's not so tough). To show you're in the know, you don't say "original issue discount," you say "OID."

Now just what is OID? Well, we already know. Birdsill is selling this paper at $37,332 in 1976 and paying back $10,000,000 at the end of 2015 in order to pay Irving for the use of his $37,332 for forty years. That difference of $10 million minus $37,332 is equal to $9,962,668. That was paid for the use of the original $37,332, plus the use of the interest that Birdsill owed each year but did not pay. That sounds a lot like compound interest. And that's how you and Irving analyzed it, too. You viewed it as interest. In the lexicon, if it walks like a duck, talks like a duck and quacks like a duck, there's a high probability it is a duck. We've got interest here.

Interest accrues over time. That's a fundamental fact of economic life. Starting in 1969, after decades of struggling with the subject, Congress purported to tax original issue discount as interest accruing over time.[42] Before we talk about what Congress did in 1969, let's consider the problem ourselves. How would we go about taxing the deal we have? We understand that there is interest. How much interest per year? Let's look at the first couple of years:

| Year | Principal | Interest |
|------|-----------|----------|
| 1976 | $37,332   | $5,600   |
| 1977 | $42,932   | $6,440   |
| 1978 | $49,372   | $7,406   |
| 1979 | $56,777   | $8,517   |
| 1980 | $65,294   | $9,794   |

This is the deal that Irving will get for the first five years. What is really going on here? What is going on is that Irving loans Birdsill (by buying Birdsill paper) $37,332. Birdsill then pays Irving $5,600, constituting 15% interest on that money. Except that, given the type of paper that Irving bought, in effect Irving, immediately upon receiving the $5,600, relends it back to Birdsill. Thus the total outstanding debt at the beginning of 1977 that Birdsill owes Irving is $42,932 (i.e., $37,332 + $5,600). Thus, Birdsill has to pay 15% on that increased amount for 1977. Once again, when the $6,440 interest is paid in 1977, Irving relends it back to Birdsill, and the loan balance increases to $49,372 ($42,932 + $6,440). Birdsill then pays 15% interest on that amount, and so it goes. How long does it go on? Well, for forty years. And what is the

**42.** For further background on the history of the original issue discount rules, see ¶ 3.02.

outstanding loan balance at the end of 40 years? Ten million dollars, of course, give or take a little due to rounding. This process is, of course, exactly the process I suggested you follow in a footnote earlier with your calculator, multiplying $37,332 by 1.15 40 times. (Just do what I say, I'm telling you; it'll turn out all right).

This is what is happening as an economic matter when a bond carries no interest and is sold at a discount. As an economic matter, the holder of the bond is relending the interest back and receiving further interest on the increased balance.[43]

So, you'd expect Congress to tax you on these amounts of interest every year, noting that the amounts increase each year due to compounding. But Congress was not that smart when it enacted the rules in force in the 1970's. Congress instead took what we might call a "dumbo" approach. Congress said that the total amount of interest in this deal is $10 million − $37,332 = $9,962,668. Then, Congress said (in its 1969 rules), for a forty year bond, we'll tax the investor on one-fortieth or 2.5% of that total interest in each of the forty years. For Irving, this cranks out to be $2.5% of $9,962,668 or $249,067 in each year.

In year 1, is this kind of a shock to Irving? Bet your bottom dollar. In year 1, Irving (after your lengthy explanation to him of how original issue discount is really interest) would expect to be taxed on the real amount of interest accrued in year 1, namely $5,600. Instead, he's hit with $249,067. (And he has no cash from the deal to pay). Is he mad, or what? At a tax rate of 40%, his taxes are $99,627. This is instead of the 40% of $5,600 or $2,240 that he expected. Boy, is he mad! Taxes were more than expected by $99,627 − $2,240 = $97,387. Wow![44]

Where did Congress come up with this straight line treatment for OID in 1969? Stupid City, that's where. You should understand that this approach of taking the total interest paid and dividing it by the number of years is not economically meaningful. That is not what happens with interest. That is not economically what was going on in our deal, as we discussed above.

So what happens now? What happens is that Irving would not buy this bond after all. Because he would not want to get hit with this freako amount of interest in the early years of the deal. So what happens with this OID bond, under the 1969 rules? Does that mean no one would buy it? Nope. Someone would buy it who does not care about receiving a freako amount of interest up front. Do you have any ideas as to who

**43.** It is mildly instructive to compare this with what would happen if Irving bought an interest bearing bond from Birdsill. If the bond offered had promised to pay $10 million in 40 years and promised to pay in cash 15% per year (i.e., $1.5 million per year) then, assuming that was the appropriate market interest rate, Irving would have given Birdsill $10 million for the bond and collected his $1.5 million per year, which he could have invested or spent. This illustrates one side-line point about OID bonds: they in effect lock you in to a pattern of relending the interest. Of course, if it is a marketable bond, which it very well could be, it could be sold at any time, thereby relieving any liquidity lockup.

**44.** Of course, you would have known that the 1969 rules were in effect, so you would have told Irving that he was going to get hit with this surprising amount of phantom income. So he would not actually have been surprised. But I am making a dramatic point, for pedagogical purposes, in the text.

might not care about that? See if you can think of something. The answer is in the next paragraph.

How about a pension fund? Pension funds, funds set aside for investment for employee pensions. The funds are not taxed on their current income, as part of the attractive deal for establishing employee pension funds, as we discussed in Stunt No. 2, above. Also some foreign investors at that time.

Okay. Here's the thing. Let's stop talking about Irving. Other than being very wealthy, he's not that interesting. What's interesting in this whole deal is not what happens to Irving but what happens to Birdsill. I told you that this stunt takes a little cranking up. But it's going to start cooking now.

Now Birdsill may have a stupid product line, but their financial people are on top of the situation. Birdsill's numbers are the same as Irving's with one important difference: Birdsill is paying the interest rather than receiving it. Thus Birdsill's overall numbers are that it received $37,332 at the beginning of year 1 and promised to pay back $10 million at the end of year 40.

Thus the total interest Birdsill is in effect paying out on this deal over the forty years is $10,000,000 − $37,332, or $9,962,668. And under the 1969 rules, Birdsill is regarded as paying this out on a straight line basis for forty years, or 2.5% of it per year. This, as we know from talking about Irving, is $249,067 per year. Now Birdsill is subject to a 40% tax. So Birdsill, still following the 1969 rules, deducts this $249,067 each year against its other income. This saves Birdsill 40% of that amount, or $99,627 in taxes per year.[45] Note that Birdsill is saving that amount in taxes in each of forty years.

Now let us say that Birdsill reinvests the amount it has saved in taxes each year at the same prevailing pre-tax interest rate of 15%. If Birdsill is in the 40% bracket, that means Birdsill's after-tax rate of return is 9%.[46] Thus Birdsill winds up with 1.09 times $99,627 after one year as a result of this. This comes to $108,593. Birdsill can keep compounding this amount at 9% a year for forty years.[47] What does Birdsill wind up with then? It's a cool $36,691,740.

Now that's just the results from reinvestment of the tax savings in year 1 compounded for forty years. Birdsill can also reinvest the $99,627 tax savings from year 2 at an after-tax return of 9% and do so for 39 years. That result cranks out to be $33,562,520. Naturally, that is less

**45.** You will of course recall why that is true. It is a fundamental concept in this course to understand why a deduction of a particular amount saves an amount in taxes equal to the tax rate times that amount, assuming the taxpayer has other income and continues to be taxed at that same rate. The reason is that taking the deduction on the return of, in this case, $249,067, means that taxable income reported to the IRS is reduced by $249,067. At a 40% rate, 40% of the amount that would have been paid in

taxes is now not paid. The tax savings, therefore, is 40% of $249,067, or $99,627.

**46.** By this time you don't need this footnote. If Birdsill is in the 40% bracket, it pays a 40% tax on its income from this investment, leaving it with 60% of its investment income. Thus it keeps 60% of 15% which is, last time I looked, 9%.

**47.** Let's say interest rates hold steady over the period to keep the math straightforward.

than year 1 because we're only doing it for 39 years instead of 40. Birdsill can do this for year 3 and year 4 on down through year 40.

What do all those tax savings and compounded reinvestments add up to for 40 years? Well, it's $396,114,090. Take a look at the OID accrual chart below.

OID ACCRUAL: COMPOUND INTEREST AND STRAIGHT LINE INTEREST COMPARED
DEDUCTING EACH AMOUNT OF INTEREST AND INVESTING THE TAX SAVINGS
15% Interest Rate; 40% Tax Rate: Savings Invested @ 9% After Tax Rate

| Year | Principal | Compound Int | St. Line Int | Tax Saved Cmp. Int. | Tax Saved St.Ln Int. | Future Value of Tax Saved Cmp Int | Future Value of Tax Saved St.Ln. Int. | Annual Gain Using St. Ln. Instead of Cmp Method |
|---|---|---|---|---|---|---|---|---|
| 1976 | $37,332 | $5,600 | $249,067 | $2,240 | $99,627 | $824,944 | $36,691,740 | $35,866,796 |
| 1977 | $42,932 | $6,440 | $249,067 | $2,576 | $99,627 | $867,778 | $33,562,520 | $32,694,742 |
| 1978 | $49,372 | $7,406 | $249,067 | $2,962 | $99,627 | $912,583 | $30,691,676 | $29,779,092 |
| 1979 | $56,777 | $8,517 | $249,067 | $3,407 | $99,627 | $959,411 | $28,057,874 | $27,098,406 |
| 1980 | $65,294 | $9,794 | $249,067 | $3,918 | $99,627 | $1,008,305 | $25,641,542 | $24,633,237 |
| 1981 | $75,088 | $11,263 | $249,067 | $4,505 | $99,627 | $1,059,303 | $23,424,724 | $22,365,421 |
| 1982 | $86,351 | $12,953 | $249,067 | $5,181 | $99,627 | $1,112,432 | $21,390,945 | $20,278,514 |
| 1983 | $99,304 | $14,896 | $249,067 | $5,958 | $99,627 | $1,167,708 | $19,525,094 | $18,357,386 |
| 1984 | $114,199 | $17,130 | $249,067 | $6,852 | $99,627 | $1,225,134 | $17,813,303 | $16,588,169 |
| 1985 | $131,329 | $19,699 | $249,067 | $7,880 | $99,627 | $1,284,693 | $16,242,853 | $14,958,161 |
| 1986 | $151,029 | $22,654 | $249,067 | $9,062 | $99,627 | $1,346,348 | $14,802,073 | $13,455,726 |
| 1987 | $173,683 | $26,052 | $249,067 | $10,421 | $99,627 | $1,410,038 | $13,480,257 | $12,070,279 |
| 1988 | $199,736 | $29,960 | $249,067 | $11,984 | $99,627 | $1,475,670 | $12,267,582 | $10,791,911 |
| 1989 | $229,696 | $34,454 | $249,067 | $13,782 | $99,627 | $1,543,118 | $11,155,035 | $9,611,917 |
| 1990 | $264,150 | $39,623 | $249,067 | $15,849 | $99,627 | $1,612,211 | $10,134,350 | $8,522,139 |
| 1991 | $303,773 | $45,566 | $249,067 | $18,226 | $99,627 | $1,682,731 | $9,197,942 | $7,515,212 |
| 1992 | $349,339 | $52,401 | $249,067 | $20,960 | $99,627 | $1,754,398 | $8,338,852 | $6,584,455 |
| 1993 | $401,740 | $60,261 | $249,067 | $24,104 | $99,627 | $1,826,866 | $7,550,697 | $5,723,831 |
| 1994 | $462,000 | $69,300 | $249,067 | $27,720 | $99,627 | $1,899,707 | $6,827,618 | $4,927,911 |
| 1995 | $531,300 | $79,695 | $249,067 | $31,878 | $99,627 | $1,972,400 | $6,164,243 | $4,191,843 |
| 1996 | $610,996 | $91,649 | $249,067 | $36,660 | $99,627 | $2,044,313 | $5,555,642 | $3,511,329 |
| 1997 | $702,645 | $105,397 | $249,067 | $42,159 | $99,627 | $2,114,685 | $4,997,292 | $2,882,607 |
| 1998 | $808,042 | $121,206 | $249,067 | $48,482 | $99,627 | $2,182,607 | $4,485,045 | $2,302,438 |
| 1999 | $929,248 | $139,387 | $249,067 | $55,755 | $99,627 | $2,246,996 | $4,015,093 | $1,768,097 |
| 2000 | $1,068,635 | $160,295 | $249,067 | $64,118 | $99,627 | $2,306,566 | $3,583,945 | $1,277,379 |
| 2001 | $1,228,930 | $184,340 | $249,067 | $73,736 | $99,627 | $2,359,797 | $3,188,396 | $828,599 |
| 2002 | $1,413,270 | $211,990 | $249,067 | $84,796 | $99,627 | $2,404,898 | $2,825,507 | $420,610 |
| 2003 | $1,625,260 | $243,789 | $249,067 | $97,516 | $99,627 | $2,439,762 | $2,492,582 | $52,820 |
| 2004 | $1,869,049 | $280,357 | $249,067 | $112,143 | $99,627 | $2,461,918 | $2,187,145 | ($274,772) |
| 2005 | $2,149,407 | $322,411 | $249,067 | $128,964 | $99,627 | $2,468,472 | $1,906,929 | ($561,543) |
| 2006 | $2,471,818 | $370,773 | $249,067 | $148,309 | $99,627 | $2,456,042 | $1,649,849 | ($806,103) |
| 2007 | $2,842,591 | $426,389 | $249,067 | $170,555 | $99,627 | $2,420,681 | $1,413,996 | ($1,006,685) |
| 2008 | $3,268,979 | $490,347 | $249,067 | $196,139 | $99,627 | $2,357,791 | $1,197,617 | ($1,160,174) |
| 2009 | $3,759,326 | $563,899 | $249,067 | $225,560 | $99,627 | $2,262,018 | $999,105 | ($1,262,913) |
| 2010 | $4,323,225 | $648,484 | $249,067 | $259,393 | $99,627 | $2,127,139 | $816,983 | ($1,310,156) |
| 2011 | $4,971,709 | $745,756 | $249,067 | $298,303 | $99,627 | $1,945,927 | $649,899 | ($1,296,028) |
| 2012 | $5,717,465 | $857,620 | $249,067 | $343,048 | $99,627 | $1,709,994 | $496,611 | ($1,213,384) |
| 2013 | $6,575,085 | $986,263 | $249,067 | $394,505 | $99,627 | $1,409,618 | $355,979 | ($1,053,638) |
| 2014 | $7,561,347 | $1,134,202 | $249,067 | $453,681 | $99,627 | $1,033,530 | $226,960 | ($806,571) |
| 2015 | $8,695,549 | $1,304,332 | $249,067 | $521,733 | $99,627 | $568,689 | $108,593 | ($460,096) |
| Totals | $9,999,882 | $9,962,550 | $9,962,680 | $3,985,020 | $3,985,072 | $68,267,220 | $396,114,090 | $327,846,870 |

↑ Principal Amount

↑ Same amount of total interest paid. (Minor difference due to rounding)

↑ Same am't of tax saved

↑ Total Gain Using St. Line Instead of Compound Method is $396,114,090 − $68,267,220 = $327,846,870

We have already talked about a lot of the numbers on this chart, so it really shouldn't be intimidating. Let's talk about each column, going from left to right:

- The left-most column is the years over which this OID note is outstanding.

- The column "principal" shows how the principal increases when the compound interest (from the next column over) is added back to the principal each year. This is Irving or whoever holds the note "relending" the interest back to Birdsill. We see ultimately the principal accumulates up to about $10 million; (we lost eighteen bucks in rounding).

- The "Compound Int" column is, of course, the amount of interest that is due each year—which increases because the previous year's interest is being added on to the principal, as we have discussed. We see the total of that interest ultimately paid down at the bottom, as $9,962,550. That amount plus the original amount of the note of $37,332 adds up to approximately the $9,999,882 face amount of the note due at the end of 40 years.

- The St. Line Int. column is the dumbo Congressional solution as to how to treat this transaction. This takes the $9,962,550 total interest and divides it by 40, giving $249,067. This is the amount of interest Congress deemed would be deductible to Birdsill every year under the 1969 rules. You can see that, comparing it to the economic reality of the Compound Int. column, it vastly overstates the amount of interest deductible to Birdsill (and included in the income of whoever holds the note) in the early years and vastly understates the amount of interest deductible to Birdsill (and included in the income of the holder) in the later years. You see that ultimately (and not surprisingly, given the way it was calculated), the same total amount of interest is deductible under the straight line method as under the compound method. This illustrates that the only difference between the two methods is the *timing* of the deduction of the interest. The total amount deducted is the same. This is illustrated in the accompanying chart:

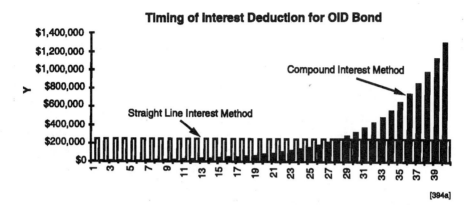

**Timing of Interest Deduction for OID Bond**

[394a]

Notice how for well over half the time the amount of interest deducted under the straight line method exceeds the amount of interest deducted under compound method. The amount of interest deducted under the compound method massively exceeds the amount of interest deducted under the straight line method during the last years of the bond.

Now we get to the intrigue. What does the fact that the timing is different come to mean? You will strongly suspect from our earlier discussions that it means a lot.

- The Tax Saved Cmp Int. column in our numerical chart shows the amount of tax saved by Birdsill if it deducts the amount of interest under the economically realistic compounding method. Thus in 1976 the tax saved is 40% of $5,600, or $2,240. In 1977, the tax saved is 40% of $6,440, or $2,576. We will see what Birdsill does with these amounts momentarily.

- The Tax Saved St.Ln.Int. column, it will not surprise you to learn, is the amount of tax saved by Birdsill if it deducts the amount of interest under the straight line method, as we have discussed above. That is 40% of the same amount of $249,067, or $99,627.

- The Future Value of Tax Saved Cmp Int. column can be explained by looking, say, at 1976. The tax saved that year, using the economically accurate compound method, is $2,240. If that amount is invested at a 9% after-tax compound rate of return for 40 years, it grows to $824,944. If the 1977 tax saved using the compound method of $2,576 is invested at 9% compound after-tax return for 39 years, it grows to $867,778. Note that this amount is greater than the year 1976 amount. This is because, while the number of years of compounding is less, 39 instead of 40, the amount you start with is larger ($2,576 instead of $2,240). Observe how, for this same reason, the amounts in this column grow every year until 2005, at which point the effect of having less years left begins to dominate over the fact that the amount you start with is increasing and the amounts you accumulate decline through the end of the 40 year period. The total future value of all these amounts of tax saved and invested is given at the bottom of the column as $68,267,220.

- The future value of tax saved St.Ln. Int. column, of course, performs the same computation for the straight line method. The Tax Saved St. Ln. Int. amount (always $99,627) is compounded at 9% after tax interest in 1976 for 40 years, then in 1977 for 39 years and so forth. We would expect to see these accumulations just decline all the way from 1976 through 1015, since we are always starting with the same amount but compounding for less years. And so we see the accumulations behave as expected. The total future value of all these amounts of tax saved and invested using the straight line method is given at the bottom of the column as $396,114,090.

The totals of the Future Value of Tax Saved Cmp Int. and Future Value of Tax Saved St.Ln Int. columns tell the final story. The total for the compound interest method is $68,267,220, which is stunningly less than the total for the straight line method of $396,114,090. As indicated in the chart, the difference is $327,846,870. Dwell on this comparison for a moment. Note also the stupifying fact that the amounts accumulated for the first two years, 1976 and 1977, in the straight line method add up to more than is accumulated in the entire 40 years in the compound method.

Thus though the total *amounts* of interest deducted were the same, the fact that straight line method allowed much larger amounts to be deducted early puts monster money in Birdsill's pocket, compared to the economically accurate compound method. Indeed the difference was a staggering $327,846,870. Given that the face amount of the underlying obligation in this transaction was $10 million, it is positively mind-boggling that the simple matter of the difference in timing of when the total amount of the interest is deducted can put over $327 million in the pocket of Birdsill (and out of the pocket of the government). This is over 30 times more than the face amount of the original obligation. Such is the raw power of the time value of money. And such is the incredible price to the government of getting the rules wrong.

For do you think that corporations and their high-powered tax counsel were aware of this effect after Congress enacted the 1969 straight line rules? Do you think that corporations, on the advice of their high-powered counsel, issued deeply discounted long term bonds as a financing tool? Does a bear—well, you know.

Congress, after getting its pocket picked by this technique for a number of years, finally figured it out and went to Smart City. Congress enacted rules in 1982 that compute OID by reference to the economically accurate view that the note holder is receiving the interest and then relending it back to the issuer of the note at further interest.[48] Thus on our deal, the deduction allowed for obligations issued after 1982 would be calculated based on the compound amount, rather than the straight line amount.

So this particular OID game is no longer available. But the analysis is still there. It was the enactment of the OID rules in 1982 that ushered in the time value of money era in federal income taxation. Once the analysis was made there, and people began to understand the enormous implications of timing in taxation, the analysis began to be applied widely in other areas of federal income taxation. This type of analysis will stand us in good stead as we examine a variety of other transactions in this field.

### 1.5.6 Stunt No. 5: Lagniappe

Now you've been so good. I'm very proud of you staggering through that previous stunt. Now you're going to get a reward. Remember, no reading this stunt until you've done No. 4.

This stunt concerns the story about how a Dutchman met an Indian, or Native American, and bought Manhattan Island for $24. The Dutchman was Peter Minuit, the leader of the local Dutch settlement, and this sale occurred in 1624. According to the author of a recent book entitled *Don't Know Much About History,*[49] "the Dutch got New York cheap."[50]

---

**48.** See ¶ 3.02.

**49.** K. Davis, *Don't Know Much About History* (1990) at 24–25. Apparently this book is named after the rock and roll song of the 60's that begins, "Don't know much about history ... but I do know that I love you" etc. etc. etc.

**50.** Id.

The title of this book, intended by the author to be amusing, may in fact be more accurate than he realizes. For if the Native American had invested that $24 in 1624 at the then prevailing rate of return and just held it, what would that $24 be worth now? Of course we need to know what interest rate or rate of return to use for this calculation. As indicated above in Stunt No. 2, the long-term rate of return on equities is 10%.[51] We may perhaps view that as the long-term equity return. Taking a more conservative approach, let us say the Native American and his heirs are able to invest this $24 at a long-term rate of return of 8%. So let us say the Native American invested this $24 in an asset that pays no dividends or interest but just appreciated 8% a year since 1624. What would the Native American's heirs have in 1993?[52]

It turns out that this computation cranks out to be a cool $51,710,-290,000,000. Rounding it off a little, what we have here is a kind of neat $51 trillion 710 billion. Now I know Manhattan Island is valuable. And I know there are a lot of people who wouldn't live anywhere else. But worth $51 trillion, it ain't. Not even close. Just ask Donald Trump. (Donald who?) And note that Manhattan Island has had a tremendous number of improvements made to it—i.e., buildings. And still it can't compare with the $24 at 8%.

So the upshot of the story is that Peter Minuit did not get Manhattan cheap. On the contrary, the Native American ate his lunch, and the Dutchman paid. It was not a Dutch treat.

The Dutch may have been the dominant navigators of the era,[53] excelling in the mathematical computations associated therewith. But they did not understand the power of the time value of money.

51. Note 16 supra.

52. Note that in this example I am not reducing the rate of return to account for taxes on the gain. This is a plausible approach. I posit that the asset just rises steadily at 8% a year but is never sold, thus not triggering any tax because (as we will learn) there has been no "realizing event," or occasion on which to impose a tax. See Chapter 4. In addition, I posit that this investment passes down from generation to generation, which—under the present American tax law—causes the gain in the hands of each generation to escape taxation—as we will learn when discussing the rules for taxing property received from a decedent in Chapter 4. Thus this footnote gives you a little introduction to these other important concepts, as well as explaining the approach in the text.

53. Viz the promulgation of the Navigation Acts by Britain's prime minister George Grenville in the 17th century, to curb Dutch hegemony on the high seas.

# Chapter 1

# HISTORY, POLICY AND STRUCTURE

*Table of Sections*

---

## ¶ 1.01   A Brief History of Income Taxation

### *(1) In General*

Taxes are a building block of civilization. They pay for "public goods", such as the cost of government administration or military defense of the state. These "public goods" are of great benefit to all the people, whether or not each person has paid any taxes. So each individual has a great incentive to avoid paying taxes and let his neighbors carry the burden.

It is not surprising, then, that in the first organized society of record, ancient Sumer, the paying of taxes carried with it great religious sanction to overcome the human disinclination to pay. The Sumerians were organized in temple-communities in which the farmers produced a food surplus paid to the priests. In Sumerian theology the priests had the power to communicate with the Gods and were themselves supernatural beings. Moreover it was also part of Sumerian theology, conveniently for the priests, that man was a slave of the Gods destined to work indefatigably for them or face the threat of drought, flood, and starvation.[1]

Even in the Golden Age of Greece the heavy taxes imposed upon the Athenian upper classes by the democratic vote of its citizens precipitated

---

**¶ 1.01**

1. Falkenstein, "La Cité-temple sumérienne," Cahiers d'histoire mondiale 791; (1954) 4 Schneider, "Die Anfänge der Kulturwirtschaft: Die sumerische Tempelstadt," Staatswissenschaftliche Beitrage (Essen, 1920). But see Oppenheim, "A Bird's-Eye View of Mesopotamien Economic History," in Polyanyi, Trade and Market in the Early Empires 27–37 (1957), indicating that there were some farming communities in Sumer that did not depend on a temple.

coups d'etat in 411 B.C. and 404 B.C.[2] The taxes imposed by the central administration in the Roman Empire were essential to financing further conquest, but ultimately their excessiveness was a significant factor in the Empire's disintegration.[3]

From the time of their earliest settlements, the American colonies of Britain evinced a healthy resistance to paying taxes to the mother country.[4] The first taxes levied by Great Britain on her colonies were the Acts of Trade and Navigation which provided for customs duties. These Acts raised little revenues for two reasons: first, they were only intended to direct the flow of commerce; second, they were widely ignored anyway. Indeed, through the mid-eighteenth century, the Americans were unique among the British colonies in being virtually exempt from taxation by the mother country. This was true notwithstanding that Great Britain incurred some significant expenses in maintaining the colonies, such as driving the French out of America during the Seven Years' War. (Most of the colonies refused to contribute troops to this war effort, flouted commercial regulations, and traded extensively with the enemy.[5])

Thus at the conclusion of the Seven Years' War, in 1763, the British came to the reasonable decision not only to lay taxes upon the colonies but actually to collect them. The Revenue Act of 1764 (the "Sugar" Act) imposed a moderate system of customs duties on the Americans. In 1765 the British promulgated the Stamp Tax which required the payment of a fee, evidenced by the affixing of a stamp, on all commercial uses of paper, such as in legal and business documents and newspapers. Such a stamp tax for raising revenue was placidly assented to in Great Britain and employed by most of the countries of Europe. However, it aroused such violent opposition in the American colonies that it was repealed the following year. In 1767 Parliament, still endeavoring to come up with a tax tolerable to the Americans, promulgated the so-called "Townshend Duties," which imposed customs on American imports of paper, paint, lead, and tea. After another uproar this was repealed. The only element of the "Townshend Duties" Parliament retained was the impost on tea, as a symbol of its power to tax the colonies.

The outcome to this point was something of a standoff. The colonies had in fact resisted taxation. Great Britain had, however, still maintained the principle that it could tax them. Great Britain had, moreover, the legitimate argument that it incurred substantial expenses in administering the colonies. To this the Americans answered with some force that since they were not represented in Parliament, it had no authority

**2.** McNeil, The Rise of the West p. 289 (1963).

**3.** Id. at 344; Palmer and Colton, A History of the Modern World (1960). The religious aspect of taxation in Renaissance Italy is displayed in the Brancacci Chapel in Florence, Italy. The frescoe "Rendering of the Tribute Money," shows the gods approving the Florentine income tax.

**4.** Except as otherwise indicated, the discussion of the taxation of the American Colonies is based on Palmer & Colton, note 3 supra, at 324–326.

**5.** 1 Morrison and Commager, The Growth of the American Republic 9 (1937).

to tax them. The British response to this was that members of Parliament did not represent merely local constituencies but spoke for the entire empire. Thus the argument ran that the Americans enjoyed "virtual representation," as did the British City of Manchester, which was also not represented in Parliament. To this the Americans replied that if Manchester was not represented it ought to be, an argument which found a sympathetic ear in Manchester. (Indeed this controversy spawned a general drive to reform the means of selecting the members of the House of Commons.)

These relatively recondite arguments were rendered moot by the Boston Tea Party. One evening in 1773 in Boston harbor a party of men in disguise boarded several ships of the British East India Company and threw a number of chests of tea overboard. Although the motivations of this act are somewhat obscure, it was apparently a protest both against the tea tax and the granting by Parliament to the East India Company of the right to sell its tea directly in the colonies, by-passing American merchants. The British thereupon closed the port of Boston (threatening the city with economic strangulation), and forbade local elections and the holding of town meetings. Although the British response here seems excessive, it must be admitted they had been tolerating a good deal from the colonies for a long time.

After this point taxation receded as an issue and other more broadly-based justifications for the American Revolution came to the fore.[6]

### (2) The American Income Tax

The dominant source of revenues of the new central government of the thirteen states, created by the adoption of the Constitution in 1789, was receipts from customs—which was of course the most inconspicuous method of taxing an undoubtedly recalcitrant populace.[7] Early in this period there were also levied, however, excise taxes on carriages, whiskey and other distilled spirits, snuff, sugar, and other items.[8]

The American people, consistent with their attitude under the British, immediately resisted these taxes. One of the more engaging manifestations of this resistance was the so-called "Whiskey Rebellion" in Western Pennsylvania in 1794 when the home of General John Neville, the regional inspector of the excise was burned to the ground.

6. Cf. "It is repugnant to reason—to suppose that this continent can long remain subject to any external power . . . There is something absurd in supposing a continent be perpetually governed by an island. In no instance hath nature made the satellite larger than its primary planet; and as England and America, with respect to each other, reverse the common order of nature, it is evident that they belong to different systems, England to Europe, America to itself." T. Paine, Common Sense (1776).

7. Except as otherwise indicated this discussion of the history of the American income tax is based on the following materials: Myers, A Financial History of the United States, (1970); Bureau of Internal Revenue, History of the Internal Revenue Service, 1791–1929 (1930); Ratner, American Taxation, Its History as a Social Force in Democracy (2d 1967); Blakely, The Federal Income Tax (1940); Paul, Taxation in the United States (1954); Annual Reports of the Commissioner of Internal Revenue.

8. The "Carriage Tax", March 3, 1791, as amended, 1 Stat. 373.

The resultant turmoil led ultimately to the occupation of several western counties of Pennsylvania by the army.[9] A somewhat more sober approach for resisting the excise taxes was the argument that they were direct taxes not apportioned among the States by population and thus violative of the new Constitution.[10] However, these taxes were held constitutional in the first of a number of Supreme Court cases on this subject.[11]

In 1797 a Stamp Tax was successfully promulgated, similar to the one which had caused an outcry 30 years earlier when imposed by the British. In 1798 a property tax was levied on houses, land and slaves. When Thomas Jefferson became President, he abolished all these taxes. They reappeared to help finance the War of 1812 and were abolished again in 1817. During this period the British set an example by enacting an income tax to help pay for the Napoleonic wars. It was abolished in 1816 but came back permanently in 1842. Moreover, in 1815 the United States' Secretary of the Treasury suggested that an income tax might ultimately be necessary. The British experience and this suggestion were, however, the only small warning clouds on the horizon and indeed there were no taxes again in the United States other than customs until the Civil War.

In addition to the other tragedies wreaked upon this country by the Civil War, it also gave rise to the first federal income tax, in 1862. This tax was graduated, providing for a levy of 3% on income up to $10,000 and 5% on income over $10,000. An exemption of $600 meant that (given the deflated dollar values of that time) only about 1% of the population was reached. The rates were increased somewhat in 1864 and later years. When the war ended, the income tax was reduced. It became a flat rate in 1867 and was repealed in 1872.

Though the income tax was gone, it was not forgotten. It became a rallying cry of the agrarian, labor, and small business organizations of the South and West. In 1892 one of the proposals of the Populist Party was a graduated income tax. Since the tax was seen as a way of raising revenues by taxing the rich, the numbers inevitably favored the proponents of the tax. These pressures in Congress finally led to the passage of the Income Tax of 1894.

The 1894 tax was 2% on individual income over $4000 (thus reaching only the highest individual incomes at that time) and 4% on corporate income. Significantly, included in income was personal property received by gift or inheritance.[12]

This income tax was, unsurprisingly, immediately challenged in the courts—as being a "direct" tax and thus violating the Constitution's

**9.** Brackenridge, History of the Western Insurrection (1859).

**10.** United States Constitution, Art. I, § 2, cl. 3. For a general discussion of this constitutional issue, see text accompanying notes 13–15 infra.

**11.** Hylton v. United States, 3 U.S. (3 Dall.) 171, 1 L.Ed. 556 (1796).

**12.** Cf. ¶ 3.08.

requirement that "direct" taxes must be apportioned among the states by population.[13] The issue was joined in the case of *Pollock v. Farmers' Loan and Trust Co.,*[14] involving a stockholders' suit to restrain payment of the corporate tax by the corporation's directors.

The logic of the opponents of the tax was weak. It would be difficult to apportion an income tax among the states by population. Each state would have to ascertain its share of the total income tax due and reapportion it among its citizens by their incomes. Even if this could be done, it would lead to an oppressive result in a state with large population and low incomes. It was unlikely the Constitution would require such an anomalous result.

This was in large measure why the prior Supreme Court decisions addressing the question had unanimously found that a tax difficult to apportion was not a direct tax. There was dictum in the *Hylton* case that only poll taxes and taxes on land were direct taxes, that a tax difficult to apportion would not be considered a direct tax by the Constitution.[15] The Court had early upheld the 1864 gross receipts tax on insurance companies on this ground.[16] The 1866 tax on the issuance of bank notes had been upheld as not a direct tax for historical reasons and because it would be difficult to apportion.[17] One ground for upholding the estate tax of 1864 was because, the Court said, it was indistinguishable from an income tax which was not a direct tax.[18]

The Court had found the income tax of 1864 valid on the grounds that it was an excise tax. Direct taxes, the Court said, could consist only of capitation taxes and taxes on real estate.[19]

Faced with this overwhelming array of argument and legal precedent, the counsel opposing the 1894 income tax salted their arguments with a little rhetoric:

> "I look upon this case with very different eyes from those of either the Attorney General or his associate who has just closed ... The act of Congress which we are impugning is communistic in its purposes and tendencies, and is defended here upon principles as communistic, socialistic—what shall I call them—populistic as ever have been addressed to any political assembly in the world ...

**13.** Article 1, Section 2, Clause 3 of the Constitution provides:

"(D)irect Taxes shall be apportioned among the several States which may be included within this Union, according to their respective Numbers ..."

Article 1, Section 9, Clause 4 of the Constitution provides:

"No Capitation, or other direct Tax shall be laid, unless in Proportion to the Census or Enumeration herein before directed to be taken."

**14.** 157 U.S. 429, 15 S.Ct. 673, 39 L.Ed. 759 (1895), reh'g denied 158 U.S. 601, 15 S.Ct. 912, 39 L.Ed. 1108 (1895).

**15.** Note 11 supra at 174.

**16.** Pacific Insurance Co. v. Soule, 74 U.S. (7 Wall.) 433, 19 L.Ed. 95 (1868).

**17.** Veazie Bank v. Fenno, 75 U.S. (8 Wall.) 533, 544–545, 19 L.Ed. 482 (1869).

**18.** Scholey v. Rew, 90 U.S. (23 Wall.) 331, 347–348, 23 L.Ed. 99 (1874).

**19.** Springer v. United States, 102 U.S. (12 Otto) 586, 602, 26 L.Ed. 253 (1880).

I do not believe that any member of this court ever has sat or ever will sit to hear and decide a case the consequences of which will be so far-reaching as this—not even the venerable member who survives from the early days of the civil war, and has sat upon every question of reconstruction, of national destiny, of state destiny that has come up during the last thirty years [Field] . . ."[20]

The Court struck down the tax. In one of its less distinguished moments in history, the Court reasoned that the tax on rental income from land was a tax on land and thus a direct tax which had to be apportioned, likewise as to a tax on income from personal property. Since so much of the income tax was invalid, the whole scheme must fall.[21]

Though a single breaker might recede, the tide was coming in. In the years following *Pollock* pressures from the agrarian, populist and Progressive groups continued to build for Congress to pass another income tax and give the Supreme Court a chance to overrule *Pollock*. It seemed likely the Court would reverse itself as the *Pollock* rationale was being eroded by subsequent decisions. The inheritance tax of 1898 was upheld on the grounds *Pollock* had not overruled *Scholey v. Rew*[22] which had found the 1864 inheritance tax valid.[23] The 1898 gross receipts tax on corporations engaged in sugar refining was sustained on the reasoning it was an excise tax and thus not within the purview of *Pollock*.[24]

In 1909 a coalition of western, progressive Republican and Democratic members of Congress appeared finally to have the votes to pass another income tax. The eastern Republicans and President Taft proposed as a compromise a corporate income tax and the Sixteenth Amendment to the Constitution sanctioning an income tax in general. The compromise was accepted. Though this appeared to be a victory for the supporters of the income tax, in fact it was a testament to the adroitness of its opponents, since the cumbersome process of the states ratifying an amendment to the Constitution would delay the imposition of an individual income tax by several years.

The Payne–Aldrich Tariff Act of 1909 resulted from this compromise, imposing a tax on corporate net income, with an exemption of $5000. It was held constitutional in *Flint v. Stone Tracy Co.*[25] (a decision which further demonstrated the limited vitality of *Pollock,* although that

**20.** Pollock v. Farmers' Loan & Trust Co., 157 U.S. 429, 532, 553, 15 S.Ct. 673, 674–675, 679, 39 L.Ed. 759 (1895) (argument of Joseph H. Choate).

**21.** Pollock v. Farmers' Loan & Trust Co., 158 U.S. 601, 637, 15 S.Ct. 912, 920–921, 39 L.Ed. 1108 (1895). Dissenting were Justices Harlan, White, Jackson and Brown. In the majority were Chief Justice Fuller, writing the opinion, and the venerable Justice Field, Justices Brewer, Shiras and Gray.

**22.** Note 18 supra.

**23.** Knowlton v. Moore, 178 U.S. 41, 20 S.Ct. 747, 44 L.Ed. 969 (1900).

**24.** Spreckels Sugar Refining Co. v. McClain, 192 U.S. 397, 24 S.Ct. 376, 48 L.Ed. 496 (1904).

**25.** 220 U.S. 107, 31 S.Ct. 342, 55 L.Ed. 389 (1911).

Thus on account of the *Flint* case the constitutionality of the corporate income tax does not depend on the Sixteenth Amendment.

question was by this time moot). In 1913 the Sixteenth Amendment, providing that Congress shall have the power to lay and collect taxes on income without apportionment among the states, was formally ratified. The 1913 Income Tax was then enacted posthaste. It imposed a 1% tax on net incomes of individuals above $3000 ($4000 for married persons) and an additional surtax of 1% on incomes above $20,000, graduated up to 6% on incomes of more than $500,000.

And still the struggle was not ended. Back into the courts went the opponents of the income tax.[26] This time they argued that the due process clause of the Fifth Amendment and the requirement that taxes must be uniform[27] were violated by the exemptions and graduated rates. However, it was the end of the line. In *Brushaber v. Union Pacific Railroad Co.*[28] Chief Justice White, a dissenter in *Pollock,* writing for the unanimous court (McReynolds not participating), held the income tax valid. The Fifth Amendment was not violated because there was not an arbitrariness that amounted to confiscation;[29] as to uniformity, that requirement was only geographical.[30] Moreover, the Court recognized broadly that the purpose of the Sixteenth Amendment was to relieve income taxes of the *Pollock* requirement of apportionment.[31]

The income tax had arrived. In the years since *Brushaber* the story has not been of its constitutionality but of its ever-broadening reach and its constantly increasing complexity. In 1920 there were 5½ million individual income tax returns in a U.S. population of 106 million. In the early 1990's there were over 90 million individual income tax returns filed annually in a U.S. population of over 200 million.[32] The Income Tax of 1913 was 14 pages[33]—compare to the immoderately-sized tome that comprises the present Internal Revenue Code.

The present extraordinarily complex income tax is the product of many forces. In the first instance there is the fact that the income tax is imposed on a very complex society. Thus a great deal of the complexity of the Internal Revenue Code will inevitably flow from that. Beyond that, there are the special interests, who—having lost the constitutional battle—still engage in hand-to-hand fighting, with respect to various code sections, to escape the brunt of the graduated rates. There are the reformers, attempting to plug the "gaps" the special interests have opened. There are the planners, who attempt to use the Code to encourage "socially desirable" behavior. And finally, the income tax is

**26.** Cf:
"In the fell clutch of circumstance,
I have not winced nor cried aloud;
Under the bludgeonings of chance
My head is bloody, but unbowed."

—William Ernest Henley, Echoes (1888). IV, In Memoriam R.T. Hamilton Bruce ("Invictus"), st. 1, 2.

**27.** Article 1, Section 8, Clause 4 of the Constitution requires that ". . . all Duties,

Imposts and Excises shall be uniform throughout the United States."

**28.** 240 U.S. 1, 36 S.Ct. 236, 60 L.Ed. 493 (1916).

**29.** Id. at 24, 36 S.Ct. at 244.

**30.** Id.

**31.** Id. at 19, 36 S.Ct. at 242.

**32.** See generally Annual Reports of the Commissioner of Internal Revenue.

**33.** 38 Stat. 166–180 (1913).

used as an instrument of national economic policy, with rate changes, rebates, credits, deductions, and surtaxes all designed to affect the country's rates of growth, inflation and unemployment.

Thus since 1913 the income tax, serving many purposes and many masters, has evolved into a massive, grotesquely complex statute. And, since each new piece of tax legislation adds materially to the Code's complexity, the end of its wanton growth is not yet in sight.

## ¶ 1.02   Theoretical Aspects of Income Taxation

Oppressive and omnipresent as the income tax is, it naturally has provoked a good deal of discussion concerning how its operation might be improved. The themes around which this discussion has revolved relate to the capacity of the tax to raise revenues, its fairness, the effect the tax has on the use of resources in the economy, and its complexity. These themes arise in the context of particular issues discussed below.

### (1) Alternatives to the Income Tax

The boldest critique of the income tax is, of course, to suggest it be done away with altogether. Assuming, however, this society is not suddenly transformed into an island paradise in which the populace gathers coconuts for sustenance, the government will continue to need to raise substantial revenues. There are other possible sources of these revenues. Examining them provides insight into the strengths of the income tax.

### (a) Printing Money

It would be possible for the government not to levy any taxes at all but simply print enough money to pay for its goods and services. Indeed, when the government runs a deficit, one of the ways it can and has financed that deficit is by printing more money.[1] The result of just printing money, however, would be a spectacular and continuing inflation. But extreme inflation is not devastating to the economy if it can be anticipated. Wages and other contracts can be indexed into the rapidly increasing price level, and the merry-go-round continues with everyone on it.[2] The tax effect results from the fact that the government will always print enough money to cause the price level to rise at a greater rate than the indexing. Thus everyone's purchasing power is decreased—which is the effect of any tax. This leads to another round of indexing and money printing, resulting in an even greater inflation, etc.[3]

---

**¶ 1.02**

1. The other major way the government finances the deficit is by borrowing from banks, or the public. See G. Ackley, Macroeconomic Theory, 423 (1961). The effect of such borrowing, or deficit financing, is similar to the effects of printing money, as discussed later in the text.

2. Holding cash would be severely disadvantaged and cash balances would be re-

duced. See Bailey, "The Welfare Cost of Inflationary Finance", 64 J.P.E. 93–95, 101 (1956).

3. This kind of volatile inflation plus indexing has characterized some Latin American countries since World War II. See Gillim, "Some Fixed Aspects of the Latin-American Free Trade Association," in 2 Shoup (Ed.), Fiscal Harmonization in Common Markets 527–529 (1967).

There are, surprisingly, certain advantages to just printing money to finance the government. The effect is impersonal; there are apparently no "vested interests" who secure loopholes to escape the inflation. There is no evasion, since there is no law to evade. There is no cost to enforcing the law, since there is no law to enforce.

But before the printing presses are cranked up, the disadvantages of just printing money should be considered. Some "vested interests" are able to index their incomes favorably against the inflation rate. Those groups who lack the political clout to index their incomes are crushed by the inflation. The uncertainty of the price level in the future makes private business transactions which cover a period of time difficult to arrange—a serious drawback in a complex economy. And for a major economy like that of the United States virulent inflation would be upsetting to international trade and the economies of other countries.[4] Thus printing money is not a realistic alternative to the income tax.

### (b) Deficit Financing

Another way for the government to raise revenues instead of imposing taxes is for it to borrow funds in the capital markets. With this technique, the government issues bonds or short-term notes which are bought by individuals and institutions. This technique, which has been used extensively since the early 1980's, to finance the country's yawning budget deficits has severe side-effects if used to extremes. Since the government is competing with private business for borrowed funds, the heavy entry by the government into the capital markets to borrow will cause interest rates to rise. This can choke off borrowing by business, which cannot afford the high interest rates. The effects will be felt first in industries like housing and automobiles which depend heavily on borrowed funds. Eventually all sectors of the economy will feel the pinch and a recession or depression can result.

Where the government is borrowing heavily, the Federal Reserve Board can take steps to mitigate the tendency of interest rates to increase. Using various techniques, such as changing reserve requirements to its member banks and buying and selling notes in the open market, the Fed can bring interest rates down, even though the government is borrowing heavily. However, these steps by the Fed tend to lead to inflation, since they involve putting more dollars out into the system. Sole or extreme reliance on government borrowing as an alternative to the income tax leads to strangulation interest rates or inflation. Deficit financing is, therefore, not a viable alternative to the income tax. One of the problems of the 90's is to reduce the U.S. federal government deficit, because of the heavy reliance on deficit financing during the 80's.

---

**4.** *Indexing the Income Tax:* As a result of the Economic Recovery Tax Act of 1981, tax brackets have been indexed for inflation since 1985. The standard deduction and the deduction for personal exemptions are also indexed to inflation. §§ 1(f), 63(d), and 151(f) as amended by § 104(a)–(c) of the Economic Recovery Act of 1981.

Indexing the tax brackets is something of an illusion since subsequent tax cuts or increases will override the effect of the indexing.

### (c) Is It A Bird? Is It A Plane? No, It's VATman!

The president rarely wears a cape in public. But he and his advisors to save the economy have at various times considered a value-added tax (VAT), which imposes a tax on the increase in the value of a product at each step in the production-distribution chain. It is ultimately paid by the consumer.[5] VATs are effective. They are used all over the world and in every country in Western Europe. VATs have the very good effect of taxing consumption and thereby discouraging consumption and increasing savings. Increasing saving is a very desirable result. Taxing income, by contrast, discourages saving (which produces income) and encourages consumption. A VAT is something that should be considered to complement the income tax.[6]

### (d) Net Worth or Wealth Taxes

In those few countries which have used it, a net worth tax imposes a levy, usually not more than 1%, on the value of property held by the taxpayer.[7] The net worth tax cannot raise a substantial amount of revenue, since the rate can never exceed the income from the property or the property will be abandoned.[8] Other problems with the net worth tax include difficulties in valuation, high cost of enforcement,[9] and lack of liquid assets on the part of the taxpayer to pay the tax.[10] In the United States the only forms of wealth tax in effect are real estate taxes and estate and gift taxes. Both of these taxes have evidenced the problems described above and neither appears capable of raising enough revenues to take the place of the income tax.[11]

### (e) Head Tax

A head tax imposes a flat amount of tax on each person in the society, regardless of income, deductions or expenses. There can be an exemption for the ill, elderly, and children. Though this tax sounds strange, there are some arguments in its favor. The law is simple. There would be almost no tax bar or tax accountants. No expensive treatises (!) would be required to explain the law. The bureaucracy needed for administering the law would be sharply reduced. The public would be

---

**5.** Thus it is a form of sales tax.

**6.** See "The VATman Cometh", The Economist, April 24, 1993, 17–18.

**7.** The net worth tax has been used in, among other countries, Germany, India, Sweden, Norway, Denmark, Finland, Columbia. See generally World Tax Series, Harvard Law School with respect to these countries.

**8.** Cf. generally Tait, The Taxation of Personal Wealth, 1967; C. T. Sandford, J. R. M. Willis, D. J. Ironside, An Annual Wealth Tax, 1975; Cooper, Taking Wealth Taxation Seriously, 34 Record of the Association of the Bar of the City of New York 24 (1979).

**9.** See Wheatcraft, "The Administrative Problems of a Wealth Tax", Brit. Tax Rev. 410–22 (1963).

**10.** Speaking more technically, it could be said that the net worth tax causes property to be converted to uses which return money income rather than imputed income, as only money income can be used to pay the tax. Thus, the old homestead, which gives a great deal of pleasure to its owners, might be sold out to be subdivided for a suburban development. Cf. A. Chekhov, The Cherry Orchard (1904).

**11.** See generally Annual Reports of Internal Revenue Service, and see Posin, Making Too Much of the Property Tax, Newsday, June 21, 1973, p. 62.

spared the periodic Congressional agony over "tax reform." Reams of editorials on the subject would not be written.

Despite all these advantages, the head tax is ultimately unacceptable as an alternative to the income tax because of its extreme regressivity. The person with little (or no) income pays the same tax as the person making $300,000 a year. It might be suggested that a correction be made for levels of income. But that then converts the head tax into an income tax. Then arguments would be advanced to allow deductions for expenses in generating the income; arguments could be made for deductions for casualty losses and medical expenses. The appeal of the head tax is its inflexibility. Once the door is opened to considering aspects of income, the whole structure of the income tax comes thundering in.

### (f) Consumption or Cash Flow Tax

The concept of taxing consumption rather than income has a long and distinguished record of support from economists and lawyers concerned with taxation. This approach in essence involves taxing a base of income reduced by saving. At first blush it might appear that this approach is regressive, as in the case of a sales or value-added tax (see ¶ 1.02(1)(c)), since people in lower brackets allocate a greater percentage of their income to consumption than do people in higher brackets. However, a consumption type tax contemplates a steeply graduated rate structure, based on levels of annual consumption, so that the overall system can be quite progressive. Moreover, deductions and exemptions can be allowed for consumption of necessities. The consumption tax may appear unfair in that, for example, a person with an income of $100,000 who consumes $10,000 worth of goods and services and saves $90,000 will be taxed at the same level as a person with an income of $15,000 who consumes $10,000 and saves $5000. However a proponent of the consumption tax could answer that the two individuals are each enjoying the same standard of living and are thus fairly taxed at the same level. At such time as the high income individual's savings are drawn down for consumption he will be taxed upon it. Moreover, the proponents argue, the consumption tax encourages saving compared to the income tax, and increased saving is needed in this society.

While the consumption tax is intellectually interesting, there appears to be no likelihood of such a tax being enacted.[12]

### (g) The "Flat Rate Tax"

Recently proposals have been made to have a "flat rate tax" system in place of the present system. The flat rate tax would involve having

---

12. The major modern economic work on this subject is N. Kaldor, An Expenditure Tax (1955). However, economists dating back to Alfred Marshall and John Stuart Mill (see J.S. Mill, Principles of Political Economy 545–46, Laughlin Ed.1884) have supported the idea. The application of this concept to the American tax system has been developed in Andrews, "A Consump-tion–Type or Cash Flow Personal Income Tax," 87 Harv.L.Rev. 1113 (1974). See also Graetz, "Implementing a Progressive Consumption Tax," 92 Harv.L.Rev. 1575 (1979); Warren, "Would a Consumption Tax Be Fairer Than An Income Tax?" 89 Yale L.J. 1081 (1980); Gunn, "The Case for an Income Tax," 46 Univ. of Chicago L.Rev. 370 (1979).

one flat rate tax, such as 20%, on all income rather than the present graduated bracket system. In addition, these proposals also contemplate doing away with many special deductions, exclusions, credits, and other special computations. (See ¶ 1.02(2)(b), relating to the Comprehensive Tax Base.)

It should be pointed out that the complexity of the Internal Revenue Code and the existence of a graduated bracket system are two independent issues. The complexity of the Internal Revenue Code does not arise from the existence of the graduated rate structure. The graduated rate structure takes about twelve pages of the Internal Revenue Code to set forth. The other pages of the Internal Revenue Code, numbering over a thousand, are concerned with various special deductions, exclusions, credits, and other special computations that are designed in many cases to promote the fairness of the income tax. As just one example, the deduction for depreciation involves some complexity. Yet it would be manifestly unfair to tax the income from an asset without allowing some form of a deduction for the cost of that asset, while it is being used. There are many examples of such necessary provisions, as illustrated throughout the pages of this book.

Nevertheless, it would be possible to simplify the Internal Revenue Code considerably. The favorable treatment of capital gains, as discussed in Chapter 4, by itself probably accounts for one-third of the size of the Internal Revenue Code. There is, obviously, much room for improvement in reducing the complexity of the Internal Revenue Code. But the American economy is a sophisticated one, with a wide variety of complicated transactions to be taxed. It is unrealistic to expect that the income tax on such a sophisticated economy can be set forth in a one or two page statute, as some of the more enthusiastic proponents of flat rate tax proposals have suggested. Thus, wholesale simplification of the Internal Revenue Code is not possible if the variety of sophisticated transactions in the society are to be taxed in a rational fashion.

A second interesting aspect of flat rate tax proposals relates to the incidence of the income tax if such proposals were adopted. It is not at all clear who would pay more taxes and who would pay less if (1) the graduated rate structure were replaced by a single percentage flat rate of tax, and (2) a wide variety of special deductions, exclusions, credits and other special computations were eliminated. If the Government is going to raise the same amount of revenue with a flat rate tax system as it raises under the present system, it is going to have to get the money from someplace. While a flat rate tax of, say, 20% may not sound very high, it will inevitably be imposed on a much broader base of income than is presently used. Thus, for example, if the deduction for interest on a home mortgage is eliminated; if Social Security payments are made fully taxable; if profits on the sale of a taxpayer's home are taxable whether or not he buys another home; if medical expenses are not deductible, etc., then that 20% rate on taxable income is very much larger indeed. The probable result of many flat tax proposals would be to lower somewhat the taxes paid by those in higher brackets and raise somewhat the taxes paid by those in middle and lower income brackets.[13] Whether that is a desirable result, and whether that is the result that is desired by the proponents of flat rate tax proposals are questions beyond the scope of this work.

### (h) "Steve and Jerry's" Tax

A variation on the flat tax was proposed by magazine magnate Steve Forbes in the 1996 presidential campaign as well as by former Governor Jerry Brown of California during the 1992 Presidential campaign. Steve and Jerry's tax drew from the ideas proposed by Robert Hall and Alvin Rabushka of the Hoover Institution at Stanford University.[14] As proposed by Jerry, the tax involved two components: a value-added tax (see ¶ 1.02.1(c) above) plus a tax on wages. The value added tax is a flat percentage imposed on business revenues. Business revenues are computed by taking gross receipts and subtracting the cost of all purchased assets. Labor costs are also deducted. Giving an immediate deduction to purchase of new assets should encourage investment. The tax on wages could be a flat rate (as Governor Brown proposed) or it could be made progressive. Had Governor Brown proposed that it be progressive he would doubtless have avoided the torrent of criticism leveled at this idea. In principle the tax on wages can be progressive. This appears to be an attractive and simple idea. The proposal by Steve Forbes was a somewhat simpler version, setting a flat percentage tax rate on all income.

The difficulty with the Hall–Rabushka–Brown proposal is that it assumes away all the problems. The income tax as presently constructed could also be simple. We could just tax all income and allow business expenses. But the problems remain. What are business expenses? How about the 3–martini lunch? What about the deduction for interest on the home mortgage? Is the public ready to give that up, whatever the overall tax scheme? What about not allowing deductions for charitable contributions? How are annuities handled? What about appreciation in value of property that is not sold? Will that be taxed or not under this new scheme? There are fundamental problems concerning the dividing line between business and personal expenses, timing issues, and embedded preferences that are not going to go away no matter what the overall income taxation principle is. Beyond that, there is still a certain amount of money the government must collect to do business and changing the form in which it is taken would not seem to lower the pain very much.

### (i) The "Marginal" Rate of Tax and The "Effective" Rate of Tax

We talk a lot in this book and in this course about the tax base. The tax base refers to what is taxed and what is not taxed. That is indeed the most complicated aspect of the field. But it is also necessary to under-

**13.** See Nordhaus, "A Proposed Flat Tax for Fat Cats," New York Times, Nov. 28, 1982, p. F3 (criticizing the flat tax proposal of Stanford University Economists Robert Hall and Alvin Rabushka).

**14.** See note 13 above.

stand the tax rate structure and how it works. The key concepts here are the *marginal* rate of tax and the *effective* rate of tax. The *marginal* rate of tax refers to the tax on the last dollar of income that the taxpayer earns. The *effective* rate of tax refers to the proportion of the taxpayer's total income that he has to pay in tax. These two rates are not the same in a system of progressive taxation.

Take a gander at § 1(a) of your favorite Code. This sets forth the tax on married couples filing joint returns. This is by far the most common return filed. You see that as income goes up, the percentage applied to the higher amounts of income goes up. The lower amounts remain taxed at the same lower level. The percentages are the *marginal* rates of tax, that are applied to the top levels of a taxpayers income. The *effective* rate of tax is the average of the marginal rates as income moves up through the brackets. Thus, where the marginal rates are always rising, as in Section 1(a), the effective rate of tax is always less than the marginal rate of tax, since it is the weighted average of the previous lower marginal rates.

Our system of "progressive taxation," as described above, can be usefully compared with "proportional taxation." Under "proportional taxation," everyone would pay the same proportion of his income, say 10%. In a 10% proportional system obviously an individual with $1 million of taxable income pays more ($100,000) than a person with $30,000 of taxable income ($3,000). But in this proportional system both of these taxpayers have a marginal and an effective rate of 10%.

However, a "progressive" system bites harder. In a "progressive" system, the higher income individual not only pays more but pays a higher percentage of his income in tax. The effective rate is higher on the higher income individual. With a progressive system, the tax system is serving, to one degree or another, to redistribute the wealth.

We are presently in an era in which the rate structure is not very progressive. There have been times in the past when the marginal rate on very high amounts of income has been as high as 70% or 90%. Obviously, if marginal rates increase steeply, effective rates also go up but not as fast.

It should also be noted that the tax rates are "indexed" for inflation, see Sec. 1(f). As a person's income goes up, he would generally move up through the brackets, attracting a higher and higher marginal rate. But if the income increase is matched by an equal amount of inflation, then the person has not had a true increase in income and therefore it would seem to be unfair to hit him with a higher marginal rate of tax. The inflation adjustment rules of Sec. 1(f) take care of that problem.

These inflation adjustment rules, however, create problems of their own. If every financial transaction in the country were indexed for inflation, this would create an increased possibility of "hyper-inflation," as all transactions would "ratchet up" to keep up with inflation, thereby creating more inflation.

### (2) Problems With the Income Tax

Although the income tax is here to stay, it could be improved. A number of criticisms have been advanced concerning the workings of the income tax. These criticisms raise a wide range of difficult problems. What the income tax does to the economy and how it might be improved are questions which have provoked a rich debate.

### (a) Allocation of Resources: Imputed Income

At the loftiest level of discussion is the assertion that the income tax distorts the allocation of resources in the economy. The argument is that the income tax imposes a cost on income but not on leisure. So, people will tend to substitute leisure for work to an excessive degree. More generally, there is said to be a "deadweight loss" with regard to taxing money income and not imputed income. Here's an example of the argument:[15]

> *Example, deadweight loss caused by income tax:* Suppose that a paralegal can earn $50 per hour. That means that $50 per hour is the value that society places on his services. If his tax rate is, say, 40% (combined federal and state), he gets after taxes only $30 per hour. Suppose that a gardener charges $40 per hour. This is, again, the value that society places on those services. Assume that the paralegal can do his gardening just as fast and efficiently as the gardener. He does not mind doing it—at least not any more than working overtime as a paralegal. Given his after tax income, the paralegal will be better off to do his own gardening. He only gets $30 per hour for working as a paralegal. So why should he work an extra hour as a paralegal to earn $30 (after tax) in order to pay a gardener to work an hour at a cost of $40? He's better off not working overtime as a paralegal but rather doing his gardening. Society is the loser, though. Society will pay the paralegal $50 an hour to work as a paralegal. But he does not choose to do it. Rather, he chooses to do work that society values at $40 per hour. This is the "deadweight loss" to society imposed by the income tax. So the argument goes. This is called the *substitution effect* brought on by the income tax. Activities generating nontaxable imputed income are substituted for activities generating taxable income. Thus the income tax discourages the paralegal from working as a paralegal.
>
> *Comment* : If the paralegal were also taxed on his imputed income of working in his garden (that's a good one—the IRS collects tax when you putter around in your begonias), then this distortion would not occur. The after-tax "income" from gardening would be 60% of $40 or $24. That $24 is less than what the paralegal gets after tax if he works as a paralegal, $30. So the paralegal goes back to the office and hires the gardener.

**15.** See, e.g., Posner, Economic Analysis of Law, 2d Ed. 373–374 (1977); cf. Aaron and Pechman Eds., How Taxes Affect Economic Behavior, (Brookings, 1981).

*Comment:* This analysis is all right as far as it goes. Unfortunately, it does not go far enough. In addition to the *substitution effect* described in the example, there is also something called an *income effect.* The income effect says the paralegal wants to maintain a certain level of income. So if the paralegal is taxed on his money income from his job, he will work overtime to make up the difference. Got to keep up those car payments. Thus the income tax encourages working as a paralegal. The gardening doesn't make the car payments. The *income effect* might be as great or greater than the *substitution effect.* We don't know. As usual, in these theoretical discussions, there is no answer.

Also, if you really want to beat this discussion to death, there are many distortions in the economy in addition to the income tax: excise taxes, monopolies, license fees, collective bargaining agreements, tariffs, government price supports and subsidies. All of these (and there are many others) distort the true price of goods and services in the economy. They all therefore lead to a distortion in the allocation of resources of the economy. The important conclusion here is that it has been shown that elimination of one of these distortions, while the rest still remain, does not necessarily improve the allocation of resources in the economy and might well worsen it. *Thus if the distortions created by the income tax were eliminated but all of the other distortions remained, the allocation of resources in the economy would not necessarily be improved and might well be worsened.*[16]

Other similar criticisms of the income tax are fallacious for the same reason. For example, it is often asserted that the income tax distorts allocation of resources in the economy because it fails to tax the income from services of a housewife (or househusband). The argument is that the housewife is benefitting herself by doing her own housework and thus should be taxed upon the fair value of that income. Such a tax would, it is argued, eliminate the distortion that is involved in taxing income received from an outside job and not taxing income arising from

---

**16.** A full-fledged treatment of the subject of the allocation of resources in the economy is beyond the scope of this work, but putting the argument a little more technically: the economy is in an efficient condition when no resource can be reallocated and no product redistributed so as to make any one individual or business firm better off without making some other individual or business firm worse off. This is the condition of so-called Paretian Optimality, Pareto, Manuel d'Economie Politique (Paris: V. Giard and E. Briere, 1909). If there is one distortion, such as for example a tax on one commodity or an income tax, the Paretian conditions are not met, since relative prices of goods and services in the economy will not reflect their true economic price. Paretian optimality can only be reached by removal of the distortion. However, if there

are *several* distortions in the economy and they cannot all be removed, removal of *one* of the conditions will not necessarily move the economy toward Paretian optimality, and may indeed worsen the situation. This result was demonstrated by Lipsey and Lancaster, "The General Theory of Second Best", 24 Rev.Econ. 11 (1956); and see also Stiglitz and Boskin, "Some Lessons from the New Public Finance", 67 Am.Econ.Rev. 295, 298 (1977); Baumol and Bradford, "Optimal Departures from Marginal Cost Pricing", 60 Am.Econ.Rev. 265–283 (1970).

This conclusion illustrates the fallacy of "piecemeal welfare economics"—that is, suggesting that certain distortions in the economy should be removed because that will improve the allocation of resources in the economy, when in fact many distortions still remain in the economy.

performing household services.[17] If she were taxed on that income, though, then one would have to allow her various deductions for expenses such as mops, brooms and detergent for performing these services. A related problem is taxing the working wife (or working husband if the wife is the primary breadwinner) on her earnings and not allowing a deductions for paying for household help. The child care credit discussed in Chapter 10, is an attempt to give some recognition to this problem, but it is inadequate. Again, since there are many distortions in the economy which interact with each other in complex ways, it cannot be said *a priori* that elimination of this particular distortion would improve the overall allocation of resources in the economy; indeed it might well worsen it.[18] Moreover, once one starts down the slippery slope of imputed income, it is difficult to know when to stop. Giving oneself a shave, painting one's porch, shining one's shoes, doing one's own tax return, all generate "income" in that sense. It is not to be expected that the Commissioner of Internal Revenue will be pushing the public to pay tax on these items any time soon.

This issue has policy implications. If the income tax is seen as truly a tax on all income, leading to distortions in the economy if all income is not reached, then great effort might be made to reach all income. Such efforts may raise severe administrative problems but it might be deemed worth undergoing these administrative problems to avoid any "distortion." See ¶ 4.05(4) for extensive discussion of the treatment of imputed income from owner-occupied housing and the related important concept of whether personal residences can be depreciated.[19]

**17.** See, e.g., Marsh, "The Taxation of Imputed Income", 58 Pol.Sci.Q. 514 (1943), Posner, note 16 supra at 374.

**18.** Note 15 supra. In addition to the reasons advanced in the text for not taxing imputed income from household services, such a tax raises the practical problem of how it would be paid. Since the income the housewife generates from performing household services is not in monetary form, she could have difficulty coming up with the cash to pay the tax. One can easily imagine an outraged housewife faced with a $1,500 tax bill on the imputed income she received for doing her own housework—to satisfy some economist's idea about allocation of resources. She could well argue that if the Service is going to tax her on this kind of income, she can pay the same way, and she can offer to come down and sweep out the offices of the Internal Revenue Service once a month.

**19.** In this note we can say a little more about imputed income of owner-occupied housing. It is often urged that it should be taxed, because if the house were rented out, it would generate taxable rental income. By living in the house the owner receives tax-free rental income (i.e., his own rent that he pays to himself). Such imputed income, it is argued, should be taxed to eliminate the "distortion" in favor of owner-occupied housing over rental housing. See, e.g., Reforming the Federal Tax Structure, Commission to Revise the Tax Structure, (Fund for Public Policy Research,) 18, (1973). But taxing imputed rent raises the difficult problem of valuation and puts a burden on the taxpayer who does not have the cash to pay the tax. Moreover, if such a tax were imposed, one would also have to allow the homeowner to deduct his/her expenses of keeping the house up, such as maintenance and depreciation. The British imposed a tax on imputed income from owner-occupied housing until 1963, when the tax was abandoned due to difficulties presented in valuation. See Goode, The Individual Income Tax 121 (1964). Compare Helvering v. Independent Life Insurance Co., 292 U.S. 371, 378–379, 54 S.Ct. 758, 759–760, 78 L.Ed. 1311 (1934) (*dicta* that taxing imputed income from owner-occupied housing is unconstitutional as being a direct tax requiring apportionment and not protected by the Sixteenth Amendment, Cf. ¶ 1.01 supra).

However, once it is realized that the way the income tax is imposed cannot have great significance for the overall allocation of resources in the economy, the income tax can be seen for what it really is: a government device for raising revenues by taxing *some forms* of income. Those forms of income which are taxed are generally those which it is comparatively easy to reach, for example wages (which can be withheld against) and market transactions in property (which do not present problems of valuation or liquidity and which are reported). But any attempt to reach novel forms of income solely for the purpose of improving the overall allocation of resources in the economy seems futile and a waste of effort.[20]

### (b) Comprehensive Tax Base

The preceding discussion has shown that allocation of resources in the economy is not helpful as a criterion for evaluating or improving the income tax. But can the criterion of fairness be usefully employed? It would seem reasonable to argue that people with about the same income should pay about the same tax, so called horizontal equity.[21] But what is income? Unless it is possible to ascertain what constitutes income it is difficult to determine whether the income tax is fair.

Those who criticize the income tax as being unfair usually start with a list of items which seem clearly to constitute income but which are, for various reasons, exempted from tax. Examples of items exempted from tax include interest from municipal and state obligations, income earned from foreign sources by U.S. citizens living in foreign countries, much of social security and railroad retirement payments, and employee death benefits. All these can be criticized as undermining the fairness of the tax system, since they all seem to constitute income.[22] Moreover, certain

---

**20.** Attempts to improve the overall allocation of resources in the economy should be distinguished from attempts to use the tax system to encourage certain specific kinds of behavior. The former are futile for the reasons stated in the text. The latter, such as accelerated depreciation (see ¶ 6.02(12)) are effective in encouraging the desired activity for the very reason that they *do* distort the taxpayer's choice in favor of the desired activity. However, for the reasons stated above, such "distortions" do not necessarily worsen the overall allocation of resources in the economy; they may indeed improve it.

**21.** It is also relatively reasonable to argue that the graduated rate structure is fair, that people with higher incomes should pay a greater percentage of that income to support the government. There are those, however, who would strongly disagree, see Friedman, Capitalism and Freedom 174 (1962). Cf. Blum and Kalven, The Uneasy Case for Progressive Taxation (1953); Steurle and Hartzmark, "Individual Income

Taxation 1947–1979," 34 Nat'l Tax J. 145 (1981); Blum, "Revisiting the Uneasy Case for Progressive Taxation," 60 Taxes 16 (1982).

It would, however, be fallacious to argue that the progressive rate structure is undesirable because it distorts the allocation of resources in the economy. See note 16, supra and accompanying text.

**22.** The most widely accepted definition of income is the so-called Haig–Simons definition, which is: "Personal income may be defined as the algebraic sum of (1) the market value of rights exercised in consumption and (2) the change in the value of the store of property rights between the beginning and end of the period in question," H. Simons, Personal Income Taxation at 50, 61–62 (1938). Another way of stating it is to say that any item which increases the net worth of the taxpayer is income. If this approach were followed, a vast array of exclusions, exemptions and special deductions in the Code would be abolished.

other items are treated favorably even though they do not escape taxation entirely, such as a lower rate on long-term capital gains,[23] or delay in payment of tax on certain transactions in property.[24] Also some deductions—such as for rapid depreciation[25] or intangible drilling costs[26] —may be argued to be unjustifiably attractive. All of these are ways in which the income tax has been regarded by critics as unfair.[27]

However, the goal of creating a comprehensive tax base and imposing a tax on all income is virtually impossible to reach. There is, for example, a vast array of federal, state and local government programs which benefit many taxpayers and therefore constitute income to them in an economic sense. These are programs such as rent subsidies, road building and maintenance, Medicare and Medicaid protection, government guarantees of loans to businesses or individuals, government scholarships and fellowships, garbage collection and so on and on. Moreover, there are more public benefits, such as dams, providing cheap electric power, flood control, and recreation, as well as schools, public institutions of higher learning, libraries, national defense. All of these confer benefits. All of these are income. But most of these are not likely subjects for imposition of tax, because to do so is either impossible or unpalatable.[28]

In addition, there are many other untaxed items of income, which do not emanate from the government: imputed income (the rental value of consumer durables owned by the taxpayer, or services performed by the taxpayer for himself[29]), transfer payments from private charities or foundations, proceeds of life insurance,[30] gifts and bequests,[31] appreciation in the value of assets that have not been sold.[32] Most of these too are unlikely candidates for imposition of tax because it would be unpalatable or impractical.[33]

Beyond even this there are non-pecuniary benefits in some jobs—e.g. the opportunity to be creative, or to exercise power—which are not taxed, although they may confer great psychic income. In contrast, the

**23.** ¶ 4.06.

**24.** This would include unrealized appreciation in value of property held (see ¶ 4.02), stock received in corporate reorganizations, (see §§ 368, 354, 355, 356, 351, D. Posin, Corporate Tax Planning: Takeovers, Leveraged Buyouts and Restructurings, Chapters 6–13, 1990, and certain other transactions in property see ¶ 4.05).

**25.** ¶ 6.02(12) infra.

**26.** ¶ 6.02(13) infra.

**27.** See Tax Revision Compendium of Papers on Broadening the Tax Base, House Committee on Ways & Means (1959); Blum, "Federal Income Tax Reform—Twenty Questions", 41 Taxes 672 (1963); Galvin, "Progress in Substantive Tax Reform", 1965 U.So.Cal.Tax Inst. 1; Blueprints for Basic Tax Reform (U.S. Treasury Dep't,

1977); Pechman, Federal Tax Policy (3rd Ed.1977).

**28.** See Bittker, "A 'Comprehensive Tax Base' As a Goal of Income Tax Reform", 80 Harv.L.Rev. 925 (1967).

**29.** See R. Goode, The Individual Income Tax, 117–125 (revised edition 1976). See also note 17 supra.

**30.** See ¶ 3.06 infra, for proceeds of life insurance.

**31.** ¶ 3.08 infra.

**32.** ¶ 4.02 infra.

**33.** See Bittker, note 28 supra, Other problems, discussed by Bittker, with creating a comprehensive tax base include treatment of various deductions, the installment method of accounting, and the extent to which the tax system should take account of family relationships.

person who has a very unattractive or hazardous job and is paid a high wage to make up for it is fully taxed on that high wage.[34]

In view of all these considerations it seems impossible to create a truly fair income tax, which reaches *all* income, and which imposes the same tax on people with about the same income. Does this mean that any attempt to make the income tax more fair is futile? Is this situation like the question of allocation of resources in the economy? That is to say is there any guarantee that any single step taken to make the income tax more fair will not, through interactions too complex to trace, make it less fair? There seems to be no study that has answered this question.[35] It is possible that any one step taken to make the income tax more fair might make it less fair because of the sheer complexity of interactions in the system.[36]

Does this then mean that no attempt should be made to make the income tax more fair? Is fairness, like allocation of resources, not useful as a guide for acting on the income tax? There does seem to be a fundamental difference between allocation of resources and fairness. Allocation of resources in the economy is not of significance to the public. The public does not grasp that concept and is not interested in it. The public is, however, very interested and believes it understands fairness.[37] Since the success of the self-assessment system ultimately depends on the confidence of the public that the income tax is roughly fair, that confidence must be maintained (or revived).

Therefore, steps to improve the apparent fairness (as opposed to improving the actual fairness which is perhaps impossible) of the income tax seem justified. The public is relatively easily satisfied in this matter. It does not demand that each person be taxed on his share of income from national defense. But the public may well demand that interest from state and municipal bonds be taxed or that tax shelters be limited.

As discussed in the preceding section, the income tax is a device for raising government revenues by taxing some forms of income: those that are relatively easily reached, visible, and relatively easily valued. Within that limited range of items of income there may be some items that seem unjustifiably exempt from taxation. They should be subject to tax to maintain the public's confidence in the system. That is why even though it is true that a comprehensive tax base cannot ultimately be achieved,[38] those pressing for the changes in the income tax that concern the public are embarked on a worthwhile course.[39]

---

**34.** See Friedman, note 21 supra, at 162.

**35.** Cf. Musgrave, "In Defense of an Income Concept," 81 Harv.L.Rev. 44 (1967).

**36.** See Bittker, "Comprehensive Income Taxation: A Response," 81 Harv. L.Rev. 1032, 1043 (1968), and see Bittker, Note 33 supra, at 983.

**37.** See e.g. P. Stern, The Rape of the Taxpayer (1972).

**38.** See Bittker, note 28 supra and accompanying text.

**39.** Cf. Galvin, "More on Boris Bittker and the Comprehensive Tax Base: The Practicalities of the Tax Reform and the ABA's CSTR:", 81 Harv.L.Rev. 1016 (1968).

Public consensus as to what is fair is, therefore, the touchstone. Although there is a perfect system that imposes a tax on all income, that system is not reachable in this world. As to this world, Professor Boris Bittker seems right when he says, "(T)he income tax structure cannot be discovered, but must be constructed."[40] And it must be constructed by working through a number of controversial issues so that the appearance of fairness can be attained even though actual fairness probably cannot be reached.

### (c)  Tax Expenditures

An important aspect of the debate on the apparent fairness of the income tax is the concept of tax expenditures. The concept involves three components: (1) the regressive effect of deductions, exclusions and certain other provisions which benefit taxpayers; (2) compilation of a list of deductions, exclusions and other beneficial provisions which are not "necessary" to arriving at true taxable income; and (3) an estimate of revenue loss from these "unnecessary" provisions. Although proponents of the tax expenditure concept tend to advance these components together,[41] they can be regarded separately.

With respect to the first component, a clear contribution of the tax expenditure concept to the debate on the fairness of the income tax is highlighting the fact that deductions, exclusions and certain other favorable provisions are regressive in that they benefit those in higher brackets more than those in lower brackets. For example, if tax-exempt interest from a state or municipal bond (to take a favorite whipping-boy) in the amount of $100 is received by a taxpayer in the 50 percent bracket, that exemption has saved the taxpayer $50 in tax liability. If that same $100 of exempt interest is received by a taxpayer in the 15 percent bracket, the exemption has saved the taxpayer $15 in tax liability.

Moreover, the tax expenditure analysis would go further to make the point that this result is functionally equivalent to selling bonds with *taxable* interest but making available high yield bonds to taxpayers in high brackets and low yield bonds to taxpayers in low brackets. Thus if the interest on state and municipal bonds were taxable, the taxpayer in the 50 percent bracket would have to receive $200 of taxable interest to end up with $100 after taxes, whereas, the taxpayer in the 15 percent bracket would need to receive only $118 of taxable interest to wind up with $100 after taxes. If both taxpayers have bought a bond for $2,360, the taxpayer receiving $118 of interest has a 5 percent rate of return; the taxpayer receiving $200 of interest has a rate of return of 8.5 percent. This is, the proponents of the tax expenditure concept argue, a bizarre result and dramatizes the inequity of excluding state and municipal bond interest from taxation.

---

**40.**  Bittker, note 28, supra at 985.

**41.**  See Surrey, "Tax Expenditures as a Device for Implementing Government Policy: A Comparison with Direct Govern-ment Expenditures," 83 Harv.L.Rev. 705 (1970); S. Surrey, Pathways to Tax Reform (1973).

A similar analysis shows the regressive effect of deductions. A deduction of $100 of home mortgage interest saves the taxpayer in the 50 percent bracket $50 in tax liability and saves the taxpayer in the 15 percent bracket $15 in tax liability. This is functionally equivalent to not allowing the deduction at all but paying a government subsidy to those with home mortgages. The terms of the hypothetical subsidy would be that those in high brackets get large subsidies and those in low brackets get low subsidies. Again, according to the proponents of the tax expenditures concept, this is a bizarre outcome.[42]

This analysis is correct and exceedingly interesting as far as it goes, but the question is what is to be done about it. This regressive effect arises inevitably from any exclusion or deduction because of the graduated rate structure. But as the discussion of the comprehensive tax base, supra, has demonstrated, it is impossible to include in taxable income all items of income in an economic sense. Imputed income from owner-occupied housing, income from unrealized appreciation in assets held, or income from national defense are, for various good reasons, not included as taxable income. Their exclusion also inevitably benefits those in high brackets more than those in low brackets. Thus, given a graduated rate structure, the only way to avoid completely the regressive effects described above is to impose a tax on a comprehensive base of all items of economic income (and to allow only the most narrowly defined business deductions). This is obviously an impossibility.

The proponents of the tax expenditure concept do not, however, advocate the elusive goal of a comprehensive tax base.[43] Rather, as the second component in the tax expenditure concept, they compile a list of *some* deductions, exclusions, and other provisions. Such a list is now published annually in The United States Government's Budget.[44] A sampling of just a few of the many items included on the list is exclusion of interest on state and municipal bonds, deductibility of interest on home mortgages, deductibility of charitable contributions, immediate deductions of research and development expenditures and so forth.[45] The implication of such a compilation is to suggest that some of these provisions should be reconsidered and perhaps abolished in light of their regressivity.[46]

**42.** Id. See also H.R.Rep. No. 94–1016 (April 7, 1976) for a further discussion of the state and local bond interest exemption and proposals for change.

**43.** For a very worthwhile exchange on this matter see Bittker, "Accounting for Federal 'Tax Subsidies' in the National Budget," 22 Nat'l Tax J. 244 (1969); Surrey and Hellmuth, "The Tax Expenditure Budget—Response to Professor Bittker," 22 Nat'l Tax J. 528 (1969); Bittker "The Tax Expenditure Budget—A Reply to Professors Surrey and Hellmuth," 22 Nat'l Tax J. 538 (1969).

**44.** As required by the Congressional Budget Act of 1974, Pub.L. 93–344, July 12, 1974; 88 Stat. 297. See also J. Pechman, Ed., Setting National Priorities: The 1979 Budget (Bookings 1978) 315–319; Congressional Budget Office Report, Tax Expenditures: Current Issues and Five Year Budget Projections.

**45.** See Special Analyses "G", Budget of the United States Government.

**46.** Surrey, note 41 supra. In some cases, according to the proponents of the tax expenditure concept, the abolished exclusion or deduction could be replaced by a system of government subsidies which

The problem with this list is that it is incomplete, as indeed it must be unless the proponents wish to support a comprehensive tax base. But the proponents of the tax expenditure concept explicitly do not wish to be viewed as advocating a comprehensive tax base.[47] Since therefore the list of tax expenditures is incomplete it lacks the moral force that a list which purports to extirpate all regressive exclusions and deductions would have.[48] Why then is the incomplete list compiled in the Budget or compiled by proponents of the tax expenditure concept better than any other list or, indeed, better than no list?[49]

The third component of the tax expenditure concept involves attaching dollar estimates of revenue loss to each of the tax expenditures listed. The items are broken down by the Budget into various categories, such as Commerce and Housing, Health, National Defense.[50] The theory of this tax expenditure budget is that it facilitates comparison of tax expenditure amounts with ordinary direct federal government expenditures for these same categories. The conclusion drawn is that the tax expenditure amounts are very large, sometimes equalling or even exceeding direct expenditures for these categories.[51] Presumably the implication is that tax expenditures are a greater drain on the Treasury than is generally realized.

However, these dollar estimates of tax expenditures are arrived at under unrealistic assumptions: It is assumed that if income from an excluded activity were suddenly subject to tax, the activity would continue at the same level; it is also assumed that if deductible expenditures were suddenly not deductible they would continue unabated. These estimates also ignore the profound effect on the economy of removing all of these tax expenditures simultaneously. For all of these reasons the estimates of the revenue loss from the Budget's list of tax expenditures are probably greatly overstated.[52]

Although the Budget in a several page discussion acknowledges these methodological shortcomings,[53] the dollar estimates continue to be published. One consequence of publishing such overstated estimates is that they tend to be picked up and used by popular writers who fail to understand the significance of the estimates.[54]

would accomplish the same goal as the exclusion or deduction without its regressive affect. See, e.g., McDaniel, "Federal Matching Grants for Charitable Contributions: A Substitute for the Income Tax Deduction," 27 Tax Law Rev. 377 (1972).

**47.**　Surrey and Hellmuth, note 43 supra, at 530.

**48.**　Cf. Blum note 27, supra.

**49.**　See Bittker, "The Tax Expenditure Budget—A Reply to Professors Surrey and Hellmuth," note 43, supra. See also, Andrews, "Personal Deductions in an Ideal Income Tax," 86 Harv.L.Rev. 309 (1972).

**50.**　See note 45, supra.

**51.**　Surrey, note 41, supra at 711.

**52.**　See e.g. Feldstein, "The Effects of the Charitable Deduction on Contributions: I and II", 28 Nat. Tax J. 81 and 209 (1975) for an analysis that suggests the Treasury's tax expenditure budget overestimates the revenue loss of the charitable contribution by more than 40 percent; see also Stiglitz and Boskin, note 16 supra at 297.

**53.**　Note 45, supra. The Budget has in recent years attempted to correct for this problem.

**54.**　See, e.g., Stern, note 37 supra, 146; Newfield and Greenfield, A Populist Manifesto 100 (1972); Cowan, "Washington and

In summary, the tax expenditure concept is subject to some methodological complexity. Notwithstanding that, it is a tool that usefully highlights the effect of various tax provisions on the overall budget process. The Budget's estimate of revenue loss attributable to tax expenditures is probably too large.[55]

### (d) Complexity

One of the most outstanding features of the present income tax is its complexity. As indicated in ¶ 1.01(2), this complexity arises from many forces: the fact that the income tax is imposed on a complex society, the impact of special interests, the impact of those who would "reform" the tax system, the impact of planners—who would use the Code to foster "sociably desirable behavior," the fact that the income tax is used as an instrument of national economic policy. Thus it is not surprising that the income tax is complex; it could not be otherwise. From this perspective it is difficult moreover to say that the income tax is "too complex" or that it is more complex than it "should" be. Obviously there are very real reasons for the income tax having evolved to its present complex state; no one is purposefully seeking a complex income tax as an end in itself.

Despite the fact that the income tax's complexity is understandable, it seems fair to say that the income tax is a deeply troubled system. The taxpayer and his advisor face annually a dizzying array of inclusions, deductions, credits, and other specialized computations and problems. While there may be good or understandable reasons for most of the provisions in the income tax, the present-day income tax, taken as a whole, is a statute that no rational person would draft as a method for collecting the nation's income taxes.[56]

Business—Closer Look at Tax Loopholes," New York Times, January 26, 1978, p. D3. Cf. Bittker, "Tax 'Loopholes' and Political Rhetoric", 71 Mich.L.Rev. 1099, (1973) for a discussion of the effect on the public of the rhetoric of the tax expenditure debate.

**55.** See in addition to the other materials cited, Woodworth, "General Policy Considerations Affecting the Choice of a Particular Tax Base," 30 National Tax Journal 225 (1977); Uilman, "Tax Policy" 29 Nat'l Tax J. 2 (1976); Thower "Preserving the Integrity of the Federal Tax System," 33 NYU Institute on Federal Taxation 707 (1975); Congressional Budget Office, Tax Expenditures: Five Year Budget Projections for Fiscal Years 1982–1986 (1981). For a very effective defense of the tax expenditure concept and description of its uses, see Surrey and McDaniel "The Tax Expenditure Concept: Current Developments and Emerging Issues," 20 Bost.Coll., Ind. & Comm'l Law Rev. 225 (1979); see also Kahn, "Accelerated Depreciation—Tax Expenditure or Proper Allowance for Measuring Net Income," 78 Mich.L.Rev. 1 (1979);

Cohen, "Tax Expenditures in Troubled Times: The Failure of Tax Incentives for Low Income Housing," 30 Univ. of S.Cal.L.Instit. on Fed'l Taxation 971 (1978).

**56.** There is a voluminous literature on the subject of Income Tax complexity. See, e.g. Eustice, "Tax Complexity and the Tax Practitioner," 8 Tax Adviser 27 (1977); Bittker, "Tax Reform and Tax Simplification," 29 Univ. of Miami Law Rev. 1 (1974); New York State Bar Assoc., Tax Section, "A Report on Complexity and the Income Tax," 27 Tax Law Rev. 325 (1972); Surrey, "The Federal Tax Legislative Process," 31 Record of New York City Bar Assoc. 515 (1976); Ginsburg, "Tax Simplification—A Practitioner's View," 26 Nat'l Tax J. 317 (1973); Comm'r of Internal Revenue Kurtz, "Tax Simplification: Some Observations from a Retrospective View of the United States Experience," Address before the Eleventh General Assembly of the Inter-American Center for Tax Administrators, reprinted in 123 Cong.Rec. S 8349 (May 23, 1977); "Evaluation of the Proposed Model Comprehensive Income Tax," Special Com-

*(e)  Recovery of Capital: A Major Theme in the Field*

*(i)  Methods of Recovering Capital*

One of the major problems running throughout the field of federal income taxation is the problem of allowing a taxpayer to recover his initial investment in an enterprise before taxing him on the profits from it. This sounds like a simple problem, but in fact it is of immense dimension. If you can see it whole and recognize the problem every time it crops up, that will help you a great deal.

Consider the problem with the following example: Taxpayer Matilda purchases a single premium life annuity. She pays $200,000 for it when she is 65 years old. The terms of the annuity are that she immediately begins receiving annual payments from it for her lifetime. The payments will be based on the taxpayer's life expectancy at age 65. Let us say that is 20 years—so that the taxpayer is expected to live to 85.[57] The payments made for 20 years will be made out of this $200,000 fund. As the payments are made, the amounts remaining in the fund will grow at 9% per year compounded. This is an after-tax interest rate.[58] A computer (not you in the coffee room) can calculate the annual payment each year that will exhaust the fund after 20 years though the remaining amounts in the fund continue to grow as the payments are made. That annuity payment so calculated is $20,100 per year.

Let us say, to keep the facts simple, that Matilda dies right on her 85th birthday. Thus the payments go for exactly 20 years.[59] Here is an

mittee on Simplification, Section of Taxation, American Bar Association, The Tax Lawyer Vol. 32, Number 3, Spring 1979. Berger, "Simple Interest and Complex Taxes," 81 Col.L.Rev. 217 (1981) (this article contains a graph showing the number of lines devoted to the interest deduction increasing.)

As several of these commentators point out, tax complexity tends to breed several effects, including "Gresham's Law" in which the bad tax practitioners tend to drive out the good tax practitioners on the theory that why should a client pay for expensive tax advice when no one can understand the law anyway. A second effect of complexity is the "Tax Lottery," or the taxpayer view that his return is unlikely to be selected for audit; if it is, the agent may not understand there is a doubtful item; if he does understand it, he or his superiors may be persuaded to compromise; if the matter goes to court, the government attorney may not understand it or the judge (or jury!) may not understand it; and then there can be appeal, etc. Ultimately if the taxpayer loses, he generally only pays what he originally owed as tax plus interest. This is in Professor Eustice's, supra, phrase the "Tax-Tag," or "Catch Me if You Can" approach taken by many taxpayers and fostered by complexity of the Code.

**57.**  It is true that the life expectancy of a female when she is born is about 77. However, once the female reaches 65, the life expectancy stretches out somewhat.

**58.**  The after-tax rate is assumed here in order to keep the numbers straightforward for purposes of the discussion. It can sometimes be the case that amounts set aside in this fashion will compound at the pre-tax rate, if they are in a pension fund for example. See Prologue.

**59.**  In a life annuity what the annuitant buys is a guarantee that the payments will go for his or her life, whatever that lifespan may prove to be. The insurance companies calculate the amount of the payment based on mortality tables. Thus if Matilda lived longer than 20 years she would continue to receive payments and get what is known in the business as a "mortality gain." If she died in less than 20 years she would undergo a "mortality loss." So that we do not fog up the discussion in the text with this, let us assume she lives her exact statistical life expectancy. For a complete discussion of annuities, see Chapter 3. See also the discussion of the *Drescher* case in Chapter 2.

interesting point: What is the total amount Matilda receives under this arrangement? Obviously it is 20 times $20,100 or $402,000. I put it to you, this is interesting. She puts in $200,000. She starts getting payments immediately and ultimately she gets a total of $402,000. Where does the extra money come from? As pointed out above, while she is getting payments, the money remaining in the account is growing. Now we get a tax question (at last).

Here is our question: How do we deduct the $200,000 cost of this transaction against the $402,000 payoff. The taxpayer has made an investment here and it has turned a profit. She put in $200,000 and when she reaches age 85, the deal finally pays off a total of $402,000. Therefore it is a profit of $202,000. If we assume a combined federal and state tax rate of 40% (33% federal and 7% state), we have a tax due on this deal of 40% of $202,000 profit or $80,800 tax. *When* we deduct the cost will not affect the overall amount of tax. The profit is always going, ultimately, to be $202,000 taxed at a 40% rate. *When* we deduct the cost will, however, affect the timing of when we pay the $80,800 tax. As we know from having been clubbed on the subject in the Prologue, *when* that $80,800 is paid has major dollar implications for the taxpayer.

Let us consider the various possibilities for deducting the cost of this annuity. The payments are coming in every year for 20 years. They are therefore presumptively taxable in full unless the taxpayer is taking a deduction of the cost of the deal to offset some or all of the payment received. So how should we time the deductions of the cost of the annuity? The theoretical possibilities are:

1) Allow the deduction of the entire cost immediately upon entering into the deal: *Immediate Deduction or "Expensing*[60]*";*

2) Allow the deductions up to the amount received on the deal each year (until the full cost of the deal has been deducted) then tax the remaining payments in full: *Open Treatment* (see also ¶ 8.03 discussing the *Logan* case);

3) Prorate the deduction of the cost of the premium over the 20 years that the annuity pays out: *Installment Treatment* ;

4) Take the deduction at the end of the 20 years after the payout has stopped: *Stupid Treatment.*

*Comment:* I say this last approach is stupid, because there is no really good reason for recovery of cost this way and no one has ever suggested that it be followed (except me of course).[61] I bring it up

**60.** We use the term "expensing" to indicate that the cost of the deal is treated as an "expense," which is to say it is immediately deductible. This is contrasted with a "capital expenditure" which is not immediately deductible (it is "capitalized"). The deduction of the capital expense may then be spread out over time (see Chapter 6).

**61.** The taxation of corporate dividends often follows the Stupid Treatment. When dividends are paid, they are often taxed in full, with no offsetting deduction of basis. Only when the stock is sold is the cost or basis of the stock deducted from the amount realized on the sale: this constitutes Stupid Treatment. However, corporate distributions of cash to shareholders

not because it is a serious candidate for the way to handle this transaction but because it actually provides a basic insight into what is going on in the deal.

5) Attribute most of the early payments to taxable interest and a small amount to non-taxable principal, with these amounts gradually altering in proportion over the term of the annuity: *Loan Amortization Treatment*. This is like a basic home mortgage. This treats the premium payment as though it were a loan from Matilda to the insurance company. It certainly looks like a loan, with the insurance company undoubtedly paying Matilda back interest and principal.

6) Deem the present value of each payment to be its cost. Deduct that cost from each payment as it comes in: *Economically Accurate Treatment*. This method is a sophisticated method carrying present value analysis to its extreme conclusion. It is by far the most economically accurate method. Naturally no one dreams of using it.

For pedagogical reasons I'd like to look at these methods in a particular order. Let us look first at alternative number 4), *Stupid Treatment*. The reason this treatment is stupid is that there is really no tax principle that justifies it. If the cost is paid at the beginning of the deal, and amounts are received over 20 years from the deal, then there is no reason to defer the deduction until the end of the deal. Nevertheless, *Stupid Treatment* helps us to understand the problem of recovery of capital. So let us see what happens under it.

There is, as we have calculated, a $202,000 gain at the end of the transaction. If we (stupidly) take the deduction for the cost of the transaction at the end of the deal, then Matilda will be taxable in full on each of the $20,100 payments as they come in each year. At a 40% rate, that produces a tax on each payment of $8,040. Thus the net cash flow is $20,100 − $8,040 = $12,060 each year. In the 20th year, Matilda also gets a $200,000 deduction, which saves her $80,000 in taxes.[62] Note that the total amount of taxes Matilda pays is still the same $80,800 that we calculated before. Matilda is paying tax of $8,040 for 20 years or $160,800. Matilda then saves $80,000 in taxes the last year so that her net tax is $160,800 − $80,000 = $80,800.

Let us now consider then what happens to Matilda on a *cash-flow basis* under *Stupid Treatment*. On a cash-flow basis, she gets $12,060 a year (after taxes) for 20 years. In the 20th year she gets $80,000 (from

are not always taxed when paid. The distributions are only taxed if they are "out of" earnings and profits of the company. If the distribution occurs when the company has no earnings and profits, it is treated as a recovery of capital and not taxed. §§ 301(c), 312, 316.

**62.** This assumes that Matilda has enough other income that she remains in the 40% marginal (federal and state) bracket even after taking this large deduction.

The astute reader may also point out that in the 20th year that deduction of $200,000 more than offsets the $20,100 of income in that year. That is true and for computational purposes I could treat the 20th year as a net deduction of $179,900. However it is mathematically the same to treat the two cash flows separately and it is clearer conceptually to do so.

taxes saved). So what is the present value of this deal to Matilda? It is clearly the present value of $12,060 per year for 20 years plus the present value of $80,000 twenty years from now. All of this is calculated at our assumed interest rate of 9%. Firing up the computer, we find that the present value of $12,060 per year for 20 years is $120,000. The present value of $80,000 twenty years from now is $14,300. Thus, the total *present value* of *Stupid Treatment* is $120,000 + $14,300 = $134,300. Let's see how that compares to some of our other possibilities.

Let us take next alternative number 3), prorating the deduction of the cost of the premium over the 20 years that the annuity pays out: *Installment Treatment*. Unlike *Stupid Treatment*, prorating has good logic behind it. It involves matching the deductions of the deal over time with the income of the deal over time.[63] To do that, then we divide $200,000 by 20 years, which gives us $10,000 per year. We subtract that $10,000 from the $20,100 annual payment. This yields us a taxable gain of $10,100 per year.[64] And what is the tax Matilda pays? That is 40% of $10,100 or $4,040. Let's just keep checking ourselves. What is $4,040 times 20—i.e. the annual tax times the number of years it is paid? Turns out it is $80,800. So Matilda is still paying the same amount in tax as in *Stupid Treatment*.

Let's take a look at the *cash flow* results of the *Installment Treatment*. This one is easy to do; as a cash matter Matilda is receiving $20,100 per year less a tax of $4,040 per year. Thus the net cash flow per year is $20,100 − $4,040 = $16,060 per year. What is the present value of that? The *present value* of $16,060 per year for 20 years is $159,800. This is substantially more than the $134,300 of *Stupid Treatment*.

Let us now look at alternative 2), allow the deductions up to the amount received on the deal each year (until the full cost of the deal has been deducted): *Open Treatment*.[65] What this means is that as the $20,100 comes in each year, the $200,000 basis or cost of the annuity is taken against each $20,100 until the $200,000 is exhausted. After the $200,000 cost is exhausted, there is of course no more deduction. The effect is that there is no tax at all on the earlier payments until the $200,000 cost deduction is exhausted. The $200,000 taken against the $20,100 per year means that for the first 9 years there is no tax on the $20,100 per year. After 9 years $180,900 of the $200,000 is exhausted. Thus $19,100 is left to apply to the $20,100 in the tenth year. Applying

---

**63.** In the major area of depreciation, we see the installment or proration method being used. It is called straight line depreciation. So-called accelerated depreciation is a variation of the proration method except that the deductions are "front-loaded" using various formulas (see Chapter 6). See also ¶ 8.03 on deferred payment sales, which is in effect what we are talking about here.

**64.** Just to check our work (as we did in junior high school algebra) we find that a

profit of $10,100 per year for 20 years = 20 × $10,100 = $202,000. So we have got the right amount of profit.

**65.** "Open Treatment," especially for property sold for payments to be received in the future, has historically been a part of the tax law, although it is not widely used today. See Chapter 8, and the discussion there of Burnet v. Logan, 283 U.S. 404, 51 S.Ct. 550, 75 L.Ed. 1143 (1931).

that means that $1,000 in the tenth year is subject to tax. The tax is 40%. Thus after nine years of tax-free receipt of $20,100 payments there is a $400 tax in the tenth year. In years 11 through 20 the payments are taxed in full. Thus in years 11 through 20, the tax is 40% of $20,100, or $8,040. Thus the after tax payments received in years 11 through 20 are $20,100 − $8,040 = $12,060. Let us check on the total amount of tax paid. It is $400 plus 10 × $8,040. That is $400 + $80,400 = $80,800. So once again we are on the money with the same amount of tax being paid as in the other above alternatives.

Let us look at the *cash flow* results of the *Open Treatment*. For the first 9 years, Matilda pays no tax on the $20,100 payments received, so there is $20,100 for years 1 through 9. In year 10 the net cash flow is the $20,100 less the $400 tax or $19,700. In years 11 through 20 the net after tax cash flow as computed in the preceding paragraph is $12,060. The *present value* of this stream of cash payments is $161,500. This is more interesting than you might think. Since the open treatment involves more up-front deductions than the prorated treatment it produces a more attractive result. But the difference is not great. It is only about $1,700 on our numbers. This is only 0.8% of the profit on the deal. The tax on that at the 40% rate is only 0.32% of the deal. This minor difference is not due to anything odd in our numbers. Rather, the reason that the difference is not that great is that the two methods are rather similar in pattern even though they are very different in concept. Both methods just spread out the cost deduction. They just do so in modestly different ways. In order to gain this miniscule amount of tax, the statute requires us to go through the very complex installment method of reporting rather than the much simpler open method.

What makes this interesting is that the Service and the statute require the much more complex installment method to be used on transactions such as the sale of property for payments to be received over time (see Chapter 8). The conventional wisdom is that the open treatment is much more favorable to taxpayers than the installment method. In fact, our present value analysis demonstrates that the difference between the two methods is *de minimis*. In that event, given the great complexity of the installment method of reporting gain on sales of property for future payments, it would seem that the installment method of reporting is a good candidate for repeal. Repeal of § 453, the installment method of reporting, would disappoint many who enjoy its elegant workings. But, as our analysis has shown, we are apparently wasting our time with it.[66]

Let us turn to alternative 1), allow the deduction of the cost immediately upon entering into the deal: *Immediate Deduction or "Expensing."* Under this method, Matilda deducts $200,000 the year she acquires the policy. This $200,000 deduction saves her 40% of that

---

**66.** You should be aware that I am in a minority of one in thinking the installment method is a waste of time. Everybody else seems to think it's a great idea, but I don't think the numbers bear that out. For further discussion of the installment method, see ¶ 8.03(2).

amount or $80,000 in taxes right away. Having then deducted her full cost, she pays tax in full on the 20 payments.[67]

From a *cash flow* standpoint, here is how *Immediate Deduction* shakes out. In the first year there is $80,000 from tax savings. Also in years 1 through 20 there is a payment of $20,100 which is subject to a 40% tax. As we have calculated, that tax is $8,040. Thus the after-tax cash flow with respect to the annual payments is $20,100 − $8,040 = $12,060, as we have calculated before. Thus the *present value* of this deal equals $80,000 plus the present value of $12,060 per year for 20 years, with a 9% interest rate. That turns out to be $80,000 + $120,000. The total is $200,000, substantially more than any of the other methods. This shows the attractiveness of an early deduction.

We now move to some more sophisticated approaches. Let us look at alternative 5), attribute most of the early payments to taxable interest and a small amount to non-taxable principal, with these amounts gradually altering in proportion over the term of the annuity: *Loan Amortization Treatment*. This is the familiar home mortgage or car mortgage schedule. Matilda is in effect the lender here. Most of what Matilda receives in the early years is taxable interest. The following table shows how this looks. Notice in particular the heavy amount of early income Matilda has. The repayment of principal by the insurance company to her is her basis or cost, which is not taxed. Notice that all the basic numbers are still the same: Cost, Profit, Tax Paid. The only thing different is present value because of the timing of the tax paid depending on the method of cost recovery.

## Loan Amortization Method of Recovery of Cost of Single Premium 20–Year Annuity @ 9% Interest Rate

| Year of Payment | Years From Present | Payment | Interest Paid at 9% on Principal | Principal Paid (Payment-interest) | Remaining Principal at End of Year $200,000 | Tax @ 40% of Interest Income | Net Cash Flow Payment-Tax | Pres. Value of Net Cash Flow |
|---|---|---|---|---|---|---|---|---|
| 1993 | 0 | $20,100 | $16,191 | $3,909 | $196,091 | $6,476 | $13,624 | $13,624 |
| 1994 | 1 | $20,100 | $15,839 | $4,261 | $191,829 | $6,336 | $13,765 | $12,628 |
| 1995 | 2 | $20,100 | $15,456 | $4,644 | $187,185 | $6,182 | $13,918 | $11,714 |
| 1996 | 3 | $20,100 | $15,037 | $5,063 | $182,122 | $6,015 | $14,085 | $10,877 |
| 1997 | 4 | $20,100 | $14,582 | $5,518 | $176,604 | $5,833 | $14,267 | $10,107 |
| 1998 | 5 | $20,100 | $14,085 | $6,015 | $170,588 | $5,634 | $14,466 | $9,402 |
| 1999 | 6 | $20,100 | $13,544 | $6,556 | $164,032 | $5,418 | $14,683 | $8,755 |
| 2000 | 7 | $20,100 | $12,954 | $7,146 | $156,886 | $5,182 | $14,919 | $8,161 |
| 2001 | 8 | $20,100 | $12,311 | $7,789 | $149,097 | $4,924 | $15,176 | $7,616 |
| 2002 | 9 | $20,100 | $11,610 | $8,490 | $140,606 | $4,644 | $15,456 | $7,116 |
| 2003 | 10 | $20,100 | $10,845 | $9,255 | $131,351 | $4,338 | $15,762 | $6,658 |
| 2004 | 11 | $20,100 | $10,013 | $10,087 | $121,264 | $4,005 | $16,095 | $6,237 |
| 2005 | 12 | $20,100 | $9,105 | $10,995 | $110,268 | $3,642 | $16,458 | $5,851 |
| 2006 | 13 | $20,100 | $8,115 | $11,985 | $98,283 | $3,246 | $16,854 | $5,498 |
| 2007 | 14 | $20,100 | $7,037 | $13,063 | $85,220 | $2,815 | $17,285 | $5,173 |
| 2008 | 15 | $20,100 | $5,861 | $14,239 | $70,981 | $2,344 | $17,756 | $4,875 |
| 2009 | 16 | $20,100 | $4,579 | $15,521 | $55,459 | $1,832 | $18,269 | $4,601 |
| 2010 | 17 | $20,100 | $3,182 | $16,918 | $38,541 | $1,273 | $18,827 | $4,351 |
| 2011 | 18 | $20,100 | $1,660 | $18,440 | $20,101 | $664 | $19,436 | $4,120 |
| 2012 | 19 | $20,100 | $0 | $20,100 | $0 | $0 | $20,100 | $3,909 |
| Totals | | | $202,006 | $200,000 | | | | $151,274 |

**67.** As in the case of the last year of *Stupid Treatment* I treat the deduction and the payment as separate items to keep the discussion simpler. This approach does not affect the results. Matilda's ability to save $80,000 in taxes from a $200,000 deduction depends, of course, on the fact that she has enough other income that she is still in the 40% bracket even after such a huge deduction.

Let us turn finally to alternative 6), deem the present value of each payment to be its cost. Deduct that cost from each payment as it comes in: *Economically Accurate Treatment*. Here's the deal. Matilda paid $200,000 for the annuity. The annuity is worth $200,000 at the time it is purchased. Its value, like the value of any investment, grows over time (see Prologue). We therefore allocate the $200,000 over the 20 payments to be received in the future. That gives each payment to be received in the future. Then as we receive each payment we would deduct that cost or basis allocated to each payment to get the net profit on each payment. So far this sounds like the prorated or installment method above. But the cost is calculated differently. The payments to be received in years 1 through 20 each have a different present value. Therefore, we need to ascertain the present value of each payment of $20,100. (Their total present value will add up to $200,000—since that is what we paid for the policy and that is what the payments are presently worth in total). We then deduct that present value from each payment as it eventually comes in. That difference gives us the taxable income associated with each payment. We then apply the 40% tax rate to each amount of taxable income, giving us the tax associated with each payment. We subtract that tax from the face amount of each payment and that gives us the net after-tax amount of each payment. We then ascertain the present value of each after-tax amount and sum them. That sum gives us the present value of the deal. This is all done in the table below.

### Economically Accurate Recovery of Cost of Single Premium 20–Year Annuity @ 9% Interest Rate

| Years Left | Payment | Present Value or Cost of Payment | Income: Payment-Cost | Tax @ 40% of Income | Net Cash Flow: Payment-Tax | Pres. Value of Net Cash Flow |
|---|---|---|---|---|---|---|
| 19 | $20,100 | $3,909 | $16,191 | $6,476 | $13,624 | $2,650 |
| 18 | $20,100 | $4,261 | $15,839 | $6,336 | $13,764 | $2,918 |
| 17 | $20,100 | $4,644 | $15,456 | $6,182 | $13,918 | $3,216 |
| 16 | $20,100 | $5,063 | $15,037 | $6,015 | $14,085 | $3,548 |
| 15 | $20,100 | $5,518 | $14,582 | $5,833 | $14,267 | $3,917 |
| 14 | $20,100 | $6,015 | $14,085 | $5,634 | $14,466 | $4,329 |
| 13 | $20,100 | $6,556 | $13,544 | $5,418 | $14,682 | $4,789 |
| 12 | $20,100 | $7,146 | $12,954 | $5,182 | $14,918 | $5,304 |
| 11 | $20,100 | $7,789 | $12,311 | $4,924 | $15,176 | $5,881 |
| 10 | $20,100 | $8,490 | $11,610 | $4,644 | $15,456 | $6,529 |
| 9 | $20,100 | $9,255 | $10,845 | $4,338 | $15,762 | $7,257 |
| 8 | $20,100 | $10,087 | $10,013 | $4,005 | $16,095 | $8,077 |
| 7 | $20,100 | $10,995 | $9,105 | $3,642 | $16,458 | $9,003 |
| 6 | $20,100 | $11,985 | $8,115 | $3,246 | $16,854 | $10,049 |
| 5 | $20,100 | $13,063 | $7,037 | $2,815 | $17,285 | $11,234 |
| 4 | $20,100 | $14,239 | $5,861 | $2,344 | $17,756 | $12,579 |
| 3 | $20,100 | $15,521 | $4,579 | $1,832 | $18,268 | $14,107 |
| 2 | $20,100 | $16,918 | $3,182 | $1,273 | $18,827 | $15,846 |
| 1 | $20,100 | $18,440 | $1,660 | $664 | $19,436 | $17,831 |
| 0 | $20,100 | $20,100 | $0 | $0 | $20,100 | $20,100 |
| Totals | | $200,000 | $202,000 | | | **$169,164** |

The payments that are furthest away in time (i.e. 19 years left) have the smallest present value ($3,909.) They therefore are allocated the lowest basis ($3,909). When time passes and they are finally paid, there will be the largest amount of income in the year of payment ($16,191).

Thus the economically accurate method involves only a small amount of taxable income in the early years, increasing as time goes on and later payments in the schedule are made.

This is the economically accurate way to recover the cost of this investment. It shows the present value of the investment to be different from any of the other methods used. It is unquestionably the economically accurate way to handle transactions with payments to be received in the future, whether annuities or any other kind of investment. Does anyone seriously suggest actually using this method? No, naturally. Why not? Beats me. I'd like to say it's too complicated, but since when has that ever been a barrier to enacting provisions into the Internal Revenue Code? Seems to me that if you're going to have a complicated Code, you at least ought to get the answers right.

Note the symbiotic relationship between the economically accurate method and the loan amortization method. Observe that the column in the loan amortization method labelled "interest paid" has the same numbers in it as the column in the economically accurate method labelled "income = payment—cost." In both cases that is what is taxed to the annuitant. But there is one major difference. In the loan amortization method the big numbers start in the early years and go down to the small amounts in the later years. This hits the annuitant with taxes earlier than in the economically accurate method. In the economically accurate method, the amounts start with the small amounts in the early years and go up to the large amounts in the later years. They are the same numbers all the way; they just occur in the opposite order.[68] This can be seen by looking at the column on the left of each chart referencing "years left" in the economically accurate method and "years from present" in the loan amortization method. The numbers are in opposite order.

Thus a sideline result that cranks out of this analysis is that the usual method in the financial community for amortizing home mortgages and other loans (as exemplified by our loan amortization model) is not correct. The payor of a home mortgage (as represented by the insurance company in our example) or a homeowner in a home mortgage should be paying small amounts of deductible interest in the early years, with these deductible amounts gradually rising. This is clearly shown by the economically accurate method.

Another effect of this analysis is to put at least a second nail into the coffin of the installment method of reporting gain. The installment method is complicated. We have already shown that it does not give a

---

**68.** A technical note: I point out for the convenience of readers who may be using their own computers or amortization tables to check my numbers that I have assumed throughout this discussion of the recovery of capital methods that payments are made at the beginning of the period for which they are attributable rather than at the end of the period. The usual approach for loan amortization is to figure that payments are made at the end of the period. I wanted, however, to have the loan amortization approach to be consistent with the other methods of recovering capital, where I used the beginning of the period. Paying at the beginning rather than the end of the period changes the numbers somewhat but in no way affects the principle being discussed.

much different answer from the much simpler open treatment. Now we also see that the installment method (whose claim to fame at least was that it was accurate) does not give the right answer either. As a matter of fact, at least on these numbers, the Open Treatment comes closer to the Economically Accurate Treatment than does the Installment Treatment

It is important to get the right answer for the present value of the arrangement. This is so taxpayers may correctly view their investment choices, without having their choices distorted by the tax rules.

The table below compares the method of recovering basis and the present value of the annuity.

**Comparison of Basis Recovery Methods for $200,000 Premium 20 Year Life Annuity at 9% Annual Interest Compounded. Total Amount Deducted in Each Case $200,000; Total Profit in Each Case $202,000; Total Tax Paid in Each Case $80,800**

| Method | Present Value |
|---|---|
| Immediate Deduction | $200,000 |
| Open Treatment | 161,500 |
| Installment Treatment | 159,800 |
| Loan Amortization | 151,274 |
| Stupid Treatment | 134,300 |
| Economically Accurate | 169,164 |

In tax, as in figure skating, timing is everything. Verify for yourself the fact that as the deduction of the cost of the premium is deferred more and more, the present value of the deal to the annuitant goes down.

As I said before, you will see these methods used (except for the Economically Accurate Treatment) throughout the field of federal income taxation. Note that Stupid Treatment is notable for grossly discouraging investment in this transaction.

As pointed out in the footnote accompanying discussion of Stupid Treatment above, corporate dividends are often taxed according to Stupid Treatment. This discourages investment in corporate stock. For example, suppose a taxpayer were faced with the choice of investing in either an annuity with the numbers above, or dividend-paying blue chip corporate stock with the same numbers (i.e. $20,100 dividends per year with little risk). The taxpayer would choose the annuity just because the basis recovery rule is unfavorable for corporate stock dividends. Is this the way to encourage investment in corporate America?[69]

69. It might be argued that corporate stock is not a "wasting asset," the way an annuity is. That is, corporate stock has a perpetual existence. So that after 20 years the annuity stops paying out whereas the corporate stock continues to pay dividends. Thus, it could be argued that Stupid Treatment is correct for corporate stock, since until the taxpayer sells the stock we do not know for how long it will produce dividends for him. That argument, while superficially appealing, does not really stand up. We do

When you see cost or basis being deducted in this field, be aware which of these methods is being used.[70]

### (ii) Application to Easements: Inaja Land

Let us apply the principles we have supposedly learned in the preceding section to the issues presented by the case of *Inaja Land*.

## INAJA LAND CO. v. COMMISSIONER[71]

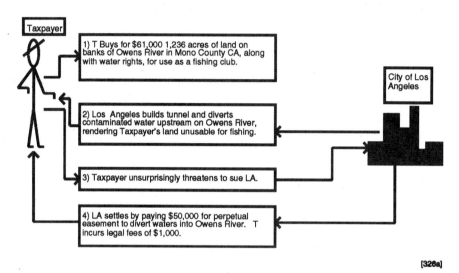

[326a]

*Question:* Is the net $49,000 settlement amount received taxable income in full or does T offset some of his basis against it to reduce or

---

not know how long an annuitant with a life annuity will live, yet we have no trouble using mortality tables to ascertain how to apply the proration or installment method to annuities (see Chapter 3). By the same token we do not know how long a taxpayer will hold the corporate stock but it is safe to say he will not hold it after he dies. Thus we could use literally the same mortality tables for calculating cost recovery for corporate stock as we do for annuities. Or better yet we could use the Economically Accurate Treatment for both. It might be objected to these approaches that the corporate stock continues in existence after the stockholder dies, whereas the annuity expires with him. Thus the corporate stock's basis should continue in the hands of the heirs. However, the heirs of the holder of corporate stock take a new basis of the fair market value of the stock when the decedent dies (see Chapter 4). This new basis in the hands of the heirs has nothing to do

with the basis of the stock in the decedent's hands; thus the basis rule we use for the decedent has no effect on the basis of the stock in the hands of the heir. This same analysis could be applied—if we wanted to make economic sense—to any other non-wasting assets, such as undeveloped land. Also (I'm really getting mad now) when you combine this treatment of dividends with the stringent rules against deducting net capital losses (see ¶ 4.06(1)), you have tax rules that severely discourage investment in the stock market. Why, in this era when everyone is screaming about how investment needs to be stimulated, doesn't anyone talk about straightening out these rules? I don't know.

**70.** This analysis feeds directly into the discussion of depreciation, at ¶ 6.02(12).

**71.** 9 T.C. 727 (1947), acq. 1948–1 C.B. 2. See also Rev. Rul. 70–510, 1970–2 C.B. 159.

eliminate taxable income?

*IRS argument:* 1) The net $49,000 is compensation for lost present or future income and consideration for release of many meritorious actions against city. Hence the $49,000 is ordinary income. 2) T has not allocated basis against the $49,000 and thus has failed in his burden to show error.

*Taxpayer argument:* 1) The language of instrument and circumstances show that the consideration was for an easement. Loss of present or future income was not considered. 2) Character of easement renders it impractical to apportion basis to it. Since sum received is less than basis of property the entire amount should be excluded from tax.

*Held:* Judgement in favor of taxpayer. 1) The payment was for an easement. 2) Since on these facts apportionment of basis is not possible. Thus full amount of payment is excluded from income.

*Comment:* Under the court's holding, taxpayer's basis in his property would be reduced by $49,000, since that amount of basis would have been used to offset the payment.

Based on our extensive discussion above, which method of cost recovery is used here? Answer: Open Treatment. Take the basis against payments as they are received.[72] No income until (and unless) basis is recovered in full. *Inaja Land* comes in for a lot of criticism for a failure to apportion just part of the basis against the $49,000 and have some of the $49,000 be income. However, as our discussion above has shown, open treatment is not so unreasonable. Moreover some kind of prorata or apportionment treatment does not give the economically correct answer either.

What approach was the Commissioner arguing for? Stupid Treatment. Everything is income first. Take deduction for full basis when (and if) property is sold. Note that the numbers are all the same here. There's $49,000 of receipts and a basis of $61,000. This is a fight about timing.

### (f) Inflation: Kerbaugh–Empire

A hallmark of modern industrial society is inflation, either low-grade or sometimes rampant. Without presenting you with a treatise on the subject it can be said that the causes of inflation appear to relate to the fact that wages and prices are "sticky downward." Workers do not like to take pay cuts (it has happened to me, but let's not get into that). Monopolistic or oligopolistic businesses may be able to resist price cuts. Large government budget deficits pump too much money into the economy. Whatever the reasons, we've got inflation, in varying degrees at varying times. What impact, if any, does that have on the federal income tax system?

---

**72.** Indeed the court cited the leading open treatment case, Burnet v. Logan, 283 U.S. 404, 51 S.Ct. 550, 75 L.Ed. 1143 (1931), discussed and graphed at ¶ 8.03.

There was actually a case that explored that problem, albeit inadvertently. That case was *Kerbaugh–Empire Co.*

## BOWERS v. KERBAUGH–EMPIRE CO.[73]

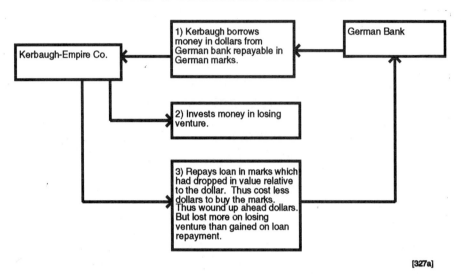

[327a]

*Question:* Did Kerbaugh–Empire have income on the loan repayment?

*IRS Argument:* Repaying the debt in depreciated marks meant taxpayer ahead on the loan transaction and thus it had income on the loan repayment.

*Supreme Court Held:* No income because the loss on the losing venture was greater than the gain on the loan repayment.

*Comment:* With all due respect the Court was dead wrong on this one. There were two transactions. They should not be combined. There was income on one and loss on the other. They occurred in different years. So it is completely wrong to say no income on loan repayment, see *Burnet v. Sanford & Brooks Co.*[74]

*Comment:* It was significant that the Court did concede that income could result from currency transactions.[75]

*Kerbaugh–Empire* opens a door into the murky problems of inflation and the income tax. What happened in this case was that there was high

**73.** 271 U.S. 170, 46 S.Ct. 449, 70 L.Ed. 886 (1926).

**74.** 282 U.S. 359, 51 S.Ct. 150, 75 L.Ed. 383 (1931), discussed and diagrammed at ¶ 9.02(1).

**75.** In modern international business transactions, companies usually protect

inflation in Germany during the period of this deal.[76] Inflation means that it takes more of the currency to buy the same product. Hence the currency is worth less. Thus marks could be bought with fewer dollars.

You do not need, however, international borrowing transactions to have inflation giving you problems with the income tax. Consider the following example:

**Example:** There is a world of just two commodities, which uses dollars as its currency. The two commodities are undeveloped land and grilled cheese sandwiches. That's all anybody wants to use or cares about. Bette buys as an investment undeveloped land subdivided into 100 plots. She buys the land for $100,000, so each plot is worth $1000. Kevin buys a load of 100 grilled cheese sandwiches. He pays $100,000, so each sandwich is worth $1,000 (they're made with Grey Poupon mustard). Immediately after these transactions, Bette sells Kevin one of her plots for $1,000 cash. Very soon thereafter, Kevin sells Bette one of his grilled cheese sandwiches for $1,000 cash.

Time passes. Over the course of the year, the land goes up in price by 30%. The grilled cheese sandwiches go up in price by 10%. At the end of the year, Bette sells Kevin one of her plots for $1,300 cash. Kevin sells Bette one of his sandwiches for $1,100. Kevin says, "Hold the phone. Suddenly, I'm short $200." The IRS says it's worse than that, fella. You just sold that sandwich for a $100 gain. At our tax rate of 33% you owe us $33. Kevin blows up.

Kevin's problem is, of course, inflation. The consumer price index in this simple economy, assuming we weight land and grilled cheese sandwiches equally, went up 20%. There is a 20% inflation rate. It costs (on average) 20% more dollars to buy products in this economy. Kevin suffered because he held property that rose in price by less than the inflation rate. Kevin suffered a loss in purchasing power. Bette's property, for whatever reasons, went up in price by more than the inflation rate. Bette enjoyed a gain in purchasing power. She no longer needs to sell a full plot of land to buy a grilled cheese sandwich.

Since the tax law in our little world is blind to this problem, it gets it wrong as to Kevin, as we have seen. And it also gets it wrong as to Bette. The IRS would say that Bette had a gain of $300 in selling her plot at the end of the year. They are saying she can buy 1.30 grilled cheese sandwiches when she sells a plot of land. But she cannot. She can buy only 1.27 grilled cheese sandwiches when she sells a plot of land.[77] She has a gain, but not as much as the IRS thinks.

themselves from currency value fluctuations by hedging in the currency markets.

**76.** This transaction took place in the early 1920's during the period of the Weimar Republic in Germany. The Weimar Republic experienced heavy inflation, which contributed to the social dislocation of the time, see e.g. B. Brecht, and K. Weill, *Die Dreigroschenoper*, ("The Three Penny Opera")(1928).

**77.** $300 (Bette's money gain) is 27% of $1,100 (the new price of grilled cheese

That is exactly the problem with inflation in our income tax. It is a massive, widespread, and distortive problem. What do we do about it?

Many people suggest that what is needed to deal with this problem is to give favorable treatment for capital gains (as we have in our present system, see Chapter 4). That is to impose a lower tax on gains from sales of property than we have on other forms of income such as salaries. Thus we would, say, cut the tax rate on sales of property in our little society from 33% to 15%. This idea is like taking a person with a cold and giving him open-heart surgery. Not only is it the wrong thing, it's also too much of it.

Let us see how cutting the tax rate would play out on our example. Kevin would pay a tax of $15 instead of $33 on his "gain." Would he still blow up? Of course. Suppose we imposed no tax at all on Kevin. Would he still blow up? Yes. Kevin's problem is that he has actually suffered a loss in purchasing power. When he sells one grilled cheese sandwich after a year, he has enough money to buy 85% of a plot of land.[78]

Suppose the price of land had remained constant. Suppose, then, the price of grilled cheese sandwiches had fallen to $85 per sandwich. On selling a grilled cheese sandwich, Kevin can now buy 85% of a plot of land. He would certainly be entitled to a $15 loss on the sale of his land, would he not? Why should this case be treated any differently from our original case?

So what do we do? Answer: we need to index the basis of assets held for the inflation rate. On our original example, the inflation rate was 20%. Thus the basis of plots of land and grilled cheese sandwiches needs to rise by 20%. Kevin now has a basis of $120 in each grilled cheese sandwich. He sells it for $110 and has a loss of $10, reflecting his true loss in purchasing power. Bette has a basis of $120 in her plots of land. She sells one for $130, she has a gain of $10, reflecting her true gain in purchasing power.

Will this be enacted? There's been talk about it, but so far nothing has been done, although the problem is severe when one considers the effects of even modest inflation over long periods of time.[79]

### (g) Other Theoretical Problems

There are other theoretical problems in income taxation more conveniently dealt with elsewhere in this work. For the issues involved in the

sandwiches, the real gain corrected for inflation).

**78.** $110/$130 = 85%.

**79.** My own personal opinion is that this issue has been befuddled by those who seek to cut the capital gains rate and give the effects of inflation as the reason. As a result, nothing gets done.

It has been suggested that loan transactions also present the inflation problem because the borrower can pay the loan back with cheaper dollars. However, the interest rate charged on the loan will incorporate an inflation factor and should take care of the problem. If it is felt that for some reason the interest rate is not handling the loan problem, the principal of the loan could be indexed for the inflation rate. If that were done, of course, interest rates would drop substantially, since they would not need to incorporate the inflation factor. The effect would be that the borrower would get a smaller deduction on repayment since repayment of principal is not deductible but repayment of interest is.

preferential treatment of capital gains, see ¶ 4.06. The debate on using various tax provisions as incentives to business is discussed at ¶ 6.02(12). The problem of treating activities which involve both business and personal aspects is considered at ¶ 6.02. The problem of the appropriate family unit on which to impose the tax is considered at chapter 15.

## ¶ 1.03   Structure of the Internal Revenue Code

There is an underlying rational structure to the Internal Revenue Code. This structure may often not be honored, but nonetheless it still is useful to comprehend it. This structure is represented in the one-page diagram that appears at the beginning of this book. Set forth below is a simplified verbal statement of the structure:

The formula for computing federal income tax liability under the Internal Revenue Code is as follows:

Steps in Computing Tax Liability

1.   Gross Income (including compensation for services and other items of income).

2.   Less: most business deductions and some non-business deductions (as provided by § 62).

3.   Yields: adjusted gross income.

4.   Less: the greater of itemized deductions or the standard deduction (itemized deductions being most non-business deductions and business deductions not allowed in step 2 above).

5.   Less: deductions for personal and dependency exemptions.

6.   Yields: taxable income.

7.   Computation of tax liability by reference to tax rate tables, and any special computations.

8.   Less: Any credits.

9.   Yields: tax owed or refund due.

It is to the various steps in this process that the succeeding chapters are addressed.

# Chapter 2

# INCOME IN GENERAL; COMPENSATION FOR SERVICES

*Table of Sections*

## ¶ 2.01 What Constitutes Income in General: *Cesarini, Old Colony Trust, Glenshaw Glass* and *Drescher*

Section 61 of the Internal Revenue Code defines gross income broadly and powerfully as "all income from whatever source derived," including, but not limited to, fifteen particular sources—ranging from obvious items like compensation for services, dividends, royalties, gross income derived from business,[1] and gains derived from dealings in property, to less likely candidates, such as alimony, pensions, and income from discharge of indebtedness. In advancing this sweeping definition of income, § 61 is the driving heart of the income tax. With § 61, Congress exerted the full measure of its taxing power, intending to tax all gains without regard to source except those specifically exempted.[2] It is with this heavy inclusive presumption that an item is income that all further analysis must contend.

A leading example of the breadth of the income concept is the case of *Cesarini v. United States.*[3] In that case taxpayers husband and wife in 1957 purchased a used piano at an auction sale for approximately $15. In 1964, while cleaning the piano, taxpayer discovered $4,467 in old currency. Taxpayers paid tax on the amount and then filed a claim for a refund

---

**¶ 2.01**

1. In a manufacturing, merchandising, or mining business, "gross income" means the total sales less the cost of goods sold, Reg. § 1.61–3(a).

2. Commissioner v. Kowalski, 434 U.S. 77, 98 S.Ct. 315, 54 L.Ed.2d 252 (1977).

3. 296 F.Supp. 3 (N.D.Ohio 1969) aff'd per curiam 428 F.2d 812 (6th Cir.1970)

of their $836.51 tax on the found money. Taxpayers argued in the alternative that the found money was 1) not income; 2) if it was income, it was income in 1957 and the statute of limitations has now run on that year and 3) if it was income, it should be taxed at the favorable capital gains rate. The court held that the found money was income in the year that it was found. The concept of income is broad enough to cover this, since Congress intended to exert the full measure of its taxing power under the Sixteenth Amendment. Regs. § 1.61–14 provides that treasure trove is income in the year when it is reduced to undisputed possession. Under Ohio state law, the money is reduced to possession when it is actually found. The court also rejected the capital gains argument.

Another major case in the income area *is Old Colony Trust Co. v. Commissioner.*

### OLD COLONY TRUST v. COMMISSIONER[4]

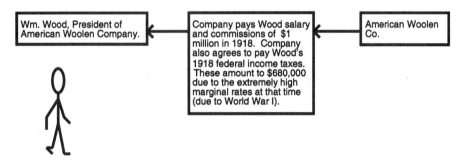

[335a]

Question: Was the payment by American Woolen of Wood's federal income taxes income to Wood?

Taxpayer's argument: He never laid hands on the money; it was sent directly to the IRS.

Held: Wood is taxable on the $680,000 that the company paid of his taxes. His wealth was increased by the payment. The fact that the payments were voluntary is irrelevant in an employer-employee setting. The payments were not a gift.

Comment: This $680,000 of federal income taxes for 1918 would, of course, be paid in 1919. Under the Court's holding, this creates further taxable income to Wood of $680,000 in 1919 (in addition to his regular salary and commissions). This additional $680,000 of income in 1919 would generate further tax to Wood of $462,400 (assuming the same effective rate of 1918). The Company would then, under its agreement with Wood, pay this additional $462,400 of income taxes for 1919 in 1920, generating additional income to Wood of $462,400 in 1920. This

4. 279 U.S. 716, 49 S.Ct. 499, 73 L.Ed. 918 (1929) 36 B.T.A. 838 (1929).

would generate additional tax liability for 1920 of $314,432, which would be payable in 1921 and so forth. Is this a problem? No.

Comment: Why did Wood and American Woolen engage in this deal? Do you think they hoped to avoid taxes by arranging affairs this way? It was a less sophisticated time. Note the case went to the Supreme Court. Compare this case to Drescher and Benaglia in Chapter 2, where once again we saw a "beleagured" upper-level employee "forced" to accept some major benefit which is thought not to be taxable.

The result in Old Colony is clearly correct. Obviously Wood's wealth was increased by this arrangement. Thus we learn that if one's debt is discharged, one is wealthier. The transaction was in the nature of compensation for services, which is explicitly taxable under § 61(a)(1).[5]

The breadth of the income concept is further illustrated in the leading case of *Glenshaw Glass.*

## COMMISSIONER v. GLENSHAW GLASS[6]

[328a]

Question: Is the ⅔ of the award that is attributable to punitive damages includible in income?

*Taxpayer argument:* The punitive damages are a windfall under the antitrust laws and thus not income under Eisner v. Macomber. *Macomber* held that "income is defined as gain derived from labor, from capital, or from both combined."[7]

*Held:* Not only are compensatory damages taxable but so are punitive damages. The punitive damages are "accessions to wealth." "Congress applied no limitations as to the source of taxable receipts ..."

*Comment:* The accession to wealth test enunciated in this Supreme Court case is broad and is a touchstone for analysis of what is income.

*Comment:* Does it really matter? Will not the parties in future negotiations on the settlement of antitrust claims take into account that

---

**5.** As *Old Colony* shows, taxpayer cannot exclude from income his employer's payment of his taxes. It is also the case that the taxpayer cannot deduct payment of his own income taxes § 275. He can deduct the payment of his state income taxes against his income as computed for federal purposes, § 164.

**6.** 348 U.S. 426, 75 S.Ct. 473, 99 L.Ed. 483 (1955), reh'g denied 349 U.S. 925, 75 S.Ct. 657, 99 L.Ed. 1256 (1955).

**7.** Eisner v. Macomber, 252 U.S. 189, 40 S.Ct. 189, 64 L.Ed. 521 (1920). See Chapter 4 for further discussion and diagram of this major case.

the plaintiff's punitive damage award is taxable. Thus will not the plaintiff hold out for more to make up for it after this case? Thus will not the defendant pay all or some of the tax?

This powerful presumption of income as exemplified by the *Glenshaw Glass* case is limited in two important respects, however. First, as the discussion in Chapter 1 has indicated, there are a number of items which are income in an economic sense which § 61 does not reach even under *Glenshaw Glass*. Second, even though an item is covered by § 61 it may be specifically excluded from income by some other provision of the Code. As will be seen, these two kinds of limitations restrict the broad sweep of § 61 with respect to the various items of gross income.

One of the most important items of gross income is, of course, compensation for the rendering of personal services. The rich variety of ways in which people are compensated for rendering services has provoked an equally rich response from the Code, Regulations, rulings, and case law. The great bulk of compensation for services is paid in the form of money wages and salaries (including bonuses, fees and commissions). These payments are clearly income and usually present no problems.

Difficulties arise, however, where the compensation is not directly in the form of wages.

For example, take a look at the case of *Drescher*:

## UNITED STATES v. DRESCHER[8]

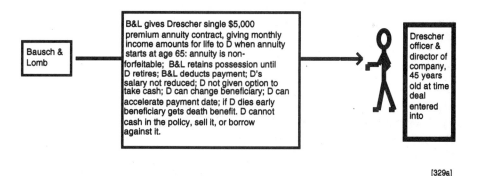

[329a]

*Question:* When is the $5,000 premium includible in Drescher's income? At time the annuity is purchased, or later on retirement at time when annuity starts paying out?

*Taxpayer Argument:* Not income at the time premium is paid

---

8.   179 F.2d 863 (2d Cir.1950), cert. de-     (1950).
nied 340 U.S. 821, 71 S.Ct. 53, 95 L.Ed. 603

because the taxpayer could not realize present cash benefits from the policy.

*IRS Argument:* Drescher was better off for having received the policy. He has income at the present time.

*Held:* Taxpayer has income at the present time. Arrangement worth less than $5,000 but more than zero. Reverse judgement in favor of taxpayer and remand.

*Comment:* Is it likely that Drescher was advised that previous cases of this kind were lost because of the annuitant's ability to realize immediate cash from the deal? Is it possible therefore Drescher consented to these fundamentally meaningless restrictions in order to attempt to avoid current taxation on the deal?

Note this case is about timing of income. The amount of income is not seriously in dispute. Anyone who thinks timing does not matter, re-read Prologue.

Further discussion: Note that the $5,000 would have grown in 20 years to be substantially more. Assuming a 7% growth or interest rate, the $5,000 would, after 20 years, have been worth $19,348. So if Drescher had lost, he would have included $5,000 in his income now and $19,348 − $5,000 = $14,348 in his income twenty years later. He would take the full $19,348 into income on retirement in 20 years because at that time he would have all the incidents of ownership of this annuity transferred to him by his employer. If he had lost and included the $5,000 now, then he would have paid tax on the $5,000 and acquired a basis of $5,000 in the policy. Then when he had to include the $19,348 into income, he would have the $5,000 basis to offset against it. This shows how basis is used to keep track of past events so that we don't count income twice.

If Drescher had won hands down and included nothing, then he would have no basis in the policy. Thus, 20 years later when he would include the whole $19,348 into income, he would have no basis to offset. In both cases the total amount included is $19,348. The question in the case is just the timing of the $5,000.

Timing does not matter right? Let's run our numbers, similar to what we did in the Prologue just to see what was at stake for Drescher. Let us assume a combined 40% tax rate (33% top federal and 7% state). If Drescher has to take the $5,000 into income immediately, his tax is $2,000. He has to pay the amount immediately. Suppose instead he does not have to take the $5,000 into income immediately but instead takes it into income 20 years hence. Assume the tax rate is still the same combined 40% rate. Thus $2,000 is his tax 20 years later. The question, as you know from reading the Prologue, is what is the present value of a $2,000 tax payment 20 years from now. Assume, as we have above, that the after-tax rate of interest that Drescher can invest his money at is 7%. We now know enough to ask the computer to crank out the answer. May I have the card, please. The present value of $2,000 20 years from now with an interest rate of 7% is $517. Thus, nearly three-quarters of the tax payable is saved. Here is another way of saying it: If Drescher wins, he needs to set aside only $517 now. If he loses he needs to set aside (i.e. pay) $2,000.[9]

Another theoretical issue as to income is the area of imputed income. Economists would argue that the value of a house that the taxpayer lives in is income to him in that it has given him shelter income. See ¶ 1.02(2)(a), note 19. In the leading case of *Helvering v. Independent Life Ins. Co.*,[10] the Supreme Court stated in dicta that taxing imputed income from owner-occupied housing is unconstitutional as being a direct tax requiring apportionment and not protected by the Sixteenth Amendment.

In *Dean v. Commissioner*[11] the court dealt with a case where a husband and wife were sole shareholders of a corporation which owned a house in which the husband and wife lived. The husband was president of the corporation although he was in military service at the time of the case. The rental value of the home was held to be income apparently in the nature of compensation to him and his wife. This was the case even though the house was transferred to the corporation at the behest of a bank which wanted the house in the corporation so it could serve as security for a loan to the corporation. A lesson from *Independent Life* and *Dean* seems to be that it's a big mistake to put your house into your closely-held corporation.

## ¶ 2.02   Fringe Benefits

### *(1) Miscellaneous Benefits Under § 132*

In addition to paying money wages or salaries, the employer may provide fringe benefits to the employee as compensation for services rendered. Under the general broad principles of § 61, the presumption is that such benefits are income. Thus, the employee has the burden of presenting some authority or other reason why any of these benefits should be excluded from income.

The Deficit Reduction Act of 1984 enacted a fairly comprehensive treatment of fringe benefits. Under these new rules, effective generally beginning January 1, 1985, gross income does not include any fringe benefit which qualifies as 1) no-additional-cost service, 2) qualified employee discount, 3) working condition fringe, or 4) de minimis fringe. Any fringe benefit not excluded by these rules or other provisions of the Code is included in income. Extensive definition and detailed special rules are provided, allowing among other things non-taxability of on-premises athletic facilities and employee parking. Detailed rules as to the

---

**9.** By the way, if you think they're fighting about small change—what's $1500 after all—remember that *Drescher* came up in 1950. Inflation has worked its toll. As a matter of fact, if there is an inflation rate of 6%, then $1500 in 1950 is worth $21,647 now.

**10.** 292 U.S. 371, 54 S.Ct. 758, 78 L.Ed. 1311 (1934).

**11.** 187 F.2d 1019 (3d Cir.1951).

taxability of personal use of the employer's copying machine are provided.

These types of excludible fringe benefits are described in more detail below:

The following fringe benefits are excludible:

*(1) A no-additional-cost service.* This is any service provided by an employer to an employee for use by the employee, if two conditions are satisfied: 1) the service is offered for sale to customers in the ordinary course of the line of business of the employer in which the employee is performing services; and 2) the employer incurs no substantial cost (including foregone revenue) in providing the service to the employee (determined without regard to any amount paid by the employee for the service).

*(2) A qualified employee discount.* This is any employee discount with respect to qualified property or services to the extent the discount does not exceed certain limits. With respect to a discount on a product, the discount cannot exceed generally the difference between the sales price of the product and its cost to the employer. With respect to a discount on a service, the discount cannot exceed 20% of the price at which the services are offered by the employer to customers. In these cases, if the discount is greater than these limits only the amount of the discount which does not exceed these limits is excludible and the balance is includible in the income of the employee.

Moreover, only certain types of property or services may qualify for this limited exclusion. As to property, the property cannot be real property or personal property of a kind which is held for investment (i.e. stocks given to an employee of a brokerage firm would not qualify). Furthermore, the discount must be offered on property or services which are offered for sale to customers in the ordinary course of the line of business of the employer in which the employee is performing services.

*(3) A working condition fringe.* This is any property or services provided to an employee of the employer to the extent that, if the employee paid for such property or services, such payment would be allowable as a deduction to the employee under section 162 or 167.

*(4) A de minimis fringe.* This is any property or service the value of which is (after taking into account the frequency with which similar fringes are provided by the employer to the employer's employees) so small as to make accounting for it unreasonable or administratively impracticable.

A special rule here provides that the operation by an employer of any eating facility for employees shall be treated as a de minimis fringe if (A) the facility is located on or near the business premises of the employer (compare the discussion of Section 119, at ¶ 2.02(2) of the text); and (B) the revenue derived from the facility normally equals or exceeds the direct operating costs of the facility. This last provision regarding eating facilities only allows for exclusion if with respect to any officer, owner, or highly compensated employee access to the facility is available to other employees on a substantially nondiscriminatory basis.

Reciprocal agreements wherein employers provide services to each other's employees will qualify for exclusion, subject to the limits described above, provided that the reciprocal agreement is embodied in a written agreement between the employers and provided that neither employer incurs any substantial additional cost (including foregone revenue) in providing the service. Thus airlines may provide travel at a discount to each other's employees and still qualify for the exclusion.

The no-additional-cost service and the qualified employee discount will be excludible with respect to any officer, owner, or other highly compensated employee only if the fringe benefit is available to other employees on a substantially nondiscriminatory basis. If these two fringes are not provided on a nondiscriminatory basis, then the fringe will still be excludible to rank and file employees but will not be excludible to the officers, owners, or other highly compensated employees.

Working condition fringe includes parking provided to an employee on or near the business premises of the employer.

In this aerobics era, a special rule provides that in any event gross income does not include the value of any on-premises athletic facility provided by an employer to his employees, their spouses and dependent children.

These rules do not apply to fringe benefits which are specifically provided for elsewhere in the statute. These rules are provided by § 132. These rules are effective starting January 1, 1985.

In addition to these rules, TRA 1984 also provided some special rules for tuition reduction plans for employees of educational institutions. The general rule here is that gross income does not include any "qualified tuition reduction." A "qualified tuition reduction" is the amount of any reduction in tuition provided to an employee of an educational institution for the education below the graduate level at the institution or at another educational institution. The tuition reduction may be provided to the employee or any retired, or disabled former employees, the surviving spouse of the employee or the spouse and dependent children of the employee.

The exclusion of the reduction in tuition will only apply to any officer, owner, or highly compensated employee if the tuition reduction plan is available on substantially the same terms to other employees on a nondiscriminatory basis. Section 117(d), effective for tuition reductions provided after June 30, 1985.

The major other fringe benefit items are discussed below.

### (2) Meals and Lodging

A major benefit employers may confer on their employees is the provision of free meals and lodging. Under the principles discussed in the preceding section and in Chapter 1, there is a general presumption that such meals and lodging are income. However, suppose a restaurant employer insists its employees take a free lunch on the premises in one-half hour so they can be available to work during the rush lunch hour? In such a case the free lunch is for the convenience of the employer and it does not seem fair to tax the employee, who has had no choice as to where and what he would like to eat. Similarly a landlord may provide an apartment building supervisor with a free apartment so that the supervisor can be easily on call 24 hours a day. Although the apartment is valuable consideration, where the employee must accept the apartment as a condition of his employment it may not be fair to tax him on it since he has not had a choice of where he would like to live.

For example, in *Herbert G. Hatt,*[1] the Tax Court was confronted with the following colorful set of facts. Herbert G. Hatt, a high-school drop-out, engaged in several odd jobs before finally meeting the love of his life Dorothy Echols, the president and majority stockholder of Johann Corporation. It was a May–December kind of deal, with Hatt being 25 at the time and Dorothy 43.

Immediately after the marriage, Hatt moved into an apartment with Dorothy in the same building used by Johann Corporation for its business. He doubtless expected it would be quiet, since the business Johann operated was a funeral home. The business telephone rang in Hatt's apartment and he answered the phone when the office was closed. He also met in the apartment with customers (presumably on a "pre-need" basis).

The court held that Hatt met the requirements of § 119, namely that with respect to lodging he must be required to accept the lodging in order to be able to properly perform the duties of his employment. Hatt was required to be on call 24 hours a day. The court also held that Hatt met the "convenience of the employer" test and the "condition of his employment test" prescribed by § 119. This was the case even though, as the court pointed out, Hatt was the president and majority stockholder of Johann and thus able to cause the corporation to assert that living upstairs was needed for the business. It was undisputed that in the Evansville area, where the business was located, the manager or some employee of every funeral home lived on the premises. (Sounds like a fun group).

These problems are also exemplified by the leading case of *Benaglia*:

¶ 2.02

**1.**   28 T.C.M. 1194, aff'd per curiam 457 F.2d 499 (7th Cir.1972).

## BENAGLIA v. COMMISSIONER[2]

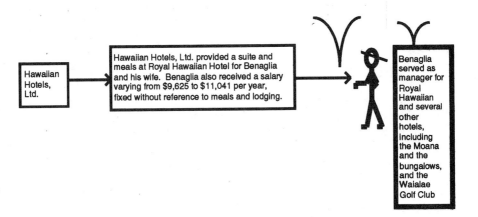

Hawaiian Hotels, Ltd.

Hawaiian Hotels, Ltd. provided a suite and meals at Royal Hawaiian Hotel for Benaglia and his wife. Benaglia also received a salary varying from $9,625 to $11,041 per year, fixed without reference to meals and lodging.

Benaglia served as manager for Royal Hawaiian and several other hotels, including the Moana and the bungalows, and the Waialae Golf Club

[330a]

*Taxpayer's argument:* Living at the hotel was for the convenience of the employer. Taxpayer could not perform his duties as manager without living on premises.

*IRS Argument:* These were significant items transferred by employer to taxpayer as employee. He did not have to pay for his own meals and lodging and was therefore wealthier because of the arrangement.

*Held:* Taxpayer could exclude these items, as they were provided for the convenience of the employer.

*Comment:* If taxpayer's presence was so necessary in the Royal Hawaiian, why was he able to manage the the Moana and bungalows, and the Waialae Golf Club without living at them?

Note that, unlike the *Drescher* case but like *Glenshaw Glass*, this case involves a now or never proposition. Either the items are taxable or they are not.

It might be asked why "convenience of the employer" should be the test here at all? Presumably, it is "convenient" for the employer to hire the employee at all or the employer would not do so. It might be answered that in-kind items which the employee must accept to help perform his job deprive the employee of choice. After all, no matter how swanky the accommodations at the Royal Hawaiian for Benaglia, the retail cash value of those accommodations would have been better. Why? Then he could have chosen the Royal Hawaiian or something more modest and saved the difference. So no taxation. Poor Benaglia and Drescher, "compelled" by their employers to accept lucious perks. Is this real?

Code § 119 now deals with this problem, providing that meals and lodging furnished by the employer are excluded from the income of the

**2.** 36 B.T.A. 838 (1937).

employee if certain tests are met. As to meals the tests are: (1) the meals must be furnished for the convenience of the employer; (2) the meals must be furnished on the business premises of the employer.[3] As to lodging, the tests are: (1) the lodging must be furnished for the convenience of the employer; (2) the lodging must be furnished on the business premises of the employer; (3) the employee must be required to accept the lodging as a condition of his employment.[4]

The Supreme Court has stated that § 119 pre-empts the field and therefore the fair market value of meals and lodging which do not literally meet these tests are income.[5]

### *(3) Group Term Life Insurance*

Under general principles the employer's payment of premiums on a life insurance policy of the employee will generally constitute income to the employee.[6] However, as an encouragement to the provision of life insurance, the Code provides that payment by the employer of premiums on an employee life insurance policy for up to $50,000 of life insurance will not constitute income to the employee.[7] Unlike the case of meals and lodging, *supra,* where the exclusion seemed grounded to a large extent on fairness, this exclusion is a clear example of using the Internal Revenue Code to encourage socially desirable behavior.[8] (Treatment of the receipt of proceeds of life insurance—as opposed to the payment of the premium—is discussed at ¶ 3.06 infra.)

The basic rule is that employer payment of the premium on a standard group term life insurance policy for its employees does not

**3.** § 119(1); Reg. § 1.119–1(a).

**4.** § 119(2).

**5.** Commissioner v. Kowalski, 434 U.S. 77, 98 S.Ct. 315, 54 L.Ed.2d 252 (1977). "Meals" must be in kind, Reg. § 1.119–1(c)(2). If a cash allowance for meals is provided, it does not meet the literal terms of § 119 and will be included in income, *Kowalski,* supra. (Cash meal allowances to state troopers). The Supreme Court in *Kowalski* specifically declined to decide whether the long-standing exclusion for supper money to employees working overtime was still viable. Although, as the Court pointed out, this exclusion is not supported by the statute, the Court seemed to hold open the possibility that the exclusion might be justified on other grounds—*Kowalski,* p. 81, note 28. One such ground could be as a courtesy of small value. The Court's statement could also be interpreted as simply an invitation to the Service not to press the issue. The Service early ruled that supper money to employees working overtime is not income, O.D. 514, C.B. 2, 90 (1920), but then did not follow its own ruling in successfully maintaining in Fogle, 18 T.C.M. 1032 (1959), that supper money was income. The Court in *Kowalski* also explicitly

declined to decide whether sporadic meal reimbursements may be excluded from income (Cf. ¶ 2.02(1) supra).

Cf. Sibla v. Commissioner, 611 F.2d 1260 (9th Cir.1980), holding that where firemen were assessed a flat amount to finance organized firehouse lunch mess whether or not they actually participated in the mess, firemen could either exclude or deduct the amount of the assessment.

If the employee brings home the bacon in the form of free groceries furnished by the employer, the rule seems to be that constitutes meals for purposes of the statute. Compare Jacob v. United States, 493 F.2d 1294 (3d Cir.1974) (groceries are meals, thus qualifying for the exclusion) with Tougher, Jr. v. Commissioner, 51 T.C. 737 (1969), affirmed 441 F.2d 1148 (9th Cir.1971), cert. denied 404 U.S. 856, 92 S.Ct. 103, 30 L.Ed.2d 97 (1971) (groceries are not meals).

**6.** Reg. § 1.61–2(d)(2)(ii)(a).

**7.** § 79. Such payments will, of course, still be deductible by the employer.

**8.** See the discussion of "tax expenditures," ¶ 1.02(2)(c) supra.

constitute income to an employee unless his coverage exceeds $50,000.[9] This exclusion has come to be of great significance in the field of labor law where the amount of group life coverage for employees is the subject of collective bargaining. The Regulations are drafted to facilitate collective bargaining.

### (4) Employee Death Benefits

Employee death benefits paid to the beneficiary or the estate of the deceased employee are included in gross income. For deaths occurring prior to August 21, 1996, there was a $5,000 exclusion.

### (5) Accident and Health Benefits

The employer may fund a health plan for employees. Provided certain requirements are met, employer contributions to such plans will not be included in the employees' income. The payments made under such plans to employees for personal injuries or sickness may also, under certain conditions, be excluded from the employees' income. As an alternative, the employer may make direct payments to employees in the event of personal injuries or sickness. Under some conditions these direct payments too may be excluded from the employees' income.[10]

### (6) Current Razzle Dazzle Executive Compensation Techniques

There is a major trend among upper level management of both large and small companies to defer their compensation under so-called "nonqualified plans," with the result of delaying the payment of taxes. As the Prologue to this book has demonstrated, deferral of taxes is money in the bank to the taxpayer. This new major move in compensation techniques is beginning to undermine the tax base and also tends to increase the disparity in compensation between very well compensated top management of companies and the rest of the employees. In addition, even though these "nonqualified plans" for top management are supposed to be at risk in the event of bankruptcy, top management is able to protect it rights in bankruptcy negotiations. This was done in the cases of the bankruptcies of Morrison Knudsen, Carter Hawley Hale, and Woodward & Lothrop. For a detailed discussion of all these techniques, see ¶ 8.04(2)(a).

## ¶ 2.03    Bargain Purchases of Stock or Other Property

The employer may confer compensation on the employee (or independent contractor) by allowing him to buy property or stock at less than its market price (a "bargain" price).[1] Where such bargain pur-

---

9. § 79(a).

10. § 104(a)(3), 105, 106.

**¶ 2.03**

1. Independent contractors may also receive stock or other property at a bargain price. The entire analysis in the text applies to independent contractors as well as employees. Note that bargain purchases of stock are provided to independent contractors in a wide variety of situations: underwriters in a "firm commitment" distribution of a new issue of securities; organizers of a corporation who take stock at less than

chases are of property of relatively "small" value, they may be regarded as courtesies and hence not taxable. Where the bargain purchase involves property of significant value, there are then two types of transactions: the property may be unrestricted or restricted.

### (1) Unrestricted Property

Where the property that is purchased at the bargain price is not subject to any restrictions (such as, for example, that the employee must render substantial future services or return the property—see (2) infra), the employee has taxable ordinary income at the time he purchased it.[2] The amount of the taxable compensation income is the value of the property less the price the employee paid for it.[3] Thus, where an employer gave an employee two new cars in exchange for two used cars, the employee had compensation income.[4]

Usually, however, the bargain purchase is of stock of the corporate employer.[5] A major issue in this area of bargain purchases of unrestricted stock or other property is whether the "bargain" is really due to services rendered or to be rendered, or whether the bargain is due to other factors, thus rendering the transaction not taxable—or indeed whether there was any bargain at all.[6]

The basis (or cost) of the property received in a bargain purchase giving rise to compensation income is the amount paid for the property increased by the amount included in income.[7]

### (2) Restricted Property

#### (a) General Rule

Compensation may be conferred on an employee (or independent contractor) by allowing him to buy property at a bargain price, which property might have to be forfeited back to the employer in the future. These transfers usually involve stock of the employer and are generally engaged in to give the employee an interest in the future growth of the

the price sold to outside investors; lawyers and other corporate consultants may also be able to buy stock at less than its market value.

**2.**  § 83(a), See also Reg. § 1.61–2(d)(2)(i).

**3.**  Id.

**4.**  Strandquist, T.C. Memo 1970–84.

**5.**  Mason v. Commissioner, 125 F.2d 540 (6th Cir.1942), cert. denied 317 U.S. 657, 63 S.Ct. 56, 87 L.Ed. 529 (1942) (cash bonus to employee required to be immediately used to purchase stock of the corporate employer at less than market value. This is a technique that can be used to circumvent state law disallowing a direct issuance of stock for future services).

**6.**  Aspegren, Jr., 51 T.C. 945 (1969) (nonacq.) (taxpayer not aware he was getting stock at a bargain not taxable); Smith, 24 T.C.M. 899 (1965) (bargain purchase of second mortgage attributable to seller's distress hence not taxable); Berckmans, 20 T.C.M. 458 (1961) (contingencies depressed the value of the stock of a company bought by its organizers; hence they did not have a bargain purchase). The SEC turns over all registration statements and offering circulars to the Internal Revenue Service so that they may be analyzed to see if compensation of underwriters and promoters has been properly reported, I.R.–454, February 16, 1962.

**7.**  Reg. § 1.61–2(d)(2)(ii). See ¶ 4.03(2), for discussion of "basis."

company; hence this discussion will hereafter be limited to transfers of stock.

At the present time there are two major ways for employers to compensate their employees by using their own stock: non-qualified arrangements under § 83; and Incentive Stock Options. These two techniques serve somewhat different purposes. Incentive Stock Options involve the employee receiving an option to purchase the stock of the employer at the fair market value of the employer's stock at the date of the grant of the option. Thus the Incentive Stock Option is only attractive if the price of the employer's stock rises after the grant of the option. The Incentive Stock Option does not involve immediate ownership of the employer's stock. Non-statutory arrangements under § 83 allow the employee to gain immediate ownership of the employer's stock at a bargain price and yet give him the possibility of avoiding immediate tax on the bargain purchase. Thus an employee who wants to vote or immediately share in dividends of his corporate employer may prefer a § 83 arrangement to an Incentive Stock Option even though there are a number of tax advantages to the Incentive Stock Option.

The discussion here will only deal further with § 83 arrangements.

Section 83 deals with the taxation of stock transferred to an employee for a bargain price and subject to restrictions. (As indicated above, if the stock were transferred for a bargain price and not subject to restrictions, the result would be immediate compensation income of the bargain element.) Typical of the restrictions on such stock transfers would be a provision that the bargain purchase must be rescinded if the employee does not perform substantial future services for the employer within a specified time.[8] Other examples of risks of forfeiture: a provision that the stock purchased at a bargain price by an underwriter participating in a public offering must be returned to the issuing company for the original purchase price if the underwriting is not successful;[9] a provision that the stock purchased at a bargain price must be returned if the total earnings of the employer do not increase.[10]

---

8. Reg. § 1.83–3(c)(1) and (2).

9. Id.

10. Id. This list is not exclusive. A substantial risk of forfeiture also exists generally when the bargain transfer is conditioned on "the occurrence of a condition related to a purpose of the transfer, and the possibility of forfeiture is substantial if such condition is not satisfied," Reg. § 1.83–3(c)(1). Reg. § 1.83–3(c)(2) gives as an example of a condition which does not constitute a substantial risk of forfeiture a requirement that the property be returned to the employer if the employee is discharged for cause or for committing a crime. But suppose the employee is discharged for cause—and the cause is that he failed to perform substantial services. As described in the text, a requirement that the stock must be returned on failure to perform substantial services does constitute a substantial risk of forfeiture.

A risk that the property will decline in value is not a substantial risk of forfeiture nor is an arrangement whereby a retiring employee is transferred stock at a bargain price on the condition he render consulting advice when asked if the likelihood that he will be asked is low. A covenant not to compete might constitute a substantial risk of forfeiture. This Reg. provides some further discussion of the factors that will be used in ascertaining whether a condition constitutes a substantial risk of forfeiture.

If the risk of forfeiture is *substantial* (and the Regulations agree that the preceding examples do generally constitute substantial risks of forfeiture),[11] then the employee does not have to include the bargain element of the transaction in his income at the time of the transaction but can postpone inclusion in income until the substantial risk of forfeiture is lifted. This makes sense from a policy standpoint. If the employee had to include the income at the time the property is received, he might have difficulty coming up with the money to pay the tax, since property subject to a substantial risk of forfeiture is not very marketable. At the time the forfeiture is lifted, the employee includes as ordinary income the value of the stock at the time the forfeiture is lifted—not the value at the time of the transfer. This income amount is reduced by the employee's purchase price.[12] See discussion infra for additional rules on valuing the stock or other property transferred. If the pattern of stock ownership of the corporation is such that it is unlikely that the forfeiture will be enforced against the employee (e.g. because the employee owns a controlling amount of stock in the corporation), then in no event will the condition be regarded as a substantial risk of forfeiture, and the employee will have to include the bargain element of the transaction in his income at the time of the transaction.[13]

As a further important qualification on this treatment, if the property is received by the employee subject to a substantial risk of forfeiture, under the criteria discussed above, but can nonetheless be transferred to a third party who will hold the property free of the risk of forfeitability, then the bargain element in the transaction must be included in the employee's income at the time of the transfer.[14] This is because, under the statute, the property in these circumstances is "transferable," and hence immediate inclusion of the bargain element in income is required notwithstanding that the property is subject to a substantial risk of forfeiture.[15]

As an example of this transferability issue, suppose an employer transfers stock to an employee at a bargain price but for a two-year period the stock can be forfeited to the employer if the employee does not perform substantial services. The arrangement further provides, however, that if the employee transfers the stock to a third party within the

---

11. Id.

12. § 83(a). This is for transfers of restricted property occurring after June 30, 1969, § 83(i). The rules for transfers of restricted property prior to that time were considerably more lenient, providing generally that no tax was imposed until the restriction was lifted, at which time only the value of the stock at the time it was transferred was ordinary income; subsequent appreciation was capital gain. Congress felt this liberal treatment provided an end-run around the rules for qualified stock options at that time, Senate Report 91–552 accompanying the Tax Reform Act of 1969, 1969–3 C.B. 423, at 500.

The rules described in this section do not apply to qualified stock options and stock purchase plans, qualified pension and profit sharing plans, qualified annuity plans, the transfer of an option without a readily ascertainable fair market value, § 83(e).

13. Reg. § 1.83–3(c)(3), containing extensive discussion and examples on this enforceability question.

14. § 83(a), 83(c)(2), Reg. § 1.83–3(d).

15. Id.

two-year period, the third party will not forfeit the stock even though the employee does not perform substantial services. Under such conditions, the bargain element of the transaction would be included in the employee's income at the time of the transaction, notwithstanding that it is subject to a substantial risk of forfeiture, because it is "transferable."[16]

As indicated above, the amount that is included in income when the substantial risk of forfeiture is lifted is the value of the stock at the time the substantial risk of forfeiture is lifted less the price the employee paid for the stock, and this amount is ordinary income.[17] Particularly if the stock is of a closely-held corporation, the question of the value of the stock at the time the risk of forfeiture is lifted will present the usual controversy between the Service and the taxpayer concerning valuation. In this area, however, the statute provides a rule which may bear heavily on the question of valuation: if at the time the substantial risk of forfeiture is lifted, the stock is still subject to some other restriction which by its terms will never lapse (a "non-lapse restriction"), the restriction will be a major factor on the question of valuation.[18]

A "non-lapse restriction" is generally a condition subjecting the stock to a permanent right of first refusal, usually in favor of the employer or the other stockholders, in the event the employee would like to sell the stock.[19] The price at which the right of first refusal may be exercised, fixed by a formula or a flat price, will be considered the value of the stock unless the Service can carry the burden of establishing a higher value.[20]

If the non-lapse restriction is cancelled by the employer, the employee has compensation income in the amount of the increase in the value of the property unless he can carry the burden of showing (1) that the cancellation was not compensatory and (2) that the employer will not take a deduction for the cancellation.[21]

If, instead of being sold, the substantially non-vested property is forfeited by the employee because of the occurrence of the forfeiting event (such as his failure to render substantial services), the tax conse-

16. According to the legislative history, if the risk of forfeiture is not legended on the stock, so that the transferee would have no notice of it, the stock is considered transferable, regardless of the intent of employer and employee, Senate Report 91–552 note 12 supra at 502.

17. As opposed to being a capital gain, see ¶ 4.06.

18. § 83(a)(1), Reg. §§ 1.83–3(h), 1.83–5(a) and (c)

19. Reg. § 1.83–3(h).

20. Reg. § 1.83–5(a)

21. § 83(d)(2), Reg. § 1.83–5(b)(1)(i)–(iii). Whether the cancellation was compensatory depends on the facts and circum-

stances, as discussed at Reg. § 1.83–5(b)(1)(iv).

The Regs. set forth further discussion and examples of non-lapse restrictions. Notable in this discussion is the fact that stock sold under an exemption to the registration requirements of the federal securities laws, such as the private placement exemption, and thus restricted as to resale, is not considered to be stock subject to a non-lapse restriction. Of course once various information, volume and holding period requirements are met, stock sold under exemptions to the federal securities laws can be freely re-sold by subsequent transferees.

quence is that the difference between the amount paid (if any) for the property and the amount received (if any) upon the forfeiture will be treated as ordinary gain or loss.[22] The Regulations describe in relatively lucid fashion the tax consequences of a number of other possible transactions with substantially non-vested and substantially vested property (such as gifts, transfers at death, forfeiture even after substantial vesting, etc.).[23]

The employer in the bargain purchase setting is allowed to deduct the amount includible in the employee's income.[24] As discussed, the employee will have income on the occasion that the substantially non-vested property has become substantially vested or because a non-lapse restriction has been cancelled. The employer's deduction is allowed under §§ 162 or 212, and hence must meet their requirements as to reasonableness, etc.

### (b) Election

Where, in connection with the rendering of services, the employee or independent contractor has made a bargain purchase of substantially non-vested property (as defined above), he may elect to include the bargain element of the transaction as compensation income immediately, rather than following the general rule of deferring inclusion in income until the property has become substantially vested.[25] Under the election, the amount includible in income would be the fair market value of the property received, determined without regard to restrictions except restrictions which by their terms will never lapse,[26] less the price paid for the property.[27] If this election is made, the substantial vesting rules described above will not apply to this property—no further amount will be included in income when the property becomes substantially vested.[28] The basis of the property subject to this election will be the amount (if any) paid for it increased by the amount included in income on its receipt.[29] The holding period of property subject to the election commences just after its receipt.[30] A gain on subsequent sale of the property will not be treated as compensatory but will be capital gain (assuming, as would usually be the case, the property is a capital asset in the hands of the employee).[31]

**22.** Reg. § 1.83–1(b)(2). This treatment does not apply where the election, discussed infra, has been made to include the substantially non-vested property in income immediately upon its receipt.

**23.** Generally Regs. §§ 1.83–1, 1.83–4.

**24.** § 83(h), Reg. § 1.83–6(a)(1).

**25.** § 83(b), Reg. § 1.83–2(a). The election must be made not later than 30 days after the transfer. Reg. § 1.83–2(b)–(f) provide rules concerning the manner of making the election and revocation.

**26.** See discussion in text accompanying notes 18–20 supra.

**27.** § 83(b)(1), Reg. § 1.83–2(a).

**28.** Id.

**29.** Reg. § 1.83–2(a).

**30.** Reg. § 1.83–4(a).

**31.** Reg. § 1.83–2(a). A loss would also be capital. Trap for the unwary: suppose the employee receives substantially non-vested stock but pays the fair market value for it, without regard to the restrictions. Making the election would then appear to be an idle gesture and therefore might not be made, since there would be no amount to include in income at the time of the transfer. However, if the stock appreciates and is later sold for a profit, that profit will be

If, instead of being sold, the property subject to the election is subsequently forfeited back to the employer, because of the occurrence of the forfeiting event, no deduction of the amount previously included in income is allowed.[32] However, a deduction would be allowed equal to the excess of the amount paid (if any) on the original bargain purchase less the amount received (if any) on the forfeiture.[33]

Thus the calculus for ascertaining whether to make the election runs as follows: If it is expected that the stock will appreciate, it is probably most attractive to make the election so that the subsequent gain will be capital. However, even though the stock is expected to appreciate, several considerations cut in favor of not making the election. First, the employee may not have the wherewithal to pay any tax immediately—and it is probably difficult to sell the substantially non-vested stock to raise the money to pay the tax. Secondly, even though the employee has the cash to pay the tax, he may still prefer to defer payment of any of his tax (so as to have use of the money or because he will later be in a lower bracket) though his gain will ultimately all be compensatory. Third, if there were a significant possibility that the stock or other property will be forfeited on account of the occurrence of the forfeiting event, making the election is disadvantageous because no deduction is allowed for the previous inclusion in income.

Thus may the humble taxpayer, closeted with his tax advisor and a crystal ball, contemplate his choice.

### (3) How Not to Pay Tax on A Billion Dollars: Deferred Compensation Goes Better With Coke

For a dazzling example of how Mr. Robert Goizueta, the chief executive of the Coca Cola company employed § 83 to defer taxes on almost $1 billion of restricted stock, see ¶ 8.04(2)(a).

## ¶ 2.04 Other Items of Compensation Income

Taxable compensation may be received other than in the form of wages in the course of a regular job. Thus the Code and Regulations cast a broad net, specifying a number of items in the nature of compensation as income: fees, commissions, tips, bonuses, severance pay, rewards, jury fees, marriage fees, pay of persons in the armed forces, and pensions.[1] As discussed below, some of these items and other items in the nature of compensation present further problems.

compensatory , since the election was not made. Letter Ruling 7829007. Presumably also under these facts the appreciation would be taken in a s compensatory income if, instead of being sold, the stock was held until it became substantially vested.

**32.** § 83(b)(1)

**33.** Reg. § 1.83–2(a). See generally, Rosenberg, "The Tax Impact of Section 83

on Planning for Executive Compensation," 32 NYU Instit. Fed'l Taxation 1031 (1974); Johnson, "Tax Models for Nonrecourse Employee Liability," 32 Tax L.Rev. 359 (1977); Nasuti "New Twists for Nonstatutory Stock Options: How They Work; How They're Viewed by IRS," 53 J. of Tax. 142 (1980).

¶ 2.04

**1.** § 61(a), Reg. § 1.61–2(a)(1).

## (1) Tips

Although the Regs. specify tips as a form of compensation, an initial question might be raised concerning this treatment since the person paying the tip is usually not legally bound to pay it. Hence it might be questioned whether the tip is a gift and hence not taxable.[2] However as the discussion of the *Duberstein*[3] case (¶ 3.08) indicates, a payment arising in a business setting can constitute income notwithstanding that there was no legal obligation to make the payment.[4] The authorities are clear that all tips are income.[5]

Taxpayers receiving tips must report them monthly to the employer, and the tips are then treated as wages subject to withholding and social security taxes. As part of the reforms enacted by the Tax Equity and Fiscal Responsibility Act of 1982, "large food and beverage establishments" must meet extensive reporting requirements with respect to their gross receipts and reported tip income of their employees. If the tip income reported by the employees is less than 8% of the gross receipts, then the employer must under most circumstances allocate additional tip income to the employees for purposes of reporting to the IRS. These reporting requirements in no way preclude the IRS from proving that the employee received a higher amount of tip income than that reported.[6]

Congress's concern with the apparently low level of taxpayer compliance in reporting tip income led to these rather stringent reporting requirements.[7] Thus does Congress attempt to penetrate the so-called "underground economy" and recover some of its lost tax revenues. There will still no doubt continue to be a rather significant number of cases in which the IRS attempts to ascertain the amount of tip income that has been received by a taxpayer. A variety of formulas, based on the percentage of sales made by the tippee and other factors have been used by the Service to estimate tip income and have been upheld in the courts.[8]

## (2) Strike Payments

Payments by a union to striking or locked out employees are, under the general weight of authority, income. This is because usually these payments are made to the striking employees without regard to their

---

2.  § 102(a) and see ¶ 3.08 infra.

3.  363 U.S. 278, 80 S.Ct. 1190, 4 L.Ed.2d 1218 (1960), conformed to 283 F.2d 949 (6th Cir.1960).

4.  ¶ 3.08 infra. See also IR–284, April 4, 1959.

5.  Reg. § 1.61–2(a)(1). Cf. Olk v. United States, 536 F.2d 876 (9th Cir.1976), rev'g 388 F.Supp. 1108 (1975) (tips to casino croupiers are income notwithstanding that croupiers are usually prohibited from rendering extra services to the tipper and only 5 to 10 percent of casino customers tip).

6.  §§ 6053(a) and 6053(c), General Explanation of the Revenue Provisions of the Tax Equity and Fiscal Responsibility Act of 1982, pp. 199–202. Form 1070 may be used for reporting tips. The taxpayer may also use a pamphlet, Treasury Document 5635, for keeping a record of tips.

7.  Id.

8.  E.g. Cesanelli, 8 T.C. 776 (1947) (percentage of sales of waiter or waitress), Meneguzzo, 43 T.C. 824 (1965) (ratio of total tips to total wages in the business).

relative need, and often picketing duties are required of the recipients.[9] However, in United States v. Kaiser[10] the Supreme Court upheld a determination by a jury that under the facts of a particular case, strike benefits were a non-taxable gift. Deferring to the lower court's fact-finding, under the principles espoused in *Duberstein*,[11] decided the same year, the Court found that the jury's determination that the payments were a gift was supported by the evidence, including the facts that the taxpayer was not a member of the union when he started to receive the payments, assistance was granted on a need basis, picketing was expected but not required.[12]

The Service, in an apparent attempt to limit the reach of Kaiser, has stated that in facts "substantially like those in the *Kaiser* case" it will regard the payment as non-taxable gifts, but that "other cases will be scrutinized to determine whether the payments constitute gross income ..." However, according to the Service, that benefits are paid only to union members will not in itself render the payments income.[13]

### (3) Imputed Compensation Income

Where the taxpayer performs services for himself, he has income in an economic sense in the amount of the value of the services he performed. This type of income is part of the larger question of "imputed income"—income arising from assets the taxpayer owns as well as services he performs for himself. This type of income presents some knotty theoretical problems, as discussed in ¶¶ 1.02(2)(a) and (b); and ¶ 4.05(4).

This issue is not, however, of only theoretical interest. It has arisen in a number of actual cases. Over the years the Service has made attempts to tax imputed income—with some success.[14] Although the Service failed in early efforts to compel a farmer to include in income the value of the farm products consumed by the farmer and his family,[15] and

---

**9.** A leading case is Woody v. United States, 368 F.2d 668 (9th Cir.1966) (Strike benefits income to member of newspaper workers union where union made no inquiry into financial need.)

**10.** 363 U.S. 299, 80 S.Ct. 1204, 4 L.Ed.2d 1233 (1960), arising out of the bitter strike against the Kohler Company in Wisconsin in the mid–1950's.

**11.** Note 3 supra.

**12.** Note 10 supra.

**13.** Rev.Rul. 61–136, 1961–2 C.B. 20, at 21.

**14.** Indeed as early as the Revenue Acts of the mid 1800's (see ¶ 1.01 supra) the Commissioner of Internal Revenue was recommending to Congress that the rental value of owner-occupied housing be included in income. Congress, however, rejected these proposals, see Smith, The United States

Federal Internal Tax History, From 1861–1870, (1914), pp. 58–76.

**15.** Morris v. Commissioner, 9 B.T.A. 1273 (1928), acq. VII–2 C.B. 75. See also T.D. 2665, March 18, 1918, disallowing deductions for expenses in raising the products consumed at home. To the same effect are the Instructions to Schedule F of Form 1040. The *Morris* court clearly perceived this as an imputed income problem in rejecting the Service's contention on the ground that "If products of a farm consumed thereon are income to the producer, it would seem to follow that the rental value of the farmer's home, the gratuitous services of his wife and children, and the value of the power derived from draft animals owned by the farmer and used without cost should also be considered. It is obvious that such items are comparable to the rental value of a private residence, which has never been regarded as income or as a

to compel the owner of a tavern to include in income the value of liquor he had consumed,[16] the Service has succeeded notably in a line of commission cases. Commissions paid to an insurance agent for selling himself insurance,[17] a real estate salesman for selling himself real estate,[18] and a stockbroker for selling himself stock[19] have all been included in income.

These cases can, perhaps, be distinguished from the usual imputed income situation on the basis that there is money and a profession involved: an employer or independent contractor has paid the taxpayer a commission for the taxpayer being his own client. Some such rationale is needed to explain the commission cases; otherwise why is not the taxpayer who cleans his own house or mows his own lawn creating income in the amount of the value of his own services?

The commission cases are the only examples thus far of imputed income being taxed to the taxpayer.[20] But might the Service begin again to test the limits of this concept? Suppose a professional tax return preparer, complying with the reporting rules,[21] prepares his own tax return? Although no commission may be involved, the taxpayer has worked for himself professionally—and the Service can easily ascertain that fact. The lack of a strong conceptual basis for distinguishing the commission cases from other examples of imputed income gives pause in this area.

### (4) Other Miscellaneous Items of Compensation Income

Unemployment compensation payments paid by state or federal governments are taxable if they exceed certain levels.

Payments by employers to employees for violation of Title VII of the Civil Rights Act of 1964 outlawing discrimination in employment based on race, religion, sex, or national origin are taxable where the underlying

factor in the determination of tax liability," *Morris,* supra at 1275. But see Dicenso v. Commissioner, 11 B.T.A. 620 (1928) (Owner of a grocery store must include in income the value of groceries he consumes).

**16.** Appeal of Sweeten, 3 B.T.A. 37 (1925) (acq.).

**17.** Commissioner v. Minzer, 279 F.2d 338 (5th Cir.1960) (commission on insurance policy on agent's life, income, not a reduction in purchase price of the policy which was barred by state law); Mensik v. Commissioner, 328 F.2d 147 (7th Cir.1964), cert. denied 379 U.S. 827, 85 S.Ct. 55, 13 L.Ed.2d 37 (1964) (waived commissions on sales to relatives, employees, and friends).

**18.** Commissioner v. Daehler, 281 F.2d 823 (5th Cir.1960) (commission paid to agent by his employer on agent's own purchase of land through employer was income to agent, not a reduction in purchase price of land, following *Minzer* note 17 supra).

**19.** Kobernat, 31 T.C.M. 593 (1972) (purchase and sale of securities for broker, his wife and their joint account). But see Benjamin v. Hoey, 139 F.2d 945 (2d Cir. 1944) where a partner in a stockbrokerage firm did not include in income that portion of his partnership net income attributable to commissions on transactions in his own account. This case may be an aberration or there may be a partnership exception to these commission cases.

**20.** See also Helvering v. Independent Life Insurance Co., 292 U.S. 371, 378–379, 54 S.Ct. 758, 759–760, 78 L.Ed. 1311 (1934), (dictum that the rental value of owner-occupied housing is not income within the Sixteenth Amendment; hence a tax upon it is a direct tax requiring apportionment among the states) (see ¶¶ 1.01 and 4.05(4)).

**21.** See § 6695.

facts show the payments are in lieu of compensation that would have otherwise been received.[22]

"Cafeteria plan" benefits are not taxed, under § 125. This does not refer to an employee lunchroom but rather to a fringe benefit compensation scheme in which an employee has the right to choose between a particular benefit and the equivalent amount of cash. Under the law prior to the enactment of § 125, such an arrangement would give rise to a tax to the employee even if he chose under the plan a fringe benefit that would otherwise have been non-taxable (such as accident and health insurance). The principle was that where cash (which is always taxable if chosen) is an alternative the employee is viewed as having taken the cash and used it to purchase the alternative benefit. Section 125 insures that employees who select the otherwise non-taxable fringe benefit under a cafeteria plan will not be taxed on it. To qualify for this treatment the cafeteria plan must be written and cannot discriminate in favor of highly compensated individuals.

**22.**  Rev. Rul. 72–341, 1972–2 C.B. 32.

# Chapter 3

# OTHER ITEMS OF INCOME AND EXCLUSIONS FROM INCOME

*Table of Sections*

The concept of income, of course, stretches well beyond the receipt of compensation for the rendering of personal services. It reaches a great many items which, though not in the nature of compensation, increase the wealth of the taxpayer.[1] As the discussion in Chapter One indicated, the outer limits of the concept of income are far from clear.[2] Nonetheless, a large number of items not in the nature of compensation has been established to be income by statute or case law. Moreover because of the broad reach of the income concept, the Code, for various reasons, specifically excludes some items from income under some circumstances. These problems are the topic of this chapter.

---

1. § 61, and see ¶ 1.02(2)(b) relating to the comprehensive tax base.

2. ¶ 1.02(2)(b) supra, relating to the comprehensive tax base.

## ¶ 3.01   Interest

### *(1) In General*

The general rule is that interest is taxable income.[1] Interest can only arise out of a bona fide indebtedness.[2] However courts will use a "substance over form" analysis to find a loan and hence interest income despite a taxpayer's assertion that the transaction is a sale and repurchase, hence giving rise to capital gain.[3]

Where the agreement is bona fide and negotiated at arm's length the Service and the courts will generally defer to the intent of the parties as to how much of a particular repayment of an indebtedness is interest and how much is principal.[4] This is clearly because the lender and the borrower have adverse interests on the question of how much of a particular loan payment is denominated "interest." To the extent the lender delays the receipt of interest income and all of the first payments are ascribed to principal, the borrower is deprived of an interest deduction.[5] Hence even a loan arrangement in which, by agreement of the parties, all repayments to the cash method taxpayer were first to be credited to the principal was respected.[6]

While this "hands-off" approach appears logical, it is not fully persuasive. Though the lender and the borrower may be at arm's length, one party or the other may have no particular motivation to negotiate on the question of the timing of the interest payment. The borrower, for example, may already be running losses, therefore have no great use for the interest deduction, and hence be willing to let the lender have that matter all his own way. Or, though the parties are at arm's length, they may not have equal bargaining power, and hence one side may be able to have the question of how the loan repayments are denominated all his

---

¶ 3.01

**1.** § 61(a)(4).

**2.** Taylor, 27 T.C. 361 (1956), aff'd 258 F.2d 89 (2d Cir.1958). But see United States v. Williams, 395 F.2d 508 (5th Cir. 1968) (dicta that "interest" as a "compensation for advance payment" could exist notwithstanding that the underlying transaction was not a loan but a prepayment of rent). Cf. Franklin, 544 F.2d 1045 (9th Cir. 1976), ¶ 8.02(4), denying an interest *deduction* in the tax shelter setting in the absence of a bona fide debt.

In the category of "last laugh" is the long-standing rule that where the taxpayer gets a refund of tax from the Treasury, the interest on that refund is taxable, I.T. 2210, C.B. IV-2, 43 (1925), Rev.Rul. 62–160, 1962–2 C.B. 139.

**3.** Comtel Corp., 376 F.2d 791 (2d Cir. 1967), cert. denied 389 U.S. 929, 88 S.Ct.

290, 19 L.Ed.2d 280 (1967), recounting the complex tale of the Zeckendorf interests' attempt to purchase the Commodore Hotel financed through what the court found in substance to be a loan from Comtel Corp., giving rise to interest income to Comtel. The maneuver of attempting to create capital gain instead of interest income is not of great significance under current law, where capital gains are not favorably treated. Still it seems well to bear the capital gain issue in mind, since it could come back to the fore if the favorable treatment of capital gains is reinstituted. See ¶ 4.06.

**4.** Rev.Rul. 63–57, 1963–1 C.B. 103; Huntington–Redondo Co. v. Commissioner, 36 B.T.A. 116 (1937) (acq.).

**5.** Rev.Rul. 63–57, note 4 supra, at 105.

**6.** Id.

own way.[7] However, the Service's "hands-off" approach as to the reporting of interest, with the exceptions noted below, is very well established.

### (2) Tax Exempt Interest

As a major refuge from the progressive rate structure for the high income taxpayer, interest on most obligations of any state, territory or possession of the United States, or any political subdivision thereof, or of the District of Columbia is exempt from taxation.[8] This exemption for interest on government obligations has been in the tax law since the first income tax statute in 1913[9] and may rest on constitutional grounds.[10] The exemption of the interest on state and municipal bonds from taxation, of course, increases the after tax yield on those bonds. The higher the taxpayer's bracket the more attractive is the tax-exempt bond because the greater is the tax being saved. Thus for a taxpayer in the 20% bracket, the yield on a tax-exempt bond paying 7% is equal to the yield on a taxable bond paying 8.75%. For a taxpayer in the 50% bracket, the yield on a tax exempt bond paying 7% is equal to the yield on a taxable bond paying 14%.

Thus has the tax-exempt state and municipal bond come to be a major target of those who would "reform" the Internal Revenue Code, as discussed in ¶¶ 1.02(2)(b) and 1.02(2)(c), relating to the comprehensive tax base and tax expenditures. Whatever the merits of the argument to tax the interest on state and municipal bonds (and there is something to be said on both sides), there are many political interests who favor the exemption—not only high income taxpayers and their advisors, but also states and municipalities themselves who can therefore issue bonds at lower interest rates, bond counsel, investment banking firms, public works contractors, etc. Hence it seems clear the exemption will remain in the tax law for the foreseeable future, as a form of revenue sharing between the federal government and the states.

Interest on obligations of the U.S. government or any agency thereof does not enjoy the exemption.[11] Nor does the interest on "arbitrage

---

**7.** The widespread custom in the home mortgage and other consumer finance areas is, of course, to have most of the early repayments denominated interest. For an analysis suggesting this treatment is in error, see ¶ 1.02(e).

**8.** § 103(a). If the "interest" is not really interest, the exemption will not apply, however. See Rev.Rul. 58–536, 1958–2 C.B. 21, (citing a number of other authorities for the proposition that where an underwriter detaches an interest coupon from a tax exempt bond as compensation for marketing the issue, collection on the coupon constitutes taxable compensation, not tax free interest; moreover, and most curiously, the "taint" remains, and any subsequent purchaser of the interest coupon also has taxable ordinary income on collection).

The Tax Equity and Fiscal Responsibility Act of 1982 imposed a 10% withholding requirement on the payers of interest and dividends subject to certain exemptions and limitations, effective for payments paid or credited after June 30, 1983.

Original issue discount on tax-exempt government securities is treated as tax-exempt interest, Rev.Rul. 73–112, 1973–1 C.B. 47.

**9.** 63 Stat. 168 (1913).

**10.** There is a debate as to whether this exemption is commanded by the Constitution. See e.g. H.R.Rept. 413, 91st Cong., 1st Sess. pt. 1 at 172–174, 1969.

**11.** Reg. § 1.103–4(b).

bonds,''—in general bonds sold by states or municipalities whose proceeds are reinvested in securities which pay a materially higher yield than the bonds sold.[12]

### (3) *Private Activity Bonds; Qualified Bonds*

In the late 1940's and early 1950's, the exemption of interest on state and local bonds began to be taken advantage of by private businesses. The typical arrangement was that the state or municipality would issue a so-called industrial development bond whose proceeds would be used to purchase or construct a facility to be leased to a private corporation. The bonds would be secured by the facility and amortized out of the rents paid by the corporation.[13] Hence the state or municipality's tax-exempt bonds were in effect being used to finance private businesses, at a lower interest rate than if the businesses had to finance themselves with taxable bonds. In the 1950's the Service began to grapple with this problem, issuing a series of rulings designed to limit the tax exemption to those industrial development bonds which were financing projects of a public nature.[14] Eventually the Service announced that it was going to issue proposed regulations that would deny the interest exemption to all industrial development bonds.[15]

At this juncture Congress stepped in for the express purpose of barring the Service's aspirations in this area.[16] Congress enacted legislation which more or less codified the Service's earlier rulings, which allowed the interest exemption for bonds financing projects of an essentially public nature.

The field is now covered heavily by § 141. One can make a career as a bond counsel shepherding bond issues through to qualify for the tax exempt interest. It's a comfy living. It could happen to you.

## ¶ 3.02   Original Issue Discount

### (1) *Background*

The present value analysis of this area has been set forth extensively in the Prologue at ¶ 1.5.5. As pointed out there, understanding original issue discount is a key to understanding the field of time value of money in taxation. This discussion complements the Prologue analysis by giving a background on the development of the legal rules in this area. The reader who has perused the Prologue's discussion of time value of money analysis of original issue discount may find the historical discussion here quite interesting. It is interesting to see how far we have come from the

---

**12.**  § 103(c).

**13.**  Senate Report No. 1014 on Tax Adjustment Act of 1968, March 15, 1968, 1968–2 C.B. 790, at 794.

**14.**  Rev.Ruls. 54–106, 1954–1 C.B. 28; 57–187, 1957–1 C.B. 65; 63–20, 1963–1 C.B. 24.

**15.**  TIR 972, March 6, 1968.

**16.**  ". . . The Committee on Finance is concerned that the Treasury Department in taking this action (denying the interest exemption) is, in effect, legislating on this subject. It does not believe that change should be made in the status of the interest on these bonds without specific legislative action on the part of the Congress.'' Senate Report, note 19 supra, at 794.

primitive attempts to understand and tax original issue discount decades ago.

Recapitulating the meaning of original issue discount: Where a corporation or other entity issues bonds or notes, the interest stated on the obligations may be insufficient, given prevailing market conditions. Hence the only way to sell the obligations may be to offer them at less than their face value. Thus a note which will be paid $100 at maturity, plus 6% interest annually may have to be sold at $97 because the 6% interest is inadequate. The extra $3, called original issue discount, is economically the same as interest: for the use of the $97 the issuer of the obligation has to pay the 6% interest annually plus the extra $3 at maturity.

Many obligations are sold with original issue discount. This is because there is inevitably a time lag between the time the debt certificates are printed up with a particular face amount and interest rate and the time the debt issue is finally marketed. In that intervening time interest rates may have increased somewhat, necessitating that the debt issue be sold at a discount from face value in order to remain competitive. (Should interest rates drop during the period between printing and sale, the issue would be marketed at a premium price in excess of the face amount. This then raises the question of how the issuer should amortize this premium as a cost of capital—see § 171 and see discussion infra). In addition to these factors, much short-term commercial paper is offered without any stated interest at all but is as a matter of course marketed at a discount from its face price. Thus for all these reasons a great many long-term and short-term debt obligations are marketed with original issue discount.

Although it has long been undisputed that original issue discount was functionally the same as interest, treatment of it has given the courts, the service and Congress a good deal of trouble over the years. As an initial matter the problem grew out of the 1939 Code which provided that favorable capital gains treatment would arise on the sale or exchange of a capital asset.[1] This led to a great deal of wrangling over whether original issue discount was a capital asset for purposes of the statute, notwithstanding its economic equivalence to interest.[2]

Matters took a bleak turn for the Service in the case of Caulkins v. Commissioner[3] in 1943 in which the Tax Court, later affirmed by the Sixth Circuit, held that the gain on retirement of ten-year non-interest bearing certificates marketed at a discount was capital under the statute. The Service, in not its finest hour, reacted to this setback by first nonacquiescing to *Caulkins* in 1943, then acquiescing in 1944, then

¶ 3.02

1. 1939 Code § 117(a), the predecessor to § 1221 of the 1954 Code.

2. See S.Rep. No. 1622, 83rd Cong., 2d Sess. p. 112 (1954).

3. 1 T.C. 656 (1943), aff'd 144 F.2d 482 (6th Cir.1944).

reinstating its original nonacquiescence retroactively 11 years later in 1955.[4]

The Supreme Court in 1965 spoke definitively on the matter in United States v. Midland–Ross,[5] dealing with pre 1954 code tax years, holding that original issue discount as the functional equivalent of interest was not a capital asset; hence gain attributable to it was ordinary income on sale of the bond. In the 1954 Code, Congress had provided the same result.[6] Although at first blush this appeared to lay the problem to rest, there still remained a debate over *when* would the discount properly be income: spread out ratably over the life of the notes (i.e., as "earned" in some sense) or only when the notes were sold or retired? The court in *Midland Ross* assumed without discussing it that the discount was income only when the notes were sold—and this was the legislative treatment in 1954. Yet, if original issue discount were to be truly treated as interest, it should be taken into income over the life of the bond.

Congress enacted some apparently reasonable rules in this area in 1969, providing for the accrual of original discount ratably over time. Thus, for example, a ten-year bond with a face amount of $100 issued at $90 would accrue $1 of taxable original issue discount per year; the basis of the bond would also go up by $1 per year to reflect this inclusion in income. (These rules are discussed in more detail at ¶ 3.02(2) below).

After these rules had been in effect for some years, it became apparent that they did not accurately reflect the economics of original issue discount. In particular, the 1969 rules did not reflect the fact that the holder of an original issue discount bond does not in fact receive the cash represented by the original issue discount until the bond matures. In effect the holder of the bond is re-lending the interest to the issuer, indeed at further interest. In short, the 1969 ratable accrual rules ignored the effects of compounding.

It can be shown mathematically (see the Prologue ¶ 1.5.5) that when account is taken of the effect of compounding, the holder of the bond has relatively small income in the early years and relatively large income in the later years of the life of the bond. Similarly, the issuer of the original issue discount bond should not deduct the OID ratably over the life of the bond, as the 1969 rules had provided. Rather, the issuer should take a relatively small deduction in the early years of the life of the bond and a relatively large deduction in the later years.

During the period after the issuance of the 1969 rules, particularly in the late 1970's (during a time of high interest rates), corporations began to take full advantage of this weakness in the 1969 rules by issuing deeply discounted bonds. They were then taking very large deductions attributable to this discount.

---

**4.** Rev.Rul. 55–136, 1955–1 C.B. 213, at 214.

**5.** 381 U.S. 54, 85 S.Ct. 1308, 14 L.Ed.2d 214 (1965).

**6.** § 1232(a)(2).

Congress responded in the Tax Equity and Fiscal Responsibility Act of 1982 by providing new rules for the taxation of original issue discount to reflect the effect of compounding. These new rules are effective for bonds issued after July 1, 1982. Corporate bonds issued after May 27, 1969, and before July 1, 1982, continue to be subject to the 1969 rules. The new rules dramatically reduce the deduction available in the early years to the issuer of an original issue discount bond. And the new rules dramatically reduce the taxable income to the holder of the OID bond in its early years. Both income and deductions are "back-loaded" by the new rules to take account of the effect of compounding. See the charts at the Prologue ¶ 1.5.5.

There were obviously many long-term bonds issued during this period between 1969 and 1982. Many of these bonds will continue to be held by institutions and the public for another decade or two or longer. The treatment of original issue discount on these bonds will continue to be governed by the 1969 rules. At the same time, of course, many new discount bonds are being issued after July 1, 1982. The discount on these bonds will be governed by the new 1982 rules.

Thus the upshot is that there are now two rather different and rather complex rules for the treatment of original issue discount both in effect at the same time. Which of the rules applies depends on the issuing date of the particular bond. Obviously as time passes, the number of bonds subject to the 1969 rules will go down and the number of bonds subject to the 1982 rules will go up. But for many years to come it will be necessary to have an understanding of both rules in this area.

First the 1969 rules will be discussed briefly, followed by the rules enacted by the Tax Equity and Fiscal Responsibility Act of 1982. Understanding the 1969 rules helps to understand the changes brought about in 1982. As I have said before, this was really the pioneering area in opening up the time value of money analysis in federal income taxation.

### (2) The 1969 Rules

As indicated above, Congress in 1969 put into place a set of rules for the treatment of original issue discount which involve the ratable accrual of original issue discount over the life of the bond, under old § 1232(a)(3)(now repealed). In particular, the holder of such a bond must include in income the ratable monthly portion of original issue discount, defined as the original issue discount divided by the number of months from issue date to maturity multiplied by the number of months such holder held the obligation. As the original issue discount is included in income, the basis of the obligation increases. If the first holder of the obligation sells it before maturity, any subsequent holder will be required to include in income the same ratable monthly portion of original issue discount. See the Prologue, ¶ 1.5.5 for some mathematical and graphical examples of how this works.

### (3) *The 1982 Rules*

As the discussion at ¶ 3.02(1) indicated, the fundamental change in the original issue discount rules effected by the Tax Equity and Fiscal Responsibility Act of 1982 was to take account of the compounding that occurs when the holder of an original issue discount bond in effect re-lends the interest to the issuer. The holder of an original issue discount bond, issued after July 1, 1982, includes in his income the ratable portion of original issue discount computed with reference to the yield to maturity determined on the basis of compounding.[7] The basis of the bond is increased to reflect this inclusion in income. This inclusion in income and upward basis adjustment is deemed to be done daily. See the mathematical and graphical analysis at Prologue ¶ 1.5.5.

The issuer of the discount bond similarly computes its deduction by reference to compounding—thus the amortization of the discount bond will give rise to a relatively small deduction in the early years of the bond and a relatively large deduction in the later years.

Where the bond is sold and the subsequent holder pays more for the bond than the basis of the original holder (as adjusted upward to reflect the daily inclusion in income), the subsequent holder will reduce his daily ratable inclusion into income of original issue discount by the ratable portion of the excess of what he paid over the basis of the seller at the time of the sale. This approach insures that the subsequent holder will have a basis equal to the face amount of the bond at maturity.

A buyer who pays less than the seller's basis for the bond will make no such correction. He will simply include the usual daily ratable amount into income and increase his basis by that same amount. At maturity, he will have a further gain.[8]

## ¶ 3.03    Dividends and Other Distributions to Stockholders

Students considering going on in the field to take corporate taxation may find this material useful. The stockholder of a corporation may receive payments from the corporation with respect to his stock. These payments may be in the form of cash, property, or additional stock of the corporation. The stockholder may also have some or all of his stock

---

7. §§ 1271–1275.

8. These new rules do not apply to obligations issued by individuals, state and local tax-exempt obligations, U.S. Treasury Bills, U.S. Savings Bonds, and (of course) bonds purchased at a premium rather than a discount.

As a historical curiosity, while passing these new original issue discount rules under the Tax Equity and Fiscal Responsibility Act of 1982, Congress also took the occasion to close up a tax avoidance maneuver known in the trade as "coupon stripping." This was actually a maneuver developed by Michael Milken, among his many other ex-

ploits. This involved the holder of a bearer bond separating the unmatured interest coupon from the bond and selling either the coupon, the bond, or both. Taxpayers engaging in this maneuver argued that they should receive certain attractive treatment with respect to the computation of the basis of the bond and the coupon. They also argued that the original issue discount rules did not apply to the coupon and the stripped bond, which allowed them to defer gain on these instruments until maturity. The Tax Equity and Fiscal Responsibility Act closed the door on this maneuver.

redeemed by the corporation, or the corporation may be liquidated. In all of these transactions, the questions are whether the stockholder has received any amount that is taxable; and if he has, whether the amount he has received is taxable as ordinary (dividend) income or as capital gain.[1] These are complex questions, a detailed treatment of which is beyond the scope of this work. Hence, only an outline will be set forth here.

An individual who is a stockholder of a corporation may receive a payment from his corporation in the form of cash (or other property) or in the form of the corporation's stock. Where the payment is in the form of cash or property, it is taxable as ordinary income to the extent of the earnings and profits of the corporation. If the amount of the distribution exceeds the earnings and profits, the excess will reduce the taxpayer's basis in his stock. This basis treatment is known (in this book) by the sobriquet "Stupid Treatment," see Chapter 1, ¶ 1.02(2)(e)(i). If the distribution exceeds both earnings and profits and the stock's basis, that excess will be treated as a gain.

If the distribution to the stockholder is of the corporation's own stock, a different set of rules are triggered. From early in the history of the tax law, stock dividends created problems for the Service and the courts. In the seminal case of Eisner v. Macomber[2] the Supreme Court held that a stockholder in receipt of a 50% stock dividend declared by Standard Oil to all shareholders had no taxable income, because no gain had been realized: " ... The essential and controlling fact is that the stockholder has received nothing out of the company's assets for his separate use and benefit; on the contrary, every dollar of his original investment, together with whatever accretions and accumulations have resulted from employment of his money and that of the other stockholders in the business of the company, still remains the property of the company, and subject to business risks ... (the taxpayer) has received nothing that answers the definition of income ... "[3]

This theme that a pro rata stock dividend does not give rise to income was eventually picked up by the Code.[4] However, there are now variations on that theme. Where the stock distribution is not pro rata—where, for example, some stockholders get a distribution of stock and the others get a distribution of cash—the stock received is taxable as a cash payment under the principles discussed above, to the extent of its fair

¶ 3.03

1. Other major transactions which corporations may engage in which have ramifications for the stockholders are the formation of the corporation, various corporate combinations (mergers, acquisitions of assets, acquisitions of stock), corporate divisions (spin-offs, split-offs, and split-ups), and recapitalizations (reshuffling of the corporation's capital structure). These transactions also present the questions for the stockholders of whether anything taxable was received, and if so whether it is taxable as ordinary income or capital gain. See generally, D. Posin, Corporate Tax Planning: Takeovers Leveraged Buyouts and Restructurings (1990).

2. 252 U.S. 189, 40 S.Ct. 189, 64 L.Ed. 521 (1920). See ¶ 4.02(1).

3. Id. at 195, 40 S.Ct. at 211.

4. § 305(a).

market value.[5] This is because, unlike in *Macomber,* the stockholder in receipt of a stock dividend which other stockholders have not received has enjoyed an increase in his percentage ownership of the corporation's assets. This is an event of economic significance and is thus an occasion to impose tax.

Where the stockholder has some or all of his stock redeemed (i.e., bought back) by the corporation for an amount greater than his basis in the stock, there is no doubt that the stockholder has taxable gain. This transaction is simply a sale or exchange of the stock, which is an occasion to impose tax.

A liquidation is a complete termination of all stockholders' interests in the corporation and generally gives rise to gain (or loss) from, in effect, a sale of the stock.

## ¶ 3.04 Rents

### (1) In General

Rent is income,[1] whether received in the form of cash or property.[2] Payments may be held to be rent, though not so denominated.[3]

For discussion of the case where a lessee makes improvements to leased property which are then received by the lessor on the termination of the lease, see ¶ 4.02(1).

## ¶ 3.05 Royalties

### (1) In General

Royalties are income.[1] Royalties can arise from books, stories, plays, copyrights, trademarks, formulas, patents, and from the exploitation of natural resources, such as coal, gas, oil, copper, or timber.[2] Royalty and other income from the discovery and exploitation of natural resources enjoy a number of favorable tax rules, on the theory that such favorable treatment will stimulate new production.[3] Payments received on the

---

**5.** § 305(b). The cash dividend is also, of course, taxable on the principles discussed above.

**¶ 3.04**

**1.** § 61(a)(5).

**2.** C.G. Meaker Co., Inc., 16 T.C. 1348 (1951) (landlord corporation's receipt of its own stock back for renewal of a lease constituted rental income in the amount of the value of the stock.).

Payments which are not even directly received at all may constitute rent to the landlord. Thus to the extent the lessee pays the property tax and insurance etc. on the leased property, the lessor will have rental income, Reg. § 1.61–8(c).

**3.** Commissioner v. Riss, 374 F.2d 161 (8th Cir.1967) (amounts in addition to rent for airplane paid as a deposit against contingency plane would have to be overhauled were rent in year it was established plane would not have to be overhauled); Kennedy, 33 T.C.M. 655 (1974) (receipts from share-cropping rent); cf. Washington Fireproof Building Co., 31 B.T.A. 824, 1934 WL 157 (1934); Waggoner v. Commissioner, 15 T.C. 496 (1950) (payments for damages above ordinary wear and tear were return of capital, not rent).

**¶ 3.05**

**1.** § 61(a)(6).

**2.** Reg. § 1.61–8(a).

**3.** These favorable rules for natural resources include: percentage depletion (allowing the taxpayer to deduct more than his original cost of the property—not

transfer of patent rights may under some circumstances constitute capital gain instead of ordinary royalty income.[4]

### (2) Advance Royalties: It's Only a Paper Moon

Analogous to the rent area, advance royalties are taxable as ordinary income on receipt.[5]

Notwithstanding this general rule it appears possible under some circumstances to structure the advance royalty transaction as a loan and thereby avoid taxation on the advance payment. In the interesting case of *Arlen*[6] the taxpayer, a songwriter, was given a $50,000 interest-free loan[7] by his publisher, repayable at $5000 a year, in exchange for the taxpayer assigning the publisher renewal rights to copyrights on his songs. The publisher could, but did not have to, apply royalties due to the taxpayer against the $5000 annual repayments. To the extent the publisher did not choose to credit the royalties against the $5000 annual payments or to the extent the royalties were insufficient to cover the annual payments, the taxpayer was personally liable for the $5000 annual payments. The loan was evidenced by negotiable promissory notes, and treated as such on the publisher's books. The taxpayer's royalty history indicated his royalties would be more than $5000 a year. The publisher did indeed amortize the loan by applying $5000 of royalties against the annual repayments.

Against the Service's challenge that the arrangement was in substance a $50,000 advance against future royalties taxable in full on receipt, the Tax Court held that the arrangement was really a loan. There was, the Tax Court found, a valid business purpose for structuring the transaction as a loan, because under the copyright law, in the event of the death of Arlen and his wife more than a year earlier than the renewal date of the copyright of any of the songs, an assignment of the copyright of such song to the publisher *might* be void. With the transaction in the form of a loan, the publisher would then be able to recoup his payment.

However, the transaction was taking place within a year of the renewal date of half the songs. Hence the assignment could not be void as to them. If Arlen *or* his wife survived only a few more years, the assignment of at least another quarter of the songs could not become void. Therefore, despite the Tax Court's finding that the entire $50,000

---

available for large oil and gas operators); election to deduct intangible drilling and development costs, and election to deduct exploration and development costs (costs which under ordinary rules would be capitalized, see ¶ 6.03(4)). See generally, Subchapter I of Subtitle A of the Internal Revenue Code. See also Miller, "Percentage Depletion and the Level of Domestic Mineral Production," 15 Natural Resources Journal 241 (1975), suggesting that percentage depletion may discourage rather than encourage natural resource production.

**4.** § 1235 and see ¶ 4.06(3)(a)(vi).

**5.** ¶ 3.04 supra. Holbrook v. United States, 194 F.Supp. 252 (D.Or.1961) (advances against author's royalties income on receipt, based on analysis of intention of the parties).

**6.** 48 T.C. 640 (1967) (acq.).

**7.** See ¶ 3.10.

was a loan, the business reason for structuring the entire transaction as a loan was not overpowering.[8]

Nonetheless, the Service acquiesced in this decision.[9] This decision meant that rather than being taxed on the entire $50,000 when received, the taxpayer was taxed on the $5000 or so royalties earned each year and paid to him and/or applied against the loan. The advantage here was in the deferral of tax liability (see the Prologue) and the spreading of the tax liability out over a number of years, possibly resulting in application of lower rates, since the taxable income would not be bunched in one year.

Several factors were crucial to the Tax Court's finding of a loan in *Arlen:* (1) The possibility of the copyright assignments becoming void, as found by the Tax Court; (2) The taxpayer's personal liability to repay the loan in the event the royalties proved to be insufficient; (3) The holding by the lender of negotiable notes of the taxpayer. These notes could, of course, have been sold to a third party for collection against the taxpayer without regard to whether the royalties were earned.

An author, composer, or artist wishing to receive a substantial payment in the nature of advance royalties tax-free would apparently have to plan the transaction to meet these conditions. Meeting these conditions, however, would be relatively difficult. It would be difficult to build into the typical royalty situation the potential failure of consideration that existed in *Arlen* with respect to the possible voiding of the copyright assignments. Probably few authors, composers, or artists would be willing to bind themselves to repay the advance payment in the event the project did not earn sufficient royalties. Most formidable of all perhaps, would be the necessity of executing negotiable notes to repay.

Notwithstanding these difficulties, the author, composer or artist who is about to receive a substantial advance payment and who is confident his royalties will earn out may be willing to meet these conditions in order to receive the advance payment as a tax-free loan. For those taxpayers with the temerity to follow him, songwriter Harold Arlen's Tax Court case may prove to be his finest melody.

## ¶ 3.06   Proceeds From Life Insurance

Although as a broad general rule proceeds from life insurance

---

**8.** Note 6 supra at 647. Therefore, notwithstanding that Harold Arlen wrote "I've Got a Right to Sing the Blues," (1932), he most certainly did not in this instance. On the contrary, he proved that though "It's Only a Paper Moon" (1933), it isn't make believe if the Tax Court believes in you. The Internal Revenue Service was, on the other hand, constrained to hum "It's Fun to be Fooled" (1934). See 48 T.C. at 642.

**9.** 1968–2 C.B. 1. Cf. Estate of Stranahan v. C.I.R., 472 F.2d 867 (6th Cir.1973)

(allowing taxpayer to accelerate future dividend income by selling stock to his son, to take advantage of a large interest deduction in the year of sale, rejecting the Service's argument that the transaction was in substance a loan to the son); Martin, 56 T.C. 1255 (1971), aff'd 469 F.2d 1406 (5th Cir. 1972) (finding a loan and disallowing the acceleration of income on similar facts). See Assignment of Income, ¶ 5.01. Cf. also § 636, regarding this issue in the oil and gas area.

contracts are taxable,[1] a very important exclusion from income is carved out for proceeds of life insurance payable by reason of death of the insured.[2] Although this exclusion almost swallows up the general rule, it should be noted that the general rule of inclusion in income will still bite in several circumstances. If, as discussed below, the proceeds of the life insurance are not paid by reason of death of the insured but prior to that time, they may be included in income.

The exclusion from income of the proceeds of life insurance paid by reason of death of the insured is of major importance to many taxpayers and to the insurance industry. The extent to which this exclusion is justified can be explored by considering an example: Suppose the insured takes out a $100,000 ordinary life policy at age 45. The insured then dies twenty years later at age 65. Using typical figures,[3] the net premiums paid after 20 years will amount to $60,000. When the beneficiary receives the $100,000 face amount of the policy, it will all be excluded from his income.[4]

If one wished to take a hard-line "tax reform" position, how much of these proceeds might be argued to be includible in the beneficiary's income? It is clear that, as in calculating the gain on any asset, the beneficiary-taxpayer is entitled to offset the cost of the asset against the proceeds received.[5] Hence, even under the most hard-nosed "tax reform" view of the matter, the most that could possibly be included in the beneficiary's income would be $40,000 ($100,000 amount received less the $60,000 cost of the policy). However, the matter is not quite so simple.

This $40,000 "profit" is made up of two elements: the pure insurance element or "mortality gain", and the accumulated interest earned on the portion of the premiums paid in as a savings element on the ordinary life policy. Looking first at the mortality gain, the insured died early in an actuarial sense. Although his life expectancy may have been age 65 when he was born, when he was 45 his life expectancy was by then to live to a considerably older age than that. Thus by dying early, the insured was a "winner" in the pure insurance lottery and his beneficiary was paid a substantial amount of mortality gain. This amount was taken from the premiums of those mortality "losers" in the pure insurance lottery who lived to ripe old ages beyond their life expectancies. Again, using typical figures, of the $40,000 profit on the life insurance policy, about $27,700 would be mortality gain paid to the beneficiary because the insured was a "winner." The balance of the $40,000 profit, $12,300, would be interest earned on that portion of the overall premium paid in as a savings element.

¶ 3.06

1.  § 61(a)(10).

2.  § 101(a)(1).

3.  These numbers are adapted from Goode, The Individual Income Tax (1964).

4.  Note 2 supra.

5.  See ¶ 4.03, for a discussion of computing gains and losses on sales or exchanges of property.

Under general income tax principles,[6] both these elements of the $40,000 profit, the mortality gain and the interest, would be income, as constituting net increases to wealth. However, it might be argued as a matter of tax policy that these two elements should be treated different-ly. It could be asserted, for example, that the death of the insured is a time of economic and emotional hardship for the family, and is therefore not an appropriate time to levy a tax. However, a number of other taxes, including federal estate taxes, can be levied at the time of the death of the family breadwinner.

Even if this hardship argument is accepted as to the mortality gain, perhaps the interest element should still be taxed. However, it is not. Not only is the interest received free of tax, it also compounds in the policy tax free.

Cutting the other way is the argument that the mortality gain proceeds are usually to replace the lost earnings of the insured, and as such they should be subject to tax as would the earnings have been. An answer to that is that since the lump-sum insurance payment is received all in one year, it will be taxed at a very high marginal rate. There are, however, attractive options, discussed below, for spreading out the payment of the insurance proceeds.

If the insured is a mortality "loser", i.e., lives beyond his life expectancy, the tax law disfavors him (but what does he care, the happy old codger). The "disfavor" comes from the fact that the long-lived insured will have paid more in premiums for pure insurance protection (taking account of foregone interest) than his beneficiary finally gets in insurance proceeds when the old rascal finally does kick the bucket. But this loss is not deductible. And the insurance premium is not deductible.

The IRS comes out about even on this: undertaxing people who die early and overtaxing people who live long. So there is no net loss in tax revenues. But individual taxpayers are playing a lottery with the Service in addition to the lottery they are playing with the insurance company.

Consider also the case of the interest element paid to the policy holder who lives past his life expectancy. At this point he can receive the face amount of a matured policy. This constitutes simply a refund of the policy-holder's savings element in the policy plus accumulated interest. The rule is that the amounts received are income to the extent they exceed the total premiums paid for the policy.[7] This treats the long-lived less generously than the short-lived in that some of the interest is taxed when received by the long-lived.[8]

---

6.  See ¶ 1.02(2)(b).

7.  § 72(e)(2).

8.  However, cutting the other way, some of the interest earned, under the terms of the policy, might have been used to pay the premium for the insurance ele-ment of the policy. In that way the policy allows in effect the deduction of premiums for term insurance. Another insured who is simply buying term life insurance may not deduct the premium as that is a non-de-ductible personal expense.

Finally, perhaps the most telling argument is that society wishes to encourage the purchase of insurance, to promote financial security. The favorable treatment of employee group term life insurance[9] suggests that policy. Hence, the argument goes, the mortality gain proceeds should be tax-free. Nonetheless, this might still suggest the interest element should be taxed.[10]

However these arguments balance out, it seems fair to say that the argument for excluding the interest element is not as strong as the argument for excluding the mortality gain. Note that even if the interest element were taxed, it would be taxed presumably only on the payment of the proceeds, not as earned and compounded over the life of the insured—still an attractive deferral treatment.

One policy argument in favor of the exclusion of life insurance proceeds is that it serves as a substitute for allowing depreciation of human capital. The idea is that an individual with a career is gradually wearing out (the author can vouch for this). This career or life that is going downhill should be allowed a deduction, since it does produce income along the way. But no such deduction is allowed directly. However, excluding the proceeds life insurance paid by reason of death of the insured, as well as the favorable treatment of pension plans (see discussion in Prologue), may in effect provide something like a deduction for the taxpayer's declining human capital.[11]

This exclusion of the interest element suggests some tax avoidance maneuvers for the very wealthy. The very wealthy often do not need the mortality gain protection of life insurance. Nonetheless they may find it attractive to purchase life insurance which provides a very small amount of mortality gain protection and a very large amount of savings and interest income. Since the interest is part of an insurance policy, it will be tax free when paid on death of the insured. The logic of this investment thus becomes similar to the logic of investing in tax-free municipal bonds—the higher the bracket, the more attractive the arrangement.[12]

Taxpayers' exploitation of this possibility through the use of so-called "Universal Life Insurance" policies, offered by many insurance companies, led Congress to enact guidelines in this area as part of the Tax Equity and Fiscal Responsibility Act of 1982. These guidelines specify the relative size of the premiums, cash surrender value and death benefits allowable for policies to qualify for the exclusion. These guidelines prevent policies that have loaded up on savings features and that offer minimal pure life insurance protection from qualifying for the exclusion.[13]

**9.** ¶ 1.02(2)(b).

**10.** Some of this discussion is based on Goode, note 3 supra.

**11.** See also the discussion of treatment of personal damages, below at ¶ 3.12(2)(b).

**12.** See ¶ 3.01(2).

**13.** § 101(f).

## ¶ 3.07   Annuities

An annuity is an arrangement whereby a taxpayer makes a premium payment, often one lump amount, to an insurance company (or other party) in exchange for which the insurance company agrees to make periodic payments to the taxpayer commencing on a particular date for the rest of the taxpayer's life.[1] This, of course, is a method for the taxpayer to guarantee himself an income for the rest of his life. The amount of the annuity payments is calculated with reference to the taxpayer's premium and his life expectancy. Thus annuities for life are the inverse of life insurance: where the taxpayer dies earlier than his life expectancy, he undergoes a mortality loss on his annuity; his beneficiaries receive, however, a mortality gain on his life insurance.[2] Where the taxpayer dies at an age beyond his life expectancy, he reaps a mortality gain on his annuity, but the payments to his life insurance beneficiaries are less than the premium payments plus interest—a mortality loss.

Income from annuities is unquestionably taxable;[3] the problem in the field is accounting for the fact that a substantial portion of amounts paid as an annuity represent a return of the taxpayer's premium which should not be taxed. (The taxable balance, of course, is interest earned on the premium.)

The problems in the field of annuities can be illustrated by the leading case of *Egtvedt*.

### EGTVEDT v. UNITED STATES[4]

Egvedt. 45 Years old. Life expectancy 28 years.

$100,000

Insurance Company

Annuity: Right to receive $5,000/yr for life.

[331a]

*Question:* How should payments under the annuity be taxed? In particular is the statutory rule that 3% of the cost of the annuity be

---

**¶ 3.07**

**1.** The annuity may also be for a fixed period, rather than life. The analysis of such limited period annuities is similar to that given in the text of life annuities.

**2.** See ¶ 3.06.

**3.** §§ 61(a)(9), 72(a).

**4.** 112 Ct.Cl. 80, 1948 WL 5013 (1948).

included in income constitutional?

*Taxpayer's argument:* The 3% rule is unconstitutional. Under the rule, 3% of $100,000 is $3,000. Thus $3,000 must be included in income. Only $2,000 is return of capital. Hence taxpayer must live 50 years (i.e., to age 95) to recover capital.

*IRS argument:* The statute is constitutional.

*Held:* The statute is constitutional.

At ¶ 1.02(2)(e) in Chapter One we have an extensive discussion of the various ways one could recover basis in the case of an annuity. It will be recalled that those various ways were:

1) Immediate deduction or expensing

2) Open treatment

3) Installment treatment

4) Stupid treatment

5) Loan amortization treatment

6) Economically accurate treatment

These are all the possible ways to recover basis in a deal that extends over time. The economically accurate method uses present value analysis (see ¶ 1.02(2)(e) and the Prologue). Under the economically accurate method, the results are that only relatively small amounts of income are reported in the earlier years of the transaction. In the later years of the transaction, large amounts of income are reported.

You should review this discussion at ¶ 1.02(2)(e) at this time. Making reference to that discussion, what type of method is the 3% rule? It is a dumb form of the proration or installment rule (No.3). Dumb in that its assumptions about life expectancy for Egvedt were wildly off the mark.

Historically, the first way annuities were handled was to provide that the first annuity payments represent entirely a non-taxable return of the premiums, until the full amount of the premium has been recovered. Subsequent payments from the annuity were then taxable in full ("open treatment" as at ¶ 1.02(2)(e)).[5] This method, while clear and giving a precise result, has the disadvantage (from the point of view of the government) of postponing the time at which the taxpayer begins to pay a tax on his annuity until he has recovered his cost. Hence, the present rule is to apply a more sophisticated version of the installment method. This of course results in some of every annuity payment being taxed.

---

**5.** See House Report No. 704, 73rd Cong., 2d Sess., p. 21 (1939–1 C.B., Part 2, pp. 554, 569–570). This method was changed in 1934 to require an annuitant to include in his annual annuity income an amount equal to 3% of the cost of the annuity, as a rough method of accounting for income and basis simultaneously, Revenue Act of 1934 (48 Stat. 680). The present refined method, discussed in the text, was adopted in 1954.

Where, as is often the case, the annuity payments are to be made for the life of the annuitant, the procedure is to exclude a certain proportion of each annuity payment ("exclusion ratio") from the annuitant's income and impose a tax on the rest. The proportion of each payment that is excluded is the same proportion that the total premium of the annuity bears to the total amount that will be paid under it.[6] With respect to an annuity for life the total amount that will be paid under it (the "expected return") is ascertained by multiplying the amount that will be received by the annuitant each year by the annuitant's life expectancy as of the date the annuity starts.[7]

To take a numerical example:

The annuitant, a male age 50, purchases a single premium annuity for $10,000, which will pay him $1,000 a year for life, payments to start immediately. Making reference to the tables at Reg. § 1.72–9, this annuitant, as an actuarial matter, may expect to live about another 25 years.[8] Hence, the expected return of the annuity is $1,000 times 25 or $25,000. The total premium was $10,000; hence the proportion of each annual payment that is excluded (the exclusion ratio) is $10,000/$25,000, or 40%. Thus, of each $1,000 payment received annually, $400 will be excluded as a return of capital and tax will be imposed on the other $600. If the annuitant lives precisely the expected 25 years, he will have excluded precisely his cost of $10,000, and have been taxed on his income of $15,000.

If the holder of a life annuity lives beyond his life expectancy, he is thereafter taxed in full on his annuity payments, since he has recovered the cost of his annuity. If the life annuitant lives less than his life expectancy, and hence does not recover his cost, he may deduct his unrecovered cost of the annuity on his final tax return.[9]

If the annuity is not for life but for a limited term, an analogous calculation is made, substituting the term of the annuity for the annuitant's life expectancy.[10]

Modifications of the basic principle for taxing annuity income are used to calculate taxable income on specialized types of annuities, such as annuities with a refund feature, temporary life annuities, increasing and decreasing life annuities, joint and survivor annuities, variable annuities and permutations and combinations of these.[11]

---

**6.** § 72(b) and (c) Reg. § 1.72–1(a). The total amount that will be paid under the annuity is of course greater than the premium because of the interest earned on the premium. Cf. the installment method of reporting gain on the sale of property, ¶ 8.03(2).

**7.** 72(c)(3)(A), Regs. §§ 1.72–4, 1.72–9.

**8.** The actual life expectancy is 25.5 years, but 25 years has been used to simplify the computations.

**9.** § 72(b)

**10.** § 72(c)(3)(B).

**11.** See generally the regulations under § 72. Where an insurance company is involved, it will generally make these calculations.

### Integrated Summary of Annuity and Life Insurance Rules

Where proceeds of an insurance policy are just simply paid to a beneficiary by reason of death of the insured, the proceeds are excluded from the beneficiary's income, § 101(a)(1). If the beneficiary leaves the proceeds with the insurance company and the company pays the beneficiary interest on the proceeds, the interest is fully taxable to the beneficiary, § 101(c).

Suppose Marvin leaves $150,000 of insurance proceeds paid to him by reason of death of his uncle with Rock Solid Insurance Company. The agreement is that Rock Solid will pay Marvin $15,000 per year for Marvin's life. At the time the contract is entered into, Marvin's life expectancy was 30 years. In that event, the original amount of proceeds is spread out over the Marvin's life and is excluded. Thus, $5,000 per year is excluded ($150,000/30). The balance of the annual payment, $10,-000, is included in Marvin's income each year. It is interest on the $150,000 and is therefore taxable.

If Marvin lives beyond his 30 year life expectancy, he can continue to exclude $5,000 of the $15,000 payment, Regs. § 1.101–4(c). This is an odd result, since it allows Marvin to exclude more than the original $150,000 of insurance proceeds. If this were a straight annuity instead of being constructed out of life insurance proceeds, Marvin would not be able to continue the exclusion, see discussion below.

Zastro Corporation purchases $5 million of "key-man" life insurance on its chief executive officer, Irving Finster, because Finster is absolutely essential to the corporation's success. Under these facts Zastro Corporation would have an "insurable interest" in Irving Finster's life. If Finster dies, Zastro Corporation would be able to exclude the insurance proceeds paid to it by the insurance company, § 101(a)(1). If Zastro bought a fully paid up policy (perhaps from Finster) on Finster's life, then it would be able to exclude only the amount it paid for the policy (its basis). Amounts in excess of the cost of the policy would be included in Zastro's income, § 101(a)(2). Thus it is much more advisable to purchase a new rather than an existing policy. If Finster is a shareholder in Zastro Corporation, then the entire proceeds of the policy are excluded from Zastro's income even if Zastro bought the policy from Finster, § 101(a)(2)(B).

George purchases an insurance policy on his life for $25,000. Seven years later he sells it to his wife Martha for $50,000. George has $25,000 income realized but no income recognized on the transaction, § 1041(a), and Martha takes George's basis in the policy § 1041(b)(2). See Chapter 4. When George dies and Martha receives the insurance proceeds of $250,000, she will be able to exclude the entire amount of the proceeds, § 101(a)(2)(A).

Friebisch purchases an annuity on his life for $200,000. His life expectancy is 40 years. The contract provides he will receive $16,000 a year for life. In effect § 72(b) spreads the $200,000 basis out over the 40 years and allows that amount to be excluded each year. The balance of the payment is included in income. Thus $5,000 a year is excluded and $11,000 per year is taxed, § 72(b)(2).

If Friebisch lives past his life expectancy he will be taxed in full on the annuity payments, thus income of $16,000 per year starting in the 41st year of the annuity. If Friebisch dies after 20 years of annuity payments, he will receive a deduction for his last taxable year of the investment in the annuity which he had not yet excluded, in this case $100,000, § 72(b)(3), Regs. § 1.72–4(a)(2) Example. This deduction will also be treated as though it arose in Friebisch's trade or business for purposes of generating a net operating loss deduction which could be carried to other years, § 72(b)(3)(C).

Suppose Friebisch and his wife had purchased the annuity described above, as a joint and survivorship annuity, with their joint life expectancy being 40 years. The same numbers would apply: exclusion of $5,000 and income of $11,000.

## ¶ 3.08　Gifts and Inheritances

### (1) Rationale for Excluding

Ever since the Income Tax of 1913, gifts and inheritances have been excluded from income.[1] Without this specific exclusion, gifts and inheritances would probably be included in income, given the general broad sweep of the concept of income. This seemingly simple exclusion raises some puzzling theoretical questions. One who receives a gift or inheritance has certainly enjoyed an increase in wealth. Why should the fact that the recipient has not worked for the gift or inheritance be a reason to exempt him from tax?[2]

Cutting the other way is the donor's circumstance. Having dominion over his wealth, he may spend it on a vacation, buy a car, confer a gift or leave it to his heirs. Why should the latter transactions give rise to an income tax? Perhaps the matter is best viewed as a question of the appropriate taxable unit. Gifts and inheritances generally occur among family members. Perhaps the taxable unit is the family[3] and gratuitous transfers among its members should not give rise to income, even as imputed income from services rendered by members of the family to each other is not taxed. That analysis is, perhaps, persuasive; except perhaps what if the gift is of $250,000 of marketable securities?

At this point you would be well-advised to make reference to Chapter 4, ¶ 4.03(2)(c)(i) regarding treatment of gifts of appreciated or depreciated property.

---

¶ 3.08

1.　102(a) is the present exclusion. The exclusion in the 1913 Income Tax was embodied in § IIB., c. 16, 38 Stat. 167.

The basis of property received by gift or inheritance is treated at ¶ 4.03(2).

2.　A federal estate and gift tax may be imposed on gifts and inheritances.

3.　See ¶ 5.02.

### (2) Definition of "Gift": Duberstein

In any event, these theoretical questions have not given taxpayers or their advisors much pause. Rather, the question in the field has been, ever since 1913, what kinds of transfers qualify as a "gift" for purposes of the exclusion? (Indeed the first case ever reported by the Board of Tax Appeals dealt with this question.[4])

The leading case on this subject, and one of the best-known cases in the field, is *Duberstein.*

## COMMISSIONER v. DUBERSTEIN[5]

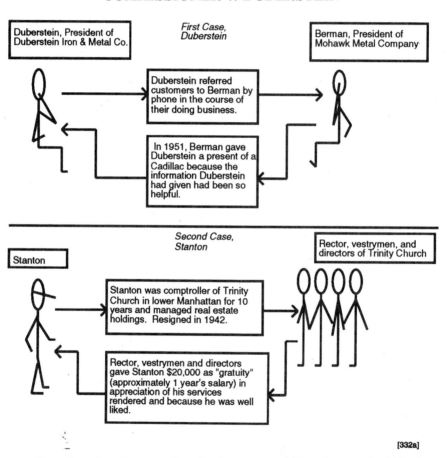

**First Case, Duberstein**

Duberstein, President of Duberstein Iron & Metal Co.

Berman, President of Mohawk Metal Company

Duberstein referred customers to Berman by phone in the course of their doing business.

In 1951, Berman gave Duberstein a present of a Cadillac because the information Duberstein had given had been so helpful.

**Second Case, Stanton**

Stanton

Rector, vestrymen, and directors of Trinity Church

Stanton was comptroller of Trinity Church in lower Manhattan for 10 years and managed real estate holdings. Resigned in 1942.

Rector, vestrymen and directors gave Stanton $20,000 as "gratuity" (approximately 1 year's salary) in appreciation of his services rendered and because he was well liked.

[332a]

*Question:* Are the transfers in these cases gifts, thus excludible from income?

**4.** Parrott, 1 B.T.A. 1, 1924 WL 6 (1924).

**5.** 363 U.S. 278, 80 S.Ct. 1190, 4 L.Ed.2d 1218 (1960), opinion conformed 283 F.2d 949 (6th Cir.1960).

*Held:* Appellate court must defer to trier of fact. As to *Duberstein* Tax Court was not clearly erroneous in its findings that the Cadillac was at bottom a recompense for services and an inducement for more services. As to *Stanton,* the District Court's finding of a gift was not explained sufficiently. Hence vacate the judgment and remand to District Court for further proceedings. The "mere absence of a legal or moral obligation" to make a transfer does not make it a gift. The transfer is income if it proceeds from "the incentive of anticipated benefit." And the most famous phrase: "A gift in the statutory sense ... proceeds from a "detached and disinterested generosity,' "citing Commissioner v. Lo-Bue. Thus the issue turns on the state of mind of the donor.

*Comment:* On remand, Stanton was found to have a gift.[6]

*Comment:* The famous phrase "detached and disinterested generosity" means that a gift does not stem from any *financial* interest. A transfer that comes from affection, indicating a high degree of *personal* interest, would be a gift.

*Comment: The donor's state of mind:* Having the question of taxability to the donee turn on the state of mind of the donor seems like a bad idea from the point of view of administration of the tax laws. Note that taxability turns not on what the donee thinks the donor thinks. It turns on what the donor actually thinks. This may be something the donee cannot find out. Indeed it may be something no one can find out. Is this any way to run a tax system?

The weakness of the *Duberstein* approach was demonstrated in the almost unbelievable case of *Harris.*

---

**6.** Stanton v. United States, 186 F.Supp. 393 (E.D.N.Y.1960), aff'd 287 F.2d 876 (2d Cir.1961), Lumbard, C.J. concurring because of the nature of appellate review but stating that he thought a contrary inference should have been drawn from the undisputed facts, id. at 877.

## UNITED STATES v. HARRIS[7]

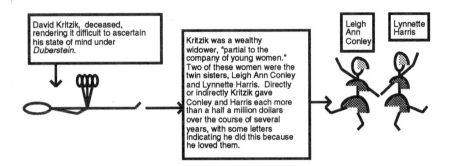

David Kritzik, deceased, rendering it difficult to ascertain his state of mind under *Duberstein.*

Kritzik was a wealthy widower, "partial to the company of young women." Two of these women were the twin sisters, Leigh Ann Conley and Lynnette Harris. Directly or indirectly Kritzik gave Conley and Harris each more than a half a million dollars over the course of several years, with some letters indicating he did this because he loved them.

Leigh Ann Conley

Lynnette Harris

In separate criminal trials, Harris and Conley were convicted of "willfully evading" their income tax obligations regarding the money. Harris was sentenced to ten months in prison, followed by two months in a halfway house and two years of supervised release. She was also fined $12,500 and ordered to pay a $150 special assessment. Conley was sentenced to five months in prison, followed by five months in a halfway house and one year supervised release. She was also fined $10,000 and ordered to pay a $4100 assessment. This case is their appeal from these convictions.

[333a]

*Questions:* Were the amounts given by Kritzik to Harris and Conley income to them? What was Kritzik's intent when he gave the money? What did Harris and Conley think Kritzik's intent was when he gave them the money—since a criminal prosecution for "willful evasion" of their income tax obligations requires Harris and Conley to believe the items are income.

*Held:*

*Case as to Conley:* Kritzik's intent is suggested by his gift tax returns in which he identified as gifts to Conley substantially less than the amounts he transferred to her, suggesting the balance was income. But he could have just underreported his gifts. He told an IRS agent in an affidavit before his death that he regarded Harris and Conley as prostitutes, but he could have been lying to avoid paying civil and criminal penalties for failure to pay gift taxes. In any event, the District Court excluded this affidavit under the hearsay rule and the confrontation clause. Even if all this proved Kritzik's intent, there was no evidence that Conley knew Kritizk's intent such that it would support a criminal prosecution of Conley. Conley picked up checks from Kritzik's office on a regular basis, but that could have been support just as well as income.

*Case as to Harris:* At trial, Harris tried to introduce as evidence three letters that Kritzik wrote. They were excluded by the District Court as hearsay, and under Fed. R. Evid. 403 because the possible prejudice exceeded their probative value. These letters were not hearsay because they were offered to prove Harris' lack of willfulness, not for the truth of the matter asserted.

7.   942 F.2d 1125 (7th Cir.1991).

In the letters Kritzik wrote that he loved Harris, loved giving things to her, and loved seeing her happy. Kritzik also wrote to his insurance company regarding jewelry he had "given" to Ms. Lynette Harris as a gift. Even if Kritzik were lying, the letters could have caused Harris to believe in good faith that the things he gave her were intended as gifts.

The conclusion that Harris should have been allowed to present letters as evidence would ordinarily lead us to remand the case for retrial. However, the current law on the treatment of mistresses provided Harris with no fair warning that her conduct was criminal. Indeed the authorities favor Harris' position that the money was a gift. With the authorities in that posture, Harris cannot possibly willfully evade tax. See Green v. Commissioner, 54 T.C.M. 764 (1987), order aff'd 846 F.2d 870 (2d Cir.1988), cert. denied 488 U.S. 850, 109 S.Ct. 131, 102 L.Ed.2d 104 (1988) (Marvin v. Marvin palimony not income); Reis v. Commissioner, 33 T.C.M. 1333 (1974) (long-term payments as a mistress to nightclub dancer Lillian Reis held a gift, despite Reis' statement that she "earned every penny" of the money).

These mistress cases are to be distinguished from out and out prostitution cases, where the payments are clearly income. Since the government does not allege that Harris received specific payments for specific sessions of sex, the prostitution cases actually support Harris' position.

Testimony showed Harris also asserted that her relationship with Kritzik was "a job," and "just making a living." She reportedly complained that she "was laying on her back and her sister was getting all the money," and described how she disliked when Kritzik fondled her naked, and made other derogatory statements about sex with Kritzik. However, this evidence at best only tells us what Harris thought of the relationship. But the test under *Duberstein* is the donor's intent not what the donee thought. If the donor thought it was a gift, it does not matter how mercenary the donee was.

"Before she met Kritzik, Harris starred as a sorceress in an action/adventure film. She would have had to be a real life sorceress to predict her tax obligations under the current law."

*Conclusion:* Remand with instructions that the indictments against Harris and Conley should be dismissed.

*Comment, doing time:* Pending the appeal, Harris and Conley served most of the sentences under the convictions that were now reversed. This was because their counsel apparently failed to show "by clear and convincing evidence that the person is not likely to flee or pose a danger to the safety of any other person" and "that the appeal is not for the purpose of delay and raises a substantial question of law or fact likely to result in reversal or an order for a new trial," 18 U.S.C.A. § 3143(b).

*Comment, "willfulness" in criminal tax cases:* "Willfulness" may work as a concept in situations of murder or arson. But in criminal prosecutions under the tax laws, the concept of willfulness can at times be troublesome. As discussed in connection with the *James* case at ¶ 3.13(2), are we to believe that potential tax evaders read the advance sheets in order to ascertain their legal position? It was very important to the court that the precedents in the field favored Harris and Conley. But suppose the precedents had not been favorable. Are Harris and Conley really reading Tax Court Memo cases before they decide not to file tax returns or not to report income? And if Harris and Conley are not to be supposed to be reading these cases, then what is the meaning of the concept of willfulness in the prosecution of criminal tax fraud cases?

*Comment: How did this mess happen anyway?*

Why this ghastly muddle of a case, leading to two women serving time for convictions that were reversed? A major root cause is the administratively unworkable standard of the *Duberstein* case. Matters were compounded severely when the issue came up as a criminal prosecution.

Beyond these conceptual difficulties, an important thing you learn from *Duberstein* is that the reach of the concept of income is pretty broad when gratuitous transfers are made in a business setting. If you don't get that from *Duberstein*, the statute now gives it to you in the employer-employee context by virtue of § 102(c). That provides in the employer-employee context that there shall not be excluded from income any amount transferred by an employer to an employee, except for *de minimis* gifts under the § 132 fringe benefit rules. In short, in the employer-employee setting § 102(c) provides a conclusive presumption of income. This would clearly change the result in *Stanton* (although not in *Duberstein*) no matter how affectionately the vestrymen regarded Stanton (and there was indeed some question about that as his departure was in fact occasioned by a bit of a tiff over the status of another employee).

Section 102(c) therefore clarifies matters in the employer-employee setting, but outside that setting there is still a confusing welter of facts that must be used to decide, under *Duberstein's* fact-based approach, whether a particular transfer is a gift.

Section 274(b) has put some clarity into the situation. It provides that no deduction is allowed for gifts to recipients in amounts of more than $25. Prior to this section, transferors were often deducting the transfer as a business expense while the transferee was calling the transaction a gift (otherwise known as having it both ways). Indeed this was attempted in *Duberstein*, with Berman deducting the Cadillac, while Duberstein attempted (ultimately unsuccessfully) to exclude it. Thus under § 274, once over the $25 threshold, taxpayers have to make up their minds. Either the transferor can take a business deduction for the transfer, in which case the transferee must take the item into income; or the transferor must forego the deduction, in which case the transferee can assert it is a gift.

After *Duberstein,* gratuitous transfers in a business setting have almost always been found to be income,[8] notwithstanding that the *Duberstein* Court later in its opinion purported not to be laying down any presumptions in the matter. The implications of *Duberstein* have radiated out into many areas, including employee death benefits,[9] tips,[10] and strike payments.[11]

Many gift cases, post *Duberstein*, have concerned family members doing business together, where gratuitous transfers between them can carry both heavy business and personal connotations. Thus in a family quarrel, a mother transferred cash and securities to her son after he had threatened both to put the family business into bankruptcy and to report her to the IRS on account of alleged violations. Subsequently, the mother successfully sued the son for conversion of the cash and securities and for punitive damages. On these facts the Second Circuit found the mother's transfer of cash and securities to the son to have been "prompted by something less than maternal affection ..." and found the transfer to be income to the son.[12] Other transfers in the family business setting have not been quite so easy to decide and the cases have gone off on their particular facts.[13]

### *(3) Gifts of Income From Property*

Instead of making an outright gift of property, the donor may confer the income from property as a gift. In such an event, the income from the property is taxable to the donee, notwithstanding that the transaction is indisputably a gift by the standards discussed above.[14] While this may seem inconsistent with the exclusion from income of the outright gift of property, discussed above, this statutory scheme makes sense. In the case of the excludable outright gift of property, there is no doubt that income subsequently derived from the property given (i.e. rent from given real estate, or interest from given money) is income to the donee.[15] That being the case, it would be consistent to say that where only the income is given, it will be taxed to the recipient. Without such a rule, of

**8.** Rhodes, 36 T.C.M. 149 (1977) (gratuitous transfer of real estate to taxpayer for his role in bringing together buyer and seller of tract of land held not a gift but income notwithstanding an agreement that taxpayer would receive no commission); Thrower, 21 T.C.M. 1540 (1962), aff'd 330 F.2d 614 (5th Cir.1964) (liquor given to members of state liquor board by distilleries did not arise from "detached and disinterested generosity,"). Cf. Mesinger, 31 T.C.M. 1127 (1972) (rent-free use of an apartment held gift where no special business favors done).

**9.** ¶ 2.02(4).

**10.** ¶ 2.04(1).

**11.** ¶ 2.04(2).

**12.** Altman v. Commissioner, 475 F.2d 876, 878 (2d Cir.1973).

**13.** E.g. Dexter v. United States, 306 F.Supp. 415 (N.D.Miss.1969) (transfer of real estate to daughter by father in exchange for daughter's past performance of services held income, not a gift); Kass, 33 T.C.M. 239 (1974) (father's transfer of stock in family corporation to son held a gift to son, who was on salary, although as a result of the transfer, son declined an offer to work for his wife's business.).

**14.** ¶ 102(b)(2).

**15.** 102(b)(1) Reg. § 1.102–1(b). This rule of inclusion in income would also cover appreciation in the value of the given property in the hands of the donee, when realized on subsequent sale. Indeed, the donee is even liable for the tax on the appreciation in the hands of the donor! See ¶ 4.03(2)(c)(i).

course, great amounts of income would be lost from taxation because they had once been the subject of a gift.

If the gift takes the form of periodic payments from specified property, it is taxable to the recipient to the extent the payments are out of income from the property and excludable to the extent the payments must be made from principal,[16] a rule consistent with the above analysis. However, according to an old Tax Court case, a gift payable "in a single lump sum in any event" out of either income or principal is not taxed to the beneficiary, though ultimately paid out of income.[17] Though the Service has acquiesced in this holding, it seems possible, given the paucity of recent authority, that the Service might choose to reconsider this question. In the meantime the lesson is clear: where a gift of income from property is contemplated, the most attractive technique is to couch the gift in terms of a lump sum payable, in any event, out of income or principal.

Where gifts of income from property or gifts of the underlying property itself are made, a more profound question can be raised: whether any gift was made at all. When, for example, a high-bracket taxpayer purports to make a gift of income or property and income to a low bracket taxpayer, the Service may attack the transaction on "assignment of income" principles and attempt to tax the income to the donor. This topic is discussed in Chapter 5.

### (4) Inheritances

#### (a) In General

Property acquired by bequest, devise or inheritance is excluded from income. In the Supreme Court case of *Lyeth v. Hoey*[18], the question presented was whether property received by the taxpayer from the estate of a decedent in compromise of his claim as an heir is taxable income. Taxpayer died in 1931 leaving as her heirs four surviving children and the taxpayer and his brother who were sons of a deceased daughter of the decedent. The decedent in her will gave the heirs small legacies. The residuary estate she gave to a complex of trusts the purpose of which was to preserve "the records of the earthly life of Mary Baker Eddy," the founder of the Christian Science religion. The heirs challenged the will on the grounds of lack of testamentary capacity and undue influence. The controversy was subsequently settled for $141,484 payable to the taxpayer. The Commissioner treated this as taxable income and assessed a tax of $56,389.

The Court disregarded state law decision in the area holding that amounts received in settlement of a will contest are income. The Court said the matter was a federal question and held that the amounts

---

**16.** § 102(b) flush language; Reg. § 1.102–1(c).

**17.** Lindau, 21 T.C. 911 (1954) (acq.).

**18.** 305 U.S. 188, 59 S.Ct. 155, 83

received in compromise were excluded from income.[19] The same policy considerations that underlie the exclusion of gifts (however they might be resolved (see ¶ 3.08(1)) underlie this exclusion.

There have, of course, been a healthy number of disputes concerning what qualifies for this exclusion. As in the gift area, though a transfer may in form qualify for the exclusion, it will be included in income if it is in substance compensation. In the leading case of *Wolder*,[20] taxpayer, an attorney, entered into a written agreement with his client to forego billing for past and future legal services in exchange for the client's bequest to him of a substantial amount of stock. Though the transfer was a bequest under New York law (and was treated as such in ancillary state court litigation) the Second Circuit, taking a leaf from the book of *Duberstein*,[21] found the arrangement to be in substance compensation.[22]

While this principle seems plain enough, a line of bequest-to-executor cases has raised some problems. An executor of course may receive a bequest tax-free. However, where the bequest is contingent upon the beneficiary's performance of services as an executor, it seems clear that the bequest is taxable compensation, and the courts have so held.[23] Where, however, the bequest is contingent only on the taxpayer's acceptance of the role of executor but is not contingent on the taxpayer's performance of the duties of executor, the Supreme Court held in the old case of *Merriam*[24] that the bequest will be excluded.

This analysis in *Merriam* was severely criticized by the Second Circuit in *Wolder* as not withstanding economic analysis,[25] but until such time as the Supreme Court reverses itself, an attractive method to pay executors is to make cash bequests to them "in lieu of all compensation or commission to which they would otherwise be entitled as executors or trustees" (the *Merriam* Court language),[26] being careful not to state further that *services* as an executor or trustee are required.[27]

L.Ed. 119 (1938).

**19.** § 102(a). It is clear that by these terms Congress meant to exclude from income all property, real and personal, which passes by reason of death of the decedent, Lyeth v. Hoey, 305 U.S. 188, 59 S.Ct. 155, 83 L.Ed. 119 (1938).

The sales proceeds of an expected inheritance from a living parent are income, Rev. Rul. 70–60, 1970–1 C.B. 11.

**20.** Wolder v. Commissioner, 493 F.2d 608 (2d Cir.1974), cert. denied 419 U.S. 828, 95 S.Ct. 49, 42 L.Ed.2d 53 (1974).

**21.** Note 5 supra.

**22.** Note 20 supra at 612. See also Rev. Rul. 67–375, 1967–2 C.B. 60. To hold otherwise would, of course, invite widespread tax avoidance by tax advisors and their elderly clients.

Where taxpayer receives an amount in settlement of a claim for compensation for services rendered the decedent, the payment is income, where the taxpayer is not an heir or legatee, Braddock v. United States, 434 F.2d 631 (9th Cir.1970).

**23.** Ream v. Bowers, 22 F.2d 465 (2d Cir.1927).

**24.** United States v. Merriam, 263 U.S. 179, 44 S.Ct. 69, 68 L.Ed. 240 (1923), (interpreting the will of Alfred C. Vanderbilt), followed by Rev.Rul. 57–398, 1957–2 C.B. 93; cf. Bank of New York v. Helvering, 132 F.2d 773 (2d Cir.1943) (although bequest formally contingent on services, underlying facts suggested none was contemplated).

**25.** Note 19 supra at 611–612.

**26.** Note 23 supra at 181.

**27.** This arrangement would seemingly mean the estate will not get an income tax or estate tax deduction for the payments, generally § 2053.

Where there is a will contest, payments in settlement are treated as though they were acquired under the will and, hence, are excludable.[28]

### (b) Transfers in Trust: Irwin v. Gavit

Some fascinating problems are presented if, say, $300,000 of securities is transferred under a decedent's will so that the decedent's spouse gets the income for life and then the remainder goes to the decedent's child. How does the exclusion of bequests of § 102 apply in that circumstance? These problems are illustrated by the case of *Irwin v. Gavit* :

### IRWIN v. GAVIT[29]

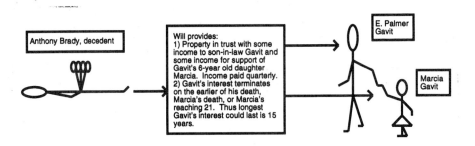

[334a]

*Question:* Are the payments to Gavit excluded as a bequest under § 102 or are they not excluded since they are income from property which was the subject of the bequest?

*Taxpayer's Argument:* The amounts left to Gavit are installment payments of a bequest of property measured by income from the property. As a bequest, the payments are therefore excluded.

*Held:* (Holmes, C. J.) Reversing lower courts, the payments to Gavit are taxable as income from the bequest. The property which was the subject of the bequest produces the income from it. "Day and night, youth and age are only types ... the distinction is not hard to draw ... this is a gift of income from a very large fund of income."

*Comment:* The Court here was interpreting the predecessor of § 102(a) which excludes bequests from income and the predecessor of § 102(b)(1) which taxes income from property which has been excluded as a bequest. § 102(b)(2) was subsequently enacted to explicitly tax income from property which is the subject of a bequest. Thus § 102(b)(2)

---

**28.** Lyeth v. Hoey, note 19 supra. If the payment comes out of estate income it may be taxable, see Delmar, 25 T.C. 1015 (1956).

**29.** 268 U.S. 161, 45 S.Ct. 475, 69 L.Ed. 897 (1925).

confirms the holding in *Gavit*.

This holding was undoubtedly correct. If Gavit had won, then not only would bequeathed property not be taxed but so would the income from it if the income were bequeathed to a different party. By contrast, there was no doubt that if property and income from it were bequeathed to the same person that only the property and not the income from it would be excluded. Thus a huge tax shelter would be created where everyone would be encouraged to leave divided interests in property to their heirs.

There is another fascinating time value of money issue in this case. After all, this whole deal does play out over a number of years. To get a handle on this problem, let us simplify the facts a little by saying that Gavit got all the income from the property and there was none paid for Marcia's support. Let us say that Gavit gets the income for life and that his life expectancy is 15 years. There are no other contingencies that cause Gavit to stop getting the income other than his own death. On Gavit's death, his daughter Marcia gets the trust corpus.

This alteration of facts clearly draws the problem as the classic one of an income beneficiary for life and a remainderman (or this case remaindergirl).

Let us also specify that the trust corpus is $500,000 of investment-grade corporate bonds, paying an interest rate of 10%, or $50,000 per year.

Now what is the problem? We have two people each with an interest in the trust property. We have Gavit with his income interest and Marcia with her remainder interest. Gavit is taxed in full on his interest and Marcia is not taxed at all on her interest either at the date of death or later when she gets her interest. Thus Marcia gets the full amount of the exclusion and Gavit gets none of it. That is the current law. That is fine, but there is another way to look at it.

The other way to look at it is to say that Gavit had a point in the case. He did have an inheritance. The inheritance was of $50,000 per year for 15 years.[30] As we know from the Prologue to this book, that deal has a value. That value is the present value of a stream of earnings of $50,000 per year for 15 years, assuming a 10% interest rate. Sip your cold coffee while I fire up my computer and get the answer. That present value is $380,300.

What about Marcia? What did Marcia really inherit? Well she inherited the right to get $500,000 in 15 years. What is that worth now? You don't need me for this one. What do you think it's going to be? I'll hit my computer again while you think about it. Turns out the value of what Marcia got is $119,700. Adds up with Gavit's interest to $500,000,

---

**30.** He might live longer or shorter than 15 years but we use his life expectancy for these discussion purposes.

of course. The income plus the remainder equals the total bequest and the total bequest was $500,000.

Thus why not have a rule that actually reflects reality? Why don't we say that Gavit inherited something with a fair market value at the date of death of $380,300 and Marcia inherited something with a fair market value at the date of death of $119,700? Since that's what really happened, it might be nice to treat it that way.[31]

Thus what we would do is say that that is what they each inherited and that neither is taxed on the value of his or her inheritance, under § 102. Their two exclusions taken together then exhaust the total $500,000 exclusion (fair market value of the corpus) to which the heirs are entitled. In short, the heirs have each inherited a slice of that $500,000 corpus.

Now what do we do? Take Gavit. He's got a basis of $380,300. Here is a critical point. If you get this point, you got it made. That $380,300 basis that Gavit has is like his capital now. He's entitled not to be taxed on it in the future just as surely as if he had purchased this right to receive $50,000 payments per year for 15 years as an annuity. So the discussion is now in terms of recovery of capital, and how you are entitled not to be taxed on your capital, see Chapter One, ¶ 1.02(2)(e).

Therefore, let's look at Gavit. He's receiving payments of $50,000 per year for 15 years. What does this look like? Looks like an annuity to me. Recall the treatment of annuities in Chapter One at ¶ 1.02(2)(e) and in this chapter at ¶ 3.07.

What we do is somehow subtract Gavit's basis against the annual $50,000 payments. Then we tax the net amount as income. In that way, Gavit is allowed to exclude his basis in his inheritance and be taxed on income from his inheritance over time.

For example, if we took the usual annuity rules, we would spread his basis of $380,300 over 15 years. That would mean he could deduct $25,333 per year against $50,000 per year. Thus he would have taxable income of $24,667 per year. If we took the economically accurate approach of recovering capital that I was pushing for in Chapter One ¶ 1.02(2)(e), then the result would be that we would be giving Gavit larger deductions of his basis in the early years and smaller deductions in the later years, as the calculations in ¶ 1.02(2)(e) demonstrate.

What about Marcia? Her basis in her remainder interest is, as we have calculated, $119,700. As in the case of Gavit, Marcia has income

---

**31.** One side-line effect of this present value analysis is to throw a light on what the parties really got. One might have thought off the top (at least I would have) that it would have been better to be Marcia than to be Gavit. After all 500,000 bucks sound like a lot more than 50 thousand bucks a year. But it turns out that what Gavit got was much more valuable. Remember, Gavit can can reinvest his income stream every year for 15 years compounded. If you are advising clients on estate planning, you might like to bear such things in mind.

over time from her interest.[32] How do we see that? Marcia's future interest of $119,700 is becoming larger as time passes. This is because as time passes, her future payment is getting closer and closer to the present. When we finally hit 15 years out and Marcia takes her remainder interest,[33] what is it worth at that time? Well of course it is worth $500,000. So Marcia, over the course of 15 years has had her interest grow to the point she has total income over the period of $500,000—$119,700 or $380,300 (no surprise there).

Question is now, how do we tax Marcia on this income? We could do it pro rata—namely, $380,300/15 = $25,353 per year. Or we could do it more economically accurately by understanding that her economic interest of $119,700 is growing by the prevailing interest rate of 10% compounded. It is the case (my computer tells me so) that $119,700 growing at 10% compounded annually cranks out to be $500,000 in 15 years. This economically accurate approach would be like the treatment of original issue discount in the Prologue. For example Marcia's interest would grow in the first year by 10% of $119,700 or $11,970.

Is Marcia taxed on this? She is not getting her hands on any money at this point. This is very much like holding appreciated property. We could therefore easily choose not to tax her on the grounds that she has not had a "realization," see Chapter 4, ¶ 4.02. However, just to be nasty about it, let's say she is taxed on it. If she is taxed on this 10% compounded increase per year, then she is entitled to raise her basis in her remainder interest by that amount. This is to insure that she will not be taxed on it again. She has in effect "earned" the right to that increase in basis by paying tax. Let's see how things work out.

Now we're ready for some complications. Suppose Gavit kicks the bucket after five years. This looks like it messes up our calculations, but in fact we can handle it. If Gavit is using the annuity system for recovering his basis, then after five years he would have deducted 5 × $25,333 = $126,665. Thus he would have $380,300—$126,665 or $253,635 of unrecovered basis. In his final tax return that is taken as a deduction, as in the annuity rules generally. So that works out.

Then, as a result of Gavit's untimely demise, Marcia gets her remainder interest early. She gets $500,000 of securities. If she is using the economically accurate or original issue discount approach for paying tax and increasing basis, she then has a basis in her remainder interest of $119,700 increased by 10% compounded annually for 5 years. Once again (I told you I'd do the math) that comes out to be a total of $192,778. So, Marcia gets $500,000 less her basis of $192,778, or $307,222 of income on the early receipt of her remainder interest.[34]

**32.** Recall the opening analysis in the Prologue. Capital grows over time; that is a fundamental economic proposition.

**33.** Assuming Gavit dies exactly on his birthday 15 years from now so as not to complicate our example. We'll give him a little drink of something.

**34.** If we had not taxed Marcia on her 10% a year compounded return, then she would have her original basis of $119,700. Then her gain on the early receipt of her

That is a way to do it instead of the approach of the current law, as exemplified by *Gavit*. One argument in favor of the *Gavit* approach is that it is less complicated. A strong argument in favor of the present value analysis approach is that it is economically accurate.

One objection that might be raised to the present-value approach is that we do not know what interest rate to apply to value the life interest and remainder. Would it depend on the type of property held by the trust? I do not see that as a big problem. We can pick some interest rate amount that is somewhat above the prevailing risk-free rate, as the Internal Revenue Code does now for many time value of money questions. See the Prologue. Doing that certainly gets you closer to an economically accurate answer than does the completely inaccurate *Gavit* approach.

### Integrated Summary of Inheritance Rules

Money or property received from a decedent by will or by intestate succession is excluded from income, § 102(a).

Amounts received in settlement of a will contest are also excluded from income under § 102(a), Lyeth v. Hoey, 305 U.S. 188, 59 S.Ct. 155, 83 L.Ed. 119 (1938), see footnote 27 above.

Nicole leaves $100,000 to her close friend Faye in thanks for Faye's companionship and support through turbulent years. This would still be excluded from Faye's income and would not trigger a *Wolder* analysis to find income.

But if Nicole had left $100,000 to Faye under a written agreement in which Faye promised to care for Nicole and provide her with therapeutic services and medicine, the $100,000 would be income to Faye, under *Wolder*. Note that § 102(c) would not apply here since Faye would not be an employee of Nicole but more in the nature of an independent contractor.

Suppose there was this same written agreement, but Nicole died suddenly without a will. If Faye then successfully sued Nicole's estate on the claim, the amounts Faye received would be income.

If Faye settled her claim with the estate for $75,000, the $75,000 would be income.

Suppose Nicole appointed Faye as executrix of her estate Nicole's will stated that Faye would receive $60,000 for these services. Again under *Wolder*, the $60,000 would be income.

Alternatively, Nicole's will provides that Faye will be the executrix of her estate and will receive a bequest of $60,000 "in lieu of compensation or commissions to which she would otherwise be entitled as executrix." In that case, *Wolder* suggests that the $60,000 would be income, but the older case of *Merriam* (note 23 above) holds that where the bequest is contingent only on the taxpayer's acceptance of the role of executrix but is not contingent on the performance of the duties of

remainder interest would be $500,000 –
$119,700 = $380,300.

executor, the bequest is excluded. As discussed in the text accompanying note 24, the Supreme Court's holding in *Merriam* was criticized in *Wolder*, but until the Supreme Court reverses itself, using the *Merriam* language quoted above is an attractive way to compensate executors.

In general suits against an estate for services rendered in which there is payment or a settlement based on any contractual theory would give rise to income to the recipient.

Section 102(c) is not necessarily applicable in *Wolder* situations because *Wolder* situations involve not only employer-employee relationships but also independent contractor relationships, to which § 102(c) has no application.

Suppose Nicole leaves $2 million in trust with income to Ronald and following Ronald's death the remainder to Denise. Assuming Ronald survives Nicole, the income paid to Ronald under the trust instrument would not be excluded. This is because where a bequest is of income from property, it is not excluded, Irwin v. Gavit, discussed above, § 102(b)(2).

## ¶ 3.09   Prizes, Scholarships and Fellowship Grants

### (1) Prizes: McDonell

Prizes and awards are included in income under § 74(a). This includes everything from the Nobel Prize and the Pulitzer prize to a door prize at a keno parlor. There are limited exceptions to the inclusion of prizes in income for prizes transferred to charities, § 74(b), and certain employee achievement awards, § 74(c). The leading prize case of *Allen J. McDonell*,[1] involved the question of whether all or any portion of expenses of a trip to Hawaii taken by the taxpayer and his wife and paid for by his employer were income to the taxpayer and if so whether the amounts were deductible by him. Taxpayer was sent as something of a chaperone for salesmen who were being sent to Hawaii as a result of having achieved certain sales quotas. He was selected out of eligible supervisors by drawing names out of a hat. At the time he was selected he was told that he and his wife were expected to go. Those selected to go received no cut in pay and did not lose vacation time. Those not chosen received no substitute benefit. Taxpayer was told he was to consider this trip an assignment and not a vacation. Taxpayer and his wife did not have spare time for swimming or shopping. The court held that taxpayer had no income on this trip, that it was taken to carry out duties assigned to the taxpayer by his employer.

### Integrated Summary of Awards Rules

Prizes are included in income with two the limited exceptions: certain prizes and awards transferred to charities and certain employee achievement awards.

¶ 3.09

1.   26 T.C.M. 115 (1967).

To qualify as an award transferred to a charity, the award must be made in recognition of religious, charitable, scientific, educational, artistic, literary or civic achievement. A line of cases holds that awards for athletic achievement does not qualify for the exclusion, even if it is transferred to a charity, because athletic achievement is not religious, charitable, scientific, etc. In such a case the award would be included in income. The transfer to the charity would then be a charitable deduction under § 170 and subject to the rules of § 170, see Chapter 7.

To qualify as an employee achievement award and thus be excludable under § 74(c), the award must be of tangible personal property under § 274(j)(3)(A). An award not qualifying here might still be excludable as a de minimis fringe benefit, see Chapter 2.

A transfer of tangible personal property is excludable as an employee achievement award (and deductible by the payor) if it meets the definition of employee achievement award under § 274(j)(3)(A), namely that it be tangible personal property and that it be (i) transferred by an employer to an employee for length of service achievement or safety achievement, (ii) awarded as part of a meaningful presentation, and (iii) awarded under conditions and circumstances that do not create a significant likelihood of the payment of disguised compensation. A an item qualifies for a length of service award only if it is received after the employee has worked for the employer for at least five years and has not received a length of service award (other than one excludable as a de minimis fringe benefit) in the current year and the four previous years.

### (2) Scholarships and Fellowship Grants

There is an exclusion for degree candidates[2] for scholarships which the individual establishes are for tuition and related expenses (such as fees, books, supplies, and equipment required for courses of instruction).[3] There is no exclusion for amounts received for teaching, research, or other services required of the student as a condition for receiving the scholarship.[4]

An exclusion is allowed for a qualified tuition reduction, which is defined as a reduction in tuition provided to an employee of an educational institution for the education of the individual or his spouse or dependents (I have my eye on this one). The exclusion is available also for tuition reduction plans at other educational institutions (these are often exchange programs). The exclusion is available to highly compen-

---

2. A "degree candidate" is a graduate or undergraduate pursuing studies or conducting research to meet the requirements for an academic or professional degree. The definition also includes a student who receives a scholarship for study at a secondary institution. Reg. § 1.117–3(e). This regulation does not mention students at elementary schools, although indeed often private elementary schools do grant substantial scholarships to students.

At the other end of the educational spectrum, a doctor in a psychiatric residency program is not a degree candidate, Bergeron, 31 T.C.M. 1226 (1972).

3. § 117(a) and (b).

4. § 117(c).

sated employees only if the reduction program does not discriminate in favor of highly compensated employees.[5]

This exclusion for scholarships raises some interesting questions. Why should tuition scholarships be excluded from income? Presumably, it is to go easy on the recipients who are struggling students. But if that is the case, note also that students who go to state universities and pay very low tuition are getting a subsidy. Not taxing them on that subsidy is, perhaps, consistent with not taxing the recipient of a scholarship. That still leaves the working student out in the cold.

The exclusion of scholarships and fellowship grants is best viewed in the context of a wide range of other assistance to education such as free schooling, low tuition at state universities, federally subsidized low-interest student loans. Since these other very real benefits are not considered income (see generally ¶ 1.02(2)(b) relating to the comprehensive tax base) perhaps the exclusion of scholarships and fellowship grants simply equalizes the situation for students receiving this particular form of educational assistance. The only problem with that analysis is what about the student who gets no scholarship but is working her way through school? Should she get to deduct her tuition payments (which is functionally equivalent to the exclusion)? Or do we mean to go harder on the student who works her way through school than the student who gets a scholarship?[6]

If a grant is in form a scholarship or fellowship but is in reality compensation for services, it will be treated as such and included in income. This is consistent with the treatment of other areas such as gifts and prizes and awards, supra, where the exclusion will be denied if the transaction is at bottom compensatory.[7]

To those who would be rude enough to suggest that the scholarships that college athletes receive are income, because of the expectation they will participate in intercollegiate sports, the Service has ruled to the contrary, because under NCAA rules once an athletic scholarship is granted for a particular year it cannot be revoked even though the recipient chooses not to play sports. Hence the theory of the ruling is that the scholarship is not awarded in exchange for playing sports. The apparent flaw in this reasoning is that if the recipient does not choose to play sports, the scholarship need not (and probably will not) be renewed for the following year. Thus, in reality, in order to keep his scholarship going from year to year, the recipient must play sports. That certainly seems to make the scholarship income.[8]

**5.**  § 117(d).

**6.**  See, e.g. Commission to Revise the Tax Structure, Reforming the Federal Tax Structure (Fund for Public Policy Research, 1973).

Cf. ¶ 6.03(3)(b) relating to the deductibility of education expenses.

**7.**  Bingler v. Johnson, 394 U.S. 741, 89 S.Ct. 1439, 22 L.Ed.2d 695 (1969).

**8.**  Rev.Rul. 77–263, 1977–2 C.B. 47. Ruling that athletic scholarships are income would tend to suggest that big time college athletes are basically underpaid professionals, perish the thought.

### Integrated Summary of Scholarship and Fellowship Grant Rules

Scholarships for tuition and books for a student who is a degree candidate at an educational institution are excluded from the students' gross income, § 117(b)(2)(A). Scholarships covering room and board are not excluded from income. Payments to the student for doing research are included in the student's income.

If the student receives a scholarship for tuition-books for, say, $5,000 but is required to do 500 hours of research to receive it (where the going rate for compensated research is $10 per hour), then the scholarship is included in income, because it is in effect payment for the research services rendered, § 117(c).

If the student receives a scholarship for room-board for $5,000 but is required to do 500 hours of research to receive it (going rate $10 per hour), then the scholarship is included in income actually for two independent reasons: 1) room-board scholarships are always included in income and 2) the room-board scholarship was in effect payment for the research services.

Suppose a student receives a $10,000 scholarship which covers $5,000 tuition and books and $5,000 room and board. Suppose further the student is required to render 500 hours of research services (value $10/hour) to get this $10,000 scholarship. If the research is deemed to be for receiving the tuition-books scholarship, then that $5,000 tuition-books scholarship is included in income. In addition the $5,000 room-board scholarship is included in income because room-board scholarships are always included in income. If the $5,000 of research services is deemed to be for receiving the room-board scholarship, then the $5,000 tuition-books scholarship is not included in income and the $5,000 room-board scholarship is still of course included in income. The moral of the story is that the educational institution should specify that the research services are required for receiving the room and board scholarship and not the tuition-books scholarship. The results above are not changed even if all students are required to render 500 hours of research in order to get their degree. As discussed above in the text, the traditional athletic scholarship does not constitute income to the recipient because failure to participate in sports does not cause the scholarship to be withdrawn for the current year.

It is fairly common that several educational institutions in an area agree to give tuition scholarships to spouses of their employees attending one of the other institutions. As long as the plan is not discriminatory, the tuition scholarships are not includible in the recipient's gross income, § 117(d)(3).

Suppose Phil, an engineer for Westinghouse goes back to Carnegie Mellon University for a Ph.D. in mechanical engineering. Westinghouse pays $15,000 toward tuition and books for the course of study on the condition that Researcher return and work for Westinghouse. As discussed above, tuition payments here would be income, because what Westinghouse is doing is paying compensation for future services, which is taxable, Regs. § 1.117–6(d)(2) and (5). Even if Researcher were not required to come back to Westinghouse, the tuition payments could be income as payment for past services.

Suppose the employee-employer relationship is not present and Robert wins the $15,000 in his state lottery (see the prologue for extensive discussion of lotteries). As discussed above, this would be income as a prize, under § 74. But suppose Robert used the funds in fact to pay his college tuition and books? Would the $15,000 then be excludable as a scholarship? Note that § 74(a) states that amounts received as prizes are income except as otherwise provided in § 117. Section 117(b)(1) seems to require that the amounts received must be in the form of a scholarship or fellowship grant as well as being used for tuition and books. Thus it may well be that even if Robert in fact uses the $15,000 to pay for tuition and books he cannot exclude the $15,000 because it was not "received . . . as a scholarship or fellowship grant."

## ¶ 3.10   Discharge of Indebtedness

### (1) General Rule and Background: Old Colony Trust; Clark; Kirby Lumber; Zarin

Before you get out of debt, of course, you have to get in debt. The way you do that is by borrowing. What are the tax consequences of borrowing? Money is, after all, flowing from one party to another. Taking an annual accounting or taking a cash flow view of the matter, the borrower could be regarded as being in receipt of income when he borrows and entitled to a deduction when he pays back the principal. The rule in fact, however, is that borrowing does not give rise to income to the borrower and repaying the debt does not give rise to a deduction.[1]

The usual reason given for this treatment is that borrowing creates an immediate offsetting deduction to repay and therefore the borrower is not wealthier than he was before the borrowing. That answer is surprisingly inadequate, however. The tax law is rife with circumstances where taxpayers are taxed in transactions where they have not enjoyed an increase in wealth. For example, the simple act of selling appreciated stock is such a case. The taxpayer is not wealthier the day after he sold the stock than he was the day before. He has just changed the form of the investment to cash.[2] The wealth came from the previous rise in the value of the stock. That previous rise in the value of the stock, which did make the stockholder richer, was not taxed. And it would never be taxed if he never sold the stock, even though he was much wealthier because of it.

---

**¶ 3.10**

**1.** The interest paid on the debt is deductible, subject to various exceptions and limitations. See ¶ 7.01(3).

**2.** In the jargon he has undergone a "realization," see ¶ 4.02.

As another example, a stockholder in a corporation who receives a distribution of cash is taxed on that distribution, even if the stock has not appreciated in the stockholder's hands. In fact the stockholder has income on the cash distribution even if the stock has gone down in price.[3]

What this discussion seems to show, if it shows nothing else, is that an increase in wealth is not necessarily the touchstone of taxation.[4]

Thus we are still left trying to explain why the borrower does not have income when he borrows. He certainly has the funds to pay the tax. We might say that the borrower has an amount realized of the amount of the loan. But then we could also say that he has a basis in the deal of the amount of the loan, since he has obligated himself to pay the loan back. Thus the reason that there is no income from borrowing is that there is no gain realized, since amount realized equals basis, see ¶ 4.03.

Whatever the confusion on the rationale, the cold rule of law on the subject is clear. The borrower does not have income on borrowing and does not have a deduction on repayment. Similarly, the lender does not have a deduction on making the loan[5] and does not have income on repayment.

Let us turn now to the question of what happens when the taxpayer is discharged from a debt. One of the early cases, *Old Colony Trust* presented an interesting set of facts, as discussed in ¶ 2.01.

*Old Colony* spawned an interesting case about 10 years later in the Board of Tax Appeals (the predecessor of the Tax Court). This was *Clark:*

---

**3.** The cash distribution is taxable as a dividend as long as the corporation has something, as an accounting matter, called "earnings and profits." These "earnings and profits" could have been earned long before the stockholder owned stock in the company. §§ 301(c), 312, 316. See ¶ 3.03.

**4.** For a discussion of just what the heck *is* the touchstone, see ¶ 4.02.

**5.** We could explain that by saying that the lender in making the loan has undertaken a capital expense in the amount of the loan. The loan is a capital asset that will create income (i.e. interest). The basis of the capital asset will be amortized against repayment of the loan principal leading to no net gain there.

## CLARK v. COMMISSIONER[6]

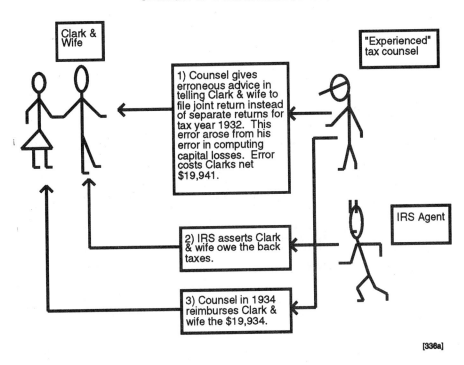

[336a]

*Question:* Was the reimbursement of the taxes by the Clark's counsel income to the Clarks?

*IRS Theory:* Counsel paid Clark's taxes and thus it is income, citing *Old Colony.*

*Taxpayer Theory:* The reimbursement was compensation for damages and thus constituted a return of capital and not income (see ¶ 1.02(2)(e) on return of capital). He took no deduction for the earlier payment.

*Held:* For taxpayer.

*Comment:* Look at *Old Colony,* discussed at ¶ 2.01, and this case. We see that the fact that a third party discharges debt of the taxpayer does not decide the question of taxability. We must know the reason for the discharge. Was it compensatory in nature, as in *Old Colony* or was it a recompense for damages as in *Clark?*

No doubt *Clark* is correctly decided. It can be viewed as a damage case. As we learn in ¶ 3.11(2), damages are taxed by what they substitute for. Here the damage payment by counsel to the Clarks was for loss of capital that he caused to the Clarks. The particular loss of capital involved (the necessity to pay federal income taxes) was not deductible. Since the obligation to pay the taxes was not deductible, the Clarks had a basis in the payment. Hence when they received the reimbursement, it

**6.** 40 B.T.A. 333 (1939), acq. 1957–1 C.B. 4.

was not taxable up to the amount of their basis. Had Counsel also paid them interest on the $19,934 (which would have been appropriate to do) the Clark's would have had income to the extent the payment exceeded their basis of $19,934.

The classic case in the field of cancellation of indebtedness is *Kirby Lumber*.

## UNITED STATES v. KIRBY LUMBER CO.[7]

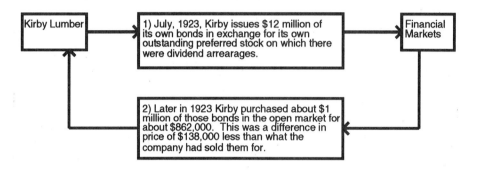

Kirby Lumber

1) July, 1923, Kirby issues $12 million of its own bonds in exchange for its own outstanding preferred stock on which there were dividend arrearages.

Financial Markets

2) Later in 1923 Kirby purchased about $1 million of those bonds in the open market for about $862,000. This was a difference in price of $138,000 less than what the company had sold them for.

[337a]

*Question:* Is the $138,000 difference in price that Kirby repurchased its own bonds for includible in Kirby's income?

*Taxpayer's Argument:* In *Bowers v. Kerbaugh–Empire* (see ¶ 1.02(2)(f)) repayment of a debt in German marks which had fallen in value did not give rise to income.

*Held:* The overall transaction was a loss in *Kerbaugh-Empire*. Here there was no diminution of assets. There was an accession to income and the difference is taxable.

*Comment:* Apparently Kirby was able to repurchase these bonds for less than their original issue price because interest rates had risen in the economy. Rising interest rates drive bond prices down because richer yields are available throughout the financial markets.

The Court made reference to *Kerbaugh-Empire*.[8] In that case, the proceeds of a loan denominated in dollars were repaid in depreciated German marks. Thus there was a profit on the repayment. The taxpayer in *Kerbaugh-Empire*, however, invested the proceeds of the loan in a losing venture and therefore the overall transaction netted to a loss. Suppose Kirby Lumber had invested the proceeds of the bonds it repurchased in a venture that lost $200,000. Would the Court have followed *Kerbaugh-Empire* and held that there was no income on the bond repurchase? Would the Court have netted the $138,000 gains on the bond repurchase against the (say) $200,000 loss on the venture to

**7.** 284 U.S. 1, 52 S.Ct. 4, 76 L.Ed. 131 (1931).

**8.** Bowers v. Kerbaugh–Empire, 271 U.S. 170, 46 S.Ct. 449, 70 L.Ed. 886 (1926).

find a net loss of $62,000? Or would it have ignored the gains on the bond repurchase altogether and found a $200,000 loss as seems to be called for in *Kerbaugh-Empire?*

We received some insight into those questions in the case of *Commissioner v. Jacobson.*[9] This case presented similar facts to *Kirby* in that the taxpayer repurchased its debt at a discount. The reason it was able to do so, however, was not because there was a general rise in interest rates. Rather, the taxpayer had come upon straitened financial circumstances. Since it was less creditworthy, its bonds were regarded as more risky by the financial markets and fell in price. *Jacobson* thus presented the *Kerbaugh-Empire* issue: the taxpayer was a loser overall but was making money on the particular repayment transaction. The Court held that there was income on the repurchase.

This is certainly the right answer. If the taxpayer is suffering other losses it may take them as appropriate. Let us ascertain tax liability one transaction at a time.

Now that we have staggered through to the truth, we find that Congress changed the rules on us anyway. Congress apparently found cases like *Jacobson* deserving of relief. Here after all is a taxpayer struggling along on the verge of collapse. It manages to pull a deal to help itself a little (repurchase its own obligations at less than face) and then the big bad IRS comes along and knocks the taxpayer back down again.

This led to the passage of § 108, which provides that cancellation of debt income (COD income in the argot) is excluded if the discharge occurs in a bankruptcy or the taxpayer is insolvent. The exclusion is temporary in that the taxpayer benefitting from it has to suffer in other ways. In particular it has to reduce other favorable "tax attributes," such as net operating loss carryovers by the amount of COD income excluded.[10] Eventually the taxpayer will pay more in tax because of the loss of these favorable attributes.

COD income and § 108 have assumed major importance in this current era of troubled leveraged buyouts. Many companies are staggering under a heavy debt load. Their very shakiness causes their debt to collapse in price. They then often repurchase their depreciated outstanding debt, tiptoeing around § 108, and still trying to keep their net operating losses alive.[11] This is a good place to remind ourselves that the provisions we study are not just for individuals. Most of the provisions we study are used as well by, for example, large publicly-held corporations.[12]

**9.** 336 U.S. 28, 69 S.Ct. 358, 93 L.Ed. 477 (1949).

**10.** 108(b). See discussion below at ¶ 3.10(2).

**11.** For a discussion of the tactics in this area see D. Posin, *Corporate Tax Planning: Takeovers, Leveraged Buyouts, and Restructurings* (1990) at the cumulative supplement Chapter 3 ¶ D.

**12.** In addition, there are specialized corporate tax provisions. See Internal Revenue Code, Subchapters C and S.

The problems in the discharge of indebtedness field were highlighted by the fascinating recent case of *Zarin.*

## ZARIN v. COMMISSIONER[13]

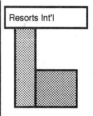

1) June, 1978, the Atlantic City casino Resorts Int'l grants $10,000 line of credit to Zarin after a credit check.
2) Zarin gets reputation as "high roller" betting house maximum on craps.
3) Resorts increases his credit line several times without further credit checks. Zarin gets complimentary services and privileges.
4) By November, 1979, Zarin's line of credit is raised to $200,000.
5) Between June, 1978, and December, 1979, Zarin loses $2,500,000 at craps table. He pays in full.
6) New Jersey Division of Gaming Enforcement files a complaint against Resorts with New Jersey Casino Control Comm'n alleging 100 casino regulation violations with respect to Zarin. The New Jersey Casino Control Comm'n issues an emergency order to Resorts making further extensions of credit to Zarin illegal.
7) Resorts evades the order through devices of "considered cleared" credit and "this trip only" credit. Both devices were later found to be illegal by the Commission and Resorts was fined.
8) By January, 1980, Zarin was gambling compulsively and uncontrollably at Resorts, spending 16 hours a day at the craps tables.
9) April, 1980, Resorts again increased Zarin's credit line without further inquiries.
10) April, 1980, Zarin delivered personal checks and counterchecks to Resorts for $3,435,000. The checks were dishonored for not sufficient funds.
10) Late April, 1980, Resorts cut off Zarin's credit.
11) November, 1980, Resorts filed suit in N.J. state court to collect the $3,435,000.
12) Zarin denied liability on grounds the debt was unenforceable under N.J. regulations designed to protect compulsive gamblers.
13) September, 1981, Resorts and Zarin settled for $500,000.
14) The IRS, living up to its reputation, asserts Zarin has $2,935,000 of cancellation of debt income.

[338a]

*Question:* Does Zarin have $2,935,000 of cancellation of indebtedness income?

*IRS argument:* Resorts' advance to Zarin of $3,435,000 in chips was a loan. The settlement for $500,000 constituted a cancellation of indebtedness.

*Held:* The debt Zarin owed to Resorts was unenforceable as a matter of New Jersey law, because of Resort's violation of the Casino Commission rules regarding extending Zarin credit. Thus the debt was not one for which the taxpayer is liable as required by § 108(d)(1)(A). Thus cancellation of the debt did not give rise to income.

*Comment:* Zarin had the defense that he was insolvent (liabilities

---

**13.**    916 F.2d 110 (3d Cir.1990).

exceed assets) at the time of the purported cancellation of debt income; thus he would not be taxable, § 108(a)(1)(B). However he filed that objection too late for consideration.

*Comment:* If Zarin subsequently failed to pay the $500,000 settlement amount, he then probably would have cancellation of debt income.

The court also held that the unenforceability of the debt meant there was a legitimate dispute as to the amount of the debt and thus that cancellation of it could not give rise to income.

The question that might be asked here is what would have happened if the facts were the same as in Zarin, except that Resorts did not violate any of New Jersey's gaming rules? The debt then would be enforceable under New Jersey law. Zarin was a resident of New Jersey. Cancellation of the debt would then appear to be income. Resorts' egregious conduct was clearly a factor in this case. So *Zarin* can certainly not be read as standing for the proposition that cancellation of gambling debts never gives rise to income.

A number of commentators have advanced some imaginative arguments that even though the gambling debt was unenforceable, Zarin still could have had income on other grounds. This would be that Zarin had a benefit of entertainment from Resorts equal to his $2.9 million cancelled debt. Since he did not pay for it, he had income of that amount. This line of reasoning finds support in the *Tufts* case (see Chapter 4). *Tufts* held that when a taxpayer benefits (in that case taking depreciation) from borrowed funds and then does not pay the debt back in full, there is still income in the amount not paid back. Another possible approach is that cancellation of the debt was in effect a punishment to Resorts for its violations of gambling regulations. As such the cancellation of the debt was tantamount to the receipt of punitive damages by Zarin, which is taxable under the leading case of *Glenshaw Glass*, see Chapter 2. Another possibility is that the cancellation of the debt was in the nature of compensatory damages to Zarin for the casino's injuries to him in preying on and aggravating his compulsion to gamble. Compensatory damages are not taxable, see ¶3.11. It could also be argued that there was no cancellation of debt because the settlement payment equalled the actual size of the debt. This argument is that the $3.5 million in chips advanced by Resorts were not really worth their face amount. The chips were not negotiable and could not be used outside the casino. Moreover, it is unlikely that Zarin could have turned the chips in for cash given the size of his debt to the casino. Another way of saying it was that there was no serious expectation that the full amount of the debt would be paid. One problem with this analysis is that if Zarin had experienced a winning streak and won the $3.5 million back, the casino would have been obligated to pay him in cash the full face value of the chips. Cutting the other way is that over an extended period of play, a winning streak of that magnitude against the house percentage was virtually impossible. There is also the intriguing argument that because Zarin was a compulsive gambler, the cancellation of $2.9 million of debt did not have that value to Zarin, putting one in mind of Garfield the Cat's question: "Are we having fun yet?"[14]

One possible problem with these imaginative approaches is that they are leaving the facts of the case and the statute behind. In point of fact the debt was unenforceable under New Jersey law. Thus it was not a true debt. Therefore there was nothing to cancel and there could not be cancellation of debt income. That's all she wrote.

It would seem, for example, to be a stretch to say that Zarin had $2.9 million of psychic income from gambling in the casino for which he should be taxed. No doubt everyone in a casino is having more fun than what they are losing or they would not be there. Shall we tax everyone who enters a casino's portals for their net psychic pleasure? And why limit it to casinos? In any event, Zarin, a compulsive gambler, would seem to be the last person to whom this argument could apply. It also seems a stretch to bring *Tufts* into this case. There was no depreciation founded on nonrecourse debt in this case. Unless one wants to read *Tufts* as saying that anyone who benefits in some way is taxed (certainly not our system), *Tufts* would seem to be inapposite. The same problem exists for the argument that the cancellation of the debt was in effect punitive damages exacted from Resorts and thus income to Zarin under *Glenshaw Glass*. This was not a punitive damages case; this was a cancellation of debt case. It is true that everything can be analogized to everything else at some level of abstraction. But our system does not go off on simply whether we can find a benefit somewhere and then tax it because in some other completely unrelated set of circumstances someone else who benefitted was taxed.

The imaginative arguments as to why Zarin did not have income also suffer from this infirmity of leaving the facts and the statute behind. To say, for example, that the cancellation of debt was compensatory damages to Zarin and thus not taxable is to ignore the facts of the case. The debt was not enforceable because of Resort's violations of regulations. The failure to enforce the debt was not intended by anyone involved to compensate Zarin for the psychological damages he suffered. It is supposition that he suffered any such damages at all. This compensatory damages argument also flatly contradicts the psychic income argument, showing the weakness of both approaches. The argument that the chips were not worth their face amount is similarly shaky. Just because the chips were not negotiable outside the casino does not mean they were not worth their face amount. In the course of play Zarin's chips were being turned over with the chips of other gamblers who were cashing chips in for their face amount at will. Did these fungible chips suddenly depreciate in value the minute they touched Zarin's fingers?

---

**14.** For further exploration of these ideas and a reprise of the rich literature this case has attracted, see Barton, Legal and Tax Incidents of Compulsive Behavior: Lessons from Zarin, 45 Tax Lawyer 749 (1992).

Zarin was playing the same game the others played with the same chips.[15]

Curiously, the one thing the commentators seem not to want to do is to take the case at face value: To have cancellation of debt income, there needs first to be a valid debt.[16] Because of Resorts' violations, the debt was not valid. Since it was not a valid debt it could not be cancelled by Resorts and there was no cancellation of debt on the settlement payment.

Here is the acid test. Take another case like *Zarin* except that the New Jersey casino does not violate any regulations. The gambler is a New Jersey resident. The debt is enforceable. Because the gambler is hysterical and because of the fear of bad publicity the casino settles a $3.5 million debt for $0.5 million. What happens to the fancy arguments now? Under the statute it's income. That is not even a particularly heartless decision unless the gambler is insolvent or bankrupt, in which case the insolvency or bankruptcy exceptions to the statute would spare him from being taxed.[17] If the gambler is worth $2 billion, who's to worry that we're taxing him on $3 million of cancellation of debt income? That being the analysis, you don't need the fancy psychic income arguments to give Zarin income. As to the arguments that this is not income, they would fall by the wayside too, on this new set of facts. Consider the arguments that settlement of the debt constitutes non-taxable compensatory damages, or that the chips aren't worth their face amount. Are those arguments going to be taken seriously in the face of having income cold under the statute? I doubt it.

### (2) Insolvent or Bankrupt Debtor

If a debtor's liabilities exceed his assets, he is insolvent. The insolvent debtor may or may not choose to file a petition under the Bankruptcy Code.[18] As mentioned above, if an insolvent debtor receives a discharge from indebtedness by virtue of a Bankruptcy Code case, the amount of income from discharge of indebtedness is excluded from the debtor's income.[19] That amount of income so excluded is applied to reduce the "tax attributes" of the debtor ("tax attributes" for this purpose being net operating losses and loss carryovers, and certain other credit carryovers, capital losses and capital loss carryovers, the basis of the debtor's assets and the foreign tax credit carryover).[20] In the alternative the debtor may elect to apply the amount of income excluded to reduce the basis in his depreciable property or real property held as inventory, rather than have the excluded amount reduce his "tax attrib-

---

**15.** Putting one in mind of the old song, "It's the wrong game with the wrong chips," which was certainly the case with Zarin.

**16.** § 108(d)(1)(A).

**17.** § 108(a)(1)(A), (B).

**18.** 11 U.S.C.A. § 301. A solvent debtor may file a petition in bankruptcy, but it would make little sense for him to do so inasmuch as he would in any event have to surrender his assets to the extent required to pay his creditors; but see the petition in bankruptcy of the solvent Manville Corporation, filed out of concern for asbestos litigation claims.

**19.** §§ 108(a)(1)(A), 108(d)(2).

**20.** §§ 108(b)(1), 108(b)(2), 1017(a)(2).

utes."[21] Subsequent disposition of property whose basis has been reduced under these provisions will give rise to income to the extent of the basis reduction, under the rules of §§ 1245 and 1250.[22]

If the debtor is insolvent but not, as in the discussion above, in a bankruptcy case, then discharge of indebtedness income will be excluded from the debtor's income to the extent that the debtor is insolvent.[23] The amount of excluded income is applied to reduce the debtor's "tax attributes" in the same way as in the case of a debtor in a bankruptcy case, described above, including the option to reduce basis of property instead of reducing "tax attributes."[24]

### Integrated Summary of Discharge of Indebtedness Rules

Suppose Borrower borrows $100,000 from Lender and then pays the debt off for $85,000. (Lender accepts the payoff because Borrower is somewhat shakey financially and Lender figures that this is the best deal he is going to get). In that event Borrower has $15,000 of cancellation of debt income (COD income in the argot). *Kirby Lumber, Zarin.*

If in the alternative Borrower pays off the debt in full just with land that cost him $60,000 and is worth $60,000, Borrower would have COD income of $40,000. Suppose the land had a value of $60,000 but a basis (or cost see ¶ 4.03(2)) in Borrower's hands of $40,000. In that event Borrower would have $40,000 of COD income and in addition $20,000 of income due to satisfying his legal obligation with appreciated property, see ¶ 4.02 and the discussion of the *Davis* case.

If Borrower does $100,000 worth of legal work for Lender who then cancels the debt, Borrower then has $100,000 of income, since he did the work and was in effect paid by the COD. If Borrower's legal work is worth only $50,000 and Lender still cancels the $100,000 debt for it, then Borrower still has $100,000 of income. It is made up of $50,000 of income as payment for his services and $50,000 of COD.

Suppose Borrower's Aunt Moneybags pays off the $100,000 loan, because Borrower is a "good boy." The nature of the third party payment must be examined. If the underlying rationale is a gift, then the repayment is excluded, § 102. If the underlying rationale is compensatory (i.e. if the aunt stated that the loan repayment was in exchange for $100,000 of legal work that Borrower had done for his aunt), then the third party-debt repayment would be income to Borrower.

Felix purchases undeveloped land for investment for $50,000. It rises in value to $100,000. Felix borrows $75,000 from Windsor Bank, secured by the property, but Felix also remains personally liable on the loan (recourse liability). Subsequently the property drops in value to $60,000. The liability is still $75,000. Felix transfers the property to Windsor and Windsor cancels the full debt of $75,000. The results to Felix are analyzed in two steps:

---

**21.** §§ 108(b)(5)(A), 1017(b)(3)(A) and (E).

**22.** § 1017(d)(1).

**23.** § 108(a)(1)-(3).

**24.** § 108(b).

1) He has COD income of $60,000 with respect to the transfer of the property. That is, the transfer of the property to the Windsor Bank has cancelled the debt to the extent of $60,000. Thus Felix has $10,000 of gain with respect to the transfer of the land ($60,000 amount realized less $50,000 basis.)

2) He has $15,000 of discharge of debt income, since the bank discharged the remaining $15,000 of this recourse debt. Since this is recourse liability, the other $15,000 of debt was not necessarily cancelled by the transfer of the land. But when in fact Windsor chose to cancel it, Felix has $15,000 of discharge of debt income. Regs. §§ 1.1001–2(a)(1), 1.1001–2(a)(2), 1.1001–2(c) Example 8.

The significance of splitting this transaction into two steps is that only the gain in the first step could qualify for capital gains treatment, since only that gain occurred with reference to the sale or exchange of property see ¶ 4.06.

The qualified real property business debt exception of § 108(a)(1)(D), providing that discharge of debt is not included in income, does not apply to exclude any of this discharge of debt from income, because that exception only applies to debt incurred with respect to real property used in a trade or business, and this property is held for investment, § 108(c)(3). For debt incurred after January 1, 1993, in order to qualify for the real property business debt exception, the debt must be qualified acquisition indebtedness—debt incurred to acquire, construct, or improve the property, § 108(c)(4).

If Felix borrowed on his property on a non-recourse basis, then the full amount of the liability would be discharged by the transfer of the property to Windsor Bank. Thus Felix would have an amount realized of $75,000, taken against his basis of $50,000 for a gain realized of $25,000. See discussion of the *Tufts* case at ¶ 4.03(2)(b)(iv). Note the nonrecourse liability situation produces the same amount of gain as the recourse liability situation—$25,000. But in the nonrecourse liability situation, the gain is computed in one step, not two steps as in the recourse liability situation. See Regs. § 1.1001–2(a)(4(I), 2(b).

In the alternative suppose Felix borrows $2 million from Venture Capital to help finance the purchase of a casino to operate in Mississippi. The riverboat is his only asset. At a time when the riverboat casino has a basis in Felix's hands after depreciation of $500,000, it runs into financial problems. Venture Capital agrees to have the $2 million debt paid off for $1 million. Assuming that Felix is solvent, the result would be that Felix has discharge of indebtedness income of $1 million, under *Kirby Lumber*. *Kirby Lumber* is the general rule and there is no applicable exception in § 108(a)(1).

If in this case Felix had borrowed his $2 million from the Lucky 7 Riverboat Casino Manufacturing Company, from whom he bought the boat, the results come out differently. Now a settlement by Felix of the $2 million debt for $1 million is treated as a reduction in the purchase price of the boat he bought from Lucky 7 and is not income to him. The basis of the riverboat in the hands of Felix would then be lowered from $500,000 (after depreciation) to $0. That lowering of the basis to $0 accounts for $500,000 of the $1 million debt discharge. And Felix would have $500,000 in income under *Kirby*. That accounts for the remainder of the $1 million debt discharge.

Suppose the facts are the same as above except that Felix has another $700,000 in debt in addition to the $2 million he borrowed. Thus he is insolvent in that his liabilities ($2.7 million) exceed his assets ($2 million—the riverboat). Then a discharge of the $2 million loan for $1 million triggers § 108(a)(1)(B) exception to the *Kirby Lumber* rule. Thus the $1 million debt discharge is excluded from income. With this exclusion, § 108(b) provides for a concomitant reduction in tax attributes. If Felix has none of the tax attributes described in § 108(b)(2)(A) through (D), then a reduction of his basis of $500,000 is required under § 108(b)(2)(E). However, as an exception to this rule, note that Felix has other liabilities (in addition to the $2 million of debt that was settled) remaining of $700,000. This would mean that the amount of those remaining liabilities is greater than his basis in the riverboat casino ($500,000 after depreciation). Section 1017(b)(2) provides that in an insolvency (or Title 11 case), the aggregate basis of the taxpayer's property shall not be reduced below the aggregate amount of the liabilities. Since in this case the amount of aggregate basis is already below the amount of the aggregate liabilities, there is no further basis reduction. There are no further tax consequences. On these facts, Felix got an exclusion from income without a concomitant reduction in tax attributes (of which he had none) or reduction in basis (which was already less than the liabilities). It might be noted that there is no strong logical relationship between the amount of liabilities and the basis of assets in the taxpayer's hands. Nonetheless, the statute uses a comparison between the two as a test for whether basis will be lowered after an exclusion of discharge of debt income.

Suppose on the facts of the preceding paragraph, Felix had a net operating loss of $100,000. In that event, the $1 million of debt discharge would be excluded from income (because Felix is insolvent) and the $100,000 net operating loss would be eliminated. There would be no reduction of basis because of § 1017(b)(2), as discussed in the preceding paragraph. In this situation, Felix could elect, under § 108(b)(5), to reduce the basis in his depreciable property (the riverboat) instead of reducing the net operating loss carryover. If the § 108(b)(5) election is made, then the § 1017(b)(2) limitation, discussed in the preceding paragraph, does not apply, see § 1017(b)(2) last sentence. Thus making this election means that $500,000 of basis is wiped out and $100,000 of net operating loss is preserved. Not making the election means that $100,-000 of net operating loss is wiped out and $500,000 of basis is preserved. Clearly on these numbers not making the election is preferable.

Suppose Felix has liabilities of $775,000 and assets of $700,000. Suppose a creditor discharges $200,000 of Felix's debt for $100,000. The result is that there is potential *Kirby* discharge of debt income of $100,000. However, Felix is insolvent by $75,000. Thus, under § 108(a)(1)(B) it appears that he can exclude the entire $100,000. However, § 108(a)(3) provides that the insolvency exclusion is limited to the amount of the insolvency. Hence on these numbers Felix excludes $75,000 and includes $25,000.

A discharge of debt can constitute a gift or income, depending on the surrounding circumstances. Where A fails to file a claim on a debt against B and the statute of limitations runs on the claim, the result it probably income. If A affirmatively renounces the debt in a setting of friendship, then the discharge would probably be a gift. Similarly a decedent in a will frequently discharges debts of relatives. These bequests, absent *Wolder* issues (discussed above) constitute non-taxable gifts and are thus exceptions to the *Kirby Lumber* doctrine.

## ¶ 3.11   Recovery of Damages to the Person or Business

### (1) In General

A taxpayer may suffer damages arising out of a personal or business tort, breach of contract, breach of fiduciary duty, violation of the antitrust laws, violation of the securities laws, violation of the civil rights laws, patent, copyright or trademark infringement, etc. Recovery of these damages must be analyzed under various special rules to determine their ultimate includibility in income.[1]

### (2) Damages From Personal Injuries

Compensatory *or punitive* damages received on account of personal injuries are excluded from income.[2] In that way this area bears a strong

---

**¶ 3.11**

1. The relationship between these special rules and the tax benefit rule (¶ 9.02(3)) is that if the analysis under these special rules indicates the recovery should be excluded from income, nonetheless the recovery will be included in income if it is attributable to a deduction taken in an earlier year which gave rise to a tax benefit. As an example of this set of facts, a taxpayer may suffer a business casualty loss, for which he properly takes a deduction in a particular year, § 165(c). The deduction benefits him. Reimbursement by insurance proceeds in a later year would then be includible in income under the tax benefit rule, notwithstanding that under the special rules for the recovery of damages the reimbursement is a non-taxable return of capital.

2. § 104(a)(2). See Redfield v. Insurance Company of North America, 940 F.2d 542 (9th Cir.1991) (Damages from viola-

tions of the Age Discrimination in Employment Act, 29 U.S.C.A. §§ 621–634 and the California Fair Employment and Housing Act, Cal.Gov't Code §§ 12900–12966 excluded under § 104(a)(2); Sparrow v. Commissioner, 949 F.2d 434 (D.C.Cir.1991) (back pay awarded in settlement of a racial discrimination claim filed under Title VII of the Civil Rights Act of 1964 included in income). If the taxpayer receives property by way of damages, the fair market value of the property will be excluded from income. The taxpayer will take a basis in the property of its fair market value at the time it was transferred in satisfaction of the damage award. If the taxpayer took a zero basis in the property he would then pay a tax on the full value of the property at such later time as he sells it. But the exclusion of § 104(a)(2) is not a deferral provision. It is a complete exemption. The only way to guarantee a complete exemption in the case of transfer of property in satisfaction of a

relationship to the exclusion of life insurance proceeds payable by reason of death of the insured. Punitive damages in connection with a case not involving physical injury or physical sickness—such as libel, slander, malicious prosecution—are not excluded.[3]

On a theoretical basis, of course, punitive damages in personal injuries cases can very well be argued to be income, as constituting a net increase to wealth rather than making the taxpayer whole, see ¶ 1.02(2)(b). Indeed even as to compensatory damages, that portion attributable to lost earnings can, as a theoretical matter, be argued to be properly subject to tax. However, the rule, as mentioned above, is for total exclusion of all damages for personal injuries except punitive damages in a case not involving personal injury or physical sickness.

Where, however, a payment for an invasion of privacy is negotiated for in advance to permit a movie or play, etc., to be made about taxpayer's life, the payment will be taxable in full, although the theory of such cases is not overly clear.[4]

In the recent Supreme Court Case of *United States v. Burke,*[5] the Supreme Court held that a payment received in settlement of a backpay claim relating to sex discrimination under Title VII of the Civil Rights Act of 1964 is not excludable from the recipient's gross income under § 104(a)(2) as damages received on account of personal injuries. The Court's reasoning was that the statute had provided for a remedy of back wages, which if paid in ordinary due course would be taxable. Thus the Court concluded it could not say that the statute redressed a tort-like personal injury.

The recent case of *Horton v. Commissioner,*[6] involved a Kentucky gas company that was liable for damages for failing to detect a gas leak in taxpayer's residence. As a result the gas company paid compensatory damages of $62,265 and punitive damages of $100,000. The Tax Court held that the punitive damages received as a result of the personal injury

---

damage claim for personal injuries is to give the recipient a basis of fair market value of the property at the time of the transfer.

**3.** 104(a) flush language.

See also Roemer v. Commissioner, 716 F.2d 693 (9th Cir.1983), decided prior to the amendment of the statute requiring inclusion of punitive damages. In *Roemer,* the Ninth Circuit reversed the Tax Court and found that the defamation action was, under California law, by its nature personal rather than business. The Court then went on to hold that punitive damages in defamation are not included in income, contrary to the present statute. See also Threlkeld, 87 T.C. 1294 (1986), judgment aff'd 848 F.2d 81 (6th Cir.1988) (Following Roemer, damage awards for both personal and professional damages are excludable under § 104(a)(2)). See also Agar, 19 T.C.M. 116 (1960), aff'd 290 F.2d 283 (2d Cir.1961)

(Dicta indicating that it is difficult to distinguish between damages to personal or business reputation).

**4.** Roosevelt, Jr. v. Commissioner, 43 T.C. 77 (1964)(amounts received by Franklin D. Roosevelt, Jr. For waiver of possible invasion of privacy claim arising from the play "Sunrise at Campobello" held income); Miller v. Commissioner, 299 F.2d 706(2d Cir.1962), cert. denied 370 U.S. 923, 82 S.Ct. 1564, 8 L.Ed.2d 503 (1962) (widow of band leader Glenn Miller received payments as an advance settlement of any liability Universal Pictures would incur because of an invasion of privacy for its making the motion picture "The Glenn Miller Story." Held: The payments were ordinary income, rejecting taxpayer's claim of a capital gain).

**5.** 504 U.S. 229, 112 S.Ct. 1867 (1992).

**6.** 100 T.C. 93 (1993).

claim were excludable under § 104(a)(2). The general test is the nature of the underlying claim, rather than on the type of damages received.

Thereafter, the Supreme Court decided the case of *Commissioner v. Schleier*[7] which presented the question of whether § 104(a)(2) of the Code authorizes a taxpayer to exclude from his gross income the amount received in settlement of a claim for backpay and liquidated damages under the Age Discrimination in Employment Act of 1967 (ADEA). Taxpayer brought suit against United Airlines for willful violation of the ADEA which "broadly prohibits arbitrary discrimination in the workplace based on age." Taxpayer succeeded at the trial court level but the decision was reversed on appeal. The case was then settled, with taxpayer receiving $145,629. Half of taxpayer's award was attributed to "backpay" and half to "liquidated damages."

The Tax Court held that the entire settlement was "damages received on account of personal injuries or sickness" within the meaning of § 104(a)(2) of the Code and was therefore excludable from income. The Fifth Circuit, relying on *Burke*, discussed above, affirmed. The Supreme Court granted certiorari because of a conflict in the circuits on the issue.

The Supreme Court held, based on *Burke*, that a recovery under the ADEA is not excludable from gross income. The Court's reasoning was that no part of an ADEA settlement arises from personal injury or sickness, as required by the language of § 104(a)(2). Even though unlawful termination of employment might cause psychological injury, the amount of damages awarded under ADEA is not attributable to that injury. Taxpayer argued that at least the liquidated damages portion of the settlement should be excluded from income. But the Court responded that it had already held that Congress intended that liquidated damages are punitive in nature and thus not personal but economic.

The Court also held that the statement in the Regs. under § 104(a)(2) that exclusion arises from damages in a tort type suit does not compel exclusion. The tort-like regulatory language is in addition to and not a substitute for the statutory requirement that the amount be received "on account of personal injuries or sickness."

In addition, the Court found that the ADEA recovery is not based on tort-like injuries, which the Court held in *Burke* was required for exclusion.

In short, the Court held that § 104(a)(2) and *Burke* establish two independent requirements that a taxpayer must meet before a recovery is excluded. First the taxpayer must demonstrate that the underlying cause is "based upon tort or tort type rights," and second, the taxpayer must show the damages were received "on account of personal injury or sickness."

Justice O'Connor wrote a dissenting opinion in which Justice Thomas joined and Justice Souter joined in part.

7. ___ U.S. ___, 115 S.Ct. 2159, 132 L.Ed.2d 294 (1995).

Subsequently, the Tenth Circuit held in *O'Gilvie v. United States*[8] that punitive damages stemming from a product liability claim are not excludable under section 104(a)(2). The court stated that four other circuits had taken that position, the Sixth Circuit being the only exception. The court asserted that the phrase 'on account of personal injuries' was ambiguous, and stated that Congress intended to exclude only those damages that 'compensate' a taxpayer for his injuries.

In December, 1995, the Fifth Circuit reversed the Tax Court in part, holding in *Robinson v. Commissioner*,[9] that punitive damages are not excludable from income.

Six days thereafter, the Tax Court declined to follow the position it had taken on punitive damages in *Horton* (see above). In *Bagley v. Commissioner*,[10] the Tax Court held that the punitive damages portion of a settlement payment received in a defamation suit was noncompensatory, and thus could not be excluded from income under § 104(a)(2). The Tax Court held that the Supreme Court had in substance overruled *Horton* in *Schleier*. The court also noted that indeed, except for the Sixth Circuit in *Horton*, all the circuit courts that have considered the issue have concluded that punitive damages are not excludable. This position was underscored by the Supreme Court's holding in O'Gilvie v. United States[11] that punitive damages received by the husband and children of a woman who died of toxic shock syndrome were not received "on account of" personal injuries, and therefore, the exclusion did not apply.

It would appear that after *Schleier* and *O'Gilvie* the Supreme Court will uphold the IRS position that all punitive damages should be taxable. The Supreme Court's two-part standard in *Schleier* for excludability under section 104 is difficult to meet.

To attempt to clarify this murky field, in 1996, Congress amended § 104 in two ways. 1) It provided that all punitive damages for personal injury or sickness—whether or not they are related to a physical injury or physical sickness are included in income, § 104(a)(2) as amended. 2) It provided that emotional distress is not treated as a physical injury or physical sickness. The legislative history explained that this provision means that damages from emotional distress based on a claim of employment discrimination or injury to reputation accompanied by a claim of emotional distress are not excluded. The legislative history went on to explain that because all damages received on account of physical injury or physical sickness are excludable from gross income, the exclusion from gross income applies to any damages received based on a claim of emotional distress that is attributable to a physical injury or physical sickness. In addition, amounts received that are not in excess of the amounts paid for medical care for emotional distress are excluded. § 104(a) flush language, as amended.

**8.**  66 F.3d 1550 (10th Cir.1995).

**9.**  70 F.3d 34 (5th Cir.1995).

**10.**  105 T.C. 396 (1995).

**11.**  ___ U.S. ___, 117 S.Ct. 452, 136 L.Ed.2d 454 (1996).

These amazingly complex provisions are summarized in the graphic below at page 151.

*Revenue Ruling 79–313*[12] dealt with the treatment of payments to be received in the future. Taxpayer was severely and permanently injured as a result of being struck by an automobile. He brought suit against the driver and the driver's insurance company proposed a settlement. Pursuant to the settlement, the company agreed to make fifty consecutive annual payments to the taxpayer. The payments were for "personal injury, pain and suffering, disability, and loss of bodily function." The amount of each payment would be increased by five percent over the amount of the preceding annual payment. The taxpayer had no right to accelerate any payment or increase or decrease the amount of the annual payment. The insurance company was not required to set aside specific assets to secure this obligation. The ruling noted that Regs. § 1.104–19(c) excludes damages based upon tort or tort type rights or received through a settlement agreement entered in lieu of such prosecution. The ruling held that all payments received by the taxpayer pursuant to the settlement agreement are excludable from gross income of the taxpayer under § 104(a)(2).

### (3) Damages From Injuries to Business; Raytheon

Injuries to taxpayers in their business do not qualify for the broad-scale exclusions of § 104(a)(2). The major principles in the field of damages from injuries to business are illustrated by the leading case of *Raytheon*:

## RAYTHEON PRODUCTION CORP. v. COMMISSIONER[13]

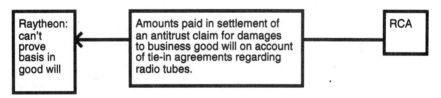

[339a]

*Question:* 1) Are the damages for a) recovery of capital for damage to good will or b) for lost profits? 2) If for recovery of capital, what is treatment if Raytheon can't prove basis?

*Held:* Damages are for recovery of capital; hence, not taxable to extent of basis. Unfortunately Raytheon cannot prove basis in good will.

---

**12.** 1979–2 Cum. Bull. 75.

**13.** 144 F.2d 110 (1st Cir.1944), cert. denied 323 U.S. 779, 65 S.Ct. 192, 89 L.Ed.

622 (1944). See ¶ 4.06(3)(b) for examples of how a basis in good will may be established.

Burden is on taxpayer to prove basis. In absence of proof, basis taken to be zero and amounts are taxable in full.

*Comment:* Raytheon's good will probably arose from its own business rather than having been purchased. Since it arose from its own business, Raytheon had no basis, since most of the costs of generating the good will would have been deducted. Allowing an exclusion from income after expenses of producing the good will had been deducted would have been an unjustified double benefit. Any capital expenditures (see ¶ 6.03(4)) involved in generating good will would, however, have gone to produce basis in the good will.

*Comment:* The transaction would be treated as a sale or exchange. Since good will is a capital asset, Raytheon would qualify for capital gain treatment. Had the damages been for lost profits, favorable capital gain treatment would not have been available. (See Chapter 4 for discussion of capital gains).

*Comment:* Compare this treatment to the complete exclusion of compensatory and punitive damages in personal injuries. However, expenses for an individual to acquire training and education are generally not deductible. Having lost the benefit of that deduction, taxpayers make up for it in part by an exclusion of damages for personal injuries.

As background, the general rule is that where a taxpayer is injured in his business, the includibility in income of the damages he receives will depend on to what the damages are attributable. The damages may be attributable to a recovery of capital, lost profits (past, present, or future); or they may be punitive damages. If the damages are attributable to a recovery of capital, they will not be income, unless the amount received exceeds the basis of the capital.[14]

On a superficial level this seems like a reasonable approach. One might be concerned, though, that the damages arise from an involuntary transaction, thus forcing the taxpayer to pay tax on gains at a time not of his choosing. The possible harshness of this is mitigated by § 1033, which allows the taxpayer to postpone the taxation of any gain if he reinvests the proceeds of his damage award in property "similar or related in service or use."[15]

---

14. In that event they will be § 1231 gain. § 1231 is a complex provision that is used to ascertain whether sales and certain other dispositions of business property are given capital gain treatment, see ¶ 4.06(3)(a)(iv). Under present law, treatment as capital gain is not of great significance, see ¶ 4.06(1). See also Boehm v. Commissioner, 146 F.2d 553 (2d Cir.1945), cert. granted 325 U.S. 847, 65 S.Ct. 1556, 89 L.Ed. 1969 (1945) (payments for loss in value of stock a return of capital where taxpayer had taken no prior deduction); IR 401, Sept. 29, 1961 (compensation to persons of Japanese ancestry, paid under the American–Japanese Evacuation Claims Act, 62 Stat. 1231, (1948) for loss of property arising from the evacuation of such persons from various western states during World War II a return of capital).

15. § 1033(a)(1). See ¶ 4.05(3).

Just in case you thought § 1033 was some kind of a backwater provision, it was recently employed to attempt to avoid $1 billion in taxes. This arose from the celebrated contract case between Texaco and Pennzoil. In late March, 1988, Pennzoil collected a staggering $3 billion from Texaco in settling its case for Texaco's interfering with Pennzoil's contract to purchase Getty Oil. The amount would be reduced by legal fees of about $400 million. Taxes on the

The difference between recovery of capital (tax-free to the extent of basis) and recovery of lost profits (fully taxable) approaches the metaphysical, inasmuch as capital is only significant because it produces profits. Hence any recovery of capital is in some sense a recovery of lost profits and any recovery of lost profits is in some sense a recovery of capital. Taxpayers, of course, are wont to argue that the damages received are a tax-free recovery of capital; the Service, of course, asserts the damages are a taxable recompense for lost profits. Lacking a meaningful economic standard for allocating between the two, the courts have rendered decisions in this area that have been somewhat erratic in rationale and result; often the approach of the underlying transaction is important.[16]

Similar agonizing problems are presented where the allocation of a damage award is between recovery of capital and punitive damages. This issue arises most frequently in the antitrust field, where statutory provision is made for punitive treble damages in civil suits.

The principle that the includibility in income of business damages received depends on to what the damages are attributable has been used to ascertain the treatment of damages for a number of other types of claims, including patent infringement (ordinary income or return of capital),[17] breach of employment contract (ordinary income),[18] and

award, regarded as lost profits, were expected to be in the $1 billion area.

Pennzoil attempted to use § 1033 as follows: It would first argue that Texaco's action in contract interference was a "theft." A theft qualifies as an "involuntary conversion," which is what is required under § 1033. Pennzoil would then purchase assets similar to those of Getty Oil. If all this held together, Pennzoil would be within the protection of § 1033 and thus be able to defer the $1 billion in taxes indefinitely (without paying any interest).

An advance ruling by the Service that this works would be required. Subsequently Pennzoil acquired 8.8% of Chevron Corporation's outstanding stock for $2.2 billion, pursuant to this plan. Chevron was not happy at this major purchase and decided to try to break Pennzoil's chops on the § 1033 issue. Chevron argued that the passive nature of the investment meant that the transaction could not qualify for § 1033. This was because Pennzoil's 49% interest in Getty Oil, which it lost to Texaco, was obviously actively managed. Thus Chevron's stock would not be similar to Getty's stock for § 1033 purposes. Pennzoil responded by raising its stake in Chevron to 9.4% and obtaining an extension of time from the Service to try to establish that the Chevron stock was similar to the Getty stock for § 1033 purposes. At this writing

the matter is still unresolved. I'll keep an eye on it for you. See D. Posin, *Corporate Tax Planning: Takeovers, Leveraged Buyouts, and Restructurings* 1084–1086 (1990).

**16.** See, e.g., *Raytheon,*supra (lost profits used to measure the damage to the good will); Specialty Engineering Co., 12 T.C. 1173 (1949) (acq.) (adopting allocation of underlying judgment); Basle v. Commissioner, 16 T.C.M. 745 (1957), aff'd per curiam 256 F.2d 581 (3d Cir.1958) (ignoring allocation of settlement agreement where taxpayer otherwise failed to prove loss of good will); Kendall, 31 T.C. 549 (1958) (acq.) (adopting allocation of condemnation award that the entire proceeds were for capital).

**17.** W.W. Sly Manufacturing Co., 24 B.T.A. 65, 1931 WL 570 (1931) (payment of patent infringer's profits to taxpayer is ordinary income to taxpayer); Big Four Industries, 40 T.C. 1055 (1963) (acq.) (damages were ordinary income, return of capital and capital gain); Mathey v. Commissioner, 177 F.2d 259 (1st Cir.1949), cert. denied 339 U.S. 943, 70 S.Ct. 797, 94 L.Ed. 1359 (1950) (damages for lost profits ordinary income).

**18.** Knuckles v. Commissioner, 349 F.2d 610 (10th Cir.1965) (taxpayer executive found incompetent by board of directors was fired but refused to knuckle under and sued for breach of employment contract. Held: amounts received were ordi-

breach of contract to purchase property (ordinary income).[19]

As discussed above, in a case of personal injury not involving a physical injury (such as libel or slander), compensatory damages are excluded from income but punitive damages are not. Thus in a libel or slander case for injury to the personal reputation, the question can arise as to the allocation of the damages between non-taxable compensatory damages and taxable punitive damages. Where the case goes to judgment, presumably the terms of the judgment would control.[20] Where, however, the case is settled, whatever evidence is available will be used to arrive at the appropriate allocation.[21] The Service has ruled that the terms of the complaint will carry great weight in making a proportional allocation.[22] However, this ruling does not exclude resort to other evidence.[23] Once the percentage of the damage award that is included in income is ascertained, the same percentage of the legal fees incident to the suit will be deductible.[24]

### Integrated Summary of Damages, Reimbursements and Similar Receipts

The following diagram should be helpful in summarizing the confusing law of taxation of damage awards.

nary income for breach of employment contract over taxpayer's claim that some of the award was non-taxable recompense for personal injury.). See also, Coats, 36 T.C.M. 1650 (1977), and Letter Ruling 7737061 (payment in settlement of suit under Title VII of the Civil Rights Act, 1964, barring discrimination in employment on the basis of race, sex, religion or national origin, 42 U.S.C.A. 2000(e–2) *et seq.* held ordinary income as a recovery of back pay).

**19.** Smith v. Commissioner, 50 T.C. 273 (1968), aff'd 418 F.2d 573 (9th Cir. 1969) (damages for breach of contract to purchase stock and real estate were ordinary income, since the sale was not com-

pleted). Republic Automotive Parts, Inc. v. Commissioner, 68 T.C. 822 (1977) (ordinary income for damages paid for suit for inducing breach of contract to distribute auto parts for a royalty).

**20.** Rev.Rul. 58–418, supra at 19.

**21.** Id.

**22.** Rev.Rul. 58–418, supra.

**23.** Id. The settlement agreement itself might serve as a guide, but it could be ignored as being self-serving with respect to the allocation for tax purposes.

**24.** Rev.Rul. 58–418, note supra; § 212(1).

*Taxation of Damage Awards*

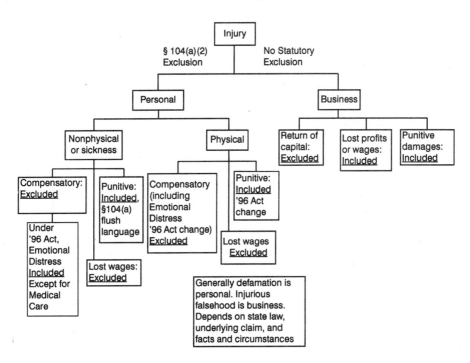

Making reference to the diagram above, a suit by a creditor for recovery of a loan that is delinquent involves a claim whose underlying nature is business. Hence recovery of the principal of the loan is a nontaxable return of capital. Recovery of delinquent interest is lost profits and is included in income. (If the debtor satisfies the claim by transferring appreciated property, the debtor has a gain to the extent the value of the property exceeds its basis.) A suit by a taxpayer for refund of overpaid federal income taxes plus interest is treated as follows. The underlying claim is still business. The receipt back of the overpaid taxes is therefore a nontaxable return of capital. The receipt of interest is included in income as lost profits.

Where damages for lost profits are paid as a result of a suit for breach of a business contract, the underlying claim is business. Hence the amounts received are includible in income as lost profits.

## ¶ 3.12  Alimony and Similar Payments

To the extent payments made incident to a divorce are income to the spouse receiving them, they are deductible to the spouse making them. This subject of alimony and similar payments made incident to a divorce is discussed in detail at ¶ 6.02(14).

## ¶ 3.13   Miscellaneous Items of Income and Exclusions From Income

### (1) In General

As earlier discussion has indicated,[1] gross income is a far-reaching and open-ended concept. In general, the presumption is that a net accretion to wealth will be included in income, whether it is from an orthodox or an unorthodox source. The statute is broad enough to cover income from sources unimagined at the time the statute was drafted. As § 61 states: "... [G]ross income means all income from whatever source derived ..." There are many exceptions, limitations and special treatments, as Chapter 2 and the other sections of Chapter 3 have shown. Beyond these topics is a range of miscellaneous transactions and events reaching across the fullness of the society which, because they apparently involve a net accretion to wealth, could be regarded as giving rise to gross income. A representative listing of these variegated items and the authority for their inclusion or exclusion from income is set forth below:

One puzzling example is illegal income.

### (2) Illegal Income: The Fantastic Saga of Wilcox, Rutkin and James

The Supreme Court's opening shot in the murky area of illegal income was *Commissioner v. Wilcox*[2] in which it held that embezzled funds were not income to the perpetrator because the perp had an obligation to restore the funds to the victim. In that sense the transaction was analyzed as being roughly like a loan (see the discussion of treatment of loans at ¶ 3.10).

This presented some policy difficulties. Why should hard-working folks pay taxes on their incomes whereas thugs and embezzlers do not have to pay? It was probably thoughts along this line that caused the Court to take a different approach to the extortionist who was the taxpayer in *Rutkin v. United States*[3]. The Court there held that the extortionist's ill-gotten gains were income. This was fine except that the *Rutkin* Court explicitly refused to overrule *Wilcox*. Thus as matters stood after *Rutkin*, income from embezzlement was not taxable but income from extortion was.

This was not a state of affairs that could continue. The *Wilcox* case was decided in 1946. The *Rutkin* decision was in 1952. It was clear after *Rutkin* to any observer of the Court that the next embezzler decision that came down the road would see *Wilcox* overruled. This proved to be the case in the celebrated case of *James v. United States*[4]. The Court in

---

**¶ 3.13**

**1.**  Chapters 1 and 2.

**2.**  327 U.S. 404, 66 S.Ct. 546, 90 L.Ed. 752 (1946).

**3.**  343 U.S. 130, 72 S.Ct. 571, 96 L.Ed. 833 (1952), reh'g denied 343 U.S. 952, 72 S.Ct. 1039, 96 L.Ed. 1353 (1952).

**4.**  366 U.S. 213, 81 S.Ct. 1052, 6 L.Ed.2d 246 (1961).

that case overruled *Wilcox* and settled the matter that illegal income was income.

There was just a teeny little loose end. The *James* case involved not only the question of whether embezzled funds were income, it also involved the prosecution of the taxpayer in that case for tax fraud. "Fraud" under the statute required willfulness. As to that issue, the Court said:

> "We believe that the element of willfulness could not be proven in a criminal prosecution for failing to include embezzled funds in gross income in the year of misappropriation so long as the statute contained the gloss placed upon it by Wilcox at the time the alleged crime was committed. Therefore, we feel that petitioner's conviction may not stand and that the indictment against him must be dismissed."[5]

This raised some really interesting questions. Are potential embezzlers reading Supreme Court cases? And if they are, how good a job are they doing of it? According to the Supreme Court, the reason that the taxpayer in *James* could not be convicted for fraud was that apparently he was supposed to have read *Wilcox*. But if he had read *Wilcox* would he not have also read *Rutkin?* But if he had read *Rutkin* would he not have realized that the reasoning in *Rutkin* had vitiated the Court's holding in *Wilcox?* What about embezzlers after *James?* Can they be prosecuted for willfully failing to pay tax? What if they have read no cases at all? What if they have only read *Wilcox?* What if they have only read *Rutkin?* What if they have read *James* but they didn't understand it? If they don't understand it, they could join the crowd. I don't understand any of it myself.[6]

### (3) Other Items of Income and Exclusion

| Item | Included or Excluded | Authority |
| --- | --- | --- |
| American Indians' Income | Generally included; some excluded pursuant to treaty or statute | Squire v. Capoeman, 351 U.S. 1 (1956); Rev.Rul. 67–284, 1967–2 C.B. 55; a number of federal statutes. |
| Barter | Often included | Receipt of property or services through barter can give rise to income under the usual rules; see Reg. § 1.6045–1(d), relating to reporting requirements for large barter exchanges. |
| Beekeeper indemnification | Included; possible non-recognition or loss | Rev.Rul. 75–381, 1975–2 C.B. 25 (Indemnification due to pesticide spraying). |
| Breeding Rights in Thoroughbred Stallions | Included | Rev.Rul. 73–173, 1973–1 C.B. 40 (Where compensation for services). |

---

**5.** *Id.* at 222–223, 81 S.Ct. at 1057.

**6.** See also the case of *Harris*, discussed at ¶ 3.08, also raising the question of willfulness in criminal tax fraud cases.

| Item | Included or Excluded | Authority |
|---|---|---|
| Campaign Contributions | Excluded unless used for personal purposes or received in exchange for political favors | Rev.Rul. 71–449, 1971–2 C.B. 77; Rev.Rul. 75–103, 1975–1 C.B. 17; Rev.Rul. 74–23, 1974–1 C.B. 17 (Income earned by contributed funds includible). |
| Child Research Reimbursements | Excluded | Rev.Rul. 67–407, 1967–2 C.B. 59 (Reimbursement of parents' expenses for living in a motel for two weeks while their child was observed in the home by researchers). |
| Contributions to Capital of Corporation | Excluded | § 118(a); see Rev.Rul. 75–557, 1975–2 C.B. 33 and § 118(b) for contributions in aid of construction of facilities by a public utility or a railroad. |
| Corporate Officers' Indemnification Insurance | Premium paid by employer excluded | Rev.Rul. 69–491, 1969–2 C.B. 22 (Insurance indemnified against errors, misstatements, wrongful acts or omissions, neglect or breach of fiduciary duty in capacity of officer or director of corporation). |
| Executor's Commissions | Excluded if waived | Rev.Rul. 66–167, 1966–1 C.B. 20; see also Breidert, 50 T.C. 844 (1968) (acq.) |
| Foreign Earned Income and Housing Expense Reimbursement | Substantial exclusion if foreign residence or presence in foreign country tests are met | § 911. |
| Gambling Winnings | Included | Winkler v. U.S., 230 F.2d 766 (1st Cir.1956) (dicta); Slavin, 43 B.T.A. 1100 (acq.) (1941) (proceeds of illegal gambling income. See also IRC § 165(d)). 20% withholding is required on most gambling winnings above $1000 from such pastimes as wagering in a parimutuel pool on horse races, dog races, jai alai, or other wagering pool or lottery, if the proceeds are 300 times as large as the amount wagered. Where multiple bets are sold on one ticket, such as Big Triple or Trifecta, the bet is considered to be the individual unit bet rather than the aggregate amount staked. Withholding does not apply to bingo, keno, and slot machines winnings. Winnings from a state-conducted lottery are only withheld against if above $5000. IRC § 3402(q), Instructions to Forms W–2G, and 5754. See also "Lottery Winnings," this chart infra. |
| Government Housing Subsidies | Generally excluded | Rev.Rul. 75–271, 1975–2 C.B. 23 (Mortgage assistance payments under § 235 of the National Hous- |

| Item | Included or Excluded | Authority |
|---|---|---|
| | | ing Act excluded) Rev.Rul. 76–75, 1976–1 C.B. 14 (Interest reduction payments under § 236 of the National Housing Act includible in income of mortgagor but also deductible). |
| Illegal Income (see above) | Included | James v. U.S., 366 U.S. 213 (1961) (embezzlement and dicta re other illegal income); Rutkin v. U.S., 343 U.S. 130 (1952) (extortion); U.S. v. Sullivan, 274 U.S. 259 (1926) (illicit liquor); Lyna Kathryn Jones, T.C. Memo 1977–329 (prostitution); Chadick v. U.S., 77 F.2d 961 (5th Cir.1935) (general graft). |
| Insurance Payments for Living Expenses | Excluded if meet statutory tests | § 123, excluding insurance reimbursements for greater than normal living expenses where taxpayer denied access to his personal residence by government authorities due to a casualty or threat of a casualty. |
| Jointly Owned Property, Income from | Apportioned to owners according to local law | Income from property owned in joint tenancy usually split evenly between the owners, see Statute of Ann. Income from property owned in tenancy in common usually split in accordance with the proportionate ownership of the parties, Mitchell, 28 B.T.A. 767 (1933) (acq.). Since tenancy by the entirety is only available to husband and wife, who ordinarily file a joint return, question of allocation of income from property owned in this form rarely arises. Woodsam Associates, Inc. v. Comm., 198 F.2d 357 (2d Cir.1952). |
| Mausoleum and Cemetery Trust Funds | Excluded | Rev.Rul. 58–190, 1958–1 C.B. 15 (laid this issue to rest by holding that amounts received by profit or nonprofit cemetery companies irrevocably set aside for the perpetual care of burial plots or mausoleum crypts are excludible from income of the cemetery company); although "Memory" or "memorial" appears in the name of many of these cemetery companies, a number of them seem to forget to use the funds set aside for perpetual care and misappropriate them for their own use, in violation of state law or their own contracts. In such a case the funds will be taxable to them. See as representative of a number of such cases Green Lawn Memorial Park, Inc. |

| Item | Included or Excluded | Authority |
|---|---|---|
| | | v. McDonald, 164 F.Supp. 438 (D.C.Pa.1958), aff'd per curiam 262 F.2d 588 (3d Cir., 1959); Hawaiian Cemetery Ass'n Ltd., d/b/a Sunset Memorial Park, 34 T.C. 1093 (1960) see also Jefferson Memorial Gardens, Inc. v. Comm., 390 F.2d 161 (5th Cir.1968) (proceeds from grave spaces and markers, sold to customers on a "pre-need" or "pay-now-use-later" plan were entirely included in income where no amount was used for care of individual plots). |
| Medicare Benefits | Hospital payments excluded; doctor payments included to extent premiums deducted | Rev.Rul. 70–341, 1970–2 C.B. 31. |
| National Research Service Awards | Excluded through 1983 | Tax Equity and Fiscal Responsibility Act of 1982 § 285. |
| Nazi Persecution Compensation Payments | Excluded | Article XI(1)(c) of the United States–Federal Republic Germany Income Tax Convention, C.B. 1966–1, 360 at 368. |
| "No Fault" Auto Insurance Payments | Excluded | Rev.Rul. 73–155, 1973–1 C.B. 50 excluded these payments on the authority of § 104(a)(3), which excludes accident and health insurance payments. |
| Parsonage, Rental Value Of | Excluded | § 107, excluding a rental allowance or the rental value of a home furnished a minister of the gospel as part of his compensation. |
| Resident of Alaska Longevity Bonus | Included | Rev.Rul. 76–131, 1976–1 C.B. 16 (Payments to residents of Alaska for more than 25 years who are over 65 not based on need, hence included in income). |
| Security payments to Guarantee Performance of Contract | Excluded | Warren Service Corp. v. Comm., 110 F.2d 723 (2d Cir.1940). |
| "Short–Swing" Profits of Insiders, Paid to Corporation | Included | Park and Tilford Distillers Corp. v. U.S., 107 F.Supp. 941 (Ct.Cl. 1952). |
| Social Security Payments | Partly included for some taxpayers | In general, as a taxpayer's adjusted gross income (as modified) and one half of the social security benefits received exceed certain base amounts, up to either 50% or 85% of the social security benefits are included in gross income. |

| Item | Included or Excluded | Authority |
|---|---|---|
| Terrorist Attack Payments | Excluded | § 104(a)(5), excluding disability income attributable to injuries sustained as a direct result of a terrorist attack (as determined by the Secretary of State) while the taxpayer was an employee of the United States outside the United States. |
| Treasure Trove (Found Property) | Included | Regs. § 1.61–14(a); Cesarini v. U.S., 296 F.Supp. 3 (N.D.Ohio 1969) (aff'd 428 F.2d 812, 6th Cir. 1970) ($4,467 found in a $15 second-hand piano income). |
| Treaty, Income Subject To | Exclusion of income by treaty prevails over other tax law | §§ 894(a), 7852(d). |
| Unsolicited Books Sent to Academics and Others | Included if contributed to charity and deducted; presumably included only to extent deduction allowed | Haverly v. U.S., 513 F.2d 224 (7th Cir.1975); Rev.Rul. 70–498, 1970–2 C.B. 6; Cf. § 170(e)(1) which now limits charitable deductions in certain cases to the basis of the property, which may be zero for unsolicited books; the Service earlier promulgated Rev.Rul. 70–330, 1970–1 C.B. 14 holding that the receipt of unsolicited books by academics and others was income regardless of whether they were contributed to charity, but this ruling was withdrawn. (Thank God for small favors). |
| Will Contest Compromise Payments | Excluded | Lyeth v. Hoey, 305 U.S. 188 (1938) (Will contest payment treated as a non-taxable bequest) see ¶ 3.08(4). |
| Workman's Compensation Payments | Excluded | § 104(a)(1). |

## ¶ 3.14　Reporting Exempt Income

A taxpayer fortunate enough to receive income exempt from taxation must still submit with his return an itemized statement showing (i) the amount of each class of exempt income and (ii) the expenses allocable to the exempt income.[1] If an expense is attributable to both a class of non-exempt income and a class of exempt income, a reasonable proportion must be allocated to each class.[2] The statement should also aver that no deduction claimed in the return is attributable to any class of exempt income.[3]

**¶ 3.14**

1. Reg. § 1.265–1(d).
2. Reg. § 1.265–1(c).
3. Reg. § 1.265–1(d).

# Chapter 4

## INCOME FROM DISPOSITIONS OF PROPERTY

*Table of Sections*

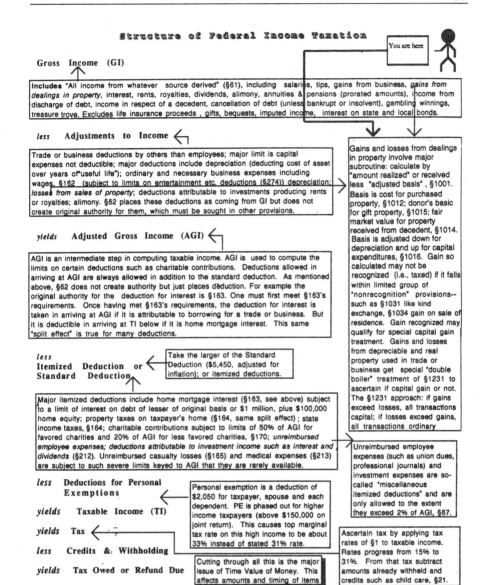

Structure of Federal Income Taxation

You are here

**Gross Income (GI)**

Includes "All income from whatever source derived" (§61), including salaries, tips, gains from business, *gains from dealings in property*, interest, rents, royalties, dividends, alimony, annuities & pensions (prorated amounts), income from discharge of debt, income in respect of a decedent, cancellation of debt (unless bankrupt or insolvent), gambling winnings, treasure trove. Excludes life insurance proceeds , gifts, bequests, imputed income, interest on state and local bonds.

*less* **Adjustments to Income**

Trade or business deductions by others than employees; major limit is capital expenses not deductible; major deductions include depreciation (deducting cost of asset over years of "useful life"); ordinary and necessary business expenses including wages, §162 (subject to limits on entertainment etc. deductions (§274) depreciation; *losses from sales of property*; deductions attributable to investments producing rents or royalties; alimony. §62 places these deductions as coming from GI but does not create original authority for them, which must be sought in other provisions.

*yields* **Adjusted Gross Income (AGI)**

AGI is an intermediate step in computing taxable income. AGI is used to compute the limits on certain deductions such as charitable contributions. Deductions allowed in arriving at AGI are always allowed in addition to the standard deduction. As mentioned above, §62 does not create authority but just places deduction. For example the original authority for the deduction for interest is §163. One must first meet §163's requirements. Once having met §163's requirements, the deduction for interest is taken in arriving at AGI if it is attributable to borrowing for a trade or business. But it is deductible in arriving at TI below if it is home mortgage interest. This same "split effect" is true for many deductions.

*less* **Itemized Deduction or Standard Deduction**

Take the larger of the Standard Deduction ($5,450, adjusted for inflation); or itemized deductions.

Major itemized deductions include home mortgage interest (§163, see above) subject to a limit of interest on debt of lesser of original basis or $1 million, plus $100,000 home equity; property taxes on taxpayer's home (§164, same split effect) ; state income taxes, §164; charitable contributions subject to limits of 50% of AGI for favored charities and 20% of AGI for less favored charities, §170; *unreimbursed employee expenses; deductions attributable to investment income such as interest and dividends* (§212). Unreimbursed casualty losses (§165) and medical expenses (§213) are subject to such severe limits keyed to AGI that they are rarely available.

*less* **Deductions for Personal Exemptions**

*yields* **Taxable Income (TI)**

*yields* **Tax**

*less* **Credits & Withholding**

*yields* **Tax Owed or Refund Due**

Personal exemption is a deduction of $2,050 for taxpayer, spouse and each dependent. PE is phased out for higher income taxpayers (above $150,000 on joint return). This causes top marginal tax rate on this high income to be about 33% instead of stated 31% rate.

Cutting through all this is the major issue of Time Value of Money. This affects amounts and timing of items

Gains and losses from dealings in property involve major subroutine: calculate by "amount realized" or received less "adjusted basis" , §1001. Basis is cost for purchased property, §1012; donor's basis for gift property, §1015; fair market value for property received from decedent, §1014. Basis is adjusted down for depreciation and up for capital expenditures, §1016. Gain so calculated may not be recognized (i.e., taxed) if it falls within limited group of "nonrecognition" provisions-- such as §1031 like kind exchange, §1034 gain on sale of residence. Gain recognized may qualify for special capital gain treatment. Gains and losses from depreciable and real property used in trade or business get special "double boiler" treatment of §1231 to ascertain if capital gain or not. The §1231 approach: if gains exceed losses, all transactions capital; if losses exceed gains, all transactions ordinary

Unreimbursed employee expenses (such as union dues, professional journals) and investment expenses are so-called "miscellaneous itemized deductions" and are only allowed to the extent they exceed 2% of AGI, §67.

Ascertain tax by applying tax rates of §1 to taxable income. Rates progress from 15% to 31%. From that tax subtract amounts already withheld and credits such as child care, §21.

## ¶ 4.01　Overview

Gains derived from dealings in property are includible in gross income. It should be noted that it is not the gross receipts received on dealings in property that are included in gross income but the "gains" derived from dealings in property—a net concept. As discussed at ¶ 2.01, normally gross income as defined by § 61 encompasses only the gross amount of wages, dividends, interest, rent, etc. received by the taxpayer undiminished by any deductions attributable to such income. Those deductions that are allowed would then be subtracted from gross income to arrive at adjusted gross income, § 62 and see ¶ 6.01. However when it comes to "dealings in property" (i.e., sales, exchanges or other dispositions, including sales of inventory), gross receipts are offset by the basis of the property to arrive at the gain; it is that gain that is included in *gross* income.[1]

When property is sold or otherwise disposed of, a complex statutory scheme involving several steps is triggered for arriving at the amount of taxable gain (or deductible loss). The several steps of the statutory scheme will first be set forth here in outline. This will be followed by a detailed discussion of each of these steps.

The first step in arriving at whether there has been a taxable gain or deductible loss is determining whether there has been a *realization,* generally a sale or other disposition of the property for consideration.[2] If there has been such a realization, the next step is to compute the *gain* or *loss realized.*[3] This is done by ascertaining the *amount realized*[4] on the sale or other disposition of the property and subtracting from it the *adjusted basis* of the property.[5] The gain realized may (on rare occasions) be *excluded* from income. And any loss might well be *disallowed.* In the case of such exclusion or disallowance, that is the end of the process.[6] Otherwise, having computed the gain realized and not excluded or the loss realized and allowed, the next step is to ascertain whether the gain or loss will be *recognized.* If a gain or loss is recognized, it will be given immediate significance on the taxpayer's tax return. If, in the alternative, the gain or loss is not recognized, it will in general be deferred until some later year.[7] Once it is ascertained that the gain or loss will be recognized, the next step is to determine the *character* of the gain or loss—whether capital or ordinary.[8] Historically capital gains are taxed under favorable rules and capital losses are taxed under unfavorable rules. Net long term capital gains are taxed under favorable rules and net capital losses are taxed under unfavorable rules. Finally, there can on occasion be a further *timing* question of the taxable year in which the gain or loss will be reported.[9]

This analysis may be boiled down to a series of questions that should be answered, in order, when analyzing the taxation of any disposition of property. These questions, and the related issues they spawn, are represented in the accompanying graphic. The issues mentioned in this graphic are the subject of the ensuing discussion. Bear in mind that this graphic is an elaboration of the subroutine on gains and losses from dealings in property which is given in the graphic on the

¶ 4.01

1. § 61(a)(3), Reg. § 1.61–6(a).

2. § 1001(a) and (b).

3. § 1001(a).

4. § 1001(b).

5. §§ 1001(a), 1011.

6. §§ 165(c), 183, 121. As discussed at ¶ 4.04 the disallowance of a broad range of losses is of major structural significance in the Code. The exclusion of gain is much

rarer and not of great structural significance. See § 121.

7. § 1001(c) and see ¶ 4.05. As discussed in ¶ 4.05, nonrecognition sometimes means permanent exemption.

8. §§ 1221, 1222, 1231, are the main authorities.

9. See ¶ 8.03.

structure of federal income taxation that appears at the beginning of this chapter and at various points in the book.

## Gains and Losses From Dealings in Property

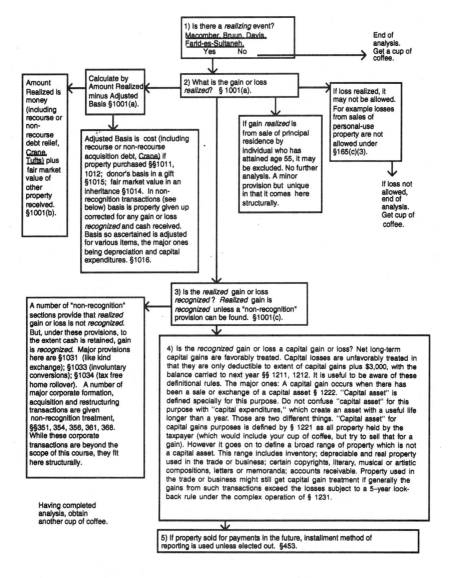

[340a]

### Steps in Taxing Dispositions of Property

(1) Has there been a realizing event? If the answer is no, that is the end of the process.

(2) What is the gain or loss realized? This is arrived at by the formula: amount realized minus adjusted basis.

(3) If there was a loss, is the loss allowed? If the loss is not allowed, this is the end of the process. (On rare occasions a gain will be excluded from income, which would also be the end of the process.)

(4) Is the realized gain or loss recognized? The gain or loss will be recognized unless a so-called "non-recognition" or deferral provision applies.

(5) What is the character of the gain or loss? Some gains and losses are capital gains and losses to which special rules apply, generally treating capital gains favorably and capital losses unfavorably.

(6) In what taxable year is the gain or loss to be reported? This is less frequently a problem than the other steps but can be a significant issue.

The workings of this structure can be illuminated by an example of a purchase and sale of marketable securities. Suppose securities are purchased on January 21, 1993 for $1000 and sold January 21, 1998 for $5000. The following is the treatment of this transaction: The sale is clearly a realizing event. The amount realized is the $5000 received; the adjusted basis is the cost or $1000. Hence the gain realized is $4000. The gain will be recognized, since no non-recognition provision applies to this transaction. The character of the gain on these facts will be a long term capital gain, thus qualifying for the favorable tax treatment of capital gains. The proper time to report this gain would be the year of sale.

This structure works comparatively simply in the case of a sale of marketable securities. If, however, the transaction had involved the sale of a mortgaged building used in the taxpayer's trade or business in consideration for which was received another mortgaged building and cash (not an uncommon transaction), many of the steps above would have been much more complex, although the underlying structure would have been the same.[10]

Each of the steps in the structure can often be resolved simply. However, each step can on occasion raise exceedingly complex problems. It is to these steps that the discussion now turns.

## ¶ 4.02   The Requirement of a Realization

### (1) In General: Macomber, Bruun, Cottage Savings

The first step in ascertaining the taxability of dealings in property is determining whether a gain or loss has been realized. The concept that income from property must be "realized" before it can be taxed is one of the most venerable in the tax law. It is clear that when property appreciates in value, the owner of that property has in some sense enjoyed income: his net wealth has increased. He could borrow against this appreciation. Or he could simply not save other funds because he

---

**10.**  For treatment of this complicated transaction, see ¶ 4.05(2)(b).

knows he has got the nest egg of appreciation already stashed away. Thus he can use the funds he would have saved for a vacation or to party it up. In that way appreciation gives rise to an immediate tangible benefit just as surely as if the taxpayer had received an increase in salary.

According to the classic definition of income advanced by the economist Henry Simons, the taxpayer holding appreciated property certainly has income. According to Simons, "Personal income may be defined as the algebraic sum of (1) the market value of rights exercised in consumption and (2) the change in the value of the store or property rights between the beginning and end of the period in question."[1] Yet the tax law has been loath to tax appreciation on property which continues to be held by the owner.

What is the reason for this? Sometimes it is said that it is difficult to make annual appraisals to ascertain how much appreciation has occurred. This should not itself be a problem, however. The price of marketable securities can be easily ascertained. Real estate (the other major asset people hold for investment) can be appraised and is appraised already for state property tax purposes.

Sometimes it is said unrealized appreciation is not taxed because the taxpayer lacks the money to pay the tax. If the appreciation is in marketable securities, however, it would be easy enough to sell some of the securities to pay the tax. Moreover, the statute certainly taxes substantial amounts of compensation income in kind, as discussed in Chapter 2. Thus the fact that unrealized appreciation is not reduced to cash does not seem to be a defense to taxing it. Furthermore, if the appreciation is in an illiquid asset such as real estate, the taxpayer could apparently borrow against the property to pay the tax. People might, however, take offense at a tax system that compels them to go into debt (particularly since most people are already in substantial debt).

However, even in the case of real estate, the rules could be tighter than they now are. Where a taxpayer holding appreciated real estate mortgages his property without personal liability, that could be an occasion for imposing a tax on the mortgage proceeds. There are several arguments to support this. First, the nonrecourse mortgage bears some of the earmarks of the sale, since the taxpayer can choose to forfeit the property to the lender without any more money changing hands between them. Also, there is no valuation problem, since the tax can be imposed on the mortgage proceeds to the extent they exceed the taxpayer's basis in the property. Nor is there a liquidity problem since clearly the taxpayer is in funds. Were such a tax to be imposed the basis of the property would be increased *pro tanto*. This issue was addressed in Woodsam Associates, Inc. v. Commissioner, 198 F.2d 357 (2d Cir.1952), where the court rejected the argument that nonrecourse financing of

¶ 4.02

1. H. Simons, *Personal Income Taxation* 50 (1938). See also ¶ 1.02(2)(b).

property held by the taxpayer was a realizing event. The *Woodsam* case and the issue it raises are discussed extensively at ¶ 4.03(2)(b)(iii) below.

However all this argument breaks down, it should be noted that the failure to tax unrealized appreciation in assets held constitutes a huge tax break to those lucky enough to hold highly appreciated assets. It should be recognized that failure to tax unrealized appreciation is a time value of money issue and triggers off our discussion of this subject in the Prologue. Let us take a quick example:

Lucy purchases undeveloped land for $100,000 when she is 20 years old. One year after she buys it oil is struck on a neighboring parcel. Her land shoots up in value to $500,000. Oil is never found on Lucy's land, but there is that potential. The land remains at the value of $500,000 for the next 40 years. Lucy sells the land when she is 61 years old. Assume a combined federal and state tax rate of 40%.

Now if Lucy had to pay tax right away on that $400,000 gain, she would pay a tax of 40% of $400,000 or $160,000.

But Lucy, under our system of not taxing unrealized appreciation, doesn't have to pay a tax on that gain right away. On our facts, Lucy holds the property for another 40 years and then pays her $160,000 tax.

Let us say that Lucy, being a planner, knows she is going to hold the property until she is 61. So she sets aside money when she was 21 that will grow to be enough to pay the $160,000 tax 40 years later. If the money grows at an after tax rate of 8%, what amount of money does Lucy have to set aside when she is 21 to have $160,000 when she is 61. Stir your coffee. Answer is $7,365. Once again we see the staggering power of time value of money.

So "mere" deferral saved Lucy $152,635. She saved 95% of her tax through "mere" deferral. That $152,635 that Lucy does not pay is $152,635 that the rest of us, who don't own appreciated assets, do have to pay.

Anybody like to reconsider the unrealized appreciation issue?

Notwithstanding this lucid analysis, the courts, the Congress, and the Service have in their combined wisdom down through the ages resolved upon the requirement that before the appreciation in value of property can be taxed, there must be a "realizing event." The property must be disposed of, usually sold or exchanged for money or other property, before the appreciation in its value can be taxed. (Similarly a decline in the value of property may only be deducted upon the "realizing event" of sale or other disposition.)

The seminal case in this area is Eisner v. Macomber.

## EISNER v. MACOMBER[2]

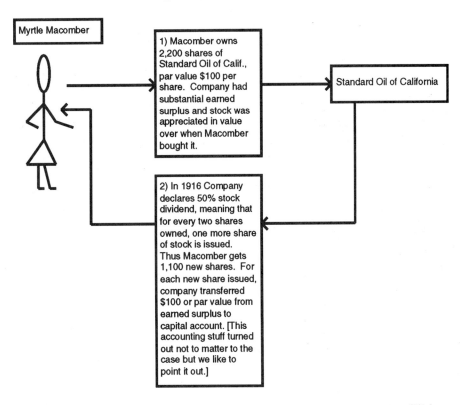

Myrtle Macomber

1) Macomber owns 2,200 shares of Standard Oil of Calif., par value $100 per share. Company had substantial earned surplus and stock was appreciated in value over when Macomber bought it.

Standard Oil of California

2) In 1916 Company declares 50% stock dividend, meaning that for every two shares owned, one more share of stock is issued. Thus Macomber gets 1,100 new shares. For each new share issued, company transferred $100 or par value from earned surplus to capital account. [This accounting stuff turned out not to matter to the case but we like to point it out.]

[341a]

*Question:* Was the stock dividend taxable to Macomber where the statute specifically taxed stock dividends?

*Held:* No. The stock dividend did not constitute a realizing event, as required by the Constitution. Hence the statute is unconstitutional here. To have income the gain must not accrue to capital, but it must be severed from the capital, derived from the capital, for the taxpayer's separate use, benefit and disposal (Holmes, Brandeis, Day and Clarke dissenting).

*Brandeis dissent:* the present transaction has the same effect as if Standard Oil had offered stock to its shareholders to be purchased pro rata and had at the same time declared a cash dividend of the price of the stock. There is no doubt that this latter transaction would have been taxable.

*Comment:* The market value of Macomber's shares before the stock dividend was about $371 per share. After the stock dividend it was about $251 per share. What would you like to make of that?

**2.**  252 U.S. 189, 40 S.Ct. 189, 64 L.Ed. 521 (1920). See also Gray v. Darlington, 82 U.S. (15 Wall.) 63, 21 L.Ed. 45 (1872) (appreciation in value of property not taxable under Income Tax of 1867); Lynch v. Turrish, 247 U.S. 221, 38 S.Ct. 537, 62 L.Ed. 1087 (1918).

As pointed out, the Supreme Court's theory in this case was that the stock dividend was not a gain severed from the capital of the corporation but simply represented the shareholder's continued investment in the corporation. Standard Oil had in fact been profitable and the stock dividend was backed by an appropriate accounting transfer from earned surplus to capital account. Nonetheless, the Court found that to tax the pro rata stock dividend would be to in effect tax the appreciation in value of the shareholder's investment, rather than to tax the income from the investment. Taxing the appreciation in the value of the capital, rather than income derived from the capital was, in the Court's view, unconstitutional; whereas there was no question that a cash dividend would have been taxable.[3]

Taxability of stock dividends is now handled by § 305, which in important respects follows the basic *Macomber* rule. The basis of stock received as a dividend is ascertained under § 307, which provides that a proportionate amount of the basis of the old stock is transferred to the new stock. In the *Macomber* case one-third of the basis of the old stock would have been allocated to be the basis of the new stock. Pro rata stock dividends, not taxable under current law, are widely used by corporations to lower the value of their stock to a more convenient trading range. The only effect of a stock dividend is to lower the price of the corporation's outstanding stock. This is for the same reason that when you cut a piece of pie into more pieces, the pieces are inevitably smaller.

It is useful to focus in detail on the meaning of *Macomber*. It is clear that the day after the pro rata stock dividend, the shareholder was no wealthier than the day before, because of the "pieces of pie" effect. The existence of the new shares in the hands of the shareholders of the corporation inevitably reduced the value of the original shares. Thus the value of the new shares plus the original shares in the hands of the shareholder was equal to the value of his original shares the day before the stock dividend—taxpayer still had the same percentage interest in the same corporation.[4]

This, however, was *not* the basis of the Court's decision. Nor could it have been. For it is also evident that if the corporation had paid a pro rata *cash* dividend, the stockholders would have been no wealthier the day after than the day before such a cash dividend was paid. The value of the stockholder's shares just after he received the cash dividend would be reduced *pro tanto* on account of the distribution of cash from the corporation. Thus in both cases—the stock dividend and the cash dividend—the shareholder's wealth does not increase on account of the transaction. But in the *Macomber* view of the world the shareholder in

---

**3.**   252 U.S. at 211, 40 S.Ct. at 194.

**4.**   It is well established in stock market trading that when a stock dividend is paid (or a stock splits), the stock price immediately drops to the appropriate new price; and the overall market value of the shareholders' holdings does not change as a result of the stock split or stock dividend. This indeed happened in the *Macomber* case, as pointed out in the graphic.

receipt of a cash dividend has experienced a taxable event, because there has been a severance of the income from the capital of the corporation—there has been a realizing event. And in the *Macomber* view such a realizing event is constitutionally required. For the Sixteenth Amendment only speaks to a tax levied on income, and, in the *Macomber* view, income only arises when there has been a severance from capital.[5]

Is it still the case that Congress is constitutionally barred from imposing an income tax on appreciation in value of assets? We get some insight into this question with the well-known case of *Helvering v. Bruun* :

### HELVERING v. BRUUN[6]

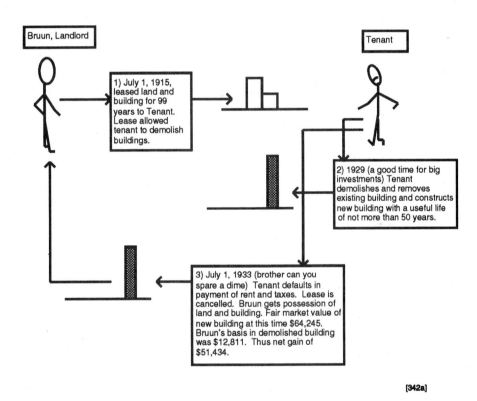

Bruun, Landlord

Tenant

1) July 1, 1915, leased land and building for 99 years to Tenant. Lease allowed tenant to demolish buildings.

2) 1929 (a good time for big investments) Tenant demolishes and removes existing building and constructs new building with a useful life of not more than 50 years.

3) July 1, 1933 (brother can you spare a dime) Tenant defaults in payment of rent and taxes. Lease is cancelled. Bruun gets possession of land and building. Fair market value of new building at this time $64,245. Bruun's basis in demolished building was $12,811. Thus net gain of $51,434.

[342a]

*Question:* Is the net gain on reacquisition of the building income to Bruun?

---

5. 252 U.S. at 211, 40 S.Ct. at 194. Indeed, in distinguishing income from capital, the Macomber Court employed the "fruit and tree" metaphor (*id.* at 206), which was traded upon heavily later in the assignment of income area for somewhat analogous purposes. See ¶ 5.02.

6. 309 U.S. 461, 60 S.Ct. 631, 84 L.Ed. 864 (1940), mandate conformed 112 F.2d 573 (C.C.A.8 1940).

*IRS Position:* Bruun has gain of $51,434 in 1933 on reacquisition of the building.

*Taxpayer Position:* The improvements became part of the realty. The gain is not derived from capital, not severed from capital. There has, in short, not been a realizing event, citing *Macomber.*

*Held:* For IRS. Gain was realized in 1933. "The fact that the gain is a portion of the value of property received by the taxpayer in the transaction does not negative its realization." The forfeiture was a realizing event.

*Comment:* Even though the new building was worth more than Bruun's basis in his old building, probably the land in 1933 (the depths of the depression) was worth less than it was in 1929. Thus did Bruun really have an economic gain of $51,434 in 1933? Probably a lot less than $51,434, if any at all. Does that mean the Court's holding is wrong? No. If there was a realizing event, then this is like the case where a corporation pays a cash dividend and concomitantly its stock drops severely in value due to other market forces. The cash dividend is still taxable as a realizing event. To realize the loss in the underlying capital it would be necessary, for example, to sell it.

There are enough ways to analyze this fact pattern to choke a horse. Think of all the ways and times we could tax a *Bruun*-type transaction with respect to the building constructed by the lessee.[7]

1) *Tax the new building at the front end and the back end.* Tax the value of the new building on signing of the lease and on termination of the lease. Take this hypo: Landlord and tenant sign a 15–year lease on undeveloped land. They agree tenant will pay rather low rent but tenant will also construct an office building at a cost of $20 million. The building will have a useful life of 30 years. If constructing the new building is part of the lease deal, then the construction of the new building looks like rent. What is the amount of the rent? This would be the value of the building at the end of the lease term. If it's worth $20

**7.** This footnote is a sidetrip for those who want to O.D. on this present value stuff. Those who are just trying to get through can pass this one up.

Consider a fancy way of treating the rental payments. On signing this 99–year lease in 1915, Bruun could be taxed on the present value of his rental payments over the lease term. Say the lease payments were $3,000 per year for 99 years. The present value of $3,000 per year for 99 years, assuming a 10% interest rate, is $29,998. We could tax him on that. Eventually, as the lease payments came in, he would get more than that, of course. He gets in total 99 × $3,000 or $297,000. Once we tax him on the $29,998, we then spread that new basis out against the lease payments in some way (see Chapter One ¶ 1.02(2)(e) on recovery of capital). For example, if we spread it out in a straight line fashion, we would deduct $29,998/99 = $303 per year. This would result in his finally being taxed on the full amount of his $297,000. Thus as the lease payments came in, Bruun would be taxed on $3,000 − $303 or $2,697 per year. He would also, as the owner of the property, be able to take other deductions with respect to the property as well, such as depreciation and maintenance. This is economically what is happening. But this is crazy, right? Nobody does this. Our tax system is not going to operate at this level of sophistication. We tax people on rents as they are paid as a cash method. We are not going to do this present value stuff. It is interesting to see how inadequately our tax system reflects true economic income.

million when constructed, then let us say it is worth $10 million at the end of the 15–year lease term (which is half the building's useful life). What is the present value of $10 million 15 years from now, with an interest rate of 10%? (Don't worry, I'm still doing the math, although I think I should get overtime). That present value cranks out to be $2,393,920. We then tax lessor on that amount at lease signing, treating the building as pre-paid rent. When the lease expires, lessor gets a building worth $10 million. We subtract his basis (i.e., the amount of gain on which he's already paid tax) of $2,393,920, giving us further income at lease termination of $10,000,000 − $2,393,920 = $7,606,080. Then (we're not through yet, sports fans) we have to let lessor depreciate the building with a basis of $10 million over the building's remaining useful life.

2) *Tax new building at the front end and during lease term.* Another way to go on this would be to once again sock lessor with the $2,393,920 on signing the lease. Then, say, lessor has income every year as the time for getting the new building approaches. What we'd be saying is that lessor's $2,393,920 is increasing in value at 10% compounded annually. That will take us to $10 million after 15 years (trust me, actually it's just the reverse of the calculation in 1) above). See the discussion of *Irwin v. Gavit* in Chapter 3. Once again there would be a $10 million basis for depreciation for the lessor at the end of the lease.

3) *Tax the building at the back end only.* Just sit around and tax lessor on nothing with respect to the building until the lease terminates. Then tax him on $10 million. Thereafter he has a basis for depreciation of $10 million.

4) *Don't tax the building at all.* Keep believing *Macomber*. There is no realization at any time during the signing or termination of the lease. Lessor has no income. Lessor also has no basis in the building and therefore gets no depreciation deduction thereafter.

Notice, very importantly, that all four of these methods involve a net of zero when we're all through. The first three methods involve $10 million taxed and $10 million deducted for a net of zero. 4) is a net of zero by having nothing taxed and nothing deducted. The only difference among them all is timing.

Which method should we use? Much of the discussion in this area and the history of the treatment of this problem has focussed on administrative convenience. It is said to be difficult to value the building many years from now. Thus 1) and 2) are discredited. In fact, however, if the estimate of the value of the building proves to be off, it could be corrected with a further offsetting deduction or inclusion in income. In any event, historically methods 3) and 4)—which do not require any advance estimates of the building value—were favored.

It looks otherwise like these methods are all pretty much the same. But what this administrative convenience approach fails to appreciate is the immense time value of money implications of the method chosen.

Let's explore that a little. Which method would the taxpayer prefer? You should be able to answer this one. The method that gives the most deferral. That's 4). You have no income on signing the lease or during the lease term or at the end of the lease. What is the price paid? It is no depreciation over the last 15 years of the building's useful life. So with 4) you have the good news (no income) early and the bad news (no depreciation) later.

Which method would the IRS prefer if they just wanted to suck as much as possible out of the taxpayer (which, of course, they don't (?)): The method which taxes the most up front. That's 2), tax up front and during the lease term. 2) is also the most economically accurate method.

How much difference does it make which method we use, applying our present value analysis?

The table below shows the present value of the unfavorable (to the taxpayer) Method 2. It will not surprise us to learn that if the taxpayer pays $4 million in tax over the course of the first 15 years of the lease and then gets $4 million in tax savings over the last 15 years of the lease, the taxpayer is under water as far as tax consequences go over the term of the lease. Indeed, this method of reporting income costs the taxpayer almost a million dollars in present value terms, or nearly 5% of the value of the entire project.

**Present Value of Method 2): determine present (negative) value of paying tax on growth in first 15 years and present (positive) value of taking depreciation deductions in last 15 years. Net the two numbers together for net present value (using 10% growth rate).**

| Annual Present Value of Building | Annual Before- Tax Growth | Tax on Annual Growth @40% | Present Value of Tax on Ann Grwth | Year No. |
|---|---|---|---|---|
| $2,393,920 | $2,393,920 | $957,568 | ($957,568) | 0 |
| $2,633,312 | $239,392 | $95,757 | ($87,052) | 1 |
| $2,896,643 | $263,331 | $105,332 | ($87,052) | 2 |
| $3,186,308 | $289,664 | $115,866 | ($87,052) | 3 |
| $3,504,938 | $318,631 | $127,452 | ($87,052) | 4 |
| $3,855,432 | $350,494 | $140,198 | ($87,052) | 5 |
| $4,240,975 | $385,543 | $154,217 | ($87,052) | 6 |
| $4,665,073 | $424,098 | $169,639 | ($87,052) | 7 |
| $5,131,580 | $466,507 | $186,603 | ($87,052) | 8 |
| $5,644,738 | $513,158 | $205,263 | ($87,052) | 9 |
| $6,209,212 | $564,474 | $225,790 | ($87,052) | 10 |
| $6,830,133 | $620,921 | $248,368 | ($87,052) | 11 |
| $7,513,146 | $683,013 | $273,205 | ($87,052) | 12 |
| $8,264,461 | $751,315 | $300,526 | ($87,052) | 13 |
| $9,090,907 | $826,446 | $330,578 | ($87,052) | 14 |
| $9,999,998 | $909,091 | $363,636 | ($87,052) | 15 |
| Totals | $10,000,000 | $4,000,000 | ($2,263,343) | |

| Basis of Building After Depreciation | Annual Depr | Tax Savings From Depr 40% Rate | Present Value At Begin of Lease of Tax Savings Due To Depreciation | Years Out |
|---|---|---|---|---|
| $10,000,006 | $666,667 | $266,667 | $122,163 | 16 |
| $9,333,339 | $666,667 | $266,667 | $116,346 | 17 |

| Basis of Building After Depreciation | Annual Depr | Tax Savings From Depr 40% Rate | Present Value At Begin of Lease of Tax Savings Due To Depreciation | Years Out |
|---|---|---|---|---|
| $8,666,672 | $666,667 | $266,667 | $110,806 | 18 |
| $8,000,005 | $666,667 | $266,667 | $105,529 | 19 |
| $7,333,338 | $666,667 | $266,667 | $100,504 | 20 |
| $6,666,671 | $666,667 | $266,667 | $95,718 | 21 |
| $6,000,004 | $666,667 | $266,667 | $91,160 | 22 |
| $5,333,337 | $666,667 | $266,667 | $86,819 | 23 |
| $4,666,669 | $666,667 | $266,667 | $82,685 | 24 |
| $4,000,002 | $666,667 | $266,667 | $78,747 | 25 |
| $3,333,335 | $666,667 | $266,667 | $74,998 | 26 |
| $2,666,668 | $666,667 | $266,667 | $71,426 | 27 |
| $2,000,001 | $666,667 | $266,667 | $68,025 | 28 |
| $1,333,334 | $666,667 | $266,667 | $64,786 | 29 |
| $666,667 | $666,667 | $266,667 | $61,701 | 30 |
| $0 | | | | |
| Totals | $10,000,000 | $4,000,000 | **$1,331,412** | |

Net Present Value of Method 2)     (**$931,930**)

The net present value of $931,930 is equal to the negative $2,263,-343 present value of taxing the appreciation in value of the building plus the $1,331,412 present value of taking depreciation later on the building.

By contrast method 4) has a net present value of zero, as far as the method of tax reporting is concerned. There is no $4 million in taxes in the early years and there is no $4 million in deductions in the later years. There is just nothing at all. Thus you don't need to be a rocket scientist to see that the net present value of reporting on this method is zero. That is $931,930 better than method 2. When the Service allows method 4) to be used, it is giving away nearly $1 million in taxes. Maybe the administrative convenience argument should be reconsidered.

Method 3), tax the building at the lease termination and then allow depreciation thereafter, was the one taken by *Bruun*. It is not quite as favorable to the taxpayer as 4), but still a lot more favorable to the taxpayer than the economically accurate method of 2). In cases prior to *Bruun* method 4) was often used on the grounds that there was no realization under *Macomber*.

After all this, Congress modified the result in *Bruun* by statute. Guess which method they took: Number 4). That is money in landlord's pockets (and money out of the pockets of the rest of us). Section 109 provides that there is no tax at all on the termination of a lease with respect to the value of property erected or other improvements made by the lessee. Under § 1019, the basis of such property so received back and not taxed under § 109 will be zero. There's number 4), do not tax or depreciate. We know that is the most favorable method for taxpayers.

The only relatively minor exception to this rule is the parenthetical language in § 109 which provides that the exclusion does not apply if the improvements by the lessee were intended as rent. If that is true (and the lease agreement would have to reflect that), then the improvements are included in income at the time of the lease termination. The amount of income would be the fair market value of the improvements. In that event the lease improvements would also be accorded a basis of their fair market value under § 1019. This is alternative 3).

So, under the statute, you usually get 4), unless the improvements are intended as rent, in which case you get 3). 1) and 2) are never heard from.

As far as the constitutional issues raised in *Bruun* are concerned, it is doubtful today that Congress would be regarded as constitutionally barred from imposing an income tax on appreciation in the value of assets. However, the issue does not usually arise because Congress has for the most part required there to be a realizing event before tax can be imposed on appreciation in the value of assets, or before a deduction will be allowed on the decline in the value of assets.[8]

Some fascinating further questions in this area were presented by the recent Supreme Court case of *Cottage Savings Assoc.*

## COTTAGE SAVINGS ASSOC. v. COMMISSIONER[9]

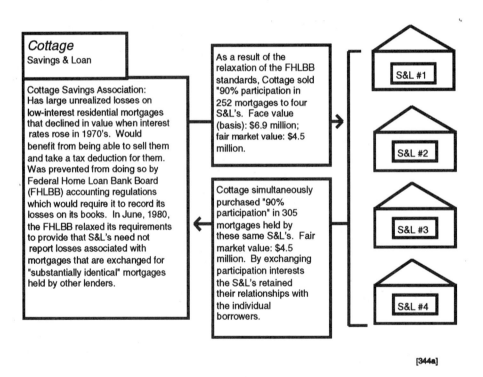

[344a]

---

**8.** See Surrey, "The Supreme Court and the Federal Income Tax: Some Implications of the Recent Decisions" 35 Ill.L.Rev. 779 (1941); Fellows, A Comprehensive Attack on Tax Deferral, 88 Mich. L. Rev. 722 (1990); Strnad, Periodicity and Accrual Taxation: Norms and Implementation, 99 Yale L. J. 1817 (1990); Shakow, Taxation Without Realization: A Proposal for Accrual Taxation, 134 U.Pa.L.Rev. 1111 (1986). See

also IRC § 951, which provides for the taxation of undistributed income of controlled foreign corporations. Compare the "mark-to-market" rule for certain tax straddles as a result of the Economic Recovery Tax Act of 1981. See § 4.06(2)(c)(vi).

**9.** Cottage Savings Assoc. v. Commissioner, 499 U.S. 554, 111 S.Ct. 1503, 113 L.Ed.2d 589 (1991).

*Question:* Did Cottage realize its losses through the transaction? For there to be a realization under § 1001(a), there must be "a sale or other disposition." The parties concede that the transactions engaged in did not constitute a "sale," because ownership was not surrendered. So did the transaction constitute a "disposition of property"?

*Service argument:* An exchange of property can only be a disposition if the properties exchanged are "materially different." Since the underlying mortgages were essentially economic substitutes, the participation interests exchanged by Cottage were not materially different from those received by Cottage from the other S & L's. In addition, property is "materially different" only if so regarded by the parties, the evaluation of the interests by the secondary mortgage market, and the views of the FHLBB.

*Cottage argument:* The participation interests exchanged were materially different because the underlying loans were secured by different properties.

*Held:* The Service has by regulations construed § 1001(a) to require that gain or loss is realized on an exchange only if the property received differs materially either in kind or in extent from the property exchanged.[10] This is a reasonable interpretation of § 1001 and we therefore defer to it. The question is what really constitutes a "material difference" for these purposes. Look, therefore, to the established case law in this area: *Macomber* (see above) and other older Supreme Court cases involving corporate reorganizations. These cases stand for the proposition that properties are "different", in the sense that is "material" for purposes of the Internal Revenue Code, so long as their respective possessors enjoy legal entitlements that are different in kind or extent. Thus if a corporate reorganization results in the shareholders surrendering stock in exchange for stock giving them "the same proportional interest of the same character in the same corporation", then the new stock received is not materially different from the stock surrendered. However, if the stock received is issued by a different corporation, or if it confers different rights and powers in the same corporation, then it is materially different. Case law does not support the Service's more elaborate approach and that approach is also administratively unworkable. Also the existence of the nonrecognition of gain or loss for like-kind exchanges for property held for productive use in trade or business or investment suggests that Congress contemplated that the exchange of similar properties would be a realization event.

The participation interests exchanged by Cottage and the other S & L's derived from loans that were made to different obligors and secured by different homes. Thus the interests did embody legally distinct entitlements. Cottage thus realized its losses. There is no reason not to

10.  Regs. § 1.1001–1.

treat the exchange of these interests as a realization, even though the FHLBB treats them as "substantially identical" for its purposes.

*Comment, is that then and this now?:* Do corporate reorganization cases decided six decades ago under law long since changed really throw light on the sophisticated transactions involved in this case? Consider, as the dissent pointed out, what was not "materially different" with regard to the properties exchanged: the retention of the 10% interests, so that the transferors could keep servicing their loans; the borrowers' lack of knowledge of the transaction; the lack of attention paid by the transferors to the factors cited by the majority as "differences," including no credit checks or appraisals; the selection of the loans to be exchanged by computer; the absence of names of the borrowers on the closing agreements. Could it not be said that if the term "material" means anything in the test of "material difference" that these differences were not "material." Thus does the dissent argue for "realities."

*Comment, but what is reality?* Isn't the *real* reality that these Savings & Loans had undergone substantial losses as a result of the drop in value of their mortgages due to the increase in interest rates? Isn't what's unrealistic in the tax field the realization requirement which prevents appreciation or depreciation in the value of assets held from being given tax effect? If that's true, then should not the realization requirement be penetrated whenever possible so to have tax results more clearly mirror true economic results? That can certainly be an interpretation of the early reorganization cases: that the Supreme Court, having enunciated the requirement of a realization in *Macomber*, then proceeded to cut back on it and find realization of gain in most of the subsequent cases.[11]

*Comment, we're talking big time:* We're not just debating doctrine here, we're talking about major transactions. The promulgation of the rules by the FHLBB in the early 80's allowing swaps of mortgage interests without requiring the recognition of accounting losses triggered the exchange of billions of dollars of depreciated mortgage interests among S & L's.

*Comment, the S & L catastrophe:* Far from allowing the nation's beleagured S & L's to exchange mortgages without recognizing accounting losses, the FHLBB should have required them to recognize unrealized depreciation in the mortgages they held. This would have put everyone on notice that the S & L industry was in deep trouble much earlier and have averted the present catastrophe. Ignoring reality in financial transactions is always hazardous.

As to other transactions, it is well established that gifts and bequests are not realizing events and therefore do not give rise to income to the transferor. The treatment of abandonment of property and the

11. See Posin, Taxing Corporate Reor-     U.Pa.L.Rev. 1335 (1985).
ganizations: Purging Penelope's Web, 133

surrender of mortgaged property has, however, presented problems in this area and is discussed in the margin.[12]

The Supreme Court has held that where a donor gives a gift on the condition that the donee pay the gift tax, a realizing event—namely a sale—has occurred. The donor has income to the extent the gift tax paid by the donee exceeds the donor's basis, Diedrich v. Commissioner, 457 U.S. 191, 102 S.Ct. 2414, 72 L.Ed.2d 777 (1982), discussed at ¶ 4.03(2)(b)(iv).

The Tax Court has ruled that a charitable contribution of property encumbered by non-recourse indebtedness is a sale that can give rise to a taxable gain, Guest, 77 T.C. 9 (1981). The topic of marital property settlements has presented difficulties and is discussed below. The requirement of a realization was suspended in the case of certain "tax straddles" under the Economic Recovery Tax Act of 1981. In this case, a "mark-to-market" rule was enacted, requiring taxpayers to treat regulated futures contracts that they hold as sold for their fair market value on the last business day of the taxable year, causing unrealized gain or loss to be taken into account. The purpose here was to foreclose tax avoidance "spread" transactions.

### (2) Marital Property Settlements and Other Satisfactions of Obligations: Davis; Farid–Es–Sultaneh

In most areas it is usually clear whether there has been a realizing event and the issue does not give rise to a dispute. It is also well established that the transfer of appreciated property to satisfy a pre-existing obligation is a realizing event. However, where property is transferred incident to a divorce or separation, some tricky questions are raised. The leading case in this area is *Davis*:

---

**12.** Abandonment of property, although not a sale or exchange, is a realizing event, Reg. § 1.165–2(b). This is usually attractive to the taxpayer, since the loss on abandonment will therefore not be subject to the limitations on capital losses, Reg. § 1.165–2(b), and see ¶ 4.06(2)(b)(ii). Special rules apply for the retirement or abandonment of depreciable property, see ¶ 6.02(12). See also CRST, Inc. v. Commissioner, 909 F.2d 1146 (8th Cir.1990) (motor carrier's operating authorities held not abandoned as a loss under § 165).

The surrender of property subject to a mortgage indebtedness in exchange for extinguishment of the indebtedness is a realizing event, with the mortgage indebtedness constituting the amount realized, whether or not the indebtedness was with personal liability (Parker v. Delaney, 186 F.2d 455 (1st Cir.1950), cert. denied 341 U.S. 926, 71 S.Ct. 797, 95 L.Ed. 1357 (1951), see ¶¶ 4.03(2)(b)(iv), 8.02(3). Surrender of property in extinguishment of a nonrecourse mortgage greater in amount than the value of the property is discussed below at ¶ 4.03(2)(b)(iv)

## UNITED STATES v. DAVIS[13]

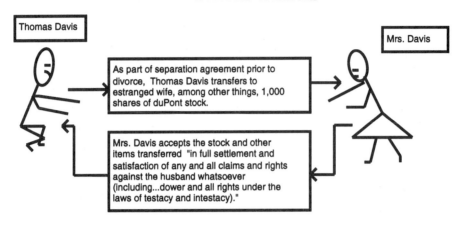

Thomas Davis

As part of separation agreement prior to divorce, Thomas Davis transfers to estranged wife, among other things, 1,000 shares of duPont stock.

Mrs. Davis

Mrs. Davis accepts the stock and other items transferred "in full settlement and satisfaction of any and all claims and rights against the husband whatsoever (including...dower and all rights under the laws of testacy and intestacy)."

[345a]

*Question:* 1) Was the transfer of duPont stock a taxable event ? 2) If so, how much taxable gain resulted?

*Taxpayer Argument:* The transaction is like a nontaxable division of property between two co-owners.

*IRS Argument:* The transaction is a taxable transfer of property in exchange for the release of an independent legal obligation.

*Held:* 1) Under controlling local law of Delaware, wife's inchoate rights in her husband's property "do not even remotely reach the dignity of co-ownership." The wife's rights are a personal liability against the husband rather than a property interest. Thus this was a realizing event, not a nontaxable division of property between two co-owners. 2) Measure gain to the husband by fair market value of what was received (satisfaction of rights) less basis in stock transferred. Difficult to value satisfaction of marital rights. Assume parties bargained at arm's length [if not further]. Hence assume marital rights are worth fair market value of property transferred.

*Comment:* Under the Court's rationale, a division of property in a community property state would lead to a different result: no tax to the husband. This would be the case because the transaction would then constitute a division of property among two co-owners. The Court conceded that under its reasoning results would vary depending on the state.[14]

**13.** 370 U.S. 65, 82 S.Ct. 1190, 8 L.Ed.2d 335 (1962), reh'g denied 371 U.S. 854, 83 S.Ct. 14, 9 L.Ed.2d 92 (1962).

**14.** Thus, *Davis* spawned two lines of cases: cases holding that in a common law state the marital property settlement is a realizing event and cases holding that in a community property-type state the marital property settlement is not a realizing event.

For common law states, see for example, Wiles v. Commissioner, 499 F.2d 255 (10th Cir.1974), cert. denied 419 U.S. 996, 95 S.Ct. 310, 42 L.Ed.2d 270 (1974); Wallace v. United States, 439 F.2d 757 (8th Cir.1971), cert. denied 404 U.S. 831, 92 S.Ct. 71, 30 L.Ed.2d 60 (1971).

For community property states, see Imel v. United States, 523 F.2d 853 (10th Cir. 1975) (property settlement non-taxable where case law had established that under Colorado law the rights of the wife in the

Davis thus applied in a mechanical way the well-established proposition that transferring appreciated property to satisfy a debt is a taxable event.[15] Thus suppose Davis had owed a debt to his lawyer (which he undoubtedly did; indeed, there was a subsidiary issue about legal fees in the *Davis* case). Suppose the debt had been $100,000. Transferring $100,000 worth of stock that happened to have appreciated from when Davis bought it at $70,000 would undoubtedly mean Davis had a realizing event. His gain would be $30,000. The question was whether it was appropriate to apply that paradigm to transfers of property incident to a divorce.

The *Davis* case leaves some other fascinating questions hanging. What about the treatment of the wife, on these facts? Although it was not before the Court, the question remains how the wife handles this transaction. The *Davis* Court did tell us that the wife would take a basis of the fair market value of the stock transferred to her. This makes some sense. Her "cost" for these purposes is the value of the property she gave up, the value of her marital rights. Those rights, the Court has found, are equal to the fair market value of the stock she received. So we seem to know everything we need to know about the wife. But we're missing one item of information. What is the wife's basis in her marital rights? Is it zero, in which case she has a gain equal to the fair market value of the stock she receives?

Another major case in this area is *Farid–Es–Sultaneh.*

---

marital property had vested at the time of the filing of the divorce suit and before the transfer); see Rev.Rul. 81–292, 1981–2 C.B. 158 (No gain or loss realized on division of jointly owned property in common law state, despite fact that each spouse took some parcels outright.).

This somewhat anomalous situation is reminiscent of the old case of Poe v. Sea-born, 282 U.S. 101, 51 S.Ct. 58, 75 L.Ed. 239 (1930) which held that the effectiveness of assignment of income (see Chapter 5) between husband and wife turned on state law. To cure this disparity Congress enacted the federal joint return.

**15.** See Kenan v. Commissioner, 114 F.2d 217 (2d Cir.1940).

## FARID–ES–SULTANEH v. COMMISSIONER[16]

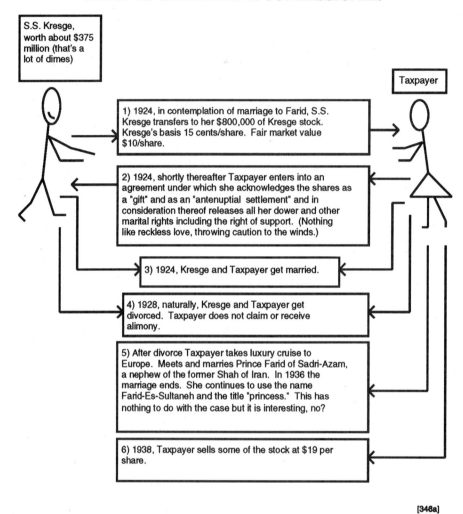

S.S. Kresge, worth about $375 million (that's a lot of dimes)

Taxpayer

1) 1924, in contemplation of marriage to Farid, S.S. Kresge transfers to her $800,000 of Kresge stock. Kresge's basis 15 cents/share. Fair market value $10/share.

2) 1924, shortly thereafter Taxpayer enters into an agreement under which she acknowledges the shares as a "gift" and as an "antenuptial settlement" and in consideration thereof releases all her dower and other marital rights including the right of support. (Nothing like reckless love, throwing caution to the winds.)

3) 1924, Kresge and Taxpayer get married.

4) 1928, naturally, Kresge and Taxpayer get divorced. Taxpayer does not claim or receive alimony.

5) After divorce Taxpayer takes luxury cruise to Europe. Meets and marries Prince Farid of Sadri-Azam, a nephew of the former Shah of Iran. In 1936 the marriage ends. She continues to use the name Farid-Es-Sultaneh and the title "princess." This has nothing to do with the case but it is interesting, no?

6) 1938, Taxpayer sells some of the stock at $19 per share.

[346a]

*Question:* How should taxpayer's gain on the sale of the stock in 1938 be calculated?

*IRS Argument:* Taxpayer's stock was acquired by gift and hence took Kresge's basis of 15 cents per share, § 1015(a).

*Held:* The stock was transferred in consideration of taxpayer's promise to relinquish her rights in his property she would acquire by the marriage. The transaction was therefore a sale. Taxpayer's basis in the stock was her cost of acquiring it. That was equal to the fair market value of her marital rights. That was equal to the fair market value of the stock at the time of the transfer. Hence her basis was $10 per share, not 15 cents per share.

16.   160 F.2d 812 (2d Cir.1947).

*Comment:* Kresge undoubtedly treated the transfer of the stock as a gift. But under the rationale of *Davis*, he should treat it as a sale. Note that *Davis* was decided 15 years after *Farid–Es–Sultaneh*.

*Comment:* How does Farid treat the transfer of her marital rights for the stock? Is it a taxable gain to her? What is her basis in her marital rights? Zero? The fair market value of the stock (so there is no gain)? Drop me a line if you get the answer.

These two marital property settlement cases are important for probing the outer contours of the realization requirement. They are correctly decided. A benefit of real legal significance was acquired by the transferor of the stock in both cases. Indeed, in Farid–Es–Sultaneh, the taxpayer's inchoate interests in the property of her husband greatly exceeded the value of the stock transferred to her.

These transactions are different from transfers of property between married or unmarried individuals that are truly gifts, for which no consideration is received. *Davis* and *Farid–Es–Sultaneh* are also different from bequests. The only possible problem with these cases was that, under *Davis,* the tax treatment of transfers in exchange for marital rights varied depending on state law. But of course that just reflected that state law really was different, and the rights of the parties to a marriage really are different in different states.

Notwithstanding that these cases are sound, Congress (having nothing better to do than to respond to non-existent problems) changed the law in this area in 1984. It provided in § 1041(a) that no gain or loss is recognized on a transfer of property to a spouse or to a former spouse (if the transfer is incident to the divorce). This overrules *Davis.* Congress provided in § 1041(b) that the basis of the property so transferred is the transferor's basis. This overrules *Farid–Es–Sultaneh.*[17] (So why did we spend so much time on cases that have been overruled? That's what makes law school law school).

Section 1041 gives a truly inaccurate answer in this area. Modify the *Farid* facts as an example. Say Kresge transferred Farid the stock on the occasion of their divorce (they were subsequently divorced). This brings the transaction within the ambit of § 1041, which applies to spouses and former spouses but not to intended spouses. On these modified facts, then, Kresge transfers $800,000 of stock with a basis of 15 cents and a fair market value of $10. This means he transferred 80,000 shares of stock with an aggregate basis of $12,000. For that he satisfied a legal obligation of at least $800,000. Why should he not be taxed on this tremendous gain of $788,000?

Put it this way. If you were advising Kresge on our facts, who wanted to make a lump sum payment to satisfy his marital obligations, what would you tell him, now that § 1041 is in effect? Pay $800,000 cash or pay with $800,000 of very appreciated stock? Look what happens. If

---

**17.** Even if the fair market value of the property is less than the basis at the time of the transfer, the basis is still the transferor's basis. Thus the rule here is different than in the straight gift area. No "notch" transaction and all that, see this Chapter ¶ 4.03(2)(c).

he pays with cash, he is still stuck with the appreciated stock that has a locked in gain of $778,000. At a 40% combined federal and state tax rate, that is a pending tax liability of $315,200. If, however, he pays with the appreciated securities, then there is no tax paid. He still has the $800,000 cash and he's got no pending tax liability.

It is true that under the basis rule of § 1041(b), the obligation for paying the $778,000 of appreciation is taken over by the wife here. So the appreciation is still subject to tax. But why allow a transferor who has under general tax principles undergone a realization to escape taxation?

For other federal income tax aspects of separation and divorce, see ¶ 6.02(14).

## ¶ 4.03   Computation of Gain or Loss Realized

Once it is ascertained that a realizing event has occurred,[1] the second step in taxing dispositions of property is to compute the amount of gain or loss realized. The Code explicitly sets forth the formula for making this computation.[2] In substance the formula is first to ascertain the "amount realized" on the transaction and subtract from it the "adjusted basis" of the property. If the result is positive, a gain has been realized; if the result is negative, a loss has been realized.[3] The critical terms in the formula are, of course, "amount realized" and "adjusted basis". The Code provides further definitions of these terms. The "amount realized" from the sale or other disposition of property is the sum of money received plus the fair market value of the property received.[4] The "adjusted basis" of the property is generally the cost of the property, adjusted further for such things as depreciation or capital expenditures.[5] Actually the ascertainment of the "amount realized" and the "adjusted basis" can be a good deal more complex than these definitions suggest; hence it is useful to discuss each of these terms in turn.

### (1) Amount Realized

Amount realized is an essential component in the formula: amount realized minus adjusted basis equals gain or loss realized. As a matter of clarity, the "amount realized" should be distinguished from the "gain realized". As the discussion above has indicated, "gain realized" is a net term; the difference between the amount realized and the adjusted basis. "Amount realized" is the gross amount of the money plus the fair market value of the property received on the transaction.[6]

---

¶ 4.03

1. As discussed in ¶ 4.02, a realizing event, although required by the statute in most cases, is not of constitutional dimension.

2. § 1001.

3. § 1001(a).

4. § 1001(b).

5. §§ 1011, 1012, 1016.

6. § 1001(b). Commissions paid on the selling of property generally reduce the amount realized, unless the taxpayer is a dealer in the property sold, in which case the commissions may be deducted as an expense. Using commissions to reduce the selling price is less attractive than deducting them as an ordinary expense, where the property sold, gives rise to a capital gain. See Reg. § 1.263(a)–2(e) (commissions on sales of securities); Hunt 47 B.T.A. 829,

Usually it will be clear what the amount realized is. Sometimes there can be a problem in ascertaining the fair market value of property received, where the property is not traded frequently and no market values exist. Valuation under these circumstances requires some species of estimation of value. There is a rich debate among the cases, the commentators and the Service concerning the best techniques to employ for this purpose—such as capitalization of future earnings, replacement value, book value, liquidation value and cash flow. Notwithstanding the existence of these various techniques, it is sometimes conceded—even by the Service—that some types of property, often involving payments contingent on future events, cannot be valued at the time of the transaction.[7] In such rare cases reporting of gain realized may be deferred to future years, as discussed at ¶ 8.03.

Also questions can arise concerning what is the amount realized in tax shelter type situations, where, for example, recourse or nonrecourse debt is involved. The tax shelter field is discussed at ¶ 8.02.

A leading case in the area of amount realized is *International Freighting Corporation, Inc. v. Commissioner.*[8] The Second Circuit, speaking through Judge Frank, held that when an employer gave stock with a fair market value greater its basis to its employees as compensation, the employer had an amount realized in the amount of the difference between the basis of the property and its fair market value. What was received that was taxed was the fair market value of the services of the employees, even though the statute (§ 1001(b)) says that the amount realized is the fair market value of the money or property received.

### (2) Adjusted Basis

#### (a) Background

Adjusted basis is the other essential component in the formula: amount realized minus adjusted basis equals gain or loss realized. It is certainly necessary to use a concept like basis or adjusted basis in computing the gain on the sale or other disposition of property. Without a concept like adjusted basis, the taxpayer would be taxed on the gross amount received on sale or other disposition of the property, without being able to subtract his previous cost of acquisition of the property or

---

1942 WL 156 (1942) (acq.) (commissions on sales of real estate); see also Godfrey v. Commissioner, 335 F.2d 82 (6th Cir.1964), cert. denied 379 U.S. 966, 85 S.Ct. 660, 13 L.Ed.2d 560 (1965) (traveling and living expenses incurred with respect to selling real estate reduced the amount realized).

Amounts received as reimbursement for real property taxes which are treated under § 164(d) as imposed on the purchaser are not considered as part of the amount realized, § 1001(b)(1).

**7.** See e.g. Dewing, Financial Policy of Corporations (1953), Vol. I, pp. 281–282, 287–292, 390–391; Perlman v. Feldmann, 154 F.Supp. 436 (D.Conn.1957).

For "open" treatment, see Rev.Rul. 68–194, 1968–1 C.B. 87. See also the classic case in this area, Burnet v. Logan, 283 U.S. 404, 51 S.Ct. 550, 75 L.Ed. 1143 (1931), discussed at ¶ 8.03.

**8.** 135 F.2d 310 (2d Cir.1943).

some other substantial expenditures made with respect to the property—a manifestly unjust result.

Hence it is intuitively apparent that a major factor in determining basis is the cost of the property to the taxpayer. However, cost is far from being the whole story. Where the property is not acquired by purchase, but in a tax-free exchange or by gift, inheritance, or other non-market transactions, techniques other than cost will have to be used to establish basis in order to compute gain or loss properly on a subsequent disposition. Moreover, once basis is established, it will often be subject to further adjustments upward or downward to account for such things as capital expenditures, depreciation, casualty losses and so forth.[9]

It should be emphasized that basis is one of the most important concepts in the tax law. The taxpayer should always know or be able to ascertain easily the basis of his property, not only for the purpose of computing gain or loss on disposition but also as a point of departure in making other adjustments to the basis. Ascertaining the basis of property is important in a number of types of transactions, besides sales or exchanges, discussed at various points in this work.[10] Indeed ascertaining the basis is important in almost every transaction involving property. The various methods for establishing basis are discussed below.

### (b) Cost Basis

### (i) In General

The dominant rule for establishing the taxpayer's basis of property is the cost of acquiring the property. More precisely, it may be stated that the basis of property is its cost, unless another rule specifically provides otherwise.[11] The cost of acquiring the property is generally the amount paid for the property in cash and/or property, plus acquisition costs.[12]

For example in *Philadelphia Park Amusement Co. v. United States*,[13] Philadelphia Park Amusement Co (PAC), in 1889, had a 50–year franchise to operate a passenger railway in Fairmount Park, Philadelphia. PAC constructed the Strawberry Bridge over the Schuylkill River for use by its streetcars. In 1934 PAC sold the bridge to the city in exchange for a 10–year extension of its franchise. Then in 1946, PAC abandoned the 10–year extension of the railway franchise and instead employed bus

---

**9.** The precise statutory formulation is: § 1011 provides that the adjusted basis shall be the basis, determined generally under § 1012. § 1012 provides that the basis shall be the cost of the property—except as otherwise provided in certain cases discussed below. § 1016 provides that once basis is established by cost or other rules, it shall be adjusted for a number of items, such as capital expenditures and depreciation, see ¶ 4.03(2)(g).

**10.** This is by no means an exhaustive list: see ¶ 6.02(12) relating to depreciation;

¶ 4.05(6), relating to wash sales of stock or securities; ¶ 4.06(2)(c), relating to holding periods for capital gains and losses; ¶ 3.02, relating to original issue discount; ¶ 2.03, relating to employee bargain purchases of property.

**11.** § 1012, and see note 8.

**12.** Reg. § 1.1012–1(a), see ¶ 6.03(4) for discussion of acquisition costs, such as brokerage fees and commissions.

**13.** 126 F.Supp. 184 (Ct.Cl.1954).

transportation for its passengers. PAC attempted to take depreciation deductions with respect to the 10–year extension of the franchise as well as a loss deduction on its abandonment. This raised the question of what was PAC's basis in the franchise, since (as we will learn) deductions for depreciation and loss with respect to property cannot exceed the taxpayer's basis in the property. (In general the rule is that the basis of property is its cost.)

The essential problem in the case was that it appeared that the fair market value of the bridge was much less than the fair market value of the 10 year extension at the time the taxpayer exchanged the bridge for the extension. This created a problem in figuring out what the taxpayer's basis in the extension was.

The court pointed out that there are two theories as to what is "cost," in cases where the property was acquired by exchange for other property. One theory of cost is that the basis of property acquired in an exchange is the fair market value of the property *given* in the exchange. The other theory is that the basis of property acquired in an exchange is the fair market value of the property *received* in the exchange. (Of course one would usually expect the two to be the same, but as pointed out that was not the situation in this case).

The court held that the proper approach is that the cost is the fair market value of the property received in the exchange.

As the court pointed out, this is a problem that rarely arises, since ordinarily the values of two properties exchanged in an arm's-length transaction are equal or presumed to be equal. Thus, the court said that the fair market value of the 10–year extension should be ascertained and that will be its basis in PAC's hands for further transactions. If, the court said, the value of the 10–year extension cannot be ascertained, one would then look to the value of the bridge. Once the value of the bridge is established it can be assumed that it was the same as that of the extension. Since the case was not prosecuted on this theory the court remands.

### (ii) Mortgages and Other Debts of the Purchaser or Seller: Crane

Where the property is purchased for a down payment plus debt obligations of the purchaser, the usual rule is that the basis is the full amount of the purchase price even though some of it is not yet paid.[14] However, where the purchaser is not personally liable on his debt obligations but they are only secured by the property purchased, problems can arise in ascertaining basis. On a theoretical level, obligations of the purchaser without personal liability should probably be included in his basis, since they do represent in some sense the "cost" of the property.

14. Edwards, 19 T.C. 275 (1952) (acq.);
Martin, Jr., 23 T.C.M. 1217 (1964).

But the problem here is that the purchaser may very well succumb to the temptation to pay a very high price for the property, financed by non-recourse obligations, in order to create a high basis from which to compute depreciation.[15] This is, of course, a classic tax shelter—a field which is now covered like a blanket by the Code.[16]

However, even prior to the onslaught of tax shelter legislation, there was an occasional judicial foray against tax shelter-type arrangements, disallowing the creation of artificially high basis with non-recourse debt.[17] And such judicial attacks on artificially high basis have continued contemporaneously with the enactment and implementation of the tax shelter legislation[18]—which, as noted, approaches the matter from the point of view of disallowing losses rather than not respecting the debt. Thus a tax shelter may founder on either the legislative or judicial shoal. See ¶ 8.02 for a detailed treatment of tax shelters.

Closely related to the question of the treatment of mortgage obligations of the buyer of property is the question of the treatment of mortgage obligations of the seller for which the buyer takes some responsibility. For example the seller may not have as yet paid off his own purchase money or other mortgage on the property before conveying the property to the buyer. If the buyer, in addition to whatever other consideration he pays for the property, assumes personal liability on the seller's mortgage, that mortgage will properly be considered to be part of the buyer's cost basis of the property.[19] Similarly the buyer's assumption of personal liability for any other non-mortgage liabilities of the seller as consideration for the property would be part of the buyer's cost basis of the property.[20]

---

**15.** See ¶ 6.02(12) for depreciation.

**16.** See §§ 465, 469 and see ¶ 8.02.

**17.** Marcus, 30 T.C.M. 1263 (1971) (contingent obligations disregarded for basis purposes.) But see Mayerson, 47 T.C. 340 (1966) (acq.) allowing non-recourse mortgage debt to be used in computing taxpayer's basis for purposes of depreciation, notwithstanding that the mortgage was for 99 years and most of the amount was due in a balloon payment at the end of the term, thus allowing the taxpayer (or his heirs) to walk away from the property after having enjoyed the depreciation deductions. Although the Service acquiesced in this case (1969–1 C.B. 21), it emphasized that its acquiescence was based on the particular facts in Mayerson and could "not be relied upon in the disposition of other cases except where it is clear that the property has been acquired at its fair market value in an arm's length transaction creating a bona fide purchase and a bona fide debt obligation," Rev.Rul. 69–77, 1969–1 C.B. 59.

**18.** Estate of Franklin v. Commissioner, 544 F.2d 1045 (9th Cir.1976), a lineal descendant of *Mayerson,* note 15 above, in which the court disallowed deductions of depreciation and interest arising from a purported sale and leaseback of a motel financed by a nonrecourse mortgage with a balloon payment at the end of 10 years because the selling price was for more than the fair market value of the property. See also Rev.Rul. 78–29, 1978–1 C.B. 62 (excluding from cost basis a very large non-recourse note where taxpayer failed to prove that the fair market value of the property being purchased at least approximately equaled the note).

**19.** United States v. Hendler, 303 U.S. 564, 58 S.Ct. 655, 82 L.Ed. 1018 (1938), reh'g denied 304 U.S. 588, 58 S.Ct. 940, 82 L.Ed. 1548 (1938). See also Old Colony Trust v. Commissioner, 279 U.S. 716, 49 S.Ct. 499, 73 L.Ed. 918 (1929) (the classic case holding that an employer's payment of an employee's taxes is income to the employee, cf. ¶ 3.10). If, however, the liabilities assumed are quite contingent and indefinite, they will not be included in basis, Rev.Rul. 55–675, 1955–2 C.B. 567.

**20.** Hendler, note 17 above.

The harder question is when the buyer takes the property from the seller subject to a mortgage on the property but does not assume personal liability on the mortgage. The considerations here are, of course, essentially the same as in the case where the buyer issues his own nonrecourse obligation in consideration for the property. In one sense nonrecourse mortgage is still a "cost" of the property, since the buyer is motivated to pay off the debt or lose the property. However where the taxpayer has issued a nonrecourse mortgage, he has an option to walk away from the property if it declines in value below the amount of the mortgage. This makes the nonrecourse mortgage different from the recourse mortgage. This difference might be something that a lawyer would seize on if it were to his client's advantage to do so.

A large proportion of commercial mortgages, financing shopping centers, apartment buildings and office buildings, are nonrecourse.[21] Thus for all these reasons it becomes important to understand the treatment of nonrecourse debt for tax purposes.

The outstanding case in this area is *Crane v. Commissioner*[22], the most important tax case ever decided. Given the immense importance of *Crane* in the field, it requires careful attention:

**21.** Indeed, part of the problem in the savings and loan catastrophe was that many of the loans made by the failed savings institutions were on a nonrecourse basis. When real estate values collapsed, the savings institutions could not proceed personally against the borrowers to recoup their losses.

**22.** 331 U.S. 1, 67 S.Ct. 1047, 91 L.Ed. 1301 (1947).

## CRANE v. COMMISSIONER[23]

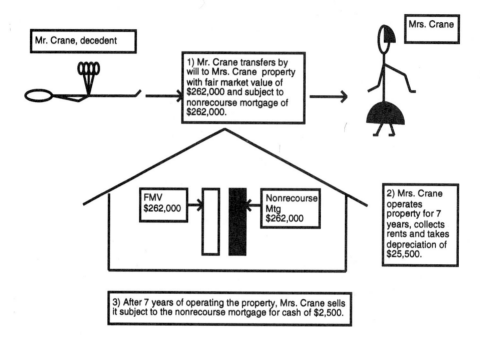

**Mr. Crane, decedent**

1) Mr. Crane transfers by will to Mrs. Crane property with fair market value of $262,000 and subject to nonrecourse mortgage of $262,000.

**Mrs. Crane**

FMV $262,000

Nonrecourse Mtg $262,000

2) Mrs. Crane operates property for 7 years, collects rents and takes depreciation of $25,500.

3) After 7 years of operating the property, Mrs. Crane sells it subject to the nonrecourse mortgage for cash of $2,500.

[347a]

*Question:* How is Ms. Crane's gain or loss computed on the sale of the property?[24]

*Comment:* This seems like a straightforward question but in fact it carries a great deal of baggage. To compute the gain we need to know the amount realized and the basis. Those numbers are not given in the facts and it is not immediately clear what they are.

*Comment:* Be clear that it is only a coincidence that the mortgage and the fair market value of the property are exactly the same amount when Mrs. Crane inherits the property. Usually this will not be the case.[25]

*Taxpayer's argument:* The gain was $2,500. The "property" sold was her equity. Her equity had a a basis of zero when it was acquired—i.e., there was no equity on acquisition. The equity was sold for $2,500. Her gain was therefore $2,500.[26]

*Comment:* Ms. Crane's having a zero basis in her property is inconsistent with her having taken $25,500 in depreciation—but hey! Let's not quibble over the small stuff.

**23.** 331 U.S. 1, 67 S.Ct. 1047, 91 L.Ed. 1301 (1947).

**24.** The numbers in this case have been simplified a little to clarify the issues.

**25.** Apparently what really happened is that the appraiser put the value of the building at the amount of the debt. Appraisers of real estate are well known to fudge their numbers somewhat for the convenience of their clients.

**26.** Taxpayer also claimed her gain was a capital gain which, under the law at that time, allowed her to exclude one-half the gain, giving her a taxable amount of $1,250. The capital gain aspect of the case is not significant and will be ignored.

*Held:* I) The first question is to determine what is the basis of the property. What is property for this purpose? Is it the physical property as Commissioner contends or the equity in the property as the taxpayer contends? It is the physical property or the owner's rights undiminished by the mortgage. This is clear for several reasons: 1) This is the ordinary, everyday usage of the term "property." Equity is something else, the value of the property above the total liens. 2) This interpretation of the word "property" is also consistent with administrative practice for estate tax purposes. In estate cases the appraised value of the property should be reported and the mortgages deducted separately. 3) In many other parts of the Code, the language has been clear in distinguishing "property" from "equity." 4) If we took equity as the property, the computation of depreciation would be a mess. It would be an unrealistically low number. It would also be complex, since the equity changes every year as the mortgage is paid off. Also the taxpayer would gain control over the timing of his deductions. If he paid off more of his mortgage his equity would go up, causing his depreciation base to go up. Depreciation from equity has never been contemplated in the tax laws. Thus the proper basis is the value of the property undiminished by the mortgage or $262,000.

II) Thus it was appropriate for the taxpayer to take depreciation from the basis of $262,000. This depreciation would cause the basis to decline under the usual rules.

III) Now we reach the question of what is the amount realized. The amount realized, under the statute, is the the sum of any money received plus the fair market value of the property received. Obviously the term "property" here means the same as the term "property" means when talking about acquisition and depreciation of the property—namely the physical property undiminished by mortgages. Since taxpayer received only $2,500 cash, she must have received something else in addition for this property. What she received as well was relief from the mortgage. Relief from a nonrecourse debt is thus part of the amount realized. If the mortgage had been with personal liability, the result was well settled prior to this case. In that event, if the buyer assumes personal liability on the mortgage, getting relief from the mortgage would constitute an amount realized in the amount of the mortgage.[27] If a mortgagor has property mortgaged on a nonrecourse basis in an amount less than the fair market value of the property, he will treat the mortgage the same way as if it was a mortgage with personal liability. This is because if he does not make his timely payments on the mortgage, he will lose the property which is, by hypothesis, worth more than the mortgage.

**Court states as follows in famous footnote 37:** "Obviously, if the value of the property is less than the amount of the mortgage, a mortgagor who is not personally liable cannot realize a benefit equal to

**27.** United States v. Hendler, 303 U.S. 564, 58 S.Ct. 655, 82 L.Ed. 1018 (1938), reh'g denied 304 U.S. 588, 58 S.Ct. 940, 82 L.Ed. 1548 (1938). Ed. note: This is in the nature of cancellation of debt income (see ¶ 3.10).

the mortgage. Consequently, a different problem might be encountered where a mortgagor abandoned the property or transferred it subject to the mortgage without receiving boot. That is not this case."

Court's analysis continues here to say that what taxpayer seeks here is a double gain. She took depreciation but seeks to have the computation of gain on the sale of the property made without reduction of basis.

*Comment:* Putting it a little more succinctly, *Crane* held, in effect, that the amount of a nonrecourse liability incurred on acquisition of property is included in the basis. (Thus the basis was $262,000). And the amount of a nonrecourse liability is included in the amount realized on sale of the property. Thus if the mortgage was still $262,000 at the time of sale, then Ms. Crane's realized amount was $262,000 + $2,500. Her adjusted basis would be $262,000 less the $25,500 depreciation she took, or a gain of $28,000.

This is depicted in the accompanying graphic:

## The Court's Decision in *Crane*

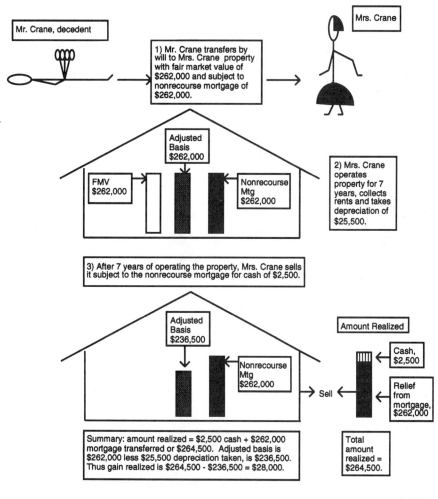

[348a]

*Comment:* It is easy to see from this graphic that the crucial lesson that comes out of *Crane* is that the mortgage must be included in both sides of the transaction. If the mortgage is not included in the basis but is included in the amount realized, then we get a taxable gain on the sale of $264,500, which has no relation to economic reality. If the mortgage is included in the basis but not in the amount realized, then we have a deductible loss on the sale of the property of $234,000 ($236,500 basis against $2,500 amount realized). This is also not a number that makes any economic sense. The only other logical possibility is to exclude the mortgage both from basis and amount realized. That would mean the basis is zero and thus no depreciation would be allowed until some of the mortgage is paid off. As the *Crane* Court pointed out, this is administratively unattractive. We don't want the depreciability of property to depend on the property's financing.

*Comment:* Note that while all this is superficially rather complicated, the underlying theory is simple. We are calculating gain on sale of property by reference to the formula: amount realized minus adjusted basis. The hassle with *Crane* is just to figure out how you compute amount realized and adjusted basis when you have property subject to nonrecourse debt.

*Comment:* Another short-hand way of describing *Crane* is to say that you treat nonrecourse debt the same way that you treat recourse debt: include the debt incurred in acquisition of the property in basis and include being relieved of the debt in amount realized.

*Comment:* Another simple way to look at it is to say that mortgages are just money going the other way. If you incur a mortgage on acquisition of property, it's like you paid money of that amount, pumping up your basis. If you get relieved of a mortgage on selling property, it's like you received money, pumping up your amount realized.

*Comment: The footnote 37 issue:* If *Crane* is the most famous tax case ever decided, then footnote 37 of the *Crane* decision is the most famous footnote in the field of federal income taxation. You can go up to a tax lawyer at a cocktail party and out of the blue you can say "I've been thinking about the footnote 37 problem," and he will know what you mean.

In footnote 37, described above, the *Crane* Court declined to consider the case of what would happen if at the time of the sale of the property, the property had a fair market value of less than the amount of the mortgage. Obviously this can only happen if the property has declined in value after a mortgage has been put on it.

This situation undermines a major ground of the Court's decision. That major ground is that a taxpayer with a nonrecourse mortgage in an amount less than the value of the property has more or less the same motivation to pay off the mortgage as a taxpayer who has a mortgage with personal liability.

What would happen in the case where the mortgage is for more than the fair market value of the property at the time of the sale of the property? This is a question that plagued the tax bar and tax academics for decades. Since we had to wait over four decades to get the answer, you can wait a few pages to get the answer too (we always like to have a cliffhanger in this course).

*Comment:* Observe that a major preoccupation of the court was that depreciation should be correctly calculated. The court felt that it would not be correctly calculated unless the mortgage were included in the basis. But as we show in ¶ 6.02(12), the usual methods of calculating depreciation—straight line or declining balance techniques—do not give the economically correct results in any event. The economically correct method of depreciation is sinking fund depreciation. It is a little ironic that after all this struggle in the *Crane* case to get depreciation right, in fact it is still calculated wrong.

*Comment:* The conventional wisdom in the literature is that the *Crane* case is bottomed on a principle of tax benefit or equity. That is, if the mortgage is in the basis for depreciation purposes, it should be in the amount realized for purposes of disposing of the property. However, the *Crane* opinion in fact does not speak in those terms. As the comments above indicate, the *Crane* Court's opinion was a very technical exercise in statutory interpretation.

The holding in the *Crane* case was elaborated in the First Circuit case of *Parker v. Delaney.*[28] The facts were similar to *Crane,* except that the property was acquired by purchase rather than by inheritance. The court had no trouble applying the principles of *Crane* and finding that when a mortgage is used to finance the purchase of property, that mortgage goes into the basis of the property. Then on subsequent sale of the property, the mortgage goes into the amount realized. Thus the gain is calculated by the amount realized minus the basis (which will be reduced by any depreciation taken).

Okay, you may say, the *Crane* case was interesting, although a little turgid. But what makes it the most important tax case ever decided? It would indeed be hard to overstate the importance of the *Crane* case to the field of federal income taxation. If Helen of Troy had the face that launched a thousand ships, Beulah Crane had the case that launched a thousand tax shelters. The *Crane* case paved the way for tax shelters, and the massive arsenal of legislation later arrayed against them. By winning the case and causing Mrs. Crane's nonrecourse debt to be included in her basis, the government gave birth to the tax shelter industry. This is an example of tunnel vision litigation strategy on the part of the government. The government has obviously lost far more money in tax shelters over the decades than they ever won in the *Crane* case. See Chapter 8 for discussion of tax shelters. *Crane's* principles are still widely used in the fields of corporate and partnership taxation, where mortgages are involved. If you wish to pursue those fields, you can do no better than to start by mastering *Crane.*

### (iii) *Mortgaging Property Held: Woodsam*

*(A) Basic Rules.* Janice purchases Blackacre, undeveloped land, for $500,000 cash. Three years later, at a time when the property is worth $1,000,000, she takes out a nonrecourse mortgage on the property for $750,000. To keep it simple let us say it is a standing mortgage. The principal remains the same and the only payments are for interest. So she puts $750,000 in her pocket, secured by the property but without personal liability. What are the tax consequences?

First, is the $750,000 taxable to Janice?

**28.** 186 F.2d 455 (1st Cir.1950), cert. denied 341 U.S. 926, 71 S.Ct. 797, 95 L.Ed. 1357. See also Blackstone Theater Co., 12 T.C. 801 (1949).

"No!" you say, laughing at my stupidity. "The transaction is obviously a loan."

But is that so obvious? Suppose, six years later when the mortgage is still in an amount of $750,000, real estate values start to sink (I have this crazy imagination). The value of the property is now $600,000. Now does the deal look like income? No?

Well, suppose Janice stops paying interest on the mortgage. She says to the bank: "The property is yours." I have nothing to lose by you taking it. I'll keep the $750,000. The bank takes the property. Janice takes a world cruise. Does it look like income now? Yes it does now.

These issues were presented in the leading case of *Woodsam*. To clarify the issues involved, the facts and numbers in *Woodsam* have been changed and simplified to pick up the numbers we have just been discussing.

## WOODSAM ASSOCIATES, INC. v. COMMISSIONER[29]

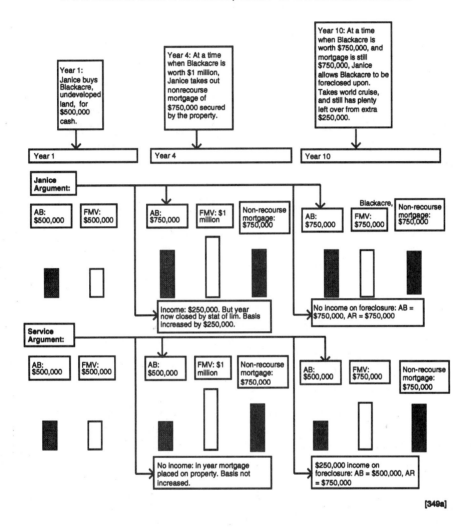

[349a]

*Question:* What is Janice's gain in Year 10?

*Janice's argument:* The mortgage of the property in Year 4 was a realizing event, giving rise to ámount realized of $750,000. Taking that against the adjusted basis yields gain of $250,000 in Year 4. Thus basis is increased in Year 4 from $500,000 to $750,000 to reflect the $250,000 income. Janice concedes that she did not pay tax on that $250,000 in Year 4, but that year is now barred by statute of limitations, so Janice doesn't want to get into that.[30] The point is that in Year 10 Janice's basis is $750,000. Thus calculate her gain as follows: Amount realized:

**29.** 198 F.2d 357 (2d Cir.1952).

**30.** Under current law, the statute of limitations is not so easily avoided. Under current law where the taxpayer takes a position in the current year that is inconsistent with a position that he took in a year closed by the statute of limitations, the closed year may be opened, see §§ 1311–1314.

$750,000 debt relief. From that subtract basis of $750,000 (for reasons argued above). Thus gain realized is $0.

*Comment, pulling a fast one:* Obviously Janice is trying to pull a fast one here with this argument. When you cut through all the funny paper flying around, what happened was that Janice bought for $500,000 and later sold for $750,000. She should therefore be taxed on $250,000, but is not taxed at all on her argument. Note how Janice extracted her gain out of the property. First she mortgaged, nonrecourse basis for $750,000. The first $500,000 of that could be viewed as a recovery of her basis or capital. The next $250,000 represents a gain. But she denies having to pay tax on the mortgaging in Year 4 because the statute of limitations is closed on Year 4.

*Held:* The mortgaging of already-held property nonrecourse is not a realizing event. Hence Janice does not have income in Year 4 on receipt of the mortgage proceeds in excess of basis. And her basis does not increase in Year 4. In Year 10, her basis is $500,000. Her amount realized is $750,000, comprised of the $750,000 debt relief. Her taxable gain is $250,000.[31]

*Comment, relationship to Crane:* Note we're learning a little more than you might think. In *Crane* we learned that acquisition debt *does* increase basis. Now we learn that mortgaging property subsequent to its acquisition *does not* increase basis. With both acquisition mortgages and after-acquired mortgages, getting relieved of them *does constitute* an amount realized.

*Comment, foreclosure:* As indicated from the discussion above, a foreclosure is treated as a sale.[32] What is the amount realized on the "sale?" It is the amount of the mortgage.

Okay, we learned the basic teaching of the *Woodsam* case, but there's more.

You're still sneering at me for thinking that the first step in the process, the placing of the mortgage on the property, might have been income right there.

I agree with you that if the mortgage had been with recourse that receipt of the mortgage proceeds could not be argued to be income. But nonrecourse financing is a little bit different. Admittedly *Crane* treated it like recourse financing for the particular purposes of its facts.

**31.** To take a variation, if the property had been worth $1 million in year 10, then Janice could have sold it for $250,000 cash plus $750,000 debt relief. Her amount realized would then be $750,000 (debt relief) plus $250,000 (cash) = $1 million. Adjusted basis equals $500,000. Thus gain is $500,000.

Incidentally, I don't recommend reading the *Woodsam* case straight up. The court succinctly summarized its holding: "... the lien of a mortgage does not make the mortgagee a cotenant; the mortgagor is the owner for all purposes; indeed that is why the 'gage' is 'mort', as distinguished from a 'vivum vadium,' " Woodsam Associates, Inc. v. Commissioner, 198 F.2d 357, 359 (2d Cir.1952).

**32.** Helvering v. Hammel, 311 U.S. 504, 61 S.Ct. 368, 85 L.Ed. 303 (1941).

But the nonrecourse mortgagor has got something going that the recourse mortgagor does not. The nonrecourse mortgagor can take a hike on the deal any time she wants. When Janice borrowed the $750,000 on a nonrecourse basis, she not only got the loan proceeds, she also in effect got an option. She got an option to sell the property to the bank for the $750,000. If real estate values shift downward, Janice has the option to call up her banker and say "Hey, Marlin, you just bought some property at $750,000 and I'm out of here." This right to sell at a particular price is called, in financial lingo a "put."[33] This is not something a borrower with recourse can do. A put can be economically attractive. For example, if real estate values continue to fall so that the property is worth $600,000, it is very economically attractive for Janice to be able to force Marlin to buy the property at $750,000. Whereas, if the property goes up in value to, say, $1,200,000, Janice does not exercise the put, but keeps the more valuable property by continuing to make her mortgage payments.[34]

That all being the case, it might be said that placing a nonrecourse mortgage on property the taxpayer holds is moving closer to a sale than placing recourse liability on the property. Why shouldn't we tax Janice at this point? She is richer. By hypothesis the property has appreciated from $500,000 to $1,000,000—or at least to $750,000. Moreover Janice obviously has got the cash to pay the tax. There's real income here.

What is stopping us from taxing Janice? We have the requirement of a realization. It is not enough that taxpayer is richer. We need something to happen for the gain to be taxed. We need a realizing event. And what is that? See our lucid discussion at ¶ 4.02. A "realizing event" is not just a sale. It could be other things as well, such as trading property, abandoning property or a foreclosure. A "realizing event" is what the courts say it is. It is not a concept that has economic content. So what about mortgaging nonrecourse? It moves you in that direction.

As stated before, we can view Janice's nonrecourse mortgaging of her property as a loan plus an option to sell (or a put). There's another way to look at it, though. We could look at it as a sale plus an option to buy it back. That is, when Janice mortgages her property on a nonrecourse basis, we could say that she has sold the property for $750,000. But she has the right to pay back the $750,000 and get the property back. This option to buy is called, in financial terminology, a "call." So now the transaction really starts to look like a taxable event.

Suppose we did tax it. What would we do then? Well, the sale plus a call model tells us. If the transaction is a sale plus a call, then let's take the sale part first. We have amount realized of $750,000 and adjusted basis of $500,000. So we have a gain of $250,000, on which tax is paid. So

33. As in "puts and calls" that are traded in the financial markets. In those cases the puts and calls are on stock or other financial instruments rather than real estate, but the principle is the same.

34. What the bank gives Janice in return for this put is a higher interest rate on the mortgage than it would charge if the loan were with recourse.

that part of the transaction is done. Then let's say that Janice does exercise her option to call the property back. Namely, she repays the $750,000. Now she owns the property all over again. What is her basis? It's got to be $750,000, since that's what she paid for it when she exercised the call. That is, as you see, just another statement of taxpayer's argument in *Woodsam*.

Now we can put it all together. We now know what do do if we wanted to treat Janice's placing a nonrecourse mortgage on property as a taxable event. We would tax Janice on the loan proceeds less her basis in the property. We would then also raise her basis in the property by the amount of that gain. That is the same thing as treating the transaction as a sale with a call which is exercised.

We could do that. We don't happen to choose to.

Which approach would the Service favor? Well, you would think the Service would favor treating the nonrecourse mortgage as a realizing event, so that it collects the tax up front. If, alternatively, the transaction is treated as a loan, then the Service gets no tax at the time of the transaction and perhaps never, if the loan is paid back. The basis in the property would remain low, so the Service would get its tax at a later time when the property sold. There again the property might be held by the taxpayer until death, with consequent tax-free step up in basis.[35] Thus the Service might never collect a tax.

But, in the *Woodsam* case the Service took the opposite approach. It favored not treating the nonrecourse financing as a taxable event. That was because the year in which the nonrecourse financing occurred was barred by the statute of limitations.

This is another example of what I call "tunnel vision" litigation policy on the part of the Service. Instead of realizing that on a time value of money basis it was better for the fisc to have nonrecourse financing be taxed, the particular litigators for the government simply sought to win their particular case on its unusual facts.

So how do *Crane* and *Woodsam* work together. The following example will illustrate.

**Example of *Crane* and *Woodsam* working together:** Michelle buys Whiteacre, undeveloped land, from Herbert for $50,000. Michelle gets the $50,000 to pay Herbert by putting down $10,000 of her own money and borrowing the other $40,000 on a nonrecourse basis from Belly–Up Savings and Loan, which issues a check to be used for payment at the closing. The transaction goes smoothly.

- Michelle's basis in Whiteacre: $50,000.

Time passes. Since Whiteacre is undeveloped real estate it is not depreciated so we don't have to worry about the basis changing on account of that.[36] After five years, Whiteacre has appreciated to a

---

**35.** 1014, and see ¶ 4.03(2)(e).　　　　**36.** See ¶ 6.02(12).

value of $100,000. At this time Michelle has paid off $10,000 of the mortgage, so the remaining mortgage is now $30,000.

- The partial pay off of the mortgage has no impact on her basis in Whiteacre: it's still $50,000.

At this time, Michelle borrows another $35,000 on Whiteacre on a nonrecourse basis.

- Impact of the after-acquired mortgage on Michelle's basis: nothing. Her basis is still $50,000.

- Over the next two years, the property drops in value from $100,000 to $85,000.

- Impact on Michelle's basis of the drop in value of the property: nothing. Her basis is still $50,000.

Two years later Michelle sells the property. She has paid off no further principal on the mortgages. She gets $10,000 at the closing and the buyer takes the property subject to the mortgages. What is her gain or loss?

Her amount realized is total debt relief of $65,000 plus $10,000 cash, for a total of $75,000. Her basis is still $50,000. Her gain is $25,000.

*Comment:* Does this make sense? Take a strict cash flow analysis: Michelle put in originally cash of $10,000. She then paid off $10,000 on the mortgage. So she put in a total of $20,000. How much cash is jingling around in her pockets now that the deal is over? She borrowed $35,000 after she had held the property. She also received $10,000 on the sale. That amount went into her pocket. Thus she got a total of $45,000. So she's ahead $25,000. That is the amount on which she is taxed.

*(B) Nice Work if You Can Get It.* And you can get it if you try. *Crane* and *Woodsam* also work together in another way that leads to some very attractive results. Unlike most of the tax advice given in this book (which is either too theoretical, obvious, or out of date), this piece of advice actually works. As we have seen, what *Crane* and *Woodsam* teach us is that debt incurred to acquire property is included in basis and debt incurred later on property is not. Both kinds of debt are included in amount realized when the property is sold or otherwise disposed of.

Here's the gimmick, illustrated by an example:

**Tax Planning Example Using *Woodsam*:** Murgatroyd acquires a small apartment building for $200,000. He puts $20,000 down and borrows the other $180,000 nonrecourse. As we know, his basis is $200,000. Three years later, the apartment building has appreciated to a value of $400,000. Murgatroyd borrows another $150,000 nonrecourse against the $200,000 of appreciation. Under *Woodsam* he is not taxed the receipt of the $150,000, and it does not go into his basis. He then uses the $150,000 to make some major capital improvements to the apartment building. As a result the

$150,000 as a capital expense does go into his basis. It can therefore be used to increase his depreciation deduction.[37] So he gets the best of both worlds: the $150,000 is not taxed but increases his basis for depreciation purposes.

*Comment:* Thus the result in *Woodsam* that the government fought so hard to achieve. Moreover, the avoidance is at the taxpayer's option. If he does not want to step up his basis by reinvesting the borrowed funds he can do that too. He could use the loan proceeds for a vacation.

*Comment:* What you need for this maneuver to work, of course, is to buy real estate which will go up sharply in value. That should be no problem (!!). See how useful this book is.

#### (iv)  The "Footnote 37" Problem: Tufts; Diedrich

*(A) "Phantom Gain".* If *Crane* is the most famous case in the history of federal income taxation, then footnote 37 of that case is the most famous footnote in the history of federal income taxation. *Crane*, as discussed above, held that acquisition nonrecourse indebtedness is included in basis and in amount realized. In footnote 37 of that opinion, the *Crane* Court declined to consider what would happen if at the time of the sale of the property, the property had a fair market value of less than the amount of the mortgage. Obviously this can only happen if the property has declined in value after the mortgage has been put on it, since no lender would lend more than the fair market value on property.

This is a highly significant issue. Since the *Crane* Court left the issue open, lawyers for taxpayers who sold property subject to nonrecourse debt of more than the value of the property argued that the amount realized could not exceed the value of the property. This thus lowered their clients' tax bill. This issue was addressed by the leading case of *Tufts*.

---

**37.**  See ¶¶ 6.03(4) and 6.02(12) for discussion of depreciation and capital expenditures.

## COMMISSIONER v. TUFTS[38]

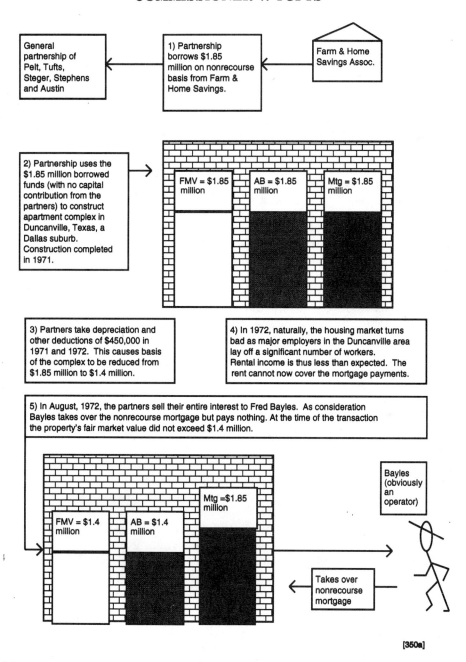

General partnership of Pelt, Tufts, Steger, Stephens and Austin

1) Partnership borrows $1.85 million on nonrecourse basis from Farm & Home Savings.

Farm & Home Savings Assoc.

2) Partnership uses the $1.85 million borrowed funds (with no capital contribution from the partners) to construct apartment complex in Duncanville, Texas, a Dallas suburb. Construction completed in 1971.

FMV = $1.85 million     AB = $1.85 million     Mtg = $1.85 million

3) Partners take depreciation and other deductions of $450,000 in 1971 and 1972. This causes basis of the complex to be reduced from $1.85 million to $1.4 million.

4) In 1972, naturally, the housing market turns bad as major employers in the Duncanville area lay off a significant number of workers. Rental income is thus less than expected. The rent cannot now cover the mortgage payments.

5) In August, 1972, the partners sell their entire interest to Fred Bayles. As consideration Bayles takes over the nonrecourse mortgage but pays nothing. At the time of the transaction the property's fair market value did not exceed $1.4 million.

FMV = $1.4 million     AB = $1.4 million     Mtg =$1.85 million

Bayles (obviously an operator)

Takes over nonrecourse mortgage

[350a]

*Question:* What was the gain realized by Tufts and the other partners on the sale of the property to Bayles?

**38.** 461 U.S. 300, 103 S.Ct. 1826, 75 L.Ed.2d 863 (1983), reh'g denied 463 U.S. 1215, 103 S.Ct. 3555, 77 L.Ed.2d 1401.

*Service's Argument:* Gain was calculated by $1.85 nonrecourse mortgage, which is amount realized, less $1.4 million adjusted basis or $450,000.

*Taxpayer's Argument:* The transaction is calculated by amount realized of $1.4 million, the fair market value of the property, less $1.4 million, the adjusted basis. Hence there is no gain or loss.[39]

*Comment, the injustice:* Observe the injustice if taxpayers prevail. They use the nonrecourse debt to pump up their basis for purposes of taking $450,000 of depreciation. Then when they sell, they don't want to hear about the nonrecourse debt to the extent it exceeds the fair market value of the property.

*Held:* The full amount of the nonrecourse mortgage is an amount realized to the taxpayers on sale of the property even though it is greater than the fair market value of the property. Thus partners had a gain of $450,000. Thus borrowing with and without recourse are treated the same way for basis and amount realized purposes. Once you take the position that recourse and nonrecourse debt are to be treated the same, then cancellation of debt principles[40] enter to put the full amount of the mortgage into income.

*Comment, cash flow:* Note the numbers crank out correctly on a cash flow basis also. The amount of gain is equal to the depreciation deduction taken ($450,000) less the amount of cash invested ($0). Since, on a cash flow basis, the depreciation deduction was unjustified, it has to be taken back into income on disposition of the property.

*Comment, time value of money:* Taxpayers in *Tufts* still got the benefit of the time value of money—although in this case it was only two years. Thus even after *Tufts*, tax shelters are alive and well. Deferral, which is money in the bank (see the Prologue), is still available. The gauntlet of anti-tax shelter legislation must be run to get a tax shelter, but this can be done. See Chapter 8.

*Comment, what about Bayles?* Why did Bayles want to take the property over when it was subject to a nonrecourse mortgage of $1.85 million and had a fair market value of $1.4 million? Answer this one and you are excused from the exam.[41]

There are a couple of possibilities. First note that Bayles has nothing to lose. The mortgage is, of course, nonrecourse. Bayles does have to make mortgage payments or face foreclosure. But he may have been able to say something to the lender Farm & Home Savings along the lines of "Don't push me. You want this property now you can have it." Having thus fended off Farm & Home, he might then hope to be a sharp enough operator to do some cosmetic fix ups and hope that the Dallas economy turns around. Then he might be lucky enough to sell the property for more than the $1.85 million mortgage and walk away a clear winner.

Alternatively Bayles might have been intending to assert under *Crane* that his basis in the property included the full amount of the

---

**39.** I have rounded the numbers for convenience.

**40.** ¶ 3.10.

**41.** I'd prefer if you didn't quote me to your instructor on this.

nonrecourse mortgage or $1.85 million. Thus Bayles would hope to take depreciation deductions from that inflated amount.

This would appear not to work, however. There is case law holding that where the amount of a nonrecourse indebtedness exceeds the fair market value of the property, the debt will not be respected for tax purposes.[42] Both depreciation and interest deductions founded on the debt will be lost.

*Comment, the role of the value of the property:* A major lesson to be drawn from all this concerns the role of the value of the property subject to a nonrecourse debt. On acquisition of the property, the value seems to matter a great deal. If the nonrecourse debt is greater than the value of the property, it will not be respected. Once valid nonrecourse financing is in place, however, we cease to care about the value of the property. On disposition of the property, the entire amount of nonrecourse debt is included in amount realized, regardless of the value of the property. The treatment of nonrecourse debt must be symmetrical.

*Comment, tax jargon:* One of the major things to gain from this course is to learn to talk like a tax lawyer, even if you don't fully understand the stuff. (I've been playing that game for years.) *Tufts* provides some major additions to tax jargon. The gain from circumstances on the pattern of *Tufts* is called "phantom gain" or "Tufts gain." That is to say, the effect on the taxpayer of a *Tufts* type pattern is, in a narrow minded sense, shocking. The taxpayer has a failed investment. He gets rid of the property. He gets nothing for it. He gets hit with a big tax. You can only explain it to your client using words like "Phantom gain," or "*Tufts* gain." Even if you pour on this gibberish, your client will not be a happy camper. You might also try to explain to your client that he got "phantom deductions" in the form of depreciation founded on the nonrecourse debt. But they usually don't want to hear about that.

*Comment, relevance for partnership taxation* : If you are considering going on in this field, a course in partnership taxation would be a likely candidate. *Tufts* gain is a major concept at some of the most critical points in that field. Have *Tufts* well in mind going in and it will help.[43]

*(B) Can You Give It Away?* How to dodge the "phantom gain" in the *Tufts* type situation? That is a question that many taxpayers and their advisors started asking before the ink on the *Tufts* decision was dry. Instead of selling the property to an erstwhile investor such as Bayles, what about giving it away? Since we're not getting anything for the property on a sale in the *Tufts* setting, let us give it away and perhaps avoid the "phantom gain." This issue was presented in the leading case of *Diedrich.*

**42.** See ¶ 8.02(4) and the discussion of the *Franklin* case.

**43.** It will indeed be noted that taxpayers in *Tufts* did business as a partnership.

## DIEDRICH v. COMMISSIONER[44]

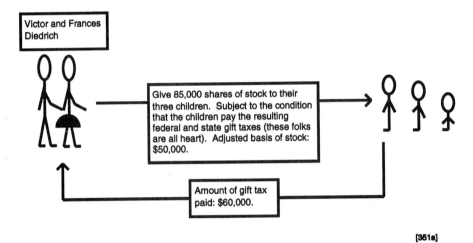

Victor and Frances Diedrich

Give 85,000 shares of stock to their three children. Subject to the condition that the children pay the resulting federal and state gift taxes (these folks are all heart). Adjusted basis of stock: $50,000.

Amount of gift tax paid: $60,000.

[351a]

*Question:* Do Victor and Frances have income to the extent that the gift tax paid by the children exceeds their basis in the stock?

*Service argument:* Victor and Frances had income of $10,000, computed by an amount realized of $60,000 gift tax paid less their basis of $50,000.[45]

*Taxpayer argument:* They have made a "net gift" of the amount by which the fair market value of the stock exceeds the gift tax paid. Thus they have no income; the amount of the gift is simply reduced by the gift tax paid by the children.

*Held:* The transaction is a part sale, part gift. The sale price is the amount of the gift tax. The donors' gain is the amount of the gift tax paid less their basis in the property. Thus uphold the Service's treatment, relying on *Crane, Bruun,* and *Old Colony.*

*Comment, relationship to* Tufts*:* The gift tax is imposed on the donor.[46] Thus this is not a nonrecourse debt situation. But the gift tax is a debt. The way that *Diedrich* informs the *Tufts* decision is to tell us that a gift of property subject to a liability is a realizing event. You will recall that the general rule for gifts is that they are not realizing events.[47] Thus it might be hoped by people in the *Tufts* fix that they could give the property away subject to the large nonrecourse liability and not have to take the liability back into income. After *Diedrich* it is

**44.** 457 U.S. 191, 102 S.Ct. 2414, 72 L.Ed.2d 777 (1982).

**45.** I have rounded the numbers for computational convenience: the actual basis was $51,073 and the actual gift tax was $62,992.

**46.** § 2502(d), the theory being apparently that if the donor has got such big bucks that he can make the gift, he can share a little of it with the government.

**47.** See ¶ 4.02.

clear that the gift of property subject to a liability is a realizing event to the donor to the extent of the liability. The balance of the value of the property above the liability (if any) is still treated as a gift. Thus the transaction is a part sale, part gift.

The significance of this case is very great and bears repeating: *Tufts* gain cannot be escaped by giving the property away, whether to a family member or a charitable organization or whomever.

I dwell on this because there is a second issue in the *Diedrich* case which gets a great deal of attention from the commentators, but that issue is not nearly as important as the *Tufts* gain issue.

*Comment, second issue, how to compute the gain:* The Service and the Court concluded that Victor and Frances had a gain of $10,000 computed by subtracting the basis in the stock of $50,000 from the gift tax liability which is the amount realized of $60,000. But is there something strange about this computation?

Take an alternate approach: Suppose that Victor and Frances had sold $60,000 of stock in order to pay the gift tax themselves and then had given the balance of the stock to their children. What would have happened then? They would have had to compute gain on the sale of that stock in the usual fashion. Since they would be selling ⅕ of their stock ($60,000 of $300,000) their basis would be ⅕ of their total basis in their stock. That would be $10,000 (⅕ of $50,000). Thus their gain would be $50,000 ($60,000 − $10,000).

Instead, according to the method employed by the Service and the Supreme Court, the gain was only $10,000. Curious, no?

With all due respect, it appears that the Court and the Service missed the boat on this one.

This faulty approach opens the door to some tax planning. As a matter of tax planning, making a conditional gift is better than selling the stock and paying the tax. Apparently there has been a great increase in conditional gifts since *Diedrich*.

### (v) Adjustment of the Purchase Price

Negotiations between the buyer and seller of property may lead to an agreement on a certain price. If subsequent negotiations may cause the price to be reduced, then obviously the cost basis will be the new lower price. Close questions can arise as to whether the whole transaction should be regarded as a reduction in purchase price or rather a discharge of indebtedness of the buyer, resulting in immediate income. See ¶ 3.10.

### (vi) Bargain Purchases of Property by Shareholders or Employees

If a corporation allows its shareholders to buy corporate property for less than the fair market value of the property, then the excess of the fair market value of the property over its adjusted basis in the hands of the corporation will be considered to be a dividend to the shareholder.[48] The basis of the property in the hands of the shareholder will be its fair market value.[49] Thus the basis in this situation is the cost of the property plus a step up to its fair market value. This is the appropriate basis, because the shareholder, having "paid the price" of a dividend treatment on the transfer, is now entitled to a fair market value basis on the property for future transactions. If the basis were not "stepped up" to account for the inclusion in income, the taxpayer would be taxed again on the income when he later sells the property.

This same general cost plus a step-up to fair market value approach is applied to the case of employees getting a bargain purchase of property from an employer. The bargain element of the purchase in this case is considered compensation and is so taxed at the time of the transfer.[50] Often the property purchased for a bargain price by the employee is subject to a condition that it might have to be forfeited back to the employer on the happening of some future contingency—such as the employee's failure to render future services to the employer. There is an elaborate statutory treatment of employee purchases of such restricted property, including specialized rules for ascertaining the amount included in income and the basis of the property. See ¶ 2.03(2) for a discussion of this area.

### (vii) Miscellaneous Problems

The basis of good will is established either by showing that the good will was purchased as part of an ongoing business,[51] or by establishing that certain non-deductible expenditures were made to attempt to improve the prospects of the business.[52]

If a sale of property involves installment payments over time bearing little or no interest, the Service may impute an amount as interest.[53] To the extent a purchaser's payments are imputed to be interest, his basis in the property purchased will be reduced.

If a purchaser obtains a number of different properties for one lump sum, the price paid must be allocated among the properties to establish the basis of each property.[54] The allocation of purchase price set forth in the sales contract is not necessarily dispositive; it may be self-serving in that, for example, too much is allocated to depreciable assets. In such a circumstance the Service may reallocate the purchase price to prevent

---

**48.** Reg. § 1.301–1(j).

**49.** Reg. § 1.301–1(h).

**50.** ¶ 2.03(2).

**51.** Grace Brothers, Inc. v. Commissioner, 173 F.2d 170 (9th Cir.1949). See also ¶ 4.06(3)(b) on the process of allocating purchase price to good will.

**52.** Cf. Cooperative Publishing Co. v. Commissioner, 115 F.2d 1017 (9th Cir. 1940) (dicta); cf. also Welch v. Helvering, 290 U.S. 111, 54 S.Ct. 8, 78 L.Ed. 212 (1933) (payments by taxpayer to creditors of a bankrupt corporation with which he was formerly associated to improve his business standing held nondeductible capital expenditures. Hence should this taxpayer subsequently sell his business, these payments would go into his basis for his good will).

**53.** § 483.

**54.** Reg. § 1.61–6(a).

substantial tax avoidance.[55] These problems arise frequently on the sale of a sole proprietorship going business, where it becomes necessary for the purchaser and seller to allocate the sales price among many types of assets. This particular problem is discussed more fully at ¶ 4.06(3)(b).

### (c) Carryover Basis

### (i) Gifts; Taft

The problems here are illustrated in the case of Taft v. Bowers. This leading Supreme Court case presented the problem as a hypothetical:

## TAFT v. BOWERS[56]

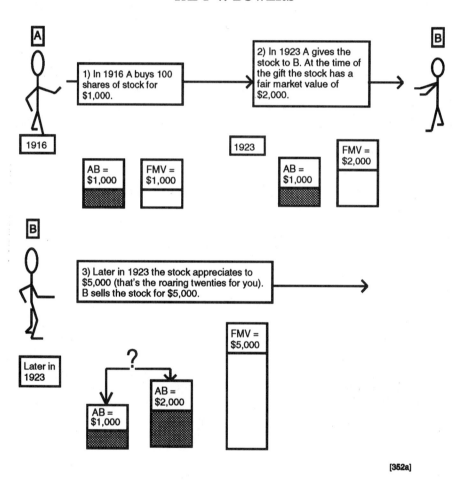

[352a]

**55.** Rev.Rul. 77–168, 1977–1 C.B. 248 (first in, first out technique required for ascertaining basis of fungible property acquired on different dates at different prices; see ¶ 4.03(2)(f) regarding special basis rules for securities); Rev.Rul. 77–413, 1977–2 C.B. 298 (basis of real property sold allocated between the 20–year possessory interest retained and the interest sold).

**56.** 278 U.S. 470, 49 S.Ct. 199, 73 L.Ed. 460 (1929).

*Question:* How much gain is B to be taxed on, $4,000 or $3,000?

*IRS Argument:* The statute [predecessor to § 1015] says that B must take A's basis and thus pay tax on $4,000—the entire amount of the appreciation of the property.

*Taxpayer Argument:* It is unconstitutional to tax me on gain that did not occur in my hands. I should not be taxed on the $1,000 the property appreciated in A's hands. Thus I should be taxed on $3,000.

*Held:* B takes A's basis and is taxed on $4,000, as the statute provides. The statute is constitutional.

*Comment:* See also ¶ 3.08 for discussion of what constitutes a "gift."

As this case illustrates, where property is transferred as a gift, the cost-of-acquisition approach discussed in the previous section cannot appropriately be used for establishing the basis of the property in the hands of the donee. Since the donee's cost is zero, this approach would give him a zero basis in the property given. But a zero basis in the property would mean that the donee would be taxed in full on the entire value of the property when he later sold it. This result is manifestly inconsistent with the exclusion of gifts from the donee's income of § 102 (see ¶ 3.08). That exclusion is more than just a mere deferral provision.

The upshot of *Taft* is that what is excluded on a gift is the donor's basis. Appreciation above that amount will be taxed eventually to the donee when he sells the property.

Another possibility for handling gifts would be to say that a gift is a realizing event (see ¶ 4.02). In that event, on the *Taft* facts, A would be taxed on $1,000 at the time of the gift. B would take a basis of $2,000. On sale of the property for $5,000, B would have a $3,000 gain.

The present rule is more favorable to taxpayers in general in that the tax on $1,000 of appreciation in A's hands is deferred until B sells the property. The present rule, however, invites taxpayers to game around. That is, if A has appreciated property, he may give it to family-member B who is in a lower tax bracket. B could then sell soon thereafter (as indeed happened in the *Taft* hypothetical). As a result, the tax on the family unit is less than if A had sold the property. Conversely, if the property has declined in value since the donor bought it, he would sell the property, and take a deduction for the loss. This deduction is more valuable to him in a higher bracket than to the donee in the lower bracket. The donor could then give the cash proceeds to the donee.

No particular larger social purpose is served by allowing taxpayers to play games of this kind. Thus it would appear that the better rule would be to make gifts a realizing event. In addition, this proposed rule would reduce the donee's administrative problems. Under the present rule, the donee has to ascertain the donor's basis, which may be difficult to do if the donor has held the property for decades. The donor's cooperation is required to ascertain the donor's basis. With the proposed rule, the donee takes the fair market value at the time of the gift. This is something the donee can establish on his own, at the time of the gift or later, without the cooperation of the donor.

The fair market value approach received a bad name as a historical matter. This is because the original rule in this area was that the donee takes a basis of the fair market value of the property given.[57] However— and this was a fatal omission—the donor did not pay tax on the appreciation in his hands at the time of the gift. As a result, this approach erred too much in the other direction. Under this flawed fair market value approach, if the donor gave the donee highly appreciated property, that appreciation would not be taxed to the donor, since the gift was not considered a realizing event. But if the donee took a basis of the fair market value at the time of the gift, then he also would never pay tax on the appreciation in the hands of the donor. The appreciation in the hands of the donor would, therefore forever escape taxation in anyone's hands. Taxpayers thus abused the rule by giving appreciated property back and forth among family members.

This carryover basis of the property in the hands of the donee is, of course, subject to further adjustments such as depreciation or capital expenditures that may occur during the period the donee holds the property.[58]

Change the facts of *Taft* somewhat and we get ourselves into a surprising muddle. Suppose that A bought the stock for $2,000 and then made the gift at a time when the fair market value was $1,000. B then sells the stock for $300. Being rationale (which is your first mistake), you would think that B would take A's basis of $2,000 and thus have a loss of $1,700 ($2,000 basis; $300 amount realized).

Not so. The statute reacts here much like an elephant might when a mouse crawls up its leg: screaming and jumping up at this savage attack. This is because on these facts A is seen as "giving away a loss." This smacks of "tax avoidance" and "trading in losses."

So the statute takes away that built-in loss. It does so by providing that, on our facts, B would take a basis of the fair market value at the time of the gift, or $1,000. Thus B's loss would be $700 ($1,000 basis; $300 amount realized) instead of $1,700. B can only deduct the loss that occurs while the stock is in B's hands. On these facts, the loss that A suffered is never deducted. Which is to say that giving away depreciated property is not a very good idea.

**57.** Wilson Brothers & Co. v. Commissioner, 124 F.2d 606 (9th Cir.1941).

**58.** The donee's holding period of the property received by gift includes the holding period of the donor, IRC § 1223(2). The holding period of property is important for the capital gains rules.

A similar carryover basis rule is used for transfers of property in corporate organizations and reorganizations. See IRC §§ 362(a) and (b) and see, Bittker and Eustice, Federal Income Taxation of Corporations and Shareholders (1987) § 14.33. The same rule is also used in the formation of partnerships, ¶ 723.

See § 4.03(2)(g) regarding adjustments to basis. The basis of the gift in the hands of the donee may also be increased by some of the gift tax paid, IRC § 1015(d)(6).

Stating the rule more generally, it is: If the donee receives property with a fair market value less than the basis at the time of the gift, then for purposes of calculating further loss in the donee's hands, the donee shall use that fair market value as his basis.[59]

The astute reader might then ask, suppose the facts are these: A buys the stock for $2,000, gives the stock to B at a time when the stock has a fair market value of $1,000. B then sells the stock for $1,500. What result to B? Now we're really in a pickle. If we take the fair market value at the time of the gift as a basis for B, that would be $1,000. But using $1,000 as a basis generates a gain when B sells the property for $1,500. But this basis of fair market value at the time of the gift rule is only supposed to be used to compute a loss for B. On our numbers he is getting a gain.

So we go back to the usual rule: B takes A's basis. That is $2,000. When B goes to sell the stock now for $1,500, he gets a loss. But when B has a loss and the property had a fair market value at the time of the gift of less than the basis, we are supposed to use that fair market value as B's basis.

So, wait a second. This is where we came in. The answer is that, on our numbers, any sale by B of the stock between the price of $1,000 and $2,000 yields no gain or loss. This is weird. This is the so-called "notch" transaction.[60]

There's a couple things to be said about this "notch" transaction. 1) If you don't like this at all, if you are getting nauseous, then tax may not be the field for you. Because there's a lot of rules like this in the field. 2) Conversely, if you like the fantasy aspect of this, then tax may be a good field for you. 3) We see here the roots of complexity. By promulgating an artificial rule divorced from economic reality—that the basis on a gift of depreciated property is the fair market value at the time of the gift—we get ourselves into further difficulty. This requires promulgation of further rules that get even more divorced from reality and more complex.

The accompanying graphic attempts to summarize the gift rules we have been discussing:

**59.** § 1015(a).     **60.** Reg. § 1.1015–1(a)(2) Example.

## GIFT RULES: ONCE MORE WITH FEELING

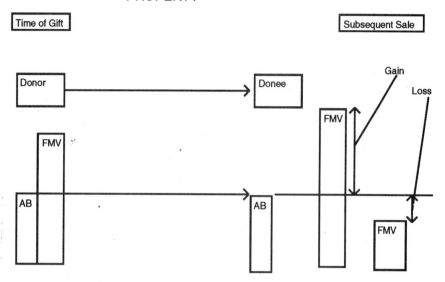

GIFT OF APPRECIATED PROPERTY

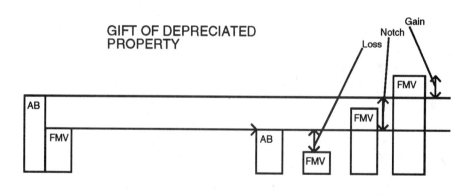

GIFT OF DEPRECIATED PROPERTY

[353a]

One final point: Where the donee is or was the donor's spouse, the donee always takes the donor's basis in a gift, if the transfer is incident to divorce.[61]

Instead of making an outright gift, a transferor may confer a benefit by selling property to a transferee at a price substantially below the property's fair market value. In such a case the transferor has effected a transaction "in part a gift and in part a sale."[62] The transferee's basis in a part gift, part sale is the greater of the amount paid by the transferee

---

**61.** § 1041(a)-(c).          **62.** Reg. § 1.1015–4.

or the transferor's basis for the property at the time of the transfer.[63] Where the property involved in a part gift, part sale is depreciated (fair market value less than transferor's basis at the time of the transfer) then as a further limitation on the part gift, part sale basis rule, the transferee's basis for determining *loss* on a subsequent sale cannot be greater than the property's fair market value at the time of the transfer.[64] Thus do the exigencies of developing a reasonable rule for a part gift, part sale combine with the prohibition against giving away losses to create a somewhat complex overall rule in this area. Some examples, adapted from the Regulations, will illustrate:[65]

> (1) A transfers property to his son for $60,000. At the time of the transfer the property has a basis in A's hands of $30,000 and a fair market value of $90,000. The basis in the hands of the son will be $60,000.

> (2) A transfers property to his son for $30,000. At the time of the transfer the property has a basis in A's hands of $60,000 and a fair market value of $90,000. The basis in the hands of the son will be $60,000.

> (3) A transfers property to his son for $30,000. At the time of the transfer the property has a basis in A's hands of $60,000 and a fair market value of $45,000. The basis of the property in the hands of the son will be $60,000 for the purpose of determining gain on a subsequent sale by the son and $45,000 for the purpose of determining loss on a subsequent sale by the son. Sales for a price between $45,000 and $60,000 will yield no gain or loss.

### (ii) Transfers in Trust

If a transfer of property to a trust is a gift, the gift rules discussed above apply for ascertaining the basis of the property in the hands of the trust.[66] If the transfer in trust is for consideration, the basis of the property in the hands of the trust is the same as the basis in the hands of the transferor, increased by the amount of gain or decreased by the amount of loss recognized to the transferor on the transfer.[67]

### (d) Substituted Basis

There is a class of transactions in which basis is established by placing the basis of property previously held by the taxpayer onto property newly held by the taxpayer. The major examples of this class of "substituted basis" transactions are tax-free exchanges of property,[68] involuntary conversions of property into other property[69] and sale and

---

**63.** This basis might be increased by a portion of the gift tax paid, (if any). § 1015(d)(6).

**64.** Reg. § 1.1015–4(a). As with the other bases derived above, this basis will be increased by any gift tax paid, Reg. § 1.1015–4(a)(2) and will be subject to fur-

ther adjustment in the hands of the transferee.

**65.** Reg. § 1.1015–4(b) Examples 1–4.

**66.** Reg. § 1.1015–1(a)(1).

**67.** § 1015(b).

**68.** § 1031, see ¶ 4.05(2).

**69.** § 1033, see ¶ 4.05(3).

purchase of a principal residence.[70] The theory of these transactions is that the taxpayer remains invested in generally the same type of property after the transaction as before the transaction; hence the transaction should not be an occasion to recognize gain (or loss).[71] The substituted basis technique is then used to insure that the gain which has escaped tax at the time of the transaction will be taxed at some later time. To the extent the taxpayer does cash out his investment and recognizes some gain, appropriate basis correction will be made. These nonrecognition transactions and their concomitant substituted basis rules are discussed more fully at ¶ 4.05.[72]

### (e) Fair Market Value Basis: Property Acquired From a Decedent

### (i) Present Rule

The basis of property acquired from a decedent is its fair market value at the date of the decedent's death.[73] This rule allows appreciation in the hands of the decedent to escape taxation forever. Contrast this with the gift rule, ¶ 4.03(2)(c)(i) above, where tax on the appreciation in the hands of the donor is only deferred but not permanently exempted. Thus a major estate planning technique is for the taxpayer to sell his loss property and hold his gain property until death. The ultimately unsuccessful attempt to "reform" this area by enacting a carryover basis rule for property acquired from a decedent is recounted at ¶ 4.03(2)(e).

The Economic Recovery Tax Act of 1981 added a significant exception to the rule that the basis of property acquired from a decedent is its fair market value at the date of the decedent's death. This rule was to forestall the maneuver whereby a taxpayer owning appreciated property would give that property to a relative who is obviously in ill health. The plan would be that upon the relative's death, he would will the property back to the donor. The donor's theory would be that he had now received the property from a decedent and could take a fair market value basis in property which had otherwise been highly appreciated in his hands. This

---

**70.** § 1034, see ¶ 4.05(4). Other substituted basis transactions include certain exchanges of life insurance policies, § 1035; stock for stock exchanges of a corporation, § 1036; certain exchanges of United States obligations, § 1037; reacquisitions of real property on default of a purchase money mortgage, § 1038; the formation and reorganization of corporations, § 358.

**71.** See ¶ 4.05.

**72.** As with the carryover basis, the substituted basis technique has very important use in the corporate organization and reorganization area. See Subchapter C, Parts III and IV.

**73.** § 1014. Where the executor of the decedent's estate elects the alternate valuation date (six months after death or the date of disposition of the property if dis-

posed of within six months after death) for estate tax purposes, the value of the property on the alternate valuation date will be the basis of the property in the hands of the heir, §§ 1014(a), 2032(a).

The holding period of property acquired from a decedent will be considered to be more than one year if it is disposed of within one year: § 1223(11).

Other exceptions to the fair market value at date of death rule for property acquired from a decedent include: (1) a gift in contemplation of death of the decedent, which is included in the estate of the decedent for estate tax purposes, where such property is sold or exchanged before the decedent's death. In such a case the donee uses a carry-over basis under §§ 1015, 1014(a); (2) items which are income in respect of a decedent pursuant to § 691.

macabre bit of tax planning has now been foreclosed by § 1014(e), which provides that in such circumstances the property will retain its original basis in the hands of the donor, if the property is received back by either the donor or his spouse.

*(ii) Property Acquired From a Decedent: The Saga of Carryover Basis*

As discussed just above, the basis of property acquired from a decedent by will or by the laws of intestate succession is the fair market value of the property at the date of death.[74] This rule allows unrealized appreciation in the hands of the decedent to forever escape income taxation.[75] The appreciation is not taxed to the decedent or his estate at death, because a bequest or inheritance is not a taxable event to the decedent, see ¶ 4.02. It is often the case that on inheritance some unrealized appreciation escapes forever income taxation.[76] This rule is, not surprisingly, of major importance in the income tax and estate tax planning of taxpayers who hold great amounts of appreciated property. In general the approach is to sell loss property before death so as to realize the loss and to hold gain property so that the heirs would benefit from the basis step-up.

To forestall the substantial income tax avoidance in this area, Congress, as part of the Tax Reform Act of 1976, enacted a carryover basis provision for property acquired from a decedent dying after December 31, 1976.[77] This provision included some important exceptions and qualifications and a significant transition rule allowing property held by the decedent prior to December 31, 1976 to be stepped up to its value at that date.[78] After the enactment of the carryover basis provision heavy lobbying pressure built up against this provision, both because of the impact it had on wealthier taxpayers and because of its great complexity. Pending its reexamination, the effective date of the carryover basis provision was in 1978 postponed to decedents dying after December 31,

**74.** An alternate valuation date, at the election of the executor, is available if also used for estate tax purposes §§ 1014(a), 2032.

**75.** The property may, of course, be subject to estate tax, but that is not relevant to the question of what is the proper treatment for purposes of income taxation. Many taxes—sales taxes, property taxes,—are imposed in the society, but their imposition does not properly excuse not imposing an income tax on the same property or transaction.

**76.** Moreover, even if the property has not in fact risen in value, it may have been subject to the allowance for depreciation deductions, which would have lowered the basis (¶ 6.02(12)) and hence it would still be property with potential, unrealized gain.

Of course, it is possible that the property has declined in value in the decedent's hands to the extent that the fair market value is less than the decedent's basis at the date of death. In that event the fair market value basis rule for inheritances is disadvantageous to taxpayers, since there will then never be an opportunity to deduct the loss.

**77.** Sections 1023, 2005, Pub.Law 94–455. See also *General Explanation of the Tax Reform Act of 1976*, prepared by the staff of the Joint Committee on Taxation, 1976–3 C.B. Vol. 2, pp. 551–563.

This attempt at reform parallels the change in the gift basis rules enacted in 1921; see text accompanying note 33 above.

**78.** Id.

1979. Subsequently it was repealed entirely.[79]

There's a lesson in here somewhere, although I am not exactly sure what it is.

### (f) Special Rules for Stock, Securities and Mutual Fund Shares

Stock and securities are acquired or transferred in a variety of unique transactions which occasion the use of special rules for ascertaining basis. Substituted and carryover basis techniques are used in the corporate organization, reorganization and division areas.[80] A substituted basis is used in wash sale transactions.[81] A cost plus taxable income approach is used for stock transferred as compensation for services.[82]

Where a taxpayer has bought identical shares of stock at different times for different prices, a problem is presented where he sells some but not all of his holdings. The size of his gain or loss and its character of being held long term or short term may well depend on which of his identical shares he is deemed to have sold. The Regulations provide that unless the taxpayer can in fact identify the particular shares sold, he will be deemed to have sold the shares he purchased earliest in time.[83] The Regulations set forth steps the taxpayer can take to insure that he can identify the particular shares he is selling, whether he holds the certificates himself or whether they are held by his broker.[84] Unless such steps are taken to identify the shares sold, the Service's "first-in first-out" rule will apply.

Similar problems are presented where the taxpayer has purchased shares of an open end mutual fund at different times for different prices. A redemption or sale of some but not all of his holdings leads to questions of which shares were redeemed or sold. Here again there are two basic possibilities. If the taxpayer can in fact identify the actual mutual fund shares disposed of, then actual cost will be used as basis. If the shares, as will often be the case, have been left by the taxpayer in the custody of a transfer agent, then the taxpayer may elect to use an average cost approach to ascertain basis.[85]

### (g) Adjustments to Basis: The Basis as History

Once basis is ascertained by any of the methods discussed above, it does not necessarily remain unchanged while the property is held by the

---

**79.** The repeal was attached to the Crude Oil Windfall Profit Tax of 1980 (§ 401(d)), a measure that was highly desired by the Carter Administration at that time.

**80.** §§ 358, 361.

**81.** § 1091 and see ¶ 4.05(6).

**82.** § 83 and see ¶ 2.03. As these authorities indicate, the cost plus taxable income approach is used to ascertain the basis of any property received as compensation for services.

**83.** Reg. § 1.1012–1(c)(1).

**84.** Reg. § 1.1012–1(c)(2) and (3).

**85.** Reg. § 1.1012–1(e), also providing for the option to treat all shares together or to maintain separate accounts for shares held for a long term and shares held for a short term.

This average cost method would, as discussed in the text, apply only to open-end mutual fund shares, Regs. § 1.1012–1(e)(1)(ii)(a). Shares of a closed-end fund, traded as they are over a securities exchange or over the counter, would be treated under the rules for stock, above.

taxpayer. On the contrary, it may well be adjusted on account of a wide variety of items while the property is held by the taxpayer, such as capital expenditures, casualty losses, and depreciation.[86]

As indicated, the basis of property may be treated specially (carried over to another taxpayer, or substituted on to another piece of property) if the property is disposed of in a nonrecognition transaction. Thus in some sense does the basis trace the history of a piece of property, always recording what has happened to it and informing what the results will be on future transactions. Applying with equal significance to all types of property from vacant land to variable annuities, and serving as a point of departure not only for calculating gain or loss on disposition but also for computing further adjustments to basis, the basis is a central concept in the tax law.

## ¶ 4.04  Disallowance of Some Losses and Exclusion of Some Gains

### (1) In General

As indicated in the above discussion, the first step in approaching sales and other dispositions of property is to determine whether there has been a realizing event. If there has been a realizing event, the second step is to compute the amount of the gain or loss realized, as discussed in the preceding section.

Gains and losses so realized and computed might still not be reflected on the taxpayer's tax return. A gain, for example, although realized and properly computed under provisions of the Code discussed above, might still be excluded from the taxpayer's income by some other provision of the Code. Similarly a loss, although realized and ascertainable in amount under the Code provisions discussed above, might not be allowed as a deduction by some other provision of the Code. If a gain is so excluded or a loss is so disallowed, then that is the end of the process for the transaction. No further issue is or need be raised with respect to recognition or characterization (as discussed below).

There is at present only one Code provision (discussed below) permanently excluding from income a realized gain from the sale or exchange of property; it applies to a narrow range of transactions and is not of great significance in terms of the structure of the Code. However, a broad range of realized losses from the sale or other disposition of property are permanently disallowed by the Code and this disallowance is of great significance in the structure of the Code.[1] Thus the discussion will deal first with the disallowance of realized losses and then with the exclusion of realized gain.

With respect to losses incurred on sales or other dispositions of property, the Code takes a two-level approach. The general rule is that

---

**86.**  § 1016, also listing a number of other adjustments to basis; see ¶ 6.03(4).

**¶ 4.04**

**1.**  See ¶ 4.04(2).

such losses are allowed.[2] However, there are provisions specifically disallowing losses incurred on certain types of transactions. These provisions are treated below. (Note that the topic of allowance of losses on sales or other dispositions of property is only a part of the larger topic of allowance of losses of all kinds—such as casualty losses or losses from bad debts, etc.).

### (2) Losses From Sales of Residence or Other Personal–Use Property

As indicated, the general rule with respect to the allowance of losses from sales or other dispositions of property is that the loss is allowed. However, an important exception to this rule is where the loss arises from the sale or other disposition of property held solely by the taxpayer for his personal use. The loss realized from sale or other disposition of the taxpayer's personal-use property is not allowed.[3] Thus the loss on sale of taxpayer's personal-use property, such as a personal residence,[4] jewelry,[5] or a horse,[6] is not allowed. The situation is not symmetrical in that gains on the sale of personal-use property are taxed.[7]

Since losses on the sale of personal-use property are not allowed, but losses on the sale of investment or business property are allowed,[8] there can naturally arise a healthy dispute over whether particular property that was sold at a loss was personal-use or investment property. This issue arises most frequently on the sale of a taxpayer's personal residence which may have been converted at some point to rental or other income-producing use. Fairly specific principles have been evolved by the courts and the Service for dealing with this problem.[9]

**2.** § 165(a). The amount of the loss allowed is limited to the basis of the property, § 165(b); this limitation is also inherent in the process of computing gain or loss realized, see ¶ 4.03.

**3.** § 165(c)(3). A loss would be allowed with respect to personal use property if it arose from a casualty above certain floor amounts. See ¶ 7.01(5)(a).

**4.** Reg. § 1.165–9, Newton, 57 T.C. 245 (1971) (loss on mortgage foreclosure of personal residence disallowed).

**5.** Winkler v. Nunan, 143 F.2d 483 (2d Cir.1944) (jewelry not bought for investment).

**6.** Clarence W. Daugette, Jr., 36 T.C.M. 252 (1977) (distinguishing between horses held for business and a personal-use horse that was not depreciated).

**7.** § 61(a)(3);      ¶¶ 4.01–4.03.      See ¶ 4.04(5) for discussion of exemption of gain on certain sales of personal residences. See ¶ 4.06 for discussion of capital gains.

**8.** Note 3 above and see ¶ 7.01(5).

**9.** The received wisdom in this field was handed down in Heiner v. Tindle, 276

U.S. 582, 48 S.Ct. 326, 72 L.Ed. 714 (1928) which involved a property that had been used as the taxpayer's personal residence for 9 years and then rented for 19 years and then sold at a loss. The Court held that the loss would be allowed since at the time of the renting the property ceased to be held for personal use and was devoted exclusively to the production of income.

This rule has now been adopted by the Regulations, Reg. § 1.165–9(b)(1). To benefit from this *Tindle* rule, the property must in fact be converted from personal to business or investment use. Renting the property out, as held in *Tindle* and Reg. § 1.165–9(b)(1), constitutes such a conversion. Putting the property up for sale does not constitute such a conversion. Unsuccessfully attempting to rent the property out does not constitute such a conversion, and a loss on property sold after an unsuccessful attempt to rent will not be allowed, Phipps v. Helvering, 124 F.2d 292 (D.C.Cir.1941) (Senator Lawrence Phipps of Colorado denied a deduction for loss on his sale of the Colorado home he vacated after his election to the United States Senate).

### (3) Losses From Sales of Property in Activities Not Engaged in for Profit

Some taxpayers engage in activities—most typically "gentleman farming" or breeding, and racing of horses—which are a hobby or recreation rather than a serious business or investment. When such activities generate losses, the difficult problem is to sort out the true farm or racehorse, etc. business which can legitimately take loss deductions from the recreational farmer or racehorse breeder who may seek to take loss deductions arising from what is for him essentially a hobby or pastime. This sorting out of the true farm, racehorse, or ski lodge, etc., business from the hobby or pastime for deduction of loss purposes is a problem which has long plagued the tax law.[10]

The present treatment of deductions from hobby-type activities not entered into for profit is discussed fully at ¶ 6.02(9). A part of that treatment is the disallowance of losses from sales of property arising from activities not entered into for profit.[11]

### (4) Disallowance of Losses Versus Nonrecognition of Losses

In addition to the two provisions discussed above disallowing losses on sales or other dispositions of personal-use property or property used in activities not entered into for profit, there are two other provisions of the Code which purport to "disallow" losses on sales or other dispositions of property. These are § 267, disallowing losses on transactions between related taxpayers, and § 1091, disallowing losses from "wash" sales of stock or securities. However, §§ 267 and 1091 do not permanently disallow the loss involved but rather, through basis adjustment, preserve the loss so that it may be taken advantage of at some later time. Thus, though couched in terms of "disallowance of loss" §§ 267 and

---

Once the property has been rented, the fact that it later becomes vacant apparently will not destroy the loss deduction, as long as personal use is not made again of the property, see McBride, 50 T.C. 1 (1968) (acq.) (loss on demolition of previously rented property allowed).

The amount of the loss allowed is the lesser of the cost of the property or the fair market value of the property at the time of conversion (reduced by depreciation taken), less the amount realized on sale of the property, Reg. §§ 1.165–9(b)(2) and 1.165–9(c), providing examples and see *Tindle* above. Of course if such property is sold at a gain, the usual basis rules apply. Presumably if property is sold at a price that would yield gain if the loss rules were applied and a loss if the gain rules were applied, then no gain or loss is realized. Cf. the "notch" transaction in the gift area, ¶ 4.03(2)(c)(i).

Even if the property is clearly held for investment-type purposes, the taxpayer must believe that there is at least some remote chance of making a profit for a loss on sale or abandonment of the property to be allowed. King v. United States, 545 F.2d 700 (10th Cir.1976) (worthless oil leases abandoned in the aftermath of the collapse of the King Resources Company and the IOS mutual fund complex of Bernard Cornfeld held deductible, as taxpayer's intent was to make a profit). Cf. Knetsch v. United States, 364 U.S. 361, 81 S.Ct. 132, 5 L.Ed.2d 128 (1960) and Goldstein v. Commissioner, 364 F.2d 734 (2d Cir.1966), cert. denied 385 U.S. 1005, 87 S.Ct. 708, 17 L.Ed.2d 543 (1967) discussed at § 6.03(6)(b).

**10.** Senate Report 91–552, 1969–3 C.B. 423, 489–491.

**11.** §§ 183(a)–(c); Reg. § 1.183–1(b). See Bessenyey v. Commissioner, 379 F.2d 252 (2d Cir.1967), cert. denied 389 U.S. 931, 88 S.Ct. 293, 19 L.Ed.2d 283 (1967).

1091 really partake more of nonrecognition transactions. They are therefore discussed at ¶ 4.05.[12]

### (5) Exclusion of Gain From Sale of Residence by Individual Who Has Attained Age 55

As the discussion above has indicated many realized losses (in general arising from sales of personal-use property) are disallowed in computing the taxpayer's taxable income. By contrast it is comparatively rare for a realized gain on dealings in property to be excluded permanently from income. At present the only such permanent exclusion of realized gain is in § 121, relating to a taxpayer who has attained the age of 55 selling his principal residence.[13] If such a gain is excluded, no further steps in the process (relating to recognition or characterization, etc.) need be taken. § 121 is elective;[14] the amount of the exclusion is limited to $125,000.[15] The exclusion can be elected only once regardless of the amount actually excluded,[16] so a qualifying taxpayer with only a small gain, say $25,000, on the sale of his principal residence may be well advised not to elect the exclusion on the transaction if he anticipates another sale of a principal residence for a possibly greater gain in the future.

An involuntary conversion of taxpayer's residence on account of a casualty or condemnation is treated as a sale for the purpose of qualifying for the benefits of the exclusion.[17] Moreover, § 121 coordinates well with both § 1033, which allows deferral of gain on involuntary conversions, and with § 1034, which allows deferral of gain on the sale and repurchase of a principal residence.[18] To the extent the taxpayer realizes more than the $125,000 of gain excluded by § 121, the balance of the gain can be deferred under §§ 1033 or 1034 if their requirements are

---

**12.** See also discussion at § 4.05(1), note 3.

**13.** To qualify for this exclusion, the property must have been owned by the taxpayer and used as the taxpayer's principal residence for periods aggregating at least 3 of the 5 years preceding the date of the sale, § 121(a)(2), Reg. § 1.121–1(c) and (d). See Rev.Rul. 80–172, 1980–2 C.B. 56 (periods of ownership and use need not be simultaneous). This provision applies to tenant stockholders in a cooperative housing corporation, § 121(d)(3) and would certainly apply to condominium ownership.

If property is held by a husband and wife as joint tenants, tenants by the entirety, or community property and the husband and wife file a joint return, then only one spouse need satisfy the age, ownership, and use requirements above § 121(d)(1), Reg. § 1.121–5.

**14.** § 121(a) and (c). The election may be made any time before the expiration of the statute of limitations on filing claims

for a refund or credit, § 121(c), and see § 6511. General rules and manner of making and revoking the election are set forth in Reg. § 1.121–4.

**15.** § 121(b), also providing a limit of $62,500 in the case of a separate return by a married individual. See also Reg. § 1.121–2(a).

**16.** § 121(b)(2), Reg. § 1.121–2(b).

**17.** § 121(d)(4). This subsection also deems a theft to be a sale for purposes of § 121. Although it may not be immediately clear how a taxpayer's principal residence could be the subject of a theft, presumably the statute would cover the case where someone makes off with taxpayer's trailer home, and he receives insurance proceeds in excess of his basis.

**18.** See ¶ 4.05 for a full treatment of §§ 1033 and 1034.

met.[19]

## ¶ 4.05   Recognition of Gain or Loss

### (1) In General

Having determined the amount of gain realized and included in income, or the amount of loss realized and allowed on the disposition of property, the task then becomes one of ascertaining whether the gain or loss will be recognized. "Recognition" of a gain or a loss means that the gain or loss will in fact be taken into account in computing the taxpayer's taxable income. The powerful presumption of the Code is that all gains or losses realized shall be recognized.[1] Indeed, most gains and losses on dealings in property are recognized without further problems. However, in an important category of transactions, Congress has provided that the gains (and sometimes losses) realized will not be recognized at the time of the transaction but will be deferred until some later time. Insuring that the deferred gain or loss will be accounted for later is accomplished by appropriate adjustment of the basis of the property involved in the transaction. Bear in mind that the gains or losses not recognized by these provisions are only deferred. The idea is that they will be recognized at a later time.

The rationale behind these nonrecognition provisions of the Code varies somewhat from provision to provision. Roughly, however, it can be said as to many of them that Congress has determined that a taxpayer who has engaged in this class of transactions has not changed the nature of his investment sufficiently to warrant a tax being imposed on his realized gain. Tax-free exchanges of like-kind property can be explained on this basis. So can the tax free treatment of certain corporate mergers and acquisitions.[2]

Some other nonrecognition provisions can be explained on the basis that the taxpayer is in a difficult spot and we should not impose a tax on him at this time. The sale of a personal residence, involuntary conversions, and transfer of property between spouses incident to a divorce[3] are of this type.

It should also be noted that these nonrecognition provisions are not always "taxpayer-friendly." For example, suppose a taxpayer owns some stock on which he has an unrealized loss. He may wish to continue to hold the stock because he believes in the company. But he may wish to

---

**19.**  § 121(d)(7), Reg. § 1.121–5(g), providing examples.

**¶ 4.05**

**1.**  § 1001(c). See also Reg. § 1.1031(a)–1(a). Of course the loss might be disallowed or the gain might be excluded as discussed in ¶ 4.04. In such an event the question of recognition of the gain or loss, of course, is never reached. For convenience in this section, when realized gains and losses are discussed, it will be assumed that the gains are not excluded from income and that the losses are allowed. (As discussed in ¶ 4.04 it is usually the case that a realized gain will not be excluded. However, a number of realized losses may in fact be disallowed).

**2.**  See D. Posin *Corporate Tax Planning: Takeovers, Leveraged Buyouts and Restructurings*, Chapters 7–9 (1990).

**3.**  See ¶ 4.02.

still get a deduction for the loss. He might strike upon the idea of selling the property (thereby creating a realizing event) and then buying it back 10 minutes later. The Code does not like tricks like that. The loss on this maneuver will not be recognized.[4]

Even supposedly "taxpayer-friendly" provisions can be seized by the Service and used to beat the taxpayer over the head. Thus the nonrecognition rule for like-kind exchanges carries a bite because it also applies to disallow the recognition of losses. As such, like-kind treatment has been imposed on taxpayers—to their surprise—in some transactions to bar a loss.[5]

The non-recognition of gain accords the taxpayer, of course, the great advantage of deferral of tax on his realized gain. As discussed in the Prologue, deferral of gain is money in the bank to the taxpayer. Time value of money issues are at the core of nonrecognition transactions.[6]

As indicated above, nonrecognition can be a double-edged sword. The taxpayer may prefer recognition of gain where he is in a relatively low marginal tax bracket at the time of the transaction or where he has another recognized loss against which to offset it. Depending upon the particular nonrecognition provision involved, the taxpayer may or may not be able to escape nonrecognition treatment when he so desires. Indeed, taxpayer scrambling to get into or out of these nonrecognition provisions has given rise to a good deal of litigation and complexity in this area.[7]

Finally, for those of you planning to take other courses in the field, it should be noted that here is where individual income taxation leaves off and corporate taxation begins. Much of corporate taxation is concerned with nonrecognition transactions. The formation of a corporation is often accomplished on a tax-free basis.[8] Some corporate mergers and acquisitions qualify to be done tax-free.[9]

---

**4.** See ¶ 4.05(6) below. If, instead, the taxpayer tries to sell the loss stock to a family member, another nonrecognition provision will bite, see ¶ 4.05(7) below.

**5.** See ¶ 4.05(2)(c).

**6.** It is indeed possible that the deferral of gain will ripen into a permanent exemption if the taxpayer dies and his heir takes a fair market value basis in the property. See ¶ 4.03(2)(e). For more on the rationale of nonrecognition transactions, see Commissioner v. Wheeler, 324 U.S. 542, 65 S.Ct. 799, 89 L.Ed. 1166 (1945), reh'g denied 325 U.S. 892, 65 S.Ct. 1182, 89 L.Ed. 2004.

**7.** It might be noted that the same results of postponing gain or loss on the various types of nonrecognition transactions could have been accomplished by providing in the Code that no gain is *realized* on them. Accounting for the deferral could

still be accomplished by appropriate basis correction. This would have had the advantage of keeping the overall structure simpler.

It should also be noted that the Code is not consistent in its use of the term "recognition". Although the provisions discussed in this section involve postponing gain or loss, some corporate tax provisions which are phrased in terms of "non-recognition" in fact allow permanent exemption from taxation. See § 1032.

**8.** Take a look at § 351.

**9.** If you have some interest in this, you might take a gander at §§ 368, 354, 356, 362, 358, D. Posin, *Corporate Tax Planning: Takeovers Leveraged Buyouts and Restructurings* Chapters 7–9 (1990).

Corporate taxation builds on the structure of individual income taxation that we have been discussing here. When there is a corporate transaction, it runs the gauntlet of the steps in this Chapter regarding whether there is a realizing event and calculating the gain or loss realized. When we get to the question of whether the gain or loss realized is recognized, we consider various corporate nonrecognition provisions at this nonrecognition step. So keep that relationship in mind and it should help in the advanced classes.

### (2) Tax–Free Exchanges of Business or Investment Property of "Like Kind"

#### (a) Overview

The granddad of all tax-free exchanges is exchanges of business or investment property of like kind, as provided in § 1031. The basic operation of § 1031 is fairly straightforward. If a taxpayer who holds property used in business[10] or for investment[11] exchanges that property for property of like kind, no gain or loss will be recognized to the taxpayer on the transaction. This will be so, notwithstanding that the taxpayer may have a substantial realized gain (or loss) on the transaction (as measured of course by the difference between the fair market value of the property he receives and the adjusted basis of the property he gives up).[12]

One can get a definitional problems up front. One question is whether a transaction is an "exchange" at all, as exemplified by the case of *Bloomington Coca–Cola Bottling Co. v. Commissioner.*[13] Section 1031 requires an "exchange" of property; a "sale" will not qualify. *Bloomington* held that if the taxpayer receives both like kind property and a small amount of money for his property, he will still be regarded as having engaged in an "exchange" of his property and thus qualify for treatment under § 1031. *Bloomington* recognized that "Border-line cases arise where money forms a substantial part" of the consideration, the implication being that if money is a substantial part, then perhaps an "exchange" has not occurred and that the transaction is instead a sale. In the event the transaction is a "sale," the nonrecognition of § 1031 would not apply.

Another question can be whether property involved in an exchange is of "like kind." This question is discussed in detail at ¶ 4.05(2)(c). The case of *Commissioner v. Crichton*[14] provides an example of the kind of

---

**10.** I.e., in a business for which expenses are deductible under § 162, see ¶ 6.02(1).

**11.** I.e., in an activity for which expenses are deductible under § 212, see ¶ 6.02(2).

**12.** Excluded from this non-recognition treatment are inventory; stocks, bonds or notes; other securities or evidences of indebtedness or interest; interests in a partnership; and certain other intangible prop-

erty, § 1031(a)(2). The exclusion of stocks and securities from non-recognition treatment under § 1031 can be regarded as the basis for the entire field of corporate reorganizations, which, as mentioned above, provides its own complex nonrecognition rules in this area. This non-recognition is mandatory, if the requirements are met.

**13.** 189 F.2d 14 (7th Cir.1951).

**14.** 122 F.2d 181 (5th Cir.1941).

problems that can be encountered. In *Crichton*, the taxpayer and her children owned, in undivided interests, a tract of unimproved country land and an improved city lot. Taxpayer effected an exchange of interests with her children. The children transferred to taxpayer their undivided interest in the city lot, worth $15,357.77. Taxpayer transferred in exchange, of equal value, an undivided ¾₂ interest in the oil, gas and other minerals in the country land. Taxpayer's basis in the mineral interest was zero, so she was looking at $15,357.77 of taxable gain. Thus she argued that the transaction fit within § 1031. Under local Louisiana law, mineral rights are interests in real and not personal property. As discussed at ¶ 4.05(2)(c), the regulations broadly hold that all real estate is "like kind." As a result, the Fifth Circuit affirmed the lower court and found that the transaction qualified as an exchange of like kind property and therefore the gain was not taxed.

Once the transaction qualifies for § 1031, the realized gain on the transaction is not recognized. Although this realized gain is not recognized at the time of the transaction, the gain is not permanently exempted from tax. Rather, the basis rules insure that the gain (or loss) will be accounted for on subsequent disposition of the new property. This is done by substituting the basis of the old property onto the new property.[15]

For example, suppose Ferdinand exchanges an office building with a fair market value of $200,000 and an adjusted basis of $120,000 for an apartment building, also with a fair market value of $200,000.[16] An apartment building is considered "like kind" to an office building for purposes of the statute, see discussion below. On the transaction Ferdinand realizes $80,000 of gain. Note that the gain is realized in that this exchange is a realizing event, as discussed at ¶ 4.02. However, because we come within the nonrecognition rule of § 1031, no gain is recognized.[17] The basis of the apartment building received is the same as that of the office building exchanged, or $120,000. Thus the unrecognized gain on the office building is preserved on the apartment building. When the apartment building is subsequently sold, the $80,000 gain will be recognized at that time. The graphic "§ 1031: A Simple Exchange" illustrates this transaction.

---

**15.** Another thing that happens is that the holding period of the property exchanged is added on to the holding period of the property received, § 1223(1).

**16.** The property received would of course have to have the same fair market value as the property exchanged or the par-

ties would not do the deal. Where the properties involved in the transaction do not have the same fair market value, money can be used to even up the deal. The treatment of that is discussed below.

**17.** § 1031(a).

**§ 1031: A Simple Exchange**

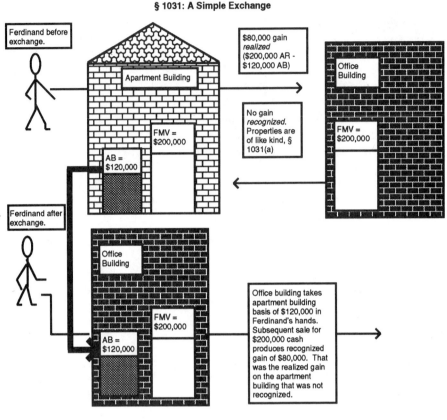

When two parties wish to exchange property, it is in fact unlikely that their two properties will have exactly the same value. Hence it is common that some cash is used to even up the transaction. The cash is often termed "boot" in the lexicon of tax professionals (as in "I'll give you my property plus cash 'to boot.' ").

Recall that the theory of § 1031 exchanges is that the taxpayer receiving like kind property has not changed his investment sufficiently to warrant paying a tax. However, where some cash is received, that theory does not hold up. The taxpayer has "cashed out" in part. Hence when some cash is received, that will trigger recognition of realized gain to the extent of the cash.[18]

Thus in our example, suppose Ferdinand exchanges his office building with a fair market value of $200,000 for an apartment building worth $180,000, and $20,000 of cash. Ferdinand will still have a realized gain of $80,000. He will recognize that realized gain to the extent of the cash, or $20,000. This will leave him with $60,000 of unrecognized gain.

**18.**   § 1031(b).

The basis in the apartment building received will preserve that unrecognized gain. To do that, the basis will be $120,000. The graphic "§ 1031: An Exchange With Cash" illustrates this transaction.

**§ 1031: An Exchange with Cash**

Ferdinand before exchange.

Apartment Building

$80,000 gain *realized* ($200,000 AR - $120,000 AB).

$20,000 gain *recognized.* Realized gain is recognized to extent of cash, §1031(b).

FMV = $200,000

AB = $120,000

Office Building

FMV = $180,000

Ferdinand after exchange.

Office Building

FMV = $180,000

AB = $120,000

Cash = $20,000

Office building takes apartment building basis of $120,000 in Ferdinand's hands. Subsequent sale for $180,000 cash produces recognized gain of $60,000. That was the realized gain on the apartment building that was not recognized.

[355a]

Note that even if the subsequent sale of the office building is not for $180,000 but for some other number, the gain preservation rules still work. That is, Ferdinand is always $60,000 under water. His gain will always be $60,000 more than it would be if his basis were $180,000. Or any subsequent loss will always be $60,000 less than it would be if his basis were $180,000. Thus for example if Ferdinand sells the office building three years later for $340,000, his gain will be $340,000 − $120,000 or $220,000. If his basis had been the fair market value of the apartment building at the time it was acquired of $180,000, then his gain on sale at $340,000 would be $160,000. Thus he is still hit with the extra $60,000 gain that he did not recognize on the earlier transaction.

The preceding example required a relatively small amount of cash to even up the transaction. But the relative values of the buildings being exchanged might require a large amount of cash to even up the transaction. In particular the cash might be for more than the realized gain. How does that play out?

To vary our example once again, suppose that Ferdinand exchanges his apartment building with a basis of $120,000 and a fair market value of $200,000 for an office building worth $110,000, and $90,000 of cash. Ferdinand still has a realized gain of $80,000. He recognizes that realized gain to the extent of the cash, or $80,000. Note: don't fall into the trap of thinking that he recognizes $90,000 of gain—i.e., the amount of the cash.

It's fundamental that you cannot recognize more gain than you realize. The realized gain is Ferdinand's true economic gain on the disposition of his apartment building. His entire realized gain is $80,000. That is all he will recognize.

What will be his basis then in the office building he receives? Observe that since Ferdinand has recognized all of his realized gain, the basis rule should not lock in any gain. The basis of the office building received should therefore be its fair market value of $110,000. This is the result the statute gives. In effect, what the statute does is give the office building the basis of the apartment building, reduced by the $10,000 that the cash received exceeds realized gain.[19] However, you can just view the matter as saying that since all the realized gain was recognized, the basis of the property received should be its fair market value. The graphic "§ 1031: An Exchange With Lots of Cash" illustrates this transaction.

**19.** § 1031(d). For more discussion of the mechanics of the basis rule, see below.

§ 1031: An Exchange with Lots of Cash

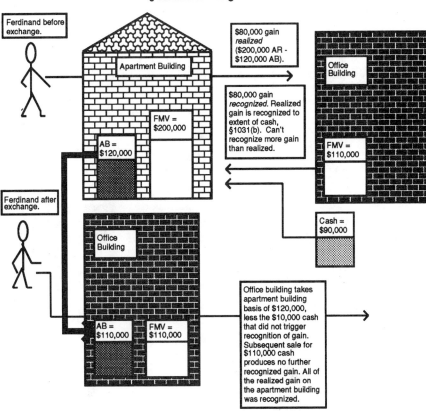

Ferdinand before exchange.

Apartment Building

FMV = $200,000

AB = $120,000

$80,000 gain *realized* ($200,000 AR - $120,000 AB).

$80,000 gain *recognized*. Realized gain is recognized to extent of cash, §1031(b). Can't recognize more gain than realized.

Office Building

FMV = $110,000

Cash = $90,000

Ferdinand after exchange.

Office Building

AB = $110,000

FMV = $110,000

Office building takes apartment building basis of $120,000, less the $10,000 cash that did not trigger recognition of gain. Subsequent sale for $110,000 cash produces no further recognized gain. All of the realized gain on the apartment building was recognized.

[356a]

Be clear with regard to these transactions involving cash: *receiving boot* triggers recognition of gain. *Giving boot* does not. The taxpayer giving boot simply adds the fair market value of the boot to the basis of the property he is receiving.[20]

It can also happen that Ferdinand would receive not only like kind property but also other property, which is not like kind. Thus in the exchange of the apartment building for the office building, Ferdinand could receive not only the office building but also a pickup truck. In that event, the pickup truck, not being like kind to the office building exchanged, is considered to be boot (or "other property" in the lexicon of the statute). As far as recognition of gain is concerned then, the pickup

**20.** §§ 1031(a) and (b), W.H. Hartman Co., 20 B.T.A., 302, 1930 WL 266 (1930) (acq.) (no gain recognized on exchanging old printing press plus money for a new printing press). This result, of course, makes sense inasmuch as the taxpayer, far from cashing out, has increased the amount of his investment in the like-kind property. This would also have the effect of increas-

ing his basis in the property received. In this circumstance, of course, gain may be recognized to the other party in the transaction, as the recipient of "boot", see Allegheny County Auto Mart, Inc., 12 T.C.M. 427 (1953), aff'd 208 F.2d 693 (3d Cir.1953) *dicta* that a taxpayer who gives boot might be able to recognize a loss on a § 1031 exchange.

truck triggers recognition of realized gain to the extent of the fair market value of the pickup truck. As far as basis is concerned, the pickup truck gets a basis of its fair market value. That is to say the basis of "other property" or "recognition property" is always its fair market value. The basis of the nonrecognition property received locks in the unrecognized gain (if any). All this is illustrated in the graphic: § 1031: An Exchange With "Other Property."

**§ 1031: An Exchange with Other Property**

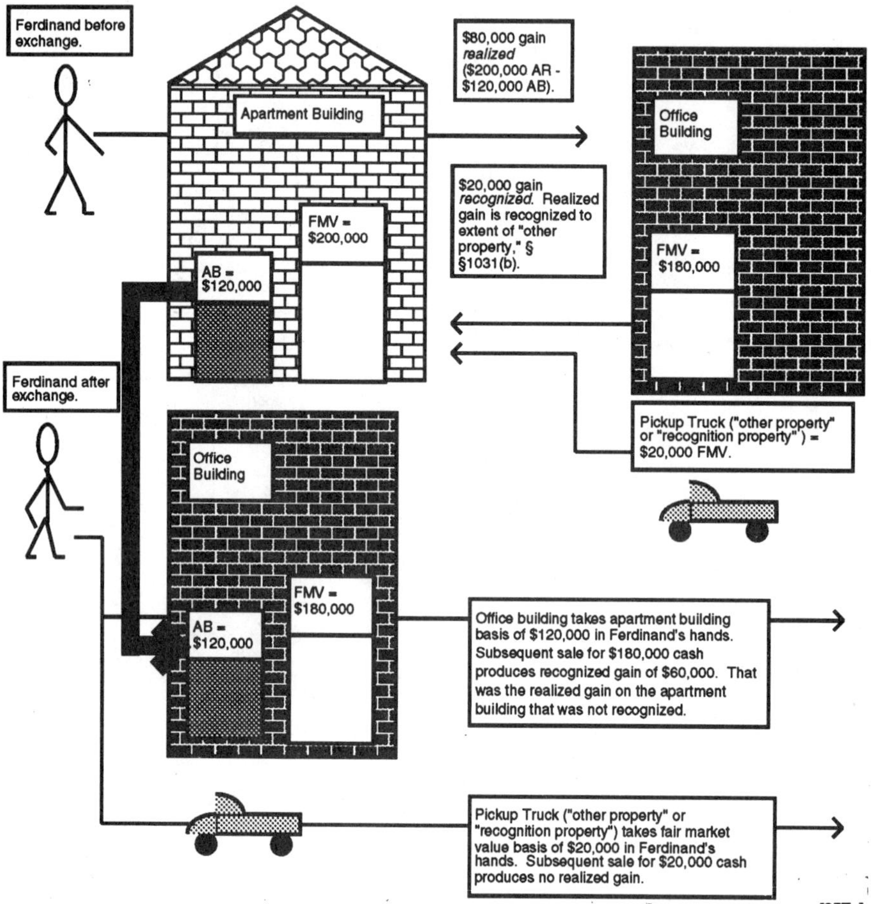

[357a]

Another possibility is that Ferdinand enters the transaction with a loss on his apartment building. Say, for example, that Ferdinand's basis in his apartment building is $200,000 and the fair market value of the apartment building is $150,000. Ferdinand exchanges the apartment building for an office building with a fair market value of $120,000 plus $30,000 cash. Ferdinand's realized loss is $50,000. But under § 1031, Ferdinand's loss is not recognized.[21] The basis rule preserves the realized loss on the apartment building; thus the basis of the office building is

---

**21.**   § 1031(c).

$170,000.[22]

*Mechanics of the Basis Rule:* The preceding analysis has shown how the basis rule in a § 1031 transaction works to lock in any realized gain that was not recognized. A further word needs to be said about how the basis rule accomplishes this task. There were two ways the statute could have been drafted to preserve the right amount of gain on the property received in a § 1031 transaction: 1) The easy way to understand; and 2) the virtually impossible way to understand. Naturally, the statute chose the second way.

The easy way to understand would have been for the statute to simply say, in English, that the basis of the nonrecognition property received will be equal to the fair market value of the nonrecognition property received less any unrecognized gain on the property exchanged.[23] As is apparent from the above analysis, this is what we are doing. And, as a matter of fact, I would even suggest that you could just do that and you would always get the right answer.

However, you should be aware that the statute does not actually do it that way, although it gets to the same result. Instead, the basis rule, as provided in § 1031(d), provides that as to the property received, "the basis shall be the same as that of the property exchanged, decreased in the amount of any money received by the taxpayer and increased in the amount of gain ... that was recognized on the exchange."[24]

Now you may ask, "What on earth is all this down and up stuff!" Well, as the saying goes, it's just so crazy it works. I will now explain why this rule is the way it is and why it works. You actually need not read this explanation. I would suggest that those interested in going on in the field of taxation should read it, however. A number of corporate and partnership tax basis rules work on this approach of going down and up. It is therefore useful for you to be familiar with it.

Those of you bailing out of this field after this course could easily skip the ensuing discussion, although you might find it interesting. You know how to get the right basis on a tax free-exchange. You don't need to know the complicated way the statute gets the same answer you can get (and it is always the same answer).

### Advanced Explanation of Mechanics of Basis Rule:
### May Be Omitted by Students Not Going on in the Field

Okay, to explain the down and up rule for those few of us still reading here: First we will explain how it works and then we will

---

**22.** § 1031(d).

**23.** If the property exchanged is loss property, then the rule would be that the basis of the property received is the fair market value of the property received increased by the amount of any unrecognized loss.

**24.** The portion of the statute I omitted in this quote states that the basis shall

go down by the amount of any loss to the taxpayer that was recognized. As we have discussed above, taxpayers do not recognize any loss on § 1031 transactions. However, § 1031(d) is also serving as the basis rule for several other nonrecognition provisions (§§ 1035, 1036, and 1037) which do recognize losses.

explain why it works. Finally, we explain the mechanics when "other property," i.e., recognition property such as the truck, is received.

### How it works

Take our first example of a simple exchange (refer to the first § 1031 graphic). According to the literal terms of § 1031(d) the basis in the office building received is the basis of the apartment building exchanged ($120,000), down by money received ($0), so we're still at $120,000 and up by gain recognized ($0), so we're still at $120,000. Thus the basis in the office building received is $120,-000, which is the correct answer. The $120,000 basis preserves the $80,000 unrecognized gain on the $200,000 apartment building. It was a strange way to get the right answer but it did work.

Take our second example of an exchange with cash (the second § 1031 graphic). According to the literal terms of § 1031(d) the basis of the office building received is the basis of the apartment building exchanged ($120,000) down by money received ($20,000), taking us down to $100,000, and up by gain recognized ($20,000), taking us back up to $120,000. Thus the basis in the apartment building received is $120,000, which is the correct answer. The $120,000 basis preserves the $60,000 unrecognized gain on the $180,000 office building. It's weird, but it's working.

Take our third example of an exchange with lots of cash. Once again according to the literal terms of the statute, the basis of the office building received is the basis of the apartment building exchanged ($120,000) down by money received ($90,000), taking us to $30,000 and up by gain recognized ($80,000), taking us back up to $110,000. This turns out to be the right answer again. The $110,000 basis is the same as the fair market value of the office building received. No gain or loss is preserved on the office building, nor should there be. All the $80,000 realized gain was recognized on the exchange. Once again, the strange basis rule worked.

### Why it works

Here is why the rule works: We start with the basis in the property exchanged. We go down by money received. What we are really doing is moving some of our basis onto the money. This is the case because money must always take a basis of its face value. (You can't have a basis of 90 cents in a dollar and then have a gain of 10 cents when you spend it). That explains why we go down by money received. We go up by gain recognized, because we always increase basis of property when we recognize gain with respect to it, so that we won't recognize the same gain again. If we pay a tax with respect to property, we're entitled to raise our basis on it.[25]

---

**25.** Recall for example the discussion of the *Woodsam* case, ¶ 4.03(2)(b)(iii) above, where the taxpayer argued that nonre- course financing should be a taxable event with a concomitant increase in basis.

Treatment of "other property"

Where "other" (i.e., recognition) property is in the deal, we in effect treat it like money, explained above. We take enough basis from the property exchanged and apply it to equal the fair market value of the recognition property. That then becomes the basis of the recognition property. In other words, the basis of recognition property (such as the truck in our example above) is always its fair market value. The remaining basis of the property exchanged is then applied to be the basis of the property received, subject to the down and up rules described above.[26]

### (b) Mortgages

Another possible form of a § 1031 exchange is the case where one or both properties is subject to a liability. Where real estate is concerned that is a likely possibility. Where property is transferred subject to a liability in a § 1031 exchange, being relieved of the liability is treated as receiving money. This is the *Crane* rule (I told you to study it). Treating the debt relief as money, you crank out your results from there, using the money rules discussed above. The following example illustrates:

**Example:** A holds for investment Whiteacre, undeveloped land with an adjusted basis of $750 in his hands and a fair market value of $1500. Whiteacre is subject to a nonrecourse liability of $500. A, in a § 1031 transaction, exchanges Whiteacre for Blackacre, owned by B, B taking Whiteacre subject to the mortgage. Blackacre has a fair market value of $1000 and is unencumbered by any liabilities.[27]

A has a gain realized on the transaction of $750. This is arrived at as follows: A's amount realized was $1000 (the fair market value of Blackacre) plus $500 (the debt relief) or $1500. His adjusted basis was $750. Hence, his gain realized is $750. Since A received boot of $500 (the debt relief), $500 of his $750 realized gain is recognized. A's basis in Blackacre is $750 (his original basis of $750 reduced by the $500 boot and increased by the $500 gain recognized). This basis of $750 makes sense. A entered this transaction with a potential gain of $750, of which $500 was recognized. He now has a basis of $750 in Blackacre which has a fair market value of $1000; the $250 unrecognized gain has been preserved.

In the circumstance that both properties in the § 1031 exchange are encumbered with liabilities and cash is also present in the transaction, matters become interesting indeed. Although such a transaction may sound esoteric at first blush, it is not such an unlikely event, particularly in the real estate area where property is often mortgaged. The treatment of such a transaction involves netting the liabilities against each other.

---

**26.** § 1031(d).

**27.** This deal makes economic sense for the parties. The economic value of Blackacre is clearly $1000 and the economic value of Whiteacre, net of liabilities, is $1000.

The party being relieved of the larger liability will have boot to the extent the larger liability exceeds the smaller.

As a policy matter it seems reasonable to treat mortgages in this way. As we have discussed above in connection with the *Woodsam* case, an argument exists that mortgaging property nonrecourse in excess of basis constitutes a realizing event. The argument is even stronger in the § 1031 setting. In the § 1031 setting, being relieved of a mortgage means that the taxpayer has withdrawn funds from the investment, at some earlier date, and now does not have to pay them back. Recognition appears to be appropriate. This analysis would hold even if the debt on the property exchanged were acquisition debt. On the acquisition debt, the taxpayer has had the advantage of borrowing money and now does not have to pay it back. Recognition seems appropriate.

Such is the basic framework of § 1031. A number of difficult definitional problems arise in the practical working out of transactions under § 1031. These problems are discussed in turn.

### (c) The Requirement That the Property Be of "Like Kind"

### (i) Real Property; Jordan Marsh

The Regulations state "the words like-kind have reference to the nature or character of the property and not to its grade or quality. One kind or class of property may not ... be exchanged for property of a different kind or class. The fact that any real estate involved is improved or unimproved is not material, for that fact relates only to the grade or quality of the property and not to its kind or class."[28] Examples of real estate exchanges in which the property was "like kind" include: city real estate for a ranch or farm;[29] exhausted timberland for virgin timberland;[30] a tenant in common interest in three parcels of property for a 100% ownership interest in one of the parcels;[31] a remainder interest in one tract of farm land for a remainder interest in another tract of farm land.[32] Note that real property in the United States and real property located outside the United States are not like kind property.[33]

In most of these examples the real estate received was put to generally the same use as the real estate exchanged. Moreover, the Regulations provide the property must be put to the same use.[34] However the Regulations' example above of an exchange of city real estate for a ranch or farm suggests possibly a broader principle. The matter therefore is somewhat unclear.[35]

**28.** Reg. § 1.1031(a)–1(b).

**29.** Reg. § 1.1031(a)–1(c).

**30.** Rev.Rul. 72–515, 1972–2 C.B. 466; see also Rev.Rul. 76–253, 1976–2 C.B. 51.

**31.** Rev.Rul. 73–476, 1973–2 C.B. 300. Cf. note 13 below.

**32.** Rev.Rul. 78–4, 1978–1 C.B. 256, compare Rev.Rul. 72–601, 1972–2 C.B. 467, holding a transfer of a life estate in one parcel of real estate in return for a remainder interest in another does not qualify as a like-kind exchange. See also Letter Ruling 7943136.

**33.** § 1031(h).

**34.** Reg. § 1.1031(a)–1(c).

**35.** Cf. ¶ 4.05(3) relating to the test of "property similarly or related in service or use" for purposes of nonrecognition of gain on reinvestment of proceeds of involuntary conversions.

An important unresolved area with respect to exchanges of real estate relates to exchanges of real property owned in fee for long term leases of real property. The Regulations provide that an exchange of real estate for a lease of real property with 30 years or more to run is an exchange of like kind.[36] However where the transaction is a sale and leaseback for more than 30 years of the same real property, caselaw is in conflict as to whether the transaction will be accorded nonrecognition.

This problem has arisen in particular where the taxpayer has a substantial unrealized loss on his business property and engages in a sale and leaseback for a long term of the property in order to gain a tax advantage by realizing the loss on the sale while in fact retaining possession of the property for his business. Where the leaseback has been for longer than 30 years, the Service has sought to impose § 1031 treatment on the transaction, thereby disallowing any loss.[37] The courts have split on whether the loss will be allowed.[38] The well-advised taxpayer seeking to realize a loss on his business property will, of course, effect the transaction with a leaseback for less than 30 years.[39] The fact that the leaseback for less than 30 years is with a related party (who might be expected to renew the lease) will not necessarily bar the loss.[40]

A leading case in this area is *Jordan Marsh.*

---

**36.** Reg. § 1.1031(a)–1(c).

**37.** § 1031(c).

**38.** Century Electric Co. v. Commissioner, 192 F.2d 155 (8th Cir.1951), cert. denied 342 U.S. 954, 72 S.Ct. 625, 96 L.Ed. 708 (1952) (applying § 1031 and disallowing the loss on a sale and 95 year leaseback); allowing the loss are Leslie Co., 64 T.C. 247 (1975) (nonacq.), aff'd 539 F.2d 943 (3d Cir.1976) (leasehold had no capital or premium value; hence the transaction was a sale and not an § 1031 exchange, discussed in the text below). City Investing Co. & Subsidiaries, 38 T.C. 1 (1962) (nonacq.) (sale and leaseback a bona fide sale; hence § 1031 not applicable). The Service announced in 1960 it would not follow *Jordan Marsh*, Rev.Rul. 60–43, 1960–1 C.B. 687 and its nonacquiescences in the more recent *Leslie* and *City Investing* indicate its opposition to these loss cases remains undiminished. See also Crowley, Milner & Co.,

76 T.C. 1030 (1981) aff'd 689 F.2d 635 (6th Cir.1982) (loss allowed on sale leaseback).

**39.** Reg. § 1.1031(a)–1(c). See also Standard Envelope Manufacturing Co., 15 T.C. 41 (1950) (loss on sale and leaseback for 24 years allowed as a bona fide sale. Transaction not attacked as being an § 1031 exchange).

**40.** This pattern was allowed in Capri, Inc., 65 T.C. 162 (1975) (10–year leaseback to related party not considered automatically renewable and hence not equivalent to 30 year leaseback).

There are a number of types of exchange transactions in the oil, gas and other mineral rights area, see e.g., Commissioner v. P.G. Lake, 356 U.S. 260, 78 S.Ct. 691, 2 L.Ed.2d 743 (1958), reh'g denied 356 U.S. 964, 78 S.Ct. 991, 2 L.Ed.2d 1071 (1958), holding that an exchange of an oil payment for an interest in realty does not involve like-kind property. For the assignment of income aspects of *P.G. Lake,* see ¶ 5.04(1).

## JORDAN MARSH CO. v. COMMISSIONER[41]

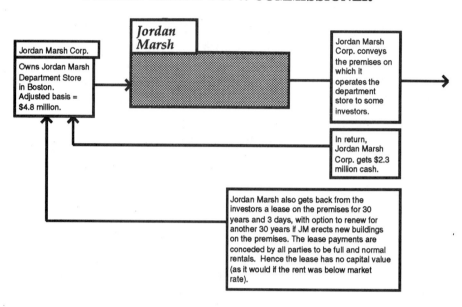

**Jordan Marsh Corp.**

Owns Jordan Marsh Department Store in Boston. Adjusted basis = $4.8 million.

**Jordan Marsh**

Jordan Marsh Corp. conveys the premises on which it operates the department store to some investors.

In return, Jordan Marsh Corp. gets $2.3 million cash.

Jordan Marsh also gets back from the investors a lease on the premises for 30 years and 3 days, with option to renew for another 30 years if JM erects new buildings on the premises. The lease payments are conceded by all parties to be full and normal rentals. Hence the lease has no capital value (as it would if the rent was below market rate).

[358a]

*Question:* Could Jordan Marsh deduct its $2.5 million loss on the department store?

*Taxpayer's argument:* The transaction was a sale followed by a lease back. Hence the sale generated a deductible $2.5 million loss.

*Service's argument:* The transaction was in substance a like-kind exchange. Under regulations, a fee ownership is like-kind to a lease for more than 30 years.[42] Thus under the rules of § 1031(a), no loss is recognized.

*Comment:* This is the kind of case you come upon in practice. Complicated as the mechanics of calculating gain and basis seem at first blush in § 1031, they are not a problem in practice. The problem is figuring out whether your deal fits into the statute at all.

*Held:* This was a sale and not a like-kind § 1031 exchange. Taxpayer cashed out in full and received full value. Also an "exchange" means a swapping of one piece of property for another, not a swap of a greater interest in a piece of property for a lesser interest. The rentals were full and normal; thus taxpayer received no capital value back in the leasehold. Thus taxpayer received nothing to which § 1031 could apply.

*Comment:* Why the taxpayer got such exquisitely poor advice as to make the leaseback for just over 30 years rather than just under 30 years in which event he could have indisputably gotten his loss without having to litigate to the Second Circuit is a tantalizing question.[43]

---

**41.** 269 F.2d 453 (2d Cir.1959).
**42.** Regs. § 1.1031(a)–1(c).

**43.** Especially in light of the earlier holding in Century Electric v. Commission-

*Comment, time value of money approach:* There was another approach that could have been taken to the case. Time value of money analysis throws a lot of light on this case. The Service could have argued that the transaction was a sham. It would start by saying that the useful life of the building is not beyond the 30 years of the lease, certainly a plausible proposition. That would mean that the residual value of the property 30 years later was limited to the land only. If we use the real estate rule of thumb that the land is one-fifth of the value of improved property, then at the time of this transaction the land was worth ⅕ of $2.3 million, or $460,000. Thus what Jordan Marsh Corporation was giving up by entering into this lease arrangement rather than continuing to own the property was the residual value of the land 30 years from now. So one might frame the question as: what is the present value of $460,000 30 years from now? That happens to be a measly $80,091 (with a 6% discount rate). Compare that to the value of being able to take at the present time a $2.5 million deduction. If we assume Jordan Marsh was in a 40% tax bracket (combined federal and state), the $2.5 million deduction saves Jordan Marsh Corp. $1 million in taxes. This all points to the transaction being a sham constructed by Jordan Marsh to get the deduction.

Economically, it might be further argued that something meaningful happened because Jordan Marsh Corp. is out of pocket the annual rent, and that would have to be factored into the analysis. However, Jordan Marsh received $2.3 million in cash. Jordan Marsh could amortize the rent for 30 years out of this fund. Jordan Marsh could set that fund aside and invest at an after-tax interest rate of, say, 6%. If that were done, the fund could support annual rental payments of $167,092 for 30 years and then be exhausted. That amount of annual rent constitutes 7% of the sales price of the property, which is within the normal range of rent for commercial real estate.[44] Thus the obligation to pay rent did not put Jordan Marsh out of pocket.

Armed with numbers like these, the Service could then have advanced cases like *Knetsch* and *Goldstein* for the proposition that the sale and leaseback were not economically purposive activity, but were motivated solely by tax considerations. See ¶ 6.03(6)(b).

So what does my argument boil down to? Note that the *Jordan Marsh* court said there was a realizing event—a sale—and therefore the loss on the property was realized. The *Jordan Marsh* court also said that the loss should be recognized. The Service agreed that there was a realizing event and thus that the loss on the property was realized. But the Service said that the loss should not be recognized because the transaction came within § 1031. This was because the long-term lease was like-kind to the fee.

---

er, 192 F.2d 155 (8th Cir.1951), cert. denied 342 U.S. 954, 72 S.Ct. 625, 96 L.Ed. 708 (1952) (exchange of fee for 95–year lease with cash was § 1031 exchange).

44. In addition to the rent, the vendees would of course get depreciation deductions on the property. The vendees were presumably not unconscious of the tax benefits.

What I am saying, however, is that there was not a realizing event at all. The transaction was a sham. The shuffling of the papers with the vendee should be ignored. Thus the loss on the property was not realized. Since there was not a realizing event, we don't even get to the question of recognition because we don't recognize a gain or loss unless we realize it.

It will be argued against this position that something did change as a result of shuffling papers with the vendee. At the end of the 30–year lease, the residual value of the property goes to the vendee instead of the taxpayer. But as we have seen above, the residual value of the property was about $80,000 on a present value basis at the time of the transaction. Are we really going to let who owns something worth $80,000 determine whether or not the taxpayer gets a $2.5 million deduction?

This is not sensible. The law, as the great Holmes said, is not an ass. To let who owns an $80,000 item drive whether a $2.5 million deduction is allowed is truly to let the tail wag the dog. That $80,000 residual value is about half one year's rent on the property, as calculated above. Particularly when the taxpayer is structuring the transaction and can throw the residual value wherever it wants, it is absurd to let the ownership of the $80,000 residual value drive the $2.5 million deduction.[45]

Having shown that economically nothing meaningful happened it now finally falls to recharacterize the transaction from a legal standpoint. $2.3 million moved to Jordan Marsh, which then had an obligation to pay it back over 30 years with interest. The residual value of the land moved from Jordan Marsh to the "vendees." Thus what we have here is a mortgage coupled with a sale of the residual value of the land. Two things happened here. Jordan Marsh borrowed money and Jordan Marsh sold a future interest in the land. Neither of these is a realizing event as to the property now. The only realizing event now would be the sale of the residual value of the land. Our analysis above has shown that to have a value of $80,091. What is its basis?

Note that the future value of the property, $80,091 is 3% of the present value, $2.3 million. Thus it seems appropriate to take 3% of the present basis against the amount realized for the future value. Three percent of the basis of $4.8 million is $144,000. Thus we would have a loss on the sale of the future value of $80,091 − $144,000 = $63,909.

**45.** It might also be argued against my position that in addition to throwing the residual value of the land to the vendee, the arrangement also deprived Jordan Marsh of the depreciation deduction, since it was now a lessee instead of the owner. Thus it might be urged that the transaction has more substance than I admit. However, that is also an empty distinction. While the transaction may have purported to deprive Jordan Marsh of the depreciation deduction, it gave to Jordan Marsh a deduction for rent. The annual rent paid by Jordan Marsh, as we have speculated in the text, would have been $167,092. Over the 30 years of the lease, that would have been 30 × $167,092 = $5,012,760. This compares favorably with the total amount of depreciation available on Jordan Marsh's remaining basis in the property of $4.8 million, which included the land and the building.

That is the amount of the loss that would be allowed—slightly less than the $2.5 million deduction that the taxpayer actually got.[46]

Would the court have bought this argument if it had been presented? I do not know. But I think it shows that time value of money analysis can provide a useful perspective on this venerable case.

Another leading case presenting a sale and leaseback was *Leslie Co. v. Commissioner.*[47] On facts similar to *Jordan Marsh,* the Third Circuit held that the leasehold had no capital or premium value. Hence there was no exchange of property on the sale of the property and the leaseback for 30 years. Thus the transaction was a sale and not an § 1031 exchange and taxpayer was able to deduct a loss on the transaction. See *Bloomington Coca–Cola Bottling C.* above.

### (ii) Personal Property

The same principles of the Regulations that govern real property like-kind exchanges govern personal property like-kind exchanges, namely, that the words "like kind" have reference to the nature or character of the property and not to its grade or quality, and moreover that one kind or class of property may not be exchanged tax free for property of a different kind or class.[48]

Thus a used car or truck exchanged for a new car or truck which will be put to the same use involves like-kind property.[49] "Like-kind" property also includes all the business assets of one telephone company exchanged for all the business assets of another telephone company;[50] exchanges of contracts of professional football (and presumably other sports) players;[51] and, it is interesting to note, an exchange of bullion-type, non-circulating gold coins of one country for an exchange of bullion-type, non-circulating gold coins of another country.[52]

**46.** The argument that *Jordan Marsh* can be recharacterized as a mortgage coupled with the sale of a future interest was first presented in the outstanding text M. Chirelstein, *Federal Income Taxation: A Law Student's Guide to the Leading Cases and Concepts* (1997).

**47.** 64 T.C. 247 (1975) (nonacq.), aff'd 539 F.2d 943 (3d Cir.1976).

**48.** Note 8 above.

**49.** National Outdoor Advertising Bureau v. Helvering, 89 F.2d 878 (C.C.A.2 1937) (disallowing a loss on the exchange).

**50.** Rev.Rul. 57–365, 1957–2 C.B. 521, citing Williams v. McGowan, 152 F.2d 570 (2d Cir.1945) ¶ 4.06(3)(b), which suggests that the mass exchange of the assets of any company for the assets of another company in the same line of business would qualify. This transaction was in effect a form of corporate reorganization—an "assets for assets" reorganization; cf. § 368(a)(1)(C), regarding the stock for assets form of reorganization.

**51.** Rev.Rul. 71–137, 1971–1 C.B. 104.

**52.** Rev.Rul. 76–214, 1976–1 C.B. 218 (Mexican 50–peso coins can be exchanged tax free for Austrian 100–corona gold coins, since both are bullion-type rather than numismatic-type coins held for investment); compare Rev.Rul. 79–143, 1979–19 I.R.B. 19 (exchange of collector-type United States gold coins for South African Krugerrands did not involve like-kind property, because value of the U.S. coins was determined by aesthetic considerations, whereas value of the Krugerrands is determined by metal content). Rev.Rul. 82–166, 1982–40 I.R.B. 9 (exchange of gold bullion for silver bullion is not like-kind, reversing earlier private letter ruling 8128102); Rev.Rul. 82–96, 1982–1 C.B. 113 (individual taxpayer who is not a dealer exchanged gold bullion held as an investment for Canadian Maple Leaf gold coins. Held: transaction qualified as

Congress has decreed that livestock of different sexes is not property of like kind, for purposes of § 1031.[53]

My friend, Marty McMahon, has explored this livestock area further; see McMahon, Taxation of Equine Sales and Exchanges, 75 Ky.L.J. 205 (1986).

### (d) The Requirement That the Property Be Held for Productive Use in Trade or Business or for Investment

In addition to being like-kind, property involved in an § 1031 nonrecognition exchange must be held by the taxpayer for productive use in his trade or business or for investment.[54] This test is applied with reference to each party to the transaction. Thus, for example, if property given up and received is held for productive use by one party, § 1031 will apply even though the property is dealer or inventory property to the other party to the transaction.[55] Also, property held for productive use in the trade or business may be exchanged for property held for investment and vice versa.[56] Thus, apparently, land held by the taxpayer for productive use in his trade or business may be exchanged tax free under § 1031 for land held by the taxpayer for investment.[57] Where the taxpayer has a plan to sell or is attempting immediately to sell property given up or received in an exchange, the property is then not held for productive use in a trade or business or for investment and § 1031 will not apply. This will be so even though the taxpayer is not a dealer with respect to the property.[58]

tax-free exchange since Canadian Maple Leaf gold coins, though legal tender, were more valuable for their gold content than face amount, hence were bullion type coins.)

See also Rev.Rul. 74–7, 1974–1 C.B. 198 (taxpayer who was not a currency dealer exchanged U.S. currency for foreign currency while on a trip and then at the conclusion of his trip reconverted his foreign currency back to U.S. currency. Held: a gain on the reconversion would not qualify as a tax-free exchange because the currency is not property held for productive use in a trade or business or for investment, see ¶ 4.05(2)(d)).

**53.** § 1031(e). The legislative history of this provision is as follows: " . . . There appear to have been representations that male calves can be traded for female calves tax free as a like-kind exchange. The importance of this arises from the fact that ordinarily the ratio of males to females in a calf crop is approximately 50–50. Since few males are normally retained in a typical cattle operation, the remaining male calves are castrated and sold as steers at ordinary income rates. If a tax-free trade of male calves for female calves were allowed, a breeding herd of females could be built up more quickly without tax consequences . . ." Senate Report 91–552, Pub.L. 91–172, 1969–3 C.B. 489.

**54.** § 1031(a).

**55.** § 1031(a), Reg. § 1.1031(a)–1(a). The other party in this case would, of course, not qualify for § 1031 treatment.

**56.** Reg. § 1.1031(a)–1(a).

**57.** The land involved would still, of course, have to be of "like kind", which seems to mean the property must be put to the same "use". Query whether the "like kind" test, which seems to require that the property involved be put to the same use, is inconsistent with the "productive use or investment test", which seems to suggest the property exchanged can be put to a different use than the property received.

**58.** Regals Realty Co. v. Commissioner, 127 F.2d 931 (2d Cir.1942). However, unproductive real estate held by one other than a dealer for future use or future realization of the appreciation in value is held for investment and not primarily for sale, Reg. § 1.1031(a)–1(b).

### (e) Three–Cornered Exchanges

At first blush, § 1031 looks like it is of limited significance. This is because it seems to require that two people get together each of whom has property that the other wants and that the two pieces of property are roughly of the same fair market value (although disparities in fair market values can be evened up through the use of "boot," as we have seen above). However, the Service has sanctioned a so-called "three-cornered deal," which has opened up the possibilities for using § 1031 to a far greater scale than had hitherto been sanctioned. In *Revenue Ruling 77–297*[59] the Service approved the following pattern, under § 1031: A enters into a written agreement with B to sell B for $100,000 a ranch (the first ranch). Pursuant to the agreement, B places $10,000 into escrow and agrees to pay at closing an additional $80,000. In addition the agreement provides that B would cooperate with A to effect the exchange should A locate suitable property. A locates another ranch (the second ranch), owned by C. B enters into an agreement with C to purchase the second ranch for $100,000. Pursuant to the agreement B placed $4,000 into escrow, agreed to pay at closing $96,000. C could not look to A for specific performance on the contract, so B was not acting as A's agent in the purchase of the second parcel of property.

At closing B purchased the second ranch as agreed. After that purchase B exchanged the second ranch with A for the first ranch.

The Service ruled that as to A the exchange of ranches qualifies for nonrecognition of gain under § 1031. As to B the transaction does not qualify for nonrecognition, since B did not hold the second ranch for productive use in a trade or business or for investment. But B did not realize gain or loss on the transaction since his amount realized equalled his basis, inasmuch as he only held the property for a short time.

The upshot is that A was able to sell his property to B under a § 1031 transaction when B did not initially own like kind property, but A was able to find and designate like kind property for B to acquire and exchange.

*Starker v. United States*[60] approved a similar pattern. A transferred appreciated real estate to B. B promised in return to locate and purchase parcels of real estate for A within five years and to pay any remaining balance in cash. As to the property that A received within the five year period, the court held § 1031 applied. In short, simultaneous transactions were not required in a § 1031 exchange.

The Tax Reform Act of 1984 substantially cut back on non-simultaneous exchanges, with new § 1031(a)(3). This section allows three-cornered transactions, but requires that the property received in the exchange must be identified within 45 days after the date the taxpayer seeking § 1031 treatment transfers his property. Moreover the taxpayer must also receive the new property either within 180 days after the date

---

**59.** 1977-2 Cum.Bull. 304.        **60.** 602 F.2d 1341 (9th Cir.1979).

he transfers his old property or by the due date of his tax return for the year of the transfer, whichever is earlier. Further rules are provided concerning the manner of identifying the property to be received.

### (3) Tax–Free Involuntary Conversions (Condemnations, Casualties) Where Proceeds Reinvested

#### (a) General Rules

Occasionally it may come to pass that a taxpayer's property may be condemned or otherwise taken against his will, or it may be subject to fire, flood, theft, or other casualty.[61] These involuntary conversions are taxable events.[62] Gain or loss on involuntary conversions is computed under the usual rules, namely that the basis of the property involuntarily converted is offset against any insurance proceeds or other compensation received.[63] Therefore, if the insurance proceeds or other compensation exceeds the taxpayer's basis in the property, the taxpayer will have a gain on the involuntary conversion. This gain, unless some nonrecognition provision applies, will of course be taxable.[64]

Taxing an involuntary conversion could be regarded as a hardship on the taxpayer inasmuch as the taxpayer, by the very nature of involuntary conversions, did not mean to cash in his investment at that particular time and sustain a tax. To alleviate this problem, Congress enacted § 1033, providing generally that if the taxpayer reinvests the proceeds of the "involuntary conversion" (essentially condemnations, threats of condemnations, casualties and thefts), within two years in other property "similar or related in service or use" then, at the election of the taxpayer, no gain will be recognized.[65]

This is, of course, analogous to § 1031 exchanges; in both instances the idea is that to the extent a taxpayer winds up invested in roughly the same kind of property as before the transaction, he will not be taxed. If the taxpayer reinvests some but not all of the proceeds from the involuntary conversion, realized gain will be recognized to the extent

---

**61.** Cf. "... time and chance happeneth to them all." Ecclesiastes 9:11.

**62.** See generally ¶¶ 4.02, and 7.01(5), regarding taxable events and casualties respectively.

**63.** ¶¶ 4.02 and 4.03, and see Rev.Rul. 73–408, 1973–2 C.B. 15.

**64.** § 1001(c).

**65.** § 1033(a)(2)(A). § 1033 does not apply to losses, and losses sustained on an involuntary conversion will be recognized. If the property is converted directly into other property similar or related in service or use (not a likely event), the nonrecognition of gain is mandatory, § 1033(a)(1). If instead of purchasing the replacement property outright the taxpayer purchases at least an 80% interest in a corporation owning such similar property, then the election to enjoy nonrecognition may still be made, §§ 1033(a)(2)(A) and (D).

Examples of property held to be "similar or related in service or use": Rev.Rul. 59–8, 1959–1 C.B. 202 (standing crop of grain replaced another standing or harvested crop of grain); Compare Maloof, 65 T.C. 263 (1975) (inventory replaced by depreciable property not qualify); Rev.Rul. 76–319, 1976–2 C.B. 242 (bowling alley burned down and replaced by billiard center not qualify). For more detailed treatment of involuntary conversions in the real estate area, see ¶ 4.05(3)(b).

If the taxpayer does not evince an "intent" to come within the rule, he will not enjoy nonrecognition, even though the replacement property is purchased within the requisite time, Feinberg v. Commissioner, 377 F.2d 21 (8th Cir.1967) (unimproved property for unimproved property not qualify for lack of intent).

that the amount realized on the conversion exceeds the cost of the new property.[66] (This too is closely analogous to the approach under § 1031). To the extent that the taxpayer does not reinvest the proceeds of the involuntary conversion, he has cashed out his investment and is therefore properly taxed *pro tanto* on his realized gain.[67] Appropriate basis rules are provided to insure that the deferred gain will ultimately be recognized on the disposition of the new property.[68]

§ 1033 only applies to defer recognition of gain on an involuntary conversion and reinvestment.[69] Losses are always recognized even though the proceeds received may be fully invested in new property.[70] It might be supposed that this is an attractive result to the taxpayer, namely that losses are always recognized immediately, whereas gains may be deferred. However, this is a mixed blessing. If a loss were not recognized on a § 1033 transaction, then the basis of the new property would inevitably be higher.[71] This would, in the case of depreciable property, lead to higher depreciation deductions against ordinary income.[72] Immediate recognition of the loss on a § 1033 pattern can, however, lead to the loss being treated as an unfavorable long term capital loss, under § 1231.[73]

The foregoing has set forth the general rules of § 1033. Particular problems have arisen in connection with involuntary conversions, especially condemnations, of real property. That topic is taken up next.

### (b) Involuntary Conversions of Real Estate

The bulk of the problems and litigation in the § 1033 field have come in the area of involuntary conversions of real property. Where real

---

**66.** § 1033(a)(2)(A). Thus for example suppose T has a building with an adjusted basis of $50,000 and a fair market value of $100,000 which is completely destroyed by fire. T receives $80,000 of insurance proceeds, $60,000 of which he uses to purchase a building similar or related in service or use to the destroyed building. T has a *realized* gain of $30,000 ($80,000 insurance proceeds amount realized minus $50,000 adjusted basis). Since T's amount realized exceeds the purchase price of the new building by $20,000, $20,000 is the amount of gain recognized. If the facts had been the same as above except that T's basis in the building was $70,000 rather than $50,000, then T would have a gain realized of $10,000. T's recognized gain would then be $10,000, since recognized gain cannot exceed realized gain.

**67.** The unreinvested proceeds here play the role of "boot." See discussion at ¶ 4.05(2)(a).

**68.** In the usual case where the taxpayer receives money on the involuntary conversion and uses it to purchase replacement property, the basis of the replacement prop-

erty is the cost of the replacement property decreased in the amount (if any) of the realized gain not recognized, § 1033(b). This is a "backward" version of the § 1031(d) rule. Indeed all substituted basis rules could be drafted in this way, which would have the advantage of making it more clear that the purpose of the substituted basis rules is to preserve unrecognized gain. Cf. §§ 358, 722. If more than one piece of property is purchased as replacement, the overall basis is allocated among them in proportion to their costs, § 1033(b).

The holding period of the replacement property includes the holding period of the converted property, § 1223(1)(A). This is for purposes of ascertaining long term capital gains.

**69.** § 1033(a), Reg. § 1.1033(a)–1(a).

**70.** Id.

**71.** See discussion at note 62.

**72.** See ¶ 4.06(3)(a)(vii).

**73.** See ¶ 4.06(3)(a)(iv) for discussion of § 1231.

property was involuntarily converted—condemned by the state or destroyed by a casualty—and the taxpayer reinvested the condemnation or insurance proceeds in other real property, the question would arise whether the replacement property was "similar or related in service or use" to the property converted in order for the transaction to qualify for nonrecognition under § 1033. The Service early on took a very strict view of what constituted property "similar or related in service or use" for these purposes. In essence, the Service took a "functional" approach, that the physical characteristics and the end use of the converted and replacement property by the taxpayer had to be similar, and some early court decisions supported that view. Thus it was held that the test is not met if unimproved real estate is converted into improved real estate, a barge is substituted for a tug, property used in a trade or business is substituted for rental property, city real estate is replaced by a farm or ranch.[74]

Dissatisfied with this restrictive view, Congress in 1958 prospectively made the "like-kind" standard of § 1031[75] applicable to § 1033 condemnations of real estate held for productive use in a trade or business or for investment.[76] This was regarded as a liberalization, since the "like-kind" standard of § 1031 had clearly allowed a wider range of transactions (including some of those enumerated above) to pass muster tax free.[77]

In the meantime, a number of cases concerning condemnations of real estate began to find their way into the circuit courts. Since these cases involved taxable years prior to 1958, the applicable standard for nonrecognition was still that the replacement property be "similar or related in service or use" to the property condemned. The Service's restrictive "functional" interpretation of this standard, discussed above, uniformly took a beating in the circuit courts in these cases. Rather, with some variations, the circuit courts held that the standard "similar or related in service or use" related to the similarity in the services or uses which the original and replacement properties bore to the taxpayer-owner. This was particularly relevant to the case where the taxpayer was a lessor and his rental property was condemned. Reinvestment of the condemnation proceeds in a different kind of rental property (such as a

---

**74.** Reg. § 1.1033(a)–2(c)(9); S.Rept. No. 1983, 85th Cong., 2d Sess. 1958–3 C.B. 993. See also McCaffrey, 31 T.C. 505 (1958), aff'd 275 F.2d 27 (3d Cir.1960), cert. denied 363 U.S. 828, 80 S.Ct. 1598, 4 L.Ed.2d 1523 (1960) (rental parking lot replaced by rental warehouse space did not meet the test).

**75.** See ¶ 4.05(2)(c).

**76.** § 1033(g) S.Rept. No. 1983, note 69 above, at 993. The "similar or related in service or use" test remains applicable to involuntary conversions of real estate not involving condemnations or the threat or imminence thereof, such as casualties and thefts. Reg. § 1.1033(f)–1(a) cross refer-

ences to § 1031 for principles in determining what is like-kind property. To the same effect is Rev.Rul. 67–255, 1967–2 C.B. 270. The like-kind standard only applies to realty which is held for productive use in a trade or business or for investment—not to realty which is inventory or for personal use, § 1033(g)(1). The reinvestment period under this rule is 3 years, § 1033(g)(4).

In a bow to the recent concern for environmental quality, Congress has decreed that condemnation of billboards and their replacement with real property may come within this like-kind rule, § 1033(g)(3).

**77.** See ¶ 4.05(2)(c).

rental office building to replace a rental apartment building) was held by the circuit courts to meet the "similar or related in service or use" standard since the new piece of property bore the same general relationship to the taxpayer as did the original property, in terms of demands made on the taxpayer by the property and the use he made of the property.[78]

Therefore the Service, always able to perceive when it is licked, threw in the towel in a revenue ruling and conceded that insofar as rental property was concerned the "similar or related in service or use" test related to the relationship the old and new property bear to the taxpayer-owner, rather than to the tenant-user.[79] Thus, to take an example from the ruling, where the taxpayer is a lessor of property used for a light manufacturing plant and the property is involuntarily converted, the reinvestment by the taxpayer of the proceeds of the conversion in a wholesale grocery warehouse which he rents out could meet the test, if the taxpayer maintained the same general lessor relationship with the property. However, where the taxpayer is a lessor as to the converted property but an owner-operator as to the replacement property, the test is not met even though the two properties are otherwise of the same kind or class.[80]

Thus in sum, the Service's restrictive view of what constituted "similar or related in service or use" for § 1033 purposes provoked both a legislative and judicial response. The legislative response was the more liberal "like kind" standard for condemnations of real estate; the judicial response was the more liberal interpretation of "similar or related in service or use" for rental property.

These two possibilities remain at the present time. The "similar or related in service or use test" applies to all involuntary conversions; the "like kind" test applies to condemnations of real property. Therefore, where real property is condemned and the taxpayer reinvests the proceeds, the transaction can be tested under either standard. Moreover

---

**78.** Liant Record, Inc. v. Commissioner, 303 F.2d 326 (2d Cir.1962), on remand 22 T.C.M. 203 (1963) (replacement of office building with three apartment buildings met test); Loco Realty Co. v. Commissioner, 306 F.2d 207 (8th Cir.1962) (replacement of light manufacturing building by warehouse and office space met the test); Pohn v. Commissioner, 309 F.2d 427 (7th Cir.1962). See also Davis v. United States, 589 F.2d 446 (9th Cir.1979).

**79.** Rev.Rul. 64–237, 1964–2 C.B. 319.

**80.** Rev.Rul. 70–399, 1970–2 C.B. 164 (rental resort hotel destroyed by fire and replaced by resort hotel which taxpayer operated himself did not meet the test. As the text discussion indicates, had this property been condemned rather than destroyed by

fire, the "like-kind" test would have applied and probably have been met).

See also Rev.Rul. 70–466, 1970–2 C.B. 165 (investment of proceeds of condemned residential housing in personal-use housing did not meet the "similar or related in service or use" test); Rev.Rul. 79–261, 1979–35 I.R.B. 13 (reinvestment of insurance proceeds from destruction of a rental office building in a new office building partly rented to tenants and partly owner-occupied met the test to the extent of the portion of the building rented to tenants); Rev. Rul. 70–144, 1970–1 C.B. 170 (lessee of a condemned building who uses his share of the proceeds to purchase property similar or related in service or use to the leased premises can qualify for non-recognition of gain).

where the converted and replacement property are rental real estate, the "similar or related in service or use" test is particularly liberal.

As an example of these possibilities consider a taxpayer whose 5000 acres of unimproved rental farmland were condemned. Taxpayer invested the proceeds of the condemnation in constructing a commercial rental building on other land he owned. The taxpayer was not responsible for maintenance of the rental farmland but was responsible for maintenance of the commercial building. Hence the transaction does not qualify under the "similar or related in service or use" test for rental property, since the services the taxpayer rendered the two pieces of property were different.[81] Moreover, the transaction does not qualify under the "like kind" test, because the leased commercial building is not "like kind" to the leased unimproved farmland.[82]

### *(4) Tax–Free Sales of Residence Where Proceeds Reinvested*

#### *(a) The Basic Rules*

Under § 1034, where the proceeds of the sale of the taxpayer's principal residence are reinvested within two years in another principal residence, then some or all of the taxpayer's gain will not be recognized.[83] § 1034 is not elective, but generally the taxpayer will want to avoid recognition of gain on the sale of his old residence and the purchase of a new residence. Since, as we have discussed, personal residences may not be depreciated, the usual reason for wishing to avoid nonrecognition—namely step-up of basis for purposes of later taking higher depreciation deductions—is not present in the § 1034 situation.

When § 1034 is employed on a house sale and purchase, the basis of the new house preserves the realized but unrecognized gain on the old house. This is done through § 1034(e) which just provides directly that the basis of the new residence is the cost decreased by any gain not recognized on the old residence. This is a much more straightforward way to achieve the result than the looney down and up rule of § 1031, discussed above.

---

**81.** Rev.Rul. 76–391, 1976–2 C.B. 243.

**82.** Id. See also Rev.Rul. 76–84, 1976–1 C.B. 219 (transaction flunked both tests because replacement property was used for personal use).

**83.** "Principal Residence" includes the land on which the residence sits for purposes of sales and purchases so long as that land is not used for any commercial purpose, Rev.Rul. 56–420, 1956–2 C.B. 519. Where taxpayer sells the land on which his personal residence sits, buys new land and moves his old house onto the new land, the transaction will come within § 1034. The cost of the new residence in this case would include the cost of the new land, the cost of moving the house, and the cost of the nec-essary construction work and other improvements made to the house during the rollover period, Rev.Rul. 54–156, 1954–1 C.B. 112. Temporarily renting out the old or new residence will not necessarily bar the use of § 1034, Reg. § 1.1034–1(c)(3); Clapham, 63 T.C. 505 (1975).

An exchange by the taxpayer directly of his old residence for a new residence will be treated as a sale of the old residence and repurchase of the new residence for purposes of § 1034, see § 1034(c). This exchange could not come within § 1031 because the residences are not property held for productive use in a trade or business or for investment, see ¶ 4.05(2)(d).

The non-recognition benefits of § 1034 may be combined with the exclusion of $125,000 of gain on sales of residences by individuals aged 55 or older, under § 121. To the extent such a taxpayer realizes more than the $125,000 of gain excludible by § 121, the balance of the gain can be deferred under § 1034. See ¶ 4.04(5). Alternatively, the taxpayer may mitigate the sting of taxation on the sale of his personal residence by spreading out the gain under § 453, where he takes back a purchase money mortgage on the sale of the property. See ¶ 8.03. Should the buyer in such a transaction default on the mortgage payments and the taxpayer reacquire the property as a consequence, the taxpayer may be able to avoid taxation on the reacquisition under § 1038. See also § 1038(e) for special rules on reacquisition of principal residences sold under §§ 121 or 1034.

§ 1034 requires that, for its benefits to be enjoyed, the new residence must be purchased within a period beginning two years before the sale of the old residence and ending two years after the sale of the old residence.[84] In particular the gain realized to the taxpayer is recognized only to the extent that the taxpayer's adjusted sales price[85] of the old residence exceeds the taxpayer's cost of purchasing the new residence. Thus the principle here is very similar to that of the involuntary conversion rule. The taxpayer's basis in his new residence is the cost of the new residence reduced by any gain not recognized on the transaction.[86] Thus is the unrecognized gain on the transaction preserved.

**84.** § 1034(a).

**85.** The "adjusted sales price" is the amount realized (see ¶ 4.03(1)) reduced by the expenses for work performed on the old residence in order to facilitate its sale, § 1034(b)(1). In order to qualify for this reduction, the expenses must have been incurred for work performed during the 90 day period preceding the day the contract for sale is entered into; the expenses must have been paid within 30 days after the date of the sale of the old residence; the expenses must not be allowable as deductions in computing taxable income and not be taken into account in computing the amount realized from the sale of the old residence, § 1034(b). For discussion of the amount realized on sale of property and treatment of commission expenses incurred therewith, see ¶ 4.03(1).

**86.** § 1034(e). The holding period of the old residence tacks onto the holding period of the new residence for the purpose of ascertaining whether a subsequent sale of the new residence could qualify as a long-term capital gain, § 1223(7). The cost of the new residence includes acquisition costs, such as brokerage fees and commissions. It also includes costs of construction, reconstruction and improvements which are made within the two-year forward and back

period described in the text, § 1034(c)(2), Regs. §§ 1.1034–1(b)(7); 1.1034–1(c)(4)(i); 1.1034–1(c)(2) providing computation and examples. Of course the cost of such capital improvements always goes into the basis of property under the usual rules, regardless of when they were made, see ¶ 6.03(4). However, only capital improvements which are made within the two-year forward and back period will be included in the cost of the new residence for the purpose of reducing the gain recognized on sale of the old residence under § 1034.

If the taxpayer constructs a new residence and some of the construction takes place within the two-year forward and back period and some of it occurs outside that period, only the cost of that construction which took place within the period will be considered as cost of the new residence for § 1034 purposes, Reg. § 1.1034–1(c)(4)(ii), Rev.Rul. 78–147, 1978–1 C.B. 261, Rev.Rul. 55–90, 1955–1 C.B. 348. If the taxpayer receives his new residence by gift or inheritance, only the cost of any reconstruction or improvements on such residence undertaken by the taxpayer will be considered as the cost of the new residence for purposes of § 1034, Reg. § 1.1034–1(c)(4)(i). The cost basis of the new residence also includes any liabilities whether with or without recourse

There is no limit to the number of times that a taxpayer may employ § 1034 to rollover his principal residence; however, generally at least two years must elapse between the dates of each sale of the principal residence for § 1034 to be applicable to each transaction.[87]

In *Lokan v. Commissioner*[88] the taxpayers sold their old home for a profit, and constructed a new home. While building the new home, they lived in a trailer next door to the new home, although some of their children slept in the house as it was under construction. The questions presented were whether they had occupied the new home within the § 1034 period and if not, could they consider the trailer and the cost of the seven and one-half acres of land surrounding it as their new home for purposes of § 1034?

The Tax Court held that taxpayers did not physically occupy the home under construction within the required period. Living in a trailer next door with one or two children sleeping in the house under construction did not constitute occupying the new house for purposes of § 1034. The court also held that while the trailer did constitute the new residence for purposes of § 1034, only one and one-half acres of the land surrounding the trailer could be included in the cost of the new residence for purposes of § 1034. The other six acres devoted to farming did not count in the cost of the new residence for § 1034 purposes.

In *Bolaris v. Commissioner*[89] the husband and wife taxpayers moved into a new home they had constructed. They had trouble selling their old home and rented it out for eight months. Eventually they sold it for a profit, within the required period to use § 1034. They attempted to deduct depreciation and maintenance expenses attributable to the period they rented the property before they sold it. The Tax Court permitted the use of § 1034 but denied the depreciation and maintenance expenses on the theory that deferred recognition of gain under § 1034 and the taking of depreciation and maintenance expenses were mutually exclusive as a matter of law.

The Ninth Circuit affirmed the Tax Court's holding that § 1034 was available to the taxpayers. The Ninth Circuit rejected the holding that

to which the property is subject at the time of the purchase. Reg. § 1.1034–1(c)(4)(i), and see ¶ 4.03(2)(b)(ii).

**87.** § 1034(d)(1). Where a subsequent sale is on account of the commencement of work by the employee at a new location, the two-year rule is waived, and § 1034 will apply to the transaction, provided the conditions of § 217(c) (relating to the 35–mile distance and the new job longevity requirements) are met, § 1034(d)(2). See ¶ 6.02(8) for discussion of § 217 and deduction of moving expenses.

If the taxpayer's principal residence is condemned, he may elect to treat the transaction under § 1034, rather than § 1033,

§ 1034(i), Reg. § 1.1034–1(h). The advantage of making such an election is questionable inasmuch as the results under the two provisions are essentially the same. If the taxpayer reinvests in a new principal residence, that would meet the "similar or related in service or use" test of § 1033 (see ¶ 4.05(3)). Moreover, by electing to be treated under § 1034, the taxpayer subjects himself to that provision's two-year rule for successive sales of personal residences; whereas by allowing the transaction to go under § 1033, the taxpayer avoids that restriction on subsequent sales.

**88.**   39 T.C.M. 168 (1979).

**89.**   776 F.2d 1428 (9th Cir.1985).

§ 1034 and taking depreciation and maintenance expenses were mutually exclusive as a matter of law. And the Ninth Circuit held further that the taxpayers had a profit motive in renting their property while they held it out for sale pursuant to § 1034. This was true even though the taxpayers rented the property for less than the mortgage payment on the property. As a result, the taxpayers could deduct their depreciation and maintenance expenses.

*Perry* [90] (otherwise known as "the case of two Lauras" inasmuch as in the case the taxpayer divorced a woman named Laura and married another woman named Laura) presented an interesting set of facts. On June 15, 1984, taxpayer, in anticipation of divorce from his first wife (Laura I) moved out of their house located in Irvine, California. On December 17, 1985, the marriage between taxpayer and Laura I was legally terminated. The marital settlement included an agreement that Laura I had exclusive use of the Irvine property for two years, that the property would be sold as soon as possible after the two years and that Laura I would have exclusive temporary use of the property pending the sale. Taxpayer married Laura II on April 18, 1987. The Irvine property was sold on March 15, 1988 for $213,000. On August 18, 1989, taxpayer and Laura II bought a home in Simi Valley, California for $400,032. Taxpayer and Laura II argued that § 1034 applied to defer their gain on the sale of the Irvine property even though taxpayer had moved out of it four years prior to its sale. The court held that the Irvine property was not the taxpayer's residence when it was sold in 1988. Under the terms of the marital settlement agreement with Laura I, taxpayer did not have the right to reside at the Irvine property. He resided at other locations for a substantial period of time before the Irvine property was sold. Since the Irvine property was not his principal residence when it was sold in 1988, taxpayer and Laura II were not entitled to nonrecognition under § 1034. (If there's anyone named Laura reading this, there's someone out in Simi Valley, California, who likes you.)

### (b) Of Imputed Income, Depreciation and Policy

As discussed above, the taxpayer's sale of his own residence is of course a taxable event.[91] If the sale is for a gain, the sting is there. However more than one taxpayer has given forth an anguished cry to discover that where the sale of his personal residence gives rise to a loss, no deduction at all is allowed, because deductions are not allowed for losses on sales of personal-use property.[92]

This seems like unfair treatment, but actually the taxpayer is getting a better shake out of this housing deal than at first appears. Consider George and Barbara who buy a house in an upscale suburb of a major metropolitan area for $270,000. Under current law, residential real estate is depreciated over about 27 years, using the straight line

**90.** 67 T.C.M. 3035 (1994).

**91.** See ¶ 4.02(1).

**92.** See ¶ 4.04(2).

method, under the ACRS system, see Chapter 6.[93] So George and Barbara could depreciate their house $10,000 per year if they were allowed to depreciate it. But they can't. As discussed in Chapter 6, the depreciation allowance for "residential real estate" applies to investment or business property, not owner-occupied housing.

It will also be recalled that taxpayers are not taxed on the imputed income of their owner-occupied housing, ¶ 1.02(2)(a). The house produces real economic income in the form of shelter, just the way ownership of a bond produces real economic income in the form of interest. So it could be said that disallowing the depreciation deduction on the house balances off not taxing the imputed income from the house. You could say that.

Another way to say it is to say that if you taxed imputed income from owner-occupied housing, you would certainly have to allow a depreciation deduction for the house that produces the income.[94]

I doubt that Congress has thought it through this way, but the situation does seem to be logical. This line of analysis brings up a deeper insight. Let me pick some numbers that work out evenly and we'll get a little surprise. Let's consider George and Barbara a little further. They live in their house for 4 years. That means for 4 years they enjoy the untaxed imputed income from their house in their marital bliss. Let's say the amount of that income annually is 4% of the value of the house, or $10,000. So at the end of 4 years, they have received $40,000 of income tax free.

But, we say, they have been punished. It has not been such a lark. They have not been allowed their depreciation deduction. On a straight line method over the statutory 27 years useful life they would have been entitled to depreciation of $10,000 per year. Thus the total depreciation they did not get is $40,000. Thus it could be said that not allowing the depreciation deduction balances off not taxing the imputed income.

Let's pursue these numbers a little further. If they had been taxed on the imputed income, and had therefore been allowed to take depreciation on their house, the basis of their house would now be $270,000— $40,000 or $230,000.

After four years suppose they sell their house for $270,000, after sales expenses[95]. So they break even. They walk and the deal is over. How do the numbers crank out?

Let's consider the two cases: 1) The real world of no tax on imputed income; no depreciation on the house; and no basis adjustment on the house; and 2) The alternate world of taxing imputed income; allowing

93. The actual statutory useful life period is 27.5 years but I drop the half year for computational convenience.

94. There are other deductions you would have to allow homeowners if you taxed them on the imputed income of their housing, such as maintenance and perhaps casualty losses. But depreciation is by far the most important deduction you would have to allow.

95. As we have learned, expenses of the sale are deductible in arriving at the gain realized, see ¶ 4.03(1).

depreciation on the house; and adjusting the basis of the house. It turns out things don't add up.

The accompanying chart lays it out:

| | | Something Is Desperately Wrong Here | | |
|---|---|---|---|---|
| | | Real World: no tax on imputed income; no depreciation for house; and no basis adjustment. | Alternate World: tax on imputed income; depreciation allowed for house; and basis adjustment. | |
| | 4 Years' Owner–Occupied Housing: | | | |
| # 1 | Income Subject to Tax | $0 | $40,000 | |
| # 2 | Imputed Income (not subject to tax): | $40,000 | $0 | |
| # 3 | Less Depreciation: | $0 | $40,000 | |
| # 4 | Taxable Income (#1–#3) | $0 | $0 | Depreciation is not an out-of-pocket expense. Thus Net After-Tax Benefit figured without subtracting depreciation. |
| # 5 | Tax (40% of #4): | $0 | $0 | |
| # 6 | Net After-Tax Benefit (#1 or #2) - #5: | $40,000 | $40,000 | |
| | Sale of House | | | |
| # 7 | Net Proceeds | $270,000 | $270,000 | |
| # 8 | Less Basis | $270,000 | $230,000 | |
| # 9 | Gain on House | $0 | $40,000 | The gain on the house is not a real benefit but just a phantom gain caused by the earlier phantom depreciation. |
| #10 | Tax (40% of #9): | $0 | $16,000 | |
| | Total After-Tax Benefit: (#6 - #10) | $40,000 | $24,000 | |

What is the problem here? The problem is that the real world case seems to be too good. And the fact of the matter is that it is too good. What has to happen in the real world case for these numbers to come out the same is for the basis of the property in the real world case to go down *even though depreciation is not allowed.* It is quite apparent from the chart that if the basis of the property in the real world case were $230,000 then the numbers would work out the same—indeed they would be the same.

There is a very big point here struggling to get out. It does not have to do just with imputed income. What we are saying here is that when we do not allow depreciation on the personal residence, the only way to really do that is not to allow the deduction *but also have the basis go down.* If you just don't allow the deduction but leave the basis the same, then when the property is sold the owner gets in effect "deferred depreciation" because his basis is still high.[96] If you are going to say that something is not depreciable, the only way to really make that so is not to allow the depreciation deduction and also make the basis go down.

This is a profoundly important theoretical point. And it is not just theoretical. We see this approach in action in the field of partnership and S Corporation taxation. There are certain situations in those fields where we wish to disallow a deduction. The approach taken is not only to disallow the deduction but also to knock the basis down, so that the taxpayer does not get the deduction in a deferred manner.[97]

To recapitulate some of the things we have discussed (or will discuss) concerning home ownership: We will see that as a theoretical matter, the deduction for interest on the home mortgage should not be allowed.[98] We have also seen that if it is allowed, the approach of allowing most of the early payments to be deemed deductible interest and most of the later payments to be non-deductible principal should be reversed. Most of the early payments should be non-deductible principal and most of the later payments should be deductible interest. This is very unfavorable.[99] We also now have shown that the basis of the taxpayer's house should go down even though he is not allowed to take a depreciation deduction. Why don't you tell this information to your parents who are financing your legal education? See how they like that. Just do me one favor. Don't mention my name.

### (5) *Other Tax–Free Transactions*

Nonrecognition-employing principles similar to those discussed above are also accorded to the exchange of insurance policies,[1] reacquisition of mortgaged real property[2]. Exchanges of common stock for common stock in the same corporation, or preferred stock for preferred stock in the same corporation are also tax free.[3] In all of these cases the deferred gain is preserved by an appropriate basis correction.

---

**96.** Of course based on all our time value of money analysis, we know that "deferred depreciation" is not as good as depreciation every year. But "deferred depreciation" is still better than no depreciation.

**97.** In keeping with my theme of trying to tune up those students who are going on in the field, take a look at § 705(a)(2)(B). That section requires that a partner's basis in his partnership interest must go down by expenditures of the partnership which are not deductible and not capitalized (such as a fine, § 162(f)). It's not enough to disallow the deduction, *the basis must also go down.* If the basis does not go down, then the partner is getting a deferred deduction for the item when he

sells his partnership interest. See also § 1367(a)(2)(D), providing the same rule for S corporations.

**98.** ¶ 7.01(3).

**99.** See ¶ 1.02(2)(e)(i), discussing the economically accurate way to recover the cost of a single premium annuity.

**1.** § 1035.

**2.** § 1038.

**3.** § 1036. The whole field of corporate reorganizations involves many kinds of exchanges of stock for stock and stock for assets tax free, with appropriate basis correction. See §§ 368, 354, 356, 361, 355.

### (6) Wash Sales of Stock or Securities

Consider a taxpayer owning 100 shares of stock in X Corporation. Taxpayer has a cost basis in the stock of $50 per share; the stock in the few months since his purchase has dropped in price to $30 per share. Notwithstanding this drop the taxpayer may still think highly of X Corporation and intend to hold the stock for a number of years. However, it would appear that the taxpayer can wrest a tax advantage from this immediate drop in the price of the stock. Suppose he engages in a "wash sale"—he sells the 100 shares of X stock and then a few days later repurchases 100 shares of X stock, thereby realizing the loss without actually giving up ownership of the X stock for any significant period. Of course had the stock risen in price after his original purchase the taxpayer would never engage in a wash sale to realize his gain! Thus it would appear generally that with marketable securities the taxpayer can realize his losses but not his gains—and all the while effectively maintain ownership of the stock or securities involved.

Naturally this power of the taxpayer to load the tax dice in his favor in the holding of marketable securities has not gone unnoticed by the Congress. The supposed neutralizer for this maneuver is the wash sale provision, § 1091, which disallows the loss deduction on the sale of old stock or securities where the taxpayer has purchased substantially identical new stock or securities within the period beginning 30 days before and ending 30 days after the sale for loss of the old stock or securities.[4]

As a theoretical matter, therefore, where the taxpayer sells stock or securities for a loss in a § 1091 situation, he clearly has a taxable event,[5] and he can calculate his loss realized under the usual rules.[6] § 1091, however, overrides these normal rules and disallows the loss so calculated on a wash sale transaction. The loss is not permanently disallowed only deferred. Appropriate correction is made to the basis of the new stock or securities to insure that the loss will ultimately be taken advantage of on a subsequent sale.[7]

---

**4.** § 1091(a), also providing a "purchase" of substantially identical stock or securities would encompass any exchange in which all gain is recognized, and would cover any option or contract to acquire substantially identical stock or securities. The loss will be allowed to one who is in the trade or business of buying and selling stock or securities or to a corporation which is a dealer in stocks or securities and the transaction is made in the ordinary course of business, §§ 1091(a) and 165(c).

**5.** See ¶ 4.02.

**6.** See ¶ 4.03.

**7.** § 1091(d), which provides the unadjusted basis of the new stock or securities is the basis of the old stock or securities increased or decreased, as the case may be, by the difference between the price at which the new stock or security was acquired and the price at which the old stock or security was sold. For example:

A buys 100 shares of stock of X Corporation, traded on the New York Stock Exchange, at $50 per share. The price soon drops to $30. A sells his 100 shares at $30. Within 30 days of the sale, A buys 100 shares of stock of X Corporation at $35. The loss on the sale of X Corporation is disallowed. However, A's basis in his new X Corporation stock is $50 plus $5 or $55. Thus should A later sell his stock for $35 he will get his loss of $20.

Had A repurchased the new X Corporation stock at $25, his basis in it would have been $45.

The strictures of § 1091 are triggered if the taxpayer purchases securities "substantially identical" to the securities sold for a loss, within the prescribed 30–day forward and back period. Stock or securities are not "substantially identical" if they are from two different issuers, even though in all other ways they may be very similar.[8] Stock or securities from the same issuer which are dissimilar in fundamental terms are not "substantially identical."[9] A well-known and effective maneuver in this area is to sell and buy stock of companies in the same industry. Thus where a taxpayer has a loss on his X Company Oil stock, he could sell it and immediately buy Y Company Oil stock, rather than wait 30 days and risk that the oil group might move upward during that period. Similarly with respect to the holding of long-term bonds, when interest rates move higher the bondholder will have significant unrealized losses. Selling such bonds and reinvesting the proceeds in bonds of another issuer of the same quality will be effective to create a deductible capital loss. At the same time the interest income will continue uninterrupted. It is true that the bondholder will have a lower basis in the new bonds and might have a gain when the bonds are ultimately retired at face. (See ¶ 4.06(3)(a)(xii) for treatment of retirement of bonds). However the bondholder on this maneuver has enjoyed the benefit of deferral—a capital loss now at the price of a capital gain many years hence.

Another effective technique for avoiding the wash-sale rules is "doubling up." A taxpayer who has a loss on some stock and would like to realize it but not actually cash out of the stock can simply buy a second lot of the stock to double his holdings. Then he would wait more than 30 days and then sell the original loss shares. That capital loss is deductible; the provisions of § 1091 have not been triggered. Taxpayer has got his loss and has not failed to have a position in the stock at any time.

Where the taxpayer has engaged in a number of purchases and sales of the same stock or securities, special rules are provided. In general the approach is to match the stock or securities sold first in time with the stock or securities bought first in time. All of this occurs under a moving 30–day forward and back period in which sales or purchases occurring within that period are matched against each other. However, an acquired share of stock or security can only be matched against a loss once. Appropriate basis rules account for these transactions.[10] All of this taken together can provide a rather interesting tableau, as the following example illustrates:

The basis of the new stock will also include acquisition costs such as brokerage fees, see ¶ 4.03(2)(b). The holding period of the new stock will include the holding period of the old stock, § 1223(4). Though a loss in sale of stock or securities may escape the limitation of § 1091, it may still be subject to the limitations of §§ 267 and 1211. See ¶¶ 4.05(7) and 4.06(2)(b)(ii) respectively.

**8.** Rev.Rul. 59–44, 1959–1 C.B. 205 (bonds with virtually the same maturity dates and interest rates issued by different local housing authorities are not "substantially identical.")

**9.** Rev.Rul. 58–210, 1958–1 C.B. 523.

**10.** Reg. § 1.1091–1(b), (c) and (d); Reg. § 1.1091–1(h).

T, who did not previously own any shares of Y Corporation stock, engages in the following transactions in Y Corporation common stock during the taxable year:

May 16      buys 1000 shares at $50 per share
June 1      sells 300 shares at $40 per share
June 20      buys 500 shares at $37 per share
June 25      sells 300 shares of those acquired on May 16 at $32 per share

Had there been only the May 16 and June 1 transactions, T would have been allowed his loss. Although the May 16 purchase comes within 30 days of the June 1 sale at a loss, the June 1 sale was of some of the original stock purchased on May 16. Nothing, of course, in § 1091 prohibits selling the original stock or securities at a loss within 30 days of their purchase. It is only when substantially identical stock or securities are purchased within the 61–day period to "wash out" the effect of the loss sale that § 1091 comes into play.

The June 20 purchase causes the June 1 loss sale to be disallowed. With respect to the June 25 sale, T has a realized loss of $18 per share on the 300 shares. Within 30 days of that June 25 sale, namely on June 20, T had bought "substantially identical" stock. Hence it might appear that the loss will be disallowed in its entirety. However 300 of the 500 shares purchased on June 20 have already been matched against the June 1 loss sale. Thus the loss on only 200 of the 300 shares sold on June 25 will be disallowed.[11]

Query what would happen if T asserted and could show by identifying the share certificates that the June 25 sale was of shares bought on June 20? Then could T assert that the wash sale rule did not apply to him, since he was buying and selling the same shares, not engaging in a wash transaction using "substantially identical" shares? Nevertheless, where the shares are fungible and T owns a block of shares from an earlier purchase, perhaps any buying and selling transactions within 30 days of one another will be deemed to be within the wash-sale rule. There is no direct authority on this matter.[12]

### (7) Losses on Sales and Exchanges Between Related Taxpayers

#### (a) In general

The taxpayer who holds property which has declined in value is often sorely tempted to realize that loss by selling the property. However

---

11. The basis for the various lots of stock would be as follows: The lot purchased on May 16 would of course take a cost basis of $50 per share (plus acquisition costs). Three hundred shares of the lot purchased on June 20 would take a basis of $47 per share (see note 92 above). The other 200 shares would take a cost basis of $37 until June 25 (Reg. § 1.1091–1(c), (d)). On June 25 these 200 shares would take a basis of $55 (note 98 above).

12. See Krane, "Losses From Wash Sales of Stock or Securities", 4 Journal of Corp. Tax. 226 (1977).

for business or other reasons the taxpayer may also wish to keep control of the property. This dilemma has often propelled taxpayers into tricky maneuvers such as selling the property and buying back substantially identical property or selling the property to a related individual or entity whom the taxpayer controls.

The maneuver of selling property and immediately buying back substantially identical property is most easily available for stock or securities, where vast accessible markets for such property exist. The disallowance of losses on such wash sales is discussed at ¶ 4.05(6). With respect to other kinds of property, such as real estate or tangible personal property, the more likely maneuver would be to sell the property to a buyer whom the taxpayer controls. Disallowance of loss on this latter maneuver is generally the object of § 267; § 267 will allow an appropriate basis correction to the buyer to preserve the loss as discussed below.

§ 267 covers all property,[13] unlike the "wash sale" provision § 1091, which covers only stock or securities. Thus should a taxpayer sell depreciated stock or securities to a related buyer whom he controls, his loss would be barred by § 267. However a taxpayer could engage in a "wash sale" of property that was not stock or securities, such as sell his depreciated rental real estate and buy similar rental real estate.[14] Such a maneuver would be effective to create a deductible loss for the taxpayer (assuming the effort of locating the new property, the closing costs etc., were worth it).[15]

### (b) "Related Taxpayers"; Constructive Ownership Rules

The related or controlled persons between whom losses on sales or exchanges are not allowed are: taxpayer and his brothers, sisters, spouse, ancestors, and lineal descendants;[16] losses are also disallowed on sales or

---

**13.** § 267(a)(1).

**14.** Indeed the taxpayer could push his luck further and sell his depreciated real estate to a buyer who would soon sell it back to him. That bald an attempt to realize a loss is, of course, likely to be disregarded as a sham.

**15.** The Service might attempt to interpret this transaction as a multi-party § 1031 transaction and bar the loss. See ¶ 4.05(2).

Another ploy with respect to marketable securities could be for the taxpayer to sell his securities at a loss on an exchange and have a family member buy the same kind of securities also in an open market transaction. While this might be effective to skirt the wash-sale rule, the Supreme Court has held that this transaction constitutes a sale at a loss to a related party, coming within the strictures of § 267, McWilliams v. Commissioner, 331 U.S. 694, 67 S.Ct. 1477, 91 L.Ed. 1750 (1947). But see United States v.

Norton, Jr., 250 F.2d 902 (5th Cir.1958) (sale of Magma Copper stock by taxpayer on New York Stock Exchange and purchase of Magma Copper stock by taxpayer's mother 28 days later did not result in disallowance of taxpayer's loss on the sale where there was no contemplation of the purchase at the time of the sale.). Cf. Merritt, Sr. v. Commissioner, 400 F.2d 417 (5th Cir.1968) (disallowing loss on taxpayer's stock which was seized by the Internal Revenue Service and then bought several months later by taxpayer's wife at a public auction, and discussing contrary authorities on this pattern), and see Hassen v. Commissioner, 599 F.2d 305 (9th Cir.1979).

**16.** § 267(b)(1) and (c)(4). Brothers and sisters may be of the half or whole blood. Transfers of loss property to a spouse incident to a divorce raise knotty questions, see Dupont, 37 T.C.M. 115 (1978) (loss allowed). Marital property settlements can also raise the threshold question of whether

exchanges between an individual and a corporation more than 50% of whose stock he owns,[17] two corporations where the same individual owns more than 50 percent of the stock of each and one or both of the corporations has been a personal holding company or a foreign personal holding company during the preceding year,[18] a grantor and a fiduciary of any trust,[19] as well as certain other related persons.[20]

In determining whether an individual owns more than 50 percent of the stock of a corporation for these purposes, constructive ownership rules are applied. Stock owned, directly or indirectly, by a corporation partnership, estate or trust is deemed owned proportionately by its shareholders, partners or beneficiaries.[21] *This is attribution from entities.* Thus for example:

A sells property at a loss to X Corporation. A actually owns 30% of the stock of X Corporation. A owns 30% of the stock of Y Corporation. Y Corporation owns 80% of the stock of X Corporation. Therefore A is deemed to own constructively 24% (his proportionate share) of the stock of X Corporation on account of his ownership of Y Corporation stock. Therefore, taking A's actual ownership of X Corporation plus his constructive ownership of X Corporation together, A is deemed to own 54% of X Corporation. Hence A's loss on sale of property to X Corporation would be disallowed. The same sort of analysis would apply if Y had been a partnership, estate, or trust.

Also, an individual is deemed to own stock owned, directly or indirectly, by his family.[22] *This is attribution from family members.* Thus for example:

there has been a realizing event at all. See ¶ 4.02(2).

**17.** § 267(b)(2). The stock ownership is measured by value. Constructive ownership rules are applied, see below. A loss on a distribution in liquidation of a corporation is allowed, however, § 267(a) parenthetical language.

**18.** § 267(b)(3), also providing that the stock ownership is measured by value.

**19.** § 267(b)(4).

**20.** The other related persons between whom sales or exchanges for a loss will be disallowed are a fiduciary of a trust and a fiduciary of another trust, if the same person is a grantor of both trusts, § 267(b)(5); a fiduciary of a trust and a beneficiary of such trust, § 267(b)(6); a fiduciary of a trust and a beneficiary of another trust if the same person is a grantor of both trusts, § 267(b)(7); a fiduciary of a trust and a corporation more than 50 percent in value of the outstanding stock of which is owned, directly or indirectly, by or for the trust or by or for a person who is a grantor of the

trust, § 267(b)(8); a person and a tax-exempt organization which is controlled directly or indirectly by such person or by members of such person's family, § 267(b)(9).

Regarding partnerships § 267 does not cover transactions between a partner and his partnership. Such transactions are governed by § 707, for which purposes the partnership is considered to be an entity separate from the partners, Regs. §§ 1.267(b)–1(b)(1)(i); 1.707–1. Any loss sale between a partnership and a person not a partner is considered as occurring between the person not a partner and the members of the partnership separately. Therefore if the non-partner and a partner are within any of the relationships described herein, no loss deduction will be allowed to the extent of the partner's interest in the transaction, Reg. § 1.267(b)–1(b)(1) and (2).

**21.** § 267(c)(1).

**22.** § 267(c)(2). An individual's "family" is defined to be his brothers and sisters (whether by the whole or half blood),

A sells property at a loss to X Corporation. A actually owns 25% of the stock of X Corporation. A's father owns 30% of the stock of X Corporation. Thus A is deemed to own constructively 30% of the stock of X Corporation on account of his father's ownership. Therefore, taking A's actual ownership of X Corporation plus his constructive ownership of X Corporation together, A is deemed to own 55% of X Corporation. Hence A's loss on sale of property to X Corporation would be disallowed.

Also if an individual actually owns stock in a corporation, or is deemed to own stock in a corporation on account of *attribution from an entity,* he will be deemed to own such additional stock in the corporation as is owned by his partner.[23] *This is attribution from partners.*

Note that attribution from partners will only occur if the individual owns some stock actually in the corporation or is deemed to own some stock by attribution *from an entity.* If the individual only owns stock in a corporation by reason of attribution from a family member, then attribution from partners will not occur. For example:

A sells property at a loss to X Corporation. A owns no stock in X Corporation. A's mother owns 10% of the stock in X Corporation. A's partner owns 48% of the stock in X Corporation. A is deemed to own only 10% of the stock in X Corporation on account of his mother's stock ownership and the loss on the sale of the property will be allowed. There is no attribution from the partner on these facts.

Alternative: A sells property at a loss to X Corporation. A owns no stock in X Corporation. A trust of which A is 50% beneficiary owns 10% of the stock in X Corporation. A's partner owns 48% of the stock of X Corporation. A is deemed to own 5% of the stock in X Corporation on account of his 50% interest in the trust. In addition, A is deemed to own 48% of the stock in X Corporation on account of attribution from his partner. Hence A is deemed to own altogether 53% of the stock in X Corporation and the loss on the sale of property will not be allowed. There is attribution from the partner on these facts.

spouse, ancestors, and lineal descendents, § 267(c)(4). See Arizona Publishing Co., 9 T.C. 85 (1947) for treatment involving community property. It is mildly interesting to note that the constructive ownership rules of § 318, used to ascertain whether a stock redemption will be treated as a sale or exchange, do not allow for attribution between siblings; they are also more restrictive in other ways.

Cf. also § 544(a)(2) which takes the more expansive approach of § 267 in ascertaining constructive stock ownership for purposes of determining whether a corporation is a personal holding company, and cf. the very limited attribution rules of § 1239, which change the character of gain from capital to ordinary on sales of depreciable property among related persons. The subtle differences among these sets of attribution rules for these various purposes can perhaps best be explained by a tax lawyer who also has an advanced degree in anthropology. For a valiant attempt in this area see Goldstein, "Attribution Rules: Undue Multiplicity, Complexity Can Create Liabilities", 15 Tul.Tax Inst. 384 (1965).

**23.** § 267(c).

It is possible to have two-step or "foxtrot" attribution in some circumstances. Where the ownership of a block of stock has been attributed to an individual from an entity, ownership of that same block can then be reattributed to another individual under the rules of attribution from family members or attribution from partners.[24] For example:

> A sells property at a loss to X Corporation. A owns no stock in X Corporation. A trust of which A's mother is sole beneficiary owns 60% of the stock of X Corporation. A's mother is therefore deemed to own 60% of the stock of X Corporation by the rules of attribution from entities. A is then deemed to own 60% of the stock of X Corporation by the rules of attribution from family members. Hence A's loss on the sale of property to X Corporation would be disallowed.

However, "foxtrot" attribution cannot occur where the first step is taken under the rules for attribution from family members or attribution from partners.[25] For example:

> A sells property at a loss to X Corporation. A owns no stock in X Corporation. A's brother-in-law owns 60% of the stock of X Corporation. By the rules of attribution from family members, A's sister is deemed to own 60% of the stock in X Corporation. Since two successive applications of the rules for attribution from family members is not allowed, A is not deemed to own any of the stock owned by his sister. Hence A is not deemed to own any of the stock of X Corporation, and A's loss on the sale of property to X Corporation is allowed.[26]

### (c)  Use of Disallowed Loss by Buyer

§ 267 is ultimately a "half-breed" provision—a cross between a pure deferral provision and a pure disallowance provision. If a loss on a sale to a related party is disallowed to the seller on account of § 267(a), the buyer will under some circumstances be able to take advantage of the disallowed loss on a subsequent transaction. Under other circumstances the disallowed loss will never be usable by the buyer, or anyone else.

---

**24.**  § 267(c)(5). It is also possible that the same block of stock can be attributed to two or more individuals simultaneously. A's wife and son might make sales of property at losses simultaneously to a corporation all of whose stock A owns. The losses on both transactions would be disallowed.

**25.**  Id.

**26.**  Another arcane variation: A sells property at a loss to W Corporation. A owns no stock of W Corporation. X Corporation owns 60% of the stock of W Corporation. Y Corporation owns 100% of the stock of X Corporation. Z Corporation owns 100% of the stock of Y Corporation. A owns 100% of the stock of Z Corporation. By the rules of attribution from entities, Y Corporation is deemed to own 60% of the stock of W Corporation. Again by the rules of attribution from entities Z Corporation is deemed to own 60% of the stock of W Corporation. By the rules of attribution from entities A is deemed to then own 60% of the stock of W Corporation, and the loss on the sale of property is not allowed. This chain of attributions is alright, since successive application of the rules for attribution from entities is not barred, § 267(c)(5).

If the buyer of property where the loss has been previously disallowed subsequently sells the property at a gain, he will only be taxable to the extent (if any) his gain exceeds the loss disallowed.[27] For example:

> A sells property with a basis in his hands of $100 to B, his son, for $50. The loss is disallowed to A. B subsequently sells the property to C for $125. B has a taxable gain of $25.[28] B's holding period starts when he purchased the property; he does not include A's holding period.[29]

If the buyer of property where the loss has been previously disallowed subsequently sells the property at a loss, he will only be able to deduct his actual loss. The previously disallowed loss will have no effect. This is because § 267(d) acts only to exempt gain to the buyer on a subsequent transaction; it does not affect the buyer's basis.[30] For example:

> A sells property with a basis in his hands of $100 to B, his son, for $50. The loss is disallowed to A. B subsequently sells the property to C, an unrelated party, for $30. B has a deductible loss of $20. The loss disallowed to A will never be used. Any subsequent disposition by C will be treated under usual rules, without reference to the fact that the property was once sold in a § 267 transaction.

If the buyer of the property in the § 267 transaction transfers the property to a third party by gift, the donee will be taxable in full if he subsequently sells the property at a gain (a sale at a loss will of course also be deductible in full).[31] For example:

> A sells property with a basis in his hands of $100 to B, his son, for $50. The loss is disallowed to A. B subsequently gives the property to C. C later sells the property for $125. C has a taxable gain of $75. C's basis for determining gain was $50 on the gifted property.[32] C's holding period of the property includes B's holding period.[33]

Suppose the buyer of the property in the § 267 transaction subsequently engages in a tax-free exchange[34] of the property. If the buyer later sells the property received in the exchange for a gain, he will only be taxable to the extent (if any) his gain exceeds the original loss disallowed the seller.[35] For example:

> A sells Blackacre with a basis in his hands of $100 to B, his son, for $50. The loss is disallowed to A. B subsequently engages in a tax-free exchange with D, receiving Greenacre in exchange for Black-

**27.** § 267(d).

**28.** Id. and Reg. § 1.267(d)–1(a)(4) Example 1.

**29.** Reg. § 1.267(d)–1(a)(4) Example 1.

**30.** Reg. § 1.267(d)–1(a)(4) Example 2.

**31.** Reg. § 1.267(d)–1(a)(4) Example 3. See ¶ 4.03(2)(c)(i) for basis rules on gifts.

**32.** Id.

**33.** Id.

**34.** ¶ 4.05(2).

**35.** Reg. § 1.267(d)–1(a)(4) Example 4.

acre. B therefore takes a basis of $50 in Greenacre.[36] B later sells Greenacre for $75. B has no gain on the sale. If B had sold Greenacre for $125, B would have had a taxable gain of $25.

Finally, it should be noted that even sales to related parties at a gain will be penalized under certain circumstances, in that such gains may be deemed ordinary rather than capital.[37] This matter is discussed at ¶ 4.06(3)(a)(vi ii).

## ¶ 4.06   Character of Gain or Loss: Capital Gains

### *(1) The Preferential Treatment of Capital Gains*

The last major step in the treatment of sales or other dispositions of property is characterizing the gain or loss as capital or ordinary. (There can occasionally be the further question of the year in which the transaction is reportable, see ¶ 8.03). This step is important because long-term capital gains are generally taxed at a lower rate than ordinary gains.[1] Concomitantly, capital losses are generally less attractive from a tax point of view than ordinary losses.[2] Thus whether a taxpayer is glad any particular transaction is capital in nature will generally depend on whether he has a gain or a loss.

The advantage of capital gains, under § 1(h) is that the tax rate on net capital gains (the excess of long-term capital gains over short-term capital losses as defined below) is capped at 28% regardless of how much other income the taxpayer has.[3] At this writing (May 1997), Congress and the President, as part of an overall budget deal, have agreed to a cut in the capital gains tax rate. So beware that by the time you read this, the rate may be lower.

For example, consider Ferdinand, an individual with enough income, including capital gains, to be in the 39.6% bracket. Ferdinand would

---

**36.** § 1031(d).

**37.** § 1239. For further background on § 267, see Cavagna, "Related-party Rule of § 267 Can, But Need Not, Upset a Client's Tax Planning," 15 Taxation for Accountants 368 (1975). See also generally Bittker, "Federal Income Taxation and the Family," 27 Stanf.L.Rev. 1389 (1975).

**¶ 4.06**

**1.** For a few years in the 1980's the favorable treatment of long-term capital gains was repealed.

The discussion in the text pertains to long-term capital gains, which is to say gains arising from the sale or exchange of capital assets held longer than a year. Short-term capital gains are generally taxed at ordinary rates. See detailed discussion below.

It should also be noted that "capital gains and losses" do not have to do with "capital expenditures." Although the terminology is similar, the two concepts do not have a great deal to do with each other. For a discussion of "capital expenditures", see ¶ 6.03(4).

**2.** This is a generalization. There are certainly times when a capital loss can be as attractive as an ordinary loss. See detailed discussion below.

**3.** Congress in 1993 tossed another of its many bones to small businesses. Under new § 1202 it provided for very favorable treatment on sale of so-called "qualified small business stock." A qualified small business is one whose gross assets are not greater than $50 million and which engages in any trade or business other than the performance of personal or financial services. Generally, the new provisions allow an individual taxpayer to exclude 50% of his gain on sale of such stock up to the greater of 10 times his basis or $10 million. The remaining 50% is still eligible for the favorable 28% maximum rate. The stock must be acquired by the taxpayer directly from the corporation itself, not in a purchase from another stockholder. The obvious intent of the statute is to encourage venture capital investment.

undertake a two-step process. 1) he would subtract his net capital gains and compute his tax on the remaining ordinary income. 2) He would then add to that tax liability a tax of 28% on the net capital gains.

Thus the capital gains are extracted and subjected to their own lower maximum tax rate. For Ferdinand, in the 39.6% bracket, being able to tax a substantial amount of his income at a rate of only 28% is very attractive indeed. This amounts to a tax break of 29% off the maximum 39.6% rate.[4]

### Here is an example:

Facts: T, a single individual taxpayer, has $35,000 of net long-term capital gain and other salary income of $150,000.

Here is what we do.

On these facts we have gross income of $185,000

Since the amount of net capital gain is $35,000, that is the amount that we are going to apply the 28% maximum rate to. The rest, $150,000, we will just apply normal rates to. The tax on $150,000 is (looking at § 1(c) since we are talking about unmarried individuals)

$$\begin{aligned}
\text{Tax on on } \$150,000 \ &= \ \$31,172 \ + \ 36\% \text{ of } (\$150,000 - 115,000). \\
&= \ \$31,172 \ + \ 36\% \text{ of } (\$35,000) \\
&= \ \$31,172 \ + \ \$12,600 \\
&= \ \$43,772
\end{aligned}$$

To that we add the tax of 28% on the $35,000 net capital gain that we broke out. If we hadn't broken it out, it would be taxed at a 36% rate.

28% of $35,000 = $9,800

Thus the total tax on T here is $43,772 × $9,800 = $53,572

The precise computation of the amount eligible for the favorable capital gains rate is more complex than this—coming into play only when so-called net long-term capital gains exceed net short term capital losses,[5] as discussed below. The ability to take advantage of this favor-

---

**4.** In rare cases it is possible that capital gains would be taxed at a rate of 15% rather than 28%. This would occur if a taxpayer did not have enough non-capital gain income to push him into the 31% bracket, but rather he remained in the lowest 15% bracket with respect to such income. In that event some or all of the net capital gains would be taxed at the 15% rate as well. The amount of net capital gains taxed at the 15% rate would be the amount of income that is still available to be taxed at the 15% rate. Most capital gains are enjoyed by taxpayers with incomes taxed at the 31% bracket or above, so this possibility does not occur often.

For possible imposition of the alternative minimum tax on capital gains, see ¶ 7.05. Corporations do not receive favorable treatment on capital gains. Partnerships, trusts and estates are taxed under the same capital gains rules as individuals, with some modifications, see e.g. Reg. § 1.1202–1(b) and (c).

**5.** As discussed below, the advantage of capital gains arises only when there has been a sale or exchange of a capital asset held longer than one year. Thus when the popular media speak of the great advantage

able rate whatever the complexities of its actual computation—is what gives capital gains their gilt-edged character in federal income taxation.[6]

It should be noted that the issue of characterizing a gain or loss as capital only arises as to recognized gains or losses. Obviously if a gain or loss is not recognized, there is no need as yet to ascertain the rules for taxing it. Moreover, the process of ascertaining whether a gain or loss is capital or not has no impact on the *amount* of the gain or loss, which is computed independently, as discussed above.

The relatively complex mechanical details of the capital gain and loss rules and the planning implications thereof will be taken up in the next section. This will be followed by a discussion of the problems in defining what particular transactions are to be subject to the capital gain and loss rules. Finally there will be a discussion of the history and policy of capital gains.

### (2) *The Rules for Taxing Capital Gains and Losses*

#### (a) *Background*

A capital gain or loss occurs if there has been a sale or exchange of a capital asset.[7] The two critical factors in this definition are "sale or exchange" and "capital asset." Both must be present for there to be a capital gain or loss, triggering the capital gain and loss rules. In analyzing a transaction, it is usually clear whether a sale or exchange has occurred (although problems on this score are discussed at ¶ 4.06(3)). Whether what was sold or exchanged was a "capital asset" can be a much more ticklish problem. "Capital assets" are defined as all property held by the taxpayer *except* inventory, depreciable or real property used in his trade or business, certain copyrights and artistic compositions, accounts receivable and certain other types of property.[8] A classic exam-

---

of capital gains, they are really referring only to long-term capital gains.

**6.** This very great advantage of capital gains taxation can be expected to generate a great deal of litigation on the question of whether various particular transactions can be treated as capital gains. It should also lead to substantial innovative tax planning to try to achieve for the taxpayer capital gains rather than ordinary income treatment. These matters are discussed further at ¶ 4.06(3).

**7.** § 1222.

**8.** § 1221(1)–(4). For the special treatment of depreciable or real property used in the trade or business, see ¶ 4.06(3)(a)(iv). More specifically with respect to some other kinds of property: a copyright, a literary, musical, or artistic composition, a letter or memorandum or similar property, held by a taxpayer whose personal efforts created such property are not capital assets. Moreover, in the case of a letter, memorandum, or similar property, even if the taxpayer's

personal efforts did not create the property, if it is held by a taxpayer for whom it was prepared, it is not a capital asset. With respect to a copyright, a literary, musical, or artistic composition, a letter or memorandum or similar property, if the basis of such property (for purposes of determining gain) is ascertained by reference to the basis of such property in the hands of another taxpayer for whom the property was not a capital asset (for the reasons described above), then the property will not be a capital asset.

*For example*, a composer gives a copyright of his composition to his son. The son, as a donee, would ascertain his basis for determining gain on future transactions of the property by reference to his father's basis in the property (¶ 4.03(2)(c)(i)). Since the father's personal efforts created the copyright, the copyright is not a capital asset in the hands of the father. Therefore the copyright is not a capital asset in the hands of the son, § 1221(3). Similar results

ple of a capital asset under this definition is stock or securities held by a taxpayer who is not a professional dealer in stocks or securities. Another classic example of a capital asset is undeveloped land held as an investment by the taxpayer. Other examples of capital assets would include the taxpayer's home,[9] paintings or other artifacts.[10] The particular reach of the definition of "capital assets" is discussed in detail at ¶ 4.06(3).

### (b) The Mechanics

The mechanics of capital gains and losses taxation are best approached as a series of steps which, if followed carefully, will lead to the correct results.[11] There are two branches in the approach. One branch of steps is followed when the taxpayer's capital gain and loss transactions add up to a net gain for the year—so called "capital gain net income." The other branch is followed when the taxpayer's capital gains and losses transactions add up to a net loss for the year. The series of steps involved when there is capital gain net income will be discussed first.

### (i) Capital Gain Net Income Rules

Now that we've chosen up sides, let's play.

Here is how we do the mechanics of capital gains and losses.

Step 1) Decide which transactions are capital gains and losses, under definitional rules discussed below. (A typical example of a capital gain is the sale of stock held for investment.)

After you have decided which transactions are capital gains and losses, you then throw them all together and net them without regard to holding period. If the net result is a gain then you apply the gain rules. If the net result is a loss, then you apply the loss rules.

---

would obtain for such property for transfers to partnerships, transfers in trusts, and transfers to controlled corporations, §§ 723, 1015(b), and 351.

Other property not considered to be a capital asset includes discount government obligations with a maturity date of less than a year, for such property bought before June 24, 1981. For positions established after that date, short-term discount government obligations are considered to be capital assets, as a change enacted by the Economic Recovery Tax Act of 1981, to forestall the so-called Treasury bill tax straddle, § 1221(5) and see ¶ 4.06(2)(c)(vi). Also not considered a capital asset are U.S. government publications, including the Congressional Record, received from the U.S. government other than by purchase, § 1221(6).

**9.** Note that if the home were sold at a loss, a deduction for the loss would not be allowed, ¶ 4.04(2). Thus the question of cap-

ital loss treatment would not arise. Sale of taxpayer's home at a gain, in addition to being eligible for capital gain treatment, is also eligible for exemption from tax or deferral of tax, see ¶¶ 4.04(2) and 4.05(4).

**10.** A loss on the sale of such assets would not be allowed at all, see note 8 above, unless the property were not held for personal use. The taxpayer's personal-use car is also a capital asset; rare, however, is the taxpayer who sells his personal-use car for a gain.

**11.** Another source for rules to be followed blindly in this area is Form 1040, Schedule D. While the Schedule D certainly yields the correct results, it is less clear what is really going on under the Schedule D approach than the approach taken in the text.

So let's say you net them together and get a gain. Then we will apply the gain rules.

Step 2) The gain rules: Separate the transactions by holding period. Assets held longer than a year before they were sold are long term gains or losses; assets held less than a year before they were sold are short-term capital gains and losses.

Step 3) Look to see if you have something called "net capital gain." If you have this "net capital gain," then you qualify for a special lower rate of tax. There is a pattern of capital gains that yields the "net capital gain." The pattern is given by the formula:

Net Long Term Capital Gains minus Net Short Term Capital Losses or

Net Capital Gain = NLTCG − NSTCL (see § 1222(11))

Note that the term "net capital gain" is a very specialized term. For example, it does not refer to short-term capital gains. If, for example, you had a pattern of transactions of $10,000 STCG and a $5,000 STCL, do you have a "net capital gain," under the statute?

No. Putting these numbers in the formula doesn't give you anything.

See:

Net Capital Gain = ($0) − ($0)

Net Capital Gain = $0.

Net Capital Gain is zero on these numbers, even though your capital gain transactions are positive. Net capital gain is very interested in long term capital gains and not at all interested in short term capital gains.

Step 4) If you have a "net capital gain," as thus defined, apply the maximum tax rate of 28% to that amount of income, even though the taxpayer's income would normally be taxed at a higher bracket on this income, such as up to the maximum bracket of 39.6%.

Step 5) Add the amount of tax generated in Step 4 above to the normal tax on the rest of the taxpayer's income. That total is the taxpayer's total tax.

The workings of this five-step process can be illustrated by an example:

**Example:** B has the following capital transactions: A long-term capital gain of $20,000; a long-term capital loss of $10,000; a short-term capital gain of $5,000; a short-term capital loss of $2,500. The only other income B has is salary of $250,000.

*Step 1:* Collecting all his capital transactions without regard to holding period, B has a capital gain net income of $12,500. The rules for capital gains apply.

*Step 2:* Grouping all his capital transactions by holding period, B has two long-term transactions—the $20,000 gain and the $10,000 loss; B has two short-term transactions—the $5,000 gain and the $2,500 loss.

*Step 3:* Look to see if B has "net capital gain." The formula is: Net Capital Gain = NLTCG − NSTCL. B has a net long-term capital gain of $10,000 and a net short-term capital loss of $0. (Since with respect to short-term transactions B has in fact a net short-term capital *gain,* obviously the amount of his net short-term capital *loss* is $0). Thus B has a Net Capital Gain of $10,000

*Step 4:* Apply the maximum tax rate of 28% to that amount of Net Capital Gain, producing $2,800 of tax liability.

*Step 5:* Add the $2,800 of tax generated in Step 4 above to the normal tax on the rest of the taxpayer's income. The tax on the rest of his income is $79,772. (Note on these examples, the rate brackets are indexed for inflation—§ 1(f)—so the Code you are using may produce slightly different results on this calculation). Thus the total tax is $82,752.

Further short examples: If C has a net long-term capital gain of $5000 and a net short-term capital loss of $1000, then the Net Capital Gain eligible for the 28% ceiling is $4000.

If D has a net long-term capital loss of $10,000 and a net short-term capital gain of $12,000, then there is no Net Capital Gain eligible for the 28% ceiling.[12]

### (ii) Capital Loss Rules

The very attractive benefit of capital gains—particularly long-term capital gains—is counterbalanced by restrictive rules when the taxpayer undergoes capital losses. The loss rules are of some complexity.

As a general overview, all capital losses occurring during the taxable year may be deducted by the taxpayer to the extent of all capital gains occurring during the year.[13] Thus if a taxpayer undergoes $1 million in

**12.** Consider the following example: Net long-term capital gain $1000; net short-term capital loss $1500. This circumstance could not arise under the rules for capital gain net income, because under Step 1 this set of facts would not give rise to a capital gain net income. This set of facts would be governed by the loss rules, discussed below.

In the 1993 Tax Act Congress added a benefit for the sale of small business stock. Under new § 1202, the treatment arises from gains of "qualified small business stock," defined as stock of a business whose gross assets do not exceed $50 million and which engages in any trade or business other than the performance of personal or financial services. If the particular requirements are met, an individual selling the stock of such a business can exclude 50% of the gain up to a maximum of 10 times the taxpayer's basis in the stock or $10 million. The includible 50% still gets the benefit of the favorable 28% maximum rate. The seller must have acquired the stock from original issuance by the company, not through any later purchases. Thus does Congress once again attempt to help small businesses.

**13.** § 1211(b)(1), Reg. § 1.1211–1(b)(1). See ¶¶ 4.04 and 4.05 for discussion of whether a loss is deductible at all.

capital losses in a taxable year, he may deduct that $1 million capital loss against $1 million of capital gains that also occurred during the year.

However, suppose the taxpayer has undergone $1 million in capital losses but has enjoyed only $500,000 in capital gains. It is here that the restrictive rules bite heavily. Congress has decreed that a taxpayer may in general deduct capital losses in excess of his capital gains only to the extent of $3000.[14] Thus in the example above the taxpayer may in general take a deduction for only $503,000 of his $1 million in capital losses in the particular taxable year. Unused capital losses may be carried over and deducted the following taxable year. The above discussion has been only an overview.

The particular technical steps that must be followed to ascertain the proper deduction for capital losses are set forth below.

The procedure is to collect all capital gains and losses transactions, without regard to how long the property was held before it was sold or exchanged and ascertain the net result. (This is the same first step as in the gains branch. It is in this step that the taxpayer ascertains whether he will be following the gain rules or the loss rules.) If all the capital gains and losses transactions taken together without regard to holding periods give rise to a loss, then it is appropriate to employ the capital loss rules. (If all the transactions taken together give rise to a gain, then the capital gain net income rules discussed above should be used).

If indeed all the transactions taken together yield a loss, then nothing should be entered in gross income. Entering nothing in gross income has the effect of allowing losses to be deducted to the extent of gains—the losses have washed out the gains.

Then the capital losses can be further deducted beyond capital gains up to a limit of $3,000. This is not much given that the taxpayer might have a net capital loss of several million dollars. Remaining losses beyond the $3,000 limit are carried forward to the following year, retaining their character as long term or short term.

Thus suppose Myrtl, with $100,000 of salary income, underwent a $300,000 short term capital loss in year 1 and had no other capital transactions. She could deduct $3,000 of that in year 1 and would carry over $297,000 of short term capital loss for the next year. If in the years thereafter she never had another capital gain or loss transaction, she would continue to carry forward this short term capital loss, deducting $3,000 per year. It would take 100 years to deduct the short-term capital loss in full. Since capital loss carryovers die with the taxpayer, the only way Myrtl would be able to deduct this loss in full is if she incurred it when she was very young.

---

14. § 1211(b)(1) and (b)(2)(B). As discussed below in the text, the precise limit is the lesser of $3000 or taxable income reduced by the zero bracket amount. Note also that this discussion applies only to non-corporate taxpayers. Corporate taxpayers may deduct capital losses only to the extent of capital gains, § 1211(a), with excess capital losses carried over to other years, § 1212(a).

### (c) Planning Implications

A study of the capital gains and losses rules suggests a number of planning techniques for the taxpayer who holds capital assets. Many of these techniques are most likely to be used at the end of the taxable year, when the taxpayer is most conscious of improving his tax position. However, many of these techniques are appropriate at any time in the year and indeed some of them, to be effective, have to be undertaken at a time other than at the end of the taxable year.

### (i) Holding Appreciated Property Indefinitely

Looking at the capital gains rules first, it might be asserted that the most obvious technique is to be sure to hold an appreciated capital asset for longer than a year before selling it, in order to be taxed at the favorable rate accorded long-term capital gains. While there is certainly merit to this idea, an even better idea is not to sell the appreciated asset at all and incur no tax on it whatsoever. The extreme version of this approach involves the taxpayer never selling the asset and dying holding it, at which point the basis of the asset is stepped up to its fair market value in the hands of the taxpayer's heirs.[15] Thus the appreciation in the asset would never be taxed.[16] Even if this extreme approach is not taken, a taxpayer may be very well advised to hold an appreciated asset well beyond one year in order to defer payment of tax as long as possible.[17] These techniques, of course, derive not from the capital gains taxation rules but from the more fundamental principle that unrealized appreciation in the value of assets held is not taxed.[18]

### (ii) Holding an Appreciated Capital Asset Longer Than One Year

Tax considerations, however, do not always rule the world. Notwithstanding that, the best tax advice, all other things equal, is to hold an appreciated asset indefinitely, the taxpayer may well at some point desire to sell his appreciated property, either because he needs the cash for business or personal use or because he feels some new investment would be superior to his old investment. In the latter instance, the new investment should be significantly superior to the old investment in order to compensate for the fact the net proceeds available for the new investment will be diminished by the tax paid on the gain from the old investment.

If the appreciated property the taxpayer wishes to sell is not a capital asset, then it does not matter how long he has held the property; the gain will be taxed at ordinary income rates, since the transaction does not involve the sale or exchange of a capital asset. Where the

**15.**  § 1014. See ¶ 4.03(2)(e) as well as note 7, above.

**16.**  There are, of course, various roll-over and nonrecognition techniques available for a taxpayer to change the property he holds without paying a tax. See ¶ 4.05.

**17.**  See ¶ 8.02(1) for a discussion of the very great advantage of deferral of tax, particularly for the high income taxpayer.

**18.**  This is the case even though unrealized appreciation is indisputably income, in an economic sense. For further discussion of this issue as it relates to the comprehensive tax base, see ¶ 1.02(2)(b).

appreciated property involved is a capital asset, the taxpayer would be well-advised to hold the property for at least a year if he can, in order to take advantage of the special capital gains deduction.

### (iii) Selling Property That Has Declined in Value

Considerations are just the reverse, of course, when the property held by the taxpayer has declined in value so that he has an unrealized loss. Just as unrealized appreciation in value of assets held is not taxed, so too is it the case that unrealized losses are not deductible.[19] Therefore the well-advised taxpayer wants to realize his losses as soon as possible so as to receive the tax benefit early. This ability of the investment-oriented taxpayer to realize losses early and postpone realization of gains is a powerful, and perfectly legitimate, tax avoidance tool.[20]

Where the property held is a capital asset, the loss picture is not as attractive as with an ordinary asset, because of the limit on amount of deduction of net loss from capital transactions. Although the unused balance of capital losses can be carried over to subsequent years, it may take many years for the full tax benefit of a large capital loss to be received. This suggests that the taxpayer with a large unrealized loss on a capital asset may want to continue to hold the asset in the hope that it will ultimately go up in value, since the tax benefit from selling the property will not be substantial.

### (iv) Combined Gains and Losses

The considerations discussed above may well be different where the taxpayer has had (or anticipates having) several capital gain and loss transactions during his taxable year. Thus where the taxpayer has already realized a large capital gain, say $50,000, he need not hesitate in realizing a large capital loss, say $35,000, insofar as the $3000 limit is concerned. He will get the full benefit of the $35,000 loss (whether it is short-term or long-term) since the excess capital loss rules only bite to the extent capital losses exceed capital gains. Capital losses are always deductible in full to the extent of capital gains. Similarly where the taxpayer has already realized a capital loss, say $40,000, he may be less hesitant to realize a capital gain, say $60,000, since a large part of the gain, $40,000, will be washed out by the loss and he will only be taxable on the balance.

The formula for ascertaining what gets the favorable capital gains rate will yield surprising results, under some circumstances. Consider a taxpayer with a long-term capital gain of $4000, short-term capital gain of $1000, and one other capital loss of $500. The $500 capital loss could be either short-term or long-term, depending on when during the taxable year the taxpayer decides to sell the property. The question is whether it matters if the taxpayer sells the property early in the tax year as a $500 short-term capital loss, or whether he sells the property late enough in

---

**19.** Cf. ¶ 4.02.

**20.** For a discussion of the surprisingly powerful effect of deferral of tax, see the Prologue and ¶ 8.02(1).

the tax year so that it becomes a $500 long-term capital loss. At first blush one might expect that it would not matter whether the $500 loss is short-term or long-term, since overall the gains exceed the losses, so the losses are fully deductible, whether short-term or long-term. However, the capital gain formula has the effect that it is more attractive if the loss is taken as a short-term loss, under these conditions.

This is the case because if the $500 loss is taken as a long-term loss, the amount available for the favorable capital gains rate is $3500–$0. (Net Long term capital gain of $3,500 minus net short-term capital loss of $0). If the $500 loss is taken as a short-term loss, the amount available for the favorable rate will be $4,000 (net long-term capital gain of $4,000 minus net short-term capital loss of $0).

Thus, the lesson that can be drawn from this is that: *It is preferable that a loss be taken as a short-term loss for any loss up to the amount of the short-term gain, where the taxpayer also has a net long-term gain.* This is because where the loss is short-term it will be consumed by the short-term gain and therefore not enter into the formula to diminish the amount eligible for the favorable capital gains rate.

The formula for computing the amount eligible for the favorable capital gains rate yields another surprising result, under other conditions. Consider a taxpayer with a long-term capital gain of $4000, a short-term capital loss of $2000, and one other capital gain of $1000. The $1000 capital gain could be either short-term or long-term, depending on when during the taxable year the taxpayer decides to sell the property. In the first instance one might expect that it would be preferable to hold the property later into the year in order to take the $1000 gain as a long-term capital gain. After all, long-term capital gains are eligible for the favorable rate. However, under these particular conditions, it does not matter whether the $1000 capital gain is taken as a long-term or a short-term gain.

This is the case because if the $1000 gain is taken as a long-term capital gain, the amount available for the favorable rate will be $3,000 ($5,000 net long-term capital gain minus $2,000 net short term capital loss). If the $1000 gain is taken as a short-term capital gain, the amount available for the favorable rate will also be $3,000 ($4,000 net long term capital gains minus $1,000 net short-term capital loss). Thus under these particular conditions, it does not matter whether the $1000 capital gain is taken as a short-term or a long-term gain.

The lesson that can be drawn from this is that: *Where the taxpayer has a short-term loss and a net long-term gain larger than the short-term loss, it does not matter whether any gain up to the amount of the short-term loss is short-term or long-term.* This is because under these conditions the gain increases the amount of the amount available for the favorable capital gains rate by the same amount whether it is short-term or long-term. It does so by either decreasing the amount of the net short-term capital loss or increasing the amount of the net long-term capital gain.

A variation of the rule above is also true: *Where the taxpayer has a short-term loss and no long-term transactions at all, it does not matter whether a gain up to the amount of the short-term loss is short-term or long-term.* This is because in either case the gain will not qualify for the favorable rate for capital gains.

The above discussion has indicated that the conventional wisdom of how capital transactions should be handled does not always hold up when capital transactions occur in particular combinations. Thus a taxpayer with several capital transactions in one year should study his position carefully before deciding on the holding period of any particular gain or loss.

*(v) Holding Period Problems; Short Sales and Short Sales "Against the Box"*

As the preceding discussion has indicated, the holding period is a key factor in determining how a taxpayer will be taxed on capital gains and losses. The length of time a taxpayer holds property is generally entirely within his control. The statutory scheme in this area clearly invites the taxpayer to decide, purely on tax considerations, how long he will hold his property. That a taxpayer has held onto property for longer than a year solely for the purpose of enjoying the favorable rate on long-term capital gains will not be a ground for the Service or the Courts to disallow the favorable treatment on the basis that the transaction was "tax-motivated" or had no "business purpose." This is in sharp contrast to some other areas of the tax law, where the taxpayer's failure to show non-tax motivations or failure to show a "business purpose" will be a reason to deny him favorable treatment.[21]

Usually there is no doubt as to whether a taxpayer has held property longer than one year to qualify for a long-term gain or loss or one year or less to qualify for a short-term gain or loss. However, occasionally a taxpayer will sell property he has held for right around one year, and it becomes necessary to count carefully months or days (if not minutes) to ascertain the proper treatment.[22]

In general, the holding period is the period the taxpayer has owned the property usually with reference to state law.[23] In determining this, consideration must be given not only to the dates on which the bare legal title passes but also to the dates on which the benefits and burdens of

**21.** Cf. Knetsch v. United States, 364 U.S. 361, 81 S.Ct. 132, 5 L.Ed.2d 128 (1960)(purchase of annuities yielding interest of 2½% financed by nonrecourse indebtedness bearing interest of 3½%, resulted in denial of deduction for the interest because nothing of "substance" was realized by the taxpayer beyond a tax advantage.) See ¶ 6.03(6)(b). Evolving a theory of when it is necessary to show more than just a tax motivation for a transaction to be respected is beyond the scope of this work. See Blum, The Importance of Form in the Taxation of

Corporate Transactions, 54 Taxes 613 (1976).

**22.** The holding period also determines whether or not property will qualify as an § 1231 asset, see ¶ 4.06(3)(a)(iv).

**23.** McFeely v. Commissioner, 296 U.S. 102, 56 S.Ct. 54, 80 L.Ed. 83 (1935), reh'g denied 296 U.S. 664, 56 S.Ct. 304, 80 L.Ed. 473 (1935); R. O'Brien and Co., Inc. v. United States, 56–1 U.S.T.C. ¶ 9261, 1956 WL 10399 (D.Mass.1956).

ownership are transferred in closed transactions.[24] This somewhat imprecise rule, grounded as it is in the vagaries of state law, can lead to some uncertainty.[25] In nonrecognition transactions, gifts, and certain other transactions, other rules will apply, usually involving lengthening the holding period to include the holding period of some other property or some other taxpayer.[26]

It is well established in the law in general that in computing a period of time "from" or "after" a particular day, the day thus designated is excluded and the last day of the period involved is included.[27] Consistent with that practice, the Service has ruled that in measuring the period property has been held for capital gains and losses purposes, the day the property was acquired is excluded and the day the property is sold is included.[28] Moreover, the holding period is measured in terms of months, not total days.[29] Thus, if A buys property on November 7, 1984, the first day of his holding period is November 8, 1984. On December 8, 1984, A has held the property for more than one month. If A sells the property on November 7, 1985, he has not held the property for more than one year. If he sells the property on November 8, 1985, he has held the property for more than one year. If B buys property on February 28 in a year which is not a leap year and sells it in the following year which is a leap year on February 29, he has not held the property for more than a year. He must sell the property on March 1st of the following year to have held the property for more than a year.[30]

Where the transaction involved is a short sale, the rules are a little more harsh. It is in fact very difficult for a taxpayer to enjoy a long-term capital gain on a short sale. Short sales usually involve securities or commodities futures traded on national or regional exchanges, although in principle they could involve any sort of property. As an example of a short sale, a seller will sell stock he does not own to a buyer, in a usual brokerage transaction. The seller will in effect borrow the stock from his broker (who has his own inventory of the stock or who borrows it from another customer or another brokerage house) for delivery to the buyer. At the time of the short sale the seller receives the proceeds of the sale,

**24.** Merrill v. Commissioner, 336 F.2d 771 (9th Cir.1964). Thus in the typical real estate transaction, the holding period would not begin at the time the parties go to contract, but could begin at the closing date, if title passes then under state law, and would certainly begin when the seller takes possession. See Rev.Rul. 54–607, 1954–2 C.B. 177.

**25.** See Morrison v. United States, 449 F.Supp. 654 (N.D.Ohio 1977).

**26.** For nonrecognition transactions, see ¶ 4.05. For gifts, see ¶ 4.03(2)(c)(i). For property acquired from a decedent, see ¶ 4.03(2)(e). For holding period rules for bargain purchases of property by employ-ees, see § 83(f) and ¶ 2.03. For the rule on worthless securities, see ¶ 7.01(6)(b).

**27.** See Sheets v. Selden's Lessee, 69 U.S. 177 (2 Wall.), 17 L.Ed. 822 (1864).

**28.** Rev.Rul. 70–598, 1970–2 C.B. 168, also providing that with respect to securities the dates of purchase and sale are the trade dates, not the dates payment and delivery are made. Where stock or a security is acquired from a corporation by the exercise of rights to acquire such stock or security, the date on which the right to acquire is exercised is included in the holding period, § 1223(6), Reg. § 1.1223–1(f).

**29.** Rev.Rul. 66–7, 1966–1 C.B. 188.

**30.** That is the clear implication of Rev.Rul. 66–7, note 29 above.

although they must be held in the brokerage account against the time when the transaction is closed. At some later date the seller closes or covers his short position by buying the stock to replace the borrowed stock. It is the seller's hope that when he covers his short position he will be buying the stock at a price which is lower than the price at which he sold short, thereby enjoying a profit. If the seller covers his position at a price higher than the price at which he sold short he has a loss.

Selling short raises a number of tax questions. The first question is when is the transaction taxable? The possibilities are that the transaction could be taxed at the time of the short sale itself, when the amount realized is received; or at the date the seller orders his broker to cover the transaction (trade date) or at the day the stock is delivered back to the lender to close the transaction. The well-established rule is that the date the stock is delivered back to the lender, or the closing date, is the date the transaction is deemed to have occurred.[31] Thus if a calendar year taxpayer is short some stock and orders his broker to cover the transaction on December 31, and the cost of the stock is fixed as of that date, but the purchased shares are not delivered to the lender until January 3 of the following year, a loss realized on that transaction would only be reportable in that following year.[32] While this rule is disadvantageous when the short seller realizes a loss, it is advantageous when he realizes a gain.

Regarding the character of gains or losses from short sales, the rule is that capital gain or loss results to the extent that the property used to cover the short sale is a capital asset in the hands of the taxpayer.[33] Thus the typical investor engaging in short sales will have capital treatment.[34]

The stickiest problem in the area of short sales is the holding period. The holding period is not, as one might expect, the length of time between the short sale and the closing of the transaction. Rather, under the Regulations, the holding period is the length of time the taxpayer

**31.** Hendricks v. Commissioner, 423 F.2d 485 (4th Cir.1970), Reg. § 1.1233–1(a)(1).

It is interesting from a theoretical point of view to consider taxing the transaction as of the time of the short sale. This presents a sort of reverse *Logan* situation (see ¶ 8.03) wherein the amount realized is known but the adjusted basis—the cost of the stock to cover the transaction—is not known. Roughly analogizing to *Logan*, the procedure could be to tax the amount realized at the time of the short sale and allow a deduction when the transaction is closed. This issue would only be significant, of course, if the short sale and the closing occurred in different taxable years. Cf. discussion in the text.

**32.** Essentially the facts of *Hendricks*, note 31 above. Note that this treatment is inconsistent with the treatment of long transactions, where the trade dates of both buying and selling securities are determinative of the timing of the transaction. See discussion above. The stated reason for this discrepancy is the supposed flexibility in delivery time of securities to cover a short position, *Hendricks*, above.

**33.** § 1233(a). Where a taxpayer has sold short, it may happen that a dividend is declared on the stock sold short. In that case, the taxpayer would have to make a payment equal to the dividend to the lender of the securities. That payment is deductible as an investment or business expense by the taxpayer, Rev.Rul. 72–521, 1972–2 C.B. 178.

**34.** See ¶ 4.06(3) for discussion of capital assets.

holds the property delivered to close the transaction.[35] Thus if a taxpayer sells X Corporation stock short on May 2, 1981 and closes the position out on May 10, 1982 with X Corporation stock bought for the purpose on May 5, 1982 (a typical pattern), the transaction will give rise to a short-term capital gain or loss.

This rule seems unjust in that the taxpayer has undergone the risks of the short position, and has had to put up margin of at least 50% of the short-sale proceeds, for more than a year and yet is denied long-term capital gain treatment should the transaction turn a profit. The only explanation of this rule appears to be that the Service, along with the other financial powers that be, does not want to encourage short selling in the securities markets.[36]

The only way for the taxpayer possibly to escape from this jardiniere is for him to close the transaction not by purchasing stock to cover his short position but by selling the short contract to someone else. The Tax Court in *dicta* has indicated that if the contract is a capital asset in the taxpayer's hands, as it likely would be, the holding period will be measured by the time elapsed between the date of the short sale and the date the contract was sold.[37] While selling the short position itself is a maneuver that may be available in the foreign exchange market and other specialized markets, it is not generally available in the securities markets and hence the typical taxpayer-investor will not easily be able to escape short-term treatment on closing his short sales.

The plot thickens in the short sale area where the taxpayer engages in a short sale "against the box." This maneuver involves selling stock short where the taxpayer already owns the same stock—thus the taxpayer is "long" and "short" at the same time. In such a situation the taxpayer clearly is not at risk, since whichever way the stock price moves, the taxpayer will have a gain on one branch of his investment and a loss on the other. A reason a taxpayer might engage in such an apparently pointless investment is to extend his holding period on a gain without risk and thus obtain a long-term capital gain.

For example, suppose a taxpayer buys 100 shares of Y Corporation stock on January 5, 1994 at $50. By July 10, 1994, the stock has appreciated to $80. The taxpayer would like to sell the stock on July 10, but doing so would result in a less favorable short-term capital gain. The taxpayer, however, fears that if he continues to hold the stock for a long-term capital gain his gain will evaporate. So on July 10, 1994, the taxpayer sells short 100 shares of Y Corporation stock. Now the taxpayer

---

**35.** Reg. § 1.1233–1(a)(3).

**36.** This rule is comparable to the rule on the major securities exchanges that short sales can only occur on an "uptick", or after an increase in the price of the stock. Thus do the securities laws and the tax laws discourage "bear raids."

**37.** LaGrange, 26 T.C. 191 (1956) (*dicta* re currency transactions).

This rule does not apply to "hedging transactions." There are special rules for commodity transactions. These matters are discussed below.

is immune from further risk on the movement of Y Corporation stock. He cannot make further gain from the movement of the stock, but he cannot lose the gain he already has.[38]

On January 6, 1995, the taxpayer closes out the short position by delivering the stock he holds long. The taxpayer's theory here is that he should have a long-term capital gain of $30 no matter what the price of the stock. As discussed above the two positions always net out to a $30 gain, no matter what the price of the stock. Both positions are long-term, under the taxpayer's theory. The long position is long-term because the taxpayer has in fact held the stock for more than a year. The short position is long-term because it has been covered by stock held for more than one year. Thus does the taxpayer secure a long-term capital gain without having borne the economic risk of the investment for the long-term holding period.[39]

Congress threw cold water on this short sale "against the box" insofar as holding periods are concerned. It provided that as to the short-sale branch of the transaction, any gain on the closing of a short sale will be short-term if at the time of the short sale, "substantially identical" property has been held by the taxpayer for less than a year[40] (as in the example above). Any loss on the short sale branch will be long-term (unattractive) under the general short sale rules discussed above. As to the long side of the short sale "against the box" transaction, Congress provided that the holding period of the stock held long at the time of the short sale commences on the date of the closing of the short sale, or on the date of any other sale or other disposition of the property, whichever

---

**38.** There will be additional transaction costs, but they will be minimal compared to the tax advantages. Moreover, the brokerage commissions themselves can be offset against the gain. See ¶¶ 4.03(1), 6.03(4).

**39.** Moreover, the taxpayer has also deferred realization of the gain until the following year.

**40.** § 1233(b)(1). "Property" for the purpose of these rules includes only stocks and securities (including stocks and securities dealt with on a "when issued" basis) and commodity futures which are capital assets in the taxpayer's hands, Reg. § 1.1233–1(c)(1), cf. Corn Products Refining Co. v. Commissioner discussed at ¶ 4.06(3)(a)(ii). There are certain restrictions on the application of these rules to commodity futures, see text below. Options to sell property or "puts" are treated as short sales and the exercise or expiration is treated as the closing of the short sale for these purposes. This rule does not apply to an option to sell which is acquired on the same day as property identified as intended for use in exercising the option, as long as

the option, if exercised, is exercised through the sale of such property, § 1233(c). Thus conventional "spreading" transactions are not subject to these special short sales rules. For more on arbitrage and spreading transactions, see the discussion below.

If the option to sell is not exercised, its cost is added to the basis of the property, id. Stock index options do not toll individual stock holding periods.

A variation on the short sale "against the box" is also precluded by § 1233. In the variation pattern, the taxpayer sells short first. The stock then declines in value giving the taxpayer an unrealized gain. To lock up the gain, the taxpayer buys the underlying stock. At such time as the taxpayer has held the long stock for more than a year he closes the short position with the long stock. Again the taxpayer's theory might be that both positions are long-term, but the statute provides that both positions are short-term. Indeed, in a particularly harsh result the statute provides that both positions will be short-term, even if the taxpayer was short for longer than a year before he bought the underlying stock.

occurs first.[41] This of course inevitably gives rise to a short-term gain or loss on the stock when it is used to close the short position.[42] Thus these short-sale rules have rendered the short-sale "against the box" technique ineffective as a method of extending the holding period of assets without any economic risk. The Regulations provide further examples.[43]

However, the short sale "against the box" is still effective in postponing a gain from one taxable year into a following taxable year. As in the examples set forth above, taxpayer's capital gain, albeit short-term in nature was successfully postponed to the following taxable year.

The Service, in a Revenue Ruling 78–182, 1978–1 C.B. 265–270, has provided an extensive analysis of the tax consequence to the holders and writers of "puts," "calls," and related transactions and combinations of transactions entered into on national options exchanges. Where such options are exercised the price of the option is added on to the price of the underlying stock.

The holding period for a commodity futures contract to qualify for a long term capital gain (or loss) is six months.[44] This special treatment can be explained in part by the fact that the bulk of trading in commodity futures involves holding periods of less than a year.[45]

**41.** § 1233(b)(2). Note that these specialized rules discussed in the text hold only for the particular conditions of the short sale "against the box," namely that the short sale has been engaged in at a time when substantially identical stock has been held for less than the long-term holding period.

Where a taxpayer engages in an "arbitrage transaction,"—for example buys warrants to purchase stock of X Company and sells the stock of X Company short, to profit from a premium in the price of the warrant—this arbitrage transaction, if clearly identified, will not affect the holding period of other X stock of X Company held by the taxpayer, § 1233(f), Regs. § 1.1233–1(f).

In ascertaining whether this rule shortening the holding period will apply, property held or sold short by the taxpayer and his spouse (unless they are legally separated) will be considered together, § 1233(e)(2)(C), Reg. § 1.1233–1(d)(3). This is a surprisingly limited ownership attribution rule, considering the large amount of taxpayer planning and maneuvering in this area. Thus where stock is held by a taxpayer and sold short by his son, the statutory rule will not apply. Similarly there is no attribution for transactions by siblings, or transactions by a taxpayer and his controlled corporation. Why a much narrower ownership attribution rule is used in this area than in other areas—such as disallowance of losses, disallowance of capital gains,

treatment of stock redemptions—remains one of those mysteries that afflict the ownership attribution rules. See ¶ 4.05(7)(b).

**42.** To the extent that the taxpayer holds more stock long than he holds short, the normal holding period rules will apply to the excess. These specialized rules apply first to the stock bought earliest in time, § 1233(b)(2).

**43.** Reg. § 1.1233–1(c)(6).

If a taxpayer engages in a short sale and then closes it during a time in which he has been long the same stock, any loss on the short sale will be long term, § 1233(d) and see Reg. § 1.1233–1(c)(4) and examples under § 1.1233–1(c)(6).

**44.** § 1222 flush language. The long-term holding period of any commodity itself is one year. It is only contracts to deliver the commodity in the future, where the commodity is subject to the rules of a board of trade or commodity exchange, that are subject to the shorter holding period. For the rules determining whether or not a commodity future is a capital asset, see ¶ 4.06(3).

**45.** The legislative history also suggests that it is only agricultural commodity futures that are to be subject to the six-month holding period, but the statute applied it to all commodity futures, See General Explanation of the Tax Reform Act of 1976, 1976–3 C.B. 1 at 439.

Hedging transactions in commodity futures are exempt from the statutory short sale rules discussed above.[46]

### (vi) Tax Straddles

Prior to the Economic Recovery Tax Act of 1981, an extremely significant tax avoidance maneuver was the so-called commodity "tax straddle." This maneuver grew out of the fact that a commodity future requiring delivery in one calendar month was not considered as property "substantially identical" to another commodity future of the same commodity requiring delivery in a different calendar month.[47] The importance of this was that transactions in the nature of the short sale "against the box" (See ¶ 4.06(2)(c)(v)) or going short and long at the same time were therefore possible in commodity futures without the holding periods being shortened by § 1233. Given the failure of § 1233 to reach these transactions, the Service, prior to the Economic Recovery Tax Act of 1981, was forced to summon up older doctrines of "substance over form," "sham transactions," lack of "purposive economic activity" to combat the proliferating commodity futures tax shelters.[48]

The Economic Recovery Tax Act of 1981 foreclosed these tax straddles. To appreciate fully the rather draconian rules imposed by that legislation it is useful to review the operations of tax straddles prior to ERTA.

The fundamental maneuver in the commodity futures tax straddle is illustrated by this example (the so-called "butterfly spread"):[49]

A has a short-term capital gain of $150,000 from the sale of real property in 1975. To minimize the tax on that transaction, A then engages in the following transaction:

(1) On August 1, 1975, A sells short 40 silver futures contracts for July 1976 delivery at total contract price of $2,000,000, and

---

**46.** § 1233(g). See also Corn Products Refining Co. v. Commissioner discussed at ¶ 4.06(3)(a)(ii); Rev.Rul. 72–179, 1972–1 C.B. 57; Regs. § 1.1233–1(b) Letter Ruling 7847004. These authorities generally define hedging for these purposes as a transaction in commodity futures entered into by one in a business to protect the business from fluctuations in the future market price of a commodity used in that business. Where "hedging" is employed as a purely tax avoidance device, it is subject to other rules. See text below.

**47.** § 1233(e)(2)(B). Reg. § 1.1233–1(d)(2), providing the example that commodity futures in May wheat and July wheat are not considered for the purposes of § 1233 to be substantially identical property.

Thus do commodity futures seem to live a charmed life under the Internal Revenue Code. They are not covered by the "wash sale" provision, § 1091 (see ¶ 4.05(6)); the long-term holding period is only 6 months (note 45 above); and futures contracts for different months are not reached by § 1233 as discussed in the text.

**48.** Rev.Rul. 77–185, 1977–1 C.B. 49, citing the venerable Gregory v. Helvering, 293 U.S. 465, 55 S.Ct. 266, 79 L.Ed. 596 (1935) (relating to corporate reorganizations) and Knetsch v. United States, 172 Ct.Cl. 378, 348 F.2d 932 (1965), cert. denied 383 U.S. 957, 86 S.Ct. 1221, 16 L.Ed.2d 300 (1966) (relating to purchase of a deferred annuity, see ¶ 6.03(6)(b) to bar a short-term capital loss on a spread on silver futures for different months).

**49.** This example is taken from Rev. Rul. 77–185, note 48 above.

simultaneously purchases 40 silver futures contracts for March 1976 delivery at a total contract price of $1,951,000.

(2) On August 4, 1975, A sells the forty futures contracts purchased on August 1 for March 1976 delivery at a total contract price of $1,825,000. On the same day A purchases 40 silver futures contracts for May 1976 delivery at a total contract price of $1,851,-000 to maintain a balanced position.

(3) On February 18, 1976, A sells the forty futures contracts purchased on August 4, 1975, at a total contract price of $2,025,000 and covers the short position established on August 1, 1975 by purchasing forty futures contracts for July 1976 delivery at a total contract price of $2,051,000. (The commission on the closing of each transaction was $2,000.)

For 1975 A reported the following transactions:

| | |
|---|---:|
| short-term gain from sale of real estate | $150,000 |
| less—short-term loss from sale of March 1976 silver futures (after commissions) | ($128,000) |
| net short-term gain | $22,000 |

For 1976 the taxpayer reported the following transactions:

| | |
|---|---:|
| long-term gain from sale of May 1976 silver futures (after commission) | $172,000 |
| less—short-term loss from short sale of July 1976 silver futures (after commission) | ($53,000) |
| net long-term gain | $119,000 |

*Taxpayer's Analysis:* Since commodity futures of different months on the same commodity are not "substantially identical property" for purposes of § 1233(b), the gain on the sale of the May 1976 silver futures is considered long-term.[50] The sale on August 4, 1975, of the March 1976 silver futures for a loss and the purchase on that date of the May 1976 futures does not come within the wash sale rules and hence the loss is recognized.[51] Thus does A convert a $150,000 short-term gain into a $22,000 short-term gain and a $119,000 long-term gain, while undergoing no economic risk in so doing. The difference between A's original gain of $150,000 and his total gain after this spread of $141,000 ($22,000 + $119,000) is due to commissions and other transactions costs. But a high bracket taxpayer saves far more in taxes than the $9000 this spread costs.[52]

On these facts, the Service ruled first that the August 4 sale and repurchase resulted in no real change of economic position and hence did not represent a closed and completed transaction. Thus the loss in 1975

---

**50.** See discussion above.

**51.** See note 78 above. The loss is taken under § 165(c)(2). See ¶ 4.04.

**52.** An additional attraction, although of lesser significance, is that the bulk of the gain has been postponed for one year.

was not allowed.[53] Therefore, when the spread was closed out in 1976 it resulted only in an economic loss of $9000. The $9000 was not allowed as a deduction, since the whole spread was entered into for the purpose of creating an artificial short-term capital loss; taxpayer had no reasonable expectation of deriving an economic gain from the spread.[54]

Notwithstanding the rather heavy weight of authority against these commodity tax shelters[55] taxpayers continued thereafter to engage in "spreads," "straddles," "paired straddles," "butterflies," "London Option Tax Shelters," "cash and carry silver spreads," "Bermuda transactions," for the purpose of securing purely tax advantages.[56]

To foreclose continued taxpayer abuse in this area, the Economic Recovery Tax Act of 1981 provided a web of rules. The major rule is that commodity futures contracts held by a taxpayer must be treated as if they were sold for their fair value on the last business day of the year (the so-called "mark-to-market rule"). Capital gain or loss resulting from a contract which was marked-to-market is treated as if 60% of the gain or loss were long term and 40% gain or loss were short term.[57] Thus, does the "mark-to-market" rule prevent taxpayers from realizing the loss on a balanced straddle transaction while postponing realization of the gain until the following year. Only the net loss on all commodities futures transactions, after being marked to the market, will be usable against other income. This mark-to the market rule applies even if the taxpayer only owns one commodities futures contract and is not in any way attempting to engage in a tax straddle. This mark-to the market rule is not a particular inconvenience to commodities futures brokers, since this same approach is used for determining investor margin requirements in commodities futures investments. Unused mark-to-market losses can be carried back for three years against mark-to-market gains, under § 1212(c).

The Economic Recovery Tax Act also provided that Treasury Bills and other short-term Government obligations issued at a discount will

**53.** Rev.Rul. 77–185, note 48 above.

**54.** Id. See also Frederick R. Horne, 5 T.C. 250 (1945) (taxpayer within a few days sold for a loss and then repurchased a membership in the New York Coffee and Sugar Exchange. Held: loss barred.) Compare the "wash sale rules," ¶ 4.05(6); Gordon MacRae, 34 T.C. 20 (1960), remanded 294 F.2d 56 (9th Cir.1961), cert. denied 368 U.S. 955, 82 S.Ct. 398, 7 L.Ed.2d 388 (1962), reh'g denied 368 U.S. 1005, 82 S.Ct. 598, 7 L.Ed.2d 548 (1962) (singer Gordon MacRae went flat and was denied interest deduction on account of lack of purposive economic activity); Goldstein v. Commissioner, 364 F.2d 734 (2d Cir.1966), cert. denied 385 U.S. 1005, 87 S.Ct. 708, 17 L.Ed.2d 543 (1967) (interest deduction denied on grounds of lack of purposive economic activity); Knetsch v. United States, note 48 above.

**55.** Id. Compare Rev.Rul. 78–414, 1978–2 C.B. 213 (sale of a futures contract on Treasury Bills gave rise to a capital gain, notwithstanding that Treasury Bills themselves are not a capital asset under § 1221(5)).

**56.** See Internal Revenue Service, "Commodity Options and Futures," IR Manual Transmittal 4236–7, May 30, 1980.

**57.** § 1256. These mark-to-market rules apply to property acquired and positions established after June 23, 1981. Taxpayers may elect, however, to have the new rules applied to all regulated futures contracts or positions which were held on June 23, 1981. Also, taxpayers may elect to mark to the market their futures contracts for the entire year of 1981, as if the 1982 rates were in effect.

be treated as capital assets, to foreclose the Treasury Bill tax straddle, see ¶ 4.06(3)(a).

When a commodity futures contract lapses, expires, or is otherwise terminated without being sold, the treatment prior to the Economic Recovery Tax Act of 1981 was that a loss on such a transaction would be an ordinary loss, since the expiration, lapse, etc. was not a sale or exchange. To prevent taxpayers from enjoying the attractive ordinary loss treatment on the lapse or expiration of commodity futures contracts during the year, The Economic Recovery Tax Act of 1981 provided, under § 1234A, that these transactions in general give rise to a capital loss.

If the taxpayer engages in a straddle transaction which does not involve regulated futures contracts, the mark-to-market rule does not apply. Rather, the losses on such a transaction are allowed only to the extent they exceed the unrealized gains on the straddle transaction (including, in consideration of whether a straddle is in effect, the transactions of certain related individuals). Losses disallowed under this rule are treated as having been incurred in the following taxable year, § 1092. The IRS will promulgate regulations applying the wash-sale and short-sale rule to straddles.

Interest and carrying charges attributable to straddles must, after the Economic Recovery Tax Act of 1981, be capitalized rather than deducted immediately as an ordinary income deduction, § 263(g).

A number of taxpayers engage in futures transactions not for the purpose of speculation, but rather to simply eliminate the risk of loss on price fluctuations in raw materials and currencies. The new mark-to-market rules and the rule requiring capitalization of carrying charges do not apply to such hedging transactions, if two conditions are met: (1) the taxpayer treats the gain or loss arising from such hedging transactions as ordinary income or loss; and (2) the taxpayer identifies the transaction as a hedging transaction before the close of the day on which he enters into it, § 1256(e). (Compare ¶ 4.06(3)(a)(ii), relating to "Corn Products" assets.) Tax shelters syndicates may not in general make use of these somewhat more attractive rules for hedging transactions.[58]

### (3) Definition of Capital Gains and Losses

As discussed earlier, the fundamental transaction that gives rise to the operation of the capital gains and losses rules is that there has to have occurred a "sale or exchange of a capital asset."[59] The key definitional terms here of course are "sale or exchange," and "capital asset." The taxpayer with a transaction that yields a gain wishes to argue, of course, that he has engaged in a "sale or exchange," and that the property so sold or exchanged was a "capital asset." By the same token the taxpayer with a transaction that yields a loss in general wishes to

---

**58.** See Bowers, "New Law Eliminates Most Tax Straddle Benefits: An Analysis of the Drastic Changes," 55 J.Tax. 338 (1981).

**59.** § 1222.

argue either that he did not engage in a "sale or exchange" or that the property involved was not a "capital asset" (or both). Note that the taxpayer seeking capital gains treatment must meet both tests to receive the favorable treatment accorded capital gains. The taxpayer seeking to avoid the restrictive capital loss rules need only fail one of the tests.

Capital gains are entirely a creation of the tax law. As discussed in more detail below, there is no underlying economic definition of capital gains. There is rather an ungainly and shifting collection of statutory and judicial rules which endow a certain group of transactions with the characteristic of being a "sale or exchange of a capital asset."

### (a) Statutory and Judicial Rules

Section 1221 defines capital asset as any property held by the taxpayer, excepting from that definition a number of broad classes of property.[60] Therefore, any property held by the taxpayer which does not come within the enumerated exceptions is a capital asset. This somewhat strange definitional approach can favor the taxpayer seeking capital gains, in a close case, since any property not specifically excepted from being a capital asset is a capital asset.[61]

The exceptions to the § 1221 general rule are:

(1) Property in the nature of inventory, or property held by the taxpayer primarily for sale to customers in the ordinary course of his trade or business.[62]

(2) Depreciable personal or real property used in the trade or business and non-depreciable real property used in the trade or business.[63]

(3) A copyright, a literary, musical or artistic composition, a letter or memorandum, or similar property held by a taxpayer whose personal efforts created such property.[64] In the case of a letter, memorandum, or similar property, if someone else prepared the material for the taxpayer who now holds it, the material is also not a capital asset.[65]

(4) Accounts or notes receivable acquired in the ordinary course of trade or business for services rendered or from the sale of

---

**60.** See also Reg. § 1.1221–1(a).

**61.** This statutory tilt in favor of the taxpayer is counterbalanced somewhat by the courts' tendency to interpret the statute against the taxpayer—not finding a capital asset in a border line case when the transaction involves a gain and finding a capital asset when the transaction involves a loss. See Corn Products Refining Co. v. Commissioner, 350 U.S. 46, 76 S.Ct. 20, 100 L.Ed. 29 (1955), reh'g denied 350 U.S. 943, 76 S.Ct. 297, 100 L.Ed. 823 (1956) (discussed below); Surrey, "Definitional Problems in Capital Gains Taxation," 69 Har.L.Rev. 985 (1956). Chirelstein, "Capital Gain and the

Sale of a Business Opportunity: The Income Tax Treatment of Contract Termination Payments," 49 Minn.L.Rev. 1 (1964).

**62.** § 1221(1).

**63.** § 1221(2). Reg. § 1.1221–1(b). See ¶ 6.02(12) regarding depreciation.

**64.** § 1221(3)(A). Reg. § 1.1221–1(c).

**65.** § 1221(3)(B). Reg. § 1.1221–1(c)(2). Where a taxpayer holds such property as a result of a gift or other nonrecognition transaction, the property will not be a capital asset as to him, § 1221(3)(C).

property in the nature of inventory described above.[66]

(5) Discount Government obligations with a maturity date less than one year from the date of issue, where the obligation was acquired before June 24, 1981. Government obligations with a maturity date of less than a year acquired after June 23, 1981, are capital assets in the hands of the holder, as a result of the Economic Recovery Tax Act of 1981.

This change in the treatment of Treasury Bills under the Economic Recovery Tax Act of 1981 was to forestall the so-called "T-bill tax straddle" in which taxpayers exploited the difference in tax treatment between T-bill futures contracts and the T-bills themselves. The IRS had ruled that gain or loss on the sale of a T-bill futures contract was a capital gain or loss, even though the gain or loss on the sale of a T-bill itself was ordinary under the statute. Taxpayers took advantage of this difference by going short and long on T-bill futures contracts. When the position moved, the taxpayer would have a loss on one leg of the transaction and a gain on the other. If taxpayer had a loss on the long side of the transaction, he would then take delivery and sell the bills themselves as a deductible ordinary loss, while having a capital gain on the short side of the transaction. If the taxpayer had a loss on the short leg of the transaction he would buy the bills and deliver them at the lower contract price, once again getting a deductible ordinary loss; while at the same time, he would have a capital gain on the other side of the transaction.

Thus, a taxpayer was always assured of a capital gain and an ordinary loss—which netted out to an attractive tax result even after consideration of commissions and transaction costs. Beyond the capital gain and ordinary loss aspects of the transaction, taxpayers could often also defer realization of their gain on the gain side of the transaction into a following year, and thereby enjoy the further advantage of deferral of income. Moreover, the realization of income could be deferred indefinitely by rolling over into a new straddle.

The "mark-to-market" rule and the new rule denominating federal, state, and local obligations issued at a discount and payable without interest at a fixed maturity date within one year from issue as capital assets effectively foreclose tax straddles of this type under these rules. The discount at the time the obligation is issued is treated as interest and taxed as ordinary gain.[67]

(6) Certain U.S. Governmental publications.[68]

Beyond these exceptions are a number of other statutory and judicial exceptions. Therefore it would be fair to say that a capital asset is property held by the taxpayer, except for the property specified in § 1221(1)–(5) and certain other property statutorily and judicially ex-

---

**66.** § 1221(4). Reg. § 1.1221–1(d).

**67.** § 1232(a)(4). Cf. ¶ 3.02 for the treatment of original issue discount.

**68.** § 1221(6), more specifically, U.S. government publications held by a taxpayer who did not purchase them at retail.

cepted. Beyond that it is also true that certain property which does not have capital asset status under these terms may still be endowed by the Code with capital asset status. These matters are all discussed below. The area is obviously far from simple. Indeed one would hardly expect it to be simple given the great stakes and pressures involved.

Before proceeding to these various definitions and exceptions, it is useful to bear in mind that all personal-use property held by the taxpayer—his home, a painting on his wall at home, his personal use car, the lawnmower used for his home—are capital assets and the sale or exchange of them at a gain would in general trigger the favorable capital gain rules. Such property is "held" by the taxpayer and is not subject to being further excluded from the status of a capital asset.[69] Note that if such personal-use property were sold or exchanged at a loss, the loss would be disallowed,[70] and hence the capital loss rules would not come into play.[71]

It is generally only when property is sold or exchanged that critical questions of the definition of a capital asset are raised. The various categories of property and transactions that are given special treatment with respect to the question of capital gain or loss status are discussed below, in turn. The large number of definitional rules in this area indicates the great taxpayer pressure (and countervailing governmental pressure) with respect to the favorable tax treatment of capital gains.

### (i) Inventory, Property Held Primarily for Sale to Customers

"Stock in trade ... inventory ... or property held by the taxpayer primarily for sale to customers in the ordinary course of his trade or business," is not a capital asset and its sale or exchange therefore yields ordinary gain or loss.[72] Thus the normal profits and losses of an ongoing business are accorded ordinary gain and loss treatment.[73]

---

**69.** In the case of the sale of the taxpayer's principal residence at a gain, tax may be deferred or forgiven altogether under certain conditions, see ¶¶ 4.05(4) and 4.04(5).

**70.** ¶ 4.04(2).

**71.** Thus the taxpayer is in a somewhat disadvantageous position with respect to his personal-use property. If he sells it at a gain, he is generally taxed on that gain (albeit at capital gain rates); if he sells his personal-use property at a loss, he gets no deduction whatsoever.

**72.** § 1221(1). "Ordinary" gain or loss in this context means "non-capital" gain or loss; the taxpayer does not receive the favorable capital gains treatment on an ordinary gain and is not subject to the restrictive capital loss rules on an ordinary loss.

A taxpayer would like to characterize a gain transaction as capital and a loss transaction as ordinary. The Service, of course,

takes just the opposite approach. Thus taxpayers and the Service will flip-flop their positions on a given type of transaction, depending on whether the particular case has yielded a gain or loss. This process tends to put a strain on the courts in their attempt to articulate consistent standards. See Comment, "The Troubled Distinction Between Capital Gain and Ordinary Income," 73 Yale Law J. 693 (1964).

**73.** One reason for this (although it can be perilous to search for reasons for according or withholding capital gains treatment) may be the lack of a "bunching" effect of gain in an ongoing business. Cf. ¶ 4.06(4), discussing the history and policy of capital gains taxation. See also Malat v. Riddell, 383 U.S. 569, 86 S.Ct. 1030, 16 L.Ed.2d 102 (1966), vac'g and remanding 347 F.2d 23 (9th Cir.1965). Corn Products Refining Co. v. Commissioner, 350 U.S. 46, 76 S.Ct. 20, 100 L.Ed. 29 (1955), reh'g denied 350 U.S. 943, 76 S.Ct. 297, 100 L.Ed.

There is a certain redundancy in the statute, inasmuch as "stock in trade," "inventory" and "property held by the taxpayer primarily for sale to customers in the ordinary course of his trade or business," all more or less amount to the same thing. Although the issue is usually clear there has been, over the years, a substantial amount of litigation over whether what the taxpayer has sold falls within this inventory-type class of property so as to give rise to ordinary gain or loss.[74]

This matter has been particularly vexing in the field of real estate. While it is hazardous to offer generalizations in this area, it could at least be said that the tendency of courts to find ordinary income on the sale of real estate will depend on the following factors: to the extent the taxpayer sells relatively many parcels in a given period of time, that will tend to suggest ordinary income treatment; to the extent the taxpayer engages in subdividing and otherwise improving the property, that will tend to suggest the taxpayer is in the real estate business and thus sales of the property will give rise to ordinary gain or loss; to the extent the taxpayer hires brokers, advertises, and engages in other promotional activity, that will tend to suggest ordinary gain or loss; to the extent the taxpayer uses the sales proceeds to buy other similar realty, that will suggest he is in the real estate business and thus give him ordinary gain or loss; beyond that, other facts and circumstances may bear on the question.[75]

For example in *Mauldin v. Commissioner*[76] the taxpayer in 1924 bought a large tract of land originally for cattle ranching. Due to a poor cattle market, he subdivided the property for residential purposes, and prior to 1940 he sold some of the lots. At that time he was undoubtedly in the business of selling real estate lots. After 1940 he made no effort to promote sales but nonetheless sold many lots due to expansion of a nearby city. The court, pointing out that indeed he sold more lots in 1945 than he did in 1940, held that at all times he had lots for sale and

823 (1956); Burnet v. Harmel, 287 U.S. 103, 106, 53 S.Ct. 74, 75, 77 L.Ed. 199 (1932).

**74.** See *Malat v. Riddell*, discussed in the text *infra*. See also Drybrough, 45 T.C. 424 (1966), aff'd per curiam 384 F.2d 715 (6th Cir.1967) (inventory sold in bulk still accorded ordinary asset treatment); compare § 337(b)(2) (regarding a bulk sale of inventory to one person in one transaction in a twelve month liquidation); Continental Can Co. v. United States, 190 Ct.Cl. 811, 422 F.2d 405 (1970), cert. denied 400 U.S. 819, 91 S.Ct. 35, 27 L.Ed.2d 46 (1970) (property treated as inventory though at one time it had been held for rent); United States v. Winthrop, 417 F.2d 905 (5th Cir. 1969) (the court, confronted with the question of whether inherited property that had been subdivided and sold gave rise to capital gain, observed: "Finding ourselves engulfed in a fog of decisions with gossamerlike distinctions, and a quagmire of un-

workable, unreliable and often irrelevant tests, we take the route of ad hoc exploration to find ordinary income.")

**75.** Id. Cf. Curtis Co. v. Commissioner, 232 F.2d 167 (3d Cir.1956) (improved property yielded capital gain; some unimproved property yielded capital gain and other unimproved property yielded ordinary income based on these various factors); Biedenharn Realty Co. Inc. v. United States, 526 F.2d 409 (5th Cir.1976), cert. denied 429 U.S. 819, 97 S.Ct. 64, 50 L.Ed.2d 79 (1976) (ordinary income found on sale of large number of lots notwithstanding lack of overt promotional activity); *Winthrop*, note 74 above sets forth a similar list of factors, 417 F.2d at 910. See Sills, The Dealer–Investor Problem Revisited: Charting a Course to Avoid the Pitfalls, 4 J.Real.Est.Tax. 24 (1976).

**76.** 195 F.2d 714 (1952).

that the volume depended on prevailing economic conditions. Notwithstanding that he was also in the lumber business after 1940, the court sustained the Tax Court's finding that taxpayer had ordinary income on the sale of his lots.

In the leading Supreme Court case of *Malat v. Riddell*[77] the Supreme Court held that the word "primarily" in the definitional phrase "... property held primarily for sale to customers in the ordinary course of (taxpayer's) trade or business ...",[78] means "of first importance." The implication of the Court's holding here is that if a taxpayer purchased and subdivided lots for the purpose of developing them and then, encountering financial difficulty, sold the lots off to various customers (approximately the facts of Malat), he would not hold the lots "primarily for sale to customers ..." Thus such a taxpayer would have capital gain or loss on the sale of the lots. The Court in fact vacated and remanded *Malat* for new findings of fact based on this standard. Taxpayer in *Malat* ultimately received capital gain on account of this standard.[79]

In the Supreme Court case of *Hort v. Commissioner,*[80] discussed also at ¶ 5.03, a lessor received a lump-sum payment from the lessee in cancellation of the lease. The taxpayer claimed a capital gain transaction, but the Court held that the amount received was ordinary income as a substitute for rent. As a corollary of the holding of ordinary income, taxpayer could not offset basis of property against the amount received.

*Metropolitan Building Co. v. Commissioner,*[81] discussed also at ¶ 5.04(2)(b), involved a case where, under a rather unusual set of facts, the sublessor released the sublease to the landlord in exchange for a payment from the sublessee. The sublessee then entered into a new lease on the same property with the landlord. Since the sublessor was paid for the release by the sublessee, the facts conjured up *Hort* and ordinary income. But since the release of the sublease was to the landlord, the facts also suggested § 1231–capital gain treatment. The Ninth Circuit struggled with this problem and heroically came up with the solution that the sublessor enjoyed § 1231–type capital gain treatment, since the release of the sublease was to the landlord. The source of the payment was held to be irrelevant.[82]

Congress in 1954 attempted to bring a modicum of rationality to the real estate area by providing, in § 1237, some objective tests to be met in order for sales of real estate to be given capital gain treatment.[83] § 1237 is not the most useful provision ever enacted into the Code. In general it

**77.**　383 U.S. 569, 86 S.Ct. 1030, 16 L.Ed.2d 102 (1966).

**78.**　Present § 1221(1).

**79.**　275 F.Supp. 358 (S.D.Cal.1966).

**80.**　313 U.S. 28, 61 S.Ct. 757, 85 L.Ed. 1168 (1941).

**81.**　282 F.2d 592 (9th Cir.1960).

**82.**　Id. at 597.

**83.**　1237 does not apply to corporations, § 1237(a). § 1237 does not apply to losses. It cannot make what otherwise would be an ordinary loss a capital loss, Reg. § 1.1237–1(a)(4). Cf. Buono, 74 T.C. 187 (1980) (acq.) 1981–5 I.R.B. 6 (Subchapter S corporation which subdivided property but ultimately sold 90% of it in one block had capital gain).

provides that capital gain will be accorded sales of real property notwithstanding the sales are from a tract the taxpayer has subdivided if: (1) No part of the tract being sold in the year in question was ever held by the taxpayer for sale in the ordinary course of his trade or business;[84] (2) In the year the property is sold from the tract the taxpayer holds no other real property for sale to customers in the ordinary course of his trade or business;[85] (3) No substantial improvement that substantially enhances the value of the parcel sold is made by the taxpayer on such tract, or is made by a contract of sale between the seller and the buyer;[86] (4) The lot or parcel sold has been held by the taxpayer for at least 5 years, unless he inherited it;[87] (5) In the year of the sale of the sixth lot, 5% of the selling price of all lots sold in that year and thereafter shall be treated as ordinary income.[88]

§ 1237 is not of great help. First of all it is not applicable if the tract involved was ever held by the taxpayer for sale in the ordinary course of his trade or business.[89] That of course begs the very question that § 1237 is designed to answer. Second, it is not exclusive. The Regulations state that the tests of § 1237 do not automatically disqualify the taxpayer from enjoying capital gain treatment on his sales of real property, if he can otherwise make out his position based on the caselaw in the field.[90] Thus § 1237 does not particularly further the cause of certainty in this area. Moreover, does this mean also that even if the taxpayer meets the tests of § 1237, the Service can make reference to the caselaw to defeat taxpayer's quest for capital gains? Finally, most anyone who could pass the relatively stringent tests of § 1237 probably would not need it. Such a person could rely on caselaw to secure capital gains treatment on his real estate sales. Anyone who really needs § 1237 to get capital gains cannot meet its tests.

Thus § 1237 is just another factor in the mush of factors in this field. The cases keep coming but clarity on the question of discriminating between sales of investment real property and sales of inventory real property must, apparently, wait another time.

The difficulties in the real estate area are in contrast to the sale and purchase of securities. The ordinary taxpayer buying and selling securities (stocks, bonds, convertibles, warrants, etc.) holds these instruments

---

**84.** § 1237(a)(1), Reg. § 1.1237–1(a)(5).

**85.** Id.

**86.** § 1237(a)(2), Regs. § 1.1237–1(a)(5). Thus the buyer as well as the seller can make improvements on the property which would prevent the application of § 1237, Reg. § 1.1237–1(c)(2)(iii). Special rules are provided to help ascertain what is a "substantial improvement," § 1237(b)(3). Reg. § 1.1237–1(c)(3)(ii). See Rev.Rul. 80–216, 1980–2 C.B. 239, regarding the applica-

bility of § 1237 to condominium conversions.

**87.** § 1237(a)(3); Reg. § 1.1237–1(a)(5).

**88.** § 1237(b)(1), Reg. § 1.1237–1(a)(5). Mitigating this already *de minimis* provision, the taxpayer may offset his selling expenses first against the ordinary income portion of the selling price, § 1237(b)(2), Reg. § 1.1237–1(e)(2)(ii) providing an example.

**89.** See discussion above.

**90.** Reg. § 1.1237–1(a)(4).

as capital assets and has capital gain or loss on their sale.[91] This is the case regardless of how many transactions the taxpayer-investor engages in; the securities will still not fall into the inventory category.[92] Securities bought and sold by registered brokers or dealers are not capital assets.[93] However, a registered broker or dealer may enjoy capital treatment on securities that he purchases if he complies with certain identification rules and does not in fact hold the securities primarily for sale to customers in the ordinary course of his trade or business.[94]

It is curious that a taxpayer can engage in virtually an unlimited number of trades with securities and still not lose capital gain and loss treatment; whereas a taxpayer who engages in a relatively few sales of real estate will probably lose capital gain and loss treatment.[95]

### (ii) "Corn Products" Assets

While the Code does not speak of a "Corn Products" asset as an asset which is considered not a capital asset, the Courts have interpreted the statute to create another category of asset which is not considered capital. The judicially-created "Corn Products" type asset arises when the taxpayer employs an asset which is *prima facie* a capital asset as an integral part of his business.

In the celebrated case of *Corn Products Refining Co. v. Commission-*

**91.** § 1221; Wood, 16 T.C. 213, 220 (1951); Kemon, 16 T.C. 1026, 1032 (1951) (despite numerous transactions, taxpayer held not to be a dealer in securities). Rev. Rul. 74–293, 1974–1 C.B. 54; Rev.Rul. 71–253, 1971–1 C.B. 228.

**92.** Mirro–Dynamics Corp. v. United States, 374 F.2d 14 (9th Cir.1967), cert. denied 389 U.S. 896, 88 S.Ct. 215, 19 L.Ed.2d 214 (1967) (though taxpayer, not a registered broker or dealer, engaged in thousands of securities transactions over a several-year period, it had capital losses on its losses).

The legislative history of § 1221(1) also shows that the phrase "to customers" was added to the predecessor of § 1221(1) to exclude from the definition of capital assets only those securities bought and sold by registered brokers or dealers. Securities traded by investors for their own account were not intended to be excluded from the definition of capital assets, H.Conf.Rep. No. 1385, 73rd Cong., 2d Sess., p. 22 (1939–1 C.B. (Part 2) 627, 632; Cf. S.Rep. No. 558, 73rd Cong., 2d Sess., p. 12 (1939–1 C.B. (Part 2) 586, 595.

Though a taxpayer is not a registered broker or dealer he may in fact be found to be a dealer for tax purposes, depending on the surrounding facts and circumstances, and thereby be denied capital gains treat-

ment on the sale of his securities, Frank v. Commissioner, 321 F.2d 143 (8th Cir.1963). (taxpayers previously had been registered brokers or dealers; their role in the transaction was to assist in raising capital; they owned a corporation which was a dealer in securities; they sold stock acquired in the transaction through this corporation to the public.) It is interesting to compare this result with the results in the securities law field, where an individual who is not a registered broker or dealer may still be regarded as a "statutory underwriter" if he participates in the offering of securities to the public, and thereby be required to meet the disclosure requirements of the Securities Act of 1933. See Securities and Exchange Commission v. Chinese Consolidated Benevolent Association, Inc., 120 F.2d 738 (2d Cir.1941), cert. denied 314 U.S. 618, 62 S.Ct. 106, 86 L.Ed. 497 (1941).

**93.** § 1236 and see legislative history to § 1221, note 92 above.

**94.** § 1236, Reg. § 1.1236–1.

**95.** In addition to the authorities discussed in this section, there has been a great deal of litigation over the capital asset status of many other kinds of property. The general principles discussed in this section would apply; but matters are often disposed of on a case-by-case basis.

er,[96] taxpayer was a manufacturer of starch, sugar and their by-products, as well as feeds and oil. Taxpayer made all these products from grain corn. Droughts in 1934 and 1936 caused a sharp increase in the price of spot corn. With only a three-week storage supply capacity, taxpayer could not buy corn at a price that would enable it to compete successfully with sugar made from cane and beets. To avoid a recurrence of this problem, taxpayer in 1937 instituted a program of establishing a long position in corn futures.[97] Then as shortages occurred and the price of corn rose, taxpayer's profits on its corn futures contracts balanced the squeeze on its profits from sugar refining. If the price of corn would drop, presumably taxpayer's losses on its corn futures would be made up by its increased profits from sugar refining. Thus, taxpayer's futures transactions were in the nature of hedging: it did not seek to make a killing in the commodities markets but rather sought to protect its business operations.[98] Taxpayer netted a profit of about $681,000 from its corn futures in 1940 and a loss from its corn futures of about $110,000 in 1942.

The problem in the case was that under the predecessor of § 1221[99] corn futures contracts were a capital asset, on a literal reading of the statute. Corn futures were "property held by the taxpayer" but were not, strictly speaking, inventory or stock in trade held by the taxpayer primarily for sale to customers in the ordinary course of its trade or business.[1] Taxpayer was not in the business of selling corn futures. The corn futures were certainly also not depreciable property used in the trade or business or real property used in the trade or business.[2] Nor were corn futures contracts even close to fitting into any of the other exceptions to the capital asset definition under the predecessor to § 1221. Thus there was an argument at that time that the corn futures were a capital asset, whose sale gave rise to capital gain or loss.

The Supreme Court, however, asserted that the definition of a capital asset must not be so broad as to defeat the purpose of Congress. The purpose of Congress, the Court felt, was clearly to deny capital gain or loss treatment to the profits and losses arising from the everyday operation of a business.[3] Thus it held that taxpayer had ordinary gain and loss on its corn futures transactions.

**96.**  350 U.S. 46, 76 S.Ct. 20, 100 L.Ed. 29 (1955), reh'g denied 350 U.S. 943, 76 S.Ct. 297, 100 L.Ed. 823 (1956).

**97.**  A corn or other commodity future is a contract to buy a fixed amount of the commodity at a fixed price at a future date. The purchaser of such a contract is said to be "long" and benefits from a rise in the price of the commodity. The seller of such a contract—who has thus agreed to sell the commodity at a fixed price on a future date—is said to be "short" and benefits from a drop in the price of the commodity. See ¶ 4.06(2)(c)(vi) for discussion of the

treatment of taxpayers who engage in "spreads" and "straddles", i.e., go long and short at the same time.

**98.**  See note 97 above.

**99.**  § 117(a) of the Internal Revenue Code of 1939, which for these purposes read approximately the same as the present § 1221.

**1.**  See § 1221(1).

**2.**  See § 1221(2).

**3.**  350 U.S. 46 at 52, 76 S.Ct. 20 at 24. See also note 5 above.

Methodologically, it might have been sounder for the Court to have interpreted the predecessor of § 1221(1) broadly not only to encompass inventory and stock in trade and property held primarily for sale to customers, etc., but also to encompass property used in the production of inventory. That could have led to the same desired and sound result but would have avoided the creation by the Court of a new class of noncapital asset property. As it was after *Corn Products,* it might be said there is a § 1221(1½) exception to capital asset treatment, which is an asset which appears on its face to be a capital asset but which is used as an integral part of the taxpayer's business.[4]

The emanations of *Corn Products* have radiated very far indeed.[5] Where taxpayer has purchased stock in a company that supplies it with material for its manufacturing business, the subsequent sale of the stock has been held to yield ordinary loss, on the basis of *Corn Products.*[6] Similarly other investments to secure business prospects have yielded ordinary treatment, even though the asset bought was *prima facie* a capital asset.[7] Notably, the *Corn Products* rule has been held not to apply to the purchase and sale of a partnership interest.[8]

Most of the cases decided in this area involve taxpayers with losses. It seems fair to surmise that taxpayers with *Corn Products* type invest-

---

4. See also § 1233(g).

5. It is still clear, however, that a purchase and sale of a commodity futures contract by a pure investor will still yield capital gain or loss, Faroll v. Jarecki, 231 F.2d 281 (7th Cir.1956), cert. denied 352 U.S. 830, 77 S.Ct. 45, 1 L.Ed.2d 51 (1956).

6. Waterman, Largen & Co. v. United States, 419 F.2d 845 (Ct.Cl.1969), cert. denied 400 U.S. 869, 91 S.Ct. 103, 27 L.Ed.2d 109 (1970) (assuring a supply of yarn to yarn seller); Booth Newspapers, Inc. v. United States, 157 Ct.Cl. 886, 303 F.2d 916 (1962) (newspaper bought stock in newsprint supplier to assure source of supply during post World War II newsprint shortage); Windle Co., 65 T.C. 694 (1976), appeal dism'd for lack of jurisdiction 550 F.2d 43 (1st Cir.1977), cert. denied 431 U.S. 966, 97 S.Ct. 2923, 53 L.Ed.2d 1062 (1977) (stock purchased with a substantial investment purpose is a capital asset even if there is a more substantial business motive for the purchase and even if the investment purpose later disappears). Union Pacific Railroad Co., Inc. v. United States, 524 F.2d 1343 (Ct.Cl.1975), cert. denied 429 U.S. 827, 97 S.Ct. 83, 50 L.Ed.2d 89 (1976) (stock of subsidiary corporations treated as noncapital assets for purposes of computing taxpayer's excess profits credit, citing *Corn Products, Booth Newspapers,* and *Waterman, Largen & Co.);* cf. Gulftex Drug Co., Inc., 29 T.C. 118 (1957), aff'd per curiam 261 F.2d 238 (5th Cir.1958) (stock bought originally to assure source of supply but subsequently held as an investment gave rise to long-term capital loss when sold).

7. Steadman v. Commissioner, 424 F.2d 1 (6th Cir.1970), cert. denied 400 U.S. 869, 91 S.Ct. 103, 27 L.Ed.2d 109 (1970) (attorney who purchased stock in music company to assure his position as general counsel had ordinary loss on his worthless stock when company went bankrupt); Rev. Rul. 58-40, 1958-1 C.B. 275 (describing three business situations in which the purchase and sale of stock, bonds, and debentures yields ordinary income treatment). Rev.Rul. 75-13, 1975-1 C.B. 67 (loss suffered by employee on employer's stock held capital notwithstanding that purchases of employer's stock were considered helpful to employee's career). Letter Ruling 7847004 (*Corn Products* will apply in currency transactions to give ordinary loss only when there is a direct relationship between the foreign currency transaction and a risk of exposure arising from the taxpayer's everyday business; moreover ordinary loss on short sales of foreign currency is allowed only where the corporation conducts its business in that country through a branch or division—not where the corporation conducts its business in the country through a subsidiary).

8. Pollack, Jr., 69 T.C. 142 (1977). See Davis, "The *Corn Products* Doctrine and its Application to Partnership Interests," 79 Colum.L.Rev. 341 (1979).

ments who have gains on them are just reporting them as capital gains. Since the assets involved are *prima facie* capital assets—i.e., shares of stock or commodity futures, etc.—the reporting of their sale as a capital gain on the taxpayer's return would not in general give rise to inquiry by the Service. It is probable that it is only when the *Corn Products*-type investment gives rise to a loss that taxpayers point out the shares of stock or commodity futures, etc. were integrally related to its business, that the motive for the purchase was predominantly business and that, therefore, the transaction should give rise to ordinary loss treatment.[9] The Supreme Court recognized these problems and narrowed the scope of *Corn Products* in *Arkansas Best v. Commissioner,*[10] where the Court dealt with a case in which stock was received by the taxpayer from a troubled bank in exchange for the taxpayer making investments in the bank. The investments were designed to preserve the taxpayer's reputation by keeping the bank from failing. The Court held the loss on the sale of the stock was capital, explicitly rejecting the broad reading *Corn Products* has received in *Booth Newspapers,* note 6 supra, and other circuit court cases. The Court's rationale was that in *Corn Products,* the corn futures were really a substitute for inventory, whereas the stock held by the taxpayer in *Arkansas Best* was not in any way inventory, since the taxpayer was not in the securities business. Thus it appeared that *Arkansas Best* was an attempt by the Supreme Court to severely cut back on the reach of *Corn Products* given the difficulties the case has presented, as discussed above.

A cute question arises as to whether the *Corn Products* doctrine applies to depreciable property. After *Arkansas Best* it appears less likely. The issue was raised in *Hollywood Baseball Association v. Commissioner,*[11] which involved the sale of professional baseball player contracts by a minor league baseball team incident to a liquidation of the business. The contracts had to be sold on demand to major league clubs. The player contracts clearly constituted depreciable property used in the trade or business of Hollywood Baseball in providing baseball games to its customers. The cost of each contract was amortizable over the life of the contract. Thus the player contracts were § 1231 assets in the hands of Hollywood Baseball.[12] The Ninth Circuit held that the *Corn Products* doctrine applied to these depreciable assets, or § 1231 assets.[13] The practical result of this holding was to deny the Hollywood Baseball club attractive benefits of § 337 on its liquidation.[14]

**9.** It is interesting to note in this connection that the *Corn Products* case itself involved a taxpayer with a net gain. Possibly the reason the transactions caught the eye of the Service was that the taxpayer in *Corn Products* first reported the transactions as ordinary income and then later changed its mind and reported them as capital gain, 350 U.S. 46 at 49, 76 S.Ct. 20 at 22.

**10.** 485 U.S. 212, 108 S.Ct. 971, 99 L.Ed.2d 183 (1988).

**11.** 423 F.2d 494 (9th Cir.1970), cert. denied 400 U.S. 848, 91 S.Ct. 35, 27 L.Ed.2d 85 (1970).

**12.** See ¶ 4.06(3)(a)(iv) below, for discussion of § 1231.

**13.** 423 F.2d 494 at 495.

**14.** See B. Bittker and J. Eustice, Federal Income Taxation of Corporations and Shareholders (1979) § 11 regarding § 337.

The implication of this holding was that the *Corn Products* doctrine even after *Arkansas Best* could possibly apply to any sale of depreciable property, since it is arguable that depreciable property used in a trade or business is always integral to that business. Thus the sale of such property would be held to always yield ordinary gain. This would effectively wipe out a major portion of the § 1231 treatment of depreciable property used in the trade or business, wherein the sale of such property often gives rise to capital gain.[15] This would undermine Congressional intent in this area. Thus, the result in Hollywood Baseball appears to be unsound[16] and it has not been followed.

### (iii) Depreciable and Real Property Used in a Trade or Business

In addition to inventory-type property and *Corn Products* assets, another major category of property is excluded from the status of "capital asset." This is depreciable property used in a trade or business and real property used in a trade or business.[17] Sales or exchanges of such business property are, however, picked up along with some other transactions and put through a special capital gain-ordinary loss treatment under § 1231. § 1231 is discussed below at ¶ 4.06(3)(a)(iv).

Prior to 1942, only depreciable property used in a trade or business was excluded from the definition of capital assets; real property used in a trade or business was considered a capital asset. This led to some difficult allocation problems where, for example, a manufacturing plant was sold. The building was not a capital asset but the land on which it stood was. This caused problems in allocating the purchase price. If the overall transaction was for a gain, the seller would want to allocate the bulk of the purchase price to the land (so as to enjoy a capital gain) and a relatively small amount of the purchase price to the building (which would give rise to ordinary gain). The buyer could very well take a contrary view, since he would want a low basis in the nondepreciable capital asset (the land) and a high basis in the depreciable asset (the building).[18]

To eliminate this allocation problem, Congress in 1942 provided that all real property—whether or not depreciable—used in a trade or business would be excluded from capital asset status.[19] This maneuver is surprisingly unsuccessful in disposing of this allocation problem under the present statutory structure. To the extent there may be recapture of

**15.** See ¶ 4.06(3)(a)(iv).

**16.** See Deltide Fishing and Rental Tools, Inc. v. United States, 279 F.Supp. 661 (E.D.La.1968) (reimbursement for rental tools lost or irreparably damaged by rental customers held eligible for capital gain under § 1231 notwithstanding the Service's argument that *Corn Products* should apply to give ordinary gain); Bernstein, " 'Primarily for Sale': A Semantic Snare," 20 Stan. L.Rev. 1093 (1968); Surrey, "Definitional

Problems in Capital Gains Taxation," 69 Harv.L.Rev. 985, 1015 (1956).

**17.** § 1221(2).

**18.** Cf. ¶ 4.06(3)(b) relating to current planning problems in the sale of a business. See ¶ 6.02(12) regarding depreciation generally. See also text accompanying note 49 below regarding the historical background of the treatment of business assets.

**19.** § 1221(2); H.R.Rep. No. 2333, 77th Cong., 2d Sess., 1942–2 C.B. 372, 414.

depreciation on the building,[20] the seller will still be interested in allocating the purchase price to the land. The buyer is still interested in allocating the bulk of the purchase price to the building for purposes of subsequent depreciation.[21]

Depreciable personal as well as real property used in a trade or business also comes within the purview of § 1221(2) and is excluded from capital asset status. (Such business real and depreciable property will be picked up by § 1231 as discussed below.) See ¶ 6.02(13)(d) for discussion of the wide variety of intangible personal property that is now subject to depreciation or amortization.

There are two critical definitional terms relating to this category of § 1221(2) property. The property must be "used"—as opposed to lying idle. And the use must be in a "trade or business"—as opposed to an investment activity or a personal activity. Not surprisingly, close questions have spawned a significant amount of litigation with respect to these two definitional terms.[22]

### (iv) Section 1231 Treatment

Although the class of "depreciable and real property used in the trade or business" is not regarded as a capital asset as discussed above, the sale or exchange of this property may give rise to capital gain or loss

---

**20.**  ¶ 4.06(3)(a)(vii).

**21.**  See discussion above.

**22.**  See Carter–Colton Cigar Co., 9 T.C. 219 (1947) (Taxpayer purchased unimproved lot for purpose of constructing on it a store, warehouse, and principal place of business. Construction plans were abandoned on account of the depression and due to the death of one of two major stockholders. On the ultimate sale of the property for a loss, taxpayer allowed to take an ordinary loss over the Service's argument that there should only be a capital loss, since the property was never "used" in the taxpayer's trade or business.); Davis, 11 T.C. 538 (1948) (Unimproved lot purchased for purpose of constructing on it a paint store ultimately sold at a loss upon discovery that the property was zoned exclusively for residential use. Held: the loss was capital, because the property could never have been used in the taxpayer's trade or business); Fackler v. Commissioner, 133 F.2d 509 (6th Cir.1943) (Renting of a multi-tenant building was a trade or business although landlord services provided through agents); Bauer v. United States, 144 Ct.Cl. 308, 168 F.Supp. 539 (1958) (*Dicta* that whether rental activity rises to the level of a trade or business so that a loss on sale of the property can be ordinary a question of fact, citing other leading cases); Alvary v. United States, 302 F.2d 790 (2d Cir.1962) (Two

rental apartment houses managed by an agent constituted a trade or business, thus taxpayer accorded ordinary loss); see Comment, "The Single Rental as a 'Trade or Business' Under the Internal Revenue Code," 23 U.Chi.L.Rev. 111 (1955).

The question of whether property is used in the trade or business generally only arises in the case of individuals. By and large corporations are assumed to use their property in their trade or business, since presumably that is the only thing a corporation can do with its property, but see International Trading Co., 57 T.C. 455 (1971), rev'd and remanded 484 F.2d 707 (7th Cir. 1973) (Corporation not allowed a loss on sale of property it held for personal use of its shareholders.)

Note therefore, that where an individual sells property at a loss, the stakes can be great indeed if a question is raised as to the use to which he put the property. If the property is regarded as "used in his trade or business," he will generally get an ordinary loss (see discussion in the text below relating to § 1231); if the property is regarded as held for investment rather than used in a trade or business, the loss will be regarded as capital and subject to the capital loss limitations; if the property is regarded as used for personal use, the loss deduction will be completely barred, see ¶ 4.04(2).

treatment under certain circumstances. This is due to the rather unusual workings of § 1231. In order to understand the rather strange—but certainly important—workings of § 1231, it is useful to look briefly at the historical conflicts that led to its enactment.[23]

The saga of § 1231 begins with the Revenue Act of 1938 which excluded depreciable personal property from the status of being a capital asset. This provision, enacted in the latter years of the depression, clearly offered relief to the taxpayer who sold his business assets at a loss—which was usually the case at that time—by providing him with ordinary loss treatment on such transactions.[24] The purpose, among others, was to encourage replacement of obsolete equipment.[25]

By 1942 economic conditions had, of course, changed dramatically. The demands of World War II caused business assets to have a significantly increased value. The government wished to encourage businessmen to dispose of business assets, particularly ships and boats, for use in the war effort. Because such assets were now deemed ordinary, sale or exchange of them gave rise to ordinary gain. Thus Congress became concerned with altering the treatment of business assets to encourage the disposal of these assets to benefit the war effort. Moreover, Congress was at this time also concerned with providing an attractive tax treatment for the proceeds of condemnations of property to be used in the war effort. And Congress was also concerned with providing attractive tax treatment for insurance proceeds where private property was destroyed on account of the war.

Most of these transactions gave rise to gains. That is to say, the amount received on sale, condemnation, or casualty of property related to the war effort was usually greater than the basis of such assets. This led to great political pressure for legislation that these business assets be put back into the status of capital assets.[26] However, there were a number of types of industries—notably the railroads—who continued to dispose of their business property at a loss. They of course would have been extremely unhappy with a return to capital status of business assets. Into this steaming caldron of the congressional consideration of this matter also came the farmers, who regularly sold their business assets—breeding and dairy livestock—at a gain. They of course favored restoring business assets to capital status.[27]

Putting all this together, Congress came up with a solution which demonstrated that the genius of the American political system was still

---

**23.** See generally, Birkeland, "Section 1231: A Fading Star for the Business Taxpayer," 60 A.B.A.J. 845 (1974).

**24.** See discussion above and accompanying text.

**25.** This is one of the first of a number of provisions in the Code designed to "stimulate investment" and hence promote economic growth. Some other examples of such provisions would include various forms of accelerated depreciation and the investment credit.

**26.** Discussion above.

**27.** See Surrey, Warren, McDaniel, Ault, Federal Income Taxation Cases and Materials, 1972 Vol. 1 p. 1017.

intact,[28] even if the integrity of the income tax was, in the process, somewhat undermined. Congress' solution, roughly speaking, was to regard all these transactions that a taxpayer may have together. If all these transactions, generally speaking, taken together give rise to a gain, then each transaction considered separately will be considered capital in character. If all these transactions taken together break even or give rise to a loss, then each transaction considered separately will be considered ordinary in character. In addition there is a preliminary treatment of casualties before all the transactions are taken together.

In particular, § 1231 works like this:

*Step 1, The Casualty Pot:* Attention is first given to all casualties the taxpayer has sustained during the taxable year with respect to three classes of property—depreciable property used in the taxpayer's trade or business and held more than one year, real property used in the taxpayer's trade or business and held more than one year, and capital assets held for more than one year which are held in connection with a trade or business or a transaction entered into for profit. The gains and losses on all of these casualty transactions[29] are netted together. If that net result is a loss, then none of these individual casualty transactions enters further into the workings of § 1231.[30] Rather, they will be treated as casualties are normally treated. That is, they will be given ordinary gain and loss treatment.[31]

If the net result on all the casualties is to break even or is a gain, then all of the casualties—gains and losses—involved in this netting process pass into consideration in the "Main Pot."[32] This

---

**28.** See V.O. Key, Politics, Parties, and Pressure Groups (1967).

**29.** A gain on a casualty would arise if, for example, the amount of the insurance proceeds received were greater than the adjusted basis of the property destroyed, see ¶ 4.03. In particular, casualties to personal-use property are only allowed as a deduction if as an aggregate they exceed 10% of the taxpayer's adjusted gross income. They must also exceed a $100 floor applied on a per casualty basis. With respect to personal-use property, only the few casualties that exceed these limits are eligible for § 1231 treatment. Casualties to business or investment property are deductible and go into § 1231 without having to meet these limits. See ¶ 7.01(5).

**30.** § 1231(a) flush language.

**31.** Casualties normally give rise to ordinary gains and losses rather than capital gains and losses, because casualties do not involve a sale or exchange, Helvering v. William Flaccus Oak Leather Co., 313 U.S. 247, 61 S.Ct. 878, 85 L.Ed. 1310 (1941)

Rev.Rul. 82–74, 1982–1 C.B. 110 (taxpayer, the lessor of an office building, paid a third party to burn it down so he could receive the insurance proceeds. Held: the taxpayer's gain—measured by the insurance proceeds less his basis in the building—did not qualify for capital gain under § 1231, since the arson was not an involuntary conversion. Outside the workings of § 1231 the receipt of the insurance proceeds did not qualify for capital gains treatment since it did not arise from a sale or exchange); and see ¶ 7.01(5).

Therefore for example, even if there is a casualty gain with respect to a capital asset (such as the taxpayer's home), the gain will be ordinary because although the asset involved was a capital asset, there was no sale or exchange, see ¶ 4.06(2)(a) relating to the definition of a capital gain or loss. (If the casualty gain on the capital asset comes to pass into the "Main Pot" of § 1231, it could then be treated as a capital gain, as discussed in the text.)

**32.** § 1231(a) flush language.

preliminary process of netting the casualties for these purposes can be conveniently termed the "Casualty Pot."

*Step 2, The Main Pot:* The "Main Pot" also involves a process of netting transactions. The transactions that are netted in the "Main Pot" are the following: (1) All casualties, if they have netted to break even or a gain in the "Casualty Pot;" (2) Sales or exchanges of depreciable property and real property used in the trade or business, held for more than one year;[33] (3) Condemnation of depreciable property and real property used in the trade or business, held for more than one year; (4) Condemnations of capital assets held more than one year which are held in connection with a trade or business or transaction entered into for profit.[34]

If all the transactions in the "Main Pot" net out to a gain, then each transaction in the "Main Pot" is considered to be a long-term capital gain or loss. These capital gains and losses arising from § 1231 are then combined with the taxpayer's other capital gains and losses arising from a sale or exchange of capital assets. All of these capital gains and losses are then treated under the normal rules for capital gains and losses, as described at ¶ 4.06(2)(b). Thus can § 1231 transform ordinary transactions into long-term capital gains and losses.

If all the transactions in the "Main Pot" net out to break even or to a loss, then each transaction in the "Main Pot" is considered an ordinary gain or loss.[35]

It is most important to note that the netting process here is only for the purpose of *characterization* of the gains or losses. The gains and losses otherwise remain as separate and distinct transactions.

That is the end of the workings of § 1231. It should be noted that depreciable and real property used in the trade or business and held for more than one year is often denominated "§ 1231 property"

---

**33.** In the case of gains from these transactions, only the gain not subject to recapture of depreciation goes into this netting process. Regs. §§ 1.1245–6(a); 1.1250–1(c). See ¶ 4.06(3)(a)(vii) for recapture of depreciation.

**34.** § 1231(a), 1231(b). The gains and losses subject to § 1231 must, of course, all be recognized, § 1231(a), Reg. § 1.1231–1(d)(4), see also ¶ 4.01. Further, the losses must otherwise be allowed. Thus not included in § 1231 are losses which are not deductible under § 267 (relating to losses on transactions between related taxpayers) or § 1091 (relating to wash sales), Regs. § 1.1231–1(d)(1), see also ¶ 4.04. If gain on the sale of § 1231(b) property is reported on the installment method of § 453 (see

¶ 8.03(2)), only the gain reportable in any particular tax year is included in § 1231 for that year, Regs. § 1.1231–1(d)(3). Of course the limitation on capital losses of § 1211 does not apply in ascertaining the amount of loss includible in § 1231, Reg. § 1.1231–1(d).

Where the taxpayer engages in a relatively small amount of rental activity, the courts have had great difficulty in resolving whether the rental property involved is § 1231 property—giving rise to the capital gain-ordinary loss results discussed in the text—or whether the rental property involved is a pure capital asset. This matter is discussed and authorities are set forth in the discussion above.

**35.** § 1231(a).

or "§ 1231 assets," because it is the main class of property that is subject to § 1231 treatment.

In the belief that "A picture shows me at a glance what it takes dozens of pages of a book to expound,"[36] the workings of § 1231 are presented on the following page. It is believed that this diagram presents the most helpful approach to § 1231.[37]

### Business Property Sales, Casualties and Condemnations
### IRC § 1231

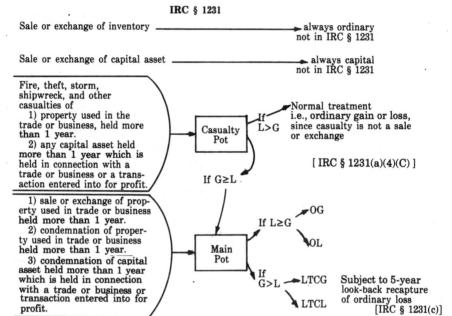

### Personal Use Property Casualties
### IRC § 165(h)

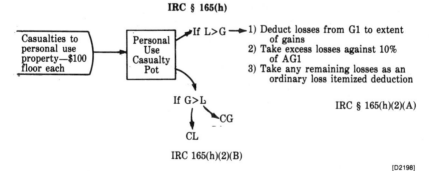

[D2198]

**36.** I.S. Turgenev, *Fathers and Sons* (1862), Ch. 15.

**37.** It should be noted that the "Casualty Pot" is also sometimes known as the "Firepot." "The Main Pot" is also some-times termed the "Big Pot," the "Hotch-pot," or the "Hodge Podge." The literate tax professional should, presumably, be familiar with all of these appellations.

Some problems of § 1231 are illustrated by the case of *Stephen P. Wasnok*[38] in which the question presented was whether the property the taxpayer disposed of constituted § 1231 property and thus produces ordinary loss or did not constitute § 1231 property in which case it produces a capital loss. The property at issue was the taxpayer's residence that he had trouble selling when he moved from Ohio to California. The court held that taxpayer's activity with respect to the property namely that he rented the property for four years, claimed depreciation and ultimately sold the property for a loss established that the property was used in a trade or business. Thus the property was not a capital asset but an asset described in § 1231. Thus the loss was put into the netting process of § 1231 and produced an ordinary loss. The loss was sustained in the year of sale of the property of 1965, when, as it happened, the taxpayer had no other income that could absorb it. The loss was not capital, which could have been carried over to other years when the taxpayer did have income that could have been cancelled out by this loss. This case is therefore unusual in that the taxpayer was arguing for what is usually unattractive for taxpayers, capital loss treatment, and the Commissioner was arguing for what is usually a a favorable treatment for taxpayers, ordinary loss. The reason the parties switched position is that the taxpayers had no taxable income to absorb the loss in the year of sale so they sought capital loss treatment to get the carryover. The Commissioner naturally opposed.

The case of *Williams v. McGowan*,[39] discussed in more detail at ¶ 4.06(b), held that the sale of a going business in a sole proprietorship form is treated as the sale of the collection of the individual assets of the business by the individual owner. As a result, § 1231 and other characterization sections come into play to characterize the gain or loss on the sale of the individual assets. The planning implications of this are discussed at ¶ 4.06(b).

Looking at the mechanics of § 1231, some examples are useful to illustrate its workings. It is assumed that all the property in the examples below has been held by the taxpayer for more than one year.

**Example: One Casualty Loss**—T owns gold bars held for more than one year for investment with a basis of $100,000 and a fair market value of $150,000. The bars are stolen and he receives insurance proceeds of $80,000. Therefore T has a deductible loss in the amount of $20,000.[40] T has no other transactions subject to § 1231. This $20,000 goes into the casualty pot. Since it is the only transaction in the casualty pot, the losses exceed the gains in the casualty pot. Therefore the $20,000 loss does not drop into the

---

**38.** 30 T.C.M. 39 (1971).
**39.** 152 F.2d 570 (C.C.A.2 1945).

**40.** § 165(c)(2). See ¶ 7.01(5) regarding computation of casualty losses.

"Main Pot." Rather, the $20,000 is given ordinary treatment and is entered on the taxpayer's tax return as an ordinary loss deduction from adjusted gross income.[41]

**Example: One Casualty Gain**—The facts are the same as in the previous Example except the amount of the insurance proceeds received is $135,000. Therefore, the transaction is now a casualty gain of $35,000.[42] This $35,000 goes into the casualty pot. Since it is the only transaction in the casualty pot, the gains exceed the losses in the casualty pot. Therefore, this $35,000 gain drops down into the "Main Pot." Since it is the only transaction in the "Main Pot," the gains exceed the losses in the "Main Pot." Hence the $35,000 gain is treated as a long-term capital gain. It is combined with T's other capital gains and losses transactions under the usual capital gains and losses rules.

**Example: One Casualty Gain, One Loss on Sale of § 1231 Property**—T has a casualty gain on the gold bars of $35,000, as in the previous Example. T has loss on sale of machinery used in his small manufacturing business of $50,000. T has no other transactions subject to § 1231. The $35,000 casualty gain first goes into the "Casualty Pot." Since it is a gain, it drops down into the "Main Pot." In the "Main Pot" it is netted against the $50,000 loss on sale of § 1231 property. Since the two transactions net to a loss, the two transactions are each treated as ordinary. Thus the casualty gain goes into gross income as $35,000 of ordinary income. The loss on the § 1231 property is taken as a $50,000 ordinary loss deduction from gross income.[43]

**Example: One Sale of § 1231 Property for a Gain, One Sale of § 1231 Property for a Loss, One Condemnation of a Capital Asset for a Loss**—X sells a building used in his trade or business for a $300,000 gain. X also sells some machinery used in his trade or business for a $160,000 loss. A plot of vacant land held by X as an investment and not used in his trade or business is condemned for a $100,000 loss.[44]

There are no casualties, so the only netting process goes on in the "Main Pot." The three transactions in the "Main Pot" net out to a gain. Therefore each transaction is considered to be long-term capital. Thus there is a long-term capital gain of $300,000, a long-term capital loss of $160,000 and a long-term capital loss of $100,-000. These are combined with X's other capital gains and losses (if any) from sales or exchanges of capital assets under the usual capital gain and loss rules.

**41.** See ¶ 6.01 regarding whether deductions are from gross income or adjusted gross income.

**42.** See ¶ 7.01(5).

**43.** See note 42 above.

**44.** A condemnation loss would result, of course, if the proceeds of the condemnation were less than the basis of the property condemned.

There are certain implications that can be drawn from this cocktail-shaker approach to § 1231 transactions. First of all it is clear that § 1231 always tilts in favor of the taxpayer. The taxpayer who has a preponderance of gains in § 1231 transactions will prefer to have all those gains and losses treated as capital rather than all as ordinary—and they will all be capital. The taxpayer who has a preponderance of losses in § 1231 transactions will prefer to have all those gains and losses treated as ordinary rather than all as capital—and they will all be ordinary.[45]

Moreover, the workings of § 1231 suggest some active planning possibilities for the taxpayer who regularly has a number of § 1231 transactions during the year. The best way to handle § 1231 transactions is to group the losses and gains in separate years. If all the § 1231 losses are taken in one year and all the § 1231 gains are taken in another year, then all the losses will be ordinary (most attractive) and all the gains will be long-term capital (most attractive). To the extent the losses and gains are mixed together, this will inevitably lead to the less than optimum result that some of the gains will be ordinary and/or some of the losses will be long-term capital.

Of course, it is often not possible to control the timing of § 1231 transactions. The sale of business property will often be dictated by business conditions which override tax considerations. Also, obviously, the timing of casualties and usually condemnations is beyond the taxpayer's control. But to the extent the taxpayer has control over the timing of his § 1231 transactions, grouping the gains and losses in separate years will lead to better results.

*(v) Copyrights, Literary or Other Artistic Compositions Created by the Taxpayer, Memoranda Held by the Taxpayer and Similar Property*

The categories of property excluded from capital asset status that have been discussed so far are inventory-type property, so-called "Corn Products" assets, and depreciable and real property used in the trade or business. In addition, the special treatment accorded by § 1231 to depreciable and real property used in the trade or business has been discussed.

Another major category of property that is excluded from capital asset status involves copyrights, literary and other artistic property and certain memoranda held by the taxpayer.[46] The several types of property

---

**45.** § 1231 treatment is sufficiently attractive that there has been interest in including certain transactions within its unique netting processes, even though those transactions would not otherwise have fit in on account of the property involved being in the nature of inventory. Thus Congress has specifically provided that property subject to § 1231 includes cut timber, and timber, coal, and iron ore royalties as well as unharvested crops § 1231(b)(2) and (4). § 1231 property also includes cattle and horses held by the taxpayer for draft, breeding, dairy, or sporting purposes, and held for more than 24 months, § 1231(b)(3)(A), as well as other livestock held by the taxpayer for these same purposes for at least 12 months, § 1231(b)(3)(B). § 1231 property does not include poultry, § 1231(b) flush language, so chicken farmers are out in the cold when it comes to enjoying the benefits of § 1231.

**46.** § 1221(3).

that are excluded from capital asset status by this portion of the definition of capital assets are: (1) copyrights, literary, musical, or artistic compositions held by the taxpayer whose personal efforts created them;[47] (2) a letter or memorandum held by the taxpayer who created it or held by a taxpayer for whom it was prepared;[48] (3) property "similar" to that described in (1) and (2) above held by a taxpayer whose personal efforts created it;[49] (4) property described in (1)–(3) above if held by a taxpayer who received the property by gift or non-recognition transaction from a taxpayer described in (1)–(3) above.[50]

This class of property cannot be subject to § 1231. This would be true even though this type of property may in fact be depreciable and may in fact be used in the taxpayer-creator's trade or business.[51] Thus sale by the taxpayer-creator would always yield ordinary income or loss. If property of this type is used in the trade or business of one who acquired it by purchase (or inheritance where the step-up of basis applies), then sale of it will be eligible for § 1231 or capital asset treatment as the case may be.

Prior to the enactment of the predecessor of § 1221(3), the treatment of the sale of a copyright or artistic composition by a taxpayer who created the property depended on the taxpayer's professional status. If the taxpayer were a professional, then the sale produced ordinary income; if the taxpayer were an amateur then the sale produced capital gain.[52] Drawing the line between professionals and amateurs produced problems; Congress therefore resolved to provide uniform ordinary income treatment for the sale of a product created by personal effort.[53]

A major definitional problem with the present statute relates to what is "similar property." The Regulations provide that "similar property" does include a theatrical production, a radio program, a newspaper cartoon strip, or any other property eligible for copyright protection (whether under statute or common law).[54] However, "similar" property

---

**47.** § 1221(3)(A).

**48.** § 1221(3)(A) and (B).

**49.** § 1221(3).

**50.** § 1221(3)(C). Conversely, a taxpayer who acquired such property by purchase could hold the property as a capital asset, or as property used in the trade or business.

**51.** Reg. § 1.1231–1(c)(1)(ii). Cf. Rev. Rul. 55–706, 1955–2 C.B. 300 (films created by a publicly-held corporation which paid fair market value for the multiplicity of skills of the many people involved in making the film were not held by the corporation as § 1221(3) property, because the corporation had not "created" the films. Thus the films were properly subject to § 1231 on their sale.)

**52.** See Senate Finance Committee Report, S.Rep. No. 2375, 81st Cong., 2d Sess. 43, 83–84 (1950); House Committee on Ways and Means Report, H.Rep. No. 2319, 81st Cong., 2d Sess. 54, 91–92 (1950).

**53.** Id., and see § 210 of the Revenue Act of 1950, 64 Stat. 906, 933.

**54.** Reg. § 1.1221–1(c)(1). "Similar property" also includes a draft of a speech, a manuscript, a research paper, an oral recording of any type, a transcript of an oral recording, a transcript of an oral interview or of dictation, a personal or business diary, a log or journal, a corporate archive, including a corporate charter, office correspondence, a financial record, a drawing, a photograph or a dispatch, Reg. § 1.1221–1(c)(2). Many of these items listed above are of significance to former holders of high public office who may wish to sell or make a charitable contribution of their personal papers. See ¶ 7.01(8) regarding the charitable contribution of such material.

does not include a patent, or an invention or design which may be protected only under the patent law and not under the copyright law.[55] Beyond that, the question of what is included in this category of non-capital assets has given rise to significant litigation.[56]

### (vi) Patents

The life of the inventor is happier than the life of the artist, writer or musician in that the inventor has an excellent chance of enjoying long-term capital gains on the creations of his muse. If an inventor transfers for consideration "all substantial rights" or certain other interests to a patent of his work, then under § 1235 he will enjoy long-term capital gains on the transaction (regardless of how long he has actually held the property), notwithstanding that the payments for the patent are (1) contingent on the productivity of the patent or (2) coterminous with the transferee's use of the patent.[57]

Payments which are contingent on use and/or coterminous with use of the transferee look at first blush like royalties, giving rise to ordinary income treatment.[58] However, even outside of § 1235, where patents, copyrights, literary or artistic and similar property are transferred for contingent payments, or payments coterminous with use, the transaction will often be regarded as a sale.[59]

Just a sale or exchange is not enough to give rise to capital gain treatment to a transaction; there must be a sale or exchange of a capital asset.[60] It is in providing both capital asset status as well as the requisite sale or exchange that § 1235 insures long-term capital gains (or long-

---

**55.** Reg. § 1.1221–1(c)(1).

**56.** See Cranford v. United States, 338 F.2d 379 (Ct.Cl.1964). In this case, taxpayer developed a format for a quiz program. He applied for copyright protection but was informed that a format for a quiz program could not be copyrighted. Taxpayer was nonetheless able to sell this format, and it ultimately became the radio program "Take It or Leave It" and the television program "The $64,000 Question." In seeking capital gain on the proceeds of the sale, taxpayer argued that since the format could not be copyrighted, it was not "similar property," under § 1221(3), and hence it was not excluded from the definition of capital asset. The court held the format was "similar property" although it was not subject to copyright, and hence the taxpayer received ordinary gain.

See also Stern v. United States, 164 F.Supp. 847 (E.D.La.1958), aff'd per curiam 262 F.2d 957 (5th Cir.1959), cert. denied 359 U.S. 969, 79 S.Ct. 880, 3 L.Ed.2d 836 (1959) (sale of movie rights to the character "Francis the Talking Mule" gave rise to ordinary income because it was "similar property" regardless of its susceptibility to copyright); Commissioner v. Ferrer, 304 F.2d 125 (2d Cir.1962) (rights of actor-turned producer Jose Ferrer in the play production of the novel "Moulin Rouge" based on the life of Toulouse–Lautrec were not covered by § 1221(3). As Judge Friendly noted, "The difficulties Mr. Ferrer must have had in fitting himself into the shape of the artist can hardly have been greater than ours in determining whether the transaction here at issue fits the rubric 'gain from the sale or exchange of a capital asset . . .' "); see Eustice, "Contract Rights, Capital Gain and Assignment of Income— the Ferrer Case," 20 Tax L.Rev. 1 (1964).

**57.** § 1235(a)(1) and (2); Reg. § 1.1235–1(a). "Patent" means a patent granted under the provisions of Title 35 of the United States Code, or any foreign patent granting rights generally similar to those under a United States patent. It is not necessary that the patent or patent application for the invention be in existence if the requirements of § 1235 are otherwise met, Reg. § 1.1235–2(a).

**58.** See ¶ 3.05.

**59.** See ¶ 3.05.

**60.** ¶ 4.06.

term capital loss), treatment for the transfers of patents within its ambit.

The purpose of this provision is to "provide an incentive to inventors to contribute to the welfare of the Nation."[61] Without this provision professional inventors, and possibly amateur inventors as well, would have the sale of their patents treated as ordinary gain.[62] § 1235 makes it clear that professional as well as amateur inventors are entitled to capital gain treatment on the sale of all substantial rights in their patents.[63] In addition to the inventor, one who purchases the inventor's interest in the patent prior to the actual reduction of the invention to practice also will have long-term capital gain on the subsequent sale of his interest in the patent. This will be true regardless of how long he has actually held the property and notwithstanding that on such subsequent sale the consideration is in the nature of royalties, payable over a period coterminous with the transferee's use or contingent on the productivity of the patent.[64] The inventor and one who purchases his interest in the patent from the inventor are considered a "holder" of the patent for these purposes.[65]

Not just any transfer of patent rights by a "holder" will qualify for the long-term capital gain (or loss) treatment of § 1235. The transfer by the "holder" of the patent must be of either (1) "all substantial rights to the patent" or (2) an "undivided interest therein which includes a part of all such rights."[66]

---

**61.** S.Rep. No. 1622 83rd Cong., 2d Sess. 439 (1954). It might be argued that inventors already receive sufficient incentive by virtue of receiving the patent itself.

**62.** Cf. Edward C. Myers, 6 T.C. 258 (1946) (amateur inventor had capital gain on the transfer of all substantial rights in a patent notwithstanding consideration was contingent on quantity of articles sold under the patent). The acquiescence in this case was withdrawn, Mim. 6490, 1950–1 C.B. 9; Rev.Rul. 55–58, 1955–1 C.B. 97 (patents sold for royalty arrangements gave rise to ordinary income for years not covered by § 1235); United States v. Zacks, 375 U.S. 59, 84 S.Ct. 178, 11 L.Ed.2d 128 (1963).

**63.** Reg. § 1.1235–1(d)(3).

**64.** § 1235(a) and (b)(2).

**65.** § 1235(b). An "inventor" for the purposes of qualifying as a "holder" is one whose efforts created the patent property and who would qualify as the "original and first" inventor, or joint inventor, within the meaning of Title 35 of the United States Code, Reg. § 1.1235–2(d)(1)(i).

In order to qualify as a "holder" the purchaser of the patent must meet a number of tests. He cannot be the employer of the inventor at the time of the transaction, nor can he be related to the inventor, as defined, § 1235(b)(1) and (2), § 1235(d), Regs. §§ 1.1235–2(d)(1)(ii), 1.1235–2.). In addition the purchaser must have purchased his interest prior to its actual reduction to practice, Reg. § 1.1235–1(d)(1)(ii). "Actual reduction to practice" for these purposes has the same meaning as it does under § 102(g) of Title 35 of the United States Code. Generally, an invention is reduced to actual practice when it has been tested and operated successfully under operating conditions. This may occur either before or after application for a patent but cannot occur later than the earliest time that commercial exploitation of the invention occurs, Regs. § 1.1235–2(e).

Thus does the statute attempt to provide incentive to inventors and to those who would invest in the promotion of the patent before its commercial use becomes established. It is only they who qualify as holders and who can therefore enjoy capital gains under § 1235.

**66.** § 1235(a). Cf. Hooker Chemicals and Plastics Corp. v. United States, 219 Ct.Cl. 161, 591 F.2d 652 (1979) (reservation of right to sell in transferee's territory did not destroy "sale").

"All substantial rights" to a patent means all rights (whether or not then held by the holder) which are of value at the time the rights to the patent are transferred. Thus "all substantial rights to a patent" would not be transferred if the grant of rights was limited geographically within the country of issuance, was limited in time to a period less than the remaining life of the patent, was limited to certain fields of use, or was limited to less than all claims or inventions covered by the patent which have value at the time of the transfer.[67]

An "undivided interest" in all substantial rights to a patent means the same factional share of each and every substantial right to the patent. An "undivided interest" therefore would not include the right to income from a patent limited geographically or limited in time to less than the remaining life of the patent.[68]

A "holder" of a patent for the capital gain purposes of § 1235 may only be an individual.[69] However, where a partnership owns the patent, each individual member of the partnership may be a holder as to his share of the patent owned by the partnership.[70]

This attractive treatment of the "holders" of patents under § 1235 is in contrast to the relatively unattractive treatment of their transferees. According to the Regulations, payments made by the transferee of patent rights in a transaction qualifying under § 1235 must be capitalized (and recovered through amortization) rather than immediately deducted.[71] Some case law has suggested techniques around this problem.[72]

### (vii) Recapture of Depreciation

Yet another way in which the tax law provides special rules for characterizing transactions is in the area of so-called "recapture" of depreciation. The necessity for the specialized recapture rules arises from the fact that property subject to the depreciation deduction[73] is often sold for gain. This is the case because the taking of depreciation

---

**67.** Reg. § 1.1235–2(b), also providing that the circumstances of the whole transaction rather than the particular terminology used in the instrument of transfer shall be considered in determining whether or not all substantial rights to the patent have been transferred in a transaction. See Estate of Klein v. Commissioner, 507 F.2d 617 (7th Cir.1974), cert. denied 421 U.S. 991, 95 S.Ct. 1998, 44 L.Ed.2d 482 (1975).

**68.** Reg. § 1.1235–2(c). See also S.Rep. No. 1622, 83rd Cong. 2d Sess. 439 (1954).

Note that this "undivided interest" approach to ascertaining capital gains treatment is fundamentally inconsistent with the approach for ascertaining capital gains treatment in the assignment of income area. In the assignment of income area "vertical cuts" are what give rise to capital

gains, whereas the "undivided interest" approach of § 1235 involves a "horizontal cut." See ¶ 5.03.

**69.** § 1235(b).

**70.** Reg. § 1.1235–2(d)(2).

**71.** Reg. § 1.1235–1(d).

**72.** Associated Patentees, Inc., 4 T.C. 979 (1945) (acq.); Allied Tube & Conduit Corp., 34 T.C.M. 1218 (1975).

See generally, Morreale, "Patents, Know–How and Trade-marks: A Tax Overview," 29 Tax Lawyer 533 (1976); Pansius, "Fruit and Roots: Transfers of Patents and the Shared Rights Test of Capital Gain," 54 Notre Dame Lawyer 846 (1979).

**73.** ¶ 6.02(12).

has caused the basis of the property to decline[74] while the fair market value of the property may not have declined as fast, or the fair market value may indeed have risen. The gain on the sale or exchange of such depreciable property will go into § 1231, where it could very well come out treated as a capital gain.[75] Thus has the taxpayer been able to take depreciation deductions, which reduce ordinary income, but pay a compensating tax at only capital gains rates. The advantage of this can be quite striking for the high bracket taxpayer.

As a numerical example: T, at all times in the tax 39.6% bracket due to high ordinary income, buys a machine for use in his trade or business for $100,000. It has a useful life under the depreciation rules of 10 years and may be depreciated under the straight line method (see ¶ 6.02(12)).

At the end of the 10 years, when the machine has a basis of 0, T sells the machine for $100,000. As a matter of economic reality nothing happened to T on this transaction in terms of value. He bought a machine for $100,000 and sold it 10 years later for $100,000 because the market for this type of machine remained strong. But while nothing happened as a matter of economic reality, the tax consequences to T of this transaction were far-reaching indeed.

Over the course of the 10 years T took $100,000 of depreciation deductions. If T was in the 39.6% combined bracket over this period, these depreciation deductions saved him $39,600 in taxes. The sale by T of the machine gives him $100,000 of gain, since his basis after the depreciation is now 0. The gain goes into § 1231 and could very well be long-term capital gain under that provision's netting processes (see ¶ 4.05(3)(iv)). The $100,000 long-term capital gain gives rise to a favorable tax rate of 28%; thus the tax on the transaction is $28,000. Thus T has a net tax savings of $11,600 ($39,600 taxes saved by the depreciation deduction less $28,000 capital gains tax paid). Thus even if the machine produces no net income, the investment has been profitable simply on account of the ability to take depreciation deductions and pay only a compensating capital gains tax.[76] T in this sense is said to have "converted ordinary income into capital gains."

This attractive pattern has long been (and still is in many cases) a basic building block of tax shelters.[77] In order to try to close up this particular advantage Congress in 1962 enacted "recapture" provisions.

Various recapture provisions apply to various types of transactions, recapturing varying amounts of the gain attributable to depreciation. The major recapture provisions are § 1245, applying generally to depreciable personal property;[78] and § 1250, applying generally to depreciable real property.

---

74. § 1016 and see ¶ 4.03(g).

75. ¶ 4.06(3)(a)(iv).

76. Beyond the advantages discussed in the text it should be noted that T has been able to defer payment of his taxes.

77. For more on tax shelters see ¶ 8.02.

78. § 1245(a)(3) and (4).

The basic theory of recapture is that the gain on the sale of depreciable property which is attributable to previously taken depreciation is deemed to be ordinary gain.

Section 1245, added to the Code in 1962, applies to personal property (i.e. not real estate) such as machinery, equipment, vehicles. Section 1245 provides that a taxpayer's gain on the sale of his property that is attributable to previously taken depreciation is taxed as ordinary income. Thus in our example above the entire amount of the $100,000 gain would be ordinary and taxed at the 39.6% rate, yielding a tax of $39,600. This makes sense inasmuch as the taxpayer took depreciation, with its tax advantages, and yet the machine did not actually decline in value economically. It is therefore only fair that he pay tax in full on the gain on sale to make up for the previous economically inaccurate depreciation deduction.

As a further example consider the same facts as above except that T only depreciates the machine for 6 years (thus $60,000 of depreciation against ordinary income and a basis in the machine of $40,000) and then sells the machine for $130,000. Then T would have realized and recognized gain of $90,000 (amount realized of $130,000 less adjusted basis of $40,000). Under the recapture rule of § 1245, The character of the gain would be as follows. $60,000 is ordinary income, not involved in the netting process of § 1231. This is because of the $90,000 gain, $60,000 was due to previously taken depreciation. This is the automatic result, without reference to § 1231. The $60,000 of gain due to previously taken depreciation does not go into § 1231 or have anything to do with the netting procedures of that section. The remaining $30,000 of gain goes into the "main pot" of § 1231 where it may turn out to be ordinary income or capital gains, depending on the other transactions in the pot. If there are no other transactions in the pot, then the $30,000 would be a capital gain under the usual § 1231 rules.

Section 1250, added to the Code in 1964, applies to real estate. It provides, in general, that the only gain recaptured on the sale of real estate is the excess of accelerated depreciation over straight line.

To illustrate what this means, consider this example. Assume T purchases an office building for $100,000 and it has a useful life under the statute of 30 years. Suppose T can properly under the statute depreciate the building on the double declining balance method. Straight line depreciation in the first year would be $3,333. Thus double declining balance would be $6,666. T then sells the building for $100,000 after one year. His gain is $100,000 amount realized less $93,334 adjusted basis or $6,666. Under the statute, the excess of accelerated depreciation over straight line for the first year is $3,333. This is the $6,666 of depreciation allowed on the accelerated method, less the $3,333 allowed on the straight line method.

Thus on the sale of this building for $100,000, $3,333 of the gain would be ordinary and $3,333 would go into the § 1231 main pot. Note that if the building were instead a machine, then § 1245 would apply to this transaction and the entire gain of $6,666 would be ordinary. That is the difference between the "strong" recapture rule of § 1245, which applies generally to personal property, and the "weak" recapture rule of § 1250, which applies generally to real estate.

In fact the present depreciation rule with respect to real estate is that it can only be depreciated under the straight line method. Therefore, while § 1250 is on the books, it does not currently apply, since under the present depreciation rules there cannot be excess of accelerated depreciation over straight line. However, we continue to discuss § 1250 because the depreciation rules frequently change and it is possible that Congress will in the future allow accelerated depreciation with respect to real estate.

Sections 1245 and 1250 generally do not affect the amount of gain or loss realized on a transaction. With respect to recognition, §§ 1245 and 1250 override some non-recognition provisions but not others. §§ 1245 and 1250, for example, override the corporate non-recognition liquidation provisions of §§ 336 and 337 and provide that the corporation will recognize ordinary gain on these transactions to the extent the gain is attributable to previous depreciation taken.[79] In these corporate transactions §§ 1245 and 1250 are doing more than characterizing gain. They are in effect creating gain, since absent these provisions the unrecognized gain to the corporation on these liquidations would never be taxed to the liquidating corporation or to anyone else.

With respect to like-kind exchanges under § 1031 and involuntary conversion rollovers under § 1033,[80] §§ 1245 and 1250 do not cause any additional gain to be recognized beyond that which would be recognized under §§ 1031 or 1033.[81] However, to the extent that realized gain is not recognized by virtue of §§ 1031 or 1033, §§ 1245 and 1250 provide that the remaining unrecognized gain subject to recapture will be preserved on the basis of the new property in the taxpayer's hands.[82]

As the previous discussion has indicated, with respect to the relationship to § 1231, the recognized gain subject to recapture comes out before consideration of § 1231. Only the recognized gain beyond that which is subject to recapture goes into § 1231.[83]

The workings of § 1245 are illustrated by the following further examples:

> **Example:** Jones sells machine A that he has used in his trade or business for $20,000. Machine A had a basis in Jones' hands before the sale of $10,000. Jones' original cost basis for machine A was $16,000, the basis having been reduced to $10,000 by the taking

---

**79.** See Bittker and Eustice, Federal Income Taxation of Corporations and Shareholders (1979), ¶ 11.61. §§ 1245 and 1250 do not override other corporate non-recognition transactions such as transfers governed by §§ 351, 332, 361, see §§ 1245(b)(4), 1250(d)(4).

**80.** ¶¶ 4.05(2) and (3).

**81.** §§ 1245(b)(3), 1250(d)(3).

**82.** Regs. §§ 1.1245–2(c)(4); 1.1250–3(d)(5).

**83.** Regs. §§ 1.1245–6(a); 1.1250–1(c)(1).

of depreciation computed on the straight-line method.[84] Jones' gain realized on the transaction is $10,000. Since no non-recognition provision applies, all the gain is recognized. Since $6,000 of the gain is attributable to previously taken depreciation, $6,000 of the gain is characterized as ordinary by § 1245. The other $4,000 of gain goes into § 1231, where it may very well come out as capital, depending on the other transactions in § 1231. Had machine A been sold for $12,000, all the $2,000 gain would have been ordinary and nothing would have passed into § 1231.

**Example:** Smith exchanges machine B that he has used in his trade or business with a fair market value of $17,000 for machine C with a fair market value of $16,000 and $1,000 cash, in a transaction subject to § 1031. Before the transaction machine B had a basis in Smith's hands of $10,000. Smith's original cost basis in machine B was $15,000, the basis having been reduced to $10,000 by the taking of depreciation computed on the straight-line method. Smith's gain realized on the transaction is $7,000 (amount realized of $17,000 minus adjusted basis of $10,000). Smith's gain recognized on the transaction is $1,000 (the amount of the "boot" received in the § 1031 exchange). This $1,000 is ordinary gain, under § 1245. Nothing passes into § 1231. Smith's basis on machine C is $10,-000.[85] The $4,000 unrecognized recapture is preserved on machine C. Smith holds machine C for one year, properly taking $1,000 depreciation on it, reducing his basis to $9,000. He then sells it for $16,500. His gain realized on that transaction is $7,500 ($16,500 amount realized less $9,000 adjusted basis). All that gain is recognized, since no nonrecognition transaction applies to the sale. With respect to the character of the gain, $5,000 of the $7,500 gain will be ordinary. This is made up of the $4,000 preserved recapture from the § 1031 transaction and $1,000 recapture from the one year's depreciation taken by Smith on machine C.[86] The rest of the gain goes into § 1231.

If the gain on the sale of property subject to recapture is reported on the installment method, recapture applies first, deeming all the gain first reported as ordinary.[87]

### (viii) Sale of Depreciable Property to a Related Party

In general, if depreciable property is sold at a gain, that gain in excess of what is recaptured at ordinary rates will likely be capital.[88] The sale will of course result in a new basis to the buyer, who can use that basis for purposes of computing depreciation. This fortuitous circumstance could naturally lead the astute tax planner to engineer the

---

**84.** ¶ 6.02(12).

**85.** ¶ 4.05(2)(d).

**86.** See Reg. § 1.1245–2(c)(4)(iii) Example (1). The treatment under § 1033 is analogous.

**87.** Reg. § 1.1245–6(d).

**88.** § 1231 will, of course, control the transaction, and if its "netting" process is positive, the gain in excess of recapture will be capital.

following transaction: Taxpayer sells real estate for a substantial capital gain to his controlled corporation, which then rents the property out, having the advantage of a high basis for purposes of depreciation. Thus does the taxpayer reap the golden harvest of capital gain and deductions against ordinary income (while, it might be noted, still retaining control of the property). Such stratagems were available until 1958 when § 1239 came upon the scene to provide ordinary income treatment on the sale or exchange between related parties of property subject to the allowance for depreciation in the hands of the transferee.

Prior to the Tax Reform Act of 1976, the "related parties" for purposes of § 1239 were husband and wife, or individual and corporation where more than 80 percent of the value of the stock of the corporation was owned by the individual, his spouse, and his minor children and minor grandchildren. The Service and taxpayers were in dispute over sales between brother-sister corporations that were more than 80 percent owned by the taxpayer. The Service maintained that such transactions were "indirectly" sales between an individual and his controlled corporation and hence within the ambit of § 1239, but the case law went the other way.[89]

The Tax Reform Act of 1976 resolved this matter decisively in the Service's favor, providing that "related persons" includes two or more corporations where 80 percent or more in value of their stock is owned by or for the same individual.[90] Moreover, the Service's legislative victory in this arena also included incorporation of the attribution rules of § 318 of the Code to ascertain whether or not 80 percent or more of a corporation's stock is owned by an individual.[91]

However, as a result of the Installment Sales Revision Act of 1980, an individual's family for purposes of the attribution rules includes only his spouse and the entity ownership attribution rules are applied without regard to the percentage limitations of § 318(a)(2)(C) (by virtue of § 1239(c)(2), effective for dispositions made after October 19, 1980).

The Committee Reports[92] provide an example of a way in which the constructive ownership rules could apply in the Section 1239 setting:[93]

An individual who owns 80 percent of the stock of a parent company will also constructively own 80 percent of the wholly-owned subsidiary;[94] hence, the two corporations will be related parties, and transactions in

---

**89.** Miller v. Commissioner, 510 F.2d 230 (9th Cir.1975); 10–42 Corp., 55 T.C. 593 (1971), nonacq. 1972–2 C.B. 4; Rev.Rul. 69–109, 1969–1 C.B. 202.

**90.** § 1239(b)(3), effective for transactions occurring after October 4, 1976. A transaction occurred on or before October 4, 1976 if there was a binding agreement on or before that date. Note, this amendment also involves a slight lowering of the stan-

dard, to 80 percent or more in value of the corporation's stock instead of the previous more-than–80–percent standard.

**91.** § 1239(c).

**92.** Staff of the Joint Comm. on Taxation, General Explanation of the Tax Reform Act of 1976 653 (1976).

**93.** § 1239(c).

**94.** § 318(a)(2)(C).

depreciable property between the parent and the subsidiary will be governed by § 1239 rules.[95]

One further controversy between the Service and taxpayers was not resolved by The Tax Reform Act of 1976 and, indeed, portended increased trouble in the future. This involves the case where an individual owns a little less than 80 percent of the number of shares of a corporation. In this event, the Service asserted that § 1239 was nonetheless triggered because such an individual owned more than 80 percent of the value of the stock on the grounds that either there were restrictions on the minority shares, or that the controlling block was worth a premium, or that the taxpayer owned options to buy more stock of the corporation. The Service's argument has some support in the statutory language,[96] and the courts have generally upheld it.[97]

This seems like a somewhat harsh result. In light of the applicability of the broader constructive ownership rules, it is now possible for an individual who only owns, say, 30% of the number of shares of a corporation to be brought up to 78% by constructive ownership, and then be subject to the argument that the value of the "control premium" would put him over 80% in value of the corporate stock. That this pattern of combining the constructive ownership rules with the "value" argument is contemplated is evidenced by the Joint Committee Explanation of the 1976 changes:

"The incorporation of constructive ownership rules into section 1239 applies generally to this section. In light of the section 318 rules, the 80–percent requirement of section 1239 will continue to be measured by reference to the value of the company's outstanding stock; however the stock which will be grouped together in measuring control will include stock considered owned by an individual under the constructive ownership rules."[98]

### (ix) Accounts Receivable

In addition to the variegated transactions described above there are a number of other transactions and types of property that are specially endowed by the Code with capital or ordinary character. Accounts receivable are, not surprisingly, regarded as ordinary assets and hence

**95.** §§ 318(a)(2)(C), 1239(c).

**96.** § 1239(b)(2), now § 1239(b)(3).

**97.** Harry Trotz, 26 T.C.M. 632 (1967) (79 percent stock ownership; control premium argument rejected; thus, taxpayer did not own more than 80 percent of stock); United States v. Parker, 376 F.2d 402 (5th Cir.1967) (80–percent stock ownership; more than 80 percent of value of stock owned because of control premium and restrictions on minority shares); Rev.Rul. 69–339, 1969–1 CB 303 (restrictions on minority shares lowered their value and therefore the majority block exceeded the 80% test);

Dahlgren v. United States, 553 F.2d 434 (5th Cir.1977), reh'g denied 557 F.2d 456 (1977); Robishaw v. United States, 616 F.2d 507 (Ct.Cl.1980) (80% test applied before transaction with corporation rather than after where taxpayer owned 79.64% before the transaction and over 80% after).

This discussion of § 1239 is adapted from Posin, "Changes in the Taxation of Corporations Effected by the Tax Reform Act of 1976" 4 J. of Corp. Tax 185 (1977).

**98.** General Explanation of the Tax Reform Act of 1976, 1976–3 C.B. 1, 653.

their sale will give rise to ordinary gain or loss.[99] This would be expected inasmuch as the sale of inventory yields ordinary income, as discussed above.

### (x) Transfers of Franchises, Trademarks and Trade Names

A transfer of a franchise, trademark, or trade name is not regarded as a sale or exchange of a capital asset if the transferor retains any significant power, right, or continuing interest with respect to it.[1] A significant power, right, or continuing interest includes various managerial powers,[2] as well as a significant right to receive payments contingent on the productivity or use of the interest transferred.[3]

### (xi) Cancellation of Lease or Distributor's Agreement

Amounts received by a lessee for the cancellation of a lease, or by a distributor of goods for the cancellation of a distributor's agreement (if the distributor has a substantial capital investment in the distributorship), are considered by the Code as amounts received in a sale or exchange for such lease or agreement.[4] This statutory sale or exchange does not, of course, guarantee capital gain or loss treatment. For such treatment the lease or distributorship must also be a capital asset in the hands of the lessee or distributor. This will depend on the individual facts of the case. The probability is that the lease or distributorship is not a capital asset but is depreciable property in the hands of the lessee or distributor used in his trade or business. In that event the statutory sale or exchange treatment of the cancellation will usually cause the transaction to be treated under § 1231, which applies to the sale or exchange of depreciable property used in the trade or business.[5]

### (xii) Retirement of Bonds

The general rule is that the collection of a claim is not a sale or exchange and therefore cannot give rise to capital gain or loss treatment.[6] However the retirement of a corporate or government bond which is a capital asset in the hands of a taxpayer is accorded sale or exchange treatment.[7] Therefore capital gain or loss will result on such transactions measured as usual by the amount received on retirement (usually the face amount), less the taxpayer's basis. Compare in this connection the discussion of original issue discount at ¶ 3.02.

---

**99.** § 1221(4).

**1.** § 1253.

**2.** § 1253(b)(2)(A)–(E).

**3.** § 1253(b)(2)(F). Such contingent payments would be deductible by the transferee, § 1253(d)(1). Any noncontingent payments in the transaction must be deducted according to particular rules, § 1253(d)(2).

**4.** § 1241.

**5.** ¶ 4.06(3)(a)(iv). Cf. Gray v. Commissioner, 642 F.2d 320 (9th Cir.1981) (payments in form for cancellation of lease of almond grove not governed by § 1241 but rather were a return of previously deducted advance rent and hence ordinary income, not capital gain.)

**6.** See Fairbanks v. United States, 306 U.S. 436, 59 S.Ct. 607, 83 L.Ed. 855 (1939).

**7.** § 1232(a)(1).

### (xiii) Worthless Securities

When securities which are capital assets in the hands of the taxpayer become worthless, the loss is treated as a loss from the sale or exchange of a capital asset on the last day of the taxable year.[8] "Securities" for this purpose are defined as a share of stock in a corporation, a right to subscribe to a share of stock in a corporation, or a bond, note, or other evidence of indebtedness issued by a corporation with interest coupons or in registered form.[9] This statutory sale or exchange, of course, leads to an unattractive result. The loss, instead of being ordinary, will be capital. Whether the capital loss is short-term or long-term will depend on whether the statutory "end of the year" holding period,[10] coupled with the period the taxpayer has actually held the security, will give rise to a short-term or a long-term holding period. In either event, of course, the result is less attractive than an ordinary loss.

### (xiv) Bad Debts

A "business bad debt" is regarded as an ordinary loss,[11] whereas a "non-business bad debt" is treated as a less attractive short-term capital loss (regardless of the period of time of the debt's existence).[12] Where a taxpayer undergoes a bad-debt loss as an investor, the loss will be treated as a non-business bad debt. For the taxpayer to enjoy a business bad-debt deduction, the debt must arise out of a business in which he is actively engaged.[13]

### (b) Planning Implications: Sale of a Going Business

As the preceding discussion has indicated, the capital gains rules are far-reaching indeed. Capital gains taxation can have significant planning impact on major transactions, such as sale of a going business, choice of the form of doing business, and on a number of corporate transactions. Problems are particularly acute where a going business is sold.

There are four major forms of doing business—the corporation, the partnership, the limited liability company, and the sole proprietorship. When an ongoing business in corporate form is sold, it may be sold in one of two basic ways: either the stock of the corporation may be sold or the assets of the corporation may be sold out the corporation. Where

---

**8.** § 165(g)(1).

**9.** § 165(g)(2).

**10.** The purpose of this "end of the year" holding period is to obviate the necessity of determining on which particular day of the taxable year the security became worthless.

**11.** § 166(a).

**12.** § 166(d).

**13.** Whipple v. Commissioner, 373 U.S. 193, 83 S.Ct. 1168, 10 L.Ed.2d 288 (1963), reh'g denied 374 U.S. 858, 83 S.Ct. 1863, 10 L.Ed.2d 1082 (1963) (losses on loans made by taxpayer to his closely-held corporation were nonbusiness bad debts, notwithstanding that he devoted time and energy to the corporation, the Court implying that the taxpayer would have had to be in the business of promoting and financing corporations to enjoy a business bad debt deduction); United States v. Generes, 405 U.S. 93, 92 S.Ct. 827, 31 L.Ed.2d 62 (1972), reh'g denied 405 U.S. 1033, 92 S.Ct. 1274, 31 L.Ed.2d 491 (1972) (test for a business debt is that the business motivation be dominant rather than just significant; on the facts, taxpayer's loan to his business found to be a nonbusiness bad debt).

the stock is sold, the transaction in general gives rise to capital gain (or loss) treatment to the shareholders.[14] Where the assets of the corporation are sold out of the corporation, the character of the gain or loss to the corporation will depend on the character of the various assets in the hands of the corporation. However, on subsequent liquidation of the corporation and distribution of the proceeds of the sale, the stockholders will in general enjoy capital gain (or loss) treatment.[15] Thus as a general matter, when the business that is sold is in corporate form, the sale will ultimately give rise to capital gain (or loss) to the shareholders.

With respect to a business in a partnership form or limited liability form, it is also generally true that the sale of a partnership interest gives rise to capital gain (or loss) treatment to the selling partner, although this may be overridden in some circumstances.[16] The character of the gain on the sale of the partnership assets by the partnership is passed through to the partners, with much the result as described below for the sale of a sole proprietorship.[17] Limited liability companies are treated the same as partnerships for tax purposes.

The sale of a going business in a sole proprietorship form is treated as the sale of the collection of the individual assets of the business by the individual owner, under the case of *Williams v. McGowan*,[18] discussed also at ¶ 4.02(3)(iv). Therefore the sale necessitates an allocation of the purchase price among the various assets of the business. As to important aspects of this allocation, the buyer and seller have adverse interests.

Often the sale of a going business sole proprietorship is negotiated for at an overall fixed price. Take the usual case where the business is operated for some years and is sold for a fixed price which is an overall gain. The task then becomes one of allocating that fixed price among the various assets of the business. These assets will involve some or all of the following: inventory, accounts receivable, cash, § 1231 assets, perhaps some undeveloped land held as an investment, covenant not to compete, and good will. Obviously, the sales price must be allocated to these types of property within some bounds of reality. However, within the bounds of reality, there may well be wide scope for negotiation between the parties as to how the sales proceeds should be allocated among their various types of property.

The seller will want to allocate the bulk of the sales price to assets which yield a capital gain, as opposed to an ordinary gain. This will conflict at least in some cases with the buyer's desire to allocate the bulk of the sales price to assets which yield ordinary gain—so as to minimize his ordinary gain or give rise to an ordinary loss, on subsequent sale.

---

**14.** This would generally be the case, unless the corporation were found to be a collapsable corporation, see § 341. See also Bittker and Eustice, Federal Income Taxation of Corporations and Shareholders (1979) Chapter 12.

**15.** §§ 1221, 331, and see Bittker and Eustice, Chapter 11.

**16.** §§ 741, 751. See also McKee, Nelson, Whitmire, Federal Taxation of Partnerships and Partners, (1977) Part V.

**17.** See McKee, Nelson, and Whitmire, Part IV.

**18.** 152 F.2d 570 (2d Cir.1945).

The buyer will also be interested in allocating a substantial amount of the sales price to depreciable or amortizable property, so as to maximize his basis for the taking of depreciation.

What this means in terms of the particular assets involved would be the following: As to inventory, an ordinary asset,[19] the seller would wish to allocate relatively less to it and the buyer would wish to allocate relatively more to it. The same could be said for accounts receivable,[20] although the value of the accounts receivable will of course be heavily influenced by their face amount.

The parties would change points of view as to, say, undeveloped land held as an investment, or any other "pure" capital asset sold as part of the business. With respect to such "pure" capital assets, the seller would wish to allocate relatively more to them, so as to maximize the amount of the gain on the sale that is characterized as capital.[21] The buyer would wish to allocate relatively less to them. This would be the buyer's approach so that he could have a low basis on his capital assets (rather than on his ordinary assets) in the event of subsequent sale. Even if the buyer does not anticipate a subsequent sale in the near future, he prefers to have a low basis on pure capital assets—such as undeveloped land—which are not depreciable.

Regarding § 1231 property, it rolls out like this. If the seller expects a gain to result from his § 1231 transactions[22] (as may well be the case), he may be happy to allocate a substantial amount of the sales price to the § 1231 assets. This would be because he would want to "tip" the workings of § 1231 to crank out to a gain, giving him capital gains. Furthermore, he would want to have more of his overall gain attributable to assets giving him capital gains. Since the buyer will often be depreciating the § 1231 property, he too may be happy to allocate a substantial portion of the purchase price to § 1231 property. Thus it would not be surprising to find in many cases a relatively great portion of the sales proceeds allocated to § 1231 property. Where, however, the seller will undergo a substantial amount of depreciation recapture on the sale of his § 1231 property, he will wish to allocate a relatively small amount of the sales price to the § 1231 property.[23]

Matters become exquisitely difficult when it comes to the covenant not to compete and good will. The giving of a covenant not to compete by

---

**19.** § 1221(1), ¶ 4.06(3)(a)(i).

**20.** § 1221(4), ¶ 4.06(3)(a)(ix).

**21.** Assuming the asset has been held for longer than one year so as to qualify for the favorable treatment. Another example of "pure" capital assets that might be sold as part of the business in addition to undeveloped land held as an investment would be stock of a closely-held corporation. This would usually be a capital asset (see

§ 1221) and, since it is not traded on a securities market, its value would be open to negotiation between the parties.

If the stock were a "Corn Products asset", see ¶ 4.06(3)(a)(ii), it would then not be a capital asset, and the parties' points of view would be reversed.

**22.** ¶ 4.06(3)(a)(iv).

**23.** See ¶ 4.06(3)(a)(vii) regarding depreciation recapture.

the seller of a business gives rise to ordinary income to the seller.[24] This is generally on the theory that compensation not to work is very similar to compensation to work, and should similarly give rise to ordinary income. As to the buyer, a covenant not to compete for a period of years is amortizable over 15 years under § 197.[25]

Good will, by contrast, is a capital asset.[26] Therefore, the sale of good will for gain yields attractive capital gains to the seller. But under the new § 197 good will can also be written off over 15 years.

Thus the seller and buyer are not adverse in their view of how much of the sales price should be allocated to these two closely-related intangible assets. The seller wants more allocated to good will (to get capital gain) and the buyer does not care (since he writes off either good will or covenant not to compete over 15 years). The result is that in these transactions we will see large amounts allocated to good will and small amounts allocated to covenants not to compete.

Therefore, with regard to some of the property that is transferred in the sale of a going business, the buyer and seller are adverse in their view of how much of the overall fixed sales price should be allocated to each of the types of property. The places in which the buyer and seller may not have adverse views is the IRC § 1231 property, and the covenant not to compete-good will dichotomy.

There is, therefore, a "three-cornered" game involved in the sale of a going business—involving the buyer, the seller, and the Service. Varying approaches have been tried by the parties involved. For example, the buyer and the seller could report the allocation of the sales price inconsistently, each allocating it the way he chooses to attain maximum tax advantage. Where that occurs the Service can be expected to contest the allocation of either or both parties. The outcome of any such litigation could be similarly inconsistent—particularly if the cases arise in different courts, as they well might.[27] If the Service challenges both parties and wins in one case, it will generally concede in the other case so as to avoid collecting two deficiencies in inconsistent cases.[28] The Service may be expected to press for a victory in the case which has the most attractive precedential value.

---

**24.** Rev.Rul. 69–643, 1969–2 C.B. 10; Ullman v. Commissioner, 264 F.2d 305 (2d Cir.1959) (covenants not to compete executed in conjunction with the sale of stock of linen supply corporations gave rise to ordinary income).

**25.** See ¶ 4.06(5).

**26.** Prior to the enactment of § 197, the traditional view of good will was that it is a capital asset because it does not come within any of the exceptions of IRC § 1221. See ¶ 4.06(3)(a). See generally Beghe, "Income Tax Treatment of Covenants Not to Compete, Consulting Agreements and Transfers of Good Will," 30 Tax Lawyer 587 (1977).

**27.** Generally taxpayers may litigate in the Tax Court by filing a timely petition. Taxpayers may litigate in federal district courts or the Claims Court by paying their tax and suing for a refund. See Pierce, "Tax Refund Litigation in District Courts: Choice of Forum, Trial Procedures and Settlement Techniques," 32 NYU Institution Fed.Tax 1289 (1974); Griswold, "The Need for a Court of Tax Appeals," 57 Harv.L.Rev. 1153 (1944).

**28.** Dixie Finance Co. v. United States, 474 F.2d 501 (5th Cir.1973). See ABA Tax Section, Final Report of Special Committee on Whipsaw, 30 Tax Lawyer 127 (1976).

The parties may well attempt to control their tax destinies in these cases by agreeing on an allocation of the purchase price of the business as part of the sales contract. The Service might respect this allocation since, as discussed above, the parties are adverse in some of their interests as to how the sales price will be allocated. However, if one party is in a substantially higher marginal bracket than the other, the parties may plan to give the tax benefits to the higher-bracket party in exchange for concessions by that higher-tax-bracket party on the sales price. In such an event, the Service can challenge the contractual sales price allocation.[29]

If, for various reasons, the allocation of the sales proceeds must be judicially determined, the greatest problem is presented in the allocation between the covenant not to compete and good will. Obviously, these two intangible assets are closely related: the good will of a purchased business may mean little if the seller opens a shop across the street. Moreover, the value of such intangible assets is obviously quite speculative compared to the value of the physical assets of the business. Therefore, it is not surprising that the problem of allocating a portion of the purchase price between a covenant not to compete and good will has spawned a good deal of litigation.[30] This litigation may be expected to continue since, as discussed above, after § 197, the parties will tend to conspire together to pick the Service's pocket.

### (4) Policy Aspects of Capital Gains Taxation

Capital gains have, for most of the time since 1921, been taxed more favorably than ordinary gains. Concomitant with this favorable treatment of capital gains has gone a restrictive treatment of capital losses.[31] The type of favorable treatment for capital gains and restrictive treatment for capital losses has varied widely over the years. As the preceding discussion of the mechanics of capital gains and losses taxation has indicated, the treatment is now exceedingly complex. This complexity no doubt results from the fact that capital gains apparently do not exist as a concept separate from the Internal Revenue Code. In short, capital gains (and capital losses) are whatever the Internal Revenue Code says they are. Lacking any economic or other touchstone for defining capital gains, it is perhaps not surprising that Congress has floundered into a sea of

---

**29.** Dixie Fin. Co. note 28, supra.

A related problem arises if one of the parties is not represented by tax counsel during the sales negotiations and therefore unwittingly agrees to an unfavorable allocation of the sales proceeds. In that event it is possible for such a party to escape from being held to that allocation. The party in such a case, however, must carry an unusually heavy burden of proof, Ullman v. Commissioner, 264 F.2d 305 (2d Cir.1959); Commissioner v. Danielson, 378 F.2d 771 (3d Cir.1967).

**30.** E.g. Proulx v. United States, 594 F.2d 832 (Ct.Cl.1979) (discussing various theories for making this allocation); Throndson v. Commissioner, 457 F.2d 1022 (9th Cir.1972) (dental practice); Better Beverages, Inc. v. United States, 619 F.2d 424 (5th Cir.1980), rehearing denied 625 F.2d 1160 (buyer carries heavy burden of establishing a significant value in covenant not to compete where sales agreement makes no allocation).

**31.** Revenue Act of 1921, P.L. No. 98, § 206(b), 42 Stat. 233; see also Revenue Act of 1924, § 206(a)(2).

complexity in defining them in the Code. Moreover, this lack of any definition of "real" capital gains makes discussion of the policy reasons for taxing capital gains favorably relatively difficult.

Nevertheless, there are a number of standard arguments that are advanced for according capital gains favorable tax treatment. Interestingly, there is no similar set of reasons for applying restrictive rules to capital losses. The literature appears to be devoid of any discussion of reasons why capital losses should be disfavored under the tax system. Apparently, all hands are content to accept the proposition that if capital gains are to be treated favorably, somehow capital losses should be treated restrictively to make up for it.[32] The lack of any serious independent reasons for restricting deductibility of capital losses may tend to undercut the reasons for favorably treating capital gains. The situation begins to partake of a game with certain benefits and costs—which taxpayers are invited to play if they so choose.

In any event, there are a number of traditional reasons advanced for the favorable treatment of capital gains. They are:

1. *The bunching of income.* This argument holds that gains from the sale of capital assets accrue over time but are only taxed at the point of sale. This, therefore, means that the gains will be bunched up in one taxable year and subjected to a higher rate of taxation, given the graduated rate structure. There are several possible answers to this argument. First of all, the sympathy for the taxpayer selling a capital asset which he may have held for many years and undergoing this bunching effect may be mitigated when it is noted that throughout the period that the taxpayer was enjoying this appreciation in the value of his capital asset, he was paying no tax at all. In short, the taxpayer holding an asset which has appreciated over many years has enjoyed the great advantage of deferral of what is, from an economic point of view, income. The taxpayer has, throughout this period, enjoyed the benefit of holding the appreciated asset. He could have borrowed against its value. He could have otherwise included it in his financial planning.

A second reason for questioning the "bunching" argument is that many taxpayers enjoy capital gains every year and therefore their income is not "bunched up" in any one particular year on account of capital gains. A third reason for questioning the "bunching" argument is that many taxpayers who enjoy capital gains are already at the highest possible marginal tax bracket—without consideration of their capital gains and, therefore, the capital gains transaction does not in fact push them into any higher bracket. Finally, it may be said as to the "bunch-

---

**32.** It might be argued that a reason for applying restrictive rules to capital losses is that capital losses are within the control of the taxpayer and therefore it is desirable to restrict the taxpayer's ability to "take advantage" of those losses. The problem with that argument is that capital losses can arise from involuntary conversions and indeed even casualty losses (see the discussion of IRC § 1231 at § 4.06(3)(a)(iv)). Moreover, losses can also arise from the sale of property which is not a capital asset, in which case the loss is deductible in full, and the timing of which would be within the control of the taxpayer.

ing" argument that many other taxpayers who have non-capital gains type income may also undergo wide fluctuations in their income. The general averaging provisions[33] provide relief for all taxpayers who may have "bunched" income.

2. *The lock-in effect.* The lock-in argument is that since gains on the holding of capital assets are only taxed on their sale or other disposition, taxpayers holding highly appreciated assets may hesitate to sell them for fear of incurring a substantial tax. The lock-in argument is always advanced somewhat gingerly, however, since it may provide a rationale for taxing accrued gains on capital assets annually rather than waiting for them to be sold at all. Moreover, the lock-in argument would appear to hold at whatever rate taxable gains are taxed at. There are no studies indicating what minimal rate of tax would have to be applied so as not to discourage taxpayers from selling their appreciated assets and reinvesting them in more productive property. One possible approach, if the lock-in effect is a serious problem, is to allow taxpayers to roll over their gains on the sale of investment assets tax-free into other investment assets. Basic rules could be provided to insure the gain is ultimately taxed at full rates when the taxpayer cashes out.

3. *Encouraging investment.* Treating capital gains favorably is often justified as an incentive to encourage investment in productive assets in the economy. The problem with this argument is that the incentive fostered by the capital gains rules is too broad. Is it part of U.S. national economic policy to encourage investment in gold bullion, paintings, antique furniture, stamps, and the like? Yet, taxpayer investment in and sale of these types of property are all granted capital gains treatment. If the tax system is to be used to foster a productive investment, apparently more refined techniques would be appropriate. Such techniques are already in the Code—for example, the investment credit, and the allowance for accelerated depreciation.[34]

4. *The inflation effect.* It is often argued that capital gains should be taxed more favorably since a significant portion of capital gains are illusory, in that they simply reflect the overall inflation rate in the economy. Since the gain due to the inflation is not "real", it should not be taxed so heavily. It might be answered as to this argument that many taxpayers suffer from this inflation effect. The taxpayer who has only compensation income may receive wage increases every year which do not actually increase his standard of living but simply keep him in step with inflation. Such a taxpayer would be moved into higher tax brackets and pay higher taxes although his wage increase was not "real." Therefore, if the problem is that inflation is pushing taxpayers into higher brackets, a general solution to that problem should be found, instead of simply solving the problem for those who enjoy capital gains.

However these arguments finally come out, one thing is clear as to capital gains: The introduction of special treatment for capital gains into

**33.** IRC §§ 1301–1305. See § 9.04.    **34.** See ¶¶ 10.02 and 6.02(12), respectively.

the Code creates a great deal of complexity. Since there is no true economic definition of capital gains, anyone who regularly engages in a particular type of transaction may hope to have that transaction deemed a capital gain. This creates a great deal of pressure to broaden the definition of capital gains.[35]

### (5) Exotic Wall Street Techniques Employed By the Wealthy To Avoid Capital Gains: Of ESOP Sales, Upreits, Equity Swaps, Shorting Against the Box, Swap Funds, DECS and the Like

To a substantial extent the policy argument above concerning how capital gains should be taxed is moot because in fact the very well-heeled often don't pay any tax at all on their capital gains. They accomplish this feat by using exotic techniques developed by Wall Street investment banking firms and law firms. Some of these techniques are legitimately in the Code, but others use the code in legal but novel or completely unanticipated ways.

Consider the case of Eli Broad, a millionaire homebuilder and a founder of the SunAmerica insurance empire.[36] Mr. Broad had a problem we all should have. He had $194 million in profits on his SunAmerica stock and he wished to raise some cash from it without the inconvenience of paying any of the $54 million in taxes he would incur if he sold the shares. A technique was made available to Mr. Broad, a technique not available to the thousands of other smaller stockholders of SunAmerica, or other investors who own SunAmercia through mutual funds. That technique is discussed below.

It appears that the trend in this country is that the payment of capital gains is becoming largely a middle class phenomenon. Those at the top of the economic ladder are sufficiently well-advised to avoid the tax. Those at the bottom of the economic ladder do not have capital gains. So, like sport utility vehicles, backyard pools, hibachis and soccer moms, paying capital gains taxes has become a characteristic of the middle class.

Here is a bird's eye view of some of the strategies employed by the very wealthy for avoiding the capital gains tax.

---

**35.** It is probably fair to say that the existence of capital gains is responsible for at least one-third of the size of the Internal Revenue Code.

See generally, McDonald, "Depreciability of Assets and the Taxation of Capital Gains," 32 Nat'l Tax J. 83 (1979); Kiefer, "Depreciability of Assets and the Taxation of Capital Gains: A Comment and Extension," 33 Nat'l Tax J. 103 (1980); Whalley, "Capital Gains Taxation and Interest Rate Changes: An Extension of Paish's Argument," 32 Nat'l Tax J. 87 (1979); Feldstein and Slemrod, "Inflation and the Excess Taxation of Capital Gains on Corporate Stock," 31 Nat'l Tax J. 107 (1978); Waggon-er, "Eliminating the Capital Gains Preference, Part I: The Problems of Inflation, Bunching and Lock–In," 48 Univ. of Colo. L.Rev. 313 (1977); Waggoner, "Eliminating the Capital Gains Preference, Part II: The Problem of Corporate Taxation," 49 Univ. of Colo.L.Rev. 9 (1977); Lokken, "The Effects of Capital Gains and Losses on the Credit for Foreign Income Taxation," 30 Univ. of Fla.L.Rev. 40 (1977).

**36.** The anecdotal material in this discussion is based on Diana B. Henriques with Floyd Norris, Wealthy, Helped by Wall St., Find New Ways to Escape Tax on Profits, New York Times, December 1, 1996, p. 1.

* Owners of a closely-held business can sell the business to their employees and not pay a capital gains tax if they reinvest the proceeds in certain investments, such as "ESOP notes," which Wall Street provides. Former Treasury Secretary William Simon and his partners sold the Avis car rental agency, which they had held less than 2 years, to the employees tax free using this technique, shielding $700 million in gain. This is under § 1042, which provides that the owner of a small business who sells at least 30% and as much as 100% of the business to an ESOP, or employee stock ownership plan may do so tax free if he has held the business for three years and reinvests the proceeds in other domestic corporate securities and does not sell them during his lifetime. The sale of a successful small business to its ESOP has become a major specialty of investment advisor firms, such as Houlihan Lokey Howard & Zukin in Los Angeles.

* Owners of real estate can swap for any other kind of real estate without paying a tax, enabling them to change their type of investment or raise cash. (A lawyer friend of mine recently swapped an office building in downtown New Orleans for a suburban, undeveloped lot, without tax). See § 1031 and ¶ 4.05(2). The origin of § 1031 was as a tax break for cash-poor farmers who needed to be able to swap fields. But it has now become a Wall Street business, with three cornered transactions (see ¶ 4.05(2)(e)) brokered by major real estate firms like Cushman & Wakefield and Merrill Lynch Realty.

The possibilities of using § 1031 have been expanded considerably when joined with some sophisticated partnership tax planning. This combines a traditional real estate investment trust (a way of investing in a diverse portfolio of real estate similar to a mutual fund for stocks) with a traditional operating partnership. This combination gives rise to a new partnership, a so-called umbrella partnership, or more briefly an "upreit" (umbrella partnership real estate investment trust). A developer can swap his property to the umbrella real estate partnership tax free, receiving a partnership share back, under § 1031. Then the real estate investment trust (REIT), which is also a partner in the umbrella partnership can market partnership shares to the public. This raises cash which can be used to rehabilitate the property the developer transferred. Thus cash has been raised; the developer's portfolio has been expanded; the property is refurbished and no taxes have been paid. Moreover, the developer-partner can borrow against his partnership share to raise money for other ventures. As long as the developer does not change his shares into the publicly marketable shares of the REIT partner, the developer will not owe capital gains taxes on the property contributed to the REIT. Total assets involved in upreits is estimated to be over $32 billion. Major real estate developers such as Sam Zell in Chicago have made use of this technique.

* Owners of the so-called qualified small business stock (generally stock of a small venture capital start up firm) can exclude half the gain

on the sale of such stock and the other half is still only taxed at the maximum 28% capital gains rate, see § 1202, ¶ 4.06(1).

\* Large shareholders can choose any of several exotic techniques to lock in their stock market profits, raise cash and not pay taxes. These techniques are discussed below.

Moreover, the language of these techniques is rich: we have upreits, DECS, swaps, Strypes, zero-cost dollars, and ACES.

Of course it should be recalled that a major capital gains tax avoidance technique is to die holding the appreciated assets, whose basis is stepped up to fair market value at death, see ¶ 4.03(2)(e). Economists estimate that one-half to two-thirds of all accumulated capital gains in the economy escape taxation through this loophole. Of course this technique has its drawbacks, including making it difficult to raise cash before one dies, and the threat that the accumulated asset could decline in value. Thus, Wall Street to the rescue.

The underlying theory of Wall Street's sophisticated techniques involves the separation of legal ownership from the economic effects of ownership. The idea is that as long as the investor remains the legal owner of the stock he does not incur capital gains taxation even if he has shed all the economic risks and benefits of ownership. Among the economic attributes that taxpayers shed include risks of price fluctuations and the receipt of dividends. These techniques are much more sophisticated than the usual hedging, or taking a counterbalancing position to one already held. These techniques not only eliminate risk, as hedging does, but they also generate cash which can be invested elsewhere.

An example of the classic deal in this area was accomplished by A. Lorne Weil, the chairman and chief executive of the Autotote Corporation, a manufacturer of wagering equipment used at tracks, casinos and betting parlors. Due in great part to the explosive rise in gambling, the company's fortunes took on a meteoric rise. In 1994, Mr. Weil's stock had appreciated to a value of $23 million, seven times their value two years earlier. It made sense for Mr. Weil to sell a substantial amount of this stock to lock in his gain and diversify his investments. Doing so, however, would have triggered the inconvenience of millions of dollars in capital gains taxes. According to information filed with the SEC, because Autotote was a public company, Mr. Weil did not sell his stock but rather swapped it to the Bankers Trust Company. In so doing he secured a place in tax history: he participated in the first genuinely new financial product of the last five decades, according to some commentators.

The deal worked like this: In 1993, Mr. Weil transferred to Bankers Trust for five years all the economic rewards and risks of owning 500,000 shares of his Autotote stock, which was worth $13.5 million at the time. Mr. Weil kept legal title to the shares. As a result the bank received any dividends paid on the stock, and received any gain in the stock's price during the five year period of the swap. In exchange the

Bank agreed to pay Mr. Weil what $13.5 million would have earned on an alternative investment, less its fee. The bank also agreed to reimburse Mr. Weil for any drop in the price of the stock over the five year period. The bank presumably covered this risk with a hedging strategy such as going short the stock, or buying puts on the stock.

Mr. Weil's strategy simulated all the effects of a sale of the stock and reinvestment of the proceeds, except for the lack of necessity to pay the huge tax on his gain. In 1996, the stock price had plummeted and was worth $500,000, down considerably from its high of $23 million. Mr. Weil suffered none of that loss since he had for all economic purposes "sold" the stock.

With this separation of legal ownership and economic attributes came the dawn of a new era on Wall Street. With the stock market as frothy as it has been, many deals have been done like this.

Another example of holding on to legal title of stock while disposing of all the economic characteristics the stock was employed in the celebrated transaction in which the Estee Lauder cosmetics company was sold to the public. Estee Lauder and her son Ronald Lauder wanted to sell 13.8 million of their shares of the business to the public. The problem was that their shares were so highly appreciated that $95 million in capital gains taxes would have been triggered by a normal sale. Instead, Mrs. Lauder and Ronald Lauder borrowed 13.8 million shares from family trust accounts and relatives and sold those borrowed shares to the public. What the Lauders did in effect was "sell short against the box," see ¶ 4.06(2)(c)(v). In this hedged position the Lauders were unaffected by the stock price and they raised cash (from the short sale). Thus they did everything one would want to do in the sale of stock, except that they paid no taxes because they still had legal title to their original 13.8 million shares.

Normal investors can also use this technique, but normal investors cannot withdraw the proceeds from their short sales until they have covered the transaction and returned the shares they have sold short. But Wall Street brokerage firms allow their very wealthy clients to immediately take out the proceeds from their short sale as a low interest loan. The Clinton Administration early in 1996 proposed legislative changes to eliminate retroactively going short against the box. The Republican leaders in Congress assured Wall Street that the proposals would not be retroactive. Since it appeared time might be running out on shorting against the box, the deals proliferated in 1996.

Another wrinkle is the swap fund. This takes advantage of § 721, which allows partners to transfer appreciated property to a partnership without incurring tax. In the 50's and 60's taxpayers attempted to swap appreciated securities into a partnership, so that each contributing partner could own a share of a diversified portfolio of securities, tax free. In the 60's the Government disallowed the swap-fund maneuver by disallowing tax free swaps with any partnership that had 80% or more of its assets invested in "readily marketable securities." Recently the maneuver has been to engage in swap fund transactions with a partnership that is close to the line, say 79% of its assets invested in readily marketable securities. Some leading Wall Street firms, such as Goldman, Sachs; Morgan Stanley, the Bessemer Trust Company, have organized swap funds under this "close to the line" approach.

In another maneuver, in late 1996, Salmon Brothers arranged a major deal for its client Western Southern Life Insurance Company, which owned shares of Cincinnati Bell that were highly appreciated. Western Southern wanted to lock in its gain and diversify its investments. The clear way to do that, of course, is to sell the stock. But as has been noted above, selling highly appreciated stock has a nasty way of attracting substantial capital gains taxes. Western Southern could, of course, have borrowed against the stock. But the traditional borrowing route is expensive, with relatively high interest rates. Substantial traditional borrowing also puts credit agencies on guard. So Salmon concocted the following ingenious scheme. Salmon sold notes exchangeable into common stock (called "DECS," for debt exchangable into common stock) to the public and transferred most of the proceeds to Western Southern. Western Southern gave notes to Salmon that mirrored the terms of the DECs Salmon sold to the public. The terms of the notes sold to the public were that they paid a fixed rate of interest, and give the noteholder a share of any future price increase in Cincinnati Bell stock. If the price of Cincinnati Bell falls, the noteholder bears all the risk. This unattractive feature means that the notes will sell in the market place for a lower price.

When the notes mature, Western Southern can pay back Salmon either with cash or with stock. If Western Southern repays with cash, it will continue to hold the Cincinnati Bell Stock. If it repays with stock, it will at that point have sold the stock and be liable for capital gains taxes. It will in that event still have had advance use of the money. As mentioned above, the whole transaction is in substance borrowing on the stock, but it is done in an inexpensive way that does not arose the ire of credit agencies. Times Mirror and American Express have also recently done deals like this.

It is this DEC technique that Merrill Lynch used to save Eli Broad millions of dollars in taxes on his block of SunAmerica stock worth $194 million. The Broad transaction, taking place in the spring of 1996, was a major event in the tax community because it was the first time the DEC technique had been used in public for an individual. Under the terms of the notes, Mr. Broad kept the right to gains on the stock after it had appreciated 35%. He had no risk on the loss side. He retained legal title to the stock and was able to vote the stock.

Some of the techniques available have been around for over a decade, but others are new. All are being used in a very aggressive fashion, given that marginal rates have risen and that the rate of audit by the Service is low.

The use of DECS-type instruments for the purpose of avoiding the capital gains tax has mushroomed over the last several years. In 1993, $1.23 billion of them were issued. In 1996, about $5.30 billion were issued. There is no reason for these instruments except to avoid capital gains taxation. So there is a great deal of capital gains tax not being paid as a result of this activity.

Another recent maneuver is the so-called zero-cost dollar. In this strategy, the holder of a single stock that has appreciated greatly sets up a hedged position made up of two option contracts on the stock. One protects him from loss. The other allows him a small participation in any gain. The taxpayer can then borrow against the position. Once again, the taxpayer has pretty well done all you ever do when you sell: insulate himself from loss and raise cash. But again unlike selling, no tax is paid.

These swap techniques are really part of the larger derivative market that has recently developed nationally and internationally. The new mathematical techniques available make possible accurate valuation and hedging strategies with respect to these complex instruments.

The result of these sophisticated techniques is that the effective capital gains rate of taxation on the super-wealthy and corporations is very low.

As to preventing these techniques, one might imagine use of older doctrines such as substance over form or the *Knetsch* case possibly being employed, see ¶ 6.03(6)(b). This would require the Service to fight these arrangements, which it does not seem to be doing. There are some difficulties, but it is possible to legislate against these techniques. For example, DECS look a lot like legitimate hedging; so it is hard to draw the line. An analysis needs to be developed where the law looks to whether the economic incidents of ownership have been surrendered. If they have, then it can be argued there has been a sale and taxes should be paid.

Finally, of course, it might be pointed out that what really brings out all these techniques is the realization requirement for triggering taxation. If investors simply had to pay tax every year on accrued gains, see ¶ 4.02, none of these other maneuvers would occur.

# Chapter 5

## ASSIGNMENT OF INCOME: WHO IS TAXED AND THE NATURE OF THE TAX

*Table of Sections*

---

## ¶ 5.01 Background

The previous chapters have considered what is included in gross income. Beyond what was said in those chapters is an additional set of problems found in that rather loosely connected body of cases and statutes that fall under the heading "assignment of income." There are two basic issues in the assignment of income field. One is who is the proper person on whom to impose a tax and the second is the character—whether capital or ordinary—of a particular item of income. While these two issues do not appear at first blush to be closely related to one another, when these two issues arise in the context of an assignment of income, the underlying concepts and problems are very similar.

Assignment of income—as the name itself implies—involves the transfer of income from one taxpayer to another before that income is received. There are two fundamental types of such assignments: gratuitous assignments and assignments for consideration.

Generally speaking the purpose of a gratuitous assignment of income is to shift income from a higher-bracket taxpayer to a lower-bracket taxpayer in the same family. The idea is to lower the tax on the income, while still keeping the income in the family. The purpose of an assignment of income for consideration is to attempt to get favorable capital gains treatment on the transaction.

Speaking a little more specifically, *gratuitous* assignments involve, for example, a cash-basis taxpayer who is owed compensation for personal services he has rendered attempting to assign the payment of that

320

compensation to a member of his family, the fact pattern of the seminal case of *Lucas v. Earl*.[1]

The purpose of such a gratuitous assignment of income is to attempt to defeat the progressive tax system. This is done by shifting income from, say, the high-bracket father to the lower-bracket child. Not surprisingly, the Service and Congress generally successfully oppose these maneuvers. In such a case the income is reattributed back to the person whose personal services earned the income.

In contrast to the personal service area, there is no problem whatsoever in gratuitous assignments of income from property. Thus Mildred can give dividend-producing stock to her son Freemantle. Freemantle, in a lower bracket, will be taxed at a lower rate on the dividends. You cannot hear a sound from the Service objecting to an outright gift of that kind. Moreover, as we discussed at ¶ 4.03(2)(c)(i), if the property transferred has appreciated in value, Freemantle rather than Mildred will also be taxed on that appreciation. Mildred's transfers were effective not only in shifting the future dividends to Freemantle but in also shifting past appreciation to Freemantle. Can't hear a thing from the Service on this one.

Thus shall we be so nasty as to draw the conclusion: those who own property can easily shift income to lower-bracket family members. Those who earn their money by the sweat of their own efforts cannot.

In this context it should be noted that allowing all gratuitous assignments of income to be effective in shifting the tax burden would not, as is commonly thought, undermine the progressive tax system. Rather, it would simply lead to another progressive system, in which the taxable unit is the family, instead of individuals. Indeed, that is precisely what happened with the advent of the joint return, which imposes a tax on the married couple. This in effect allows all gratuitous assignments of income between the married partners.

Assignments of income for *consideration* spring not from a desire to split income but from an urge to enjoy capital gains treatment on what would otherwise be ordinary income.[2]

Consider, for example, a taxpayer who owns property on which there is a lease, producing periodic rental payments to the taxpayer. For various business reasons the lessee wishes to be discharged from the lease. After negotiations the lessee pays the taxpayer a lump sum in exchange for cancellation of the lease. The taxpayer may be regarded as having effected an assignment of his rights on the lease for consideration. The question in cases of this nature is whether the transaction can give rise to capital gain rather than ordinary income.[3]

---

**¶ 5.01**

1. 281 U.S. 111, 50 S.Ct. 241, 74 L.Ed. 731 (1930).

2. For a general discussion of capital gains income see ¶ 4.06.

3. These are essentially the facts Hort v. Commissioner, 313 U.S. 28, 61 S.Ct. 757, 85 L.Ed. 1168 (1941), discussed at note 3, ¶ 5.03 infra and accompanying text.

Similarly, the taxpayer could sell the right to receive future dividends, interest, royalties, or trust income—all with the hope of receiving capital gain in lieu of what would otherwise have been ordinary income. The Service would be expected to oppose such maneuvers,[4] as discussed below.

Both of these types of assignments—the gratuitous assignment and the assignment for consideration—raise far-reaching questions in the tax law. Almost all types of income can be subject to them. Many of the areas are now covered by statute. There are, however, hoary cases, whose principles still bite. The doctrine of assignment of income spills out into many fields, including the taxation of trusts, family partnerships, collapsible corporations.[5] A classic case like *Old Colony Trust Co. v. Commissioner*[6] is fundamental to the field; ultimately the assignment of income area is a child of the great case of *Gregory v. Helvering*[7] and the doctrine of substance-over-form.

## ¶ 5.02   Gratuitous Assignments of Income: Birth of a Metaphor

The early cases in the assignment of income field almost uniformly related to gratuitous assignments of income. The case which contributed the most in particular to the assignment of income field is without doubt *Lucas v. Earl*,[1] decided by the Supreme Court in 1930. This case is famous not because of the originality of *Earl*'s results nor because of the brilliance of its analysis, nor even because it was the first assignment of income case (although it was). *Earl* gave to the field something far more important than any of that. *Earl* gave to the field a metaphor. In dealing

---

**4.** Id.

**5.** Cf. J. Peschel and E. Spurgeon, *Federal Taxation of Trusts, Grantors, and Beneficiaries* (1978) Part III regarding grantor trusts; § 482, allowing the Secretary of the Treasury to allocate income, deductions, credits or allowances among related taxpayers involves assignment of income principles, see generally Fuller, "Section 482 Revisited," 31 Tax L.Rev. 475 (1976). § 446(b), allowing the Secretary of the Treasury to compute income under an accounting method that clearly reflects income involves assignment of income principles. Commissioner v. South Lake Farms, Inc., 324 F.2d 837 (9th Cir.1963).

**6.** 279 U.S. 716, 49 S.Ct. 499, 73 L.Ed. 918 (1929) (employer's payment of employee's income taxes income to the employee). See Chapter 2.

**7.** 293 U.S. 465, 55 S.Ct. 266, 79 L.Ed. 596 (1935) (Although taxpayer complied with the literal terms of the reorganization-statute its provisions were held not to apply because the taxpayer was engaging in an artifice to avoid paying taxes). See Commis-

sioner v. Court Holding Co., 324 U.S. 331, 65 S.Ct. 707, 89 L.Ed. 981 (1945) (which raises the closely-related question of which taxpayer sold property, see Commissioner v. South Lake Farms, Inc., note 6 supra.)

**¶ 5.02**

**1.** Note 2, ¶ 5.01 supra. See also Helvering v. Eubank, 311 U.S. 122, 61 S.Ct. 149, 85 L.Ed. 81 (1940) reh'g denied 312 U.S. 713, 61 S.Ct. 609, 85 L.Ed. 1144 (1941) (commissions on insurance policy renewals taxable to the person who originally sold the policies); Burnet v. Leininger, 285 U.S. 136, 52 S.Ct. 345, 76 L.Ed. 665 (1932); Poe v. Seaborn, 282 U.S. 101, 51 S.Ct. 58, 75 L.Ed. 239 (1930) (Married couple residents of state with community property law allowed to split their income. This led to a rash of states adopting community property laws, culminating in the establishment of the federal joint tax return for husbands and wives in 1948. See Bittker, "Federal Income Taxation and the Family," 27 Stanford Law Review 1389 (1975) at 1404–1414.)

with a taxpayer's gratuitous assignment to a family member of compensation income for services he had rendered, Justice Holmes, speaking for the Supreme Court, said that the income tax can "not be escaped by anticipatory arrangements and contracts however skillfully devised ... by which the fruits are attributed to a different tree from that on which they grew."[2]

Of course, once the income was taxed to Earl, the subsequent transfer of funds to the wife would be excluded from her income as a gift.

Ironically, the metaphor was not so apt in this first case; presumably the "tree" was the taxpayer himself, and the "fruit" was his compensation income. The metaphor was more readily applicable to subsequent cases through the years.

A related case is *Commissioner v. Giannini*[3] which dealt with a taxpayer who declined compensation for services the Board of Directors had voted him as President and Director of Bancitaly Corporation. The taxpayer told the Board that he would not accept the compensation and suggested that the Board do something worthwhile with the money. The Board thereafter granted the money to the University of California to establish a Foundation of Agricultural Economics, named after the taxpayer. The taxpayer did not report any of the $1,357,607 so transferred to the regents of the University of California as income.

The Commissioner, in his usual role as grinch, assessed a tax on the amount. The Commissioner's argument, straight out of *Earl,* was that the actual receipt of money or property is not always necessary to constitute taxable income. A taxpayer "realizes" income when he directs the disposition of it in a manner that it reaches the object of his bounty. Taxpayer responded that he had absolutely and unconditionally refused the property offered him. Thus it could not be "diverted" or assigned to an object of his bounty.

The court held that the taxpayer did not direct the disposition of the funds and therefore that he was not taxed on them.

A couple of revenue rulings raise similar issues, although they do not come out the same way.

In *Revenue Ruling 66-167*[4] the Service dealt with the case where a taxpayer declined to seek amounts he could have received as fees and commissions in serving as the sole executor of his wife's estate. The

---

**2.** 281 U.S. 111 at 115, 50 S.Ct. 241 at 242.

During this period the Supreme Court also used the "fruit and tree" metaphor in the wholly unrelated field of criminal procedure, barring the use of "tainted" evidence derived from an illegal or unconstitutional search or other procedure—"fruit of the poisonous tree," Nardone v. United States,

308 U.S. 338, 60 S.Ct. 266, 84 L.Ed. 307 (1939); see also Silverthorne Lumber Co. v. United States, 251 U.S. 385, 40 S.Ct. 182, 64 L.Ed. 319 (1920). Apparently the Court was in an agricultural mode during this period.

**3.** 129 F.2d 638 (9th Cir.1942).

**4.** 1966-1 Cum.Bull. 20.

Service held that such waived fees and commissions were not includible in taxable income.

In *Revenue Ruling 74–581*[5] the Service addressed the treatment of payments received for services performed by a faculty member or a student of a university's school of law in their clinical programs. (So listen up). The policy at the school was that all fees to which the faculty member is entitled because of his work as an assigned attorney under the Criminal Justice Act would be assigned over to the law school. As a matter of practice the checks were paid by the court to the faculty member who then endorsed them over to the law school.

The Service ruled that the payments were not income to the faculty member. The ruling noted that there are a number of other similar cases in which it has ruled that the person rendering services does not have income. These include fees for representing indigent defendants where the fees are turned over to the employer, a legal aid society; checks received by a physician from patients which he is required to endorse over to the hospital.

In 1937 the Supreme Court decided the well-known *Blair v. Commissioner,*[6] involving the assignment by a father to his children of fixed annual dollar amounts of income to be paid from his life interest in a trust. The Court held the assignments to be of property and to be valid for tax purposes. Thus the children rather than the father were taxable on the assigned income, as it was received.

Employing the fruit and tree metaphor in *Blair,* the father's life interest in the trust income would be regarded as the tree—the underlying property. Since the father did not assign a fixed amount of income for just a few years but a fixed amount of income for the full term of his life interest, the assignment was valid for tax purposes. The father, in effect, chopped down some of his fruit and some of his tree and *gave some of his fruit and some of his tree to his children.* Such a "vertical cut" was effective to shift the tax liability on the assigned income to the children.

A related case is *Estate of Stranahan v. Commissioner*[7] which involved a decedent Frank Stranahan who had entered into a closing agreement with the IRS under which it was agreed that the decedent owed the IRS $754,815 for interest due to deficiencies in federal income, estate and gift taxes. In order to get the full benefit of deducting this large amount of interest the decedent accelerated the receipt of some income. He assigned his son the anticipated receipt of $122,820 in stock dividends from his Champion Spark Plug Company stock. As consideration, the son paid the decedent $115,000 by check, dated December 22, 1964. Decedent reported this amount as income on his 1964 return and was thus able to deduct his interest payments to the IRS in full.

**5.** 1974–2 Cum.Bull. 25.

**6.** 300 U.S. 5, 57 S.Ct. 330, 81 L.Ed. 465 (1937).

**7.** 472 F.2d 867 (6th Cir.1973).

The Tax Court held that the dividends paid to the son under this agreement in 1965 were taxable to the decedent's estate in 1965, not 1964. The Tax Court found that the agreement entered into with the son was in reality a loan by the son to the father and therefore decedent had no income in 1964 (since receipt of loan proceeds is not taxable).

The Sixth Circuit reversed, holding that the transaction was legally enforceable and not a sham. Valuable consideration was part of the transaction. Thus the transaction was economically realistic, with substance, and should be respected, notwithstanding that it concededly was entered into for the purpose of lowering federal income taxes.

The subsequent decision of the Supreme Court in *Harrison v. Schaffner*[8] (1941) suggests this *Blair-Stranahan* analysis is correct. In *Schaffner* the life income beneficiary of a trust assigned to her children fixed dollar amounts to be paid the following year out of the income of the trust. The Court found that this assignment of income for one year was not "a substantial distribution of trust property"[9] and hence that the assigned income was taxable to the donor rather than the donees.

Employing the fruit and tree metaphor in *Schaffner*, the donor's assignment of a fixed amount of income was not for a period coextensive in time with her own life interest but only for one year. Thus the donor in *Schaffner* can be regarded as having assigned only the "fruit," rather than a portion of the underlying property or "tree." The assignment was a "horizontal cut" and did not shift the tax burden to the donees.

The landmark *Helvering v. Horst*,[10] decided in 1940, was a prototype fruit and tree situation. Donor, the owner of negotiable bonds, detached from them negotiable interest coupons shortly before their due date and gave them to his son who collected the interest in the same year. The Supreme Court, explicitly employing the fruit and tree metaphor,[11] held that the interest was taxable to the donor. The analysis was clear: the donor had given only the "fruit"—the coupon—rather than the "tree"— a bond. Thus the assignment was only a "horizontal cut" and therefore the income remained taxable to the donor.[12]

---

8. 312 U.S. 579, 61 S.Ct. 759, 85 L.Ed. 1055 (1941).

9. Id. at 583, 61 S.Ct. at 762.

10. 311 U.S. 112, 61 S.Ct. 144, 85 L.Ed. 75 (1940).

11. Id. at 117, 118, 61 S.Ct. at 147, 148.

12. Although *Schaffner* and *Horst* both involved "horizontal cuts" and therefore the assigned income was taxable to the donor, there is an interesting difference between the two cases. *Schaffner* involved an asset—the life interest in the trust income—that was in some sense wasting, or wearing out. Once the asset stopped throwing off income, because of the death of the life tenant, it would necessarily have a value of zero. The bond involved in *Horst*, however, was not a wasting asset. Once it stopped throwing off income—at maturity—the principal amount of the bond would still remain to be paid back. Putting it another way, if the life estate in the trust had been purchased from the life tenant by another (so that the purchaser would have an estate *pur autre vie*), the purchaser would be able to amortize the cost of the estate (computed by reference to the life expectancy of the seller) against the income payments. Of course the purchaser of a bond in the bond market *cannot* amortize the cost of the bond against the interest payments. What this all boils down to mean is that the assignment of income in *Schaffner*, even though it was only for one year, necessarily involved an assignment of capital or "tree" as well as income, or "fruit."

Thus by 1941 the courts' theoretical approach to gratuitous assignments of income was well-established: gifts of fruit, or "horizontal cuts" in the donor's property would be ineffective to transfer the tax on the income to the donee; gifts of the tree, or "vertical cuts" in the donor's property coextensive in time with the donor's own interest, would be effective to transfer the tax on the income to the donee. There is a rationale. To the extent the donor assigns vertical cuts he loses the power to reassign income from that vertical cut. Thus the assignment will be respected for tax purposes.

Some modern applications of these principles include the case of *Susie Salvatore*[13] in which taxpayer contracted to sell her service station to Texaco and thereafter gave one-half of the service station to her children. The court held that the taxpayer was taxable on the full amount of the proceeds of the sale, not one half the amount.

Also, in Revenue Ruling 69–102, 1969–1 Cum. Bull. 32, the Service addressed the tax consequences of the maturity and surrender for their cash surrender values of an endowment life insurance contract that he sold to a charity for less than its full value and an annuity contract that he transferred to his son as a gift. Consistent with the earlier case law, the Service held that the taxpayer had ordinary income for the taxable year in which the recipients surrendered the contracts.

These principles have further found their modern incarnation in such diverse fields as income from a business, compensation for personal services, dividend income, income from property, royalty income, income from sale of crops.[14]

The *Schaffner* court did not make this distinction between wasting and non-wasting assets. Cf. § 273, disallowing a deduction for the shrinkage in value of a life or term interest acquired by gift, bequest or inheritance. See also Early v. Commissioner, 445 F.2d 166 (5th Cir.1971), cert. denied 404 U.S. 855, 92 S.Ct. 100, 30 L.Ed.2d 96 (1971).

13.   29 T.C.M. 89 (1970).

14.   See, e.g., Rev.Rul. 55–2, 1955–1 C.B. 211 (tax on accounts receivable for personal services could not be shifted); Rev. Rul. 74–32, 1974–1 C.B. 22 (tax on income for personal services could not be shifted); Hyman v. Nunan, 143 F.2d 425 (2d Cir. 1944) (L. Hand, J.) (tax on dividend income could not be shifted); Montgomery v. Commissioner, 230 F.2d 472 (5th Cir.1956) (transfer of business property to avoid liability in tort action effective to shift tax burden on subsequent income); Rev.Rul. 74–32, supra (income from sale of property could not be shifted); Commissioner v. Sunnen, 333 U.S. 591, 68 S.Ct. 715, 92 L.Ed. 898 (1948), on remand 168 F.2d 839 (8th Cir.1948) (gift of royalty payments to wife ineffective to shift tax burden where donor retained ultimate power to cancel the payments); United States v. Lawhon, 499 F.2d 352 (5th Cir.1974), cert. denied 419 U.S. 1121, 95 S.Ct. 804, 42 L.Ed.2d 820 (1975) (involving actual fruit and trees, taxpayer can be taxable on proceeds of orange sales though his children owned the orange groves); Rev.Rul. 71–130, 1971–1 C.B. 28 (vertical cut of a royalty interest shifted the tax burden to the donee).

Also a significant gratuitous assignment of income case during this period was Helvering v. Clifford, 309 U.S. 331, 60 S.Ct. 554, 84 L.Ed. 788 (1940), mandate conformed 111 F.2d 896 (C.C.A.8 1940) (Creator of a short-term trust was taxable on the trust income in view of the fact that he retained control over the investment policies and administration of the trust corpus, and the trust income was payable to his wife. Although *Clifford* is obviously in the same family of cases as those described in the text, the Court specifically declined to consider whether the case came within the ambit of *Lucas v. Earl*.)

See also Corliss v. Bowers, 281 U.S. 376, 50 S.Ct. 336, 74 L.Ed. 916 (1930) (income

## ¶ 5.03  Assignments of Income for Consideration

The development of the case law in the area of assignments of income for consideration was much slower than for the gratuitous assignments. However the two lines of cases soon effected a dramatic merger. In *Burnet v. Harmel*[1] an advance payment or "bonus" received by the owner of property in consideration for the assignment of the right to exploit oil reserves was held to be ordinary income, in the nature of rent, rather than an amount received on sale of property rights yielding capital gain.

In the major case of *Hort v. Commissioner,*[2] discussed also at ¶ 4.06(3)(a)(i), a lessor received a lump-sum from the lessee in cancellation of the lease. Against the taxpayer's claim of a capital gain, the Supreme Court held that the amount received in cancellation was ordinary income, since it was a substitute for rent.[3]

Assignment of income doctrine reached its apotheosis in the case of *Commissioner v. P.G. Lake,*[4] decided in 1958. Taxpayer in *Lake* owned a working interest in an oil and gas lease—that is he had the right to develop and sell the oil and gas reserves on certain property over the term of the lease.[5] Since the oil and gas is inventory to the taxpayer, its sale over the term of the lease would have yielded him ordinary income.[6] Taxpayer, however, assigned a portion of the anticipated future revenues from the oil and gas sale up to $600,000 to a third party in exchange for a lump sum of $600,000. The taxpayer's $600,000 assignment of income was payable out of 25% of the revenue attributable to the taxpayer's

from a revocable trust taxed to the grantor); Burnet v. Wells, 289 U.S. 670, 53 S.Ct. 761, 77 L.Ed. 1439 (1933) (income of an irrevocable trust which was used to pay the premiums on the grantor's life insurance held taxable to the grantor).

See §§ 671–679, discussed at ¶ 5.04(3) for the present statutory treatment of *Clifford*-type trusts.

**¶ 5.03**

1. 287 U.S. 103, 53 S.Ct. 74, 77 L.Ed. 199 (1932).

2. 313 U.S. 28, 61 S.Ct. 757, 85 L.Ed. 1168 (1941), see text accompanying note 4, ¶ 5.01 supra.

3. In characterizing the gain by reference to what the payments substitute for, *Hort* bears a close relationship to the damages field, ¶ 3.11.

Taxpayer in *Hort* also had the temerity to assert, as an alternative argument, that the cancellation payment should give rise to a loss, since it was for less than the difference between the present value of the future lease payments and the fair rental value of the property for the unexpired period of the lease. The Court quite properly rejected that argument on the ground

that taxpayer's proper tax benefit in this event simply lay in reporting less gross income in the future.

Another possible basis for the ordinary income holding in *Hort*, although it was not employed by the Court, could have been that the transaction did not constitute a sale or exchange but rather was just an extinguishment of taxpayer's claim, since the property (the lease) did not survive the transaction. Compare ¶ 4.06(3)(a)(xii) regarding the treatment of the retirement of debt instruments.

4. 356 U.S. 260, 78 S.Ct. 691, 2 L.Ed.2d 743 (1958), reh'g denied 356 U.S. 964, 78 S.Ct. 991, 2 L.Ed.2d 1071 (1958).

5. In the oil and gas field the typical arrangement is that the owner of land will convey an oil and gas lease—the right to develop and sell the oil and gas reserves over a term of years—to the lessee. The consideration to the lessor is usually a royalty or fraction of the gross revenues produced (often one-eighth). See K. Miller, Oil and Gas Federal Income Taxation, (1982) Ch. 13.

6. § 1221 and see ¶ 4.06(3)(a)(i).

working interest; it was expected to pay out over three years (and did so); and it specified payment of 3% interest on the unpaid balance remaining from month to month. After the $600,000 plus interest was paid, the taxpayer would receive the entire gross revenues from his working interest for himself for the balance of the lease term.

In oil and gas tax law parlance, the taxpayer on these facts had "carved out" an "oil payment"—the right to receive a specific sum of money out of the proceeds of the sale of oil and gas.[7] The question was whether the assignment of such a "carved out" interest gave rise to ordinary income or capital gain.

That the Supreme Court held that the assignment of income in *Lake* gave rise to ordinary income is not so surprising; but the way in which the Court reached that result effected a quantum jump in the development of assignment of income doctrine. The first ground of the Court's opinion was that the $600,000 received was a substitute for what would have been received in the future as ordinary income.[8] Although this appeared to partake of *Hort*, this was in fact a considerable expansion of *Hort*, since the lump-sum payment made in lieu of the ordinary income in *Lake* came from a third party; whereas in *Hort* the lump-sum payment was simply an acceleration of payments from the original payor. As another way of looking at the matter, the property involved in *Lake*—the oil payment—survived the transaction and was in the hands of the third party. Whereas in *Hort,* the property involved—the lease— was extinguished by the transaction.[9] Thus the transaction in *Lake* looked considerably more like a sale or exchange of property than did the transaction in *Hort*. Yet still the Court found the payment in *Lake* to be a substitute for ordinary income.

Striking though this aspect may have been, it was not the most significant feature of the Court's opinion. The Court went on to cite major *gratuitous* assignment of income cases, to buttress its opinion— *Clifford,*[10] *Schaffner,*[11] and most particularly *Horst.*[12] The gratuitous assignment of income cases, of course, dealt not with the character of consideration received on the assignment but with the question of the taxable person.[13] By introducing the gratuitous assignment of income cases into the *Lake* analysis, the Court necessarily infused the assignment of income for consideration area with the whole theoretical framework developed in the gratuitous assignment of income area—viz., "vertical cuts," "horizontal cuts," "fruit and tree," etc.[14]

Veritably, the theory of the gratuitous assignment of income area adapted exceedingly well to the assignment of income for consideration cases. The "carved out" oil payment in *Lake* could certainly be regarded

**7.** Anderson v. Helvering, 310 U.S. 404, 410, 60 S.Ct. 952, 955, 84 L.Ed. 1277 (1940). See also note 19 infra.

**8.**　356 U.S. at 264, 78 S.Ct. at 693.

**9.**　See note 3 supra third paragraph.

**10.**　See ¶ 5.02.

**11.**　Id.

**12.**　¶ 5.02, text accompanying note 6. See *Lake* opinion at 267.

**13.**　¶ 5.02.

**14.**　Id.

as a "horizontal cut" (and it since has been[15]) or a sale of "fruit" and not the "tree," hence giving rise to ordinary income rather than capital gain. This seems to be the clear import of the Court's opinion in *Lake*. Conversely, where a taxpayer owns a working interest or a royalty and sells a percentage of it coextensive in time with his own interest (a "vertical cut" or sale of "fruit and tree" together), the result should be a capital gain. This was in fact the Service's position in I.T. 4003,[16] quoted with approval by the Court in *Lake*.[17]

Thus since *Lake* the two types of assignment of income are subject to the same analysis; and the ripples of *Lake* are felt on a wide range of types of assignment of income down to the present time.[18] Ironically, considering *Lake*'s great importance to the field, the actual results on *Lake*-type facts were changed by the Code for transactions after August 7, 1969. After that date, an oil payment or production payment[19] carved out and sold as in *Lake* will be treated as a mortgage loan on the property.[20] This was done to eliminate tax advantages arising from "ABC" and similar-type transactions involving interests in mineral property.[21]

---

**15.** E.g. Lyon and Eustice, "Assignment of Income: Fruit and Tree as Irrigated by the P.G. Lake Case," 17 Tax Law Rev. 295 (1962).

**16.** I.T. 4003, 1950–1 C.B. 10, 11, declared obsolete by Rev.Rul. 70–277, 1970–1 C.B. 280. Although I.T. 4003 was since declared obsolete along with a number of other rulings as part of the Service's program of declaring obsolete pre–1953 rulings, see Rev.Proc. 67–6, 1967–1 C.B. 576, its spirit would seem to live on after its quotation by the Supreme Court in *Lake*.

**17.** 356 U.S. at 265 note 5, 78 S.Ct. at 694 note 5, see ¶¶ 3.05 and 4.06(3)(a)(vi) regarding the disposition of interests in licenses and patents. See also Rev.Rul. 71–130, 1971–1 C.B. 28 (Gratuitous assignment by a husband and wife of one-half of a one-eighth royalty interest to an irrevocable trust for the benefit of their minor children effective to shift the tax burden on the assigned interest to the trust—illustrating again the merger of the theories of gratuitous assignments and assignments for consideration); Rev.Rul. 55–526, 1955–2 C.B. 574 (allowing capital gain on the sale of a royalty interest, since it constitutes property).

**18.** See ¶ 4.06 for general treatment of capital gains.

A variation on the theme is the assignment of future dividend, rent, or other income not for the purpose of getting capital gain but to accelerate the income into the year of the assignment when the taxpayer has a large offsetting loss. The Service's response to this has been to treat the trans-action as a loan. Compare Estate of Stranahan v. Commissioner, 472 F.2d 867 (6th Cir.1973) (assignment of future dividends effective to accelerate income) with Martin, 56 T.C. 1255 (1971) (assignment of future rents treated as a loan). See also Johnston, 35 T.C.M. 642 (1976) (assignment of rental income to preserve Subchapter S status held a loan). Cf. discussion of *Arlen*, ¶ 3.05(2) where taxpayer sought treatment of advance royalties as a loan.

**19.** A "production payment" is a right to a specified share of the production from minerals in place or the revenues therefrom (thus in the nature of a royalty), but it must have an expected economic life shorter than that of the mineral interest it burdens. It may be limited by a dollar amount, quantity of mineral, or period of time. Hence the definition includes the oil payment, text accompanying note 7 supra. Reg. § 1.636–3.

**20.** § 636(a). Reg. § 1.636–4 (effective date).

**21.** Actually an ABC transaction involved somewhat the reverse of the facts in *Lake*, although both are covered by § 636. In an ABC transaction, A, the owner of a working interest in an oil and gas lease (the right to develop and sell the oil and gas reserves over a lease term, note 5 supra), would sell that interest to B less a retained production payment (a royalty limited by dollar amount or time, etc., to being less than the underlying working interest note 19 supra). A would then sell to C the production payment. This is attractive to A

## ¶ 5.04   Application of Assignment of Income Doctrine

The principles forged in the early assignment of income cases have come to radiate out into a large number of fields today—sometimes intact, sometimes modified by subsequent cases or statute. Some of these topics have already been discussed, but it is useful to summarize them.

### (1) Oil, Gas, and Other Minerals

As discussed above, under current law where a production payment is carved out of underlying mineral property and assigned for consideration, the transaction will be treated as a mortgage loan on the property. Thus the "carve out" will not give rise to income to the assignor. The income used to pay off the production payment will be treated as the repayment of the loan by the assignor and the assignee. Similarly, where the underlying mineral property is sold less a retained production payment, the retained production payment will be treated as a mortgage loan on the property (this to preclude the so-called ABC transaction).[1] Where, however, the cut is "vertical" and the assignment is, for example, of a royalty interest coextensive in time with the underlying property, the transaction will be considered a sale of property with the potential of yielding capital gain under the usual rules.[2]

The same analysis applies in a gratuitous assignment. If the gift is a "vertical cut" of the mineral interest, it will be effective to transfer the

---

because he gets capital gain on the two sales. This is because even after *Lake*, A would presumably get capital gain on the sale of the working interest, since that is the sale of the "tree," albeit he did retain the "fruit." The subsequent sale of the production payment or "fruit" should also give rise to capital gain, since A is now selling everything he has in the property. As for B, this arrangement is attractive, since he has been able to purchase the working interest for a reduced price. B also gets the attractive intangible drilling and development expense deduction ( § 263, Reg. § 1.612–4) and may qualify for percentage depletion ( §§ 613, 613A). Most important also to B is the fact that the income paying off the production payment would not be included in B's income, even though the production payment has helped finance B's purchase of the working interest. C includes in income the income of the production payment but may amortize his cost of the production payment against it.

Section 636 takes the fun out of ABC transactions, particularly for B, who would have paid a premium to A for the tax advantages. Under § 636 the retention by A of the production payment, on his sale of the working interest to B, is treated as a purchase money mortgage loan. A's sale of the production payment to C is then treated as a sale of the mortgage to C (Reg.

§ 1.636–1(a)(2)). The income paying off the production payment is included in B's income, as a discharge of his mortgage obligation to C. B gets no deduction for the payment to C, since it is a non-deductible repayment of a loan (except for the interest).

Section 636 also removes a tax benefit that grew directly out of *Lake*. A taxpayer with a working interest in mineral property might be limited in the amount of depletion he could take either because he is running losses or because of the 50% limit of § 613. By carving out and selling a production payment, under *Lake*, he could increase current depletable income. Converting this transaction to a loan, of course, eliminates this maneuver.

See Joyce and Del Cotto, "The AB (ABC) and BA Transactions: An Economic and Tax Analysis of Reserved and Carved Out Income Interests," 31 Tax Law Rev. 121 (1976); Wilkinson, "ABC Transactions and Related Income Tax Plans," 40 Texas Law Rev. 18 (1961).

**¶ 5.04**

1. Note 21 supra and accompanying text.

2. There is nothing in § 636 to preclude this, and see also note 16 and accompanying discussion in text of *Lake*. See also ¶ 4.06 for capital gains and losses.

tax burden to the donee.[3] "Horizontal cuts" will not be effective to transfer the tax burden to the donee.[4]

### (2) Leases

#### (a) Gratuitous Assignments

Consistent with the analysis developed above, a gratuitous assignment of a lease by the owner of the underlying property will in general not be effective to shift the tax burden on the rent to the donee.[5] Perhaps if the only interest the taxpayer has is the lease (i.e., he does not own the underlying property), a gratuitous assignment of the lease would be effective to shift the tax burden. This might be the case because the taxpayer would not be engaging in a "horizontal cut" but would be assigning everything he had.[6]

#### (b) Assignments for Consideration—Cancellation of the Lease by Landlord or Tenant

Where the tenant pays the landlord to cancel the lease, it is clear that the landlord realizes ordinary income under *Hort*.[7] Where a landlord pays a tenant to cancel a business lease, the payment is generally given § 1231 treatment, since the tenant is disposing of his entire interest in the property—a vertical cut.[8] Suppose, however, the lessee sublets part

---

3. Rev.Rul. 71–130, ¶ 5.03.

4. § 5.02.

5. Iber v. United States, 409 F.2d 1273 (7th Cir.1969) (gratuitous assignment of lease to a 10–year trust failed to shift tax burden, notwithstanding that had the underlying property been assigned, the incidence of tax apparently would have been shifted pursuant to the grantor trust rules, note 24 infra, the court citing *Earl, Horst,* and *Schaffner* ); Rev.Rul. 58–337, 1958–2 C.B. 13 (same facts and same result); Galt v. Commissioner, 216 F.2d 41 (7th Cir. 1954), cert. denied 348 U.S. 951, 75 S.Ct. 438, 99 L.Ed. 743 (1955) (gratuitous assignment of lease failed to shift tax burden where taxpayer retained reversionary interest in the property); United States v. Shafto, 246 F.2d 338 (4th Cir.1957) (assignment of five-year lease failed to shift tax burden); but see Lum v. Commissioner, 147 F.2d 356 (3d Cir.1945) (gratuitous assignment of lease was effective to shift tax burden because assignee received rights as "landlord"; questionable whether this older decision would hold up but perhaps this could be pursued by taxpayers in the Third Circuit). If the assignment of the lease fails to shift the tax burden it would seem to follow *a fortiori* that assignment of just the rent from the lease would also be ineffective, see Midwood Associates v. Commissioner, 115 F.2d 871 (C.C.A.2 1940).

6. Cf. *Lum* note 5 supra.

7. § 5.03 supra. See also Reg. § 1.61–8(b).

8. Where the landlord pays the tenant to cancel the lease, the initial question is whether the transaction is a sale or exchange. § 1241 deems the transaction to be a sale or exchange, consistent with earlier case law. Having established that there is a sale or exchange, the next question is whether there has been a sale or exchange of *property*, rather than of just income from the property—i.e., the *Lake*-type question. It is clear that a leasehold of land constitutes property to the tenant, without regard to the term of the leasehold, Rev.Rul. 72–85, 1972–1 C.B. 234. See also Reg. § 1.1250–1(e)(3) and House Report 749, Eighty-eighth Congress, 1964–1 C.B. (Part 2) 125,401 deeming a leasehold real property for purposes of recapture of depreciation (¶ 4.06(3)(a)(vii); but see Reg. § 1.1031(a)–1(c) (providing that a lease must have 30 years or more to run to be considered real estate for purposes of a tax-free exchange for other real estate) (see ¶ 4.05(2))).

Having established that a leasehold is property, the next question is whether it is the kind of property that can qualify for capital gains-type treatment. If the leasehold was not used in the taxpayer-tenant's trade or business but was, for example, of personal use property, it would constitute a capital asset in the taxpayer's hands and its sale would give rise to a capital gain, clearly

of his lease and receives a payment in cancellation of the sublease. Is he regarded as a landlord, to whom the payment is ordinary income under *Hort,* or a tenant, to whom the payment is given § 1231 treatment? This delicious issue was presented in *Metropolitan Building Co. v. Commissioner,*[9] discussed also at ¶ 4.06(3)(a)(ii), where, under a rather unusual set of facts, the sublessor released the sublease to the landlord in exchange for a payment from the sublessee. The sublessee then entered into a new lease on the same property with the landlord. Since the sublessor was paid for the release by the sublessee, the facts conjured up *Hort* and ordinary income. But since the release of the sublease was to the landlord, the facts also suggested § 1231 treatment as discussed above. The Ninth Circuit struggled with this problem and heroically came up with the solution that the sublessor enjoyed § 1231-type treatment, since the release of the sublease was to the landlord. The source of the payment was held to be irrelevant.[10]

*Metropolitan,* however, should not be taken as standing for the proposition that the cancellation of a sublease always gives rise to a capital gain to the sublessor. The *Metropolitan* court did not speak to the question of what would happen if the release of the sublease had been to the sublessor rather than the landlord. In a case where the sublessee pays the sublessor for a release from the sublease and then does not do further business with the landlord (presumably a more common set of facts than in *Metropolitan* ), the pattern is vintage *Hort* and presumably ordinary income would be the result.[11]

### (c) Assignments for Consideration—Third Party Transactions

Where a tenant sells a lease used in his trade or business to a third party, the transaction will receive § 1231 treatment.[12] If a landlord sells

---

implied by Rev.Rul. 72–85 supra, and see §§ 1221, 1222. (A loss on the sale of such property would not be allowed. See ¶ 4.04(2). See also ¶ 4.06(3) for treatment of sale of property not used in a trade or business but held for investment.) If the leasehold is used in a trade or business, its sale will give rise to § 1231 treatment, since the leasehold is depreciable property used in a trade or business. Rev.Rul. 72–85 supra, § 1231(b)(1). If the taxpayer were in the business of selling leases, his gain on sale of the lease would be ordinary, Rev. Rul. 72–85 supra § 1221. The basis of the leasehold for purposes of depreciation or sale would be its acquisition cost (see ¶ 6.03(4)).

As a further note on the sale or exchange aspect of this transaction, § 1241 allows payment made for a partial cancellation of a lease to qualify as being received in a sale or exchange, if the cancellation relates to a severable economic unit—such as a portion of the premises covered by the lease, or a reduction in the lease term, Reg.

§ 1.1241–1(b). Such partial cancellations have been held to involve property and hence to give rise to capital gain, Rev.Rul. 56–531, 1956–2 C.B. 983 and cases cited therein. Note that this is a somewhat more liberal approach than *Lake.* § 1241 specifically does not preempt the field, 1.1241–1(a), hence other types of partial lease cancellations could give rise to sales or exchanges and capital gain (or loss). See Rev. Rul. 56–531 supra. See also Modiano–Schneider, Inc., 32 T.C.M. 19 (1973).

9.  282 F.2d 592 (9th Cir.1960).

10.  Id. at 597.

11.  Indeed the Tax Court held that *Hort* applied in *Metropolitan,* (31 T.C. 971 (1959)) only to be reversed by the Ninth Circuit.

12.  Rev.Rul. 72–85, and authorities discussed therein. If the lease is for personal-use property, gain on the sale will be a capital gain; a loss will not be allowed, see discussion at note 8 supra.

a lease of his underlying property, a classic *Lake*[13] situation is presented: an interest of lesser duration in time than the underlying interest is being carved out and sold. *Hort,*[14] although it involved an extinguishment rather than a sale of a lease, is also relevant for its concept of a substitute for ordinary income in the landlord-tenant situation. Thus the landlord would get ordinary income on the sale of a lease of his property.

Finally, in the real estate setting, the landlord might try an "ABC" type transaction, as described in ¶ 5.03 supra, relating to the oil and gas area. This would involve selling the property for cash plus a right to receive a "production payment" or a payment in the nature of a royalty up to a fixed amount, payable out of the profits of the property in future years. The theory would be that the seller had retained an economic interest in the property and hence that the buyer would not be taxed on the income attributable to the "production payment." In fact, however, a very good argument can be made that the transaction is in substance a purchase money mortgage in favor of the seller and hence that the buyer should be taxed on the proceeds of the "production payment" before paying them over to the seller.[15]

Note that the buyer and the seller of real estate have somewhat adverse interests as to whether such a transaction shall be treated as the sale of property less a retained economic interest or as a purchase money mortgage in favor of the seller. If the transaction is treated as a sale of property less a retained economic interest, the buyer is not taxed on the proceeds of the production payment;[16] the seller, however, receives ordinary income on the pay-out of the production payment. If the transaction is treated as a purchase money mortgage in favor of the seller, then the buyer is taxed on the proceeds of the production payment. When the proceeds are then paid to the seller, they will be part of the purchase price of the property and the seller will generally get capital gain on them.

In the classic ABC transaction, the best of both worlds is attained by arranging to have the seller sell his retained production payment to a third party soon after he sells the property. (Whence the nomenclature "ABC", since three parties are involved). The seller can now claim to get capital gain on the sale of the production payment, since he is now disposing of his entire remaining interest in the property and hence cannot possibly be engaging in a "horizontal cut" or sale of fruit only. Thus does the seller get capital gain while the buyer excludes the proceeds of the production payment. The buyer of the production payment amortizes his cost against the payment proceeds, and A, B, and C

13. § 5.03.

14. Id.

15. As discussed in ¶ 5.03 supra, this purchase money mortgage analysis is now imposed by statute on "ABC" transactions involving oil and gas and other mineral property.

16. Reasoning by analogy from the old mineral interest cases, summarized in ¶ 5.03.

each go home happy, no doubt the envy of the rest of the letters of the alphabet.[17]

These are essentially the facts of *Bryant v. Commissioner*,[18] involving the sale of a farm, in which the Fifth Circuit held that the buyer could not exclude the proceeds of a production payment, to be satisfied out of future farm profits, reserved by the seller (the seller's tax liability was not at issue). The court cited three factors that influenced it to hold that the transaction was in substance a sale of the entire property with a mortgage in favor of the seller: (1) the production payment was limited to a specific amount and was included in the total figure that the parties, as a factual matter, regarded as the purchase price; (2) the production payment was expected to be satisfied in a short time and for a certain sum; and (3) interest was to accrue on the unpaid balance of the production payment.[19] Not stated as part of the court's reasoning but possibly also influencing the outcome was the fact that the seller's subsequent sale of the production payment was to a *Clifford* trust formed by the buyer.[20] If these factors were otherwise, perhaps an ABC transaction could still be effected in the real estate area; *Bryant* certainly has not totally closed the door here.[21]

### (3) *Trusts*

Assignment of income problems can arise in two ways in the trust area. On the creation of the trust the question is whether the transfer by the grantor of income-producing property to the trust is effective to shift the tax burden on the property from the grantor to the trust. Historically the most nettlesome problems in this area have arisen where the trust is a short-term or grantor trust.[22] The second assignment of income problem in the trust area occurs when the trust beneficiary seeks to assign his rights to the trust income.

### (a) *Creation of the Trust*

The tax consequences of the creation of a short-term trust have been a matter of controversy from the early days of assignment of income

---

**17.** The transaction could perhaps be made even stronger if the seller of the property retains an already existing lease. Subsequent sale of the lease could be very strongly argued to give rise to capital gain, since it is well established that a lease is property; see Rev.Rul. 72–85. For "ABC" transactions in the mineral property area see ¶ 5.03 supra.

**18.** 399 F.2d 800 (5th Cir.1968).

**19.** Id. at 805–806.

**20.** Id. at 802.

**21.** See discussion of other authorities in *Bryant*.

A field closely related to this is whether there has been a sale or exchange at all or rather a license. See ¶¶ 3.05, 4.06(3)(a)(xi).

The purchase of a corporation, of course, may also be financed by income which the corporation itself produces—the so-called "bootstrap acquisition," see Boone v. United States, 470 F.2d 232 (10th Cir.1972) (purchase of a life insurance company financed by 84% of future premium income); in such corporate transactions the buyer or seller may be threatened with dividend treatment if the transaction is not structured carefully, see B. Bittker and J. Eustice, Federal Income Taxation of Corporations and Shareholders (1979) ¶ 9.25.

**22.** Also known by the sobriquet "Clifford Trust," see ¶ 5.02 supra.

doctrine.[23]

Most significant for the purposes of this discussion is the fact that a grantor is regarded as the owner of the trust property if he or his spouse retains a reversionary interest in the trust corpus or income which has a value of more than 5% of the trust property.[24]

What is the practical significance of this 5% rule? The time value of money considerations crank out that the reversionary interest cannot take place for 39 years, assuming an 8% discount rate. If the trust instrument provides, for example that the reversion will take place after 15 years, the reversionary interest will have a value of 31% of the trust corpus or income.

If the trust instrument provides that the reversion to the grantor will take place on the death of an income beneficiary (other than the death of a minor child), the trust will automatically be treated as a grantor trust, and the income of the trust property will be taxable to the grantor.[25]

### (b) Related Topics

### (i) How to Pay for Law School (?): Below Interest Loans

Another method of shifting income from higher-bracket family members to lower-bracket family members has historically been the use of interest-free loans. To take a random case, suppose Buford's mama wishes to pay Buford's law school tuition and expenses but is finding it onerous to do so. Let's say law school costs $20,000 a year. Suppose Buford's mama has $250,000 cash investments. The maneuver is that she lends it to Buford without requiring Buford to pay interest. Buford has two choices at this point: He could either abscond to Puerto Rico (who needs law school with that kind of coin in your pocket), or Buford could invest the funds in corporate bonds paying 8% per year interest. That cranks out to the $20,000 Buford needs every year for law school. Buford is in a lower tax bracket than his mama. So Buford pays a lower tax than his mama would on the money. After the end of his three-year sojourn in law school, Buford should repay his mama the $250,000 (she hopes).

If all this works out as Buford's mama would like, Buford has a law degree, and she has paid for the degree with funds taxed at a reduced rate.

Before Buford writes home with this suggestion, be aware that the gloomy old Code has taken the zip out of this one, too. It has done so in a way that is both interesting in itself and that shows the power of the statute to recharacterize transactions.

---

**23.** See note 9, ¶ 5.02 supra, and see Henning, "Treatment of the Grantor Trust as a separate entity," 32 Tax Law Rev. 409 (1977).

**24.** § 673(a).

**25.** § 673(b).

What the statute does is to say that if Buford and Buford's mama try this maneuver described above, they will not get the result they expect. Instead, the transaction will be deemed to something different. It will be deemed to be that Buford is paying interest to his mama at a higher than market rate ("applicable federal rate"). Buford's mama is then deemed to be giving Buford that interest back as a gift.[26] Gifts of course are not deductible. Buford is also getting interest in fact on the $250,000. Buford can deduct the interest payments he is deemed to be making to his mama against the interest he is in fact receiving on the $250,000. The interest deduction Buford takes for these deemed payments cannot exceed the interest income Buford is receiving on the $250,000.[27]

All this is sorted out in the accompanying series of graphics:

## Treatment of Gift Loans with Below-Market Interest #1

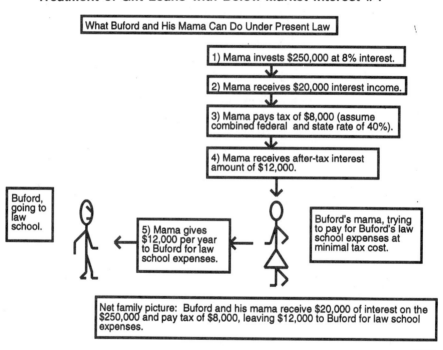

What Buford and His Mama Can Do Under Present Law

1) Mama invests $250,000 at 8% interest.

2) Mama receives $20,000 interest income.

3) Mama pays tax of $8,000 (assume combined federal and state rate of 40%).

4) Mama receives after-tax interest amount of $12,000.

Buford, going to law school.

5) Mama gives $12,000 per year to Buford for law school expenses.

Buford's mama, trying to pay for Buford's law school expenses at minimal tax cost.

Net family picture: Buford and his mama receive $20,000 of interest on the $250,000 and pay tax of $8,000, leaving $12,000 to Buford for law school expenses.

[360a]

---

**26.** § 7872(a).

**27.** Because § 163(d) limits the deduction for investment interest to the amount of investment income received.

## Treatment of Gift Loans with Below-Market Interest #2

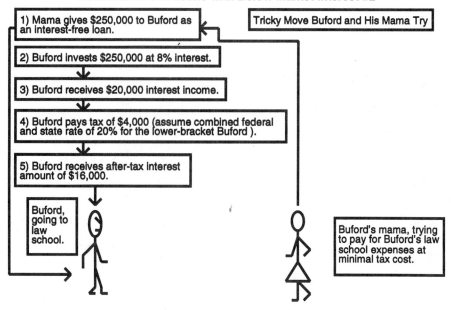

1) Mama gives $250,000 to Buford as an interest-free loan.

Tricky Move Buford and His Mama Try

2) Buford invests $250,000 at 8% interest.

3) Buford receives $20,000 interest income.

4) Buford pays tax of $4,000 (assume combined federal and state rate of 20% for the lower-bracket Buford ).

5) Buford receives after-tax interest amount of $16,000.

Buford, going to law school.

Buford's mama, trying to pay for Buford's law school expenses at minimal tax cost.

Net family picture:  Buford and his mama receive $20,000 of interest on the $250,000 and pay tax of $4,000, leaving $16,000 to Buford for law school expenses.

[361a]

**Treatment of Gift Loans with Below-Market Interest #3**

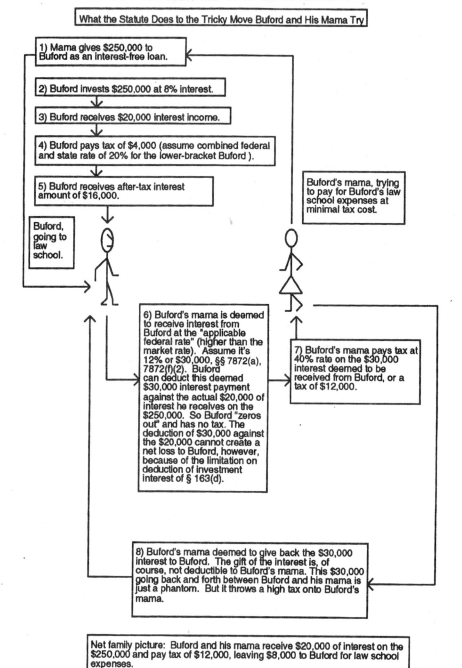

What the Statute Does to the Tricky Move Buford and His Mama Try

1) Mama gives $250,000 to Buford as an interest-free loan.

2) Buford invests $250,000 at 8% interest.

3) Buford receives $20,000 interest income.

4) Buford pays tax of $4,000 (assume combined federal and state rate of 20% for the lower-bracket Buford ).

5) Buford receives after-tax interest amount of $16,000.

Buford, going to law school.

Buford's mama, trying to pay for Buford's law school expenses at minimal tax cost.

6) Buford's mama is deemed to receive interest from Buford at the "applicable federal rate" (higher than the market rate). Assume it's 12% or $30,000, §§ 7872(a), 7872(f)(2). Buford can deduct this deemed $30,000 interest payment against the actual $20,000 of interest he receives on the $250,000. So Buford "zeros out" and has no tax. The deduction of $30,000 against the $20,000 cannot create a net loss to Buford, however, because of the limitation on deduction of investment interest of § 163(d).

7) Buford's mama pays tax at 40% rate on the $30,000 interest deemed to be received from Buford, or a tax of $12,000.

8) Buford's mama deemed to give back the $30,000 interest to Buford. The gift of the interest is, of course, not deductible to Buford's mama. This $30,000 going back and forth between Buford and his mama is just a phantom. But it throws a high tax onto Buford's mama.

Net family picture: Buford and his mama receive $20,000 of interest on the $250,000 and pay tax of $12,000, leaving $8,000 to Buford for law school expenses.

A summary of this series of graphics is to say that you can do # 1. But if you try to do # 2, which is much better than # 1, you get # 3, which is much worse than # 1.

The only way the interest can be taxed to Buford instead of his Mama is for them to give Buford the $250,000 outright. So get on the phone and tell Buford's mama about this new tax ploy you've learned.[28]

Actually the below interest loan provisions are just sort of an elaborate preventive. Because of their punitive effect they just scare everyone away. So no one ever does transactions under them. That being the case, it could be said that you don't have to learn these provisions. All you have to know is that it's a bad idea to do low interest loan deals. I don't actually recommend that approach, however. I think you ought to know how it works because you're a tax lawyer and there it is.

### (ii) Unearned Income of Children

As a further restriction on assigning income from higher-income to lower-income family members, the Code provides that all net unearned income (above a floor amount of $500 plus the greater of another $500 or expenses of the income) of a child under 14 years is taxed at the rate the income would be taxed at if the income were received by the parent. This is the case regardless of the source of the assets producing the income. Unearned income is income from investment property. Income the under–14 child earns through rendering his own personal services (such as babysitting or playing professional tennis) would be taxed to the child at his own rate. Thus the child could pay income at two different rates of tax depending on the source of his income. Thus can the child's tax return become even more complex than the parent's.

This rule cuts back on the parents' ability to shift income-producing property to a lower-bracket child in order to lessen the overall tax on the family.[29] This provision is like the joint return in that it moves our system closer to the idea that the taxable unit is the family rather than single individuals.

### (c) Alimony

The payment of alimony and child support is another major statutory example of assignment of income. One party to the dissolving marriage is allowed to shift income to the other lower-bracket party. The subject of alimony is treated in detail at ¶ 6.02(14).

## ¶ 5.05   Assignment of Income Without Tears

The trouble with assignment of income doctrine is that it is a song without end.[1] The whole area of capital gains can be looked on as an application of assignment of income doctrine. That is, most any asset has value because it is capable of producing a stream of ordinary income

---

**28.** For further discussion of the expenses of law school, see ¶ 6.03(3)(b)(ii).

**29.** § 1(g).

**¶ 5.05**

**1.** Cf. Lyon and Eustice, "Assignment of Income: Fruit and Tree as Irrigated by the P.G. Lake Case," 17 Tax Law Rev. 295 (1962).

either at the present or in the future.[2] Hence the proceeds from the sale of that asset are in some sense a substitute for ordinary income, conceivably triggering *Lake*-type discussions of "carve-outs," "vertical and horizontal cuts," "fruit and tree," etc. Similarly, where the assignment of income is gratuitous, the problem that is raised is what is the appropriate family unit on which to impose a tax. Indeed, as discussed above, the joint return is a congressionally-sanctioned assignment of income from the wage earner to his spouse.[3] Family partnerships present assignment of income problems.[4] The field of corporate taxation is rife with assignment of income issues ranging from the viability of the corporation as a taxable entity to questions of the character of taxable gain in the collapsible corporation area.[5]

Thus when Justice Oliver Wendell Holmes planted the tree in *Lucas v. Earl*,[6] he doubtless did not know how great a tree would grow, how far its branches would reach, and where its fruit would fall.

2. See ¶ 4.06(4).

3. See discussion of Poe v. Seaborn, ¶ 5.02 supra. See also Bittker, "Federal Income Taxation and the Family," 27 Stanford Law Review 1389 (1975).

4. See McKee, Nelson & Whitmire, Federal Taxation of Partners and Partnerships, (1977) Chapter 14.

5. Cf. § 482, allowing the Service to allocate income, deductions and credits among taxpayers under common control in order to clearly reflect income.

6. ¶ 5.02, supra.

# Chapter 6

# BUSINESS DEDUCTIONS

*Table of Sections*

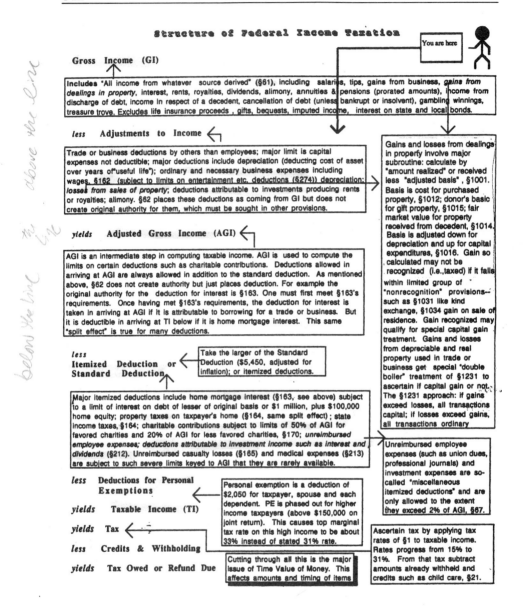

## ¶ 6.01   Structural Issues in General

### (1) Putting the Tax Code on the Back of an Envelope

It is in the area of deductions that the "pop culture" critics of the income tax founder most egregiously. These "pop culture" critics include some politicians, a large number of newspaper columnists, and a huge number of people who horse—collar me at cocktail parties to tell me how they are going to reform the federal income tax. Since I have had it up to my *keister* with these people, will you pardon me if I get a few things off my chest?

The main thing these experts like to do is to explain how the present Internal Revenue Code and Regulations (which together constitute some 10,000 pages) can be reformed to fit on the back of an envelope. Now I would be the first to admit that the Code and Regulations run, at times, to the prolix. Nevertheless, the idea that the rules of a reasonable income tax system in a sophisticated economy such as ours could be reduced to the back of an envelope is absurd.

Let's take the typical proposal from one of these "experts." Let's say it's a well—known nationally syndicated newspaper columnist. These guys usually say something like "Let's take income and just apply one flat rate of tax, say, 15%, and that'll be it." (Some politicians have thrown out ideas like this too, see the discussion of "Steve and Jerry's Tax," in Chapter 1. Already we are in limbo.) The complexity of the Internal Revenue Code stems not from the progressive rate structure. That only takes a few pages in § 1.

What's complex is not the rate structure but the base to which the rate structure is applied.

This leads us to the next "reform" proposal (give me a nickel for every time I've heard this one—and I'll pay tax on all those nickels too). The "expert" says: "Just put a tax on income and allow no deductions." That is rich.

Take a simple case. A neighborhood grocery store is owned by the owner as a sole proprietor. Over the course of a year the grocery store generates $1,000,000 of sales. Shall we tax that $1,000,000 at 30 or 40 percent or whatever it is? Say we tax it at 40%. That's a tax of $400,000. The cost of goods sold is $600,000. This grocery store has employees. Expenses there run $90,000. What about utilities? There's another $45,000. Rent is another $80,000. There's insurance; there's property taxes—another—another $10,000. Putting all the expenses together with the income, this business made $275,000 this year. They'll have a tough time paying tax of $400,000. You think there's a taxpayer revolt now; try presenting this business with a tax bill of $400,000.

We have to allow the expenses of generating the income, don't we? Otherwise we are just imposing a mindless tax on the volume of economic activity. Compare this to someone who sells stock he bought at $1,000,000 for $2,000,000. To whom is it more fair to give the tax bill of $400,000?

The idea of an income tax is inextricably bound up with the idea of fairness. It's based on ability to pay. Income is a net concept. But to gauge the ability to pay we really have to allow as a deduction from income the legitimate expenses of producing that income. Soon as the tax expert admits that (as he has to), he can throw away the envelope.

There's a lot of complex transactions out there. Suppose somebody constructs a building in 1993 for $40 million to produce rental income of $4 million per year over the next 30 years. Do we allow the deduction of the $40 million in the first year? Recall the Prologue. Allowing that deduction up front is much more valuable to the taxpayer than spreading that $40 million deduction out over the period the building produces income. It's probably fairer to require the building to be deducted over the period it is producing income. That's depreciation. Well that takes a few rules to specify, doesn't it? Our expert is off his envelope again.

So our expert is still struggling. He says, "Okay, allow business deductions. I admit there'll be some complications." But it's more than just complications. Let's say the expert and I are arguing about this matter over lunch. That immediately leads to two questions: 1) who is going to pick up the tab; and 2) can whoever picks up the tab deduct it in arriving at the amount of his taxable income?

Suppose (just to fantasize for a moment) that I pick up the tab. Isn't explaining the tax law (or trying to) part of my job? Or is that just too nebulous? Do we need some rules in this area? Don't we have a problem—once we decide to allow business deductions—in figuring out just what it is that constitutes business deductions? Drawing the line between deductible business expenses and non—deductible personal expenses is complicated.

How about taxing an annuity, a subject we've talked about a couple of times already (see the Prologue and Chapter 3). Taxpayer pays a premium in 1993 and then in 2003 he begins receiving payments for 20 years. How do we tax that? No deduction at all for the premium? Obviously wrong. We have to deduct the premium somehow along the time that the income comes in. That gets complicated. How is that to be simplified?

The statute is always going to be complicated. That is not something to run away from. Step up to it. Enjoy it. The complexity is part of the attraction of the field. And it could put some money in your pocket.

Now even though the statute is always going to be complicated, there is some simplification we can do. We can look at the "deep structure" of the Internal Revenue Code. We've talked about this before. And we have our diagram that attempts to depict the field on one page that appears at the beginning of this book, at the beginning of this chapter, and other chapters in this book. There's a deep structure to the field of federal income taxation. It does not change, though some individual provisions change. Understanding that deep structure will help you.

### (2) The Deep Structure of the Tax System

Okay, we're in a position, having fought our way through the discussion of income, to look at the deep structure of this field. A taxpayer has income. Income is defined as gross receipts or gross income (§§ 61), less the deductions necessarily required to produce that income. That is what we mean by income.

Despite the apparent complexity of the subject, there's amazingly only two things that the taxpayer can do with his income. He can consume it, or he can invest it. Another term for investing is to make a capital expenditure. You cannot name me an expenditure that does not come under one of those two categories.

How do we handle those two basic types of expenditures? In a "pure" income tax, what we would do is provide no deductions for either consumption or saving. In a "pure" income tax, we are taxing income and we do not reduce income by expenditures for consumption or capital expenditures.[1] (Section 262 provides no deduction for personal, living or family expenses; § 263 provides no deduction for capital expenditures.)

There is one further qualification, with regard to capital expenditures. To understand it first consider that the term capital expenditure is broader than you might think. Thus if you buy a building, you've made a capital expenditure; if you buy gold, you've made a capital expenditure; if you buy a computer, you've made a capital expenditure; if you buy stock, you've made a capital expenditure; if you spend money to produce an invention that gains a patent, you've made a capital expenditure; if you buy an annuity, you've made a capital expenditure; if you put your money in a savings bank account, you've made a capital expenditure.

What do all these transactions have in common? They all create an asset of one kind or another that produces income in the future. Now there are two kinds of capital expenditures. One kind produces a wasting asset and the other kind produces an asset that theoretically lasts forever. Consider the examples of capital expenditures in the previous paragraph. Which of them produced a wasting asset and which produced an asset that theoretically lasts forever. Take a look. Don't just jump to the next paragraph. Put the coffee down and take a look.

Okay, I'll bet you got them all. The following examples are capital expenditures that produce wasting assets: building, computer, patent, annuity. The others are assets that theoretically last forever. We make this distinction. On both of these kinds of capital expenditures we do not allow an immediate deduction (§ 263). On wasting assets, we allow a deduction of their cost or basis spread out over the period of their useful lives (major example here is depreciation under § 168). How we ascertain their useful lives could be a matter of controversy, but I'm talking deep structure and theory right now. On assets that last forever we do not allow a deduction over time for the cost or basis. This would be the case even if the asset is producing a stream of income over time. An example of this is stock that pays dividends. We do not allow a deduction of the cost of the stock over time even though the stock is producing taxable dividends over time.

Keep this deep structure in mind. This is the real economics of an income tax system. What you want to understand is how our system at

1. For discussion of the consumption tax, as compared to the income tax, see Chapter 1.

various times departs from this deep structure. If you understand this deep structure, it will also help you to understand how various deductions fit into the picture. It will also help you to understand what people are arguing about, and why particular arguments—that sound silly off the top—are made.

Let's just take one example that hits close to home. Why can't you deduct the cost of your legal education? There's no doubt you can't. I don't care who you are, what your family circumstances, what your reasons for going to law school. You cannot deduct the cost of your legal education and that is it.[2]

What is the reason for this? The layman—which you are rapidly ceasing to be—would think it is just another one of "those arbitrary rules." But in fact this rule grows out of the deep structure of the federal income tax. The cost of legal education prepares you for a new profession, a profession you cannot enter without this education. Thus it creates an asset that produces income over time. Thus it is a capital expense and not deductible when paid.

Now we move to the second step in analyzing capital assets. Is this a wasting asset or an asset that lasts forever? It would appear it is wasting—that is that your legal career only lasts at most your lifetime. However, the Service regards it as not wasting. Thus no deduction for your legal education over time.

You could argue about that. You could say that the tax law ought to allow you to write off the cost of your legal education over time. Now you are making an educated argument. You know what you are talking about. (The argument loses, of course).

Take some other examples. The deduction for interest on the taxpayer's home mortgage is a good example. The cost of borrowing for business is deductible. That's part of the cost of doing business. But the interest cost on the home mortgage is a personal consumption item. It should not be deductible in the pure income tax. But we do allow it to be deducted in our income tax (see Chapter 7). Why is that? We could debate that. The home mortgage interest deduction raises major policy questions. That's because it violates the deep structure of a pure income tax.

Here's another one. Employer contributions to so-called qualified pension plans are excluded from the employee's income (see the Prologue and Chapter 8). That violates the deep structure. You can see it clearly if you bear in mind that exclusions are equivalent to deductions. That exclusion for pension contributions is the same thing as if the employee received the amount of money and then put it into the pension fund himself and was allowed to take a deduction.

This pension contribution is savings. In effect, this treatment of pension plans gives the employee a deduction for saving. As we said

2.  See ¶ 6.03(3)(b).

before, in a "pure" income tax we do not give the taxpayer a deduction for saving. But we do in our system.

Keep in mind as we go along where in the deep structure we are. Keep in mind as we are going along whether the particular deduction violates the deep structure of federal income taxation.

### (3) The Statutory Structure of the Tax System

Once a taxpayer has ascertained the amount of his gross income, including items of compensation for services he has rendered, other items to be included in income, gains from dealings in property, including whether some of his transactions and property qualify for the favorable capital gains treatment, it is time for the taxpayer to consider his deductions. There are two kinds of deductions, which are illustrated by the following schema: (you may also wish to refer to the graphic at the beginning of this Chapter)

Steps in Computing Taxable Income

1.  Gross income

2.  Less: deductions allowed above the line as provided by § 62.

3.  Yields: adjusted gross income

4.  Less: the greater of itemized deductions or the standard deduction

5.  Less: deductions for personal and dependency exemptions.

6.  Yields: taxable income[3]

It can be seen from this schema that deductions are allowed in two sets: Those deductions that are taken from gross income to arrive at adjusted gross income, and those deductions taken from adjusted gross income to arrive at taxable income. This latter group of deductions is also called itemized deductions (see Chapter 7). It is § 62 of the Code that directs whether particular deductions will be allowed as deductions from gross income or from adjusted gross income. Section 62 itself creates no deductions, nor does it bar any. It simply directs where particular deductions shall be taken. Deductions that are taken from gross income are said to be taken "above the line"; deductions that are taken from adjusted gross income are said to be taken "below the line," in the argot of tax professionals.

There are several reasons why it is important to ascertain whether a deduction is above the line or below the line. Deductions taken above the line are allowed in full. Deductions taken below the line—so-called itemized deductions—are only allowed to the extent they in the aggregate exceed the standard deduction. The standard deduction is in essence a floor amount which is allowed as an itemized deduction to all taxpayers. Taxpayers may deduct their particular itemized, or below the line,

---

**3.** Sections 61, 62 and 63. A taxpayer in the business of selling goods would have a preliminary step of ascertaining gross re- ceipts less cost of goods sold to arrive at gross income from that business.

deductions only to the extent their sum exceeds the standard deduction.[4] Therefore, a deduction which is taken above the line will always be allowed in full. Whereas a deduction which is taken below the line, will only be allowed if the taxpayer has enough other itemized deductions so that his total itemized deductions exceed the standard deduction.

In addition, adjusted gross income (AGI) is sometimes used to make further computations—the major ones being to ascertain a floor for the medical expense deduction, and the casualty loss deduction to personal-use property and a ceiling for the charitable contributions deduction.[5]

Adjusted gross income serves as a more sensible measure for limiting these other deductions than does gross income. Suppose, for example, Adelle Furgeson who owns her own auto parts business generates $100,000 of revenues but has $70,000 in expenses. She suffers, let us say, a personal casualty loss to her home of $15,000. The casualty loss deduction (as discussed in Chapter 7 at ¶ 7.01(5)) only allows casualties to personal-use property to the extent they exceed a floor of 10% of adjusted gross income. If the 10% floor were keyed to *gross income* rather than adjusted gross income, Adelle would then be able to deduct only $5,000 of her $15,000 loss. (10% of $100,000 = $10,000; hence $5,000 of $15,000 is in excess of the floor). Compare Adelle's case to that of Bennett Fargsworth who works as an accountant in a small company at a salary of $30,000 with no business deductions. If we're still using gross income and Bennett suffers a $15,000 personal casualty, he would be able to deduct $12,000 of it. This is the excess of $15,000 over 10% of $30,000 or $3,000. Thus although Adelle and Bennett have the same net income of $30,000, Adelle can only deduct $5,000 of her casualty whereas Bennett can deduct $12,000, if gross income is used as the measure.

When the casualty loss is keyed to adjusted gross income rather than gross income, this anomaly drops out. Adjusted gross income takes account of Adelle's expenses. They both have $30,000 of net income or adjusted gross income. The 10% rule appropriately gives them each the same floor for calculating their deductible casualty loss. Thus so-called "horizontal equity" is insured.

The concept of adjusted gross income performs this important task of insuring horizontal equity in a less than perfect fashion. As discussed at various points in this chapter and Chapter 7, the deductions allowed in arriving at adjusted gross income do not perfectly reflect the expenses of producing gross income. For example alimony payments are allowed as a deduction in arriving at adjusted gross income, although alimony payments do not generate any gross income.[6] Similarly a number of deductions, called miscellaneous itemized deductions, are not allowed in arriving at adjusted gross income. Examples of these would include union dues, work clothing expenses. This is the case even though these expenses have produced gross income (see Chapter 7 ¶ 7.02). Thus AGI is

4. 63(c).

5. See generally Chapter 7.

6. Putting the alimony deduction above the line could be justified on choice of taxable person grounds, see ¶ 6.02(14).

a little ragged in producing a concept of net income to assist in calculating various limits on deductions. But that is one of the ideas behind it.

To qualify as a deduction above the line, a deduction must specifically fit within § 62, otherwise the deduction is allowed only below the line. Whether a particular deduction can be taken above the line will depend on the particular facts. For example, interest on a loan is allowed as a deduction by § 163. But the deduction for interest will only be allowed above the line if the loan giving rise to the interest payment was taken for the purpose of conducting the taxpayer's own business or for producing rental or royalty income for the taxpayer. If the loan was taken to purchase a home, then the deduction for interest allowed by § 163 can only be taken below the line, since there is nothing in § 62 that allows it to be above the line. Similarly, the deduction for casualty losses can only be taken above the line if the casualty was sustained by business or investment-type property; if the casualty was to non-business or personal property, it may only be deducted below the line.[7]

It is only after it is ascertained that a particular item is deductible under one of the specific Code provisions discussed below that the item is tested under § 62 to determine whether it is deductible above or below the line.

## ¶ 6.02   Deductions Arising Out of Business and Profit Seeking Activity

### (1) Common Business Expenses

### (a) Ordinary and Necessary Business Expenses

Section 162(a) allows for the deduction of "all the ordinary and necessary expenses paid or incurred during the taxable year in carrying on any trade or business." There are a number of qualifying words in that phrase, but the phrase "trade or business" is not one of them. This is because Congress, in § 212, provided that there shall also be allowed as a deduction "all the ordinary and necessary expenses paid or incurred during the taxable year—(1) for the production or collection of income; (2) for the management, conservation or maintenance of property held for the production of income ..." §§ 162 and 212, therefore, provide for the two major types of business activity as defined by the Code: business activity that constitutes a trade or business; and business activity that constitutes investment (or production-of-income activity that does not rise to the level of a trade or business).

Thus, a taxpayer who is an employee, or who runs his own business, is engaging in a trade or business (that of either being an employee of a particular kind or of running a particular business). However, a taxpayer who buys stocks and bonds or who holds a piece of real estate for rental

---

7. § 165, discussed at ¶ 7.01(5). Note that a deduction for casualties to *personal-use* property is subject to a $100 per casualty floor, and further that, as discussed above, such casualties are only deductible to the extent that in the aggregate they exceed 10% of the taxpayer's adjusted gross income.

income is not engaging in a "trade or business" but is rather engaging in "profit-seeking" or "investment" activity.[1]

The taxpayer who is engaging in a "trade or business" deducts his ordinary and necessary business expenses under § 162(a); the taxpayer who is engaging in "profit-seeking" or "investment" activity takes his ordinary and necessary business expenses as a deduction under § 212. Since the deduction is allowed whichever kind of activity the taxpayer is engaging in, it often will not matter whether the taxpayer is deemed to be engaged in a trade or business or rather in profit-seeking/investment activity. But on occasion it will matter which kind of activity the taxpayer is engaging in.[2] Moreover, the Code often speaks in terms of "trade or business" activity on the one hand and investment or profit-seeking activity on the other, and it is useful to know that those terms are referring to the activities described in §§ 162 and 212, respectively.[3]

The important limiting words in the phrase "ordinary and necessary business expenses" have come to be "ordinary" and "necessary." Obviously, the great mass of expenses incurred by a taxpayer in running a business—wages, rent, utilities, repairs, etc.—are deductible under § 162(a) without question.

However, what if a dealer in stock takes out a life insurance policy on the life of the President of the United States because he fears the President's death would adversely affect the stock market, and he attempts to deduct the premium as an ordinary and necessary business expense? The Board of Tax Appeals (the predecessor of the Tax Court), when confronted with this question, held that that expense was not ordinary or necessary, because it did not appear that other persons in the same business, when confronted with similar conditions, incurred such expenses.[4] Similarly, it was held that an attorney who paid hush money to an accuser whose charges were harming his professional reputation could not deduct the payments as an ordinary and necessary business expense.[5]

These cases apparently do rest on the ground that the expenses in question were not ordinary and/or necessary. Thus the deduction is denied even though the expenses are legitimately incurred incident to the taxpayer's trade or business. In short, not *all* expenses related to the

¶ 6.02

**1.** See ¶ 6.02(2).

**2.** See ¶ 6.02(10), relating to the deduction for an office in the home.

**3.** See e.g. §§ 167(a) and 168 relating to the deduction for depreciation, discussed at ¶ 6.02(12).

**4.** Goedel v. Commissioner, 39 B.T.A. 1, 1939 WL 263 (1939); to the same effect is Rev.Rul. 55–714, 1955–2 C.B. 51 (denying the manager of an entertainer a deduction

for life insurance premiums on policy on the entertainer's life).

**5.** Bonney v. Commissioner, 247 F.2d 237 (2d Cir.1957), cert. denied 355 U.S. 906, 78 S.Ct. 333, 2 L.Ed.2d 261 (1957). See also Reffett, 39 T.C. 869 (1963) (contingent fees paid to witnesses in damage suit were not ordinary); But see Rev.Rul. 63–275, 1963–2 C.B. 85 (research expenses of faculty members, including travel, are ordinary and necessary business expenses—thank God for small favors).

taxpayers trade or business are deductible. Only those which are "ordinary and necessary" are deductible.[6]

A major limit on the deductibility of expenses has to do with salaries. To be deductible, salaries or other compensation for personal services must be reasonable, § 162(a)(1). One should be clear. The Service is not in the business of limiting the size of salary payments as a matter of public policy.

Rather, the Service uses the weapon of "reasonable compensation" to limit shifting income between related taxpayers who are trying to reduce their total tax burden. Nevertheless, given the great attention that has attended the high salaries of corporate executives in recent years, one may wonder whether the Service could use the "reasonable . . . compensation" weapon of § 162 to curb high salaries as a matter of public policy. Without a directive from Congress, the Service was most unlikely to attempt this even though the approach has support in the statutory language.[7]

In 1993, Congress gave the Service just such a directive, enacting § 162(m), which applies to publicly held corporations. It denies a deduction to such a corporation for a salary in excess of $1 million if the recipient is one of the corporation's 5 highest-paid executives. If the salary in excess of $1 million is based "on the attainment of one or more performance goals," then the deduction is allowed in full. "Performance goals," under the statute are required to be developed in advance by outside directors and to be approved by a majority of the corporation's shareholders. The legislative history states that performance criteria that could be used could include the company's sales, earnings or share price.

This provision raises some interesting questions about corporate governance that shade off into a course in corporations. It sounds like an effective curb on excessive salaries to require approval by outside directors and shareholders of performance criteria. But in practice outside directors are frequently not very far "outside," and can receive many perks from management in their role as outside directors. Similarly shareholders often passively vote for whatever management proposes,

---

**6.** Some mildly interesting *dicta* on what is "ordinary and necessary" is provided in Welch v. Helvering, 290 U.S. 111, 115, 54 S.Ct. 8, 9, 78 L.Ed. 212 (1933) ("life in all its fullness must supply the answer to the riddle"); Deputy v. du Pont, 308 U.S. 488, 496, 60 S.Ct. 363, 367, 84 L.Ed. 416 (1940) ("it is the kind of transaction out of which the obligation arose and its normalcy in the particular business which are crucial and controlling").

**7.** The Service does have an older case as a weapon if it wanted to use it. In Patton v. Commissioner, 168 F.2d 28 (6th Cir. 1948), the Service successfully limited the deduction of the salary of a bookkeeper to $13,000 instead of the $46,000 that was being paid. The $46,000 was paid in accordance with an arrangement that gave the bookkeeper 10% of the business's net sales. The Service succeeded even though the bookkeeper was not related to the controlling partners of the enterprise, and there was no suggestion that the transaction constituted a gift. The result was that the $33,000 disallowed amount was taxed to the partnership, since no deduction was allowed. The $33,000 was also taxed to the bookkeeper because he in fact received it. The Service made out very well indeed.

often without even realizing what they are voting for. Thus perhaps the question of excessive salaries for management is a corporate governance question rather than a tax question.

These ideas seem to be borne out by a recent study by Graef Crystal, a corporate compensation expert in San Diego. There are a number of directors who sit on many boards of the Fortune 1,000 companies. These include people like Frank C. Carlucci, the former Defense Secretary who as of 1996 sat on 14 corporate boards. Another such director is former Labor Secretary Ann D. McLaughlin, who sits on 11 boards. Joseph A. Califano, Jr., a former Secretary of Health, Education and Welfare, sits on nine companies' boards. Others sit on as many as 15 boards.

Indeed, in 1995, 68 directors of Fortune 1,000 companies sat on nine or more corporate boards, according to Directorship, a Greenwich, Conn., consulting firm. The question is how much scrutiny can a director give a company (when there are 4 to 11 meetings a year) sitting on so many boards? The study by Mr. Crystal looked at the performance of the 256 companies whose boards have one or more of these 68 directors and found no statistically significant difference in performance. Mr. Crystal did find, however, that those 256 companies paid their chief executives and their directors more than did other companies. (For example HFS paid its directors a total of $417,000 in 1995, comprised of fees, stock, stock options and pensions). See generally Judith H. Dobrzynski, When Directors Play Musical Chairs.

As to closely-held corporations, § 162(m) does not deal with excessive salaries for management. In that area, the Service is still fighting with its traditional tools. Common examples of unreasonably high compensation being paid which would be subject to challenge by the Service would include: excessively high salaries paid to the controlling shareholders of a closely-held corporation for the purpose of minimizing the corporation's tax; excessive salaries paid to members of the family employed in the family business, for the purpose of deflecting income to lower-bracket family members;[8] wage payments between taxpayers who are also engaging in other transactions such as the purchase and sale of property, where a capital expense may be disguised as a deductible wage payment.[9]

The employees in these "suspect" situations may very well be rendering substantial services, in which case their employers are entitled to deduct their compensation in full. The most difficult case arises where the employee in this situation is rendering substantial services, but appears to be overpaid for those services. Then the courts and the Service must engage in the agonizing process of determining how much of the employee's compensation was "reasonable" and how much was "unreasonable," for the purpose of disallowing as a deduction to the employer the unreasonable amount. A large number of factors have been adduced by all hands concerned to try to settle this matter, and the

**8.** Cf. Chapter 5 on the doctrine of assignment of income.

**9.** See generally Regs. §§ 1.162–7 and 8.

number of litigated cases is exceedingly large. The major factors seem to be the level of compensation paid other employees in comparable jobs, whether the payments are pro rata to stock holdings, level of employer earnings, the type of work performed.

Problems can arise if the compensation is contingent on earnings, and the earnings grow to a surprising degree over the years. The result may be compensation that appears to have grown to an unreasonable level, but the regulations provide that if the contingent compensation agreement was arrived at pursuant to a free bargain between the parties, the resulting very high level of compensation will be allowed as a deduction.

Demonstrating that a contingent compensation arrangement was arrived at under a free bargain where, as is usually the case in these cases, the corporation is a family corporation or otherwise closely-held, can be difficult indeed.

For example, the case of *Harolds Club v. Commissioner*,[10] involved a contingent profit arrangement in a family setting. The two sons of Raymond Smith owned all the stock of Harolds Club casino. Raymond was an effective manager and his sons entered into an agreement where by Raymond would receive an annual salary of $10,000 plus 20% of the profits. Thereafter, as will come as no surprise, gambling proved to be extremely popular. Harolds Club profits increased dramatically, leading Raymond to receive as total salary under the contingent arrangement, $350,000 to $560,000 during 1952–1956. The question was whether this salary was reasonable. Competitors testified that they thought he was worth what he was paid.

The Ninth Circuit noted that under the regulations, contingent compensation, generally speaking, should be allowed as a deduction even though it is unusually large if it is paid pursuant to a "free bargain" between the employer and the individual, Reg. § 1.162–7(b), and if the contract was reasonable at the time when it was made. The Ninth Circuit affirmed the Tax Court's disallowance of the deduction on the grounds that there was no "free bargain," since it found that Raymond dominated his sons. (Apparently Raymond was a little too effective as a manager).

See also Reg. § 1.404(a)–1(b), providing that contributions to qualified pension, profit sharing, and other deferred compensation plans may be deducted only if the contribution, when taken together with the other compensation of the employee, constitutes reasonable compensation; Kennedy v. Commissioner, 671 F.2d 167 (6th Cir.1982) (compensation arrangement was reasonable when made).

Often on the occasion of a merger or takeover, upper-level executives may be displaced. They often land on their feet, however, assisted

---

10.   340 F.2d 861 (9th Cir.1965).

in their descent by a golden parachute, or large severance pay. The Tax Reform Act of 1984 limited the deduction of these payments when they are found, under the statute, to be "excess parachute payments."[11]

Beyond the "ordinary and necessary" limitation, there are other very important grounds for denying a deduction under § 162(a), discussed elsewhere in this work. They are that the deduction may be denied under § 162 because the expenditure is, in fact, personal in nature,[12] a capital expenditure (which may sometimes be amortized over time)[13] or that the expenditure violates public policy.[14] Moreover, special rules are provided for particular areas such as travel and entertainment expenses, educational expenses, fines and penalties, etc. These special topics are discussed below.

*(b) Travel and Transportation Expenses: Flowers; Hantzis; Andrews; Correll*

Section 162(a)(2) allows the deduction of travelling expenses, including amounts expended for meals and lodging other than amounts which are "lavish" or "extravagant" while away from home in the pursuit of a trade or business.[15] Surprisingly nettlesome problems are presented by this statutory provision.

The leading case in this area is *Flowers*:

---

**11.** § 280.

**12.** 6.03(3).

**13.** 6.03(4).

**14.** 6.03(5).

**15.** See Moffit, 31 T.C.M. 910 (1972) allowing deductions for meal expenses on a business trip under § 212.

## COMMISSIONER v. FLOWERS[16]

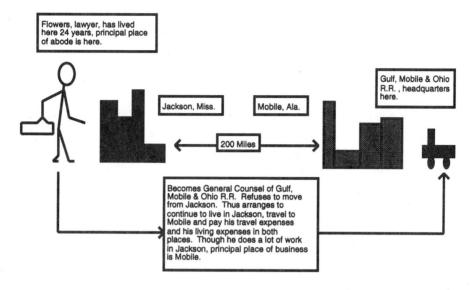

Flowers, lawyer, has lived here 24 years, principal place of abode is here.

Jackson, Miss.    Mobile, Ala.

Gulf, Mobile & Ohio R.R. , headquarters here.

200 Miles

Becomes General Counsel of Gulf, Mobile & Ohio R.R. Refuses to move from Jackson. Thus arranges to continue to live in Jackson, travel to Mobile and pay his travel expenses and his living expenses in both places. Though he does a lot of work in Jackson, principal place of business is Mobile.

[364a]

*Question:* Were Flowers' travel expenses (including transportation, meals and lodging in Mobile) deductible?

*IRS Argument:* "Home" under § 162(a)(2) is principal place of business. Thus taxpayer not away from home when in Mobile and hence no deduction for travel.

*Held:* Three-part test for determining whether a travel expense is deductible under § 162(a)(2): 1) The expense must be reasonable and necessary; 2) The expense must be incurred while away from home; 3) The expense must be incurred in pursuit of business. Taxpayer flunks third test; the expenses were not incurred in pursuit of business. It was his own choice to live in Jackson. This is just a long commute and therefore not deductible as being personal expenses under § 262.

*Comment:* "Travel expenses" in tax law is defined as not only expenses of travel but also meals and lodging at the destination, § 162(a)(2).

*Comment:* A short lesson of this case is that if you want to live in Jackson, MS, you have to pay for it.

*Flowers* gets a lot of attention because it is a Supreme Court case. Prior to *Flowers* there was a split in authorities as to the definition of "home" under the statute. The Tax Court and the Service defined it as the taxpayer's place of business. Other cases had defined it as the taxpayer's residence. Thus the issue was squarely presented in *Flowers.*

**16.** 326 U.S. 465, 66 S.Ct. 250, 90 L.Ed. 203 (1946), reh'g denied 326 U.S. 812, 66 S.Ct. 482, 90 L.Ed. 496 (1946).

While the *Flowers* Court purported to decline to rule on this question, implicit in and necessary to its holding is the idea that the taxpayer's home for tax purposes is his place of business, agreeing with IRS. That one's home is where one's business is has come to be the principal idea in this area.[17]

Under the terms of the statute, a deduction is allowed for "traveling expenses ... while away from home in the pursuit of a trade or business." Another case which probes the meaning of "away from home" is *Rosenspan v. United States*.[18] In this case, taxpayer Robert Rosenspan was a jewelry salesman working on a commission basis, paying his own traveling expenses without reimbursement. He traveled for some 300 days a year by car in the midwest, staying at hotels and eating at restaurants (sounds like fun). He used his brother's home in Brooklyn as his residential address. Often when he was in New York, he stayed at a hotel rather than wearing out his welcome at his brother's house. At one point he changed his registration of his automobile to the address of a cousin in Cincinnati. He did not claim that he had a permanent abode or residence in Brooklyn or anywhere else.

The court disallowed a deduction for Rosenspan's meals and lodging while in his sales territory because he did not have a home to be away from, as required by the statutory language. Rosenspan in effect carried his home on his back. He did not have any possible duplication of expenses which is part of the rationale for being able to deduct expenses while away from home in pursuit of a trade or business.

A further illustration that, perhaps, hits somewhat closer to home is afforded by *Hantzis*.

---

**17.** Note that Flowers could not deduct his expenses in Jackson because when he was there he was not in pursuit of his trade or business, for which main posting was in Mobile.

Cf. Daly v. Commissioner, 631 F.2d 351 (4th Cir.1980), on reh'g 662 F.2d 253 (1981) (salesman who lived in Virginia and stayed overnight in his territory of Delaware, Pennsylvania, and New Jersey was away from home on these occasions and could deduct meals and lodging expenses).

**18.** 438 F.2d 905 (2d Cir.1971), cert. denied 404 U.S. 864, 92 S.Ct. 54, 30 L.Ed.2d 108 (1971), reh'g denied 404 U.S. 959, 92 S.Ct. 306, 30 L.Ed.2d 281 (1971).

## HANTZIS v. COMMISSIONER[19]

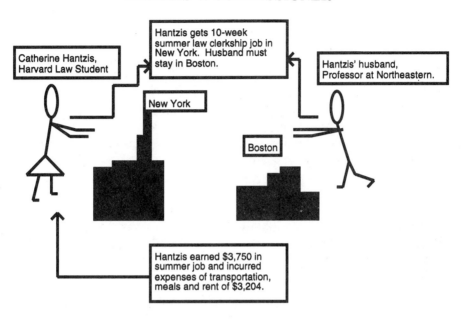

Catherine Hantzis, Harvard Law Student

Hantzis gets 10-week summer law clerkship job in New York. Husband must stay in Boston.

Hantzis' husband, Professor at Northeastern.

New York

Boston

Hantzis earned $3,750 in summer job and incurred expenses of transportation, meals and rent of $3,204.

[365a]

*Question:* Were Hantzis' transportation, meals and lodging in New York deductible under § 162(a)(2) as traveling expenses while away from home in pursuit of a trade or business?

*IRS argument:* Deduction should be disallowed on grounds that 1) expenses were not incurred "in the pursuit of a trade or business." 2) taxpayer's tax home was New York and thus she was not away from home when she incurred the expenses.

*Held:* No deduction. 1) Taxpayer did incur the expenses in the pursuit of a trade or business, but 2) she was not away from her tax home.

*Comment:* Since Hantzis had no business reason to maintain a home in Boston, she could not argue that her tax home was Boston and that she was on temporary employment in New York (see discussion below).

*Comment:* As did the Supreme Court in *Flowers*, the court purports to say that it is not holding that the tax home is the place of business. Yet, as in *Flowers*, that is necessarily part of the decision.

*Comment:* The court in *dicta* mentions the necessity for duplicative expenses to gain the deduction.

Another interesting case is *Andrews v. Commissioner*[20] involving a second home that Edward W. Andrews and his wife Leona maintained at Lighthouse Point, Florida. The Andrews attempted to deduct the Lighthouse Point home as traveling expenses while away from home in the pursuit of a trade or business.

**19.** 638 F.2d 248 (1st Cir.1981), cert. denied 452 U.S. 962, 101 S.Ct. 3112, 69 L.Ed.2d 973 (1981).

**20.** 931 F.2d 132 (1st Cir.1991).

Andrews was president and chief executive officer of Andrews Gunite Co., which was engaged in the swimming pool and construction business in New England. Andrews was also engaged in business in Florida, being a large builder of swimming pools and also raising, breeding and racing horses. The horse business was profitable. Andrews used the Lighthouse Point house as his personal residence during the racing season in Florida. Andrews claimed deductibility in full as lodging expenses for the expenses of his Lighthouse Point house, including depreciation of the house and furniture as well as deducting tax, mortgage interest, utilities and insurance. All these deductions were taken in connection with his horse racing business.

The Tax Court found that Andrews spent six months in Florida on the race horse business and six months in Massachusetts in the pool business. The Tax Court concluded that Andrews therefore had two tax homes and was not away from either one when he was at the other one. Thus the court denied Andrews deduction of his Florida meals and lodging expenses.

The First Circuit remanded the case to the Tax Court with instructions to ascertain which home was Andrews' tax home, so that he could deduct expenses of the other as being away from home. The court noted that generally time spent at a location will be determinative of which is the taxpayer's principal place of business for deciding where is his tax home. Then expenses at the other location would be deductible. But it was now up to the Tax Court to make the excruciating decision in this case, when the taxpayer spent six months of the year at each location.

*Flowers* and *Hantzis* are further examples of the more general idea that inherently personal living expenses are not deductible. They are not deductible even if they are increased because of the taxpayer's work or business. In that sense *Flowers* and *Hantzis* are straight out of the book of the older case of *Smith*,[21] which held that expenses of a nurse for a child of a married couple are not deductible even though the nurse is needed so the wife could work.

*Flowers* and *Hantzis* may also be seen as great big commuting cases. It is well established that the cost of commuting is not deductible.[22] Most

---

**21.** See later in this chapter ¶ 6.03(3).

**22.** Regs. §§ 1.162–2(e), 1.212–1(f). See Coombs, 67 T.C. 426 (1976), aff'd in part, rev'd in part 608 F.2d 1269 (9th Cir.1979) (employees at a nuclear test site in Nevada who were compelled to travel 65 miles to nearest lodging could not deduct their "commuting" expenses).

The bar against the deductibility of commuting expenses is lifted if the taxpayer has to carry such bulky tools and equipment that he must incur additional expenses to bring his equipment with him. Such additional expenses would be incurred if, for example, because of having to transport bulky equipment the taxpayer took his private car rather than public transportation. Fausner v. Commissioner, 413 U.S. 838, 93 S.Ct. 2820, 37 L.Ed.2d 996 (1973), reh'g denied 414 U.S. 882, 94 S.Ct. 43, 38 L.Ed.2d 130 (1973) (deduction denied to airline pilot who had to transport flight bags because he would have taken his automobile to the airport whether or not he had to transport the bags; therefore, he did not incur any additional expenses on account of the bags); Rev.Rul. 75–380, 1975–2 C.B. 59; Kallander v. United States, 526 F.2d 1131 (Ct.Cl.1975) (same as *Fausner* and same result); McCabe v. Commissioner, 688 F.2d 102, 49 A.F.T.R.2d 1192 (2d Cir.1982) (po-

commentators regard nondeductibility of commuting expenses as an appropriate result. Commuting expenses are seen as inherently personal and barring their deduction as a fundamental principle of federal income taxation.

However, in my opinion (not that anyone has asked for it), when the matter is viewed from an economic approach, non-deductibility of commuting expenses does not make sense. Put the non-deductibility of commuting expenses against the deductibility of interest on a home mortgage and see where that takes us. From the standpoint of function, commuting and the home mortgage interest payment are substitutes for one another. The more affluent individual can live closer to work in a fancy neighborhood if he chooses and is able to deduct the interest on his large home mortgage. Compare that to the lower-income individual who is compelled to live further away from his job. He is able to to spend less on a house and less on deductible home mortgage interest. He must spend more on commuting expenses which he cannot deduct. Anyone like to go out into an outlying suburb of a major metropolitan area and defend all this?

Another leading case in this area is *Correll.*

## UNITED STATES v. CORRELL[23]

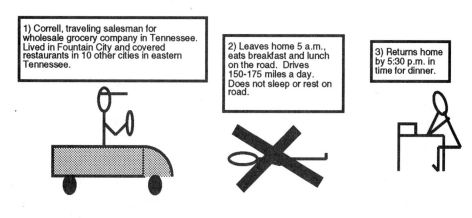

1) Correll, traveling salesman for wholesale grocery company in Tennessee. Lived in Fountain City and covered restaurants in 10 other cities in eastern Tennessee.

2) Leaves home 5 a.m., eats breakfast and lunch on the road. Drives 150-175 miles a day. Does not sleep or rest on road.

3) Returns home by 5:30 p.m. in time for dinner.

[366a]

*Question:* Can taxpayer deduct cost of breakfast and lunch on the road as being "traveling expenses while away from home pursuing his trade or business" under § 162(a)(2)?

liceman could not deduct expenses of driving to work in order to be able to carry his revolver, as he was required to by his employer, since the necessity for driving was occasioned by where he chose to live); Cf. Green, 74 T.C. 1229 (1980) (blood donor could deduct cost of traveling between her home and hospital because her body was the container in which the blood was transported).

**23.** 389 U.S. 299, 88 S.Ct. 445, 19 L.Ed.2d 537 (1967).

*IRS Argument:* Has consistently promulgated the rule that to qualify for travel "away from home" the trip must require sleep or rest.

*Taxpayer Argument:* "Away from home" in § 162(a)(2) should mean outside the greater metropolitan area in which a taxpayer resides.

*Held:* Find in favor of IRS "sleep or rest" rule. Words "meals and lodging" together in the statute suggest that taxpayer can only deduct meals where lodging also involved on trip.

*Comment:* Briefs of amici curiae in favor of the taxpayer were filed by the Bureau of Salesmen's National Associations, and the Manufacturing Chemists' Association.

The *Correll* case owes its place in the pantheon to the fact that it is a Supreme Court case that affirms the Service's long-held sleep or rest rule as a definition of deductible "travel expenses" under § 162(a)(2). It is the black letter law on the subject.[24]

This sounds like a fairly reasonable definition. However, it appears that it comes down harder on the less affluent. Correll was working some grueling hours, leaving home at 5 a.m. to get to his appointed rounds on time.

Is this the work-style of an affluent, high-paid salesman? Not likely. Why didn't Correll stay over night on the road to take some of the pressure off himself. Probably because he couldn't afford it. He was obviously paying his own expenses, or he wouldn't be litigating this matter. So another high-powered, very well-paid salesman in Correll's shoes would stay overnight on the road and as a result would be able to deduct his meals (in addition to deducting his lodging). Like in *Flowers*, a seemingly neutral principle seems to in fact come down harder on the less affluent.

Where the taxpayer travels between various business locations during the day, he can deduct the cost of such traveling expenses (automobile expenses, public transportation expenses) as ordinary and necessary business expenses under § 162(a). Since such taxpayers would not be "away from home" they could not deduct any expenses for meals.

While it is necessary to be away from home overnight in order to be "away from home" for purposes of deducting traveling, meals and lodging expenses, it is possible to stay away from home too long, in which case the taxpayer's home will be deemed to have moved with him. In such an event, the taxpayer will not be able to deduct his expenses inasmuch as he is no longer "away from home." The Service's approach here has been to distinguish between "temporary" employment—in which case the taxpayer is "away from home" and can deduct his meals and lodging expenses—and employment for an "indeterminant" period—in which case the taxpayer's home moves to his place of employment and he cannot deduct his meals and lodging expenses. The Service has ruled

**24.** See also Rev.Rul. 75–170, 1975–1 C.B. 60 (railroad employees); Barry v. Commissioner, 435 F.2d 1290 (1st Cir.1970) (napping on side of the road in car did not qualify).

that where employment at a particular location is anticipated to be, or turns out to be, for a year or more, the employment is not temporary but permanent.

This one-year rule works out very well for law professors and other academics who visit at another institution for a year. They can deduct their transportation, food and lodging expenses because they are still deemed to be away from home. Such are the little bones we get from academic life.[25]

The final logical extreme of all these possibilities is the peripatetic or itinerant taxpayer who for reasons of business seems to have no home at all but is continuously on the road throughout the year. Where the facts demonstrate that this is the case, the taxpayer is regarded as "carrying his home on his back" and therefore cannot deduct any of his meals and lodging expenses. This is a ridiculous result and demonstrates the weakness of the *Correll* approach.[26] Traveling expenses (air-fare, gasoline, etc.) in such a case could, however, be deducted.

Taxpayers with two or more places of business may deduct the cost of traveling from the major business site to the minor business site.[27] Where a married couple have their business or place of employment in two widely separated locations, no deduction for living expenses at either location is allowed.[28] This rule appears rather harsh even under *Correll*; it would seem that a married couple could be regarded as having a tax home at one of the two business locations and deduct the other.

It is interesting from an analytical standpoint to put the principles discussed in this section together with the principles involved in taxing meals and lodging provided by the employer, discussed at ¶ 2.02(2). Putting all these principles together, the following pattern emerges: If the taxpayer receives meals and lodging from his employer on the employer's business premises, and meets certain other requirements, the value of the meals and lodging will be excluded from the taxpayer's income. If, however, the taxpayer obtains and pays for his meals and lodging some distance away from the employer's business premises, he

**25.** Rev.Rul. 74–291, 1974–1 C.B. 42; Peurifoy v. Commissioner, 358 U.S. 59, 79 S.Ct. 104, 3 L.Ed.2d 30 (1958) reh'g denied 358 U.S. 913, 79 S.Ct. 227, 3 L.Ed.2d 234 (construction workers); Wills v. Commissioner, 411 F.2d 537 (9th Cir.1969) (baseball player Maury Wills of the Los Angeles Dodgers did not meet the temporary employment test because his work was seasonal; Six v. United States, 450 F.2d 66 (2d Cir.1971) (remand of question of whether actress Ethel Merman's engagement in New York musical "Gypsy" (ironic in this context) was of sufficient duration not to be temporary). Hasselback, "Tax Implications of a Visiting Professorship," 52 Taxes 499 (1974).

**26.** Rev.Rul. 73–529, 1973–2 C.B. 37; Rosenspan v. United States, 438 F.2d 905 (2d Cir.1971), cert. denied 404 U.S. 864, 92 S.Ct. 54, 30 L.Ed.2d 108 (1971) reh'g denied 404 U.S. 959, 92 S.Ct. 306, 30 L.Ed.2d 281 (1971).

**27.** Sherman, 16 T.C. 332 (1951) (acq.); Rev.Rul. 55–109, 1955–1 C.B. 261; Folkman v. United States, 615 F.2d 493 (9th Cir. 1980).

**28.** Foote, 67 T.C. 1 (1976).

See generally Riepen, "Extraordinary Commuting Expenses: Deductibility of Transportation Expenses Between Residence and Temporary Place of Business," 51 S.Cal.L.Rev. 499 (1978); Chod, "Travel, Transportation and Commuting Expenses: Problems Involving Deductibility," 43 Missouri L.Rev. 525 (1978).

cannot deduct their cost, and thus the value of the meals and lodging will be included in his income. If the taxpayer, however, should have to travel on business away from home and stay overnight, he can deduct the cost of his meals and lodging, and therefore their value in effect will be excluded from his income. Finally, if the taxpayer travels away from where he lives to a job location for a long period of time, his tax home will be deemed to have moved with him to the new job location and he will not be able to deduct the cost of his meals and lodging—their value will therefore in effect be included in his income. The question is whether all this really makes any sense.

### (2) The Dichotomy Between Deduction and Capital or Personal Expenses

(a) Necessary Rental and Similar Payments; Starr's Estate; Fitzpatrick

The classic case of *Starr's Estate* presents a good introduction to the problems in this area.

### STARR'S ESTATE v. COMMISSIONER[29]

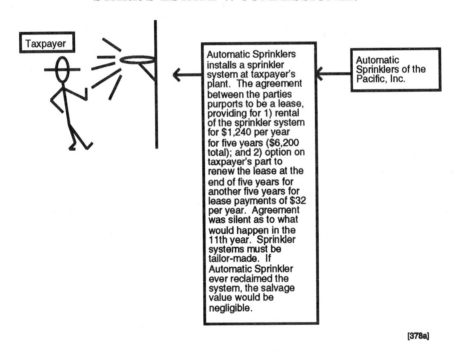

[378a]

*Question:* Were the payments under the agreement rent or an installment purchase of the sprinkler system?

---

**29.**   274 F.2d 294 (9th Cir.1959).

*Held:* For tax purposes, the payments were an installment purchase of the sprinkler system even though title did not pass under the agreement under state law. The value to the lessor in the sprinkler system was exhausted by this arrangement. The court remanded the case for consideration of interest as being deductible to taxpayer. The normal purchase price of the system was $4,960, while the total price here was $6,200, suggesting $1,240 as interest over the 5 years.

*Comment:* Thus the annual payments were not deductible as paid but were rather capital expenses. Depreciation would then be allowed, since the sprinkler system and the attendant building are wasting assets.

*Comment:* Under the numbers given, the arrangement implies that the interest rate was 7.93%, which is a reasonable rate. This further confirms that the economic reality of the situation was an installment purchase with interest.

*Comment:* The court stated the Commissioner allowed depreciation of $269 per year, finding that the sprinkler system had a 23–year useful life. That $269 over 23 years assumes that the purchase price is $6,200 $(23 - \$269 = \$6,200)$. However, if we follow the court's approach that $1,240 of the $6,200 is interest, then the purchase price is $4,960. It is therefore only $4,960 that should be depreciated over the 23 years. That churns out to be a depreciation deduction of $216 per year. The moral of this story is that you do not add the interest to your basis for depreciation purposes.

Let us pursue the installment purchase idea a little. What are the numbers on the installment purchase theory? The interest deduction for the first year is 7.93% of the purchase price of $4,960, or $393. Interest in subsequent years would be less because the principal would be declining as it is paid off. See the prologue in general for further discussion of the treatment of interest as compounding over time. It would, in short, be wrong to just deduct ⅕ of the interest per year. After five years, when the purchase price is paid, there would be no further payments and of course no interest deduction. Looking at depreciation, the $216 deduction, which is taken on a straight-line method, would continue for the full 23 years. This is comprised of the five years of the installment purchase agreement and the subsequent 18 years.

What do these numbers come to in the first year? In the first year the interest is $393 and the depreciation is $216. This gives a total deduction the first year if the installment purchase approach is followed of $609. That is considerably less than a deduction of the full amount of the payment under the contract of $1,240. That is what the fighting was about.

The court, however, at the end of its opinion seems to down-play the significance of this difference. How much difference does this really make? If you formulate the question, I'll do the dirty math. The question is what is the present value of being able to deduct $1,240 per year for five years?[30]

That's the lease theory. Then we need to compare that with the present value of deducting interest for five years and depreciation for 23 years. That's the installment purchase theory. We need, of course, a chart:

Comparison of Lease and Installment Purchase Theory of *Starr's Estate*. Assume combined federal and state tax rate of 40% ; before tax interest rate of 7.93% and after tax interest rate of 4.76%. 7.93% interest rate arrived at by computation from numbers in the case. 4.76% interest rate is the after-tax rate of interest (i.e. 60% of 7.93%),

| | | LEASE (TP View) | | INSTALLMENT PURCHASE (IRS View) | | | | | |
|---|---|---|---|---|---|---|---|---|---|
| | Payment | Tax Savings from Ded Payment | Present Value of Ded Payment | Interest | Tax Savings from Ded Interest | Present Value of Int Ded | Depreciation | Tax Savings from Ded Depr | Present Value of Depr Ded |
| Year | | | | | | | | | |
| 1 | $1,240 | $496 | $473 | $393 | $157 | $150 | $216 | $86 | $82 |
| 2 | $1,240 | $496 | $452 | $326 | $130 | $119 | $216 | $86 | $79 |
| 3 | $1,240 | $496 | $431 | $254 | $101 | $88 | $216 | $86 | $75 |
| 4 | $1,240 | $496 | $412 | $176 | $70 | $58 | $216 | $86 | $72 |
| 5 | $1,240 | $496 | $393 | $91 | $36 | $29 | $216 | $86 | $68 |
| 6 | | | | | | | $216 | $86 | $65 |
| 7 | | | | | | | $216 | $86 | $62 |
| 8 | | | | | | | $216 | $86 | $59 |
| 9 | | | | | | | $216 | $86 | $57 |
| 10 | | | | | | | $216 | $86 | $54 |
| 11 | | | | | | | $216 | $86 | $52 |
| 12 | | | | | | | $216 | $86 | $49 |
| 13 | | | | | | | $216 | $86 | $47 |
| 14 | | | | | | | $216 | $86 | $45 |
| 15 | | | | | | | $216 | $86 | $43 |
| 16 | | | | | | | $216 | $86 | $41 |
| 17 | | | | | | | $216 | $86 | $39 |
| 18 | | | | | | | $216 | $86 | $37 |
| 19 | | | | | | | $216 | $86 | $36 |
| 20 | | | | | | | $216 | $86 | $34 |
| 21 | | | | | | | $216 | $86 | $32 |
| 22 | | | | | | | $216 | $86 | $31 |
| 23 | | | | | | | $216 | $86 | $30 |
| Total | | | $2,162 | $1,240 | | $445 | $4,960 | | $1,190 |
| | | Total Present Value of Treatment as Lease | $2,162 | | Total Present Value of Treatment as Installment Sale (sum of total present value of interest deduction and total present value of depreciation). | | | | $1,635 |

Thus the difference between treating it as a lease and as an installment sale is $2,162 − $1,635 = $527. Small change, you say? Well

**30.** We ignore the payment of $32 per year for the second five years as being *de minimis.*

calling it a lease increases the present value by 32%. Any time you can increase asset value by 32% you are doing something significant. This is the case notwithstanding that the court in Starr's Estate suggested that the attack on leases may not be worthwhile in terms of revenue.

Another aspect of the case is the treatment of Automatic Sprinklers, the company that manufactured and installed the sprinkler system. If the transaction is treated as a lease to Starr's Estate (attractive for Starr's Estate as we have seen), then the payments would be rental payments to Automatic Sprinklers as the lessor. These would be taxable, of course. The relevant offsetting deduction would be a deduction for depreciation of the sprinkler system, which was found in the case to have a useful life of 23 years. Thus there would be a relatively small deduction for Automatic Sprinklers each year of $216. From the point of view of the Internal Revenue Service, then, the lower taxes paid by Starr's Estate if the transaction is called a lease would be offset by the higher taxes paid by Automatic Sprinklers.

If, on the other hand, the transaction is regarded as an installment sale over five years, then as we have seen, Starr's Estate pays a higher tax. However, Automatic Sprinkler is then favored with a lower tax because on an installment sale over five years Automatic Sprinklers is allowed to offset its cost of the sprinkler over five years instead of 23 years (see Chapter 8). Thus on an installment sale Starr's higher tax is offset by Automatic Sprinkler's lower tax.

Therefore it appears to all break even for the government. It would appear that the government should allow the parties to call a transaction a lease or a sale as they like, since the revenues more or less break even. Except for what? The analysis that the tax revenues break even either way assumes that the parties are in the same tax bracket. This might well not be the case of course. If Automatic Sprinkler is running losses from the rest of its business, it will be happy to style the deal as a lease. The higher income will still not be taxable to Automatic Sprinkler and Starr's Estate will have lower income. If Starr's Estate has losses and Automatic Sprinkler has high income, then the parties will style the deal as an installment sale.

Part of the negotiation between the parties will be to split the tax gains they get by styling the deal in the most favorable way. The government cannot sit by and let the taxpayers deal to their own advantage in this way.

Having said all that, it must also be said that much of the preceding analysis is now irrelevant. This is because of the rules allowing rapid depreciation (or cost recovery) provided by the ACRS system (see ¶ 6.02(12)).

These rules allow very short useful lives for depreciation. As the *Starr's Estate* table above indicates, if depreciation occurs over 5 years instead of 23 years, the difference between the lease approach and the installment sale approach would be erased.

So under current law none of this matters very much anymore. But the principles of immediate deduction versus capital expenditure highlighted by this discussion remain important.

*White v. Fitzpatrick*[31] involved a transfer of property from husband to wife with a resulting lease or license back. Taxpayer was engaged as a sole proprietor in the manufacture of chokes for use on barrels of shotguns. He had a patent on the device, which he transferred to his wife for the full term of the patent for consideration of $10. The wife then licensed the patent back to taxpayer, with royalties at $1 on each device marketed. Taxpayer filed a gift tax return declaring the fair market value of the patent he transferred to be $10,000. For the next four years, taxpayer paid his wife $60,000 as royalties.

At about the same time the wife also purchased the property on which the company was located for $16,800 and then leased it back to her husband orally. The next day the taxpayer made a gift to his wife of $16,175 to cover the purchase price and filed a gift tax for that amount. Rental payments were $1,500 a year plus a one time $5,000 "adjustment in rent."

During the tax years in question, taxpayer deducted both the royalty and rent payments as business expenses.

It will be noted that if these two transactions are allowed to stand, the income from the patent is shifted to the wife from the husband. (Husband takes deduction and wife has income). This case arose out of tax years prior to the filing of the joint return, so the arrangement was effective in shifting income from the husband to the wife, who was presumably in a lower tax bracket.

Recognizing this, the Second Circuit affirmed the district court and disallowed the deduction of the payments to the wife. The court said that "underlying reality ... contradicts this appearance of complete assignment. Though title to the properties might reside in the wife, control rests with the husband as effectively as if he had never made the gift of the patent or the money to buy the property." Thus considerations of family relations override the form of a transaction, compare *Harolds Club* above at ¶ 6.02(1)(a). Compare also assignment of income problems in Chapter 5.

#### (b) *Education Expenses*

#### (i) *The Law; Hill; Coughlin*

A case that illustrated the problems in this area is *Hill v. Commissioner*[32] which involved school teacher Nora Payne Hill. Ms. Hill taught school in Virginia for 27 years. For the tax year in question, she attended

---

**31.** 193 F.2d 398, cert. denied 343 U.S. 928, 72 S.Ct. 762, 96 L.Ed. 1338 (1952).

**32.** 181 F.2d 906 (4th Cir.1950).

summer school at Columbia University in New York City, incurring expenses of $239.50, which she deducted. The laws of the state of Virginia required that to retain her teaching certificate she must either present evidence of college credits in professional or academic subjects earned during the life of the certificate or pass an examination on selected books. Ms. Hill held the highest certificate issued to public school teachers in Virginia. The court noted that to satisfy this requirement she took two courses, one on short story writing, which was in her field, and the other on abnormal psychology which, the court noted, "would be most useful to a teacher whose pupils were adolescents."

The Fourth Circuit reversed the Tax Court, which had held the expenses were personal, and found that these expenses were incurred in carrying on a trade or business and were both ordinary and necessary. The expenses also were not personal. Hence the court held the expenses were deductible. The court regarded it as irrelevant that the state requirements could be satisfied by a test instead of taking the courses. Indeed the court opined that taking the courses was a better way to satisfy the requirement (although that observations was not necessary for its decision).

*Hill* can be usefully compared with the case of *Coughlin v. Commissioner*[33] in which a tax lawyer attended the Fifth Annual Institute on Federal Taxation of New York University. (It could happen to you). In so doing, he incurred expenses of tuition, travel, board and lodging of $305. Taxpayer argued that his expenses were deductible as an ordinary and necessary expense incurred in the practice of his profession. Analogizing to *Hill*, the court held that these expenses were to enable taxpayer to keep sharp the tools he actually used in his going trade or business.

The area of education expenses is now blanketed by regulations, which provide several inter-related tests to determine the deductibility of education expenses.

Education expenses are deductible if they (1) maintain or improve skills required by the individual in his employment or other trade or business or (2) meet the express requirements of the taxpayer's employer, or the requirements of applicable law as a condition to the retention by the taxpayer of his employment or rate of compensation.[34] Even if the education expenses meet either test (1) or test (2), they will still not be deductible unless further they (3) are not expenditures made by an individual for education to meet the minimum educational requirements for qualification in his employment or other trade or business; or (4) do not lead to qualifying the taxpayer for a new trade or business.[35] Thus, to be deductible, educational expenses must pass either test (1) skill maintenance; *or* test (2) required by employer or by law; and then pass both test (3) not required to meet minimum educational standards or

33.   203 F.2d 307 (2d Cir.1953).
34.   Reg. § 1.162–5(a).
35.   Reg. § 1.162–5(b)(2) and (3).

qualifications in taxpayer's trade or business; *and* test (4) not qualify taxpayer for a new trade or business.

The theory of these regulations (if there be one) is that educational expenses to maintain existing skills or which are required by the employer or other state or federal law are analogous to expenses to keep a piece of machinery used in taxpayer's trade or business running. Such expenses are clearly deductible as an ordinary and necessary expense of doing the taxpayer's business. Expenses which cause the taxpayer to meet minimum educational requirements for his trade or business, or which prepare him for a new trade or business, are analogous to capital expenses and therefore cannot be deducted.[36]

Examples of skill-maintenance educational expenses which would pass test (1) as well as tests (3) and (4) would be refresher courses or courses dealing with current developments in the taxpayer's professional field.[37] Examples of educational expenses that would meet test (2) expenses required by employer or law would be explicit (and reasonable) employer requirements that certain courses be taken from time to time for job retention or state statutes requiring professionals to take a certain number of courses to retain professional licensing. The Regulations provide some detailed examples of test (3) which must be passed by all educational expenses to be deductible, namely that the expenses do not qualify the taxpayer to meet the minimal education requirements of his trade or business.[38]

Examples of the test (4) that must also be passed by all educational expenses to be deductible, namely that the expenses do not qualify for the taxpayer for a new trade or business, would be a general practitioner of medicine who takes a two-week course reviewing new developments in several specialized fields of medicine. The expenses would be deductible because they maintain or improve his skills (test (1)) and do not qualify him for a new trade or business.[39]

An example of educational expenses that flunk test (4) would be an engineer who studies law at night and receives a bachelor of law degree. This expenditure would flunk test (4) in that it prepares him for a new trade or business, and may, depending on the facts, also be disqualified

---

**36.** A problem with this theory is that educational expenses which are treated as capital should then be amortizable over the taxpayer's anticipated career or lifetime, but such amortization has been absolutely disallowed, Sharon v. Commissioner, 591 F.2d 1273 (9th Cir.1978), cert. denied 442 U.S. 941, 99 S.Ct. 2883, 61 L.Ed.2d 311 (1979) (cost of law school and bar review course may not be amortized over taxpayer's professional life because such costs were "personal" expenses.)

**37.** Reg. § 1.162–5(c)(1); Carroll v. Commissioner, 418 F.2d 91 (7th Cir.1969) (policemen studying philosophy in college could not deduct); compare Glasgow, 31

T.C.M. 310 (1972), aff'd per curiam 486 F.2d 1045 (10th Cir.1973) (minister could deduct expense of college courses in history, literature, psychology, and other liberal arts subjects on theory that such courses assisted him in serving his congregation; a questionable holding which probably should not be relied upon); Ford, 56 T.C. 1300 (1971), aff'd per curiam 487 F.2d 1025 (9th Cir. 1973) (teacher of English and social studies could deduct expenses for studying linguistics and anthropology).

**38.** Reg. § 1.162–5(b)(2)(iii), relating to secondary school teachers.

**39.** Reg. § 1.162–5(b)(3)(i), Example (3).

because it does not pass either tests (1) or (2).[40] Indeed, even if an employee is absolutely required by his employer to obtain a law degree in order to keep his nonlegal job, nevertheless, the expenses of the legal study would be nondeductible even though the employee does not intend to practice law, since the expenses do as an objective matter prepare him for a new career.[41] This rule has caused, for example, Internal Revenue Service agents who attended law school at night to improve their skills in their existing jobs to be unable to deduct the expenses of their legal education.[42]

The major problem with test (4) is differentiating between expenses that simply prepare an employee for a change of duties that does not constitute a new trade or business, in which case the expenses are deductible, and expenses which do qualify the employee for a new trade or business, in which case the expenses are not deductible.[43]

The fact that a course of educational study leads to the granting of a degree does not in itself cause the educational expenses to flunk any of tests (1) through (4).[44]

Expenses of travel for education are not deductible.[45]

### (ii) The Economics: What Does It Really Cost to Go to Law School?

So what does it finally cost to go to law school? You probably don't need me to tell you anything about that. But let me try to put a little perspective on it. It costs you your tuition, books, travel and living expenses. Of course you would have had living expenses anyway, but perhaps they are higher at law school. What else does it cost? The standard economic analysis here is that going to law school (or any vocationally-oriented school) also costs you your "opportunity cost," to

---

**40.** Reg. § 1.162–5(b)(3)(i), Example (1).

**41.** Reg. § 1.162–5(b)(3)(i), Example (2).

**42.** See Weiler, 54 T.C. 398 (1970).

**43.** Reg. § 1.162–5(b)(3)(i). The Regulations throw a moderate amount of light on this subject by providing that all teaching and related duties are considered to involve the same trade or business and educational expenses relating to such shifts—as from teacher of one subject to another, teacher to guidance counselor, or teacher to principal—are deductible.

See also the following cases holding that education expenses were not deductible because they involved qualifying the taxpayer for a new trade or business: Davis, 65 T.C. 1014 (1976) (cost of Ph.D. for social worker); Burnstein, 66 T.C. 492 (1976) (cost of becoming a social worker not deductible to teacher of handicapped children); Sharon v. Commissioner, 591 F.2d 1273 (9th Cir. 1978), cert. denied 442 U.S. 941, 99 S.Ct. 2883, 61 L.Ed.2d 311 (1979) (cost of Califor-

nia bar review course not deductible by New York lawyer); Antzoulatos, 34 T.C.M. 1426 (1975) (cost of intern becoming a registered pharmacist not deductible). It is the author's experience (based on an audit) that expenses of attending a graduate study program leading to a Master's degree in Taxation are deductible, where the taxpayer has engaged in the practice of tax law prior to the commencement of the graduate study, on the theory that such training improves existing skills but does not prepare the taxpayer for a new trade or business. However, were a taxpayer to complete law school and then immediately embark upon graduate tax study, it is likely that such expenses would not be deductible since the taxpayer would not have established the trade or business of being a tax lawyer prior to commencement of the graduate study.

**44.** Reg. § 1.162–5(a) and see authorities in Note 23 supra.

**45.** 274(m)(2).

use the jargon. That is, it costs you what you could have earned had you gotten a job instead of going to law school. You are out of pocket that money, too, so the analysis goes. That analysis is OK as far as it goes. The problem is that it assumes you could have gotten a job with your B.A. in sociology or art history, or whatever degree you have. But you might not have gotten a job at all if the economy is in rocky shape.[46]

Indeed it is the case that when the economy is rocky, law school applications soar. What is happening here is that people are obviously going to law school because they can't get a job, not in spite of the fact that they can get a job.

The other economic aspect of legal education is the fact, as discussed in the previous section, that its cost cannot be deducted or amortized over time. This seems unjustified since it is creating an asset (your career) which will produce income over time. However, the tax code is treating you better than you think. As you labor to gain your legal education, you are in receipt of imputed income (as discussed in Chapters 1, 2). That is, you are performing educational services on yourself. This imputed income is not taxed. So even though you cannot deduct your legal education expenses, you also are not taxed on your imputed income.[47] Don't you feel better now? Next time your brother-in-law at a family reunion rags you around the cheese dip for being an impoverished law student, tell him you've got imputed income. That'll hold him for at least a half an hour.

#### (3) Expenses for the Production of Income, or for the Maintenance of Investment Property: Higgins; Gilmore; Estate of Baier; Surasky; Myer J. Fleischman; Horrmann; Lowry

As discussed above, § 212 allows individuals to deduct all the "ordinary and necessary expenses paid or incurred during the taxable year—(1) for the production or collection of income; (2) for the management, conservation or maintenance of property held for the production of income ..." The reason it takes two Code sections to provide the deductions for expenses incurred in all of these business-type activities is that the Supreme Court in the 1941 case of *Higgins v. Commissioner*[48] upheld the Service's position that expenses incurred in profit-seeking or investment-type activity were not deductible under the predecessor of § 162. Congress nullified that holding by enacting the following year the predecessors of §§ 212(1) and 212(2).[49] Sections 162 and 212, therefore, embodying as they do the same "ordinary and necessary" language, are

---

**46.** See Kramer, Legal Education in an Era of Change: Will Legal Education Remain Affordable, by Whom and How?, 1987 Duke L. J. 240 (1987).

**47.** Also, particularly if you go to a low-tuition state school, you've got a subsidy in that your legal education costs more to provide you than you are paying for it. This subsidy is not taxed.

**48.** Higgins v. Commissioner, 312 U.S. 212, 61 S.Ct. 475, 85 L.Ed. 783 (1941), reh'g denied 312 U.S. 714, 61 S.Ct. 728, 85 L.Ed. 1145 (1941).

**49.** S.Rep. No. 1631, 77th Cong., 2d Sess., reprinted in 1942–2 C.B. 504, 570.

generally interpreted in a parallel fashion insofar as the standards that must be met for the deduction to be allowed.[50]

The same standards generally apply as to whether an expense is ordinary and necessary; and the same standards apply to determine whether an expense will be disallowed because it is personal in nature, a capital expense, or violative of public policy.[51]

There are some differences between §§ 212 and 162, however. Importantly, since the deductions under § 212 are, by definition, not attributable to a "trade or business," they are only deductible above the line if they are attributable to property held for the production of rents or royalties.[52] *Hence as an extremely important structural point, most deductions under § 212 only come off "below the line," i.e., as deductions from adjusted gross income in arriving at taxable income. Moreover, those deductions under § 212 that come off "below the line" are also subject to the 2% floor on itemized deductions as described at ¶ 7.02.*[53]

As one example of how all this goes together, the expenses of renting a safe deposit box in order to store stock certificates—which yield dividend income and not rents or royalties—would be deductible under § 212 but could be taken only below the line.[54] Moreover, those expenses would only be deductible at all to the extent they, together with the other miscellaneous itemized deductions of the taxpayer, exceeded 2% of the taxpayer's adjusted gross income. Similarly, the expenses of other profit-seeking activities, or investment activities engaged in by the taxpayer, which do not rise to the level of being a trade or business, which produce income other than rents or royalties would only be deductible below the line and would run the gauntlet of the 2% floor (as discussed at ¶ 7.02).[55]

For expenses to be deductible under § 212(1) or 212(2), they must be reasonable in amount and must be reasonably related to the profit-seeking activity.[56] Expenses can be deductible under § 212 even though the profit-seeking activity is fruitless and the taxpayer is in fact running losses.[57]

A major case in this area is *Gilmore.*

**50.** See Bingham's Trust v. Commissioner, 325 U.S. 365, 65 S.Ct. 1232, 89 L.Ed. 1670 (1945).

**51.** See Regs. §§ 1.212–1(d), 1.212–1(f), 1.212–1(n).

**52.** See ¶ 6.01.

**53.** § 67.

**54.** ¶ 7.01(1).

**55.** Another difference between §§ 212 and 162 is that § 212 expenses can be deducted only by individuals; however, corporations can apparently deduct their expenses in such investment activities under § 162 without challenge. There are also limitations on § 212 expenses with respect to the computation of net operating loss carryovers under § 172, and use of taxpayer's dwelling unit for business purposes under § 280A (see ¶ 6.02(10).)

**56.** Reg. § 1.212–1(d); Lykes v. United States, 343 U.S. 118, 72 S.Ct. 585, 96 L.Ed. 791 (1952), reh'g denied 343 U.S. 937, 72 S.Ct. 768, 96 L.Ed. 1344 (1952) (legal expenses not deductible simply because taxpayer would use income-producing property to pay the judgment if the case were lost—compare the *Gilmore* case note 20, infra).

**57.** Regs. § 1.212–1(b).

## UNITED STATES v. GILMORE[58]

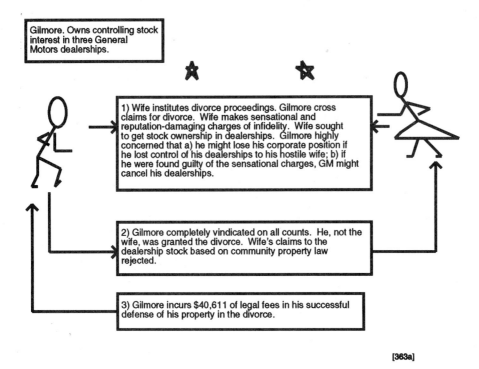

[363a]

*Question:* Are Gilmore's legal fees deductible, under § 212(1) and (2)?

*IRS argument:* The entire amount of fees is nondeductible as a personal or family expense under § 262.

*Taxpayer argument:* The expenses were necessary to protect his property held for the production of dividend and salary income from his wife's claims.

*Held:* (Harlan, J.) For IRS. The deductibility of § 212 deductions depends on the origin of the claim, which was here personal—the divorce. This limitation has been present on § 162 deductions and the same limit is followed for § 212. Characterization as business or personal depends on the origin not on the consequences of the litigation.

*Comment:* The legal fees were apparently larger because the taxpayer had to defend this property.

*Comment:* Surprisingly, the taxpayer in Gilmore was subsequently allowed to add the legal expenses of the divorce litigation to the basis of his property, a highly questionable treatment which is not consistent

**58.** 372 U.S. 39, 83 S.Ct. 623, 9 L.Ed.2d 570 (1963).

with the original *Gilmore* case.[59]

The Court said that to allow the deduction for the divorce litigation expenses means that if two taxpayers are each sued in an automobile accident the deductibility of their litigation costs would turn on the "mere" character of the assets each happened to possess. What is wrong with that? Deductibility of a particular expense always turns on the particular circumstances of a taxpayer. Notwithstanding that, the "origin of the claim" theory is regarded as a good rule in the field.[60]

But, the "origin of the claim" theory cannot be defended as logical or consistent with the "deep structure" of federal income taxation (see the beginning of this Chapter, ¶ 6.01). Rather, it should be clear that if substantial assets are held, they are going to on occasion have to be defended against the claims of estranged spouses and others. The cost of that defense is properly deductible as a cost of holding that property. To fail to allow the deduction is to fail to accurately reflect the true cost of holding the asset.

The "origin of the claim" doctrine does two things which are attractive from the Service's point of view: 1) provides a bright line distinction as to what is deductible and what is not; and 2) narrows the scope of the deduction.

Sections 212(1) and 212(2) allow a fairly broad range of deductions incident to profit-seeking activity, such as investment advisory fees, office rent, clerical help, and custodial fees with respect to such activity or with respect to income-producing property.[61] Brokerage fees, paid incident to the purchase or sale of stock, securities, real estate, or other property cannot be deducted but must instead be added to the cost of the property purchased or subtracted from the selling price of the property sold.[62]

Subsequent examples of litigation under § 212 include *Bowers v. Lumpkin*[63] in which the court held that legal expenses to defend title to property are not deductible under § 212. The case of *Estate of Baier v. Commissioner*[64] held that legal expenses incident to the disposition of a capital asset (a patent) cannot be deducted under § 212 but are capital expenses and are thus deducted from the amount realized on the sale of the asset. Thus in effect the legal fees are deducted against favorably taxed capital gains rather than less favorably taxed ordinary income. The rationale was that the origin of the claim lay in the dispute concerning the disposition of the patent.

---

**59.** See Gilmore v. United States, 245 F.Supp. 383 (N.D.Cal.1965). See also Nadiak v. Commissioner, 356 F.2d 911 (2d Cir. 1966) (applying the *Gilmore* origin-of-the-claim test to a deduction claimed under IRC § 162).

**60.** See also United States v. Patrick, 372 U.S. 53, 83 S.Ct. 618, 9 L.Ed.2d 580 (1963), a companion case to Gilmore in which the Court disallowed deduction of legal expenses of a husband in arriving at a property settlement incident to a divorce.

**61.** Reg. § 1.212–1(g).

**62.** Reg. § 1.263(a)–2(e).

**63.** 140 F.2d 927, cert. denied 322 U.S. 755, 64 S.Ct. 1266, 88 L.Ed. 1585 (1944).

**64.** 533 F.2d 117 (3d Cir.1976).

In *Surasky v. United States*[65] taxpayer was a shareholder of Montgomery Ward & Co. In connection with a proxy fight with respect to the company, taxpayer contributed $17,000 to a shareholders' committee to help wage the fight for one side. Taxpayer was not an officer, director or employee of Montgomery Ward and did not seek such a position, although he did believe he would make more money if the shareholders' committee drive was successful. The taxpayer eventually received substantial dividends on his stock and eventually sold his stock for a substantial capital gain. The Fifth Circuit reversed the lower court decision and held that the contributions were deductible even if they were not proximately related to the production of income. Thereafter the Service, in Revenue Ruling 64–236[66] ruled that it would follow the *Surasky* opinion except to the extent that the court indicates that deductible proxy fight expenditures need not be proximately related to the production of income.

*Myer J. Fleischman* [67] presented the question of the deductibility of legal expenses incurred in defending a wife's lawsuit to set aside their antenuptial contract. The taxpayer tried to distinguish his facts from those of *Gilmore* (see above) on the grounds that the legal expenses did not spring out of the marriage relationship but from rights excluded from that relationship. Nevertheless the court found the wife's rights here were also grounded in the marriage relationship. The court found the legal expenses were not deductible, relying on *Gilmore*.

In the interesting case of *William C. Horrmann*[68] the taxpayer bought and lived in a house and then put it up for sale, intending never to live in it again. The property was held out for sale for three years. Taxpayer sold the property in 1945 for $20,800. At the time he bought the property its value was $60,000 and at the time he abandoned it as a personal residence the value was $45,000. The question was whether taxpayer could take deductions for depreciation, maintenance and a capital loss with respect to the property. The court found that the taxpayer had attempted, albeit unsuccessfully, to rent the property during the time it was for sale. Because of the attempts to rent, taxpayer was entitled to take depreciation with respect to the property for the three years it was held for sale.

Similarly, with respect to maintenance expenses, the court found that the property was held for the production of income and therefore the maintenance expenses were deductible. As to the question of deduction of the long term capital loss, the court held that the standard was not whether the property was "held for the production of income," but rather whether holding the house was a "transaction entered into for profit." The court as to this issue held that the property had not been converted from personal use to a transaction entered into for profit and denied the deduction for the long-term capital loss.

**65.**  325 F.2d 191 (5th Cir.1963).      **67.**  45 T.C.439 (1966).

**66.**  1964–2 Cum.Bull. 64.      **68.**  17 T.C. 903 (1951).

*Lowry v. United States*[69] is a leading case also presenting the question of deductibility of sale of real estate used at one time as a residence. The case involved taxpayers, who ceased to use their summer house as residential property in 1967 and immediately offered it for sale without attempting to rent it. The question was whether they converted it into "income producing property," thereby entitling them to deduct the maintenance expenses incurred after it was put on the market and prior to its sale in 1973. Notwithstanding the taxpayer's failure to attempt to rent the property, the court ruled that it had been converted from personal to business use. Since the house was part of a cooperative community on Martha's Vineyard, it was not practical to try to rent it. Moreover, citing Reg. § 1.212–1(b) the court said that income for purposes of § 212 deductions is not confined to recurring or rental income but applies also to gains from dispositions of property.

Indeed, the court pointed out that under that regulation, maintenance expenses of property held for investment are deductible even if the property is not producing income, there is no likelihood of current income and there is no likelihood of gain upon sale of the property. Rather the determination of whether the prior residence has been converted depends on the taxpayer's purpose in light of all the facts and circumstances. Here the taxpayer was knowledgeable in real estate and sought to take advantage of the boom in recreational real estate prices.

### (4) Miscellaneous Business and Pleasure Travel Expenses: Rudolph

Often a taxpayer may be forced to attend a business meeting or convention in Acapulco, Las Vegas, or New Orleans (try the Jazzfest in April).

As the taxpayer packs his bags and prepares to undertake the burdens of this trip, he may wonder whether the Internal Revenue Service will be so rude as to question that the expenses of the trip may be fully deductible. This question relates to the third test set forth in the *Flowers* case,[70] namely, that the expense must be incurred in pursuit of the taxpayer's business. Obviously in this situation, there is no question of where the taxpayer's home is or that the taxpayer is away from home. But the fact that business and pleasure may very well be combined on the same trip raises some of the more nettlesome questions in the tax law.

A leading case in this area is *Rudolph*.

**69.**   384 F.Supp. 257 (D.N.H.1974).

**70.**   See ¶ 6.02(3).

## RUDOLPH v. UNITED STATES[71]

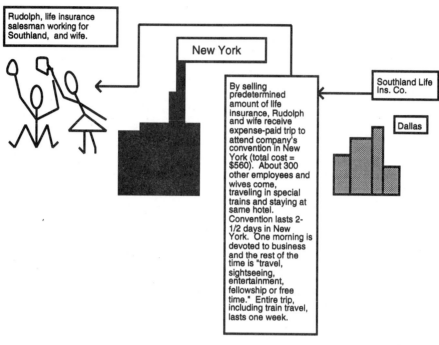

[367a]

*Question:* Was the cost of the trip income to Rudolph as a bonus under § 61? If it was income, were the expenses deductible to Rudolph as a business expense under § 162(a)(2)?

*Taxpayer's argument:* He was a trapped organization man compelled to attend conventions.

*Held:* Dismissed the writ of certiorari as improvidently granted, thereby letting the lower court findings stand. These findings were that the dominant purpose of the trip was for the company to afford a pleasure trip in the nature of a bonus. Thus it was income. From Rudolph's point of view it was a pleasure trip. Thus the expenses were not deductible.

*Dissent* (Douglas, J., joined by Black, J.): Other professionals are able to attend conventions without attracting tax. Why single out insurance agents?

*Comment:* Note the methodology: First the question of income and then the question of deduction.

*Comment:* One answer to Douglas is that this "convention" was held out as a reward for selling a certain amount of life insurance. Neverthe-

**71.** 370 U.S. 269, 82 S.Ct. 1277, 8 L.Ed.2d 484 (1962), reh'g denied 371 U.S. 854, 83 S.Ct. 15, 9 L.Ed.2d 93 (1962).

less, there is no doubt conventions present one of the toughest problems around for untangling business and pleasure.

*Rudolph* is still good law on the income side of mixed business and pleasure travel. For purposes of ascertaining deduction, the rules are now much more complex. For purposes of deductibility, the expenses of such trips are divided into two parts: the expense of traveling to and from the destination; and the expenses of lodging, meals, etc. incurred at the destination. With respect to the expenses for traveling to and from the destination, the Regulations provide an all or nothing approach. The expenses of traveling to and from the destination are fully deductible if the trip is "related primarily" to the taxpayer's trade or business, and the expenses are not deductible at all if the trip is "primarily personal in nature." These determinations are made by reference to time spent on business or pleasure.[72]

As to the second type of expenses—the expenses incurred at the destination—the approach is to allocate those expenses. The expenses allocable to business activities while at the destination are deductible; the expenses allocable to personal activities while at the destination are not deductible. This allocation approach is followed regardless of whether the expenses of getting to and from the destination were deductible or not.[73]

Since foreign travel for business purposes has been regarded by Congress with a particularly jaundiced eye, such travel must also meet the tests of § 274(c). § 274(c) disallows deductions for that portion of the travel which is not allocable to the taxpayer's trade or business or profit-seeking activity.

Section 274(c) bites, therefore, in particular as to the travel to and from the destination. It is already true, as discussed above, that expenses incurred at the destination are only deductible to the extent they are allocable to business activities. However, where the business travel is to a foreign destination, to the extent some of the taxpayer's time at the foreign destination is spent on personal activities, some portion of the expenses for traveling to and from the destination will be disallowed by virtue of § 274(c).[74] This restriction of § 274(c) on travel to and from a foreign destination does not apply if the travel does not exceed one week, or if the taxpayer spends less than 25 percent of his total time on non-business activities.

Expenses of foreign conventions (defined as conventions held outside of the U.S. and its possessions, Canada, and Mexico) are deductible only if it is "as reasonable" for the meeting to be held outside this North American area as within it.[75]

The expenses of a spouse, dependent, or other individual accompanying the taxpayer is not on a business trip are only deductible if the

**72.** Reg. § 1.162–2(b)(1) and (2).

**73.** Id. See also Cannon, 24 T.C.M. 1074 (1965).

**74.** § 274(c)(2); Reg. § 1.274–4(f)(5), and see Reg. § 1.274–4(g) for further qualifications.

**75.** § 274(h), as amended by HR 5973, which repealed restrictive rules enacted in 1976 regarding subsistence, expense limitations, air fare limitations, and other special reporting requirements. Expenses of a convention on a cruise ship are deductible up to $2000 per person per year, only if the cruise ship is registered in the U.S. and all ports of call are in the U.S., Highway Revenue Act, 1/6/83.

spouse, dependent or other individual is an employee of the person or business paying the expenses, the travel of the spouse, dependent, or other individual is for a bona fide business purpose and such expenses would otherwise be deductible by the spouse, dependent, or other individual.[76]

Business travel expenses must meet the substantiation requirements of § 274(d) discussed infra.

### (5) Entertainment, Amusement and Recreation Expenses: Sutter; Cohan; Sanitary Farms

Once a taxpayer has returned home from an invigorating business trip to the Bahamas, which he hopes will be deductible, he may choose to entertain some business associates and their wives with dinner and an evening at the theater, which he would also like to charge off on his tax return. The expenses of entertaining business associates has presented one of the most difficult problems in the tax law. Obviously it is very difficult to separate the pleasure component from the business component where a taxpayer pays the bill for actual or potential customers, or other business associates at dinner, the theater, or other recreational activities.

How should we handle this? If taxpayer is at home and just goes out to dinner alone, he cannot deduct the cost of that dinner. But if he takes a client out for dinner, then should he be able to deduct not only the client's dinner but also his own? Isn't that going too far? He would have had to eat dinner in any case. Isn't the theoretically proper approach to the taxpayer's own dinner to allow him to deduct it only to the extent it exceeds what he would have otherwise paid for dinner?

The Service took that position originally. In 1921 the Service promulgated a regulation allowing a deduction for the cost of meals and lodging away from home. That deduction was limited to the extent the cost exceeded "any expenditure ordinarily required for such purposes when at home."[77]

This is the logical approach but it proved difficult to administer. Thus to simplify matters the Treasury asked Congress in 1921 to allow a deduction for the entire amount of such meals and lodging expenses.[78] Congress responded in 1921 with language[79] that later became § 162(a)(2). This historical perspective is helpful to see why the rules in this area seem to be too generous.

---

**76.** § 274(m)(3).

See Postlewaite, "Deduction of Expenses for Conventions and Educational Seminars," 61 Minn.L.Rev. 253 (1977); Shaddock, "The Tax Consequences of a Spouse's Convention Expenses," 29 Baylor Law Review 585 (1977).

**77.** Treas. Reg. 45 (1920 ed.), Art. 292, 4 Cum. Bull. 209 (1921).

**78.** Statement of Dr. T.S. Adams, Tax Adviser, Treasury Department, in Hearings on H.R. 8245 before the Senate Committee on Finance, 67th Cong., 1st Sess., at 50, 234–235 (1921).

**79.** § 214(a)(1) of the Revenue Act of 1921, c. 136, 42 Stat. 239.

If this is true for food, then what about Knicks games, the theater, The Final Four, country clubs and nightclubs? The same issue is presented there. If the taxpayer takes a client to such events on business, can the taxpayer deduct not only the client's expenses but his own? This problem was presented in the well-known case of *Sutter*.

## SUTTER v. COMMISSIONER[80]

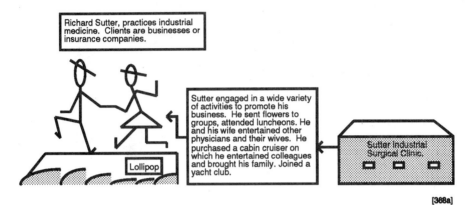

Richard Sutter, practices industrial medicine. Clients are businesses or insurance companies.

Sutter engaged in a wide variety of activities to promote his business. He sent flowers to groups, attended luncheons. He and his wife entertained other physicians and their wives. He purchased a cabin cruiser on which he entertained colleagues and brought his family. Joined a yacht club.

Lollipop

Sutter Industrial Surgical Clinic.

[368a]

*Question:* Can Sutter deduct his promotion and entertainment expenses, including maintenance and depreciation on his cruiser, under § 162 as ordinary and necessary business expenses?

*Held:* Giving the flowers is not deductible at all. As to luncheons, entertaining and maintenance and depreciation on cruiser, expenses are only deductible for business. Costs of entertaining taxpayer and/or his family are not deductible even in business setting unless they are different from or in excess of what taxpayer would have incurred for his own personal use. Burden of proof on this matter is on taxpayer, citing *Cohan*, see below.

*Comment:* This imposes the same rule on entertainment expenses that the Service originally attempted to impose in the meals and lodging area, as discussed above.

The same administrative difficulties that attended the Service's original rule in the meals and lodging area has caused the Service to by and large ignore the *Sutter* rule. Thus the Service has generally allowed taxpayers to deduct their own expenses in full incurred in a business setting.[81]

Another major theme in the travel and entertainment area has been

---

**80.** 21 T.C. 170 (1953).

**81.** Contra *Moss v. Commissioner*, 758 F.2d 211 (7th Cir.1985), cert. denied 474 U.S. 979, 106 S.Ct. 382, 88 L.Ed.2d 335 (1985) (pig theory of lawyer trying to deduct all his lunch expenses, including those of lunches with associates in his own firm because he thought all his lunches were in a business setting. Held: disallowed.)

the irksome problem of keeping records. Some taxpayers solve the problem by not keeping any, as illustrated in the major case of *Cohan*.

## COHAN v. COMMISSIONER[82]

New York

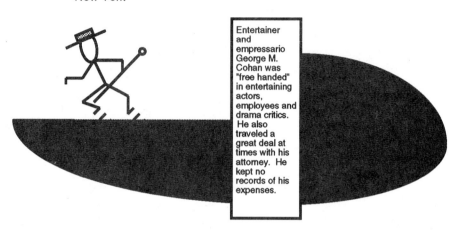

Entertainer and empressario George M. Cohan was "free handed" in entertaining actors, employees and drama critics. He also traveled a great deal at times with his attorney. He kept no records of his expenses.

[369a]

*Question:* Given that Cohan had some real travel and entertainment expenses, can he deduct any of them given that he did not keep records.

*Held:* Reversed Board of Tax Appeals holding that in the absence of records Cohan can deduct nothing. Remanded to BTA holding that "absolute certainty in these matters is usually not possible ... the Board should make as close an approximation as it can ..." With the further proviso that the Board can estimate the amounts conservatively against the taxpayer given that the inexactitude is of the taxpayer's own making.

*Comment:* The opinion by Learned Hand noted that the taxpayer "naively" admitted to entertaining drama critics.

*Comment:* This case, decided in 1930, over time led up to game-playing by taxpayers. Taxpayers without records would give high estimates of their business expenses, expecting to be cut down by the Service, which began to take this factor into account in cutting back the estimates. Since most returns were not audited at all, most of these inflated estimates went through unchallenged. This is an example of how the unrelenting pressure of taxpayers to lower their tax bill on an annual basis can degrade rules that are not designed to stand up to that pressure.

Those who cry for simplification in the tax system rarely address the problem of substantiating travel and entertainment expenses in the

**82.**   39 F.2d 540 (2d Cir.1930).

business setting. I won't take any "back of the envelope" proposal seriously unless it deals with this issue.

The net result of all these developments in the 1920's and 30's was that things were kind-of wide open in this area. As long as there was a colorable case that the meals or travel and entertainment activities had to do with "business," not only were the client's expenses deductible but so were the taxpayer's. This wide open attitude reached its apotheosis in the famous case of *Sanitary Farms Dairy.*

## SANITARY FARMS DAIRY, INC. v. COMMISSIONER[83]

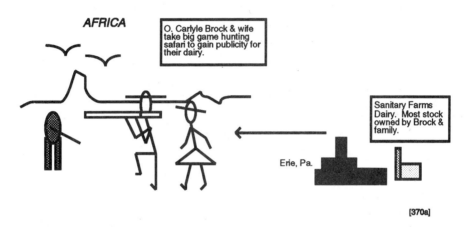

*Question:* Are the expenses of a big-game hunting African safari undertaken by the controlling shareholder deductible to an Erie, PA dairy as advertising expenses?

*Held:* Yes.

*Comment:* You've got to be kidding!

*Comment:* The court in dicta said "there is a little bit of the hunter in all of us."

*Comment:* Not only was the cost of the trip deductible to the dairy but it was not income to Brock (an avid big-game hunter) and his wife. Just a sideline benefit of his job. You know how it goes in the dairy business. Just scuffle, scuffle, scuffle.

*Comment:* It was cases like this that inspired comedian Mel Brooks to style himself as a tax expert who announced he had cut his own tax bill from $90,000 to $1.40 by deducting World War II under travel expenses.

After cases like *Sanitary Farms,* it became apparent that stricter

---

**83.**  25 T.C. 463 (1955).

rules were necessary to qualify for these business deductions. The business nexus of such activities should be much more clear.

Theoretically, the matter should have been dealt with under § 162, or § 212 where appropriate, in simply determining whether the particular expense was, under the circumstances, an ordinary and necessary business expense. However, in the early 1960s, the probably accurate public impression was that there were widespread abuses in the area of deductibility of business entertainment.[84] As a result, Congress enacted § 274(a), applying strict standards to business-oriented entertainment, amusement and recreation. In addition, rules for the substantiation of such expenses were required by new § 274(d), thus overruling *Cohan*. Consequently, expenses for business-oriented entertainment, amusement, and recreation must meet the usual standards of § 162 or 212, and must further run the gauntlet of potential disallowance under § 274(a) as well as be substantiated by § 274(d).

§ 274 deploys a set of rules of stupifying complexity. It is set forth in the accompanying flow-chart. The major points of the chart are discussed further in the text.

---

**84.** See Staff of House Ways and Means Comm., 90th Cong., 1st Sess., Legis- lative History of the Revenue Act of 1962, Pt. 1.

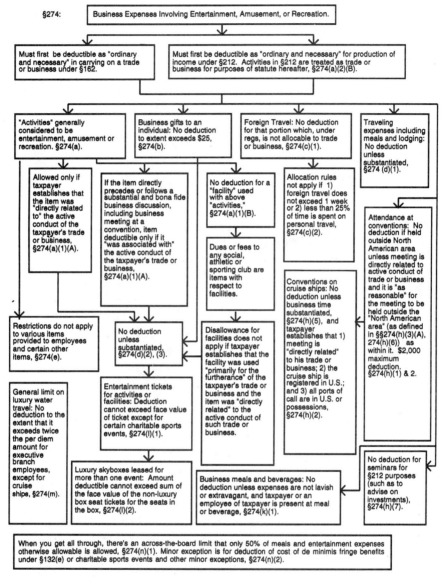

[371a]

There will be a quiz on this at noon.

The flow-chart depicts what can only be described as a nightmarish statutory scheme. Note, for example, that for a taxpayer to be able to deduct a luxury skybox, he must undergo six levels of statutory analysis. (I'd rather just stay home and watch on TV).

And the Regs. do what is known in football as "pile on." The Regs. under § 274 reach a new high of opacity in defining the various terms of art in the statute.

As the flow-chart indicates, § 274(a) disallows deductions with respect to activities which are of a type generally considered to constitute entertainment, amusement, or recreation, unless the taxpayer establishes that the item was directly related to—or, in the case of an item directly preceding or following a substantial and bona fide business discussion, that the item was associated with—the active conduct of a taxpayer's trade or business. The two major tests here are that the entertainment, etc. item must be "directly related" to the active conduct of the taxpayer's trade or business, or that the entertainment, etc. activity must be "associated with" the active conduct of the taxpayer's trade or business, if the item directly precedes or follows a substantial and bona fide business discussion.[85] The Regulations, setting a new standard in turgidity, go on to explain the "directly related to" and the "associated with" tests, elaborate on various other terms in § 274(a), as well as give a few examples.[86] As a rough generalization, it could be said that the Regulations apply strict standards in the explanation of the rules of § 274(a).

Expenses for entertainment, amusement, and recreational facilities—such as country clubs, sporting lodges, and other entertainment clubs—are subject to severe limitations on deductibility. The general rule is that no deduction is allowed with respect to a facility used in connection with entertainment, amusement or recreation, even though such deduction would qualify as an ordinary and necessary business expense under § 162.[87] This disallowance of expenses with respect to entertainment, etc. facilities applies to dues or fees to any social, athletic or sporting club.[88] Clubs operated solely to furnish lunches in a business setting are exempted from this disallowance.[89] And in a significant further exception, if the taxpayer establishes that in the case of a club, the facility was used primarily for the "furtherance of the taxpayer's trade or business" and that the amount paid was "directly related" to the active conduct of such trade or business, the disallowance will not apply.[90]

A number of relatively minor business-oriented entertainment expenses are exempted from these disallowance rules, including business meals, food and beverages for employees, expenses for goods, services, facilities and recreation for employees (under certain conditions), expenses for business meetings, and certain other expenses.[91]

As with expenses for travel, expenses for entertainment, amusement, and recreation which survive the gauntlet of § 274(a) can still

---

85. Expenses incurred under § 212 are treated as incurred under § 162 for the purposes of § 274,.§ 274(a)(2)(B).

86. Reg. § 1.274–2(c), (d), (e). Reg. § 1.274–2(b)(1) defines entertainment, amusement or recreation.

87. § 274(a)(1)(B).

88. § 274(a)(2)(A).

89. Reg. § 1.274–2(e)(3)(ii).

90. § 274(a)(2)(C).

91. § 274(e). Reg. § 1.274–2(f)(2).

only be deducted if they are substantiated in accordance with the requirements of § 274(d), discussed infra.

### (6) Limits on Deductibility of Business Meals: Sutter Lives

The tax legislation of 1986 and 1993 enacted rules to provide restrictions on the deductibility of business meals. As indicated in the flow-chart a few pages earlier, the rules are set forth under § 274(k). Once the deductible amounts are established under § 274(k), only 50% of them may actually be deducted, under § 274(n). Under the § 274(k)(1) rules no deduction is allowed for the expense of any food or beverage unless (A) the expense is not lavish or extravagant under the circumstances, and (B) the taxpayer (or an employee of the taxpayer) is present at the furnishing of such food or beverages. Under § 274(k)(2) these restrictions do not apply if the general restrictive rules of § 274(a) do not apply to the expense by reason of § 274(e)(2) (taxpayer treating the expenses as compensation for withholding purposes), (3) (reimbursed expenses), (4) (recreational expenses for employees other than highly compensated employees), (7) (items made available to the public), (8) (entertainment sold to customers), or (9) (expenses includible in income of persons who are not employees).

As also indicated in the flow-chart above, there is a broad backstop rule providing that after all the tests and computations of other entertainment, amusement and recreation rules, in any event only 50% of the established deduction is allowed in many cases. This new rule has been alluded to several times above.

In particular, under § 274(n)(1) only 50% of deductions otherwise allowed are allowed for any expense for food or beverages and any activity which is of a type generally considered to constitute entertainment, amusement, or recreation, or with respect to a facility used in connection with such activity.

This 50% restriction does not apply to certain relatively minor expenses, under § 274(n)(2). If the employee is reimbursed for business meals, then he is not subject to these rules. Rather the employer would be. The employer can also deduct in full the cost of food qualifying as a de minimis employee fringe benefit. Thus, little lunches, dinners, and parties for employees are deductible in full by the employer.

This general disallowance of 20% of meal and entertainment expenses may be seen as a limited reincarnation of the *Sutter* rule. In the *Sutter* case, discussed above at ¶ 6.02(5), the court allowed deduction of the taxpayer's own entertainment expenses in the business setting only to the extent the expenses exceed what the taxpayer would have paid for himself had business not been involved. Suggesting the taxpayer would have spent only 20% of the expenses on himself had business not been involved is a rather generous approach. But nevertheless, in watered-down form, *Sutter* lives.

### (7) The Substantiation Requirement for Travel, Entertainment, and Business Gifts

In the leading case of *Cohan*[92], discussed also above at ¶ 6.02(5), performer and producer, George M. Cohan spent substantial amounts of money on business travel and business entertainment but had no records whatsoever to substantiate his expenditures. The Service admitted that Cohan had spent significant sums in this fashion but attempted to disallow the deductions because of the lack of any substantiation. Judge Learned Hand, speaking for the Second Circuit, held that Cohan under these circumstances was entitled to some deduction which, in the absence of documentation, would have to be estimated. The Court seemed to concede that the estimate could be relatively small in comparison to what Cohan might have actually spent, but it was wrong, in the Court's view, to disallow all expenses because of the lack of substantiation.

This relatively attractive *Cohan* rule continues to hold sway for deductions under § 162. However, with respect to travel, entertainment, and business gift expenses, the *Cohan* rule has been superseded by the stringent substantiation requirements of § 274(d).

The basic rule of § 274(d) is that no deduction will be allowed for any traveling, entertainment, amusement, or recreation expense or any expense for business gifts unless the taxpayer can substantiate these expenses.[93]

The Regulations describe in great detail what is required to meet the substantiation standard of § 274(d). Substantiating an item by adequate records means the taxpayer must maintain an account book, diary, statement of expense or similar record in which each element of an expenditure is recorded at or near the time of the expenditure and in addition provide documentary evidence—such as receipts, bills, or similar evidence. Taken together, the account book and the documentary evidence will meet the requirement of providing "adequate records" for purposes of § 274(d).[94]

Exempted from the substantiation requirements are expenses relating to food and beverages for employees, certain expenses treated as compensation, certain items available to the public,[95] items relating to entertainment sold to customers, and items relating to recreational expenses for employees.[96]

**92.** Cohan v. Commissioner, 39 F.2d 540 (2d Cir.1930). Compare Raytheon Production Corp. v. Commissioner, 144 F.2d 110 (1st Cir.1944), cert. denied 323 U.S. 779, 65 S.Ct. 192, 89 L.Ed. 622 (1944), holding that a damage award attributable to destruction of good will was taxable in full, inasmuch as the taxpayer failed to prove the cost of its good will. For discussion of damage awards, see ¶ 3.11.

**93.** See also Reg. § 1.274–5(a).

**94.** Reg. § 1.274–5(c)(2). See Dowell v. United States, 522 F.2d 708 (5th Cir.1975), cert. denied, 426 U.S. 920, 96 S.Ct. 2626, 49 L.Ed.2d 374 (1976) (expenditures must be substantiated individually). Reg. § 1.274–5(c)(3).

**95.** § 274(e)(1)–(10), also providing certain other exceptions.

**96.** Reg. § 1.274–5(c)(7). Also exempted from the substantiation and other rules of § 274 are expenses which are deductible in any event without regard to the relation-

Where an employee incurs expenses for the benefit of his employer and is reimbursed for them, the employee may omit both the expenses and the reimbursement from his tax return, if he makes an adequate accounting of the expenditures to the employer.[97] This shifts the requirement to substantiate the travel and entertainment, etc. expenses under § 274(d) to the employer.

The Service is empowered to promulgate rules regarding reimbursement arrangements, per diem allowances and mileage allowances which can take the place of requiring the employee to meet the substantiation standards of § 274(d), and the accounting requirement in the case of employees under reimbursement arrangements.[98]

Thus, in sum, entertainment expenses must meet the requirements of § 162 (the business expense); then meet the standards of § 274(a); and finally be adequately substantiated.

### (8) Moving Expenses

Moving expenses incident to a taxpayer being transferred to a new job assignment present a difficult theoretical question in that both personal and business elements are present to a high degree. Obviously, the taxpayer could not pursue his job if he did not move to the new job location. At the same time, it may be argued that moving the taxpayer's family and personal effects is "inherently personal" and therefore non-deductible.[99] Thus moving expenses present much the same theoretical problems that travel and entertainment expenses present: they have a strong business and personal component. As we have seen, supra, the matter was resolved in the case of entertainment expenses by applying the very stringent standards of § 274(a), coupled with the substantiation requirements of § 274(d). Thus does the Code try to walk the fine line between allowing reasonable and legitimate business entertainment expenses and disallowing personal expenses for entertainment. In the moving expenses area, the approach is to allow some of the expenses in full, and impose some dollar limitations on certain other expenses incident to the taxpayer's moving to a new job location.[1]

To qualify for any deduction at all for moving expenses under § 217, the moving expenses must be incurred in connection with the commencement of work by the taxpayer as an employee or as a self-employed individual at a new principal place of work.[2] The term "commencement of work" includes the beginning of work by the taxpayer as an employee

---

ship to the taxpayer's business, such as interest, property taxes, and casualty losses. See Reg. § 1.274–6.

**97.** Reg. § 1.274–5(e)(4); Reg. § 1.274–5(e)(2)(i). If the reimbursement exceeds the expenses, the employee must include the difference in his income, Reg. § 1.274–5(e)(2)(ii). See also Lewis v. Commissioner, 560 F.2d 973 (9th Cir.1977) (excessive allocation to personal use under reimbursement agreement).

**98.** Reg. § 1.274–5(f).

**99.** See the discussion of the personal expense limitation on deductions, ¶ 6.03.

**1.** § 217. See also § 82, which provides that amounts the taxpayer receives as reimbursement for moving expenses will be included in income, regardless of the extent to which the taxpayer's moving expenses are deductible under § 217.

**2.** § 217(a).

or as a self-employed individual for the first time or after a substantial period of unemployment or part-time employment; the beginning of work by a taxpayer for a different employer or, in the case of a self-employed individual, in a new trade or business; or the beginning of work by a taxpayer for the same employer in the same business at a new location.[3] To qualify as being in connection with the commencement of work, the move must bear a "reasonable proximity both in time and place to such commencement," and in general the expenses have to be incurred within one year of the date of the commencement of the work.[4]

The new principal place of work must be at least fifty miles farther from the former residence than was the former principal place of work.[5] The taxpayer must be a full-time employee for at least thirty-nine weeks during the twelve month period immediately following his arrival in the general location of his new principal place of work.[6]

"Moving expenses" means, for purposes of the § 217 deduction: (A) moving household goods and personal effects from the former residence to the new residence; (B) traveling (including meals and lodging) from the former residence to the new residence; (C) traveling (including meals and lodging) after obtaining employment, from the former residence to the general location of the new principal place of work and return, for the principal purpose of searching for a new residence, (D) meals and lodging while occupying temporary quarters in the general location of the new place of work during any period of thirty consecutive days after obtaining employment, (E) expenses incident to the sale of the taxpayers old residence and the purchase of the taxpayer's new residence.[7]

Moving expenses (A) and (B) may be deducted in full. Expenses (C) and (D) may not exceed together $1,500. Expenses (E) (relating to residence sale and purchase expenses) may not be deducted in an amount greater than $3,000 less the amount deducted for expenses (C) and (D).[8]

A taxpayer may choose, therefore, whether to take expenses (C), (D), or (E) against the $3,000 limit. To the extent that the expenses (E) are not deducted because of this dollar limit, they are reflected in the computations relating to the taxpayer's sale of his old residence and

---

**3.** Reg. § 1.217–2(a)(3).

**4.** Id.

**5.** § 217(c), also providing that if the taxpayer had no former principal place of work, the place of work must be at least fifty miles from his former residence.

**6.** An alternative test that may be met here is that during the twenty-four month period immediately following the taxpayer's arrival at the general location of his new principal place of work, he is a full-time employee or performs services as a self-employed individual on a full-time basis in the new location for at least seventy-eight weeks, of which at least thirty-nine are during the first twelve months following his

arrival in the new location. § 217(c)(2). These tests are waived if the taxpayer is unable to satisfy them by reason of death, disability, involuntary separation (other than for willful misconduct) from the service of the employer, and certain other conditions.

**7.** § 217(b); Reg. § 1.217–2(b), providing further definition and examples, and requiring that in addition to the dollar limits discussed below, "moving expenses" must also meet the general requirement of being reasonable.

**8.** § 217(b)(3).

purchase of his new residence. Under the usual rules for such expenses, selling expenses of the old residence are deducted from the amount realized, thus reducing any capital gain the taxpayer may have on the sale of the old residence; purchase expenses of the new residence are added to the basis of the new residence and will, therefore, reduce any gain the taxpayer may have on the subsequent sale of the residence.[9] Therefore, taxpayers are generally well advised to take the expenses (C) and (D) to the full extent possible (i.e., up to the sublimit of $1,500), since they will not be allowed anywhere else. Note, however, that often residence sale and purchase expenses will not have an impact on the taxpayer's tax liability immediately if the taxpayer recognizes no gain on the sale of his old residence because of the operation of § 1034.[10]

### (9) Activities Not Engaged in for Profit

One of the areas viewed with the greatest suspicion by the tax law is where the taxpayer piles up large deductions while enjoying himself excessively. While no one would question the deductibility of expenses incurred in the running of a dry cleaning business, grocery store, or investing in stocks and bonds—no matter how much the taxpayer may enjoy these business activities—there is apparently something inherently suspect about a farm to which the taxpayer repairs on weekends or the raising of horses for breeding or racing purposes, or any other activity which appears to partake of the sweet life.

From early in its history, the tax law has purported to be able to differentiate between business and profit-seeking activities on the one hand and activities not entered into for profit on the other, with a concomitant disallowance of losses generated by the latter activities.[11] Taxpayers' success in having deductions arising out of these fun-type activities allowed ultimately led Congress to enact § 183, which disallows deductions under certain conditions which are attributable to an "activity not engaged in for profit."

The particular limiting rules of § 183 are triggered when the taxpayer engages in an "activity not engaged in for profit." Thus a great deal turns on the definition of that phrase. The Code and Regulations set forth a large number of factors that are to be used in arriving at a conclusion as to whether an activity is engaged in for profit or not. Briefly stated, these factors are, first that the activity should be one other than one for which deductions are allowed under § 162 or 212. In addition, also important are the manner in which the taxpayer carries on the activity, the expertise of the taxpayer or his advisers, the time and effort expended by the taxpayer in carrying on the activity, the expecta-

---

9. See ¶ 4.03. In no event, however, may a taxpayer secure a double benefit by taking residence sale and purchase expenses both under § 217 and reflecting them in his residence sale and purchase computations. To the extent that residence sale and purchase computations are taken under § 217, they may not be reflected in the residence sale and purchase computations. § 217(e).

10. See ¶ 4.05(4).

11. See e.g. Thacher v. Lowe, 288 Fed. 994 (S.D.N.Y.1922).

tion that assets used in the activity may appreciate in value, the success of the taxpayer in carrying on similar or dissimilar activities, the taxpayer's history of income or losses with respect to the activity, the amount of occasional profits, if any, which are earned, the financial status of the taxpayer, and the elements of personal pleasure or recreation involved in the activity.[12] In addition to these factors, the Regulations also inform that "the determination whether an activity is engaged in for profit is to be made by reference to objective standards, taking into account all of the facts and circumstances of each case."[13]

This melange of factors and considerations is possibly illuminated by several examples in the Regulations, which include deeming an inherited farm, writing and publishing philosophical pamphlets, dog and horse breeding, as "activities not engaged in for profit" when the taxpayer had other sources of substantial income.[14] On the other hand, an inherited farm operated by a taxpayer in a fairly serious fashion, an independent oil and gas wildcat driller, and a chemist with his own workshop were found by the Regulations, under the particular facts set forth, to be "activities engaged in for profit" notwithstanding that significant losses were incurred over the years.[15] The bottom line is that where the activity is "recreational," as that term is usually defined—i.e., farming or horse and dog racing, etc.—and the losses from the activity are taken against taxpayer's substantial other income, the taxpayer is very likely to be deemed to have an "activity not engaged in for profit."[16]

Once it is established that a taxpayer is indeed involved in an "activity not engaged in for profit," the rules specifying the amount and type of deductions allowed are clear. Potential deductions are divided into three categories:[17] (1) deductions that are allowable without regard to whether or not the activity is engaged in for profit—i.e., mortgage interest, property taxes; (2) deductions that would be allowable if the activity were engaged in for profit but which do not result in adjustments to the basis of the property—i.e., ordinary and necessary business expenses, under § 162 or 212; (3) deductions that would be allowed if the activity were engaged in for profit but which do result in an adjustment

---

**12.** § 183(c); Reg. § 1.183–2(b). Reg. § 1.183–2(a).

**13.** Reg. § 1.183–2(a).

**14.** Reg. § 1.183–2(c) Examples (1)–(3). See as a significant case in this area Brannen, 78 T.C. 471 (1982), judgment aff'd 722 F.2d 695 (11th Cir.1984) (limited partnership tax shelter investment in a "spaghetti western" movie found to be not engaged in for profit at the partnership level and hence individual partners' deductions barred. See ¶ 8.02).

**15.** Reg. § 1.183–2(c) Examples (4)–(6). Cf. Dreicer v. Commissioner, 665 F.2d 1292 (D.C.Cir.1981), on remand 78 T.C. 642 (1982) (even though taxpayer may believe likelihood of profit is small, as long as tax-

payer has intent to make profit, the activity is not within § 183).

**16.** See Reg. § 1.183–2(b)(8). Cf. Gertrude Gorod, 42 T.C.M. 1569 (1981) (ten years of fruitless effort to rent lower level of a duplex in run-down area of Malden, Mass. did not constitute an activity not engaged in for profit, and hence maintenance and depreciation deductions could be taken); Miles, 45 T.C.M. 1333 (1983) (ineptly run chicken farm, where taxpayer failed to heat henhouse during winter and allowed chickens to roam freely over 45 acres so that he could not find their eggs (characterized by the court as "open-range chicken farming"), was an activity not entered into for profit.)

**17.** 183(b); Reg. § 1.183–1(b)(1).

to the basis of the property—primarily the deduction for depreciation or cost recovery.[18]

The treatment of these deductions is that with respect to "activities not engaged in for profit," deductions in category one will always be allowed in full. Deductions in category two will only be allowed to the extent the gross income from the activity exceeds the deductions in category one attributable to the activity not engaged in for profit. The deductions in category three will only be allowed to the extent that the gross income from the activity not engaged in for profit exceeds the deductions in category one and category two.[19]

As an example, consider the case of a horse farm owned by an executive who has $100,000 of income from salary. He tends his horse farm generally on weekends and enjoys himself. Members of his family help out. The horse farm is an activity "not engaged in for profit." The horse farm generates $25,000 of gross income; there are mortgage interest and property taxes attributable to the horse farm property of $11,000; supplies and maintenance are $13,000; and depreciation or cost recovery on buildings and equipment of the horse farm is $5,000. The computation of the amount of these deductions that will be allowed is illustrated by Table 6–1.

If more than one piece of property is eligible for the depreciation deduction, the Regulations prescribe rules for allocating the depreciation deduction and appropriate basis adjustment.[20]

## Table 6–1

Limitations on Deductions of Activity Not Engaged in for Profit

| | | |
|---|---|---|
| 1. | Gross income from horse farm | $25,000 |
| 2. | Level one deductions, mortgage interest, and property taxes (allowed without limit) | 11,000 |
| 3. | Gross income less level one deductions | $14,000 |
| 4. | Level two deductions, supplies and maintenance (do not affect basis) | 13,000 |
| 5. | Gross income less level one and two deductions (line three less line 4) | $1,000 |
| 6. | Depreciation on buildings and equipment | 5,000 |
| 7. | Amount of depreciation allowed as a deduction (line 6 up to limit of line 5) | $1,000 |
| 8. | Total deductions allowed with respect to horse farm (lines 2 + 4 + 7) | $25,000 |

---

**18.** See ¶6.02(12). Also allowed here would be the deduction for casualty losses to business property (which is not subject to the 10% of adjusted gross income limit, see ¶7.01(5)).

**19.** Reg. § 1.183–1(b).

**20.** Regs. § 1.183–1(b)(2), 1.183–1(b)(3).

The taxpayer is assisted by a presumption that if he turns a profit from the activity for three or more of the taxable years in a period of five consecutive taxable years ending with the taxable year in question, the activity will be presumed to be an activity engaged in for profit. In computing whether a profit has been turned, the activity is treated as though it were an activity entered into for profit, so that all appropriate deductions are taken account of in full.[21] Where the activity consists in major part of the breeding, training, showing or racing of horses, the taxpayer need only show a profit in two out of a period of seven consecutive taxable years in order to get the advantage of the presumption.[22]

This presumption suggests that taxpayers may be able to do a little planning by way of bunching up income in order to turn a perhaps small profit in several years of the five or seven year measuring period. Thus, a few judicious sales of property might be enough to tip the scales in the taxpayer's favor in two or three years out of the appropriate measuring period. When contemplating such planning, however, it should be borne in mind that the presumption here is not conclusive; the Treasury is still empowered to determine that, notwithstanding that a profit has been turned in the qualifying number of years of the five-or seven-year period, the activity is still an activity not engaged in for profit.[23] If the taxpayer were to run huge losses in the activity in two years and very small profits in the activity in three years, the Treasury may very well be able to rebut the presumption and impose the § 183 limitations upon the activity.[24]

Taxpayers hoping to benefit from the presumption may elect to stay a determination of whether the presumption applies and report their activities as though they were entered into for profit.[25] If over the five or seven years that the taxpayer so reports his activity the presumption does not come into effect or is rebutted, the statutory period for the assessment of any deficiency attributable to treating the activity as one not engaged in for profit is extended to cover the years in question.[26]

To the extent that deductions are allowed under § 183, they will be allowed below the line as itemized deductions, since nowhere in § 62 are deductions arising from an activity not engaged in for profit mentioned,

---

**21.** § 183(d); Reg. § 1.183–1(c)(1). The net operating loss deduction of § 172 is not taken into account in computing whether a profit has been turned for the purposes of this presumption.

**22.** § 183(d), last sentence.

**23.** § 183(d).

**24.** Faulconer, 45 T.C.M. 1084 (1983), judgment rev'd 748 F.2d 890 (4th Cir.1984) (small profits in profit years and large losses in loss years plus other surrounding facts allowed IRS to overcome presumption for

Buck Island and Westover Farms, Virginia horsefarm.)

Where the taxpayer is engaging in more than one activity which may be arguably regarded as an activity not engaged in for profit, it may be possible to combine or fragment such activities in order to get the benefit of the presumption, or indeed to escape the reach of § 183 altogether. Regs. § 1.183–1(d) deals with these issues.

**25.** § 183(e).

**26.** § 183(e)(4).

see Brannen, 78 T.C. 471 (1982), judgment aff'd 722 F.2d 695 (11th Cir.1984).

### *(10) Office in the Home; Soliman*

The deductibility of expenses attributable to a taxpayer using a portion of his home as an "office" for the carrying on of business or profit-seeking activities has long vexed the courts, Congress and the Service. Much as in the case of entertainment expenses (discussed at ¶ 6.02(5)), § 162's stricture that only ordinary and necessary business expenses could be deducted proved inadequate to deal with apparent widespread taxpayers' abuse in this area.[27]

Congress, therefore, enacted § 280A(a), providing relatively stringent rules. Section 280A(a) also provides rules for the treatment of the rental of vacation homes, and certain other business uses of residential property. These issues are discussed at ¶ 6.02(11).

With respect to the home office issue, it is first clear that deductions which are generally allowed without regard to whether the taxpayer has an office in his home will continue to be allowed.[28] This would include such deductions as mortgage interest, property taxes and casualty losses above the 10% of adjusted gross income and $100 floors.[29] Where § 280A bites is in the area of deductions that are only allowed if the taxpayer is engaged in a trade or business, or profit-seeking activity—such as maintenance expenses, utility expenses, rent, and depreciation or cost recovery. It is these deductions, then, that are at stake in the home office area.

With respect to these deductions, they are only allowed to the extent they are allocable to a portion of the taxpayer's residence which is exclusively used on a regular basis (A) as the principal place of business for any trade or business of the taxpayer; (B) as a place of business which is used by patients, clients, or customers in meeting or dealing with the taxpayer in the normal course of his trade or business; or (C) in the case of a separate structure which is not attached to the taxpayer's residence, in connection with the taxpayer's trade or business. Moreover, where the taxpayer's trade or business involves him being an employee, he may only take business deductions attributable to his home office if the use of the home office is for the convenience of the taxpayer's employer.[30]

These rules bar deductions attributable to a home office where the taxpayer does not conduct a trade or business in the home office, but is

**27.** Cf. Bodzin v. Commissioner, 509 F.2d 679 (4th Cir.1975), cert. denied 423 U.S. 825, 96 S.Ct. 40, 46 L.Ed.2d 41 (1975) (attorney for the Internal Revenue Service not allowed to deduct rent attributable to study where he had adequate office space at work.)

**28.** § 280A(b).

**29.** As to casualty losses it does matter whether the taxpayer can deduct them as part of a home office business, because if he can the casualty losses will be allowed "above the line" and thus be business casualties not subject to the $100 and 10% of AGI floors.

**30.** § 280A(c).

only engaging in profit-seeking activity. Thus, exclusive use of a study or den for the purpose of making investments in the stock market by a taxpayer who is not in the trade or business of investing in securities would not qualify; nor would exclusive use of a study or a den in the home by a teacher to prepare for class qualify, unless it could be shown that the employer provided no work space and required the teacher to prepare lessons at home.[31]

Taxpayers who can take business-type deductions (maintenance, utilities, rent, depreciation, etc.) attributable to their home office are generally taxpayers who are self-employed and use the office as their principal place of business, or taxpayers who may have more than one trade or business, one of which is operated from their home office.[32]

Allowing taxpayers who regularly meet patients, clients, or customers in the home to also qualify as having a home office (even though the office may not, in fact, in some cases be the taxpayer's principal place of business) indicates that Congress was prepared to relax its standards somewhat where it could be objectively shown that the taxpayer was making extensive business use of a portion of his home. Allowing taxpayers business-type deductions where they have a separate structure used in their trade or business, even though it may not be their principal place of business, again relaxes the standard where there is a more objective test.

It should be emphasized, however, that where the taxpayer is an employee, he will not in any event be allowed to take business-type deductions with respect to a portion of his home used as an office, unless that usage is for the convenience of the employer, as well as being the employee's principal place of business.[33]

Even if the taxpayer qualifies as having a home office by meeting one of the three alternative tests described above, the situation is no particular bargain. The business deductions attributable to such home

---

**31.** Thus, the taxpayer in Bodzin, supra, would have also lost under these new rules. Cf. Moller v. United States, 553 F.Supp. 1071 (Ct.Cl.1982), judgment rev'd 721 F.2d 810 (Fed.Cir.1983), cert. denied 467 U.S. 1251, 104 S.Ct. 3534, 82 L.Ed.2d 839 (1984) (very active securities investment qualified as trade or business for purposes of § 280A; expenses allowed for offices in two different homes); Drucker, 79 T.C. 605 (1982), judgment rev'd 715 F.2d 67 (2d Cir.1983) (concert violinist playing for the Metropolitan Opera Orchestra could not deduct room at home set aside for practice, since it wasn't the principal place of his trade or business, notwithstanding that the Met provided him with no practice space).

**32.** § 280A(c)(1)(A). See Edwin Curphey, 73 T.C. 766 (1980) (doctor with principal place of business at hospital had principal place of business at home office with respect to his real estate business); John Green, 78 T.C. 428 (1982) (home office deduction allowed where office was used only to receive telephone calls).

**33.** Indeed, even if the employer provided the employee with no work space, the employee might arguably be denied a home office deduction because notwithstanding that he makes significant use of his home office, the home office is still likely not to be the employee's principal place of business, if the employee transacts substantial amounts of business on the employer's premises or elsewhere. Nor is it likely that such an employee would meet clients or customers in his home office, or have a separate structure attributable to his business. Cf. Weightman, 42 T.C.M. 104 (1981) (part of room can be a home office; on these particular facts other requirements for a home office not met).

office may not exceed the gross income derived from the use of the home office less any deductions allocable to such use which would be allowed whether or not the taxpayer had a qualifying home office.

As an example, suppose a taxpayer generates $15,000 of gross income from a small consulting business, operated out of his study in his home. If the mortgage interest and property taxes attributable to his study are $5,000, then there is a balance of $10,000 against which deductions for maintenance, utilities, and depreciation attributable to that study may be taken. To the extent the deductions for maintenance, utilities, and depreciation exceed $10,000 they will not be allowed. The Service has promulgated regulations specifying the order in which allowed deductions will be taken.[34]

The Supreme Court in the case of *Commissioner v. Soliman*[35] recently tightened the standards in the home office area. The case concerned an anesthesiologist who spent 30 to 35 hours per week administering anesthesia and postoperative care in three hospitals, none of which provided him with an office. He also spent two to three hours per day in a room in his home that he used exclusively as an office.

According to the Court the taxpayer's home office was not his principal place of business. The treatment of patients at the hospitals was more important than the administrative work he did at home.

Moreover, the hours he spent at home were insufficient to render the home office the principal place of business in light of the circumstances of the case. Thus taxpayer was denied deductions associated with the business use of his home.

### (11) Rental of Vacation or Other Homes

Taxpayers who rent vacation or other homes which they also use for personal purposes are limited in the deductions they may take by § 280A. The fact that § 280A also simultaneously provides rules for limiting deductions with respect to qualifying home offices and certain other business uses of residential property causes the statute here to be virtually unintelligible.

Rental homes are best analyzed, under § 280A, by dividing them into four categories:

1. Rental homes that are not used by the taxpayer for personal purposes at any time during the taxable year. These are simply investment properties owned by the taxpayer and are not subject to any of the restrictions on deductibility under § 280A. The taxpayer may take

---

34. The order of deduction is: (1) deductions that would be allowed regardless of use as a home office, i.e., mortgage interest and property taxes attributable to the home office; (2) deductions that do not cause basis adjustments (maintenance); (3) deductions that do cause a basis adjustment (depreciation and casualties), Reg. § 1.280A–2(i)(5); Reg. § 1.280A–3(d)(3). See generally Lang, "When a House Is Not Entirely a Home: Deductions Under Internal Revenue Code § 280A for Home Offices, Vacation Homes, etc." 1981 Utah L.Rev. 275 (1981).

35. 506 U.S. 168, 113 S.Ct. 701, 121 L.Ed.2d 634 (1993).

deductions with respect to these properties under the usual rules under § 162 or 212, as well as §§ 167 and 168, relating to depreciation or cost recovery.

Under § 280A(d)(3), renting a dwelling to any person (including relatives according to the legislative history) for use as the tenant's principal residence shall not be treated as using the dwelling for personal purposes. This makes it possible for a taxpayer, for example, to buy a home, rent it to his elderly parents for fair rental and take all deductions including depreciation in full.

2. Rental homes used for personal purposes for a period which does not exceed the greater of fourteen days, or 10 percent of the number of days during such year for which the unit is rented at a fair rental.[36] Taxpayers with units which fall into this category may take deductions which are allowable without regard to business use of property—such as mortgage interest, property taxes and casualty losses above the prescribed limits—in full.[37] Deductions which may only be taken if they are attributable to property used in business or profit-seeking activity—such as maintenance, utilities, depreciation and casualty losses without regard to the 10% of adjusted gross income and $100 floors—may only be taken to a limited extent, based on usage. The usage limit as to these deductions is that they may be taken only in proportion to the number of days the property is rented out, divided by the total number of days the property is used for rental and personal purposes. Thus, if property is rented out for three hundred days and used personally for twenty-five days, $\frac{300}{325}$ of the business type deductions may be taken.[38]

3. Rental homes used for personal purposes for a number of days which exceeds the greater of fourteen days or 10 percent of the number of days during the year for which the unit is rented at a fair rental.[39] This is the type of unit on which the restrictions of § 280A bear most heavily; and, not surprisingly, it is the type of unit of most interest to taxpayers who wish to make some tax hay out of a vacation home of which they make substantial personal use. Taxpayer dreams of renting a little cottage by a lake in Maine and using it as a vacation home all summer, followed by a two week rental, thereupon to deduct all expenses associated with the vacation home founder on the shoals of § 280A.[40]

---

**36.** § 280A(d)(1). Thus, for example, if a vacation home were rented for 300 days during the year and used by the taxpayer for 25 days during the year, it would fall into this category since the number of days of personal use did not exceed 10 percent of the number of days it was rented.

**37.** § 280A(b).

**38.** § 280A(d) and (e). It should be noted that § 280A is a disallowance provision. It only comes into play to the extent that the taxpayer otherwise establishes allowable deductions under § 162, 212, 167, or 165, etc. See Bolton, 77 T.C. 104 (1981), judgment aff'd 694 F.2d 556 (9th Cir.1982),

apparently rejecting the approach of § 280A(e).

**39.** § 280A(d) as discussed in the text supra, § 280A(d)(3), added in 1981, provides that renting a dwelling unit to any person (including relatives, according to the legislative history) for use as the tenant's principal residence shall not be treated as using the dwelling unit for personal purposes.

**40.** For whatever anecdotal evidence is worth, the author has received more requests for free tax advice from friends and acquaintances in the area of vacation homes than in any other area.

Rental home units in this category are subject to the same usage restrictions on deductions as units in category 2 described above.[41] In addition to the usage limit, units in this category are subject to an income limit. Business-type deductions, such as maintenance, utilities, and depreciation which meet the usage limit are still subject to the further income limit that they cannot be deducted to the extent that they exceed the gross rental income derived from renting the property less the deductions that would be allowed regardless of business use (such as mortgage interest, property taxes, and casualty losses that are allocable to the business use).[42]

Thus, for example, if a rental vacation unit in this category produced $10,000 of rental income, and there were $8,000 of mortgage interest and property taxes allocable to business use of that unit, then only $2,000 of maintenance, utilities, and depreciation could be deducted.[43]

4. Rental homes rented for less than fifteen days. If a taxpayer makes personal use of his vacation or other rental home and does rent it but for less than fifteen days, then no deductions whatsoever attributable to the rental use (i.e., maintenance, utilities, depreciation) will be allowed. But the rental income so generated is excluded from gross income.[44] This rule simplifies calculations for taxpayers who engage in relatively short-time rentals of their property. However, it does bestow a windfall on taxpayers who can rent their vacation units for a very high rental during a short period.[45]

As discussed above, an important limitation on the deductions attributable to rental of a vacation or other home relates to the number of days that a unit is rented out versus the number of days that a unit is used for personal purposes. Where the vacation home is part of a condominium complex, a rental pool arrangement may be set up in which the condominium owners split the rent generated from the rental of their units without regard to which particular unit is actually rented. In such arrangements, the Service has provided in regulations that the limit on deductions relating to days of personal use versus days of rental use will be computed by reference to the number of days a taxpayer's unit is *actually* rented.[46]

Thus, taxpayers contemplating purchasing condominium units involved in such pools, should attempt to purchase units which will be the ones that are actually rented. While the overall rental income of the pool will be split evenly among the owners of the units, only those owners

**41.** § 280A(d) and (e).

**42.** § 280A(c)(5).

**43.** The mortgage interest, property taxes and casualty losses which are "allocable" to the business use of the unit is that proportion of those expenses which is equal to the proportion of the year that the unit is rented out, Bolton v. Commissioner, 694 F.2d 556 (9th Cir.1982).

**44.** § 280A(g).

**45.** An example of this would be a condominium overlooking the running of the bulls at Pamplona, see E. Hemingway, *The Sun Also Rises* (1927) *passim.*

**46.** Reg. § 1.280A–3(e)(4); to similar effect is Fine v. United States, 647 F.2d 763 (7th Cir.1981); Letter Ruling 800903.

whose units are actually rented will be able to take maintenance, utilities, and depreciation, etc. deductions with respect to their units.

### (12) Depreciation and Accelerated Cost Recovery

#### (a) Background

#### (i) Rationale for Depreciation

Taxpayers are entitled to take a depreciation deduction with respect to certain property used in the trade or business or for the production of income.[47] The rationale of the depreciation deduction is that the property the taxpayer is using in his trade or business, or profit seeking activity, is wearing out and that deterioration is a cost of doing business which is appropriately reflected on the taxpayer's tax return.

Put differently, the deduction for depreciation is simply a way of reflecting the fact that the taxpayer is always entitled to a deduction for a return on his capital, and should only be taxed to the extent his income exceeds the cost of his investment. Therefore, the taxpayer may deduct an aliquot part of the cost of an asset spread out over the asset's useful life against the income generated by the asset.[48]

By the same reasoning, depreciation will not be allowed for property which does not wear out over time or through use. Thus, no depreciation is allowed for undeveloped land, securities or stocks, gold, collectibles, or good will. Basis is recovered on such property when it is sold or otherwise disposed of (see ¶ 4.03).[49] Another way of stating the same theory is that depreciation is a method for matching income produced by the asset with the cost of the asset.

In any event, this theoretical justification for depreciation is eroded in fact by a number of considerations. First of all, it is often true that depreciable property, in particular real property, goes up in value over time rather than declines in value to zero or to a hypothetical salvage value. Furthermore, the deduction for depreciation is often an instrument of national economic policy. Rapid methods of depreciation are often allowed, and artificially shorter useful lives may be used with the intention of stimulating investment in new depreciable property.

Thus, for all these reasons, the deduction for depreciation should not be viewed as an attempt to seriously represent what is happening to the value of the property being depreciated, but rather as an artificial method for the taxpayer to do what every taxpayer is entitled to do—namely, ultimately to recover the cost of his investment.[50]

---

**47.** § 167(a).

**48.** Cf. Lischer, "Depreciation Policy: Whither Thou Goest," 32 Sw.L.J. 545 (1978).

**49.** The purchase price of improved real estate must be allocated between the land, which cannot be depreciated, and the improvements, which can be depreciated. Reg. § 1.167(a)–5.

**50.** Yet another way of interpreting depreciation is that it provides a "reserve" set aside for the taxpayer to reinvest in new property once his old property wears out. However, given inflation and technological change, it is not at all clear that the cost of new property the taxpayer would buy would bear any particular relationship to the cost

As we would expect from our discussion of time value of money issues in the Prologue, the taxpayer generally wants to depreciate his property as rapidly as possible. This will involve choosing a so-called accelerated method of depreciation if it is available for the particular asset, and using the shortest useful life allowed for the particular asset. In taking rapid depreciation, the taxpayer benefits from a deferral of his tax liability. This is usually attractive, for the tax dollars saved can be reinvested in the taxpayer's business or otherwise used by the taxpayer.[51]

The deduction for depreciation is the obverse side of the requirement that capital expenditures may not be deducted immediately.[52] Where an expenditure must be capitalized rather than deducted immediately, it may then be subject to the allowance for depreciation and recovered over a period of years. It follows, then, that as the deduction for depreciation is taken on a particular asset, the basis of that asset goes down by the amount of depreciation taken.[53] However, depreciation is not "optional" in the sense that even if the taxpayer chooses not to take his deduction for depreciation—because he may already be running operating losses for the year—the basis of the property involved will still go down by at least the minimum amount of depreciation allowable on the property.[54]

This basis adjustment means, of course, that if the property has not in fact been declining in value during the period the depreciation was taken, when the property is finally sold there will be a substantial taxable gain. This gain appears to just balance the books since the taxpayer has been enjoying a depreciation deduction over the time the property was held. But in fact the taxpayer may well wind up ahead of the game, because the deduction for depreciation has been taken early, whereas the gain on the sale of the property is taxed later.

### (ii) Inflation Problems

Balanced against the benefit of deferral that depreciation affords the taxpayer is the effect of inflation. Depreciation provides a deduction for taxpayer's original cost of the property. This approach fails, however, to take account of inflation. Say a company buys a machine that costs $5,000 and properly depreciates it over 10 years. Suppose also that the

---

of the property he has depreciated. See discussion below.

It should also be noted that publicly-traded corporate taxpayers may take accelerated forms of depreciation for purposes of computing their tax liability and slower or straight-line forms for computing their profits as reported to stockholders. While this ability to simultaneously tell bad news to the tax man and good news to the shareholders has been criticized, it still remains a practice that can be engaged in as long as it is disclosed. Cf. SEC Reg. S–X, 17 CFR § 210.3–16(*o*)(1975).

"Depreciation" as used in this discussion also covers the term "amortization," which often refers to the writing off of the cost of intangible assets, such as patents, copyrights, franchise agreements, leases. Amortization is generally done only on a straight-line basis.

**51.** For a fuller discussion of the advantages of deferral of income, see the Prologue and ¶ 8.02(1).

**52.** ¶ 6.03(4).

**53.** § 1016(a)(2).

**54.** § 1016(a) (flush language).

inflation rate is 10% a year over the ten years and that the cost of replacing the machine increases by that inflation rate. At the end of 10 years taxpayer would have taken $5,000 in depreciation deductions to fully recover his original cost. There is just one tiny problem. With the inflation rate of 10% a year, replacing the machine now costs $12,969.

Should depreciation take account of inflation? It is clear that in the inflationary environment of this example we are not adequately taking account of the taxpayer's cost of doing business. It would appear that his replacement cost of the asset is at least as relevant as his historical cost.

It would appear, therefore, that by understating his true cost of doing business (his replacement cost) we are overstating his profits. Therefore, we are overtaxing him. Moreover, this problem is not limited to the relatively high inflation rate posited by the example. Even if inflation is 3% over the course of the ten-year period—which is about as low as it gets over a 10-year period—the cost of replacing the $5,000 machine would be $6,720. If the useful life were 20 years, with 3% inflation, the cost of replacing the machine would be $9,031.

It is often suggested that the way to cope with this problem is to index the original cost of the machine for inflation. Then one would calculate the depreciation deduction based on that indexed cost. While this idea sounds nice in theory, it is not so clear how it would actually work. Consider the chart below:

Depreciation of an Asset That is Indexed For Inflation

Inflation Rate = 10% Per Year

| Year | Original Basis After Inflation Adjustment | Depreciation Taken St. Line |
|------|-------------------------------------------|------------------------------|
| 1 | $5,000 | $500 |
| 2 | $5,500 | $550 |
| 3 | $6,050 | $605 |
| 4 | $6,655 | $666 |
| 5 | $7,321 | $732 |
| 6 | $8,053 | $805 |
| 7 | $8,858 | $886 |
| 8 | $9,744 | $974 |
| 9 | $10,718 | $1,072 |
| 10 | $11,790 | $1,179 |
| Total | | $7,969 |

We see that by taking 10% of the indexed original cost of the asset each year for 10 years as depreciation gives us a total amount of depreciation of $7,969. Yet the replacement cost of the machine after 10 years is $11,790. While it is true that using the indexed original cost basis gave us more depreciation than using the non-indexed original cost (i.e., $5,000), this indexing procedure did not produce enough depreciation to recompense the taxpayer for his replacement cost of the machine.

There are other approaches that could be tried. It is often glibly asserted in the financial press that depreciable assets should be indexed to reflect inflation. We now see that coming up with a sensible approach there is not so simple.

The tax law does not index the basis of assets for depreciation (or for any other reason) at the present time. Thus it seems fair to say that not enough depreciation is being allowed. However, this effect is offset by the fact that the present Accelerated Cost Recovery System (ACRS), discussed in the next section, allows for very rapid depreciation. This is accomplished by the use of relatively short useful lives and the use of accelerated methods of computing depreciation. These result in a large amount of the total depreciation being taken very early in the life of the asset. These large deductions early have the effect of deferral of tax. As we have learned at exhausting length (see the Prologue), deferral of tax is money in the bank to the taxpayer. Hence these accelerated methods make up (or perhaps more than make up) for the failure to index the basis of the asset for inflation.

### (iii) Basic Methods of Depreciation

The basic method of computing depreciation is to deduct a portion of the asset's basis each year over a period of years. The three variables in making this calculation, as a general rule, are: the basis of the asset, the period over which the deductions are to be taken, and the method of computing how much will be deducted each year. The basis of the asset is generally determined under rules discussed elsewhere in this work (¶ 4.03(2)); usually the basis of a business asset is the cost of the asset. The period over which the depreciation deductions will be taken is determined by reference to rules promulgated by the IRS and the Congress. There are various methods for computing the amount of depreciation that will be taken in each year. The ACRS system promulgated by the Economic Recovery Tax Act of 1981, discussed below, provides new, simplified, and attractive rules for making these calculations.

An illustration of the basic workings of computing depreciation can be given by the following example: an asset has a cost basis of $100.00. Reference to the appropriate rules determines that this asset is properly depreciated over a period of ten years—the "useful life." If the "straight line" method of depreciation is used, then 10% of the basis of the property will be deductible each year for the useful life of the property, leading to a deduction of the total amount of the basis of the property at the end of the ten-year period.

Thus, the taxpayer would take, in this example, a depreciation deduction of $10.00 per year for ten years. His basis would go down by $10.00 per year for ten years. At the end of ten years his basis would be zero, and there would be no more depreciation taken, even though the property might be used in further years. If the taxpayer were to sell the property after five years, his basis for computation of gain or loss on the sale would be $50.00. The rate of deduction for each year for straight-line depreciation is determined by dividing 100% by the number of years in the useful life. Thus, in the example above, had the useful life been five years, the rate of depreciation taken per year would have been 20%; a useful life of fifty years would have given rise to a rate of 2%, etc.

Instead of using the "straight line" method described above, the taxpayer may sometimes use one of the various methods of accelerated depreciation. One of the most attractive aspects of the Economic Recovery Tax Act of 1981 (from the point of view of taxpayers) is that it allows very rapid methods of computing depreciation to be used. Most methods of accelerated depreciation are derived by reference to the straight-line method.

One well accepted accelerated method of depreciation is the 200% declining-balance method. Using the original example above, the 200% declining-balance method would involve using a rate of depreciation that was twice that used under the straight-line method. Thus, the taxpayer would, in the first year, take a depreciation deduction of $20.00. In subsequent years the taxpayer would continue to use a rate of 20% but importantly, the 20% rate would be applied to the *remaining* basis on the taxpayer's property at the beginning of the year, rather than to the original basis. Thus, the depreciation taken in the second year under the 200% declining-balance method would be $16.00 (20% of the remaining basis of $80.00). In the third year the amount of depreciation taken would be $12.80 (20% of the remaining balance of $64.00). Thus, it can be seen that the 200% declining-balance method yields much greater depreciation deductions in the early years of the useful life of the property.

However, the mathematics of the 200% declining-balance method is that in the later years of the useful life it will yield less depreciation than the straight-line method. This is because the 20% rate of depreciation is applied to an ever decreasing basis, whereas the 10% rate under the straight-line method is always applied to the original basis. Moreover, it is inevitable that the 200% declining-balance method will yield smaller depreciation deductions than the straight-line method in the later years of the useful life because the overall amount of depreciation that can be taken under *either* method is only $100.00. To the extent that the 200% declining-balance method yields greater deductions in the earlier years, obviously, in the later years it will yield smaller depreciation deductions, because there will simply be less depreciation left to be taken.[55]

As a matter of fact, the problem is somewhat more complex than that. The mathematics of the 200% declining-balance method will actually lead to the result that not all the depreciation will be taken. The method, in short, never leads to the basis getting to zero, since it always involves computation of 20% of a smaller and smaller amount. The approach, therefore, is to switch from the 200% declining-balance meth-

**55.** § 167(b).

od to the straight-line method at some point during the useful life to be able to take all the depreciation and bring the basis to zero. A comparison of the amounts of depreciation taken over a ten-year useful life with an asset with a cost basis of $100.00, including the switch from 200% declining-balance to straight-line, is set forth in the accompanying chart.

**Comparison of Straight–Line and 200%
Declining-Balance Depreciation**

| Straight–Line: IRC Sec. 167(b)(1) | | | 200% Declining–Balance IRC Sec. 167(b)(2) | | |
|---|---|---|---|---|---|
| Basis at Beginning of Year | Year | Am't of Depreciation Taken | Basis at Beginning of Year | Year | Am't of Depreciation Taken |
| 100.00 | 1.00 | 10.00 | 100.00 | 1.00 | 20.00 |
| 90.00 | 2.00 | 10.00 | 80.00 | 2.00 | 16.00 |
| 80.00 | 3.00 | 10.00 | 64.00 | 3.00 | 12.80 |
| 70.00 | 4.00 | 10.00 | 51.20 | 4.00 | 10.24 |
| 60.00 | 5.00 | 10.00 | 40.96 | 5.00 | 8.19 |
| 50.00 | 6.00 | 10.00 | 32.77 | 6.00 | 6.55* |
| 40.00 | 7.00 | 10.00 | 26.21 | 7.00 | 6.55 |
| 30.00 | 8.00 | 10.00 | 19.66 | 8.00 | 6.55 |
| 20.00 | 9.00 | 10.00 | 13.11 | 9.00 | 6.55 |
| 10.00 | 10.00 | 10.00 | 6.55 | 10.00 | 6.55 |
| 0.00 | 11.00 | | 0.00 | 11.00 | |

* Switching to straight-line when it becomes more attractive, Sec. 167(e)(1).

Similarly to the 200% declining-balance method of depreciation, it is possible to use other accelerated methods such as 125%, 150%, 175% methods of depreciation. These methods work like the 200% method in that the rate of depreciation that is used is a percentage of the rate that would be employed in the straight-line method.

In addition to the straight-line method, and the accelerated depreciation methods, there is also the "sum-of-the-years-digits" method. In this method the amount of depreciation that may be taken in each year is determined by a fraction, the numerator of which is the number of years left in the useful life of the property and the denominator is a number which is the sum of all the numbers making up the useful life of the property.

For example, using the same facts as in figure 1 above, the amount of depreciation that could be taken in the first year under the sum-of-the-years-digits method would be $\frac{10}{55}$ times 100, or 18.18. The number 10 is the number of years left in the useful life of the property. The number 55 is the sum of the numbers 1 + 2 + 3 + 4 + 5 + 6 + 7 + 8 + 9 + 10. In the second year of use of the property the amount of depreciation that could be taken would be $\frac{9}{55}$ times 100, or 16.36. In the third year of the use of the property the amount of depreciation that is taken under the sum-of-the-years-digits method is ⁹⁄₅₅ times 100, etc. It can be seen intuitively that this method will ultimately recover all the depreciation. This is because the various numerators of the fractions used will be the digits in the useful life of the property—10, 9, 8, etc. The denominator is also made up of a sum of these same digits.

*(b) The Myth That Accelerated Depreciation Stimulates Investment in Plant and Equipment*

We can use the time value of money concepts developed in the Prologue to explore the "received wisdom" that accelerated depreciation encourages investment in new plant and equipment. As the chart above illustrates, the same total amount of depreciation is taken in the straight-line method and the 200% declining-balance method. Nevertheless it is virtually universally believed that if machinery may be depreciated under, say, the double declining-balance method, this will stimulate investment in plant and equipment compared to limiting depreciation to the straight-line method.

In fact running the numbers shows that this effect is so weak as to be negligible.

Consider the case of Jennifer, a sole proprietor, the owner of a widget factory. Jennifer is considering purchasing a widget redactor that would increase the income from her business. The machine costs $50,-000. The widget redactor has a useful life of 10 years and produces income after maintenance expenses of $11,000 per year. Jennifer is in a tax bracket (combined federal and state) of 40%. Given the level of risk of the income from the widget business the relevant after tax rate of return for analyzing the present value of the income stream from the widget redactor is, let us say, 12%.[56]

The question is whether Jennifer should invest in the machine. The proper approach is to ascertain what the present value of the machine is to Jennifer, given the numbers set forth above. If the present value of the machine is more than $50,000, Jennifer should buy the machine. If the present value is less than $50,000, Jennifer should not buy the machine.

The accompanying table illustrates the calculations:

**56.** It should be emphasized that in this example this rate of return is a subjective matter. It depends on the point of view of Jennifer. In other examples where we have used present value analysis (in the Prologue especially) we have used an objective after-tax interest rate. That is because in those examples we were dealing with virtually risk-free returns on high-grade bonds. In this example, we are dealing with the necessarily at least somewhat risky return on a business. When risk is involved the judgment of what rate of return is required depends on the particular individual. Some people are much more risk-averse than others. Most everyone is at least somewhat risk-averse. When risk is present, people (and businesses) require a higher rate of return to make up for it.

Present Value of $50,000 Machine Compared Using
Straight–Line and 200% Declining–Balance Depreciation

Straight Line

| Year | Income From Machine | St.-Ln. Depre- ciation | Income After Depre- ciation Deduction | Tax on Income From Machine at 40% Rate | Net Cash Flow: Income From Machine Minus Tax | Present Value of Cash Flow From Machine at 12% Rate |
|---|---|---|---|---|---|---|
| 1 | $11,000 | $5,000 | $6,000 | $2,400 | $8,600 | $7,679 |
| 2 | $11,000 | $5,000 | $6,000 | $2,400 | $8,600 | $6,856 |
| 3 | $11,000 | $5,000 | $6,000 | $2,400 | $8,600 | $6,121 |
| 4 | $11,000 | $5,000 | $6,000 | $2,400 | $8,600 | $5,465 |
| 5 | $11,000 | $5,000 | $6,000 | $2,400 | $8,600 | $4,880 |
| 6 | $11,000 | $5,000 | $6,000 | $2,400 | $8,600 | $4,357 |
| 7 | $11,000 | $5,000 | $6,000 | $2,400 | $8,600 | $3,890 |
| 8 | $11,000 | $5,000 | $6,000 | $2,400 | $8,600 | $3,473 |
| 9 | $11,000 | $5,000 | $6,000 | $2,400 | $8,600 | $3,101 |
| 10 | $11,000 | $5,000 | $6,000 | $2,400 | $8,600 | $2,769 |
| Total | $110,000 | $50,000 | $60,000 | $24,000 | $86,000 | **$48,592** |

Double Declining Balance

| Year | Income From Machine | Double Declining– Balance Depreciation | Income After Depreciation Deduction | Tax on Income From Machine at 40% Rate | Net Cash Flow: Income From Machine Minus Tax | Present Value of Cash Flow From Machine at 12% Rate |
|---|---|---|---|---|---|---|
| 1 | $11,000 | $10,000 | $1,000 | $400 | $10,600 | $9,464 |
| 2 | $11,000 | $8,000 | $3,000 | $1,200 | $9,800 | $7,813 |
| 3 | $11,000 | $6,400 | $4,600 | $1,840 | $9,160 | $6,520 |
| 4 | $11,000 | $5,120 | $5,880 | $2,352 | $8,648 | $5,496 |
| 5 | $11,000 | $4,096 | $6,904 | $2,762 | $8,238 | $4,675 |
| 6 | $11,000 | $3,277 | $7,723 | $3,089 | $7,911 | $4,008 |
| 7 | $11,000 | $3,277 | $7,723 | $3,089 | $7,911 | $3,578 |
| 8 | $11,000 | $3,277 | $7,723 | $3,089 | $7,911 | $3,195 |
| 9 | $11,000 | $3,277 | $7,723 | $3,089 | $7,911 | $2,853 |
| 10 | $11,000 | $3,277 | $7,723 | $3,089 | $7,911 | $2,547 |
| Total | $110,000 | $50,001 | $59,999 | $24,000 | $86,000 | **$50,148** |

Difference in present value as percentage of cost of machine = 3.11%

On these numbers Jennifer would invest in the machine if allowed
to take accelerated depreciation and would not invest in the machine if
limited to straight-line depreciation. Thus these numbers seem to prove
that a government policy allowing accelerated depreciation *does* stimulate investment in plant and equipment.

But psssst! I've got a little secret for you. I cooked the numbers to
put us on the knife edge. As the chart indicates, the difference in the
present value between the two methods constitutes about 3% of the
purchase price of the machine. I suggest this is not a big difference.
Rather than being on the knife edge as we are in this example, it is much
more likely the case that the machine is either worthwhile to purchase
or not regardless of the method of depreciation.

Another way of looking at our numbers is to say that if the machine costs less than $48,592, it should be purchased regardless of depreciation method and if it costs more than $50,148, it should not be purchased regardless of depreciation method.[57] Only if the price of the machine happens to fall within this 3% range between $48,592 and $50,148 does method of depreciation have any impact on the decision to purchase the machine.

This 3% range becomes even more irrelevant when it is recalled that the numbers going into these ten-year calculations are not exactly written in stone. How do we know that the machine will produce net income of exactly $11,000 per year for 10 years? How do we know that the combined federal and state tax rate will remain at 40% for the next 10 years? How about this 12% discount rate—which depends on the risk of the taxpayer's business and on the prevailing interest rates in the economy? Is all that going to remain the same for 10 years? All these numbers are "soft" estimates. The sponginess of these numbers washes out this 3% differential.

For example, if the projected income from the machine is $11,500 per year instead of $11,000 per year, then the present value of the machine when straight-line depreciation is used is $50,287; and the present value when double declining-balance is used is $51,843. Thus the machine should be bought regardless of depreciation method. By the same token if the projected income from the machine is $10,500 per year, then the the present value of the machine when straight-line depreciation is used is $46,897; and the present value when double declining-balance is used is $48,453. Thus the machine should not be bought regardless of depreciation method.

What this seems to show is that we are going through a great deal of complexity in the statute with regard to these accelerated methods of depreciation in order to have a minimal impact on investment.

I have another little secret for you. Insofar as I am aware, I am in an extreme minority among those interested in tax policy (i.e., 1) that believes the proposition that accelerated depreciation methods provide little economic stimulus to investment. I believe I have proven that here. But if you go around saying that to theorists in the field you may get some odd stares.

### (c) "Sinking Fund" Depreciation

We can squeeze a little more blood out of the example in the previous section. The question now before us is whether there is a really correct way to calculate depreciation. Economists have approached the matter using so-called "sinking fund" depreciation.[58] If we were quite sure of the revenue from the machine as being $11,000 per year, we

---

**57.** I note that if the machine does cost a little less or a little more than $50,000, that will change our depreciation numbers slightly and feed back to effect a slight change in our present value calculations. That minor effect does not detract from the point being made in the text.

**58.** See e.g. Samuelson, Tax Deductibility of Economic Depreciation to Insure Invariant Valuations, 72 J. Pol. Econ. 604 (1964).

could treat the purchase of the machine as though we had lent money on a mortgage. Both the mortgage lender and the purchaser of a machine are doing the same thing, essentially. They are investing their money with the expectation of getting a return plus the principal back. If we are the lender on a mortgage, the treatment is that most of the early payments are allocated to (taxable) interest. This is because interest is calculated on the unpaid balance of the loan and that unpaid balance is necessarily the largest at the beginning of the loan. Most of the later payments are allocated to (nontaxable) recovery of principal. If you or any relative has had a home mortgage, you know that from the point of view of the borrower most of the early payments are allocated to (deductible) interest and most of the later payments are allocated to (nondeductible) repayment of principal.

If we follow that approach with the machine—with the purchaser of the machine treated like the lender—then most of the $11,000 in the early years is taxable return and most of the $11,000 in the later years is nontaxable recovery of capital. The way that we make most of the payment in the later years not taxable is to allow the deduction for depreciation. Thus under this economic approach we *back-load* the depreciation. From that point of view, straight-line is actually too fast.

If I've lost you (which I've got a feeling I have) let me illustrate the matter with another fearless chart, derived from the chart above. We have $11,000 per year, before taxes, for 10 years income from the machine. The machine cost $50,000. This means our internal rate of return on the machine is 17.68%. Another way of putting it is that $11,000 per year for 10 years discounted at a rate of 17.68% equals $50,000.

Now as each year goes by, the machine becomes less valuable. At the beginning we could expect 10 years of income from the machine. The value of the machine at the beginning of 10 years is obviously the discounted present value of 10 years of income from the machine. After the first year is over and we have pocketed our income from the machine, there are only 9 years left.

What is the value of the machine now? If we really believe that this machine was only good when we started for a total of 10 years of income at $11,000 per year, then after the first year the machine is only good for 9 more years of income at $11,000 per year. Hence the machine is after one year only worth the discounted present value of 9 years of income at $11,000 per year. What has been lost? Obviously the tenth year of income of $11,000. What is that worth? It is clearly the discounted present value of $11,000 10 years from now. Another way of saying it is that after the first year's usage, the tenth year's payment has dropped off the chart. Thus we could say that the machine has declined in value by the present value of that tenth year's payment. Then we could say that that is the appropriate amount of the depreciation deduction for the first year. After the second year's usage and pocketing of income from the second year, the machine now only has eight years left on it. The machine has now dropped by the value of the $11,000 payment nine years from now. Therefore that is the amount of depreciation we would take in the second year. We continue with the back year dropping off until we have depreciated the entire value of the machine. This is depicted in the accompanying chart. The crazy lines indicate that the value of the machine each year has dropped by the present value of the last year's payment for the previous year.

To put "sinking fund" depreciation in a nutshell (suitable for exam-taking purposes), you can say that the back end payment drops off every year.

Notice that if you follow the depreciation line across you see that the amount of depreciation allowed is small in the earlier years and builds up to be large. As I pointed out earlier, depreciation is "back loaded" under the sinking fund approach. If you follow this approach, then what you say is that of each $11,000 annual income, the depreciation amount as calculated in the chart is a deduction from the $11,000 and the balance of the $11,000 annually is taxable.

| "Sinking Fund" Depreciation | | Start of Year 1 Present Value | Start of Year 2 Present Value | Start of Year 3 Present Value | Start of Year 4 Present Value | Start of Year 5 Present Value | |
|---|---|---|---|---|---|---|---|
| Year | Income | Value | Value | Value | Value | Value | |
| 1 | $11,000 | $9,347 | $9,347 | $9,347 | $9,347 | $9,347 | |
| 2 | $11,000 | $7,943 | $7,943 | $7,943 | $7,943 | $7,943 | |
| 3 | $11,000 | $6,750 | $6,750 | $6,750 | $6,750 | $6,750 | |
| 4 | $11,000 | $5,736 | $5,736 | $5,736 | $5,736 | $5,736 | |
| 5 | $11,000 | $4,874 | $4,874 | $4,874 | $4,874 | $4,874 | |
| 6 | $11,000 | $4,142 | $4,142 | $4,142 | $4,142 | $4,142 | |
| 7 | $11,000 | $3,519 | $3,519 | $3,519 | $3,519 | | |
| 8 | $11,000 | $2,991 | $2,991 | $2,991 | | | |
| 9 | $11,000 | $2,541 | $2,541 | | | | |
| 10 | $11,000 | $2,160 | | | | | |
| Machine's Value | | $50,002 | $47,843 | $45,302 | $42,311 | $38,791 | |
| Annual Change in Value or Depreciation: | | | $2,160 | $2,541 | $2,991 | $3,519 | |

| Year | | Start of Year 6 Present Value | Start of Year 7 Present Value | Start of Year 8 Present Value | Start of Year 9 Present Value | Start of Year 10 Present Value | Start of Year 11 Present Value |
|---|---|---|---|---|---|---|---|
| 1 | | $9,347 | $9,347 | $9,347 | $9,347 | $9,347 | |
| 2 | | $7,943 | $7,943 | $7,943 | $7,943 | | |
| 3 | | $6,750 | $6,750 | $6,750 | | | |
| 4 | | $5,736 | $5,736 | | | | |
| 5 | | $4,874 | | | | | |
| 6 | | | | | | | |
| 7 | | | | | | | |
| 8 | | | | | | | |
| 9 | | | | | | | |
| 10 | | | | | | | |
| Value | | $34,659 | $29,776 | $24,040 | $17,290 | $9,347 | $0 |
| Depreciation | | $4,142 | $4,874 | $5,736 | $6,750 | $7,943 | $9,347 |

This is analogous to the approach that was followed in the Prologue with the treatment of original issue discount. You may find it helpful to review that treatment at this time.

Thus we have shown that as a matter of economic analysis, straight-line depreciation (reasonable as it seems) actually allows depreciation to go too fast. Depreciation should be back-loaded.

Consider, from that perspective, the fact that most businesses finance the purchase of their depreciable plant and equipment with borrowed funds. The borrowed funds generate of course a deductible interest payment. As we have discussed above, the deduction for interest is front-loaded to the borrower. Thus the business that borrows to finance the purchase of depreciable plant and equipment is winning two ways. It is able to take the deduction for interest on a front-loaded basis, and it is able to take the deduction for depreciation faster than is warranted economically.

When you add the extremely rapid methods of depreciation now allowed by the so-called ACRS system (see below), you have really got a major subsidy for investment in plant and equipment. This is more or less intentional—although Congress may not have realized the full impact of the incentives it was creating.

Indeed the argument could be advanced that the excessively rapid depreciation deduction is creating tax-free income. If that is the case, then there could be grounds for denying the deduction for interest on the debt used to finance the investment in the plant and equipment. See § 265(a)(2), discussed at ¶ 6.03(6)(a).

The ACRS system is discussed in the next section.

### (d) The ACRS System; Sharp

The Economic Recovery Tax Act of 1981 established a far simpler system than the previous system for ascertaining the proper rules for depreciating various types of property. The system was substantially changed in 1986.

Under the Accelerated Cost Recovery System (ACRS) it is no longer necessary to make reference to complex rules with respect to establishing the "useful life" of property, the "salvage value" of property, and the rules for new as compared to used property. Indeed, so radical is the change in methods of calculating depreciation that new terminology is introduced. Property under the new system is said to be undergoing "accelerated cost recovery" rather than "depreciation", although the two concepts are fundamentally the same. The ACRS system simply represents a system of very rapid depreciation under simplified rules for determining the useful life of the property involved. The terms "cost recovery" and "depreciation" will be used in this discussion more or less interchangeably.

This new system of depreciation is both a creature of the "supply side" school of economics and a response to various technical criticisms of the depreciation system by the tax bar. As the Senate Finance Committee stated in its report:

The Committee believes that present rules for determining depreciation allowances and the investment tax credit need to be replaced because they do not provide the investment stimulus that is essential for economic expansion.

The Committee also believes that present rules are unnecessarily complicated . . .

The Committee heard copious testimony that the present rules are too complex. These rules require determinations on matters, such as useful life and salvage value, which are inherently uncertain and, thus, too frequently result in unproductive disagreements between taxpayers and the Internal Revenue Service. Current regulations provide numerous elections and exceptions which taxpayers— especially small businesses—find difficult to master and expensive to apply. The Committee believes that a new capital cost recovery system should be structured which de-emphasizes the concept of useful life, minimizes the number of elections and exceptions, and so is easier to comply with and to administer . . .

The Committee Bill replaces the present system of depreciation with the Accelerated Cost Recovery System (ACRS). ACRS permits costs for most tangible depreciable property using accelerated methods of cost recovery over predetermined recovery periods generally unrelated to, but shorter than, present law useful lives. The methods of cost recovery and recovery periods are the same for both new and used property.[59]

The ACRS system of § 168 is mandatory, although it allows some elections to be made within the system. It applies to most tangible depreciable property. Those few types of property not covered by § 168 are covered by older § 167. Intangible property is covered to a large degree by § 197.

*Recovery periods.* Under ACRS property is assigned to one of several classes of recovery periods. Salvage value is disregarded. The same schedules are employed for new and used property. Most personal property is recovered over 3, 5, or 7 years. Automobiles are particularly assigned to the 5–year class. Residential real property is written off over 27.5 years and nonresidential real property over 39 years.

*Methods of Depreciation.* As to methods of depreciation, residential real property (i.e. rental apartment buildings and rental housing) and nonresidential real property (i.e. office buildings, factories and the like) can be depreciated only on the straight line method (as an attack on tax shelters, see Chapter 8). Property in the 3, 5, 7, or 10 year classification can be depreciated by the 200% declining balance method, with a switch

**59.** Senate Finance Committee Report No. 97–144; accompanying the Economic Recovery Tax Act of 1981, reprinted in 1981–2 C.B. 412 at 425.

to straight line when that method yields more depreciation. Property recovered over 15 and 20 years uses the 150% declining balance method, switching to straight line when it becomes more attractive. Property in the 3 to 10 year classes may be depreciated over the 150% rather than 200% for all property within a particular class put into service in the year of the election (an election few will make). Moreover, property within the 3 to 20 year classes may be depreciated on the straight-line method for all property within a particular class (once again an election few would make and one wonders why the election is available at all). An extended useful life election is also available.

*Conventions.* There are certain "conventions" or rules for treating property that is acquired during the year as acquired at a particular point in the year. The ACRS system uses the "half-year convention.," which means that for administrative convenience all property is treated as though it were placed into service at the midpoint of the year regardless of when it was actually put into service. The result is one-half year of depreciation is allowed whether an asset is placed in service on the first day or the last day of the taxpayer's taxable year. To balance off, there is a half year of depreciation at the end of the asset's recovery period as well.

Assets under ACRS that are sold are also treated under a half-year convention for the year of sale.

*Bonus Depreciation: § 179.* Congress keeps believing that if it throws more depreciation at taxpayers it will stimulate the economy. As a result, in addition to the very attractive depreciation rules described above investment in personal property might also qualify for § 179 bonus depreciation. Section 179 allows an immediate deduction of the cost of some depreciable personal property in the year in which it is put into service. This is a small change item inasmuch as the maximum amount of bonus depreciation is $18,000 in 1997.[60]

Moreover, this ceiling is lowered by one dollar for every dollar of § 179 property placed in service during the year in excess of $200,000. Thus large businesses do not get the benefit of § 179; it belongs to small businesses and individuals. The basis of property depreciated under § 179 is reduced to reflect the § 179 depreciation and then such basis as is left is depreciated under the usual ACRS rules.

*Other Limits on Depreciation: Luxury Cars and "Listed" Property.* A maximum of $12,800 adjusted for inflation for years after 1988 may be deducted with respect to cars over the usual five year period. Thereafter a maximum of $1,475 can be depreciated in each year following the first five years until basis is exhausted, under § 280F.

Also under § 280F, ACRS deductions are limited with respect to other "listed property" where there is a business use of 50% or less.

---

**60.** The amount deductible increases over the next several years under the following schedule: 1998: $18,500; 1999: $19,- 000; 2000: $20,000; 2001: $24,000; 2002 $24,000; 2003 and thereafter $25,000.

"Listed property" includes: passenger automobiles, entertainment property, computers not used exclusively at a regular business establishment (watch that home computer), and cellular phones. Use of "listed property" by an employee is not regarded as business use unless the use is for the convenience of the employer and is required as a condition of employment. Listed property which is used for business 50% of the time or less is depreciated under an alternative depreciation system.[61] This involves longer useful lives and less rapid methods of depreciation.

The computational approach to the complex rules described above is to first compute any § 179 bonus depreciation, then compute regular ACRS depreciation and finally see if any limits of § 280F bite.

The case of *Sharp v. United States*[62] presented some interesting depreciation problems. Taxpayers Hugh and Bayard Sharp were equal partners in a partnership which purchased a Beechcraft airplane at a cost of $45,875. They made additional capital expenditures to the plane, bringing its total basis to $54,273.50. During the period of ownership the plane was used by the partnership 73.654% for personal use and 26.346% for business. (One rarely sees a percentage allocation out to this level of accuracy). Thus the partnership was only allowed to take depreciation on 26.346% of the basis of the plane, or $14,298.90. Thus over the five years of use from 1948 to 1953, only $13,777.92 of depreciation was allowed. (Note these were on depreciation rules that predated ACRS). The plane was sold in 1954, with the question being the amount of gain or loss realized by the partnership.

The taxpayers calculated as follows: basis $54,273.50 less $13,777.92 basis yields adjusted basis of $40,495.58. The selling price of the airplane was $35,380. Hence the taxpayers compute a loss of $5,115.58. They do not seek to deduct the loss (that *would* be overreaching).

The government treated the plane as though it were two assets, a business asset and a personal asset. The government calculated the basis of the business asset was $14,298.90 less the depreciation allowed of $13,777.92, producing and adjusted basis of $520.98. The government then also allocates 26.346% of the amount realized on the sale of the plane as attributable to the business asset. This yields $9,321.21 and thus the government concludes that the taxpayers had a gain of $8,800.23 on the sale. Since they were equal partners, they would each be responsible for one-half the gain. (As to the personal asset portion of the plane the numbers would be: $26,058.79 amount realized less adjusted basis $39,974.60 or a loss of $13,915.81. The loss, being personal, is not deductible.)

The court upheld the government's allocation theory. Otherwise the taxpayer would have been able to deduct the cost of the business portion of the plane to a greater degree than actual economic depreciation and not have to pay tax on the difference on sale.

---

**61.** § 168(g).

**62.** 199 F.Supp. 743, affirmed 303 F.2d 783 (3d Cir.1962).

### (13) Other Business Deductions

#### (a) Depletion

Various Code provisions encourage the exploration for and development of natural resources. The depletion allowance is a way for owners of mineral deposits to recover their cost, which they as the owner of a wasting asset are assuredly entitled to do.

There are two kinds of depletion allowances: cost depletion and percentage depletion.[63] Cost depletion, allowed for all mines, oil and gas wells, other natural deposits, and timber, is computed with respect to the taxpayer's adjusted basis (which will usually be his cost) in the mineral property. In particular, the computation of cost depletion involves spreading the taxpayer's adjusted basis over the amount of the mineral deposit and taking the aliquot amount of the adjusted basis as a deduction as the mineral deposit is sold. Thus, if 10 percent of the deposit is recovered and sold, the taxpayer can deduct 10 percent of his adjusted basis attributable to the mineral deposit.[64] If, after working the deposit for a while, the taxpayer determines that the estimated amount of the mineral deposit was incorrect and must be changed, the change in the estimate is made and the taxpayer's remaining adjusted basis is spread over the new estimated amount of the deposit. Once the taxpayer's basis goes to zero under cost depletion, no further depletion deduction is allowed, even though the taxpayer may continue to extract and sell more of the deposit. Cost depletion, therefore, is a reasonable way to allow a taxpayer to recover his cost in a wasting mineral deposit, where it is difficult to estimate the precise amount of the mineral deposit that can be economically exploited.[65]

Percentage depletion is keyed to the taxpayer's income from the mineral property and in that sense is unique among allowances in the nature of depreciation. In particular, the taxpayer is allowed to take a percentage, varying from five to twenty-two percent depending on the mineral involved, of his gross income from the property as a deduction for depletion.[66] The attractive aspect of percentage depletion is that even after the taxpayer has recovered his cost of the mineral property involved, if he continues to be able to exploit the mineral property and generate additional income from it, he continues to be able to take percentage depletion. Percentage depletion, in short, is not limited by the taxpayer's cost of the property.

**63.** §§ 612 and 613.

**64.** § 612.

**65.** In the case of timber, this approach must be refined to take account of the fact that new trees may be growing to at least in part replace the trees that are cut. Reg. § 1.611–3(b)(2).

**66.** § 613(b). The gross income from the property against which this percentage is calculated means the taxpayer's gross income less any rents or royalties paid or incurred by the taxpayer in respect of such mineral property, § 613(a). This makes sense in that the rents or royalties paid by the taxpayer in connection with the property are themselves subject to depletion by the payee and therefore their exclusion prevents the same income from being depleted twice. Moreover, the depletion allowance shall not in any event exceed 50 percent of the taxpayer's taxable income from the property (computed without the depletion allowance).

This exceedingly attractive aspect of percentage depletion has led to heavy criticism and has also been defended as an incentive for needed mineral exploration.[67] Congress has responded to this controversy by limiting the use of percentage depletion for oil and gas under complex rules.[68]

Taxpayers may use cost or percentage depletion, whichever gives them the most attractive result for the particular taxable year.[69] There are a number of questions in the depletion area relating to whether a taxpayer has an economic interest in minerals so that he may take depletion, allocation of depletion among various owners, separation or aggregation of properties eligible for depletion, minerals which qualify for depletion, and other issues. There is a rich lode of cases and authorities on these questions.[70]

### (b) Intangible Drilling and Development Costs

As a further boost to the exploration for and development of oil and gas wells, taxpayers are allowed to deduct immediately so-called intangible drilling and development costs with respect to such wells.[71] Deduction of intangible drilling costs (IDCs in the argot of the trade) is optional, and a taxpayer electing not to deduct his IDCs may treat them as a capital expense to the property involved which can be recovered by depreciation. It is usually the case that the IDC deduction is available on property which is eligible for the percentage depletion allowance, the size of which is not affected by the basis of the property. Faced with this embarrassment of riches, the taxpayer will, in such circumstances, almost always elect to take the deduction for IDCs immediately. A variety of questions surround the IDC deduction, including the party eligible to take the deduction, expenses which qualify for this attractive treatment, and procedures for making a valid election.[72]

An analogous immediate deduction for mining exploration and development expenditures is also allowed.[73]

### (c) Bond Premium

Because of the volatility of the credit markets, a taxpayer may pay more for a bond than its face amount. This excess amount is known as bond premium. Payments on the bond would then, as an economic matter, not all be interest; some of such payments would represent return of the taxpayer's bond premium. To recognize that economic fact,

**67.** Cf. Galvin, "The 'Ought' and 'Is' of Oil and Gas Taxation" 73 Harv.L.Rev. 1441 (1960).

**68.** § 613A.

**69.** §§ 611–613.

**70.** See Burke & Bowhay, Income Taxation of Natural Resources (1981).

See ¶ 5.04(1) regarding the treatment of "carved-out production payments" in the oil and gas area.

**71.** § 263(c); Reg. § 1.612–4. The IDC deduction also applies to geothermal wells.

**72.** See Note 35 supra.

**73.** §§ 616 and 617, which do not apply to oil and gas wells, which already enjoy the IDC deduction. This immediate write-off of capital expenditures is not allowed for expenditures incident to operations of a mine.

the Code allows a taxpayer to amortize his bond premium over the life of the bond.[74] In the absence of such a treatment, the taxpayer with bond premium would report too much interest income and then take a capital loss when the bond is paid off.

### (d) Purchased Intangibles: Section 197; Newark Morning Ledger

A major change to the business deduction area was effected by the 1993 Tax Act. The act provided that 100 percent of the cost of good will, going-concern value, and other intangibles that have been purchased are amortized (written off) over 15 years (§ 197(a), (c)). This is a major change, especially as to the exceedingly important asset of good will, which heretofore was not amortizable at all for tax purposes. (Good will can be written off for **financial** as opposed to tax purposes over 40 years.) A large number of extremely important assets are covered by this new rule. It would be difficult to overestimate the importance of this new rule in business transactions and, for example, corporate takeovers.

There are some extremely large numbers potentially riding on the treatment of good will and other intangibles in the takeover field. For example, in the Time/Warner merger, 80 percent of the $14 billion Time paid to acquire Warner was attributable to good will for financial accounting purposes; ninety percent of the $13 billion Philip Morris paid for Kraft was attributable to good will for financial accounting purposes. In these two cases the ability to write off good will of that magnitude for tax purposes over 15 years would result in deductions approaching $1 billion per year.

The previous rule barring the amortization of good will led taxpayers to engage in evasive maneuvers to try to have various intangible assets acquired to be deemed to be something other than good will. The most prominent of these cases was the celebrated *Newark Morning Ledger v. United States*.[75]

In *Newark Morning Ledger* the taxpayer bought eight newspapers from Booth Newspapers, Inc. for $328 million. It allocated $67.8 million of the purchase price to subscriber lists and claimed deductions for amortization of these lists. The Service took the position that amortization of the lists was not proper because the subscriber lists were inseparable from good will. The taxpayer's position was that once it proved the value and the useful life of the subscriber lists, it could amortize them. The taxpayer asserted good will is a residual concept only.

In a 5–4 decision, the Supreme Court held that the deduction was allowed. The Court asserted that "good will has no determinate useful life of specific duration." the Court said that in this case the taxpayer carried the burden of showing the subscriber lists have a limited useful

---

**74.** § 171, which is elective except in the case of tax-exempt securities. Market premium as well as original issue premium may be amortized. Amortization of the bond premium reduces the basis of the bond, § 1016(a)(5).

**75.** 507 U.S. 546, 113 S.Ct. 1670, 123 L.Ed.2d 288 (1993).

life. The taxpayer must also be able to prove the value with reasonable accuracy.

The decision was hailed in the financial press as one that would have a multibillion-dollar effect on large takeovers where a great deal of the consideration paid is for good will.

In response to this and other cases, congress enacted new Code § 197 providing, as stated above, that intangibles can be amortized over 15 years. In particular new § 197 mandates 15–year straight-line amortization for all purchased intangibles. Such intangibles include:

* Good will and going-concern value
* Covenants not to compete
* Customer lists, favorable contracts with suppliers or customers (but not accounts receivable)
* Workforce in place
* Books and records and databases
* Patents, copyrights, know-how, formulas, processes
* Franchises, trademarks, trade names
* Licenses, permits, and other rights granted by government

This 15–year straight-line amortization treatment is obviously much more favorable than prior law for assets such as good will, which could not be amortized at all for tax purposes. But it is much less favorable than prior law for other assets. An example here would be a covenant not to compete, which generally runs no more than five years. Indeed, it would violate the law and/or public policy of most if not all states for a covenant not to compete to last as long as 15 years. But it is clear, under the statute, that even though a covenant not to compete expires after, say, five years, it must still be amortized over 15 years unless taxpayer disposes of his entire interest in the business, § 197(f)(1)(B).

From a policy point of view it might be argued that allowing good will to be amortized is questionable, given that advertising expenditures are immediately deductible. Advertising expenditures are supposed to preserve and build up good will. It therefore might be argued that if the good will is being built up by (deductible) advertising expenditures, it should not be amortizable at all. An answer to that is that one can still make deductible repairs to an asset (such as a blast furnace) that is itself being depreciated.

### (e) Miscellaneous Rapid Write–Offs

A number of other types of capital expenditures are allowed rapid amortization by the Code, generally in order to encourage these expenditures as being socially desirable. Examples of such expenditures include research and experimental expenditures,[76] expenditures for pollution-

---

**76.** § 174.

control facilities,[77] newspaper, magazine, and other periodical expenditures,[78] expenditures to remove architectural and transportation barriers to the handicapped and elderly.[79]

Also see § 195, allowing amortization of expenses in connection with starting up a business, and § 194, relating to amortization of reforestation expenditures.

### (14) Alimony and Similar Payments; The Marriage Tax

#### (a) Alimony and Property Settlements

Breaking up is hard to do and the tax law does not make it any easier with a set of complex rules governing the taxability of payments between parties incident to a divorce or a separation. In the discussion which follows, the husband will be deemed the one to pay alimony or other payments to the wife, in accordance with the statutory language; however, obviously the wife may make alimony or other payments to the husband, so the usage here is for convenience.[80] Further as to terminology, the terms "husband" and "wife" may be used here to refer to the parties even though they may be divorced.[81]

While a divorced husband and wife may hope to sever all aspects of their relationship, when it comes to their tax liability, they often remain inextricably intertwined. The basic rule is that alimony payments are includable in the wife's gross income,[82] and are deductible to the husband above the line.[83]

There are a couple of ways to look at the fact that the payments are deductible "above the line." It could be viewed that this is inconsistent with the idea that deductions above the line should be business-like deductions to assist us in arriving at net income or adjusted gross income. Alimony is apparently an intensely personal deduction. Arguing the other way, the statutory arrangement here could be seen as simply a way of choosing the taxable individual. If the husband is just a conduit for some of his income going to the wife, then it is appropriate to net out the alimony above the line, so that it has no further impact whatsoever on his return.

There are only two possibilities under the statute regarding payments in the nature of alimony: 1) the payments can be deductible to the payor and income to the payee (in which case the tax burden of the payments falls on the payee); or 2) the payments can be not deductible to the payor and not income to the payee (in which case the burden of the payments falls on the payor).[84]

---

**77.** § 169.

**78.** § 173.

**79.** § 190.

**80.** See § 7701(a)(17), providing that the same statutory rules shall apply where the wife makes payments to the husband.

**81.** Id.

**82.** § 71.

**83.** §§ 215, 62(a)(10).

**84.** The avaricious reader might like to know if there is a possibility that a payment could be deductible to the payor and not income to the payee. The answer is: not a chance. The only two choices under the statute are those given in the text.

It is important to understand that taxpayers are invited by the statute to engage in tax planning in this area. The underlying economics of the divorce situation are usually that the higher-income spouse makes payments to the lower-income spouse. Thus Goldie Hawn, Joan Lunden, and Roseanne Arnold make payments to their estranged husbands.[85]

What is usually desired by both partes and their tax advisors, therefore, is that the payments be deductible to the payor and income to the payee (i.e., 1) above. This is more attractive than if the payments are not deductible to the payor and not income to the payee. The reason for this is clear. If the payments are deductible to the higher-bracket payor that saves the estranged couple more in taxes than it costs to have the payments income to the lower-bracket payee.[86] Thus the parties have more after-tax income to divide among themselves. No matter how much the estranged couple hate each other, they can certainly get together on that great American pastime: beating the government out of some taxes.

Not every payment the payor spouse makes to the payee spouse is deductible to the payor and income to the payee (thereby throwing the tax burden onto the payee, which is where we usually want it). Only payments which meet the statute's technical definition of "alimony or separate maintenance payments" are treated this way. Payments which do not meet the definition of "alimony or separate maintenance payments" are not deductible to the spouse and not income to the payee (thereby throwing the tax burden onto the payor). By choosing to have the payments come within or without the statutory definition of "alimony or separate maintenance payments," the parties can decide on whom to throw the tax burden. This is illustrated in the accompanying graphic.

---

**85.** Jane Fonda gave her ex husband, former student leader Tom Hayden a lump-sum property settlement.

**86.** In some unusual cases it might be that the parties prefer that the burden of the tax fall on the payee. This could be true if the payee is in a higher bracket than the payor. The payee might, for example, have responsibility for raising several children and thus be deemed by the court to require high payments from the payor even though the payee has more income than the payor.

The Tax Burden of Payments Between
Divorced or Separated Spouses

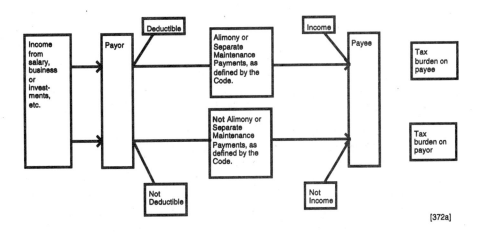

[372a]

Thus the technical definition of "alimony or separate maintenance payments" is critical here in ascertaining on whom the tax burden falls. The Code here proceeds in a rather technical fashion. The Code first states that "alimony or separate maintenance payments," as illustrated above, are income to the recipient and deductible to the payor.[87] As previously discussed, this treatment is usually what the parties want. To qualify for this attractive status of being income to the recipient and deductible to the payor, the payments, as illustrated above, must meet the elaborate technical definition of "alimony or separate maintenance payments." The statute defines "alimony or separate maintenance payment" to mean any payment that:

1) is in cash;[88]

2) is made under a divorce or separation instrument;

3) the divorce or separation instrument does not specify that the payment is not deductible to the payor and not income to the recipient (i.e., the parties can choose to throw the burden of the payments onto the payor rather than the payee by just so specifying in the instrument);

4) if payor and payee are divorced or legally separated, they may not be members of the same household at the time of payment;

5) payments must be terminable at death of payee spouse.[89]

In addition, the statute also states that if any part of the payment which otherwise meets the above definition is fixed by the divorce or

---

87. §§ 71(a), 215(a).

88. A check is of course all right. What they mean here is not "in kind," like a dozen frozen turkeys.

89. § 71(b)(1).

separation instrument to support children, it will not be treated as alimony or separate maintenance but rather as child support. Child support, not being "alimony or separate maintenance," is not deductible to the payor and is not income to the payee (tax burden therefore on payor).[90] Once again we see the parties specifically able to choose who will bear the tax burden of the payments. Also, if any amount specified in the instrument will be reduced on the happening of a contingency relating to a child, then that amount will be treated as child support rather than alimony (burden on payor).[91]

As another example, *I.T. 4001*[92] dealt with the situation that a husband paid premiums on a life insurance policy assigned to his former wife and with respect to which she is the irrevocable beneficiary and also a life insurance policy not assigned to the wife and with respect to which she is only the contingent beneficiary. The question was whether those payments are alimony (i.e. income to the wife and deductible to the husband). The Service ruled that the premiums on the policy which was assigned to the wife and with respect to which she was the irrevocable beneficiary were alimony under the statute but that the payments on the policy which was not assigned to her and with respect to which she was only the contingent beneficiary are not alimony (and thus not deductible to the payor and not includible in the income of the payee).

There is also an odd rule that alimony payments may not be "front loaded." The rule is that if the payments in the second year exceed payments in the third year by more than $15,000, then that excess is recaptured in the third year. Then if the alimony payments in the first year exceed the average of the payments in the second and third year (after reducing the second year excess payments as ascertained above) by more than $15,000, that excess amount is also recaptured in the third year. By "recapture" it is meant that that excess is taken back into the income of the payor and is a deduction to the payee.[93]

**90.** § 71(c)(1).

**91.** § 71(c)(2).

In the leading case of Commissioner v. Lester, 366 U.S. 299, 81 S.Ct. 1343, 6 L.Ed.2d 306 (1961), which influenced the enactment of the present statute, the written agreement incident to the divorce provided that the payments made by the husband to the wife shall be reduced by one-sixth in the event that any of the three children marry, become emancipated, or die. Although the arrangement seemed to suggest that one-half of the payments to the wife was for child support, the Supreme Court held that the agreement did not adequately "fix" one-half of the payments for child support, and therefore the payments were entirely alimony and fully deductible to the husband. This case is notable for its discussion of the statutory scheme governing alimony and similar payments. The court stated that the statutory scheme gives the husband and wife the power to allocate the tax burden between them to their mutual advantage.

**92.** 1950–1 Cum.Bull. 27.

**93.** § 71(f). If the payments cease during the three-year period due to the death of either spouse or the payee's remarriage, the recapture rule does not apply, § 71(f)(5).

This strange concern with front-loading of alimony payments (not regarded as a widespread tax shelter) apparently arose out of the great concern of one member of the Senate over this issue. The real problem in the field is, of course, not the front-loading of alimony but the failure to pay it at all.

A problem, of course, may arise if one of the parties is advised as to tax consequences of the divorce agreement and the other party is not. This can lead to an agreement which heavily favors the well-informed side. (Nasty).

### (b) Property Settlements; Davis

Often, instead of alimony or in addition to alimony, the parties to a divorce will enter into a property settlement. The leading case in this area is *United States v. Davis*,[94] which is also discussed at ¶ 4.02.

In *Davis*, the husband transferred to his estranged wife 1,000 shares of appreciated DuPont stock. In consideration the wife transferred "in full settlement and satisfaction of any and all claims and rights against the husband whatsoever (including . . . dower and all rights under the laws of testacy and intestacy).

This posed the questions: was the transfer of duPont stock a taxable event? 2) If so, how much taxable gain resulted?

The taxpayer argued the transaction is like a nontaxable division of property between two co-owners. The Service argued the transaction is a taxable transfer of property in exchange for the release of an independent legal obligation.

The Supreme Court held that under controlling local law of Delaware, the wife's inchoate rights in her husband's property "do not even remotely reach the dignity of co-ownership." The wife's rights are a personal liability against the husband rather than a property interest. Thus this was a realizing event, not a nontaxable division of property between two co-owners.

The Court then held that the measure gain to the husband is by fair market value of what was received (satisfaction of rights) less basis in stock transferred. The Court conceded it is difficult to value satisfaction of marital rights. The Court thus assumed that the parties bargained at arm's length. Hence the Court assumed that the marital rights are worth the fair market value of property transferred.

Under the Court's rationale, a division of property in a community property state would lead to a different result: no tax to the husband. This would be the case because the transaction would then constitute a division of property among two co-owners. The Court conceded that under its reasoning results would vary depending on the state.

Congress changed the law in this area in 1984. It provided in § 1041(a) that no gain or loss is recognized on a transfer of property to a spouse or to a former spouse (if the transfer is incident to the divorce). This overrules *Davis*. Congress provided in § 1041(b) that the basis of the property so transferred is the transferor's basis.

**94.** 370 U.S. 65, 82 S.Ct. 1190, 8 L.Ed.2d 335, rehearing denied 371 U.S. 854,     83 S.Ct. 14, 9 L.Ed.2d 92 (1962).

*(c) The Marriage Tax: Once More With Feeling*

There is a substantial controversy regarding status for filing a return. This is the so-called "marriage tax" or sometimes the "single person tax." Historically, this issue has oscillated back and forth depending on the particular rate schedules in place at the time. The idea is that depending on the particular rate schedules in place at the time, sometimes it appears that the tax law favors married people and sometimes it favors single people.

The tax rates that were in effect in 1992 give a particularly good example of this effect. Examine the accompanying table.

### Married and Single Persons' Tax for 1992

| Taxable Income | Tax on Married Couple (Sec. 1(a)) | Tax on Single Person (Sec. 1(c)) | Difference: The Single Person Tax |
|---|---|---|---|
| $10,000 | $1,500 | $1,500 | $0 |
| $20,000 | $3,000 | $3,072 | $72 |
| $30,000 | $4,500 | $5,872 | $1,372 |
| $40,000 | $6,982 | $8,672 | $1,690 |
| $50,000 | $9,782 | $11,560 | $1,779 |
| $60,000 | $12,582 | $14,660 | $2,079 |
| $70,000 | $15,382 | $17,760 | $2,378 |
| $80,000 | $18,270 | $20,860 | $2,591 |
| $90,000 | $21,370 | $23,960 | $2,591 |
| $100,000 | $24,470 | $27,060 | $2,591 |
| $110,000 | $27,570 | $30,160 | $2,591 |
| $120,000 | $30,670 | $33,260 | $2,591 |
| $130,000 | $33,770 | $36,360 | $2,591 |
| $140,000 | $36,870 | $39,460 | $2,591 |
| $150,000 | $39,970 | $42,560 | $2,591 |
| $160,000 | $43,070 | $45,660 | $2,591 |
| $170,000 | $46,170 | $48,760 | $2,591 |
| $180,000 | $49,270 | $51,860 | $2,591 |
| $190,000 | $52,370 | $54,960 | $2,591 |
| $200,000 | $55,470 | $58,060 | $2,591 |
| $210,000 | $58,570 | $61,160 | $2,591 |
| $220,000 | $61,670 | $64,260 | $2,591 |
| $230,000 | $64,770 | $67,360 | $2,591 |
| $240,000 | $67,870 | $70,460 | $2,591 |
| $250,000 | $70,970 | $73,560 | $2,591 |
| $260,000 | $74,070 | $76,660 | $2,591 |
| $270,000 | $77,170 | $79,760 | $2,591 |
| $280,000 | $80,270 | $82,860 | $2,591 |
| $290,000 | $83,370 | $85,960 | $2,591 |
| $300,000 | $86,470 | $89,060 | $2,591 |

Note that these calculations do not take account of the fact that above $150,000 the personal exemption is gradually phased out (see Chapter 7). This phase-out in substance causes the marginal rate (and thus the effective rate) to go up somewhat on incomes above the $150,000 level.

What does this all mean? Well, suppose Jack and Jill are living together without being married (remember the old days?). Jack fell down and broke his *keister* so Jill is the only one making any money. Jill's 1992 income as an advertising agency executive is $140,000. We see from our trusty table that Jill is paying a tax of $39,460. Jill decides to make an honest man out of Jack and so they get married. As we see from our trusty table, this puts Jill's income on the married person's table. Jill and Jack's taxes are now $36,870. So they save $2,591 in taxes. Not bad for a night's work.

Comes now Little Boy Blue. He plays a trumpet with a small jazz band on Iberville St. in the French Quarter in New Orleans. In 1992, he makes $140,000 per year. But LBB is not just another hophead musician. He knows from taxes. He knows Jill and Jack from the old days, and one afternoon over po'boys and iced tea on Canal he points out that Jill and Jack are now paying less taxes than he, since he is single.

"Pshaw," says Jack, massaging his keister. "Two can't live as cheaply as one. We should get a tax break."

"You should get a job," says LBB.

To everyone's surprise, Jack does get a job. With his background in water-hauling, he gets a job as an upper-level manager with the Orleans Parish Sanitary District. The salary is $70,000.

Meanwhile Jill's been taking a hit. Advertising revenues are off; the Olympics Triplecast tanked, and her salary plummets to $70,000. As a married couple with income of $140,000, their taxes are still $36,870.

They meet their old friend LBB one afternoon for beignets and *cafe au lait* on Bourbon St. LBB, always with a keen eye for the bottom line, says "You should get divorced." Is he right?

This supposed tax penalty of marriage arises from the fact that in the case where the husband and wife have approximately equal amounts of taxable income, the joint return tax rate schedule will impose a heavier tax on the couple than if each of them had filed as unmarried individuals. Moreover, the married couple in this circumstance cannot avoid this effect by filing separately, because they will then be subject to the tax rate schedule for married individuals filing separately which would impose approximately the same tax as the joint return tax rate schedule. In Jack and Jill's case, if they filed as married individuals filing separately, they would each incur a tax liability of $18,414, for a total joint tax liability of $36,828. This is approximately the same as the liability for married individuals filing jointly.

This has led from time to time to a public outcry to "do away with the tax on marriage" by allowing married persons who both have income to file as though they were unmarried individuals.

The problem with that idea is that a married couple so filing will have a lesser tax liability than another married couple where only one of the parties earns all the income—even though the two couples have the same total amount of income. Thus if Jack and Jill, each with their $70,000 of income, are each allowed to file as single individuals, they will have a tax liability of $17,760. This would crank out, as our trusty table helps us compute, to a total joint tax liability of $35,520. The problem is this would violate the principle that two married couples with the same income ought to pay the same tax. Thus if Jack Spratt and his wife earn $140,000 on the wife's salary as a chef, their tax liability is $36,870. Why should the Spratts pay more than Jack and Jill? Dispirited as we are by this conundrum, we are relegated to just sitting in a corner and eating our Christmas pie.

## ¶ 6.03   Limitations on Deductions

### (1) In General

Notwithstanding the detailed treatment of a wide variety of deductible items, described above, there are a number of expenditures which appear to arise out of business or profit-seeking activity whose deductibility can still be in question. There are several broad principles that may apply to such items, which have the effect of preventing them from being deducted even though they are expenditures arising out of business or profit-seeking activity. The major principles here are that in the case of compensation for personal services, the compensation must be "reasonable"; expenditures may also be nondeductible because they are personal in nature, are capital expenditures, or violate public policy. In addition to these broad limits, there are also some more specialized disallowance provisions. Taken together, these limits on deductions cover a wide variety of expenditures and transactions as the ensuing discussion indicates.

### (2) The Limit of Reasonable Compensation for Services

#### (a) In General

The wages of an employee, of course, are deductible as an ordinary and necessary business expense.[1] However, the wages, salary, or other compensation for personal services must be "reasonable"; to the extent that compensation for personal services is unreasonable, it will not be allowed as a deduction.[2] In the usual case, the question of unreasonable compensation does not arise, since the employer and employee are at arms length, and whatever bargain they strike will be respected for tax purposes by the Service. Where the parties are related, as by family or by virtue of other business associations, the possibility that inflated compensation is being paid to maximize the employer's tax deduction becomes real, and such arrangements draw intense scrutiny from the Service.

¶ 6.03

1. See ¶ 6.02(1).

2. § 162(a)(1); a similar limitation is generally held to exist for wages deducted pursuant to § 212, see ¶ 6.02(2).

Detailed discussion of the area of reasonable compensation for services is given at ¶ 6.02(1).

### (b) The Problems of the Double Tax on Corporate Dividends

Let us look briefly at the vexing case of the closely-held corporation. Corporations (other than so-called S–Corporations) pay a corporate tax at a top rate of 35% on income above $10 million, under § 11. Once corporate income is taxed, it then may be distributed to shareholders as a dividend. Dividends paid by corporations are not deductible to the corporation in arriving at its taxable income. Salaries paid by the corporation are deductible. Both dividends and salaries are, however, taxable to the shareholders. Assuming, for simplicity, a flat corporate rate of 35% and a flat shareholder rate of 39.6% (these are the top rates for corporations and shareholders), the situation may be represented by the diagram accompanying this discussion.

Double Tax on Corporate Dividends Illustrated

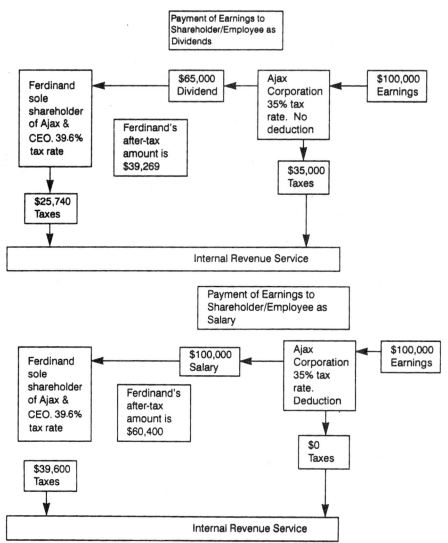

Thus the imposition of the corporate tax rate on dividends left Ferdinand with $21,131 less ($60,400 minus $39,269) than if the payment is treated as salary. The corporate tax reduced Ferdinand's rate of return by 35%. Thus we get a very vexing problem in the administration of the tax laws with regard to closely-held corporations whose shareholders also serve as executives or employees of the corporation. The corporation will make payments to these shareholder/employees. As illustrated above, if the payment is called "dividends," there is the double tax. If the payment is called "salary," there is only the single shareholder-level tax.

With Ferdinand owning all the stock, the payments are just money to him. He does not really care what they are called. The bottom line is that Ferdinand wants $100,000 out of his company. When the payment comes out of Ajax, it has to be called something. If you were advising Ferdinand, what would you suggest the payment be called? (Since Ferdinand owns all the stock, Ajax will be doing just what he wants). In that case, hey! Let's call the payment salary. This company never pays dividends!

The Service is, unfortunately, aware of this little gambit. They challenge excessive salary payments. Since § 162 provides that compensation must be reasonable, the Service will challenge salary payments that are too high and disallow the deduction for "unreasonable" compensation. The Service will recharacterize unreasonable compensation as dividends. The payments will then pick up the extra corporate tax. Taxpayers, of course, resist. There is a plethora of cases on the subject. One of the major sources of evidence in such cases is what other companies in similar industries pay for comparable services.

Shareholders of closely-held corporations also engage in other maneuvers to try to extract money out of their corporation and avoid the corporate level tax. They may rent property to the corporation and charge an excessive rent. Rent, like salary, is deductible. They may lend money to the corporation and charge a very high rate of interest. Interest is deductible. Another move is to put children or other relatives on the payroll. This again is a way to try to extract funds and also shift income to someone who may be in a lower tax bracket. The Service is vigilant.[3]

The fact that unreasonable compensation is not deductible to the employer does not necessarily affect the taxability of such unreasonable compensation to the employee. First of all, taxpayers are taxable on *all* compensation received, whether reasonable or unreasonable. Second, if

---

3. This double tax on corporate dividends is of significance to large publicly-held corporations as well. With the publicly-held corporation, you do not have the issue of executives trying to take dividend payments out as salary. Usually executives of publicly-traded companies do not own a large enough percentage of the stock so that substantial payments to them could be denominated dividends.

The problem with the double taxation of dividends in the publicly-held company is that it encourages companies to raise money by selling debt or bonds instead of stock in order to raise money. The interest payments on debt is deductible whereas the dividends on stock are not deductible. This leads to excessive amounts of debt in the economy ("overleveraging," in the argot). Companies with large amounts of debt are, of course, more likely to go bankrupt than companies without it. The payment of in-

terest on debt is legally enforceable whereas the payments of dividends on stock is not.

This problem that the tax system encourages debt-financing has been the subject of intense study by the American Law Institute and the Treasury Department. One obvious answer is to make dividends deductible to the corporation. That has a major problem in that it causes a large loss in tax revenue. It is simply impossible to lift the double tax on dividends and not lose revenue. The impossibility of the task has not prevented large expenditures of time in studies trying to figure out how to accomplish it. Making dividends deductible also could have the effect of increasing shareholder pressure for corporations to pay dividends. Corporate executives and their advisors may not like this since they would prefer to retain the funds for purposes of reinvestment.

the unreasonable compensation may not be deducted by the employer on the grounds that it is, for example, a dividend, then the unreasonable compensation will be deemed a dividend to the employee. If a simultaneous sale of property is going on between the employer and the employee, the excessive compensation may be deemed a payment for the property, a result which is unattractive to the payor-employer—who therefore cannot deduct the payment—but could be attractive to the payee-employee, who might be able to treat the payment as a capital gain.[4]

### (3) The Limit of Personal Expenses

#### (a) Miscellaneous Personal Expenses: Smith

A fundamental principle of the federal income tax system is that no deduction is allowed for personal, living, or family expenses.[5] This seemingly self-evident and simple proposition is, in fact, fraught with difficulty. Virtually every expenditure a taxpayer makes can be viewed as having both a personal or family component, and hence be regarded as nondeductible, and as having a business expense component, and hence be regarded as deductible. Even such apparently personal items as food and shelter have their business component, since obviously a taxpayer cannot work without nourishment and protection from the elements. Even such a purely personal expense as a tennis vacation could be regarded as having a business aspect, since without such recreation and incentive, the taxpayer may very well perform less effectively at his trade or business. Thus, lines must be drawn and rules must be made, to prevent all expenses of living from being deductible in full.

The leading case in trying to unpack this problem is *Henry C. Smith:*

---

4. For elaboration of these principles see Sterno Sales Corp. v. United States, 170 Ct.Cl. 506, 345 F.2d 552 (1965) (unreasonable compensation still taxable to employee as compensation); Regs. § 1.162–8 (unreasonable compensation deemed payment for property). For general discussion, see Mayson Manufacturing Co. v. Commissioner, 178 F.2d 115 (6th Cir.1949); Hoffman "Heeding Significant Factors Improves the Odds for Reasonable Compensation," 50 J Tax. 150 (1979); Ford and Page, "Reasonable Compensation: Continuous Controversy," 5 J.Corp.Tax. 307 (1979).

5. § 262. See Halperin, "Business Deductions for Personal Living Expenses: A Uniform Approach to An Unsolved Problem," 122 Univ. of Penn.L.Rev. 859 (1974).

## SMITH v. COMMISSIONER[6]

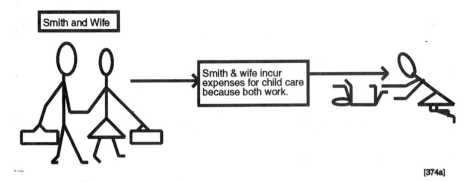

[374a]

*Question:* Are the child care expenses deductible as an ordinary and necessary business expense?

*Taxpayer's argument:* A "but for" test: "But for" the nurse, the wife could not leave the child and pursue her job.

*Held:* Expenses are personal in nature, not the ordinary accompaniment of business pursuits. Thus not deductible under § 262.

*Comment:* The Board of Tax Appeals (the predecessor of the Tax Court) asserted that medical care, clothing and food also meet the "but for" test in that without them one cannot work. Those expenses, of course, would be incurred whether the second spouse works or not. The child care expenses are only incurred if the second spouse works.

*Comment:* While the issues raised in *Smith* are still quite lively, Congress did have some pity on working couples with children by providing for a credit for child care expenses, see Chapter 10.

The *Smith* case has come under criticism for its analysis. As the comment above indicates that test is faulty. However, as the brief above indicates, another ground of the *Smith* case's holding was that the nursemaid expenses are personal in nature. However you feel about child care, the idea of inherently personal non-deductible expenditures is certainly a very real concept. The working person has a variety of increased expenses for food, clothing, and commuting. None of these is deductible.

Some of the cases and commentary in this area take the approach that there is something almost mystical about this concept of expenses that are "inherently personal" even if they are derived from business. In fact the tax system would not fall down if expenses of increased food, clothing, commuting, haircuts and so forth on account of employment were deductible. What would happen is that the tremendous number of people who have those kind of expenses would deduct them; the tax rate would be increased to make up for the lost revenue; and we would be

**6.** 40 B.T.A. 1038, 1939 WL 83 (1939), aff'd without opinion 113 F.2d 114 (2d Cir. 1940).

back more or less to square one. In fact that is probably a superior way to handle things. That is because those people who stay home and do not have these kinds of employment-related expenses would be hurt by a regime of allowing these deductions and increasing the tax rates. And those people should pay higher taxes, since they are not out-of-pocket work-related expenses. The people who are working should be able to deduct their increased expenses from doing so. This would more accurately reflect their true income.

In any event, following this "inherently personal" principle, it is clear that items such as food, clothing, shelter, are not deductible.[7] Also not deductible are other more optional but such inherently personal expenditures as haircuts (even though more haircuts may be required because the taxpayer is employed), dentures, health spa expenses, hearing aids.[8]

The "inherently personal" principle has been inadequate to deal with a wide variety of expenses that contain heavy personal and business elements, such as travel and entertainment, and these expenses are subject to specialized rules, discussed earlier in this chapter.

### (b) Education Expenses

Expenses for education are often barred because they are in the nature of capital expenses or personal expenses. As a result, they form a subcategory of limitations on deductions. Detailed discussion of education expenses is given at ¶ 6.02(2)(b).

### (4) The Limit of Capital Expenditures: Welch, Mt. Morris Drive–In; Midland Empire; Morton Frank; Indopco

It is fundamental to the federal income tax system that no deduction is allowed for capital expenditures, which are in general defined as the cost of acquisition, construction or erection of buildings, machinery and equipment, furniture and fixtures and similar property having a useful life substantially beyond the taxable year.[9] Instead of being deducted immediately, capital expenditures are added to the basis of the property involved and, if the property is depreciable, depreciated or amortized over the property's useful life.[10] If the property is not depreciable (such as stock or securities or undeveloped land), then the tax benefit of a capital expenditure will only be enjoyed upon sale or other disposition of

---

**7.** The cost of acquiring and maintaining uniforms is deductible as a business expense if the uniforms are specifically required as a condition of the taxpayer's employment and the uniforms are not suitable for ordinary wear, Rev.Rul. 70–474, 1970–2 C.B. 35. Cf. Sanner, 28 T.C.M. 476 (1969) (gray suit required to be worn by state driver's license examiners not deductible because it was suitable for ordinary wear); Pevsner v. Commissioner, 628 F.2d 467 (5th Cir.1980), reh'g denied 636 F.2d 1106 (1981) (Yves St. Laurent clothing bought by saleswoman to work in a boutique not a deductible expense even though she lived simply and did not wear them off the job.)

**8.** Reading, 70 T.C. 730 (1978), aff'd 614 F.2d 159 (8th Cir.1980) (living expenses in general); Moscini, 36 T.C.M. 1002 (1977) (food); Drake, 52 T.C. 842 (1969) (acq.); Sparkman v. Commissioner, 112 F.2d 774 (9th Cir.1940) (dentures); Rev.Rul. 78–128, 1978–1 C.B. 39 (health spa expenses); Bakewell, 23 T.C. 803 (1955) (hearing aid).

**9.** § 263(a); Regs. §§ 1.263(a)–2(a), 1.263(a)–1(b).

**10.** See ¶ 6.02(12); § 1016.

the property, where the higher basis will result in a smaller gain or a larger loss on the transaction.

The rationale for this treatment of capital expenditures can probably be best understood as an accounting concept: where an asset produces income over a period of time, expenses producing that asset should be written off over that same period. Where the income-producing asset is not a "wasting" asset, then no such write-off of the expenses to produce it is appropriate. Failure to allocate expenses of producing, acquiring, etc. a capital asset in this way would constitute a failure to accurately compute income.[11]

While it is clear that brokerage fees incident to acquiring property are added to the basis of the property, it has also been held that legal, appraisal, and similar fees involved in the acquisition of property are capital expenses, which can only be amortized if the underlying property is depreciable property.[12]

An early leading case in the area of capital expenditures was *Welch v. Helvering:*

**11.** § 446(b), requiring that the taxpayer use a method of accounting that accurately reflects income.

**12.** Woodward v. Commissioner, 397 U.S. 572, 90 S.Ct. 1302, 25 L.Ed.2d 577 (1970) (litigation expenses incident to the purchase of stock); United States v. Hilton Hotels Corp., 397 U.S. 580, 90 S.Ct. 1307, 25 L.Ed.2d 585 (1970) (appraisal fees incident to the purchase of stock). See also Commissioner v. Idaho Power Co., 418 U.S. 1, 94 S.Ct. 2757, 41 L.Ed.2d 535 (1974) (depreciation on construction equipment taxpayer used to build its own facilities had to be capitalized and added to the basis of the newly-constructed facilities, which had a much longer useful life than the construction equipment).

Cost of investment advice is, however, deductible, Bagley, 8 T.C. 130 (1947).

## WELCH v. HELVERING[13]

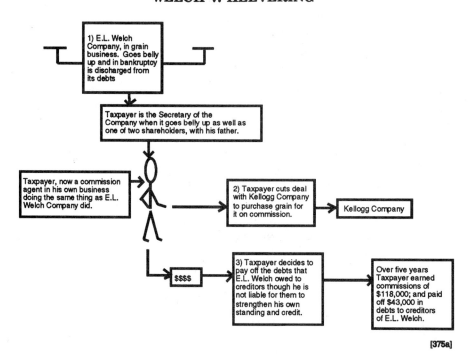

[375a]

*Question:* Is taxpayer's payment of Welch Company debts deductible to taxpayer as "ordinary and necessary" business expenses under § 162?

*Service argument:* Payments are not deductible as ordinary and necessary but were capital expenditures for the development of reputation and good will.

*Held:* The payments were not deductible for two reasons: 1) the payments were "necessary" but not "ordinary"; 2) the payments were capital expenditures establishing good will, agreeing with Service's argument.

*Comment:* The second argument concerning good will has come to be one for which *Welch* is famous.

*Comment:* Since taxpayer in *Welch* was continuing a business in which he and his father were already engaged, he might have been regarded as just "repairing" his already existing good will. Therefore the payments might have been regarded as immediately deductible as "ordinary and necessary."

*Comment:* Note that the taxpayer's payment of debts was always substantially less than his income from commissions each year. This

13. 290 U.S. 111, 54 S.Ct. 8, 78 L.Ed. 212 (1933).

suggests he carefully scaled his repayments so that he always had a net profit. This might suggest the payments are deductible expenses of doing business.

*Comment:* Curiously, although this case is famous, the weight of subsequent cases of *voluntary debt repayment* is to allow an ordinary and necessary expense deduction.

The result in this case was that taxpayer could add the debt repayment amounts to his basis in his good will. Good will, however, is regarded as an asset with an indefinite useful life. Hence there is no depreciation or amortization of good will. Thus the only way taxpayer would ever get the tax benefit of these expenditures would be if he would sell his business, including the good will. This was, of course, something he might well never do. This had to be a bitter pill to swallow, given that the alternative result was immediate deduction of the payments. This was, essentially, a case of now or never for the taxpayer.

Amounts paid or incurred for *incidental repairs* which do not add to the value or substantially prolong the useful life of the property are not capital expenditures and are deducted immediately.[14] Allowing the deduction for repairs is like allowing the deduction for casualty losses. (Indeed the repair may be occasioned by a casualty loss). In both the breakdown requiring the repair and the casualty loss, the property involved has undergone some unexpected damage reducing its value. In both cases a deduction is appropriate. Indeed, a breakdown which is not repaired might very well qualify as a casualty loss.

In any event, while it is usually clear whether a particular expenditure is a deductible repair or a replacement which must be capitalized, the borderline is far from distinct. There is a great wealth of litigation in this area.[15]

Note that the difference between finding something to be a repair and to be a capital expense is one of timing. The repair is immediately deductible ("currently deductible" in the argot), whereas a capital expense is only deductible at some time in the future. As we have learned from the Prologue and elsewhere in this book, the question of timing can be of towering importance to the taxpayer (and the government). The leading case of *Mt. Morris Drive-In Theatre Co.* illustrated the excruciating problems that can arise in trying to distinguish a repair from a capital expense.

---

**14.** Reg. § 1.263(a)–1(b), see also Reg. § 1.162–4.

**15.** See, e.g., United States v. Times-Mirror Co., 231 F.2d 876 (9th Cir.1956) (cost of microfilming back issues of a newspaper deductible); United States v. Wehrli, 400 F.2d 686 (10th Cir.1968) (repairs not deductible if part of a larger plan of capital investment); Red Star Yeast and Products Co., 25 T.C. 321 (1955) (acq.) (new sewer and drains capital expenditures).

## MT. MORRIS DRIVE–IN THEATRE CO. v. COMMISSIONER[16]

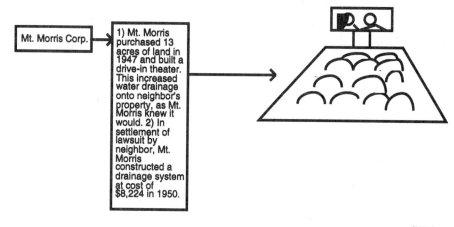

Mt. Morris Corp.

1) Mt. Morris purchased 13 acres of land in 1947 and built a drive-in theater. This increased water drainage onto neighbor's property, as Mt. Morris knew it would. 2) In settlement of lawsuit by neighbor, Mt. Morris constructed a drainage system at cost of $8,224 in 1950.

[376a]

*Question:* Was the $8,224 cost of the drainage system immediately deductible or a capital expense?

*Held:* Capital expense. Mt. Morris knew it would have to build a drainage system when it bought the property.

*Concurrence Raum, J.:* This was a capital expense regardless of whether the need for it was foreseen at the time of the acquisition of the land.

*Dissent Rice, J.* This expenditure did not improve the property or extend its useful life. It was a currently deductible repair.

It would appear, at first blush, that the Tax Court got it right. The drainage system would last longer than a year. But of course so does any repair. But still, the expenditure made the property better suited for its use and foreclosed a lawsuit.

As indicated in the discussion above, what was at stake in this case was the timing of the deduction for the drainage system. The $8,224 would either be deducted immediately as a repair (as taxpayer argued) or added to the basis of the property. The drainage system would then be depreciated over its appropriate useful life. The land on which the drive-in theater was built could of course not be depreciated because land is not a wasting asset. However improvements and structures to the land can be depreciated. Apparently the drainage system would fall into that category. Hence the stakes in *Mt. Morris* were that the taxpayer would take an immediate deduction for the cost of the drainage system, or write it off over time.

As we know from the Prologue to this book and extensive other discussion as well, this timing issue is money in the bank to the taxpayer. Just to demonstrate the point once again, let us assume a combined 40% federal and state tax rate and an after-tax interest rate of

16. 25 T.C. 272 (1955).

7%. Let us also assume that the drainage system is appropriately written off over thirty years at a straight-line rate. This means that ⅟₃₀ or 3.33% of the cost of the drainage system is deducted per year.

What is the present value to the taxpayer Mt. Morris Drive–In of each of these two methods of recovering the $8,224 cost? For the immediate write-off, the present value is clear: With a 40% tax rate, the deduction reduces taxable income by $8,224 and thus reduces tax by 40% of that amount, or $3,290.

Figuring the present value of writing it off on a straight-line basis over 30 years is a little more complex but nothing we can't handle after all we've been through together. (I do the math; you do the thinking). If 3.33% of the cost is deducted each year for 30 years, then that means that $274 per year is deducted. That $274 per year deduction saves, at a 40% tax rate, taxes of $110 per year for 30 years. Therefore (I'm sure you're way ahead of me) we want to know the present value of $110 per year for 30 years with an after-tax interest rate of 7%. That present value cranks out to be $1,365. That is a difference of $3,290–$1,365, or $1,925. That difference is 23% of the original investment of $8,224. Thus changes in tax timing amount to a 23% rate of return on the original investment.

We probably feel that *Mt. Morris* was correctly decided. It is useful to compare it to the leading case of *Midland Empire*.

## MIDLAND EMPIRE PACKING CO. v. COMMISSIONER[17]

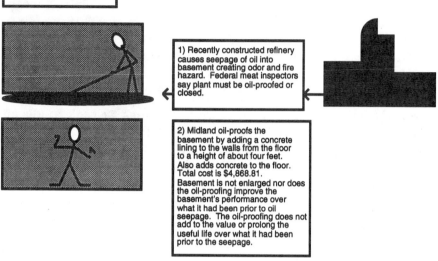

Midland Empire Packing Co. For 25 years has used its basement for curing hams and bacon and storing meat.

1) Recently constructed refinery causes seepage of oil into basement creating odor and fire hazard. Federal meat inspectors say plant must be oil-proofed or closed.

2) Midland oil-proofs the basement by adding a concrete lining to the walls from the floor to a height of about four feet. Also adds concrete to the floor. Total cost is $4,868.81. Basement is not enlarged nor does the oil-proofing improve the basement's performance over what it had been prior to oil seepage. The oil-proofing does not add to the value or prolong the useful life over what it had been prior to the seepage.

[377a]

*Question:* Is the expense of oilproofing the basement a repair or a capital expenditure?

*IRS argument:* The expenditure is for a capital improvement and should be recovered through depreciation.

*Held:* The expense of oilproofing is a repair and hence deductible immediately as an ordinary and necessary expense.

*Comment:* Court states it is not required to reach the question of whether the expenditure is deductible as a business loss under § 165.

Can *Mt. Morris* and *Midland Empire* be reconciled? One way to reconcile the cases is is to note that the problem encountered in *Mt. Morris* (the drainage) was foreseeable, whereas the problem encountered in *Midland* (the seepage from the new refinery) was not. The only problem with that approach is that foreseeability has never been a test in the field. But perhaps it is some kind of subliminal test. Suppose we overlay the facts of *Mt. Morris* onto *Midland*. That is, suppose that when Midland bought its plant, the refinery was already in place and generating a seepage problem into Midland's property.

It would seem that oil-proofing the basement at the time of purchase to combat a pre-existing seepage problem would constitute a capital expense. Have we discovered something in the capital expense/repair area? The secret test of foreseeability?

*Advertising expenses* are deductible, even if they are "institutional"

17. 14 T.C. 635 (1950), acq., 1950-2 C.B. 3.

advertising expenses designed to create good will.[18]

The ability to deduct advertising expenses immediately raises some troubling questions. Take this hypothetical. Suppose Pan–World Airlines runs a shuttle in the very competitive Boston–New York–Washington corridor. Pan–World has $100 million to spend to improve its competitive position in this market. It can spend the money on a new fleet of planes that provide more reliable and safer service than its older fleet. Or it can keep its older fleet and advertise the "Great Pan–World Shuttle—Come Fly with Us!" Pan–World's management figures that both plans—the new fleet of planes or the advertising campaign—will increase before tax profits by 15%. As an economic matter the two plans are equivalent. But the advertising is deductible immediately. By contrast the new fleet of planes constitutes a capital expenditure whose cost can only be recovered over a number of years. Because of the different tax rules, the advertising is more profitable than buying the new planes. Thus it will not be surprising if management chooses to go with the advertising.

Is that the result we want? Does this have anything to do with why the plant and equipment in this country is aging while the advertising is the slickest in the world?

If the advertising is not for a particular product but to create good will or a reputation, the expenses are nondeductible capital expenditures; expenditures to preserve existing good will or reputation are immediately deductible.[19]

Expenses of searching for a job are deductible if the taxpayer is searching for employment in his already-existing trade or business. If the taxpayer has a trade or business but searches for employment in a new trade or business, expenses of searching for the new job are not deductible, even if the taxpayer succeeds in finding a job in the new trade or business. If the taxpayer has no pre-existing trade or business, job-seeking expenses are not deductible, even if he is successful in finding a job.[20]

The case of *Morton Frank*[21] illustrates the nettlesome problems of deductibility of expenses for searching for a new business. In *Frank*, taxpayer traveled through many states to examine newspapers and radio

---

**18.** Reg. § 1.162–20(a)(2); see also Sanitary Farms Dairy, Inc., 25 T.C. 463 (1955) (acq.), discussed above at ¶ 6.02(5)(expenses of taxpayer's African big game photography safari deductible as advertising expense to taxpayer's controlled corporation, a dairy in Pennsylvania, no part of the cost of the trip taxable to taxpayer; cases like this give all taxpayers hope, but the opportunity has long since gone.

**19.** Rev.Rul. 76–203, 1976–1 C.B. 45 (moving company could deduct payments to customers for fire losses).

**20.** Rev.Rul. 75–120, 1975–1, C.B. 55, also holding that unemployed taxpayers may in general deduct the expenses of search for a job in the trade or business of their last previous employer. If the break in employment is too long, however, the taxpayer may lose the deduction for job seeking expenses, see Canter v. United States, 173 Ct.Cl. 723, 354 F.2d 352 (1965) (four-year break was too long for taxpayer to get deduction).

See ¶ 2.04(4), relating to employer reimbursement of employee moving and job-seeking expense.

**21.** 20 T.C. 511 (1953).

stations for possible purchase. He had previously been employed by several small newspapers. After a substantial amount of travel he took a job with the Arizona Times in Phoenix and then traveled more, looking at newspapers to purchase. Eventually taxpayer and his wife purchased a newspaper in Canton, Ohio. Taxpayer and his wife claimed a deduction for their traveling and telephone expenses and legal fees in the course of this search. None of these claimed expenses had anything to do with taxpayer's employment at the Arizona Times.

The court held that the taxpayer could not deduct any of these expenses of searching for the new business venture. The expenses of investigating and looking for a new business and trips preparatory to entering a business are not deductible as an ordinary and necessary business expense. The word "pursuit" in the statutory phrase "in pursuit of a trade or business" is not used in the sense of "searching for" but in the sense of "in the course of." Instead of being deductible, expenses of searching for a new business or investment are considered acquisition expenses and are added to the basis of the property acquired.[22] Under the court's analysis, if the search for a new business is not successful, the expenses are not deductible, on the theory that the taxpayer is not engaged in a trade or business and that there was no transaction entered into for profit.[23]

To clarify this area Congress enacted § 195 to deal with "start-up" expenses. Under § 195, a taxpayer can elect to amortize start-up expenses over a period of not less than 60 months from the month in which the business begins.[24] To employ § 195, the taxpayer must actually enter the trade or business (no breaks for losers).

The purchase of small items, such as pens, small tools, office equipment, which have a relatively short useful life, may be deducted immediately, notwithstanding that technically speaking, the cost of such items is a capital expense.[25]

The Supreme Court recently decided a leading case in this area. While the underlying transaction involved dealt with an innovative, sophisticated corporate transaction,[26] the circumstances also generated the leading case in the field of capital expenses. The question was whether the expenses of planning this tricky transaction are deductible immediately or whether they are non-deductible capital expenditures.

---

**22.** Woodward v. Commissioner, 397 U.S. 572, 90 S.Ct. 1302, 25 L.Ed.2d 577 (1970).

**23.** Frank, 20 T.C. 511 (1953) (as discussed in the text, unsuccessful search for a newspaper or radio station); Bick, 37 T.C.M. 1591 (1978) (same result as to expenses for investigating business possibilities in Europe); Richmond Television Corp. v. United States 345 F.2d 901 (4th Cir. 1965), rev'd and remanded on another issue 382 U.S. 68, 86 S.Ct. 233, 15 L.Ed.2d 143

(1965), on remand 354 F.2d 410 (4th Cir. 1965) (expenses of preparing to start up a new business must be capitalized).

**24.** § 195(b)(1).

**25.** Regs. §§ 1.162–3, 1.162–6, 1.162–12.

**26.** See D. Posin, *Corporate Tax Planning: Takeovers Leveraged Buyouts and Restructurings* (1990)(and supps) at 131–135 ("The National Starch–Unilever Pattern").

Ironically, the question of whether the expenses of planning this innovative transaction are deductible became more famous than the transaction itself.

## INDOPCO v. COMMISSIONER[27]

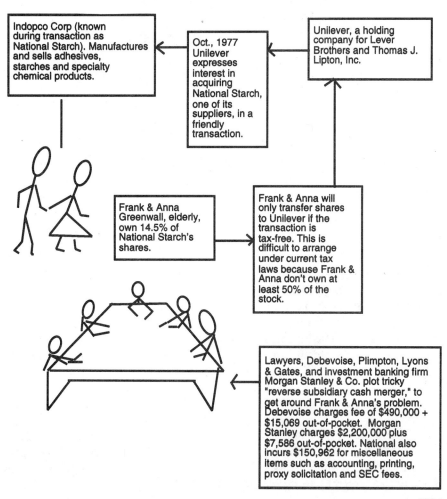

Indopco Corp (known during transaction as National Starch). Manufactures and sells adhesives, starches and specialty chemical products.

Oct., 1977 Unilever expresses interest in acquiring National Starch, one of its suppliers, in a friendly transaction.

Unilever, a holding company for Lever Brothers and Thomas J. Lipton, Inc.

Frank & Anna Greenwall, elderly, own 14.5% of National Starch's shares.

Frank & Anna will only transfer shares to Unilever if the transaction is tax-free. This is difficult to arrange under current tax laws because Frank & Anna don't own at least 50% of the stock.

Lawyers, Debevoise, Plimpton, Lyons & Gates, and investment banking firm Morgan Stanley & Co. plot tricky "reverse subsidiary cash merger," to get around Frank & Anna's problem. Debevoise charges fee of $490,000 + $15,069 out-of-pocket. Morgan Stanley charges $2,200,000 plus $7,586 out-of-pocket. National also incurs $150,962 for miscellaneous items such as accounting, printing, proxy solicitation and SEC fees.

[379a]

*Question:* Are the expenses of planning this tricky transaction capital under § 263 or deductible under § 162?

*Taxpayer's Argument:* Based on recent case law, the test for capital expenditures is whether an asset was created or enhanced. No asset was created or enhanced here. Deductibility under § 162 is the rule rather than the exception.[28]

---

27. 503 U.S. 79, 112 S.Ct. 1039, 117 L.Ed.2d 226 (1992).

28. Brief for Petitioner 16, citing *Commissioner v. Lincoln Savings & Loan As-*

*Held:* While an expenditure that creates or enhances a separate and distinct asset should be capitalized, it does not follow that only expenditures that create or enhance separate and distinct assets are to be capitalized. While the presence of a future benefit is not controlling it is undeniably important in deciding if an expenditure is capital. The expenses of planning this merger with Unilever created substantial future benefits for National Starch, including access to Unilever's technology, synergy with Unilever's own products, convenience of having one shareholder rather than 3500.

*Comment:* One of the reasons the tab for this transaction was so high was that a new tricky maneuver had to be invented to accommodate the desires of the Greenwalls.

Thus we see the Court in *INDOPCO* adopting a sophisticated financial approach to ascertaining what is a capital expenditure. This is to be contrasted with a literal, asset-based approach. The Court seems to have made the right choice. The asset approach would not have given a clear answer, since the concept of what is an asset is nebulous.[29]

### (5) The Limit of Public Policy

#### (a) Background

A troublesome area of the tax law has been the status of bribes, kickbacks, and fines, which are regularly paid by taxpayers incident to the conduct of their trade or business, or profit-seeking activity. These payments may be made by taxpayers whose businesses are otherwise legal—for example a kickback paid by an optician to an eye doctor who recommends patients to him—or they may be made by taxpayers whose entire *modus operandi* is beyond the pale of law and order.[30] Since the federal income tax purports to be literally an "income" tax, not a tax on gross receipts, the argument can be made that such payments should be deductible at least if regularly made by taxpayers incident to their trade or business or profit-seeking activity. However, allowing the deduction of bribes, kickbacks or fines for violating public health and safety regulations may be too outrageous to be countenanced.[31] Congress more or less dealt with this problem by enacting in 1969, § 162(c) dealing with illegal

*soc.,* 403 U.S. 345, 91 S.Ct. 1893, 29 L.Ed.2d 519 (1971)(additional premiums paid by bank to federal insurers are capital expenditures because they created a separate and distinct capital asset).

**29.** See Johnson, The Expenditures Incurred by the Target Corporation in an Acquisitive Reorganization are Dividends to the Shareholders, Tax Notes 463, 478 (1991).

This case has created a furor in investment banking and merger and acquisition circles, since it means that fees involved in this kind of work become more expensive to clients on an after-tax basis.

**30.** Illegal income is subject to tax, ¶ 3.13(2).

**31.** See Tank Truck Rentals, Inc. v. Commissioner, 356 U.S. 30, 78 S.Ct. 507, 2 L.Ed.2d 562 (1958) (fines paid by trucking company which consistently violated the State Highway weight regulations not deductible); Cf. Commissioner v. Tellier, 383 U.S. 687, 86 S.Ct. 1118, 16 L.Ed.2d 185 (1966) (). See also Mazzei, 61 T.C. 497 (1974) (taxpayer hoodwinked into putting money into a box that was supposed to reproduce money could not deduct his loss).

bribes, kickbacks, and other payments; § 162(f) dealing with fines and penalties; and § 162(g) dealing with treble damages under the anti-trust laws. These are discussed in turn.

### (b) Illegal Bribes, Kickbacks and Other Payments

There are three types of illegal payments whose deduction is barred under § 162(c): (1) illegal payments to government officials or employees; (2) other illegal payments; (3) kickbacks, rebates, and bribes under medicare and medicaid.

As to the first category, no deduction is allowed under § 162(a) for any payment made directly or indirectly to an official or employee of any government, or any agency of any government, if the payment constitutes an illegal bribe or kickback. If the payment is to a foreign official or employee of a foreign government, the question of whether the payment is regarded as illegal will be ascertained by reference to the Federal Corrupt Practices Act of 1977. Payments to facilitate nondiscretionary administrative acts are deductible. Payments to foreign political figures to get business are not deductible. The burden of proof for establishing whether a payment is illegal (or would be illegal by reference to the Federal Corrupt Practices Act of 1977 in the case of foreign payment) is upon the Service.[32]

As to the second category, illegal payments to parties other than domestic or foreign government officials or employees are also not deductible. The test of illegality here is whether the payment is illegal under any law of the United States or any law of a state, but importantly, only if the state law is generally enforced. The term illegality is stretched, however, in that a payment which subjects the payor not only to a criminal penalty but also to the loss of a license or privilege to engage in a trade or business will be regarded as illegal for purposes of barring the deduction. Illegal payments specifically include a kickback in consideration of the referral of a client, patient or customer. The burden of proof of establishing that the payment is illegal rests, as in the case of illegal payments to government officials, with the Service.[33]

---

**32.** § 162(c)(1). The Service has undertaken to have taxpayers assist in meeting this burden by asking taxpayers questions regarding questionable payments. See general ABA Tax Section, "Letter to Commissioner of Internal Revenue on Revision of '11 Questions' "32 Tax Lawyer 7 (1978); see also Special Subcommittee of the Committee on Practice and Procedure, New York State Bar Association Tax Section, Report on the Internal Revenue Service "slush fund" investigation, 32 Tax L.Rev. 161 (1977).

**33.** 162(c)(2). Case law has generally held that this statutory bar to deductibility does not reach illegal discounts or rebates to taxpayers customers, but only reaches illegal payments to third parties in the na-

ture of kickbacks or referral fees. See, e.g., Max Sobel Wholesale Liquors v. Commissioner, 630 F.2d 670 (9th Cir.1980).

See Alex v. Commissioner, 628 F.2d 1222 (9th Cir.1980); Rev.Rul. 77–243, 1977–2 C.B. 57 (allowing customer rebates to be subtracted from gross receipts in arriving at gross income); Boucher, 77 T.C. 214 (1981), decision aff'd 693 F.2d 98 (9th Cir.1982) (fact that state does not enforce law does not make illegal payments deductible).

The theory of the authorities in general that allow the illegal customer discount or rebate is that such a discount or rebate is a subtraction from gross receipts in arriving at gross income, and not a deduction; therefore, the transaction is not covered by the

As for kickbacks, rebates, and bribes under Medicare and Medicaid, no deduction is allowed for such payments whether or not the payments are illegal.[34]

Finally, there is the question of payments that are themselves legal but that may have something to do with illegal activities. The Supreme Court case of *Commissioner v. Tellier*[35] held that legal expenses incident to unsuccessful defense of prosecution for fraud in the sale of securities could be deducted.

The Court found that the payments were expenses of his securities business, under *Gilmore*. Moreover the Commissioner conceded the expenses were ordinary and necessary. Thus the only ground on which they could be disallowed would be that allowing the deduction would be against public policy. The Court rejected that argument, asserting that the federal income tax is a tax on net income, not a sanction against wrongdoing. Indeed income from criminal activity is taxed. The Court cited *Commissioner v. Sullivan*[36] that deductions for rent and wages paid by operators of a gambling enterprise are deductible even though the business itself and the specific rent and wages payments were illegal under state law. The Court distinguished *Tank Truck Rentals v. Commissioner*[37] (disallowing deductions claimed by taxpayers for fines and penalties imposed on them for violating state penal statutes) on the grounds that allowing a deduction in those circumstances would directly dilute the punishment involved.

### (c) Fines and Penalties

No deduction is allowed for any fine or similar penalty paid to a government for the violation of law, even if such fine could be otherwise established to be an ordinary and necessary business expense.[38] This codifies the *Tank Truck Rentals*[39] holding that payments for fines are not deductible whether or not the fines arise from intentional or inadvertent violations. This statutory bar to deductibility extends also to payments pursuant to a conviction or plea of guilty or *nolo contendere* for a crime; civil penalties imposed by Federal, State or local law, including additions to tax and other tax penalties; payments in settlement of the taxpayer's actual or potential liability for a fine; payments forfeited as collateral posted in connection with a proceeding which could result in the imposition of a fine or penalty.[40]

statute, Rev.Rul. 82–149, 1982–33 I.R.B. 5 (illegal price rebates may be subtracted from gross sales in arriving at gross income).

See Chu and McGraw, "The Deductibility of Questionable Foreign Payments," 87 Yale L.J. 1091 (1978).

**34.** § 162(c)(3). Under § 280E, no deduction is allowed for amounts paid with respect to illegal trafficking in drugs.

**35.** 383 U.S. 687, 86 S.Ct. 1118, 16 L.Ed.2d 185 (1966).

**36.** 356 U.S. 27, 78 S.Ct. 512, 2 L.Ed.2d 559.

**37.** 356 U.S. 30, 78 S.Ct. 507, 2 L.Ed.2d 562.

**38.** § 162(f).

**39.** Tank Truck Rentals, Inc. v. Commissioner, 356 U.S. 30, 78 S.Ct. 507, 2 L.Ed.2d 562 (1958).

**40.** Reg. § 1.162–21. These rules, however, do not bar the deduction of legal fees and related expenses paid or incurred in

### (d) Treble Damage Payments Under the Antitrust Laws

If the taxpayer is convicted in a criminal proceeding of violating the antitrust laws, or pleads guilty or *nolo contendere* to an indictment or information charging such a violation, no deduction is allowed under § 162(a) for two-thirds of any payment for damages paid under the treble damage provisions of the Clayton Act. If the treble damage payment arises out of a private cause of action against the taxpayer without a concomitant criminal proceeding as described above, then the entire amount of damages paid will be deductible.[41]

### (e) Expenses to Influence Legislation and Elections

A long-standing rule of the tax law has been that expenses for the passage or defeat of legislation, political contributions and other lobbying expenditures were not deductible.[42] Congress has refined this principle in certain respects.

Ordinary and necessary expenses, including traveling expenses and the cost of preparing testimony, paid or incurred in direct connection with appearances before members of Congress or committees of Congress, as well as the cost of submission of statements to members of Congress or committees of Congress, are deductible if incurred in connection with the taxpayer's trade or business. Such expenditures are also deductible if paid or incurred for the purpose of communicating with any state legislative body or its members. Similarly, ordinary and necessary expenditures, including travel expenses, carried on for the purpose of engaging in direct communication between the taxpayer and an organization of which he is a member are deductible if the communication is with respect to legislation of direct interest to the taxpayer in his trade or business and to the organization.[43]

Beyond these limited allowances for deductions, Congress has codified the long-standing judicial rule that expenses for participation in, or intervention in, any political campaign on behalf of any candidate for public office are not deductible. Also not deductible are expenses in

---

defending a prosecution or civil action arising from the violation of law. Reg. § 1.162–21(a)(2).

**41.** § 162(g). In the absence of a criminal proceeding § 162(g) would not apply and the full amount of the damage payment would be deductible under the usual rules. Apparently, the reason only two-thirds of the treble damages paid is not deductible is that the amount of the actual damages paid were earlier reported in income and therefore the taxpayer is certainly entitled to a deduction when the actual damages are repaid.

**42.** Cammarano v. United States, 358 U.S. 498, 79 S.Ct. 524, 3 L.Ed.2d 462 (1959)

(expenses of liquor and beer dealers to defeat anti-liquor legislation not deductible).

**43.** § 162(e); Reg. § 1.162–20, providing extensive discussion. Experts, whether employees or self-employed, may deduct the cost, including travel, of testifying before legislative committees in area of their expertise, Reg. § 1.162–20(c)(2)(ii)(b)(2). It is perhaps unfortunate that although business interests and "experts" may deduct their expenses of testifying before congressional committees, an ordinary citizen who wishes in good faith to speak to a matter of public concern before a congressional committee may not deduct expenses for doing so, even if he is invited.

connection with any attempt to influence the general public, or segments thereof, with respect to legislative matters, elections, or referendums.[44]

Congress in 1966 enacted legislation to prevent taxpayers from circumventing the long-standing rules against deductibility of political contributions by providing that even indirect contributions to political parties will not be deductible. Such indirect contributions would include (1) advertising in a convention program of a political party, or in any other publication if any part of the proceeds of such publication benefits (or is intended to benefit), a political party or political candidates; (2) admission to any dinner or program, if any part of the proceeds of such dinner or program directly or indirectly benefits a political party or a political candidate; (3) admission to an inaugural ball, gala, parade, or concert, or similar event which is identified with a political party or a political candidate.[45]

### (6) Other Limits

#### (a) Expenses and Interest Relating to Tax Exempt Income: Tax Arbitrage

Since interest on state and local bonds is tax exempt[46] it has occurred to enterprising taxpayers in the past that they might borrow say one million dollars at, say, 12 percent interest, and use the funds to buy one million dollars worth of state bonds on which the 9% interest is tax-free. The taxpayer uses the bonds as security for the loan. If the taxpayer is in the 39.6 percent bracket, his deduction for interest[47] reduces his effective rate of interest on the loan to 7.24 percent.[48] Since the bonds pay 9 percent, the taxpayer has a sure-fire winning investment, courtesy of the Internal Revenue Code.

Congress has taken the fun out of this maneuver by providing that no deduction shall be allowed for interest on indebtedness incurred to purchase tax-exempt obligations.[49] While that simple prohibition may dispose of matters in an obvious case like the one described above, taxpayer's financial affairs may be sufficiently complex to make it difficult to determine whether taxpayer has borrowed funds to carry tax-exempt obligations, or whether taxpayer has simply by happenstance incurred an indebtedness while at the same time owning tax-exempt obligations. For example, would it be argued that any taxpayer with a

---

**44.** § 162(e)(2). See Rev.Rul. 74–407, 1974–2 C.B. 45 (corporate expenses for preparing a brochure for shareholders suggesting they contact their congressman with respect to pending tax legislation not deductible). See Krebs, "Grassroots Lobbying Defined: The Scope of Section 162(e)(2)(B)," 56 Taxes 516 (1978).

**45.** § 276; Reg. § 1.276–1, providing extensive discussion.

**46.** ¶ 3.01(2).

**47.** ¶ 7.01(3).

**48.** How do I get that, you ask. Well if the $1 million is borrowed at 12%, then interest of $120,000 must be paid. Taking a deduction for $120,000 means taxpayer's income is reduced by $120,000. Since taxpayer is in the 39.6% bracket, his taxes are reduced by 39.6% of $120,000 or $47,520. Thus you could say that the net amount of after-tax interest that is paid is $120,000 − $47,520 = $72,480. That certainly seems to suggest that the after-tax interest rate on the borrowing is 7.24%.

**49.** § 265(a)(2).

mortgage on his home should be denied a deduction for the interest on that mortgage to the extent that he happened simultaneously to own tax-exempt bonds? A variety of other examples could be adduced in which the taxpayer has incurred mortgage or other indebtedness in connection with a wide variety of investments while at the same time owning some tax-exempt bonds.

Matters are not simplified by the fact that the statute requires a subjective test: The question is whether the taxpayer incurred the indebtedness *for the purpose* of purchasing tax exempt obligations. The Service has attempted to sort this matter out by issuing Rev.Proc. 72–18,[50] which discusses various methods for ascertaining whether indebtedness has been incurred for the purpose of purchasing or carrying tax-exempt obligations. If the borrowed funds can actually be traced to the purchase of the tax exempt obligations, that would certainly establish the tainted purpose. If the tax-exempt securities are used as collateral for an indebtedness, that is very strong evidence that a tainted transaction has occurred. Borrowing funds for purposes of financing a trade or business or for financing a personal transaction, such as the purchase of a house, would generally not be regarded as tainted, even though the taxpayer simultaneously owns tax-exempt securities. However, a transaction in which taxpayer ostensibly borrows funds in order to buy stock as an investment and simultaneously owns tax-exempt securities would be suspect.

These rules, while making it more difficult, certainly do not close the door on a taxpayer who wants to borrow funds to buy tax-exempt securities and is willing to go to a significant amount of effort to camouflage the transaction. In light of all these difficulties and possibilities for abuse by enterprising taxpayers, it might be better to allow borrowed funds to be used to purchase tax-exempt securities on the theory that widespread taxpayer transactions of this type would drive down the yield of such securities and deny the taxpayers their benefits.

In addition to the fact that apparently the market would cure the supposed abuse in this area, there are some other reasons to question the wisdom of § 265(a)(2). There are a variety of other ways, unimpeded by the Code, for borrowing to produce tax-exempt income. For example, anyone who has a home mortgage and an IRA (which is a lot of people) is in effect borrowing to produce tax-exempt income. As an economic matter the individual is borrowing money and investing in something which produces tax-free income. Indeed, you do not even have to stretch to talk about an IRA.

Anyone who is borrowing money for his or her home mortgage is already borrowing money and deducting interest to produce tax-exempt income. The tax-exempt income in this case is the imputed income that comes from owner-occupied housing. See Chapters 1, 2 and 7. Once again anyone who borrows money and buys stock that increases in price is

**50.** Rev.Proc. 72–18, 1972–1 C.B. 740.

borrowing money, deducting the interest and getting tax-exempt income from the transaction. Consider anyone who borrows money while having a pension fund or life insurance policy that has an inside buildup of insurance value (see Prologue). There again is the phenomenon of borrowing and deducting interest while enjoying tax-free income.

I could go on (but I am sure you don't want me to). The bottom line is that § 265(a)(2) is like trying to plug up a tidal wave with a bottle cap. The economic phenomenon of "tax arbitrage"—borrowing and deducting interest for the purpose of investing for tax-exempt income—is widespread.[51]

However, before we hit the hysteria button, let us recall once again, that the market has a way of curing these things. Take owner-occupied housing. While it is true that borrowing to buy a house is in effect tax arbitrage, it is also true that this advantage is exploited by many people, driving up the price of owner-occupied housing. Thus in effect the imputed income of owner-occupied housing is reduced to an after-tax rate. In case you think I'm spinning moonbeams, consider this. Suppose we changed the tax laws so that people were taxed on their imputed income from owner-occupied housing.

In other words, when you bought a house, one of the things you had to consider in your budget (in addition to the mortgage payments and property taxes) was the "imputed income tax." Once that were imposed, the price of housing would generally drop in the economy across the board. That shows that the lack of tax on imputed income has caused the price of housing to rise. If the price is up because of a lack of tax on imputed income, then the rate of return from getting the imputed income (i.e., the shelter of the house) is down. The bottom line is that the tax arbitrage effect of borrowing to buy a house is eliminated by the market.

Notwithstanding this excellent analysis that I have provided, Congress does not appear to be listening. It has enacted several other provisions designed to foreclose tax arbitrage, ignoring the fact that the market will cure the problem. Some of these other "anti-arbitrage" provisions are § 264(a)(2), disallowing deduction of interest on debt incurred to carry a single-premium insurance or annuity contract. § 163(d) limits deduction of interest on debt incurred to finance investments. The amount that can be deducted is limited to the amount of the taxpayer's investment income. (Investment income for these purposes means income from dividends, royalties, rents, interest and gains from sale of investment property).

Any amounts of investment interest disallowed are carried forward to subsequent years where they may qualify for deduction. This provision shows a concern with timing. Congress does not want to see taxpayers, for example, borrowing to buy a stock that pays no dividends

51. See Shakow, Confronting the Problem of Tax Arbitrage, 43 Tax L.Rev. (1987).

(or vacant land) and getting an immediate interest deduction. Meanwhile the taxable gain from the growth stock or vacant land would occur at some later date, giving the taxpayer a time value of money advantage (I told you this time value of money stuff would help—see Prologue).

Another example of anti-arbitrage legislation is the so-called passive loss rules of § 469. These limit the deduction of losses from "passive" or investment activities (other than portfolio investments in the financial markets). The limit is that the losses from such activities can only be deducted to the extent of the income from such activities. Once again a major focus is timing. We do not like to see early deductions producing later income.

Other expenses relating to carrying tax-exempt securities—such as safe deposit boxes, investment advice—which would otherwise be deductible under § 212—are not deductible.[52] These items are not nearly as significant in amount as interest on indebtedness.

As to tax-exempt income other than interest—such as life insurance proceeds, gifts, and scholarships—expenses attributable to such tax-exempt types of income are not deductible, regardless of under what provision they would otherwise be deductible.[53]

### (b) Sham or Uneconomic Transactions: Knetsch

To jump into this topic, try out the leading case of *Knetsch*.

---

**52.** § 265(a)(1).

**53.** § 265(a)(1). See also § 264(a), barring a deduction for life insurance premiums in the context of taxpayer's business where taxpayer is directly or indirectly a beneficiary under the policy. Thus the deductibility of life insurance premiums is often dead twice, from § 265(1) and § 264(a).

## KNETSCH v. UNITED STATES[54]

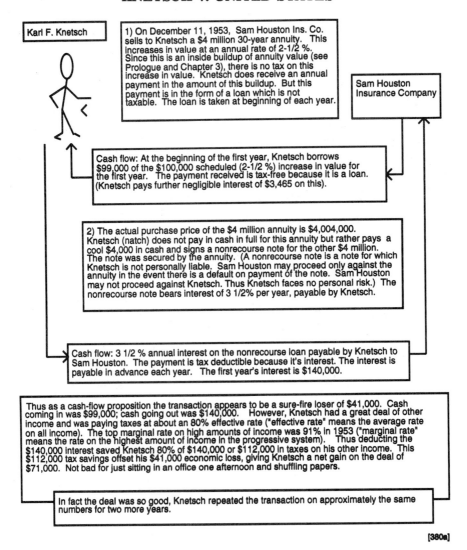

Karl F. Knetsch

1) On December 11, 1953, Sam Houston Ins. Co. sells to Knetsch a $4 million 30-year annuity. This increases in value at an annual rate of 2-1/2 %. Since this is an inside buildup of annuity value (see Prologue and Chapter 3), there is no tax on this increase in value. Knetsch does receive an annual payment in the amount of this buildup. But this payment is in the form of a loan which is not taxable. The loan is taken at beginning of each year.

Sam Houston Insurance Company

Cash flow: At the beginning of the first year, Knetsch borrows $99,000 of the $100,000 scheduled (2-1/2 %) increase in value for the first year. The payment received is tax-free because it is a loan. (Knetsch pays further negligible interest of $3,465 on this).

2) The actual purchase price of the $4 million annuity is $4,004,000. Knetsch (natch) does not pay in cash in full for this annuity but rather pays a cool $4,000 in cash and signs a nonrecourse note for the other $4 million. The note was secured by the annuity. (A nonrecourse note is a note for which Knetsch is not personally liable. Sam Houston may proceed only against the annuity in the event there is a default on payment of the note. Sam Houston may not proceed against Knetsch. Thus Knetsch faces no personal risk.) The nonrecourse note bears interest of 3 1/2% per year, payable by Knetsch.

Cash flow: 3 1/2 % annual interest on the nonrecourse loan payable by Knetsch to Sam Houston. The payment is tax deductible because it's interest. The interest is payable in advance each year. The first year's interest is $140,000.

Thus as a cash-flow proposition the transaction appears to be a sure-fire loser of $41,000. Cash coming in was $99,000; cash going out was $140,000. However, Knetsch had a great deal of other income and was paying taxes at about an 80% effective rate ("effective rate" means the average rate on all income). The top marginal rate on high amounts of income was 91% in 1953 ("marginal rate" means the rate on the highest amount of income in the progressive system). Thus deducting the $140,000 interest saved Knetsch 80% of $140,000 or $112,000 in taxes on his other income. This $112,000 tax savings offset his $41,000 economic loss, giving Knetsch a net gain on the deal of $71,000. Not bad for just sitting in an office one afternoon and shuffling papers.

In fact the deal was so good, Knetsch repeated the transaction on approximately the same numbers for two more years.

[380a]

*Question:* Was the interest Knetsch paid on the nonrecourse note deductible?

*Service argument:* The transaction was a sham. There was no economic substance to the transaction. No economic gain could be achieved without regard to tax consequences. Thus the indebtedness is not real and the interest deduction should be denied.

*Taxpayer's argument:* The transaction meets the letter of the law.

*Held:* The transaction was a sham entered into solely for the purpose of reducing Knetsch's taxes. The deduction of interest is denied.

**54.** 364 U.S. 361, 81 S.Ct. 132, 5 L.Ed.2d 128 (1960).

*Dissent:* Justice Douglas: It is true that the taxpayer was bound to lose on the annuity. Yet as long as the transaction itself is not "hocus pocus", the interest seems deductible.

*Comment:* The contract called for a monthly annuity of $90,171 at maturity (when Knetsch would be 90 years old). If Knetsch had held the annuities to maturity and continued every year to borrow the net appreciation less $1,000, the amount of the annuity at maturity would be $43 per month.

*Comment:* Knetsch was investing long and borrowing short. That is, he was locking the insurance company in to a 2–½% interest rate for 30 years. If prevailing interest rates dropped to 1%, then Knetsch could have paid off his nonrecourse loan with other funds borrowed on a nonrecourse basis at 1% and the transaction would then have been profitable to Knetsch thereafter. Is a basis of the court's decision the taking of judicial notice that interest rates will not fall for the next 30 years?

*Comment:* Suppose Knetsch had won this case. Other high-income taxpayers would have flocked to these annuities driving down the rate of return on them and driving up the interest rate on the nonrecourse borrowing, to the point that the tax benefit would be eliminated. But perhaps there were not enough high-income taxpayers to have that effect.

*Comment:* This maneuver is now foreclosed by § 264(a)(2), which was effective the year after Knetsch engaged in this transaction.

In the author's opinion (not that anyone has asked for it), the *Knetsch* case cannot withstand analysis. As pointed out in a comment above, if interest rates had dropped sometime over the ensuing 30 years, the transaction would have turned profitable. Is not Knetsch allowed to engage in a risky or stupid investment without losing his interest deduction. Or do we just go off on the fact that we "know" (as we assuredly do) that he was just trying to evade taxes? Unfortunately for that line of analysis, a lot of transactions are entered into for the purpose of minimizing or eliminating taxes. Buying tax-free municipal bonds is a transaction that springs easily to mind (see Chapter 3). Are we to impose a tax on the interest received because we "know" the taxpayer bought them to minimize taxes? Employing the S Corporation form for doing business to avoid the corporate tax is invited by the statute. Shall we deny those benefits as soon as someone elects to take them? Engaging in a tax-free rollover of a personal residence (see Chapter 4) avoids taxes. The list goes on.

This issue is not mooted by the enactment of § 264(a)(2) denying the deduction on the particular facts of *Knetsch. Knetsch* has come to stand for a general proposition that transactions without a "business purpose" or that do not have "economic substance" may lose their tax benefits. Rather than launching a jurisprudence of "business purpose", would it not have been better to allow transactions that meet the letter of the law and let Congress enact any changes it likes (which it is doing anyway)?

As a result of *Knetsch* and similar cases the courts have evolved significant judicial doctrines for the barring of deductions and other tax benefits on transactions that appear to satisfy all statutory criteria. These doctrines, known variously as sham transaction, substance over form, step transaction, business purpose, give the courts and the Service a relatively formidable arsenal to apply to carefully structured transactions where it appears that the taxpayer may be trying to pull a fast one. The problem is that the scope of these doctrines is most uncertain.

On the other hand there certainly is a broad class of transactions where taxpayers seem to be extracting tax benefits not contemplated by the statute. Perhaps, indeed, the best ready test for whether these doctrines will apply is whether the taxpayer appears to be extracting, in a dramatic fashion, a tax benefit not contemplated by the particular statutory provision involved.

In a similar vein, in *Goldstein,*[55] taxpayer won $140,000 in the Irish Sweepstakes and, on the advice of her son, purchased one million dollars of United States Treasury Notes paying interest of 1.5 percent, borrowing one million dollars from two different brokerage houses at 4 percent to finance the transaction. The notes were pledged as collateral for the borrowing. The court denied the interest deduction on the ground that the transaction had no substance or purpose aside from the taxpayer's desire to obtain the tax benefit of a large interest deduction to offset the Sweepstakes winnings.

---

**55.** Goldstein v. Commissioner, 364 F.2d 734 (2d Cir.1966), cert. denied 385 U.S. 1005, 87 S.Ct. 708, 17 L.Ed.2d 543 (1967).

See generally, Bittker and Menikoff, "Restructuring Business Transactions for Federal Income Tax Purposes," 1978 Wisc. L.Rev. 715 (1978).

# Chapter 7

---

## ITEMIZED DEDUCTIONS AND
## PERSONAL EXEMPTIONS

*Table of Sections*

---

## ¶ 7.01   Itemized Deductions

### *(1) In General*

As discussed at the beginning of Chapter 6, deductions may be classified into two categories: deductions taken "above the line" and deductions taken "below the line." Deductions taken above the line are those deductions which are taken from gross income to arrive at adjusted gross income. Deductions taken below the line are deductions taken from adjusted gross income to arrive at taxable income. Deductions taken below the line are called "itemized deductions."[1] It is § 62 of the Code that provides the rules for whether the particular deductions will be taken above the line or below the line.

It should be noted that to the extent that the deductions discussed in this chapter do not relate to business or profit-seeking activity, they represent an exception to the general structural principle of the Code that personal or living expenses are not deductible.[2]

These deductions, such as that for interest on the home mortgage, charitable contributions, medical expenses, casualty losses, and state and local taxes, have come under criticism because they are not required for a theoretically sound income tax. Indeed they are considered "tax expenditures" that are allowed for a policy reason and cost tax revenues to promote certain policies or assist taxpayers in some way. As discussed

---

**¶ 7.01**

1. As an exception to the generalization in the text, the deductions for personal and dependency exemptions are taken be- low the line but are not regarded as "itemized deductions," § 63(d).

2. § 262.

in Chapter 1, one of the criticisms of "tax expenditures" is that they help higher-income bracket taxpayers more than lower-income bracket taxpayers.

As a partial response to this criticism, Congress in 1990 enacted § 68, which limits the amount of itemized deductions that upper income bracket taxpayers may take. Section 68 is directed to taxpayers who have adjusted gross income that exceeds $100,000 (on a joint return, as adjusted upward for inflation). The amount of itemized deductions such taxpayers can actually deduct is reduced by 3% of the excess of adjusted gross income over $100,000.[3] Thus for example if a taxpayer has adjusted gross income of $400,000 and itemized deductions otherwise allowable of $75,000, the itemized expenses allowed to be deducted would be reduced by $9,000 to $66,000. This is computed by taking 3% of $300,000, which is the amount that the taxpayer has in excess of $100,000. That $9,000 is then subtracted from $75,000 to yield $66,000.[4]

One might only wonder why Congress bothered with this *de minimis* provision. This does not raise much revenue; it hits relatively few taxpayers. If there is really a theoretical problem with itemized deductions, this provision is not doing much about it.

Also important as to deductions taken below the line is that they will only have an impact on the computation of the taxpayers taxable income to the extent their total exceeds the taxpayer's standard deduction.[5]

### (2) Expenses of Tax Advice and Litigation

Expenses in connection with the determination, collection, or refund of any tax are deductible.[6] This includes taxes of federal, state or municipal authorities, and includes income, estate, gift, property or any other tax. Also deductible are expenses paid or incurred for tax counsel or expenses paid or incurred in connection with preparing tax returns or in connection with any proceeding involved in determining taxpayer's tax liability or contesting his tax liability.[7] In major planning areas, such as divorce settlements (see ¶ 6.02(14)) or estate planning, that proportion

---

**3.** An alternate limit in the statute is that itemized deductions will be reduced by 80% of the total of itemized deductions if that is lesser than the 3% limit. This 80% limit will only rarely be triggered.

**4.** In ascertaining the amount of itemized deductions for this purpose, the medical expense deduction, the deduction for casualty losses, and the deduction for investment interest are not included. These deductions are subject to their own limits as discussed elsewhere in this chapter.

**5.** Therefore, taxpayers may attempt to argue that a particular deduction should be taken above the line if they do not expect that their total deductions below the line will exceed their standard deduction. Excess

itemized deductions may be subject to tax under the alternative minimum tax, see ¶ 7.05.

**6.** 212(3). Reg. § 1.212–1(e); see Rev. Rul. 68–662, 1968–2 C.B. 69 (legal expenses incident to unsuccessful defense of criminal tax case held deductible); compare Wassenaar, 72 T.C. 1195 (1979) (graduate of LL.M. program in taxation of New York University could not deduct a year's tuition, meals, and housing as an expense of preparing his tax return; anyone who has eaten the food at Hayden Hall for a year is probably entitled to some satisfaction but this was not the way). Merians, 60 T.C. 187 (1973) (acq.).

**7.** Reg. § 1.212–1(*l*).

of the legal advice which is properly allocable to tax planning is deductible.[8]

### (3) Interest

There is a major housing program going to be proposed by the President. Since I'm so well-connected in Washington, I have some inside dope. Here's how it will work. It's going to be massive. It's going to come to a total of about $89 billion a year. This is big time. Here's some other facts about it. Fifty-six percent of this, or $50 billion, is going to go to the richest 20 percent of Americans. The poorest 20% will get $15 billion.

How do you think the public will react to this proposal? How do you react to it? How will the New York Times editorial page react to it? How will this go down in the talk shows and the call-in programs?

Well, I was just funning you. The President is not going to make a proposal like this. No. Why not? Because he does not have to. We already have this program in effect. This is the effect of allowing taxpayers to deduct the interest on their home mortgage.[9] Wealthy taxpayers have bigger homes, bigger mortgages and are in higher brackets so they benefit more from the mortgage interest deduction.

This is one of the more spectacular effects of tax expenditures (see Chapter 1). Let's talk a little about the interest deductions generally and then we'll return to the intriguing subject of the home mortgage interest deduction.

The first question is whether a particular arrangement gives rise to deductible interest at all. For example, in *Revenue Ruling 69–188*,[10] the Service ruled that a "loan processing fee" or "points" was deductible as interest on a loan because it did not pay for any particular services from the lender but was a payment solely for the use or forbearance of money

In the leading case of *J. Simpson Dean*,[11] taxpayer obtained an interest-free loan from a corporation he controlled. The government's theory of taxation is that the taxpayer has enjoyed an economic benefit from the free use of borrowed funds (which could after all be invested to earn interest). The taxpayer's alternative to the interest-free loan was of course to borrow money at interest. By giving the taxpayer an interest free loan the controlled corporation would have to forego earning interest on the money itself. Thus it looks like income. However, the court held the arrangement was not income because had the taxpayer borrowed the funds elsewhere he would have 1) had income from investing the funds and 2) had an offsetting deduction of the interest he paid on the borrowed funds. Since the deduction for interest paid offsets the

---

**8.** Rev.Rul. 72–545, 1972–2 C.B. 179; *Merians* note 6 supra.

**9.** The Economist, "America's Cities," May 9th, 1992, 21, at 24. The Economist continues, "Reduce subsidies for the well-off and the money can be found to repair crumbling housing—and then to sell it off to give people a stake in the places they live in."

**10.** 1969–1 Cum.Bull. 54.

**11.** 35 T.C. 1083 (1961).

interest earned on the borrowed funds, the court held that the taxpayer has no income on the receipt of an interest-free loan from his controlled corporation. (In this connection see ¶ 5.04(3)(b) on low interest loans, § 7872, and assignment of income.)

Interest can deductible if it arises from business or investment activity. It is not deductible if it arises from personal activity.[12] Interest is deductible from gross income at arriving at adjusted gross income (i.e., above the line) if it is attributable to indebtedness incurred in connection with business, or for the production of rental or royalty income.[13] However, if interest is attributable to profit-seeking activity which does not produce rental or royalty income—such as interest on a stock brokerage margin account, which produces dividend income—the interest is only deductible as an itemized deduction.[14]

The way matters stack up now in the Code, there are basically four kinds of interest.

1) *Interest arising out of a trade or business.* This is where Willie Taxpayer borrows money to finance the purchase of supplies for his restaurant operated as a sole proprietorship. No doubt that is a cost of Willie doing business and no doubt that interest is deductible. Moreover, no doubt it is deductible "above the line" as a deduction from gross income in arriving at adjusted gross income.[15] Note, in the nasty department, the above-the-line deduction of trade or business interest is denied to interest incurred in the performance of services by the taxpayer. Thus, while such employee trade or business interest is deductible, it is deductible only "below the line."[16]

2) *Investment interest.* Willie also has investments in the stock market. He borrows some money against some of the stocks he owns in order to finance the purchase of other securities. He can deduct the interest on this borrowing up to the extent of his investment income, including gains on sales of his investment property. Any interest disallowed because in excess of investment income can be carried forward to the next taxable year.[17] As an override to these rules, interest on debt incurred to carry tax-exempt bonds and some other tax-exempt investments is not deductible.[18] Investment interest is deductible above the line if attributable to rental or royalty income.

3) *Interest incurred in a passive activity.* Willie borrows to invest in an apartment building which he does not actively manage. The deduc-

---

**12.** § 163(a).

**13.** § 62(a)(1) and (5).

**14.** § 62(a)(5). See ¶ 6.01 for discussion of the significance of taking deductions from gross income to arrive at adjusted gross income, or from adjusted gross income to arrive at taxable income.

**15.** § 62(a)(1).

**16.** § 62(a)(1). This is "nasty" of course because deductions that come below the line will not get used at all unless the taxpayer itemizes his deductions (i.e., has enough itemized deductions to exceed the standard deduction).

**17.** § 163(d).

**18.** See Chapter 6, ¶ 6.03(6)(a).

tion for interest on the debt incurred to buy the apartment building is limited to the amount of income derived from the investment. Disallowed amounts are carried forward.[19]

4) *Interest incurred to finance purchase of personal-use property or services.* This category breaks into two parts. Interest for personal-use purposes—typically credit card interest on personal items such as clothing, dining out, and travel—is considered to be "personal interest" and is not deductible. Interest on automobile loans is similarly not deductible. Home mortgage interest is the sole exception here. It is a major interest payment item for taxpayers and it is deductible subject to certain dollar and price limits.[20]

These four types of interest and how they fit into the structure of the Code are depicted in the accompanying diagram:

**19.** § 469. Often these passive-loss or shelter-type investments are made in the form of a partnership, which passes the losses through to the individual partners. See Chapter 8.

**20.** § 163(h).

**Interesting Interest**

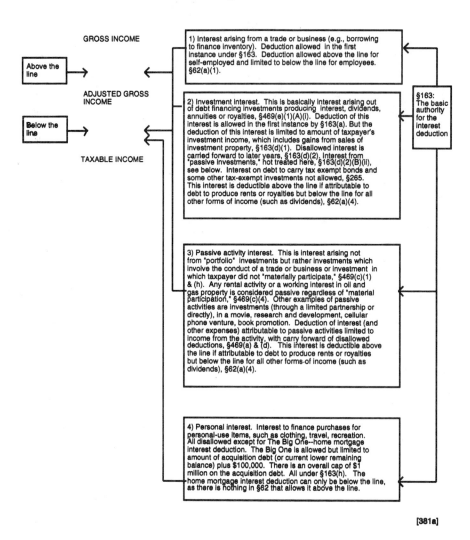

[381a]

Let us discuss in a little more detail the home mortgage interest deduction. The rules allow only qualified residence interest to be deducted. Qualified residence interest is defined as interest on debt secured by a principal or second residence of the taxpayer. This interest is deductible notwithstanding the general rule providing that personal interest is not deductible. Qualified residence interest is limited to *acquisition debt* and *other debt*.

1) Acquisition debt is debt to acquire or substantially improve a principal or second residence (up to a total debt of $1 million). 2) Other debt is debt (not in excess of $100,000) secured by a principal or second residence. Thus the maximum qualified residence debt for a taxpayer would be $1,000,000 plus $100,000.

As far as the acquisition debt is concerned (1 above), the amount that can be borrowed is limited to the taxpayer's basis in his house. This is his original purchase price plus amounts spent on improvements. Thus if the taxpayer's home goes up in value after he buys it, he cannot borrow against it and treat that borrowing as acquisition indebtedness. But such borrowing may qualify as "other debt," see the discussion below. A second limitation with regard to the acquisition debt is that refinancing the old mortgage will qualify only up to the amount of the balance of the old mortgage just prior to the refinancing. Thus a homeowner who has paid off part of his debt can only refinance (say to take advantage of lower interest rates) up to the amount of the remaining debt balance. (He may go above that debt by as much as $100,000 under (2), the other debt rules). A third overall limit is that the total amount of home mortgage acquisition debt may not exceed $1,000,000. If it does, only the amount up to $1 million qualifies for the interest deduction. (To that $1 million can be added the other debt of up to $100,000 in home equity debt, if the value of the house will support it in the eyes of the bank).

This $100,000 other debt provision makes possible the popular home equity loan, or home equity line of credit, in which typically a bank lends the homeowner up to $100,000 on a second mortgage. All of the interest on the loan would be deductible regardless of the use to which the proceeds were put. § 163(h)(3). Thus, to take a nasty little example (remember I didn't make these rules), your parents could borrow on their house to finance your legal education and deduct the interest. Whereas, as pointed out above, interest on student loans taken directly by you is not deductible.

Bear in mind, as mentioned above, the deduction for home mortgage is allowed not only on the taxpayer's principal residence but also on one other second residence. This provision gave a little jolt to the depressed vacation home market. These new rules do not apply to mortgages taken out before October 1987. (Thus your grandfather's old mortgage is grandfathered).

By and large the interest on the home mortgage is the largest single itemized deduction for taxpayers. Absent the mortgage interest deduction most people would not build up enough itemized deductions to exceed the standard deduction (of $5,000 for joint returns, indexed upward for inflation). As the comments at the beginning of this section indicated, the home mortgage interest deduction represents a major tax expenditure which much more heavily subsidizes the well-to-do than it does the poor. At the same time, any attempts to change or limit it appear to be politically out of the question. People (including the author) build their financial lives around the mortgage interest deduction.

The advantage to deducting interest on the home mortgage is even greater when it is recalled that home ownership produces major amounts of imputed income (see Chapters 1, 2, and 6.03(6)). To review the concept of imputed income briefly: if you buy a bond, it produces taxable interest income. If you buy a house it produces in-kind income—namely shelter. However, the shelter income the house produces is not taxable. We call this income "imputed income." We could also call it "in-kind income from the house the taxpayer owns."

So let's look at it. The taxpayer who has borrowed money to purchase a house has borrowed money to produce tax-free income. He should, therefore, as a theoretical matter be barred from taking the deduction since he is not paying any tax on his income.[21] Another way to demonstrate the inequity is to compare the homeowner with a tenant. The tenant pays rent which produces the imputed income of shelter from his apartment. But the tenant cannot deduct his rent.

Another take on the situation is to say that not taxing imputed income from owner-occupied housing causes resources to be directed to that tax-free source of income. Resources are therefore directed away from taxable sources of income such as corporate bonds.

Note also that it is higher-income people that benefit the most from the exclusion of imputed income from owner-occupied housing. Higher-income people have fancier houses—which generate more imputed income. And higher-income people are in higher tax brackets; hence the exclusion saves them more money. Put that together with the fact, as discussed at the beginning of this section, the mortgage interest deduction favors higher-income people and you have a powerful effect.

All of this can be easily summarized in one succinct piece of tax advice: If you are rich, buy a big house. (And you can quote me).

In case you hoped this discussion was over, may I point out that the same analysis applies to other consumer durables? But the interest deduction rules are different.

For example with the next largest ticket item after houses, namely cars, interest on an automobile loan cannot be deducted. There is unquestionably imputed income with respect to cars. A car that one owns confers valuable transportation services. Thus when a taxpayer borrows money to buy a car, she is borrowing money to acquire an asset that produces tax-free income. As we have seen from the discussion above, when one borrows money to produce tax-free income, the appropriate response at first blush appears to be to deny a deduction for the interest on the loan. This is because it is too much to allow the benefit of

**21.** Cutting the other way is the argument that a homeowner who owns his home free and clear is getting an advantage of imputed income without any offsetting limitation on deduction. Thus it could be argued the mortgaged homeowner should also be able to enjoy imputed income without any offsetting limitation on deduction. However, that argument appears to be unpersuasive. That argument seems to be saying in substance that since homeowner who owns his house free and clear is getting away with a major benefit, let us also give the benefit to the (much larger) group of homeowners who have mortgages.

What all this boils down to say is that the exclusion of imputed income from owner-occupied housing is a large tax benefit that should, as a theoretical matter, be closed but that will, as a practical matter, not be closed.

the deduction—which is supposed to be an expense of producing income—when the income is not taxed.

The problem here again is what about the person who owns her car outright. That person is also in receipt of imputed income but is not suffering any offsetting penalty. Thus, the argument goes, the person who has borrowed to buy the car should also not suffer an offsetting penalty and should be able to deduct the interest on the loan.

But the analysis can get away from you if you look too long at it. Consider Melanie, who borrows money from the dealer to buy a new expensive car for $30,000. Let us say Melanie has also got $30,000 worth of marketable securities, securities which she chose not to sell to buy the car outright. So Melanie's position is that she owns a $30,000 car; she owes $30,000 on it; and she has $30,000 of securities. The rule under current law, as we know, is that Melanie cannot deduct the interest on her auto loan, because that is "personal interest."[22]

Now let's consider Judy who also has $30,000 of marketable securities. Judy also wants to buy a $30,000 car. But instead of selling the securities she borrows $30,000 against them, using them as collateral for the loan.[23] She then walks over to her friendly Jaguar dealer and plunks down the cash.

What is the result? Judy, like Melanie, is in receipt of tax-free imputed income from the car. Judy, unlike Melanie, can apparently deduct the full amount of her interest on the indebtedness. This is because her indebtedness is not personal interest but rather investment interest.[24] But no, you say. Judy's interest is personal because she used the loan proceeds to buy the car.

You'd have a point. The Service in 1987 issued guidelines for allocating interest expenses in view of the varying rules on deductibility of various kinds of interest. The basic principle is that interest expense on debt is allocated in the same manner as the debt to which the interest relates. Debt is allocated by tracing the use of the proceeds of the debt to specific expenditures. The example I gave would clearly cause the interest to be regarded as personal.

Okay. Try this one. Judy and Melanie each have $30,000 cash. Melanie buys a car for $30,000 borrowing the entire purchase price. She then uses her $30,000 cash to buy marketable securities. Judy uses her $30,000 in the bank to buy the car outright. She then borrows $30,000 to finance the purchase of marketable securities, using the securities to secure the loan. Is Judy's interest personal and non-deductible now? Do the debt-tracing rules work now? No.

---

**22.** § 163(h).

**23.** I recognize that Judy cannot borrow 100% of the value of the securities, unless they are T-Bills. The reader who is worried about this could just assume that Judy has $60,000 of securities and borrows 50% of their value.

**24.** Deduction of investment interest has its own limitations, § 163(d), but these limits are not triggered if the investment income is greater than the investment interest.

What is the moral of this muddle? First we see here an example of why the rule used to be that interest is always deductible. As an economic matter it is really impossible to say what debt is financing what acquisition. That being the case, it then becomes impossible to compare the taxpayer who has borrowed to buy a car or a house with the taxpayer who has supposedly bought the car or house outright. Unless the taxpayer who has supposedly bought the car or house outright has no other indebtedness, you cannot really say that he has bought the car, house, or anything else outright. It would appear that you have to come back to say that not taxing imputed income at least on big ticket items like houses and cars is a distortion. But it does not make a whole lot of sense to try to use the interest deduction rules—which are themselves fraught with theoretical difficulties—to try to make the distortion more even-handed. No matter what you do with the interest deduction, it is still going to be the case that failure to tax imputed income from big-ticket consumer durables is a distortion, in that income from other investments is taxed.

*Policy.* There is a reason for the peculiar propensity of the recent legislation to encourage borrowing against the home. The drafters of the recent legislation wanted to limit the deduction of non-business interest. At the same time, they did not want to limit the home mortgage deduction, because of the political uproar that would cause. They feared, however, that sharp-planning taxpayers, having lost the deduction for non-business or personal interest, would begin refinancing their houses for ready cash and continue to take the interest deduction. Seeing the handwriting on the wall, the drafters decided to beat the sharp-planning taxpayers to the punch by providing specific rules for second mortgages or refinancings.

Whether, as a matter of national economic policy, the tax system should favor the leveraging of the family home is another question.[25]

After all this "blood, sweat and tears," it turns out that the benefit of being able to deduct interest on the home mortgage is not at all as great as it seems. This is because the residential real estate market responds to this subsidy by a general rise in prices. Thus, the homeowner is able to deduct his mortgage interest, but he is paying more (and has to borrow more) to buy his house. So the homeowner is not really much better off due to being able to deduct the interest on his mortgage, but he is more deeply in debt.

There is no doubt this price effect from deductibility of the home mortgage occurs. We see a similar effect in a small way when home mortgage rates change. When rates are down, housing prices tend to go up. When rates are up, housing prices tend to be depressed.

As discussed in detail (you might say excessive detail) in the prologue, interest has a special role in the tax law. It is particularly bound

**25.** See Interview of the author in Washington Post story "Surprises Are in Store As Deductions Dwindle," by Ann Swardson, November 5, 1986.

up with the concept of time and time value of money. This impacts even the simple question of deductibility of interest. Prepaid interest—i.e., interest paid before the time period to which it is attributed—generally must be capitalized. For example, under § 263A(b) construction-period interest must be added to the basis of the property under construction, rather than deducted immediately.

In the past, tax shelter arrangements in the real estate area would employ non-recourse debt which is in excess of the fair market value of the property being financed by the debt. In such a case, the interest deduction may be disallowed on the theory that the indebtedness is not bona fide because the debtor, having no equity in the property, has no motivation to pay off the debt.[26] Reference here should also be made to ¶ 6.03(6)(b) relating to disallowance of deductions in connection with sham or uneconomic transactions.

Other problems in the area of determining whether a bona fide indebtedness exists include the question of debt versus equity in the closely-held corporation,[27] leases with an option to purchase which may be deemed to be a purchase on credit.[28]

### (4) Taxes; Cramer

A wide variety of taxes may be deducted. These are: real property taxes (state, local and foreign); personal property taxes (state and local); income, war profits, and excess profits taxes (state, local and foreign); the windfall profits tax.[29] These taxes may be deducted whether or not they are attributable to a trade or business, profit-seeking activity, or personal activity.[30] These taxes are allowed as a deduction "above the line" under two conditions: (1) they are attributable to a trade or business carried on by the taxpayer; or (2) they are attributable to profit-seeking activity of the taxpayer which produces rent or royalty income.[31] If these taxes are not deductible above the line but only below the line,

**26.** Estate of Franklin v. Commissioner, 544 F.2d 1045 (9th Cir.1976) (purchase of motel by limited partnership followed by lease back of the property to the original owner financed by nonrecourse liability to be paid in installments; held on the facts taxpayer failed to carry the burden of showing the nonrecourse debt did not exceed the fair market value of the property.) Beck v. Commissioner, 678 F.2d 818 (9th Cir.1982) (same as *Franklin* ). See ¶ 8.02(4).

**27.** As discussed also in Chapter 6, stockholders of a closely-held corporation generally prefer to have the investment in the corporation denominated as debt rather than stock, so as to provide their corporation with an interest deduction on payments with respect to their investment. The Service naturally has opposed these efforts, see e.g. Fin Hay Realty Co. v. United States, 398 F.2d 694 (3d Cir.1968); Plumb, "The Federal Income Tax Significance of Corporate Debt: A Critical Analysis and a Proposal," 26 Tax L.Rev. 369 (1971). See § 385.

**28.** Rev.Rul. 55–540, 1955–2 C.B. 39 (providing extensive guidelines); Cal–Maine Foods, Inc., 36 T.C.M. 383 (1977) (purported lease with option to purchase was respected).

See Green v. Commissioner, 367 F.2d 823 (7th Cir.1966) (presenting the related question of whether a sale would be treated as a loan).

**29.** § 164(a).

**30.** Id.

**31.** For elaboration of these structural issues see ¶ 6.01; and see also § 62.

they will only benefit the taxpayer to the extent he has excess itemized deductions.[32]

The deduction for taxes which are not attributable to the taxpayer's trade or business or profit-seeking activity can be criticized on the grounds that it is an unjustified erosion of the tax-base.[33] It can be defended on the ground that it effects a rough revenue sharing between the states and the federal government; to the extent states and localities raise property taxes, the taxpayer's federal tax bill will be decreased. The problem with this argument is that it is not necessarily those states which may be most in need of federal funds that impose higher state and local taxes.

In any event, the primary beneficiaries of the deduction for taxes unrelated to business or profit-seeking activity are homeowners who can deduct their property taxes. Moreover the deduction for property taxes on more expensive homes will send the owner over the standard deduction with respect to his itemized deductions and thereby cause him to benefit in full from other itemized deductions, such as charitable contributions, medical expenses, casualty losses, etc.

On the sale of real property, the property tax is apportioned between the buyer and seller according to the number of days in the tax year that each owns the property.[34]

In recent years some states have attempted to shift the deduction for property taxes from landlords to tenants by imposing the tax directly on the tenant.[35] The Service, grasping almost immediately the adverse revenue effects, ruled solidly against this.[36]

A tax refund is includable in gross income to the extent that the deduction of the tax in a previous year conferred a tax benefit.[37]

An interesting case in the real estate tax area is *Cramer v. Commissioner*,[38] in which the Tax Court held that 1) where a daughter paid her mother's real estate taxes, the payments were not deductible to the daughter, since she had no legal obligation to pay them and had no legal

---

**32.** Id. State, local, and foreign taxes not explicitly described in the text may be deducted if attributable to carrying on a trade or a business or profit-seeking activity, § 164(a). This would allow, for example, state stock transfer taxes and unemployment compensation taxes to be deducted. Federal taxes, including income or profits and excess profits, estate and gift, and certain other taxes may not be deducted, § 275. Foreign income taxes may, at the taxpayer's election, be taken as a tax credit rather than deducted, see §§ 901–908.

**33.** See ¶¶ 1.02(2)(b) and (c).

**34.** § 164(d), reversing the rule of Magruder v. Supplee, 316 U.S. 394, 62 S.Ct. 1162, 86 L.Ed. 1555 (1942), requiring the purchaser to capitalize his share of property taxes.

**35.** Were this maneuver to be successful, all parties would be ahead. The tenant would deduct that portion of his rent attributable to property taxes. It is true that the landlord would then lose the deduction for property taxes, but the portion of the rent attributable to property taxes would not then be included in his income in the first instance: he would simply be a collection agent for the state. See Kee and Moan, "The Property Tax and Tenant Equality," 89 Harv.L.Rev. 531 (1976).

**36.** Rev.Rul. 79–174, 1979–1 C.B. 99 (New York State).

**37.** See ¶ 9.02(3).

**38.** 55 T.C. 1125 (1971).

or equitable interest in her mother's property. Her payments were in substance gifts to her mother; 2) where a taxpayer had sold property and provided owner financing and retained title under state law, her payment of property taxes that the buyer let fall in arrears were imposed on her and deductible.

### (5) Casualties and Other Losses

#### (a) Casualties

Losses are allowed to individual taxpayers if they are incurred in a trade or business or incurred in a transaction entered into for profit, to the extent not compensated for by insurance. Losses of all kinds incurred in a trade or business or profit-seeking activity producing rents or royalties are allowed above the line.

Losses incurred with respect to personal-use property are only allowed if the loss arises from a casualty and then only if the loss exceeds certain limits.[39] The limits are first that the amount of an individual loss to personal-use property is deductible only to the extent that it exceeds a $100 floor amount. The second limit is that the aggregate of all these personal-use casualties, after subtraction of the $100 floor, is only deductible to the extent it exceeds 10% of the taxpayer's adjusted gross income.[40]

An example will illustrate the operation of these limits:

Mr. Hardluck has an adjusted gross income of $50,000. He suffers three different casualties during the year to his personal residence, uncompensated for by insurance. He suffers a fire with damage of $2,000, windstorm damage of $2,500, and a theft with damage of $3,000. His casualty loss deduction would be computed as follows: After taking out the $100 floor on each of these casualties the amount of the loss that might be deductible is $1,900, $2,400 and $2,900, respectively. Adding these amounts up yields $7,200. Ten percent of Hardluck's adjusted gross income is $5,000. Therefore the amount of his allowable casualty loss deduction is $2,200 ($7,200 − $5,000).

Note that the character of the deduction would be determined under § 1231, if the property which suffered the casualty had been held longer than one year. (see ¶ 4.06(3)(a)(iv)).

The floor of 10% of adjusted gross income was added to the Code by the Tax Equity and Fiscal Responsibility Act of 1982, effective for tax years beginning after 1982. This floor means that the overwhelming majority of casualty losses to personal-use property will not be deductible. Rare indeed will be the taxpayer who has aggregate casualty losses,

---

**39.** Insurance premiums on personal-use property are not deductible. If they were deductible that would mean the taxpayer would be able to take a deduction to produce the tax-free imputed income that arises from consumer durables (see Chapter 1).

**40.** §§ 165(a), (c), (h). If an area in which a taxpayer lives is declared a Federal Disaster Area, the taxpayer may deduct a casualty loss attributable to the disaster in the year preceding the year the casualty was sustained, subject to the 10% and $100 limits, § 165(i).

uncompensated for by insurance, that will exceed 10% of his adjusted gross income. And even if that floor amount is exceeded, the deduction is good only to the extent of that excess. Moreover, if the taxpayer does finally surmount these limits to get a deduction with respect to a casualty to personal-use property, it will still only do him some good if his total itemized deductions exceed his standard deduction (see ¶ 7.03).[41]

This high floor limit on casualty losses to personal-use property will increase the pressure by taxpayers to show that a particular casualty loss was to business or investment property (deductible without regard to the 10% floor) rather than to personal-use property. Given the great stakes, vigorous litigation may be expected where the facts show a close case.

The allowance of a deduction for losses incurred in a trade or business or incurred in profit-seeking activity is consistent with the general theory of income taxation that a taxpayer should be allowed to deduct losses arising out of his business or investment activities.[42] Such business or profit-seeking activity losses, other than casualties, are discussed infra.[43]

The allowance of a limited deduction for a casualty to personal-use property is an exception to the usual rule that no deductions are allowed with respect to property used by the taxpayer only for personal purposes. Thus, a taxpayer may not depreciate or take maintenance deductions with respect to property used for personal purposes, such as his home or personal-use car, lawnmower, television set, etc. However, should a casualty be sustained to any such items of personal-use property, a deduction would be allowed as discussed above, if aggregate personal casualties exceed 10% of adjusted gross income.

Apparently the theory underlying allowance of the limited deduction for casualties to personal-use property is that the major casualty deprives the taxpayer of disposable income in circumstances which did not yield him personal satisfaction or utility. Therefore, it could be argued, the major casualty loss is fairly deducted in arriving at a true measure of the taxpayer's taxable income. The contrary view would hold that even substantial casualty losses are part of the risks of living and it is not the place of the Internal Revenue Code to cure all the world's problems.[44] These countervailing considerations are probably what led Congress to arrive at the conclusion in 1982 that casualty losses to personal-use property could be deducted, but only to the extent they exceed 10% of adjusted gross income.

"Casualty" losses include losses from fire, storm, shipwreck, or other casualty, or from theft.[45] There is a refreshing paucity of cases

---

**41.** For more on these structural matters, see ¶ 6.01. See also ¶ 4.04(2), relating to losses on sales and other dispositions of property.

**42.** See ¶ 1.02(2).

**43.** ¶ 7.01(5)(b).

**44.** See ¶ 1.02(2)(b), relating to the comprehensive tax base and (c) relating to tax expenditures.

**45.** § 165(c)(3). See James A. Wilson, 43 T.C.M. 699 (1982) (theft occurred when live-in girlfriend of taxpayer stole $10,000

litigating the question of what is a "fire," "storm," or "shipwreck," this being one of the few areas over the years on which taxpayers and the Service could agree. However, the litigation over what is an "other casualty" is ample indeed. There is also a fair amount of dispute over what is a "theft."

After surveying a wide range of disparate cases, the Service attempted to get control of the question of what is an "other casualty" by ruling that "other casualties" must be analogous to fires, storms or shipwrecks. In particular, according to the Service, an "other casualty" must be "sudden" (as opposed to gradual or progressive); "unexpected" (as opposed to anticipated); and "unusual" (as opposed to commonly occurring).[46] Earthquakes and floods have been found to be casualties.[47] Losses from a severe drought may constitute a casualty.[48] Gradual deterioration from rust or dutch elm disease is not sufficiently sudden to be a casualty.[49] There was an epic battle with regard to termite damage, the Service finally ruling that the dietary propensities of termites are such that the damage they cause occurs too gradually to constitute a casualty.[50]

Casualties need not arise only from the vagaries of weather, fire and pestilence; they may also arise from more mundane events or even the taxpayer's own actions. Thus, in the latest of a surprisingly long line of cases in which husbands somehow manage to destroy their wives' diamond rings, it has been held that a husband accidentally throwing his wife's diamond ring down a garbage disposal was a casualty.[51] Damage to taxpayer's automobile arising even from taxpayer's own faulty driving (so long as it is not due to the willful act or willful negligence of the taxpayer) can constitute a casualty.[52]

"Theft" as a type of casualty loss has been broadly defined by the Regulations to include, but not necessarily be limited to, larceny, embezzlement, and robbery.[53] The difference between thefts and other casualties is that thefts are deductible in the year when discovered, whereas

necklace and other articles from him, even though he did not press charges).

**46.** Rev.Rul. 72–592, 1972–2 C.B. 101.

**47.** Grant v. Commissioner, 30 B.T.A. 1028, 1934 WL 342 (1934); Rev.Rul. 76–134, 1976–1 C.B. 54.

**48.** Ruecker, 41 T.C.M. 1587 (1981) (death of lawn and shrubbery on account of strict water rationing rules arising from a drought held to be a casualty; not clear if the fact if the area was declared a federal disaster area was essential to the decision).

**49.** Appleman v. United States, 338 F.2d 729 (7th Cir.1964), cert. denied 380 U.S. 956, 85 S.Ct. 1090, 13 L.Ed.2d 972 (1965) (Dutch elm).

**50.** Rev.Rul. 63–232, 1963–2, C.B. 97 (citing the leading authority Our Enemy the Termite, by T.E. Snyder; compare Her-

bert H. Nelson, 27 T.C.M. 158 (1968) (attack of voracious beetles a casualty); Rev. Rul. 79–174, 1979–1 C.B. 99 (same).

**51.** Carpenter, 25 T.C.M. 1186 (1966); See also John P. White, 48 T.C. 430 (1967) (acq.) (accidental slamming of a car door on wife's hand, breaking her ring and causing her to lose the stone, a casualty); but see Keenan v. Bowers, 91 F.Supp. 771 (E.D.S.C. 1950) (flushing of wife's diamond ring down the toilet not a casualty); compare Kielts, 42 T.C.M. 238 (1981) (loss of 2.47 carat diamond from setting of ring while going about daily chores a casualty because violent blow of which taxpayer was unaware had apparently dislodged the stone).

**52.** Reg. § 1.165–7(a)(3); see also Shearer v. Anderson, 16 F.2d 995 (2d Cir. 1927).

**53.** Reg. § 1.165–8(d).

fire, storm, shipwreck, or "other casualties" are deductible in the year when sustained.[54]

The rule for determining the amount of the deduction on a casualty loss is as follows: taxpayer may deduct the lesser of (a) his basis in the property or (b) the decline in the fair market value of the property due to the casualty.[55] The amount so calculated is subject to the $100 and 10%-of-adjusted-gross-income limits discussed above where the casualty is to personal-use property.[56] If the casualty is to property used in a trade or business or property held for the production of income, and the property is totally destroyed, then the deductible loss is the amount of the basis regardless of whether the fair market value is greater or less than the basis.[57] This more liberal treatment of business property reflects the fact that business property is often subject to the allowance for depreciation and therefore the basis will be recoverable by the taxpayer even if there is never a casualty. If property is converted from personal to business or profit-seeking use before the casualty, the basis for use in computing the casualty loss is the lesser of the property's adjusted basis in the taxpayer's hands or the fair market value of the property at the time of the conversion.[58]

If a casualty does not completely destroy the property, the same principles apply, with minor modifications. The amount of the casualty is still the lesser of the property's adjusted basis or the decline in the fair market value of the property.[59] As an example,

> **Example:** An automobile used in business has a basis of $3,600 in taxpayer's hands and a fair market value of $2,000. The automobile is damaged in an accident and after the accident it has a fair market value of $1,500. The amount of the casualty loss is $500 (the lesser of the decline in fair market value or the adjusted basis of the property).[60]

The amount of any deduction taken as a casualty loss on property which is not completely destroyed reduces the basis by the amount deducted.[61]

Where several related types of property are damaged by a casualty, the Regulations take two different approaches, depending on whether the property is used in a trade or business or profit-seeking activity on the one hand, and used for personal purposes on the other. Thus, for

---

54. § 165(e) (thefts); § 165(a).

55. Reg. § 1.165–7(b)(1).

56. §§ 165(c)(3), and (h).

57. Reg. § 1.165–7(b) (flush language).

58. Reg. § 1.165–7(a)(5).

59. This approach will be taken with respect to property used in the taxpayer's trade or business or profit-seeking activity, as well as personal-use property. The rule that amount of a loss is always the adjusted basis for business property only holds where the business property is completely

destroyed, Reg. § 1.165–7(b)(1) (flush language).

60. See Reg. § 1.165–7(b)(3). Example (1). This example in the text assumes no compensation by insurance. Also if the automobile were personal-use property, the $100 floor and the 10% of adjusted gross income limit would have to be applied after making this computation to determine how much (if any) of this loss is deductible.

61. § 1016(a)(1).

example, if damage by a casualty has occurred to a building and ornamental or fruit trees all used in the trade or business, the computation of the amount of the deductible casualty is made by reference to each individual type of property and separate losses are determined for the building and the trees. However, if the building and the trees are used for personal purposes, the value of the building and trees and the bases of the building and trees are aggregated and an overall computation is made, using the rule discussed above to ascertain the amount of the deductible casualty.[62]

Fair market value of property before and after the casualty must generally be ascertained by competent appraisal.[63] The cost of repairs is evidence, but not dispositive, of the question of the loss of value on account of the casualty.[64]

To the extent taxpayer is compensated by insurance for his loss, the amount of the casualty will not be deductible.[65] Thus, in the example above, where the taxpayer's loss was $500, if he had received insurance proceeds of $300, his deductible loss would only be $200. Indeed, it is quite possible that the taxpayer would receive insurance compensation in an amount greater than his adjusted basis for the property, in which case the taxpayer does not have a casualty loss, but a casualty gain. For example,

> **Example:** Taxpayer owns a painting with a cost basis of $5,000. It has a fair market value of $25,000. It is destroyed by a fire and the taxpayer receives insurance proceeds of $15,000. The taxpayer has a $10,000 gain on the casualty. The fact that the insurance proceeds did not compensate him fully for his loss with respect to the fair market value of the property is irrelevant. The appreciation in the value of the painting was never taken into the taxpayer's income.[66]

Where the taxpayer's loss is deductible in one year and he anticipates an insurance recovery in the following year, he may deduct the loss in the year the casualty is sustained only to the extent (if at all) it exceeds the likely recovery.[67] If a taxpayer declines to press a claim for fear that his insurance rates will rise, he may deduct his loss, even

---

**62.** Reg. § 1.165–7(b)(2)(i) and (ii), again subject to the $100 and 10% limits.

**63.** Reg. § 1.165–7(a)(2)(i).

**64.** Reg. § 1.165–7(a)(2)(ii). The appraisal fees would be deductible as expenses of determining a tax liability, § 212(3); Blackburn, 44 T.C.M. 1124 (1982) (repair costs allowed as a measure of damages only if repairs are made).

**65.** § 165(a).

**66.** For the characterization of gains and losses on casualties, see ¶ 4.06(3)(a)(iv).

The legal fees and other expenses incurred in securing compensation for the loss are considered part of the loss, Spectre, 25 T.C.M. 519 (1966).

**67.** Reg. § 1.165–1(d)(2)(i), also providing that the balance of the loss may be deducted only upon the taxpayer establishing by objective evidence, such as the execution of a release, that he has abandoned the insurance claim.

though had he pressed his claim he would have been compensated in full.[68]

### (b) Other Losses:

Losses other than casualty losses are only deductible if they are attributable to the taxpayer's trade or business or profit-seeking activity.[69] The allowance of a deduction for business losses relates primarily to losses on sales of property. But a business loss can arise from other transactions, such as a breach of contract that goes uncompensated. The loss deduction should not be confused with the case where a business is running operating losses, which are produced by other deductions, such as the deduction for ordinary and necessary business expenses,[70] depreciation,[71] or bad debts,[72] etc. A net operating loss so produced has significance in that it may be carried over to other years to be deducted against taxable income in those other years.[73]

The disallowance of losses from sales of personal-use property is of major structural significance in the Code. This rule wipes out a raft of losses frequently undergone by taxpayers. For example, one virtually always has a loss on the sale of one's personal automobile. This loss is not deductible under § 165(c)(3). The sale of household effects at a garage sale for far less than their original cost also does not give rise to a deduction for the same reason. And most significantly, in this era when residential real estate prices are falling in many areas of the country, loss on sale of one's house is not deductible. Before one bemoans the fact of the disallowance of these losses, bear in mind that if these losses, were allowed to all taxpayers, then tax rates would have to be higher to make up for the lost revenue. (There is, as has often been noted, no free lunch.)

It is at the borderline between non-deductible losses on personal use of property and deductible losses on business or investment use that we find litigation tension. This tension might particularly be expected to occur where large losses have occurred. One of the toughest areas here is losses on residential real estate that has also been used for investment or business purposes. Taxpayers of course may well have a mixed motive in buying residential real estate. They may well think about the potential for appreciation when they buy their home. If the taxpayer uses the property solely as a principal residence, the fact that he or she had profit potential also in mind would not be enough to sustain a deduction if the

**68.** Hills v. Commissioner, 691 F.2d 997 (11th Cir.1982), reh'g denied 697 F.2d 1094 (1983) (discussion of other authorities); contra Bartlett v. United States, 397 F.Supp. 216 (D.Md.1975) and Axelrod, 56 T.C. 248 (1971).

**69.** § 165(c).

**70.** § 162(a).

**71.** §§ 167, 168.

**72.** § 166. Losses on sales of property deductible under § 165 may also, of course, contribute to producing a net operating loss.

**73.** § 172; see Davies, "The Net Operating Loss Deduction: Inequity Among Taxpayers," 10 Tax Advisor, 530 (1979).

property were later sold for a loss. If some business or investment use is made of the property, the chances are better, but success is not guaranteed.[74]

In allowing losses on sales of business and investment property to be deducted, the loss deduction of § 165(a) plays an integral part in the scheme for taxing gains and losses on the sales and other dispositions of property, discussed at ¶ 4.04. In addition to losses on sales and other dispositions of property, a loss may be sustained as a result of a casualty, discussed at ¶ 7.01(5)(a). A deductible loss under § 165(a) may also arise if securities held by the taxpayer become worthless during the taxable year, discussed at ¶ 7.01(6).

Abandonment of business or investment property will also give rise to a deductible loss under § 165(a). Since abandonment is not a sale or exchange, the loss on abandonment, even of a capital asset, is deductible against ordinary income without regard to the restrictions that attend capital losses.[75]

The major areas of dispute with respect to abandonment are (1) whether the property has been abandoned or sold, given the more favorable treatment to taxpayers of abandonment[76] and (2) whether property has been abandoned or is just temporarily not being used by the taxpayer.[77] As with casualty losses, other losses otherwise deductible may only be deducted to the extent not compensated for by insurance or otherwise.[78]

Losses from gambling transactions are allowed only to the extent of gains from such transactions.[79] This appears at first blush to be a relatively liberal treatment of gambling losses; since most gamblers are not engaged in a trade or business or even profit-seeking activity but rather are simply indulging in personal recreation—for which ordinarily no deduction is allowed whatsoever. However, this relatively liberal treatment of gambling losses is balanced by the fact that any net income from gambling is taxable.[80]

---

**74.** See Gevirtz v. Commissioner, 123 F.2d 707 (2d Cir.1941) (loss deduction denied when vacant land purchased to construct apartment buildings in fact used for construction of a large personal residence); Weir v. Commissioner, 109 F.2d 996 (3d Cir.1940), cert. denied 310 U.S. 637, 60 S.Ct. 1080, 84 L.Ed. 1406 (1940) (loss on sale of shares in coop apartment building in which taxpayer lived held deductible because the shares produced taxable dividend income).

**75.** ¶ 4.06(2)(b)(ii). Abandonment of depreciable property used in the taxpayer's trade or business similarly does not come within § 1231 because it is not a sale or exchange, and therefore will not run the

risk of being treated as a capital loss. See ¶ 4.06(3)(a)(iv).

**76.** Cf. Bloomington Coca–Cola Bottling Co. v. Commissioner, 189 F.2d 14 (7th Cir.1951) (plant held sold rather than abandoned).

**77.** See Reg. § 1.165–2(a). The Regulations provide rules regarding a loss deduction on account of the demolition of buildings, Reg. § 1.165–3.

**78.** § 165(a).

**79.** § 165(d).

**80.** Cf. ¶¶ 6.03(3), 3.13(3). See generally Epstein, "The Consumption and Loss of Personal Property and the Internal Revenue Code," 23 Stanf.L.Rev. 454 (1971).

### (6) Bad Debts and Worthless Securities: Whipple

### (a) Bad Debts

Any debt which becomes worthless during the taxable year is deductible, whether or not the debt arises out of the taxpayer's trade or business, profit-seeking activity, or personal activities.[81] In thus allowing a deduction for a bad debt which arises out of personal activity—such as a loan to a family member—this rule is surprisingly liberal.

As with the deductions for interest, taxes, and casualties and other losses, if the bad debt is attributable to the taxpayer's trade or business or to profit-seeking activity that produces rental or royalty income, it is allowed as a deduction from gross income in arriving at adjusted gross income ("above the line").[82] If the bad debt does not meet these tests, it will be allowed as an itemized deduction ("below the line"), and therefore will only benefit the taxpayer to the extent he has excess itemized deductions.

A major area of dispute is whether the taxpayer has a true indebtedness which can be deducted at all. This is particularly troublesome where the debt is owed to members of the family. While there may be a presumption that intra-family transfers are gifts rather than loans, that presumption may be rebutted if there is a real expectation of repayment and intention to enforce the collection of the indebtedness.[83] If amounts are invested with the expectation they will be returned, with a profit, on the happening of some contingency—such as the success of a business venture—and the contingency does not occur, then the taxpayer has a loss, deductible under § 165, rather than a bad debt.[84] If the transaction arises out of personal activities, the taxpayer is better off having it characterized as a bad debt rather than a loss since losses from personal activities are not deductible under § 165.[85]

If the transaction arises out of profit-seeking activity, the taxpayer is better off having it characterized as a loss, since losses incurred in connection with profit-seeking activities are deductible in full;[86] whereas bad debts incurred in profit-seeking activities are generally restricted to being deducted as a short-term capital loss.[87] If the transaction arises out of the taxpayer's trade or business, it will not matter whether it is characterized as a loss or a bad debt, since both are deductible in full.[88]

---

**81.** § 166(a).

**82.** § 62; See ¶6.01 for further discussion of structural issues.

**83.** Van Anda's Estate, 12 T.C. 1158 (1949), affirmed per curiam 192 F.2d 391 (2d Cir.1951) (on facts, no valid debt to wife); compare T. Albert White, 30 T.C.M. 64 (1971) (transfer to child created a debt although deduction disallowed because the debt was not worthless).

**84.** See Canelo, 53 T.C. 217 (1969), aff'd per curiam 447 F.2d 484 (9th Cir. 1971) (attorney's payment of litigation costs which would be reimbursed on successful termination of litigation; held was not a debt).

**85.** ¶7.01(5)(b).

**86.** § 165(c).

**87.** § 166(d) and see discussion infra.

**88.** §§ 165(c), 166(a).

The amount allowed as the deduction on a bad debt is the basis of the debt.[89] This will be the amount of money loaned, if the taxpayer is the original creditor. If the taxpayer acquired the debt by purchase, the basis will, of course, be the amount he paid to acquire the obligation— which could be less or more than its face amount. Similarly, if the taxpayer acquires the debt by gift or inheritance, the appropriate basis rule will apply.

There is a great deal of litigation concerning the tax year that a debt becomes worthless so that it may be deducted.[90] The Service will play its own version of three-card monte with the taxpayer in forcing him to pick the correct year in which the debt became worthless while the spectre of the running of the statute of limitations hangs over the taxpayer's head.[91] A wide variety of factors may be used to indicate that a debt has become worthless: insolvency of the debtor, bankruptcy, refusal to pay, death, subordination.[92]

The taxpayer may elect to charge off part of a debt where it becomes clear that the debt will not be fully paid.[93] The *pas de deux* between the taxpayer and the Service is to a somewhat different tempo in the case of partially worthless debts. The taxpayer has somewhat more control as an initial matter since he may elect to take a deduction for partial worthlessness by charging off the unrecoverable amount on his records.[94] However, since it is not desirable to give the taxpayer unfettered discretion as to when he decides to take a deduction for partial worthlessness, the Service must be satisfied that the debt has become partially worthless.[95]

Instead of fighting it out with the Service for each bad debt deduction, taxpayers may establish a reasonable reserve for bad debts where they have a significant number of credit transactions.[96]

---

**89.** § 166(b).

**90.** The problems here are acknowledged by § 6511(d)(1) which provides for a seven-year statute of limitations for claims relating to bad debts and worthless securities, instead of the usual three years.

**91.** See Denver & Rio Grande Western Railroad v. Commissioner, 279 F.2d 368 (10th Cir.1960) (taxpayer failed to prove the year in which a debt became worthless).

**92.** See e.g., Zeeman v. United States, 275 F.Supp. 235 (S.D.N.Y.1967), modified and remanded 395 F.2d 861 (2d Cir.1968); Schultz, 30 T.C. 256 (1958), rev'd on other grounds 278 F.2d 927 (5th Cir.1960) (running of statute of limitations not dispositive); Los Angeles Shipbuilding & Drydock Corp. v. United States, 289 F.2d 222 (9th Cir.1961).

**93.** § 166(a)(2).

**94.** Reg. § 1.166–3(a)(2)(i).

**95.** § 166(a)(2); Reg. § 1.166–3(a)(2)(i) and (iii). See also Brimberry v. Commissioner, 588 F.2d 975 (5th Cir.1979) (in light of the Service's discretion to disallow election for partial worthlessness, taxpayer has a heavier burden of proof than in the case of total worthlessness).

**96.** § 166(c); Reg. § 1.166–1(b); Reg. § 1.166–4(c); See also Black Motor Co. v. Commissioner, 41 B.T.A. 300 (1940) (acq.), aff'd on other grounds 125 F.2d 977 (6th Cir.1942) (providing a widely-used formula based on previous year's accounts receivable and bad debt losses for estimating reserves).

Bad debts which are deducted and then subsequently paid must be taken into income pursuant to tax-benefit principles discussed in Chapter 9.[97]

If a nonbusiness debt becomes worthless during the year the taxpayer is entitled to only treat it as a short-term capital loss.[98] A nonbusiness debt is a debt incurred in connection with profit-seeking activity of the taxpayer, or personal activity of the taxpayer. It is not a debt incurred with respect to the trade or business of the taxpayer.[99] This treatment of nonbusiness bad debts is restrictive in the sense that a taxpayer may only claim them as a short-term capital loss; but the treatment is liberal in the sense that taxpayers may take a deduction at all for a debt which may be incurred solely with respect to personal activities—so long as the debt is bona fide.[1] Nonbusiness bad debts are also unattractive in that they may not be deducted as partially worthless, and they may not be treated by reserves.[2]

Given that business bad debts are deductible in full, whereas nonbusiness bad debts may only be deducted as a short-term capital loss, it is not surprising that there has been a substantial amount of litigation as to whether a particular debt is business or nonbusiness. The leading case in this area is *Whipple*.

---

**97.** ¶ 3.12. Where the taxpayer is using a reserves method, it may be necessary to take unused reserves back into income, where the taxpayer goes out of business.

**98.** § 166(d).

**99.** § 166(d)(2).

**1.** For the restrictions applicable to short-term capital losses, see ¶ 4.06(2)(b)(ii).

**2.** § 166(d)(1)(A).

## WHIPPLE v. COMMISSIONER[3]

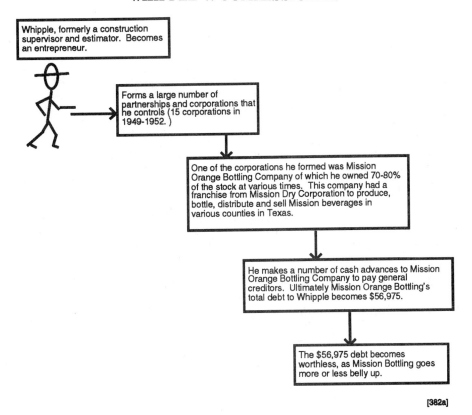

[382a]

*Question:* Is the $56,975 loss undergone by Whipple deductible as a "trade or business" bad debt under § 166(a) (giving rise to a full ordinary income deduction) or a nonbusiness bad debt under § 166(d) (giving rise to a very limited capital loss deduction).

*Taxpayer's Argument:* His many activities in promoting business constituted a trade or business. Hence the loss was deducted in full as arising out of a trade or business.

*Held:* It is well-established that full-time service to a corporation does not alone amount to a trade or business. That being the case, full-time service to many corporations also cannot constitute a trade or business. Taxpayer might have had an argument if he were developing these businesses for subsequent sale to others, but he was not. Thus his return here is an investment return. Thus his deduction is limited to a nonbusiness bad debt.

*Comment:* Presumably taxpayer was reporting the gains on the sale of others of his other business ventures as capital gains. Thus he apparently sought the best of all worlds: capital gains on his gains and

**3.** 373 U.S. 193, 83 S.Ct. 1168, 10 L.Ed.2d 288 (1963), reh'g denied 374 U.S. 858, 83 S.Ct. 1863, 10 L.Ed.2d 1082 (1963).

ordinary losses on his losses. This favorable treatment would give tax incentives to promoters of small businesses—which may be what we want to do. But it is obviously up to Congress to make that decision.

If you find *Whipple* a little frustrating, bear in mind that the distinction between capital gains and losses and ordinary gains and losses is fundamentally arbitrary. See the discussion in Chapter 4. *Whipple* can be viewed as another example of a case (in the loss area) of drawing that arbitrary line.[4]

### (b) Worthless Securities

If a security which is a capital asset becomes worthless during the taxable year, the resulting loss is treated as a sale or exchange on the last day of the taxable year of a capital asset.[5] A "security" for these purposes means a share of stock or right to receive a share of stock in a corporation, or a bond, debenture, note or other evidence of indebtedness issued by a corporation or by a government, with interest coupons or in registered form.[6]

The artificial holding period, extended to the end of the year in which the security becomes worthless, obviates the necessity of determining on what day of the taxable year the security became worthless (a great help in that it is usually difficult enough to determine in what year a security became worthless let alone what day). Worthless securities are therefore treated less attractively than nonbusiness bad debts, and much less attractively than business bad debts, in that they *may* wind up being long-term capital losses.[7] This relatively unattractive treatment of worthless securities may lead taxpayers to try to assert that their loss on a worthless evidence of indebtedness should be treated under the bad debt rule.[8] However, lest there be any doubt about it, the statute explicitly provides that the bad debt rule shall not apply to a debt which is evidenced by a security as defined under the worthless security rules.[9]

Determining when a security has become worthless presents the same problems as determining when a debt has become worthless.[10] It has been held that a taxpayer does not have to be "an incorrigible optimist" and wait until the last possible moment to deduct an investment as worthless; however, the taxpayer cannot be "a Stygian pessimist" and deduct the investment at the first sign of difficulty. This literary mouthful is not particularly helpful in the great mass of cases in which there is a significant amount of debtor difficulty but taxpayer may very

---

**4.** See also United States v. Generes, 405 U.S. 93, 92 S.Ct. 827, 31 L.Ed.2d 62 (1972), reh'g denied 405 U.S. 1033, 92 S.Ct. 1274, 31 L.Ed.2d 491 (1972) (loans by an employee to a family corporation created nonbusiness debt where the taxpayer could not show that his dominant motive in making the loan was protection of his job). See also Reg. § 1.166–9, dealing with the deductibility of losses of guarantors, endorsers, and indemnitors; Reg. § 1.166–6 dealing with treatment of the mortgagee or pledgee

on the sale of mortgaged or pledged property.

**5.** § 165(g).

**6.** § 165(g)(2).

**7.** For the disadvantage of long-term capital losses, see ¶ 4.06(2)(b)(ii).

**8.** ¶ 7.01(6)(a).

**9.** § 166(e).

**10.** United States v. S.S. White Dental Manufacturing Co., 274 U.S. 398, 403, 47 S.Ct. 598, 600, 71 L.Ed. 1120 (1927).

well expect to be paid on his debt.[11] In such cases, it is exceedingly difficult to determine in which year the security finally becomes worthless.[12]

### (7) Medical Expenses: Ochs

Amounts paid for medical care and medical insurance of the taxpayer, his spouse, and dependents are allowed as a deduction, to the extent uncompensated for by insurance or otherwise. A major barrier to getting any benefit from this deduction is that expenses for medical care are only deductible to the extent they exceed 7½% of the taxpayer's adjusted gross income. "Medical care" for these purposes covers a wide variety of medical and dental treatments and medicaments. The term is sufficiently vague to invite dispute, and taxpayers have not been too ill to litigate the matter extensively with the Service. In particular, the Code provides that the term "medical care" means amounts paid "for the diagnosis, cure, mitigation, treatment or prevention of disease, or for the purpose of affecting any structure or function of the body; for transportation primarily for and essential to medical care referred to above; or for insurance covering medical care." Closely related to this ability to deduct premiums for health insurance is the fact that insurance premiums paid by an employer are excluded from an employee's gross income.[13] The exclusion of premiums if paid by the employer does not have to run the daunting gauntlet of the 7½% floor. Thus the message from the statute is that employer-financed health insurance is favored over employee-financed. This could be understandable as a paternalistic nudge to encourage expenditures on health insurance.[14] The Regulations further elaborate the definition of "medical care". Congress changed the law in 1990

---

**11.** Ruppert v. United States, 22 F.Supp. 428, 431 (Ct.Cl.1938), cert. denied 305 U.S. 630, 59 S.Ct. 94, 83 L.Ed. 404 (1938).

**12.** See Morton v. Commissioner, 38 B.T.A. 1270, 1938 WL 165 (1938) (nonacq.), aff'd 112 F.2d 320 (7th Cir.1940) (extensive discussion); Reg. § 1.165–5(b) and (c); Austin Co., 71 T.C. 955 (1979) (sale of assets and liquidation of debtor supported claim of worthlessness). See generally Natbony, "Worthlessness, Debt–Equity, and Related Problems," 32 Hastings L.J. 1407 (1981).

**13.** § 106.

**14.** § 213(e)(1). Reg. § 1.213–1(e)(1)(ii). See also Edward A. Havey, 12 T.C. 409 (1949) (travel to the shore and Arizona not deductible although doctor recommended the trips for the taxpayer's health; the trips were not specifically linked with a change of climate). Compare with Rev.Rul. 76–332, 1976–2 C.B. 81 (cosmetic surgery deductible; Congress has since overturned this); Rev.Rul. 73–201, 1973–1 C.B. 140 (legal abortions and vasectomies deductible); Reg. § 1.213–1(e)(1)(iii) (allowing expenditures which would ordinarily be treated as non-deductible capital outlays to be immediately deductible if they qualify as a medical expense, providing the examples of eyeglasses, seeing eye dog, artificial teeth and limbs, a wheelchair, crutches, an inclinator or an air conditioner which is detachable from the property and purchased only for the use of a sick person).

In the case of a capital expenditure, which, unlike the items described above, effects a permanent improvement to the property—such as a swimming pool that otherwise is deductible as a medical expense because of taxpayer's heart disease—the deduction is allowed to the extent the cost of the improvement exceeds the increase in value (if any) of the property as a result of the improvement. To the extent that, because of these rules, the cost of the improvement is not deductible, it will be added to the taxpayer's cost basis of his property); see Feld, "Abortion To Aging: Problems of Definition in the Medical Expense Tax Deduction," 58 B.U.L.Rev. 165 (1978).

to provide that the cost of elective cosmetic surgery is no longer deductible as a medical expense. Congress through this change in the law was saying, "if you want a facelift, that's fine; but don't expect the tax law to help you pay for it."[15]

> "Amounts paid for operations or treatments affecting any portion of the body including obstetrical expenses and expenses of therapy or X-ray treatments are deemed to be for the purpose of affecting any structure or function of the body and are therefore paid for medical care. Amounts expended for illegal operations or treatments are not deductible. Deductions for expenditures for medical care allowable under Section 213 will be confined strictly to expenses incurred primarily for the prevention or alleviation of a physical or mental defect or illness. Thus, payments for the following are payments for medical care: hospital services, nursing services (including nurses board where paid by the taxpayer), medical, laboratory, surgical, dental and other diagnostic and healing services, X-rays, medicine and drugs ... artificial teeth or limbs, and ambulance hire. However, an expenditure which is merely beneficial to the general health of an individual such as an expenditure for a vacation, is not an expenditure for medical care."[16]

If the taxpayer regularly runs significant medical expenses approaching or exceeding the 7½% floor each year, he would be well advised to, if possible, put off payment of medical expenses for one year so as to bunch two or more years' deductible expenses into a single year for the purpose of exceeding the 7½% floor.

The leading case of *Ochs* illustrates the kind of borderline problem that can arise in the medical deduction area. This case came before a distinguished panel of the Second Circuit that included Augustus Hand and Jerome Frank:

**15.** § 213(d)(9).

**16.** Reg. § 1.213–1(e)(1)(ii). Cf. Rose France, 40 T.C.M. 508 (1980), aff'd per curiam 690 F.2d 68 (6th Cir.1982), (no medical expense deduction for dance lessons to 66–year-old widow; though the Service won't dance, it will call the tune).

## OCHS v. COMMISSIONER[17]

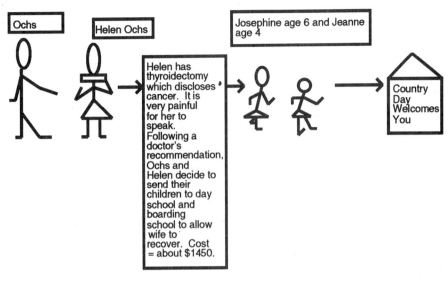

[383a]

*Question:* Are the expenses of sending the children to school deductible as a medical expense?

*Taxpayer's argument:* It is medically necessary for wife to recover to send the children away from school.

*Held:* Children's schooling expenses were nondeductible family expenses under § 262.

*Dissent by Judge Frank:* This leader of the "legal realism" school asserted that the deduction should be allowed. Congress never thought of this problem when it enacted the medical expense deduction. If the wife were sent away to a sanitarium, the expense would be deductible. This is a meaningless distinction. "The cure ought to be the doctor's business, not the Commissioner's . . ."

*Comment:* It was taken for granted by all that in order to raise young children you need to be able to scream.

Medical expenses are inherently personal. But the statute allows a deduction for "medical care," defined as an expense for the "cure, mitigation, treatment or prevention of disease."[18] The expenses in *Ochs* certainly seem to fall within that definition. One way to interpret the court's opinion is to say that the expenditures were for "medical care" but that § 213 is overridden by § 262's disallowance of personal expenditures.

This holding is consistent with the idea, discussed in Chapters One and Two, that the imputed income of taxpayers' household services which they do for themselves is not taxed. It is also the case that if taxpayers pay for someone else to perform those services that payment is

---

**17.** 195 F.2d 692 (2d Cir.1952), cert. denied, 344 U.S. 827, 73 S.Ct. 28, 97 L.Ed 643 (1952).

**18.** § 213(d).

not deductible. Thus is the second spouse working outside the home for taxable income discouraged. This case does nothing to change that even though the taxpayers had a medical necessity for incurring the child care expenses.

As pointed out above, the limit imposed on the amounts paid for medical care which can be deducted is that it is only deductible to the extent it exceeds 7½% of the taxpayer's adjusted gross income.[19] The effect of this very high floor is that few people will take the medical expense deduction. Generally, only very wealthy, ill people who carry no health insurance will be taking this deduction

The only drug expenditures that qualify for deduction are expenditures for prescription drugs and insulin.[20]

Medical expenses cannot be deducted if they are compensated for by insurance or otherwise, and this rule holds true even if the taxpayer is not reimbursed in the same year in which he pays his medical expenses. If the taxpayer does take a deduction for payment of medical expenses in one year (because, perhaps, it is unclear whether he will be reimbursed), reimbursement of those expenses in the following year must be included in his income to the extent that the expenses were allowed to be deducted under the rules of § 213.[21]

As indicated above, the taxpayer may deduct expenses for medical care of his dependents.[22] Medical expenses are considered support in ascertaining whether the taxpayer has met the support tests for determining dependency status.[23]

As a policy matter, allowing medical expenses to be deducted can be criticized as an erosion of the comprehensive tax base. The medical expense deduction can be defended on the ground that medical expenses reduce the taxpayer's discretionary income to be spent on consumption that increases his personal satisfaction.[24] In terms of tax expenditure analysis, the medical expense deduction is less vulnerable than other itemized deductions to criticism that it favors higher-bracket taxpayers, because of the 7½% percent floor.[25]

### (8) Charitable Contributions

#### (a) In General

Charity may begin at home but to the extent the taxpayer supports charities outside the home, he may receive a tax deduction as an

---

**19.** § 213(a).

**20.** § 213(b).

**21.** Reg. § 1.213–1(g)(3)(ii). The approach of the Regulations here is to attribute the reimbursed amounts first to the portion of the medical expenses that were deductible, rather than to the amounts that were nondeductible because of the five-percent floor.

**22.** See ¶ 7.04 for discussion of dependents.

**23.** Reg. § 1.152–1(a)(2)(i). See also § 152(a).

**24.** ¶ 1.02(2)(b).

**25.** See ¶ 1.02(2)(c). See also Andrews, "Personal Deductions in An Ideal Income Tax," 86 Harv.L.Rev. 309 (1972); Newman, "The Medical Expense Deduction: A Preliminary Postmortem," 53 So.Calif.L.Rev. 787 (1980).

itemized deduction. In order to receive the deduction the gift must be to a qualified charitable organization.

Deductions for charitable contributions are subject to certain percentage limits of the taxpayer's adjusted gross income and must meet several other standards, as discussed below.[26]

The organizations that are qualified to receive a deductible charitable contribution are in general qualified organizations that are nonprofit organizations organized exclusively for religious, charitable, scientific, literary, or educational purposes, or to foster amateur sports, or for the prevention of cruelty to children or animals.

The restriction that charitable organizations cannot generally engage in lobbying was held constitutional even though veteran's groups are allowed to receive deductible contributions while carrying on lobbying.[27] The IRS may properly revoke the status of a school to receive deductible charitable contributions if the school practices racial discrimination.[28]

The taxpayer's transfer must be a contribution or gift, as opposed to a payment in consideration for value received, in order to qualify for the charitable deduction.[29] Guidance in this area can be provided by the leading case of *Duberstein*,[30] holding that gifts must arise out of "detached and disinterested generosity." In *Singer*,[31] the court asserted that the appropriate test is whether a substantial benefit is expected from the contribution, meaning by that that the benefit to be received would be greater than benefits that inure to the general public. Fostering the donor's public image would not in itself bar the deduction.[32] If the taxpayer receives consideration of a value less than the amount he contributes, the excess can qualify as a deductible contribution.[33]

In order to be deductible within a particular taxable year, "payment" of the charitable contribution must be made within that year.[34]

**26.** § 170.

**27.** Regan v. Taxation with Representation of Washington, 461 U.S. 540, 103 S.Ct. 1997, 76 L.Ed.2d 129 (1983).

**28.** Bob Jones University v. United States 461 U.S. 574, 103 S.Ct. 2017, 76 L.Ed.2d 157 (1983).

**29.** § 170(c).

**30.** Commissioner v. Duberstein, 363 U.S. 278, 80 S.Ct. 1190, 4 L.Ed.2d 1218 (1960), conformed to 283 F.2d 949 (6th Cir.1960), discussed at ¶ 3.08(2).

**31.** Singer Co. v. United States, 196 Ct.Cl. 90, 449 F.2d 413 (1971) (sewing machine company's sale of sewing machines to schools at a discount was not a charitable contribution but a marketing plan, held deduction denied; bargain sales to churches, hospitals, and government agencies allowed as a charitable deduction).

**32.** Id. at 423.

**33.** Oppewal v. Commissioner, 468 F.2d 1000 (1st Cir.1972) (payment to school deductible to extent it exceeded cost of educating taxpayer's children); Rev.Rul. 68-432, 1968-2 C.B. 104 (same approach as to membership fees of charitable organizations); Rev.Rul. 67-246, 1967-2 C.B. 104 (same approach of partial deduction for tickets to charitable events where price paid is more than value of attending the event).

**34.** § 170(a)(1); ordinarily, a contribution is made at the time delivery is effected, Reg. § 1.170A-1(b); Mann v. Commissioner, 35 F.2d 873 (D.C.Cir.1929) (pledges not deductible); Reg. § 1.170A-1(e) (transfers contingent on the happening of a precedent event not deductible unless the possibility that the transfer will not become effective is so remote as to be negligible).

The charitable contribution must be of "property"; contribution of services will not qualify.[35] If the charitable contribution is of property other than money, the general rule is that the amount of the contribution is the fair market value of the property at the time of the contribution.[36] This means that the taxpayer is generally well advised to sell depreciated property, in order to realize a loss, and contribute the proceeds, but to contribute appreciated property and not sell it and contribute the proceeds, to avoid realizing a gain.[37]

The advantage of contributing appreciated property to charity rather than selling it can be illustrated with an example:

> **Example: Contribution of Appreciated Property for Fun and Profit.** T buys stock in Xidex Corporation for $25,000. It has appreciated since her original purchase ten times and is now worth $250,000. T wishes to contribute the stock to the law school from which she graduated. T has two choices. She can sell the stock and contribute the proceeds or she can just contribute the stock directly.

> What happens in each case?

> *Alternative 1) Sell stock and contribute proceeds:* If T sells the stock and contributes the proceeds, it lays out like this: Sale of the stock yields a taxable gain of $225,000 ($250,000 FMV less $25,000 AB). If T's combined federal and state capital gains rate is 35% (28% federal and 7% state), T's tax is $78,750. T has left after paying the tax $250,000 (the gross proceeds of the sale)[38] less the $78,750 tax, or $171,250. It is that $171,250 that T can contribute to her law school as a result of liquidating her investment in Xidex Corporation. T then gets a charitable deduction for contributing that $171,250 to her law school.[39] That deduction saves T (in a 50% combined state and federal bracket for ordinary income) $85,625. How does this all wind up? T's law school has received $171,250, and T's taxes

---

**35.** Reg. § 1.170A–1(g), providing, however, that unreimbursed expenditures made incident to the rendering of services to a qualified organization are deductible, including the out-of-pocket costs of transportation and meals necessarily incurred in performing donated services. See also Orr v. United States, 343 F.2d 553 (5th Cir.1965) (depreciation not allowed on automobile and airplane used by taxpayer on charitable business); Babilonia v. Commissioner, 681 F.2d 678 (9th Cir.1982) (parents of Olympic figure skater Tai Babilonia could not deduct cost of skating lessons and travel expenses of Tai and her mother as unreimbursed expenditures made incident to the rendering of services to the U.S. Olympic Committee).

**36.** Reg. § 1.170A–1(c)(1); see below for an important limitation on this principle where the transfer is of property that would not have yielded long-term capital gain if sold by the taxpayer.

**37.** This maneuver is possible because a gift is not a taxable event, see ¶ 4.02(1). Although the general rule is that using appreciated property to satisfy a pre-existing obligation is a taxable event, using appreciated property to satisfy a pre-existing charitable pledge does not trigger imposition of tax, Rev.Rul. 55–410, 1955–1 C.B. 297.

**38.** Don't get confused on this one. While T's taxable gain on the transaction was $225,000, T of course actually received $250,000 for the sale. That money is in the bank until T has to pay some of it for her taxes.

**39.** This assumes T's adjusted gross income is large enough so as not to trigger limitations on charitable contributions keyed to gross income (see discussion below at ¶ 7.01(8)(b)).

have been reduced by $85,625. The combined benefit is $171,250 + $85,625 or $256,875.

*Alternative 2) Contribute the stock:* Suppose in the alternative T just gives the stock to the law school. The gift is not a realizing event, thus T does not recognize or pay tax on her $225,000 gain on the stock. Notwithstanding that, T can take a deduction for the full value of the stock, or $250,000. This deduction saves T (in a 50% bracket for federal and state on ordinary income) $125,000 in taxes. How does all this wind up? T's law school has received stock with a value of $250,000. It being a tax-exempt entity, it can sell that stock without paying any tax on the gain transferred from T. Thus the law school's true benefit is $250,000. T has saved taxes of $125,000. The combined benefit is $250,000 + $125,000 or $375,000.[40]

*Comment:* This is a truly amazing result. The total benefit is greater than the value of the property. The result here is often described as a double benefit. The double benefit is that T gets not to pay tax on the appreciation and yet take a deduction for the full fair market value of the property. In fact the benefit is triple. In addition to the double benefit described above, T gets a larger deduction when she contributes the unsold property than when she contributes the after-tax cash on selling the property. Note that in 1) when T sells the stock, T gets a deduction of $171,250 on contributing the after-tax proceeds. But in 2) contributing the stock, T gets a deduction of $250,000, the full value of the stock.

That is why the advantage is more than just the tax saved on the appreciation. On our numbers, the tax saved on just the appreciation is 35% of $225,000 gain or *$78,750.* In fact, however, we see that 2) contributing the stock is better than 1) selling the stock by the amount of $375,000 minus $256,875 or *$118,125.* Where did the extra $39,375 come from? It comes from the larger deduction that T gets on contributing the $250,000 of stock in 2) rather than contributing the $171,250 cash in 1). The deduction in 2) is larger than the deduction in 1) by $78,750. In the 50% bracket, that extra $78,750 deduction saves the taxpayer an additional $39,375 in taxes.

Thus for tax planning purposes contributing appreciated property to charity is even more advantageous than is commonly realized.

As a policy matter, the question is whether it really makes sense to confer such a great advantage on the contribution of appreciated property compared to selling the property and contributing cash.

This is why Congress limited the amount that can be deducted for contributions of appreciated property to 30% of the taxpayer's adjusted gross income rather than 50% (as discussed below). This is not a particularly serious limitation and in any event the excess deduction not allowed can be carried forward five years.

---

**40.** Some of the zip could be taken out of this transaction by the alternative minimum tax (AMT), as discussed later in this chapter.

Where a charitable contribution is of property that would yield ordinary income or short-term capital gain if sold, the amount of the charitable contribution is limited to the taxpayer's basis in the property.[41]

Taxpayers often sell appreciated property to a qualified charity for less than the fair market value of the property. To the extent the sale is for less than the fair market value of the property, the taxpayer is in some sense making a charitable contribution. The problem in these bargain sales to charities, is ascertaining how much gain the taxpayer has on the transaction and what is the amount of his charitable contribution.

For determining the taxpayer's gain on the transaction, the rule is that the adjusted basis for determining gain from the bargain sale is that portion of the adjusted basis which bears the same ratio to the adjusted basis as the amount realized bears to the fair market value of the property.[42] The amount of the taxpayer's charitable contribution is the difference between the property's fair market value and the sales price to the charity. These principles are illustrated by the following example:

> **Example:** Suppose that appreciated long-term capital gain property with a fair market value of $1,000 and an adjusted basis of $300 is sold to a qualifying charitable organization for $600. The adjusted basis for computing the gain on this transaction would be $180, i.e., 60 percent of $300, since the property was sold for 60 percent of its fair market value. The gain, therefore, on the transaction is computed as $600 amount realized, less $180 adjusted basis equals $420. This $420 would be taxed as a long-term capital gain. The amount of the deductible charitable contribution is $1,000 minus $600 equals $400.

Note that if the contributed property had been inventory, rather than long-term capital gain property, then the computation of gain would be the same as above, but the gain would be ordinary. The amount of the charitable contribution would, however, be only $120 (that portion of the basis that was not allocated to computing the gain on the bargain sale, in accordance with § 170(e)(1)(A)).

---

**41.** § 170(e)(1)(A). Thus a broad class of assets will only give rise to a deduction of the taxpayer's basis if a subject of charitable contribution. For example, contribution of the taxpayer's inventory will only give rise to a deduction of the taxpayer's basis. See ¶ 4.06(3) for rules defining what types of property are capital assets which would be exempt from this rule if held for the long-term holding period. This rule, combined with § 1221(3) denying capital asset status to, among other things, letters and memoranda of the taxpayer, means that political figures may not secure a large charitable contribution deduction for the transfer of their personal papers to a library or a museum, etc. It was the question of whether former President Nixon had contributed his Vice Presidential papers before the effective date of this rule, involving backdated documents, that created his major tax problem in the old Watergate days.

**42.** § 1011(b).

Congress has provided complex and restrictive rules governing the contribution of remainder interests, income interests and other partial interests in property to qualified charities, § 170(f).

## (b) Percentage Limits

Taxpayers are subject to a wide variety of limits on the amounts they may deduct as charitable contributions, depending on the type of charity, the type of property contributed, and the type of transfer. These matters are dealt with in turn.

The various limits are expressed as a percentage of the taxpayer's "contribution base" for the taxable year. The contribution base is the taxpayer's adjusted gross income, computed without regard to any net operating loss carryback.[43]

With respect to types of charities, the Code creates two types: those to whom the taxpayer may contribute up to 50 percent of his charitable contribution base, and those to whom the taxpayer may contribute up to only 30 percent of his charitable contribution base. The so-called 50–percent charities include churches or associations of churches, schools and colleges, hospitals, medical schools or medical research organizations, organizations receiving a substantial part of their support from the state or federal government or the general public, the state or federal government, certain private foundations.[44] So-called 30–percent charities are those organizations qualified to receive deductible charitable contributions but that do not qualify as 50–percent charities.[45]

Where the taxpayer makes contributions to both 50–percent charities and 30–percent charities in the same taxable year, the amount of the contributions to the 50–percent charities are taken against the limit first. Then if the contributions to the 50–percent charities have not exhausted the limit on 50–percent charities, the contributions to the 30–percent charities, up to 30 percent of the charitable contribution base, or the remaining amount on the 50–percent limit whichever is less, are allowed.[46] As an example:

> **Example of Charitable Contribution Limits:** Taxpayer's charitable contribution base is $100,000. He contributes $25,000 to a 50–percent charity and $35,000 to a 30–percent charity. The $25,000 contribution to the 50–percent charity is deductible in full. Only $25,000 of the $35,000 contributed to the 30–percent is deductible, since the limit to the 30–percent charities for this taxpayer is the lesser of $30,000 or the remaining $25,000 of the 50% limit.

Contributions to 50–percent charities which exceed 50–percent of the taxpayer's charitable contribution base may be carried forward for five years.[47] Contributions to 30–percent charities in excess of the allowable limit for a particular taxable year may not be carried forward.[48] In determining whether there is to be a carryover, contributions to the 50–percent charities in the particular tax year are taken first against the 50–percent limit before consideration of contributions to the

---

**43.** § 170(b)(1)(F).

**44.** § 170(b)(1)(A); Reg. § 1.170A–9.

**45.** § 170(b)(1)(B).

**46.** § 170(b)(1)(B).

**47.** § 170(d)(1), providing various restrictions.

**48.** Id.

30–percent charities.[49] Thus, for example, if the taxpayer's charitable contribution base is $100,000 and he contributes $45,000 to a 50–percent charity and $25,000 to a 30–percent charity, there will be no carryover because the entire contribution to the 50–percent charity is taken out first against the 50–percent limit.

As mentioned above, if the taxpayer contributes capital gain property, it may be deducted only to the extent it does not exceed 30–percent of the taxpayer's charitable contribution base.[50] "Capital gain property" means for these purposes any capital asset, and § 1231(b) asset, the sale of which at the time of contribution would have resulted in a long-term capital gain.[51] The amount of the contribution of capital gain property which is allowed under the 30–percent limit is then applied to the 50–percent or 30–percent limits, depending on which type of charity is receiving the contribution.[52] Moreover, in determining whether the 50–percent or 30–percent limits have been exceeded, contributions of capital gain property are taken account of after all other contributions.[53] To the extent that contributions of capital gain property exceed the 30–percent limit, they are carried forward for five years and treated under these same rules for the five years.[54]

Charitable contributions are allowed as a deduction only if substantiated according to detailed rules set forth in the Regulations.[55]

The burden rests with the taxpayer to establish that the charity qualifies for the receipt of deductible contributions, consistent with the general rule that the burden of proof in civil tax litigation rests with the taxpayer. The Service promulgates a cumulative list of Exempt Organizations to assist taxpayers who may be making contributions to other than the very well known charitable organizations.

## ¶ 7.02   Floor on Miscellaneous Itemized Deductions

As discussed in Chapter 6 at ¶ 6.01, there are two kinds of itemized deductions: "miscellaneous itemized deductions" (as defined by the statute), and "the rest of them" (for want of a better term). The difference between them is that "miscellaneous itemized deductions" are only deductible to the extent that they exceed 2% of the taxpayer's adjusted gross income. Thus they are said to be deductible subject to a 2% floor.[1] The "rest of them" are deductible in full.

---

**49.**  § 170(d)(1).

**50.**  § 170(b)(1)(C)(i).

**51.**  § 170(b)(1)(C)(iv).

**52.**  This restriction only applies if the contribution of capital gain property is not subject to § 170(e)(1)(B), relating to certain contributions of tangible personal property and certain contributions to private foundations discussed supra. See § 170(b)(1)(C)(i).

**53.**  § 170(b)(1)(C)(i).

**54.**  § 170(b)(1)(C)(ii).

**55.**  § 170(a)(1);   Reg.   § 1.170A–1(a)(2)(i), 1.170A–1(a)(2)(ii). When required by the District Director, a charitable contribution must be substantiated by a statement from the organization to which the contribution was made, Reg. § 1.170A–1(a)(2)(iii). See Prop.Reg. § 1.170A–13(a) and (b) (April 1983). Compare ¶ 6.02(7) regarding the substantiation requirement for travel, entertainment and business gifts.

¶ 7.02

**1.**  § 67.

"Miscellaneous itemized deductions" includes unreimbursed employee expenses (such as travel or professional journals), expenses of investment advice for investing in stocks and bonds.[2]

The itemized deductions that are not subject to the floor include home mortgage interest,[3] state and local taxes on the home,[4] losses on personal-use property,[5] charitable deductions,[6] medical expense deductions,[7] moving expenses.[8]

This statutory treatment is depicted in the accompanying graphic.

2. Investment advice for investments that produce rents or royalties would not, however, be in this category. Investment expenses related to producing rent or royalty income are taken above the line, and are thus not itemized expenses, § 62(a)(4).

3. The deduction for home mortgage interest is subject to some limits under § 163. It is the amounts that survive those limits that can be deducted in full thereafter without regard to the 2% floor. See ¶ 7.01(3).

4. Allowed by § 164.

5. The casualty loss deduction for personal-use property is subject to its own limits and floors of § 165(c) and (h), see ¶ 7.01(5). The amounts (if any) that finally get through those limits are then deductible in full below the line without regard to the 2% miscellaneous itemized deduction floor.

6. Charitable deductions are subject to their own limits in § 170, as discussed in ¶ 7.01(8). It is the amounts that survive those limits that are then deductible in full below the line without regard to the 2% floor.

7. The medical expense deduction is subject to severe restrictions of its own as provided in § 213, see ¶ 7.01(7). It is only the amounts (if any) that survive those limits that can then be deducted in full below the line without being subject to the 2% floor.

8. Moving expenses are subject to their own limits under § 217. It is only the amounts that survive those limits that can then be deducted in full below the line without regard to the 2% floor.

2% Floor on Miscellaneous Itemized Deductions

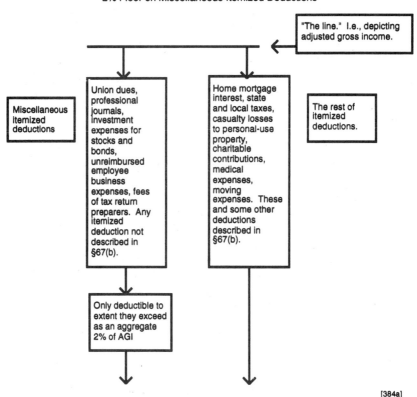

[384a]

One thing that emerges from contemplating this statutory scheme is that below-the-line deductions have been a serious target of Congress in recent years. The 2% floor raises about $20 billion over five years. The deductions not subject to the floor have been subjected to their own limits. There is only one big one that stands virtually unscathed. That is the deduction for interest on the home mortgage. As discussed at ¶ 7.01(3), it is not subject to much in the way of limits in its own right and it is not subject to the 2% floor. When it comes to deductions below the line, the home mortgage interest deduction is truly The Big Guy.

## ¶ 7.03   The Standard Deduction

All individual taxpayers are entitled to deduct a fixed amount from adjusted gross income in arriving at taxable income, whether or not they have any itemized deductions at all. This fixed amount, called the standard deduction, is adjusted for inflation. It currently stands at about $6,200 for married couples filing joint returns and $3,250 for single individuals. In effect, a married couple that uses the standard deduction is simply not taxed on its first $6,200 of income.

Thus it is only when itemized deductions exceed $6,200 for the married couple that the itemized deductions confer a tax benefit. And then the benefit is only to the extent of that excess. This structure and how it fits together with the 2% floor on miscellaneous itemized deductions is depicted in the accompanying graphic.

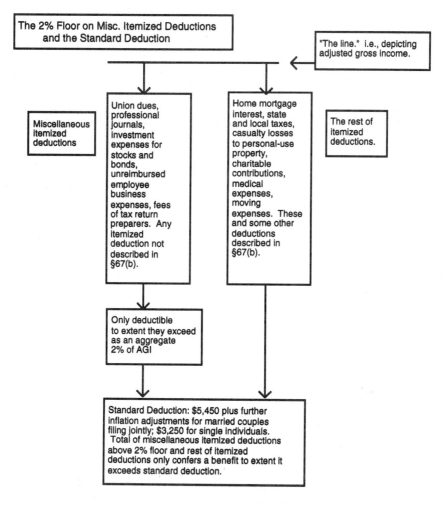

[385a]

Thus, taxpayers with relatively small amounts of itemized deductions are spared the agony of computation and substantiation and may simply take a free ride on the standard deduction.

As indicated in the earlier discussion on structure of the Internal Revenue Code,[1] taxpayers who do not expect to have excess itemized deductions—i.e., itemized deductions in excess of the standard deduction—prefer to have such deductions taken above the line (as deductions from gross income in arriving at adjusted gross income) so that they will get a full benefit from the deduction. Obviously, taxpayers are not free to move deductions from below the line to above the line, but must abide by

¶ 7.03

1.  ¶ 6.01.

the rules of § 62 in ascertaining which deductions go above the line. It is only in a close question that a taxpayer may make an attempt to argue that a deduction is above the line if he does not expect to have excess itemized deductions.

Congress has similarly played this game when in 1976 it moved the deduction for alimony from below the line to above the line, to insure that taxpayers would always get the full benefit of their alimony deduction.[2]

Married taxpayers 65 or older receive an additional standard deduction of $1,200. They also get a tax credit of 15% of their first $7,500 of retirement income. This retirement income credit phases out as their income increases. Elderly taxpayers who are single receive similar but reduced benefits. As long as we are discussing older folks, it might be noted that up to 85% of social security benefits are taxed if the recipient's income exceeds $44,000 for married couples or $34,000 for single individuals (counting half of their Social Security payments).[3]

## ¶ 7.04   Personal and Dependency Exemptions

Having worked out his itemized deductions and run the gauntlet of the 2% floor on miscellaneous itemized deductions, the taxpayer is allowed to deduct a $2,350 personal exemption for himself and his spouse. In addition he is allowed to deduct a $2,350 exemption for any dependents.[1]

The idea of these relatively large deductions for personal and dependency exemptions is to assist families, as part of the "family values" that we hear so much about in the political sphere these days. In fact approximately the same result as is accomplished by personal and dependency exemptions could be achieved by altering the rate structure so that it kicks in at a higher level of income. (But that wouldn't sound so nice and "family.")

The fact that personal and dependency exemptions are simply a substitute for manipulating the rate structure is indeed recognized by the statute. Beginning in 1991, the personal and dependency exemptions are phased out for higher income taxpayers. For a joint return, total exemptions are diminished by 2% for each $2,500 that the taxpayer's adjusted gross income exceeds $150,000. The effect of this is to increase the top marginal rate of tax on higher-income people. As their income goes up above $150,000, their tax rate is going up because they are slowly losing the dependency deduction. As a result the top marginal rate on high-income people is raised above the top 39.6% rate stated in the statute.[2] Moreover, high-income people with large families get hit harder by this approach. This is because with larger families, they have a larger total deduction for dependency exemptions. Thus they lose more as they go over the threshold.

---

2.   ¶ 6.02(14). For further discussion of these structural matters see ¶ 6.01.

3.   § 86.

**¶ 7.04**

1.   §§ 151, 152.

2.   § 1.

All of this is a tricky way of raising taxes on high-income people without appearing to do so. In this era when no politician wants to be caught dead suggesting that taxes should be raised (when in fact taxes do have to be raised), we may see more of the legislative legerdemain in the future.

This raises the question of whether an already complex income tax statute is now intentionally being used to befuddle the public as to the level of taxes it is paying. So far this has happened only to upper-income people. But it could happen to you.

## ¶ 7.05　Alternative Minimum Tax

One of the more absurd provisions of the income tax law is the alternative minimum tax. The basic idea behind the AMT is that it is a backstop to the regular tax. We need a backstop, apparently, because all too many individuals (and corporations) are seen by Congress to cleverly wiggle through various attractive provisions of the Code. As a result many very high-income individuals and corporations contrive (with their advisors such as you will become) to pay virtually no tax at all. Consider a high-income taxpayer Buford Harrington who invests heavily in state and local municipal bonds (see ¶ 3.01(2)), as well as equipment eligible for accelerated depreciation (see ¶ 6.02(12)) and deducts intangible drilling costs for oil and gas exploration (see ¶ 6.02(13)). Buford is not feeling a great deal of pain come April 15.

The basic idea of the AMT is to establish a second tax system that defines income more broadly. It includes in its base many of the items that the regular tax system exempts. For example it adds back to its base the excess of accelerated depreciation over what would be deducted using less attractive methods and longer useful lives. It also adds back to the base the the inside interest build up on life insurance policies (see the Prologue) as well as benefits of incentive stock options. In addition certain deductions such as those for medical expenses and state and local taxes are diminished in computing the base. Then the AMT applies a fairly low rate to this broader base. The individual caught within the maw of the AMT then in effect pays the greater of his regular tax or the AMT.

Thus the various provisions that give rise to avoiding tax remain in effect, but any individual who uses them very extensively will pick up some tax under the AMT. The top AMT rate is now 28%, which is significantly less than the top statutory regular tax rate of 39.6%.[1]

The AMT misses a few things, though. Notably absent are the widespread advantages of the ability to deduct home mortgage interest, contributions to pension plans, employee fringe benefits, tax-free state and municipal bond interest, Buford, if he is playing his cards right, is still feeling pretty good.

### ¶ 7.05

1. § 55(b)(1). Bear in mind that the top marginal rate for high-income people (who are the target of the AMT) is actually higher than 39.6% because of the phase-out of the personal and dependency exemptions, as discussed at ¶ 7.04.

# Chapter 8

# TAX PLANNING

*Table of Sections*

---

## ¶ 8.01  Introductory

As the Service, the courts, and Congress, weave their web of rules regarding the taxpayer's liability, the taxpayer, of course, is not inert. The taxpayer may legitimately arrange his affairs to minimize his tax liability; indeed, at many junctures, the Code invites him to do so. While tax planning approaches are discussed throughout this work, there are certain broad areas of tax planning for individuals that merit special attention. They are the subject of this chapter.

## ¶ 8.02  Tax Shelters

### (1) The Building Blocks of Tax Shelters

"Tax shelters" have long been a major tax planning technique. While they are now heavily restricted by statute, there still remain some possibilities for decreasing tax liability by engaging in tax shelter investments. Before turning to the network of rules that restrict tax shelters, it is useful to discuss how tax shelters work.

The following are the basic building blocks of all tax shelters:

*Business Activities Combined on a Tax Return*

In general, an individual files a tax return which combines all of his business activities for the year. Money lost on one activity will be subtracted from money gained on another, and the net results will be the individual's taxable income for the year. This simple truism provides one of the fundamental building blocks for tax shelters. If the individual's return were bifurcated—e.g., losses incurred in real estate could not be taken against salary earned as an executive—tax shelters would be limited.[1] The concept of a high-income taxpayer engaging in activities which produce tax losses against which he offsets his high income is central to the tax shelter.[2]

### The Limited Partnership

The limited partnership has proved to be the ideal vehicle for constructing a tax shelter. The customary arrangement is that the general partner puts together the arrangement and provides the skills and managerial know-how for conducting the partnership business. The limited partners are investors. This form is attractive for doing tax-shelter business for several reasons. First, a project (be it a movie, apartment building, equipment leasing, farming) envisioned as a tax shelter is usually too large for any one investor to finance. By conducting the project as a limited partnership, shares can be sold. Second, from the point of view of the typical high-income investor, it is all well and good to incur *tax* losses; but no one wants real, substantial, unlimited losses. Hence, a vehicle—such as the limited partnership—which limits the liability of the investor to the amount he invests is preferred.

These two features—the possibility of selling shares in the investment and limiting the investors' liability—are characteristic of the corporation as well as the limited partnership. However, the corporation is singularly inappropriate as a tax-shelter vehicle because the tax losses incurred by a corporation cannot be passed through to the shareholders but remain with the corporation to be carried over to the corporation's other taxable years.[3] Thus the third reason that the limited partnership is the favorite vehicle for a tax-shelter investment is that the tax losses it generates are passed through to the partners.

The losses incurred by regular corporations (not S Corporations) can be carried over to other years. Indeed a corporation's net operating loss carryovers can themselves become an attractive asset of the corporation which other corporations would seek to acquire. See D. Posin, *Corporate Tax Planning: Takeovers Leveraged Buyouts and Restructurings* Chapter 13 (1990).

In order to employ the partnership for these purposes, a number of technical requirements must be overcome. These are covered in the

---

1. Cf. § 183 disallowing deductions, except to the extent of income, from "activities not engaged in for profit." While § 183 might arguably be used to attack tax shelters, Reg. § 1.183–2 has tended to limit the scope of § 183 to activities which contain a sporting, hobby, or recreational element. Cf. Goldstein v. Commissioner, 364 F.2d 734 (2d Cir.1966), cert. denied 385 U.S. 1005, 87 S.Ct. 708, 17 L.Ed.2d 543 (1967). See also ¶ 6.02(9).

2. Indeed barring the deduction of losses in one activity from gains in another in certain circumstances is the approach of the "passive loss" rules' attack on tax shelters, discussed below.

3. So-called S Corporations do allow losses to be passed through to the shareholders much like a partnership. However, the S Corporation does not lend itself to being a tax shelter vehicle. This is mainly because the S corporation cannot exploit debt the way a partnership can to pump up basis for depreciation purposes. See discussion below.

partnership tax course which, if you're interested in this kind of maneuvering, you might like to take.

*Increase of Basis by Nonrecourse Financing*

Thus far, based on the first two building blocks, there is a high-income taxpayer buying a share in a limited partnership which will generate tax losses that are passed through to a taxpayer and against which he may offset his other income. At this point it might well be asked, "What's so great about that?" If the taxpayer has invested $50,000 in a share of a limited partnership, he will presumably only be allowed to deduct an amount equal to his basis of $50,000.[4] If the taxpayer is in the 40–percent bracket, this will only save him $20,000 in taxes—not an impressive result, particularly if the taxpayer ultimately winds up out of pocket the full $50,000!

However, the taxpayer's basis is not necessarily restricted to $50,000 even though he has only paid $50,000 for his limited partnership share. If the limited partnership purchases property subject to a purchase money mortgage (or a mortgage to a third party), even though the loan was secured only by the property itself (be it apartment building, movie, railroad rolling stock, etc.), the partner's basis can be increased by his share of the loan if certain technical requirements are met.

This result applies the rule articulated by the Supreme Court in *Crane v. Commissioner*.[5] In *Crane*, which did not involve a partnership, the Court held that when property subject to nonrecourse debt is inherited, the heir includes in her basis the amount of that nonrecourse debt. You have doubtless already encountered *Crane* at ¶ 4.03(2)(b)(ii). This rule was justified on the ground of administrative convenience. If the heir's basis were limited only to her equity interest, then her basis would change every year as she amortized the mortgage, creating nightmarish problems in the calculation of depreciation.[6]

As discussed in Chapter 4, the *Crane* approach was later applied to property purchased subject to an unassumed mortgage.[7]

An example will illustrate the effect of employing the *Crane* approach:

> A limited partner pays $50,000 for his 10% share of a partnership. The partnership arranges a $2.5 million loan to finance construction of an apartment building, the loan secured only by the building. If various technical requirements of partnership tax law are met, the limited partner would be entitled to increase his basis in the partnership by $250,000, to a total basis of $300,000, although he had only contributed $50,000. Such 80 or 90 percent nonrecourse

---

4. § 165(b). The partner's basis in a limited partnership share is the amount of money he pays for his share plus the adjusted basis of the property he contributes to the partnership. § 722. A partner only can deduct as losses an amount equal to his basis in the partnership share. § 704(d).

5. 331 U.S. 1, 67 S.Ct. 1047, 91 L.Ed. 1301 (1947).

6. Id. at 9–10, 67 S.Ct. at 1052–1053.

7. Parker v. Delaney, 186 F.2d 455 (1st Cir.1950), cert. denied 341 U.S. 926, 71 S.Ct. 797, 95 L.Ed. 1357 (1951).

debt financing is common in limited partnerships in the tax shelter field.

*Early Deductions*

At this point in our discussion, the tax shelter is all dressed up with no place to go. Based on the previous building blocks, there is a high income limited partner who, although he has only contributed $50,000 in the partnership, has a basis that has been "artificially" increased to $300,000. Thus he has a tremendous potential for incurring tax losses. The final step in this tableau is a lot of deductions early in the life of the investment which would create a substantial net operating loss for the partnership, these losses to be then passed through to the partners. In certain kinds of businesses, large early deductions are available—whether by government policy to encourage that business, or by happenstance. It is these businesses, then, that have been typically the subject matter of the limited partnership tax shelter.

Thus, for example (recall that the discussion here is on how tax shelters work prior to the network of restrictive legislation discussed below), in the real estate area substantial deductions for interest (including prepaid interest)[8] and taxes[9] were available during the period the project was being constructed. Since the project produced no income during the construction period, these early deductions produced substantial losses in the construction period which passed through to the partners When the project was operating, normal operating expenses, of course, were deducted[10] along with the deductions for real estate taxes, interest on the nonrecourse loan, and accelerated depreciation. The deductions for interest and accelerated depreciation had the attractive feature of being large in the early years of the project.

As discussed at ¶ 6.02(12), even straight-line depreciation is actually too fast from an economic standpoint ("sinking-fund depreciation" being what is appropriate). Thus accelerated depreciation is way too fast. Where the taxpayer borrows to invest in depreciable plant and equipment, an interesting situation is created. Since the depreciation he takes on this plant and equipment is excessive, that investment is in effect producing tax-free income. As a result, you could look at the situation of borrowing to invest in depreciable plant and equipment as borrowing to invest in an arrangement that produces tax-free income. If that analysis is taken, then there are grounds for denying or at least delaying the interest deduction. This would be on the authority of § 265(a)(2), discussed at ¶ 6.03(6)(a).

In the oil and gas area, in addition to deductions for interest on the nonrecourse loan and some of the other deductions discussed above, there was the unique election to deduct immediately expenditures for

---

**8.** See ¶ 7.01(3) for restrictions on deductibility of construction interest and prepaid interest.

**9.** § 164.

**10.** § 162.

intangible drilling and development costs, expenses which under the usual rules would be capitalized.[11]

In the heyday of tax shelters, where a movie was the subject of the limited partnership arrangement, a notable deduction was depreciation calculated by using the "income forecast" method, which led to an early write-off of the cost of the film.[12] An alternative arrangement in the film area—the so-called Production Company—involved a limited partnership providing financing for a film by contributing its partners' capital plus the proceeds of a substantial nonrecourse loan to the distributor or independent producer in exchange for a fee, part of which was contingent on the success of the film. The partnership then deducted currently the costs of making the film, on the theory that the partnership had no ownership interest in the film. This approach was also applied to books and records.

Similarly, the areas of farming and sports franchises were used as the subject matter for tax shelters because of the availability of rapid deductions—e.g., feed costs in livestock farming to the cash method taxpayer, player contracts in sports franchises written off over a short period of time.

### Winding Up

After the project has operated for several years, the shelter effect begins to wane—largely because, as indicated in the preceding discussion, many of the key deductions have their greatest effect in the early years of the project. Thus, there comes a time when it is attractive to the investor to sell out his interest and reinvest his funds in another shelter or some other project. It is upon this sale of his interest that a tax may be incurred. This is because (as discussed in Chapter 4) *Crane* also held that when property is sold subject to a nonrecourse indebtedness, the taxpayer has an amount realized in the amount of the nonrecourse indebtedness.[13] This will often give rise to a gain because accelerated

---

**11.** Intangible drilling and development costs include expenditures related to oil and gas property for wages, fuel, repairs, hauling, supplies "incident to and necessary for the drilling of wells and the preparation of wells for the production of oil or gas," Reg. § 1.612–4. This regulation goes on to provide a rather detailed discussion of what constitutes intangible drilling and development costs. See ¶ 6.02(13)(b).

**12.** Because it is difficult to estimate the useful life of a film, the normal method for calculating depreciation was not applied. Rather, the "income forecast" method was used. Under the "income forecast" method, depreciation was calculated for a particular year as follows: The cost of the film is multiplied by the income received in the year and divided by the total estimated income of the film. Since a great percentage of the total estimated income of the film is

assumed to be received in the first year or two of the film's life, this method results in a rapid write-off of the cost of the film. Rev.Rul. 60–538, 1960–2 C.B. 68; Rev.Rul. 64–273, 1964–2 C.B. 62.

**13.** Crane v. Commissioner, note 10. The "phantom gain" in these circumstances cannot even be given away, see Guest, 77 T.C. 9 (1981) (charitable contribution of property subject to a nonrecourse mortgage constitutes a bargain sale to a charity), Rev.Rul. 81–163, 1981–1 CB 433 (same). See discussion at ¶ 4.02.

As discussed at ¶ 4.03(2)(b)(iv), the Court in *Crane* in its celebrated "footnote 37" explicitly declined to rule on the question of what would happen if the nonrecourse debt were for a greater amount than the fair market value of the property transferred (or foreclosed upon). The Court's res-

depreciation and deductions analogous to it (such as the deduction for intangible drilling costs, and film depreciation using the "income forecast method") have drastically lowered the basis of the property in question. This gain upon selling out has been subjected to varying treatment over the years and has depended also on the type of property involved. Historically taxpayers have received the favorable capital gains treatment on selling out.

### Deferral

Deferral of tax is not really an additional building block of tax shelters but arises out of the operation of the other factors discussed. Deferral is still a major aspect of current tax shelters.

Consider the case where the depreciation deductions in Year 1 shelter ordinary income, and then the gain attributable to those deductions is recaptured at ordinary income rates in Year 10. That postponement of tax for ten years is of great importance for two reasons:

(1) The tax imposed ten years later may be less. This could arise for instance if, as often is anticipated, the taxpayer is in a lower tax bracket ten years hence. Moreover, if the taxpayer holds the property until death, then basis of the property is stepped up to fair market value in the hands of taxpayer's heirs, and the deferral becomes a complete exemption. § 1014, see ¶ 4.03(2)(e).

(2) More significantly, even if the taxpayer is in the same bracket ten years later, the use for ten years of the money that would have gone to pay the tax is of tremendous value. As discussed in the Prologue, there are many ways to illustrate the powerful effect of this deferral.

## (2) The "At Risk" Limitations

### (a) In General

The "at risk" rules have severely limited the effectiveness of tax shelter investing. The "at risk" rules take a dead-eye aim at the single most important building block of tax shelters—the use of nonrecourse financing. The fundamental rule is that a taxpayer,[14] who runs a net loss on an activity for the taxable year, may deduct that loss against his other income only to the extent that he is "at risk" (i.e., invested with personal liability) in the activity.[15] It can be seen that this rule strikes directly at the classical tax shelter as described in the preceding section. As an example:

ervation of judgment on this matter provided grist for the mill of a great number of academic papers. As discussed in Chapter 4, the Supreme Court in Commissioner v. Tufts, 461 U.S. 300, 103 S.Ct. 1826, 75 L.Ed.2d 863 (1983), reh'g denied 463 U.S. 1215, 103 S.Ct. 3555, 77 L.E.2d 1401 (1983) resolved this question by deciding that where property encumbered by a nonrecourse mortgage is sold, the amount realized on the sale includes the amount of the mortgage notwithstanding that the mortgage exceeds the fair market value of the property.

14. "Taxpayer" refers in the statute to individuals, Subchapter S corporations, and most closely-held corporations, § 465(a)(1). The discussion in the text will focus primarily on the treatment of individuals.

15. §§ 465(a), 465(d).

**Example:** Taxpayer invests $10,000 cash in an activity and incurs a $90,000 nonrecourse liability to further finance the activity. The gross income from the activity for the first year is $3,000. The deductions of interest, depreciation, property taxes, and maintenance with respect to the activity for the first year, come to a total of $15,000. Taxpayer thus has a net loss on the activity of $12,000, only $10,000 of which may be taken as a deduction against taxpayer's other income (such as salary, dividends, etc.). The $2,000 net loss that could not be deducted, plus any net loss sustained in any future years, may be held "in suspense" and used at such time as taxpayer further invests with personal liability in the activity, or otherwise increases his amount "at risk" as by not making withdrawals against future gross income generated by the project.[16]

Consider again the example above. Suppose early in the second year of the investment, the taxpayer distributes to himself $5,000 from the activity. A problem is now presented because the taxpayer in the first year of the investment took a deduction for $10,000, which was his amount "at risk" at that time. Now, with the distribution of the $5,000 the taxpayer has only invested with personal liability, a net amount of $5,000. Yet, he has taken a deduction from the activity in the amount of $10,000. To deal with this problem, the "at risk" rules provide a "recapture" rule. The rule is that in any year that the taxpayer comes to have less at risk than the net loss taken from the activity against other income, the taxpayer must include in his income the amount by which his cumulative net loss deductions exceed the amount he has at risk in the activity. In such a situation, the recaptured net loss deductions are held in suspense and may be used at such time in the future that the taxpayer puts more at risk in the activity.[17] As an example:

**Example:** Taxpayer puts at risk $10,000 in an activity and also incurs a $90,000 nonrecourse debt to finance the activity. In the first year of the investment the gross income from the activity is $3,000 and the deductions attributable to the activity total $15,000. The taxpayer, therefore, has a net loss from the activity of $12,000, of which $10,000 may be deducted against other income. Early in the second year of the investment, taxpayer distributes to himself $5,000 in cash. Taxpayer also sustains in the second year of the investment a net loss of $4,000. The $4,000 net loss deduction sustained in the second year will not be allowed but will be held in "suspense" for possible use in future years. In addition, the taxpayer will include $5,000 in income in order to reduce the net loss deduction taken on the activity to $5,000, which is his net amount at risk in the property. The $5,000 net loss so recaptured into income will then be put in suspense and may be deducted in such future year as the taxpayer has more at risk in the activity. Therefore, on these facts, the taxpayer now has $11,000 of net losses "in sus-

16. § 465(a)(2).                    17. § 465(e).

pense." ($2,000 from first year + $4,000 from second year + $5,000 recaptured).

If in the third year of the investment, the taxpayer breaks even and also puts $3,000 additional "at risk" into the activity, he will be entitled to deduct $3,000 of the suspended net losses from the activity against other income.

In any year that the taxpayer has net income from the activity, his amount "at risk" in the activity will be increased by the amount of that net income (unless he withdraws the amount of the net income).

Thus it can be seen from the foregoing discussion that the "at risk" amount is a running account which is increased by the amounts the taxpayer invests with personal liability in the property, and the net income (if any) generated by the activity, and is decreased by net losses from the activity deducted against other income and cash withdrawn from the activity.

The "at risk" amount is very much akin to a partner's basis in the partnership, which continually adjusts to reflect these transactions, and limits the amount that ultimately the partner may deduct as a loss.

It might also be noticed that the "at risk" rules bear some resemblance to the rules governing "activities not engaged in for profit" and the rules governing offices in the home and vacation homes. In all these areas lines of activity are segregated and deductions limited, to some extent, by the amount of income generated by the activity.[18]

The preceding discussion has described the basic "at risk" rules. Critical to the operation of those rules, of course, is the definition of "activity." Obviously, the degree to which "activities" for the purposes of the statute are defined broadly or narrowly will affect the extent taxpayers will be able to amalgamate losses and income, or be forced to separate them and put up more "at risk" in the loss activities to gain the loss deduction. The statute lists a number of activities which have traditionally been the subject of tax shelter investments: the holding, producing or distributing of motion picture films or video tapes; farming; equipment leasing; exploring for or exploiting oil and gas resources; exploring for or exploiting geothermal deposits.[19] Holding real estate is also a separate activity.[20]

With respect to each of these lines of business, the statute explicitly provides that a taxpayer's activity with respect to each activity shall be treated as a separate activity.[21] This means, for example, that the income from one film or videotape may not be offset against the loss from another film or videotape; the income from each farm may not be offset against the net loss from each farm, etc.

---

**18.** For activities not engaged in for profit, offices in the home, and rental of vacation homes, see ¶¶ 6.02(9), (10), (11).

**19.** § 465(c)(1).

**20.** § 465(c)(3).

**21.** § 465(c)(2).

There are, of course, a wide variety of lines of business other than the five explicitly mentioned in the statute. The major contribution of the Revenue Act of 1978 to the "at risk" rules was to provide that the "at risk" rules apply to all activities including real estate in addition to those explicitly mentioned in the statute. In so expanding the reach of the "at risk" rules, Congress did not provide guidelines for segregating the many other areas of business in which taxpayers engage into separate activities. Rather, it authorized the Service to promulgate regulations for the aggregation or separation of activities in the areas of business not explicitly mentioned in the statute.[22]

The accompanying chart illustrate the workings of the classic tax shelter. You can see that in the chart depicting the classic tax shelter the rate of return based on cash flow is extremely high in the early years. Then things go badly in the later years, which is why the taxpayer wants to sell the burned out tax shelter. But even sale gives poor results, because under *Tufts* the taxpayer still has substantial back end gain. The ability to take a large proportion of the deductions in the early years gives the taxpayer the advantage of the time value of money.

Congress enacted several reforms to curb these unduly attractive results. They first cut back on depreciation, allowing only straight-line for real estate. Congress also enacted the "at risk" rules, as explained above. The effect of these changes is to reduce substantially the cash flow rate of return. Things also do not go so badly at the end. The result is that the taxpayer is not able to "front load" his deductions and thus does not gain the advantage of time value of money.

---

**22.** § 465(c)(3)(C). The legislative history makes clear that "tax shelter characteristics" will be used to help define separate activities. Such characteristics would include substantial nonrecourse financing and other novel financing techniques, accelerated deductions, mismatching of income and deductions, and the method of marketing the activity as an investment. H.Rep. No. 95–1445, reprinted in 1978–3 C.B. (Vol. 1) 181, 244. To the extent a taxpayer participates in a line of business as a trade or business in which he actively participates in the management, all activities involved in that trade or business will be treated as one activity for the purposes of the "at risk" rules. Also, if a trade or business is carried on by a partnership or Subchapter S corporation and 65 percent or more of the losses for the taxable year is allocable to persons who actively participate in the management of the trade or business, then the trade or business shall constitute one activity. § 465(c)(3)(B).

Tax Shelter Example

**HOW THE CLASSIC TAX SHELTER WORKED**

Taxpayer puts up $10,000 and borrows $90,000 nonrecourse
She buys a building for $100,000
Here are the numbers:
1) The building has a useful life of 30 years and may be depreciated using the double-declining-balance method.
2) The loan carries an interest rate of 10% and is paid off over 30 years.
3) Annual payment on the loan (principal and interest) is $9,547.
4) The building produces rental income revenues of $15,000 per year.
5) Other out-of-pocket expenses are :$3,000 property taxes; $2,000 maintenance.
6) Taxpayer is in the 50% tax bracket.

| A | B | C | D | E | F | G | H | I | J |
|---|---|---|---|---|---|---|---|---|---|
| | | Maintenance & Property | Mortgage | Portion of Mortgage Payment That is Deductible | Depre-ciation | Taxable Income | Tax Savings | Net Cash Flow | Cash Flow Annual Rate of Return on Initial |
| Year | Revenues | Taxes | Payment | Interest | (DDB) | =B−(C+E+F) | 50% of G | =B−C−D+H | $10,000 |
| 1 | $15,000 | $5,000 | $9,547 | $9,000 | $6,667 | ($5,667) | $2,833 | $3,286 | 33% |
| 2 | $15,000 | $5,000 | $9,547 | $8,945 | $6,222 | ($5,168) | $2,584 | $3,037 | 30% |
| 3 | $15,000 | $5,000 | $9,547 | $8,885 | $5,807 | ($4,693) | $2,346 | $2,799 | 28% |
| 4 | $15,000 | $5,000 | $9,547 | $8,819 | $5,420 | ($4,239) | $2,120 | $2,573 | 26% |
| 5 | $15,000 | $5,000 | $9,547 | $8,746 | $5,059 | ($3,805) | $1,903 | $2,356 | 24% |
| 6 | $15,000 | $5,000 | $9,547 | $8,666 | $4,722 | ($3,388) | $1,694 | $2,147 | 21% |
| 7 | $15,000 | $5,000 | $9,547 | $8,578 | $4,407 | ($2,985) | $1,492 | $1,945 | 19% |
| 8 | $15,000 | $5,000 | $9,547 | $8,481 | $4,113 | ($2,594) | $1,297 | $1,750 | 18% |
| 9 | $15,000 | $5,000 | $9,547 | $8,374 | $3,839 | ($2,213) | $1,107 | $1,560 | 16% |
| 10 | $15,000 | $5,000 | $9,547 | $8,257 | $3,583 | ($1,840) | $920 | $1,373 | 14% |
| 11 | $15,000 | $5,000 | $9,547 | $8,128 | $3,344 | ($1,472) | $736 | $1,189 | 12% |
| 12 | $15,000 | $5,000 | $9,547 | $7,986 | $3,121 | ($1,107) | $554 | $1,007 | 10% |
| 13 | $15,000 | $5,000 | $9,547 | $7,830 | $2,913 | ($743) | $372 | $825 | 8% |
| 14 | $15,000 | $5,000 | $9,547 | $7,659 | $2,719 | ($377) | $189 | $642 | 6% |
| 15 | $15,000 | $5,000 | $9,547 | $7,470 | $2,538 | ($7) | $4 | $457 | 5% |
| 16 | $15,000 | $5,000 | $9,547 | $7,262 | $2,368 | $370 | ($185) | $268 | 3% |
| 17 | $15,000 | $5,000 | $9,547 | $7,033 | $2,368 | $599 | ($299) | $154 | 2% |
| 18 | $15,000 | $5,000 | $9,547 | $6,782 | $2,368 | $850 | ($425) | $28 | 0% |
| 19 | $15,000 | $5,000 | $9,547 | $6,506 | $2,368 | $1,126 | ($563) | ($110) | -1% |
| 20 | $15,000 | $5,000 | $9,547 | $6,202 | $2,368 | $1,430 | ($715) | ($262) | -3% |
| 21 | $15,000 | $5,000 | $9,547 | $5,867 | $2,368 | $1,765 | ($883) | ($430) | -4% |
| 22 | $15,000 | $5,000 | $9,547 | $5,499 | $2,368 | $2,133 | ($1,067) | ($614) | -6% |
| 23 | $15,000 | $5,000 | $9,547 | $5,094 | $2,368 | $2,538 | ($1,269) | ($816) | -8% |
| 24 | $15,000 | $5,000 | $9,547 | $4,649 | $2,368 | $2,983 | ($1,492) | ($1,039) | -10% |
| 25 | $15,000 | $5,000 | $9,547 | $4,159 | $2,368 | $3,473 | ($1,736) | ($1,283) | -13% |
| 26 | $15,000 | $5,000 | $9,547 | $3,620 | $2,368 | $4,012 | ($2,006) | ($1,553) | -16% |
| 27 | $15,000 | $5,000 | $9,547 | $3,028 | $2,368 | $4,604 | ($2,302) | ($1,849) | -18% |
| 28 | $15,000 | $5,000 | $9,547 | $2,376 | $2,368 | $5,256 | ($2,628) | ($2,175) | -22% |
| 29 | $15,000 | $5,000 | $9,547 | $1,659 | $2,368 | $5,973 | ($2,987) | ($2,534) | -25% |
| 30 | $15,000 | $5,000 | $9,547 | $870 | $2,368 | $6,762 | ($3,381) | ($2,928) | -29% |
| | | | | | $99,994 | | | | |
| Adj Basis at Crossover | | $28,422 | | | | | | | |
| Balance of Mtg at Crossover | | $65,057 | | | Switch to straight line | | | Crossover point | |
| Sale of property at crossover point for $100,000 yields cash of $34,943 and taxable gain of $71,578, *Tufts* | | | | | | | | | |

It is useful to point out the relationship between the at risk rules and the limits on activities not engaged in for profit (¶ 6.02(9)). When the not-for-profit rules apply, no net loss from an activity is deductible, whether or not the taxpayer has amounts invested at risk in the activity. This is a harsher rule than the "at risk" approach, which allows net losses to be deducted against other income to the extent the taxpayer is at risk in the activity. In the case of Brannen,[23] the Tax Court used the not-for-profit rules to bar a loss deduction even where the taxpayer had amounts invested at risk in a movie tax shelter. This case, as well as the cases discussed below at ¶ 8.02(4) show the power of the courts to reach on occasion harsher results than those mandated by the at-risk rules.[24]

### (b) The Collapse of the Savings & Loan Industry

It should be noted that where financing is provided from outside lending institutions such as banks and savings and loans, the "at risk" rules do not apply.[25] Thus with regard to financing from those sources, taxpayers may continue to play the shelter game with nonrecourse debt and no "at risk" limit on their deductions.

It appears that this provision, which was enacted in the 1986 tax act, put a great deal of pressure on savings and loans to provide tax-shelter financing. These loans all looked good on the books. Note that there is a certain lack of restraint present with nonrecourse financing. The borrower is delighted to borrow more than the real value of the property on a nonrecourse basis. This can be facilitated by accommodating appraisers. The lender, particularly if it is already being run and regulated in a rather loose fashion, just likes to book big loans. Unfortunately, with the collapse of real estate values, savings and loans found themselves foreclosing on property that was now valued at far less than the outstanding debt. Since the financing was nonrecourse, S & L's were unable to proceed personally against the borrowers. It appears clear that this nonrecourse financing provision in the "at risk" rules contributed to the S & L catastrophe. This provision is still on the books.

### (3) Passive Activity Losses

### (a) In General

Congress continued its onslaught against tax shelters in 1986 with the enactment of a complex scheme of rules limiting deduction of so-called "passive activity losses" against other income. It is useful in understanding the relationship of the passive loss rules and the "at risk" rules to compare what they are aimed against. The "at risk" rules, discussed above, took aim at the fundamental building block of tax shelters of the use of nonrecourse debt to pump up basis for depreciation purposes. The passive activity loss rules, by contrast, take aim at the building block that taxpayers generally report all their income and losses in various lines of business or investments together on one return. The passive activity loss rules segregate losses generated from passive activities and bar them from being deducted against other income.

---

**23.** 78 T.C. 471 (1982), judgment aff'd 722 F.2d 695 (11th Cir.1984).

**24.** Compare to this case Lemmen, 77 T.C. 1326 (1981) (acq.) (managed cattle breeding arrangement was entered into for profit, amount of purchase price allocated to depreciable herd cut back.)

**25.** § 465(b)(6).

A "passive activity" is defined as any activity which involves the conduct of any trade or business or § 212–type activity, and in which the taxpayer does not materially participate. In addition, "passive activities" always include rental activity, regardless of whether the taxpayer materially participates in the rental activity. Thus, no matter how actively the taxpayer may manage a piece of rental property he owns, it will still be considered a passive activity.[26]

As a limited exception to this treatment of real estate, if a taxpayer actively participated in rental real estate activities during the year, then up to $25,000 of the net losses arising from that activity may be deducted against other "non-passive" income. This $25,000 exception is phased out to 0 by 50% of the amount by which the adjusted gross income (computed without regard to passive losses) of the taxpayer for the taxable year exceeds $100,000.[27]

The losses and credits generated from all such passive activities taken together can only be taken against the income and tax liability generated from such passive activities taken together. They cannot be deducted against income and tax liability arising from other activities not deemed to be passive.[28] Any unused passive activity losses and credits are carried forward to the next year where they may be applied against passive activity income and tax liability for that year. This carryforward continues indefinitely.[29] Thus the "phantom" losses that tax shelters produce with depreciation from a basis inflated by nonrecourse debt is not usable against other income. But it does remain to offset the later phantom gain on selling the property. The phantom gain is produced by the decline in basis of the property subject to the depreciation.

Portfolio or investment income, i.e., income from interest, dividends, annuities, or royalties not derived in the ordinary course of a trade or business, is not considered to be income from a passive activity for these purposes. Expenses, including interest, properly allocable to such portfolio income is also not taken into account for these purposes.[30] The gain or loss from the disposition of property producing such portfolio income is also not regarded as a passive activity for these purposes.[31]

A passive activity does not include a working interest in oil or gas property.[32] An interest as a limited partner in a limited partnership is generally treated as a passive activity.[33]

If an activity changes from being passive to being active, any unused deduction allocable to such activity is offset against the income from the

26. § 469(c)(2).

27. § 469(i).

28. § 469(a), (c)(6).

29. § 469(b).

30. Interest on debt incurred to finance investment income is only deductible to the extent of investment income, § 163(d).

31. § 469(e)(1).

32. § 469(c)(3).

33. § 469(h)(2).

activity for the taxable year.[34]

If during a tax year a taxpayer disposes of his entire interest in a passive activity or former passive activity, then the following rules apply: If all realized gain or loss is recognized, any loss from such activity which has not previously been allowed as a deduction is not treated as a passive activity loss.

However, this treatment does not apply if the disposition is to a related party. Also, if the loss arising from the disposition is a capital loss, the capital loss rules will be applied before the application of these rules.[35]

### (b) Relationship Between the "At Risk" Rules and the Passive Activity Loss Rules

With this tide of legislation sweeping against tax shelters, one may ask just what is the relationship between the "at risk" rules and the passive loss rules. Basically, the approach is that the "at risk" rules are applied first. Any loss that sneaks through the "at risk" rules is then clobbered by the passive loss rules. Any loss that manages to get through both we just throw down the stairs. (Just kidding; losses that get through both the "at risk" rules and the passive loss rules are allowed.)

### (4) Judicial and Administrative Limitations: Franklin

In addition to the juggernaut of legislation against tax shelters over the past couple of decades, there has been substantial action on the judicial and administrative fronts. For example, the leading case of *Estate of Franklin*[36] involved a sale of a motel to a limited partnership followed by a leaseback of the property to the original owner. The purchase price was to be paid in installments over ten years, plus a balloon payment at the end, for which the partnership had no personal liability. The annual rental payments on the leaseback just equaled the amount of the installment obligations. Thus no money was changing hands over the ten-year period, yet the partnership purported to own the property for purposes of depreciation and interest deductions.

The Ninth Circuit held, following *Crane*,[37] that such an arrangement involving nonrecourse debt could be a valid sale and therefore support depreciation and interest deductions by the purchaser. However, the Court held that in this instance the taxpayer had failed to carry the burden of showing that the nonrecourse debt did not exceed the fair market value of the property.[38] Where the nonrecourse debt exceeds the fair market value of the property, the Court stated, payments on the principal yield no equity in the property.[39] Since the taxpayer had no equity in the property, the depreciation deduction would be denied

---

**34.** § 469(f)(1).

**35.** § 469(g).

**36.** Estate of Franklin v. Commissioner, 544 F.2d 1045 (9th Cir.1976).

**37.** Crane v. Commissioner, 331 U.S. 1, 67 S.Ct. 1047, 91 L.Ed. 1301 (1947); see text accompanying notes 10–12 supra.

**38.** Estate of Franklin v. Commissioner, 544 F.2d 1045, 1048 (9th Cir.1976).

**39.** Id.

because " 'depreciation is not predicated upon ownership of the property *but rather upon an investment in property.' "[40]

The interest deduction also requires that the borrower have an equity in the property. The nonrecourse debt has no economic significance if it is for an amount greater than the value of the property securing it, since the borrower has no motivation to pay off the debt. Hence, since there was no bona fide indebtedness the interest deduction was disallowed.[41] *Franklin,* therefore, resolved the question left open by *Crane* of what would happen if nonrecourse mortgage debt were used to buy property with a fair market value less than the debt. *Crane* and its progeny had held that where the value of property is equal to or worth *more* than the nonrecourse debt, the nonrecourse debt would support deductions for depreciation and interest because the taxpayer would have an equity interest in the property and hence have a motivation to pay off the debt.[42] *Franklin* now held that where the nonrecourse mortgage debt is of an amount greater than the fair market value of the property, the debt will not support deductions for depreciation and interest.[43]

The question might fairly be asked, "Why would a taxpayer purchase property for nonrecourse mortgage debt in excess of the fair market value of the property?" The answer appears to be that the *Franklin* court was using the concept of fair market value of the property without regard to the tax considerations. Obviously, no sane purchaser would pay more for property, whether using nonrecourse debt or not, than the property is worth. But where the purchaser, because he is in a high tax bracket, can enjoy substantial tax advantages on the purchase of the property, it may be rational for him to pay more than the property is worth in an economic sense.

Indeed, the facts in *Franklin* suggest that this was the case. Evidence was introduced in the lower court that the motel property involved

**40.** Id. at 1049 (quoting Mayerson, 47 T.C. 340, 350 (1966)) (emphasis in original). See also Narver, Jr., 75 T.C. 53 (1980), opinion aff'd 670 F.2d 855 (9th Cir.1982) (nonrecourse debt not valid where promoter bought and resold property at "inflated" price through his controlled entities): Beck v. Commissioner, 678 F.2d 818 (9th Cir. 1982) (same), Thompson v. Commissioner, 631 F.2d 642 (9th Cir.1980), cert. denied 452 U.S. 961, 101 S.Ct. 3110, 69 L.Ed.2d 972 (1981).

**41.** Id.

**42.** See, e.g., Bolger, 59 T.C. 760 (1973) (acq.), in which taxpayer bought property from a seller, leased it to a user and paid for the purchase by incurring nonrecourse liability to an institutional lender, secured by the property and an assignment of the lease. Lease payments were made directly to the lender. Thus, Bolger owned the property via the vehicle of nonrecourse debt,

reported the lease payments as income and took the large depreciation and interest deductions. The Tax Court upheld this arrangement, following *Crane,* because the amortization of the mortgage increased taxpayer's equity in the property. See Mayerson, 47 T.C. 340 (1966) (acq.); Rev.Rul. 69–77, 1969–1 C.B. 59; see also Hudspeth v. Commissioner, 509 F.2d 1224 (9th Cir. 1975); American Realty Trust v. United States, 498 F.2d 1194 (4th Cir.1974).

**43.** The other end of the *Crane* transaction—namely the sale of the property subject to a nonrecourse indebtedness—has been the subject of great controversy, where the amount of the nonrecourse indebtedness exceeds the value of the property. For discussion, including the decision of the Supreme Court in the *Tufts* case on this question, see footnote 13 supra.

had been purchased by the seller the previous year for about half the selling price to the taxpayer.[44] Moreover, the property was insured for only about half this selling price.[45]

*Franklin* achieves a result similar to, but by no means identical with, the results under the at-risk rules. Under the at-risk rules, a nonrecourse liability is still considered part of the basis of property for purposes of computing depreciation and interest deductions and ascertaining basis. However, if depreciation, interest and other deductions give rise to net losses in excess of amounts at risk, such losses will not be allowed (although they may be carried over and allowed if more amounts are put at-risk).[46] Thus, under the at-risk rules, the nonrecourse liability will be included in the basis of the property and the basis will be reduced by the full amounts of depreciation taken. This is not as harsh as the *Franklin* approach of disregarding the nonrecourse liability for *all* purposes, including computation of depreciation, and deduction of interest, where the amount of the debt exceeds the fair market value of the property.

*Franklin* is therefore of great significance. All that is required to achieve its draconian results is for the Service to assert successfully that the taxpayer has failed to carry his burden of showing that the nonrecourse liability is not greater than the economic fair market value of the property. Since tax considerations tend to bid up the price of real estate shelter property beyond its economic value, the threat *Franklin* poses looms large indeed.[47]

The Service, never one to procrastinate when a favorable decision is rendered, issued a ruling hard on the heels of *Franklin*, applying its rationale to a film tax shelter financed with nonrecourse debt.[48] The film shelter originated in 1974 and thus was not subject to the at-risk rules. Employing the same rationale as *Franklin* and citing it, the Service said that the nonrecourse note used to purchase the film would be disregarded in determining depreciation and interest deductions because the note was for an amount significantly greater than the economic fair market value of the film.

In addition to *Franklin* and rulings issued pursuant to it, the Service has maintained a steady administrative pressure on tax shelters

---

44. Estate of Franklin v. Commissioner, 544 F.2d 1045, 1048 n. 4 (9th Cir.1976).

45. Id. The *Franklin* court did not in fact make a substantive finding that the property had been purchased for more than its economic fair market value. Rather the court simply held that the taxpayer had failed to carry the burden of showing that the purchase price including the nonrecourse debt did not exceed the economic fair market value of the property.

46. See ¶ 8.02(2).

47. Would the Service have the temerity to try to apply *Franklin* even in areas where the "at risk" and passive loss rules do apply in an attempt to achieve *Franklin*'s harsh results?

48. Rev.Rul. 77–110, 1977–1 C.B. 58, see also Rev.Rul. 79–432, 1979–2 C.B. 289. See also Narver, 75 T.C. 53 (1980), aff'd 670 F.2d 855 (9th Cir.1982) (where property resold by a promoter for a price far in excess of fair market value, financed by a nonrecourse note, court held there was in substance no sale and the depreciation and interest deductions were disallowed.)

by using audit procedures to highlight them, aggressive litigating postures toward them, proposed practice rules to limit tax shelter opinion letters and the like.

### (5) Tax Shelters Without Tears

What is the problem? Why are we having so much trouble with tax shelters? Historically, we see the decision in the *Crane* case,[49] followed by the flowering of tax shelters followed by the huge, complex outpouring of legislative, judicial and administrative actions against tax shelters. It is fair to say that the system of administration of the tax laws has been engaged in a massive campaign against tax shelters for several decades.

The question is whether it had to be this way. Once *Crane* was decided the way it was, could the response to tax shelters have taken a different course?

It seems clear that things could have been different. As we have seen, the amount of depreciation allowed in the early years of an investment is, from the point of view of economic analysis, always overstated. Even straight-line depreciation overstates the amount that should be allowed in the early years (and necessarily understates it in the later years). See ¶ 6.02(12). This leads to deferral of income which is the essence of tax shelters.

As our discussion of depreciation has shown, the economically correct method of depreciation is "sinking fund" depreciation. It will be recalled that under that method, depreciation is backloaded—with small amounts of depreciation in the early years and large amounts in the later years.

If that method of depreciation had been applied historically, the strength of the tax shelter type of investment would have been seriously if not mortally impaired. There would have been no deferral. We would not have had to enact the massive phalanx of antitax shelter rules that we now have. The tax law would have been much simpler.

There was a better way once, but it's too late now.

## ¶ 8.03    Deferred Payment Sales: Logan

### (1) In General

Where a taxpayer sells property for deferred payments to be paid over a period of years in the future, he is automatically put on the installment method of reporting, unless he elects otherwise.[1] The installment method of accounting for such sales in effect spreads the taxpayer's gain out over the period for which he will receive the payments. This approach is generally attractive because it results in deferral of gain and

---

**49.** ¶ 4.03(2)(b)(ii).

**¶ 8.03**

**1.** § 453(d)(1). For rules barring the installment method on sales between cer-

tain related parties, see discussion below.

is used by most taxpayers. As we have pointed out at great length elsewhere, deferral of gain is money in the bank to the taxpayer. See see the Prologue and ¶¶ 1.02(2)(e); 3.08(4)(b); 6.02(12).

The question may be asked whether it is appropriate to defer gain in this situation and thereby put money in the pocket of the selling taxpayer. The idea behind installment sales treatment is that the seller who has sold for notes of the buyer is not necessarily in funds to pay the tax. The buyer's notes cannot be easily sold for cash. That does make sense, but if that is the problem, then it would be appropriate to charge the seller interest on his deferred tax liability. It is one thing to be concerned about the seller's liquidity; it is another to put money in the seller's pocket just because he has chosen to use the installment method of reporting.[2] Without an interest charge on the deferred tax liability, the statute encourages sellers to use the installment method of reporting even if they do have the funds (say from other sources) to pay the tax on the sale immediately. This misallocates resources. We are encouraging the seller to keep his funds loaned to the buyer rather than perhaps put his funds elsewhere based on financial market conditions.

If the deferred payment sales arrangement is not reported on the installment method, then the so-called closed method approach is used. The fair market value of the deferred payment claims is included in the cash basis taxpayer's amount realized in the year of the sale. The amount realized so computed will be taken against the taxpayer's basis in the property to ascertain taxpayer's gain or loss in the year of sale. This is the method used by the Service in the celebrated *Logan* case. See the graphic below.[3]

In the rare case, the claims are so speculative in value that no fair market value may be placed upon them. The payments could be difficult

---

**2.** The statute does impose an interest charge on the deferred tax liability in the case of sales for a price above $150,000, where the buyer has a total face amount of obligations from such sales exceeding $5 million, § 453(a). In addition, borrowing against such obligations is considered to be a payment, triggering tax. This provision was enacted to combat what was perceived as sharp tax planning in the case of the Campeau/Federated Department stores leveraged buyout. See D. Posin, *Corporate Tax Planning: Takeovers, Leveraged Buyouts and Restructurings* Chapter 3 ¶ C (1990).

**3.** If the property sold is a capital asset, the gain (or loss) will be capital (a characterization which has little importance now, see ¶ 4.06). If the claims are subsequently paid at face, the difference between the face amount and the fair market value will be treated as ordinary income, regardless of whether or not the underlying property sold was a capital asset.

If any claim is not paid off (or paid off at less than the amount at which it was valued), then the taxpayer has a bad debt loss, which will generally give rise to a short-term capital loss, unless the sale of the property was incident to the taxpayer's trade or business. See Warren Jones Co. v. Commissioner, 524 F.2d 788 (9th Cir.1975), rev'g 60 T.C. 663 (1973) (land contract included in amount realized notwithstanding its fair market value was steeply discounted from its face amount); § 166(d) (short-term, capital loss on nonbusiness bad debts); see also ¶ 7.01(6) for bad debts and worthless securities generally.

Accrual method taxpayers are treated similarly except that the initial valuation of the installment notes to the accrual method taxpayer is at their face amount.

to value because they are contingent on events based in the future that are hard to predict. For example the payments could be a percentage of the royalties produced by a copper mine in an era when copper prices are volatile. The payments could also be difficult to value because the debtor is staggering on the edge of bankruptcy. In such cases the transaction may be reported as "open." Under "open" treatment, the payments received as the years go by will first be applied against the basis of the property and no gain will be reported until the year in which the cumulative payments exceed that basis. Payments in excess of that basis will be reported as capital gain if the underlying property sold was a capital asset.[4]

This "open" treatment is, therefore, attractive in that gain is deferred until basis is recovered. In Congress's view, "Only in rare and extraordinary cases will property be considered to have no fair market value."[5]

The issues involved in "closed," "open" and "installment" treatment are illustrated by the classic case of *Burnet v. Logan.*

**4.** Cf. Burnet v. Logan, 283 U.S. 404, 51 S.Ct. 550, 75 L.Ed. 1143 (1931), see graphic below.

**5.** Reg. § 1.1001–1(a); Senate report accompanying Installment Sales Revision Act of 1980, page 24; McCormac v. United States, 191 Ct.Cl. 483, 424 F.2d 607 (1970) (contingent payments valued); compare Wiggins' Estate, 72 T.C. 701 (1979) (open transaction allowed for contracts that lacked ascertainable fair market value). See also United States v. Davis, 370 U.S. 65, 82 S.Ct. 1190, 8 L.Ed.2d 335 (1962), reh'g denied 371 U.S. 854, 83 S.Ct. 14, 9 L.Ed.2d 92 (1962) (value of extinguishment of marital rights determined by reference to value of property given up; discussed on other issues at ¶ 4.02(2)).

## BURNET v. LOGAN[6]

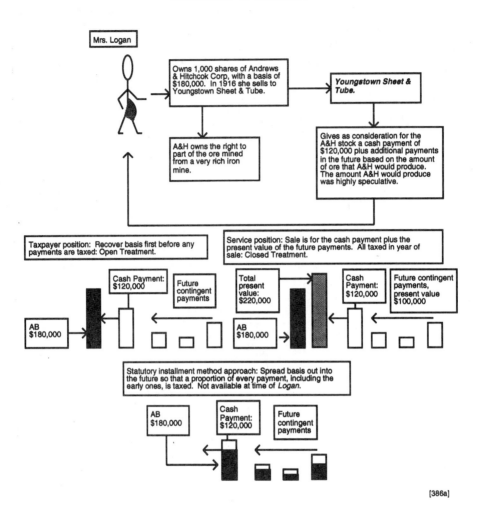

[386a]

*Question:* How are the payments to be received in the future taxed? As indicated in the graphic, the possibilities are: 1) The payments are untaxed until basis is recovered first, or 2) The cash payment and the present value of the future payments are taxed in the year of sale. A third possibility, not considered by the *Logan* Court, is the installment method of the current statute, discussed below.

*Taxpayer position:* Use open treatment. No gain in year of sale nor until basis recovered.

*Service position:* Use closed treatment. Estimate future payments will come in at $9,000 per year for 45 years, based on the amount of ore

---

**6.** 283 U.S. 404, 51 S.Ct. 550, 75 L.Ed. 1143 (1931). The facts in this graphic have been simplified from the original case.

supposedly left at the deposit. These payments had a present value of $100,000. This $100,000 present value plus the $120,000 cash payment gave Mrs. Logan an amount realized in the year of sale of $220,000. Taking that $220,000 against Mrs. Logan's basis of $180,000 gave her a gain in year of sale of $40,000.

*Held:* Open treatment should be used. The arrangement is too speculative to be valued. Thus nothing is included in income for 1916, the year of sale.

*Comment, the three methods:* Note the extreme difference between the Service's approach and the taxpayer's approach. The Service's approach gives the gain as early as possible and the taxpayer's approach gives the gain as late as possible. The installment method approach gives a result in between the other two. It provides for ratable inclusion of income as payments are made. These are the three major approaches to contracts for future payments. As discussed further below, the open treatment has pretty well gone out with the buggywhip. The installment method is by far the most widely used. The closed method is rare but can be elected under the statute.

*Comment, time value of money analysis applied to* Logan: What happens as each payment for the next 45 years comes in under *Logan*? The total of $9,000 per year for 45 years has been valued by the Service as being worth $100,000 on a present value basis.[7] Note that without discounting the total worth of the payments is 45 × $9,000 or $405,000. Since the total value of the payments on a present value basis is $100,000, then each payment, having been valued at its present value, would take a basis of its present value at the year of the sale. Then as each payment came in at $9,000, the excess of $9,000 over the basis of the payment would be income. This is shown in the accompanying chart.

---

7. This implies an interest rate of 8.8%. These numbers have been simplified from the actual numbers of *Logan*. The principle is the same.

Logan cost recovery

### Time Value of Money Analysis Applied to *Logan*

| Year | Amount of Payment | Present Value or Basis of Payment | Amount Included in Income as Payment Rec'd | |
|---|---|---|---|---|
| \multicolumn{5}{l}{Present Value of $9,000 Payments Paid Annually for 45 Years.} |
| 1 | $9,000 | $8,272.06 | $727.94 | $9,000 minus basis of payment |
| 2 | $9,000 | $7,603.00 | $1,397.00 | |
| 3 | $9,000 | $6,988.05 | $2,011.95 | |
| 4 | $9,000 | $6,422.84 | $2,577.16 | |
| 5 | $9,000 | $5,903.34 | $3,096.66 | |
| 6 | $9,000 | $5,425.87 | $3,574.13 | |
| 7 | $9,000 | $4,987.01 | $4,012.99 | |
| 8 | $9,000 | $4,583.65 | $4,416.35 | |
| 9 | $9,000 | $4,212.91 | $4,787.09 | |
| 10 | $9,000 | $3,872.16 | $5,127.84 | |
| 11 | $9,000 | $3,558.97 | $5,441.03 | |
| 12 | $9,000 | $3,271.11 | $5,728.89 | |
| 13 | $9,000 | $3,006.54 | $5,993.46 | |
| 14 | $9,000 | $2,763.36 | $6,236.64 | |
| 15 | $9,000 | $2,539.86 | $6,460.14 | |
| 16 | $9,000 | $2,334.43 | $6,665.57 | |
| 17 | $9,000 | $2,145.61 | $6,854.39 | |
| 18 | $9,000 | $1,972.07 | $7,027.93 | |
| 19 | $9,000 | $1,812.56 | $7,187.44 | |
| 20 | $9,000 | $1,665.96 | $7,334.04 | |
| 21 | $9,000 | $1,531.21 | $7,468.79 | |
| 22 | $9,000 | $1,407.37 | $7,592.63 | |
| 23 | $9,000 | $1,293.53 | $7,706.47 | |
| 24 | $9,000 | $1,188.91 | $7,811.09 | |
| 25 | $9,000 | $1,092.75 | $7,907.25 | |
| 26 | $9,000 | $1,004.36 | $7,995.64 | |
| 27 | $9,000 | $923.13 | $8,076.87 | |
| 28 | $9,000 | $848.46 | $8,151.54 | |
| 29 | $9,000 | $779.84 | $8,220.16 | |
| 30 | $9,000 | $716.76 | $8,283.24 | |
| 31 | $9,000 | $658.79 | $8,341.21 | |
| 32 | $9,000 | $605.51 | $8,394.49 | |
| 33 | $9,000 | $556.53 | $8,443.47 | |
| 34 | $9,000 | $511.52 | $8,488.48 | |
| 35 | $9,000 | $470.14 | $8,529.86 | |
| 36 | $9,000 | $432.12 | $8,567.88 | |
| 37 | $9,000 | $397.17 | $8,602.83 | |
| 38 | $9,000 | $365.04 | $8,634.96 | |
| 39 | $9,000 | $335.52 | $8,664.48 | |
| 40 | $9,000 | $308.38 | $8,691.62 | |
| 41 | $9,000 | $283.44 | $8,716.56 | |
| 42 | $9,000 | $260.51 | $8,739.49 | |
| 43 | $9,000 | $239.44 | $8,760.56 | |
| 44 | $9,000 | $220.08 | $8,779.92 | |
| 45 | $9,000 | $202.28 | $8,797.72 | Adds to $405,000. |
| Total: | $405,000 | $100,000.00 | $305,000.00 | |

Did the Service and the taxpayer handle open treatment this way in *Logan*? I don't know, but I doubt it. We have only been applying sophisticated time value of money techniques to taxation from the last decade or so. *Logan* was decided in 1931. Probably what the taxpayer and the Service did was to divide the $100,000 that was reported as income from these payments in the year of sale by 45, yielding $2,222. Then they would have said that $2,222 was the basis of each payment as it came in. That would then give income in each year of $9,000 − $2,222, or $6,778. 45 years of income of $6,778 gives us $305,000. So this straight-line method also gives us a total of $305,000 income reported as the payments come in. But we know from the Prologue and other areas where we have discussed time value of money that the straight-line method is the wrong way to do it.[8]

*Comment, estate taxes:* One of the confusing aspects of this case was that this future payment contract was, in the facts of the case, valued in the estate of Mrs. Logan's mother. But, the Court said, that valuation had to be accomplished for estate tax purposes.

*Comment, planning for closely-held businesses:* When a closely-held business is sold, there can be great dispute about what the value should really be. By definition the stock is not publicly traded, so the valuation problem can be acute. One technique for accomplishing such a sale that the buyer and seller might both agree upon is to make part of the consideration a percentage of gross revenues for a period of years.[9] This is then a contingent payment contract which might be difficult or easy to value depending on how volatile the revenues of the business are.

*Comment, open treatment under current law:* You can't hardly get it any more. If the payment is for a contingent amount and the maximum payment is not fixed but the period of time is fixed, then the Service can compel the basis to be recovered ratably over the fixed time period. If the maximum amount of the payback is fixed but the time period is not fixed, then each payment received will be taxed in the same proportion that the maximum payment on the contract bears to the seller's basis.[10] If both the maximum price and the period of payments are not fixed, then the regulations spread the basis recovery out more or less arbitrarily over a period of 15 years.[11] With all of these techniques, if it comes out wrong at the end of the contract, the seller simply takes a further deduction for loss or reports more income for gain to even things up.

Can the seller under a contingent payment deal avoid these techniques and still get the old attractive *Logan* deal? The seller might try to say that he is "electing out" of these techniques in the same way that the seller under the usual installment method (which is not contingent) can elect out of installment treatment.

See if we can keep from getting confused on this one. The normal sale for fixed payments over a fixed period of time can be reported either under the installment method or—if the seller elects out of the install-

---

**8.** See also e.g. ¶ 6.0(12)(c), discussing "sinking fund" depreciation and ¶ 1.02(2)(e), discussing recovery of capital.

**9.** Keying the royalty percentage to *net* income would not be a good idea, since games can be played in arriving at net income.

**10.** Regs. § 15A.453–1(c).

**11.** Senate report to accompany Installment Sales Revision Act of 1980, pp. 23–24, also admonishing once again that only in rare and extraordinary cases may the "open" or *Logan* method of reporting be used.

ment method—it can be reported as a closed transaction. (Review the graphic above on *Logan*). Transactions with a contingent selling price are treated the same way. They are either on the installment method (using the techniques described above) or the seller can elect out of the installment method. What happens to contingent deals where the seller elects out of the installment method? The philosophy of the statute is that they should be then reported on the most unattractive method of being closed in the year of sale. However perhaps the seller on a contingent payment deal—particularly if selling price and pay-out period are both not fixed and the payments are hard to estimate—might hope to get the most attractive treatment of all, open (*Logan*) treatment. Given the legislative history, and the attitude of the Service, the chances of that are not good. If the facts of *Logan* came up today, they would not get *Logan* treatment.

### (2) The Installment Method of Reporting

As we have described in the previous section, the installment method of reporting involves spreading the seller's gain out over the period in which the payments are to be made. This section discusses the installment approach in more detail, since it is used in the overwhelming majority of deferred payment sales. See also ¶ 1.02(2)(e)(i) where I argue that the installment method in present value terms differs little from open treatment and is basically a waste of time. However, even if I am right about that (and I have been wrong in print before), you still have to learn the installment method, since it is widely used, whereas open treatment is almost never available.

An "installment sale," under the statute, is a disposition of property where at least one payment is to be received after the close of the taxable year in which the disposition occurs.[12] The installment method may be used where only a single payment is to be made, provided that payment is made in a year following the close of the year of sale.[13] In an installment sale, the taxpayer is on the installment method of reporting automatically, unless he elects out of it.[14]

The computation of the installment method is as follows: The proportion of each payment that is received is taxed as the proportion that the gross profit bears to the total contract price.[15] For example:

---

**12.** § 453(b)(1). This discussion pertains primarily to casual sales of real and personal property; dealers who sell property on the installment method use analogous rules. See § 453(b)(2).

**13.** Applying the installment method to such a one-payment sale does not spread the taxpayer's gain over more than one year, but it does have the effect of deferring the gain until the year in which the payment is actually made. Absent the installment method, such a sale with one deferred payment would probably be valued and taxed to the taxpayer in the year of the sale. See text above. Prior to the Installment Sales Revision Act of 1980, two or more payments were required in order to qualify for installment method treatment. See also Rev.Rul. 82–227, 1982–52 IRB (using installment method on year-end stock sale to choose which year to be taxed on sale).

**14.** § 453(a) and (d).

**15.** § 453(b) and (c).

**Example:** T sells a plot of vacant land for $100,000 to be paid in five installments of $20,000 in the year of sale and $20,000 in each of the four following years. Adequate interest is separately stated and paid. The basis of the land in T's hands is $40,000. To compute the installment method for this transaction, it is first determined that the gross profit on this transaction is $60,000. The ratio of the gross profit to the contract price ($60,000/$100,000) is 60 percent. Therefore, 60 percent of each $20,000 payment, or $12,000 is taxed to T on the receipt of each payment. When the five payments have been made, T will have been taxed on his $60,000 of gain.

If the property is sold subject to a mortgage of the seller's, either with or without personal liability, only the excess of the mortgage, if any, over the seller's basis will be considered a payment in the year of sale. For purposes of computing the ratio, the contract price will exclude the mortgage except to the extent the mortgage exceeds the seller's basis.[16] As an example:

**Example:** T sells a plot of vacant land for $50,000 plus the assumption by B of a $50,000 mortgage on the property. The $50,000 purchase price is to be paid in five installments of $10,000 in the year of sale and $10,000 in each of the four following years. Adequate interest is separately stated and paid. The basis of the land in T's hands is $40,000. To compute the installment method for this transaction, it is first determined that the gross profit on the transaction is $60,000 ($50,000 cash plus being relieved of $50,000 mortgage yields total amount realized of $100,000 less the basis of $40,000, gives a gross profit of $60,000). The contract price is $60,000 ($50,000 purchase price plus $10,000 excess of mortgage over basis). Thus $60,000/$60,000 or 100% of each payment will be taxed to T.

The payment in the first year is $20,000 ($10,000 cash plus $10,000 excess of mortgage over basis). The payment in each of the next four years is $10,000. Thus the total amount taxed to T will be $60,000, which is the amount of his gain. The higher percentage applied to the payments (compared to the example above) makes up for the fact that in this example being relieved of the mortgage in the year of sale was for the most part not taxed.

This procedure not only establishes the timing for the reporting of a taxpayer's gain, but it also establishes the basis in the installment notes that the taxpayer holds. The rule is that taxpayer's basis in his installment notes is the face amount of the note less the amount which would be reportable as income were the note satisfied in full.[17] Thus, should the taxpayer sell the note before it is satisfied, he can calculate his gain (or

**16.** Reg. § 1.453–4(c). The contract price is reduced by commissions and other costs of the sale under the usual rules. See ¶ 4.03(1).

**17.** § 453B(b).

loss) since the installment method has established his basis in each note.[18]

The installment method may be employed where some gain is recognized in a tax-free exchange. In such a transaction the approach is to apply the installment sale rules to the taxable part of the transaction. Thus, the gross profit is the recognized gain and the contract price is the total amount of the consideration received less the fair market value of the non-recognition property received.[19] In making all these computations, the installment obligations are valued at face.[20]

The Installment Sales Revision Act of 1980 also tightened the rules on a transaction whereby the taxpayer would, for example, sell appreciated property to his or her spouse on the installment method and the spouse would shortly thereafter sell the property to a third party. The effect of this transaction would be that the taxpayer would be able to report the gain on the installment method. The spouse, who would get full payment immediately, would have no gain to report since the spouse's basis was the fair market value of the property. Thus, did the family group in effect get to report the transaction on the installment method while at the same time obtaining the total sales price immediately.[21]

The Installment Sales Revision Act of 1980 neatly solved this problem by providing that the second sale will trigger recognition of gain by the first seller.[22] This rule applies only to a second sale within two years after the date of the first sale, except in the case of marketable securities, where the rule applies without a time limit.[23] This rule of acceleration of recognized gain applies only where the first sale is to a "related party," defined to include spouses, children, grandchildren, parents, a 50–percent or more owned corporation (applying the attribution rules of § 318), partnerships, trusts and estates that are related to the taxpayer under the corporate stock ownership attribution rules.[24]

## ¶ 8.04 Deferred Compensation: A Survey

### (1) In General

Employee compensation can take a wide variety of forms, as indicated in Chapter 2. In addition, employee compensation may be in the form

---

**18.** Not only will sale of the note trigger gain or loss but so will distribution, transmission, gift, or other disposition, § 453B(a).

**19.** See ¶ 4.05.

**20.** § 453(f)(6); Senate report accompanying the Installment Sales Revision Act of 1980, page 19.

**21.** See Senate Report accompanying Installment Sales Revision Act of 1980, page 17.

**22.** § 453(e).

**23.** §§ 453(e)(2), 453(f)(2). § 453(e)(6) and (7) provide certain exceptions, includ-ing the exception that the rules won't apply if it is established to the satisfaction of the Service that the two transactions did not have as one of their principal purposes the avoidance of federal income tax.

**24.** § 453(f)(1), Senate report accompanying Installment Sales Revision Act of 1980, page 16.

The installment method is not available on sales of depreciable property to related taxpayers covered by § 1239, see § 453(g) and see ¶ 4.06(3)(a)(viii).

of various deferred arrangements. This is an area in which taxpayers and their employers may engage in significant planning to defer the employee's current tax liability, provide the employer with a tax deduction and ensure retirement security for the employee. A complete treatment of this complex subject is beyond the scope of this work; only an outline of the planning possibilities in this area will be presented.[1]

The difference between qualified and nonqualified deferred compensation plans is fundamental to this area. Qualified plans are so-called because they meet a variety of explicit rules relating to employee participation and benefits. When these rules are met, qualified plans receive the attractive treatment that the employee is not taxed when his benefits are earned, but only when they are received; the earnings of the plan are not subject to tax as they are accumulated, but only when distributed; and the employer gets a current deduction for contributions to such plans. See also the discussion in the Prologue.

Nonqualified arrangements do not have to meet these broad requirements with respect to employee participation, benefits and funding, but the price they pay is a somewhat less attractive tax treatment as a result. Nonqualified or contractual deferred compensation plans are particularly useful for compensating the executive, or other highly compensated individual—such as an entertainer or athlete—where the employer may be willing to undergo a tax disadvantage to confer unusual benefits on the object of its bounty.

For more detailed discussion, see ¶ 8.04(2)(a) below.

### (2) Non–Qualified Plans

#### (a) Current Razzle–Dazzle Executive Compensation Techniques

Using the nonqualified technique described above, John Welch Jr., chief executive officer of General Electric in 1995 deferred taxes on $1 million of salary. By so doing he will increase his compensation substantially within five years. Mr. Welch was not alone. J.F. McDonnell, the chairman of McDonnell Douglas corporation deferred $2.5 million. Michael H. Jordan of Westinghouse deferred $1.8 million. John L. Clendenin of BellSouth has nearly $10 million in his deferral accounts.[2] There is no ceiling on how much money can be sheltered using these nonqualified techniques. Roberto C. Goizueta, the chief executive officer of Coca Cola has accumulated $1 billion in Coca Cola stock that will not be taxed until after he retires. Readers of this book need no introduction to the extremely attractive effect of deferring large amount of tax for a significant number of years, see the Prologue.

**¶ 8.04**

1. See Fischer, "Deferred Compensation: Born Again—For Now," 37 NYU Inst. on Fed.Tax. Section 28 (1979); Greene, "Compensating the Executive in Cash; Payment Now or Payment Later," 1978 So.Calif.Tax Inst. 193.

2. The anecdotal information in the text comes from Christopher Drew and David Cay Johnston, Special Tax Breaks Enrich Savings of Many in the Ranks of Management, The New York Times, October 13, 1996, p. 1.

The size of this movement should not be underestimated. Many large companies, such as I.B.M., Tenneco, and Merrill Lynch have expanded their plans to include as many as hundreds or even thousands of employees. Owners of small business are setting up nonqualified plans, which are allowing them to save for their retirement without including their employees. The employees would have to be part of any § 401(k) plan or qualified plan set up.

The total number of employers who had notified the IRS that they have nonqualified plans has swelled from less than 1,000 at the beginning of 1982 to over 24,000 at the end of 1996. And there are a number of employers who have established plans who have not notified the IRS.

A major reason the number of nonqualified deferral plans has exploded is the increased restrictions Congress has enacted with respect to qualified plans. Congress enacted ERISA which was intended to expand and protect the retirement funds of workers. ERISA, and subsequent legislation limited how much executives could save in qualified plans. In particular Congress in 1986 cut the maximum that one person could contribute to a 401(k) or supplemental retirement program from $30,000 to $7,000, because of the large amounts of tax the government was losing with these deferral plans. In 1988 and 1993, Congress cut the amounts that executives could receive from regular pension plans from up to $250,000 to $150,000. These changes substantially lowered the federal budget deficit. Then, Congress began to raise marginal tax rates, with signatures from President Bush and President Clinton, from a maximum of 28% in 1991 to a maximum of 39.6% in 1993. This was coupled with the denial of deduction to the employer for annual executive salaries about $1 million. All of this spurred the rush to nonqualified plans.

It should be noted that because these are nonqualified plans, as discussed above, the setting aside of this money for deferred taxation to the executive does not result in deferred taxation to the employer. The corporate employer and its shareholders pay taxes on the money and thus the employer and it shareholders are subsidizing the executive's tax deferral.

The Government has not challenged this practice on the theory that the money set aside and its growth is taxed to the company, so that the Treasury is not losing tax revenues. The idea is that it is not for the Treasury to police how the company and its employees distribute the tax burden. The problem with that theory is that many companies are now buying life insurance policies on their employees. Since the inside buildup of life insurance is not taxed, see ¶ 3.06, the arrangement, taken altogether is costing the Treasury substantial revenues. According to one survey about 300 of the largest 1,000 companies are now using life insurance to finance their nonqualified deferred compensation arrangements. There are several techniques that employ life insurance. The major one operates as follows: the company takes out a policy on its employees. The company pays the premium and names itself as a beneficiary. The company keys the policy's investment return to fixed interest rates or to mutual funds. When the employee is ready to withdraw his deferred money, the company borrows from the policy or cashes it in for its cash surrender value. Another option is for the company to pay the deferred money out of its own funds and hold the policy until the death of the employee, at which time it collects the proceeds tax free.

Moreover, companies are not required to inform their shareholders how much compensation top executives are deferring. These plans appear to amount to a pay raise to top management and as such, critics say, should be reported. It appears that the rise of the use of nonqualified plans has significantly changed the way executives are compensated. It is estimated that in 1980 executives at large companies received 90% of their retirement benefits from regular qualified company pension plans, participated in by most employees and limited as to amounts (as discussed above). But by 1996, astonishingly, only about 30% of executive retirement benefits came from company plans and the rest came from nonqualified plans that only top management participates in. Indeed, under federal rules, only top management can participate in these plans. Since the amounts in nonqualified plans are subject to the claims of general creditors, federal law does not allow rank and file employees to participate in these plans. Also these nonqualified plans are not backed up by the federal pension insurance fund.

A survey of the 1,000 largest public companies by Compensation Resource Group Inc. showed that 74% of the companies offered nonqualified plans for top executives. Sometimes executives are allowed to defer the money for just a few years, rather than for retirement. This is to be compared with IRA's and §§ 401(k) and 403(b) plans which require a penalty of 10% on withdrawals before age 59½. Beyond that, the deferred money is often awarded a very high interest rate by the company. BellSouth has paid interest rates to its deferred amounts of from 8 to 22 percent over the last 10 years.

To return to Mr. Welch, he received an interest rate of 14% on the deferred $1 million of his $2 million salary. After 5 years at that rate the $1 million would have compounded to $1,925,415. Receiving that amount at a 40% tax rate five years later would leave Mr. Welch with $1,155,249. If he had taken the deferred $1 million immediately and paid taxes, he would have had only about $600,000. The best, after tax, secure interest rate he could hope to receive on that $600,000 would be, say, 5%. After five years the $600,000 would compound, at that interest rate, to $765,769. Thus the gain from being able to defer and receive the artificially high interest rate is $389,480 ($1,115,249 less $765,769). Since deductible compensation is capped at $1 million (see ¶ 6.02(1)(a)), these maneuvers also preserve the companies involved the possibility of being able to deduct the payments later, when they are paid. Thus by choosing to defer payments with nonqualified plans, executives save their companies taxes. For example a company in the top corporate bracket of 35% saves $350,000 by being able to deduct $1 million in deferred salary. Companies can be willing to give some of these tax savings back to the executive who agrees to defer some of his salary. Companies may also pay the cost of insurance that eliminates the risk of using nonqualified deferred compensation plans.

Using these techniques has enabled a great many top management people to defer a great deal of income, as indicated above. But the unquestioned giant in the field of executive compensation is Roberto C. Goizueta, the chief executive of the Coca–Cola Company. He has by all accounts done an excellent job as the chief executive officer of Coke. His accomplishments in the deferred compensation field, though, are the stuff of legend. Mr. Goizueta was born in Cuba and educated at Yale. Since 1979, according to company proxy statements, Mr. Goizueta has received total compensation of more than $1 billion. Not counting stock options. And one might want to count stock options, since Coca–Cola's stock price has appreciated 52 times since he took charge. The $1 billion is also not counting his § 401(k) plan and his regular pension worth $3 million a year. But the really interesting part is that he has paid taxes on this billion dollar package at a rate of 5%. This makes a nice comparison with a typical middle class family with $50,000 of income and two children, which pays 17% of its income in taxes.

Basically, Mr. Goizueta employed § 83, discussed at ¶ 2.03. He has received a total of 17.2 million Coke shares on the condition that he not sell them or borrow against them before he retires. He has also received two cash payments based on the price of Coke stock. The restrictions on the stock do not affect his power to vote the shares or receive dividends on them (which amounted to $4.9 million in 1995). As long as the restrictions are not lifted, Mr. Goizueta does not have to pay taxes. With the stock recently trading around $50, Mr. Goizueta checks in at right around $1 billion of deferred compensation. As we know from the prologue, deferral of tax is like money in the bank. Mr. Goizueta's has accomplished a great deal as chief executive officer of Coke. His career also demonstrates that deferred compensation goes better with Coke.

Another aspect of these nonqualified plans is that they take top management out of the same pension plans as the rest of the employees. As Sylvester J. Schieber of Watson Wyatt Worldwide, a benefits consulting group, said, "Senior management is no longer in the same puddle with the rest of the work force, and if the puddle dries up, senior management is not much affected."[3] Although nonqualified plans supposedly do not have the safeguards of qualified plans, the fact is that the power of top management is such that their nonqualified plans are protected in bankruptcy proceedings even as the rank and file's § 401(k) plans, in which they may be required to invest in the company's stock, go broke.

---

**3.** The anecdotal information on treatment of pension benefits in bankruptcy is based on Diana B. Henriques and David Cay Johnston, Managers Staying Dry as Corporations Sink, The New York Times, October 14, 1996, page A1.

An example is the widely publicized bankruptcy of Morris Knudsen construction company. The company had a distinguished reputation for building major projects in difficult places, such as the 726 foot Hoover Dam across the Colorado River and the Trans–Alaska oil pipeline. It also had an outstanding reputation for taking care of its employees. But soon after Mr. William J. Agee (the ex-corporate raider with Bendix who had a widely publicized relationship with Mary Cunningham, a former Bendix executive whom he eventually married) took charge of the company, the company fell on hard times. Workers' regular pension benefits were frozen and further years of service did not count toward future benefits. Instead, only a § 401(k) plan was available for retirement for new employees. Mr. Agee, meanwhile, moved the company headquarters from its traditional location in Boise Idaho to Carmel, California, closer to Mr. Agee's mansion in Pebble Beach. Thereafter, the board set up a deferred-compensation plan for Mr. Agee and 100 of his top executives. Six months later, the company reported surprising losses on its new mass-transit manufacture contracts, that had been initiated by Mr. Agee. In February, 1995, the board demanded Mr. Agee's resignation. For about a year the company resisted its creditors but eventually it filed for protection of the bankruptcy laws in connection with a purchase of the company by another smaller construction company. The company's stock shrank virtually to $0, and the § 401(k) plans that had bought mostly the company's stock similarly dissolved. A year before the bankruptcy filing, however, the company's creditors agreed to let the company pay Mr. Agee and its other executives the $4.4 million in their supposedly more risky nonqualified plan.

Another story is presented by Carter Hawley Hale. The Carter Hawley Hale § 401(k) was different from the the Morris Knudsen in that the employees of Carter Hawley Hale could only buy the company's stock in it. Through the 80's, as the company's stock soared. More than 14,000 employees participated in the § 401(k), as a supplement to their relatively small regular pension plans. Ultimately the company went bankrupt and was eventually purchased by Federated Department Stores, with rank and file employees losing at least 90% of their value in their 401(k)'s. The supplemental pension and savings plans set up for Philip M. Hawley, the president and chief executive officer and other top executives had more options than just the company's stock, including an account that paid 10% interest. During the bankruptcy these supplemental pensions and deferred compensation plans of top management were preserved.

Still another example is the department store chain Woodward & Lothrop. When this chain (with its flagship store known affectionately as "Woodies" in the Washington D.C. area) went bankrupt, it stopped paying deferred compensation and supplemental pension benefits to retired executives and widows of retired executives. Some lost hundreds of thousands of dollars of pension benefits. In total some 33 retired executives lost pension benefits of $8 million. This group hired a lawyer and after an arduous process, the Bankruptcy Court allowed only $4.1

million of their claim and classified the group as general unsecured creditors, putting them last on the list to get paid. The group hopes to collect 70% of that claim or about $2.8 million out of the original $8 million.

The Pension Benefit Guaranty Corporation, the federal agency that insure pension benefits, announced, in August, 1995, that the regular pension fund for rank and file employees of Woodward & Lothrop would be protected. In addition the deferred compensation of the top 14 executives was also fully protected. The company argued that it needed to retain essential management during the reorganization and so it won the court's approval to reinstate the special benefits of 13 top management; the benefits of a 14th were guaranteed by A. Alfred Taubman, the chairman of Woodward & Lothrop and its largest shareholder. (One might be so impudent as to ask whether the job market for executives of a company that has gone bankrupt is really so robust that they need to have all their pension benefits preserved to keep them on the job).

These cases are not unique. Giving the lie to the idea that nonqualified benefits go to the end of the creditors line are the the bankruptcy filings of R. H. Macy & Company, now owned by Federated; Dow Corning, the silicon-products company combatting liability claims for breast implants;[4] Am International, a manufacturer of graphics and mailroom equipment; First American Health Care, the leading home health care provider; Insilco, the manufacturer of Rolodex office products; Federated Department Stores and its sister chain Allied Stores. In all these cases, according to bankruptcy records collected by New Generation Research of Boston, all or substantial amounts of supplemental or deferred nonqualified compensation for top executives were preserved or reinstated in connection with the bankruptcy proceeding.

In addition to relying on the top management's own bargaining power in the bankruptcy proceeding, other devices are being employed to safeguard nonqualified deferred compensation. A popular device is the so-called "rabbi trust," (the model was created for a rabbi of a Jewish congregation in Brooklyn). Under a rabbi trust, the company sets the executive's deferred money aside in a separate account. Although the money still belongs to the company and is subject to its creditors, the account is nonetheless considered to be safer than relying on just the company's promise to pay. In addition, executives can purchase insurance to protect deferred compensation or supplemental benefits from a company's unwillingness or inability to pay in the future. Some companies may even reimburse the executive for the cost of the insurance. Executives of PG & E and CSX corporation have purchased such insurance.

The upshot of these trends is that life seems to be getting tougher for middle management and rank-and-file employees. In the bankruptcy setting, top management may negotiate for its own benefits as the rank-

---

4. See Daniel Q. Posin, Silicone Breast Implant Litigation and My Father-in-Law: A Neo–Coasean Analysis, 70 Tulane Law Review 2565–2582 (1996).

and-file are being squeezed. Also the heavy use of § 401(k) plans that encourage or require investment in the company's stock means that middle management and rank-and-file employees may have their retirement funds too heavily invested in the stock of one company.

The original thesis of the pension law was to provide that if management wanted to save for their retirement on a tax-deferred basis, they had to develop a plan that covered most employees. With these nonqualified plans, that link is being broken and less provision is now being made for rank-and-file employees.

It can be argued that by limiting the amounts that executives can save in regular pension plans, the government created this problem and perhaps those limits should be liberalized. Another approach would be to remove the tax advantages of deferred compensation, through, for example, legislatively imposing the doctrine of constructive receipt on nonqualified arrangements.

It is not known how much money has been deferred in nonqualified plans, restricted stock plans or other ways. But the amount is doubtless substantial. There is a substantial specialty of consultants, accountants, lawyers, financial planners and others advising large and small business how to compensate top management without including other employees.

### (b) Incentive Stock Options

A stock option is a right granted by a company to an employee to purchase the stock of the company from the company at a particular price for a particular period of time. If the company's stock rises to a price above the option price, the employee has a sure-fire winning deal. This is a form of compensation.

Another rose from the bouquet presented to taxpayers by the Economic Recovery Tax Act of 1981 was the so-called Incentive Stock Option. Similarly to the older qualified and restricted stock options, under the incentive stock option there is no tax on the grant or the exercise of the option. When the employee sells the stock he receives on exercise of the option he is taxed at a capital gains rate.

To qualify for this attractive treatment, the incentive stock option arrangement must meet a series of conditions at the level of the corporate employer, and the employee must satisfy certain holding period requirements.

With respect to the employer, the option must be granted under a plan which is approved by the stockholders within 12 months before or after the plan's adoption by the employer. The option itself must be granted within 10 years of the date that the plan is adopted or approved by the shareholders, whichever is sooner. The option must be exercisable only within a period of ten years after the date it is granted. The option price must equal or exceed the fair market value of the stock to which it is subject when the option is granted. The option must be not transferrable other than at death and it may be exercised only by the employee during his life. If the employee owns more than 10% of the company's stock he is not eligible for the option unless the option price is at least 110% of the fair market value of the stock, and the option may not in this case be exercised more than 5 years after it is granted. The option cannot be exercisable while there is an outstanding incentive stock option that has been granted to the employee in an earlier year. Employees may be granted incentive stock options for stock per year for no more than $100,000 fair market value of the stock, plus a carryover of one half of the amount of stock options that could have been granted in a previous year (the unused carryover amount may be carried over for 3 years).

At the employee level the employee who has acquired stock by exercising an incentive stock option must hold the stock for at least one year and cannot dispose of the stock within two years after the option was granted, in order to qualify for capital gains rates on disposition of the stock. If either of these holding period requirements is not met, the gain on disposition of the stock will be taxed at ordinary income rates. The gain, whether capital or ordinary, on the disposition of the stock is measured by the amount realized on the sale of the stock and the price paid for the stock pursuant to the option.[5] To the extent the gain on the disposition of the stock is ordinary, because of failure to comply with the holding period requirements, the employer will be entitled to a deduction.[6]

Stock options issued under previous stock option arrangements may qualify for treatment as incentive stock options.[7] An incentive stock option cannot be exercised if there is outstanding an incentive stock option that was granted to the employee at an earlier time.[8] The employee can pay for the stock on exercise of the option with other stock of the corporation.[9] The transfer of stock to an employee upon his exercise of the option must be reported to the Service by the employer.[10]

### (3) Qualified Plans

A pension, profit-sharing, or stock bonus plan which meets a wide variety of rules receives the attractive tax treatment that employer contributions to the plan are immediately deductible to the employer and not includable in the income of the employee until the benefits are received. Moreover, earnings on the amounts contributed by the employer to the plan accumulate tax-free until distributed to the employee. See the Prologue for a numerical example of the immense benefits that are conferred by qualified plans.[11]

5. § 422.

6. § 421(b).

7. ERTA § 251(c)(1)(A). Temp.Reg. § 14a.422A–1 details the rules for electing incentive stock option treatment for options granted after 1975 and before 1981.

8. §§ 422A(b)(7), 422A(c)(7).

9. Section 422A(c)(5)(A). Pyramiding of ISO stock without tax cost with an employer's stock which is increasing in value is not possible, Technical Corrections Act of 1982, § 102(j)(6).

10. § 6039.

11. §§ 404(a) (employer contributions); 402(a)(1) (employees).

In order to qualify for these attractive tax benefits the plan must be "qualified", which means it must meet requirements related to the following areas:

Minimum participation standards must be met; this requires that while not every employee must be covered, a certain minimum number must be covered to insure that the plan confers relatively broadly based benefits and does not just benefit a few highly-placed employees.[12] The plan must not involve any discriminatory contributions or benefits; this again is to insure that highly-placed or highly-compensated employees do not obtain excessive benefits under the plan.[13] Benefits must vest within certain time periods to prevent an employee working for a long period of time and receiving no benefits.[14] In addition to vesting pursuant to specified schedules, benefits must also accrue according to specified schedules; accrual is necessary first before benefits can vest. Accrual applies only to defined benefit plans.[15] There are limits on the benefits and contributions that may accrue to participants in qualified plans. The particular amounts are adjusted upward by the Service.[16] To ensure employer ability to pay benefits, minimum funding standards are also provided.[17]

Employees are taxed only the receipt of the benefits from the plan, and they have various options as to how they will be taxed on them. An employee can elect to report the lump sum under a ten-year forward averaging method, to avoid the impact of the progressive tax rate schedule.[18] The employee can elect to tax the distribution attributable to contributions before December 31, 1973 as long-term capital gain and the balance treated under the ten-year forward averaging rules.[19] The employee may choose to have his distribution paid to him and taxed as an annuity.[20] The employee may choose to roll over a distribution from his pension plan into another qualified plan, an annuity plan, or an IRA, tax free.[21]

Significant rules protecting employee's rights with respect to vesting and other matters were enacted by The Employee Retirement Income and Security Act of 1974 (ERISA). The Tax Equity and Fiscal Responsibility Act of 1982 (TEFRA) enacted a number of restrictive rules relating to maximum plan benefits and contributions and "top-heavy" plans (plans which provide more than 60% of benefits to key employees) as well as other matters.

### (4) H.R. 10 Plans, and Individual Retirement Accounts

Self-employed individuals can adopt a so-called H.R. 10 plan. If the various rules of such plans are complied with, the self-employed individ-

**12.**　§§ 401(a)(3), 410.

**13.**　§ 401(a)(4).

**14.**　§§ 401(a)(7), 411. This was an important result of The Employee Retirement Income Security Act of 1974 (ERISA).

**15.**　§ 411(b)(1).

**16.**　§ 415.

**17.**　§ 412.

**18.**　§ 402(e).

**19.**　Id.

**20.**　§ 72(c) and (f).

**21.**　§ 402(a)(5), (6), (7).

ual will be treated as an employee for purposes of fitting within the structure of qualified plans described above.

Individual retirement accounts are another way for individual tax-payers to defer compensation until their retirement years.[22] The taxpay-er may set aside up to $2,000 per year ($2,250 for a married couple only one of whom works) in an IRA. The income earned by the account is not taxed as long as it accumulates in the IRA. The amounts contributed to the plan may be deducted if the taxpayer is not covered by an employer plan. Alternatively, if the employee is covered but has adjusted gross income of less than $25,000 ($40,000 for a married couple filing a joint return) the amounts contributed may be deductible. Amounts later withdrawn are included in income; there is an exclusion for those funds that were not deductible when contributed.

## ¶ 8.05 A Bird's Eye View of Sophisticated Estate Planning

While the subject of estate planning is beyond the scope of the basic course in federal income taxation as it is usually conceived, it seems that it is useful to convey to beginning students some of the sophisticated techniques that are employed in the estate planning area. These are matters that the student is likely to run into with respect to parents or other relatives. Also, the tax avoidance in this area raises policy ques-tions of interest to a student of the field of federal taxation. An informed attorney should have some knowledge of the basic principles of estate planning (or as the late Professor David Kadane used to say "never let your client get out the door without asking if he has a will.")

The basic principle is that if one dies with an estate above $600,000, a tax is levied on that excess. (At this writing—May, 1997—it is possible that this threshold will be raised, as part of the 1997 budget deal). The rate starts in at 37% and rises to 55%. The basic maneuvering in the field is to keep assets out of the estate so that they do not trigger the tax. There are a large number of techniques available to the well-advised for doing that.

Corporate executives, for example, are able to transfer millions of dollars of stocks and stock options to their children and not pay estate tax on them. Investors can put a wide variety of property, including stock, vacation homes into partnerships for their children, causing the property to be valued for taxation purposes at 30% to 70% less than their fair market value. Moreover, further appreciation in the value of these assets in the partnership does not attract the estate tax. A taxpayer can purchase a share of his children's inheritance which protects the inheri-tance from the estate tax. Moreover, some taxpayers can put their financial affairs together in such a complex fashion that the Service may sometimes give up trying to penetrate the legal miasma to collect the taxes.

The estate tax is so easy to avoid; indeed, less that two percent of adult deaths triggers payment of the estate tax. The rest of adult deaths

**22.** § 408.

are of either people who were too poor to trigger it or were sufficiently well-advised to avoid it.

The estate and gift tax law allows individuals to give tax-free gifts of up to $10,000 per year to as many people as they want. A married couple can give $20,000 annually to as many people as they want. In addition, each taxpayer can transfer up to $600,000 tax free at death. Gifts during life that exceed the $10,000 limit can be not taxed but they will reduce the $600,000 death exemption dollar for dollar.

One of the basic estate planning techniques is to set up a trust that holds property and avoids having the estates of the husband and wife put together when one spouse dies and leaves property to the other. Thus the couple can pass on $1.2 million in assets without attracting the estate tax.

In the executive compensation area, a major device is the transferable stock option. Stock options have long been a way to compensate executives, giving them the option to buy the company's stock at less than market value, see discussion above. Indeed if the company's stock appreciates greatly, this right to buy stock at a low price becomes extremely valuable indeed. Where the stock option has the feature that it is transferable to the executive's children, either directly or in trust, it can become a powerful means to transferring great amounts of wealth without triggering gift or estate tax. The Service has not provided guidelines on how to value stock options, so taxpayers are, not surprisingly, valuing them at virtually no value. Once the option is transferred the child can exercise the option to great profit, and no further gift or estate tax is triggered to the parent. It is the case that the exercise of the option causes the parent to have to pay income tax, under the assignment of income doctrine, see ¶ 5.02. That in itself can be an estate planning technique as the payment of income taxes by the parent enriches the child who does not have to pay the tax and reduces the parent's estate for estate tax purposes.

As an example of this technique, Eugene M. Isenberg chief executive of Nabors Industries, a Houston oil drilling and exploration company, transferred options to buy 2.25 million Nabors shares to trusts for his two daughters and grandchildren. In October and November of 1996 these options were exercised and produced a gain of $29.7 million. Mr. Isenberg did have to pay income tax on the gain. The transfer of these options had conditions attached that made it less valuable for gift tax purposes, so that a lesser gift tax was paid. The condition was that over the term of the trusts, Mr. Isenberg must get back the value of the assets he transferred plus a rate of interest.

*The house as real and tax shelter.* Another maneuver has withstood IRS challenge for some time. This is transferring the family house or a vacation home to a trust with the donor parent holding a life interest and the (usually minor) children with a remainder interest. The trust lapses, say, in 30 years. The value of the house to the children for gift tax purposes is calculated as only the present value of their remainder interest. When the children eventually come into ownership of the house in fee simple, they pay no further tax. During the life of the trust, they get no income from the house (conveniently ignoring the fact that they are living in the house and thus receiving shelter income). The children's remainder interest in a $500,000 house 30 years from now is $49,689 (assuming an 8% interest rate for the calculation). That is all that is charged for gift tax purposes. The gift is valued at the time it is made. Obviously the house has a fair market value of far more at the time of the gift and will be much more valuable 30 years from now when it actually passes to the children. If the parents die before the 30 year term of the trust, the value of the house would be included in their estate. Much of the advantage of the maneuver is then lost, but as the saying goes, there is no harm in trying. One maneuver is also to set up the term of the trust for a period that is substantially less than the life expectancy of the grantor, or person setting up the trust. When the trust period lapses on the home, the children then own the home. The parents can still stay in the home and pay rent. Or they can move out, at a time when the children are grown and that is something they just might want to do.

All of this can be done twice in that the Service permits two personal residence trusts; so the family vacation home can also be transferred this way and avoid estate taxes.

Another problem dealt with by the estate planning is the case of the small family business that has become immensely profitable and is now extremely valuable. An example is the Telect Company, located in Spokane, Washington, started by Bill and Judi Williams.[1] which manufactures fiber optic telephone equipment. Starting as a very small business the company now has 700 employees and annual revenues of $72 million. The question for the family is how to pass on the family business to their children without incurring a tax so large it would cause them to have to sell the business to outsiders to pay it. To solve the problem, the family engaged in a current hot estate planning technique.

The approach allows a those who own a family partnership or corporation to give minority interests in it away and have the value of the gifts discounted by as much as 40%. The reason the Service has grudgingly accepted this technique is that it is the case that a minority interest in a closely-held business is less valuable than its proportionate share because the minority lack control and can be exploited to some extent subject to somewhat loose standards of fiduciary duty. For the same reason some people will pay a "control premium" to gain control of a company a minority interest can be discounted. The Service has long accepted this analysis in valuing minority interests when unrelated people own the business, the Service has resisted it for family members,

---

¶ 8.05

1. Anecdotal information in this discussion is based on Christopher Drew and David Cay Johnston, For Wealthy Americans, Death is More Certain Than Taxes, The New York Times, December 22, 1996, p. A1.

because of the obviously possibility of collusion (say for example to avoid gift taxes).

The issue of valuing transfers of minority interests in family corporations was litigated for several decades and the Service started losing cases recently. They kept fighting until they incurred the ire of the Tax Court and were forced to pay a taxpayer's legal expenses. Thereafter the Service ruled, in 1993, that transfers of minority interests in family partnerships and corporations could be discounted for estate and gift tax valuation purposes.

This ruling, in turn, has led to some aggressive tax planning. Many taxpayers are creating partnerships, transferring vacation homes, securities, and other investments in to them and then giving minority interests in the partnership to their children, discounting the value by 30 to 70 percent.

Recently, 91–year old Charles C. Clark of San Antonio put $2 million of securities into a partnership in 1992 and 1993. He then gave ownership interest in the partnership to 11 relatives, including children, in-laws and grandchildren. For estate and gift tax purposes he discounted the value of the gifts by 30%. The Service disallowed the discounts arguing that Mr. Clark had no valid business reason for the transfers. The Service asserted the transaction was a sham, undertaken only to obtain tax advantage. One flaw in the taxpayer's approach would seem to be that the stocks in the portfolio transferred are publicly traded (indeed including such major companies as Microsoft, Coca–Cola and Walt Disney). Thus the discount rationale, which applied originally to the illiquid shares of a closely held business, does not hold up. Similarly the minority-ownership-in-business rationale also does not seem to apply to vacation homes or primary residences.

As a further spin on this technique is to have the wealthy patriarch of the family transfer his assets to trusts in the Bahamas in favor of children or other relatives. This has the further virtue from the taxpayer's point of view of making it hard for the Service to get records, given the Bahamian bank secrecy laws. If the Service cannot reach the records in full, it is likely to throw in the towel in a case.

# Chapter 9

## TAX ACCOUNTING

*Table of Sections*

---

## ¶ 9.01 In General

The term "tax accounting" is somewhat misleading. Tax accounting is not like financial accounting (you will be relieved to hear), with balance sheets and income statements. Rather, the subject of tax accounting is really timing. The question in the field of tax accounting is just *when*, i.e., in what year, is an item included in income or deductible. Thus the field of tax accounting might better be termed tax timing.

So to be absolutely clear about that matter (not to say tedious), the field of tax accounting is not concerned with the validity or amounts of income or deduction items. The only question in tax accounting is in what year does the item properly occur.

At first blush, it sounds like *when* something is included in income or deductible is no big deal. But you know much better than that from the Prologue. As you know from the Prologue, timing in federal income taxation can be of immense significance, particularly where long periods of time are involved. Since this chapter's focus is on timing it should be considered to be closely related to the Prologue. The difference is that in this chapter we focus on the particular statutory and case law rules regarding timing. In the Prologue we focussed on the broader economic significance of timing and the time value of money.

Another difference between this chapter and the Prologue is that timing can be important because marginal and/or effective rates of tax[1] change from one year to the next. These changes can occur from change in the law or changes in the taxpayer's income. This was not something that we paid much attention to in the Prologue (where we just happily

¶ 9.01

1. See Chapter One for discussion of marginal and effective rates of tax.

ran numbers on out to the horizon). Thus the matter of timing can be of great significance if the effective rate of tax is different between the two years.

The Code attempts to get a grip on the elusive topic of timing by providing as an opening statement that taxable income shall be computed under the method of accounting on the basis of which the taxpayer regularly computes his income in keeping his books.[2] Thus while the Code does not directly employ financial accounting concepts on the issue of timing, it will borrow some of the concepts of financial accounting. After the Code borrows some of these principles, it alters them for its own purposes.

This creates a major tension in the financial world. Tax accounting and timing principles often diverge from financial accounting and timing principles, even for major publicly traded corporations. This creates a lot of tension and complexity in the financial world.[3]

Having in its opening statement given the taxpayer the right to ascertain timing questions based on the taxpayer's method of financial accounting, as discussed above, the Code then characteristically takes some of what it promises back. It says further that if the method of accounting used by the taxpayer does not "clearly reflect income" (major words in the field), then the Service may use some other method that does clearly reflect income.[4]

Given the large stakes on the question of timing, one could easily expect substantial conflicts between the Service and taxpayers on the timing of income or deduction items. And it is true that this area of the tax law is no less devoid of litigation than any other area.

It is interesting to note that in financial accounting, the precise timing of borderline items into one year or the next does not result in any change of liabilities to the corporation. But the choice of taxable year for a borderline item in the tax field can have a direct effect on increasing or decreasing the taxpayer's tax liability. Thus one might suppose that the problems of timing in the financial world are less intense than in the tax world. This would be especially so because footnotes on a company's financial records can explain why certain timing decisions were made.

However, one can make too much of this difference between tax and financial accounting. While allocation of borderline items on the financial books does not literally have a direct effect on a company's liabilities, it can have a significant effect on the profits the company reports. This in turn can have a significant effect on the company's stock price. The variation in the stock price can affect the company's cost of capital, or

**2.** § 446(a).

**3.** As a very recent example of this growing out of the S & L catastrophe, see

the *Cottage Savings Ass'n* case in Chapter 4.

**4.** § 446(b).

the level of dividends it must pay to support its stock price. Thus timing principles in the financial world are rather well developed, and the tax law makes some use of them.

## ¶ 9.02  Transactional Problems

There is a fundamental tension in the field of tax accounting. It is between the legal rule that taxable income is reckoned up on an annual basis and the economic fact that many complex business transactions span more than one year. We explore the implications of this tension in the following material.

### (1) Annual Accounting: Sanford & Brooks

Most individual taxpayers compute their income on the basis of the calendar year.[1] Alternatively, we could wait until the individual dies and then collect all the income taxes due on the individual's income for his lifetime at his death. But the government, as is well known, does not like to wait (time value of money and all that). By nailing the taxpayer every year, however, certain distortions are created. Business transactions are not always organized to fit neatly within one year. But the overall thrust of the law in this area is not transaction-oriented. Instead, it's an annual accounting concept. This keeps things simple. Except when there are exceptions. Which make things complicated. This is all illustrated nicely by the leading case of *Sanford & Brooks*:

¶ 9.02

1. § 441(a) and (b). Business firms often use a fiscal year, say September 1 through August 31 of the following year. The fiscal year may be geared to the company's seasonal business. Thus Toys R Us would have a fiscal year ending January 31.

## BURNET v. SANFORD & BROOKS CO.[2]

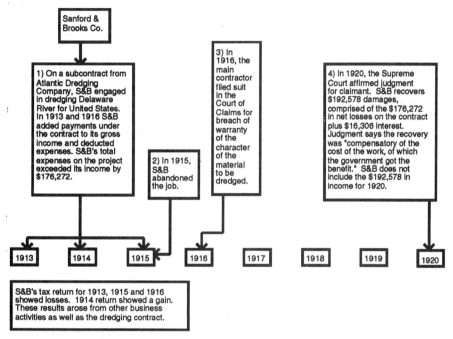

Sanford & Brooks Co.

1) On a subcontract from Atlantic Dredging Company, S&B engaged in dredging Delaware River for United States. In 1913 and 1916 S&B added payments under the contract to its gross income and deducted expenses. S&B's total expenses on the project exceeded its income by $176,272.

2) In 1915, S&B abandoned the job.

3) In 1916, the main contractor filed suit in the Court of Claims for breach of warranty of the character of the material to be dredged.

4) In 1920, the Supreme Court affirmed judgment for claimant. S&B recovers $192,578 damages, comprised of the $176,272 in net losses on the contract plus $16,306 interest. Judgment says the recovery was "compensatory of the cost of the work, of which the government got the benefit." S&B does not include the $192,578 in income for 1920.

1913   1914   1915   1916   1917   1918   1919   1920

S&B's tax return for 1913, 1915 and 1916 showed losses. 1914 return showed a gain. These results arose from other business activities as well as the dredging contract.

[387a]

*Question:* Should an annual accounting concept be applied and therefore the $192,578 is income in 1920; or should a transaction accounting concept be applied and therefore the $192,578 is offset by the $176,272 losses and $16,306 interest in earlier years?

*Comment:* A clear implication of the annual accounting concept is that the losses in the earlier years would then stand. If the transaction approach is applied, then there would be no income in 1920 and no losses in the earlier years. Taxpayer would file amended returns to eliminate those losses.

*Comment:* Taxpayer preferred the transaction approach because it was not getting immediate benefit from the losses in the earlier years but would have to pay taxes on the damages in 1920. The Service preferred the annual accounting approach for the same reason.

*Held:* Apply annual accounting concept. Receipts from the conduct of a business are included in the taxpayer's return regardless of whether the particular transaction results in net profit. Annual accounting was a familiar concept at the time of the adoption of the 16th amendment providing for the income tax. Sixteenth Amendment does not require transaction accounting.

The taxpayer obviously had a strong argument on the grounds of equity. But if we are going to be that fair to each individual taxpayer, exploring the implications over several years of each transaction undertaken, we are going to have a very complex tax code indeed.

**2.** 282 U.S. 359, 51 S.Ct. 150, 75 L.Ed. 383 (1931).

After *Sanford & Brooks,* Congress did act to deal with such problems. It enacted § 172, which now allows losses incurred in one year to be carried back 3 years and then forward 15 years. The provision is much broader than anything needed by Sanford & Brooks. The losses under § 172 need not arise out of transactions that are related to profitable results in later years. Rather, any losses incurred in one year may be carried to a total of 18 other years and taken against any profits in those other years.

Thus we begin to understand the roots of complexity of the tax statute. By attempting to treat taxpayers like *Sanford & Brooks* more fairly we enact a provision which makes the statute more complex. But perhaps this is worthwhile. The statute now treats generally of the cyclical or volatile business that may have high income in some years and losses in others. By allowing the losses to be carried to the income years, we make the treatment of the cyclical firm more akin to that of the firm which enjoys steady income over the years.

**For example,** Variable Corporation has the following income and loss pattern over a four year period: year 1 $50,000 loss; year 2 $200,000 income; year 3 $50,000 loss; year 4 $200,000 income. The total net income over the four year period is $300,000. Without a provision like § 172 allowing carryover of losses, Variable Corporation would have incur $56,250 in tax liability in years 2 and 4 (using the corporate tax rates of § 11). This would mean a total tax liability over the four-year period of $112,500. Compare that to Stochastic Corporation, which has income of $75,000 per-year for the four years. That also comes to $300,000 of income over the four years. Using again the corporate tax rates of § 11, we find that Stochastic's annual tax is $13,750. Stochastic's total tax over the four-year period is $55,000. Though the two companies have the same amount of income over the four-year period, Variable's total tax is $112,500 and Stochastic's total tax is $55,000, a staggering difference of $57,500! Should Variable really be taxed more than Stochastic? Of course not, you say.

Do we cure the problem by allowing Variable to carry its $50,000 losses forward to its $100,000 income years? You might think so, but let's run the numbers. By carrying forward its losses Variable now has $150,000 of income in each of years 2 and 4. That of course still cranks out to be total income of $300,000. Under § 11, we find that Variable's income in each of years 2 and 4 is $39,250. That's a total tax over the period of $78,500. That's still $23,500 more than Stochastic pays! So allowing the carryover improved the situation. But we still have a significant problem!

Why is that? Why has the carryover not solved the problem? Anybody that can answer that is excused from the exam. Think about it; the answer is in the footnote.[3]

---

**3.** Hi. I'm sure you don't need this help but here it is anyway. While allowing the losses to carry over to the income years ameliorated the problem, we still have a progressive rate structure. Even with allowing the carryover of losses, Variable's income is still bunched up compared to Stochastic's. Being bunched up punched

*Comment:* We have to a significant extent abandoned the simplicity of the annual accounting method by enacting § 172. But even with the addition of that complex provision, we still have not managed to treat Variable the same as Stochastic. Thus we got the worst of all worlds: still not treating the two companies the same and a complex statute.

Section 172 may only be used by businesses (including sole proprietors). A salaried employee generally does not incur expenses greater than his income. But if he does, he cannot carry them over to other years.

Another change to the Code also ameliorates the problems encountered by the taxpayer in *Sanford & Brooks.* This is § 186, enacted in 1969, which provides that damages for breach of contract or fiduciary duty or antitrust violations will be excluded from income if the loss giving rise to the damages did not generate a tax benefit.

### *(2) Claim of Right: North American Oil; Lewis*

*North American Oil* is the leading case illustrating transaction problems:

### NORTH AMERICAN OIL CONSOLIDATED v. BURNET[4]

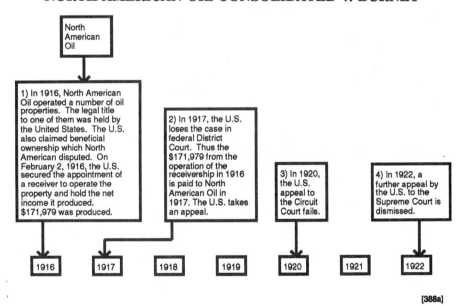

1) In 1916, North American Oil operated a number of oil properties. The legal title to one of them was held by the United States. The U.S. also claimed beneficial ownership which North American disputed. On February 2, 1916, the U.S. secured the appointment of a receiver to operate the property and hold the net income it produced. $171,979 was produced.

2) In 1917, the U.S. loses the case in federal District Court. Thus the $171,979 from the operation of the receivership in 1916 is paid to North American Oil in 1917. The U.S. takes an appeal.

3) In 1920, the U.S. appeal to the Circuit Court fails.

4) In 1922, a further appeal by the U.S. to the Supreme Court is dismissed.

[388a]

*Question:* In what year is the $171,979 from the operation of the

Variable up into the higher progressive corporate rates, causing Variable still to have to pay a higher corporate income tax over the four-year period.

4.  286 U.S. 417, 52 S.Ct. 613, 76 L.Ed. 1197 (1932).

property by the receiver included in income to North American Oil?

*Taxpayer argument:* The money is taxable in 1916. If not taxable in 1916, it is taxable in 1922.

*Service argument:* The money is taxable in 1917.

*Comment:* In this ambiguous set of facts, do you think that the taxpayer and the Service arrived at their respective conclusions as to when the money is taxable based on their respective views of the integrity and underlying jurisprudence of the federal income tax? If not, then how *did* they arrive at their respective conclusions as to year of taxability?

*Comment:* Three guesses and the first two don't count. The taxpayer was in a much higher bracket in 1917 than in either 1916 or 1922. 1917 was a very high bracket year. See the discussion of *Old Colony Trust* in Chapter 3.[5] Thus taxpayer comes up with the conclusion that the taxable year is anything but 1917. Conversely, the Service arrives at the conclusion that 1917 is the right year. Having decided ahead of time what their conclusions will be, they then construct their argument. Tax law is no different from any other practice of law.

*Held:* (Brandeis, J.) The funds were not taxable as income to the company in 1916, because at that time there was no assurance that the company would receive the funds at all. There was no "constructive receipt" (see below) in 1916, because at no time in that year could the company demand the funds. The company was taxable on the funds in 1917, the year when the District Court entered a final decree vacating the receivership. It does not matter for these purposes whether the company was on a cash or accrual method of accounting (see below). The funds were not income in 1922 when the litigation was finally terminated. "If a taxpayer receives earnings under a claim of right and without restriction as to its disposition, he has received income which he is required to return [i.e., report on his tax return], even though it may still be claimed that he is not entitled to retain the money, and even though he may still be adjudged liable to restore its equivalent." If in 1922, the Government had ultimately prevailed and the taxpayer were obliged to refund the money received in 1917, it would then properly take a deduction for 1922.

Brandeis in *North American Oil* invented a concept, the "Claim of Right," that had not been in existence prior to this case. But after all, he was Louis Brandeis. The apparent elements of this new concept are that 1) the taxpayer actually receives the funds and 2) the taxpayer does not concede that there is any other valid claim to the funds, even though in fact others may dispute the taxpayer's right to the funds. These elements would distinguish this transaction from borrowing money, where an obligation to repay is of course recognized by the recipient of the

5. Also note that the top bracket on corporations in 1916 was 2%. In 1917, at the height of World War I, the top bracket on corporations ranged up to 60%. In 1922, the top corporate bracket was 12.5%.

funds. When funds are received under a claim of right, the taxpayer is in receipt of income which may then be taxed. If an adverse claim later proves valid, the approach is to take a deduction in the year the funds are repaid.

As in *Sanford & Brooks*, we see here the annual accounting concept prevailing over transactional analysis in the courts. From the point of view of administering the tax laws, it appears the Service should not have to wait until this interminable litigation finally drags to a conclusion before it collects its taxes.

Beyond that, if we take the transactional approach in this particular case, the question could arise as to just when is the litigation over. Even after an appeal to the Supreme Court is dismissed, who knows what other judicial or legislative moves the government might try which would keep at least a minor cloud hanging over the ultimate resolution of the underlying dispute. Rather than sitting around trying to decide whether there is still life in this controversy or not, it is more efficient to employ the claim-of-right doctrine and then take a deduction later if necessary.

The *North American Oil* analysis sounds good, but would there be any problems if North American did have to pay back the funds in 1922. Would that be so simple to deal with? While that did not happen in the *North American Oil* case, we do have a case where that did happen. The case is *Lewis*.

## UNITED STATES v. LEWIS[6]

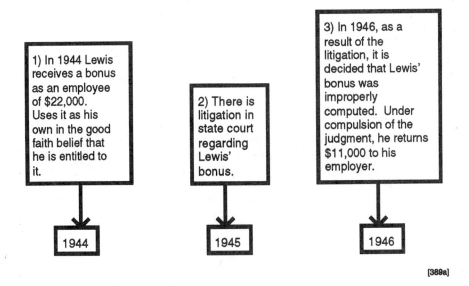

[389a]

**6.**   340 U.S. 590, 71 S.Ct. 522, 95 L.Ed.   S.Ct. 741, 95 L.Ed. 1356 (1951).
560 (1951), reh'g denied 341 U.S. 923, 71

*Question:* Should taxpayer take the deduction for the repaid $11,000 in 1944 or in 1946?

*Service's argument:* Taxpayer should deduct the $11,000 in 1946.

*Taxpayer's argument:* He should deduct the $11,000 in 1944, by filing an amended return with his recomputed taxes.

*Comment:* Obviously Lewis was in a higher bracket in 1944, so the deduction meant more to him then. That is why the Service and Lewis squared off the way they did.

*Held:* (Black, J.): Relying on *North American Oil*, the amount is deductible in 1946. The bonus was held by taxpayer under a claim of right. Nothing in the holding of the *North American Oil* court permits an exception just because a taxpayer is mistaken in his belief as to his claim of right. Income taxes must be paid on an annual accounting method, citing *Sanford & Brooks* (see above). The claim-of-right doctrine is a rule of finality and "is now deeply rooted in the tax system."

*Comment:* This does not seem to really be a claim-of-right case. The claim-of-right doctrine described by the Court in *North American Oil* seemed to contemplate that there were adverse claims to the funds at the time they were received by the taxpayer. But the taxpayer did not concede their validity. In the case of *Lewis,* there was no adverse claim to the money he received at the time he received it.

In any event, assuming as the Court does that Lewis received the funds under a claim-of-right, as in *North American Oil*, the *Lewis* case presents the next question: what happens on repayment? In *dicta* the *North American Oil* Court said that the deduction there would be appropriate in the year of repayment. This would employ the annual accounting method instead of transactional analysis. Since the annual accounting method is embedded in the statute,[7] the Court properly applied it rather than improvising new transactional analysis theory.

It can be useful to compare this area to the assignment of income area, discussed in Chapter 5. It could be argued that the Supreme Court was willing to improvise there and formulate rules restricting the ability of taxpayers to shift income to lower-bracket members of the family. Yet the Court is not willing to improvise in the assignment of income area. But one factor explains the Court's approach in both these lines of cases: They came out against the taxpayer.

We could have lived with the results in *North American Oil* and *Lewis.* When an amount has to be repaid in a different year (which does not happen that often, let's face it), sometimes the annual accounting approach would help a taxpayer and sometimes hurt him. This would of course depend on the applicable tax rates when the taxpayer receives the money and when he has to repay it. The annual accounting approach

7. See the discussion above at ¶ 9.02(1).

would not always be biased against taxpayers. So we could have lived with this simple approach. But naturally we don't.

The result in *Lewis* was seen to be a problem. If there is a problem, then with good old American know-how we can fix it. And a statutory provision was enacted to fix it. But the price to pay was increasing the complexity of the statute.

Three years after the decision in *Lewis*, Congress enacted § 1341. This allows a taxpayer who receives an amount under a claim-of-right which he must later repay to reduce his taxes in the year repaid by the larger of the following: 1) the tax savings if the deduction is taken in the year repaid or 2) the tax savings if the deduction were taken in the year the amount was received.[8]

The accompanying graphic illustrates the operation of § 1341 by showing how it would work in *Lewis*.

## APPLICATION OF § 1341 TO LEWIS

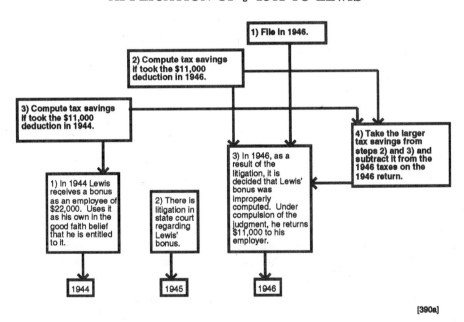

[390a]

A case construing § 1341 was *Joseph P. Pike*.[9] The taxpayer, an attorney who practiced insurance law, in 1957 sold stock he owned in the Cardinal Life Insurance Company for a gain of about $20,000. A special counsel of the state of Kentucky came to the conclusion that, for various reasons, the $20,000 properly belonged to the Cardinal Company. Taxpayer did not agree with this result, but to protect his reputation in the

---

**8.** There is a *de minimis* rule that none of this kicks in unless the amount involved exceeds $3,000.

**9.** 44 T.C. 787 (1965).

insurance industry, he paid the $20,000 to the Cardinal Company in 1958. He then sought to employ § 1341 to take the tax savings as if the deduction were taken in the year of receipt of the $20,000, 1957. The court held that § 1341 was not available to the taxpayer because it was not "established" under the terms of § 1341(a)(2) that the taxpayer did not have an unrestricted right to the item. He was not compelled by legal process to repay the item. Rather, taxpayer repaid the item out of his belief that the continued controversy would damage his reputation. Hence the $20,000 was deductible in 1958 as an ordinary and necessary business expense under § 162.

It might be noted that this case also conjures up the case of *Welch v. Helvering*[10] on the question of whether a payment to safeguard one's reputation is deductible at all.

Section 1341 was also interpreted by *Van Cleave v. United States.*[11] Taxpayer was president and majority stockholder of VanMark Corporation which adopted a by-law requiring corporate officers who received from the corporation income determined by the IRS to be excessive and therefore not deductible to the corporation (i.e. unreasonable compensation, see ¶ 6.02(1)) to pay the amount deemed excessive back to the corporation. In addition, the taxpayer had a separate agreement with the corporation to repay nondeductible compensation. In an audit, the Service determined that $57,500 of taxpayer's salary for tax year 1974 was excessive and disallowed it as a deduction to the corporation. Taxpayer paid this amount back in 1975. The Service on audit of 1975 allowed the deduction in 1975 but disallowed the use of § 1341 to take the deduction against 1974's income.

The district court disallowed the use of § 1341 because the payment was voluntary in the sense that taxpayer was the controlling stockholder of the employer and thus could have caused the corporation to abrogate the repayment agreement. The government did not pursue this argument, which appears to be flawed. There was a valid agreement with the employer, a separate legal entity, that the compensation should be repaid.

The government's argument was that § 1341 only applies if it appeared that the taxpayer had an unrestricted right to the excess salary. The government asserted that taxpayer had more than an *appearance* of an unrestricted right but actually had an unrestricted right, contingent on the happening of an event in a subsequent year. The court rejected the argument and held that § 1341 was available to the taxpayer. The fact that taxpayer's ultimate right to the compensation was not determined until the occurrence of a subsequent event does not mean that he had, in the statutory sense, an unrestricted right to the compensation when he received it.

10.  See ¶ 6.03(4).

11.  718 F.2d 193 (6th Cir.1983).

### *(3) The Tax Benefit Rule*

### *(a) In General: Alice Phelan Sullivan Corp.*

There is another transactional pattern that gets into tension with the annual accounting concept. It is kind of the reverse of *Lewis* and similar to *Sanford & Brooks.* A taxpayer may recover an item for which he took a deduction in an earlier year. Thus a loan previously deducted as a bad debt[12] may in fact be paid in a later year, or an amount deducted for medical expenses[13] may be reimbursed by insurance in a later year. Ordinarily repayment of a loan or health insurance payments do not give rise to income.[14] On equitable principles, however, it would appear that the fact that these transactions gave rise to earlier deductions should cause the later recovery to be included in income. If so, what is the appropriate treatment on recovery where the earlier deduction produced no tax benefit because the taxpayer, on account of other losses, had no taxable income in the year the earlier deduction was taken?

The problems in this area are exemplified by the case of *Alice Phelan Sullivan Corporation.*

### ALICE PHELAN SULLIVAN CORP. v. UNITED STATES[15]

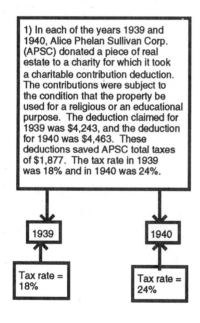

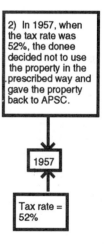

[391a]

---

**12.** Deductible under § 166. See ¶ 7.01(6)(a).

**13.** Deductible under § 213 above certain limits. See ¶ 7.01(7).

**14.** The interest on loans will, of course, be income. See ¶ 3.01.

**15.** 381 F.2d 399 (Ct.Cl.1967).

*Question:* Should Alice Phelan Sullivan Corp. take the return of the property in 1957 back into income?

*Service's argument:* The entire amount of $8,707 that was previously claimed as a charitable contribution in 1939 and 1940 should be added back into taxpayer's income in 1957, generating taxes of $4,528.

*Comment:* Since the applicable corporate tax rate was much higher in 1957 than in 1939 and 1940, adding the same amount back in 1957 generates more taxes ($4,528) than were saved by the deductions in 1939 and 1940 ($1,877).

*Taxpayer's argument:* The present assessment can be no more than the tax saved on the original deal, or $1,877, relying on the *Perry* case which had held to that effect.

*Held:* 1) A transaction which returns to a taxpayer his own property cannot be said to give rise to income. 2) But the principle is well-engrained in our tax law that the return of property which has been the subject of a deduction must be treated as income in the year of recovery. 3) This latter principle is limited by the "tax benefit rule," which holds that the returned item may be excluded from income to the extent that the initial use as a deduction did not actually provide a tax saving. 4) But where the full use of a deduction was made, giving rise to a tax saving, then the amount of the saving is immaterial. The recovery is viewed as income to the full extent of the deduction previously allowed, basing the opinion on § 111 and the regulations thereto, which have broadened the tax benefit concept beyond the statutory limitations. Using the annual accounting concept of *Sanford & Brooks* (see above), the taxpayer takes the full amount of the deduction back into income at the higher current rate.

*Comment:* The taxpayer's basis in the property once it has been returned would equal the amount included in income, or $8,707.

*Comment:* There is a third alternative, which is to have the property come back into income not at the value used when it was deducted—but at its current value. This could well be different from the $8,707 value that it had at the time it was donated. Neither the parties nor the court appeared to consider this possibility. But it would seem highly relevant if the property were now worth $75,000 or $25.

The tax benefit rule is one of the venerated principles in the field of federal income taxation. In the early controversies on the matter, the Service took the hard-nosed position that the recovery of previously deductible items gave rise to income, and the recovery did so regardless of whether the earlier deduction had produced a tax benefit.[16] § 111, however, whose predecessor was enacted in 1942, has now pre-empted the field and takes the more reasonable view that recovery of such

---

**16.** G.C.M. 22163, 1940–2 C.B. 76.

deductible items gives rise to income only to the extent that the earlier deduction produced a tax benefit for the taxpayer. This is the essence of the tax benefit rule: that recovery of a previously deductible item gives rise to income only to the extent the previous deduction produced a tax benefit.

The tax benefit rule is sometimes viewed as having two aspects: the inclusionary aspect and the exclusionary aspect. They are really two sides of the same coin. The inclusionary aspect states that if a deduction in an earlier year generated a tax benefit, then the later recovery will be taxed, as in *Alice Phelan Sullivan*. The exclusionary aspect states that if a deduction in an earlier year generated no tax benefit (because there would have been no taxable income even without the deduction), then a later recovery of the item will be excluded from income.

Reasonable as it sounds, the tax benefit rule still leads to anomalous results. This is curious given that it is an equitable principle. The anomaly of the tax benefit rule of § 111 and *Alice Phelan Sullivan* is highlighted when it is compared with its sister provision, § 1341, discussed above. The tax benefit rule "looks forward"—an amount deducted in an earlier year that generates a benefit is included in income in a later year, when it is recovered. § 1341 "looks backward"—dealing with the problem of an erroneous inclusion of income in an earlier year which must be deducted in a later year, when it is paid back. Rather than focusing on the amounts includible and deductible, § 1341 focuses on the tax liabilities involved, giving the taxpayer the option of selecting the tax result in either the year of inclusion or the year of deduction, whichever is more favorable.[17] Thus, under § 1341, the taxpayer gets the best possible deal regardless of the tax rates in the two years involved. By contrast, the taxpayer in the maw of § 111 and the tax benefit rule is playing a lottery. He may do well or poorly depending on the tax rates in the years involved in his transaction.

The Regulations are clear that the tax benefit rule does not apply to deductions for depreciation, depletion, or amortization.[18]

Thus suppose for example business property is depreciated for several years, but the depreciation deductions produce no tax benefit because the taxpayer, on account of other losses, has no taxable income for those years. On a subsequent sale of the property for an amount in excess of its depreciated basis, the entire amount of the gain will be income notwithstanding that the depreciation deductions produced no

**17.** Both of these provisions are related to §§ 1311–1314, which allow for adjustments to be made in tax liability for years barred by the statute of limitations where, generally, for an open year the taxpayer or the Service has successfully maintained a position inconsistent with a position taken in the barred year. See Coleman, "Mitigation of the Statute of Limitations—Sections 1311–1314," 31 N.Y.U.Inst.Fed.Tax 1575 (1973). See Stone v. White, 301 U.S. 532, 57 S.Ct. 851, 81 L.Ed. 1265 (1937), reh'g denied 302 U.S. 777, 58 S.Ct. 260, 82 L.Ed. 601 (1937) (defense of equitable recoupment available to Service or, presumably, taxpayers.) See also Ames, "The History of Assumpsit," 2 Harv.L.Rev. 53 (1888).

**18.** § 1.111–1(a).

tax benefit.[19] Taxpayer's only solace here would be the net operating loss carryover rules (if applicable), discussed above.

The tax benefit need not and usually does not occur in the year the deduction is taken. Thus if a deduction for a bad debt, etc., is taken in a year in which the taxpayer already has operating losses, the deduction would produce no tax benefit in that year. However the deduction could increase the taxpayer's operating loss carryovers to other years.[20] Thus, where a deduction increases an unexpired carryover, which *might* benefit the taxpayer in another year, recovery of the deducted item produces income. (Net operating losses can be carried back three years (which can be waived) and forward 15 years.)

The tax benefit rule has also been held specifically to apply to deductions and subsequent recoveries of casualty losses,[21] embezzled funds,[22] and bonuses,[23] among many other items.[24] The tax benefit rule is an outstanding example of how a narrowly-drawn statutory concept has, through judicial, administrative and legislative elaboration, come to be broadly applicable.

Section 186 has extended the theory of § 111 to provide that damages for breach of contract or fiduciary duty or antitrust violations will be excluded from income if the loss giving rise to the damages did not generate a tax benefit.

### (b) Equitable Applications: Hillsboro

As discussed in the preceding section, the tax benefit rule has a life of its own. It has grown from a narrow conceptual base to encompass transactions far beyond those originally imagined. It has spawned substantial case law, broad regulations, and additional legislation. And the vigor is still there. In a recent pair of cases, the Supreme Court raised the ante once again, applying the tax benefit rule as a broad equitable principle to rationalize transactions that would have otherwise led to unjustified advantage to taxpayers.

---

**19.** This example suggests the possibility that the taxpayer might try to elect not to take the depreciation deduction during the loss years. However, depreciation is essentially not elective, although various methods of depreciation may be elected. Under § 1016(a) (flush language) the basis of property subject to the deduction for depreciation must go down by at least the minimum amount of depreciation allowed regardless of whether the deduction is actually taken or does any good. See ¶ 6.02(12).

**20.** See discussion above at ¶ 9.02(1).

**21.** Reg. § 1.165–1(d)(2)(iii).

**22.** Tennessee Foundry & Machinery Co., 48 T.C. 419 (1967), aff'd on other grounds 399 F.2d 156 (6th Cir.1968) (receipt of insurance proceeds includible in income because in substance a recovery of previously-deducted embezzlement loss.).

**23.** Larchfield Corp. v. United States, 373 F.2d 159 (2d Cir.1966) (bonus recovered as settlement of a derivative suit).

**24.** In the case where an insolvent accrual method taxpayer is discharged from an indebtedness he previously deducted, income will result only to the extent the taxpayer is solvent following the discharge. Haden Co. v. Commissioner, 118 F.2d 285 (5th Cir.1941), cert. denied 314 U.S. 622, 62 S.Ct. 73, 86 L.Ed. 500 (1941). See ¶ 3.10(2).

Thus in the case of *Hillsboro National Bank v. Commissioner*,[25] the taxpayer corporation had paid certain taxes that were imposed on its shareholders and had properly taken a deduction for them, under § 164(e). In a later year the taxes were refunded directly to the shareholders. In that later year the Service then attempted to make the corporation take the amount of the refund back into income. The corporation's argument was that it had not received the refund. Hence application of the tax benefit rule was inappropriate since the rule only taxes "recoveries," in the terms of the statute.[26]

The Court, however, described the rationale of the tax benefit rule more broadly, characterizing its purpose as being the achievement of "rough transactional parity in tax ... and to protect the Government and the taxpayer from the adverse effects of reporting a transaction on the basis of assumptions that an event in a subsequent year proves to have been erroneous ... when ... the later event is indeed fundamentally inconsistent with the premise on which the deduction was initially based."[27]

## ¶ 9.03  Accounting Methods

### *(1) Overview*

In general taxpayers may elect to use any method of accounting that clearly reflects income and is regularly used in keeping their books. The two major methods of accounting are the cash method and the accrual method.

Taxpayers using the accrual method of accounting generally accrue items as income when all the events have occurred that establish the right to receive the income and the amount of income can be determined with reasonable accuracy. Taxpayers using the accrual method of accounting generally may not deduct items of expense in a year prior to the time of economic performance.

More detail on the two methods of accounting and variations on the theme is set forth below.

### *(2) The Cash Method*

### *(a) In General*

Taxpayers using the cash method of accounting generally recognize items of income when they are actually received or deemed to be received (constructively received). Under the cash method items are deducted when paid. This is the system used by most individuals. The conventional wisdom is that the cash method is simpler than the accrual method

---

**25.** Decided with United States v. Bliss Dairy, 460 U.S. 370, 103 S.Ct. 1134, 75 L.Ed.2d 130 (1983), on remand 704 F.2d 1167 (9th Cir.1983).

**26.** § 111(a).

**27.** It should be pointed out that the above approach by the Court to the tax benefit rule was strong *dicta*. It actually decided the case based on an interpretation of § 164(e) that the corporation should not be taxed on the refund because it had not actually received it.

but that the accrual method is more accurate than the cash method. In fact, as the Prologue indicates, when time value of money issues are paramount, the cash method may well also be more accurate than the accrual method as well as being simpler.

This is not to say that the cash method is without its difficulties. One major problem with the cash method is that it does not mean what it says. Suppose, for example, that a migrant farm worker is paid by his employer with a bushel of apples. Does the worker have income notwithstanding that what he received was not cash? There is not a shadow of a doubt that the worker has income in that setting under the cash method. Under the cash method of accounting "all items which constitute gross income (whether in the form of cash, property, or services) are to be included for the taxable year in which actually or constructively received."[1]

This causes a bit of a muddle right off the top. Suppose that our migrant farm worker, instead of receiving apples, receives a promise from the owner to pay him at a later date. Is this worker now in receipt of income on the receipt of this piece of paper? If he is, then what is the meaning of the accrual method of accounting?

Note also that the Regs. allude to "constructive" as well as actual receipt of income. Thus apparently a taxpayer can have income on the cash method even though he has not *actually* received any income. He may *constructively* receive it.

So it would seem that what the Regs. are telling us here is that under the cash method the taxpayer might have income even though he does not receive cash and/or does not receive anything at all. We will struggle some more with these problems.

For example, the case of *Charles F. Kahler*[2] presented the excruciating question of when did a cash basis taxpayer realize income represented by a check delivered December 31, 1946 after banking hours?

The court held the check was income in the year it was received, asserting that, according to the regulations, all items of gross income shall be included in the taxable year in which received by the taxpayer, and that where services are paid for other than by money, the amount to be included as income is the fair market value of the thing taken in payment. Thus the court treated the check like it was a bushel of apples. The court felt that it was immaterial that the check was delivered too late to cash.

Why are taxpayers and the Commissioner fighting about in what year is something income, in these cases? Because the taxpayer is clearly fighting to put the item in a low-bracket year and the Commissioner is fighting to put it in a high-bracket year.

¶ 9.03

1. Reg. § 1.446–1(c)(1).
2. 18 T.C. 31 (1952).

In *Jay A. Williams*[3] taxpayer was a cash basis timber broker who received on May 15, 1951, as compensation for his services an unsecured, non-interest-bearing promissory note in the amount of $7,166.60, payable 240 days thereafter. At the time the note was issued, taxpayer knew that the maker of the note would be unable to pay anything on it because he was short of funds. Upon receipt of the note, taxpayer attempted on 10 or 15 occasions to sell it to various banks or finance companies, but he was unable to do so. Eventually he received $6,666.66 from the maker of the note in 1954.

The court held that it is unquestioned that promissory notes or other evidences of indebtedness received as payment for services constitute income to the extent of their fair market value. Taxpayer argued that the note was not received as payment but merely as an evidence of indebtedness.

The court asserted that a note received only as security, or as an evidence of indebtedness and not as payment may not be regarded as income at the time of receipt. Moreover, the court said, even if the taxpayer had failed to show that the note was not intended as payment, in fact because the maker was without funds, bore no interest, and was unsecured, it did not have a fair market value and thus it is not the equivalent of cash in the year of receipt. It would appear that this latter argument about lack of fair market value is sounder than arguments that draw from something as possibly amorphous as the intent of the maker of the note.

In *Cowden v. Commissioner*[4] the Fifth Circuit gave a very helpful discussion of the cash method. The taxpayer in April 1951 in entered into an oil, gas and mineral lease under which he would be paid various amounts over 1951–1953. The payor was willing and able to make the payments immediately and it was Cowden who negotiated to delay some of the payments. The Tax Court held that since the payor was willing and able to make the payments, the contract rights to receive the payment were income in the year they were negotiated. The Fifth Circuit said that while it is true that the parties may enter into any legal arrangement they see fit even though the form they use is selected with the hope of reducing taxes, it is also true that if the consideration which one of the parties receives is the equivalent of cash, it will be subject to tax. Thus the question is whether the undertaking by the lessee to make future bonus payments was, when made, the equivalent of cash. The court said it is not necessarily the case that only negotiable instruments are cash equivalents—in fact some negotiable instruments are not if the maker's solvency is in question. On the contrary, according to the court, if a promise to pay of a solvent obligor is unconditional and assignable and is of a kind that is frequently transferred to lenders or investors at only a normal discount for the time value of money, such promise is the equivalent of cash and taxable as cash. Thus the court remanded for the

3. 28 T.C. 1000 (1957).                    4. 289 F.2d 20 (5th Cir.1961).

Tax Court to consider whether the lessee's undertaking was a cash equivalent, primarily a fact question.

### (b) Constructive Receipt

The doctrine of constructive receipt speaks to the situation where the taxpayer has the choice of receiving income in a particular year or delaying it.[5] In that situation, the doctrine of constructive receipt holds that a taxpayer may not avoid paying tax on income in a particular year by declining to choose to receive it. For example, suppose royalties on the sale of a book have been earned in Year 1 and are due and payable in Year 1. The publisher offers to send the money to the author in December of year 1. The author may respond that he would rather wait until January of Year 2 before receiving them.[6] In that event the royalties would be deemed to have been received by the author in Year 1.[7] To take another case, suppose a lawyer bills a client for services rendered in Year 1. The client is slow to pay (as they often are) and so does not pay until Year 2. This would *not* be a case of constructive receipt inasmuch as the lawyer did not have the power to receive the money in the earlier year.

The doctrine of constructive receipt serves a useful purpose in buttressing the annual accounting concept for cash method taxpayers. Without this doctrine, taxpayers and their controlled or related payors would be able to unjustifiably gain the advantage of deferral of tax. Other taxpayers, who are employees of larger institutions, would probably not have such choices.

But how far does this doctrine really reach? Is an individual who is the chief executive officer and controlling shareholder of a small corporation in constructive receipt of the corporate earnings, because he has the power to pay all the earnings out as dividends to himself?

The answer to that one is no.[8] The doctrine does not reach that far, although it is troublesome why it does not. What it would take would be for the chief executive officer and controlling shareholder of the closely-held corporation to bring about board action to authorize or set aside the funds for the payment of dividends. If he then declined to take the set-aside funds at that point, he would apparently be in constructive receipt of the dividends.[9]

The doctrine, therefore, can be easily avoided by the controlling shareholder of a small corporation so that he may time the payment of dividends to a year when he is in a lower bracket.

---

**5.** We have discussed at length the benefits of delaying tax in the Prologue.

**6.** I hear this has been done.

**7.** This assumes the Service finds out about this little informal arrangement. One of the problems in this field is the difficulties of finding out what taxpayers and their controlled or friendly payors are up to.

**8.** See Amend, 13 T.C. 178 (1949), acq., 1950–1 C.B. 1.

**9.** The minority shareholders of the corporation would not be in constructive receipt of their dividends, since they do not have the power to receive their dividends at will.

An interesting constructive receipt case was presented in *Paul v. Hornung*,[10] involving one of the great football players of the late 50's and early 60's. Hornung, a triple-threat player (both on and off the field), was an All–American quarterback at Notre Dame, and then played for the Green Bay Packers in their heyday. On December 31, 1961, Hornung played in the National Football League championship game in Green Bay, Wisconsin, between the Green Bay Packers and the New York Giants. He scored 19 points and established a new NFL scoring record. After the game, at 4:30 p.m., Hornung was informed he had won the Sport Magazine award as the outstanding player in the National Football League and would be awarded a new Corvette automobile. The editor of Sport Magazine did not have the key or the title to the Corvette with him. Hornung did not demand immediate possession of the car but he did accept the award. The car had been purchased by Sport Magazine and was in New York in the hands of the Chevrolet dealer. As far as Sport Magazine was concerned, the car was available to Hornung. However, it was Sunday and the New York City Chevrolet dealer was closed. Hornung was informed on December 31 that there would be a luncheon in New York the following Wednesday at which time he would receive the car. He attended the luncheon, posed for photographs and received the car. He was not required to attend the luncheon or pose for photographers to receive the car. For his 1962 income tax return Hornung reported the acquisition of the car, and the sale of the car for $3,331.04. He did not report the fair market value of $3,331.04 of the car as income in 1962 or any other year.

Hornung argued that he should have the value of the car as income in 1961, under the doctrine of constructive receipt. He was in a lower tax bracket in 1961. The doctrine of constructive receipt is ordinarily asserted by the Commissioner against the taxpayer to accelerate income into an earlier year. Thus it was somewhat unusual for a taxpayer to assert it in order to change the year that he himself had earlier reported income. Indeed one would think the doctrine should be unavailable to the taxpayer on some grounds of estoppel. However, the court held that the doctrine could, in principle, be asserted by the taxpayer.

Nevertheless, the court held that in this case Hornung did not have unfettered control over the automobile in 1961, since the car was still in the hands of a dealer in New York. Moreover, at the time the award was announced in 1961, nothing was given or presented to Hornung to evidence his ownership of the car. Hence the car was income in 1962.

The other side of the coin, when is a year-end item deductible, was explored in *Revenue Ruling 54–465*[11] in which the Service ruled that a charitable contribution in the form of a check is deductible (under § 170(a)) in the taxable year in which the check is delivered provided the check is honored and paid and there are no restrictions as to time and manner of payment. In fact the rule has come to be that the payment is

---

**10.**  47 T.C. 428 (1967).           **11.**  1954–2 Cum.Bull. 93.

deductible in the year that one puts the check in the mail,[12] provided that it is subsequently honored and paid in due course. Amounts charged on a credit card are deductible when they are charged on the card.[13]

The case of *Vander Poel, Francis & Co., Inc.* also offered some ideas on the related subject of "constructive payment." It quoted with approval a passage from the highly regarded Mertens, Law of Federal Income Taxation which said in substance that a payment which is found to be constructively received in an earlier year than it actually was may not actually also be constructively paid in that same earlier year. The jurisprudence of the statute is that it tries to reach all income, whereas deductions are a matter of legislative grace. Thus, it could occur that a payment would be constructively received in an earlier year but not be regarded as constructively paid in that earlier year.

### (c) Accounts Receivable

In at least a partial answer to our apple picker discussed above, it is clear that bills, or amounts due from employers, customers or clients are not income to a cash-method taxpayer. These items only become income when they are received in cash or in kind. (The apples are income; the piece of paper-I.O.U. is not.) Were these bills or accounts receivable income to the cash-method taxpayer, the difference between the two methods of accounting would be eliminated in a major respect.

If the taxpayer is on the accrual method, then accounts receivable are regarded as income even though the cash or its equivalent has not been received. The amount of income is the face amount of the accounts receivable.[14] When the money comes in on the receivable, there is no further income to the accrual-method taxpayer, since he has already been taxed on the item. If the receivable is ultimately not paid (there are a few deadbeats out there), then the accrual method taxpayer takes a deduction for bad debts (see Chapter 7).

### (d) Application: Executive Compensation Arrangements

The basic principles of cash-method accounting we have been discussing are used to undergird some high-powered arrangements for compensating top executives, athletes and other high-income individuals on salary.[15]

What is interesting about these arrangements for highly-compensated individuals and their tax advisors is that they do not have to be made available to rank and file employees (and generally they are not).

These particular executive compensation arrangements are called "nonqualified" arrangements. This distinguishes them from ordinary

---

**12.** Witt's Estate v. Fahs, 160 F.Supp. 521 (S.D.Fla.1956).

**13.** Rev. Rul. 78–38 1978–1 C.B. 68; Rev. Rul. 78–39, 1978–1 C.B. 73.

**14.** There can be a deduction of some amount as a "reserve" for bad debts (not all accounts receivable are ultimately paid).

**15.** See also Chapter 8, which discusses pensions and other deferred compensation methods.

pension plans which are (and must be) available to rank and file employees. A nonqualified executive compensation arrangement is a highly attractive arrangement with excellent tax advantages for the recipient.

The basic structure of a nonqualified arrangement is that there is a contractual agreement to make payments to the executive in the future. However—and this is the key—the agreement is not represented by notes or secured in any way. Thus the arrangement cannot be said to be the equivalent of cash (it's not apples, to use our farm worker example above). The arrangement does not give rise to taxable income to the employee until the payments under the contract are made.[16] This result is important because it might have been thought that under the doctrine of constructive receipt such an arrangement might have given rise to taxable income to a cash-basis taxpayer upon being entered into. However, where the contractual arrangement is not evidenced by notes, or funded or secured in any way, the cash-basis taxpayer has not received "cash or its equivalent" and is therefore not taxed on the arrangement at the time it is entered into.[17]

If the deferral under such a contractual arrangement is to be for a substantial period of time, an interest or earnings element is generally included in the arrangement. This may take the form of ordinary interest which is credited to the employee's account, or so-called "phantom stock plans" and "stock appreciation rights" may be used in which amounts are credited to the employee's account based on the performance of the employer's stock or an index of the general stock market.

The attractiveness of these contractual, nonqualified arrangements to the employee is balanced by the fact that the employer may not take a deduction for compensation paid or accrued under such nonqualified plans until the amounts are includable in the gross income of the employee.[18]

Thus, it is difficult to shift income from one taxpayer to another,[19] but it is easier to shift income from one year to another. Should it not be the other way around?

### (e) Prepaid Expenses

As discussed in the Prologue and in Chapter 6, taxpayers are very anxious to deduct expenses early to gain the advantages of deferral. Cash- and accrual-method taxpayers follow the same rules with regard to

---

**16.** Rev.Rul. 60–31, 1960–1 C.B. 174, modified by Rev.Rul. 70–435, 1970–2 C.B. 100.

**17.** Rev.Rul. 60–31, 1960–1 C.B. 174. See also Rev.Rul. 72–25, 1972–1 C.B. 127 (where the employer funded its deferred compensation liability with an annuity contract; held the deferred compensation agreement does not create an escrow account or trust or fund or any other form of asset segregation and therefore the employ-ee is not currently taxable on the arrangement).

**18.** § 404(a)(5). While this rule is to be expected for a cash-method taxpayer it is a significant restriction on an accrual-method taxpayer. Most employers of any significant size would be on the accrual-method of accounting.

**19.** See Chapter 5.

capital expenses (see Chapter 6). They also follow the same rules with respect to deductibility of expenses that are paid early—so-called prepaid expenses. These include items such as rent, salaries, insurance premiums. Such prepaid expenses are deductible only to the extent the service paid for is used during the taxable year.

A heavy item here is interest. Taxpayers like to prepay interest on a loan in a year when their other income is high in order to knock down their tax bracket. With a literal application of the cash method, this technique would work. The Code now chills out that maneuver with § 461(g), which provides that cash-method taxpayers must capitalize prepaid interest. To "capitalize" prepaid interest means not to deduct it but treat it as a capital expense. Then the taxpayer may deduct the interest over the period of time to which it is allocable.[20]

An example of the problems in the prepaid expense area is the case of *Commissioner v. Boylston Market Ass'n*,[21] which held that a taxpayer who prepaid his insurance premiums in one year to cover several years could take these payments as deduction prorated over the several years life of the policy. The court rejected the Commissioner's weird argument that the taxpayer could not take the prorated amount in a particular year of the proration because the taxpayer had not made a cash payment of sufficient size in that year. Thus *Boylston Market* illustrates the point that a taxpayer can create an asset, in that case prepaid insurance premium, by the expenditure of cash. Then the expenditure is written off over the life of the asset.

Similarly *Cathcart*[22] dealt with the question of whether taxpayer was entitled to deduct points withheld from mortgage proceeds in the year taxpayer obtained his mortgage. The court recognized that, by revenue ruling and statute, taxpayers who prepay points on their home mortgages with funds not obtained from the lender are entitled to deduct the entire amount in the year paid. But the court said that where the points are *withheld* from the mortgage proceeds by the lender, they are not deductible in the year the mortgage was obtained but must be prorated over the life of the mortgage.

The results in *Cathcart* were elaborated on in *Revenue Ruling 87–22*,[23] in which the Service dealt with case in which a taxpayer refinanced his old home mortgage with a principle balance of $80,000 with a new mortgage loan of $100,000, the extra $20,000 to be used to pay for improvements on his house. The Service ruled that $80,000 of the new mortgage loan was not incurred in connection with the purchase or improvement of the taxpayer's principal residence and $20,000 of the new mortgage loan was incurred in connection with the improvement of the taxpayer's principal residence. Thus 80% of the points on the new

---

**20.** "Points" incurred in acquiring a home mortgage are excepted from this rule and may be immediately deducted, § 461(g)(2). Once again that home mortgage interest lives a charmed life.

**21.** 131 F.2d 966 (C.C.A.1 1942).

**22.** 36 T.C.M. 1321 (1977).

**23.** 1987–1 Cum.Bull. 146.

mortgage loan were not immediately deductible but rather had to be prorated over the life of the loan and 20% of the points on the new mortgage loan were immediately deductible, under under § 461(g)(2).

### (3) The Accrual Method

#### (a) In General

As indicated above, the accrual-method of accounting generally involves accruing items as income when all the events have occurred that establish the right to receive the income and the amount of income can be determined with reasonable accuracy.

The conventional wisdom is that the cash method is fine for individuals and some small businesses. However, when businesses become larger and more sophisticated, the more accurate accrual method is needed. After our discussion in the Prologue of time value of money issues, this conventional wisdom could be questioned. Some of the tricky taxpayer maneuvers discussed there were made possible by accrual-method accounting and were cured by cash-method accounting.

The weakness in accrual-method accounting is that, in the phrase, it "does not follow the money." Since it "does not follow the money," it is weak on dealing with transactions that extend over longer periods of time.

It is the essence of accrual-method accounting to recognize income items before they are received and recognizing expense items before they are paid. Rather, items like accounts receivable (see discussion above) and accounts payable are recognized at the time the rights with respect to the item become fixed, even if no cash has yet changed hands.

For example in *Spring City Foundry Co. v. Commissioner*[24] the Supreme Court addressed a case where an accrual method taxpayer had sold goods in 1920 on credit. Before the purchaser could pay, it went bankrupt and it was clear before the end of the year that the taxpayer would not be paid in full. The taxpayer argued, among other things, that the partial worthlessness of the purchaser's obligation reduced the amount that the taxpayer need report in gross income. The Court held that in the accrual method the total amount which the taxpayer has a right to receive is included in gross income. If some part of the obligation subsequently becomes uncollectible, that is something which may be deducted under the appropriate statutory section.

Similarly in *Revenue Ruling 70–151*[25] the Service dealt with the situation that an accrual method taxpayer instituted suit against the United States in the Court of Claims for damages for alleged breach of contract. The taxpayer was awarded a judgment in 1968 and the United States filed a petition for writ of certiorari in 1969 and it was denied in 1969. Congress made no appropriation for the amount of the judgment

---

**24.** 292 U.S. 182, 54 S.Ct. 644, 78 L.Ed. 1200 (1934), rehearing denied 292 U.S. 613, 54 S.Ct. 857, 78 L.Ed. 1472 (1934).

**25.** 1970–1 Cum.Bull. 116.

in 1969. The Service ruled that the right to receive the sum due as a result of the judgment became fixed in 1969 and thus was properly included in the taxpayer's income in 1969 even though Congress did not in 1969 appropriate funds to pay the sum. While one can understand the principle of this ruling, it seems particularly hard on the taxpayer when it is the United States itself that is not paying its debt in a timely fashion.

### (b) Income

There is a significant override to accrual-method accounting. That concerns the case where the accrual-method taxpayer receives the cash in advance of when it is due. In that case, the taxpayer is put on the cash method and taxed in full on the amount received.

To take an example, suppose rent on property is paid 3 years in advance. The lessor would have to take the full amount received into income immediately, even though he is on the accrual method. The accrual method lessee, however, would not be able to deduct the entire amount in the year of payment. Rather he would be required to treat the advance payments as a capital asset which is amortized over the three years of the advance payment at ⅓ per year. This is a heads-the-Service-wins-tails-the-Service-wins approach to this transaction. Well, after all, we have to raise some money, don't we?

See for example *New Capital Hotel, Inc.*[26] in which the Tax Court dealt with a $30,000 advance payment received by the petitioner lessor, an accrual method taxpayer. The payment was received in 1949 but was to be applied as rent in 1959. The Court held the payment was includible in income in 1949. The Court stated that the $30,000 was paid as advance rental for the year 1959; it was not a security deposit. It was intended to be rent, was described in the lease as rent and was primarily rent. Since it is received in 1949, it is taxable in 1949 even though the rent is to be applied for use of the property in 1959.

But how far can the concept be pushed? Like the cash method (see discussion above), the accrual method can only be pushed so far. What happens if a sale of property for a particular price is booked by the taxpayer in Year 1, but the closing date or date of title passing is in Year 2. Does accrual-method accounting mean that the sale price is taken into income in Year 1?

The short answer is no. The accrual of income is not allowed or required until the property contracted for has been transferred. This is the case even though a binding contract for the transfer of the property has been entered into in an earlier year. The same principle holds for services. Suppose the taxpayer in Year 1 enters into a binding contract to perform services in Year 2. This taxpayer is not taxed on the fee for the services until they are performed.[27]

**26.** 28 T.C. 706 (1957), affirmed per curiam 261 F.2d 437 (6th Cir.1958).

**27.** Lucas v. North Texas Lumber Co., 281 U.S. 11, 50 S.Ct. 184, 74 L.Ed. 668

While this seems to violate the accrual method, this approach could be explained on a realization basis. That is, it could be said that the gain was not *realized* until title passed. See Chapter 4 for discussion of the realization requirement. Whether it makes one feel better to bottom one's treatment of this transaction on the artificial accrual-method accounting approach or the artificial realization requirement is a matter of personal taste. I say both accrual-method accounting and the realization requirement are "artificial," because neither actually reflects the economics of what is happening in this transaction. Under economically-accurate time value of money analysis, the taxpayer should be taxed on the present value of the payments to be made in the future, see the Prologue. That is the most economically accurate approach, but we are nowhere near adopting it.

Since we decline to follow the economically accurate approach, we are left to haggle about legal rules that may not seem to have too much point. But that's what lawyers do, isn't it?

See ¶ (e) below for further specialized treatment of the prepaid income area.

### (c) Deductions: General Dynamics

Under the accrual method, expenses are deducted when "all the events" occur which fix the taxpayer's liability. In particular under the "all events test," two issues must be established: 1) the fact of liability; and 2) the amount of the liability can be determined with reasonable accuracy.[28]

For example in the case of *Schuessler v. Commissioner*[29] the accrual method taxpayer was in the business of selling furnaces with a guarantee that he would turn the furnaces on and off each year for five years. The taxpayer in 1946 took a deduction of $13,300 as a reserve to represent the estimated cost of carrying out this guarantee for furnaces sold that year. The court upheld the deduction on the grounds that it more accurately reflected income than a system in which taxpayer would sell equipment in one year, be taxed on an inflated price because he obligated himself to provide services and then take a deduction in the later years when he performed the services.

A leading Supreme Court case in this area is *General Dynamics*.[30] In this case, a major defense contractor, General Dynamics, an accrual-method taxpayer, provided health benefits to its employees as a self-insurer, paying its employee health benefits out of its own funds. The company still employed a private carrier to administer the plan.

(1930).

**28.** § 461(h)(3)(B). See also United States v. Anderson, 269 U.S. 422, 46 S.Ct. 131, 70 L.Ed. 347 (1926) (munitions manufacturer incurred a profits tax on munitions manufactured in 1916 which was due and paid in 1917; held: tax deductible in 1916).

**29.** 230 F.2d 722 (5th Cir.1956).

**30.** United States v. General Dynamics Corp., 481 U.S. 239, 107 S.Ct. 1732, 95 L.Ed.2d 226 (1987).

Since the filing and processing of claims took time, there was a delay between the providing of health services and the payment of those claims by General Dynamics. Thus some of each year's claims would not be paid until the following year or two, because some claims would not be filed until after the year the services were provided. General Dynamics asserted it could deduct the amount of claims which were not filed in the year they were incurred. The company estimated the amount of those claims based on its actuarial experience.

The Supreme Court, speaking through Justice Marshall, held that these delayed claims could not be deducted in the year incurred because the "all events" test was not satisfied. Claims which have not yet been filed, in the Court's view, might never be filed. This could be due to employees' error or procrastination, or confusion over the coverage or fear of disclosure to the employer of the nature or type of services rendered. The Court did not wish to accept statistical evidence as a basis for allowing a deduction to an accrual-method taxpayer. Historically it has been true that the courts and the Service have not accepted statistical evidence to support additions to reserves for estimated expenses.

The stakes in this case may seem relatively minor—a delay of a year or two in taking a deduction. But recall from the Prologue that an accrual-method taxpayer taking the full face amount of a deduction years in advance of when the item has to actually be paid can gain some outstanding benefits. If large amounts are involved even a one-or two-year difference can mean significant tax savings.

In the interesting Supreme Court case of *Hughes Properties*,[31] the Court held, in contrast with *General Dynamics*, that an accrual-basis casino can accrue its liability at the end of the year for progressive slot machine jackpots which had not yet been won by any player.

### (d) Current Law: Economic Performance

*Schuessler, General Dynamics* and *Hughes* were decided on the "all events test." After these cases, the statute was amended to toughen up the standards for ascertaining when an accrual-method taxpayer may take a deduction. In particular the statute now provides that the "all events" test shall not be treated as met any earlier than when "economic performance" occurs with respect to the item in question.[32] Under these new rules, taxpayer in *Schuessler* and *Hughes* would now lose. Moreover, these new economic performance rules prevent some of the wild abuses in the time value of money area that are described in the Prologue. Thus under these rules it is clear that reserves for estimated future expenses such as personal injury claims, refunds, maintenance and service contracts, and cancellations may not be taken.[33]

In particular the "economic performance" standard provides that:

---

**31.** United States v. Hughes Properties, Inc., 476 U.S. 593, 106 S.Ct. 2092, 90 L.Ed.2d 569 (1986).

**32.** § 461(h)(1).

**33.** Taking such reserves is a standard practice in financial accounting, so once again we see a discrepancy between financial and tax accounting.

*Services provided to the taxpayer:* If the liability of the accrual-method taxpayer arises out of providing services to the taxpayer, economic performance occurs when the person provides such services. Thus even though the taxpayer is contractually liable to pay or in fact does pay for the services in an earlier year, economic performance (and thus deductibility) occurs only in the later year when the services have been provided.[34]

*Property provided to the taxpayer:* If the liability of the accrual-method taxpayer arises out of providing property to the taxpayer, economic performance occurs when the person provides such property. Thus even though the taxpayer is contractually liable to pay or in fact does pay for the property in an earlier year, economic performance (and thus deductibility) occurs only in the later year when the property has been provided.[35]

*Property used by the taxpayer* (i.e., rented): If the liability of the accrual method taxpayer arises out of providing the use of property to the taxpayer, economic performance occurs when the taxpayer uses the property. Thus even though the taxpayer is contractually liable to pay or in fact does pay for the use of the property in an earlier year, economic performance (and thus deductibility) occurs only in the later year or years when the property is used.[36]

*Services and property provided by the taxpayer:* If the liability of the accrual method taxpayer requires him to provide services or property to someone else, economic performance occurs when the taxpayer provides such property or services. Thus even though the taxpayer is contractually obligated in an earlier year to provide property or services, there is no deduction of expenses of providing the property or services until the year these are provided.[37]

*Workers' compensation and tort liabilities:* If the liability of the accrual method taxpayer requires a payment to another person arising out of a workers compensation act or a tort claim, economic performance occurs as the payments to such person are made. Thus the taxpayer is put on the cash method. The accrual-method taxpayer cannot gain the huge advantage of taking an up-front deduction for the full face amount of a workers compensation or tort claim that is to be paid out over time.[38]

The Service is also given the power to promulgate regulations dealing with other items.[39]

**34.** § 461(h)(2)(A)(i).

**35.** § 461(h)(2)(A)(ii), thus codifying the result in the older Supreme Court case of Lucas v. North Texas Lumber, 281 U.S. 11, 50 S.Ct. 184, 74 L.Ed. 668 (1930).

**36.** § 461(h)(2)(A)(iii).

**37.** § 461(h)(2)(B).

**38.** § 461(h)(2)(C). See the Prologue.

**39.** § 461(h)(2)(D).

There are some exceptions. Economic performance is not required where it occurs within the shorter of (1) a reasonable period after the close of the tax year in which the expense is accrued or (2) 8½ months after the close of that year. In addition, (a) the item is recurring in nature and the taxpayer consistently treats items of the kind as incurred in the tax year in which the all events test (not including the eco-

### (e) *Prepaid Income: American Automobile Association; Schlude*

The economic performance rules described in the preceding section govern the case of advance deductions for the accrual-method taxpayer. But what of the case of advance income for the accrual-method taxpayer? From a tax accounting standpoint it is awkward when an accrual method taxpayer is paid in advance of the time that all the events have occurred to fix his liability.

The statutory scheme under which the Service operates here gives it a great deal of discretion. It is a discretion the Service has not shrunk from exercising.

Section 446(b) provides, as discussed above at ¶ 9.01, that if the method of accounting used by the taxpayer "does not clearly reflect income," the computation of taxable income shall be made under method as in the opinion of the Service does clearly reflect income.

The Service, has historically argued that advance payments to accrual method taxpayers are income when received, even though the payments have not yet been earned. One of the leading cases in this area is *American Automobile Association*.

---

nomic performance test) is satisfied, and (b) the item is either not a material item or its accrual in the year before economic performance results in a more proper match against income than would accruing it in the year of economic performance. § 461(h)(3).

### AMERICAN AUTOMOBILE ASSOCIATION
### v. UNITED STATES[40]

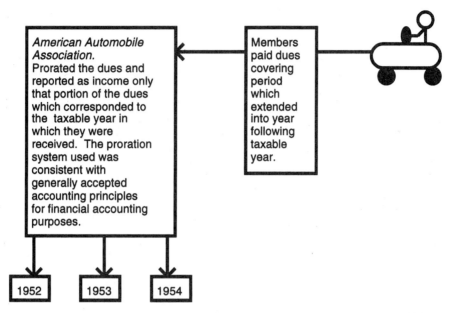

[392a]

*Question:* In what year are dues paid in advance reportable as income by American Automobile Association?

*Service's argument:* The entire amount of advance dues should be reported as income in the year received.

*Taxpayer's argument:* The proration system they used comported with generally accepted accounting principles, as proven by expert testimony.

*Held:* The taxpayer's proration of dues did not necessarily correspond to the times when members might need services. Thus the taxpayer's method did not clearly reflect income. The exercise of the Service's discretion in rejecting the Association's accounting system was not unsound.

This is an example of hardball by the Service, with the Court not stopping it. There might be a number of approaches to clearly reflecting income for advance payments for the accrual-method taxpayer. But plainly, requiring the full inclusion of advance payments does not reflect income. It is plain that a variety of expenses incurred by AAA (utilities, rent, local taxes) that are fairly attributable to these advance payments would not be deductible until later years. Thus the government's approach clearly does not reflect income.

This issue came up again in the well-known case of *Schlude:*

**40.** 367 U.S. 687, 81 S.Ct. 1727, 6
L.Ed.2d 1109 (1961), reh'g denied 368 U.S.
870, 82 S.Ct. 24, 7 L.Ed.2d 70 (1961).

## SCHLUDE v. COMMISSIONER[41]

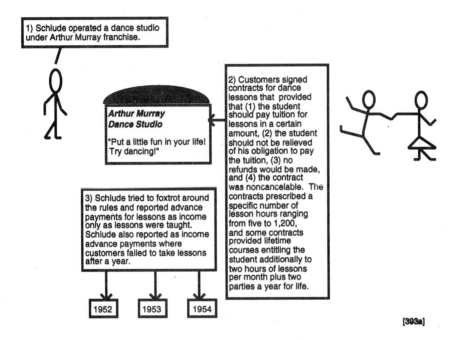

1) Schlude operated a dance studio under Arthur Murray franchise.

**Arthur Murray Dance Studio**

"Put a little fun in your life! Try dancing!"

2) Customers signed contracts for dance lessons that provided that (1) the student should pay tuition for lessons in a certain amount, (2) the student should not be relieved of his obligation to pay the tuition, (3) no refunds would be made, and (4) the contract was noncancelable. The contracts prescribed a specific number of lesson hours ranging from five to 1,200, and some contracts provided lifetime courses entitling the student additionally to two hours of lessons per month plus two parties a year for life.

3) Schlude tried to foxtrot around the rules and reported advance payments for lessons as income only as lessons were taught. Schlude also reported as income advance payments where customers failed to take lessons after a year.

1952    1953    1954

[393a]

*Question:* Was it proper for the Service, exercising its discretion under § 446(b), to stop the music and reject the studio's accounting system as not clearly reflecting income and to include as income in the year received the advance payments for dance lessons?

*Held:* Relying on the *American Automobile Association* case, the Court invokes the "long-established policy ... in deferring, where possible, to congressional procedures in the tax field," and, as in that case, cannot say that the Commissioner's rejection of the studio's deferral system was unsound.

Also the system employed by the taxpayer was artificial, as it was in *American Automobile Association,* in that the advance payments related to services which were to be performed only upon customers' demands without relation to fixed dates in the future.[42]

*Comment:* This case would seem to follow consistently from *American Automobile Association.* It suffers from the same problem in that it appears that there are a number of expenses allocable to performing under the contract in future years which cannot be deducted in advance,

**41.** 372 U.S. 128, 83 S.Ct. 601, 9 L.Ed.2d 633 (1963).

**42.** See also Commissioner v. Indianapolis Power & Light Co., 493 U.S. 203, 110 S.Ct. 589, 107 L.Ed.2d 591 (1990) (cash deposits made to public utility by less creditworthy customers were not advance payments of utility bills taxable under *AAA* and *Schlude* but rather were in essence non-taxable loans to the utility).

to match the advance payments.[43]

Consider once again the asymmetry of the treatment of advance receipts and advance expenditures. Suppose that one of the customers in the *American Automobile Association* case was a limousine company that wished to have AAA protection for its vehicles. The company pays its dues 3 years in advance. After the AAA case, AAA must take that 3 years' advance payment into income in the year received. However, the limousine company cannot deduct the three years dues up front but must wait until "economic performance" has occurred. This would mean that it could deduct the advance payments for the AAA protection only in the year to which the dues are attributable—i.e., write the advance payment off over three years.

As another example, *Artnell Co. v. Commissioner*[44] addressed the question of whether prepayments for services (proceeds of advance sales of tickets for Chicago White Sox baseball games and revenues for related future services) must be treated as income when received or whether inclusion in income can be deferred by the accrual method taxpayer until the games were played and other services rendered. The court in *Artnell*, running counter to the previous cases in the field, such as *Automobile Club of Michigan, American Automobile Association* and *Schlude* (see above), concluded that there must be situations where the deferral technique will so clearly reflect income that the Supreme Court will find an abuse of discretion if the commissioner rejects it. The court thus remanded the case for a further hearing in the tax court to ascertain whether the taxpayer's deferral method of accounting did clearly reflect its income.

On remand indeed the Tax Court held that the taxpayer's method of accounting was more supportable than that of the Commissioner and upheld the taxpayer's method of deferring income. The government did not petition for certiorari in *Artnell*.

Subsequently, the Commissioner propounded *Rev. Proc. 70–21*[45] in which it held that if there is prepayment of income for services to an accrual method taxpayer for services to be rendered within the current and a succeeding year, income must be included in the current year only to the extent that services are rendered in that year. However, no deferral is allowed if the prepayment is for services to be rendered beyond the reach of the succeeding year ("the two-year rule"). In that latter case, immediate inclusion is required for prepaid income for services to be rendered.

A couple of narrow exceptions to this stringent treatment of prepaid expenses have been enacted over the years. Congress overturned the holding on the particular facts of *American Automobile Association* with § 456, which allows deferral of prepaid dues of some membership organi-

---

**43.** The author, as an awkward teenager, once took dance lessons from an Arthur Murray studio. It did not help much.

**44.** 400 F.2d 981 (7th Cir.1968).

**45.** 1970–2 Cum.Bull. 501.

zations. And § 455 allows the deferral of prepaid newspaper and magazine subscriptions.[46]

**46.** § 455 thus allows the so-called newsletter tax shelter, in which heavy start-up promotion costs are deducted but the subscription income coming in is in large measure deferred. This can be attractive for investors to deduct the promotion costs up front against other high income. The author, in his more adventurous days, once wrote a newsletter which was constructed as a tax shelter. Thus you could say that the author once was a tax shelter. The subject of the newsletter: naturally, taxes.

# Chapter 10

# CREDITS

*Table of Sections*

## ¶ 10.01   In General

Once a taxpayer has computed his tax liability, his task is still not done. He may be entitled to certain credits against the tax liability that he owes. Credits are subtractions directly from the tax bill; whereas deductions, by contrast, are subtractions from income. Thus, a credit of $100 reduces the taxpayer's tax liability by $100. A deduction of $100 reduces a 31–percent bracket taxpayer's tax by $31 and a 15–percent bracket taxpayer's tax liability by $15. If the taxpayer has no taxable income, neither a credit nor a deduction will do him any good unless (as is sometimes the case) it can in effect be carried to other taxable years. Also a credit may be constructed to pay a refund and become in effect a negative income tax for poor people.

Because credits provide dollar-for-dollar tax savings, they are often seen as more equitable than tax deductions, whose impact depends on the taxpayer's tax bracket. However, that would be an overly simple view of the issue. As a practical matter, taxpayers are never given a credit of 100 percent of any particular expenditure that they might make. Obviously, if a 100–percent credit were available for, say, child care, every taxpayer would make the expenditure, since he would get *all* his money back from the government. Thus, credits are always keyed to a percentage of amounts expended for the particular activity in question. However, the ability to undertake a level of expenditure great enough to take advantage of the credit will depend on the taxpayer's income. Therefore, credits, as well as deductions, can often be best taken advantage of by those with higher incomes.

## ¶ 10.02   Child etc. Care Credit: *Smith*

In the leading case of Henry C. Smith (as discussed in Chapter 6),[1] a husband and wife employed nursemaids to take care of their young child so that both could work. The Board of Tax Appeals held that the couple could not deduct the expenses of the nursemaids on the grounds that such expenses were inherently personal, and "of a character applicable to human beings generally" and therefore not deductible. *Smith* has been criticized on the basis that the expenses for child care would not have been incurred had not both parents been working. However, the court's reasoning that such expenditures are non-deductible, personal expenditures appears to be sound. Granted that additional expenses were incurred on account of the wife's working, this could also be said about a variety of personal expenses incident to the holding of a job: such as more haircuts, finer clothes, commuting expenses, lunches out. The position that all incremental increases in personal expenses incident to holding a job should be deductible would not appear to be tenable.

The question of the treatment of child care expenses can also be seen as part of the larger issue of imputed income. Consider two couples: the Joneses and the Garcias. In the case of the Joneses, Judy Jones, works and makes $50,000 per year; Willie Jones does not work but stays home and takes care of the kid and the house. In the case of the Garcias, Manny Garcia works and makes $50,000 per year. Ana Garcia also works, making $15,000 per year, and they hire a housekeeper to take care of the kid and the house at an annual salary of $10,000 per year. As an economic matter, the Garcias are $5,000 per year better off than the Joneses. But the Garcias are taxed in full on the $15,000 earnings of Ana. If the Garcias are in the 40% bracket (combined federal and state rate), the tax on Ana's earnings is $6,000. Subtracting the $6,000 tax and the $10,000 child care expenses from Ana's earnings, we find that the Garcias are actually losing $1,000 a year from Ana's job.

Thus does the tax system discourage the lower-earning spouse from going to work. If historically and culturally women are usually the second lower-income wage earner in the family, then the effect can be seen as a women's issue: the tax system discourages women from working outside the home.

We can push the analysis further. Let us say that the value of Ana Garcia's work in the home is worth $10,000 (reasonable given what the Garcias pay for a housekeeper/babysitter). Thus in terms of value to society, it is better if Ana works outside the home where her services are worth $15,000 rather than in the home where her services are worth $10,000. Yet the taxation of Ana's earnings coupled with no deduction for child care expenses means that Ana will stay home. Economists call

1. Henry C. Smith v. Commissioner, 40 B.T.A. 1038, 1939 WL 83 (1939), aff'd per curiam 113 F.2d 114 (2d Cir.1940).

this a "deadweight" loss to the society. The tax system has distorted Ana's behavior so that she works in a lesser-valued activity.

Lest you think this is all just some more idle chatter on my part, Congress has actually tried to respond to this problem. While the response is not complete, it shows some thinking along these lines.

The response was a credit for the care of children and others in the taxpayer's household incident to the holding of a job by the taxpayer. The credit is 30% of employment-related expenses for taxpayers with adjusted gross incomes of $10,000 or less. The percentage credit decreases by 1% for each $2000 (or fraction thereof) increase in adjusted gross income. The credit does not decrease below 20%. Therefore, taxpayers with adjusted gross income of $28,000 or more receive a credit of 20% of employment-related expenses.[2]

The following table illustrates the amount of the percentage credit at various levels of adjusted gross income. The credit is 30% for adjusted gross income of $10,000 or less.

| AGI Over | % Credit |
|---|---|
| $10,000 | 29% |
| $12,000 | 28% |
| $14,000 | 27% |
| $16,000 | 26% |
| $18,000 | 25% |
| $20,000 | 24% |
| $22,000 | 23% |
| $24,000 | 22% |
| $26,000 | 21% |
| $28,000 | 20% |

The maximum amount of employment-related expenses that may be taken into account in computing the credit is $2,400, if there is one child or other qualifying individual in the home and $4,800 if there are two or more children or other qualifying individuals in the home.[3] Thus, for example a taxpayer with an adjusted gross income of $18,000 and one child in the home who incurred $3000 of employment-related expenses would get a credit of $600 (25% of $2,400). If this same taxpayer had two qualifying individuals in the home, the credit would be $750 (25% of $3000).

A "qualifying individual" for these purposes means (A) a dependent of the taxpayer who is under the age of thirteen and with respect to whom the taxpayer is entitled to a dependency deduction;[4] (B) a depen-

---

2. § 21.

3. § 21(c).

4. It is possible for an individual to be a dependent of a taxpayer without the taxpayer being entitled to a dependency deduction for that individual. A "dependent" of

the taxpayer is one who is in one of the generally familial relationships with the taxpayer described in § 152(a), and for whom the taxpayer provides more than half the support. For the individual to give rise to a dependency deduction to the taxpayer,

dent of the taxpayer who is physically or mentally incapable of caring for himself; (C) the spouse of the taxpayer if physically or mentally incapable of caring for himself.[5]

"Employment-related expenses," to which the credit is keyed, means amounts paid to enable the taxpayer to be gainfully employed which are for household services and expenses for the care of a qualifying individual whether the expenses are for care inside or outside the home, as long as the qualifying individual regularly spends at least eight hours a day in the taxpayer's household.[6]

The amount of the employment-related expenses incurred during any taxable year which may be taken into account in making this computation cannot exceed, in the case of an unmarried taxpayer, the taxpayer's earned income; or in the case of a married couple, the earned income of the spouse with the lesser amount of earned income.[7] This rule is relaxed where one spouse is a student or incapable of caring for himself. In either of those events, such spouse shall be deemed to be gainfully employed and to have earned income of not less than $200 per month, where there is one qualifying individual in the household; or $400 a month where there are two or more qualifying individuals in the household. Thus, for example, if one spouse is working and earning $25,000 a year and the other spouse is incapable of caring for himself, and they have one ten-year-old child in a day care center, the spouse incapable of caring for himself will be deemed to have earned income of $400 per month for the purpose of the earned income limit. (There would be two qualifying individuals in this instance—the child and the spouse incapable of caring for himself.) In this case up to $4,800 of employment-related expenses could be taken into account in computing the credit (assuming the expenses were in fact incurred).[8]

An unmarried taxpayer is treated as maintaining a household only if he furnishes over half the cost of the household; a married couple is deemed to maintain a household only if the couple furnishes over half of the cost of the household for the taxable year.[9]

If a child who is under the age of fifteen or who is physically or mentally incapable of caring for himself receives over half of his support during the calendar year from his parents who are divorced or legally separated and the child is in the custody of one or both of his parents for more than one-half the calendar year, then the child is treated as being a

---

he not only has to be a "dependent" but must meet several other tests. See ¶ 7.04.

**5.** § 21(b).

**6.** § 21(b)(2). A liberal result in this area was reached by the Tax Court in finding that the expenses of sending a child to camp for eight weeks, plus one-third of the cost of a school trip to Washington, D.C., qualified as employment-related expenses, Zoltan, 79 T.C. 490 (1982). This result was reversed by the statute, § 21(b)(2) flush language.

**7.** § 21(d)(1).

**8.** § 21(d)(2).

**9.** § 21(e), also providing that married couples must generally file a joint return (to prevent the dollar limit from being multiplied).

qualifying individual with respect to that parent who has custody for a longer period during the year.[10]

No credit is allowed for amounts paid by the taxpayer to a person for whom the taxpayer is allowed a dependency deduction or who is a child of the taxpayer under the age of nineteen.[11]

## ¶ 10.03   Other Credits

The statute provides other credits. They are an interesting grab-bag. They include: credit for the elderly and the permanently and totally disabled,[1] foreign tax credit (of great importance to large companies doing business abroad),[2] credit for clinical testing expenses for certain drugs for rare diseases or conditions,[3] credit for producing fuel from a nonconventional source,[4] certain uses of gasoline and special fuels,[5] alcohol used as a fuel,[6] credit for increasing research activities,[7] low income housing credit,[8] enhanced oil recovery credit,[9] expenditures to provide access to disabled individuals,[10] targeted jobs credit.[11] If the business credits cannot be used in the taxable year, they can be carried back three years and forward 15 years.[12]

## ¶ 10.04   Speculations on an Investment Tax Credit

Tax ideas come in cycles. Periodically there surfaces the idea of bringing back the investment tax credit to stimulate the economy. Historically, the investment tax credit has worked roughly as follows: business firms get to subtract 10% of the amounts they invest in new plant and equipment from their tax bill.

It is strange that people want to bring the ITC back because the results with the credit when it was in place beginning in the late 1970's were not particularly good.

There are two kinds of credits: a one-time credit and a permanent credit.

The problem with a one-time credit is that businesses do not have time to plan for the investment before the credit runs out.

The problem with a permanent credit is that it distorts investments by directing them into the areas favored by the credit. Most particularly, it directs investments into plant and equipment instead of into worker retraining. One would think that the decision as to whether to invest in

**10.** § 21(e)(5). Cf. ¶ 7.04, relating to rules for determining which parent gets the dependency deduction in a case of divorce or separation.

**11.** § 21(e)(6). This one stings. I could use it.

### ¶ 10.03

**1.** § 22.

**2.** §§ 27, 901.

**3.** § 29.

**4.** § 29.

**5.** § 32.

**6.** § 40.

**7.** § 41.

**8.** § 42.

**9.** § 43.

**10.** § 44.

**11.** § 51.

**12.** §§ 38, 39.

plant and equipment or worker retraining ought to be made by the market rather than have the decision biased by the tax code to favor plant and equipment. This might be particularly true of an Administration that says it "puts people first."

Another problem with the credit is that in many cases it pays firms for doing what they are already doing, investing in new plant and equipment. To combat this problem, some economists, including those advising President Clinton, have favored an "incremental credit." This would provide a credit for investment in plant and equipment only above a certain threshold level. This seems to have the attractive feature that it encourages spending in new plant and equipment at a much smaller cost then a credit for all such expenditures.

But as the policy-maker employs an incremental credit, he begins to see that he has a tiger by the tail. One problem is to establish the "base year," the year against which the "incremental" expenditures will be measured. Whatever year or period is chosen, companies who happen to have made large investments during that period will be unfairly penalized. Moreover, as the economy expands, the "base" becomes smaller relative to overall investment. Thus the size of the credit swells, adding to the budget deficit.

To combat this problem, a "floating base" might be tried. But a floating base gives perverse results. In a boom year, when the economy is expanding, firms rapidly outrun the floating base. As a result, the credit throws off large benefits to business firms. But in a recession year, firms stay near the base. As a result, the credit's benefits diminish sharply. The credit thus magnifies the business cycle, stimulating investment in boom years and depressing investment in recession years. This is not exactly what we want.

An incremental credit also invites game-playing by business firms and their sophisticated advisors. How is the incremental credit, with or without a floating base, to be handled in the case of mergers or split-ups of companies?

Also, when coupled with accelerated depreciation, and deduction of interest on borrowing to purchase plant and equipment, the credit can yield benefits that may exceed the original price of the plant and equipment.

Putting these conceptual problems together with the credit's indifferent historical record, it may be safe to say that the investment credit is an idea whose time has come and gone.

## ¶ 10.05 Earned Income Tax Credit

The Revenue Reconciliation Act of 1993 enlarged greatly the Earned Income Tax Credit, § 32. An analysis of this country's welfare system, including Aid to Families with Dependent Children, now must take account of the effects of the EITC. The thrust of the EITC is to help people who work at low wages and have family responsibilities. The

EITC provides for a credit against taxes owed. The maximum amount of the credit is $3,370. If on the taxpayer's particular numbers the credit exceeds the taxes owed, the balance is paid to the taxpayer as in effect an income subsidy. The amount of the credit is tied to the taxpayer's income and the number of his children.

While the precise calculation is complex an example may be helpful. In the typical case of a taxpayer with two children the income subsidy is paid for taxpayer's wages up to $8,425, where the taxpayer receives the maximum subsidy of $3,370. The subsidy then remains at the maximum for earnings levels up to $11,000. Then the subsidy diminishes as earnings go higher, ultimately becoming zero at earnings of $27,000. At $10,000 of earnings, the taxpayer's tax liability would be zero under normal computations (taking account of the standard deduction and personal exemptions). At $20,000 of earnings, the taxpayer's tax liability would be around $700. The subsidy or credit would be diminished at this higher level of earnings to be about $1,475. Thus the taxpayer would receive net $775 from the government.

The Earned Income Credit is a very interesting and powerful technique. It employs the relatively efficient tax system to mount a welfare program. This is much more efficient than employing the bureaucracy of welfare agencies. The recipients just fill out a tax return. While the computation of the credit is complex, the IRS can do it for them automatically once they fill out their returns.

In making these calculations, if a taxpayer has more than $2,200 of unearned income (i.e., interest, dividends, net rental, royalty, net passive income and net capital gains), no credit is allowed. For calculating the phaseout of the credit losses from these items are not used to reduce income.

The odd structure of the credit is designed to encourage work rather than discourage it as usual welfare programs do. The amount of the subsidy rises with wages. Then it remains constant over a wide range of income. It is only phased out at the higher levels of income. But the way the subsidy phases out, there is little incentive to cut back on work to increase the subsidy. For example, on our numbers above, if the taxpayer has earnings of $27,000, he gets no subsidy. If he cuts back on work and his earnings drop to $11,000, he increases the subsidy by $3,370. But to do so he has lost $16,000 of earnings, which yield after tax $13,600. Thus it makes no sense for the taxpayer to give up $13,600 to gain a subsidy of $3,370.

President Clinton has talked about "ending welfare as we know it." The cleverly designed EITC has the potential to do just that for many taxpayers. The EITC also shows power of the tax system to reach out and control behavior and deal with issues far beyond what one would normally consider to be taxation.

## ¶ 10.06   Other Proposed Credits

At this writing (May 1997), two other credits have been proposed as part of the 1997 budget deal between the Republican-controlled Congress and President Clinton. One credit, which seems likely to be enacted, is a $500 per-child tax credit. In general, the way such a credit would work is that after a taxpayer has figured his tax liability, he subtracts $500 for each child from that tax liability. Thus if a taxpayer has three children and his tax were $4,000 without regard to the per-child credit, the taxpayer would subtract $1,500 from his tax liability to yield a net tax liability of $2,500. Unless special provisions are made, therefore, this credit only helps taxpayers with some significant income and therefore some significant tax liability.

Another credit being discussed is a credit for some portion of payment of college tuition expenses. Once again, such a credit only helps taxpayers with some significant tax liability (who are paying to send a child to college). Further, it may not help much at all, since the likely result of this will be to cause colleges to reduce their loan and scholarship aid offers to students because colleges will be taking account of the availability of the credit.

Another thing that can be said about these two credits is that they scream "Middle Class Family," because you need income, children, and college bound children to take full advantage of them. Whether this is the best tax policy is a question. (On a personal level, I am not knocking these credits since "Middle class family" is exactly the boat I am in.)

# Appendix A

# THE PRESIDENT AND MRS. CLINTON'S 1996 TAX RETURN AND ACCOMPANYING PRESS RELEASE

| FORM 1040 | U.S. Individual Income Tax Return | 1996 | (99) | IRS Use Only – Do not write or staple in this space. |
|---|---|---|---|---|

Department of the Treasury – Internal Revenue Service

For the year Jan. 1 – Dec. 31, 1996, or other tax year beginning    , 1996, ending    , 19    OMB No. 1545-0074

**Label** (See page 11.)

Your first name and initial / Last name
**William J. Clinton**

Your social security number ▓▓▓▓▓▓▓▓

If a joint return, spouse's first name and initial / Last name
**Hillary Rodham Clinton**

Spouse's social security number ▓▓▓▓▓▓▓▓

Use the IRS label. Otherwise, please print or type.

Home address (number and street). If you have a P.O. box, see page 11.    Apt. no.
**1600 Pennsylvania Avenue, N.W.**

City, town or post office, state, and ZIP code. If you have a foreign address, see page 11.
**Washington, DC 20500**

For help finding line instructions, see pages 2 and 3 in the booklet.

**Presidential Election Campaign** (See page 11.)

| | Yes | No |
|---|---|---|
| Do you want $3 to go to this fund? | X | |
| If a joint return, does your spouse want $3 to go to this fund? | X | |

Note: Checking "Yes" will not change your tax or reduce your refund.

**Filing Status**

Check only one box.

1. ☐ Single
2. ☒ Married filing joint return (even if only one had income)
3. ☐ Married filing separate return. Enter spouse's soc. sec. no. above & full name here ▶
4. ☐ Head of household (with qualifying person). (See instructions.) If the qualifying person is a child but not your dependent, enter this child's name here ▶
5. ☐ Qualifying widow(er) with dependent child (year spouse died ▶ 19 ). (See instructions.)

**Exemptions**

6a ☒ Yourself. If your parent (or someone else) can claim you as a dependent on his or her tax return, do not check box 6a
b ☒ Spouse

No. of boxes checked on lines 6a and 6b   **2**

c Dependents:

| (1) First Name   Last name | (2) Dependent's social security number. If born in Dec. 1996, see inst. | (3) Dependent's relationship to you | (4) No. of mos. lived in your home in 1996 |
|---|---|---|---|
| Chelsea V. Clinton | ▓▓▓▓▓▓▓▓ | Daughter | 12 |
| | | | |
| | | | |
| | | | |
| | | | |

No. of your children on line 6c who:
• lived with you   **1**
• did not live with you due to divorce or separation (see instructions)

Dependents on 6c not entered above

If more than six dependents, see the instr. for line 6c.

Add numbers entered on lines above ▶   **3**

d Total number of exemptions claimed

**Income**

Attach Copy B of your Forms W-2, W-2G, and 1099-R here.

If you did not get a W-2, see the instr. for line 7.

Enclose, but do not attach, any payment. Also, please enclose Form 1040-V (see the instructions for line 62).

| | | |
|---|---|---|
| 7 | Wages, salaries, tips, etc. Attach Form(s) W-2 | **200057** |
| 8a | Taxable interest. Attach Schedule B if over $400 | **28606** |
| b | Tax-exempt interest. DO NOT include on line 8a ... 8b   6280 | |
| 9 | Dividend income. Attach Schedule B if over $400 | **5141** |
| 10 | Taxable refunds, credits, or offsets of state and local income taxes (see instructions) | **2214** |
| 11 | Alimony received | |
| 12 | Business income or (loss). Attach Schedule C or C-EZ | **742852** |
| 13 | Capital gain or (loss). If required, attach Schedule D | **100066** |
| 14 | Other gains or (losses). Attach Form 4797 | |
| 15a | Total IRA distributions ... 15a     b Taxable amount (see inst.) | 15b — |
| 16a | Total pensions and annuities ... 16a     b Taxable amount (see inst.) | 16b |
| 17 | Rental real estate, royalties, partnerships, S corporations, trusts, etc. Attach Schedule E | |
| 18 | Farm income or (loss). Attach Schedule F | |
| 19 | Unemployment compensation | |
| 20a | Social security benefits ... 20a     b Taxable amount (see inst.) | 20b |
| 21 | Other income. | |
| 22 | Add the amounts in the far right column for lines 7 through 21. This is your total income ▶ | **1078936** |

**Adjusted Gross Income**

If line 31 is under $28,495 (under $9,500 if a child did not live with you), see the instr. for line 54.

| | | | |
|---|---|---|---|
| 23a | Your IRA deduction (see instructions) | 23a | |
| b | Spouse's IRA deduction (see instructions) | 23b | |
| 24 | Moving expenses. Attach Form 3903 or 3903-F | 24 | |
| 25 | One-half of self-employment tax. Attach Schedule SE | 25   13835 | |
| 26 | Self-employed health insurance deduction (see inst.) | 26 | |
| 27 | Keogh & self-employed SEP plans. If SEP, check ▶☐ | 27 | |
| 28 | Penalty on early withdrawal of savings | 28 | |
| 29 | Alimony paid. Recipient's SSN ▶ | 29 | |
| 30 | Add lines 23a through 29 | | **13835** |
| 31 | Subtract line 30 from line 22. This is your adjusted gross income ▶ | | **1065101** |

For Privacy Act and Paperwork Reduction Act Notice, see page 7.     Form **1040** (199

Form 1040 (1996)  William J. and Hillary Rodham Clinton                                          Pa~

| | | | |
|---|---|---|---|
| **Tax Compu-tation** | 32 Amount from line 31 (adjusted gross income).................................... | 32 | 1065101 |
| | 33 a Check if: ☐ You were 65 or older, ☐ Blind; ☐ Spouse was 65 or older, ☐ Blind. | | |
| | Add the number of boxes checked above and enter the total here ................ ▶ 33a | | |
| | b If you are married filing separately and your spouse itemizes deductions or you were a dual-status alien, see instructions and check here ............................ ▶ 33b ☐ | | |
| | 34 Enter the larger of your: { Itemized deductions from Schedule A, line 28, OR Standard deduction shown below for your filing status. But see the instructions if you checked any box on line 33a or b or someone can claim you as a dependent. ● Single – $4,000 ● Married filing jointly or Qualifying widow(er) – $6,700 ● Head of household – $5,900 ● Married filing separately – $3,350 } ....... | 34 | 545644 |
| | 35 Subtract line 34 from line 32 ....................................... | 35 | 519457 |
| **If you want the IRS to figure your tax, see the Instructions for line 37.** | 36 If line 32 is $88,475 or less, multiply $2,550 by the total number of exemptions claimed on line 6d. If line 32 is over $88,475, see the worksheet in the inst. for the amount to enter.................... | 36 | 0 |
| | 37 Taxable income. Subtract line 36 from line 35. If line 36 is more than line 35, enter -0- ...... | 37 | 519457 |
| | 38 Tax. See instructions. Check if total includes any tax from a ☐ Form(s) 8814 b ☐ Form 4972 ........................................ ▶ | 38 | 172122 |
| **Credits** | 39 Credit for child and dependent care expenses. Att. Form 2441....... | 39 | | |
| | 40 Credit for the elderly or the disabled. Attach Schedule R ........... | 40 | | |
| | 41 Foreign tax credit. Attach Form 1116 .............. | 41 | | |
| | 42 Other. Check if from a ☐ Form 3800 b ☐ Form 8396 c ☐ Form 8801 d ☐ Form (specify) | 42 | | |
| | 43 Add lines 39 through 42 ........................................ | 43 | |
| | 44 Subtract line 43 from line 38. If line 43 is more than line 38, enter -0- ................ ▶ | 44 | 172122 |
| **Other Taxes** | 45 Self-employment tax. Att. Sch. SE .................................. | 45 | 27669 |
| | 46 Alternative minimum tax. Attach Form 6251................... | 46 | |
| | 47 Social security and Medicare tax on tip income not reported to employer. Attach Form 4137 ......... | 47 | |
| | 48 Tax on qualified retirement plans, including IRAs. If required, attach Form 5329................ | 48 | |
| | 49 Advance earned income credit payments from Form(s) W-2 ............. | 49 | |
| | 50 Household employment taxes. Attach Schedule H ........................ | 50 | |
| | 51 Add lines 44 through 50. This is your total tax ............................... ▶ | 51 | 199791 |
| **Payments** Attach Forms W-2, W-2G, and 1099-R on the front. | 52 Federal income tax withheld from Forms W-2 and 1099........... | 52 | 53463 | |
| | 53 1996 estimated tax payments and amount applied from 1995 return .. | 53 | 152200 | |
| | 54 Earned income credit. Attach Schedule EIC if you have a qualifying child. Nontaxable earned income: amount ▶ and type ▶ | 54 | | |
| | 55 Amount paid with Form 4868 (request for extension) .............. | 55 | | |
| | 56 Excess social security and RRTA tax withheld (see inst.) .......... | 56 | 4 | |
| | 57 Other payments. Check if from a ☐ Form 2439 b ☐ Form 4136 ... | 57 | | |
| | 58 Add lines 52 through 57. These are your total payments ............................. ▶ | 58 | 205667 |
| **Refund** Have it sent directly to your bank account! See inst. and fill in 60b, c, and d. | 59 If line 58 is more than line 51, subtract line 51 from line 58. This is the amount you OVERPAID ...... | 59 | 5876 |
| | 60a Amount of line 59 you want REFUNDED TO YOU ....................................... ▶ | 60a | |
| | b Routing number ▢ c Type: ☐ Checking ☐ Savings | | |
| | d Account number ▢ | | |
| | 61 Amount of line 59 you want APPLIED TO 1997 ESTIMATED TAX ▶ | 61 | 5876 |
| **Amount You Owe** | 62 If line 51 is more than line 58, subtract line 58 from line 51. This is the AMOUNT YOU OWE. For details on how to pay and use Form 1040-V, see instructions......................... ▶ | 62 | |
| | 63 Estimated tax penalty. Also include on line 62 ... | 63 | | |

| | |
|---|---|
| **Sign Here** Keep a copy of this return for your records. | Under penalties of perjury, I declare that I have examined this return and accompanying schedules and statements, and to the best of my knowledge and belief, they are true, correct, and complete. Declaration of preparer (other than taxpayer) is based on all information of which preparer has any knowledge. |

| | | | |
|---|---|---|---|
| Your signature ✗ William J. Clinton | Date 4-14-97 | Your occupation U.S. President | |
| Spouse's signature. If a joint return, BOTH must sign. ✗ Hillary Rodham Clinton | Date | Spouse's occupation Attorney | |

| | | | |
|---|---|---|---|
| **Paid Preparer's Use Only** | Preparer's signature ▶ Robert L Jones CPA | Date 4/14/97 | Check if self-employed ☐ | Preparer's social security no. |
| | Firm's name (or yours if self-employed) and address Hariton, Mancuso & Jones, P.C. 11140 Rockville Pike Rockville, MD | | EIN | ZIP code 20852 |

**SCHEDULES A&B**
**(Form 1040)**

Department of the Treasury
Internal Revenue Service

Name(s) shown on Form 1040

## Schedule A – Itemized Deductions

▶ Attach to Form 1040.    ▶ See Instructions for Schedules A and B (Form 1040).

OMB No. 1545-0074

**1996**

Attachment
Sequence No. 07

Your social security number

**William J. and Hillary Rodham Clinton**

| | | | | | |
|---|---|---|---|---|---|
| **Medical and Dental Expenses** | | Caution: Do not include expenses reimbursed or paid by others. | | | |
| | 1 | Medical and dental expenses (see page A-1)....................... | 1 | | |
| | 2 | Enter amount from Form 1040, line 32.... | 2 | | | |
| | 3 | Multiply line 2 above by 7.5% (.075)............................. | 3 | | |
| | 4 | Subtract line 3 from line 1. If line 3 is more than line 1, enter –0–........................ | | 4 | 0 |
| **Taxes You Paid** (See page A-1.) | 5 | State and local income taxes.................................. | 5 | 38225 | |
| | 6 | Real estate taxes (see page A-2)............................... | 6 | | |
| | 7 | Personal property taxes...................................... | 7 | 20 | |
| | 8 | Other taxes. List type and amount ▶ | 8 | | |
| | 9 | Add lines 5 through 8........................................ | | 9 | 38245 |
| **Interest You Paid** (See page A-2.) Note: Personal interest is not deductible. | 10 | Home mortgage interest and points reported on Form 1098.......... | 10 | 3263 | |
| | 11 | Home mortgage interest not reported on Form 1098. If paid to the person from whom you bought the home, see page A-2 & show that person's name, ID no. & address ▶ | 11 | | |
| | 12 | Points not reported on Form 1098. See page A-3................. | 12 | | |
| | 13 | Investment interest. If required, attach Form 4952. (See page A-3)................................ | 13 | | |
| | 14 | Add lines 10 through 13....................................... | | 14 | 3263 |
| **Gifts to Charity** If you made a gift and got a benefit for it, see page A-3. | 15 | Gifts by cash or check. If any gift of $250 or more, see pg. A-3 ........ | 15 | 609300 | |
| | 16 | Other than by cash or check. If any gift of $250 or more, see page A-3. If over $500, you MUST attach Form 8283 ...................... | 16 | | |
| | 17 | Carryover from prior year.................................... | 17 | | |
| | 18 | Add lines 15 through 17...... Carryover to next year..... –76749 | 18 | 532551 |
| **Casualty and Theft Losses** | 19 | Casualty or theft loss(es). Attach Form 4684. (See page A-4.)............................... | | 19 | 0 |
| **Job Expenses and Most Other Miscellaneous Deductions** (See page A-5 for expenses to deduct here.) | 20 | Unreimbursed employee expenses – job travel, union dues, job education, etc. If required, you MUST attach Form 2106 or 2106-EZ. (See page A-4.) ▶ | 20 | | |
| | 21 | Tax preparation fees......................................... | 21 | | |
| | 22 | Other expenses – investment, safe deposit box, etc. List type and amount ▶ Boston Harbor Trust Co. _____ 10828  Midlife Investments _____ 3  Tax Prep. & Acctng Services ____ 8910 | 22 | 19741 | |
| | 23 | Add lines 20 through 22...................................... | 23 | 19741 | |
| | 24 | Enter amount from Form 1040, line 32.... | 24 | 1065101 | | |
| | 25 | Multiply line 24 above by 2% (.02)............................. | 25 | 21302 | |
| | 26 | Subtract line 25 from line 23. If line 25 is more than line 23, enter –0–........................ | | 26 | 0 |
| **Other Miscellaneous Deductions** | 27 | Other – from list on page A-4. List type and amount ▶ | | 27 | 0 |
| **Total Itemized Deductions** | 28 | Is Form 1040, line 32, over $117,950 (over $58,975 if married filing separately)?  NO. Your deduction is not limited. Add the amounts in the far right column for lines 4 through 27. Also, enter on Form 1040, line 34, the larger of this amount or your standard deduction.  YES. Your deduction may be limited. See page A-5 for the amount to enter. | } ........▶ | 28 | 545644 |

KFA   For Paperwork Reduction Act Notice, see Form 1040 Instructions.      Schedule A (Form 1040) 19

Schedules A&B (Form 1040) 1996 | OMB No. 1545-0074 | Page

Name(s) shown on Form 1040. Do not enter name and social security number if shown on other side.

**William J. and Hillary Rodham Clinton**

Your social security number

## Schedule B – Interest and Dividend Income

Attachment Sequence No. 08

**Note:** If you had over $400 in taxable interest income, you must also complete Part III.

**Part I Interest Income** (See page B-1.)

1 List name of payer. If any interest is from a seller-financed mortgage and the buyer used the property as a personal residence, see page B-1 and list this interest first. Also, show that buyer's social security number and address ▶

| Payer | Amount |
|---|---|
| 1st Fidelity Bank Trustee | 8727 |
| Boatmen's Nat'l Bank of Arkansas | 1311 |
| Boatmen's Nat'l Bank of Arkansas | 1381 |
| Boston Harbor Tr. Co. | 4353 |
| Mercantile Bank of Central Arkansas | 846 |
| Midlife Investments | 2 |
| NationsBank | 4782 |
| Riggs Bank N.A. | 7204 |

**Note:** If you received a Form 1099-INT, Form 1099-OID, or substitute statement from a brokerage firm, list the firm's name as the payer and enter the total interest shown on that form.

2 Add the amounts on line 1 ........... | 2 | 28606
3 Excludable interest on series EE U.S. savings bonds issued after 1989 from Form 8815, line 14. You MUST attach Form 8815 to Form 1040 ........ | 3 |
4 Subtract line 3 from line 2. Enter the result here and on Form 1040, line 8a ..... ▶ | 4 | 28606

**Part II Dividend Income** (See page B-1.)

**Note:** If you had over $400 in gross dividends and/or other distributions on stock, you must also complete Part III.

5 List name of payer. Include gross dividends and/or other distributions on stock here. Any capital gain distributions and nontaxable distributions will be deducted on lines 7 and 8

| Payer | Amount |
|---|---|
| ▶ 1st Fidelity Bank Trustee | 2949 |
| Boston Harbor Tr. Co. | 2192 |

**Note:** If you received a Form 1099-DIV or substitute statement from a brokerage firm, list the firm's name as the payer and enter the total dividends shown on that form.

6 Add the amounts on line 5 ........... | 6 | 5141
7 Capital gain distributions. Enter here and on Schedule D* .......... | 7 |
8 Nontaxable distributions. (See the inst. for Form 1040, line 9.) ..... | 8 |
9 Add lines 7 and 8 ............. | 9 |
10 Subtract line 9 from line 6. Enter the result here and on Form 1040, line 9 ..... ▶ | 10 | 5141

\* If you do not need Schedule D to report any other gains or losses, see the instructions for Form 1040, line 13.

**Part III Foreign Accounts and Trusts** (See page B-1.)

You must complete this part if you (a) had over $400 of interest or dividends; (b) had a foreign account; or (c) received a distribution from, or were a grantor of, or a transferor to, a foreign trust. | Yes | No

11a At any time during 1996, did you have an interest in or a signature or other authority over a financial account in a foreign country, such as a bank account, securities account, or other financial account? See page B-1 for exceptions and filing requirements for Form TD F 90-22.1 ....... | | X
b If "Yes," enter the name of foreign country ▶
12 During 1996, did you receive a distribution from, or were you the grantor of, or transferor to, a foreign trust? If "Yes," see page B-2 for other forms you may have to file ....... | | X

KFA For Paperwork Reduction Act Notice, see Form 1040 instructions.      Schedule B (Form 1040) 199

**SCHEDULE C-EZ**
**(Form 1040)**

Department of the Treasury
Internal Revenue Service

## Net Profit From Business
(Sole Proprietorship)

▶ Partnerships, joint ventures, etc., must file Form 1065.

▶ Attach to Form 1040 or Form 1041.          ▶ See Instructions on back.

OMB No. 1545-0074

**1996**

Attachment
Sequence No. **09A**

Name of proprietor

Hillary Rodham Clinton

Social security number (SSN)

▨▨▨▨▨▨▨▨▨▨

**Part I     General Information**

**You May Use
This Schedule
Only If You:**

- Had business expenses of $2,500 or less.
- Use the cash method of accounting.
- Did not have an inventory at any time during the year.
- Did not have a net loss from your business.
- Had only one business as a sole proprietor.

**And You:**

- Had no employees during the year.
- Are not required to file Form 4562, Depreciation and Amortization, for this business. See the Instructions for Schedule C, line 13, on page C-3 to find out if you must file.
- Do not deduct expenses for business use of your home.
- Do not have prior year unallowed passive activity losses from this business.

**A**  Principal business or profession, including product or service

Author

**B**  Enter principal business code
(see pg. C-6) ▶ 6883

**C**  Business name. If no separate business name, leave blank.

**D**  Employer ID no. (EIN), if any
▨▨▨▨▨▨▨▨▨

**E**  Business address (including suite or room no.). Address not required if same as on Form 1040, page 1.

City, town or post office, state, and ZIP code

**Part II     Figure Your Net Profit**

| | | |
|---|---|---|
| **1**  Gross receipts.<br>Caution: If this income was reported to you on Form W-2 and the "Statutory employee" box on that form was<br>checked, see Statutory Employees in the Instructions for Schedule C, line 1, on page C-2 and check here . . ▶ ☐ | **1** | 742852 |
| **2**  Total expenses. If more than $2,500, you must use Schedule C. See Instructions . . . . . . . . . . . . . . . . . . . . . . . . | **2** | |
| **3**  Net profit. Subtract line 2 from line 1. If less than zero, you must use Schedule C. Enter on Form 1040, line 12,<br>and ALSO on Schedule SE, line 2. (Statutory employees do not report this amount on Schedule SE, line 2.<br>Estates and trusts, enter on Form 1041, line 3.) . . . . . . . . . . . . . . . . . . . . . . . . . . . . . . . . . . . . . . . . . . | **3** | 742852 |

**Part III     Information on Your Vehicle.** Complete this part ONLY if you are claiming car or truck expenses on line 2.

**4**  When did you place your vehicle in service for business purposes? (month, day, year) ▶ _____ .

**5**  Of the total number of miles you drove your vehicle during 1996, enter the number of miles you used your vehicle for:

**a**  Business _____   **b**  Commuting _____   **c**  Other _____

**6**  Do you (or your spouse) have another vehicle available for personal use? . . . . . . . . . . . . . . . . . . . . . . . . . . . . . . . . . ☐ Yes   ☐ No

**7**  Was your vehicle available for use during off-duty hours? . . . . . . . . . . . . . . . . . . . . . . . . . . . . . . . . . . . . . . . . . . ☐ Yes   ☐ No

**8 a**  Do you have evidence to support your deduction? . . . . . . . . . . . . . . . . . . . . . . . . . . . . . . . . . . . . . . . . . . . . . . ☐ Yes   ☐ No

**b**  If "Yes," is the evidence written? . . . . . . . . . . . . . . . . . . . . . . . . . . . . . . . . . . . . . . . . . . . . . . . . . . . . . . . . . ☐ Yes   ☐ No

For Paperwork Reduction Act Notice, see Form 1040 instructions.          Schedule C-EZ (Form 1040) 1996

SCHEDULE D
(Form 1040)

Department of the Treasury
Internal Revenue Service

Name(s) shown on Form 1040

## Capital Gains and Losses

▶ Attach to Form 1040.          ▶ See Instructions for Schedule D (Form 1040).
▶ Use lines 20 and 22 for more space to list transactions for lines 1 and 9.

OMB No. 1545-0074

**1996**

Attachment
Sequence No. **12**

Your social security number

William J. and Hillary Rodham Clinton

**Part I** Short-Term Capital Gains and Losses – Assets Held One Year or Less

| (a) Description of property (Example, 100 sh. XYZ Co.) | (b) Date acquired (Mo., day, yr.) | (c) Date sold (Mo., day, yr.) | (d) Sales price (see page D-3) | (e) Cost or other basis (see page D-3) | (f) LOSS If (e) is more than (d), subtract (d) from (e) | (g) GAIN If (d) is more than (e), subtract (e) from (d) |
|---|---|---|---|---|---|---|
| | | | | | | |
| | | | | | | |
| | | | | | | |

| | | | |
|---|---|---|---|
| 2 | Enter your short-term totals, if any, from line 21 ................ | 2 | |
| 3 | Total short-term sales price amounts. Add column (d) of lines 1 and 2 ........................... | 3 | |
| 4 | Short-term gain from Forms 2119 and 6252, and short-term gain or loss from Forms 4684, 6781, and 8824 ...................... | 4 | |
| 5 | Net short-term gain or loss from partnerships, S corporations, estates, and trusts from Schedule(s) K-1 .. BOSTON HARBOR TR. CO | 5 | 26074 |
| 6 | Short-term capital loss carryover. Enter the amount, if any, from line 9 of your 1995 Capital Loss Carryover Worksheet ................ | 6 | |
| 7 | Add lines 1 through 6 in columns (f) and (g) ....................... | 7 ( ) | 26074 |
| 8 | Net short-term capital gain or loss. Combine columns (f) and (g) of line 7 ................................ ▶ | 8 | 26074 |

**Part II** Long-Term Capital Gains and Losses – Assets Held More Than One Year

| | | | | | | |
|---|---|---|---|---|---|---|
| | | | | | | |
| | | | | | | |
| | | | | | | |

| | | | |
|---|---|---|---|
| 10 | Enter your long-term totals, if any, from line 23 ................ | 10 | |
| 11 | Total long-term sales price amounts. Add column (d) of lines 9 and 10 ........................... | 11 | |
| 12 | Gain from Form 4797; long-term gain from Forms 2119, 2439, and 6252; and long-term gain or loss from Forms 4684, 6781, and 8824 .................................. | 12 | |
| 13 | Net long-term gain or loss from partnerships, S corporations, estates, and trusts from Schedule(s) K-1 ... BOSTON HARBOR TR. CO. | 13 | 73992 |
| 14 | Capital gain distributions ............................................. | 14 | |
| 15 | Long-term capital loss carryover. Enter the amount, if any, from line 14 of your 1995 Capital Loss Carryover Worksheet ................ | 15 | |
| 16 | Add lines 9 through 15 in columns (f) and (g) ...................... | 16 ( ) | 73992 |
| 17 | Net long-term capital gain or (loss). Combine columns (f) and (g) of line 16 ................................ ▶ | 17 | 73992 |

**Part III** Summary of Parts I and II

| | | | |
|---|---|---|---|
| 18 | Combine lines 8 and 17. If a loss, go to line 19. If a gain, enter the gain on Form 1040, line 13. Note: If both lines 17 and 18 are gains, see the Capital Gain Tax Worksheet on page 24 .......................... | 18 | 100066 |
| 19 | If line 18 is a loss, enter here and as a (loss) on Form 1040, line 13, the smaller of these losses: | | |
| a | The loss on line 18; or | | |
| b | ($3,000) or, if married filing separately, ($1,500) ............................................. | 19 ( ) | |
| | Note: See the Capital Loss Carryover Worksheet on page D-3 if the loss on line 18 exceeds the loss on line 19 or if Form 1040, line 35, is a loss. | | |

For Paperwork Reduction Act Notice, see Form 1040 Instructions.          Schedule D (Form 1040) 1996

KFA

| SCHEDULE SE | Self–Employment Tax | OMB No. 1545-0074 |
|---|---|---|
| (Form 1040) | | **1996** |
| Department of the Treasury<br>Internal Revenue Service | ▶ See Instructions for Schedule SE (Form 1040).<br>▶ Attach to Form 1040. | Attachment<br>Sequence No. **17** |

| Name of person with self-employment income (as shown on Form 1040)<br>Hillary Rodham Clinton | Social security number of person with<br>self-employment income  ▶ | |

### Who Must File Schedule SE

**You must file Schedule SE if:**

● You had net earnings from self-employment from other than church employee income (line 4 of Short Schedule SE or line 4c of Long Schedule SE) of $400 or more, OR

● You had church employee income of $108.28 or more. Income from services you performed as a minister or a member of a religious order is not church employee income. See page SE–1.

**Note:** Even if you had a loss or a small amount of income from self-employment, it may be to your benefit to file Schedule SE and use either "optional method" in Part II of Long Schedule SE. See page SE–3.

**Exception:** If your only self-employment income was from earnings as a minister, member of a religious order, or Christian Science practitioner, and you filed Form 4361 and received IRS approval not to be taxed on those earnings, do not file Schedule SE. Instead, write "Exempt–Form 4361" on Form 1040, line 45.

### May I Use Short Schedule SE or MUST I Use Long Schedule SE?

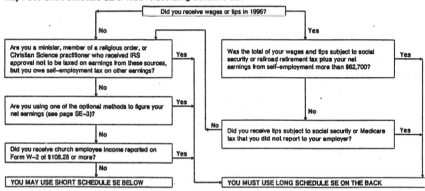

**YOU MAY USE SHORT SCHEDULE SE BELOW**          **YOU MUST USE LONG SCHEDULE SE ON THE BACK**

**Section A – Short Schedule SE.** Caution: Read above to see if you can use Short Schedule SE.

| | | |
|---|---|---|
| 1  Net farm profit or (loss) from Schedule F, line 36, and farm partnerships, Schedule K–1 (Form 1065), line 15a ......... | **1** | — |
| 2  Net profit or (loss) from Schedule C, line 31; Schedule C–EZ, line 3; and Schedule K–1 (Form 1065), line 15a (other than farming). Ministers and members of religious orders see page SE–1 for amounts to report on this line. See page SE–2 for other income to report. ...... | **2** | 742852 |
| 3  Combine lines 1 and 2 ........................... | **3** | 742852 |
| 4  Net earnings from self-employment. Multiply line 3 by 92.35% (.9235). If less than $400, do not file this schedule; you do not owe self-employment tax ...................... ▶ | **4** | 686024 |
| 5  Self-employment tax. If the amount on line 4 is:<br>● $62,700 or less, multiply line 4 by 15.3% (.153). Enter the result here and on Form 1040, line 45.<br>● More than $62,700, multiply line 4 by 2.9% (.029). Then, add $7,774.80 to the result. Enter the total here and on Form 1040, line 45. | **5** | 27669 |
| 6  Deduction for one–half of self-employment tax. Multiply line 5 by 50% (.5).<br>Enter the result here and on Form 1040, line 25 .................... | **6** | 13835 | |

For Paperwork Reduction Act Notice, see Form 1040 Instructions.          Schedule SE (Form 1040)

KFA

## THE WHITE HOUSE

### Office of the Press Secretary

**For Immediate Release**  April 14, 1997

### STATEMENT BY THE PRESS SECRETARY

The President and Mrs. Clinton's 1996 federal income tax return shows $199,791 in Federal Income Tax on an Adjusted Gross Income of $1,065,101, of which $200,000 was the President's salary. The return shows that the Clintons made an overpayment on their taxes during 1996 of $5,876. The Clintons have elected to apply this overpayment to their 1997 income taxes.

In addition to the President's salary, the Clintons' income included royalty income in the amount of $742,852 from Mrs. Clinton's book, It Takes A Village; interest and dividend income and capital gains reported by Boston Harbor Trust Company, the Trustee of the Clintons' blind trust; other interest and dividend income; a refund of 1995 taxes paid by the Clintons to the State of Arkansas; and residual payments.

The return reports dividend and interest income of $12,000 from the "Henry G. Freeman, Jr., Pin Money Fund," established under a 1912 will for whoever is, at a given time, the spouse of the President of the United States. Mrs. Clinton intends to contribute this income to charitable entities, as she has in prior years.

The return also reports $609,300 in charitable contributions by the Clintons. The contributions were derived primarily from the proceeds of Mrs. Clinton's book. As you know, all income from the book (net of taxes and minor administrative expenses) is being donated to charity.

The President today also filed a federal income tax return on behalf of his daughter, Chelsea, which shows $1,969 in tax on income of $13,101.

-30-30-30-

*

# Appendix B

# RESEARCHING FEDERAL TAXATION ON WESTLAW®

*Analysis*

## Section 1.   Introduction

*Federal Taxation* provides a strong base for analyzing even the most complex problem involving federal taxation. Whether your research requires examination of statutes, administrative materials, case law or expert commentary, West books and WESTLAW are excellent sources.

WESTLAW expands your library, giving you access to decisions from federal courts and documents from the U.S. Congress, as well as to articles and treatises by well-known commentators. To help keep you up-to-date with current developments, WESTLAW provides frequently updated federal databases. With WESTLAW, you have unparalleled legal research resources at your fingertips.

## Additional Resources

If you have not used WESTLAW or have questions not covered in this appendix, see the *WESTLAW Reference Manual* or call the West Group Reference Attorneys at 1–800–REF–ATTY (1–800–733–2889). The West Group Reference Attorneys are trained, licensed attorneys, available 24 hours a day to assist you with your WESTLAW or West book search questions.

## Section 2.   WESTLAW Federal Databases

Each database on WESTLAW is assigned an abbreviation called an *identifier*, which you use to access the database. You can find identifiers for all databases in the online WESTLAW Directory and in the print *WESTLAW Database Directory*. When you need to know more detailed information about a database, use Scope. Scope contains coverage information, related databases and valuable search tips. To access Scope, click the **Scope** button while in the database.

The following chart lists WESTLAW databases that contain information pertaining to federal tax law. For a complete list of federal tax law databases, see the online WESTLAW Directory or the print *WESTLAW Database Directory*. Because new information is continually being added to WESTLAW, you should also check the Welcome to WESTLAW screen and the WESTLAW Directory for new database information.

## WESTLAW Federal Taxation Databases

| Database | Identifier | Coverage |
|---|---|---|
| Combined Tax Materials | FTX–ALL | Varies by individual database |
| Cases & Releases | FTX–CSRELS | Varies by individual database |
| **Federal Case Law** | | |
| Cases | FTX–CS | Begins with 1789 |
| Supreme Court Cases | FTX–SCT | Begins with 1790 |
| Courts of Appeals Cases | FTX–CTA | Begins with 1891 |
| District Courts Cases | FTX–DCT | Begins with 1789 |
| Court of Federal Claims | FTX–FEDCL | Begins with 1856 |
| Tax Court Cases | FTX–TCT | Board of Tax Appeals decisions: 1924–1942 |
| | | Tax Court decisions: 1942–present |
| | | Tax Court memorandum decisions: 1954–present |
| **Federal Statutes and Regulations** | | |
| U.S. Code Annotated | FTX–USCA | Current data |
| Tax Code Before Tax Reform Act of 1986 | FTX–USC–OLD | Pre–Tax Reform Act of 1986 |
| Rules | FTX–RULES | Current data |
| Materials on the Tax Reform Act of 1986 | FTX–TRA86 | Begins with 1986 |

| Database | Identifier | Coverage |
|---|---|---|
| Code and Regulations | FTX–CODREG | Varies by database |
| Code of Federal Regulations | FTX–CFR | Current data |
| Federal Register | FTX–FR | July 1980 |
| Final, Temporary and Proposed Regulations | FTX–REG | Varies by database |
| Treasury Decisions | FTX–TD | Begins with August 1980 |
| Public Laws | FTX–PL | Tax Equity and Fiscal Responsibility Act of 1982, Tax Reform Act of 1984, Tax Reform Act of 1986 |
| Congressional Research Service | FTX–CRS | Begins with 1989 |
| General Accounting Office Reports | FTX–GAO | Begins with January 1994 |
| Legislative History–U.S. Code, 1948 to Present | LH | Begins with 1948 |
| **Federal Administrative Materials** | | |
| Combines FTX–CB, FTX–NR, FTX–GCM, FTX–AOD, FTX–TM, FTX–ISP, FTX–MSSP, FTX–WD and FTX–EXEMPT | FTX–RELS, | Varies by individual database |
| Combines FTX–WD, FTX–CB and FTX–NR | FTX–CBWD | Varies by individual database |
| Combines FTX–GCM, FTX–AOD and FTX–TM | FTX–MEMOS | Varies by individual database |
| Delegation Orders | FTX–DO | Begins with 1954 |
| Executive Orders | FTX–EO | Begins with 1954 |
| Industry Specialization Program | FTX–ISP | Begins with 1992 |
| Internal Revenue Manual | FTX–IRM | Current data |
| International Acts | FTX–IA | Begins with 1955 |
| IRS Actions on Decisions | FTX–AOD | Begins with 1967 |
| IRS Announcements and Notices | FTX–ANN | Notices: begins with 1980 |
| | | Announcements: begins with 1988 |
| IRS Cumulative Bulletins | FTX–CB | Begins with 1954 |
| IRS Exemption Rulings | FTX–EXEMPT | Begins with January 1994 |
| IRS General Counsel Memoranda | FTX–GCM | Begins with 1962 |
| IRS Market Segment Specialization Program | FTX–MSSP | Begins with 1993 |
| IRS News Releases | FTX–NR | Begins with January 1981 |
| IRS Publications | FTX–IRSPUBS | 1996 |
| IRS Publications (Retired) | FTX–IRSPUBS–OLD | 1984–1995 |
| IRS Technical Memoranda | FTX–TM | Begins with 1967 |
| IRS Written Determinations | FTX–WD | Begins with 1954 |
| Revenue Procedures | FTX–RP | Begins with 1954 |
| Revenue Rulings | FTX–RR | Begins with 1954 |
| Treasury Department Orders | FTX–TDO | Begins with 1954 |
| **Texts and Periodicals** | | |
| Akron Tax Journal | AKRONTJ | Selected coverage begins with 1987 (vol. 4); full coverage begins with 1993 (vol. 10) |
| American Journal of Tax Policy | AMJTP | Selected coverage begins with 1988 (vol. 7); full coverage begins with 1994 (vol. 11) |
| Boston University Journal of Tax Law | BUJTXL | Selected coverage is from 1990 (vol. 8) to 1991 (vol. 9) |
| Corpus Juris Secundum: Internal Revenue | CJS–FTX | 1996 edition |
| Employee Fringe and Welfare Benefit Plans | EMPFRINGE | 1996 edition |

| Database | Identifier | Coverage |
|---|---|---|
| Federal Bar Association Section of Taxation Report | FEDBASTXR | Selected coverage begins with 1991 (vol. 1991–Winter) |
| Federal Tax Practice (Casey) | CASEY | Current through the December 1995 cumulative supplement |
| Law of Federal Income Taxation (Mertens) | MERTENS | Current through January 1996 monthly update |
| Law of Tax–Exempt Organizations, The | JW–TAXEXEM | Current through 1993 cumulative supplement |
| Limited Liability Companies | LLC | Current through 1994 |
| Partnership Taxation, 5th Edition | PTNRTAX | Current through June 1995 |
| PLI Tax Law and Estate Planning: Estate Planning and Administration Course Handbook Series | PLI–EST | Begins with September 1984 |
| PLI Tax Law and Estate Planning: Tax Law and Practice Course Handbook Series | PLI–TAX | Begins with September 1984 |
| Practising Law Institute | PLI | Begins with September 1984 |
| Subchapter S Taxation | SUBSTAX | Current through April 1995 cumulative supplement |
| Taxation–Law Reviews, Texts & Bar Journals | TX–TP | Varies by publication |
| Tax Law Review | TAXLR | Full coverage begins with 1988 (vol. 44, no. 1) |
| Tax Lawyer | TAXL | Selected coverage begins with 1982 (vol. 35) |
| Virginia Tax Review | VATXR | Selected coverage begins with 1987 (vol. 7); full coverage begins with 1993 (vol. 13) |

**Warren, Gorham & Lamont Publications**

| | | |
|---|---|---|
| Warren Gorham Lamont Publications | WGL | Varies by publication |
| Warren Gorham Lamont Tax Journals | WGL–TAXJ | Varies by publication |
| Banking Law Journal, The | WGL–BLJ | Full coverage begins with 1987 (vol. 104) |
| Journal of International Taxation, The | WGL–JITAX | Full coverage begins with 1990 (vol. 1) |
| Journal of Partnership Taxation | WGL–JPTAX | Full coverage begins with 1985 (vol. 1) |
| Journal of Real Estate Taxation, The | WGL–JRETAX | Full coverage begins with 1985 (vol. 12) |
| Journal of Taxation, The | WGL–JTAX | Full coverage begins with 1985 (vol. 62) |
| Real Estate Law Journal | WGL–RELJ | Full coverage begins with 1986 (vol. 14) |
| Real Estate Law Report | WGL–RELR | Full coverage begins with 1990 (vol. 19) |
| Taxation for Accountants | WGL–TXACCT | Full coverage begins with 1985 (vol. 34) |
| Taxation for Lawyers | WGL–TXNLAW | Full coverage begins with 1985 (vol. 13) |

**Directories and Dictionaries**

| | | |
|---|---|---|
| West's Tax Law Dictionary | DI–TAX–WT | Current data |
| Shepard's® Tax Dictionary | DI–TAX–SH | Current data |
| TaxSource Directory | TAXSOURCE | Current data |
| West's Legal Directory–Taxation | WLD–TAX | Current data |

**News and Information**

| | | |
|---|---|---|
| Accountant, The | ACCNT | Begins with January 1995 |
| Accounting and Finance | ACCFIN | Begins with May 1994 |

| Database | Identifier | Coverage |
|---|---|---|
| Accounting & Tax Database (DIALOG) | ACCT & TX–DB | Begins with August 1971 |
| Accounting & Tax Database–Current (DIALOG) | ACCT & TX–DB–C | Most recent 12 to 24 months |
| Accounting Technology | ACTTCH | Begins with January 1995 |
| Accounting Today | ACCTDY | Begins with January 1994 |
| CMA–The Management Accounting Magazine | CMAMAM | Begins with February 1994 |
| CPA Journal, The | CPAJ | Begins with January 1989 |
| European Accountant | EUROACCT | Begins with January 1995 |
| Internal Auditor | INTAUDITOR | Begins with February 1994 |
| International Accounting Bulletin | INTERACB | Begins with January 1995 |
| National Public Accountant | NATPUBACNT | Begins with January 1994 |
| National Tax Journal | NATAXJ | Begins with March 1994 |
| Practical Accountant Magazine | PRCTACNTM | Begins with January 1995 |
| Tax Adviser, The | TAXADVSR | Begins with January 1994 |
| Taxation News | TAXNEWS | Varies by source |
| Tax Executive | TAXEXEC | Begins with January 1989 |
| Tax Notes Today (DIALOG) | TNT | Begins with January 1987 |
| WESTLAW Topical Highlights–Federal Tax | WTH–FTX | Current data |

**BNA Materials**

| | | |
|---|---|---|
| Daily Tax Report | BNA–DTR | Begins with January 1986 |
| Daily Tax Report (most recent two weeks) | BNA–DTR–NEW | Most recent two weeks |
| BNA Daily News from Washington (DIALOG) | BNA–DNEWS | Begins with June 1990 |
| BNA Daily News from Washington–Current (DIALOG) | BNA–DNEWS–C | Most recent 12 to 24 months |
| BNA Highlights and Contents | BNA–TOC | Current data |
| BNA Pension & Benefits Reporter | BNA–PEN | Begins with 1986 |
| BNA Pensions & Benefits Daily | BNA–PBD | Begins with March 1987 |
| BNA's Taxation Database | BNA–TX | Begins with January 1986 |
| BNA Tax Conferences & Meetings | BNA–TXCONF | Begins with January 1988 |
| BNA Tax Updates | BNA–BTU | Current issue |
| BNA Washington Insider | BNA–BWI | Begins with September 1987 |
| BNA Washington Items | BNA–DC | Begins with January 1987 |
| Legislative Tracking Calendars | BNA–TRACK | Begins with January 1986 |

**Tax Management Portfolios and Journals**

| | | |
|---|---|---|
| Tax Management Portfolios–All | TM–ALLPORT | Active portfolios |
| Tax Management Portfolios–Compensation Planning Series | TM–CP | Active portfolios |
| Tax Management Portfolios–Estates, Gifts and Trusts Series | TM–EGT | Active portfolios |
| Tax Management Portfolios–Foreign Income Series | TM–FOR | Active portfolios |
| Tax Management Portfolios–Real Estate Series | TM–RE | Active portfolios |
| Tax Management Portfolios–The Tax Reform Act of 1986 | TM–TRA86 | Active portfolios |
| Tax Management Portfolios–U.S. Income Series | TM–US | Active portfolios |
| Tax Management Journals–All | TM–ALLJNL | Begins with January 1987 |
| Tax Management Compensation Planning Journal | TM–CPJ | Begins with January 1987 |
| Tax Management Estates, Gifts and Trusts Journal | TM–EGTJ | Begins with January/February 1987 |
| Tax Management Memorandum | TM–TMM | Begins with January 1987 |

| Database | Identifier | Coverage |
|---|---|---|
| Tax Management Real Estate Journal | TM–REJ | Begins with January 1987 |
| Tax Management Weekly Report | TM–TMWR | Begins with January 1987 |

## Section 3.  Menu–Driven WESTLAW: EZ ACCESS®

EZ ACCESS is West's menu-driven research system. It is ideal for new or infrequent WESTLAW users because it requires no experience or training on WESTLAW.

To access EZ ACCESS, click the **EZ ACCESS** button. Choose the research task you wish to perform and follow the simple instructions on each menu. For more information on browsing documents, see the *WESTLAW Reference Manual* or the *WESTLAW User Guide*.

## Section 4.  Retrieving a Document with a Citation: Find and Jump

### 4.1  Find

Find is a WESTLAW service that allows you to retrieve a document by entering its citation. Find allows you to retrieve documents from anywhere in WESTLAW without accessing or changing databases or losing your search result. Find is available for many documents, including case law (federal and state), the *United States Code Annotated®*, the *Code of Federal Regulations*, the *Federal Register*, federal rules, federal public laws, and texts and periodicals.

To use Find, simply access the Find service and type the citation. Following is a list of examples:

| To Find This Document | Access Find and Type |
|---|---|
| 26 U.S.C.A. § 401 | **26 usca 401** |
| 26 C.F.R. § 1.61–12 | **26 cfr 1.61–12** |
| Public Law No. 104–191 | **pl 104–191** |
| *U.S. v. Hill*, 113 S.Ct. 941 (1993) | **113 sct 941** |
| Tax Court Rule 221 | **tax ct rule 221** |
| Rev. Rul. 95–44 | **rev rul 95–44** |
| Revenue Procedure 95–27 | **rev proc 95–27** |
| Private Letter Ruling 95–18–004 | **plr 9518004** |
| Technical Advice Memorandum 94–51–001 | **wd 9451001** |

For a complete list of publications and their abbreviations that can be retrieved with Find, consult the Find Publications List. Click the **Pubs List** button after accessing Find.

### 4.2  Jump

Use Jump markers (> or ▶) to go directly from a case or law review article to a cited case, USCA® section or article; from a headnote to the corresponding text in the opinion; or from an entry in a statute index database to the full text of the statute.

### Section 5.   Natural Language Searching: WIN®—WESTLAW is Natural·

**Overview:** With WIN, you can retrieve documents by simply describing your issue in plain English. If you are a relatively new user, Natural Language searching makes it easier to retrieve cases on point. If you are an experienced user, Natural Language gives you a valuable alternative search method.

When you enter a Natural Language description, WESTLAW automatically identifies legal phrases, removes common words and generates variations of terms in your description. WESTLAW then searches for the concepts in your description. Concepts may include significant terms, phrases, legal citations or topic and key numbers. WESTLAW retrieves the 20 documents that most closely match your description, beginning with the document most likely to match.

### 5.1   Natural Language Searching

Access a database, such as Federal Taxation–Courts of Appeals Cases

(FTX–CTA). If the Terms and Connectors Query Editor is displayed, click the **Search Type** button and select **Natural Language**. At the Natural Language Description Editor, type a Natural Language description such as the following:

**are damages for back pay excludable from gross income**

### 5.2   Next Command

WESTLAW displays the 20 documents that most closely match your description, beginning with the document most likely to match. If you want to view additional documents, use your right mouse button to select **Next 10 Documents** or choose **Next 10 Documents** from the Browse menu.

### 5.3   Browsing a Natural Language Search Result

**Best Mode:** To display the best portion (the portion that most closely matches your description) of each document in your search result, use your right mouse button to select **Next Best** or click the **Best>** button.

**Standard Browsing Commands:** You can also browse your Natural Language search result using standard WESTLAW browsing commands, such as citations list, Locate, page mode and term mode. When you browse your Natural Language search result in term mode, the five portions of each document that are most likely to match your description are displayed.

### Section 6.   Terms and Connectors Searching

**Overview:** With standard Terms and Connectors searching, you enter a query, which consists of key terms from your research issue and connectors specifying the relationship between these terms.

Terms and Connectors searching is useful when you want to retrieve a document for which you have specific information, such as the title or the citation. Terms and Connectors searching is also useful when you want to retrieve documents relating to a specific issue. If the Natural Language Query Editor is displayed, click the **Search Type** button and select **Term Search**.

### 6.1  Terms

**Plurals and Possessives:** Plurals are automatically retrieved when you enter the singular form of a term. This is true for both regular and irregular plurals (e.g., **child** retrieves *children*). If you enter the plural form of a term, you will not retrieve the singular form.

If you enter the non-possessive form of a term, WESTLAW automatically retrieves the possessive form as well. However, if you enter the possessive form, only the possessive form is retrieved.

**Automatic Equivalencies:** Some terms have alternative forms or equivalencies; for example, *5* and *five* are equivalent terms. WESTLAW automatically retrieves equivalent terms. The *WESTLAW Reference Manual* contains a list of equivalent terms.

**Compound Words and Acronyms:** When a compound word is one of your search terms, use a hyphen to retrieve all forms of the word. For example, the term **along-side** retrieves *along-side, alongside* and *along side*.

When using an acronym as a search term, place a period after each of the letters in the acronym to retrieve any of its forms. For example, the term **e.s.o.p.** retrieves *esop, e.s.o.p., e s o p* and *e. s. o. p.* Note: The acronym does *not* retrieve *employee stock ownership plan*, so remember to add additional alternative terms to your query such as **"employee stock ownership plan"**.

**Root Expander and Universal Character:** When you use the Terms and Connectors search method, placing a root expander (!) at the end of a root term generates all other terms with that root. For example, adding the ! symbol to the root *deduct* in the query

**deduct! /5 loss**

instructs WESTLAW to retrieve such words as *deduct, deducted, deductability* and *deduction*.

The universal character (*) stands for one character and can be inserted in the middle or at the end of a term. For example, the term

**s****holder**

will retrieve *shareholder* and *stockholder*. Adding three asterisks to the root *elect* in the query

**elect****

instructs WESTLAW to retrieve all forms of the root with up to three additional characters. Terms like *elected* or *election* are retrieved by this query. However, terms with more than three letters following the root, such as *electronic,* are not retrieved. Plurals are always retrieved, even if more than three letters follow the root.

**Phrase Searching:** To search for a phrase, place it within quotation marks. For example, to search for references to the alternative minimum tax, type "**alternative minimum tax**". When you are using the Terms and Connectors search method, you should use phrase searching only if you are certain that the phrase will not appear in any other form.

### 6.2  Alternative Terms

After selecting the terms for your query, consider which alternative terms are necessary. For example, if you are searching for the term *exempt,* you might also want to search for the term *non-exempt.* You should consider both synonyms and antonyms as alternative terms. You can also use the WESTLAW thesaurus to add alternative terms to your query.

### 6.3  Connectors

After selecting terms and alternative terms for your query, use connectors to specify the relationship that should exist between search terms in your retrieved documents. The connectors you can use are described below:

| Use: | To retrieve documents with: | Example: |
|---|---|---|
| & (and) | both terms | **fraud! & fine** |
| or (space) | either term or both terms | **abstention abstain\*\*\*** |
| /p | search terms in the same paragraph | **368(a) /p reorganiz!** |
| /s | search terms in the same sentence | **gambl! /s income** |
| +s | one search term preceding the other within the same sentence; especially useful when searching in the title field (ti) where both parties have the same name | **ti(kurzman +s kurzman)** |
| /n | search terms within "n" terms of each other (where "n" is a number) | **charitable /3 organization** |
| +n | one search term preceding the other by "n" terms (where "n" is a number) | **estate +3 tax** |
| "   " | search terms appearing in the same order as in the quotation marks | **"net operating loss"** |
| Use: | To exclude documents with: | Example: |
| %<br>(but not) | search terms following the % symbol | **attorney lawyer /5 client /s privileg! % sy,di(work-product)** |

### 6.4  Restricting Your Search by Field

**Overview:** Documents in each WESTLAW database consist of several segments, or fields. One field may contain the citation, another the title, another the synopsis, and so forth. Not all databases contain the same fields. Also, depending on the database, fields of the same name may contain different types of information.

To view the fields and field content for a specific database, see Scope or choose **Fields** from the Browse menu. Note that in some databases, not every field is available for every document.

To retrieve only those documents containing your search terms in a specific field, restrict your search to that field. To restrict your search to a specific field, type the field name or abbreviation followed by your search terms enclosed in parentheses. For example, to retrieve a case in the U.S. Court of Appeals for the Federal Taxation–Courts of Appeals Cases database (FTX–CTA) entitled *Baker v. LeBoeuf, Lamb, Leiby & Macrae,* search for your terms in the title field (ti):

**ti(baker & leboeuf)**

The fields discussed below are available in WESTLAW databases you might use for researching federal practice issues.

**Digest and Synopsis Fields:** The digest (di) and synopsis (sy) fields, added to case law databases by West's attorney-editors, summarize the main points of a case. The synopsis field contains a brief description of a case. The digest field contains the topic, headnote, court and title fields and includes the complete hierarchy of concepts used to classify the point of law, including the West digest topic name and number and the key number. Restricting your search to these fields limits your result to cases in which your terms are related to a major issue in the case.

Consider restricting your search to one or both of these fields if

- you are searching for common terms or terms with more than one meaning, and you need to narrow your search; or

- you cannot narrow your search by moving to a smaller database.

For example, to retrieve cases that discuss the deductibility of net operating losses, access the Federal Taxation–Cases database (FTX–CS) and type

**sy,di(deduct! /p net /3 operat! /3 loss)**

**Headnote Field:** The headnote field (he) is a part of the digest field, but does not contain the topic number, hierarchical classification information, key number or title. The headnote field contains only the one-sentence summary of the point of law and any supporting citations given by the author of the opinion. A headnote field restriction is useful when you are searching for specific statutory sections or rule numbers. For example, to retrieve headnotes that cite 26 U.S.C.A. § 1312, type the following query:

**he(26 +s 1312)**

**Topic Field:** The topic field (to) is also a part of the digest field. It contains hierarchical classification information, including the West digest topic name and number, and the key number. You should restrict search terms to the topic field in a case law database if

- a digest field search retrieves too many documents, or

- you want to retrieve cases with digest paragraphs classified under more than one topic

For example, the topic Internal Revenue has the topic number 220. To retrieve United States district court cases that discuss the accrual of liability for estate taxes, access the Federal Taxation-District Courts Cases database FTX-DCT and type a query like the following

to(220) p liab! p accru! p estate 3 tax!

To retrieve West headnotes classified under more than one topic and key number, search for your terms in the topic field. For example, to search for cases discussing deductions, which may be classified to 220, Internal Revenue, or 371, Taxation, among other topics, type a query like the following

to(deduct!)

For a complete list of West digest topics and their corresponding topic numbers, access the Key Number service, click the **Key Number Service** button in the Welcome to WESTLAW window

> *Note* Be aware that slip opinions, cases not to be reported by West, and cases from topical services do not contain the digest, headnote or topic fields

**Prelim and Caption Fields:** When searching in a database containing statutes, rules or regulations, restrict your search to the prelim (pr) and caption (ca) fields to retrieve documents in which your terms are important enough to appear in a section name or heading. For example, to retrieve federal statutes relating to accelerated cost recovery, access the Federal Taxation-United States Code Annotated database (FTX-USCA) and type the following

pr,ca(accelerat! 3 cost)

## 6.5  Restricting Your Search by Date

You can instruct WESTLAW to retrieve documents *decided* or *issued* before, after, or on a specified date, as well as within a range of dates. The following are examples of queries that contain date restrictions:

da(aft 1995) & 6501(a)

da(1995) & self-employ! s health p deduct!

da(11 21 96) & tals! 3 return

You can also instruct WESTLAW to retrieve documents *added to a database* on or after a specified date, as well as within a range of dates. The following are examples of queries that contain added-date restrictions:

ad(aft 1990) & sy(qualif! p 501(c)(3))

**ad(aft 1–1–96 & bef 10–1–96) & tax-exempt /5 bond**

## Section 7.   Verifying Your Research with Citators

**Overview:** A citator service is a tool that helps you ensure that cases are good law; retrieve cases, legislation or articles that cite a case or statute; and verify the spelling and format of citations.

For citations not covered by the citator services, including persuasive secondary authority such as restatements and treatises, use a technique called WESTLAW as a citator to retrieve cases that cite your authority (see Section 7.4).

### 7.1   KeyCite[SM]

KeyCite is the new case history and citation verification service from West. KeyCite integrates all the case law on WESTLAW, helping you trace the history of a case, retrieve a list of all cases and secondary sources that cite a case, and track legal issues decided in a case.

KeyCite provides a listing of both direct and negative indirect history for any case within the scope of its coverage. For citation verification, the KeyCite display provides the case; title; parallel citations, including many looseleaf citations; court of decision; docket number; and filing date.

With KeyCite you no longer need to use other citator services in order to guarantee that you have the most up-to-date information. You can also use KeyCite to check unpublished cases.

You can use KeyCite to check case history. The History of the Case display traces the direct history of the case for the same parties and fact situation. It also displays negative indirect history, which consists of cases outside the direct appellate line that may have a negative impact on the precedential value of an earlier decision. The display also includes related references, which are opinions involving the same parties and facts but resolving different issues.

In addition to case history, KeyCite shows you Citations to the Case, listing all sources that cite a decision. These sources are available as soon as they are added to WESTLAW, giving you the most current citing information available.

### 7.2   Shepard's Citations

For case law, Shepard's provides a comprehensive list of cases and other documents that have cited a particular case. Shepard's also includes explanatory analysis to indicate how the citing cases have treated the case, e.g., "followed," "explained."

For statutes, Shepard's Citations provides a comprehensive list of cases citing a particular statute, as well as information on subsequent legislative action. The federal court rule divisions for each of the statute citators currently available on WESTLAW provide a comprehensive list of cases citing a particular federal court rule. Federal court rule divisions include:

| | |
|---|---|
| Supreme Court Rules | Federal Rules of Criminal Procedure |
| Federal Rules of Evidence | Federal Rules of Civil Procedure |
| Bankruptcy Rules | Federal Rules of Appellate Procedure |

In addition to citations from federal, state and regional citators, Shepard's on WESTLAW includes citations from specialized citators such as *Federal Tax Citations.*

### 7.3 Using WESTLAW As a Citator

Using WESTLAW as a citator, you can search for documents citing a specific statute, regulation, rule, agency decision or other authority. For example, to retrieve documents citing 26 C.F.R. § 148.1–5, access the Federal Taxation–Courts of Appeals Cases database (FTX–CTA) and type a query like the following:

**26 +5 148.1–5**

### Section 8.   Research Examples

### 8.1   Retrieving Law Review Articles

Recent law review articles are often a good place to begin researching a legal issue because law review articles serve 1) as an excellent introduction to a new topic or review for a stale one, providing terminology to help in query formulation; 2) as a finding tool for pertinent primary authority, such as cases and statutes; and 3) in some instances, as persuasive secondary authority. For example, you need to gain more background information on the factors the federal courts have considered in determining what is a justiciable case or controversy.

*Solution*

- To retrieve recent law review articles relevant to your issue, access the Journals & Law Reviews database (JLR); select Natural Language searching; then enter a description like the following:

  **are punitive damage awards taxable**

- If you have a citation to an article in a specific publication, use Find to retrieve it. For more information on Find, see Section 4.1 of this appendix. For example, to retrieve the article found at 72 Denver University Law Review 215, access Find and type

  **72 denv u l rev 215**

- If you know the title of an article, but not which journal it appeared in, access the Taxation–Law Reviews, Texts & Bar Journals database (TX–TP) and search for key terms from the title in the title field. For example, to retrieve the article "Taxability of Punitives in Personal Injury Cases Comes Up for Scrutiny" type the following Terms and Connectors query:

  **ti(taxability & punitives)**

## 8.2　Retrieving Federal Statutes

You need to retrieve federal statutes dealing with penalties for failing to furnish information regarding tax shelters.

*Solution*

- Access the Federal Taxation-U S Code Annotated database (FTX-USCA) Search for your terms in the prelim and caption fields using the Terms and Connectors search method

  **pr,ca(penal! & fail! p "tax shelter")**

- When you know the citation for a specific section of a statute, use Find to retrieve the statute. For example, to retrieve 26 U.S.C.A. § 6707, access the Find service and type

  **26 usca 6707**

- To look at surrounding statutory sections, use the Table of Contents service. Select a Jump marker in the prelim or caption field. You can also use Documents in Sequence to retrieve the section following § 6707 Click the **Docs in Seq** button.

- When you retrieve a statute on WESTLAW, it will contain an Update message if legislation amending or repealing it is available online. To display this legislation, select the Jump marker in the Update message.

> Because slip copy versions of laws are added to WESTLAW before they contain full editorial enhancements, they are not retrieved with Update. To retrieve slip copy versions of laws, access the United States Public Laws database (US-PL), then type **ci(slip)** and descriptive terms, e.g., **ci(slip) &** *[term]*. Slip copy documents are replaced by the editorially enhanced versions within a few working days. Update also does not retrieve legislation that enacts a new statute or covers a topic that will not be incorporated into the statutes. To retrieve this legislation, access US-PL and enter a query containing terms that describe the new legislation.

## 8.3　Retrieving Federal Court Rules

Suppose you've misplaced your rules pamphlet and you need to check the Federal Rules of Civil Procedure.

*Solution*

- Access the Federal Taxation-Rules database (FTX-RULES) and search for key terms in the caption field

  **ca(timely 3 filing)**

To determine the abbreviation for the Federal Rules of Civil Procedure, as well as the Federal Rules of Evidence, Rules of the U.S. Supreme Court, rules of the U.S. courts of appeals and other rules, access Scope.

*Note*: Local rules of the U.S. district courts and U.S. bankruptcy courts are contained in the state court rules database (XX–RULES, where XX is the state's two-letter postal abbreviation) for the state in which the court sits. Access the appropriate database and search for the rule abbreviation in the citation field (ci), e.g., **ci(usdct)**. To determine the rule abbreviation, access Scope.

- When you know the rule number, use Find to retrieve the rule. For example, to retrieve Rule 54 of the Rules of Practice and Procedure of the United States Tax Court, access Find and type

**tax ct rule 54**

- When you retrieve a court rule on WESTLAW, it will contain an Update message if documents amending or repealing it are available online. To display these documents, select the Jump marker in the Update message. Note: Slip copy documents, legislation enacting a new statute or rule, and legislation covering a topic that will not be incorporated into the statutes cannot be retrieved with the Update service. To retrieve these materials, run a descriptive word search in the US–PL or US–ORDERS database.

## 8.4 Using the Citator Services

One of the cases you retrieve in your case law research is *United States v. Monsanto*, 109 S.Ct. 2657 (1989). You want to see whether this case is good law and whether other cases have cited this case.

> *Solution:* Use KeyCite to retrieve direct history and negative indirect history of *Monsanto*. While viewing the case, click the **KeyCite** button.

## 8.5 Following Recent Developments

As the taxation specialist in your firm, you are expected to keep up with and summarize recent legal developments in this area of the law. How can you do this efficiently?

*Solution*

One of the easiest ways to stay abreast of recent developments in taxation law is by accessing the WESTLAW Topical Highlights–Federal Tax database (WTH–FTX). The WTH–FTX database summarizes recent legal developments, including court decisions, legislation and changes in the area of taxation law. Some summaries also contain suggested queries that combine the proven power of West's topic and key numbers and West's case headnotes to retrieve additional pertinent cases.

- When you access WTH–FTX, you will automatically retrieve a list of documents added to the database in the last two weeks.

- To read a summary of a document listed, double-click the citation of the document.

- To view the full text of a document, access Find while viewing the list and type the document citation, e.g., **1997 wl   1786.**

- To search this database, choose **New Search** from the Search menu. At the Terms and Connectors Query Editor, type your query. For example, to retrieve references discussing tax-sheltered annuities, type a query like the following:

  **tax /3 shelter! /s annuity**

# Table of Cases

**References are to Paragraph Numbers**

## E

Early v. Commissioner—5.02, n. 12.
Edwards v. Commissioner—4.03, n. 14.
Egtvedt v. United States—3.07; 3.07, n. 4.
Eisner v. Macomber—2.01; 2.01, n. 7; 3.03; 3.03, n. 2; 4.02; 4.02, n. 2.
Estate of (see name of party)
Eubank, Helvering v.—5.02, n. 1.

## F

Fackler v. Commissioner—4.06, n. 22.
Fairbanks v. United States—4.06, n. 6.
Farid-Es-Sultaneh v. Commissioner—4.02; 4.02, n. 16.
Faroll v. Jarecki—4.06, n. 5.
Faulconer v. Commissioner—6.02, n. 24.
Fausner v. Commissioner—6.02, n. 22.
Feinberg v. Commissioner—4.05, n. 65.
Ferrer, Commissioner v.—4.06, n. 56.
Fine v. United States—6.02, n. 46.
Fin Hay Realty Co. v. United States—7.01, n. 27.
Fleischman v. Commissioner—6.02; 6.02, n. 67.
Flint v. Stone Tracy Co.—1.01; 1.01, n. 25.
Flowers, Commissioner v.—6.02; 6.02, n. 16.
Fogle v. Commissioner—2.02, n. 5.
Folkman v. United States—6.02, n. 27.
Foote v. Commissioner—6.02, n. 28.
Ford v. Commissioner—6.02, n. 37.
France v. Commissioner—7.01, n. 16.
Frank v. Commissioner, 321 F.2d 143—4.06, n. 92.
Frank v. Commissioner, 20 T.C. 511—6.03; 6.03, n. 21, 23.
Franklin's Estate v. Commissioner—3.01, n. 2; 4.03, n. 18; 7.01, n. 26; 8.02; 8.02, n. 36, 38, 44.

## G

Galt v. Commissioner—5.04, n. 5.
General Dynamics Corp., United States v.—9.03; 9.03, n. 30.
Generes, United States v.—4.06, n. 13; 7.01, n. 4.
Gevirtz v. Commissioner—7.01, n. 74.
Giannini, Commissioner v.—5.02; 5.02, n. 3.
Gilmore, United States v.—6.02; 6.02, n. 58.
Gilmore v. United States—6.02, n. 59.
Glasgow v. Commissioner—6.02, n. 37.
Glenshaw Glass Co., Commissioner v.—2.01; 2.01, n. 6.
Godfrey v. Commissioner—4.03, n. 6.
Goedel v. Commissioner—6.02, n. 4.

Goldstein v. Commissioner—4.04, n. 9; 4.06, n. 54; 6.03; 6.03, n. 55; 8.02, n. 1.
Gorod v. Commissioner—6.02, n. 16.
Grace Bros. v. Commissioner—4.03, n. 51.
Grant v. Commissioner—7.01, n. 47.
Gray v. Commissioner—4.06, n. 5.
Gray v. Darlington—4.02, n. 2.
Green v. Commissioner, T.C. Memo. 1987-503—3.08.
Green v. Commissioner, 367 F.2d 823—7.01, n. 28.
Green v. Commissioner, 78 T.C. 428—6.02, n. 32.
Green v. Commissioner, 74 T.C. 1229—6.02, n. 22.
Green Lawn Memorial Park, Inc. v. McDonald—3.13.
Gregory v. Helvering—4.06, n. 48; 5.01; 5.01, n. 7.
Guest v. Commissioner—4.02; 8.02, n. 13.
Gulftex Drug Co., Inc. v. Commissioner—4.06, n. 6.

## H

Haden Co v. Commissioner—9.02, n. 24.
Hammel, Helvering v.—4.03, n. 32.
Hantzis v. Commissioner—6.02; 6.02, n. 19.
Harolds Club v. Commissioner—6.02; 6.02, n. 10.
Harris, United States v.—3.08; 3.08, n. 7.
Harrison v. Schaffner—5.02; 5.02, n. 8.
Hassen v. Commissioner—4.05, n. 15.
Hatt v. Commissioner—2.02; 2.02, n. 1.
Haverly v. United States—3.13.
Havey v. Commissioner—7.01, n. 14.
Hawaiian Cemetery Ass'n, Ltd. v. Commissioner—3.13.
Heiner v. Tindle—4.04, n. 9.
Helvering v. _____ (see opposing party)
Hendler, United States v.—4.03, n. 19, 27.
Hendricks v. Commissioner—4.06, n. 31.
Higgins v. Commissioner—6.02; 6.02, n. 48.
Hill v. Commissioner—6.02; 6.02, n. 32.
Hills v. Commissioner—7.01, n. 68.
Hillsboro Nat. Bank v. Commissioner—9.02; 9.02, n. 25.
Hilton Hotels Corp., United States v.—6.03, n. 12.
Holbrook v. United States—3.05, n. 5.
Hollywood Baseball Ass'n v. Commissioner—4.06; 4.06, n. 11.
Hooker Chemicals and Plastics Corp. v. United States—4.06, n. 66.
Horne v. Commissioner—4.06, n. 54.
Hornung v. Commissioner—9.03; 9.03, n. 10.
Horrmann v. Commissioner—6.02; 6.02, n. 68.
Horst, Helvering v.—5.02; 5.02, n. 10.

# Table of Internal Revenue Code Sections

References with parens in the note column denotes which group of footnotes

| UNITED STATES CODE ANNOTATED 26 U.S.C.A.—Internal Revenue Code | | | UNITED STATES CODE ANNOTATED 26 U.S.C.A.—Internal Revenue Code | | |
|---|---|---|---|---|---|
| | | This Work | | | This Work |
| Sec. | Sec. | Note | Sec. | Sec. | Note |
| 119(2) | 2.02 | 4 | 163(h) | 7.01 | 20 |
| 121 | 4.01 | 6 | | 7.01 | 22 |
| | 4.04 | | 163(h)(3) | 7.01 | |
| | 4.04 | 17 | 164 | 2.01 | 5 |
| | 4.05 | | | 7.02 | 4 |
| 121(a) | 4.04 | 14 | | 8.02 | 9 |
| 121(a)(2) | 4.04 | 13 | 164(a) | 7.01 | 29 |
| 121(b) | 4.04 | 15 | | 7.01 | 30 |
| 121(b)(2) | 4.04 | 16 | | 7.01 | 32 |
| 121(c) | 4.04 | 14 | 164(d) | 4.03 | 6 |
| 121(d)(1) | 4.04 | 13 | | 7.01 | 34 |
| 121(d)(3) | 4.04 | 13 | 164(e) | 9.02 | |
| 121(d)(4) | 4.04 | 17 | | 9.02 | 27 |
| 121(d)(7) | 4.04 | 19 | 165 | Ch. 4 | |
| 123 | 3.13 | | | 4.02 | 12 |
| 125 | 2.04 | | | 6.01 | 7 |
| 132 | 2.02 | | | 6.02 | 38(2) |
| | 3.08 | | | 6.03 | |
| 141 | 3.01 | | | 7.01 | |
| 151 | 7.04 | 1 | | 7.01 | 72 |
| 151(f) | 1.02 | 4 | 165(a) | 4.04 | 2 |
| 152 | 7.04 | 1 | | 7.01 | |
| 152(a) | 7.01 | 23(2) | | 7.01 | 40 |
| | 10.02 | 4 | | 7.01 | 54 |
| 162 | Ch. 4 | | | 7.01 | 65 |
| | 4.05 | 10 | | 7.01 | 78 |
| | 6.02 | | 165(b) | 4.04 | 2 |
| | 6.02 | 38(2) | | 8.02 | 4 |
| | 6.02 | 55 | 165(c) | 4.01 | 6 |
| | 6.02 | 59 | | 4.05 | 4(2) |
| | 6.02 | 85 | | 7.01 | 40 |
| | 6.03 | | | 7.01 | 69 |
| | 8.02 | 10 | | 7.01 | 86 |
| | 9.02 | | | 7.01 | 88 |
| 162(a) | 6.02 | | | 7.02 | 5 |
| | 6.03 | | 165(c)(2) | 4.06 | 40(2) |
| | 7.01 | 70 | | 4.06 | 51 |
| 162(a)(1) | 6.02 | | 165(c)(3) | 4.01 | |
| | 6.03 | 2 | | 4.04 | 3 |
| 162(a)(2) | 6.02 | | | 7.01 | |
| 162(c) | 6.03 | | | 7.01 | 45 |
| 162(c)(1) | 6.03 | 32 | | 7.01 | 56 |
| 162(c)(2) | 6.03 | 33 | 165(d) | 1.1 | 3 |
| 162(c)(3) | 6.03 | 34 | | 3.13 | |
| 162(e) | 6.03 | 43 | | 7.01 | 79 |
| 162(e)(2) | 6.03 | 44 | 165(e) | 7.01 | 54 |
| 162(f) | 6.03 | | 165(g) | 7.01 | 5(2) |
| | 6.03 | 38 | 165(g)(1) | 4.06 | 8(3) |
| 162(g) | 6.03 | | 165(g)(2) | 4.06 | 9(3) |
| | 6.03 | 41 | | 7.01 | 6(2) |
| 162(m) | 6.02 | | 165(h) | 7.01 | 40 |
| 163 | Ch. 4 | | | 7.01 | 56 |
| | 6.01 | | | 7.02 | 5 |
| | 7.02 | 3 | 165(i) | 7.01 | 40 |
| 163(a) | 7.01 | 12 | 166 | 7.01 | 72 |
| 163(d) | 5.04 | 27 | | 9.02 | 12 |
| | 6.03 | | 166(a) | 4.06 | 11(2) |
| | 7.01 | 17 | | 7.01 | |
| | 7.01 | 24 | | 7.01 | 81 |
| | 8.02 | 30 | | 7.01 | 88 |

| UNITED STATES CODE ANNOTATED | | | | UNITED STATES CODE ANNOTATED | | |
|---|---|---|---|---|---|---|
| 26 U.S.C.A.—Internal Revenue Code | | | | 26 U.S.C.A.—Internal Revenue Code | | |
| | | This | Work | | This | Work |
| Sec. | | Sec. | Note | Sec. | Sec. | Note |
| 1221(3) (Cont'd) | | 7.01 | 41(2) | 1233 | 4.06 | |
| 1221(3)(A) | | 4.06 | 47(2) | | 4.06 | 40 |
| | | 4.06 | 48(2) | | 4.06 | 47 |
| | | 4.06 | 64 | 1233(a) | 4.06 | 33 |
| 1221(3)(B) | | 4.06 | 48(2) | 1233(b) | 4.06 | |
| | | 4.06 | 65 | 1233(b)(1) | 4.06 | 40 |
| 1221(3)(C) | | 4.06 | 50(2) | 1233(b)(2) | 4.06 | 41 |
| | | 4.06 | 65 | | 4.06 | 42 |
| 1221(4) | | 4.06 | 20(2) | 1233(c) | 4.06 | 40 |
| | | 4.06 | 66 | 1233(d) | 4.06 | 43 |
| | | 4.06 | 99(2) | 1233(e)(2)(B) | 4.06 | 47 |
| 1221(5) | | 4.06 | 8 | 1233(e)(2)(C) | 4.06 | 41 |
| | | 4.06 | 55 | 1233(f) | 4.06 | 41 |
| 1221(6) | | 4.06 | 8 | 1233(g) | 4.06 | 4(2) |
| | | 4.06 | 68 | | 4.06 | 46 |
| 1222 | | 4.01 | | 1234A | 4.06 | |
| | | 4.01 | 8 | 1235 | 3.05 | 4 |
| | | 4.06 | 7 | | 4.06 | |
| | | 4.06 | 44 | | 4.06 | 57(2) |
| | | 4.06 | 59 | | 4.06 | 62(2) |
| 1222(11) | | 4.06 | | | 4.06 | 65(2) |
| 1223(1) | | 4.05 | 15 | 1235(a) | 4.06 | 64(2) |
| 1223(1)(A) | | 4.05 | 68 | | 4.06 | 66(2) |
| 1223(2) | | 4.03 | 58 | 1235(a)(1) | 4.06 | 57(2) |
| 1223(4) | | 4.05 | 7(2) | 1235(a)(2) | 4.06 | 57(2) |
| 1223(6) | | 4.06 | 28 | 1235(b) | 4.06 | 65(2) |
| 1223(7) | | 4.05 | 86 | | 4.06 | 69(2) |
| 1223(11) | | 4.03 | 73 | 1235(b)(1) | 4.06 | 65(2) |
| 1231 | | 3.11 | 14 | 1235(b)(2) | 4.06 | 64(2) |
| | | Ch. 4 | | | 4.06 | 65(2) |
| | | 4.01 | | 1235(d) | 4.06 | 65(2) |
| | | 4.01 | 8 | 1236 | 4.06 | 93 |
| | | 4.05 | | | 4.06 | 94 |
| | | 4.06 | | 1237 | 4.06 | |
| | | 4.06 | 16(2) | | 4.06 | 83 |
| | | 4.06 | 29(2) | | 4.06 | 86 |
| | | 4.06 | 31(2) | 1237(a) | 4.06 | 83 |
| | | 4.06 | 32(3) | 1237(a)(1) | 4.06 | 84 |
| | | 4.06 | 34(2) | | 4.06 | 85 |
| | | 4.06 | 45(2) | 1237(a)(2) | 4.06 | 86 |
| | | 4.06 | 51(2) | 1237(a)(3) | 4.06 | 87 |
| | | 4.06 | 88(2) | 1237(b)(1) | 4.06 | 88 |
| | | 5.04 | | 1237(b)(2) | 4.06 | 88 |
| | | 7.01 | | 1237(b)(3) | 4.06 | 86 |
| | | 7.01 | 75 | 1239 | 4.05 | 22(2) |
| 1231(a) | | 4.06 | 30(2) | | 4.05 | 37(2) |
| | | 4.06 | 32(2) | | 4.06 | |
| | | 4.06 | 34(2) | | 4.06 | 97(2) |
| | | 4.06 | 35(2) | | 8.03 | 24 |
| 1231(b) | | 4.06 | 34(2) | 1239(b)(2) | 4.06 | 96(2) |
| | | 4.06 | 45(2) | 1239(b)(3) | 4.06 | 90(2) |
| | | 7.01 | | | 4.06 | 96(2) |
| 1231(b)(1) | | 5.04 | 8 | 1239(c) | 4.06 | 91(2) |
| 1231(b)(2) | | 4.06 | 45(2) | | 4.06 | 93(2) |
| 1231(b)(3)(A) | | 4.06 | 45(2) | | 4.06 | 95(2) |
| 1231(b)(3)(B) | | 4.06 | 45(2) | 1239(c)(2) | 4.06 | |
| 1231(b)(4) | | 4.06 | 45(2) | 1241 | 4.06 | 4(3) |
| 1232(a)(1) | | 4.06 | 7(3) | | 4.06 | 5(3) |
| 1232(a)(2) | | 3.02 | 6 | | 5.04 | 8 |
| 1232(a)(3) (repealed) | | 3.02 | | 1245 | 3.10 | |
| 1232(a)(4) | | 4.06 | 67 | | 4.06 | |
| | | | | | 4.06 | 79(2) |
| | | | | 1245(a)(3) | 4.06 | 78(2) |

# Table of Treasury Regulations

References with parens in the note column denotes which group of footnotes

# Table of Revenue Rulings

References with parens in the note column denotes which group of footnotes

# Index

References are to paragraph numbers

†